A Bibliography of William Morris

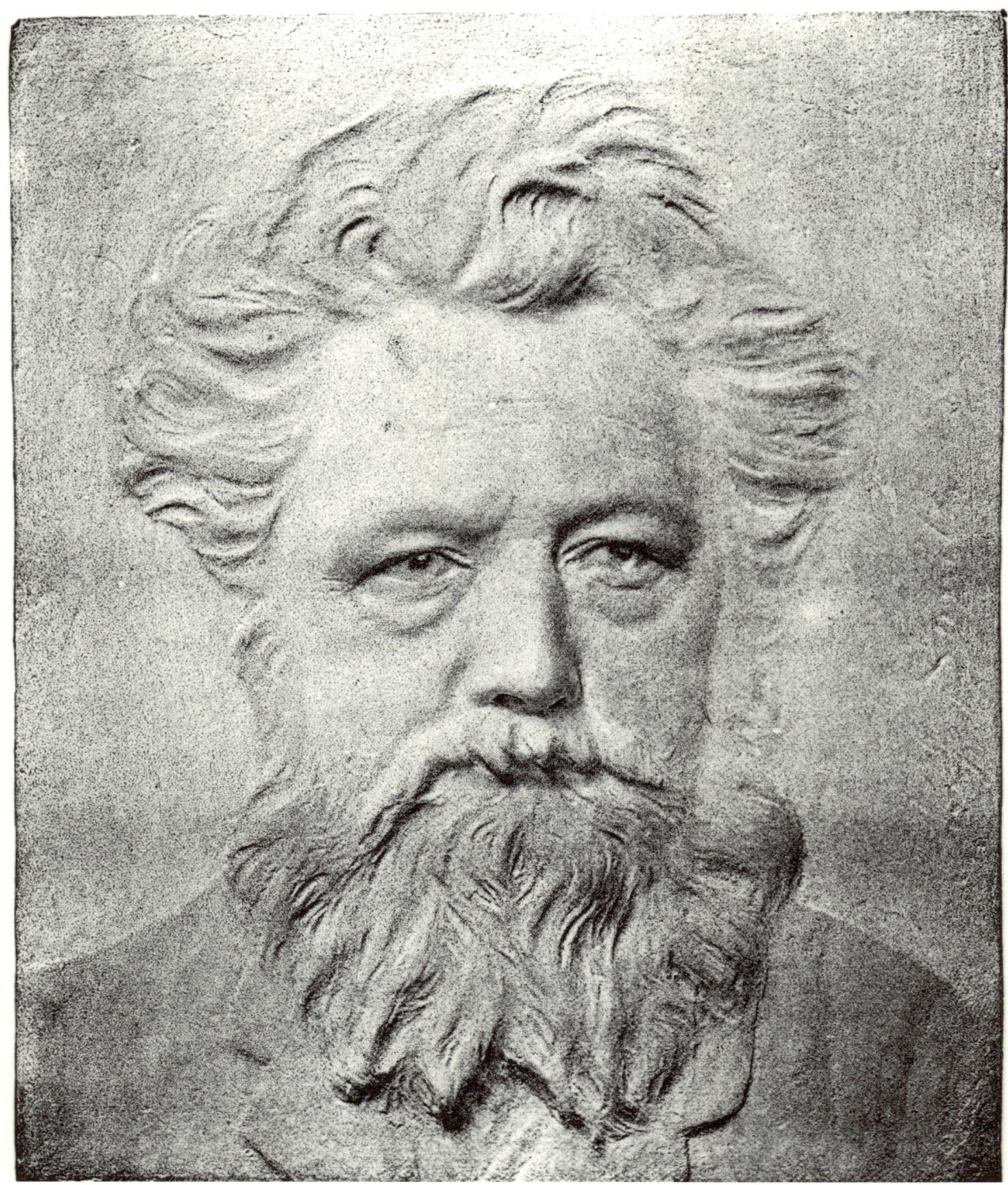

A Bibliography

OF

William Morris

Eugene D. LeMire

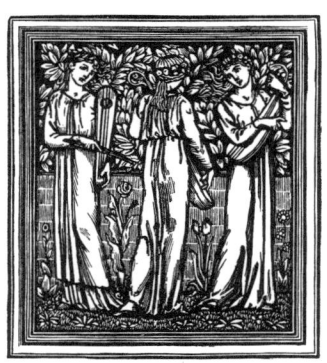

OAK KNOLL PRESS
THE BRITISH LIBRARY
2006

First Published by Oak Knoll Press in 2006
310 Delaware Street, New Castle, Delaware, USA
Web:http://www.oakknoll.com
and
The British Library
96 Euston Road, London,
NW1 2DB, UK

ISBN: 1-58456-173-4 (Oak Knoll Press)
ISBN: 0-7123-4926-x (The British Library)

Title: A Bibliography of William Morris
Author: Eugene LeMire
Book design, and composition by Wesley B. Tanner/Passim Editions
Publishing Director: J. Lewis von Hoelle

Copyright: © Eugene Lemire, 2006 All rights reserved.

Library of Congress Cataloging-in-Publication Data
and the British CIP Record is available from the publishers.

ALL RIGHTS RESERVED:
No part of this book may be reproduced in any manner without the
express written consent of the publisher, except in the case of brief
excerpts in critical reviews and articles. All inquiries should be
addressed to: Oak Knoll Press, 310 Delaware St., New Castle, DE 19720
Web: http://www.oakknoll.com

This work was printed and bound in the United States of America
on archival, acid-free paper meeting the requirements of the American
Standard for Permanence of Paper for Printed Library Materials.

FRONTISPIECE:
Figure 1. Portrait of Morris from a sculpture by J. A. Smith
from which plaster plaques were made and sold
at the Royal Academy, 1891

TITLE PAGE:
Vignette from A-4.05 *The Earthly Paradise*, 1st edn., vol. 3 (title page)

To Margaret

Contents

List of Illustrations	ix
Acknowledgements	xiii
List of Abbreviations	xv
Abbreviations of Libraries, Private Collections, and Institutions cited	xxii
Introduction	xxvii
Organization	l
Some Definitions	liii
Fields and Field Titles	liv
Areas Not Included	lx
A: The Original Editions with Posthumous Editions to 1915 and First Editions to the Present	3
B: Morris's Contributions to Books	171
C: Morris Collections and Selections	280
D: Morris in Periodical Publications	307
E: Forgeries, Piracies, and Sophistications	355
Appendices	
Appendix I: Interviews	369
Appendix II: Ephemera	371
Index	377

Illustrations

Figure 1.	Portrait of Morris from a sculpture by J. A. Smith from which plaster plaques were made and sold at the Royal Academy, 1891	*Frontispiece*
Figure 2.	A-1.01: *The Oxford and Cambridge Magazine*, title page of the bound volume	2
Figure 3.	A-2.01: *The Defence of Guenevere* (1st edn.) title page	5
Figure 4.	A-2.04: *Defence of Guenevere* (KP, Kelmscott Press edn.) head title in Border 2	9
Figure 5.	A-3.01: *Jason* (1st edn.) title page	15
Figure 6.	A-3.02: *Jason* (2nd edn., 1st American) title page	17
Figure 7.	A-3.09: *Jason* (1st Morris book in LPL, Longmans Pocket Library) title page	22
Figure 8.	A-4.01: *EP* (*The Earthly Paradise*, 1st edn., vol. 1 (of 3)) title page	26
Figure 9.	A-4.03: *EP* (2nd edn., 1st American) title page	29
Figure 10.	A-4.08: *EP*, substitute title page inserted in vol. 3, part 4, for use in A-4.01	32
Figure 11.	A-4.17: *EP* (KP edn.) opening: engraved title & Prologue begins	41
Figure 12.	A-4.18: *EP* (Silver Library Edn.) title page	43
Figure 13.	A-5.01: *Grettis Saga* (1st edn.) opening: poem (verso) & facing title page	47
Figure 14.	A-6.01: *Volsunga Saga* (1st edn.) title page	52
Figure 15.	A-7.01: *Lovers of Gudrun* (1st edn.) opening: frontis. & title page	55
Figure 16.	A-7.01: *Lovers of Gudrun* (1st edn.) binding	56
Figure 17.	A-7.01: *Lovers of Gudrun* (1st edn. RB, Roberts Brothers): ledger entry	56
Figure 18.	A-8.01: *Love is Enough* (1st edn.) title page	57
Figure 19.	A-8.01: *Love is Enough* (1st edn.) binding	58
Figure 20.	A-8.02: *Love is Enough* (1st edn., American issue) binding	59
Figure 21.	A-9.01: *Three Northern Love Stories* (1st edn.) title page	62
Figure 22.	A-12.01: *Sigurd* (1st edn.) title page	69

Illustrations

Figure 23.	A-12.05: *Sigurd* (KP edn.) opening: frontis. & head title	73
Figure 24.	A-15.01: *Wake, London Lads* (1st edn.) fly sheet	77
Figure 25.	A-16.01: *The Decorative Arts* (1st edn.) title page	78
Figure 26.	A-16.01: *The Decorative Arts* (1st edn.) handbill ad for the lecture	79
Figure 27.	A-17.02: *The Art of the People* (Seymour edn.) title page	81
Figure 28.	A-17.03: *The Art of the People* (Hillacre edn.) title page	82
Figure 29.	A-21.01: *Hopes and Fears for Art* (1st edn.) title page	85
Figure 30.	A-23.03: *Chants for Socialists* (2nd edn., 1st complete) wrapper title	91
Figure 31.	A-24.01: *Summary . . . Principles of Socialism* (1st edn.) wrapper title	93
Figure 32.	A-25.01: *Art and Socialism* (1st edn.) title page	94
Figure 33.	A-25.01: *Art and Socialism* (1st edn.) wrapper front cover	95
Figure 34.	A-26.02: membership card, Hammersmith Branch, SL (Socialist League)	97
Figure 35.	A-31.02: *Useful Work v. Useless Toil* (Freedom Library) wrapper title	106
Figure 36.	A-31.05: *Useful Work v. Useless Toil* (Kerr edn.) wrapper title	107
Figure 37.	A-37.02: *True and False Society* (2nd edn.) wrapper title	112
Figure 38.	A-40.01: *The Odyssey* (1st edn. vol. 1 of 2) title page	114
Figure 39.	A-45.01: *John Ball and . . .* (1st edn) title page	119
Figure 40.	A-45.02: *John Ball and . . .* (KP edn.) engraved title & facing head title	121
Figure 41.	A-45.04: *John Ball and . . .* (Mosher edn.) title page	122
Figure 42.	A-48.01: *Roots of the Mountains* ('Superior' edn.) title page	133
Figure 43.	A-48.01: *Roots of the Mountains* ('Superior' edn.) chintz binding	135
Figure 44.	A-49.01: *Monopoly* SP (The Socialist Platform, 1st edn.) wrapper title	138
Figure 45.	A-49.01: *Monopoly* SP (The Socialist Platform, 1st edn.) opening: cartoon & head title	139
Figure 46.	A-50.01: *News from Nowhere* (1st edn., American) opening: frontis. & title page	140
Figure 47.	A-50.02: *News from Nowhere* (2nd edn., 1st English) title page	141
Figure 48.	A-50.02: *News from Nowhere* (2nd edn., 1st English) original paper wrapper bound in with the half citron levant binding	142

Illustrations

Figure 49.	A-50.02: *News from Nowhere* (2nd edn., 1st English) half citron levant binding	143
Figure 50.	A-50.05: *News from Nowhere* (KP edn.) opening: frontis. & head title	145
Figure 51.	A-52.01: *The Saga Library* (1st edn., vol. 1 of 6) title page	150
Figure 52.	A-52.01: *The Saga Library* (1st edn., vol. 1 of 6) binding	151
Figure 53.	A-54.01: *The Glittering Plain* (KP edn.) head title	154
Figure 54.	A-56.01: *Under an Elm-Tree* (1st edn.) wrapper title	161
Figure 55.	A-56.02: *Under an Elm-Tree* (2nd edn.) wrapper title	162
Figure 56.	A-59.01: *Poems by the Way* (KP edn.) head title in Border 1	167
Figure 57.	A-63.01: *The Order of Chivalry* (KP edn.) frontis. & head title	174
Figure 58.	A-66.01: *Gothic Architecture* (KP edn.) last page, with colophon	177
Figure 59.	A-68.01: *Socialism: Its Growth & Outcome* (1st edn.) title page	178
Figure 60.	A-70.03: *Amis & Amile* (3rd edn., Broc.) title page	182
Figure 61.	A-70.03: *Amis & Amile* (3rd edn., Broc.) binding	183
Figure 62.	A-73.01: *Emperor Coustans and . . .* (KP edn.) opening: engraved title & head title	187
Figure 63.	A-74.01: *Wood beyond the World* (KP edn.) colophon & 1st KP mark	188
Figure 64.	A-74.01: *Wood beyond the World* (KP edn.) opening: frontis. & head title	189
Figure 65.	A-74.02: *Wood beyond the World* (trade edn.) title page	190
Figure 66.	A-74.03: *Wood beyond the World* (RB edn.) title page	191
Figure 67.	A-74.03: *Wood beyond the World* (RB edn.) RB ledger entry	191
Figure 68.	A-74.03: *Wood beyond the World* (RB edn.) binding	192
Figure 69.	A-77.02: *Beowulf* (2nd edn.) title page	197
Figure 70.	A-79.01: *Old French Romances* (Allen edn.) title page	200
Figure 71.	A-80.01: *Well at the World's End* (KP edn.) opening: frontis. & head title	203
Figure 72.	A-80.02: *Well at the World's End* (2nd edn., vol.1 of 2) title page	204
Figure 73.	A-84.01: *Water of the Wondrous Isles* (KP edn.) head title	213
Figure 74.	A-85.01: *Some German Woodcuts* (KP edn.) head title of Preface	217
Figure 75.	A-86.01: *The Sundering Flood* (KP edn.) head title	219

Illustrations

Figure 76.	A-86.01: *The Sundering Flood* (KP edn.) map as pastedown inside the front cover	220
Figure 77.	A-88.01: *A Note by Morris* . . . (KP edn) opening: frontis. & head title	225
Figure 78.	A-89.02: *John Ball* (only, Little Leather edn.) binding, front cover	226
Figure 79.	A-89.03: *John Ball* (only, Haldeman-Julius) wrapper title	227
Figure 80.	A-90.03: *Gertha's Lovers* (Broc. edn.) title page	229
Figure 81.	A-93.01: *History of Over Sea* (Broc. edn.) title page	231
Figure 82.	A-101.02: *A Dream* (Avon edn.) wrapper title	239
Figure 83.	A-104.01: *Communism* (Fabian Tract) wrapper title	242
Figure 84.	A-113.01: *Art, Labour, and Socialism* SPGB (Socialist Party of Great Britain)	248
Figure 85.	A-122.01: *Sir Peter Hardon's End* (Bib. edn.) wrapper, outer pages	253
Figure 86.	A-122.01: *Sir Peter Hardon's End* (Bib. edn.) wrapper, inner pages	254
Figure 87.	A-132.01: *Morris on Art Matters* (1st edn.) wrapper title	264
Figure 88.	B-3: *Lectures on Art* (1st edn.) title page	272
Figure 89.	C-5: *Defence of Guen.: A Book of Lyrics* (1st edn.) epigraph & facing title page	283
Figure 90.	C-9: *Pre-Raphaelite Ballads* (1st edn.) spread title	286
Figure 91.	C-16.05: *Story of the Unknown Church* (Finch edn.) title page	292
Figure 92.	C-29: *Atalanta's Race and* . . . (LCBEL, Longmans Class Books . . .) binding	300
Figure 93.	C-30: *Prose and Poetry* (OUP) title page	301
Figure 94.	D-43: *1st Annual Report SPAB* title page	310
Figure 95.	E-2: *All for the Cause* . . . (forgery) wrapper title	357
Figure 96.	E-5: *The God of the Poor* (forgery) title page	360
Figure 97.	Appendix II-2.02: *Morris Exhibit* (Boston) wrapper title	372
Figure 98.	Appendix II-7: *Sidonia* (prospectus) Morris text	373
Figure 99.	Appendix II-7: *Sidonia* (prospectus) 2nd KP mark	374
Figure 100.	Appendix II-11: [*Morris to Webb*] (letter, keepsake) Morris text	375

Acknowledgements

There are many people, particularly the staff of the many libraries where this research was conducted, to whom only a general thanks is possible. But others contributed aid and support beyond their daily duty. First of these is Margaret LeMire, without whose help, encouragement, patience under pressure, and skill in command of a computer this work could never have been done. Others to whom I owe thanks are Gary Aho, Professor of English, Univ. of Massachussetts at Amherst (rtd.); Chad and Suzanne Andersen, Melbourne; the late Freeman Bass of London, Collector; Helen Berger and her late husband Sanford, Carmel, California; Philip R. Bishop, proprietor of Mosher Books of Lancaster, Pennsylvania; Ronald Briggs, Salisbury, former Secretary, The William Morris Society, UK (rtd.); Leslie Caelli, Special Collections, Baillieu Library, University of Melbourne; Amy Cooper Cary, Rare Books, University of Iowa Libraries; Peter Cormack, Curator, William Morris Gallery; Joseph Dunlap, Librarian, Columbia University (rtd.); Peter Faulkner, Emeritus Honorary University Fellow, Exeter University; Colin Franklin, collector and bibliographer; the late William E. Fredeman, Emeritus Professor of English, UBC; Brian Gerrard, Rare Books, Monash University, Melbourne; Kenneth Goodwin, Professor of English, University of Queensland; Dr. John Gorman, San Diego, California; Ken Hounslow, Flinders University (rtd.); Dr. Margaret Hood, research assistant; Elizabeth James, Curator of Printed Books, BL; Danielle Kovacs, Curator, Special Collections, W. E. B. Du Bois Library, University of Massachusetts at Amherst; Norman Kelvin, Distinguished Professor of English, City University of New York (rtd.); Lorraine Janzen Kooistra, English Department, Nipissing University, Ontario; Mark Francis Lasner of Washington, DC; David LeMire, Adelaide; Dr. Marc LeMire, Adelaide; Ian McBain, Deputy Librarian, Flinders University; David McKitterick, Librarian, Trinity College, Cambridge; Ian Morrison, Senior Librarian, Heritage Collections, State Library of Tasmania; J. Moseley, Curator, St. Bride's Printing Library; Paul Naidich, Publications Editor, Special Collections, The University of California at Los Angeles; Dr. Brenda Niall, Monash University; Frances O'Neill of Heritage Victoria; Terry O'Neill, Monash University, Melbourne; William S. Peterson, Professor of English, University of Maryland (rtd.); John William Pye, of John William Pye Rare Books, Brockton, Massachusetts; Roger Simpson, Norwich; Merete Smith, Assistant Curator of Rare Books, Baillieu Library, University of Melbourne (rtd.); Peter Stansky, Emeritus Professor of History, Stanford University (rtd.); Susan Otis Thompson, Librarian, Butler Library, Columbia University (rtd.); Andrew Tuft of the Library Store, Flinders University; Jean-François Vilain, Collector, of Philadelphia; and Kim Scott Walwyn, OUP (rtd.); Susan Woodburn, Special Collections, Barr Smith Library, University of Adelaide.

Institutions

My special thanks to The Australian Research Grants Commission which funded this project through its first three years, when such assistance was particularly valuable.

Acknowledgements

I wish also to thank some publishers for permission to reprint previously published work:

Thoemmes Press, Bristol, for permission to reprint portions from my Introductions to the Thoemmes reprints of James Leatham's *William Morris: Master of Many Crafts* (Bristol, 1994) and Morris's *The Hollow Land and other Contributions to The Oxford and Cambridge Magazine* (Bristol, 1996).

The Bibliographical Society of Australia and New Zealand, for permission to reprint portions of my article 'A New Bibliography of William Morris', and a review of John Collins' *The Two Forgers: a Biography of Harry Buxton Forman & Thomas James Wise*, both printed in the Society's *Bulletin*, respectively, 17.4 (Fourth Quarter, 1993): 181–92, and 17.1 (1st Quarter, 1993): 47–52.

The Book Collector, and its editor, Nicolas Barker, for permission to use passages from my article, 'William Morris in America: a Publishing History from Archives', published in *The Book Collector*, 43.2 (Summer, 1994), 201–28.

Princeton University Press and Prof. Norman Kelvin for permission to quote from *The Collected Letters of William Morris*. 5 Parts in 4 vols. (Princeton, New Jersey: Princeton University Press, 1984–96).

The Society of Antiquaries of London, owners of the Morris copyright, for permission to quote from Morris's letters.

Special Collections, Information Division, The University of Melbourne, provided the images for Figures 4, 11, 23, 40, 43, 50, 53, 56, 57, 63, 71, 73–5, and 77, along with permission to use them here.

The Flinders University Library's photographer, Ashton Claridge, provided images and permission for their use for Figures 15–17, 20, 49, 52, 66–8, 85–6, and 92.

Except for the frontispiece, Figure 1, photographed by the British Library, all the remaining images were done by Margaret LeMire.

I am indebted to Oak Knoll Press for the enthusiasm and professionalism with which the book was undertaken and carried through, and particularly to Bob Fleck, John Lewis von Hoelle, and Geoffrey Matheson, all of whom played important roles. My thanks also to Wesley B. Tanner of Passim Editions, Ann Arbor, who did the design and composition and 'saw the book through the press' as the Victorians would have said.

Eugene D. LeMire
Emeritus Professor of English
The Flinders University of South Australia

Abbreviations List

ORGANISATIONS CITED, SPECIAL TERMS, WORKS, LIBRARIES AND ARCHIVAL COLLECTIONS USED

Other bibliographical terms used are defined in *Glaister's Glossary of the Book*, 2nd edn. rev. (Berkeley and Los Angeles: University of California Press, 1979).

ACES	The Arts and Crafts Exhibition Society.
ACES Essays	*Essays by Members of the Arts and Crafts Exhibition Society*, ed. William Morris (London: ACES, 1893; rptd. 1899, 1903).
ACES Cat.	*Arts and Crafts Exhibition Society. Exhibition Catalogues,* 5 vols. (London: The Society, 1888–90, 1893, 1896).
ALS	autograph letter signed.
American Book Design	Susan Otis Thompson, *American Book Design and William Morris* (New York: R. R. Bowker Company, 1977; rptd. 1996 with 'Foreword' by Jean-François Vilain).
Am. Lit. Gaz. and PC	*American Literary Gazette and Publishers' Circular* (Philadelphia) 1st and 15th each month until 18 Jan. 1872 when it was incorporated into *The Publishers' Weekly* (see *Pub. Weekly*, below).
Art of the Book	*William Morris and the Art of the Book*, ed. Paul Needham (New York: The Pierpont Morgan Library, 1976). This is the catalogue for an exhibition held at the Pierpont Morgan Library, New York, Sept.–Nov. 1976.
Bib.	*The Bibelot: A Reprint of Poetry and Prose for Book Lovers, chosen in part from scarce editions and sources not generally known.* A reprint series owned, managed, and edited from 1895 to 1915 by T. B. Mosher. Under its masthead Mosher pbd. monthly issues of literary texts, complete in either 1 or 2 issues. These were collected into annual volumes issued in January of the following year.
Bishop	Philip R. Bishop, *Thomas Bird Mosher: Pirate Prince of Publishers: A Comprehensive Bibliography & Source Guide to The Mosher Books, Reflecting England's National Literature & Design*, with an Introduction by William E. Fredeman (New York and London: Oak Knoll Books & The British Library, 1998). Mosher's publisher's devices and the decorative blocks in his Morris books are referred to here by 'Bishop No.', the numbers

Abbreviations List

	attached to each by Bishop (pp. 72–3), following the pattern established by S. C. Cockerell for the KP.
Bowers	Fredson Bowers, *Principles of Bibliographical Description*, New York: Russell & Russell Inc., 1962 (1949).
BLC	*The British Library Catalogue.*
Broc.	The Brocade Series, a series of 50 titles, including 9 Morris titles, selected, edited, and published from 1895 to 1905 by Thomas B. Mosher of Portland, Maine.
BSR	*The Bookseller* (London).
BSR (US)	*The Bookseller* (US).
Cary	Melbert B. Cary, *A Bibliography of The Village Press Including An Account of the Genesis of the Press by Frederic W. Goudy and a Portion of the 1903 Diary of Will Ransom, Co-Founder* (New York: Press of the Woolly Whale, 1981; 1st pbd. 1938).
Chiswick Arch.	Chiswick Press Archive, Dept. of Manuscripts, The British Library, BL (Add.) MS 50912–25; 41960A, B, and C; 41895–96, 41928, 41956.
Christie's Catalogue	*The Estelle Doheny Collection . . . Part VI Printed Books and Manuscripts Concerning William Morris and His Circle*, to be sold on 19 May, 1989 (New York: Christie, Manson and Woods International Inc., 1989).
Cockerell	S. C. Cockerell, 'A Short Description of the Kelmscott Press' and 'An Annotated List of All the Books Printed at the Kelmscott Press in the Order in Which They Were Issued', 1st pbd. in *A Note by William Morris on His Aims in Founding the Kelmscott Press* (London: Kelmscott Press, 1898) and reprinted in Sparling (the latter is the version used here; see below).
Cockerell Papers	The diaries and correspondence of Sydney Carlyle Cockerell, 151 vols. BL (Add.) MS 52623–52773.
Colbeck Collection	*A Bookman's Catalogue: The Norman Colbeck Collection of Nineteenth-Century and Edwardian Poetry and 'Belles Lettres' in the Special Collections of the University of British Columbia*, ed. and compiled by Norman Colbeck, 2 vols. (Vancouver: University of British Columbia Press, 1987).
Collins	John Collins, 'Harry Buxton Forman and William Morris: A Preliminary Enquiry', *The Book Collector.* 21 (Winter, 1972), 502–23.
Commonweal	*The Commonweal, the Official Journal of the Socialist League*, 1885–90.
Coupe	Robert L. M. Coupe, *Illustrated Editions of the Works of William Morris in English: A Descriptive Bibliography* (London and New Castle, Del.: The British Library and the Oak Knoll Press, 2002).
CW	*The Collected Works of William Morris*, 24 vols. Edited and Introduced by May Morris. (London: Longmans, Green and Co., 1910–15).

Abbreviations List

DF	The Democratic Federation, the name changed to the Social Democratic Federation at the Annual Conference of 4 Aug. 1884.
Dunlap 1	Joseph R. Dunlap, 'The Road to Kelmscott: William Morris and the Book Arts before the Founding of the Kelmscott Press', Ph.D. thesis (New York: Columbia University, 1972).
Dunlap 2	*The Book That Never Was* (New York: Oriole Editions, 1971).
Eng. Cat.	*The English Catalogue of Books* (London, compiled from *Pub. Circ.*, see below).
Enquiry	John Carter and Graham Pollard, *An Enquiry into the Nature of Certain Nineteenth Century Pamphlets* (London: Constable and Company, Limited, 1934); Second Edn., which is the version used here, ed. Nicolas Barker and John Collins (London: Scolar Press, 1983).
EP	*The Earthly Paradise*.
Faulkner	P. Faulkner (ed.), *William Morris: The Critical Heritage* (London: Routledge and Kegan Paul, 1973).
FL	The "Freedom" Library, a series of publications originating from the publishers of *Freedom, A Journal Of Anarchist Communism*.
FP	fine paper.
Gaskell	Philip Gaskell, *A New Introduction to Bibliography* (Oxford: The Clarendon Press 1985; 1st pbd. 1972).
Goodwin	Kenneth L. Goodwin, *A Preliminary Handlist of Manuscripts and Documents of William Morris* (London: WMS, 1983).
Gordon	Walter Kelly Gordon, 'A Critical Selected Edition of William Morris's "Oxford and Cambridge Magazine (1856)"', Ph.D. thesis (University of Pennsylvania, 1960).
Ham. Min. Book	The Hammersmith Minute Books, SL and HSS, BL (Add.) MS 45891–45893.
Hatch	Brenton L. Hatch, *A Checklist of the Publications of Thomas Bird Mosher of Portland, Maine* (Amherst: University of Massachusetts Press, 1966).
HBF	Harry Buxton Forman, *The Books of William Morris Described with Some Account of His Doings in Literature and in the Allied Crafts* (London: Hollings, 1897; rptd. 1969).
Henderson	Philip Henderson (ed.), *The Letters of William Morris to His Family and Friends* (London: Longmans, Green and Co., 1950).
HSL	The Hammersmith Socialist Library, a series of publications issued by the Hammersmith Socialist Society.
HSR	*Hammersmith Socialist Record*. ed. Sam Bullock (London: The Hammersmith Socialist Society, 1891–3), the 'monthly sheet' of the Society.

Abbreviations List

HSS	Hammersmith Socialist Society.
IISH	International Institute of Social History, Amsterdam.
JC	John Johnson Collection, MS e. 3., New Bodley Library, Oxford University.
Juvenilia	Florence S. Boos (ed.), *The Juvenilia of William Morris: with a Checklist and Unpublished Early Poems* (New York and London: The William Morris Society, 1983).
JWMS	*Journal of the William Morris Society* (London: WMS, 1961–). Title altered in 2002 to *The Journal of William Morris Studies*.
Kilgour	Raymond L. Kilgour, *Messrs. Roberts Brothers: Publishers* (Ann Arbor: University of Michigan Press, 1952).
KP	Kelmscott Press.
KP Biblio.	William S. Peterson, *A Bibliography of the Kelmscott Press* (Oxford: The Clarendon Press, 1985 rptd. with corrections; first issued 1984). The numbering system used here to describe the various decorative borders and ornaments of the KP books is the same as that used and added to by Peterson (see his p. xxxiii). It is taken from the chronological numbering of borders (with an 'a' added to the number for verso borders) first used in Cockerell's 'An Annotated List of All the Books Printed at the Kelmscott Press . . .', first pbd. in *Note by William Morris on His Aims in Founding the Kelmscott Press*. (Hammersmith: KP, 1898; rptd. in Sparling (see below for the version used here).
KP Hist.	William S. Peterson, *The Kelmscott Press: A History* (Oxford: The Clarendon Press, 1991).
Larremore	Thomas A. Larremore, 'An American Typographical Tragedy—the Imprints of Frederick Conrad Bursch' [in 2 parts, I. *The "Literary Collector" Periods* [and] II. Hillacre House] *The Papers of the Bibliographical Society of America* 43 (1st and 2nd Quarter 1949), 1–38, 111–72 (New York: The Society, 1949).
LCBEL	Longmans Class Books of English Literature, a series begun in 1905 and extending through the 1920s.
LCC.	London County Council.
LeMire	Eugene D. LeMire, 'Introduction' to *The Hollow Land and Other Contributions to the 'Oxford and Cambridge Magazine'* (Bristol: Thoemmes Press, 1996).
Lethaby	W. R. Lethaby, *Philip Webb and His Work*. (Oxford: Oxford University Press, 1935; rptd. 1980).
Letters	Norman Kelvin (ed.), *The Collected Letters of William Morris*, 4 vols., 5 Parts (Princeton: Princeton University Press, 1984–96).
Longmans Accts.	Unpbd. Longmans MS accounts in the W. H. Smith and Son Bequest, Library of the William Morris Society, Kelmscott House, 26 Upper Mall, Hammersmith, Lon-

	don. These accts. include several annual accounts from the New York branch.
Longmans Arch.	Archives of the House of Longman, 1794–1914, The Library, University of Reading, UK; published on microfilm by Chadwyck-Healey, 37 reels, 1981. Both the original archive and the microfilm version are used here, the latter with references to reel numbers.
LP	large paper.
LPL	Longmans Pocket Library, a series begun in 1905 and running through the 1920s. It includes fourteen Morris titles in eighteen volumes.
Mackail	J. W. Mackail. *The Life of William Morris*, 2 vols. (London: Longmans, 1899; many times reprinted).
Memorials	GB-J [Georgiana Burne-Jones], *Memorials of Edward Burne-Jones*, 2 vols. (London: Macmillan and Co., Limited, St Martin's Street, 1912).
MM	*William Morris: Artist, Writer, Socialist*, 2 vols. ed. May Morris (Oxford: Basil Blackwell, 1936; rptd. New York, 1966).
'Morris in America'	Eugene D. LeMire, 'William Morris in America: A Publishing History from Archives', *The Book Collector*, 43/2 (Summer, 1994), 208–28.
NAAA	The National Association for the Advancement of Art and Its Application to Industry.
Nowell-Smith	Simon Nowell-Smith, *International Copyright Law and the Publisher in the Reign of Queen Victoria* (Oxford: The Clarendon Press, 1968).
NUC	*National Union Catalogue*, Library of Congress.
OUP	Oxford University Press.
Pearson	Richard Pearson, 'William Morris, 1834–96', in vol. 4.3 of *The Index of English Literary Manuscripts* (London: Mansell, 1993), 473–747.
Peterson	William S. Peterson (ed.), *The Ideal Book: Essays and Lectures on the Arts of the Book by William Morris* (Berkeley and Los Angeles, California: The University of California Press, 1982).
Proctor	Robert Proctor's MS Notebook for a Morris Bibliography, BL Case 43.
Pub. Circ.	*The Publishers' Circular* (London, 1837–).
Pub. Weekly	*Publishers' Weekly*. Successor to *The American Literary Gazette and Publishers' Circular*. Philadelphia, pbd. on the 1st and 15th each month until Jan. 18, 1872 when it is incorporated into *The Publishers' Weekly* and pbd. in New York.
PW	The Poetical Works of William Morris: an unnumbered series of eleven uniform volumes, the first ten issued by Longmans, Green and Co. in 1896 and the eleventh, *Beowulf*, in August 1898.

Pye	John William Pye, *A Bibliography of American Editions of William Morris* (Brockton, Mass.: John William Pye Rare Books, 1993).
Quaritch Catalogue	*A Catalogue of Books and Pamphlets from the library of Maurice Buxton Forman, with an introduction by Graham Pollard: Cat. No. 926.* Offered for sale by Bernard Quaritch Ltd. 5–8 Lower John Street, Golden Square, London, W1R 4AU (London: Bernard Quaritch, 1973); items acquired at the Solomon Sale, Sotheby's, 1972.
Quinn Catalogue	*Complete Catalogue of the Library of John Quinn, Sold by Auction in Five Parts.* 5 vols. (New York: The Anderson Galleries, 1923–4) rptd. in 2 vols., 1924. The copy used here is the second reprint in 2 vols. (New York: Lemma Corporation, 1969).
Ransom	Will Ransom, *The Private Presses and Their Books* (New York: Philip C. Duschnes, 1963; 1st pbd. 1923).
R and T	Reeves and Turner, 196, Strand. After 6 Sept. 1893 the address changes to 6 Wellington Street, Strand.
R and T Arch.	Archives of Messrs Reeves and Turner, 196, Strand, and of William Reeves, 185, Fleet Street and later 83 Charing Cross Road; in the Collection of Mr William Reeves, Bookseller, No. 1a Norbury Crescent, Norbury, London. Since these archives were consulted in Norbury, they have been deposited in the BL. Being as yet uncatalogued, they are currently arranged in 32 boxes as Deposit 9356.
RB	Roberts Brothers of 143 Washington Street, Boston. Moved in 1885 to Roberts House, 3 Somerset Street, Boston.
Roberts Arch.	The Roberts Brothers Archive, The Houghton Library, Harvard University, Cambridge, Mass.
Rpts. Bib.	Reprints from "The Bibelot", a Mosher series of 12 titles, of which 6 are by Morris, selected, edited, and published from 1897 to 1902 by Thomas B. Mosher of Portland, Maine.
Scott	Temple Scott [I. H. Isaacs], *A Bibliography of the Works of William Morris* (London: Geo. Bell & Sons, 1897; reprinted 1977).
SDF	The later name of The Democratic Federation (see DF, above).
Sequel	Nicolas Barker and John Collins, *A Sequel to 'An Enquiry into the Nature of Certain Nineteenth Century Pamphlets' by John Carter and Graham Pollard: The Forgeries of H. Buxton Forman & T. J. Wise Re-examined* (London & Berkeley: Scolar Press, 1983).
SL	The Socialist League.
SLA	Socialist League Archive, The International Institute of Social History, Amsterdam. Also on microfilm. Unless otherwise indicated, references here are to the microfilm edition, pbd. in 37 reels by International Research Publications.

'SL Leaflets'	Eugene D. LeMire, 'The Socialist League Leaflets and Manifestoes: An Annotated Checklist', *The International Review of Social History*, 22/1 (1977), 21–9.
Smith Arch.	The files of the Morris Estate, now held in the Library of the William Morris Society, having been given to the Society by W. H. Smith and Son, in whose strongroom the files had been kept from the time when C. H. St John Hornby was a trustee to the Estate. Hornby was also founder of the Ashendene Press and a director of W. H. Smith and Son.
Socialist Diary	Florence Boos, ed. *William Morris's Socialist Diary* (London and New York: London History Workshop Centre, 1985; 1st pbd. 1981).
Sonnenschein Arch.	The Swan Sonnenschein & Co. Archive at the University of Reading.
SP	The Socialist Platform: a series of SL pamphlets (1885–90) of which Morris and Bax were the general editors as well as contributors.
SPAB	The Society for the Protection of Ancient Buildings.
Sparling	Henry Halliday Sparling, *The Kelmscott Press and William Morris, Master-Craftsman* (London: Macmillan and Co., Limited, 1924); two articles by Cockerell first pbd. in *A Note by William Morris on His Aims in Founding the Kelmscott Press* (KP 1898) are here reprinted.
SPGB	The Socialist Party of Great Britain.
Tanselle 1	G. Thomas Tanselle, 'The Bibliographical Description of Patterns', *Studies in Bibliography*, 23 (1970), 71–102.
Tanselle 2	'The Identification of Type Faces in Bibliographical Description', *Studies in Bibliography*, 60 (1966).
t.e.g.	top edge gilt.
Thompson	Edward P. Thompson, *William Morris: Romantic to Revolutionary* (London: Lawrence and Wishart, 1955; revised, Merlin Press, 1977); the revised version is used here unless otherwise indicated.
TL	The Torch Library, a series of publications issued by the publishers of *The Torch: A Revolutionary Journal of Anarchist-Communism*.
Tributes	*Tributes to William Morris on the Publication of 'The Earthly Paradise'* (New York: Roberts Brothers, 1869).
Two Forgers	John Collins, *The Two Forgers: A Biography of Harry Buxton Forman & Thomas James Wise* (New Castle (DE): Oak Knoll Books, 1992).
Unpublished Lectures	*The Unpublished Lectures of William Morris*, ed. and comp. by Eugene D. LeMire (Detroit: Wayne State University Press, 1969); with a Calendar and a Bibliography of Morris's public speeches appended.

Abbreviations List

V and A	The Victoria and Albert Museum, London.
Vallance	Aymer Vallance, *William Morris: His Art, His Writings, and His Public Life. A Record* (London: George Bell and Sons, 1897).
Walsdorf	John J. Walsdorf, *William Morris in Private Press and Limited Editions: A Descriptive Bibliography of Books By and About William Morris, 1891–1981* (Phoenix, Arizona.: Oryx Press, 1993).
WC	World's Classics, Oxford University Press.
WMG	William Morris Gallery, Walthamstow, London.
WMS	William Morris Society, Kelmscott House, Upper Mall, Hammersmith.

LIBRARIES, PRIVATE COLLECTIONS, AND INSTITUTIONS USED

AUSTRALIA

The symbols given are those used by NUCOS; the first letter indicates the nation, state, or territory; the following letters refer to a particular library or collection.

ABN	Australian Bibliographical Network (computerised)

Australian Capital Territory

ANL	Australian National Library
ANU	Australian National University Library

New South Wales

NNC	University of Newcastle Library
NPar	NSW Parliamentary Library
NU	University of Sydney, Fisher Library

South Australia

SFU	Flinders University Library
SPar	South Australian Parliamentary Library
SSL	State Library of South Australia
SU	University of Adelaide, Barr Smith Library

Abbreviations List

Victoria

VMoU	Monash University Library
VPar	Parliamentary Library of Victoria
VSL	State Library of Victoria
VU	University of Melbourne, Baillieu Library

Western Australia

WMDU	Murdoch University Library, Perth

Private Collection (Australia)

LeM	Eugene D. LeMire, Adelaide

USA AND CANADA

The symbols given are those used by the *National Union Catalogue* (*NUC*): the first letter indicates the state; the following letters indicate a particular library or collection.

California

CSfU	The University of San Francisco
CLU	University of California at Los Angeles, including the Emery Walker Collection and the MacKenzie Bell Collection (neither abbreviated)
CLU-C	University of California at Los Angeles, William Andrews Clark Memorial Library
CSmH	Henry E. Huntington Library, San Marino, California
CSt	Stanford University Libraries, Palo Alto
Cst-H	Stanford University, Hoover Institution
CU-B	University of California, Berkeley, The Bancroft Library

Connecticut

CtY	Yale University, New Haven

District of Columbia

DLC	US Library of Congress: General collection, Copyright Division, Pennell-Whistler Collection

Abbreviations List

Illinois

IEN	Northwestern University, Evanston

Massachusetts

MH-H	Harvard University, Cambridge, Houghton Library
MU	University of Massachusetts, Amherst (including the Collection of Cedric L. Robinson, Windsor, Conn.)

Michigan

MiD	Detroit Public Library
MiDW	Wayne State University Library, Detroit

New Jersey

NjP	Princeton University, Princeton; including Seeley G. Mudd MS Collection; Firestone Library; Janet C. Troxell Pre-Raphaelite Collection.
NjR	Rutgers, The State University of New Jersey, including the Symington Collection, with Wise-Forman correspondence.

New York

NN or NYPL	New York Public Library
NNBerg	New York Public Library, Berg Collection
NNCButler	Columbia University, Butler Library
NNPM	Pierpont Morgan Library

Pennsylvania

PPRF	Rosenbach Foundation, Philadelphia

Texas

TxU, HRC	University of Texas, Humanities Research Centre, Austin

PRIVATE COLLECTIONS (USA)

California

BGR	Sanford and Helen Berger Morris Collection, Kelmscott-on-the-Sea, Carmel. This Morris collection is now deposited in CSmH (see above)

New Hampshire

Dede	Donald Dede, Keene, New Hampshire

Abbreviations List

Pennsylvania

Bsp	Philip R. Bishop T. B. Mosher Collection, Millersville, Pa.
J-F V	Jean-François Vilain, Philadelphia

Canada

CaBVaU	University of British Columbia, Vancouver
An-C-TU	University of Toronto Library

Private Collection, Canada

Fdmn	The late Professor William E. Fredeman, Vancouver

The United Kingdom

Key to symbols used in K. L. Goodwin: *A Preliminary Handlist of Manuscripts and Documents of William Morris.*

Camb: Fitz	The Fitzwilliam Museum, Cambridge
Camb: Trin	Trinity College Library, Cambridge University
Camb: U	Cambridge University Library
Chelt: Walker	Cheltenham Municipal Museum and Art Gallery, The Emery Walker Collection.
Kelm	Kelmscott Manor, Kelmscott, Oxfordshire
BL (Ash.)	The British Library, The Ashley Library
BL (Add.)	The British Library, Additional Manuscripts
BL (MMB)	The British Library, The May Morris Bequest (Additional Manuscripts)
BL (RSG)	The British Library, William Morris Papers (The Robert Steele Gift) (Additional Manuscripts)
BL (RSG: Supp.)	The British Library, William Morris Papers (The Robert Steele Gift: Supplementary Volumes, Additional Manuscripts)
BL (HSSP)	The British Library, Hammersmith Socialist Society Papers (Additional Manuscripts)
BL (GBS)	The British Library, Bernard Shaw Papers (Additional Manuscripts)
BL (Cock.)	The British Library, The Cockerell Papers (Additional Manuscripts)

Abbreviations List

Bodl	Bodleian Library, Oxford
MML	Marx Memorial Library, London
StB	St Bride Printing Library (City of London Libraries)
WMG	The William Morris Gallery and Brangwyn Gift, Walthamstow
WMS	The William Morris Society, Kelmscott House, Hammersmith, London

Private Collection, London

Bass	Freeman Bass, Esq. (decd.), London

SCOTLAND

ABCL	Aberdeen Central Library
Aberd: Univ	University of Aberdeen, King's Library, James Leatham Arch.

THE NETHERLANDS

IISH	International Institute of Social History, Amsterdam: Max Nettlau Collection, Amsterdam
IISH, ASL	The Archives of the Socialist League, International Institute of Social History, Amsterdam
IISH, ASP	Andreas Scheu Papers, International Institute of Social History, Amsterdam
Amst: MEA	Marx-Engels Archives, International Institute of Social History, Amsterdam

Introduction

By the time of his death in October 1896, William Morris was both the most influential and the most famous 'bookman' of his age, being not only a writer of original verse and prose but also a translator, calligrapher, type and book designer, rubricator, printer, collector, and publisher. Two book-length bibliographies—the first by 'Temple Scott' (I. H. Isaacs) and the second by Harry Buxton Forman—appeared in the year after his death.[1] Despite scholarly advances—the discovery and identification of previously unpublished manuscripts, the unearthing of fugitive publications, the attribution to Morris of anonymous leaflets, pamphlets, and articles in periodicals—the general reader as well as the historian, critic, or collector has had no post-1897 revised and supplementary account of the original editions and no account of the texts first issued after 1897.

Though more than a century has passed since Morris's death and the publications of the first bibliographies, the purposes of a new bibliography remain the same as for Scott and Forman: to list and describe the Morris oeuvre as completely and accurately as possible. But now this requires the bibliographer to supplement and correct the Morris canon as inherited, to bring it into accord with what scholarship and the publishing industry have made of it both before and since 1897.

The term canon itself implies a primary interest in the texts that Morris created. The varied audience that shares an interest in Morris's publications determines what is included, how the canon is defined or limited. The textual critic and the editor are served by putting in order, with some distinguishing detail, the various editions, issues, and impressions of each title, including any variants within the entries. Such an account can also provide the general reader with a guide to the texts, through what is sometimes a bibliographical thicket of changing or exchanged titles, ambiguous or doubtful attributions, and uncertain or demonstrably incorrect dates of issue. The term canon also implies some strictures that apply here: where there has been uncertainty about authorship, only publications attributed to Morris with the authority of fact and argument are included. So, this bibliography is limited to those texts we know beyond reasonable doubt the author wrote, and only to complete versions of them. Except in the rare early cases when Morris approved of selected American editions (when without copyright no authorial intervention could be enforced anyway) abridged editions are not included. Where there has been disagreement, as with the disputed authorship of

---

1. See Temple Scott, *A Bibliography of the Works of William Morris* (London: Geo. Bell and Sons, 1897, rptd. in 1977; hereafter referred to as Scott, on which pseudonym see Appendix I-17); and H. Buxton Forman, *The Books of William Morris Described, with Some Account of His Doings in Literature and in the Allied Crafts* (London: Hollings, 1897, rptd. 1969; hereafter referred to as HBF).

three pieces in *The Oxford and Cambridge Magazine*, or where publications are attributed to Morris here for the first time—as is the case with 'The Meaning of Socialism' and several other pieces—a brief summary of the facts and argument for the attribution, with references, appears in the relevant entry.

A further limitation of the Morris canon also applies: only the work that Morris wrote for the public is listed and described, including those items that for one reason or another did not reach the public until after his death. Unless publication was approved by Morris, personal letters to his family and friends and internal organizational memoranda pursuant to business or political activities are excluded, even though in a number of instances such materials have been published posthumously. There are several examples of Morris granting such approval, one being T. J. Wise's production of a privately printed pamphlet, *Letters on Socialism* (see A-76.01). But letters to the press are included, each with a separate entry in Section D: Contributions to Periodicals. Being collections that include letters to the press, Philip Henderson's edition of *The Letters of William Morris to His Family and Friends* (London: Longmans, 1955) and Norman Kelvin's *The Collected Letters of William Morris* (5 parts in 4 vols.) Princeton: The Princeton University Press, 1984–96), are both entered in Section C: Collections and Selections (C-34 and 38, respectively). Lectures written and delivered, often on a number of occasions, even those never published by Morris, so far as is known, or never published entire, are included. The fact of public delivery is itself taken here as sufficient indication of the author's intent to bring these works before the public.

Besides the central concern to update, correct, and extend the Morris canon, decisions must be made, and revised, in response to standard bibliographical questions relating to textual matters and, therewith, the books as material objects: 'what Morris works were published in the period 1856 to 1915?' which leads on to, ' what do we need to know about them and their history?' 'Which questions need evidence of a directly bibliographical sort (from the books themselves) or a collateral kind (from archives, trade journals, biographies, diaries, correspondence, etc.) be collected?' and 'in what degree of detail?' 'To what sorts of readers should the work be addressed?' Taking that last question as an example of a typical difficulty illustrates that there are no single, all-purpose answers to these questions. And it is well to be aware of the larger and more complex constituency of readers, as described by Carter and Pollard:

> Collectors . . . form only a small minority, though a respected minority, among those for whom bibliography is a necessary tool. Students, scholars, critics, biographers, bibliographers, historians—any of these may for one purpose or another have need to rely on the accurate description and classification of the published editions of a piece of literature. They will not be concerned whether its first edition is worth a shilling or a pound.[2]

Some readers will be concerned to know whether the copy of *News from Nowhere* they have in hand has all the pages and parts of the first edition published in Boston in 1890, while others will

---

2. *The Firm of Charles Ottley, Landon & Co.: Footnote to 'An Enquiry'* (London: Rupert Hart-Davis, 1948), 14.

wonder whether their copy includes the considerable revisions made by Morris for the second edition when it was revised, set, printed, and issued in London in 1891. Others will want to know whether it derives directly and without change from the original text as published serially in *The Commonweal, the Official Journal of the Socialist League*, 1885–90 (hereafter referred to simply as *Commonweal*), as was the 1st edn. Such readers as these, and others, as represented by their interests and their bibliographical questions, have remained my constant companions throughout, bearing from beginning to end upon the necessary decisions of what to include, and how much, where, and how to record it. Inevitably, choices set limits, but limits must be set in order to define the task and to achieve an exhaustive account within the limits defined. This Introduction concludes with the detail of the general organization, formulary, and definitions, these being the ways adopted here to deal with both a complex readership and the special problems posed for the bibliographer by Morris's variety and his unconcern for bibliographical tidiness.

The larger historical background affecting the Morris canon and the ways it has come before the public are the central parts of this introduction: copyright regulations governing the issue of Morris's books in England and the USA; Morris's relations with the publishers and printers of his original editions; the extension of coverage here to 1915, 20 years after Morris's death, thus including the posthumous Morris books issued by the Estate, those issued as contributions to the revolution in printing, and those that were subjects of forgery, piracy, or sophistication.

The question of copyright, the legal protection of Morris's intellectual property, is obviously a crucial factor in the transmission of Morris's works on both sides of the Atlantic both before and after his death. Since intellectual property rights were a basic consideration in many of the decisions of what to publish and when, questions of copyright impinge repeatedly in the body of the bibliography, making an early explanation and comparison of the British and US laws necessary to an understanding of the legal-economic background to Morris's enterprise in the making and marketing of his books.

In the USA, the absence until 1891 of an international copyright law led to the development of an informal or extra-legal system, a sort of 'gentlemen's agreement' between publishers. The agreement was that whichever American publisher first publicly undertook to publish a foreign (usually English) author was considered to have established an exclusive right to publish that author's works. Since foreign authors generally had no copyright in the USA, they had no say in the matter, the agreement being protective only of the American publisher's 'right', not the author's. This agreement ensured that for the last half of Morris's life his American books, from *The Life and Death of Jason* in 1867 to *The Wood beyond the World* in 1895, were published, with only four exceptions,[3] by the same publisher, Roberts Brothers of Boston. Their connection with Morris and, following his death, with the Morris Estate, ended when the Roberts Brothers firm went out of business in 1897,

---

3. These included two school anthologies: *Atalanta's Race and other Tales from 'The Earthly Paradise'* (see C-2); *The Life and Death of Jason*. Abridged by A. F. Blaisdell (New York: Clark & Maynard, [1885]); an anthology for the general reader: *William Morris: Poet, Artist, Socialist: A Selection from His Writings together with a Sketch of the Man* (see C-4); and Morris and Bax's collaboration, *Socialism: Its Growth and Outcome* (see A-68.01). Morris seems to have known and approved of all of these, and the general anthology had his active cooperation. Each was formally registered for copyright by its US publisher.

selling their list and other assets, such as warehoused stocks of books, etc., to another well-known Boston firm, Little, Brown and Company, which is still a presence among American publishers. In 1899 Longmans of New York bought the plates of twelve volumes set in Boston for Roberts and continued to print from some of them for years thereafter.[4]

Though the first US International Copyright Act, the Chace Act, became law in 1891, neither Morris nor his first American publisher went through the difficult and expensive process required to gain copyright there. The basic difference between the British and the American systems was that in America copyright could only be established by going through certain procedures. In Britain copyright was much simpler and less expensive. An author's intellectual property had, and still has, the automatic protection of the law both before publication (in perpetuity) and afterwards for the periods specified in copyright legislation and altered from time to time by legislation. In both jurisdictions copies of publications were required by law to be deposited in certain government institutions: in Britain the British Library (in Morris's time and the century thereafter called The British Museum) and various other United Kingdom national and university libraries, in the USA in the Library of Congress. But only in the USA was that deposit a requirement for copyright. In Britain, until a work was published, or sold, the 'right to copy', that is to publish, unless sold or leased, was the property of the author and his or her heirs and assigns, and that was by law protected. In America nothing was copyright until the applications were lodged, the fee paid, and the required two copies, printed in the United States, deposited in the Library of Congress. In Morris's later years and for the twenty years after his death, American law provided protections roughly equal to those of British law: twenty-eight years, extending to forty-two years if the author or his immediate family survived the first allotted span. After passage of the US Chace Act, authors seeking copyright in both countries had to make arrangements for a simultaneous issue in both countries (since Britain had matching legislation to apply to foreign authors, in practical terms American). And it follows that any of the Morris titles previously published in England were ineligible for copyright in the USA. All this renders it doubtful whether Morris and his earliest British publishers thought American sales would justify the trouble. And the 'gentlemen's agreement' made it needless for Roberts Brothers to register copyright. It being impossible for Morris, in the era of the 'gentlemen's agreement' to order a proper audit of his pre-1891 accounts, it is doubtful whether either he or his advisers could have known precisely how many of his books were sold in the US. Roberts' usual strategy of first importing English sheets and selling them in an American binding before investing in an American setting suggests that Morris's American sales were profitable.

But while Roberts never applied for copyright on their Morris books, the firm made efforts to be seen to be fair to the foreign authors whose works they published. The Roberts notepaper accompanying Morris's royalty payment on 25 January 1886 had a quotation as a heading: "'There must be an

---

4. The twelve sets involved eleven titles, with 8° and 12° versions of *The Glittering Plain* (Ledger Book, 1894–9, Roberts Arch.).

international copyright agreement. England has done her part, and I am confident the time is not far distant when America will do hers. It becomes the character of a great country, firstly, because it is justice; secondly, because without it you can never have, and keep, a literature of your own." — Charles Dickens, from a Speech.'

Roberts' frequent use of the phrase 'Author's Edition' in their Morris books from 1871 on, and in the books of other English authors, was modelled on that of Baron Tauchnitz, who initiated his Tauchnitz International Editions in 1841 with royalty contracts negotiated with his authors prior to publication. His bibliographers say he tried, 'through various phraseology [including 'Author's Edition'] on the title, [to ensure] some protection for writers in an obstinately protectionist country [the USA] that refused to acknowledge foreign copyrights'.[5]

One defect of Morris's dependence on F. S. Ellis, his English publisher at this time, for all the arrangements with Roberts was that he was unaware, as he would not have been in later years, of what the words 'Author's Edition' were intended to signify. Forman says, 'I do not understand the words "Author's Edition"; nor did Morris, who first showed me the book and told me with an amused air that he had not been consulted about it.'[6] What it meant, or was intended to mean was expressed in a sentence from a pamphlet published by Roberts titled, *Tributes to William Morris*, a sentence which probably would have surprised the poet, had he read it: 'Mr. Morris's Poems are published in America by arrangement with him, and he receives a stated copyright on all sold'.[7]

In England, copyright on Morris's earliest titles, one after another, began to lapse in 1903 as the copyright limits defined in the 1842 Copyright Act were reached. That Act specified that copyright remained for seven years after the author's death or forty-two years after publication, whichever was longer. Applied to Morris's first publications—*The Oxford and Cambridge Magazine* (1856) and *The Defence of Guenevere and Other Poems* (1858)—the forty-two years ended in 1898 and 1900, respectively, but the seven years copyright after his death extended that for both to 3 October 1903.

As a writer whose interests always took a practical turn, Morris was from the first engaged with the existing commercial institutions, the companies of publishers and printers that provided the necessary services by which the writer's work makes its way to the market and then the public. Over the forty years of his career as a 'bookman', from the days of *The Oxford and Cambridge Magazine* of 1856 until his death in 1896, he had arrangements with one American and four successive English publishers and their associated printers for the manufacture and marketing of his major works. The contractual agreements with his major publishers obviously left unrestricted Morris's writing for the various organizations, like the Society for the Protection of Ancient Buildings (SPAB), the Socialist

---

5. William B. Todd and Ann Bowden, *Tauchnitz International Editions in English 1841–1955: A Bibliographical History* (New York: Bibliographical Society of America, 1988), p. 51. Here the abbreviation for pages in footnote references is omitted throughout, except when the source is a bibliography, where confusion can result from the presence of item numbers as well as page numbers.
6. HBF, pp. 148–9.
7. *Tributes to William Morris on the Publication of 'The Earthly Paradise'* (New York: Roberts Brothers, 1869), 2; hereafter referred to as *Tributes*.

League (SL), or the Eastern Question Association (EQA), who published his work for them in their usual organs or in pamphlet or leaflet form.

In Boston, as already noted, Roberts Brothers published a selection of Morris's books, using various printers to begin with, but mainly Welch, Bigelow and Co. of the University Press, Cambridge, Mass. The publisher continued that association, finally settling on John Wilson and Son, who in 1879 succeeded Welch, Bigelow at the University Press.

In London, which included the rest of Great Britain and its Dominions for all practical and legal or copyright purposes during the period from 1856 through 1915, Morris's main publishers and printers were as follows: (1) 1856–67: Bell and Daldy and their printer, the Chiswick Press; (2) 1868–85: F. S. Ellis, who began as a one-owner operation (1868–71), but also worked with partners as Ellis and Green (1872), then as F. S. Ellis again (November 1872–3), and Ellis and White (1873–85). His chosen printer was known, first, as Strangeways and Walden (1868–71), then John Strangeways (1872–81), and finally, as Strangeways and Sons (1882–96 and after Morris's death); (3) 1885–June 1896: Reeves and Turner, who used various printers: Strangeways, The Ballantyne Press, and The Chiswick Press; and (4) June 1896–1938: Longmans, Green and Co., who usually employed either the Ballantyne or the Chiswick Press for their Morris books, depending on whether a popular or a de luxe edition was called for. Longmans became Morris's regular publisher in June 1896, and continued in that role under direction of the Morris Trustees into the nineteen-thirties, though they declined to undertake publication of May Morris's two-volume collection of her father's fugitive and unpublished writing.[8] After long delays searching for another publisher, the project was undertaken by Sir Basil Blackwell, whose Shakespeare Head Press issued it in two volumes in 1936. When May Morris died in 1938, the only surviving heir of the Estate set up by her father, the Estate was wound up with the remaining property being disposed of in her will, where she passed on the Morris copyright to The Society of Antiquaries of London.

The first business connection Morris made with a major publisher was occasioned by his sponsorship as an undergraduate of *The Oxford and Cambridge Magazine*. In the mid-1850s, many, perhaps most publishers were still also proprietors of new and used bookshops. Bell and Daldy was such a firm, and as a specialist provider of university textbooks to Oxford and Cambridge had a distinct advantage for Morris and his friends, given the anticipated audience for their magazine. The senior partner was the same George Bell who became more widely known later as the head of George Bell and Sons.[9] In 1854, two years before he became publisher of the *Magazine*, Bell acquired a Cambridge bookshop from J. & J. J. Deighton, Booksellers to the University, which then became Deighton, Bell & Co. Later in the same year the additional work following from that led Bell to take a partner, Frederick R. Daldy, in the publishing side of the

---

8. *William Morris: Artist, Writer, Socialist*, 2 vols. ed. May Morris (see A-130.01; hereafter referred to as MM).
9. On George Bell and his businesses see Edward Bell's *George Bell, Publisher: A Brief Memoir* (London: Printed for private circulation at the Chiswick Press, 1924); and 'Obituary: George Bell', *The Bookseller*, No. 397 (Dec. 1890), 1375–7 (hereafter referred to as *BSR*).

business, to restyle the firm Messrs. Bell and Daldy, and to aim at supplying textbooks to both the ancient universities.

Besides their direct access to both Oxford and Cambridge University staff and students, Bell and Daldy had another advantage that Morris would probably have been aware of when considering them as possible publishers of *The Oxford and Cambridge Magazine*. George Bell had a longstanding commercial and personal relationship with the two Charles Whittinghams (the uncle and the nephew). Their Chiswick Press, generally acknowledged at the time as the best of the Victorian commercial printers, regularly did Bell's personal printing as well as Bell and Daldy's work, which included Morris's *Magazine* and his first two books of poetry. His experience then with the Chiswick Press led Morris and Burne-Jones in 1867 to choose that firm to print the two trial sheets—one in Whittingham's adapted Caslon and the other in the Basle type—for the abortive folio first edition of *The Earthly Paradise* (*EP*),[10] and in 1888–9 to print *The House of the Wolfings* and *The Roots of the Mountains*, Morris's main experiments leading to the 'typographical adventure'[11] of the Kelmscott Press.

In 1858, having failed in the previous year to arrange publication of *The Defence of Guenevere and Other Poems* through Macmillan,[12] Morris entered into an agreement for publication with Bell and Daldy. The terms of their contract have not been found, but they seem most likely to have been based on the standard royalty contract, with the publisher putting up the capital for the venture and the author being paid a percentage on copies sold, usually after the publisher had recovered expenses. The *Defence* did not sell well, and of an edition of five hundred copies, Mackail says, 'some two hundred and fifty were sold and given away, and the remainder of the edition stayed long on the publisher's shelves'.[13] The result, Mackail implies, was a considerable loss to the publisher.

So, in 1867 when Morris produced his next book, *The Life and Death of Jason*, Bell and Daldy proved unwilling to repeat all aspects of the experience of nine years previous. They changed their agreement with Morris to an 'on commission' basis.[14] This eliminated their own risk by requiring the author to put up the capital, the publisher acting as the organizing and marketing agent for a fixed percentage, or 'commission' of the expenses involved, the commission usually being between ten and fifteen percent. The new arrangement, however, proved to be the undoing of the relationship of the publisher George Bell with Morris precisely at the verge of his greatest popular successes as a poet. Mackail explains how that happened:

> When the first edition of "Jason" was published in 1867, Morris gave a copy to his friend F. S. Ellis, remarking that it was hard luck to have to publish a poem at one's own expense. Bell and Daldy, the pub-

---

10. See Joseph R. Dunlap, *The Book That Never Was* (New York: Oriole Editions, 1971), 28 (hereafter referred to as Dunlap 2).
11. Morris used this phrase to describe his plans to establish the KP when he wrote to recruit William Bowden to help in establishing the Press (see *Letters*, iii. 252). On Bowden see the *Printer* field in A-50.02.
12. See Morris to Alexander Macmillan (*The Collected Letters of William Morris*, ed. Norman Kelvin (i. 30, 32; hereafter referred to as *Letters*).
13. J. W. Mackail, *The Life of William Morris*, i. 130; hereafter referred to as Mackail.
14. Mackail implies such a change was made (see the passage quoted). But Forman says, 'up to that time [the publication of *Jason*], Morris had risked his own money on his poetic ventures' (HBF, p. 47), which is clearly incorrect so far as *The Defence of Guenevere* is concerned.

lishers of the Oxford and Cambridge Magazine and of "The Defence of Guenevere", had brought "Jason" out, and in view of their experiences with the earlier volume it was not surprising that they should decline to undertake any risk. But when the first edition was exhausted, as it was within a few months, Mr Ellis had become his adviser, and the publishers paid a substantial sum for the right to print a second. After this second edition, "Jason" was transferred to Ellis, who had already entered into an agreement to publish "The Earthly Paradise".[15]

This remark by Morris to Ellis is what reveals that his *Jason* was published 'on commission'. Morris may not have been aware beforehand that when a book proves unexpectedly popular and profitable, 'on commission' arrangements could be to the author's advantage, since the publisher's share was based on expenses, not on sales as it is in royalty agreements. It was for this reason that G. B. Shaw came eventually to publish all his books 'on commission'. But he is an exception to the general belief that it is only because the tyro author is driven by the need to get published that 'on commission' contracts were made, and are still.[16]

Frederick Startridge Ellis had a much longer tenure as Morris's publisher, from 1867 to 1885, when he retired from business. As well as a publisher, he was a dealer in and scholar of rare books and manuscripts, the author of two studies of medieval books of hours. He wrote the catalogue of the Huth collection (a large and valuable library assembled by Henry Huth, 1815–78, and his son Alfred, 1850–1910) and edited several of the medieval books issued in Kelmscott Press editions. Introduced to Morris by Swinburne, and well acquainted with the Pre-Raphaelites—he became Rossetti's publisher in 1870—Ellis soon became one of Morris's closest friends. When Rossetti gave up his half share in the lease of Kelmscott Manor, Ellis became co-tenant with Morris, an arrangement that lasted from mid-1874 to 1884, when deteriorating health forced Ellis to withdraw, and in 1885 to retire from business. Sharing with Morris the enjoyments of the place—the fishing in the River Thames flowing past one side of the property and the glories of the Tudor manor house—Ellis joined the inner circle that surrounded the poet in his later years and finally became one of the three executors of the Morris Estate. Oswald Doughty says of him that 'By all he was respected for his personal integrity, geniality and kindly nature, and his clients invariably became his friends.'[17]

As the publisher of the first edition of *The Earthly Paradise*, it fell to Ellis to overcome the difficulties posed by Morris's unforeseen extensions of the poem after 1868 when the first volume was issued, announcing that the work would be completed in two volumes. Before the end of 1869, the growth of some of the stories under the poet's hand, particularly 'The Lovers of Gudrun', had made a third volume necessary, posing some difficult problems.[18] The great success of the poem was the central feature of Ellis's time as Morris's publisher. While no new edition, other than Roberts' Bos-

---

15. Mackail, i. 194.
16. See Philip Gaskell, *A New Introduction to Bibliography* (Oxford: The Clarendon Press, 1985 (1972), 300; hereafter referred to as Gaskell.
17. Oswald Doughty, *The Letters of Dante Gabriel Rossetti to His Publisher, F. S. Ellis* (London: Scholartis Press, 1928), xiv.
18. On those problems see the *Notes* in A-4.01.

ton setting, was done in Ellis's term, he published the first edition in twenty-two separate issues between 1868 and 1885, dividing it in various ways: the *editio princeps* in three volumes with its six-volume large-paper (LP) variant, the four-volume alternative to the original three-volume version, both later called the 'Library Edition', and in the ten-part 'Popular' version of 1872. Other than the *Jason* reprints and *The Earthly Paradise*, Ellis first published the *Grettis* and *Volsunga Sagas, Love is Enough, The Æneids, Sigurd the Volsung, Three Northern Love Stories, The Decorative Arts,* and *Hopes and Fears for Art*. When he retired from business at the end of 1885, having shown some early symptoms of tuberculosis, Ellis's relationship with Morris was as close as ever.

As the change to Ellis from Bell and Daldy is related to the publication of *Jason* and its immediate popularity, so that book's popularity also fixed the attention of more than one American publisher on Morris. Thus it is no coincidence that Morris's books began to be published in Boston, Mass., at about the same time as Ellis became his English publisher. For some years Roberts Brothers had confined their business primarily to the production and sale of 'blank books', that is, diaries and photo albums, the latter being new at that time and especially popular in the Civil War period.[19] In 1863, at the suggestion of their manager, Thomas Niles, brother-in-law to Lewis A. Roberts, the owner and later a silent partner of Niles, the firm embarked on the publication of poetry and fiction; and under Niles' guidance soon gained considerable stature. Eventually its list included Morris, the Rossettis, and George Meredith from England and some major Americans: Edward Everett Hale, Louisa May Alcott, and Emily Dickinson.

Niles died in 1894, and the manager who succeeded him, Eugene D. Hardy, complained to Sydney Cockerell in 1897 that Morris would never answer their letters. But an explanation of that may lie in the way Roberts came to acquire Morris as an addition to their list. Niles' statement, referring to their 1870 edition of *The Earthly Paradise*, a declaration used repeatedly in Roberts' advertising, was that previously quoted here: 'Mr. Morris's poems are published in America by arrangement with him, and he receives a stated copyright on all sold.'[20] This sorts rather oddly with Hardy's letter to Cockerell of 15 February 1897, in response to the latter's questioning the basis of the royalty payments made by the publisher to the poet:

> We have never had any arrangement with Mr. Morris. As a rule we reprinted from English copies, in the absence of any copyright laws, between the two countries, and we have paid him often an outright sum based on the profits of our sales . . . . We pay this royalty gratuitously . . . . We always regretted that Mr. Morris would not answer our letters. We sent him money regularly for years and he has accepted it.[21]

19. There is a considerable literature on the firm of Roberts Brothers, for which see Eugene D. LeMire, 'William Morris in America: A Publishing History from Archives', *The Book Collector*, 43/2 (Summer 1994), 201–28; hereafter referred to as 'Morris in America'. The standard history of the firm is by Raymond Kilgour, *Messrs. Roberts Brothers: Publishers* (Ann Arbor: University of Michigan Press, 1952). Little, Brown and Co. have made available what remains of the Roberts records by depositing them in the Houghton Library, Harvard University. The Rare Books and Manuscripts Dept. of the Butler Library, Columbia University, has a collection of some 1,500 items, mostly correspondence to and from or related to Roberts Brothers.

20. *Tributes*, 2.

21. From the 'Roberts Letter Book. 18 Nov. 1895 to 4 Nov. 1897', (Roberts Archive, Box 7, The Houghton Library, Harvard University; hereafter referred to as Roberts Arch.).

The only requirement for Roberts Brothers was the informal 'gentleman's agreement' which applied only to Roberts' relationship with other American publishers, as already discussed. Neither Morris nor Ellis had a legal right to negotiate the royalties, which were paid 'gratuitously', or to demand an audit of sales. Though in 1867 Ticknor and Fields were contending with Roberts to be the first American publisher to issue *Jason*, Roberts won the race by getting an early copy of the book from England where it was published in early June 1867. Roberts completed printing in July, thus making publication possible in early August, only two months after the English first edition appeared. Ticknor and Fields acknowledged defeat. This was the process by which Roberts came to have an informal but exclusive 'right' to publish Morris's books for the American market from 1867 until 1897 and the winding up of the firm.[22]

But it needs to be noted that there was more connection and cooperation between the English publisher and the American than appears in Hardy's letter. Clearly Ellis, whose publishing experience told him that Roberts held all the cards where copyright was concerned, decided, like Morris cashing Roberts' 'lean and attenuated' cheques,[23] that something was better than nothing. With Niles' victory over Ticknor and Fields, and perhaps even before that, contact was obviously established between him and Ellis, who cooperated with Roberts on many occasions, exporting competitively-priced English sheets to be put out in Roberts bindings, some with the Roberts imprint. Ellis was able to sell Roberts a set of plates of the *Jason* second edition, when Bell and Daldy, then Morris's London publisher, and Niles both underestimated the probable sales of that book and distributed the type of their first printings without first making stereo moulds.[24] The same relations between the trans-Atlantic publishers, cordial and cooperative, appear to have applied after Ellis was succeeded by Reeves and Turner in 1885.

After 1897 the story of Morris's American books becomes part of the working relationship between Longmans of London, Longmans of New York, and the Morris Estate. But the record of Roberts' output of Morris—fifty-eight issues of fourteen Morris titles and one commissioned exhibition catalogue—confirms the primacy of their role in introducing Morris to American readers. In 1898, when Little, Brown and Co. bought out Roberts' list and stock,[25] they continued to sell the

22. Besides *Jason* (US setting in 1870, see A-3.02) and an exhibition catalogue, *The Morris Exhibit at the Foreign Trade Fair, Boston, 1883–84* (1883, see Appendix II-2.02), Roberts published American settings of *The Earthly Paradise* (1868–70, see A-4.03, 4.07, and 4.10); *The Lovers of Gudrun* (1870, as a separate issue printed from the Roberts *EP* forms, see A-7.01); *Love is Enough* (1873, see A-8.03); *Sigurd the Volsung* (1876, see A-12.03); *The Decorative Arts* (1878, see A-16.02); *The Æneids* (1879, see A-11.03); *Hopes and Fears for Art* (1882, see A-21.02); *The House of the Wolfings* (1890, see A-47.02); *News from Nowhere* (1890, see A-50.01); *The Glittering Plain* (1892, see A-54.03); *Poems by the Way* (1892, see A-59.03); and *The Wood beyond the World* (1895, see A-74.03). Roberts issued the English 2nd edn. of *The Defence of Guenevere and Other Poems* (1875, 1883, and 1891, see A-2.03 for all of these), using imported sheets bound in a Roberts binding. There seems never to have been a Roberts setting of that book.

23. Ellis wrote to Cockerell on 5 July 1899: 'All I remember about the Royalty from Roberts was that W.M. used to receive a lean and attenuated cheque from them occasionally whereat he grumbled & stuffed it in his breeches pocket. So far as my memory serves me about £2. 11. 2. was the average amount [a cheque foil dated 23 Jan. 1897, was for £17. 1s. 2d. as recorded in the Roberts Letter book]. I fancy it was supposed to be 10 per cent on the profits but as there was not the slightest means of checking accts, there was nothing to be said' (The diaries and correspondence of Sydney Carlyle Cockerell (hereafter referred to as Cockerell Papers), BL (Add.) MS 52715).

24. Kilgour argues convincingly that in England printing at this time was cheaper than in the USA (see Kilgour, 29).

25. See *One Hundred and Twenty-Five Years of Publishing: 1837–1962* (Boston: Little, Brown and Company, 1962), 20.

remaining Roberts books for a short interval, mostly in Little, Brown bindings; but they made no Morris books themselves. After Longmans' New York Branch took over the American publications, they bought the twelve Roberts sets of Morris plates[26] in May 1899, and brought out Morris's two posthumously published romances, *The Water of the Wondrous Isles* (1897) and *The Sundering Flood* (1898). These are US editions, composed and printed by John Wilson and Son at the University Press, Cambridge, Mass., but intended for sale on both sides of the Atlantic. Longmans was able to issue them under a registered American copyright and with simultaneous publication in London to qualify for British copyright.[27]

In England the story of Morris's publishers is more complicated. In 1885, when Ellis retired from business, Morris negotiated a contract with Reeves and Turner,[28] who were to be his regular publisher for the next decade, until four months before he died. In this move, he was probably influenced by Ellis, who had been his adviser for nearly twenty years, especially in matters concerning book-collecting and publishing, and (to an unknown extent) by Harry Buxton Forman, Morris's bibliographer and also a defender of the Pre-Raphaelite poets, including Morris, when they were attacked by Robert Buchanan in 'The Fleshly School of Poetry'.[29] Forman, who rose to be the second highest official in the Postal Service, was a Morris collector and an early enthusiast who volunteered in the *Earthly Paradise* period to read proofs of Morris's books. His edition of Shelley's *Collected Poems* (1876), was for many years the standard edition. This and his several other highly-regarded scholarly editions of Keats and Shelley were published by Reeves and Turner. Forman seems to have offered to act as an intermediary to provide an introduction when Morris was beginning his negotiations with William Dobson Reeves in 1885. Morris wrote to Forman on 28 October : 'Thanks for your kind offers. I am just writing to Reeves to begin the intercourse on

---

26. There were no American stereos of *The Defence of Guenevere*, *Gudrun*, *The Decorative Arts*, or *The Morris Exhibit*; but there were two sets of *The Glittering Plain*, one from the American setting and the other the photolithographic plates made from the Kelmscott Press (KP) edn. for the printing of the American facsimile.

27. Except in the USA, there seem to have been no Morris editions or reprints in English originating elsewhere in the English-speaking world during Morris's lifetime or within the extended period through 1915 covered here. The explanation seems to be that, other than in the USA and its dependencies, English-speaking countries in this period were either current or former parts of the British Empire; and these were supplied with English books by their English publishers.

28. Sources of information about the Reeves firm are not plentiful, there having been a patriotic effort during the Second World War to get publishers and printers to donate accumulated out-of-date records to the war effort for their value as cellulose fibre to the munitions industry. The detail of Reeves and Turner's work for Morris is to be seen here and in Forman's bibliography; and there is an interview with William Dobson Reeves, the sole surviving partner after Osborne Turner's death in 1887, in the series 'Booksellers of To-Day', in *The Publishers' Circular*, 16 June 1890, p. 749–50 (hereafter referred to as *Pub. Circ.*). William Dobson Reeves (1825–1907), of 196, Strand, was the father of another bookseller-publisher a few steps away and across the street, William Reeves of 185 Fleet Street, who also published Morris. The latter was a printer as well as a publisher and distributor of Socialist publications in the 80s and 90s, and the little that remains of his records shows the younger Reeves acting as distributor of SL publications. In 1993, a surviving 'William Reeves, Bookseller' was discovered operating mainly as a dealer in music books from his warehouse at No. 1 Norbury Crescent, Norbury. His archives include a full run of catalogues of his great-grandfather William Dobson Reeves' firm of Reeves and Turner and a few records from his grandfather, William Reeves of 185 Fleet Street (more recently, these records have been deposited in the Music Department of the BL). It was the current Mr Reeves who provided the information that the Reeves and Turner records he inherited are all that remains after the paper drives of the war years (for more on the Reeves-Morris relationship, see the *Printer* and *Notes* fields in A-50.02).

29. See Forman's 'The "Fleshly School" Controversy', *Tinsley's Magazine*, 10 (Feb. 1872), 89–102.

my part: I shall be glad to meet you in his shop when I can get about but at present I am leg-fast with gout'.[30]

There was no serious difficulty about the contract beyond Morris's request that a clause be changed to allow him to end the agreement without penalty by giving 'due notice', and on 24 November Morris wrote to Reeves and Turner: 'Dear Sirs, I return the agreement signed finding it quite satisfactory.'[31]

The next decade proved to be as productive as the last. Reeves was less innovative than Morris wished to be, but he was a gentleman and an honest man, judging by his contemporaries' comments,[32] and he seems to have been happy to implement Morris's growing interest in the later 1880s and early 90s in a new kind of book-making. In 1890, Morris got what he had wanted for some time, a new and cheaper one-volume edition of *The Earthly Paradise* for which he created a floral design to be gilt-stamped on its cloth binding. The new printer, The Ballantyne Press, had been engaged earlier, in 1888, for the first edition of *Signs of Change*. This involved a change from the medium-sized London establishment of Strangeways, Morris's regular printer for nearly twenty years, to a much larger Edinburgh firm, formerly printer of Sir Walter Scott, that had set up a London branch in 1878. After this first book, Ballantyne gradually took over much of the Morris work, except for the period of the late 80s and early 90s when Morris returned to the Chiswick Press to produce the works with which he made his early experiments in the art of making books. He tried his hand at book design, type selection (helping to revive the scribal or calligraphic inheritance of oblique stress, greater blackness, and shorter, inclined, fully bracketed serifs), selecting paper, and designing bindings. These early trials are best seen in *The House of the Wolfings* and *The Roots of the Mountains*. From 1891 to 1896 the Chiswick Press produced the first 'popular' editions of those Morris titles for which the *editiones princepes* were issued from the Kelmscott Press. The period of Ballantyne's greatest involvement with Morris's books came after Longmans became his publisher in June 1896.

In the late 1880s as he approached the founding of the Kelmscott Press, Morris for obvious reasons became more than ever involved with all aspects of book making and publishing, making decisions normally considered the province of the publisher. With *The Odyssey* (1887) Morris began to specify the production details of his own books and, notably, took direct control of discussions with the printer, deciding on design, on what sort and size of paper was to be used, the size of print runs, and what price should be charged. The *editio princeps* of his translation of *The Odyssey* was first issued in two large (and different), hand-made paper versions, one on Dickinson's and the other on Dutch Van Gelder Zonen, each in two volumes and each with its own de luxe binding. The two volumes were paginated continuously for convenience when printing the one-volume popular edition issued a month after the second volumes of the first edition. All this is a notable departure from ordinary practice, large and fine paper copies

30. *Letters*, ii. 476.
31. *Letters*, ii. 495.

32. See W. C. Hazlitt, *Confessions of a Collector* (1897), 131, see especially his Chapter viii, 128–33.

previously being restricted to small numbers, as an extra to the ordinary books, mainly to be distributed as gifts or sold to collectors at a premium price.[33]

For *The House of the Wolfings* (1888) Morris revived after many years of disuse the Chiswick Press version of the Basle roman type design. *The Roots of the Mountains* (1889) provided the occasion for introducing two of his Morris and Company cotton prints—'Honeysuckle' and 'Little Chintz'—as binding material for the 'Superior Edition'. For each of these latter two books he wrote an original lyric poem as a title-page epigraph, as he said, 'just to fill up the great white lower half'.[34]

But if Reeves himself was not the innovator that Morris was, there is no sign of anything but willing cooperation in his somewhat diminished role. There are clear indications that increasingly Morris made the decisions. But the good feeling for each other is maintained. This is an aspect of Morris that is not often enough realized, perhaps because there was so much of conflict on the political side of his life. That there was a personal element in his business dealings can be seen in his comment in a letter to his daughter Jenny, when he was seeing his translation of *The Odyssey* through the press: 'I am getting on fast enough with the Homer as far as my part is concerned; but Strangeways is rather hanging fire: I am going to call on him on my way to Merton today, and shall have a chaffing-match with the old-gentleman, as we are on good terms'.[35]

But Morris's urge to control more of the process, to produce better designed and better made books, gradually outgrew even the warm attachments to the printer Strangeways and, eventually, to his publisher. In the later stages of the Kelmscott Press, Morris took over as his own publisher. On 23 November 1889 he wrote to Andreas Scheu, an Austrian colleague and friend from the Socialist League, in reply to an appeal for assistance in Scheu's search for employment. Here he indicates his inclination to make more of the book business, starting with his own publications:

> I will of course set myself to work to see if anything can be done in getting you some place worthy of your capacity . . . . I wish you were my publisher, as I really think something might be done with my books, more than has been done, and I am thinking of bringing out a cheap edition of the Earthly Paradise in one vol. But I am rather tied to old Reeves at present.[36]

Six months later it had become public knowledge that Morris was thinking of a change of publishers. That underlies his comment in July 1890, when he writes to Georgiana Burne-Jones: 'I have undertaken to get out some of the Sagas I have lying about. Quaritch is exceedingly anxious to get hold of me, and received with enthusiasm a proposal to publish a Saga Library: item he will give me money (or perhaps I ought to say old books)'.[37]

---

33. Colin Franklin observes that all the early Morris books published by Ellis had only twenty-five LP copies. See his *Printing and the Mind of Morris* (London: privately printed for the author at the Rampant Lions Press, 1986), 17. The later editions tended to have more, like the 125 copies for each vol. of The Saga Library.

34. Morris, as quoted in HBF, p. 140. He also used a separate printing of *The Roots of the Mountains*' title page, adorned with his lyric, as a separate advertising leaflet or prospectus for the book (see Appendix II-3).

35. *Letters*, ii. 623.

36. *Letters*, iii. 129.

37. *Letters*, iii. 175. The reference to payment in 'old books' is based on Quaritch's trade in rare books, for which Morris was a frequent customer.

But while the *Saga Library* went smoothly enough, the joint venture with Quaritch as publisher of Kelmscott Press books did not end happily. Mackail says: 'By the end of 1892 Morris had made up his mind to add the trade of publisher to that of printer. "There is really no risk in it", he said in summing up the situation: "I shall get more money; and the public will have to pay less".'[38]

Morris's move to take over the publishing function for the Kelmscott Press books was also influenced by his disagreement with Quaritch over discounts to the trade, where Quaritch undercut Morris's trade price for the Chaucer. In response to this, Morris refused to supply Quaritch with more copies except at a lesser discount until his own trade customers had been supplied. Quaritch wrote his son on 20 August 1894, that, 'Mr. Wm Morris will call on me tomorrow; he is laying down the law to me about the Chaucer, —and I must submit. This has cooled my ardour to obtain the transfer of his publications from Reeves and Turner. Mr. Morris's success has turned him into a despot'.[39]

Bernard Quaritch was not the only publisher who wanted to 'get hold' of Morris, and until some time late in 1895 or early 1896,[40] when the decision was made to commit to Longmans, there were several other publishers who took opportunities to do particular things with Morris; and it seems that Reeves, having softened the let-out clause for Morris and being already partly retired,[41] saw in that no reason for a rupture in their relations, acting as Morris's regular publisher but more and more merely as a marketing agent until replaced by Longmans.

Looking about for a new publisher, Morris tried several. Besides Quaritch's publication of *The Saga Library* (six volumes, 1891–1906), Lawrence and Bullen published the English popular edition of *The Wood beyond the World* (1895) after the Kelmscott Press first edition. George Allen produced the volume *Old French Romances* (1896), a collection of four translations from medieval French, all previously published in three Kelmscott Press volumes. And as early as 1888, Morris gave permission for Henry Halliday Sparling to edit his *Volsunga Saga* translation for The Camelot Series of the publisher Walter Scott.

Morris had, of course, many occasional publishers besides the major ones during his career. Some were individuals like James Leatham, to whom Morris gave permission to publish at will *A King's Lesson* and *Under an Elm-Tree*. Leatham issued the first separate editions of these two titles in 1891 and went on printing them, in new editions each time, until he died in 1945. He added two more Morris pamphlets to his output with *A Factory as it Might Be* in 1907 and *The Revolt of Ghent*, c. 1911. Morris's first Socialist lecture pamphlet, *Art and Socialism*, came of an initiative by two Leek

---

38. Mackail, ii. 281.

39. Quoted from Bod. MS Eng. lett. c. 435, f. 194 in William S. Peterson, *A Bibliography of the Kelmscott Press*. Soho Bibliographies 24 (Oxford: The Clarendon Press, 1985 (rptd. with corrections, first pbd. in 1984); hereafter referred to as *KP Biblio*.), p. 110.

40. S. C. Cockerell's MS Diary for 1895 records on Mon. 23 Dec. a trip with Morris into the City to discuss with C. J. Longman the possible transfer of Morris's publishing (BL (Add.) MS 52772).

41. William Dobson Reeves, by then 68 years old, announced that the firm would 'carry on their publications from the first floor of 5 Wellington Street, Strand' from 4 Sept. 1893. The announcement seems to imply a retirement from the bookshop side of the business. The only Morris publication to carry the new address in its imprint was the 'Fourth Edition' of *News from Nowhere* in 1895 (see A-50.02, under *Later impressions of this edn.*).

Introduction

members of the Democratic Federation (DF), Ethelbert Edward Minton, a bank clerk, and William Larner Sugden, an architect.

A substantial number of Morris texts came from the many political, conservationist, and artistic associations with which he had major and enduring commitments. The Society for the Protection of Ancient Buildings (SPAB); The Kyrle Society; the Social Democratic Federation (SDF, earlier the DF), the Socialist League, the Arts and Crafts Exhibition Society (ACES), and the Hammersmith Socialist Society (HSS) all published Morris items, both separate titles and periodical articles. Relevant detail with respect to these is in the Section A or Section D entries.

But all Morris's relations with his publishers and printers led ultimately to his last major publishing decision: to sign a contract with Longmans, Green, and Company. A publisher of a different order of magnitude and probably among the first companies of the Victorian age to qualify as what we would now describe as a 'multinational', it was always and remains still a family company, never listed on the stock exchange, and it has always been controlled by direct descendants of the founder, notwithstanding the policy of importing 'new blood' by occasionally appointing directors from outside the family, but within the firm. The profound contrast between Morris's previous publishers and Longmans immediately raises the question of what brought it on. Mackail's comment in his first Notebook may or may not have been carefully considered: 'He transferred publishing to Longmans at Walker's advice, but did not care himself what firm he went to, except that he objected to Macmillan'.[42] To go from the sort of publishers Morris had worked with through his writing career, with each of whom there was a considerable personal rapport, to the oldest (excepting the presses of the two ancient universities) and largest concern in the business, with a history going back to 1724,[43] was clearly a major change, and not one that appears immediately and obviously consistent with the interests of Morris as a great innovator in the design, printing, and publishing of books.

Another motive was at work here. Morris had some significant warnings of declining health, his serious illness of 1890 being an especially clear one. It has been noted that in the years of the Kelmscott Press, 'a matter of record is his deep worry about the health of his daughter Jenny, who had suffered from her teenage years from severe epilepsy'.[44] It is clear that Morris was a man with a talent for business as well as having fair and friendly relations with those with whom he did business. His concern for and foresight in providing for his family can be seen clearly in his arrangements for what amounted to the gradual sale of Morris and Co. to the Smith brothers, in his setting up through his will of a family trust, in his careful choice of the trustees, and in the latitude of the powers given them to administer the Estate.

---

42. From Mackail's MS Notebook 1 in the Morris Collection (Walthamstow: William Morris Gallery, 1958, J 163, p. 9; hereafter referred to as WMG).

43. *The Bookman's Directory* (1893) says that Thomas Longman founded the firm, c. 1723, on the premises at 39 Paternoster Row (including the ship device) of William Taylor, 'and there the firm has prospered for 170 years, having relations with nearly all the eminent English men of letters.'

44. See Charles Harvey and Jon Press, *William Morris: Design and Enterprise in Victorian Britain* (Manchester: Manchester University Press, 1991), 215. Chapter 7 of this book provides the most thorough account we have of Morris's astute arrangements for the handling of his family's finances after his death.

The somewhat surprising turn to Longmans in the last months of his life began with an agreement made probably late in 1895, to come into effect in June 1896. As previously noted, Cockerell's Diary entry for Monday, 23 December 1895 records a trip to see C. J. Longman about transferring Morris's publishing.[45] The move can best be understood in terms of Morris's effort to provide for those dependent on him, to put his affairs in the best order possible for the time when he would no longer be there to make decisions. There is some validation of Morris's foresight in that he died on 3 October 1896, only four months after the shift to Longmans in June.

While there was no obvious strong personal connection, direct or indirect, to attract Morris to Longmans in the way he had been drawn to Ellis and then to Reeves and Turner, in Morris's time Longmans enjoyed a very high reputation in the trade for its seniority, its size, and its professionalism. Long before its connection with Morris and with the Morris Estate, the company enjoyed great respect from its competitors. In Morris's time this was reflected in the position in the minds of his contemporaries occupied by C. J. Longman, then head of the firm. Editor of *Fraser's Magazine* and *Longmans Magazine*, until he appointed Andrew Lang to edit the latter, publisher of *The Edinburgh Review*, he was formidable, popularly known as 'the Lion of Paternoster Row'. He did a term as President of the Publishers' Association, founded in 1896, chairing a committee set up by the association to investigate the debasement of the common currency of trade terminology, to redefine in more precise ways such words as 'edition', 'impression', 'issue'—the meanings of which were often debated in the trade journals.[46]

Another aspect of Longmans' reputation must have been the attentive, precise, and thorough way (it could be called the 'businesslike' way), the firm conducted its financial relations with authors. Morris would never have seen it, but Roberts Brothers' bookkeeping in the private accounts of the firm was sufficiently detailed and careful in relation to the records of printing, which had an internal relevance to the Firm. But the same cannot be said of the way they calculated Morris's annual royalties. Being fully aware that there was no legal copyright in Morris's case, and therefore no legal obligation involved in their payments to him, the writer of the longhand scrawl across ledger-book entries that represents Roberts' calculation of royalties never deals in any other than round figures, either in the amounts to be paid or in the number of copies on which the payment is based. As an example of the range of attitudes possible, the contrast between that and the Longmans accounts could hardly be overstated.

But then, publishing was the core business of Longmans. Unlike the bookseller-publishers previously engaged by Morris, Longmans did not involve itself in the retail side by conducting new, used, or rare book shops. Nor did it do any printing. The Longmans royalty book makes it clear

---

45. See Note 40.

46. In the event the committee recommended that the Association commit itself to a set of definitions that were remarkably close to those developed by such modern bibliographical authorities as Fredson Bowers and W. W. Greg, though it is doubtful the definitions of the Publishers' Association Committee had any more effect on usage in the market place than those of Bowers or Greg. But subsequent Longmans books are notable for including on the verso of their title pages a 'Bibliographical Note' which provides at least the basic facts of previous publication, but not always with clear distinctions between edns., impressions, issues, and states.

that the arrangement with Morris, which continued with the Trustees after his death, provided for specific royalty amounts to be settled for each title published and for each new edition of each title, with a separate but equally detailed accounting for American sales.[47] Examples of the variation in royalties between different issues can be seen in Longmans' accounts for 1897, covering the period from 19 December 1896 to 20 December 1897: the one-volume *Earthly Paradise* received a royalty payment of 100*s*. per 100 copies sold; *John Ball* (cheap edn.), 16*s*. 8*d*. per 100 copies; *The Well at the World's End*, published in two volumes, attracted royalties of £28 per 100 copies sold, or £17. 18*s*. 5*d*. for the 64 copies sold that year; and *The Water of the Wondrous Isles*, published in the same year, yielded the highest total amount, £64. 16*s*. 0*d*. from 864 copies sold at £7. 10*s*. 0*d*. royalty per 100 copies sold. The point here is the distinctions being made on the basis of the sales potential of new authorial content, as against that of the known popularity of certain titles perennially reprinted, both affecting the amount of risk and the likely return involved in the publisher's investment. And the accounting shows in exquisite detail how these figures are calculated and recorded in eight columns after each issue of each title then on the market, filled in with a copperplate hand starting with the number of copies 'on hand' on 19 December 1897, plus the number 'printed' in the year, minus the copies 'given away', or 'sold to America' to arrive at the number of copies 'sold' multiplied by the royalty per 100 copies, with the sum payable worked out to the last penny. The New York branch of Longmans submitted the same balance sheet in American dollars for its sales. Both of the accounts were accompanied by signed certificates from each printer who had worked on Morris books during the year to attest to exactly how many copies had been printed of each title. On seeing these full year's accounts from Longmans, Ellis exclaimed that, 'I fear the bard never got such beautifully elaborate statements from me'.[48] It was by a general professionalism of which the accounts are a particular example that Longmans gained the confidence of Morris and his chief advisers, who would certainly have included Ellis, Cockerell, and Emery Walker, a friend and neighbour of Morris with expertise in printing and publishing, sometime editor of *The English Illustrated Magazine*.

The Longmans initiatives began as soon as the new contract with Morris came into effect in June, 1896, with the announcement of a new series called 'The Poetical Works of William Morris' in ten volumes, the first four of which were devoted to *The Earthly Paradise*.[49] But the role of Longmans in Morris's publishing extends far beyond this first project and Morris's death several months

---

47. See the Ledger Book of royalty payments, 1903–7, in the *Archives of the House of Longman*, 1794–1914, at Reading University Library, hereafter referred to as Longmans Arch. By persistent negotiation, Cockerell got the American payments changed from a specially discounted American rate to an equivalent amount for American sales of each book as was paid for the same books sold in Britain.

48. Letter of 31 Mar. 1899 (Cockerell Papers, BL (Add.) MS 52715). The accounts for 1897 show totals of £198. 12*s*. 1*d*. from Longmans of London and £51. 12*s*. 1*d*. from Longmans of New York, a total of £250. 10*s*. 7*d*., clearly a sum worth considering. And the publishing profits grew with the Estate's and Longmans' publishing initiatives: by 1903 the annual royalty cheque had nearly doubled to £520. 0*s*. 6*d*. (accounts in the W. H. Smith Bequest Archives, William Morris Society Library, Kelmscott House; hereafter referred to as Smith Arch.).

49. This series was announced by the *Pub. Circ.*, 65/1566 (4 July 1896), 6; and advertised by Longmans in the following week's number, 65/1567 (11 July 1896), 33.

later. Longman's involvement extended through the remaining years of the Morris copyright on his published works, and all but the last of the significant publishing initiatives of the Trustees of the Morris Estate.

To include those publications, as well as others still to be discussed, Section A, the descriptions and history of the Morris books in their original editions, is enlarged to include the books issued from Morris's death through 1915, the year when the last two volumes of *The Collected Works of William Morris* were issued.[50] That year provides a convenient and a fitting place to end the full publication histories of each title while continuing to list any posthumous first editions from then to the present. The extension provides for appropriate attention to the posthumous editions both from the public domain and under the remaining protection of the original separate titles still covered by copyright and *The Collected Works*, still the standard and most inclusive collection of Morris's texts, with many items first appearing there. The main reason for extending original edition coverage to the twenty years after his death is the number, significance, and quality of the Morris books produced in that additional twenty years, books about which little is generally known. The first Morris bibliographers could only cover the books published in part of the year after his death, when their books went to press.

The two decades after Morris's death[51] added on to the Section A's account of the original editions is also the conclusion of the Estate's effective use of the copyright. The flow of copyright editions in this period is representative of both the Estate's exercise of its control and the Trustees' willingness to break new ground in the publication of previously unpublished or fugitive work. The books themselves were prepared with close reference to the author's tastes and principles, not only in respect of their printing, type, paper, and binding, but also in the preparation of the texts (while Morris was never a great reviser, he—with some gritting of teeth—accepted the removal of solecisms from his texts when they were pointed out by others).

These initiatives were devised and carried through by the Trustees of the Estate of whom, in accordance with Morris's will, there were three. Jane Morris, Morris's widow, died in 1914 and was succeeded by her daughter May. Mrs Morris took no part in the daily business of the Estate, nor did she work on the preparation of the new publications; but she was consulted before any substantial decisions were made. Sydney Cockerell, later the director of the Fitzwilliam Museum at Cambridge, was the former secretary to the Kelmscott Press, the principal executor, and the person chiefly responsible for the texts produced by the Estate. F. S. Ellis, Morris's friend, already discussed, the third Trustee, was succeeded after his death in 1901 by Robert Proctor of the British Museum, an expert on fifteenth-century printed books. When he died in 1903 while hiking over a glacier in the Austrian Tyrol, C. H. St. John Hornby, a director of W. H. Smith and Sons and founder of the Ash-

---

50. Edited by May Morris in 24 vols. (London: Longmans, Green and Co, 1910–15; hereafter referred to as *CW*.

51. 'Original editions' normally applies only to books published in an author's lifetime. The expression 'effective use of copyright' used here refers to the time when the copyrights covering most of the Morris titles were still enforceable in Britain. As previously noted, Morris's individual works began to emerge into public domain in 1903. Except for May Morris's collection, *William Morris, Artist, Writer, Socialist*, the Estate's major initiatives ended with the completion of *CW*.

endene Press, succeeded him. The death of May Morris in 1938 brought on the winding up of the Estate. By the provisions of her will, the Morris copyright passed then to The Society of Antiquaries of London. The copyright is effective still insofar as the control of unpublished or recently issued work is concerned.

The Morris Estate supported the publication of the last thirteen titles, including seven by Morris, issued by the Kelmscott Press and supervised by S. C. Cockerell. The seven by Morris were four posthumous first editions and three Kelmscott Press reprints of previously published works: the last five volumes of the eight-volume Kelmscott Press *Earthly Paradise* still unpublished at the time of his death, two Kelmscott reprints of earlier titles: *Sigurd the Volsung* and *Love is Enough*, first editions of his last two prose romances: *The Water of the Wondrous Isles* and *The Sundering Flood*, and two short Kelmscott books on books: *Some German Woodcuts of the Fifteenth Century* and *Note by William Morris on His Aims in Founding the Kelmscott Press*.[52] All this was done before the closure of the Press in 1898.

Then, from 1898 to 1903 the Trustees produced fourteen volumes containing eighteen Morris titles, all printed by the Chiswick Press in Golden type, on Kelmscott Press paper, bound in one of the two typical Kelmscott Press bindings,[53] and all done as part of a project to complete Morris's plan to print all his own books in his own Kelmscott Press type. The project began gradually with Cockerell's issue, one by one, of a series of five uniform octavo volumes containing six fugitive Morris lectures and one essay. Called the 'Golden type octavo edition' by May Morris, each volume was popularly priced at *2s. 6d.*, making necessary several impressions of various volumes to meet demand.

Buoyed by their success, the Trustees then committed themselves to a much larger programme, an eight-volume limited issue set of miscellaneous works—verse and prose translations, romances, lectures and essays—which May Morris called the 'Golden type quarto edition'. As part of that, the Trustees created two new titles, the first being the seventh volume of the eight-volume set: *Architecture, Industry, and Wealth: Collected Papers* (1902) and second *The Hollow Land and Other Contributions to the Oxford and Cambridge Magazine* (1903), published separately in a size and binding designed to range with the Golden type octavo set. Though priced at the high end of the market at 2 guineas per volume for the eight-volume set, the sheer quality of production—design, paper, type, and binding—combined with the rarity of some of the fugitive texts and the limitation of the print run to 315 copies (316 actually, the Chiswick Press having always made one extra copy for their archive) of which 299 were for sale, 69 of those in the United States, all this meant that the books sold out immediately to subscribers. With the Trustees putting up the money and Longmans being engaged only on a 'commission' basis, the result was a handsome profit to the estate after all

---

52. The first of these books on books is based on the abortive catalogue of Morris's rare book collection, and reprints the text of his article in *Bibliographica* as an Introduction. The second was the last book printed by the KP. After these titles were issued, it was considered inappropriate to call posthumous reprints 'KP' books because they would have had none of Morris's original design work either in their make-up or ornaments.

53. Quarter dark blue holland spines with printed paper labels and light grey paper-covered boards.

expenses, including the £100 fee the two editors, Cockerell and Proctor, were paid.[54] These post-Kelmscott Press books, all but two of which are new editions of works previously published, could only to be issued without prohibitive losses while copyright was still effective.

The five and eight-volume sets were all of a standard of production as near as possible to that of the Kelmscott Press. But it is not only their physical make up that makes these books significant. The texts were all edited by Sydney Cockerell, who enlisted the aid of Robert Proctor well before 1901, when the latter became a Trustee. Called by Carter and Pollard, 'the greatest typographical scholar of his age',[55] Proctor was an admirer of Morris as well as a curator employed in the British Museum Library (for which Ellis was for several years the official buyer of rare books), who brought a scholarly rigour to all aspects of the Morris texts as he and Cockerell prepared them for the press.[56] His view of their editorial responsibilities was expressed succinctly in a letter to Cockerell concerning their editing of *The Hollow Land and Other Contributions to the Oxford and Cambridge Magazine* (dated 28 September 1902):

> As to punctuation, etc., my view which was formed in the copying process is this: that there are two alternatives before us: one is to produce an exact reprint of the original, misprints, mispunctuations (which often make sheer nonsense) and all, and state publicly that it is so. The other is to do for our author what he would have done for himself, as far as may be; at any rate to give the matter the best presentation, and not to handicap it by irrelevant difficulties. And this I think is our duty, because if we don't do it nobody else can, but anybody after October 1903 can issue facsimile reprints to his heart's content. One can hardly imagine anyone less likely to take trouble about proof-reading and correction than W. M. at 22; the work he did not do then we should do now as far as lies within our power.[57]

Finally, from 1910 to 1915 the Estate, working in an equal partnership, i.e. half shares in the profits, with Longmans providing the capital, issued the twenty-four volumes of *The Collected Works of William Morris*.[58] Though the 1842 copyright act was revised in 1911, further extending the rights of the author and his 'heirs and assigns', the planning and prospectus for *The Collected Works* were completed by 1910 and therefore within the context of the 1842 Act. But only the first four volumes of *The Collected Works* were issued in 1910, following C. J. Longman's advice to the Trustees: 'if such an edition as this is ever to be put on the market, it ought to be put on very shortly, as the copyrights are beginning to run out'.[59]

54. The editors' fees were adjusted upward from £80 (see *Notes* in A-47.04).

55. *An Enquiry into the Nature of Certain Nineteenth-Century Pamphlets* (London: Constable and Company, Limited, 1934, p. 136). The 2nd edn., used here, was edited and completed for the press by Nicolas Barker and John Collins (London: Scolar Press, 1983; hereafter referred to as *Enquiry*).

56. The standard biographical essay on Proctor is Pollard's 'Robert Proctor' in *The Library*, 5 n.s. (Jan. 1904), 1–34. Evidence in the Longman Arch. and in Cockerell's correspondence indicates that the two editors worked together preparing the text and settling any outstanding questions—attributions of items in *The Oxford and Cambridge Magazine*, for example—and that the texts were finally typed for the printer by Proctor.

57. From Cockerell's correspondence with Proctor in the Cockerell Papers, BL (Add.) MS 52743.

58. Correspondence between Longmans and the Trustees indicates that Longmans undertook all expenses for the production and marketing of the *CW* (see *Notes*, A-126.01).

59. Smith Arch. The *EP*, Morris's most successful book, which formed vols. 3–6 (1910–11) of the *CW*, was 1st pbd. 1868–70. It follows that in 1910 the 1st vol., first issued in 1868 and comprising the first 2 parts as later arranged and named, entered the public domain.

All this was done, of course, in addition to a heavy schedule of new editions and reprints of the existing books, all funded and produced through Longmans, and all under the watchful eye of the executors, especially of S. C. Cockerell, whose correspondence with C. J. Longman is a model of how to keep a publisher trying to do better.

Almost all these Longmans books were issued after Scott's and Forman's bibliographies went to press, and — except for the Kelmscott Press books[60]— they have had little focused bibliographical attention. But they are in several cases *editiones princepes* and in all cases the official editions, published with the copyright authority of the Estate before the proliferation of cheap copies in public domain could make such lavish productions uneconomic.

A certain self-effacing reticence has obscured much of the work done by other trustees and their associates in the Morris circle. The title page of each *Collected Works* volume announces that May Morris provided the Introduction, but neither the texts themselves nor the editorial machinery give an account of the extent of her contribution. Every text that she edited involved collecting and comparing the existing manuscripts with the various printed versions in order to determine her father's final intent wherever there was a textual difficulty. She also struggled with C. J. Longman over the time required for her work[61] and with Magnússon and St. John Hornby for control of the issues in which the different parties had an interest and a conflict over degrees or areas of responsibility. Before production began, she consulted about each volume's design and printing with Bernard Newdigate, the manager of the Arden Press, the printing subsidiary of W. H. Smith and Son.

Other contributors to this posthumous second flowering of Morris publications were the publishers and printers, working mainly in private but some in public or commercial presses, who were inspired by Morris. They worked towards a revolution, a new era in type and book design. To them, Morris not only wrote but demonstrated by example that books, like the other objects with which we surround ourselves, can also have a clarity and beauty that enhances their use, that concentration on all aspects of design, materials, and craftsmanship can issue in books of a wonderful beauty not always in conflict with the function of communicating texts.

The printers and publishers referred to here were not by any means all slavish imitators of the Morris style in book-making, which has been described as 'pure revivalist' or 'arts-and-crafts'. The critical responses in America and Britain to the Kelmscott Press books have always produced opinions at both extremes, positive and negative. But the inspiration of the revolutionary practitioners was more tolerant. Besides the romantic arts-and-crafts revival of Old Face type designs and woodcut ornaments, with an obvious debt to the products of the earliest days of printing, American admirers of Morris, working in both private and commercial presses, tended towards classical and aesthetic restraint and clarity (like T. B. Mosher). Others were more inclined to the modern style,

---

60. William S. Peterson's two studies, taken together, provide a very detailed treatment of the KP books and their background. See his *KP Biblio.* and *The Kelmscott Press: A History* (Oxford: The Clarendon Press, 1991); hereafter referred to as *KP Hist.*
61. The original plan, as described in Longmans' Prospectus, was for 24 vols. issued, 'in six quarterly instalments of four volumes each, to be issued in three-month intervals', i.e. it was to be completed in less than 2 years. Mainly because of May Morris's editing, the full set was six years in the making (see *Series* and *Publication* fields in A-126.01).

art-nouveau, which influenced little other than the decoration of books. But, whether like or unlike Morris in style, the printers' versions of Morris texts expressed some homage to his independent approach to the art of making books.

Susan Otis Thompson has written a detailed account of Morris's influence in *American Book Design and William Morris*,[62] showing that the American fine-art-printing productions of Morris texts by printers inspired by the Kelmscott Press reflect all three main styles that together made the revolution in printing and book-making.

Some printers were interested in Morris texts for reasons that had something to do not only with book design or printing, but also to cater to the burgeoning trade in first and limited editions. Thomas Bird Mosher was obviously appealing to the discerning reader by his informed and tasteful choice of texts, a restrained aesthetic style, minimal decoration, and mainly Caslon Old Face type. But he was also determined to make money, with a distinctly American marketing strategy that combined the prices of mass-produced products with good printing in limited editions. The Bibelot separates are single-text editions, usually first separate editions, issued first in monthly paperback pamphlets, not merely fascicles of a journal because in most cases they stand alone, including only such extra comment as is relevant to the main text. Generally the text is complete in one issue, and no Morris text required more than two. They become parts of a serial only when collected into an annual volume under The Bibelot masthead in January of the year following the separate issues. The monthly pamphlets cost five cents a copy, ten cents if the text ran to two parts. In the various Mosher series—there were fourteen besides the Bibelot separates—the buyer could choose optional fine paper and binding, and enjoy the added value of expressly limited editions,[63] printed in one or another of the regular series, plus The Bibelot separates, that Mosher invented to increase his customers' options.

Mosher found in Morris his greatest publishing interest of all, producing more issues of his work than that of any other writer.[64] Sometimes called 'the Portland pirate' because he regularly reprinted the texts of English works never copyrighted in America, he was sufficiently mindful of the law never to violate the US International Copyright Act of 1891.[65] He made a significant contribution to the transmission of Morris's texts in the USA, being from 1896 to 1914 both an indicator of and a stimulus to the growth of Morris's reputation there. His first Morris book, *The Story of Amis and Amile*, was issued in Portland, Maine, in August 1896, two months before Morris's death

---

62. New York: R. R. Bowker Company, 1977 (rptd. 1996 with 'Foreword' by Jean-François Vilain); hereafter referred to as *American Book Design*). See also Will Ransom's *The Private Presses and Their Books* (New York: Bowker, 1963, first pbd. in 1923; hereafter referred to as Ransom). Thompson's notes, with Ransom's, are useful guides to Morris books by American printers (with English printers included in the latter).

63. When *A Dream of John Ball* appeared in Mosher's Old World Series in 1902, for example, it was available as one of 925 copies on Van Gelder handmade paper for $1, bound either in japan vellum or 'Old Style Blue Paper Boards' with yapp edges for $1.25,

in a 'flexible leather binding' for $1.50, or as one of 100 numbered copies printed on japan vellum for $2.50 (see Philip Bishop, *Thomas Bird Mosher: Pirate Prince of Publishers: A Comprehensive Bibliography & Source Guide to The Mosher Books Reflecting England's National Literature & Design*: (New Castle, Del. and London: Oak Knoll Press and The British Library, 1998), p. 58; hereafter referred to as Bishop).

64. See Bishop, p. 476.

65. For the one exception to this rule, see William Fredeman in Bishop, p. 20.

(it had been published originally two years earlier at the Kelmscott Press as *Of the Friendship of Amis and Amile*). But besides Mosher's 48 issues of twenty-one Morris titles—the last of which, *Sir Peter Harpdon's End*, appeared in 1914—many other American Morris books were issued in the twenty years after his death.

American producers of Morris texts included such figures as Ralph Fletcher Seymour at the Aldebrink Press (see A-17.02), Frederic Goudy at the Village Press (see B-16.02, A-83.04 and 105.01), Frederic M. Burr at the Hillside Press (see A-96.04 and 102.03), Clark Conwell at the Elston Press (A-102.01, C-14 and 15), and G. Putnam's Sons (see A-109.01). For the copyright reasons already discussed, it was not until 1903 that British printers and publishers, including the private presses, had the option of using Morris's earliest publications: his contributions to *The Oxford and Cambridge Magazine*, and his first volume of poetry, *The Defence of Guenevere and Other Poems*. John Lane of the Bodley Head (see A-2.07 and 111.01); James Finch (see A-95.02, 96.03, 101.03, and C-16.05); and James Thomson at the Avon Press in Wimbledon (see A-101.02, C-16.04 and 23, whose books in form and content replicate those of Mosher's Bibelot editions), Alexander Moring at The De la More Press (see A-2.08), and Blackie and Son (see A-2.12 and 109.02) acted on the opportunity to print Morris's earliest pieces in de luxe editions when the copyright lapsed.

Because so little is known about them—they are largely ignored by students of Morris—the books from Mosher, the private presses and the wider circle of 'fine-art' publishers have not been exhaustively and systematically catalogued or described in a formulary intended to disclose the make-up of each book.[66] But they are Morris books as well as being one of the indirect results of Morris's 'typographical adventure' and their inclusion here is, in the simplest terms, because they are Morris primary sources, not only collectors' items but also part of the history of Morris's texts.

Readers not well acquainted with bibliographical scholarship may require some explanation of another group of publications belonging to the twenty-year interval after Morris's death. Being forgeries, piracies, or sophistications of genuine Morris texts, these appeared posthumously (necessarily so, considering that a living Morris would certainly have exposed the fraudulent abuse of his copyright had he known of it). These made their appearance in the years shortly before turn of the century, years that also saw Morris's emergence as a collectors' item, as the enthusiasm of book dealers and their customers for early modern first editions—especially those in limited print runs—swept bookshops and auction rooms on both sides of the Atlantic. This was the atmosphere when Forman wrote and published *The Books of William Morris described* (1897), much the more comprehensive and detailed treatment of the two 1897 bibliographies. Besides the value of Forman's marshalling there of factual information, information now otherwise unavailable, from the printers and publishers of the original editions, a fair modern assessment would rate his work as a landmark in author bibliography, in his time a relatively recent invention. The detail of his descriptions (less systematic than a modern formulary, but remarkably comprehensive), his facsimile reprints (usually reduced in size)

---

66. But see John Walsdorf's *William Morris in Private Press and Limited Editions: A Descriptive Bibliography of Books By and About William Morris, 1891–1981* (Phoenix, Ariz.: Oryx Press, 1983; hereafter referred to as Waldorf).

of nearly all the title pages of the *editiones principes* and many of the later editions as well as the first, and his effort to include details of later editions, impressions, issues, and variants wherever there was any difference worth recording, all this results in a remarkably comprehensive account of the original Morris editions and their publishing history from their beginning through the first half of 1897.

But Forman's bibliography had also a secret purpose: to provide a spurious provenance for forged (hence also pirated) first editions and sophisticated copies of legitimate editions. The basics of the fraud were revealed in 1934 by John Carter and Graham Pollard. At the time they thought (though they made no accusation against him) that Thomas James Wise, assisted only by some minor accomplices, was its only begetter. From our vantage point, over sixty-five years after Carter and Pollard's first exposure of the fraud, it is possible to see a good deal more of it—the mainspring of which has since been named 'creative forgery'—than was visible when their *Enquiry* was published in 1934. The years following this initial disclosure have been punctuated by a series of further revelations, making the tale seem, as Barker and Collins have said in their *Sequel to 'An Enquiry'*, more and more like 'Frankie and Johnny': 'This story has no moral, this story has no end.'[67] Obviously, the scholarly writing concerning this complex swindle is voluminous. In 1985 William E. Fredeman counted 'more than twenty separate publications and at least a hundred articles, not counting various reviews and numerous exhibition, sales, and booksellers' catalogues',[68] all devoted to the often brilliant exposures of this most intricate and endlessly surprising enterprise in the production of manufactured rarities, mainly false 'Victorian' first edition pamphlets, in which Morris's titles form only a part, though a central one. The forensic analysis of paper and type, much developed since the original *Enquiry*, added to the more familiar techniques of descriptive and analytic bibliography, have produced in this instance a new direction and methodology for modern bibliography. These, plus the disclosure of letters exchanged between Wise and Forman, have been the means of distinguishing the 'creative forgeries', genuine texts that claim, directly or indirectly, through false or deliberately ambiguous imprint dates, to be first editions or first separate editions.

This is not the place to survey the history of the frauds and their exposure,[69] but it is an opportunity to correct the Morris canon by providing details of the Morris documents now known to be falsified in one way or another and by pointing out just where and how Forman and Wise distorted the record. Frequent references in Section A direct attention to the descriptive listing in Section E: Forgeries, Piracies, and Sophistications.

Organization

The attempt to compile a complete and orderly account of the Morris canon and its history encounters some complications along the way, and something needs to be said here of the nature of these

---

67. *A Sequel to 'An Enquiry into the Nature of Certain Nineteenth-Century Pamphlets'* (London: Scolar Press, 1983), 182. Hereafter referred to as *Sequel*.
68. 'The Story of a Lie: A Sequel to "A Sequel"', *Review*, 7 (1985), 267.
69. That survey has already been done: see Professor Fredeman's article, cited in the note above.

and the way they are addressed both in the general organization and in the arrangements for recording the facts in the various fields, particularly in Section A, where the detail requires some care in definition and organization.

Section A, the core of the book, is where from the beginning in 1856 to 1915, all separate publications appear, from a single flysheet or broadsheet to the twenty-four volumes of *The Collected Works*, with the publishing histories of subsequent editions, impressions, and issues, and including any variant states,[70] along with posthumous first editions from 1915 to the present. Section D: Morris in Periodicals, consists of Morris's first publications in periodicals (here the term 'periodicals' includes all serials) and extends from the first, his contributions in 1856 to *The Oxford and Cambridge Magazine*, to the present. In other words, included here are all first periodical publications, both original and posthumous, that, at the time of publication, were additions to the Morris canon. Though a book made from a first printing in a magazine is included in Section A, the reverse is not true: a piece first published as a separate edition and then reprinted in a journal is not listed in Section D.[71] There is no attempt at publication histories for periodical publications, nor any effort to record every instance where Morris items are reprinted in journals.

Three periodicals were so closely associated with Morris that they have been included in Section A as Morris titles: *The Oxford and Cambridge Magazine*, *The Commonweal*, and *The Hammersmith Socialist Record* (*HSR*). But Morris's original contributions to those journals are listed in Section D.

Morris's personal letters are excluded here as not having been written for publication. But both Henderson and Kelvin's editions of Morris letters are included in Section C, since they collect and reprint letters to the press, obviously written for publication, as well as those that are personal and usually unpublished. There are also 'finding list' entries for both in the Section of Abbreviations because of their importance as sources of collateral evidence regarding Morris's publications.

Besides these there are three shorter lists. Section B: Morris's Contributions to Books (1856–96), is limited to those items originally written for the books in which they appear. Consequently, this list ends with Morris's death in 1896.[72] Section C: Collections and Selections, consists of anthologies of Morris materials from 1856 to 1915 intended to be representative of the Morris oeuvre and collections built around particular interests, such as poetry or prose. It also includes collections of fugitive publications from 1916 to the present, but it does not include Morris items selected for inclusion in collections or anthologies not oriented around Morris. A Morris text as part of a larger collection of titles not by Morris, as the *Volsunga Saga* is in vol. 49 of the Harvard Classics, is excluded, as are indi-

---

70. An exception to the 1915 limit applies in order to provide a complete account of Morris books published in specific, named series. For example, post-1915 Morris titles in the Pocket Library or the Longmans Class Books in English Literature are included.
71. An exception to this occurs when a Morris piece was issued by more than one periodical at or about the same time. In that case finding list details for all the contemporary journal printings are included in the Section D entry.
72. There is one exception to this rule, B-20, 'Justice and Socialism', an extensive set of notes for a lecture. This was not published until Paul Meier included the set in *La Pensée Utopique de William Morris* (Paris: Éditiones Sociales, 1972), 835–40.

vidual poems reprinted in general or school anthologies or periodicals after their initial appearance. Section E: Forgeries, Piracies, and Sophistications, treats of the fraudulent publications of genuine writings by Morris. Two appendices are added for items that should be noted but do not fit conveniently elsewhere. Appendix I is a listing of Interviews with Morris (1856–96) which, while they contain quotations from Morris, are not his responsibility. Appendix II: Ephemera is a list of Morris texts, published by Morris and his Estate, written for a specific, limited, or 'ephemeral' purpose, such as advertising.

Authorship problems arise not only with the anonymous contributions to *The Oxford and Cambridge Magazine* (reviewed in the *Notes* field to the Section A entry for the *Magazine*, A-1.01), but also because many short items, especially leaflets written by Morris and others for the Social Democratic Federation, the Socialist League, the Eastern Question Association, and the Society for the Protection of Ancient Buildings, were published anonymously. Only those cases are included here for which there is convincing evidence of Morris's authorship, and the reasons for the attribution to Morris are included in the entry for the item concerned. Then, there is Morris's tendency frequently to publish the same work under different titles or in a different context—the untitled song sung to Hylas in *Jason* becomes 'A Garden by the Sea' in *Poems by the Way*; 'Hands' in *The Oxford and Cambridge Magazine* is later used as the Prince's song in 'Rapunzel' in *The Defence of Guenevere and Other Poems*; *Labour and Pleasure versus Labour and Sorrow* in a later version becomes *The Beauty of Life*; *The Labour Question from the Socialist Standpoint* becomes *True and False Society*. Throughout this bibliography the focus remains always on the substance of the individual work, whatever changes occur in the title or context. The headings following the code number for each entry in Sections A, B, C, and E are the short forms most commonly used for the work in question, and variant titles, where they occur, are explained in the *Edition* field of the relevant record.

Morris also, contrariwise, tended frequently to issue different works under the same title, or titles so similar as to create confusion: *What Socialists Want* refers to two works: a complete lecture and an unsigned leaflet, both issued by the Socialist League and both written by Morris. Here it is entered as two titles because it refers to two works. *Early England* and *Medieval England* (the latter also sometimes called 'Feudal England') are quite different, being originally conceived as the first two lectures in a trilogy to be called 'England as it was, as it is, and as it may be'. Such cases are reported in summary in the *Edition* field. On call for lecturing not only to Socialist groups but also in support of his many other causes, Morris eventually learned to economize his work by reusing parts of previous lectures, sometimes with new titles, repeating the beginning and the outline of the original, but adding fresh topical references for the particular audience, in its place and time. Other confusions are begotten by journal reports of his speeches or publication of his articles or letters to the newspapers under headings different from the author's, these journal headings being later quoted as if they were his own. There are instances, not included here, where all that remains of a lecture or speech is the title, the MS text being so far undiscovered, or the text having never been written out, an approach that Morris adopted increasingly towards the end of his public life. But the purpose of the bibliography being to list and give details of Morris's work written for publication, titles are omitted here if there is, so far discovered, neither some form of publication in whole or part nor a contemporary account published with some textual detail. Where a contemporary account, say, in shorthand, is all that remains of a text, it is listed, generally in Section D, since it was in journals that such accounts originally appeared.

Section A is organized on the same pattern used by Forman, whose intention at least was to introduce the history of each title at the point where it first appears in the chronology of Morris's works. What results is a history of individual titles within a history of Morris's oeuvre.

To do this requires a system of organization that allows the reader to find a way within the sequence without the inconvenience of constant references to the index. Two chronologies are involved. The first is the chronology of the Morris works, as determined by the date of each title's first publication. The second is the chronology of that title's publication history, its editions, impressions, and issues from the *editio princeps* through to the end of 1915. Though an index is appended, a more immediate orientation to these chronologies is available in the entries. A numbering system organizes Section A (as well as Sections B, C, and E) by a two-part number that allows the reader to see with a glance at an entry heading just where in the two chronologies any entry fits. The whole number, to the left of the point, attaches to a specific title in the sequence of texts. The number to the right of the point refers to the second chronology, which places the particular issue in the sequence of issues of that title. This sequence always starts with .01 (that form of 1 being computer sortable wherever decimal points and values larger than one digit are involved), a number which always belongs to the *editio princeps* as Forman uses that term: the first issue of the first impression of the first edition. The idea of a double chronology was used (though not always consistently) by Forman[73] but he used a single sequence of whole numbers that includes all titles and all issues up to his time of writing.

Some Definitions

It is in fitting authentic titles, dates, and other publication details to particular texts, clarifying muddles both by setting out the necessary facts and by explanation, that a new bibliography of Morris will find its sternest test as well as its most general usefulness. The field titles and their sequence in Section A (with application to Sections B, C, and E, and the two appendices as well) have been adopted as a way of allowing for fact, explanation, and source references while clearly distinguishing between them, whether taken directly from the books or from collateral sources. The technical terms used are the common language of bibliography, here in some cases adapted to the special problems of Morris's publications.[74]

---

73. As T. J. Wise pointed out in his anonymous review of Forman's book, this sequence of issues of a particular title is not always maintained (see *The Athenæum*, No. 3664 (15 Jan. 1898), 80–1). But Forman's intent to follow the double chronological sequence is clear enough.

74. These matters are covered in Gaskell. The approach and formularies used here derive from Gaskell and, where greater detail is necessary, from Fredson Bowers, *Principles of Bibliographical Description* (Princeton: Princeton University Press, 1949).

Some minimal definitions are necessary at the outset:

Edition here is used as a bibliographical term: it means all the copies of a book derived from the same setting of type, whether from original type, stereotype plates, photolithography, in microform, printed from computer tape, direct computerized setting, or other forms of reproduction. If half or more of a published text is reset, the resulting text is a new edition. An impression is all of the copies of a book printed from the same setting of type and issued at a particular time. It is a subset of the edition from which its setting is derived, and, given Victorian technological resources like making moulds from which new plates could be made, there can be any number of impressions from one original setting.

Issue is a word that has two meanings, both employed here. In standard English usage issue means simply any separate publication, or, as a verb: to bring forth or to publish. But in bibliography it is also a technical term referring to a group of copies, part of a single impression, brought forth or published either after the first release, or issue, or released at the same time but incorporating some alteration designed for a particular part of the market. This bibliographical usage is expanded in the relevant entries.

Bibliographically, issues are of two types, either or both being subsets of a particular impression. Any publicized later release of copies either held back or not sold after the first release or issue is called a reissue. A second type of issue, called special issue, occurs when some copies are changed deliberately to cater for a particular section of the market, as for example when Roberts sometimes sold English sheets in American bindings with the place of publication and publisher altered to 'Boston: Roberts Brothers'. A single impression may have several reissues or special issues, though it is still common in the book trade, as it was with the Victorians, to call issues or impressions 'editions' and to number them accordingly.

A *variant* or variant state exists when a particular impression is changed in some respect during the printing process as for example by stopping the press to correct misspellings (see the Kelmscott Press *Gothic Architecture*, A-66.01) discovered during the printing, or when the paper is changed for LP copies of an impression, or when the original edition binding material, lettering, or design changes from the original for some copies of the same impression. The first is a textual variant; the latter two are paper and binding variants. A paper variant embodies a change in quality or size of the paper used, as for 'large' or 'fine paper' (LP or FP) copies; and a binding variant comes about by changes to some copies either in the ways mentioned above or when the number of volumes in which the work is bound is altered.

Fields and Field Titles

After the field titles, printed in italics, is any information derived either from the book itself or from collateral sources (in the latter case it is followed by a source reference in parentheses). The first field in each entry is a transcription of the title page (without a field title unless otherwise specified in square brackets) as it appears in the book being described. The title-page transcription is in quasi-facsimile, and in general follows the Soho Bibliography conventions: whatever the size or type design of the original, here the type is Adobe Garamond and the size 10.5 point. But where the style of the original title page is readily reproduced, it is: lower and upper cases are rendered as they are, as are small caps, italics, underlining, and bold type. Details more difficult to reproduce are noted in square brackets within the transcription, here including the use of coloured or gothic types; publishers' marks; ornamental head-piece or tail-piece woodcuts; and vignettes.

A head title is a page with a title heading followed by the beginning of the text. A wrapper title appears on a pamphlet which has no title page except that on the wrapper. This frequently occurs with pamphlets that are self-wrapped, i.e. where the wrapper leaf is conjunct with the last leaf containing text.

Besides the title page, the only other quasi-facsimile transcripts are colophons, which replace the *Printer* field wherever there is a colophon; and under *Contents*: dedications; headings and illustration labels; half titles (but only where non-standard half titles are used); statements of limitation; printers' imprints; chapter and section heads, and incipits and explicits. Details of publisher, place, printer, series, or limitation, when available from other fields, such as the title transcription, are not repeated as separate fields elsewhere in the entry. Transcriptions always follow a colon and end with a semi-colon. Publications not seen are marked with an asterisk in the heading, following the code number.

Some fields, notably Collation, Contents, and *Technical Notes* examine the books in sufficient detail to determine the particular features of each edition, so that by comparison of a number of copies it becomes possible to describe each edition in terms of a complete or 'ideal' copy, that is, the book as intended by the writer and publisher to reach the public. Such variations as a change of paper or of binding are described under *Technical Notes*. Variations in the dimensions of type area are a useful indicator of whether a book is a new impression or a new setting, hence a new edition. Leaf size is a reliable indicator of the size of the book and, through comparisons, of the difference between ordinary and LP copies. All three of these fields necessarily appear, like the collational formula, wherever the edition changes. Successive impressions and issues are usually the same as the first issue of the edition to which they belong, except for minor corrections to the title page, as in the date of publication. Consequently, one or more of these fields are often omitted after the first issue entry unless changes are made in a new impression with a special issue.

Edition: the Edition field provides, first, any edition information contained within the book itself, such as Pocket Edition, without special punctuation. Edition names not in the book itself but taken from the names in common use, or in advertisements, publishers' records, or bibliographical lists are given within quotation marks (this comes first only when there is no edition information given in the book). Then appears the present compiler's reconstruction of the place of the particular text in the sequence of editions, issues, and impressions. This being an editorial extrapolation is provided in square brackets from the evidence available either from the book itself, from collateral material, or from both (with any relevant source reference identified in parenthesis). Any variants, such as large paper, fine paper, or textual variants are noted under this field title. Then, where applicable, any previous publications of parts of the contents are recorded. This only applies to the collections made by Morris himself, which all are simply defined as Morris books and appear in Section A: *The Defence of Guenevere and Other Poems, Three Northern Love Stories and Other Tales, Hopes and Fears for Art, A Dream of John Ball and A King's Lesson, Signs of Change,* and *Poems by the Way. Old French Romances* is included in Section A as a Morris title because it was done while he was alive, with his active cooperation, and later was included as a Morris title in May Morris's *The Collected Works of William Morris,* Volume XVII. All other collections made by others from Morris's works, whether before or after his death, are recorded in Section C, which is a comprehensive list of collections, selections, and anthologies through 1915. This list continues to the present with collections of fugitive pieces.

All editions, all first impressions, and all distinctive or special issues have separate entries or, in the language of computers, records. Variants, being parts of particular editions and impressions, are not noted and described in separate entries, that is they do not have separate records in Section A. They are described under the editions or impressions in which they occur. The publishing history of each book is complete up to the publication being described in the individual entry. Hence under *Edition* any previous publications, as for example in periodicals, are also listed.

The orientation of letterpress on title pages, colophons, printer's imprints, and illustration labels is assumed to be horizontal and is specified only when otherwise; and the position on the page of display headings, titles, etc., is assumed to be centred and only noted when it differs from that.

Translation: this, like several other fields, appears in an entry only when the nature of the publication makes it relevant, to indicate the fact of translation and the language of the original, but only when the information is not on the title page. As stated previously, there is no attempt here to list or describe translations of Morris's texts into other languages.

Collaborators, Editors, and Illustrators: this is another field included only where it applies and where the information is not available elsewhere in the entry. The names and roles are given of those who made significant contributions to the publication described in the entry. Included here are those who, like E. Belfort Bax, collaborated with Morris in *Socialism: Its Growth and Outcome,* or S. C. Cockerell and Robert Proctor, who selected and edited the fugitive texts included in *Architecture, Industry, and Wealth,* though their names appear nowhere in the volume. As usual, the information is from the book unless set within square brackets.

Though a year of issue is usually included in both the title page and colophon transcriptions, there is always further information on dates of issue in the *Publication* field as part of the attempt to establish a day of issue.

Series: this field is used only in entries where it is relevant for the identification and description of the various publisher's series in which Morris books appear. Books in a series may have some or all of these uniform features: bindings, spine labels, paper, make-up of pagination, leaf size, type area, type, positioning of running heads, footnotes, preliminaries, and end-matter. Most of the Morris series books were created by either T. B. Mosher or Longmans, Green and Co., but Morris's texts found their way into some of the most famous publishers' series in the period covered here: Oxford's

Introduction

World's Classics and Standard Authors series, Dent's 'Everyman's Library', and Routledge's 'Muses Library'. Some series were created specifically for Morris's books (one example is Longmans 'The Poetical Works of William Morris') while other Morris books are parts of a larger sequence involving other writers. The Longmans' series Class Books of English Literature has five Morris titles (one of which, *The Earthly Paradise*, is abridged with passages rendered in prose; hence it is not entered here). Longmans Pocket Library has fourteen Morris titles in eighteen volumes. Mosher issued Morris books in seven of his fourteen series (counting the Bibelot separates as a series).

The details common to a series, including both information available from the book itself and from collateral sources, are given in the *Series* field in the entry for the first Morris book included in the series. To avoid needless repetition, the full series details are given only in the first entry, with cross references to this site in the entries of other titles in the series. This allows the descriptions of later publications in the same series to focus on those details that are unique to the books in question. The series number given after the *Series* field title assists the reader to locate particular titles in multi-volume collections like *The Collected Works of William Morris*, which is generally but not always chronological, or in a series like the 'Golden type quartos', where the chronological sequence of individual volumes is not given in the books.

Place: the place of publication is assumed to be London; so this field only appears in an entry when the publication is issued either in another place or in another place as well as London. In the latter case both London and the other place or places are cited. The place is always the city, or cities in the case of simultaneous publication, from which the publisher issues the book; and as an aid to identifying copies the publisher's imprint is transcribed in full, with addresses as they appear in the book.

Collation: This field appears only in the entries that record a new edition, that is, a new setting, or where a change in format is made to publish an existing setting in a different number of volumes. For example, the 'Popular' ten-part edition of *The Earthly Paradise* as issued by Ellis and Green in 1872 was printed from the same plates as the original three-volumes (1868–70), but each of the ten-part volumes, obviously, is divided differently from the earlier version. The same plates were used again in 1886 when Reeves and Turner issued the same setting in five volumes by combining pairs of parts from the ten-part issue, a change which requires another amendment of the collation.

The *Collation* is an analytical account in bibliographical shorthand of the way the letterpress of a book is constructed. As Bowers says, 'as far as possible it must reflect and record the presswork' of the book as it is (Bowers, p. 228). It combines several elements in a sequence, the first being a statement of general paper size (for example cr. 8° or pott 4°) which also serves to indicate format (folding) where that coincides with the number of leaves in a normal gathering. Where the general size, say 8°, differs from the number of leaves in the gathering the difference is noted, as in '8° in 12s', which means 8° size in a 12° folding. This is followed wherever necessary by a note on any variation from the standard signature usage, as for example in a reprint where more than one signature is used or where 8° forms are rearranged for 12° imposition without altering the signatures (the original signatures are obsolete in the new format, but the page numbers remain correct and can serve the purpose of the signatures). A colon follows and introduces a collational formula listing all the gatherings in the book, including any unsigned gatherings, cancellations (with any replacements), interruptions or errors in the sequence, etc., or printed inserts that are obviously part of the letterpress of the book (as distinct, for example, from leaves or gatherings of publisher's advertising not conjunct with any of the book's text and having no demonstrable connection with the printing of the particular book. As Fredson Bowers says, the collation 'is concerned only with the sheets of the book and does not include end papers, binders' leaves, inserted advertisements not conjugate in the gatherings, or inserted among conjugate advertisements, or any inserted plates'. The principle behind these exclusions is the function of the collational formula, which is to provide an analytical account of the printing, the letterpress, of the book as it was intended by the author and publisher to be in an 'ideal copy'. But besides the excluded non-integral matter, some insertions such as engraved plates may be conjugate with others printed as part of the regular sequence of gatherings, establishing that both the letterpress and the engraved plates were printed on the same press at the same time. Other inserted printed or engraved leaves (such as the 'Addenda and Corrigenda' leaf or the map facing p. 191 in *The Saga Library*, vol. 2) of a similar sort, on the same paper, though not belonging to the regular sequence of gatherings, are parts of the intended printing of the book and consequently are recorded in the collation formula. Both the integral and non-integral insertions are here described in the *Contents*. Inserted leaves are each noted in the collational formula by marking their exact position, e.g. A–B^8 (B5+1), and where they constitute a gathering by the use of the symbol χ.

A statement of signing follows the formula, but this appears only for those books in which there is some variation from the standard form, where the signatures appear (and only appear) on the first page of each gathering. The standard signing—\$1 signed (\$ = 'all')— is assumed and therefore requires no statement. After a statement of the total of leaves, derived from all the gatherings, the pagination statement follows, with inferred page numbers in square brackets. The sum of any pages not numbered and not inferable (because not related to any printed sequence of page numbers in the book) begins the series in italicized arabic numerals with square brackets.[75] Pagination statements end with a total in square brackets, and that total, of course, always equals twice the number of leaves. Concluding the section, when required, is a note on any non-integral insertions or additions such as wrappers, or advertisements attached to the base copy (for the meaning of 'base copy', see below).

Contents: this provides a sequential account of all the pages of the book as described in the pagination formula in the *Collation*, including also in their appropriate places any non-integral insertions, such as plates and advertisements. Pages or parts thereof transcribed in quasi-facsimile—printers' imprints, statements of limitation, incipits and explicits, and chapter or section headings—are preceded by a colon and followed by a semi-colon. The series of Morris titles published by the Kelmscott Press are described, as they are in Peterson's *A Bibliography of the Kelmscott Press*,

75. See Gaskell, 332.

with the numbering system for paper, ornaments, initials, frames, etc., invented by S. C. Cockerell in his 'Short Description of the Kelmscott Press' and applied in his 'Annotated List of the Books printed at the Kelmscott Press' (hereafter referred to as Cockerell). In a similar fashion, the head and tail-pieces, press marks, and ornaments in T. B. Mosher's Morris books are described according to the numbering scheme devised by Philip Bishop in *Thomas Bird Mosher: Pirate Prince of Publishers*. Plates are included under *Contents*, but ornamentation—like end papers, binding, and wrappers—is included under *Technical Notes*.

Technical Notes: this field is concerned with the physical make-up and design of the book under a series of sub-field titles: *paper*: includes colour, sort (machine or handmade), any edging ornamentation, such as t.e.g. (top edge gilt), the paper name if there is one, and any watermark; *leaf size*: always with height (vertical) first, in millimetres, and whether trimmed, lightly trimmed, or deckle edged; *printing*: whether and where coloured inks are used; *type*: designs specified only when named; *lines-to-page*: whether leaded, with the line count from a typical page; *pagination*: this is assumed to be in arabic numbers at the outer margins of the headlines, and only noted when it differs from that; *headlines, shoulder titles*, or *shoulder notes*: position and content specified; *end-papers*: number, colour, and any maps, designs, or letterpress specified; *binding: wrapper*: colour, material, and blocking noted, with transcriptions of any letterpress. Where a series is involved, features that are common to the series are cross-referenced to this field (and occasionally others) in the entry for the first Morris book in the series.

The description of wrappers presents complications that require further detail. Their presence is briefly noted at the end of the *Collation* field as something added to but not integral to the pamphlet. But full description is considered a subset of binding and placed in that part of the sequence in the *Technical Notes* field, where the printed contents, colour, and method of attachment (sewn, stapled, or glued) is specified. In some cases, a wrapper may provide the only 'title page' the pamphlet has, and the transcription of the title that begins such an entry is labelled 'wrapper title', the description of the whole binding or wrapper being provided as usual under *binding: wrapper* in the *Technical Notes*. A pamphlet described as self-wrapped has no separate wrapper. The first leaf has the title page on its recto and the last leaf, being conjunct with the first, concludes the printed text. Dust wrappers, where they appear, are described immediately after the binding, but there has been no special effort made to compile an exhaustive list of dust wrappers.

Publication: the dates of publication provided are intended to record the day of issue or, failing that, the interval within which the day of issue lies, or, failing that, the specific date considered to be as close as has yet been found to the day of issue, such as the date printing was finished, with supporting documentation noted. Dates given in colophons are normally some time before issue, binding usually coming some time after the printing was finished. Such dates are identified as colophon dates or finished printing dates. This field also provides print run and price, along with any changes from the original price.

Notes: these are provided only where there is a aspect of the book that requires explanation that cannot adequately or conveniently be dealt with under the field titles. For example, a representative selection of entries lists the costs involved in producing the particular edition or impression, taken from printers' or publishers' archives, and in some instances it has been possible to give details of the agreements for royalties between author and publisher. The *Notes* field is also used to present an overview of F. S. Ellis's strategy to accommodate the changes of the original publishing plan for *The Earthly Paradise*, to make the case for Morris's authorship in instances of disputed authorship or attributions made here for the first time, or, in Section E, to summarize the evidence in the more complex cases of forgery, piracy, or sophistication of the publication described in the entry.

Register of Copies Consulted: this is not intended to be an exhaustive list of all copies seen, let alone all those located. The generally agreed minimum of 7 copies of each edition have been consulted where that was possible.

Base copy: the 1st copy noted in the *Register of Copies Consulted* is the book used as the basis for the description in an entry, though occasionally some details of an 'ideal copy' must be supplied from other copies (often when describing original bindings). There may be a use in repeating that an asterisk following the entry number indicates editions, impressions, or issues not seen.

Later impressions (or issues): this field is used to list those routine impressions or reissues, usually of the more popular books, that do not vary in any significant way from the 1st issue of an edition or impression and therefore do not justify a separate entry. These lists come at the end of the entry which sets the pattern, and to which the reader can refer for more detail. The summary entries include only the publisher, date, edition name and number, impression, or issue, print run, and price.

Areas Not Included

1. This is a primary bibliography. Secondary sources, such as scholarly or critical publications on Morris or his works are not included. The secondary Morris bibliography has been listed and annotated in two book-length surveys: Gary Aho, *William Morris: A Reference Guide* (Boston, Mass.: G. K. Hall & Co., 1985) and David and Sheila Latham, *An Annotated Critical Bibliography of William Morris* (London: Harvester Press, 1991). In *The Journal of the William Morris Society* (hereafter referred to as *JWMS*), the Lathams continue to provide a biennial update of the Morris secondary material, titled 'William Morris: An Annotated Bibliography'. Produced 'usually' in the odd years, the last instalment, No. 11, was published in 15/4 (Summer, 2004), i–xii. It covers the years 2000–2001.

2. Since the concern of this bibliography is with Morris's published works, his calligraphic manuscripts—which are individual works of art, often of texts not his own—appear here only when the text is by Morris and where facsimile editions of the Morris originals, such as *A Book of Verse* (1981), have been published. Where these facsimiles exist, they are treated as original editions in the chronological sequence of published titles.

3. No translations of Morris into foreign languages are included.

Introduction

4. For the years after 1915 there is no attempt to list or describe editions, issues, or impressions after the first.

5. Musical settings of Morris lyrics are included only when they are first editions or first separate editions of Morris's text, as is the case, for example, with 'All for the Cause' (1887) with music by E. Belfort Bax, or 'A Death Song' (1887) with music by Malcolm Lawson.

6. Internal memoranda or circular letters from Morris to his fellow members of various organizations in which he had official functions are not included here. Though they were often printed for circulation, they are so limited in both function and audience as not to be properly classed as publications. Those printed documents, such as *To Socialists* (see A-28.01), which address a more general audience and have a less ephemeral purpose, are included as publications.

7. Manuscripts are neither listed nor discussed except in cases where they bear on questions of authorship or dating. Finding lists of the Morris manuscripts and their locations are provided in Ken Goodwin's *A Preliminary Handlist of Manuscripts and Documents of William Morris* (London: William Morris Society, 1983; hereafter referred to as Goodwin) and Richard Pearson's 'William Morris: 1834–1896' in *The Index to English Literary Manuscripts*, Vol. 4.3 (London: Mansell, 1993).

A Bibliography of William Morris

THE

OXFORD AND CAMBRIDGE

MAGAZINE

FOR 1856.

CONDUCTED BY MEMBERS OF THE TWO
UNIVERSITIES.

LONDON:
BELL AND DALDY, FLEET STREET.
1856.

Figure 2. A-1.01: *The Oxford and Cambridge Magazine*, title page of the bound volume

A

The Original Editions with Posthumous Editions to 1915 and First Editions to the Present

Besides the original separate publications, from bound volumes to single sheet leaflets and those issued posthumously through 1915, when the *Collected Works of William Morris* was completed, this list includes separate publications of posthumous first editions to the present. Publication histories of each title are provided through 1915.

A-1.01: The Oxford and Cambridge Magazine

[annual vol.:] THE | OXFORD AND CAMBRIDGE | MAGAZINE | FOR 1856. | [printer's ornament] | [thin wavy rule] | CONDUCTED BY MEMBERS OF THE TWO | UNIVERSITIES. | [thin wavy rule] | LONDON: | BELL AND DALDY, FLEET STREET. | 1856.
wrapper title: [Jan. no., all within a typographical border:] [aligned left] No. 1. [centred] January, [right] 1856. | THE | [ornamental 3-line caps, 'O', 'C', and 'M', in neo-gothic type] Oxford and Cambridge | Magazine. | CONDUCTED BY MEMBERS OF THE | TWO UNIVERSITIES. | Contents | [list of 9 items] | LONDON: | BELL AND DALDY, FLEET STREET. | [printer's imprint, below compartment, aligned flush left] | PRINTED BY C. WHITTINGHAM [aligned right] TOOKS COURT, CHANCERY LANE.
Edition: annual vol.: [1st impression, 1st edn.] The 1st number had a 2nd impression, see *Notes*, below. The 12 monthly numbers of the *Magazine* were bound as a vol. in Jan. 1857. The vol. title page with title and contents for the bound vol., and a cancellans leaf for pp. 465–6 were included with the last issue, Dec. 1856. Morris, being editor of the 1st issue, used the occasion of a 2nd impression, required when the 1st impression was exhausted, to insert an expanded version of the review of Kingsley's *Sermons for the Times*. The addition, by making use of waste space, made no difference to the number of leaves in the gathering or the sequence in the collation. The only sign distinguishing the change in the second impression is the greater length of the review of *Sermons for the Times* on pp. 61–2, which leaves no waste space.

On the disputed attributions to Morris, see the *Notes*, below. Morris's contributions were 1st collected and pbd. separately in 1903 as *The Hollow Land and Other Contributions to the Oxford and Cambridge Magazine* (see C-20).
Collation: (collected edn., 1856): Jan.: cr. 8°: [A]² B–R⁸ S² (–S2) T–2C⁸ 2D² (–2D2) 2E–2I⁸ (± 2I‚₇) 2K–3A⁸ 3B⁴ 3C–3E⁸ 3F⁶ 390 leaves pp. [i–iii] iv [1] 2–776 [= 780] + wrapper (from which the Jan. title page is transcribed, above). The two singletons, S² (–S2) and 2D² (–2D2), are the last leaves of the issues in which they appear.

Because of misplaced lines it was decided after the copies had been printed and released, to cancel pp. 465–6 of the August issue, and a cancellans was provided at the end of the December number for readers to correct their defective copies. No copy thus corrected has been seen.
Contents: (collected edn. for 1856): p. [i], title page; p. [ii]: blank; pp. [iii]–iv, headed: CONTENTS.; p. [1], text begins; pp. 2–776, text completed with explicit: THE END. | [thin rule] | [printer's imprint] CHISWICK PRESS: C. WHITTINGHAM, TOOKS COURT, | CHANCERY LANE.
Technical Notes: *paper*: plain white machine-made; *leaf size*: cut flush, 215 x 137 mm.; *pagination*: continuous through all 12 issues as in the annual bound copies, the standard number of pages being 64, enlarged to 66 in nos. 4 and 6, 72 in no. 11, and 60 in no. 12; *binding*: bound vol. for 1856: blue cloth-covered boards with printed paper spine label: THE | OXFORD | AND | CAMBRIDGE | MAGAZINE | FOR 1856.; *wrapper*: monthly issue in green paper wrap-

per: p. [*1*], see title transcription, above; pp. [*2–4*], ads; *ornamentation*: it is not clear how much part Morris had in the design of the *Oxford and Cambridge Magazine*, but he would have had, as the source of funds, an ultimate veto power. The ornaments used in printing the magazine—a full ornamental typographical border on each monthly wrapper, ornamental initials to start each contribution, and the head-piece repeated on the 1st page of each issue—were made for the Chiswick Press from designs by Charlotte and Eleanor Whittingham, daughters of the owner-director, Charles Whittingham (the nephew). 'Nearly all' were cut in wood by Mary Byfield (see Joseph R. Dunlap, 'The Road to Kelmscott: William Morris and the Book Arts', 22 (hereafter referred to as Dunlap 1)), and most are reproduced in HBF, pp. 22, 24.

Publication: 1856, No. 1, Jan., 750 copies printed on 18 Dec. 1855, for issue on 1 Jan. 1856 with a 2nd impression of 500 copies printed on 18 Jan. 1856; Nos. 2–9, Feb.–Sept., 1,000 copies each; Nos. 10–12, Oct.–Dec., 750 copies (Chiswick Press Archive, Department of Manuscripts, BL (Add.) MS (hereafter referred to as Chiswick Arch.)). Monthly copies priced 1*s*. Bound annual vol., 13*s*.

Register of Copies Examined: BL: (base copies: 2 copies: Copy 1: C.59.10 and Copy 2: Ashley 3679); LeM (AMS facsimile reprint, 1972, from Northwestern Univ. copy); Camb U (T 718.c.1.).

Notes: The *Oxford and Cambridge Magazine* is included in this list of Morris's separate publications because, though a periodical, it is also, like *Commonweal* and *The Hammersmith Socialist Record*, a Morris pbn., he being its 'begetter', its financier, its 1st editor, and its main contributor. But after setting the pattern with his 1st issue, Morris decided not to continue as editor. An entry in the diary of Margaret Price (sister of Cormell Price) for 9 Jan. 1856 says: 'Morris does not like being editor of the O. and C. Magazine, so gives Fulford £100 a year to be editor.' (Quoted by G. Burne-Jones, *Memorials of Edward Burne-Jones*, i. 127; hereafter referred to as *Memorials*).

Since the death of Morris the identification of his contributions has been the most problematic of the scholarly issues connected with the *Oxford and Cambridge Magazine*. Before printing what he calls his 'Morris list', H. Buxton Forman refers to 2 other lists that were in circulation when he published his bibliography. There were others besides these, and there were several marked copies that made various attributions, usually to people with some connection to the *Magazine*. The difficulty is that the lists do not agree, and most are demonstrably wrong in one or more of their attributions. 3 items variously attributed to Morris—'Ruskin and "The Quarterly"', 'The Two Partings', and 'A Night in a Cathedral'—are at the centre of the difficulty, with the 1st being sometimes seen as a collaborative effort of Morris and Burne-Jones, the 2nd and 3rd being sometimes attributed to William Fulford.

The evidence now available on the attributions is reviewed in the 'Introduction' to the Thoemmes Press reprint of *The Hollow Land and Other Contributions to the Oxford and Cambridge Magazine* (see xiii–xxvii; hereafter referred to as LeMire). The conclusions reached there reinforce those of J. W. Mackail as embodied in his list of Morris's contributions in *The Life of William Morris* (see Mackail, i. 92). The list declines the attribution to Morris of any of the three contested pieces. The reasons behind that judgement can be briefly summarised. In response to a query from E. T. Cook and A. Wedderburn, editors of *The Works of John Ruskin*, Mackail described Morris's role in 'Ruskin and *The Quarterly*' as limited to that of consultant to Burne-Jones, who actually wrote the essay, a fact that, as Burne-Jones' son-in-law, Mackail was in a position to know. As regards the 2 stories—'The Two Partings' and 'A Night in a Cathedral'—in his Notebooks, now in the WMG (MS J163-6), used as he prepared *The Life of William Morris*, Mackail refers to both stories as by then known definitely to be by Fulford, expressed with such certainty as to suggest he had at hand some incontrovertible evidence now unavailable. His conclusion is reinforced by a recent discovery that the 2 lyrics incorporated in 'The Two Partings' were both published by Fulford in the 1st vol. of his poems, *Songs of Life* (1859). This undoubted fact directly contradicts Forman's version of what he calls 'the Morris list', throwing into some doubt whether Morris had much to do with it.

Mackail says:

> The full list is as follows: the poems being distinguished by having their titles printed in italic:
>
> January: The Story of the Unknown Church. (A tale.) *Winter Weather*.
>
> February: The Churches of North France. No. 1. Shadows of Amiens.
>
> March: A Dream. (A tale) 'Men and Women.' By Robert Browning. [a review].
>
> April: Frank's Sealed Letter. (A tale.)
>
> May: *Riding Together*.
>
> July: Gertha's Lovers. (a tale.) c. 1–3. *Hands*.

August: "Death the Avenger and Death the Friend."
Svend and His Brethren. (A tale.)
Gertha's Lovers, c. 4, 5.
September: Lindenborg Pool. (A tale.)
The Hollow Land. (A tale.) c. 1, 2.
The Chapel in Lyoness.
October: The Hollow Land, c. 3.
Pray but One Prayer for Me.
December: Golden Wings. (A tale.) (Mackail, i. 92).

There were 2 engraved photographic reproductions of Thomas Woolner's medallions of Tennyson and Carlyle offered for separate sale to subscribers for later binding with the magazine, but these are not integral to the *Magazine* as printed.

A-2.01: The Defence of Guenevere

THE | DEFENCE OF GUENEVERE, | AND OTHER POEMS. | BY WILLIAM MORRIS | [publisher's mark of Aldine anchor and dolphin crossed with a bell] | LONDON: | BELL AND DALDY, 186, FLEET STREET. | 1856.

Edition: [1st impression, 1st edn.] In addition to the main body of poems published here for the 1st time, Morris reprints 4 of his 5 verse contributions to the *Oxford and Cambridge Magazine*: 'Pray but One Prayer for Me' (reprinted here as 'Summer Dawn'), 'Riding Together', 'The Chapel in Lyoness', and 'Hands' (reprinted as the song sung by the Prince in 'Rapunzel'). The only Morris poem from the *Magazine* not reprinted here is 'Winter Weather.'

Collation: fcap 8°: [A]⁴ B–Q⁸ R⁴ 128 leaves pp. [i–vii] viii [1] 2–248 [= 256] + errata slip, loosely inserted.

Contents: p. [i], half title; p. [ii], blank; p. [iii], title page; p. [iv], blank; p. [v], dedication: TO MY FRIEND, | DANTE GABRIEL ROSSETTI, | PAINTER, | I DEDICATE THESE POEMS.; p. [vi], blank; pp. [vii]–viii, [headed] CONTENTS. | [30 poem titles, printed as a list]; tipped in slip inserted before p. 1, facing p. viii, headed: ERRATA | [list of 5 errors and their page nos., see HBF, p. 36]; pp. 1–18: THE DEFENCE OF GUENEVERE.; pp. 19–42: KING ARTHUR'S TOMB.; pp. 43–56: SIR GALAHAD, A CHRISTMAS MYSTERY.; pp. 57–64: THE CHAPEL IN LYONESS.; pp. 65–109: SIR PETER HARPDON'S END.; pp. 111–34: RAPUNZEL.; pp. 135–47: CONCERNING GEFFRAY TESTE NOIRE.; pp. 148–54: A GOOD KNIGHT IN PRISON.; pp. 155–8: OLD LOVE.; pp. 159–62: THE GILLIFLOWER OF GOLD.;

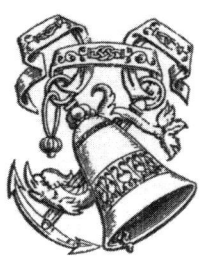

Figure 3. A-2.01: *The Defence of Guenevere* (1st edn.) title page

pp. 163–5: SHAMEFUL DEATH.; pp. 166–8: THE EVE OF CRECY.; pp. 169–73: THE JUDGEMENT OF GOD.; pp. 174–7: THE LITTLE TOWER.; pp. 178–81: THE SAILING OF THE SWORD.; pp. 182–6: SPELLBOUND.; pp. 187–93: THE WIND.; pp. 194–8: THE BLUE CLOSET.; pp. 199–201: THE TUNE OF THE SEVEN TOWERS.; pp. 203–214: GOLDEN WINGS.; pp. 215–22: THE HAYSTACK IN THE FLOODS.; pp. 223–5: TWO RED ROSES ACROSS THE MOON.; pp. 226–30: WELLAND RIVER.; pp. 231–3: RIDING TOGETHER.; pp. 234–6: FATHER JOHN'S WAR-SONG.; pp. 237–8: SIR GILES' WAR-SONG.; pp. 239–40: NEAR AVALON.; pp. 241–5: PRAISE OF MY LADY.; p. 246: SUMMER DAWN.; p. 247: IN PRISON.; p. 248, text completed with explicit: THE END. | [thin rule] | CHISWICK PRESS:—PRINTED BY C. WHITTINGHAM | TOOKS COURT, CHANCERY LANE.

Technical Notes: *paper*: cream machine-moulded, no watermark; *leaf size*: trimmed, 170 x 106 mm.; *printing*: *running titles*: all rectos and versos, relevant poem title, in italics; *endpapers*: 1 free end and paste-down, front and back, paste-downs and facing free ends plain matt brown and blank, reverse sides of free ends plain white and blank, front and back; *binding*: at least three different states of the binding appear in what may indicate 3 different batches sent to the binder: All are in brown textured cloth and all are in the Colbeck Collection (CaBVaU); the BGR collection (now in the CSmH) has 2 of the 3 bindings: (BGR 1st, base copy): 'diagonal wave' No. 106ae' (G. Thomas Tanselle, 'The Bibliographical Description of Patterns', *Studies in Bibliography*, 23 (1970), 71–102; hereafter referred to as Tanselle 1), blind-stamped thick-thin rule borders front and back and top and bottom of spine; (2nd copy) a 'moire' patterned cloth with a thin-rule border blind-stamped on the front within the same thick-thin rule borders, with typographical ornaments blind stamped at each corner and in the centre; *spine*: 1st copy: gilt-stamped: THE | DEFENCE | OF | GUENEVERE | [thin rule] | MORRIS | [printer's leaf] | LONDON | BELL & DALDY; 2nd copy: gilt-stamped: Morris's Poems | [printer's leaf]; the 3rd variant (VU copy) is bound in a mid-brown herring-bone pattern (Tanselle No. 120 'crisscross'), thick-thin rule compartments front and back and at the head and foot of the spine; spine is as copy 1 except the tail-piece leaf ornament has, as Norman Colbeck puts it, a larger ornament below the author's name, 'with tail turning to the right' (*Colbeck Collection*, p. 578); *ornamentation*: Chiswick Press ornaments above and below each half title, and above the head title of all poems with ornamental head-pieces and illuminated initial letters; various ornamental tail pieces after each poem and on last page of text or on the following page (pp. 18, 110). 'Sir Galahad', 'Concerning Geffray Teste Noire', 'The Haystack in the Floods', 'Welland River', 'Riding Together', 'Father John's War-Song', 'Praise of My Lady', 'Summer Dawn', and 'In Prison', all end without ornament.
Publication: 1858 [issued 27 Feb.–13 Mar.] (*Pub. Circ.*, 21/492 (15 Mar. 1858), 117). Mackail says Mar. (i. 135).
Register of Copies Examined: Fdmn (base copy); SPar; BGR (3 copies, including 2 of the 3 variant bindings); VU (Baill E R 38A, 3rd variant binding); An-C-TU (M677 D44 1858); MU (ER); BL (4 copies: 1568 / 4495. and C.58.c.10.; Ashley 1212 and 1213).
Notes: Morris, letter to Alexander Macmillan, 25 Oct. 1857: 'Having a volume of poems which I intend bringing out, I wish to know if you would undertake to publish them, and on what terms?' Again, on 7 Nov. 1857: 'Your letter to me was somehow mislaid so I have only just seen it. I send you some of the poems on the chance of their being any good, though I should tell you that I scarcely thought it likely you would undertake to publish them at your own risk: I suppose in case of no other arrangement being possible, you would not object to publishing them at my own expense.' (*Letters*, i. 30)

But Macmillan did object, as indicated in Morris's letter of 21 Nov. [1857]: 'Three of the four manuscripts I sent you reached me today, the other (called "Arthur's Tomb") is missing, would you be good enough to see if you have it, and if so send it to me—Thanking you for the trouble you have taken—' (*Letters*, i. 32).

Of the 500 copies printed, 250 'were sold and given away', and the rest 'stayed long on the publisher's shelves' (Mackail, i. 130).

The 3 bindings perhaps represent different batches of sheets from the same impression sent at intervals to the binder. 'Morris's Poems' were sent 'to Messrs Bone and Son' so it may be conjectured that Bell and Daldy held some copies of the original edn., unbound, and released them some time after the 1st batch, which is consistent with the situation as described by H. B. Forman: 'The Defence of Guenevere of 1858 must have sold very slowly; for it was still to be had at Messrs. Bell and Daldy's after they had moved to York Street, Covent Garden, and published the Jason' (HBF, p. 41) in 1867.

From *A Bookman's Catalogue: the Norman Colbeck Collection* (hereafter referred to as *Colbeck Collection*): 'Dark brown cloth, spine gilt, edges uncut, drab brown endpapers, publisher's 24 page catalogue at end dated July 1859. It is probably not the 1st binding batch, which normally were without ads at end; but it has the main features of early copies—the smaller ornament below author's name on spine, with tail turning to the left'. There were 3 other copies of *Guenevere* in Colbeck's collection of which the 4th had a 'larger spine ornament with tail turning to right' (ii. 578).

A-2.02: The Defence of Guenevere

THE | DEFENCE OF GUENEVERE, | AND OTHER POEMS. | BY WILLIAM MORRIS. | [thin rule] | (*Reprinted without alteration from the edition of 1858.*) | [thin rule] | LONDON: | ELLIS & WHITE, 29, NEW BOND STREET. | 1875.

Edition: [1st issue, 1st impression, 2nd edn.] Besides the regular copies, Forman says, 'there were twenty-five copies on Whatman's paper, of demy 8° size' (HBF, p. 37). While not a deliberate facsimile reprint, and with the new printer omitting all of the Chiswick Press ornamental head and tail pieces, this, as Forman points out, is very close to the 1st edn., even to leaving uncorrected 4 of the 5 errors in the 1st edn. errata slip (of which none was provided in the new edn.). It seems likely that the text was set from a copy of the 1st edn. minus the errata slip (HBF, p. 37).

Collation and *Contents*: as in A-2.01, except for the change in the imprint date to 1875 and the printer's imprint, p. 248: [thin rule] | PRINTED BY ROBERT ROBERTS, BOSTON, LINCOLNSHIRE.

Technical Notes: *paper*: LP copies: cream-white Whatman hand-laid, no watermark; ordinary copies: machine-laid with dandy roll laid lines; *leaf size*: LP: uncut size avg. 190 x 128 mm.; ordinary copies: trimmed, t.e.g., 188 x 122 mm.; *printing*: as in A-2.01; *end-papers*: single free end and paste-down, plain white and blank, front and back; *binding*: plain dark blue or green unblocked cloth; *spine*: printed paper label: [within a thin-rule compartment] THE | DEFENCE | OF | GUENEVERE | AND OTHER POEMS | BY | W. MORRIS | 8s.; and 25 LP copies printed in demy 8° and bound in grey paper-covered boards with cream paper spine and printed paper spine label; *ornamentation*: all of the Chiswick Press head and tail-pieces of the 1st edn. are omitted here.

Publication: 1875 [issued 16–31 Mar.]; *print run*: 250 copies (?); *price*: 8s. (*Pub. Circ.*, 38/901 (2 Apr. 1875), 241).

Register of Copies Examined: LeM (base copy); VU (3 copies: SpC [E], B821.85De, and (Ba SpC | BX 821.8 Morris, with bookplate of Sir Ernest Scott); BL (1568 / 1186 / 1889); NNPM (Ms 8990); MU (Spec. Coll. PR 5078 D4 1875a); CSt (821.6 M87dg); BGR; Fdmn.

Notes: inserted in an NNPM copy of this book (MS 8990) is an autographed letter signed and dated 'May 5, 1875' from F. S. Ellis to an unknown correspondent (probably Harold Pierce of Philadelphia). Ellis presents an LP copy (the 1st edn. had no LP variant) to the American collector to continue his run of Morris's LP copies. He explains that the new edn. was to be one of a collected edn. of Morris's poetry, but such a collection was not done until the Longmans issue of The Poetical Works in 1896.

Later impressions of this edn.: (this list excludes the American issues, for which see A-2.03 below).

1.* Ellis: 1883: [2nd impression, 2nd edn.]; *print run*: unknown; *price*: 8s.

2.* Reeves and Turner: 1889: [3rd impression, 2nd edn.]; *print run*: unknown, but the number had to be adequate to cover the Roberts Brothers (hereafter referred to as RB) import, which later practice suggests might have been 250 copies for the 1st American issue.

A-2.03: The Defence of Guenevere (imported shts. RB)
Title page duplicates A-2.02.

Edition: [2nd issue, 1st American, of the English 1st impression, 2nd edn.] 250 copies (? if the same as the imported 1891 copies; see Roberts Arch., Book E, p. 251) of the English 1st impression, 1st edn., were exported in sheets to Roberts Brothers of Boston in 1875 and issued in a Roberts binding (thus stamped on the spine), but with the original Ellis and White publisher's imprint and Robert Roberts printer's imprint (see *Publishers' Weekly*, successor to *The American Literary Gazette and Publishers' Circular*, 8/204 (11 Dec. 1875), 917; hereafter referred to as *Pub. Weekly*). See this field in A-2.01 for previous pbns. of several poems.

Collation: this Roberts-bound book is the same edn. in all respects as A-2.02, except for the end-papers and binding, for which see *Technical Notes*, below.

Technical Notes: *end-papers*: 2 free ends and paste-down, front and back, plain white and blank except paste-down and facing free end are dark matt brown; *binding*: plain unblocked dark green cloth with chamfered edges; *spine*: gilt-stamped with single lines of alternating ovals and vertically spaced (3) dots at head and foot, the letterpress being between horizontal thin rules: | THE | DEFENCE | OF | GUENEVERE | [chain-line rule] | BY | [in swash caps] WILLIAM MORRIS | [plain text] ROBERTS BRO'S[.]

Publication: 1875 [issued 1 May] (see *Pub. Weekly*, above); *print run*: probably the same number as in 1891 (see below): 250 copies imported from Ellis and White; *price*: $2.00.

Register of Copies Examined: LeM (base copy); NNPM (LP copy: MS8990M); CSt (Felton PR 5074/D31, 1875); MU (Spec. Coll. PR 5078 D4 1875a).

Notes: this is the only Roberts Morris title for which RB never produced an American setting. The American publisher chose instead on three occasions to import small numbers of copies in sheets and bind them in an American binding.

Later issues: American issues only:

1.* RB: 1883: [2nd American issue, imported sheets from the English 2nd edn.]; *print run*: probably 250, as on the 3rd occasion (see below); *price*: $2.00.

2.* RB: 1891: [3rd American issue of imported sheets from the English 2nd edn.] (see Roberts Arch., Book E, p. 255); *print run*: 250 copies imported; *price*: $2.00.

A-2.04: The Defence of Guenevere (KP)

THE DEFENCE OF GUENEVERE, | AND OTHER POEMS. BY WILLIAM | MORRIS.

Edition: 'Kelmscott Press Edition' [1st impression, 3rd edn.] Corrections by the author made here, including an alteration in 'Summer Dawn', were incorporated in later Longmans edns. (see HBF, pp. 39–40). See this field in A-2.01 for previous pbns. of several of the poems collected here.

Collaborators, editors, and illustrators: spine titling hand-lettered by Herbert M. Ellis.

Series: 5th title, 3rd by Morris, produced by the KP.

Colophon: HERE ends The Defence of Guenevere, and | other Poems, written by William Morris; and | printed by him at the Kelmscott Press, 14, | Upper Mall, Hammersmith, in the County of | Middlesex; & finished on the 2nd day of April, | of the year 1892. | [¶] Sold by Reeves & Turner, 196, Strand, London. | [KP printer's mark 1]

Collation: small 4° in 8s: [a]² b–l⁸ m⁶ [$4 (–b1 k2 m4) signed] 88 leaves pp. [4] [1] 2–169 [170–2] [= 176].

Contents: pp. [1–2], blank; p. [3], half title, here used as the title page, see above; p. [4], headed: [flush left] A TABLE OF THE CONTENTS OF | THIS VOLUME. | [list of titles, see A-2.01]; p. [1], 1st chapter head title, text begins; pp. 2–169, text completed; p. 170, colophon: see above, followed by printer's mark 1; pp. [171–2], blank.

Technical Notes: *paper*: Flower paper 1; *leaf size*: untrimmed deckled edges, avg. 203 x 142 mm.; *printing*: printed in red and black: all shoulder notes, marginal glosses, poetic refrains, character names in dialogue, and stage and scene directions in red; *type face*: Golden type; *shoulder notes*: all rectos and versos, short titles of the relevant poems; *endpapers*: (the standard KP practice): 3 free ends and a pastedown, plain white and blank, front and back; *binding*: the 1st KP use of limp natural vellum with green silk ties, short title hand-lettered by Herbert M. Ellis in gothic script up the spine: 'Guenevere'; *ornamentation*: full borders 2 and 1; 1 corner ornament; 10-line initials for each of the 30 poems; 19 6-line initials.

Publication: 2 Apr. 1892 [finished printing, issued on '19 May 1892']; *print run*: 300 paper copies and 10 on vellum; *price*: 2gns. and 'about' 12gns., respectively (Cockerell, p. 150).

Register of Copies Examined: VU (2 copies: SpC L base copy, LP from Poynton Collection, with Morris's signature pasted in from another source; SpC 19F, also Poynton Coll.); BGR; CSt (Z239.2/K29 M87d Gunst); NNPM (MS 76893, KP edn. with inserted letter to Herbert M. Ellis referring to spine lettering); BL (C.43.e.5.); CSmH; SSL.

Notes: NNPM copy: with ALS from Morris to Herbert M. Ellis 9 June 1892, thanks him for lettering 'Guenevere' on the spines of all copies with a pen and black ink. This is the only KP book so treated.

May Morris discusses Morris's corrections to the text for the KP edn., both those made and those merely projected (*CW*, vol. I. xxii–xxxi).

A-2.05: The Defence of Guenevere

This title page duplicates A-2.02 except that the new publisher's imprint and the date are changed: LONGMANS, GREEN, AND CO. | LONDON, NEW YORK, AND BOMBAY | 1896.

Edition: [2nd English issue, 3rd impression, 2nd edn.] This issue is made up of the remaining Reeves copies (see A-2.02 for the details) purchased by Longmans when Morris switched to that firm as his main publisher. The only changes are in the publisher's imprint, the date, the binding, and the spine label.

Series: The Poetical Works of William Morris. This series is indicated only on the printed paper spine label. This title is one of a uniform set of 10 unnumbered vols. all issued in 1896 as part of Longmans 1st initiative as Morris's publisher. The number increased to 11 vols. with the addition of *The Tale of Beowulf* in 1898; for series details and the titles included, see this field in A-4.16.

Technical Notes: *binding*: bound in plain black unblocked cloth; *spine*: printed paper spine label: [within thin-rule compartment] THE | POETICAL | WORKS OF | WILLIAM | MORRIS | [thin rule] | THE | DEFENCE | OF | GUENEVERE | AND OTHER POEMS | [below compartment] Six Shillings Net.

Publication: in June 1896, an unknown number of remaining Reeves and Turner copies were acquired by Longmans in sheets when they took over Morris's publishing from Reeves and Turner. Longmans had these newly bound and issued with a new title page sometime between the 18th and the 25th of July 1896 (*Pub. Circ.*, 65/1569 (25 July 1896), 84); *price*: 6s. net, the original standard price for all the vols. in the series.

Register of Copies Examined: BGR (base copy).

A-2.06: The Defence of Guenevere

THE | DEFENCE OF GUENEVERE | AND OTHER POEMS | BY | WILLIAM MORRIS | Reprinted from the Kelmscott Press Edition, as revised | by the Author | LONGMANS, GREEN, AND CO. | LONDON, NEW YORK, AND BOMBAY | 1900 | *All rights reserved*.

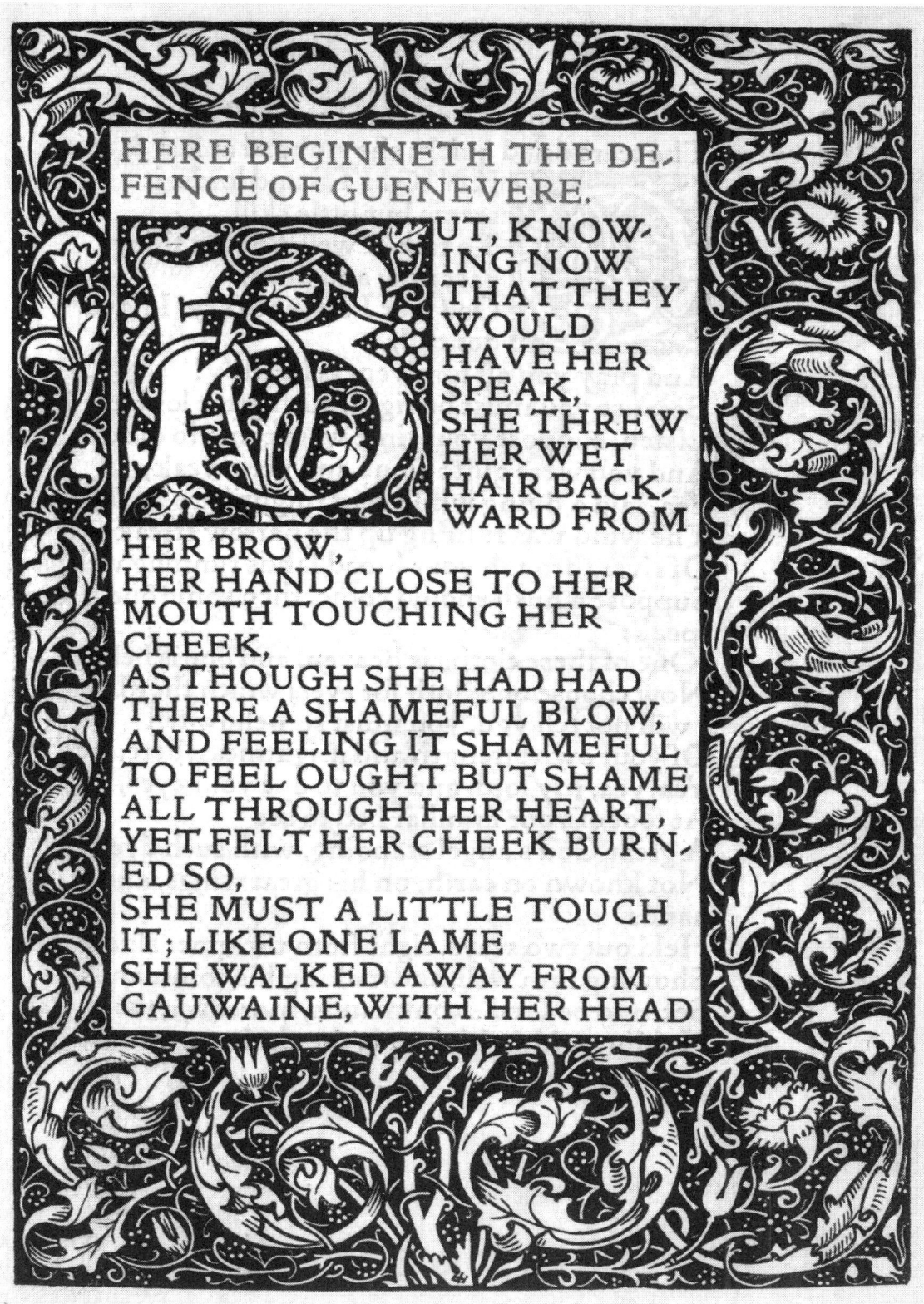

Figure 4. A-2.04: *Defence of Guenevere* (KP, Kelmscott Press edn.) head title in Border 2

Edition: 'Best Edition' in Longmans Arch. and advertising [1st impression, 4th edn.]. Longmans Arch. indicates resetting, though Morris's corrections are minor and not always well advised (see *Notes*, below).

Collation: cr. 8°: π⁴ A–P⁸ Q⁶ 130 leaves pp. [i–vi] vii–viii [1] 2–248 [249–52] [= 260].

Contents: p. [i], half title; p. [ii], headed: Bibliographical Note; p. [iii], title page; p. [iv], blank; p. [v], dedication: as in A-2.01; p. [vi], blank; p. vii–viii, headed: CONTENTS; p. [1], headed: THE DEFENCE OF GUENEVERE | [text begins]; pp. 2–248, text completed with explicit: THE END | Printed by BALLANTYNE, HANSON & CO. | Edinburgh & London; pp. [249–50], ads; pp. [251–2], blank.

Technical Notes: *paper*: cream-white 'antique wove' (Longmans Arch.) machine-made with dandy roll laid lines; *leaf size*: trimmed, 191 x 121 mm.; *printing*: this new setting has a smaller leaf size, type and type area than the 2nd edn., but it remains a very close line-by-line copy of that edn.; *binding*: plain black unblocked cloth; *spine*: printed paper spine label: [within thin rule compartment] | THE | POETICAL | WORKS OF | WILLIAM | MORRIS | [thin rule] | THE | DEFENCE | OF | GUENEVERE | AND OTHER POEMS | [below compartment] | *Five Shillings Net*.

Publication: 1900 [18 May]; *print run*: 1,000 copies (Unpublished Longmans Accounts for 1900, Smith Arch.; hereafter referred to as Longmans Accts.); *price*: 6s. net; reduced to 5s. net, along with all the other titles in the series Poetical Works of William Morris, in July 1900 (*Pub. Circ.*, 6 (Jan. 1899–Dec. 1900), 446).

Register of Copies Examined: SU (2 copies: base copy: 821.85 M877 [Q] 1900 and 821.85 M877 [Q8] 1908).

Notes: the 1st impression of this new edn. begins a two-part group, all derived from this setting. The 1st impression (1900), the 4th (1908), and the 6th (1915) were called the 'Best Edition', having larger paper and belonging to, and ranging with, the set 'The Poetical Works of William Morris'. The 2nd impression in 1903 started another sequence called the 'Cheap Edition' and including the 3rd impression (1905) and the 5th (1909) done on smaller and cheaper paper but using moulds to reproduce the same setting as the 'Best' sequence. The same setting was small enough in type area to serve for the Pocket Library version in 1916 (see A-2.12).

This edn. merits consideration as incorporating all of Morris's revisions, done for the Kelmscott Press edn., and F. S. Ellis's re-editing of the 1875 (2nd edn.) text specifically for this 1900 edn. Ellis wrote to Cockerell while he was in the process (13 Apr. 1900) to discuss what he was doing. He was conscious that this would be the most widely used version of the corrected text, the KP edn. being limited to 300 copies on paper and 10 on vellum, all being too expensive for the general audience. In his editing, he followed the KP edn. closely, but also used Morris's corrected printer's copy of the second edn. He found many changes by Morris in the punctuation, some of which were problematic themselves. For example, there were difficulties with Morris's inconsistent use of quotation marks and his introduction of new errors, several of which are cited. Moreover the errors of the 1st edn., listed on the errata slip inserted in 1858, had never been dealt with thoroughly. All these matters Ellis undertook to decide. This 4th edn. is the result.

Later impressions of this edn.: Longmans:

1. 1903 [issued 20 June]: New Edition. 'Cheap Edn.' [2nd impression, 4th edn.]; *print run*: 2,000 copies; *price*: 1s. 6d. net; *binding*: plain unblocked blue buckram; *spine*: printed paper label: THE | DEFENCE | OF | GUENEVERE | AND OTHER POEMS | BY | WILLIAM MORRIS; this copy with the original brown paper wrapper, spine printed as the paper label except for one line of gothic type: and other Poems | [thin rule];

2. 1905 [4 Mar.]: 'Cheap Edition' [3rd impression, 4th edn.]; *print run*: 1,000 copies; *price*: 1s. 6d.;

3. 1908 [7 Feb.]: 'Best Edn.' [4th impression, 4th edn.]; *print run*: 500 copies; *price*: 6s. net;

4. 1909 [2 June]: 'Cheap Edition' [5th impression, 4th edn.]; *print run*: 1,000 copies; *price*: 1s. 6d. net;

5. 1915 [15 Sept.]: New Impression. 'Best Edn.' Reprinted from the Kelmscott Press Edition, as revised by the Author. [6th impression, 4th edn.]; *print run*: 250 copies; *price*: 6s. net;

6. For impressions of this title in the Pocket Library series, see A-2.12.

A-2.07: The Defence of Guenevere (Bodley Head)

[The title page has a full ornamental border within thin-rule compartment, engraved from a pen-and-ink design:] THE • DEFENCE • OF • GUENEVERE | AND • OTHER • POEMS | • BY • WILLIAM • MORRIS • | ILLUSTRATED • BY • JESSIE • M • KING | JOHN • LANE • THE • BODLEY • HEAD | LONDON • AND • NEW • YORK • MDCCCCIV

Edition: [1st impression, 5th edn.]

Collation: cr. 8°: [A]⁸ (A2+1) B⁸ (B1+1) (B2+1) (B3+1) (B7+1) (B8+1) C⁸ (C6+1) (C7+1) D⁸ (D2+1) E⁸ (E2+1) (E6+1) (E7+1) F⁸ (F4+1) G–H⁸ (H5+1) I⁸ (I1+1) K–L⁸ (L1+1) (L3+1)

(L4+1) (L8+1) M⁸ (M3+1)) N⁸ (N1+1) (N3+1) (N7+1) O⁸ (O2+1) P–Q⁸ R⁴ [$2 (–C2 N1 R2) signed] 132 leaves + 24 inserted plates, included in the pagination = 156 leaves pp. [2] [1–9] 10–310 [=312].

Contents: pp. [*1–2*], blank; p. [1], half title: [within full ornamental border, engraved letterpress from hand-lettering] • DEFENCE • OF • GUENEVERE | AND • OTHER • POEMS; pp. [2–3], blank; p. [4], frontis.; p. [5], title page; p. [6], blank; p. [7], dedication: as A-2.01 with small tailpiece at foot; p. [8], blank; pp. [9]–10, contents, with headpiece; pp. 11–14, list of 97 illus., headings, head-pieces and tail-pieces; p. [15], 2nd half title; p. [16], blank; p. [17], 1st chapter head, text begins; pp. 18–309, text continues, with frequent illus. and blanks on pp. [24, 28, 38, 42, 44, 46, 56, 60, 68, 76, 86, 92, 96, 100, 104, 112, 148, 152, 154, 158, 186, 192, 198. 202. 212. 220. 234. 240. 250, and 258]; p. 310, text ends, with tail-piece and explicit: THE END.

Technical Notes: *paper*: plain white machine-made for letterpress, heavily coated for inserted plates; t.e.g.; no watermark; *leaf size*: trimmed, 188 x 127 mm.; *printing*: running titles: relevant poem title, in caps all rectos and versos; *end papers*: 1 free end and pastedown, front and back, all plain white and blank; *binding*: dark red cloth with gilt-stamped design on the front of a lady in a golden gown with arms extended and forms to the left and right (that reproduce the design on the back) with title and author at the foot, all within a gilt thin-rule compartment; *spine*: gilt-stamped with ornaments above and below the title and author: THE • DEFENCE | OF • GUENEVERE | AND • OTHER | POEMS • BY | WILLIAM • | MORRIS • | [ornament] | [at foot] JOHN LANE | [ornament]; the back has a single tail-piece gilt-stamped at the head with a framed cross topped by a flaming brand; *ornamentation*: 39 head-pieces, 28 tail-pieces, 2 full borders, 1 part border, and 24 full page illus. All the ornamentation and illustration is engraved from pen-and-ink drawings.

Publication: 1904 [the imprint date is 1904, but the common practice was to print the next year's date on books issued near the end of a year. This edn. was issued '14–21 November 1903'] ('Publications of the Week', *Pub. Circ.*, 79 (21 Nov. 1903), 568); *print run*: not known; *price*: 5s. net.

Register of Copies Examined: BL (base copy: C.109.p.5.); VU (Ba SpC Morg 821.8 Morris); ANL (821.85).

A-2.08: The Defence of Guenevere (ed. Steele)

THE DEFENCE OF | GUENEVERE AND | OTHER POEMS BY | WILLIAM MORRIS | EDITED BY ROBERT | STEELE | ALEXANDER MORING LIMITED | THE DE LA MORE PRESS 298 | REGENT STREET LONDON W 1904

Edition: [1st impression, 6th edn.]

Collation: small 8°: [a]⁸ (a4+1) b–c⁸ d⁴ B–R⁸ 156 leaves, pp. [2] [i–xii] xiii–lvi [lvii–lviii] 1–255 [256] [-2] [= 312] + one inserted plate. The plate is inserted as frontis. (described here under *Contents*) facing A5. It is counted in the pagination of the book, but it is not integral to the book as printed (it is printed on different paper), so the leaf assigned to the frontis. must be deducted from the total to make the book's page count equal half the leaf count.

Contents: pp. [*1–2*], blank; pp. [i–ii], blank; p. [iii], series title: [flush left, top] THE KING'S POETS; p. [iv], blank; p. [v], heraldic device as ensign of the series: THE KING'S POETS; p. [vi], blank; p. [vii], half title: [top, flush left] THE DEFENCE OF GUENEVERE; p. [viii], blank; p. [ix], blank recto of inserted frontis.; p. [x], inserted frontis., photographic process block reproducing a painting, with the photographer's name in copperplate, below left: *Hollyer, Photo.* | [label in copperplate, centred] *King Arthur's Tomb,* | *by Dante Gabriel Rossetti.* | *Reproduced by permission from a platinotype by The New Gallery.*; p. [xi], title page; p. [xii], 3-line epigraph, from Keats 'Ode to a Nightingale', (chosen by Steele? Not used by Morris for any of his edns.): ". . . . THE SAME THAT OFT-TIMES HATH | CHARM'D MAGIC CASEMENTS OPENING O'ER THE FOAM, | OF PERILOUS SEAS IN FAËRY LANDS FORLORN."; pp. xiii–li, introduction; p. [lii], blank; p. liii, dedication: [top, flush left] TO MY FRIEND DANTE | GABRIEL ROSSETTI PAINTER | I DEDICATE THESE POEMS; p. [liv], blank; pp. lv–lvi, contents list, unheaded; p. [lvii], 2nd half title (as the 1st, above); p. [lviii], blank; pp. 1–236, text; p. [237], section half title, [upper left] NOTES; p. [238], blank; pp. 239–55, Steele's notes; p. [256], printer's imprint: RICHARD CLAY & SONS, LIMITED, | BREAD STREET HILL, E.C., AND | BUNGAY, SUFFOLK.

Technical Notes: *paper*: cream-white machine-laid paper with dandy roll laid lines; *leaf size*: trimmed, t.e.g., 150 x 114 mm.; *pagination*: centred on direction line; *end-papers*: single free end and paste-down, plain white and blank, front and back; *binding*: three-quarter 'vellum', i.e. vegetable parchment, with plain unblocked grey paper-covered boards with 5 ornamental raised bands on the spine and a printed brown paper label between the 1st and 2nd bands: THE | KING'S POETS | [thin rule] | [red] The Defence | of | Guenevere | [thin rule] | [black] WILLIAM

MORRIS; a 2nd binding, in red cloth, has not been seen; *ornamentation*: frontis. engr. from Rossetti's *King Arthur's Tomb*. Series logo designed by Blanche McManus (see Jean-François Vilain, 'Foreword' to *American Book Design*, pp. xiii–xiv).
Publication: 1904 [issued '1–7 May'] (*Pub. Circ.*, 80 (7 May 1904), 515); *print run*: not known; *price*: 2s. 6d. net, cloth; 3s. 6d. half japan vellum.
Register of Copies Examined: LeM (2 copies, base copy presented as a prize for an essay on 'Character in Shakespeare' and awarded to Julia Drummond by Professor Gollancz, 1904); BL (012209.h. 1/25).
Later issues and impressions of this edn.:
1.* 1906, Phila. Pa., by G. W. Jacobs;
2.* 1907, London: King's Poets No. 25; Chatto and Windus;
3.* 1907, Boston: John W. Luce and Co.

A-2.09: The Defence of Guenevere (+ Hollow Land, *CW* I)

THE COLLECTED WORKS | [details common to the set, see A-126.01] | VOLUME I | THE DEFENCE OF GUENEVERE | THE HOLLOW LAND | [publisher's imprint, see A-126.01] | MDCCCCX
For the full title and all details common to the set, particularly *Technical Notes*, see the entry for the *CW*, A-126.01.
Edition: 'Collected Works' edn. [1st impression, 7th edn.]
Series: vol. 1 of 24.
Collation: medium 8°: a⁸ (a2+1) b⁸ c⁴ B–2A⁸ 2B⁴ [$2 (–c2 L2) signed] 208 leaves pp. [i–vi] vii–xxxvii [xxxviii–xl] 1–145 [*The Defence of Guenevere* ends] [146–8] 149 [text of *The Hollow Land* begins] 150–372 [373–6] [= 416] +1 inserted plate, noted in the formula, but not included in the book's pagination; described here under *Contents*.
Contents: p. [i], blank; p. [ii], notice of limitation (see this field in A-126.01); pp. [iii–iv], blank; inserted plate, recto blank, as frontis., photographic reproduction of a drawing in a blind-stamped compartment, name of the plate maker in copperplate, below right: *Emery Walker Ph. sc.* | [label, centred, in copperplate] *William Morris, | From an early drawing by himself*; p. [v], title page; p. [vi], blank; p. vii, headed: CONTENTS; p. viii, list ends; p. ix, headed: INTRODUCTION | [text begins]; pp. x–xvii text continues]; [xviii], illus. labelled: FACSIMILE OF A DRAFT PAGE OF GOLDEN WINGS; pp. xix–xxxiv, Intro. completed, including within it: pp. xxvj–xxxj: scene for *Sir Peter Harpdon's End* ; p. [xxxviii], blank; p. [xxxix], half title; p. xl, dedication: TO MY FRIEND | DANTE GABRIEL ROSSETTI | PAINTER | I DEDICATE THESE POEMS; p. 1, headed: THE DEFENCE OF GUENEVERE | [text begins]; pp. 2–372, text completed; p. [373], blank; p. [374], printer's imprint, as in A-126.01; pp. [375–6], blank.
Technical Notes: only the detail specific to this title is provided here; *shoulder notes*: all rectos and versos, short titles of the relevant items; *spine label*: the 1st five lines as in this field in A-126.01, thereafter: THE | DEFENCE OF | GUENEVERE | THE HOLLOW | LAND
Publication: 1910 [issued 4 Nov. 1910] (Longmans Arch.); for *print run* and *price*, see A-126.01.
Register of Copies Examined: LeM (base copy); see also this field in the entry for *The Collected Works*, A-126.01.
Notes: 12 Aug. 1897: Cockerell, clearing out Kelmscott House after Morris's death, notes in a letter to Mrs Morris that he has found a 1st edn. copy of *Guenevere* with some corrections, presumably in Morris's hand. No evidence has so far been found to suggest that these corrections were ever approved for use. It appears that Morris started revisions at some point (see below), but decided finally not to make changes (Cockerell Papers, BL 52738). A letter from May Morris to Cockerell (Smith Arch.), 25 May 1910, queries the time and circumstances of these Morris corrections as she engages with the preparation of this 1st vol. of the *CW*. The corrections were on separate longhand sheets different from Morris's usual paper and inserted in a copy that Morris gave to her mother. A letter of 29 May 1910 shows that May decided that the corrections were made for the 1875 edition, but were not used.

May wonders whether they were consciously abandoned or merely forgotten for the KP edition. Finally, later letters in the Smith Arch. show her decision was to reject the corrections; but she printed them in the Introduction to vol. I of the *CW*, describing them as coming from 'an interleaved copy' (I. xxv). She has corrected the errors listed on the errata slip inserted in the 1st edition and later mentioned by H. B. Forman, but is worried about the flatness of her introduction (Cockerell read and approved all her introductions before their submission). This has led her to be more personal and 'perhaps . . . sentimental'. She also worries about whether some unpublished 'songs and fragments' written in this early period should go in this 1st vol. or at the end. They were saved for printing in vol. 24, *Scenes from the Fall of Troy and Other Poems*.

18 June 1910: She wants to know how closely her father went over *The Defence of Guenevere* for the KP edition. She will follow his wishes wherever they can be determined.

Old and new fragments will not be mixed in the *CW*, vol. I, but she will incorporate appropriate fragments in her general Introduction; this led her to include there the excised scene from *Sir Peter Harpdon's End*.

A-2.10: The Defence of Guenevere (Muses Library)
THE | DEFENCE OF GUENEVERE | AND OTHER POEMS | BY | WILLIAM MORRIS | WITH AN INTRODUCTION BY | JOHN DRINKWATER | [Routledge mark, with monogram 'R'] | LONDON | GEORGE ROUTLEDGE & SONS, LTD. | NEW YORK: E. P. DUTTON & CO.
Edition: [1st impression, 7th edn.]
Series: The Muses Library.
Collation: 12° in 8s: [a]⁸ b⁴ A–O⁸ 124 leaves pp. [i–xxiv] 1–224 [= 248].
Contents: p. [i], half title: [top left, in gothic] The Muses Library | THE | DEFENCE OF GUENEVERE; p. [ii], ad, includes notice of vols. 1 and 2 of *EP* in The Muses Library; p. [iii], title page; p. [iv], blank; p. v, dedication page: TO | OLIVER W. F. LODGE | THIS EDITION OF | THE DEFENCE OF GUENEVERE | IS | DEDICATED.; p. vi, statement of the places and dates of Morris's birth and death; pp. vii–viii, contents (see A-2.01); pp. ix–xxiii, introduction; p. [xxiv], blank; pp. 1–222, text; pp. 223–4, index of 1st lines and printer's imprint: The Edinburgh Press, 9 & 11 Young Street.
Technical Notes: *paper*: plain white machine-made, t.e.g.; *leaf size*: trimmed, 150 x 94 mm.; *running heads*: individual poem titles in italic caps, all rectos and versos; *end-papers* and *binding*: see this field in A-3.11, the entry for the *Jason* edn., 1st of the 3 Morris titles in this series.
Publication: n.d. [issued 1–8 June 1912] ('Books of the Week', *Pub. Circ.*, 96 (8 June 1912), 751); *print run*: unknown; *price*: 1s. net; Drinkwater's introduction is signed and dated: Birmingham, 1911
Register of Copies Examined: BL (base copy: 011604. de.17.); but this copy has a library binding. For that see *Technical Notes* in A-4.20.

A-2.11: *The Defence of Guenevere (Collins)
DEFENCE OF GUENEVERE | WILLIAM MORRIS | [vignette of a youth playing a lyre] LONDON AND GLASGOW | COLLINS' CLEAR-TYPE PRESS
Edition: [1st impression, eighth edn.; as it was Collins' practice to make use of the letterpress for a first issue in later publications, parts of the setting issued here appear again in several later Collins selections from Morris's *Defence* (see the relevant Collins entries in the C-List, which include a book titled *The Life and Death of Jason*, which also includes—as is first indicated on the Contents page—*The Defence of Guenevere*, see C-25). This book was issued in 2 bindings, standard and deluxe. Most of the details of this description are taken from Coupe, pp. 42–4].
Series: The Cameo Poets
Collaborators, Editors, and Illustrators: illus. by P. B. Hickling; end papers design signature only partially decipherable as 'Sheeh'; title page vignette possibly by A. A. Dixon ('indistinct initials' says Coupe, p. 44).
Collation: pp. 1–252.
Contents: the *Defence of Guenevere* poems, with 4 Hickling colour illustrations: frontispiece and 3 in the text.
Technical Notes: *leaf size*: 153 x 103 mm.; *end papers*: colour illustrations of a scene with Cupid and Psyche, front and back; *binding*: in 2 forms, ordinary and deluxe: the ordinary copies in grey-green cloth-covered boards, with a floral compartment on the front containing: [in gilt] Guenevere | [floral ornament in a blue background] | [plain] Morris; the deluxe version: maroon leather with ornamental scroll compartments on the front and spine around the title and author, and a.e.g.; *ornamentation*: besides the pictures, each poem has a rectangular landscape as head-piece, 10 designs inserted without reference to content, and tail-pieces, in 9 designs, used wherever space allows.
Publication: Coupe's copy is a presentation dated 'xmas 1912' which he reckons is 'around' the date of publication (p. 42).
Register of Copies Located: see Coupe, pp. 42, 43.

A-2.12: The Defence of Guenevere (Blackie)
[within full border, with ornamental initial 'E']: EARLY • POEMS OF | WILLIAM • | [ornamental rule] | MORRIS • | [ornamental rule] | ILLUSTRATED • BY • | FLORENCE • HARRISON | [ornamental device] | BLACKIE • & • SON • LTD • LONDON | GLASGOW • AND • BOMBAY • • | 1914
Edition: [1st impression, 8th edn.]
Series: A Gresham Book, so described in *150 Years of Publishing: Blackie and Son, 1809–1959*.
Collation: 4°: [1–2]⁴ (1₂+1) 3–25⁴ (3₁+1) (5₃+1) (7₂+1) (10₁+1) (12₃+1) (13₁+1) (15₂+1) (18₁+1) (19₄+1) (21₃+1) (22₂+1) (23₁+1) (24₃+1) (25₁+1) (26₄+1) 26⁶ [$1 (+ 26ᵃ 26ᵇ) signed] 106 leaves pp. [i–xvi] 1–194 [195–6] [= 212] + 16 inserted colour plates, including the frontis., with protective tissues on which the scenes being illustrated are quoted; these are not counted in the book's pagination though noted in the formula and

described in their appropriate places in the *Contents*. 12 black and white illus. are integral and counted in the pagination.

Contents: p. [i], illus. of lady strewing roses; p. [ii], blank; p. [iii], half title: [illuminated large 'E'] EARLY | [3 fleurons] POEMS | OF WILLIAM | MORRIS [fleuron] | [ornamental bottom border]; p. [iv], ad; 1st inserted colour plate facing p. [v], photographic reproduction of a painting of Lancelot and Guenevere's kiss, as frontis., to face title page; as with all the colour plates, the picture is glued to a tipped in leaf of heavier paper, blank overleaf, which has a tissue guard printed on the side overleaf from the picture with the text illustrated by the picture; all of the colour plates are similarly treated; the 12 'black plates', not described here, have no protective tissues, the relevant quotations appear below the pictures, and they are counted in the book's pagination, being printed on leaves that are normal parts of the gatherings; p. [v], title page; p. [vi], ornamental scene of door and bells with bell ringer; p. vii–viii, headed: CONTENTS [see the list in A-2.01 which is reproduced here with some changes in the order of the poems in the original *Defence of Guenevere*]; pp. ix–xi, headed: LIST OF COLOURED PLATES; p.[xii], engraved tail-piece of a maiden standing before a door; pp. xiii–xiv, headed: LIST OF BLACK PLATES; pp. [xv], black and white scenic ornament; p. [xvi], blank; p. 1, text begins with ornamental border around the title; p. 2, text; 2nd inserted colour plate, to face p. 2, reproduction of a painting of the 'choosing cloths'; pp. 3–22, text; 3rd inserted colour plate, to face p. 22, of Lancelot and Guenevere at the tomb of Arthur; pp. 23–36, text; 4th inserted colour plate, facing p. 36, Christ speaking to Galahad; pp. 37–58, text; 5th inserted colour plate, facing p. 58, Sir Peter Harpdon beats Sir Lambert; pp. 59–78, text; 6th inserted colour plate, facing p. 78, Sir Peter Harpdon's lady reflects; pp. 79–86, text; 7th inserted colour plate, facing p. 86, Rapunzel sings from the tower; pp. 87–100; 8th inserted colour plate, facing p. 100, the ladies of the 'blue closet' watch for the coming of Arthur; pp. 101–22, text; 9th inserted colour plate, facing p. 122, Fair Jehane wears her wreath; pp. 123–36, text; 10th inserted colour plate, facing p. 136, a portrait of Dame Alice; pp. 137–50, text; 11th inserted colour plate, facing p. 150, three maids await the return of *The Sword*; pp. 151–6, text; 12th inserted colour plate, facing p. 156, the wind, as a maid, whirls about; pp. 157–66, text; 13th inserted colour plate, facing p. 166, ghosts in the white moonlight at the Seven Towers; pp. 167–74, 14th inserted colour plate, facing p. 174, Godmar threatens Jehane in 'The Haystack in the Flood's; pp. 175–82, text; 15th inserted colour plate, facing p. 182, a crusader knight, in prison, reflects in 'Riding Together'; pp. 183–92, text; 16th inserted colour plate, facing p. 192, the earthly lover prays for some sign from her deceased lover 'up in the stars'; pp. 193–4, text completed; p. [195], black and white tail-piece; p. [196], printer's imprint: PRINTED IN GREAT BRITAIN | *At the Villafield Press, Glasgow, Scotland*

Technical Notes: *paper*: cream-white machine-made, t.e.g.; *leaf size*: trimmed, 254 x 186 mm.; *end-papers*: one free end and paste-down, front and back, facing free end and paste-down grey with dark grey line drawing of fairy trumpeter, knight and ladies, opposite sides of free ends plain white and blank, front and back; *binding*: pale blue cloth, back plain and unblocked; front gilt-stamped: EARLY POEMS OF | WILLIAM MORRIS | [2 floral framed compartments, separated by a gilt armoured knight with sword]; [left compartment]: ILLUSTRAT- | ED BY | [right compartment]: FLORENCE | HARRISON; *spine*: gilt-stamped: [floral border with thick-thin rules above and below] | EARLY | POEMS OF | WILLIAM MORRIS | [floral border repeated] | ILLUSTRAT- | ED BY | FLORENCE HARRISON | [floral design] | [thick-thin rules above publisher's name:] BLACKIE & SON | LIMITED | [floral border repeated]; as originally sold there was a dark blue dust jacket with the same ornament and letterpress as the binding; some copies were sold with a glassine jacket in a box with the dust wrapper pasted on the top and side (see Coupe, p. 49); *ornamentation*: title in ornamental border; head and tail pieces, colour frontis. and 15 colour plates inserted and 12 black and white illus. integral to the book.

Publication: 1914 (date advanced) [2,000 copies issued '17 October 1913'] (Blackie's Publishers Arch., Glasgow, General Stock File E–G); *price*: 12s. 6d. net.

Register of Copies Examined: LeM (base copy); VU (E); BL (11650.i.45.); CaBVaU.

Later issue of this edn.:

1. *1914, New York: Dodge Publishing Company, 214–220 East Twenty-Third Street (see Coupe, p. 48).

A-2.13: The Defence of Guenevere (LPL)

THE DEFENCE OF | • • GUENEVERE • • | AND OTHER POEMS | BY WILLIAM MORRIS | POCKET EDITION | LONGMANS, GREEN, AND CO. | 39 PATERNOSTER ROW, LONDON | FOURTH AVENUE & 30TH STREET, NEW YORK | BOMBAY, CALCUTTA, AND MADRAS | 1916 | All rights reserved

Edition: Pocket Edition. [7th impression from stereo plates of the 4th edn.] For the significance of this edn. which includes Morris's revisions for the KP version, see *Notes* in A-2.06. Only those fields that require addition or correction are included here.

Series: Longmans Pocket Library (hereafter referred to as LPL). For further series detail of matters common to the LPL series, binding, etc., common to all books in this series, see this field in the record of the 1st book pbd. in the series, A-3.09. Though issued later than the 1915 limit of the original editions described here, like several later publications it is included in order to provide a complete account of the series, here the Morris edns. in The Pocket Library. Other post-1915 reprints of this title in this series, with dates and print runs, are noted in the *Publication* field, below.

Contents: as in A-2.09, except for the printer's imprint, p. 248: [thin rule] | PRINTED IN GREAT BRITAIN BY RICHARD CLAY & SONS, LIMITED | BRUNSWICK ST., STAMFORD ST., S.E., AND BUNGAY, SUFFOLK

Technical Notes: these are common to the series (see this field in A-3.09) or to the Fourth Edition (see A-2.06).

Publication: 1916 [issued '31 Aug. 1916'] (Longmans Arch. and Bibliographical Note on the verso of the title page); *print run*: 500 copies; *price*: 2s. cloth, 3s. lthr.

Register of Copies Examined: BL (base copy: 012203. c.17/29); LeM.

Post-1915 impressions in this series:

1.* 20 Oct. 1916; *print run*: 1,000 copies by Richard Clay & Sons;

2.* 11 May 1921; *print run*: 1,000 copies;

3.* Apr. 1926; *print run*: 1,000 (?) copies.

A-3.01: Jason

THE LIFE AND DEATH | OF JASON | A POEM | BY WILLIAM MORRIS. | [Bell and Daldy device of a bell crossed with an Aldine anchor-with-dolphin] | LONDON: | BELL AND DALDY, | YORK STREET, COVENT GARDEN. | 1867.

Edition: [1st impression, 1st edn.]

Collation: cr. 8°: [A]² B–Z⁸ 2A⁶ 184 leaves pp. [4] [1] 2–363 [364] [= 368] + tipped in Errata slip and 1 leaf of ads. Neither is counted in the book's pagination nor noted in the formula, but they are described here in their appropriate places under *Contents*.

Contents: p. [1], half title; p. [2], blank; p. [3], title page; p. [4], blank; tipped in errata slip with 10 corrections facing p. [1]; p. [1], text begins with 13-line prose Argument, a precis of the entire story; pp. 2–263, text completed with explicit: THE END. | [thin rule] | CHISWICK PRESS:—

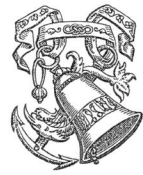

Figure 5.   A-3.01: *Jason* (1st edn.) title page

PRINTED BY WHITTINGHAM AND WILKINS, | TOOKS COURT, CHANCERY LANE.; p. [364], blank; leaf inserted facing p. [364], printed on the recto to advertise as 'in preparation', the contents of *The Earthly Paradise*: prologue, epilogue, and 24 titles of tales, not all conforming to the tales as published.

Technical Notes: *paper*: cream machine-moulded, with dandy roll laid lines, vertical chain lines, no watermark; *leaf size*: lightly trimmed, 190 x 123 mm.; *printing*: lines numbered by tens inside right margins; *running titles*: all versos: *THE LIFE AND DEATH* | [all rectos] *OF JASON*.; *end-papers*: one free end and paste-down, plain white and blank, front and back; *binding*: plain red unblocked cloth; *spine*: printed label: [within a thin-rule compartment] THE | LIFE | AND | DEATH | OF | JASON | A POEM | BY | WILLIAM | MORRIS | [below frame] BELL AND DALDY.

Publication: 1867 [copies were issued '3 June 1867'] (Chiswick Arch.); HBF says (p. 45) this book was 'finished' in January 1867, probably meaning that it was printed by then and issued sometime thereafter. May Morris took 'finished' to mean 'issued' (*CW*, II. xxviii). But Mackail, who says the 1st issue was 'June, 1867' (i. 183), the reviews (see *The Times*, 9 June 1867), and Morris's correspondence (see *Letters*, i. 51) all suggest a date such as the Chiswick Arch. records; *print run*: 500 copies; *price*: 7s. 6d.
Register of Copies Examined: LeM (base copy); BGR (5 copies (a, b, c, d, & e) no binding variants: 'a'. inscribed 'E. B. Jones | from his friend | the Author'. Pasted on free end paper, book plate of E. B.-J., with his marginal note on p. 145 in pencil: 'wrong numbering from here to end of book' (line 281 is numbered 280). This copy lacks the errata slip, which has been torn out (stub remains), the corrections having been made in the text in pen by B.-J. The bindings of all 5 BGR copies and the LeM copy are plain unblocked red (cherry) cloth, with paper label (no price printed); 'b' Has Buxton Forman's book-plate & signature ('Shelley' book-plate with date '19 March 1874') and contains tipped-in letter (*Letters*, i. 75) from Morris to Forman dated 'March 9, 1869'; 'c' inscribed to 'J. F. Robertson/ with the Author's kind regards'; 'd' and 'e' have nothing distinctive, but all copies have the ad. for the *E.P.*, then 'in preparation', 24 tales + Prol. & Epilogue (but neither the titles nor their sequence fully correspond with this title as first pbd.).
Notes: Chiswick Arch. records total cost of production as £59. 7s. 6d., exclusive of binding.

This being the 1st of Morris's books to achieve a very considerable success with the reading public, it caused some upset of its publishers' preconceptions in both England and America. When Morris submitted the fair copy of *Jason* early in 1867, Bell and Daldy, recalling the market failure of *The Defence of Guenevere*, offered an 'on commission' contract involving no risk to themselves and an assured percentage of the expenses of production and marketing. But no provision was made for the possibility of sales beyond the 500 copies originally ordered. Neither stereo plates nor moulds were made, and the type was distributed immediately after printing. Consequently, when the book sold out very quickly, there was no alternative to resetting. Morris seized the opportunity to make what Mackail calls 'numerous corrections' (i. 185). After the 2nd edn. of *Jason* was issued, Morris changed his English publisher from Bell and Daldy to F. S. Ellis who was a close friend and sufficiently confident of Morris's ability to risk the expenses of production.

Originally, Morris intended 'The Deeds of Jason' (his first title) to be one of the tales in *EP*. But, as Mackail says, 'the story . . . capable of almost indefinite expansion in detail, grew on his hands till it became obvious that it had outgrown its destined place' (i. 183).

A-3.02: Jason (RB)

THE LIFE AND DEATH | OF | [3-line swash caps] JASON. | *A POEM* | BY WILLIAM MORRIS | BOSTON | ROBERTS BROTHERS | 1867
Edition: [1st issue, 1st impression, 2nd edn., 1st American].
Collation: 12° in 6s, 2 sigs.: [1]⁴ 2–26⁶ 27² [$1 and 3 signed –1] 156 leaves pp. [4] [1–4] 5–307 [308] [= 312].
Contents: pp. [1–4], ads; p. [1], half title; p. [2], blank; p. [3], title page; p. [4], blank; p. 5, 1st chapter head title, text begins; pp. 6–307, text completed with explicit: THE END.; p. [308], blank.
Technical Notes: *paper*: cream-white machine-moulded with dandy roll laid lines, no watermark; *leaf size*: trimmed, 174 x 114 mm.; *printing*: *running titles*: as in A-3.01; *endpapers*: 2 free ends and paste-down, front and back, plain white and blank except paste-down and facing free end in dark matt brown; *binding*: red or green cloth, textured 'sand' (Tanselle I, no. 408) with Oxford-rule compartment blind-stamped front and back; *spine*: rounded spine gilt-stamped: [thick-thin rule] | [drop cap initial 'J'] JASON | A | POEM | BY | William Morris | [ornamental device] | [thin-thick rule] | *ROBERTS BROS* | [thick-thin rule]
Publication: 1867 [issued '1–15 Aug.'] (*American Literary Gazette & Publishers' Circular* (hereafter referred to as *Am. Lit. Gaz. & PC*), 9/8 (15 Aug. 1867), 213–14); Cost Book A indicates this 1st impression comprised 2,000 copies, from which came the 1,000 copies for a 'Second Edition' (Roberts Arch.) issued in America in 1870; *price*: $1.50 for ordinary copies, but prices varied considerably depending on bindings, of which RB made 3 available besides the cloth described above: 'Morocco antique, $5; calf, $4.50; and half-calf, $3.75'.
Register of Copies Examined: LeM (2 copies, 1st, base copy, and 2nd issue); BGR (2 copies); MH (microfilm, Mas 1009).
Notes: 'printed by Geo. C. Rand & A[very] 1867 Jason. total cost = $705.32' (Roberts Arch., Cost Book A. 72). The 1st American issue followed a similar course to the English. Being the 1st Morris book published by Roberts Brothers of Boston and therefore the basis of the RB claim to an exclusive right to publish Morris in the USA, a distinct urgency attached to its early issue. RB set their own edition from an

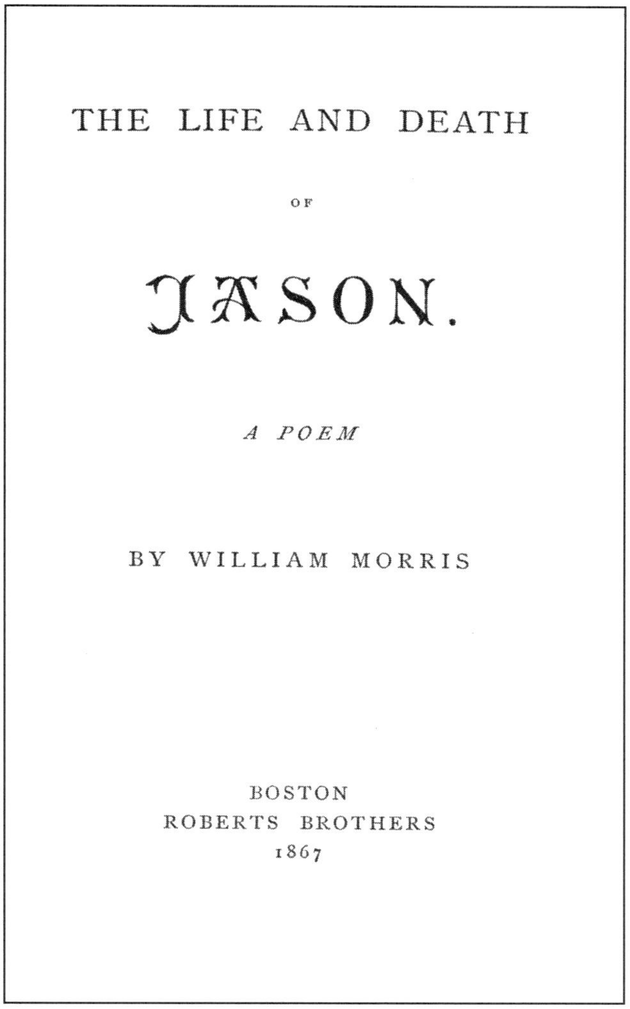

```
THE LIFE AND DEATH

OF

JASON.

A POEM

BY WILLIAM MORRIS

BOSTON
ROBERTS BROTHERS
1867
```

Figure 6. A-3.02: *Jason* (2nd edn., 1st American) title page

advance copy of the English 1st edition and had 2,000 copies printed by Aug. 1867, only two months after the English 1st edition. The 2,000 American copies were published in 2 issues, in 1867 and 1868 respectively, the latter called the 'Second Edition'. The size of the 1st printing was obviously thought adequate to the likely demand, so again, like the English 1st edition, neither stereo plates nor moulds were made. Consequently, when another printing was called for in 1870, RB arranged to import plates or moulds, from which stereo plates could be made of the English 'Second Edition, Revised'. This much is clear from comparison of an English copy with one from the American impression, seen in the light of the record of the production made by the Roberts firm. In Roberts Arch., Cost Book A, this reprint is called the 'Stereo Edn.', no doubt referring to the imported stereo plates (all the Roberts plates of Morris titles are indi-

cated by the notes on their sale to Longmans in 1899) from which issues after those of 1867 and 68 were printed.

Obviously, everything is the same in the 2 original issues except for the preliminaries, including ads, which are reset to accord with the American publisher. The American printer's imprint is 'Cambridge: Presswork by John Wilson and Son', the term 'Presswork' being intended, perhaps, to suggest machining only, something less inclusive than 'Printed by' would have conveyed.

The lessons learned by RB from their 1st issue of a Morris title are evident in all but the two last RB publications and the last vol. of *EP*, the success of which was already assured by the previous vols. After *Jason*, American publications of Morris titles usually began with an issue of imported English sheets (or sheets derived from imported plates in this instance) in an American binding. This was followed by an American edition when the popularity of the initial publication justified it. The only case where sales did not justify, in Thomas Niles' view, the larger investment was *The Defence of Guenevere and Other Poems* for which there never was a Roberts setting. Also, after *Jason*, when an American setting was ordered moulds were made as a matter of course.

Later issues and impressions of this edn.: RB:

1. 1868: Second Edition [2nd issue, 1st impression, 2nd edn., 1st American]; *print run*: 1,000 copies remaining of the 1st impression; *price*: $1.50.

A-3.03: Jason

[title as in A-3.01 except for the introduction of a line after the author's name]: SECOND EDITION, REVISED; [and a changed imprint date]: 1868

Edition: Second Edition, Revised. [1st impression, 3rd edn., 2nd English] Plates made from this edition were used for subsequent impressions by Bell and Daldy in October 1868, thereafter by F. S. Ellis (HBF, p. 47) and by Roberts. Since the book had to be reset after the 1st impression sold out, Morris used the opportunity to make revisions, notably to the way the general 'Argument' at the beginning of the text of Book I was given a separate page before the beginning of the text, and by introducing a short summary or argument at the beginning of each book.

Collation: 8°: [A]² B–2A⁸ 186 leaves pp. [4] [1] 2–367 [368] [= 372].

Contents: p. [1], half title; p. [2], printer's imprint: LONDON: PRINTED BY W. CLOWES AND SONS, STAMFORD STREET | AND CHARING CROSS.; p. [3], title page; p. [4], headed: ARGUMENT. | [13 lines of text];

p. [1], headed: THE LIFE AND DEATH OF JASON. | [ornamental thin rule] | BOOK I | [2-line summary of the 1st chapter] | [text begins]; pp. 2–367, text completed with explicit: THE END. | [printer's imprint, as above]; p. [368], blank.

Technical Notes: as in A-3.01, except: books I–III, V–VIII, X–XII, and XV–XVII start new pages, and those that do not are preceded by a thin rule; *end-papers*: one free end and paste-down, plain white and blank, front and back; *binding*: plain red unblocked cloth; *spine*: printed paper label: [within a thin-rule compartment] THE | LIFE | AND | DEATH | OF | JASON | A POEM | BY | WILLIAM MORRIS | [below frame] BELL AND DALDY.

Publication: 1868 [issued '16–31 Dec. 1867'] (*Pub. Circ.*, 30/727 (31 Dec. 1867), 985); *print run*: 500 copies; *price*: 7s. 6d.

Register of Copies Examined: SPar (base copy); BGR.

Later impression of this edn. by Bell and Daldy:
1. 1868 [2–14 Nov.]: 'Third Edition', 2nd impression of A-3.03, 3rd edn., 2nd English; *print run*: 500 copies (HBF, 47); *price*: 7s. 6d.

A-3.04: Jason

THE | LIFE AND DEATH OF JASON | A POEM. | [the three-musicians woodcut vignette] | BY WILLIAM MORRIS, | AUTHOR OF THE EARTHLY PARADISE. | *FOURTH EDITION.* | London: F. S. Ellis, 33 King Street, Covent Garden. | MDCCCLXIX. | [*All Rights reserved.*]

Edition: Fourth Edition. [actually the 3rd impression, 3rd edn., 2nd English.] 25 LP copies as well as the ordinary copies. This is the 1st impression of this title to bear the imprint of F. S. Ellis and the 1st impression of *Jason* to have the title page vignette of the three musicians, a woodcut 1st used in the original issue of *EP*, Part I.

Collaborators, Editors, and Illustrators: Forman attributes the three-musicians design and the engraving to Morris (HBF, p. 51), but, Dunlap says, 'Vallance (p. 378) and May Morris (*CW*, III. xi) attribute the design to Burne-Jones and the engraving to Morris'. For an account of this woodcut, see Dunlap 2, 40–2 and Aymer Vallance, *William Morris: His Art, His Writings, and his Public Life. A Record*, 378 (hereafter referred to as Vallance).

Contents: as in A-3.03, except for the new title page and the printers imprint: STRANGEWAYS AND WALDEN, Printers, 28 Castle St. Leicester Sq.

Technical Notes: as A-3.03, except: LP copy: *paper*: Whatman's hand-laid; *leaf size*: untrimmed, avg. 222 x 141 mm.; *binding*: grey paper-covered boards with a printed spine label; ordinary copies: same paper and binding as A-3.03, but light red or pink spine label slightly larger: [within a thin-rule compartment] THE | LIFE | AND | DEATH | OF JASON | Poem | by William Morris. | [below compartment] Price 8s.; ads, not integral, a single leaf tipped in on the free end-paper.

Publication: 1869 [issued '15–30 Oct. 1869'] (*Pub. Circ.*, 32/771 (1 Nov. 1869), 688); *print run*: 1,000 ordinary and 25 LP copies; *price*: ordinary copies, 8s., no price announced for the LP copies.

Register of Copies Examined: MU (base copy: PR 5076 A1 1869a) l. p. copy: signed by Morris, with his presentation inscription to Robert Banner dated 'Jan. 24th, 1885'; NNU 821.85 /Jl /2:; MH; CtY.

Notes: begun under Ellis with the 1st vol. of the *EP* in June 1868, this issue extends to this title Ellis's practice of printing 25 LP copies on Whatman hand-made paper besides the ordinary copies. These special copies, obviously intended primarily for presentation, continued to be printed for all 1st editions issued by Ellis, plus the 'Eighth Edition' of *Jason*, until Morris began his design experiments with Reeves in his translation of the *Odyssey* (2 vols., 1887), when two LP variants in much larger print runs were issued well before the 1st ordinary copies appeared.

Later issues of this impression by Ellis:
1. 1869: 'Fourth Edition', see next entry, below; *print run*: 1,000 copies; *price*: 7s. 6d. (these copies sufficed for the 'Fifth', Sixth', and 'Seventh' 'editions' (see HBF, p. 48 and A-3.04, below);
2. Ellis & Green: 1870: 'Fifth Edition' [2nd issue, 3rd edn.] see 'Fourth Edition'; *print run*: remaining copies from the 'Fourth Edition'; *price*: see above;
3. 1872: 'Sixth Edition' [3rd issue, 3rd edn.] see 'Fourth Edition'; *print run*: remaining copies from the 'Fourth Edition'; *price*: see above;
4. 1877: 'Seventh Edition' [4th issue, 3rd edn.] see 'Fourth Edition'; *print run*: remaining copies from the 'Fourth Edition'; *price*: see above.

A-3.05: Jason (imported plates, RB)

THE LIFE AND DEATH | OF | JASON. | A Poem. | BY WILLIAM MORRIS. | Author's Edition. | BOSTON: | ROBERTS BROTHERS. | 1871

Edition: Author's Edition [3rd impression, 1st American, of the 3rd edn., 2nd English] Done with plates made from the English 'Second Edition. Revised', it was set by Wm. Clowes and Sons and supplied to RB by Ellis. The setting of this American impression, called the 'Stereo Edn.' in

Roberts Cost Book A and printed in America, is identical with the English 'Second Edition, Revised', dated 1868 (see A-3.03), except for changes in the preliminaries, the omission of the English version's line numbers, a change of format from 8° to 12° (making another collation necessary here), and the American binding. That the English plates were imported is a conclusion forced by the printing being done in Boston, the comparison of the settings, the unusual absence in this case of any account of composition expenses in the RB 'Cost Books', and the reference to the cost of '8 boxes', shipping boxes being a necessary expense in all cases of imports from or exports to England by RB.

The account of this American impression in 'Morris in America' is incorrect, as is that of John William Pye in his *Bibliography of American Editions of William Morris* (p. 16; hereafter referred to as Pye). There was only one edition, i.e. one setting, of *Jason* done in America, and the 1st (and only) impression of that provided sufficient copies for the 'Second Edition' (actually a 2nd issue) in Apr. 1868. The 2nd and all subsequent reprints by RB—1877, 1886, and 1893—were from the English plates of the 'Second Edition, Revised', the actual plates, rather than sheets being imported on this occasion. These plates became obsolescent in the UK when Morris revised the English edn. in 1882. The American impressions were machined, but not composed, at John Wilson's works in Cambridge, Mass.

Collation: 8° in 12s, with 8° sigs.: [1⁴ 2–16¹² c⁸] 192 leaves pp. [8] [1] 2–367 [368–76] [= 384].

Contents: changes of this RB edn. from the English 'Second Edition, Revised', the plates from the latter being the basis of this reprint: pp. [*1–2*], ads of Morris books pbd. by RB; p. [*3*], half title, reset on a single line; p. [*4*], verso of half title, omits English printer's imprint and inserts ad for Roberts' edn. of *EP*; p. [*5*], title page reset; p. [*6*], printer's imprint: Presswork by | JOHN WILSON AND SON, | Cambridge. [Mass., from plates made in England by Wm. Clowes and Sons, Stamford Street and Charing Cross]; p. [*7*]: ARGUMENT. | [prose summary of the poem in 13 lines, from English setting]; p. [*8*], blank; p. [1], identical setting except for omission of line number on the outer margin, here and throughout; pp. 2–367, text completed with explicit: THE END. | [thin rule] | Cambridge: Presswork by John Wilson and Son; p. [368], blank; pp. [369–76], ad for RB pbns.

Technical Notes: *paper*: cream machine-laid with dandy roll laid lines; *leaf size*: trimmed, 175 x 116 mm.; *end-papers*: 2 each, front and back, dark brown matt free ends and facing paste-down, 3 other sides all plain white and blank; *binding*: dark red, blue, or green cloth, textured 'sand' (Tanselle 1, no. 408); Oxford rule border blind-stamped front and back; *spine*: gilt-stamped: [ornamental border at the head, alternating ovals and lines of 3 vertical dots, all between thin rules] | THE | LIFE | AND | DEATH | OF | JASON | [ornamental rule] | BY | [in swash caps] WILLIAM MORRIS | Boston | ROBERTS BROTHERS | [at the foot, ornamental border repeated from the head].

Publication: 1871 [issued 'Nov. 1870'] (*Am. Lit. Gaz. & PC*, 16/2 (Dec. 1870), 126); *print run*: 500 copies; *price*: $1.50.

Register of Copies Examined: LeM (base copy); MU (Spec. Coll.PR5076/A1, 1871); BGR.

Later issues and impressions of this edn.: RB:

1. 1877: [2nd American impression, 3rd edn., 2nd English]; *print run*: 280 copies;

2. 1886: [3rd American impression, 3rd edn., 2nd English]; *print run*: 280 copies;

3. 1893: [4th American impression, 3rd edn., 2nd English]; *print run*: 280 copies;

4.* Longmans, NY: 1900: Ninth Edition; [2nd issue, 4th American impression, 3rd edn., 2nd English]; *print run*: 100 remaining RB copies of the 'Fourth Edition' purchased by Longmans NY and pbd. with a new title page; *price*: $1.50;

5. Longmans, NY: 1903: [5th American impression, 3rd edn., 2nd English]; *print run*: 230 copies;

6. Longmans, NY: 1909 [6th American impression, 3rd edn., 2nd English]; *print run*: not known.

A-3.06: Jason

THE | LIFE AND DEATH OF JASON | A POEM | [three-musicians vignette] BY | WILLIAM MORRIS, | AUTHOR OF THE EARTHLY PARADISE. | *Eighth Edition, revised by the Author*. | LONDON: | ELLIS AND WHITE, 29 NEW BOND STREET, W. | 1882. | [All Rights reserved.]

Edition: Eighth Edition, revised [1st issue, 1st impression, 4th edn., 3rd English].

Collaborators, Editors, and Illustrators: the three-musicians vignette has been recut here by George Campfield, the original having burnt in a fire at Strangeways.

Collation: cr. 8°: [A]² B–2A⁸ 2B⁶ 192 leaves pp. [4] [1] 2–376, + separately paginated, but integral, sequence of ads: [1]2–4 [= 384].

Contents: p. [*1*], half title; p. [*2*], blank; p. [*3*], title page; p. [*4*], headed: ARGUMENT. | [13 lines of prose text]; p. [1], head title | [one and a half lines, as argument, in italics] | [text begins]; pp. 2–376, text completed with explicit: THE END. | [thin rule] | LONDON: | Printed by Strangeways

& Sons, Tower Street, Upper St. Martin's Lane.; pp. [377–80], integral, separate pagination sequence: pp. [1]–4, ads for Ellis and White's Publications.
Technical Notes: *paper*: cream-white machine-laid, with dandy roll laid lines, no watermark; *leaf size*: untrimmed, avg. 192 x 124 mm.; *printing*: *headlines*: all versos: THE LIFE AND DEATH | [all rectos] OF JASON; *pagination*: as in A-3.01; *end-papers*: 1 free end and paste-down, plain white and blank, front and back; *binding*: as A-3.01, except *spine*: altered label: [within a thin-rule compartment] THE | LIFE | AND | DEATH | OF | JASON. | [thin rule] | W. MORRIS. | [thin rule] | EIGHTH EDITION. | [below compartment] 8*s*.; the 25 LP copies are bound in quarter holland with plain unblocked blue paper-covered boards, ordinary copies in plain dark red or green unblocked cloth, and, like the LP copies, with printed spine label: THE LIFE | AND | DEATH | OF | JASON. | W. MORRIS. | EIGHTH EDITION. | 8s.
Publication: 1882 [issued '2–16 Jan. 1882'] (*Pub. Circ.*, 45/1064 (16 Jan. 1882), 14); *print run*: 2,000 ordinary and 25 LP copies; *price*: ordinary copies, 8*s*. The LP copies were probably used as presentation copies, hence no price was advertised (HBF, p. 49).
Register of Copies Examined: VU (E, base copy); CSt (821. / M87Lj); SU (821.85 M877 l Z22t; LeM; BGR.
Later issues and impressions of this edn.:
1. Reeves and Turner (R and T): 1889; *print run*: the number of copies issued is unknown;
2. Longmans: 1896: Eighth Edition [2nd issue, 1st impression, 4th edn., 3rd English] part of the series, 'The Poetical Works of William Morris'; *print run*: remaining copies of the preceding R and T issue.

A-3.07: Jason (KP)

THE LIFE AND DEATH OF JASON, | A POEM. BY WILLIAM MORRIS.
Edition: 'Kelmscott Press Edition' [revised by Morris; 1st impression, 5th edn., 4th English].
Collaborators, Editors, and Illustrators: 2 illus. by Burne-Jones.
Series: 34th title, 14th by Morris, pbd. by the KP.
Colophon: Here endeth The Life and Death of Jason, written | by William Morris, and printed by the said William | Morris at the Kelmscott Press, Upper Mall, Ham- | mersmith, in the County of Middlesex, and finished | on the 25th day of May, 1895 [2 printer's flower ornaments No. 3] | [KP printer's mark, No. 2] | Sold by William Morris at the Kelmscott Press

Collation: large 4° in 8s: [a]⁴ b–z⁸ 2a⁴ [$4 (–b1 h3 k3 l3 p2, 4 q3 2a2–4) signed] 184 leaves pp. [8] [1] 2–353 [354–60] [= 368].
Contents: pp. [1–4], blank; p. [5], title page; p. [6], headed: ARGUMENT | [18 lines of prose summary beginning with a 6-line floriated initial 'J']; p. [7], blank; p. [8], frontis. woodcut illus. with border 14a; p. [1], within border (no. 14) 1st chapter head, text begins; pp. 2–[354], text completed with explicit: [printer's leaf ornament] And now is all that ancient story told | Of him who won the guarded fleece of Gold.; p. [355], endpiece illus. by Burne-Jones; p. [356], blank; p. [357], colophon (see above); pp. [358–60], blank.
Technical Notes: *paper*: Batchelor's hand-made KP Perch paper; *leaf size*: deckled edges, lightly trimmed, avg. 288 x 210 mm.; *printing*: printed in black and red, red for chapter titles, shoulder notes, and speakers' names in poetic dialogues; *type face*: Troy type, with a few words in Chaucer type; *shoulder notes*: on all rectos and versos except chapter heads, sub-heads for adjacent text; *end-papers*: standard KP treatment: 3 free ends and pastedown, front and back, plain white and blank; *binding*: limp cream vellum with 3 green silk ties; *spine*: gilt-stamped across: THE LIFE | & DEATH | OF JASON | BY | WILLIAM | MORRIS; *ornamentation*: 2 full borders: 14a and 14, each used twice, once for each of the 2 illus.; 18 half borders: pp. 152 and 159 and one for each chapter head title except the 1st; 5 part borders, one 15-line initial, 16 8-line initials, 21 6-line initials, and 324 drop cap initials.
Publication: 25 May 1895 [finished printing, issued '5 July 1895']; *print run*: 200 copies on paper, 6 on vellum; *price*: paper 5*gns.*, vellum 20*gns.* (Cockerell, p. 160).
Register of Copies Examined: CSt (base copy: Z239.2/ K29M87Lj f Bender); BGR (Burne-Jones bookplate; presentation in Morris's longhand: 'to Edward Burne-Jones from WM | June 30th 1895'; BL (C. 43. f. 10.); VU (E).
Notes: William S. Peterson quotes Morris's response to an interviewer (Temple Scott) who raised the question of the prices of the KP books and their effect on sales. Using the KP *Jason* as his example, Morris explains that the small print run, 200 copies, made the 5*gns.* price necessary to recover costs (see Appendix I-17 and William S. Peterson, *The Ideal Book: Essays and Lectures on the Arts of the Book by William Morris*, 113; hereafter referred to as Peterson).

A-3.08: Jason (PW)

THE | LIFE AND DEATH OF JASON | A POEM |

[three-musicians woodcut vignette] | BY | WILLIAM MORRIS | AUTHOR OF 'THE EARTHLY PARADISE' | NINTH EDITION | LONGMANS, GREEN, AND CO. | 39 PATERNOSTER ROW, LONDON | NEW YORK AND BOMBAY | 1897 | *All Rights Reserved.*
Edition: Ninth Edition. 'New Edition' in Longmans Arch. [also called at the time the "Cheaper Library Edition"; [new set; 1st impression, 6th edn., 5th English].
Series: The Poetical Works of William Morris (hereafter referred to as PW). For series details, see this field in A-4.16.
Collation: cr. 8°: [A]² B–2A⁸ 2B⁴ 190 leaves pp. [4] [1] 2–376 [= 380].
Contents: p. [*1*], half title; p. [2], ad; p. [3], title page; p. [4], precis, headed: ARGUMENT | [13-line prose precis]; p. [1], headed: THE | LIFE AND DEATH OF JASON | BOOK I | Jason, having grown up to manhood in the woods, | is warned of what his life shall be. | [text begins, divided into 17 books]; pp. 2–376, text completed with explicit: And now is all that ancient story told | Of him who won the guarded Fleece of Gold. | THE END | Printed by BALLANTYNE, HANSON & Co. | Edinburgh & London.
Technical Notes: *paper*: cream-white 'antique' machine-made with dandy roll laid lines; *leaf size*: trimmed, 190 x 127 mm.; *printing*: lines counted by tens at the right hand margins; *running titles*: all versos, centred: THE LIFE AND DEATH | [all rectos] OF JASON; *end-papers*: 3 free ends and paste-down, plain white and blank, front and back; *binding*: plain unblocked black cloth with printed paper label, printed within a thin-rule compartment: THE | POETICAL | WORKS OF | WILLIAM | MORRIS | [thin rule] | THE LIFE | AND | DEATH | OF | JASON | [below compartment] *Five Shillings Net.*
Publication: 1897 ['17–24 April'] (*Pub. Circ.*, 65/1569 (25 July 1897), 84); Longmans Arch., where this new setting is described, dates this 'April 1897'; *print run*: 500 copies (Longmans Arch.); *price*: 5s. net.
Register of Copies Examined: VU (base copy: E); CSt (821. / M87Lj); LeM.
Later issues and impressions from this edn. in this series.: Longmans:
1. 1902 [14 Dec. 1901] (Longmans Arch.): Tenth Impression [2nd impression, 6th edn., 5th English] PW edn.; *print run*: 500 copies; *price*: 5s.;
2.* 1907 [17 Aug.] (Longmans Arch.]: Eleventh Impression [3rd impression, 6th edn., 5th English]; *print run*: 500 copies; *price*: 5s.

A-3.09: Jason (LPL)

THE LIFE & DEATH | OF JASON | [in italic swash caps] *A POEM* | BY | WILLIAM MORRIS | AUTHOR OF 'THE EARTHLY PARADISE' | POCKET EDITION | LONGMANS, GREEN, AND CO. | 39 PATERNOSTER ROW, LONDON | NEW YORK, BOMBAY, AND CALCUTTA | 1907 | All rights reserved
Edition: Pocket Edition [1st impression, 7th edn., 6th English].
Series: 'Longmans Pocket Library'; since *Jason* is the 1st of the Morris books included in this series, this entry records details of the series. When the last Morris title, *Hopes and Fears for Art*, was added in 1919, the number of Morris books in the Pocket Library had grown to 14 titles in 18 vols. Between the 1st (*Jason*, 1907) and the last (*Hopes and Fears*) were *Poems by the Way* (1910); *News from Nowhere* (1912); *John Ball and a King's Lesson* (1913); *The Roots of the Mountains* (2 vols., 1913); *The House of the Wolfings* (1913); *The Glittering Plain* (1913); *The Wood beyond the World* (1913); *The Well at the World's End* (2 vols., 1913); *The Sundering Flood* (2 vols., 1913); *The Water of the Wondrous Isles* (2 vols., 1913); *The Pilgrims of Hope and Chants for Socialists* (1915); and *The Defence of Guenevere* (1916).

Books in the series are uniform in design, price, size and binding except for *The Pilgrims of Hope and Chants for Socialists* which, though of the same height as the others, had to be made squarer in order to accommodate Morris's long lines of verse without turning. Except for one title, *News from Nowhere*, available in paperback as well as the standard cloth or lthr., the bindings are uniform dark green cloth or lthr., t.e.g., with 2 versions of the Longmans ship device on each, one blind-stamped on the front and the other gilt-stamped on the spine. Titles and the author's name are gilt-stamped across the spine. Dust wrappers seem to have been regularly sold with each vol. (though not all the wrappers have been seen). At least 2 designs were used, one with and one without the C. M. Gere drawing of Kelmscott Manor on the front, originally done for the KP edition of *News from Nowhere*. Both have titles up the spine and across the front, with the price prominently displayed on the front and advertisements only on the back. The price per vol. varied with the choice of binding: 2s. net in cloth, 3s. net lthr. and 4s. and 6s. for those published in 2 vols. (the paperback *News from Nowhere* cost 1s.). In some cases texts were new set (this is specified in the *Edition* field in each Pocket Library entry). Longmans announced that, 'though the size of the pages on which the vols. are printed

Figure 7. A-3.09: *Jason* (1st Morris book in LPL, Longmans Pocket Library) title page

is only 6 1/2 inches x 4 1/8 inches [165 x 105 mm., but that varies for *The Pilgrims of Hope and Chants for Socialists*: 165 x 115 mm.], yet the type is clear, and the matter can easily be read' (Longmans *Notes on Books*, 10/206 (June 1907), 268).
Collation: fcap 8°: π² A–U⁸ X⁶ 168 leaves pp. [4] [1] 2–331 [332] [= 336].
Contents: p. [1], ad for Longmans Pocket Library (books by authors other than Morris); p. [2], headed: ARGUMENT | [15 lines of text in bourgeois type]; p. [3], title page; p. [4]: *BIBLIOGRAPHICAL NOTE* | [4 lines of text]; p. [1], headed: THE | LIFE AND DEATH OF JASON | BOOK I | [2-line summary, in italics]; pp. 2–331, text completed with explicit: THE END | Printed by BALLANTYNE, HANSON & CO. | Edinburgh & London; p. [332], blank.
Technical Notes: *paper*: cream-white machine-wove, with t.e.g.; *leaf size*: trimmed, 158 x 111 mm.; *printing*: running titles: all rectos and versos: THE LIFE AND DEATH OF JASON; *end-papers*: one free end and paste-down, plain white and blank, front and back; *binding*: dark green cloth or lthr. *spine*: gilt-stamped ship design below gilt lettering: THE LIFE | & • DEATH | OF • JASON | [abstract versions of the Longmans swan mark as line-fillers] | WILLIAM | MORRIS | [thin rule] | [Longmans 'Sign-of-the-Ship mark'] | [thin rule] | LONGMANS; front blind-stamped with Longmans' ship device in an ornamental oval frame.
Publication: 1907 [issued '13–20 July'] ('Books of the Week', *Pub. Circ.*, 87 (20 July 1907), 76); *print run*: 3,000 copies (Longmans Arch.); *price*: paper, 2s.; lthr., 3s.
Register of Copies Examined: LeM (base copy, bookplate of G. Irwin-Carruthers.); NN; BL (012203. e. 17/8); SU (821.85 M877l (Q7) Z22).
Notes: the entry from the Longmans Arch. says the 3,000 copies were printed by 25 June 1907, with the type set and

moulds made by Ballantyne, at a total cost, without binding, of £55. 5s. 1d.
Later impressions of this Pocket Edn.: Longmans:
1. 1914: [Dec. 12 (Longmans Arch.) 2nd impression, 7th edn. 6th English]; *print run*: 1,044 copies;
2. 1920 [31 Dec. 1919 (Longmans Arch.) 3rd impression, 7th edn. 6th English]; *print run*: 1,000 copies.
3.* 1926 [Feb., (Longmans Arch.) 4th impression, 7th edn, 6th English]; *print run*: unknown; *price*: 2s.

A-3.10: Jason (*CW* II)

THE COLLECTED WORKS | [details common to the set, see A-126.01] | VOLUME II | THE LIFE AND DEATH OF JASON | [publisher's imprint, see A-126.01] | MDCCCCX

For the full title of this vol., and the details common to the set, especially those under *Technical Notes*, see A-126.01, the entry for the *CW*.
Edition: 'The Collected Works' [1st impression; 8th edn., 7th English].
Series: vol. 2 of 24.
Collation: medium 8°: a⁸ (a1+1) b⁶ (b5+1) B–T⁸ U⁶ [$2 (–U2) signed] 164 leaves pp. [i–vi] vii–xxviii [1] 2–295 [296–300] [= 328] + 2 inserted plates, not counted in the pagination, but described here under *Contents* and noted in the formula.
Contents: p. [i], blank; p. [ii], notice of limitation, see A-126.01; pp. [iii–iv], blank; 1st inserted plate as frontis., within a blind-stamped compartment, with the name of the plate maker, below right, in copperplate: *Emery Walker Ph. sc.* | [label, centred, in copperplate] *William Morris | From a photograph made in 1870*; p. [v], title page; pp. [vi–vii], headed: CONTENTS; pp. ix–xxviii: INTRODUCTION, including, pp. [xxii–xxiv], illus. integral to the letterpress, labelled: FACSIMILE OF VERSES TO PREFACE JASON IN THE EARTHLY PARADISE and p. [xxv], illus., labelled: FACSIMILE PAGE FROM THE JASON MANUSCRIPT; 2nd inserted leaf, to face p. xxvi, a photo reproduction of a drawing, within a blind-stamped compartment, with the name of the plate maker, below right, in copperplate: *Emery Walker Ph. sc.* | [label, centred, in copperplate] *Miss Jane Burden | From a pencil drawing by William Morris made in 1858*; p. xxvii, Intro. completed; p. xxviii, headed: BIBLIOGRAPHICAL NOTE; p. [1], half title: THE LIFE AND DEATH OF JASON | ARGUMENT | [21 lines of prose]; p. 2, headed: THE LIFE AND DEATH OF JASON | [text of Book 1 begins]; pp. 3–295, text continues, books 1–17; p. 296, text ends with explicit: THE END; p. [297], blank; p. [298], printer's imprint (see A-126.01); pp. [299–300], blank.
Technical Notes: paper, leaf size, printing, position (but not content) of headlines, running titles, shoulder titles, endpapers, and binding are all common to the series and are described in this field in A-126.01, the entry for the set, treated as a single work. Only those details specific to this vol. are included here: *shoulder titles*: all rectos and versos: Book I–XVII; *spine label*: [5 lines common to the set, see 126.01] | THE | LIFE & DEATH | OF JASON
Publication: 1910 [issued 4 Nov.] (Longmans Arch.); *print run* and *price*: see A-126.01.
Register of Copies Examined: LeM (base copy, copy 729); for the full list of copies consulted, see this field in A-126.01.
Notes: the passage of poetry printed in type and in facsimile in May Morris's 'Introduction', pp. [xxvi–xxviii], is Morris's 'link' between *Jason* and the framework of *EP* as it would have been according to his original plan to include 'The Deeds of Jason' as the 1st tale in *EP*. It seems not to have been pbd. before this.

A-3.11: Jason (Muses Library)

THE LIFE AND | DEATH OF JASON | A POEM | BY | WILLIAM MORRIS | WITH AN INTRODUCTION BY | JOHN DRINKWATER | [Routledge bookmark] | LONDON | GEORGE ROUTLEDGE & SONS, LTD. | NEW YORK: E. P. DUTTON & CO.

Edition: The Muses Library [1st impression, 9th edn., 8th English].
Collaborators, Editors, and Illustrators: [edited, with] Introduction by John Drinkwater.
Collation: 8°: [a]⁸ b⁴ B–Y⁸ Z⁴ 184 leaves pp. [i–vii] viii–xxii [xxiii–xxiv] [1–3] 4–344 [= 368].
Contents: p. [i], half title; p. [ii], blank; p. [iii], title page; p. [iv], blank; p. [v], dedication: TO | ALFRED NOYES | WITH A SENSE OF A LARGE INDEBTEDNESS | AND IN COMMON REVERENCE | OF A GREAT NAME; p. [vi], Morris's birth date and death date, with the names of the houses where he was born and died; p. [vii], headed: INTRODUCTION | [text begins]; pp. viii–xxii, INTRODUCTION completed: [signature below right] John Drinkwater. | [below left, indented] Birmingham, 1910; p. xxiii, headed: *CONTENTS*; p. [xxiv], blank; p. [1], blank; p. 2, headed: ARGUMENT | [16 lines of prose summary of the story]; p. 3, headed: THE LIFE AND DEATH | OF JASON | BOOK I | [text begins]; pp. 4–344, text ends with explicit: [indented] And now is all that ancient story told | Of him who won the guarded Fleece of Gold. | THE

END. | [printer's imprint] WILLIAM BRENDON AND SON LTD. | PRINTERS, PLYMOUTH

Technical Notes: *paper*: plain white machine-made, t.e.g.; *leaf size*: trimmed, 150 x 94 mm.; *printing*: *running titles*: [all rectos and versos] THE LIFE AND DEATH OF JASON; *end-papers*: 1 free end and paste-down, plain white and blank, front and back; *binding*: plain unblocked blue cloth or blue leather-covered boards; *spine*: gilt-stamped with an Art-Nouveau tree design with branches forming 2 compartments, at the head: MORRIS | JASON | THE | MUSES | LIBRARY | [2nd compartment, at the foot, below the tree] ROUTLEDGE

Publication: n.d. [1910, issued c. '1–14 Dec. 1910'] (accession stamp, BL copy); John Drinkwater's Introduction is dated 'Birmingham 1910'; *print run*: unknown; *price*: 1s. net.

Register of Copies Examined: BL (base copy: 011604. de. 9.); NNC (B82 SD85 H 1910, signed by the editor); CaBVau; BGR.

Later impression of this edn.: Routledge and Dutton: 1. 1911 [2nd impression, 9th edn., 8th English]: *print run*: unknown; *price*: 1s. net.

A-3.12: Jason (Everyman)

[full floral border] THE LIFE | and DEATH | of [fleuron] JASON | [swash letters] by [plain type] WILLIAM | MORRIS. [fleuron] | [central fleuron] | LONDON: PUBLISHED | by J. M. DENT & SONS LTD | AND IN NEW YORK | BY E. P. DUTTON & CO

Edition: 'Everyman Edn.' [1st impression, 10th edn., 9th English].

Collaborators, Editors, and Illustrators: Introduction by 'E. R.' [Ernest Rhys].

Series: Everyman's Library, edited by Ernest Rhys.

Collation: small 8°: π⁶ A–T⁸ 158 leaves pp. [i–xii] [1] 2–304 [= 316].

Contents: p. [i], half title; p. [ii], ad; p. [iii], blank; p. [iv], full border, around an epigraph with a floral ornament: A rom- | ance, | and it | me took | to read | & drive | the night | away | [signed] CHAUCER; p. [v], title page within 2nd full border, a mirror image of the 1st; p. [vi], blank; pp. vii–viii, text begins, headed: INTRODUCTION; p. ix, text ends: [initialled, below right] E. R. [Ernest Rhys] | [dated, left] *December 1911*; p. x: BIBLIOGRAPHY IN BRIEF [Morris's works + Mackail's *Life*]; p. xi: CONTENTS; p. [xii], blank; p. [1], text begins; pp. 2–304, text completed with printer's imprint: THE TEMPLE PRESS, PRINTERS, LETCHWORTH

Technical Notes: *paper*: cream machine-moulded, t.e.g.; *leaf size*: trimmed, 173 x 106 mm.; *printing*: *headlines*: [all rectos and versos] The Life and Death of Jason; line count in 10s all versos on the right margins, all rectos outside margin; *end-papers*: 1 free end and facing paste-down, front and back, with a floral design printed in light green over the free end and facing paste-down, with a scroll on the versos with the Everyman epigraph: EVERYMAN, | I WILL GO WITH | THEE, | TO BE THY GUIDE | IN THY MOST NEED | TO GO BY THY SIDE; reverse sides of free ends plain white and blank, front and back; *binding*: the series was advertised as, 'in four styles of binding: cloth, flat back, coloured top; lthr., round corners, gilt top; library binding in cloth, & quarter pigskin'; this copy, library binding: red top edge, textured blue cloth (Tanselle 1, no. 102, 'rib'), unblocked back, front blind-stamped at centre with publisher's device: [within the branches of a single flowering plant] J. M. | DENT & | SONS LTD; *spine*: flat, gilt-stamped full length with floral ornaments except at the head, also gilt-stamped: THE [fleuron] | LIFE & | DEATH | of JASON | BY [fleuron] | WILLIAM | MORRIS | [at the foot] J. M. DENT | E. P. DUTTON; *price*: 1s. net, cloth; 2s. lthr.

Publication: [1912 'December, 1911'] the date of Rhys' introduction; an unknown number of copies were issued 17–24 Feb. 1912, in London ('Books of the Week', *Pub. Circ.*, 96 (24 Feb. 1912), 249). Under the copyright law in 1899, the US required deposit in The Library of Congress within 30 days (see Simon Nowell-Smith, *International Law and the Publisher in the Reign of Queen Victoria*, 65–6; hereafter referred to as Nowell-Smith).

Register of Copies Examined: LeM (base copy); CaBVaU; BL (12206. p. 1/409.) Fdmn; BGR.

A-3.13: Jason (ed. Maxwell)

THE LIFE AND DEATH | OF JASON | BY | WILLIAM MORRIS | EDITED WITH INTRODUCTION AND NOTES BY | E. MAXWELL | OXFORD | AT THE CLARENDON PRESS | 1914

Edition: [2nd issue (or impression?), 11th edn, 10th English] This version of *Jason* is set, except for its prelims and notes, from an edition by E. Maxwell, used earlier in the 2 Oxford Press collections: the *Prose and Poetry (1856–1870) by William Morris* (see C-30), and the Oxford World Classics collection, restricted to Morris's poetry *The Defence of Guenevere, The Life and Death of Jason, and Other Poems* (see C-31), both of which retain his textual notes. Here the text is preceded by a new introduction by E. Maxwell,

whose copy text is the 2nd edn. revised of 1868 (see A-3.03), with 'alternate readings' from the 1st edn. in footnotes and other notes as endnotes omitted in the earlier Oxford collections. Maxwell's text must have been made available for both earlier versions. The Oxford *Prose and Poetry (1856–1870)*, has the 1st impression of the setting used in Maxwell's *Jason* described here, the signatures, pagination, type, and type area being reproduced exactly, the pagination beginning with p. [313] in both. This all suggests that this later version made use of the plates from the earlier collection. The World Classics version is a different setting, but retains the Maxwell text and textual notes.
Collaborators, Editors, and Illustrators: Edited with Introduction and Notes by E. Maxwell.
Printer: Horace Hart, Printer to the University.
Collation: Small 8°: [a]^8–b^8 c^4 Y–2O^8 2P^6 2Q–2R^8 [$2 (–c1) signed] 170 leaves pp. [i]–xxxii [313] 314–618 [619–20] [[=340] [= 340]. Other than preliminaries and endnotes, pagination is that of the earlier OUP *Prose And Poetry (1856–1870) By William Morris* (see C-30). The body of this book is obviously printed from the same plates as the *Jason* text in the earlier collection of Morris's *Prose and Poetry*.
Contents: p. [i], half title; p. [ii], list of 3 'editions of Morris published by Oxford University Press' including this one, *Prose and Poetry (1856–1870)*, and *The Defence of Guenevere, The Life and Death of Jason, and Other Poems*, No. 183 of The World's Classics; p. [iii], title page; p. [iv], publisher's imprint: OXFORD UNIVERSITY PRESS | LONDON EDINBURGH GLASGOW NEW YORK | TORONTO MELBOURNE BOMBAY | HUMPHREY MILFORD M.A. | PUBLISHER TO THE UNIVERSITY; pp. [v–vi], headed: CONTENTS.; p. [vii]: headed: INTRODUCTION | [text begins]; pp. [viii]–xxx, Introduction completed; p. [xxxi], 2nd half title: THE LIFE AND DEATH OF JASON | A POEM | 1867 | (First published in 1867. Reprinted here from the second edition, | revised, 1868. The alternate readings given at the foot of the page | are those of the first edition); p. [xxxii]: ARGUMENT | [13 lines of prose summary]; pp. [313]–322, text [end of gathering c]; pp. [323]–588, text completed, pp. 589–618, notes; pp. [619–20], blank.
Technical Notes: *paper*: white machine-made; *leaf size*: trimmed, 183 x 126 mm.; type area: 138 x 85 mm.; lines to page: set solid, 40 ll. (p. 372); *end-papers*: 1 free end and paste-down, plain white and blank, front and back; *binding*: black cloth-covered boards with blind-stamped double thin-rule compartment, front and back; *spine*: gilt-stamped: [double thin-rule] | WILLIAM | MORRIS | JASON | MAXWELL | OXFORD | [double thin rule]
Publication: 1914 [issued '2 October' (OUP Arch., LB 3531); *print run*: 2,000 copies; *price*: 2s. 6d.
Register of Copies Examined: BL (base copy: 011649.g.17., with BL accession stamp: '7 Oct. 14').

A-3.14: Jason (Headley Bros.)

The life and death | of | [in red] JASON | [in black] A METRICAL ROMANCE | BY | WILLIAM MORRIS | Decorated by Maxwell Armfield | London | [in red] HEADLEY BROTHERS | [in black] Bishopsgate, E.C.
Edition: [1st impression, 12th edn., 11th English]. Robert Coupe finds another issue of the same book by its printer, the Swarthmore Press Ltd., Ruskin House, 40 Museum Street, W.C.1, done probably at the same time as the Headley Bros. and bound in pale blue buckram. A third came out in New York, pbd. by Dodd, Mead and Company, bound in purple and issued in 1917 (see Coupe, p. 74).
Printer: Swarthmore Press.
Collation: Crown 4° in 8s: [1]^6 (1$_2$+1) 2^8 (2$_4$+1) 3–7^8 (7$_7$+1) 8–10^8 (10$_5$+1) 11–14^8 (14$_4$+1) 15–17^8 (17$_3$+1) 18–24^8 190 leaves, pp. [i–iv] v–x [1] 2–16 (+2) 17–30 (+2), 31–44 (+2) 45-60 (+2) 61–78 (+2) 79–108 (+2) 109–20 (+2) 121–28 (+2) 129–34 (+2) 135–46 (+2) 147–68 (+2) 169-92 (+2) 198-203 (+2) 209-18 (+2) 219–74 (+2) 275–84 (+2) 285–320 (+2) 321–22 (+2) 323–30 (+2) 331-2 [= 332 + 10 + 38 = 380] + 6 inserted colour plates noted in the formula and described in the *Contents*, but not counted in the book's pagination. The 19 leaves added to the pagination statement are black and white line drawings printed on leaves integral to the ordinary gatherings; these are not included in the book's pagination but here added to the total here.
Contents: p. [i], half title; p. [ii], blank; inserted frontis. labelled above, within the frame: Jason; p. [iii], title page; p. [iv], blank; p. v, headed: Note on the Drawings; p. vi, 'Note' ends, initialled: M.A.; p. [vii]: List of Drawings; p. viii, list ends; p. ix, headed: Contents; p. x: Argument [17 lines of prose summary]; p. [1], headed: [12-line ornamental head-piece, Minoan style] | Book One | [text begins]; pp. 2–8, text; inserted plate facing p. 9, labelled at the top within the frame: "Chiron raised his arm and drew him back"; pp. 9–98, text; inserted plate facing p. 98, labelled in the List of Drawings: "Linceus set his eager face, and loosed the dove which down the west wind flew"; pp. 99–142, text; inserted plate to face p. 142, labelled in the List of Drawings: Medea and the dragon; pp. 143–204, text; inserted plate to face p. 204, labelled at the top: Circe; pp. 205–250, text; inserted plate to face p. 250, labelled: "There-

with she turned from him her face divine, and reached the shallop over Argo's side"; pp. 251–332, text completed with explicit: THE END. | [triangular tail piece, Minoan style] | [thin rule] | Headley Brothers, Bishopsgate, E.C. and Ashford, Kent

Technical Notes: *paper*: machine-wove, t.e.g.; *leaf size*: trimmed, 247 x 188 mm.; *printing*: *running heads*: [all rectos and versos] THE LIFE AND DEATH OF JASON; *end-papers*: 1 free end and paste-down, front and back, pale mauve with designs extending across the opening of facing free end and paste-down; *binding*: mauve cloth-covered boards with white-stamped Minoan-style design of a fleece below the title on the front, back plain and unblocked; *spine*: white-stamped: THE LIFE | & | DEATH | OF | JASON | WILLIAM | MORRIS | HEADLEY
Publication: n.d. [1915, issued '11–18 Dec.'] (*Pub. Circ.*, 103 (19 Dec. 1915), 633); *print run*: unknown; *price*: 7s. 6d. net.
Register of Copies Examined: BL (base copy: 11650. i. 55.)
Notes: ad by Headley Brothers: 'William Morris's famous epic of the doughty deeds of Jason is here presented in a new dress. The Artist in illustrating the text has made use of the latest knowledge acquired by the Minoan excavations. These examples of Greek art have never been utilised before for modern book illustrations . . . [Armfield's] linework is based upon the open linework of the period—the finest at present known . . . . 7s. 6d. net' (*Pub. Circ.*, 103 (2 Oct. 1915), 345).

A-4.01: The Earthly Paradise (1st vol.)

THE | EARTHLY PARADISE | A POEM. | [the three-musicians woodcut vignette] | BY | WILLIAM MORRIS, | AUTHOR OF THE LIFE AND DEATH OF JASON. | London: *F. S. ELLIS, 33 King Street, Covent Garden.* | *MDCCCLXVIII.* | [All Rights reserved.] (last square brackets in the original)
Edition: [1st impression, 1st edn.] Later called 'Parts I and II', but no indication of part or vol. is shown in this edn. (for more detail on the division into parts, see the *Notes*, below). Besides the ordinary copies, 25 LP copies, each in 2 vols., were issued at the same time on Whatman handmade paper (HBF, p. 52). The same 2-vol. LP copies were produced with Parts III and IV. Thus, when the poem was pbd. complete there were 25 LP sets of 6 vols. as well as the ordinary 3-vol. series, later called 'The Library Edition'.
Collaborators, Editors, and Illustrators: the vignette of three musicians, designed by E. Burne-Jones and as originally cut by Morris, is here used for the 1st time on the title-page and as a tail-piece. It was later destroyed by fire at Strange-

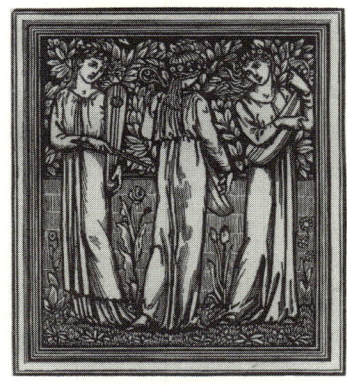

Figure 8. A-4.01: *EP* (*The Earthly Paradise*, 1st edn., vol. 1 (of 3)) title page

ways and re-cut by George Campfield (for an account of the design and the woodcut, see Dunlap 2, 40–1).
Collation: cr. 8°: [A]⁴ B–2U⁸ 2X⁴ 344 leaves pp. [i–vii] viii [1] 2 [3] 4–676 [677–80] [= 688].
Contents: p. [i], half title; p. [ii], blank; p. [iii], title page; p. [iv], printer's imprint: LONDON: | STRANGEWAYS AND WALDEN, PRINTERS, | 28 Castle St. Leicester Sq.; p. [v], dedication: TO | MY WIFE | I DEDICATE THIS BOOK.; p. [vi], blank; pp. [vii]–viii: [7-line dropped head] A TABLE OF CONTENTS. | [thin rule] | [list of preliminaries, months, and 12 tales]; pp. 1–676, text; p. [677], three-musician vignette repeated; p. [678], printer's imprint repeated (street number omitted); pp. [679–80], blank.
Technical Notes: *paper*: thin white machine-wove, no watermark; *leaf size*: trimmed, 183 x 120 mm.; *printing*: *running titles*: [all versos] THE EARTHLY PARADISE. |all rectos,

title of the relevant tale or month; *end-papers*: 1 free end and paste-down, plain white and blank, front and back; *binding*: plain dark green unblocked cloth-covered boards; *spine*: a printed paper label: [within thin-rule compartment] THE | EARTHLY | PARADISE. | [thin rule] W. MORRIS | [below compartment] *Price 14s.*; 25 LP copies in 2 vols. on Whatman hand-made paper, demy 8°, bound in quarter white holland with blue paper-covered boards; *spine*: printed paper labels: THE EARTHLY | PARADISE. | W. MORRIS. | I [II]. The LP vols. have the same page nos. as the original vol., i.e. pagination is continuous through the 2 vols., when the 3-vol. set was complete making up a 6-vol. LP set in which each 2 vols.—1 and 2, 3 and 4, and 5 and 6—are paged continuously, corresponding to the pagination as set for the ordinary copies.

Publication: 1868 [issued '1–14 May'] (*Pub. Circ.*, 31 (15 May 1968), 270); but see 'the end of April' (Mackail, i. 193) and 'Now Ready' (*The Bookseller* (1 May 1868), 337; hereafter referred to as *BSR*); *print run*: 1,000 copies; *price*: 14s.

Notes: of all Morris's books, *EP* has the most complicated publishing history, never fully explicated. The complications were brought about by the way the poem developed in the lengthy course of its initial composition, from 1865 through 1870 (see Mackail, Chapter 6, and Dunlap 2, 11–13). Conceived from the first as a cycle of tales—Northern, Eastern, and classical—with a framework tale designed to provide for 2 tales for each month of a fictional year, it was originally planned to appear in a single large folio vol. with copious wood-cut ornaments by Morris and illus. by Burne-Jones. But the poem went through a series of authorial changes that continued even after the first part of the cycle had been published in 1868. First, trial pages made it clear to both poet and illustrator that the ornamented folio was over-ambitious at the time in that it required nothing less than that new era in typography, book design, and production that came about with the Kelmscott Press in the 1890s. Second, *The Life and Death of Jason*, which began as part of the projected cycle, under the title 'The Deeds of Jason' (the MS of which is preserved in the Huntington Library), had to be hived off and published separately in 1867 when it outgrew its allotted niche. Subsequently the length of the remaining tales again proved too much, and the single-vol. project was abandoned in favour of 2 vols. The new plan became explicit in the 1st published vol. of Apr. 1868, where 12 projected tale titles appear as an ad for 'the second and concluding volume' then 'in preparation'. But this plan also failed when 'The Lovers of Gudrun', the 6th story of this 2nd vol., the last tale for the month of November, stretched to nearly 200 pages, thus forcing another revision of the plan. The 2nd vol. being then over 500 pages, with still another 6 tales remaining to be told, a 3rd became necessary to complete the design.

These changes resulted in several moves by Morris's publisher, F. S. Ellis, to market effectively a long and complex work that enjoyed both critical acclaim and large sales as soon as the 1st published vol. appeared. Though priced at a relatively expensive 14s. per copy (and later increased to 16s., 8s. for each vol., when the instalment was divided into 2), this 1st instalment went through 3 English impressions—1,000 copies in Apr., 750 in June, and 1,250 in Aug.—in its 1st year, 1868, besides being reset in Boston for a 2nd edn. that went through 2 impressions—1,000 in Aug. and 1,000 in Oct.—before the year's end. When the 2nd vol. was published in early Nov. 1869 (but dated 'MDCCCLXX' on the title page), it had no vol. number, being announced on the title page as 'Part III'. At the same time, the 'Fifth Edition' of the 1st vol. (actually the 4th impression done from stereo plates of the 1st edn., see HBF, p. 53) appeared in 2 vols. differentiated for the 1st time as 'Part I' and 'Part II'. Part III announces that the 'purchasers of Parts I. and II. in one vol. (as originally issued) will find a new title page for that volume in Part IV'. The new title page thus promised differs from the original only in the addition of a line identifying the vol.'s contents as 'Parts I. & II.' and in a change of publication date to an inaccurate 'MDCCCLXX'. There was also included a new spine label to substitute for the original: 'The Earthly Paradise. | W. Morris. | I. & II.' Forman says, 'how it was arranged for the copies containing the new title page and label to get into the hands of purchasers of the original volume of 1868, I was never able to fathom.' What he 'was never able to fathom' was that anyone who bought the 1st vol. as originally published, that was later to be called Parts I and II, would have to buy Part IV to have the complete poem, and Part IV includes the new title page for the 1st vol. Ellis's strategy of using 'Parts' rather than 'Volumes' to name the segments of the poem had the effect of putting into the hands of the purchaser of the original 1st vol. as well as those who bought the 2-vol. 'Fifth Edition' of that 1st vol.—both of which required the later 2 vols. to complete the poem—a complete and uniform set, or the means to create one, coherently numbered, whether in 3 vols. or 4.

So the original edition of *EP* (1868–70) appeared in both 3 vols. and 4 vols., with the last 2 vols. serving equally appropriately to complete either set, and with both sets being later named 'The Library Edition'. In addition, from the same 1st edn. setting, 25 LP copies were printed, 2 for each vol. of the original 3-vol. version. Hence, when the poem was issued complete in late 1870, it existed in 3 vols., in 4 vols., and in 6 vols. in the LP version.

Temple Scott says, 'some copies (probably 500) of the first edition of the first part contain cancel leaves—notably pp. 75–6; on p. 75, l. 20, was a ludicrous misprint of 'my' for 'thy'' (Scott, p. 4). So at least one of the corrections may have been made with a cancel in the later copies of the 1st impression, 1st edn.. But this copy and the others consulted do not show evidence of any cancels on pp. 75–6. Morris himself wrote to an unknown correspondent that the errors 'will be corrected in a second edition' (*Letters*, i. 63).

Register of Copies Examined: LeM (base copy); BGR; BL (2 copies: 11648. eee. 49. and the 2-vol. LP copy: Ashley 3681).

Later issues and impressions of this version of the 1st edn.:
Ellis:
1. 1868 [June]: Second Edition [2nd impression, 1st edn.]; *print run*: 750 copies; *price*: 14s.;
2. 1868 [Aug.]: Third Edition [3rd impression, 1st edn.]; *print run*: 1,250 copies; *price*: as above;
3. 1869 [1–15 Jan.]: Fourth Edition [2nd issue, 3rd impression, 1st edn.]: *print run*: remaining copies of the 'Third Edition'; *price*: as above.

A-4.02: The Earthly Paradise (vol. I, imported shts. RB)

The title page duplicates A-4.01, except for a new publisher's imprint substituted for Ellis's: *Boston*: Roberts, [*sic*] Brothers. | MDCCCLXVIII | [All Rights reserved.] (last square brackets in the original)

Edition: later called, by RB, 'English Edition'. [2nd issue, 1st American, 1st impression, 1st edn.] Imported in sheets by Roberts Brothers and sold in an American binding with Roberts' imprint but in addition to the English printer, Strangeways', imprint. Except for the publisher's imprint, and the American binding, this vol. duplicates A-4.01. The only fields included here are those that require correction or addition.

Contents: as in A-4.01, including the printer's imprint, pp. [iv] and [678].

Technical Notes: as A-4.01, except *leaf size*: trimmed, 209 x 146 mm.; *binding*: 3/4 white cloth binding with tan paper-covered boards, front gilt-stamped on plain dark red or green unblocked cloth with chamfered edges; *spine*: gilt lettering between RB ornamental borders of alternating dots and ovals between thin rules: THE | EARTHLY | [swash initial] PARADISE | [ornamental rule] | BY | [swash caps] WILLIAM MORRIS | [publisher's device of a globe with the 6 months of tales told in this vol. around the circumference] | [above the lower border] ROBERTS BROTHERS.

Publication: 1868 [issued 10 June], an unknown number of copies imported from the 1,000 printed for the English 1st edn. were issued in Boston on 10 June 1868 (*Am. Lit. Gaz. & PC*, 10 (1 June 1868), 62); *price*: $3.00.

Register of Copies Examined: CU-B (PR5075/1868).

Later imports by RB, in shts., of this English 1st edn.:
1. 1869: Third Edition [2nd issue, 1st American, 3rd English impression, 1st edn.];
2. 1871: Sixth Edition [2nd issue, 1st American, 5th English impression, 1st edn.].

Later imports of this vol. in shts. are listed under A-4.15.

A-4.03: The Earthly Paradise (RB, vol. I of 3-vol. set)

THE | EARTHLY PARADISE | *A POEM*. | By WILLIAM MORRIS, | AUTHOR OF "THE LIFE AND DEATH OF JASON." | *From the Third London Edition.* | BOSTON: | ROBERTS BROTHERS. | 1868.

Edition: [1st impression, 2nd edn., 1st American] The 1st USA setting, the English 3rd impression was used as copytext. This is the 1st vol. of the American 3-vol. set, but like the first 4 English issues without specification of vol. or part. The American publisher, again like the English, still expected to issue the whole poem as a 2-vol. set and included a list of tales for 'the second and concluding volume'.

Collation: 12° gathered in 12s but with 8° sigs.: [1–18¹² 19⁶] 222 leaves pp. [8] 1–430 [431–6] [= 444]. 1st sig. on 5ʳ of each odd numbered 12° gathering; 2 sigs. for each even-numbered 12° gathering: on 1ʳ and 9ʳ of the gathering. The misplacing of pp. 81–4 after pp. 85–8 in the base copy confirms that the imposition is 8° with each sheet a double 4° to allow half of the sheet to be combined with the preceding or following gathering. 12° gatherings are formed with 2 sigs., 8 and 4-leaf gatherings alternating with 4 and 8-leaf gatherings, the 4 leaves being cut to form 2 separate 2-leaf sections which could by mistake be reversed, as was done in this case.

Contents: p. [1], half title; p. [2], blank; p. [3], title page; p. [4], copyright statement and printer's imprint: AUTHOR'S EDITION. | UNIVERSITY PRESS: WELCH, BIGELOW, & CO., | CAMBRIDGE.; p. [5], dedication: TO | MY WIFE | I DEDICATE THIS

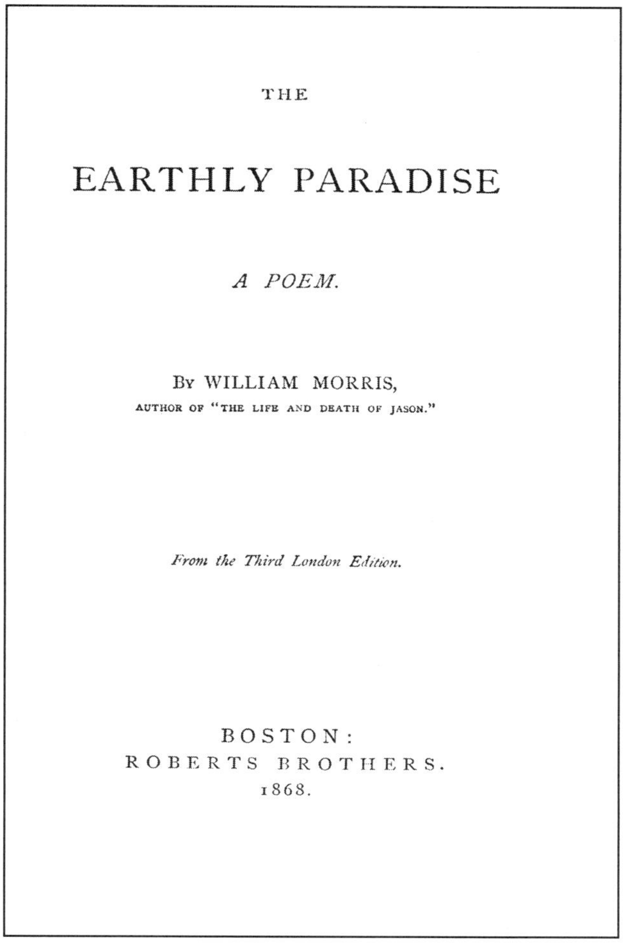

Figure 9. A-4.03: *EP* (2nd edn., 1st American) title page

BOOK.; p. [*6*], blank; p. [*7*], [headed]: A TABLE OF CONTENTS. | [french rule] | [list completed]; p. [*8*], blank; p. 1, text begins; pp. 2–430, text completed: [thin rule] | Cambridge: Printed by Welch, Bigelow, & Co.; p. [431], ad for 'The second and concluding volume of The Earthly Paradise', with a list of 12 titles and an epilogue projected; p. [432], ads. Bound in at the end of this copy is a 6° gathering, separately paginated and printed on plain machine-made paper, advertising 'Messrs. Roberts Brothers' List of Publications.'
Technical Notes: *paper*: cream-white 'antique wove' machine-laid paper, no watermark, dandy roll laid lines; *leaf size*: trimmed, 174 x 116 mm.; *printing*: *running titles*: [all versos] THE EARTHLY PARADISE. | [all rectos: in italic caps, the relevant tale title, intercalary lyric, or link]; *end-papers*: 2 free ends and paste-down, with dark matt-brown paste-down and facing free end, remaining sides plain white and blank; *binding*: t.e.g., plain dark red unblocked cloth, bevelled edges; *spine*: gilt-stamped with RB ornamental border of egg and dot design between thin rules, top and bottom: THE | EARTHLY | PARA-DISE | [ornamental rule] | BY | [swash caps] WILLIAM MORRIS | [Roberts' *EP* globe encircled with the months, Mar.–Aug., pertaining to the tales of this vol.] | ROBERTS BROTHERS

Publication: 1868 [issued 13 Aug.] (Cost Book A, Roberts Arch.); *print run*: 1,000 copies issued; *price*: $2.25 (Roberts Arch. and ads).
Register of Copies Examined: LeM (base copy); CaBVaU; NjP.
Notes: 'the American Edition, was printed from advance sheets of the English edition of F. S. Ellis . . . [RB] sold two thousand copies in two years' (Raymond L. Kilgour, *Messrs. Roberts Brothers: Publishers*, 56; hereafter referred to as Kilgour). *The American Literary Gazette* explains the differences in make-up and marketing between the imported version and this 1st American edition: 'Sept–Oct 1868: Roberts edn.: 16mo vellum cloth, gilt top, bevelled boards. Price $2.25.'; 1st version (from imported English sheets): 'Crown 8° Edition. (Third revised (English)). Green vellum cloth, gilt top, bevelled boards, Price $3.00'. In Sept. Roberts is selling the first 2 vols. as 2 sets, from imported English shts. and from the American setting: '$6.00, 8° & $4.50 for the 16° (*Am. Lit. Gaz. & PC*, 11/9 (1 Sept. 1868), 214).
Later issues and impressions of this edn.: (RB):
1. 1868 [issued 10 Oct.] (Roberts Arch.): [2nd impression, 2nd edn., 1st American]; *print run*: 1,000 copies; *price*: $2.25.
Other impressions of American sets, see A-4.11.

A-4.04: The Earthly Paradise (Parts I and II in 2 vols.)

Title page as A-4.01, except addition above the publisher's imprint: Part I [II] | *FIFTH EDITION.*; and change of the imprint date: MDCCCLXX.
Edition: FIFTH EDITION. [4th impression, 1st edn.] The original 1st vol. was issued here for the 1st time divided into 2 vols. A new title page was inserted in the last vol. of the edn., Part IV (see A-4.08), to be excised and inserted in the original 1st vol. to make it clear that it contains both Parts I and II of a 4-part, 3-vol. set.
Collation: vol. 1, Part I: cr. 8°: [A]⁴ B–Y⁸ Z⁴ 176 leaves pp. [*8*] [1] 2–343 [344] [= 352].
vol. 2, Part II: cr. 8°: [A]⁴ B–Y⁸ 172 leaves pp. [*8*] [1] 2–336 [= 344].

Contents: the contents are the same as the 1-vol. version, 1st impression, 1st edn., except changes to the title pages (see above). Both vols. end with the three-musicians woodcut vignette, but the dedication is omitted from vol. II, and a 2nd half title added: THE | EARTHLY PARADISE. | MAY, JUNE, JULY, AUGUST.; text begins on p. 2.

Technical Notes: *paper*: machine-laid paper, thicker and rougher than the paper used in the previous impressions, with dandy roll laid lines; *leaf size*: as in A-4.01; *binding*: the same as earlier impressions except the printed paper label adds new detail: THE | EARTHLY PARADISE. | W. MORRIS. | Fifth Edition. | I. [II] | [below compartment] Price 8s.

Publication: 1870 [issued '15–30 Nov. 1869'] (*Pub. Circ.*, 32/773 (8 Dec. 1869), 793); *print run*: 1,000 copies (HBF, p. 53); *price*: 16s. for the 2 vols., 8s. for each (*Pub. Circ.*, 32/773 (8 Dec. 1869), 793).

Register of Copies Examined: BGR.

Later impression of this edn.:

1. Ellis: 1871: 'Sixth Edition.' [5th impression, 1st edn.]; *print run*: unknown; *price*: 8s.

A-4.05: The Earthly Paradise (Part III)

THE | EARTHLY PARADISE | A POEM. | [the three-musicians woodcut vignette] | BY | WILLIAM MORRIS, | AUTHOR OF THE LIFE AND DEATH OF JASON. | PART III. | *London: F. S. ELLIS, 33 King Street, Covent Garden.* | MDCCCLXX. | [All Rights reserved.] (last square brackets in the original)

Edition: PART III. [1st impression, 1st edn.] Besides the ordinary copies, there were 25 copies printed for private circulation in 2 vols. on hand-laid paper and watermarked 'C. Ansell, 1869' (MH copy).

Collation: cr. 8°: [A]⁴ B–2L⁸ 268 leaves pp. [8] [1] 2–526 [527–8] [= 536].

Contents: pp. [1–2], F. S. Ellis's ads for Morris books pbd. or 'in preparation'; p. [3], half title; p. [4], blank; p. [5], title page; p. [6], printer's imprint: LONDON: | STRANGE-WAYS AND WALDEN, PRINTERS, | Castle St. Leicester Sq; p. [7], headed: CONTENTS. | [thin rule] | [list of 6 titles, 2 each under] SEPTEMBER | OCTOBER | [and] NOVEMBER; p. [8], blank; p. [1], 2nd half title: THE | EARTHLY PARADISE. | [thin rule] | SEPTEMBER, OCTOBER, | NOVEMBER; pp. 2–526, text completed; p. 527, three-musicians woodcut vignette; p. 528: printer's imprint repeated, as above.

Technical Notes: *paper*: cream machine-laid 'antique wove' paper with dandy roll laid lines, no watermark; *leaf size*: trimmed, 187 x 127 mm.; *printing*: *running titles*: all versos: THE EARTHLY PARADISE | all rectos: [in italics, title of the relevant tale or the appropriate month if an intercalary lyric]; *end-papers*: 1 free end and paste-down, plain white and blank, front and back; *binding*: plain unblocked dark green or blue cloth-covered boards with printed paper label: [within thin-rule compartment] THE | EARTHLY | PARADISE | [thin rule] | W. MORRIS. | [thin rule] | PART III. | [below compartment] *Price* 12s.

Publication: 1870 [The English issue was 15–30 Nov. 1869, simultaneous with the 1st issue of the 2-vol. version of Parts I and II (see the previous entry)] (*Pub. Circ.*, 32/773 (8 Dec. 1869), 793); *print run*: 2,000 copies printed (HBF, p. 58), of which 1,000 were exported to Boston (see the next entry); *price*: 12s.

Register of Copies Examined: LeM (base copy); BGR (2 copies, Am & Eng.); S Par; VU(E); VPar; VSL; MH.

Later issues and impressions of this edn.:

1. Ellis: 1870 [issued 15–31 Jan.]: SECOND EDITION. [2nd issue of remaining 1st impression copies]; *price*: 12s.;
2. Ellis: 1870 [issued Aug.] THIRD EDITION. [2nd impression, 1st edn.]; *print run*: 500 copies; *price*: 12s.;
3. R and T: 1891 [issued Mar.]: SEVENTH EDITION; *print run*: unknown: *price*: 12s.;
4. Longmans: 1896 [issued July]: SEVENTH and EIGHTH EDITION. [re-issue of R and T remaining copies from those printed in 1885 and 1891] i.e. from the 1st edn., called the 'Library Edition', but also issued as 'Cheaper Library Edition' and here as part of the new Longmans series, PW. When the unsold Morris shts. were purchased by Longmans in 1896, they were given new title pages, a Longmans binding, and a reduction in price to 6s. After this re-issue, from 1896 to the new setting of 1900, when Longmans rptd. the EP vols., the plates of each carried corrections incorporating the revisions Morris made for the 1-vol. edn. issued in 1890 and the KP edn. of 1896–7.

A-4.06: The Earthly Paradise (Part III, imported shts., RB)

Title page as in the previous entry, except for a change of the imprint date: MDCCCLXX.

Edition: PART III. [2nd issue, 1st American, made of imported English sheets from the 1st impression, 1st edn.] The 2nd vol. of the 3-vol. set is called by RB the 'English Edition'. In this case 1,000 sets of English sheets from the 2,000 printed by Strangeways for the 1st impression (see A-4.05) were imported by RB and combined with the imported 1st edition of the 1st vol. and later with Part IV, also made from imported sheets, to make a complete set of *EP* in imported sheets with American bindings, when complete the set being called the 'Deluxe Edition' (described in Pye, pp. 22–3 and in Cost Book A, Roberts Arch.). Since this issue duplicates the previous entry except for minor changes, the only fields included are those necessary to record the changes.

Contents: p. [ii], copyright statement: AUTHOR'S EDITION.; p. [528], the English printer's imprint has been excised, along with Ellis's publisher's imprint.

Technical Notes: *binding*: 100 copies imported in the English binding and 900 copies have the standard RB binding in dark green cloth (see this field in A-4.02), except that on the front the months on the circumference of the gilt-stamped globe are those included in this book: SEPTEMBER | OCTOBER | NOVEMBER.; another binding besides those described in A-4.02, in light green cloth, no chamfered edges; *spine*: gilt-stamped: THE | [arched over a half globe] Earthly | [straight text] PARADISE | [thin rule] | By | William Morris | VOL. 2 | AUTUMN. | [in gothic] Boston | [plain type] ROBERTS BROTHERS

Publication: 1870 [imported Dec. 1869] (Roberts Arch.): 'Deluxe Edition' [2nd issue, 1st American, 1st edn.]; *print run*: 1,000 copies imported (Cost Book A, Roberts Arch.); *price*: $3.00.

Register of Copies Examined: LeM (base copy); SPar (set of 3 vols. Part III, being 2nd vol., is 1st edn.).

Later imported issue of this edn.:

1. RB: 1891 [issued 10 Mar.]: 'English Edition.' (Roberts Arch.); *print run*: 376 copies imported; *price*: $3.00.

A-4.07: The Earthly Paradise (vol. II, Part III, RB)

THE | EARTHLY PARADISE | A POEM. | BY WILLIAM MORRIS, | AUTHOR OF 'THE LIFE AND DEATH OF JASON.' | PART III. | BOSTON: | ROBERTS BROTHERS. | 1870.

Edition: PART III. 'Author's Edition.' [1st impression, 2nd edition, 1st American] Part III, vol. II of the complete 4-part series in 3 vols. 'Author's Edition' does not distinguish a particular edn., being used regularly with various books to indicate an existing copyright arrangement between publisher and author (see the general Introduction discussion of copyright). In 1871, this American setting was combined with the 1st and 3rd vols. in their American editions to form the RB 'Cheap Edition' as described in the Cost Books and in advertising.

Collation: 12° with 8° sigs.: [1–18¹²] 216 leaves pp. [6] [1] 2–382 (pagination restarts for integral advertising matter) [1–3] 4–36 (restarts again) [1] 2–4 [5–8] [= 432]. sigs. as in A-4.03, alternating between 2 sigs., on 4ʳ and 12ʳ of odd-numbered gatherings, and 1 sig., on the 8ʳ of each even-numbered gathering.

Contents: p. [1], half title; p. [2], blank; p. [3], title page; p. [4]: AUTHOR'S EDITION. | [thin rule] | University Press: JOHN WILSON & SON, CAMBRIDGE.; p. [5], headed: A TABLE OF CONTENTS. | [french rule] | [list of 6 tales, 2 each under the months of 'September' 'October' and 'November']; p. [6], blank; p. [1], 2nd half title: THE EARTHLY PARADISE. | [french rule] | SEPTEMBER, OCTOBER, NOVEMBER.; p. 2, 1st chapter head: [dropped head] SEPTEMBER. | [text begins]; pp. 3–382, text completed with explicit: THE END. | [thin rule] | [printer's imprint] University Press: Welch, Bigelow & Co. Cambridge; following the text, but part of the same gathering, and continuing in a 2nd gathering are the *Tributes to William Morris*, also issued as a free pamphlet for advertising purposes, separately paged (36 pages), another 4 pages, separately paged, of quotations from English journals on *EP*, and another 4 pages, without page nos., of other RB advertising.

Technical Notes: as in A-4.03, variant binding in apple-green cloth as well as that of vol. I, Parts I and II, in plum.

Publication: 1870 [issued 12 Jan.] (Cost Book A, Roberts Arch.); *print run*: 1,500 copies; *price*: $1.50.

Register of Copies Examined: LeM (base copy); BGR.

Notes: In 1870 Wilson took over the printing from Welsh, Bigelow and acquired existing stocks of *EP* along with the stereo forms created by Welsh, Bigelow. As a result an anomaly was created with two different printers imprints, Wilson on the verso of a new title page, Welsh, Bigelow at the end of the last form. The new title page appears in both the remaining stock and the 1871 Wilson reprint of 500 copies.

Later impression of this edn.: RB:

1. 1871: 'Author's Edition.'; *print run*: 500 copies; *price*: $1.50.

A-4.08: The Earthly Paradise (vol. III, Part IV)

THE | EARTHLY PARADISE | A POEM. | [three-musicians woodcut vignette] | BY | WILLIAM MORRIS, | AUTHOR OF THE LIFE AND DEATH OF JASON. | PART IV. | *London*: F. S. ELLIS, 33 *King Street, Covent Garden*. | MDCCCLXX, | [All Rights reserved.] (last square brackets in the original)

Edition: PART IV. [1st impression, 1st edn.] 3rd vol. of 3-

vol. set or 4th vol. of 4-vol. set. Besides the ordinary copies, there were, as with vols. I and II, 25 LP copies in 2 vols. on hand-laid paper. The whole *EP* was thus being made as a 6-vol. LP set with pagination starting or re-starting in vols. I, III, and V. Bound in at the end of this 1st impression is a revised title page for the purchasers to insert into their original 1-vol. version of the 1st vol.

Collaborators, Editors, and Illustrators: on the three-musicians woodcut vignette, see Dunlap 2, 40–2.

Collation: cr. 8°: [A]⁴ (– A4) B–2E⁸ 2F⁶ (2F6+1) 226 leaves pp. [6] [1] 2–442 [443–6] [= 452] + a single leaf, probably printed on the missing A4, is tipped into this 3rd vol. after the last leaf of 2F. It was intended to be excised and inserted in the 1st vol. as a replacement title page. It includes the note 'Parts I and II' and is dated, inappropriately for vol. 1, 'MDCCCLXX'. The original vol. 1 title page lacked the part designation (not devised until the projected second vol. outgrew its limits and had to be made into 2). The original 1st vol. contained what became Parts I and II, and was dated, correctly, 'MDCCCLXVIII'. The title page inserted in vol. 3 was probably printed at the same place and time as the rest of vol. 3, but it is not integral to either vol. 1, its intended place, or vol. 3, where it first appeared. The inserted leaf is described here in its actual place in the *Contents*. It was clearly Ellis's reasonable assumption that the buyers of part 4 of a poem would already own parts 1 and 2.

Contents: p. [1], half title; p. [2], blank; p. [3], title page; p. [4], imprint: LONDON: | STRANGEWAYS AND WALDEN, PRINTERS, | Castle St. Leicester Sq.; p. [5], CONTENTS | [thin rule] | [list for Dec., Jan., Feb., Epilogue, and L'Envoi]; p. [6], blank; p. [1], 2nd half title: THE | EARTHLY PARADISE | [thin rule] | DECEMBER, JANUARY, | FEBRUARY.; pp. 2–442, text completed with explicit: THE END. | LONDON: | Printed by STRANGEWAYS AND WALDEN, Castle St. Leicester Sq.; p. [443], repeat of the three-musicians woodcut vignette as on title page; p. [444], blank; p. [445], inserted title page facing p. [445], see *Collation*, above, reproduces the original title page of vol.1 except for the insertion after the authorial note: PARTS I. & II.; and a new date in the place of the original: MDCCCLXX; p. [446], blank; extra spine label to replace the one on the 1st vol., loosely inserted before the extra title page: THE | EARTHLY | PARADISE. | [thin rule] | W. MORRIS. | [thin rule] | I. & II.

Technical Notes: *paper*: cream machine-laid, no watermark, with dandy roll laid lines; *leaf size*: trimmed, 190 x 124

Figure 10. A-4.08: *EP*, substitute title page inserted in vol. 3, part 4, for use in A-4.01

mm.; *printing*: *running titles*: all versos: THE EARTHLY PARADISE. | [all rectos, tale titles in italics, all caps]; *endpapers*: 1 free end and paste-down, plain white and blank, front and back; *binding*: plain dark green unblocked cloth; *spine*: printed paper label: [within thin rule compartment] THE | EARTHLY | PARADISE. | [thin rule] | W. MORRIS. | [thin rule] | IV. | [below compartment] Price 12s.; Besides the ordinary copies, there were, as with vols. I and II, 25 LP copies on demy 8° hand-laid paper, watermarked: J. Whatman 1870 (MH copy); published as 2 vols. in quarter-holland, light blue paper-covered boards, with white holland spine and printed spine label: THE | EARTHLY | PARADISE | W. MORRIS | V [VI] and page numbering continuous through the 2 vols.

Publication: 1870 [issued '1–15 Dec.'] (*Pub. Circ.*, 33/798 (17 Dec. 1870), 1014); *print run*: '1,500 ordinary copies printed' and 25 LP copies' (HBF, p. 68); *price*: ordinary copies 12s.

Register of Copies Examined: LeM (base copy); SPar (set of 3 vols. Part 4, being 1st edn).
Notes: 'uniform with Part III . . . the first page of the advertizements [*sic*] in Volsunga Saga . . . announces that in October will be published the fourth and concluding portion of The Earthly Paradise. I do not think it was really ready much before December; but at all events it was out well before Christmas' (HBF, p. 65).
Later issues and impressions of this edn.: Ellis:
1. 1870: SECOND EDITION.; *print run*: 500 copies; *price*: 12*s*.;
2. 1871: THIRD EDITION.; *print run* and *price*: as above.

A-4.09: The Earthly Paradise (vol. III, imported shts. RB)

Title page as in A-4.08, except changed imprint date: 1871.
Edition: PART IV. [2nd issue, comprising imported sheets from the English 1st impression, 1st edn.] (described in Roberts Cost Book A).
Series: 'Part IV' completes the sets of the *EP* in imported English sheets in American bindings, being the 3rd vol. of the 3-vol. set.
Technical Notes: *paper*: t.e.g.; bindings in dark green or plum cloth with chamfered edges; *spine*: gilt-stamped as in A-4.08, globe circumscribed with the 3 months covered here: DECEMBER | JANUARY | FEBRUARY
Publication: 1871 [issued Feb.] (Roberts Arch.); *print run*: 500 copies imported; *price*: $3.00.
Register of Copies Examined: CU-B (with Henry James's autograph).

A-4.10: The Earthly Paradise (vol. III, Part IV RB)

THE | EARTHLY PARADISE | *A POEM.* | BY WILLIAM MORRIS, | AUTHOR OF 'THE LIFE AND DEATH OF JASON.' | PART IV. | BOSTON: | ROBERTS BROTHERS. | 1871.
Edition: 'Author's Edition.' called the '6-quire edn' or '16mo. edn..' in Cost Book A and advertised as the 'Cheap Edition' [1st impression, 2nd edn., 1st American of Part IV.].
Series: 'Part IV', completes the American setting of the 3-vol. set.
Collation: 12°, with 8° sigs.: [1–17¹²] [2 sigs., on 4ʳ and 8ʳ of each gathering] 204 leaves pp. [6] [1] 2–401 [402] [= 408] (for an explanation of this format, see this field in A-4.03).
Contents: prelims as in A-4.03, except p. [4], copyright note: 'AUTHOR'S EDITION.' | [printer's imprint] UNIVERSITY PRESS: | JOHN WILSON & SON, CAMBRIDGE.; p. [5], headed: A TABLE OF CONTENTS. | [french rule] | [6 tale titles arranged, 2 each under the months] DECEMBER | JANUARY | FEBRUARY | EPILOGUE | L'ENVOI; p. [6], blank; p. [1], 2nd half title; THE EARTHLY PARADISE. | [french rule] | DECEMBER, JANUARY, FEBRUARY.; p. 2, text begins; pp. 3–400, text continues, with last section, 'L'Envoi' in italics; p. 401, text completed with explicit: THE END. | [thin rule] | University Press: John Wilson & Son, Cambridge; p. [402], blank.
Technical Notes: as in A-4.03, except *binding*: in green or plum cloth; Roberts Brothers gilt-stamped globe encircled by months: DECEMBER | JANUARY | FEBRUARY
Publication: 1871 [issued '19 Jan.'] (Cost Book A, Roberts Arch.); *print run*: 1,000 copies; *price*: $1.50.
Register of Copies Examined: LeM (base copy); BGR.
Later impression of this edn.: RB:
1. 1871 [issued 1 Feb.] (*Am. Lit. Gaz & PC.*, 16/7 (1 Feb. 1871), 131): 'Second Edition'; *print run*: 500 copies; *price*: $1.50.

A-4.11: The Earthly Paradise (3-vol. set, RB)

Title pages of this complete 3-vol. set duplicate A-4.10, except: PARTS I. AND II. [III and IV].
Edition: 'Cheap Edition' [textually all the vols. are successive impressions, this one the 3rd of the 2nd edn., 1st American], 1st complete set issued by RB in the American setting: 4 parts in 3 vols. The successive sets RB pbd. were advertised variously as '16mo', and 'Cheap Edition' (this being the latter) different only in binding, paper, and price. The 1st vol., like the original English edn. imported in sheets (see A-4.02), contains both Part I and Part II. Since this issue duplicates the 3 vols. described in A-4.03, 4.07, and 4.10, only those fields that have changed are included.
Technical Notes: *binding*: dark blue and dark red (maroon or 'plum') cloth; blind-stamped continuous ornamental border along the head and foot, of crosses superimposed on circles all within thick rules, extending around the edges of the front, spine, and back; gilt globe on the front with appropriate months for the contents of each vol. around the circumference; *spine*: gilt-stamped: THE | [lettered as an arc over a segment of an inclined hemisphere] EARTHLY | [below the globe segment, prtd. straight] PARADISE | [thin rule] | BY | WILLIAM MORRIS | Vol. I [II and III] | SPRING—SUMMER [AUTUMN and WINTER] | [in gothic] BOSTON | ROBERTS BROTHERS; a rpt. of the RB pamphlet *Tributes* is inserted in vol. II.
Publication: 1871 [issued '1 February 1871'] (*Am. Lit. Gaz.*

& PC, 16/7 (1 Feb. 1871), 131); *print run*: 600 copies; *price*: $4.50 the set.

Register of Copies Examined: LeM (base copy); BGR; MiU; NJP; CaBVaU.

Notes: Roberts' ad for their EP 3-vol. sets: 'The Work Complete in Three Volumes. Crown 8°. [English edn.] green vellum cloth, bevelled boards; price, $9. 16mo. [American 'de Luxe edn'] green [or] wine vellum cloth, gilt top, bevelled boards; price $6.75. 16mo [American 'cheap edn'], cloth, neat; price $4.50 . . .. Special notice.—To enable everybody to possess a copy of Mr. Morris's "New Storehouse of Treasure-Stories of Enchantment and delight," the Publishers, on the completion of the Work, issue a new and Cheaper Edition, printed on white laid paper, and bound neatly in plain cloth. There will thus be three distinct editions of the Work; priced at $3.00, $2.25, and $1.50 per volume, respectively' (Am. Lit. Gaz. & PC, 16/7 (1 Feb. 1871), 131).

Later issues and impressions of this edn. : RB:

1. 1874 [Apr.]: '6-quire edn' in Cost Book A; *print run*: 280 sets;
2. 1878 [19 Oct.]: '6-Quire Edn.'; *print run*: 280 sets, plus 100 extra copies of vols. 1 and 2, 'to complete sets of nice 16mo Ed' with left over copies of the 'Fine Edition' (Cost Book A, Roberts Arch.);
3. 1884 [29 Oct.]: '16mo edn', *print run*: 280 sets; *price*: see *Notes*, above;
4. 1888 [27 July]: 'Cheap edn', *print run*: 280 sets; *price*: see *Notes*, above;
5. 1893 [13 Jan.]: 'Cheap Edn.', *print run*: 280 sets; *price*: see *Notes*, above.

A-4.12: The Earthly Paradise (10 Parts)

THE EARTHLY PARADISE | A POEM. | BY | WILLIAM MORRIS, | AUTHOR OF THE LIFE AND DEATH OF JASON. | POPULAR EDITION. | IN TEN PARTS. | *Part 1.* | PROLOGUE—THE WANDERERS. | ATALANTA'S RACE | LONDON: | ELLIS AND GREEN, | 33 KING STREET, COVENT GARDEN, W.C. | MDCCCLXXII. | [*All Rights reserved.*]

Brackets are in the original. The subsequent title pages are the same in all the Parts down to line 7, the part number. The remainder of the title page is special to each Part:

Part II. | [aligned left] THE MAN BORN TO BE KING. | THE DOOM OF KING ACRISIUS. | THE PROUD KING.

Part III. | [aligned left] THE STORY OF CUPID AND PSYCHE. | THE WRITING ON THE IMAGE. | THE LOVE OF ALCESTIS.

Part IV. | [aligned left] THE LADY OF THE LAND. | THE SON OF CRŒSUS. | THE WATCHING OF THE FALCON. | PYGMALION AND THE IMAGE. | OGIER THE DANE.

Part V. | [aligned left] THE DEATH OF PARIS. | THE LAND EAST OF THE SUN AND WEST OF THE MOON.

Part VI. | [aligned left] ACONTIUS AND CYDIPPE. | THE MAN WHO NEVER LAUGHED AGAIN. | THE STORY OF RHODOPE.

Part VII. | [aligned left] THE LOVERS OF GUDRUN.

Part VIII. | [aligned left] THE GOLDEN APPLES. | THE FOSTERING OF ASLAUG. | BELLEROPHON AT ARGOS.

[Title pages of Parts II to VIII all end with imprint, date, and copyright notice as in Part I]

Part IX. | [aligned left] THE RING GIVEN TO VENUS. | BELLEROPHON IN LYCIA. | LONDON: | Ellis and Green, | 29 New Bond Street, W. | (Late 33 King Street, Covent Garden). | MDCCCLXXII.

Part X. | [aligned left] BELLEROPHON IN LYCIA. | THE HILL OF VENUS. | EPILOGUE. 'L'ENVOI'. | LONDON: | F. S. Ellis, 29 New Bond Street, W. | (Late 33 King Street, Covent Garden). | MDCCCLXXII.

Edition: 'Popular Edition. In Ten Parts. Part I.' etc. Until 1896, the 'Popular Edition' series title applies to both the 10-part and the later 5-part series. From 1896, Longmans called the 5-part series the 'Cabinet Edition'. This 10-part issue is the 1st impression of this series, but the mixture of impressions of the 1st edn. setting within individual parts has in this case and A-4.13 become such as to make detailed distinctions both difficult and probably pointless.

Collation: Part 1: 8°: [A]^4 B–I^8 K^4 72 leaves pp. [8] [1] 2–136 [= 144].

Part 2: 8°: π^4 K*^{4} L–Y^8 Z^4 108 leaves pp. [4] 137–343 [344] [= 216] pagination continues from Part 1:.

Part 3: 8°: [A]^2 B–L^8 82 leaves pp. [4] [1] 2–160 [= 164].

Part 4: 8°: [M]^8 N–Y^8 88 leaves pp. [2] 161–334 [= 176] pagination continues from Part 3.

Part 5: 8°: [A]^2 B –L^8 82 leaves pp. [4] [1] 2–160 [= 164].

Part 6: 8°: π^2 M–Y^8 90 leaves; pagination continues from Part 5: pp. [4] 161–336 [= 180].

Part 7: 8°: [title page tipped in, printed perhaps on the missing L8, excised from that gathering and tipped in at the beginning] π^2 (–π2) Z–2L^8 (–L8) 96 leaves; pagination continues from Part 6: pp. [2] 337–526 [= 192].

Part 8: 8°: [A]^2 B–M^8 90 leaves pp. [4] [1] 2–176 [= 180].

Part 9: 8°: π² N–X⁸ 74 leaves pagination continues from Part 8: pp. [4] 177–320 [= 148].
Part 10: 8°: π² Y–2E⁸ 2F⁶ 64 leaves pagination continues from Part 9: pp. [4] 321–442 [443–4] [= 128].
Contents: duplicates 1st edn., of which this is a rpt., in the 3-vol. format—A-4.04, .05, and .08— except for adjustments in the prelims and end matter: the three-musicians woodcut vignette is used as a frontis. only in Parts I and II and as a tail-piece to Parts II and X; pagination reproduces that of the 4-vol. format; contents pages appear only in Parts I, III, IV, and VIII, repeating those of the 1st 4-vol. set; the publisher's imprint address is changed in Part IX to LONDON: | ELLIS AND GREEN, | 29 NEW BOND STREET, W. | (*Late of 33 King Street, Covent Garden*). | MDCCCLXXII.; the publisher's name is changed in Part X: LONDON: | F. S. ELLIS, 29 NEW BOND STREET, W. | (*Late 33 King Street, Covent Garden*). In all parts the printer's imprint appears on the verso of the half title: LONDON: | PRINTED BY JOHN STRANGEWAYS, Castle St. Leicester Sq.
Technical Notes: common to the set: *paper*: cream-white machine-wove paper, no watermark; *leaf size*: trimmed, 170 x 116 mm.; *printing, running heads*, see this field in A-4.01; *pagination*: as in the 4-vol. 1st edn. (see A-4.04, 4.05, and 4.08); *binding*: dark green cloth-covered thin boards with a blind-stamped thin-rule compartment front and back; gilt-stamped on front: THE | EARTHLY PARADISE | [titles of the tales in the Part, in italic caps with thin rules between titles]; *spine*: gilt-stamped: THE | EARTHLY | PARADISE | W. MORRIS | I [II–X]; *end-papers*: 1 free end and paste-down, rougher, flecked paper, otherwise plain white and blank, front and back.
Publication: 1872 (Parts 1 and 2) [issued 1–15 Feb.]; (Part 3) [16–30 Mar.]; (Part 4) [1–15 May]; (Part 5) [1–15 June]; (Part 6) [1–15 July]; (Part 7) [2–15 Aug.]; (Part 8) [16–31 Aug.]; (Part 9) [1–15 Oct.]; (Part 10) [1–15 Nov.] (*Pub. Circ.*, 35/826 (16 Feb. 1872), 112, etc.); *print run*: Parts 1 and 2 = 2,000 copies; Part 3 = 1,250 copies; all other parts = 1,000 copies (HBF, p. 71); *price*: retail, 3s. 6d. each, i.e. 2s. 8d. net (later reduced to 2s. 6d).
Register of Copies Examined: SU (base copy: 821.85/M877e [in store] Z22); BGR (2 copies: (a) and (b)); NN; CaBVaU; SSL (5-part version) (storage, 821 M8773).
Later impressions of this edn.: Longmans:
1. 1902 [8 Nov.]: Part 2 of 10, 'Popular Edition'; *print run*: 1,500 copies;
2. 1903 [9 Sept.]: Part 2 of 10, 'Popular Edition'; *print run*: 250 copies;
3. 1903 [17 Oct.]: Part 3 of 10, 'Popular Edition'; *print run*: 1,000 copies;
4. 1904 [17 May]: Part 7 of 10, 'Popular Edition'; *print run*: 250 copies;
5. 1904 [21 Sept.]: Part 2 of 10, 'Popular Edition'; *print run*: 250 copies.

A-4.13: The Earthly Paradise (5-vol. set)
THE | EARTHLY PARADISE | A POEM. | BY | WILLIAM MORRIS, | AUTHOR OF THE LIFE AND DEATH OF JASON. | IN FIVE VOLUMES. | VOL. I [II, III, IV, V] | THE WANDERERS. | ATALANTA'S RACE. | THE MAN BORN TO BE KING. | THE DOOM OF KING ACRISIUS. | THE PROUD KING. | LONDON: | REEVES AND TURNER, 196 STRAND. | MDCCCLXXXVI. | [*All Rights Reserved*]
Last brackets in the original. The subsequent title pages are the same in all the vols. down to the vol. number, and the remainder of the title pages is special to each Part:
VOL. II. | THE STORY OF CUPID AND PSYCHE. | THE WRITING ON THE IMAGE. | THE LOVE OF ALCESTIS. | THE LADY OF THE LAND. | THE SON OF CRŒSUS. | THE WATCHING OF THE FALCON. | PYGMALION AND THE IMAGE. | OGIER THE DANE. | [imprint, date, and copyright notice as in vol. I]
VOL. III. | THE DEATH OF PARIS. | THE LAND EAST OF THE SUN AND WEST OF THE MOON. | ACONTIUS AND CYDIPPE. | THE MAN WHO NEVER LAUGHED AGAIN. | THE STORY OF RHODOPE | [imprint as in vol. I] | MDCCCLXXXIX. | [*All Rights Reserved*]
VOL. IV. | THE LOVERS OF GUDRUN. | THE GOLDEN APPLES. | THE FOSTERING OF ASLAUG. | BELLEROPHON AT ARGOS. | [imprint, date, and copyright notice as in vol. I]
VOL. V. | THE RING GIVEN TO VENUS. | BELLEROPHON IN LYCIA. | THE HILL OF VENUS. | EPILOGUE. | L'ENVOI. | [imprint, date, and copyright notice as in vol. I]
Edition: 'New Edition.' 'In Five Volumes'; advertised as the 'Popular Edition' [but still the 1st edn. setting] this being a recombination of the 10-Part set (see A-4.12) in a 5-vol. format, the 1st Morris pbn. to be issued by R and T. From 1896, Longmans continued the 5-part set, calling it the 'Cabinet Edition'. Since this merely recombines the 10-part version, probably in the first instance by combining the remaining unsold sheets of the 10-part version with any new impressions required being printed from

the plates made by 'Strangeways & Walden, Printers, 28 Castle Street, Leicester Square', the letterpress here largely duplicates A-4.12, though the mixture of imprint dates in the vols. suggest the copy described here is a mixed set of various impressions. But all derive from the 1st edn. Only details of altered fields are included here.

Collation: vol. 1: small 8°: [A]² B–Y⁸ (–M) Z⁴ [$1 (+ K4) signed], 174 leaves pp. [4] [1] 2–343 [344] [= 348].

vol. 2: small 8°: [A]² B–Y⁸ (–M⁸) 170 leaves pp. [4] [1] 2–334 [335–6] [= 340].

vol. 3: small 8°: [A]² B–Y⁸ 170 leaves pp. [4] [1] 2–336 [= 340].

vol. 4: small 8°: π² Z–2L⁸ (–2L8) B–M⁸ 185 leaves pp. [4] 337–526 [= 194] [1] 2–176 [176 + 194 = 370] signing and pagination here begin continuous with the 1st edn. vol. 3 (& vol. 3 here) and change to 1st edn. vol. 4 vol. numbers, signatures, and pagination after p. 526, 2L7).

vol. 5: signing and pagination here duplicate the latter part of the 1st impression, 1st edn. vol. 4: small 8°: π² N–2E⁸ 2F⁶ (–F6) 135 leaves pp. [4] 177–442 [= 270].

Contents: except for minor variations in the prelims and end matter, the contents follow those of the 1st edn. in 4 vols. (see A-4.04, .05, and .08); vol. I may be taken as representative: p. [1], half title; p. [2], as frontis., three-musicians vignette; p. [3], title page, see above; p. [4], dedication; p. 5, contents; pp. [1]–343, text; p. [344], tail-piece, three-musicians vignette.

Technical Notes: *paper*: machine-made; *leaf size*: 165 x 115 mm.; *binding*: dark blue or dark red cloth, title gilt-stamped on front and spine.

Publication: '1886' vol. I: [issued 1–15 Mar.] (*Pub. Circ.*, 49/1164 (15 Mar. 1886), 280); vol. II: [16–31 Apr.] (ibid., 49/1167 (1 May 1886), 446); vol. III: [16–31 May] (ibid., 49/1169 (1 June 1886), 560); vol. IV: [16–30 June] (ibid., 49/1171 (1 July 1886), 738); vol. V: [17–31 Aug.] (ibid., 49/1175 (1 Sept. 1886), 969); *print run*: not known; *price*: 5s. each vol. (*English Catalogue of Books* (hereafter referred to as *Eng. Cat.*).

Register of Copies Examined: SSL (base copy: 821 M8773); NjP.

Later issue and impression of this edn.:

1. R and T: 1889: Parts 1, 2, 4, and 5 rptd.; *print run*: unknown;

2. Longmans: 1896, reissue of remaining R and T copies with Longmans imprint on the title page.

A-4.14: The Earthly Paradise (1 vol.)

THE | EARTHLY PARADISE | A POEM | BY | WILLIAM MORRIS | [the three-musicians woodcut vignette, 2nd version] | LONDON | REEVES AND TURNER, 196 STRAND | 1890.

Edition: 'Cheap Edition' [1st impression, 3rd edn., 2nd English] The text is revised by Morris, and his revisions incorporated in later edns, including the KP edn..

Collaborators, Editors, and Illustrators: for the originators of title-page vignette used here, see this field in A-4.01. Gilt floral design for the binding by Morris. Forman proof-read this vol. (see *Notes* below).

Collation: 8°: π⁴ A–2E⁸ 228 leaves pp. [i–vii] viii [1–2] 3–445 [446–8] [= 456] + 1 inserted leaf of ads. before π not noted in the formula or counted in the pagination, but described under *Contents*.

Contents: [1] inserted leaf facing the half title with R and T ads for 'Mr William Morris's Works'; p. [i], half title; p. [ii], printer's imprint: [1st line in gothic] Ballantyne Press | BALLANTYNE, HANSON AND CO. | EDINBURGH AND LONDON; p. [iii], title page; p. [iv], bibliographical note; p. [v], dedication: TO | MY WIFE | I DEDICATE THIS BOOK; p. [vi], blank; pp. [vii]–viii, headed: CONTENTS.; p. [1], 'An Apology' (title quoted from the Contents, here under the general title only); p. [2], blank; p. 3, text begins; pp. 4–445, text completed with printer's imprint: [thin rule] | PRINTED BY BALLANTYNE, HANSON AND CO. | EDINBURGH AND LONDON; pp. [446–8], blank.

Technical Notes: *paper*: white machine-wove, no watermark: some copies all edges dyed red; *leaf size*: trimmed, 211 x 143 mm.; *printing*: double columns, with a 2 mm. separation between columns throughout, except for full width titles and 'Argument'; *running titles*: all rectos and versos: title of the current tale, all caps, complete on each page; *end-papers*: 1 free end and paste-down, plain white and blank, front and back; *binding*: 'a choice of leathers from 12s 6d' (R and T ad, see *Notes*, below); ordinary copies: red, olive green, or white cloth with a gilt Morris design of 'sprigs of myrtle' (HBF, p. 71) within a double thin-rule compartment, with flowers at each corner, the same design gilt-stamped on the front and blind-stamped on the back; *spine*: gilt-stamped in a scroll design of 'bay and tulip' (ibid.), with title within top border of bay leaves, and bottom border of dots above bay leaves: THE | EARTHLY | PARADISE | BY | WILLIAM | MORRIS | [at foot] 1891; in copies dated 1898 and thereafter the backs are plain; HBF reports without comment (p. 72) that copies dated '1890' on the title page are dated '1891' at the foot of the spine. The BGR copies include one with 1896 on the

title page and 1891 on the spine. From 1898 no date appears on the bindings.
Publication: 1890 [issued 17–29 Nov.] (*Pub. Circ.*, 53/1277 (1 Dec. 1890), 1568); *print run*: not known; *price*: cloth 7s. 6d.; lthr. from 12s. 6d. (see *Notes*, below).
Register of Copies Examined: LeM (base copy: 3 copies); MiU; MU (PT5075/A1, 1890); SSL (2 copies: 821.8 M8773); SU (RC 821.85/M877e/1890); VU (821.85E); BGR; BL (Ashley Lib. 3683).
Notes: Morris to Scheu on 23 Nov. 1889: 'I wish you were my publisher as I really think something might be done with my books, more than has been done, and I am thinking of bringing out a cheap edition of The Earthly Paradise, in one vol; But I am rather tied to old Reeves at present' (*Letters*, iii. 129). Morris to Emery Walker, 21 Aug. 1890: 'Have made a design for the binding of the cheap E.P' (*Letters*, iii. 195). HBF *Catalogue*: p. 511: has a letter from Morris thanking Forman for proof reading this vol. R and T advertises it as, 'just ready, a new and complete reissue, in 1 vol., 8°, fully gilt, ornamental binding, from a special design by the Author, 7s. 6d. May be had in a variety of lthr. bindings from 12s. 6d. upwards' (*Reeves and Turner, a Catalogue of Books*, No. 403, Dec. 1890).
Later issues and impressions of this edn.:
1. Reeves: 1896 [Dec. 1895] '1891' on spine: 'Cheap Edn.'; *print run*: unknown; *price*: 7s. 6d.;
2. Longmans: 1896 [1 July]: NEW EDITION 'Cheap Edition'; *print run*: 2,000 copies; *price*: as above;
3. Longmans: 1898 [17 Dec.]: 'Cheap Edition'; *print run*: 1,000 copies; *price*: as above;
4. Longmans: 1900 [21 July]: 'Cheap Edition'; *print run*: 1,000 copies; *price*: as above;
5. Longmans: 1903 [31 Dec. 1902]: 'Cheap Edition'; *print run*: 1,000 copies; *price*: as above;
6. Longmans: 1905 [6 May]: 'Cheap Edition'; *print run*: 1,000 copies; *price*: as above;
7. Longmans: 1907 [19 July]: 'Cheap Edition'; *print run*: 1,500 copies; *price*: as above;
8. Longmans: 1910 [8 Oct.]: 'New Impression'; *print run*: 1,750 copies; *price*: as above.

A-4.15: The Earthly Paradise (3-vol. set, imported shts. RB)

[The title pages of this set are those of the imported English sheets and duplicate A-4.02, 4.06, and 4.09, except for the changes to the edn. note and publisher's imprint. What follows is specific to this set:] 'Vols. I and II [Parts 1–3] Ninth Edition.' 'Vol. III [Part IV] Seventh Edition' | LONDON: | REEVES AND TURNER, 196 STRAND. | BOSTON, U. S. A.: ROBERTS BROTHERS. | 1891.
Edition: English 3-vol. 'Library Edition'; called 'English Edition' by Roberts Brothers and issued in Boston, in Mar. 1891, with imported sheets in a US binding and with the RB imprint combined with R and T's. After the purchase of the RB business in 1898, Little, Brown and Co. continued selling the stock taken over. The title page edition numbers, 'Vols. I and II [Parts 1–3] Ninth Edition.'; 'Vol. III [Part IV] Seventh Edition' recorded here refer to the English sequence. Since this issue duplicates A-4.02, 4.06, and 4.09, only those fields that require correction or addition are included.
Contents: printer's imprint: [in gothic] BALLANTYNE PRESS: | [plain type] BALLANTYNE, HANSON AND CO. | EDINBURGH AND LONDON.
Technical Notes: *binding*: the ordinary copies are as in this field in A-4.11 except a later BGR copy has light blue cloth with the Little, Brown and Company monogram gilt-stamped on the spine, being probably from left-over RB sheets imported in 1891 and bound after Little, Brown bought out the RB business in May 1898. This later binding has a different gilt stamping below the half globe, on the spine, after the last word of the title: PARADISE | [thin rule] | By | WILLIAM MORRIS | VOL. I. [II. and III.] | SPRING–SUMMER [AUTUMN and WINTER] | LITTLE, BROWN | AND COMPANY.
Publication: '1891' [issued 10 Mar.] (Roberts Arch.); *print run*: 322 copies of vols. I and II, and 376 copies of vol. III. The uneven numbers imported suggest that RB was perfecting sets with some left-over copies of odd vols.; *price*: $9.00 the set.
Register of Copies Examined: see this field in A-4.02, 4.06, and 4.09.

A-4.16: The Earthly Paradise (4 vols. PW)

THE | EARTHLY PARADISE | A POEM. | [three-musicians woodcut vignette, later version] | BY | WILLIAM MORRIS, | AUTHOR OF THE LIFE AND DEATH OF JASON. | PART I. [II.–IV.] | *NINTH EDITION*. [or *SEVENTH EDITION*. or *EIGHTH EDITION* for vols. III. and IV.] | LONGMANS, GREEN, AND CO. | LONDON, NEW YORK, AND BOMBAY. | 1896. | *All rights reserved*.
Edition: unlike the complete sets of *EP* issued by RB from 1871 on, the English never issued the Library Edition in complete matched sets as such. In this instance, as with the versions issued by Morris's earlier English publishers, sets

of the standard 'Library Edition' are typically mixed editions, with the individual vols. being printed and issued separately. Here the 'Ninth Edition.' (vols. 1 and 2) is combined with the 'Seventh Edition.' vols. 3 and 4. The copies issued on this occasion are a re-issue by Longmans of R and T copies printed in 1885 and re-issued in 1891, i.e. from the 1st edn., called the 'Library Edition', but now advertised as 'Cheaper Library Edition', with new title pages and reduced in price. Longmans continued the practice of producing new impressions of individual vols. whenever the stocks of a particular vol. ran low. Since this issue duplicates A-4.04 in Parts I and II, and 4.05 and 4.08 in Parts III and IV, only those fields are included that require addition or correction.

Series: 4 vols. earlier called 'The Library Edition', are here part of a new series, 'The Poetical Works of William Morris' (PW), the series being indicated only on the printed paper spine labels. But except for the title pages and spine labels, the letterpress of this book is that of the remaining R and T copies acquired by Longmans in sheets. The change of publisher and this series, the 1st Longmans initiative, were announced in the *Pub. Circ.*, 65/1567 (11 July 1896), 33: 'Messrs. Longmans, Green & Co will in future be the publishers of all the works of William Morris, both verse and prose. They propose to issue at an early date a popular library edition of his poems, in ten vols., of which 'The Earthly Paradise' will fill four.' One week later the same trade journal records in 'Publications of the Week' (65/1569 (18 July 1896), 84) the issue of all 10 vols. Given the short time involved, the evidence of cancel title pages being used for various titles in the series, and the fact that *EP* edn. is identified as the 'Ninth Edition', repeating the R and T description, it is likely that, except for one new book, the combined edn. titled *Poems by the Way. Love is Enough*, the books of this new series began with remaining stock purchased from R and T, Longmans having fitted out each copy with a new title page with the Longmans imprint and dated 1896. These copies had also a new binding and printed paper spine label, where the series name appears at the top. But Longmans made haste to renew the supply with a new impression of 2,000 copies of *EP*, issued after the series had been made available with the older copies. The original series is recorded in the *Pub. Circ.* 'Publications of the Week':

Morris, (W.)—Poems by the Way. Love is Enough. cr. 8°, pp. 344, 6s. Longmans.
_____—The Æneids of Virgil, done into English verse. 2nd edit. cr. 8°, pp. 382, 6s.   Longmans.
_____—The Defence of Guenevere and Other Poems. From the edition of 1858, without alteration. cr. 8°, pp. 248, 6s. Longmans.
_____—The Earthly Paradise. 9th edit. 4 vols. cr. 8°, pp. 1650, each 6s. Longmans.
_____—The Life and Death of Jason: a Poem. 8th Edit. revised by the author. cr. 8°, pp. 376, 6s. Longmans.
_____—The Odyssey of Homer, English verse. cr. 8°. pp. 458, 6s. Longmans.
_____—The Story of Sigurd the Volsung and the Fall of the Niblungs. 5th edit. cr. 8°, pp. 346, 6s. Longmans (*Pub. Circ.*, 65/1569 (25 July 1896), 84).

In August 1898, Longmans added *The Tale of Beowulf*, the 11th vol. in the 'Poetical Works' series, the only indication of which, in this as in the other vols, is on the printed paper spine label. For this initial publication, only the publisher's imprint and dates of publication are changed in all cases except for the one new title, *Poems by the Way. Love is Enough*, which for the first time combines these two earlier titles.

The *Eng. Cat.* says that the price of each vol. in the series was reduced from 6s. to 5s. in July 1900 (see vol. 6 (1898–1900), 446).

Technical Notes: spine: new spine label: [within thin-rule compartment] THE | POETICAL | WORKS OF | WILLIAM | MORRIS | [thin rule] | THE | EARTHLY | PARADISE | VOLUME I [–IV] | [below compartment] *Six Shillings*.

Publication: 1896 [issued July]: 'Poetical Works'; *print run*: issued in an unknown number of Reeves and Turner copies purchased and given new title pages by Longmans who issued their 1st impression of the 4 vols. later the same year and early the next; *price*: 6s. each vol. (Longmans Arch.).

Register of Copies Examined: since the English sets were not issued as such, the constituent volumes are made up of whatever issues in this series came to hand.

Later issues and impressions of this edn.: the Longmans rpts. listed below for 1896 and 1897, Longman's 1st impressions, were done on plates corrected to incorporate Morris's revisions for the 1890 1-vol. edn.. This list includes all subsequent issues of 'The Library Edition' and 'Poetical Works' versions, which became less and less distinguishable, some issues being described in ads under both headings:
1. 1896 [17 Oct.]: vols. I and II (of IV): TENTH EDITION. 'Library Edition'; *print run*: 500 copies; *price*: 6s.;
2. 1896 [7 Nov.]: vol. III (of IV): EIGHTH EDITION;

print run: 500 copies; *price*: 6s.;

3. 1897 [27 Jan.]: vol. IV (of IV): 'Poetical Works of William Morris'; *print run*: 500 copies; *price*: 6s. (Longmans Arch.);

4. 1902 [4 Oct.]: vol. I (of IV): ELEVENTH IMPRESSION, 'Library Edition'; *print run*: 500 copies; *price*: 5s.;

5. 1902 [6 Dec.]: vol. III (of IV): NINTH EDITION, 'Library Edition'; *print run*: 500 copies; *price*: 5s.;

6. 1903 [18 Mar.]: vol. II (of IV): ELEVENTH EDITION, 'Library Edition'; *print run*: 500 copies; *price*: 5s.;

7. 1904 [6 July]: vol. IV (of IV): 'Ninth Edition', 'Library Edition'; *print run*: 500 copies; *price*: 5s.;

8. 1912 [May]: vol. I (of IV): 'Cheap Edition', 'Library Edition'; *print run*: 250 copies; *price*: 5s.;

9. 1912 [Aug.]: vol. III (of IV): 'Cheap Edition', 'Library Edition'; *print run*: 250 copies; *price*: 5s.;

10. 1915 [Dec. 1914]: vol. II (of IV):'Cheap Edition', 'Library Edition'; *print run*: 250 copies; *price*: 5s.

A-4.17: The Earthly Paradise (8-vol. KP set)

THE EARTHLY PARADISE. BY WILLIAM | MORRIS. VOLUME I. [II–VIII. KP printer's leaf ornament No. 2] PROLOGUE: THE | WANDERERS. [KP printer's leaf ornament No. 1] MARCH: ATALANTA'S | RACE. THE MAN BORN TO BE KING. [KP printer's flower ornament No. 3]

vols. II–VIII repeat the 1st title page as far as the vol. number. Thereafter the title-pages are specific to each vol.:

VOLUME II. [two KP printer's leaf ornaments No. 2] APRIL: THE | DOOM OF KING ACRISIUS. THE PROUD | KING.

VOLUME III. [KP printer's leaf ornament No. 2] MAY: THE STORY | OF CUPID AND PSYCHE. THE WRITING | ON THE IMAGE. [KP printer's leaf ornament No. 2] JUNE: THE LOVE OF | ALCESTIS. THE LADY OF THE LAND.

VOLUME IV. [KP printer's leaf ornament No. 2] JULY: THE SON | OF CRŒSUS. THE WATCHING OF THE | FALCON. [KP printer's leaf ornament No. 1] AUGUST: PYGMALION AND | THE IMAGE. OGIER THE DANE.

VOLUME V. [KP printer's leaf ornament No. 1] SEPTEMBER: | THE DEATH OF PARIS. THE LAND EAST | OF THE SUN AND WEST OF THE MOON. | [KP printer's leaf ornament No. 2] OCTOBER: THE STORY OF ACONTIUS | AND CYDIPPE. THE MAN WHO NEVER | LAUGHED AGAIN.

VOLUME VI. [KP printer's leaf ornament No. 2] NOVEMBER: | THE STORY OF RHODOPE. THE LOVERS | OF GUDRUN.

VOLUME VII. [KP printer's leaf ornament No. 1] DECEMBER: | THE GOLDEN APPLES. THE FOSTERING | OF ASLAUG. [KP printer's leaf ornament No. 2] JANUARY: BELLEROPHON | AT ARGOS. THE RING GIVEN TO VENUS.

VOLUME VIII. [KP printer's leaf ornament No. 2] FEBRUARY: | BELLEROPHON IN LYCIA. THE HILL OF | VENUS. [KP printer's leaf ornament No. 1] EPILOGUE. L'ENVOI.

Edition: 'Kelmscott Press Edition' [4th edn., 3rd English] The copytext being the revised 1-vol. 'popular' 2nd English edn., with further revisions by Morris for the KP version.

Collaborators, Editors, and Illustrators: some border designs were finished by R. Catterson-Smith (see 'Note' in colophon for vol. 8). William H. Hooper was the main engraver of the KP borders and initials (see *KP Hist.*, p. xxix).

Series: 41st title, 17th by Morris, pbd. by the KP.

Colophons: (vol. 1 and vol. 4 are given in full; repeated wording in succeeding vols. is indicated by ellipses).

[vol. 1:] Printed by William Morris at the Kelmscott Press, | and finished on the 7th day of May, 1896.

[vol. 2:] . . . finished on the 24th day of August, 1896.

[vol. 3:] . . . finished on the 24th day of August, 1896.

[vol. 4:] Printed by the Trustees of the late William Morris at | the Kelmscott Press, and finished on the 25th day of | November, 1896.

[vol. 5:] . . . finished on the 24th day of | December, 1896.

[vol. 6:] . . . and finished on the 18th day of | February, 1897.

[vol. 7:] . . . and finished on the 17th day of | March, 1897.

[vol. 8:] . . . at | the Kelmscott Press, Upper Mall, Hammersmith, in |the county of Middlesex, and finished on the 10th day | of June, 1897.

Collations: all vols. are medium 4° in 8s:

vol. I: a⁴ b–n⁸ o⁴ [$4 (–a2, 4 b1 h1) signed] 104 leaves pp. [8] [1] 2–193 [194–200] [= 208].

vol. II: [a]⁴ b–h⁸ i⁶ [$4 (– b1–3) signed] 66 leaves pp. [8] [1] 2–121 [122–4] [= 132]

vol. III: [a]⁴ b–l⁸ m⁶ [$4 (–b1 b3 h3 h4 i3 i4) signed] 90 leaves pp. [8] [1] 2–169 [170–2] [= 180].

vol. IV: [a]⁴ b–i⁸ k⁶ [$4 (–b1–3 e4 g3) signed] 74 leaves pp. [8] [1] 2–137 [138–40] [= 148].

vol. V: [a]⁴ b–q⁸ r⁴ [$4 (–b1–3 n4 r2) signed] 128 leaves pp. [8] [1] 2–241 [242–8] [= 256].

vol. VI: [a]⁴ b–o⁸ p⁶ [$4 (–a b2 b3) signed] 114 leaves pp. [8] [1] 2–217 [218–20] [= 228].

vol. VII: [a]⁴ b–n⁸ o⁶ [$4 (–4 b1 b3 g1 m1) signed] 106 leaves pp. [8] [1] 2–203 [204] [= 212].

vol. VIII: [a]⁴ b–m⁸ n⁶ [$4 (–b1–3) signed] 98 leaves pp. [8] [1] 2–186 [187–8] [= 196].

Contents: vol. 1: pp. [1–2], blank; p. [3], title page; p. [4], dedication: TO MY WIFE I DEDICATE THIS BOOK.; pp. [5–6], headed: [top, flush left] THE EARTHLY PARADISE | [text of what is called 'An Apology' in other edns.]; p. [7], blank; p. [8], engraved title and argument within full border; p. [1], head title and text begins within full border; pp. 2–90, tale completed; p. 91, intercalary lyric, title as a shoulder note: March; pp. 92–4, 'March' lyric completed; p. [95], blank; p. [96], engraved title within full border: [all flush left] Atalanta's Race. | [in red] The Argument | [prose text] | [verse text begins]; p. [97], text continues within full border; pp. 98–121, tale completed; p. 122, 3rd tale engraved head title: The Man Born To Be King. | [in red] Argument | [prose text] | [poem begins]; p. 123, text continues within woodcut border; pp. 124–93, text completed with explicit: END OF VOL. I. | [colophon, see above]; pp. [194–200], blank.

vol. 2: pp. [1–6], blank; p. [7], title page; p. [8], blank; p. [1], text of 'April' begins; p. 120, text ends; p. 121, colophon, see above; pp. [122–4], blank.

vol. 3: pp. [1–6], blank; p. [7], title page; p. [8], blank; p. [1], text of 'May' begins; p. 168, text ends; p. 169, colophon, see above; pp. [170–2], blank.

vol. 4: pp. [1–6], blank; p. [7], title page; p. [8], blank; p. [1], text of 'July' begins; p. 136, text ends; p. 137; colophon, see above; pp. [138–40], blank.

vol. 5: pp. [1–6], blank; p. [7], title page; p. [8], blank; p. [1], text of 'September' begins; p. 240, text ends; p. 241, colophon, see above; pp. [242–8], blank.

vol. 6: pp. [1–6], blank; p. [7], title page; p. [8], blank; p. [1], text of 'November' begins; p. 216, text ends; p. 217, colophon, see above; pp. [218–20], blank.

vol. 7: pp. [1–6], blank; p. [7], title page; p. [8], blank; p. [1], text of 'December' begins; p. 202, text ends; p. 203, colophon, see above; p. [204], blank.

vol. 8: pp. [1–6], blank; p. [7], title page; p. [8], blank; p. [1], text of 'February' begins; p. 186, colophon, see above; pp. [187–8], blank.

Technical Notes: details common to the set: *paper*: Apple paper; *leaf size*: deckled edges, lightly trimmed, avg. 235 x 163 mm.; *printing*: in red and black, red for shoulder notes, quoted passages, the title of the relevant tale, and for the heading of 'The Argument'; *type face*: Golden type; *end-papers*: standard KP treatment: 3 free ends and pastedown, front and back, plain white and blank, of the same paper as the body; *binding*: limp natural vellum with red or green silk ties, with title, author, and vol. gilt-stamped on the spine: THE | EARTHLY | PARADISE | BY | WILLIAM | MORRIS | VOL. I [II, III, IV, V, VI, VII, and VIII]. But vol. 1 is the only one stamped in 12-point (Pica) caps, all the other vols. being in 9-point (Bourgeois) caps, the same variation of vol. 1 from the rest applies in all copies seen. Details are generally common to all the 8 vols. of the set, though ornamentation differs between vols.; *ornamentation*: vol. 1: borders: nos. 27a and 27, 28a and 28, and woodcut title; one 3/4 border (used before all intercalary lyrics); ornamental initials: total = 291: 11-, 10-, 6-, and 4-line; vol. 2: borders: nos. 29a and 29, 28a and 28; one 3/4 border, ornamental initials: total = 190: 12-, 10-, 6-, and 4-line; vol. 3: borders: nos. 30a and 30, 27a and 28, and 29; two 3/4 borders, ornamental initials: total = 232: 12-, 10-, 6-, and 4-line; vol. 4: borders: nos. 31a and 31, 29a and 29, 28a and 28, 30a and 30; two 3/4 borders; ornamental initials: total = 131: 10-, 6-, and 4-line; vol. 5: borders: nos. 29a and 29, 27a and 27, 28a and 28, 31a and 31, two 3/4 borders; ornamented initials: total = 205: 12-, 10-, 6-, and 4-line; vol. 6: borders: nos. 27a and 27, 30a and 30; one 3/4 border; ornamented initials: total = 213, 10-, 6-, and 4-line; vol. 7: borders: nos. 29a and 29, 31, 30a and 30, 27a and 27; two 3/4 borders; ornamented initials: total = 243: 10-, 6-, and 4-line; vol. 8: borders: nos. 28a and 28, 29a and 29; one 3/4 border; ornamented initials: total = 186: 10-, 6, and 4-line; and KP press mark, no. 1.

Publication: vol. I: 1896 [24 July]; vol. II: 1896 [issued 17 Sept.]; vol. III: 1896 [5 Dec.]; vol. IV: 1896 [22 January 1897]; vol. V: 1896 [9 Mar. 1897]; vol. VI: 1897 [11 May]; vol. VII: 1897 [29 July]; vol. VIII: 1897 [27 Sept.] (Cockerell, pp. 164–8); *print run*: (all 8 vols.) 225 paper copies and 6 vellum; *price*: paper 30s. per vol., vellum 7gns. per vol. Vols. 4–8 issued by the Trustees of the Morris Estate.

Register of Copies Examined: VU (L, 2 copies; base copy is the presentation copy to Georgiana Burne-Jones, vol. I signed and dated by Morris on the recto of the 3rd free end of the front end papers, top right in longhand in ink: *to Georgie | from | Will. | August 24, 1896.*

Notes: the borders printed in the KP edition of *EP* were designed by William Morris, except the 1st of vols. II, III, and IV, which were designed by R. Catterson-Smith under William Morris's direction, to match the facing borders; Catterson-Smith also finished the initial words 'Whilom' and 'Empty' for the *Water of the Wondrous Isles*. All the other letters, borders, title-pages, and ornaments used at

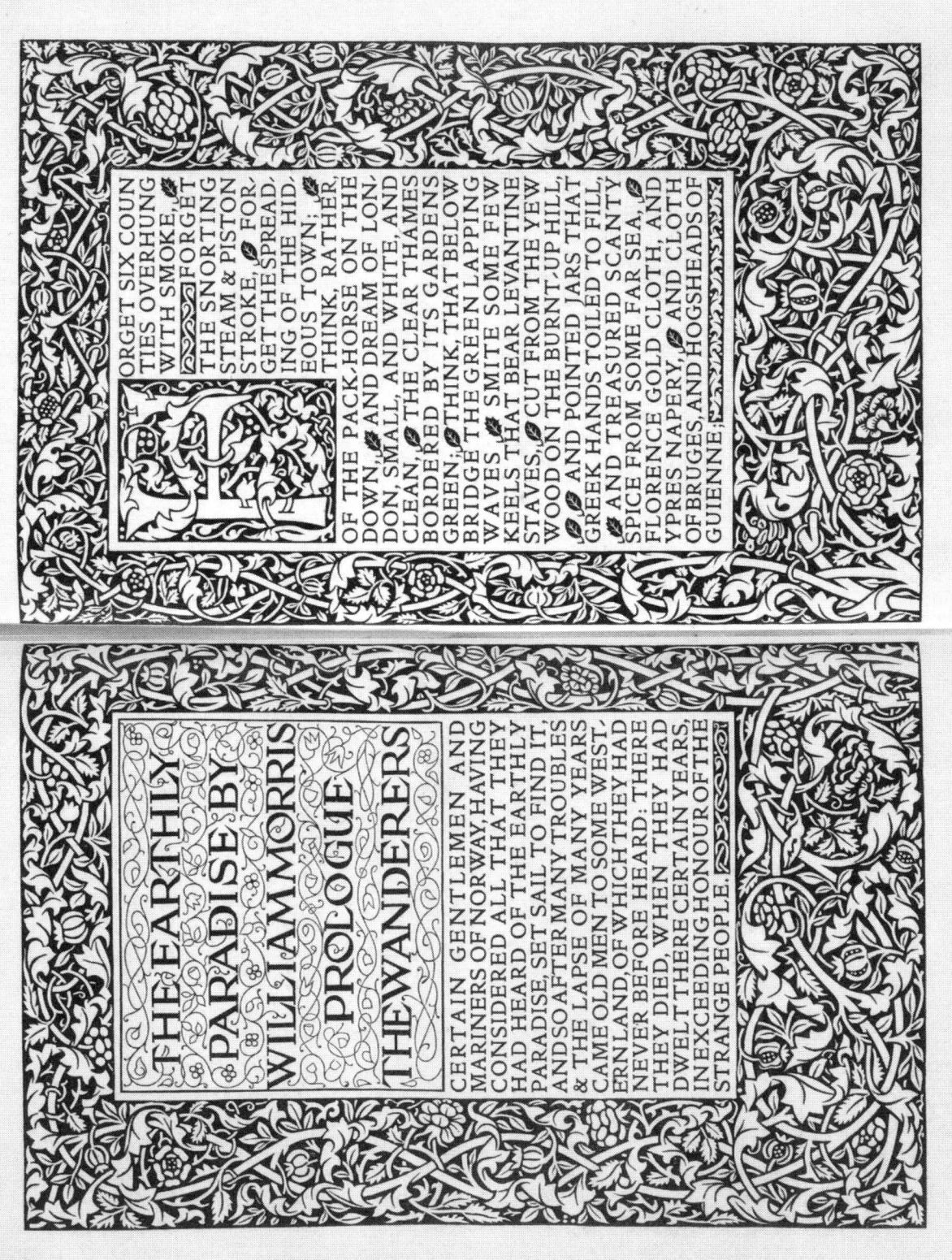

Figure 11. A-4.17: *EP* (KP edn.) opening: engraved title & facing head title

the KP, except the Greek type in *Atalanta in Calydon*, were designed by Morris.

Forman (HBF, p. 72) says the copy text for the KP edn. was the 1890 Reeves and Turner revised 1-vol. edn.. The revisions made in 1890 and those introduced in the KP edn. were incorporated in Longmans later edns., except in America.

A-4.18: The Earthly Paradise (Silver Library + 12-part variant)

THE EARTHLY | PARADISE: A POEM | BY WILLIAM MORRIS | IN FOUR VOLUMES | VOL. I [II, III, IV] | [Silver Library bookmark in ornamented compartment: ship in full sail, date of Longmans' founding to the left] 1724 | LONGMANS, GREEN, AND CO. | 39 PATERNOSTER ROW, LONDON | NEW YORK AND BOMBAY | 1905

Title pages of the other 3 vols. of the Silver Library duplicate this except for the vol. numbers. The 12-part 'New Edition' title pages differ only in a part number in place of vol. number and by adding the title or titles of each part, as follows: PART I | PROLOGUE: THE WANDERERS; PART II | ATALANTA'S RACE | THE MAN BORN TO BE KING; PART III | THE DOOM OF KING ACRISIUS | THE PROUD KING; PART IV | THE STORY OF CUPID AND PSYCHE | THE WRITING ON THE IMAGE; PART V | THE LOVE OF ALCESTIS | THE LADY OF THE LAND | THE SON OF CRŒSUS | THE WATCHING OF THE FALCON; PART VI | PYGMALION AND THE IMAGE | OGIER THE DANE; PART VII | THE DEATH OF PARIS | THE LAND EAST OF THE SUN AND | WEST OF THE MOON; PART VIII | THE STORY OF ACONTIUS AND CYDIPPE | THE MAN WHO NEVER LAUGHED | AGAIN; PART IX | THE STORY OF RHODOPE | THE LOVERS OF GUDRUN; PART X | THE GOLDEN APPLES | THE FOSTERING OF ASLAUG; PART XI | BELLEROPHON AT ARGOS | THE RING GIVEN TO VENUS; PART XII | BELLEROPHON IN LYCIA | THE HILL OF VENUS

Edition: 'Silver Library Edition' in 4 vols. and 'New Edition.' in 12 parts. [1st impression, 5th edn., 4th English] Though differing in paper, number of vols., binding, and title page, both of these versions originate in the same setting, which incorporates the revisions of the text made by Morris for the 1-vol. edn. of 1890 and for the KP edn..

Collaborators, Editors, and Illustrators: Introduction to the Silver Library Edition (I. ix–xvi) signed: 'J. W. Mackail.' The same Introduction as used also for the 12-part version is not signed. The half-tone portrait photograph of Morris used as the frontis. in both versions was made by '*Emery Walker, Ph. sc.*'

Collation: Silver Library in 4 vols. The differences in the number of leaves of the gatherings here are the consequence of the division of these vols. into the 12-part version, all copies of both versions being printed at the same time.

vol. 1: 8°: π^8 ($\pi1+1$) A–M^8 N^4 O–P^2 Q–Y^8 Z^2 170 leaves pp. [i–viii] ix–xvi 1–323 [324] [= 340] + 1 inserted plate not counted in the book's pagination, but noted in the formula and described here under *Contents*.

vol. 2: 8°: π^4 A–F^8 G–H^4 I–P^8 Q–R^2 S^4 T–Y^8 Z^4 2A^2 162 leaves pp. [8] 1–312 [313–16] [= 324].

vol. 3: 8°: π^4 A–I^8 K–L^2 M^4 N–2I^8 2K^4 2L^2 250 leaves pp. [8] 1–489 [490–2] [= 500].

vol. 4: 8°: π^4 A–N^8 O–P^4 Q–2D^8 212 leaves pp. [8] 1–412 [413–16] [= 424].

Collation: New Edition, in 12 parts:

Part I: 8°: [a]^2 ([a1] +1) b^4 A–F^8 54 leaves pp. [i–iv] v–xii 1–96 [= 108]; + 1 inserted plate, not paginated but noted in the formula and described under *Contents*.

Part II: 8°: π^2 G–M^8 N^4 O^2 56 leaves pp. (continue from Part I) [4] 97–204 [= 112].

Part III: 8°: π^2 P^2 Q–Y^8 Z^2 62 leaves pp. (continue from Part II) [4] 205–323 [324] [= 124].

Part IV: 8°: π^2 A–F^8 G^4 54 leaves pp. [4] 1–104 [= 108].

Part V: 8°: π^2 H^4 I–P^8 Q^2 64 leaves pp. (continue from Part IV) [4] 105–228 [= 128].

Part VI: 8°: π^2 R^2 S^4 T–Y^8 Z^4 2A^2 46 leaves pp. (continue from Part V) [4] 229–312 [313–16] [= 92].

Part VII: 8°: π^2 A–I^8 K^2 76 leaves pp. [4] 1–148 [= 152].

Part VIII: 8°: π^2 L^2 M^4 N–S^8 56 leaves pp. (continue from Part VII) [4] 149–256 [= 112].

Part IX: 8°: π^2 T–2I^8 2K^4 2L^2 120 leaves pp. (continue from Part VIII) [4] 257–489 [490–2] [= 240].

Part X: 8°: π^2 A–E^8 42 leaves pp. [4] 1–80 [= 84].

Part XI: 8°: π^2 F–N^8 O^4 70 leaves pp. (continued from Part X) [4] 81–216 [= 140].

Part XII: 8°: π^2 P^4 Q–2D^8 102 leaves pp. (continued from Part XI) [4] 217–412 [413–16] [= 204].

Contents: Silver Library Edition: vol. I: p. [i], half title; p. [ii], blank; inserted leaf as frontis., recto blank, reproduction of a portrait photograph within a blind-stamped compartment and labelled, below, with photographic reproduction of Morris's longhand signature: *William Morris* | [plate maker, in copperplate] *Emery Walker Ph. sc.*; p. [iii],

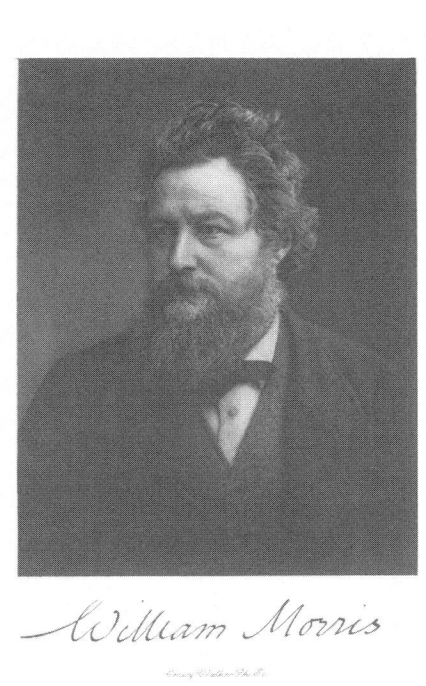

Figure 12. A-4.18: EP (Silver Library Edn.) title page

title page; p. [iv], blank; p. [v], dedication: TO | MY WIFE | I DEDICATE THIS BOOK; p. [vi], blank; p. vii: CONTENTS; p. [viii], blank; p. ix: INTRODUCTION begins; pp. x–xv, text of the Introduction continues; p. xvi, Introduction ends: [signature, below right] J. W. MACKAIL; p. 1, text begins; pp. 2–324, text completed with printer's imprint: END OF VOL. I | Printed by Ballantyne, Hanson & Co. | Edinburgh and London
Contents: Silver Library, vol. II, III, and IV: as vol. I, above, except: Introduction removed and vol. numbers changed on half titles, title pages, and text endings.
Contents: New Edition in 12 Parts; this version omits the 'contents' pages, printing the tale titles on the front cover and head title of each Part, otherwise the same as the Silver Library title page (see above); the tales follow the title (see above).

Technical Notes: *paper*: Silver Library: ordinary white machine-made (Longmans Arch.); *leaf size*: trimmed, 187 x 129 mm.; 12 Part: special cream-white 'antique wove' machine-made, as used in Mackail's *Life of William Morris*, and for which the executors paid an extra penny per pound of paper (Longmans Arch.); *leaf size*: trimmed, 188 x 127; *printing*: *running titles*: [same both versions, both rectos and versos] INTRODUCTION; [thereafter all versos] THE EARTHLY PARADISE | [all rectos, the relevant tale title or appropriate intercalary lyric title, all caps]; *end-papers*: Silver Library: one free end and paste-down front and back, each vol. with free end and facing paste-down in a repeating pattern of vines forming compartments with alternating Longmans ships and swans against a background sea of wavy brown lines; reverse side of free ends plain white and blank; New Edition in 12-Parts: 1

free end and paste-down, plain white and blank, front and back; *binding*: Silver Library: plain red-brown cloth with front blind-stamped thin-rule border; *spine*: gilt-stamped across: THE | EARTHLY | PARADISE | [thin rule] | WILLIAM | MORRIS | VOL. • I [II, III, IV] | [at foot, the full-rigged ship abstracted from the title page device, with date of Longmans' foundation] 17 | 24 | [caption between rope rules] THE SILVER | LIBRARY [dolphin device] | [below lower rope rule] LONGMANS & Cº;

binding: New Edition in 12 Parts: quarter dark blue holland with light blue paper-covered boards; *spines*: stamped in red: E. P. | [vol. no. in roman]; printed on front: THE EARTHLY PARADISE, BY | WILLIAM MORRIS. PART I [II–XII] | [titles of the tale or tales in the vol.] | [at the foot] PRICE ONE SHILLING NET [except Parts IX and XII] PRICE TWO SHILLINGS NET

Publication: 1905: Silver Library [vols. 1 and 2: issued 27 Jan.] (Cockerell Papers, BL (Add.) MS 52642); vols. 3 and 4 dates unknown; 1905: New Edition: [Parts 1 and 2: issued 12 Jan.; Part 3: 21 Jan.; Part 4: 25 Jan.; Part 5: 15 Feb.; Part 6: 22 Feb.; Parts 7 and 8: 8 Mar.; Parts 9 and 10: 22 Apr.; Parts 11 and 12: 20 May] (Impression Books, Longmans Arch.); *print run*: 3,000 copies of each of 12 parts, from which 411 sets were bound in 4 vols. for the Silver Library. For this 1st issue of the 12-part series, Part 1 had 1,249 copies bound; Part 2, 1,000 copies; Parts 3–12, approx. 750 copies. From the 1st impression 78 sets of the 12-Part series and 261 of the 4-vol. Silver Library Edition were sold in quires to Longmans of New York; *price*: 1s. net per part, except Parts 9 and 12: 2s. net per part; Silver Library, 3s. 6d. per vol. net (Longmans ad).

Register of Copies Examined: LeM (2 copies; base copies: 1 of each version), Fdmn (3 copies of the New Edition, 1 of the Silver Library).

Notes: Cockerell's Diary (Cockerell Papers), 28 July 1904, records that he discussed a new setting of the *EP*, considered necessary because of the worn condition of the existing plates. On 26 Aug. he and Hornby decided to accept Longman's terms for the new edn.. The terms were that the Trustees agreed to pay half the costs (the printing being estimated by Ballantynes at £196. 5s. 8d.), to be paid by yielding half of their royalties until the half costs were paid, the royalties being, for the Silver Library Edition, 15% for the first 2 vols, and 12 1/2% for the last 2. The New Edition in 12 Parts, Longmans offered 10% for the 1s. parts.

How these matters were resolved is made clear in Longmans description of the series in their trade magazine, Longmans *Notes on Books*, Mar. 1905, p. 127.

Later impression: Longmans:
1. 1913 'New Edition' Part II (of XII); *print run*: 2,000 copies.

A-4.19: The Earthly Paradise (4 vols. *CW* III–VI)

THE COLLECTED WORKS | [title details common to the set, see A-126.01] | VOLUME III [VI] | THE EARTHLY PARADISE | A POEM | I [II, III, IV] | [publisher's imprint, see A-126.01] | MDCCCCX

For the full title and details common to the series, especially *Technical Notes*, see the entry for the *CW*, A-126.01.

Edition: '*The Collected Works*' edn. [1st impression, 6th edn., 5th English].

Collation: vol. 1 of *EP*, vol. III of *CW*: all vols. medium 8°: a^8 (a3+1) b^8 B–S^8 [$2 signed] 152 leaves pp. [i–viii] ix–xxxii 1–265 [266–72] [= 304] +1 inserted plate, noted in the formula but not included in the book's pagination; described here under *Contents*.

vol. 2: a^8 (a2+1) (a4+1) (a5+1) (a8+1) b^2 B–R^8 [$2 (–b2) signed] 138 leaves pp. [i–vi] vii–xx 1–255 [256] [= 276] +4 inserted plates, noted in the formula but not counted in the book's pagination; described here under *Contents*.

vol. 3: a^4 b^8 (b1+1) (b5+2) c^8 (c6+2) (c7+2) B–$2C^8$ [$2 (–a2 b2) signed] 220 leaves pp. [4] [i–viii] ix [x] xi–xxxvi 1–396 [397–400] [= 440] +4 inserted plates noted in the formula but not counted in the book's pagination; described here under *Contents*.

vol. 4: a^8 (a2+1) (a6+1) b^8 B–Y^8 [$2 (–b2) signed] 184 leaves pp. [i–viii] ix–xxxii 1–332 [333–6] [= 368] +2 inserted plates, noted in the formula but not counted in the book's pagination, described here under *Contents*.

Contents: vol. 1 (vol. III of *CW*): pp. [i–iii], blank; p. [iv], limitation notice (see A-126.01); pp. [v–vi], blank; an inserted plate as frontis., reproduction of a portrait of Morris, in a blind-stamped compartment, the artist named below left in copperplate: *G. F. Watts, R.A. pinx* | [the plate maker, below right, in copperplate] Walker & Boutall, ph. sc. | [labelled, centred, in copperplate] *William Morris, | aet 37*; p. [vii], title page; p. [viii], blank; p. ix: CONTENTS; p. x, three-musicians woodcut vignette, reproduction of the 1st version as cut by Morris from a design by E. Burne-Jones; pp. xi–xxviii, INTRODUCTION, including, p. xxix, photographic facsimile of p. 94 of Morris's MS fair copy, labelled FACSIMILE FROM THE MANUSCRIPT OF THE EARTHLY PARADISE; p.

xxx, BIBLIOGRAPHICAL NOTE; p. [xxxi], dedication: TO MY WIFE | I DEDICATE THIS BOOK; p. [xxxii], blank; pp. 1–2, [An Apology, as titled in other edns]; p. 3, headed: PROLOGUE: THE WANDERERS | THE ARGUMENT | [10 lines of prose in caps] | [text begins]; pp. 4–[266], text completed with explicit: THE END OF THE FIRST PART OF | THE EARTHLY PARADISE; p. [267], blank; p. [268], printer's imprint (see this field in A-126.01); pp. [269–72], blank.

vol. 2 (vol. IV of *CW*); p. [i], blank; p. [ii], limitation statement (see this field in A-126.01); pp. [iii–iv], blank; 1st inserted plate as frontis., photolitho reproduction of a painting in a blind-stamped compartment, with the artist's name below left in copperplate: *Dante Gabriel Rossetti, pinx.* | [below right the plate maker, in copperplate] *Emery Walker Ph. sc.* | [label, centred, in copperplate] *The Water-Willow | (a Portrait of Mrs. William Morris)*; p. [v], title page; p. [vi], blank; p. vii: CONTENTS; p. [viii], blank; 2nd inserted plate to face p. ix, photographic reproduction of a woodcut labelled in copperplate: PSYCHE AT THE ENTRANCE TO HADES, DESIGNED BY | EDWARD BURNE-JONES AND ENGRAVED ON WOOD BY | WILLIAM MORRIS; pp. ix–x, Introduction begins; 3rd inserted plate reproducing a woodcut, to face p. x, oriented vertically, labelled: PSYCHE IN CHARON'S BOAT, DESIGNED BY EDWARD BURNE-JONES AND ENGRAVED BY WILLIAM MORRIS; p. [xi], photographic facsimile, integral with the letterpress, labelled: FACSIMILE FROM THE MANUSCRIPT OF THE EARTHLY PARADISE: DRAFT PAGE OF CUPID AND PSYCHE; pp. xii–xvi, Introduction continues; 4th inserted plate in a blind-stamped compartment, facing p. xvii, reproduction of a drawing with the artist named in copperplate, below left: *F. L. Griggs del. 1910* | [below right, in copperplate, the plate maker] *Emery Walker Ph.sc.* | label centred in copperplate] *Kelmscott Manor | looking East*; pp. xvii–xx, Introduction concludes; p. 1, text begins; pp. 2–255, text completed with explicit: THE END OF THE SECOND PART | OF THE EARTHLY PARADISE; p. [256], printer's imprint (see this field in A-126.01).

vol. 3 (vol. V of *CW*): pp. [1–4], blank; pp. [i–iii], blank; p. [iv], limitation notice (see this field in A-126.01); pp. [v–vi], blank; 1st inserted plate as frontis. in blind-stamped compartment, photo reproduction of an oil painting, with an inscription printed by hand on the top of the painting: [flush left] JANE MORRIS A.D. 1868. *D. G. Rossetti pinxit Conjuge clara poetâ, et præclarissima vultu, denique picturâ clara sit illa meâ* | [plate maker's name below right, in copperplate] *Emery Walker Ph. sc.*, | [label, centred] *Mrs. William Morris | from the painting by D. G. Rossetti | 1868*; p. [vii], title page; p. [viii], blank; p. ix: CONTENTS; p. [x], blank; pp. xi–xviii, Introduction continues; 2nd inserted plate. facing p. xviii, photo reproduction of a drawing with the name of the artist below right: *F. L. Griggs del. 1910* | [plate maker below right] *Emery Walker Ph. sc.* | [label in copperplate, centred]: *Kelmscott Manor | from the garden door*; pp. xix–xxxii, Introduction continues; 3rd inserted plate between pp. xxxii and xxxiii, on a s. sh. folded to form 2 leaves, the opening of which, other sides being blank, is a reproduction of a MS page labelled in copperplate: *Facsimile from the draft manuscript of "The Lovers of Gudrun."*; pp. xxxiii–xxxiv, Intro. continues; 4th inserted plate, oriented vertically between pp. xxxiv and xxxv, s. sh. folded, as the previous plate, to form 2 leaves in the opening of which, other sides being blank, is a reproduction of a MS page, labelled: Facsimile from the manuscript of "The Earthly Paradise:" "The Ring given to Venus"; pp. xxxv–xxxvi, Intro. concludes; pp. 1–396, text of Vol. III completed with explicit: THE END OF THE THIRD PART | OF THE EARTHLY PARADISE; p. [397], blank; p. [398], printer's imprint (see this field, A-126.01); pp. [399–400], blank.

vol. 4 (vol. VI of *CW*): p. [i], blank; p. [ii], limitation statement (see this field in A-126.01); pp. [iii–iv], blank; 1st inserted plate as frontis., within a blind-stamped compartment, photo reproduction of a chalk drawing signed and dated '1871', with the artist's name below left in copperplate: *D. G. Rossetti, del.* | [the plate maker's name below right] *Emery Walker Ph. sc* | [label in copperplate, centred] *"Jenny"*; p. [v], title page; p. [vi], blank; p. [vii], headed: CONTENTS; p. [viii], blank; p. ix, Introduction begins; 2nd inserted plate, to face p. xiii, reproduction of a chalk drawing, in a blind-stamped compartment, including D. G. Rossetti's signature device and the date, 1871, on the drawing with the artist's name below left in copperplate: *D. G. Rossetti, del.* | [below right, the plate maker] *Emery Walker, Ph. Sc.* | [centred label, in copperplate] *"May"*; pp. xiii–xxiv, Intro. continues; p. [xxv], photo reproduction in a thin-rule compartment of a Morris MS page labelled: Facsimile of an unpublished "Hill of Venus" MS.; pp. xxvi–xxxii, Intro. concludes; pp. 1–[333], text completed with explicit: THE END OF THE EARTHLY PARADISE; pp. [334], printer's imprint (see this field, A-126.01); pp. [335–6], blank.

Technical Notes: paper, leaf size, printing, position (but

not content) of headlines, running titles, end-papers, and binding are all common to the series and are described in this field in A-126.01, the entry for the set. Included here are only those details that are specific to the 4 vols. of this edn.: *headlines*: not used; *shoulder notes*: all rectos and versos: relevant titles of sections or tales, *spine label*: COLLECTED | WORKS | OF WILLIAM | MORRIS | VOLUME III [–VI] | THE | EARTHLY | PARADISE | I [–IV]
Publication: 1910 [vols. 1 and 2 issued 4 Nov.]; 1911 [vols. 3 and 4 issued 28 Mar.] (Longmans Arch.); *print run and price*: see A-126.01.
Register of Copies Examined: LeM (base copy); for other copies see this field in the entry for the *CW* (A-126.01).

A-4.20: The Earthly Paradise (vol. I of III, projected, Routledge)

THE | EARTHLY PARADISE | A POEM | BY | WILLIAM MORRIS | WITH AN INTRODUCTION BY | JOHN DRINKWATER | VOL. 1 | MARCH TO JUNE | [publisher's device of an ornamented 'R'] | LONDON | GEORGE ROUTLEDGE & SONS, Limited | NEW YORK: E. P. DUTTON & Co.
Edition: 'The Muses Library Edition' [1st impression, 7th edn., 6th English] vol. I, Mar. to June of 3 vols. projected; vols. 2 & 3 seem not to have been completed, though the 2nd vol. is announced in the advertisements included in The Muses' Library version of *The Defence of Guenevere*.
Series: 'The Muses Library', 3 Morris titles were published (or planned for publication) in this series. Besides this one, not completed, there were issued edns. of *Jason* (see A-3.11) and *The Defence of Guenevere* (see A-2.10), both introduced by John Drinkwater.
Collation: small 8°: [A]⁶ B–Y⁸ Z² [$1 (+W) signed 184 leaves pp. [i–vii] viii–xii [1] 2–355 [356] [= 368].
Contents: p. [i], half title: [top, flush left, in gothic, underlined with a thin rule] The Muses Library | THE EARTHLY PARADISE | (MARCH TO JUNE); p. [ii], note: Uniform with this volume | The Life and Death of Jason | by the same author and editor | also The Defence of Guenevere and Other Poems (In Preparation); p. [iii]: title page; p. [iv], bibliographical note on Ellis's 3-vol. 1st edn. of the poem; p. [v], headed: CONTENTS | [list completed of 8 story titles involving 4 months]; p. [vi], dedication: TO R. CATTERSON-SMITH | THE FRIEND OF WILLIAM MORRIS | THIS EDITION OF | THE EARTHLY PARADISE | IS DEDICATED | [with a 4-line stanza from Browning's 'Memorabilia' as an epigraph]; p. [vii] headed: Introduction | [text begins]; pp. viii–xii, intro. completed and signed: [below right] JOHN DRINKWATER | [below left] Birmingham, 1911; pp. [1]–355, text; p. [356], printer's imprint: Printed by | London and Norwich Press, Ltd. | London and Norwich.
Technical Notes: *paper*: plain white machine-made; *leaf size*: trimmed, 144 x 97 mm.; *lines-to-page*: 44 lines without head or direction lines; *end-papers*: free end and pastedown, plain white and blank, front and back; *binding*: (from WMDU copy) dark blue cloth-covered boards, plain and unblocked, front and back, gilt-stamped on spine: art nouveau floral design as background to the letterpress, growing up the spine, with 3 double thin-rule compartments: [top] MORRIS | THE EARTHLY | PARADISE I | [middle] THE MUSES' | LIBRARY | [bottom] ROUTLEDGE
Publication: 1911 [issued 13–20 Oct.] ('Publications of the Week', *BSR*, 57/147 n.s. (20 Oct. 1911), 1462); but see 7–14 Oct. ('Books of the Week', *Pub. Circ.* (14 Oct. 1911), 584); *print run*: not known.
Register of Copies Examined: BL (base copy: 011604. de. 12.); WMDU (QM 824.829 M8778E).

A-5.01: Grettis Saga

GRETTIS SAGA | [thin rule] | THE STORY | OF | GRETTIR THE STRONG | TRANSLATED FROM THE ICELANDIC | BY | EIRÍKR MAGNÚSSON, | TRANSLATOR OF 'LEGENDS OF ICELAND'; | AND | WILLIAM MORRIS, | AUTHOR OF 'THE EARTHLY PARADISE.' | LONDON: | F. S. ELLIS, KING STREET, COVENT GARDEN. | MDCCCLXIX.
Edition: [1st impression, 1st edn.] Besides the ordinary copies, there were 25 demy 8° LP copies on Whatman hand-laid paper (HBF, p. 56). The prelims of this book include as an epigraph an untitled sonnet, facing the title page, later rptd. in all edns. and HBF, p. 57.
Collaborators, Editors, and Illustrators: Forman says the map of the 'west parts of Iceland', inserted here between the contents and the 1st chapter, was 'engraved on wood by Morris' (HBF, p. 55). But the same map appears in the 1900 edn. signed with the name of the plate maker, '*Walker & Boutall sc.*', and '*Philip Webb inv.*', i.e. invenit = designed this, which indicates clearly enough that at that time Webb was considered to be the maker of the map. But the 2 later edns. of this title do not include the signatures, and May Morris makes no attribution of the map, as she usually does in such cases, in her list of illus. to vol. VII of the *CW*, p. xiii. There is a difficulty in the notion of making a wood-

> A life scarce worth the living, a poor fame
> Scarce worth the winning, in a wretched land,
> Where fear and pain go upon either hand,
> As toward the end men fare without an aim
> Unto the dull grey dark from whence they came:
> Let them alone, the unshadowed sheer rocks stand
> Over the twilight graves of that poor band,
> Who count so little in the great world's game!
>
> Nay, with the dead I deal not; this man lives,
> And that which carried him through good and ill,
> Stern against fate while his voice echoed still
> From rock to rock, now he lies silent, strives
> With wasting time, and through its long lapse gives
> Another friend to me, life's void to fill.
>
> WILLIAM MORRIS

GRETTIS SAGA.

THE STORY
OF
GRETTIR THE STRONG

TRANSLATED FROM THE ICELANDIC
BY
EIRÍKR MAGNÚSSON,
TRANSLATOR OF 'LEGENDS OF ICELAND;'
AND
WILLIAM MORRIS,
AUTHOR OF 'THE EARTHLY PARADISE.'

LONDON:
F. S. ELLIS, KING STREET, COVENT GARDEN.
MDCCCLXIX.

Figure 13. A-5.01: *Grettis Saga* (1st edn.) opening: poem (verso) & facing title page.

cut first, a function Morris might have performed, when it was known in advance that the design would be used to make a plate. Walker and Boutall's plates were made by the photolithographic process which would work at least as well with the original design on paper, thus eliminating the steps of transfer to wood and hand engraving. It is possible of course that in order to get the effect of a woodcut, the plate maker might use a printed copy from a woodcut to produce the plate. Walker said that Morris was convinced of the efficacy of the photographic plate for printing when Walker demonstrated to him that he could not tell the difference between a copy printed from a photographic plate and one from an original woodcut.

Collation: cr. 8°: [a]^8 b^4 (b4+2) B–U^8 χ^2 166 leaves, pp. [i]–xxiv [1] 2–306 [307–8] [= 332] + a map on 2 leaves not counted in the book's pagination, but noted in the formula and described here in the appropriate position under *Contents*.

Contents: p. [i], half title; p. ii, untitled sonnet as an epigraph to the book; p. iii, title page; p. [iv], blank; p. [v]: PREFACE. | [thin rule] | [text begins] | [footnote, separated by thin rule and divided into 2 columns by a vertical thin rule]; pp. vi–xvi, text completed: [signed aligned right] EIRÍKR MAGNÚSSON, WILLIAM MORRIS. | [aligned left] *London,* | *April,* 1869.; pp. xvii–xviii, dropped head: CHRONOLOGY OF THE STORY. | [thin rule] | [list, by year, of historical events of the story]; p. xix–xxiv, headed: *CONTENTS.* |list of 95 chapters and 6 appendices] | [thin rule]; pp. [*1–4*] inserted single sheet folded to form 2 leaves, 1st and last pages blank, facing pages with a map within a compartment, labelled in a smaller compartment, within the left margin: A MAP OF THE WEST | PARTS OF ICELAND, | WITH THE CHIEF | STEADS NAMED IN | THE STORY; p. [1], headed: THE STORY OF | GRETTIR THE STRONG. | [3-line 'argument', in italics, formatted in hanging indent] | CHAP. I. | [text, with footnote in 2 cols. separated by thin rules, as p. [v], above]; pp. 2–272, text completed with explicit: GOOD PEOPLE HERE THE WORK HATH END: | MAY ALL FOLK TO THE GOOD GOD WEND!; p. 273, headed: NOTES AND CORRECTIONS. | [thin rule] | [note on abbreviations] | [thin rule] | [notes begin]; pp. 274–81, notes completed; p. [282], blank; p. 283, headed: INDEX I. | [thin rule] | PERSONAL NAMES. | [index begins]; pp. 284–90 index of personal names completed; p. 291, headed: INDEX II. | [thin rule] | LOCAL NAMES. | [index begins]; pp. 292–6, index completed; p. 297, headed: INDEX III. | [thin rule] | [headed] THINGS. | [index begins]; pp. 298–302, index of things completed; p. 303, headed: PERIPHRASTIC EXPRESSIONS IN THE SONGS. | [thin rule] | [index begins]; p. 304, index ends with a thin rule; p. 305, headed: PROVERBS AND PROVERBIAL SAYINGS THAT | OCCUR IN THE STORY. | [thin rule]; p. 306, list ends: [thin rule] | [thin rule] | LONDON: STRANGEWAYS AND WALDEN, Castle St. Leicester Sq.; pp. [307–8], blank.

Technical Notes: *paper*: cream-white 'antique' machine-wove, with dandy roll laid lines, no watermark; *leaf size*: ordinary copies: 191 x 125 mm., LP: 219 x 144 mm.; *printing*: *type area*: 132 x 81 mm.; *running titles*: [section heads used as verso running heads for Preface, Contents, and Indices; the saga text has on all versos:] THE STORY OF | [all rectos] GRETTIR THE STRONG; *end-papers*: 1 free end and paste-down, plain white and blank, front and back; *binding*: ordinary copies: plain unblocked dark olive cloth; *spine*: printed paper label: [thick-thin rule, top and bottom] | *GRETTIS SAGA* | [thin rule] | THE STORY OF GRETTIR | THE STRONG | [thin rule] | E. MAGNUSSON | AND | W. MORRIS | [thin rule] | 8s.

Publication: 1869 [issued 1–15 May]; the signature at the end of the 'Preface' adds a date, 'April, 1869'; no formal record of issue appears in *Pub. Circ.*, but Ellis announced it as 'ready' in the 15 May issue (*Pub. Circ.*, 32/760 (15 May 1869), 296).

Register of Copies Examined: VPar (base copy); VSL (s439.6/B34); SSL (Y7470); BL (2348.b.3.); VU; CSt (Spec.Coll. Felton PR5081.G7); LeM (Prior facsimile). In all respects other than its title page, paper, binding, and the absence of signatures of the original choirs, the George Prior Publishers edn. of 1980 is a facsimile of this 1st edn.

Notes: Morris's 1st book-length saga translation, the *Grettis Saga*, has a pbn. record that is among his shortest. Only 4 issues, each a new edn., were made from its 1st pbn. in 1869 through 1915, the end of the pbn. histories recorded here. Besides the 1st edn. of 1869, the issues were the Longmans new edn. of 1900, the Golden type quarto edn. of 1901, and the *CW* edn. of 1911. Obviously, the book was never a popular success: print runs of these 4 edns. were, respectively, 500, 500, 1,000, 315, and 1,050.

This 1st edn. was the occasion for Morris to defend Magnússon's role in their joint translation. In so doing, he defined the nature of their collaboration:

> I have noticed that Mr. Vigfusson in his recently published Prolegomena to the Sturlunga Saga, speaks of me as the sole translator of the English versions of the Grettis Saga and the Gunnlaugs Saga Ormstungu, omitting to mention the name of Mr. Eiríkr Magnússon, my collaborateur. As a matter of fact, when we set about these joint works, I had just begun my study of the Icelandic under Mr. Magnússon's mastership, and my share in the translation was necessarily confined to helping in the search for the fittest English equivalents to the Icelandic words and phrases, to turning the translations of the 'vísur' into some sort of English verse, and to general revision in what might be called matters of taste; the rest of the work, including notes, and all critical remarks, was entirely due to Mr. Magnússon's learning and industry.
>
> I should explain that the Gunnlaugs Saga, which was first printed in the Fortnightly Review, when republished in our 'Three Northern Love Stories' went through a very careful revision, in which we both shared.
>
> Mr. Magnússon's responsibility and labour was, therefore, much greater than mine in these works, though if his pleasure in that labour was half as much as mine, it was great indeed. The recollection of the great services he rendered me in the matter, and indeed, I think, to the public in general, makes me venture to trouble you with this letter (to the Editor of *The Athenæum*, 12 May 1879, rptd. *Letters*, i. 513–14).

Later impression of this edn.:
1. Post-1915 facsimile reprint by George Prior Publishers, London, 1980 (see also under *Edition*, above).

A-5.02: Grettis Saga

GRETTIS SAGA | THE STORY OF | GRETTIR THE

Original and Posthumous Editions

STRONG | TRANSLATED FROM THE ICELANDIC | BY | EIRÍKR MAGNÚSSON | AND | WILLIAM MORRIS | *NEW EDITION* | LONGMANS, GREEN, AND CO. | 39 PATERNOSTER ROW, LONDON | NEW YORK AND BOMBAY | 1900 | *All rights reserved*
Edition: NEW EDITION [1st impression, 2nd edn.] The prelims of this book include as an epigraph the same untitled sonnet prtd. in A-5.01.
Collaborators, Editors, and Illustrators: Edited by F. S. Ellis; Walker and Boutall supplied the plate of 'A Map of the West Parts of Iceland, with the Chief Steads Named in the Story'. On the origin of this map see this field in the previous entry.
Collation: cr. 8°: [a]⁸ b⁴ (b4+2) B–U⁸ χ² 166 leaves pp. [i–iv] v–xxiv [1] 2–280 [281–2] 283–306 [307–8] [= 332] + a map on 2 leaves not counted in the book's pagination, but noted in the formula and described here in the appropriate position under *Contents*.
Contents: see this field in A-5.01, except p. 306, appendices end with printer's imprint at the foot: Printed by BALLANTYNE, HANSON & Co. | Edinburgh & London; pp. [307–8], Longmans ads, headed: WORKS BY | WILLIAM MORRIS.
Technical Notes: *paper*: cream-white machine-wove 'antique' (Longmans Arch.) with dandy roll laid lines; *leaf size*: trimmed, 190 x 125 mm.; *printing*: *running heads*: [all versos] THE STORY OF | [all rectos] GRETTIR THE STRONG; *end-papers*: 1 free end and paste-down, plain white and blank, front and back; *binding*: plain black unblocked cloth; *spine*: printed paper spine label: THE STORY OF | GRETTIR | THE STRONG | [thin rule] | E. MAGNÚSSON | AND | W. MORRIS | [thin rule] | Five Shillings. Net
Publication: '1900' [issued 8 May]; *print run*: 1,000 copies (Longmans Arch.); *price*: 5s. net (Longmans *Notes on Books*, 9/181 (31 May 1900), 235); issued in America, 23–30 June ('Publications of the Week', *Pub. Weekly*, 57/1483 (30 June 1900), 1244).
Register of Copies Examined: SU (base copy: 839.6 G83M); BGR; BL (12403.f.35.)

A-5.03: Grettis Saga (Golden 4°)

[aligned left] THE STORY OF GRETTIR THE STRONG TRANSLATED | FROM THE ICELANDIC BY EIRIKR MAGNUSSON AND | WILLIAM MORRIS.
Edition: 'Golden type quarto edition' [1st impression, 3rd edn.].
Collaborators, Editors, and Illustrators: [Edited by S. C. Cockerell and R. Proctor], with 'A Map of the west of Iceland . . .'. On the origin of this map see this field in A-5.01.
Series: 3rd vol. of the Golden type quarto series edited by Cockerell and Proctor for the Morris Estate. For further detail common to the series, see this field and *Notes* in A-47.04.
Colophon: Here ends The Story of Grettir the Strong, translated from the Icelandic by | Eiríkr Magnússon and William Morris. First printed in 1869, and now re- | printed at the Chiswick Press with the Golden type designed by William | Morris for the Kelmscott Press, and finished on the 3rd day of August, 1901. | Published by Longmans, Green and Co. of London, New York & Bombay.
Collation: 4°: π² [a]–2a⁴ 2b² 100 leaves pp. [4] [i–ii] iii–xiv [xv–xvi] 1–177 [178–80] [= 200].
Contents: p. [1], blank; p. [2], map, unsigned, labelled: A MAP OF THE WEST | PARTS OF ICELAND, | WITH THE CHIEF | STEADS NAMED IN | THE STORY.; pp. [3–4], blank; p. [i], title page; p. [ii], blank; p. iii, headed: [flush left] PREFACE. | [text begins]; pp. iv–viii, text completed, signed: [below right] Eiríkr Magnússon. | William Morris. | [left] London, April, 1869.; p. ix, headed: [flush left] CHRONOLOGY OF THE STORY. | [dates and events, flush left, in hanging indents, as a list]; p. x, Chronology ends; p. xi, headed: [flush left] CONTENTS. | [list begins]; pp. xii–xiv, contents concluded; p. [xv], blank; p. [xvi], epigraph, in red, an untitled sonnet signed below right: WILLIAM MORRIS.; p. 1, headed flush left, in red: THE STORY OF GRETTIR THE STRONG, TRANSLATED | BY EIRÍKR MAGNÚSSON AND WILLIAM MORRIS. | [5-line summary, in black, of Chapters I–XIII] | text begins; pp. 2–146, text completed with explicit: GOOD PEOPLE, HERE THE WORK HATH END: | MAY ALL FOLK TO THE GOOD GOD WEND!; pp. 147–76, a series of 6 appended sections of notes and indices; p. 177, text ends, colophon, see above; pp. [178–80], blank.
Technical Notes: other than the title, collation, and colophon, the only item specific to this vol. is the content of the *shoulder notes*: all rectos and versos, either title of subsection or: Grettir the Strong | Chapter [+ roman number]. For all details common to the series, see this field in A-47.04, the 1st publication in the series.
Publication: '3 August 1901' [colophon date, issued for sale 27 Nov.]; *print run*: 315 copies (Chiswick Arch.); *price*: 2gns.

Register of Copies Examined: LeM (base copy); VU(L); BL (C. 43. f. 16.)

A-5.04: Grettis Saga (*CW* vol. VII)
THE COLLECTED WORKS | [for title details common to the set, see A-126.01] | VOLUME VII | THE STORY OF GRETTIR THE STRONG | THE STORY OF THE VOLSUNGS | AND NIBLUNGS | [publisher's imprint, see A-126.01] | MDCCCCXI
Edition: 'Collected Works' edn' [1st impression, 4th edn. of both texts included] The prelims of this book include as an epigraph an untitled sonnet, used in all the original edns. of this text and here facing p. [xxxvi], text rptd. in HBF, p. 57.
Collaborators, Editors, and Illustrators: with a 'map of the west parts of Iceland' on the origins and design of which, see this field in A-5.01.
Series: The Collected Works of William Morris: vol. 7 of 24; for details of this set, see this field in A-126.01.
Collation: medium 8°: [a]⁸ (a2+1) b–c⁸ (c8+1) B–2I⁸ [$2 (–b2 c2 F2) signed] 272 leaves pp. [i–vi] vii–xlvii [xlviii] 1-279 [280, *Grettis Saga* ends] [281, *Volsunga Saga* begins] [282] 283–490 [491–6] [=544] +2 inserted plates noted in the formula but not included in the book's pagination; described here in *Contents*. The *Collation* here includes both titles combined in this book.
Contents: p. [i], blank; p. [ii], limitation certificate (see this field in A-126.01); pp. [iii–iv], blank; 1st inserted plate as frontis. in a blind-stamped compartment, to face p. [v], reproduction of a photograph with the plate maker's name below right, in copperplate: *Emery Walker Ph. sc.* | [label centred in copperplate] *William Morris* | *(1876)*; p. [v], title page; p. [vi], blank; p. vii, headed: CONTENTS | [list begins]; pp. viii–xiii, contents completed; p. [xiv], blank; p. xv, headed: INTRODUCTION | [text begins]; pp. xvi–xxxiv, introduction completed, including some unpbd. verse, 'Baldur's Dream' (pp. xxi–xxiv) and 'The Lay of Thrym' (pp. xxiv–xxxii), both complete Icelandic poems translated by Morris and Magnússon, and 'Bibliographical Note to the Story of Grettir the Strong', and another to the *Volsunga Saga*; p. xxxv, 1st half title: GRETTIS SAGA: THE STORY OF | GRETTIR THE STRONG: TRANS- | LATED FROM THE ICELANDIC BY | EIRÍKR MAGNÚSSON | & WILLIAM MORRIS; p. xxxvi, untitled sonnet, as epigraph, signed, below right: WILLIAM MORRIS; pp. xxxvii–xliv, headed: PREFACE | [text begins]; p. xlv, Preface ends with signatures: [below right] EIRÍKR MAGNÚSSON. | WILLIAM MORRIS. | [flush left] London, April 1869.; pp. xlvi–xlvii, headed: CHRONOLOGY OF THE STORY | [text begins as a list]; p. xlvii, chronology concludes; p. [xlviii], blank; 2nd insertion, fold-out map, unsigned, within an ornamental compartment (see this field in A-5.01) titled within an inner compartment: A MAP OF THE WEST | PARTS OF ICELAND, | WITH THE CHIEF | STEADS NAMED IN | THE STORY; p. 1, text begins; pp. 2–227, text completed with formulaic ending (see this field in A-5.01); pp. 228–79, 8 appendices, headed 'Notes and Corrections' (pp. 228–37); 'Additional Notes and Corrections by Eiríkr Magnússon' (pp. 237–40); 3 indexes to 'personal names' (pp. 241–53); 'local names' (pp. 254–64); and 'things' (pp. 264–75); 'Periphrastic Expressions in the Songs' (pp. 275–7); and 'Proverbs and Proverbial Sayings That Occur in the Story' (pp. 278–9); p. 279, text ends; p. [280], blank; p. [281], 2nd half title: VÖLSUNGA SAGA: THE STORY OF THE | VOLSUNGS AND NIB- LUNGS, WITH CER- | TAIN SONGS FROM THE ELDER EDDA. | TRANSLATED FROM THE ICE- LANDIC | BY EIRÍKR MAGNÚSSON & WILLIAM | MORRIS; p. [282], blank; p. 283, headed: PREFACE | [text begins]; pp. 284–6, Preface completed; p. 287, headed: THE NAMES OF THOSE WHO ARE MOST | NOTE- WORTHY IN THIS STORY | [list begins]; p. 288, list ends; p. 289, headed: A PROLOGUE IN VERSE; p. 290, verse ends, signed: WILLIAM MORRIS; p. 291, headed: Chapter I, text begins; pp. 292–396, text completed: [verse] NOW MAY ALL EARLS | BE BETTERED IN MIND, | MAY THE GRIEF OF ALL MAIDENS | EVER BE MIN- ISHED, | FOR THIS TALE OF TROUBLE | SO TOLD TO ITS ENDING.; p. 397, headed: CERTAIN SONGS FROM THE ELDER | EDDA, WHICH DEAL WITH THE STORY OF THE VOLSUNGS | [text begins]; pp. 398–480, text completed; pp. 481, headed: NOTES TO THE VÖLSUNGA SAGA | [Notes begin]; pp. 482–90, Notes completed; pp. [491–6], end matter, see A-126.01.
Technical Notes: paper, leaf size, printing, headlines, running titles, shoulder titles (form), end-papers, and binding are all common to the series and are described in this field in A-126.01, the entry for the set. Included here are only those details that are specific to this vol.; *shoulder notes*: all rectos and versos, specific to each tale or song, using the relevant title, in shortened versions where necessary; *spine label*: the first 5 lines are common to the set, see A-126.01. The part specific to this vol. is thus: GRETTIR THE | STRONG | THE VOLSUNGS | & NIBLUNGS
Publication: 1911 [issued 14 June] (Longmans Arch.); for *print run* and *price*, see A-126.01.
Register of Copies Examined: LeM (base copy); for other

copies see this field in the entry for the Collected Works (A-126.01).

Notes: letters from May Morris to S. C. Cockerell, Nov. 1910, refer to a error made in printing vol. VII. Though the specific vol. is not mentioned, the context and the date point to the vol. of translations from the Icelandic done in collaboration by Morris and Magnússon, where Magnússon's role is not mentioned as co-author on the title page, but only on the 2 half titles. A meeting was arranged for May Morris to discuss a possible cancel leaf with Longmans editor, Mr Kelk, but there is no evidence of a cancel being made.

Magnússon wanted to make changes to the text, but May Morris and her advisers resisted the suggestion. In the end, Magnússon's revisions appeared as 'Additional Notes and Corrections by Eiríkr Magnússon' (vii. 237–40). They are explained in May Morris's Introduction in a way relevant not only to the particular instance but also to a general principle applicable to her editing of these vols.:

> Some additional notes and corrections recently made by Mr. Magnússon for the Grettis Saga and Volsunga Saga appear in the present volume. If the original collaborators had re-published their translations after this lapse of time, they would doubtless have made alterations and corrections of the mistaken or doubtful passages in the text; but I have not felt justified in presenting it in altered form. These translations of the sagas appear here as forming part of my father's works, and as such they must stand, with text unaltered from that of the first edition, in the case of the Grettis saga incorporating the corrections noted on pp. 273–8 of the 1869 edition, but making no pretence of special or recent scholarship. These corrections had already been included in the 1900 reprint. Mr. Magnússon's additional notes, which follow the original notes to each saga, will supply much useful information to those who may be reading the text with a view to comparing it with other translations (VII. xxxiij).

A-6.01: Volsunga Saga

VÖLSUNGA SAGA. | [thin rule] | THE STORY | OF THE | VOLSUNGS & NIBLUNGS | WITH CERTAIN SONGS | FROM THE | ELDER EDDA. | TRANSLATED FROM THE ICELANDIC | BY | EIRÍKR MAGNÚSSON, | TRANSLATOR OF "LEGENDS OF ICELAND"; | AND | WILLIAM MORRIS, | AUTHOR OF "THE EARTHLY PARADISE." | LONDON: | F. S. ELLIS, KING STREET, COVENT GARDEN. | MDCCCLXX.

Edition: [1st impression, 1st edn.] Besides the ordinary copies, 12 LP copies on Whatman hand-made paper were printed in demy 8°, with another 12 on Whatman's cr. 8°.

Collation: cr. 8° and demy 8°: [a]⁸ b² B–S⁸ T² 148 leaves pp. [i–v] vi–xx, [1] 2–275 [276] [= 296].

Contents: p. [i], half title; p. [ii], blank; p. [iii], title page; p. [iv], blank; pp. [v]–xi, headed: PREFACE | [text begins]; p. [xii], blank; pp. xiii, headed: CONTENTS. | [thin rule] | [list begins]; pp. xiv–xvi, contents concluded; p. [xvii–xviii], headed: THE NAMES OF THOSE WHO ARE MOST | NOTEWORTHY IN THIS STORY. | [thin rule] | [list begins]; pp. xix–xx, A PROLOGUE IN VERSE. | [6 stanzas, signed below right] WILLIAM MORRIS.; p. [1], headed: THE STORY OF | THE VOLSUNGS AND NIBLUNGS. | [thin rule] | Chap. I. | Of Sigi, the Son of Odin. | [text begins]; pp. 2–163, text completed, followed by an explicit in verse, aligned left.: NOW MAY ALL EARLS | BE BETTERED IN MIND, | MAY THE GRIEF OF ALL MAIDENS | EVER BE MINISHED, | FOR THIS TALE OF TROUBLE | SO TOLD TO ITS ENDING.; p. [164], blank; p. [165], 3rd half title: CERTAIN SONGS | FROM | THE ELDER EDDA, | WHICH DEAL WITH THE STORY OF THE VOLSUNGS.; p. [166], blank; pp. [167]–76, headed: PART OF THE SECOND LAY OF | HELGI HUNDING'S-BANE.* | [thin rule] | [text begins]; pp. 177–81, headed: PART OF THE LAY OF SIGRDRIFA.; pp. 182–202, headed: THE LAY CALLED THE SHORT | LAY OF SIGURD.; pp. [203]–7, headed: THE HELL-RIDE OF BRYNHILD; pp. [208]–214, headed: FRAGMENTS OF THE LAY OF | BRYNHILD; pp. 215–28, headed: THE SECOND OR ANCIENT LAY | OF GUDRUN.; pp. 229–42, headed: THE SONG OF ATLI.; pp. 243–9, headed: THE WHETTING OF GUDRUN.; pp. 250–9, headed: THE LAY OF HAMDIR.; pp. 260–70, headed: THE LAMENT OF ODDRUN.; p. [271–2], headed: Notes. | [thin rule]; p. [273]–5, headed: ALPHABETICAL LIST OF PERSONS, PLACES, | AND THINGS IN THE STORY. | [thin rule] | [list begins]; pp. 274–5, list completed with printer's imprint at foot: LONDON: | STRANGEWAYS & WALDEN, Printers, 28, Castle Street, Leicester Square.; p. [276], blank.

Technical Notes: *paper*: cream-white machine-laid, with dandy roll laid lines; no watermark; 12 certified copies on Whatman hand-made in demy 8° and another 12 copies on Whatman hand-made in cr. 8° but uncertified (HBF, p. 64); *leaf size*: ordinary copies: 191 × 125 mm., LP (from Fdmn untrimmed copy): 219 × 144 mm.; *printing*: running

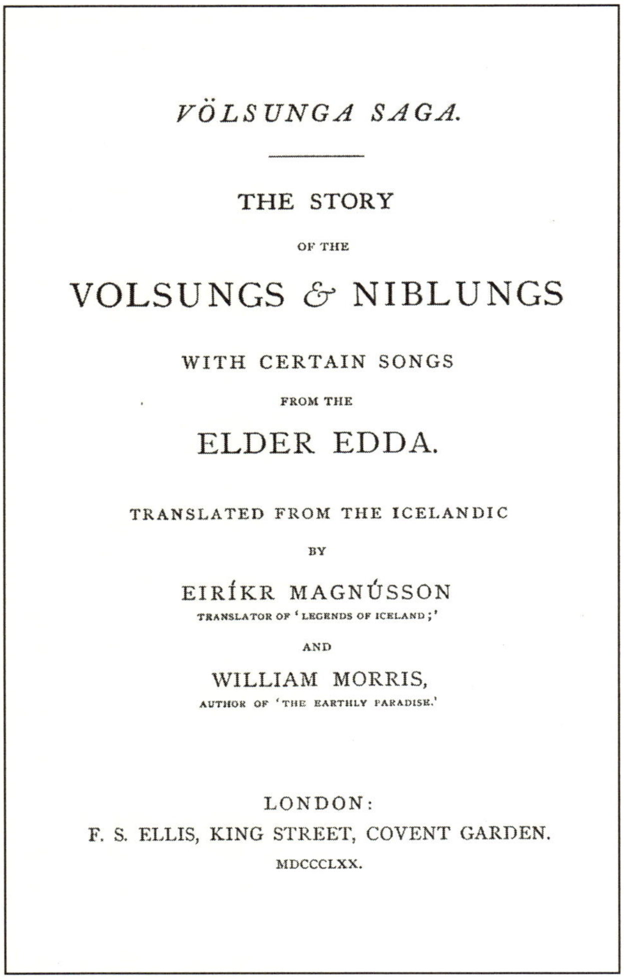

> VÖLSUNGA SAGA.
>
> THE STORY
> OF THE
> VOLSUNGS & NIBLUNGS
> WITH CERTAIN SONGS
> FROM THE
> ELDER EDDA.
>
> TRANSLATED FROM THE ICELANDIC
> BY
> EIRÍKR MAGNÚSSON
> TRANSLATOR OF 'LEGENDS OF ICELAND;'
> AND
> WILLIAM MORRIS,
> AUTHOR OF 'THE EARTHLY PARADISE.'
>
> LONDON:
> F. S. ELLIS, KING STREET, COVENT GARDEN.
> MDCCCLXX.

Figure 14. A-6.01: *Volsunga Saga* (1st edn.) title page

titles: used throughout, section titles or the text title all rectos and versos); *end-papers*: 1 free end and paste-down, front and back, paste-down: small nonpareil pattern, free end plain white; *binding*: green cloth with a gold-stamped design by Philip Webb (Forman says it is by Morris, HBF, p. 64). but see *Notes*, below) of 'flowers and flying birds on the front' and 'on the back . . . birds and rabbits'.
Publication: 1870 [issued 7 May] (*BSR* (2 May 1870), 431); *print run*: 750 copies (HBF, p. 63); *price*: 12s.
Register of Copies Examined: SPar (base copy); MU (Spec. Coll. PR5081, V6 S8, 1870a, LP copy, one of two sets of twelve, one of demy 8vo and one crown 8vo size, the demy 8vo copies being certificated); BL (2 copies: Ashley Lib.1215: "One of twelve copies printed upon Whatmans hand-made paper" (3:167) "crown octavo" and 2346.b.3); LeM (Prior copy). In all respects other than its title page, paper, binding, and the absence of signatures and the orig-

inal choirs, the George Prior Publishers edn. of 1980 is a facsimile of the ordinary 1st edn.
Notes: according to both Scott (p. 30) and Vallance (379), the ornamental cloth binding was designed by Philip Webb. Of the binding, Forman says: 'The book was issued in a peculiarly fine green cloth, stamped in gold all over the sides and back from a most beautiful design by Morris' (HBF, p. 64). Aymer Vallance says, 'the pattern on the side consists of flowers and flying birds on an arabesque ground; while that on the back, with conventional birds and rabbits, may be taken, from the severely decorative point of view, to mark the highest point of the designer, Mr. Philip Webb's capacity in this line. There were twelve large paper copies of the book, the title-page in some few instances, of which one was Mr. F. S. Ellis's copy, being ornamented with colour-ornaments by Morris's own hand' (Vallance, 379).
Later impression of this edn.:
1. Ellis: 1879 [2nd impression, 1st edn.]; *print run*: unknown; *price*: 12s.

A-6.02: Volsunga Saga
[2 and a half line dropped cap "V"] VOLSUNG SAGA: THE STORY OF | THE VOLSUNGS AND NIBLUNGS, | WITH CERTAIN SONGS FROM | THE ELDER EDDA. EDITED, WITH | INTRODUCTION AND NOTES, BY H. HALLIDAY SPARLING. | TRANSLATED FROM THE ICELANDIC BY EIRÍKR | MAGNÚSSON (TRANSLATOR OF "LEGENDS OF | ICELAND"); AND WILLIAM MORRIS (AUTHOR OF | "THE EARTHLY PARADISE"). | [french rule] | WALTER SCOTT | LONDON: 24 WARWICK LANE | PATERNOSTER ROW | 1888
Edition: [1st impression, 2nd edn.].
Series: The Camelot Series. This series was advertised as: 'New Comprehensive Edition [of] favourite prose works . . . . In shilling Monthly Volumes. Crown 8vo' (*BSR*, 6 Mar. 1888, p. 313). *Volsunga Saga* was the 24th in the series, which included works by Carlyle, Whitman, Thoreau, DeQuincy, Shelley, and Swift.
Place: Newcastle-on-Tyne, London, and New York.
Collation: cr. 8°: [a]–c^8 d^2 001–0017^8 0018^6 168 leaves pp. [i–v] vi–lii [1] 2–276 [277–84] [= 336].
Contents: p. [i], half title: [in modern gothic] The Camelot Series. | EDITED BY ERNEST RHYS. | THE STORY OF THE VOLSUNGS.; p. [ii], blank; p. [iii], title page; p. [iv], blank; pp. [v], headed: CONTENTS; pp. vi–viii: contents completed; p. [ix], Introduction begins

with woodcut head-piece and a 5-line illuminated drop cap initial "I"; pp. x–xxxvii, Introduction completed with appended signature, below right: H. HALLIDAY SPARLING.; p. [xxxviii], blank; p. [xxxix]: TRANSLA-TORS' PREFACE | [thin rule] | [text begins], pp. xl–xlv, 'Preface' completed; p. [xlvi], blank; p. [xlvii], 2nd half title; p. [xlviii], blank; p. [xlix]: THE NAMES OF THOSE WHO ARE MOST | NOTEWORTHY IN THIS STORY.; p. l, list of 'Names' etc. completed; p. [li], headed: A PROLOGUE IN VERSE. | [french rule] | [verse begins]; p. lii: [verse ends] | [signed, below right] WILLIAM MORRIS.; p. [1], headed: THE STORY OF | THE VOLSUNGS AND NIBLUNGS. | [thin rule] | CHAP. I. | *Of Sigi, the son of Odin.* | [text begins]; pp. 2–159, text completed with explicit in verse, aligned left, as in the previous entry, p. 163; p. [160], blank; p. [161], 3rd half title: CERTAIN SONGS | FROM | THE ELDER EDDA, | WHICH DEAL WITH THE STORY OF THE VOLSUNGS.; p. [162], blank; pp. 163–71, headed: PART OF THE SECOND LAY OF | HELGI HUND-ING'S-BANE.* | [thin rule] | [text begins]; pp. 172–75, headed: PART OF THE LAY OF SIGRDRIFA.; pp. 176–96, headed: THE LAY CALLED THE SHORT | LAY OF SIGURD.; pp. 197–201, headed: THE HELL-RIDE OF BRYNHILD; pp. 202–8, headed: FRAGMENTS OF THE LAY OF | BRYNHILD; pp. 209–22, headed: THE SECOND OR ANCIENT LAY | OF GUDRUN.; pp. 223–36, headed: THE SONG OF ATLI.; pp. 237–43, headed: THE WHETTING OF GUDRUN.; pp. 244–52, headed: THE LAY OF HAMDIR.; pp. 253–62, headed: THE LAMENT OF ODDRUN.; pp. 263–5, headed: ALPHABETICAL LIST OF PERSONS, PLACES, | AND THINGS IN THE STORY. | [thin rule] | [list begins]; p. [266], blank; pp. 267–75, headed: BOOK LIST. [a bibliography by Sparling] | [french rule] | [list begins]; p. 276, list ends: [thin rule at foot] *Printed by* WALTER SCOTT, *Felling, Newcastle-on-Tyne.*; pp. [277–84], ads.
Technical Notes: *paper*: white machine-wove, no watermark; *leaf size*: untrimmed, avg. 172 x 119 mm.; *printing: running titles*: prelims and end-matter: the appropriate section titles for all rectos and versos: CONTENTS, INTRODUCTION, PREFACE, INDEX, and BIBLIOGRAPHY; the 2 main titles are divided, the 1st, versos: *THE STORY OF THE* [and rectos:] *VOLSUNGS AND NIBLUNGS.*; the 2nd, verso: *SONGS FROM THE EDDA*; rectos, the title of the relevant lyric; *end-papers*: 1 free end and paste-down, front and back, plain white and blank; *binding*: plain unblocked dark blue cloth; *spine*: printed paper label: [all within red thin-rule compartment] Camelot Series | [thin rule] | THE STORY | OF THE | VOLSUNGS | Edited by | H. HALLIDAY SPARLING

Publication: '1888' [issued Jan.] (*BSR*, 6 Feb. 1888, p. 150); *print run*: unknown; *price*: 1s.

Register of Copies Examined: LeM (base copy, lacks the 1st two leaves of the adverts); BL (12205.ff.61); CU-B; TxU; MU; CtY.

Later issues and impressions of this edn.:
1. Walter Scott: n.d. [1896?] (ad, *BSR*, No. 458 (10 Jan. 1896), 81);
2. issued as No. 31 in The Scott Library, in London, Newcastle-on-Tyne, and New York, 3 East 14th Street.

A-6.03: Volsunga Saga (Golden 4°)

[aligned left] VOLSUNGA SAGA: THE STORY OF THE VOLSUNGS | AND NIBLUNGS, WITH CERTAIN SONGS FROM THE | ELDER EDDA. TRANSLATED FROM THE ICELANDIC | BY EIRIKR MAGNUSSON AND WILLIAM MORRIS.

[bound in with] THREE NORTHERN LOVE STORIES AND OTHER TALES.

Edition: 'Golden type quarto edition' [1st impression, 3rd edn.] In this vol. the 2 titles are handled individually, with separate pagination and signatures. Since they are separate except for the binding, only the 1st title is described here (see also A-9.01).

Collaborators, Editors, and Illustrators: [edited by S. C. Cockerell and Robert Proctor, though their work is not specified in the book].

Series: 4th vol., unnumbered, in the 8-vol. 'Golden type quarto series'.

Colophon: Here ends The Story of the Volsungs and Niblungs, with some Songs from | the Elder Edda; translated from the Icelandic by Eiríkr Magnússon and | William Morris. First printed in 1870, and now reprinted at the Chiswick | Press with the Golden type designed by William Morris for the Kelmscott | Press and finished on the 20th day of September, 1901. Published by Long- | mans, Green and Co. of London, New York and Bombay.

Collation: 4°: [a1]⁴ a2² [here a2 refers to a gathering, not a leaf] b–p⁴ 62 leaves pp. [i–ii] iii–xii 1–112 [= 124].

Contents: p. [i], half title (that serves as title page); p. [ii], blank; p. iii, headed: [flush left] PREFACE. | [text begins]; pp. iv–v, Preface completed; p. [vi], blank; p. vii, heading: [top, flush left] THE NAMES OF THOSE WHO ARE

MOST NOTE- | WORTHY IN THIS STORY. | [names, as a list]; p. viii, names concluded; p. ix–x, heading: [flush left] CONTENTS | [list begins].; p. xi–xii, heading: [in red, flush left] A PROLOGUE IN VERSE BY WILLIAM MORRIS.; p. 1, 1st chapter head, text begins; pp. 2–66, text completed with explicit (see this field in A-6.01); p. 67, headed: [in red, flush left] CERTAIN SONGS FROM THE ELDER EDDA, WHICH | DEAL WITH THE STORY OF THE VOLSUNGS. | [1st song title, heads the 1st of 2 cols., followed by text (for the other song titles, see this field in A-6.01)] PART OF THE SECOND | LAY OF HELGI HUND- | ING'S-BANE; pp. 68–99, 'songs' completed; p. [100], blank; p. 101, heading: [flush left] NOTES.; p. 102, 'Notes' concluded; p. 103, heading: [top, flush left, 1st of 2 cols.] INDEX. [followed by a list]; pp. 104–11, index continues; p. 112, index concludes with colophon in one column format; see the *Colophon*, above.
Technical Notes: paper, printing (including colour), position (but not content) of shoulder notes, end-papers, and binding are all common to the series and are described in this field in A-47.04, the 1st pbn. of the series.
Publication: 20 Sept. 1901 [printing finished, issued 20 Dec. 1901] (Chiswick Arch. and Longmans Arch.); *print run* and *price*: see this field in A-47.04.
Register of Copies Examined: LeM (base copy).

A-6.04:* Volsunga Saga (Norroena Society)
THE VOLSUNGA SAGA. TRANSLATED FROM THE ICELANDIC BY EIRÍKR MAGNÚSSON AND WILLIAM MORRIS, WITH INTRODUCTION BY H. HALLIDAY SPARLING, SUPPLEMENTED WITH LEGENDS OF THE WAGNER TRILOGY BY JESSIE L. WESTON, AND OLD NORSE SAGAS KINDRED TO THE VOLSUNG AND NIBLUNG TALE. HON. RASMUS B. ANDERSON, LL. D., EDITOR-IN-CHIEF. J. W. BUEL, PH. D., MANAGING EDITOR. LONDON, NEW YORK, [ETC.] NORROENA SOCIETY, 1906.
Edition: [1st impression, 4th edn. of the Morris-Magnússon text].
Series: vol. 6 (of 15?). From the half title: 'Norroena, the history and romance of northern Europe: a library of supreme classics printed in complete form'.
Publication: 1906; *print run*: 'Of the Viking edition there are but six hundred and fifty sets made for the world.'
Register of Copies Located: CU-B (Bancroft Main Stack: PT 722 | ES. N6; 1907n6); CaBVaU.
Later impressions of this edn.:

Norroena:
1.* 1907: Memorial of Rasmus B. Anderson, editor-in-chief [2nd impression, 4th edn.]; *print run*: 'Three hundred and fifty complete sets'; *price*: unknown;
2.* 1911: Anglo-Saxon Classics, Imperial Edition [3rd impression, 4th edn.]; *print run*: 350 sets, numbered; *price*: unknown.

A-6.05: *Volsunga Saga (Harvard Classics)
Edition: [1st impression, 5th edn.]
Collaborators, Editors, and Illustrators: ed. by Charles W. Eliot.
Series: vol. 49 of The Harvard Classics.
Publication: 1910.
Register of Copies Located:, BL (12209. ppp. 9/49)

A-6.06: Volsunga Saga (*CW* VII)
This is a combined edn. of *The Grettis Saga* and *Volsunga Saga* pbd. as vol. VII of *CW*. For the title page, collation, contents, and all details specific to this vol., see A-5.04. For details common to the set see A-126.01.
Edition: [1st impression, 6th edn. for both texts included].
Publication: 1911 [issued 14 June] (Longmans Arch.); for *print run* and *price*, see A-126.01.
Register of Copies Examined: see this field in A-126.01.

A-7.01: The Lovers of Gudrun (RB)
THE | LOVERS OF GUDRUN. | *A POEM.* | BY WILLIAM MORRIS. | REPRINTED FROM 'THE EARTHLY PARADISE.' | BOSTON: | ROBERTS BROTHERS. | 1870.
Edition: [1st impression, 1st separate edn.] The text is the last section from Part 3 of *EP*, extracted from the printing of the 2nd edn., 1st American, retaining the original pagination, here bound in with a separate gathering of *Tributes to William Morris*, separately paginated and printed by Roberts Brothers. It too was issued separately as a free advertising handout.
Collaborators, Editors, and Illustrators: frontis. of Gudrun standing between 'the doorposts where the dragons played', reproduces in half-tone a design by Hammatt Billings.
Collation: 8° in 12s, (8° sigs. only): [1¹² (1,+1) 2–5¹² 6¹⁰] 70 leaves pp. [i–ii] [245] 246–382 [= 140] + 1 engraved plate noted in the formula and described in the *Contents*, but not included in the book's pagination; and 2 separate gatherings—36 leaves and 4 leaves—of Roberts Brothers advertising not included in the formula or pagination statement but described in the *Contents*. Pagination is that of Part 3 of

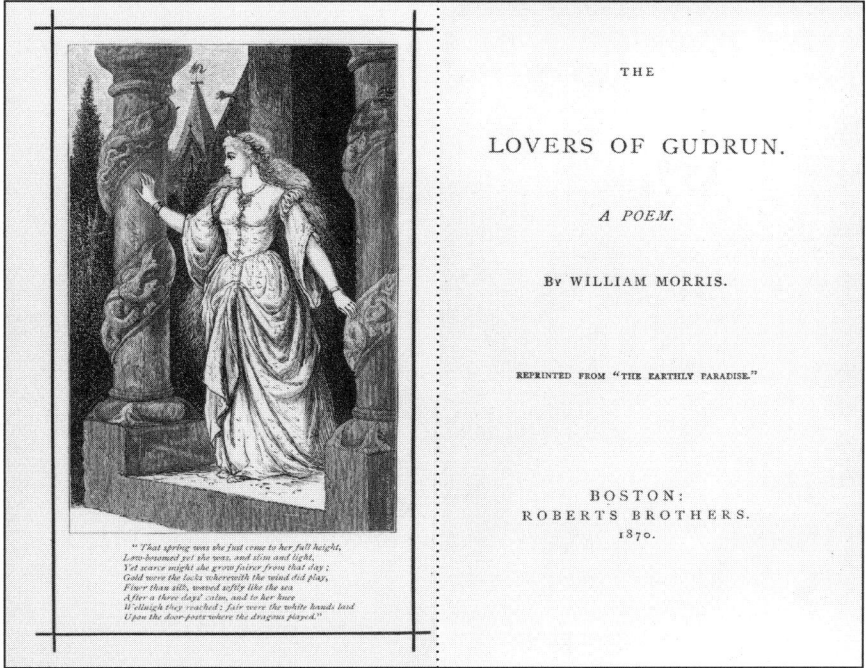

Figure 15. A-7.01: *Lovers of Gudrun* (1st edn.) opening: frontis. & title page

the American 3-vol. 4-Part *Earthly Paradise*.
Contents: frontis. inserted to face the title page, engraved design by Hammatt Billings, of Gudrun standing between the entrance pillars of the hall at Bathstead; p. [i], title page; p. [ii], headed: PUBLISHERS' NOTE. | "The Lovers of Gudrun" is one of the six stories | comprising the Third Part of the "Earthly Paradise," | and is reprinted from that volume for the convenience | of tourists and others. The publishers have not thought it necessary to make any changes in the paging. | [printer's imprint] UNIVERSITY PRESS: WELCH, BIGELOW, & CO. | CAMBRIDGE.; p. [245], 1st chapter headtitle, text begins; pp. 246–382, text completed with explicit: THE END. | [thin rule] | Cambridge: Printed by Welch, Bigelow, & Co.; pp. [1–3] 4–36 [37–40]; the separately printed ads. consist of the Roberts pamphlet of 36 pages: TRIBUTES TO WILLIAM MORRIS, ON THE PUBLICATION OF *THE EARTHLY PARADISE*. (also issued as a separate pamphlet for free distribution), and a separate 4-page list of: MR. WILLIAM MORRIS'S WORKS.
Technical Notes: *paper*: cream machine-wove with dandy roll laid lines; no watermark, *leaf size*: trimmed, 175 x 119 mm.; *printing*: *running titles*: [all versos] THE EARTHLY PARADISE. | [all rectos] THE LOVERS OF GUDRUN. (appended *Tributes*, not described here); *pagination*: as in the 1st impression, 2nd edn., 1st American, i.e. the 1st prtd. page no. is p. 246; *end-papers*: paste-down and 2 free ends, front and back: dark matt brown paste-down and facing free end, reverse side and 2nd end-paper, plain white, front and back; *binding*: red, green, brown, or blue sand-textured cloth (see *Notes*, below); HBF, p. 60, says it was issued in 'red, in blue, and in green cloth watered-silk grained', but no such bindings have been seen; top right of front cover gilt-stamped with the title in large ornamental letters with an ornament of a circle within which the customary Roberts Aldine device of a boy blowing soap bubbles, sitting astride a smaller globe representing the earth; title gilt-stamped on spine: THE | LOVERS | OF | GUDRUN | [crossed gilt torches]. Toronto copy has been re-bound with a library binding, but it has a printed paper spine label which appears to be derived from the earlier binding: [double thin rule] THE | LOVERS | OF | GUDRUN | WILLIAM | MORRIS | [thin rule] | LONGMANS | [double thin rule]. This suggests that Longmans of NY re-issued this title with its own spine label but without change to the title page, after Longmans became Morris's publisher in 1896, and purchased the remaining stock of Roberts Brothers from Little, Brown and Co. after May 1898. That would match the arrangements made by Longmans with respect to several other titles which they acquired by purchase from the printed stock of the previous publisher. Other than the spine label, the Toronto copy is indistinguishable from the 1st issue of this title. No reference to a separate issue has been found.
Publication: '1870' [issued May] (date of order, Longmans Arch., Cost Book A). RB advertises the book as one that 'will be published in the Month of May' (*Am. Lit. Gaz. & PC*, 15/1 (2 May 1870), 6) and on 1 June (*Am. Lit. Gaz. & PC*, 15/3, p. 80) it is 'announced' as ready 'with a frontispiece from a design by Billings'; *print run*: 500 copies (Longmans Arch., Cost Book A); *price*: $1.00.
Register of Copies Examined: LeM (base copy); An-C-TU (M677 E38 1870); BGR; CtY (proof sheets).

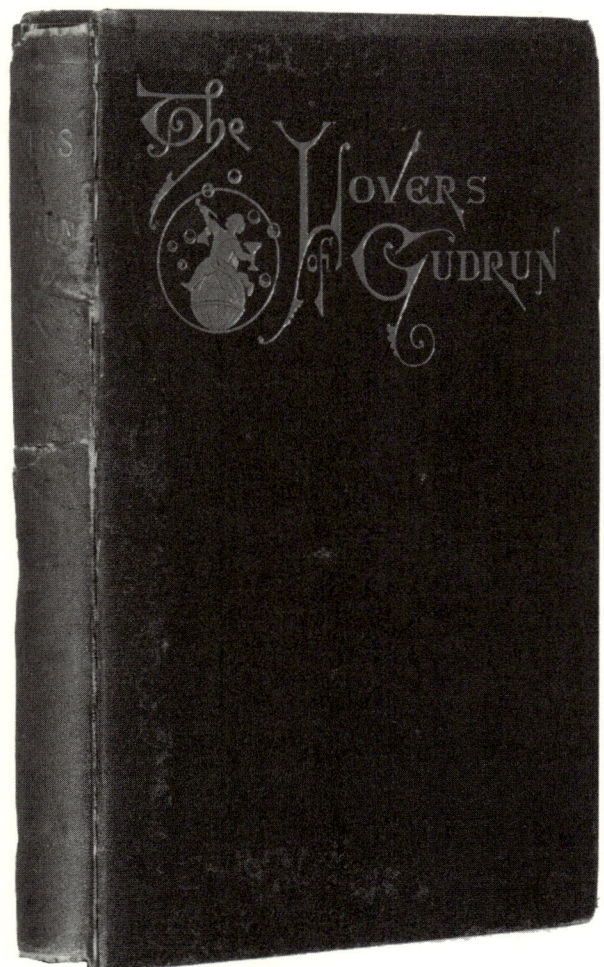

Figure 16. A-7.01: *Lovers of Gudrun* (1st edn.) binding

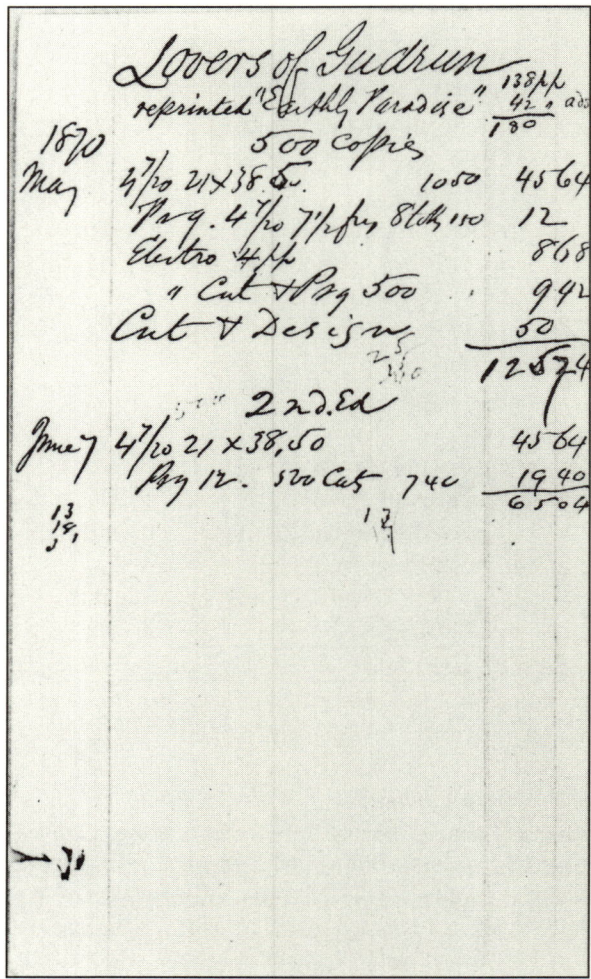

Figure 17. A-7.01: *Lovers of Gudrun* (1st edn. RB, Roberts Brothers): ledger entry

Later impression of this edn.:

1. RB: '1870' [order dated 7 June]: '2nd edn..' (Cost Book A, Roberts Arch.) [2nd impression, 2nd edn., 1st American; *print run*: 500 copies; *price*: $1.00.
Notes: printed from *EP* as set for Roberts Brothers, with the same 8° signing for gatherings that are duodecimo, having all the signatures of the 8° and keeping also the *EP* pagination; RB letter to Forman, 9 Feb. 1897 (in RB Letter Book: MH-H, Little Brown Arch.): 'sending electro' (Forman had enquired 'for an edition projected by F. S. Ellis, 1869', see Goodwin, 47). RB continues, 'We always keep the book [*Lovers of Gudrun*] in stock although it has not had a very large sale of late years. We have on hand today about 30 copies bound. Red, green or brown, last colour changed from blue, and about 75 in sheets folded . . . cloth bound at 2/4 cash net on 1/6 sheets.' But it would clearly have been a violation of copyright for Forman to import the American copies for sale in England, and no evidence that he did so has turned up.

Under 'Messrs. Roberts Brothers, Boston': '"The Lovers of Gudrun" by William Morris. This is perhaps the finest poem in the "Earthly Paradise", and is to be issued small enough for the pocket' (*Am. Lit. Gaz & PC.*, 15/1 (2 May 1870), 6.

In their ad in this issue RB announces *Gudrun* in a list of books which they will publish 'during the month of May'. They describe the book as '16mo, cloth, neat Price $1. This Poem, generally acknowledged by all critics to be the masterpiece of the author, and one of the great poems of this century, is published in this separate form for the convenience of tourists, of seaside and wayside ramblers.'

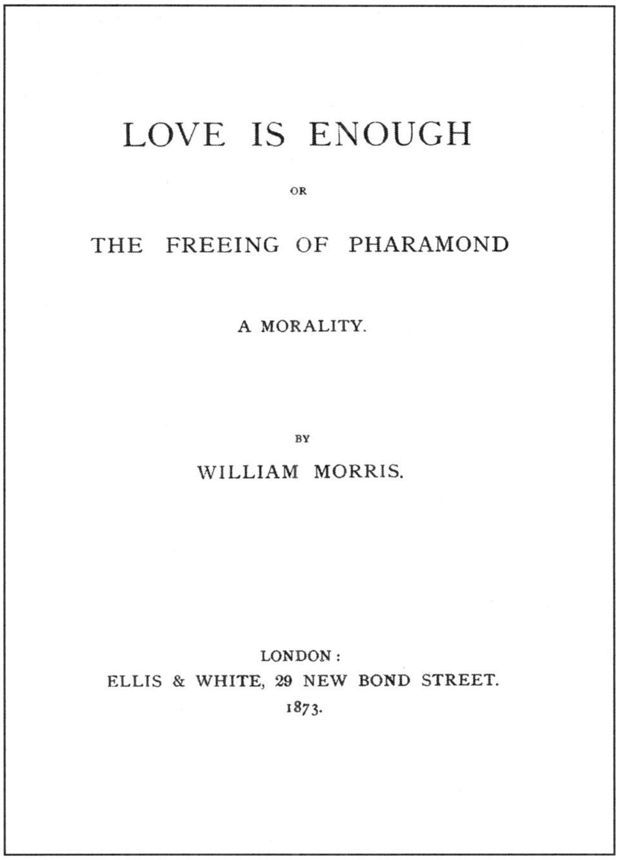

A-8.01: Love is Enough

LOVE IS ENOUGH | OR | THE FREEING OF PHARAMOND | A MORALITY. | BY | WILLIAM MORRIS. | LONDON: | ELLIS & WHITE, 29 NEW BOND STREET. | 1873.

Edition: [1st issue, 1st impression, 1st edn.] Besides the ordinary copies, 25 LP copies were prtd. on Whatman's handmade demy 8° paper 'for private circulation only', 4 copies on vellum (HBF, pp. 80–1).

Collation: square cr. 8°: [A]⁴ B–I⁸ K⁴ 72 leaves pp. [8] [1] 2–134 [135–6] [= 144].

Contents: pp. [1–2], blank; p. [3], half title; p. [4], blank; p. [5], title page; p. [6], imprint: LONDON: | PRINTED BY JOHN STRANGEWAYS, | Castle St. Leicester Sq.; p. [7], headed: DRAMATIS PERSONÆ; p. [8], blank; p. [1], headtitle and text begins; pp. 2–134, text completed with explicit: THE END. | [printer's imprint, as above]; pp. 135–6, ads. The LP copies have a limitation notice on the verso of the half title: *Twenty-five copies printed on large paper for | Private Circulation only*; the remaining details are given for the LP copies by Forman, except that the three-musicians woodcut vignette is used as a tail-piece at the end of the LP copy.

Technical Notes: *paper*: cream machine wove, no watermark; *leaf size*: lightly trimmed, 191 x 143 mm.; *printing*: *headlines*: *running titles*: all versos and rectos: LOVE IS ENOUGH.; *end-papers*: 1 free end and paste-down, plain white and blank, front and back; *binding*: plain dark blue unblocked cloth, gilt-stamped on front with Morris flower design, intertwining branches of myrtle from the left and willow from the right, enclosing title in 3-line caps, the same size and design as on the spine; gilt-stamped title up the spine: LOVE IS ENOUGH.

Publication: 1873 [issued 16–31 Nov. 1872] (*Pub. Circ.*, 35/845 (9 Dec. 1872), 814); *print run*: 1,500 ordinary copies, 25 LP, 4 on vellum; *price*: ordinary copies: 7s. 6d.

Register of Copies Examined: LeM (base copy); VSL (S822.8/M83L); VU (B821.85.Le); BGR; VMoU (820.8 M877 A6/Lo); MU (LP copy with autograph letter by Ellis: Spec Coll. PR5078/L6 1873a); CSt (Spec.Coll.Felton PT5078.L6).

Notes: Morris wrote to F. S. Ellis, [Nov.] 1872 about the vellum for the 4 copies:

'Vellum to be ready (Fri) in a week, I find it no use to try for any thing but what we saw before, white, thick, the same on both sides, copiously dressed; they have no idea of any thing else; so I thought I had better order it; price stiffish

Figure 18. A-8.01: *Love is Enough* (1st edn.) title page

2s. 9d. per sheet & Strangeways wants 60 sheets, so countermand it if you think it too dreadful [at] £2.15 copy: but you can get God Almighty's price for them I know: only I thought I would tell you at once' (*Letters*, i. 173–4).

The dating of this letter is based on Buxton Forman's statement that the regular edn. was through the press in Nov. 1872. It seems reasonable to assume the 4 vellum copies of the book, as well as the 25 on Whatman hand-made paper, were printed at the same time as the ordinary copies. See HBF, pp. 79–81.

Love is Enough was never popular. The 1st impression of 1,500 copies covered the export of sheets to America and the British sales through the rest of the term of Ellis as Morris's publisher and the entire term of Reeves and Turner, there being some copies left still when Longmans took over in 1896. In Boston confidence based perhaps on the sales of *EP* led to a simultaneous issue of the 'English Edition' from copies imported in sheets, and the 'Popular Edition', an American setting of 1,500 copies. 12 years later, in 1885, Reeves and Turner took over from Ellis the cop-

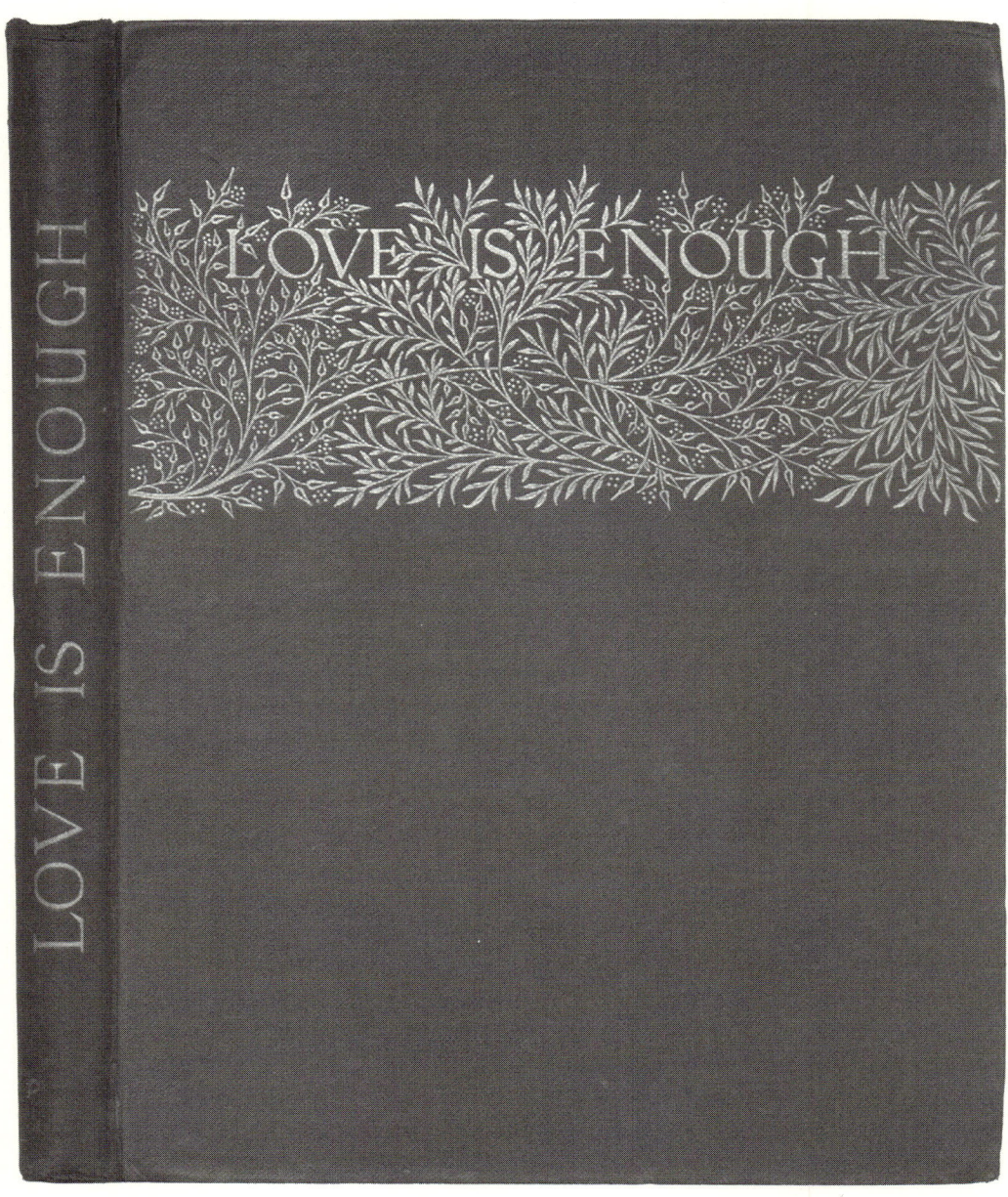

Figure 19. A-8.01: *Love is Enough* (1st edn.) binding

ies remaining of the 1st impression of 1,500 and continued to advertise and sell these 'Third Edition' copies through the 15 years the firm remained publishers of Morris. The only change made was the revision of the title page in 1889 to indicate the change of publisher and date. The original Morris-designed binding was used through the life of this edition.

When Longmans, Green and Co. became Morris's publisher in June 1896, *Love is Enough* was combined in a single vol. with *Poems by the Way*, a book treated here as a separate title (A-81.01) with references to that entry under each of the separate titles. After that initiative there is no record of any further reprints of either the English or the American edns, except for the new settings done for the KP and *CW* edns.

Later issues of this edn.:
1. Ellis: 1873 [issued 17–31 Jan.]: Second Edition. [3rd issue, 2nd English, 1st impression, 1st edn.], *print run*: copies remaining from the 1st impression of 1,500 copies; *price*: 7s. 6d.;
2. Ellis: 1873: Third Edition. [4th issue, 3rd English, 1st edn.]; *print run*: copies remaining from the 1st impression; *price*: as above;
3. R and T: 1889: Third Edition. [5th issue, 4th English, 1st impression] this with R and T's imprint and a new date on copies remaining from the 1st impression, by Ellis; *price*: as above.

A-8.02: Love is Enough (imported shts. RB)

title page reproduces A-8.01 except for the place of pbn., publisher's imprint, and date: BOSTON: | ROBERTS BROTHERS. | 1873.
Edition: [2nd issue, 1st American, 1st impression, 1st edn.] Made up of imported shts. of the English 1st impression, 1st edn. in an American binding, issued in Boston at the same time as the 1st impression of the 1st American edn. (see A-8.03). Since this is another issue of sheets already described in A-8.01, only certain fields, where contents are altered, are included here.
Printer: John Strangeways, 28 Castle St. Leicester Sq.
Collation: as in A-8.01.
Contents: as in A-8.01, except the publisher's imprint on the title page is changed (as above). The printer's imprint, p. 134, is omitted, as is the appended leaf of Ellis and White ads (pp. 135–6).
Technical Notes: as in A-8.01, except: *paper*: t.e.g.; *leaf size*: 180 x 136 mm.; *end-papers*: 1 free end and paste-down, front and back, facing free end and paste-down in dark matt

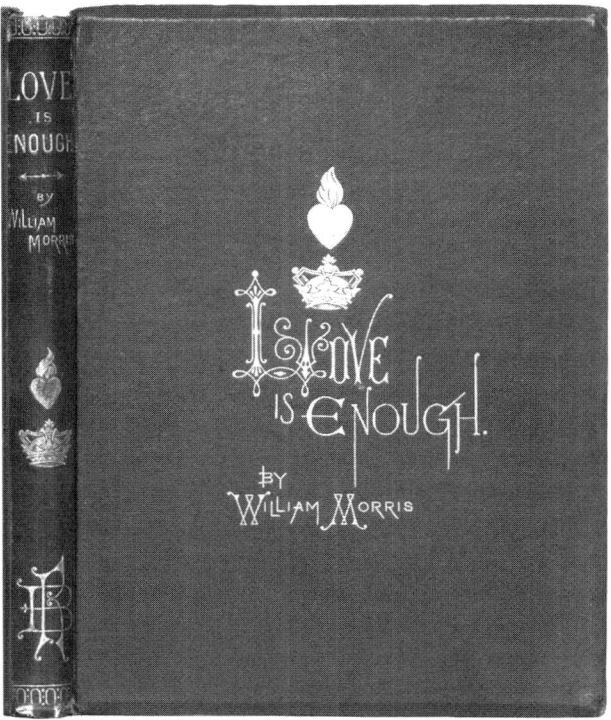

Figure 20. A-8.02: *Love is Enough* (1st edn., American issue) binding

blue, free end overleaf plain white and blank; *binding*: dark green or maroon unblocked cloth with bevelled edges; front: gilt title and author below crown and flaming heart: [in 6-line swash caps] LOVE | IS ENOUGH | BY | WILLIAM MORRIS; *spine*: gilt-stamped: [standard RB ornamental border of alternating ovals and 3 dots aligned vertically, all above a thin rule] LOVE | IS | ENOUGH | [french rule with darts at both ends] | BY | [aligned left, swash caps] WILLIAM | [aligned right, swash caps] MORRIS | [burning heart and crown design from front repeated in smaller size] | [monogram] R [superimposed on] B [both in the swash letters of the front title] | [ornamental border of top repeated]
Publication: 1873 [issued 18–23 Jan.] ('Books Just Published', *Pub. Weekly*, No. 54 (23 Jan. 1873), 85); *print run*: probably 500 copies, all the imported copies came from the 1st English impression of 1,500 copies; *price*: $2.00.
Register of Copies Examined: LeM (base copy); BGR; MU.
Notes: 'Roberts Brothers will inaugurate the publishing business for 1873 by issuing in January: "William Morris. Love is Enough. Two Editions. The English Edition, Square, 8vo, cloth, gilt top, bevelled boards, Price: $2.00. Roberts Brothers "Popular Edition". 16mo, cloth. Price . . . $1.25"' (*Pub. Weekly*, No. 26 (26 Dec. 1872), 706).

A-8.03: Love is Enough (RB)

LOVE IS ENOUGH; | OR | THE FREEING OF PHARAMOND. | [in gothic] A MORALITY | BY WILLIAM MORRIS, | AUTHOR OF "THE EARTHLY PARADISE," "THE LIFE AND DEATH OF JASON," ETC. | BOSTON: | ROBERTS BROTHERS. | 1873.

Edition: AUTHOR'S EDITION., 'Popular Edition' [1st impression, 2nd edn., 1st American].

Collation: 12° (obsolete 8° sigs. only): [1–5^{12} 6^{10}] 70 leaves pp. [1–8] 9–140 [=140] + 2 appended separate gatherings not included in the formula or the pagination but described in their appropriate places in the *Contents*.

Contents: p. [1], half title; p. [2]: [RB Aldine cherub-on-globe mark]; p. [3], title page; p. [4], copyright note and printer's imprint: AUTHOR'S EDITION. | Press of | JOHN WILSON AND SON, | [in gothic] Cambridge.; p. 5, headed: DRAMATIS PERSONÆ.; p. [6], blank; p. 7, 1st chapter head and text begins; pp. 8–140, text completed with: [thin rule] | Cambridge: Press of John Wilson & Son.; + 2 appended separately paginated, not integral gatherings of ads.: pp. [1]–36 headed: TRIBUTES | TO | WILLIAM MORRIS, | ON THE PUBLICATION OF | THE EARTHLY PARADISE.; pp. [1]–4; ads, headed: MR. WILLIAM MORRIS'S WORKS.

Technical Notes: *paper*: white machine-made, no watermark; *leaf size*: trimmed, 174 x 113 mm.; *printing*: running titles: [all rectos and versos] LOVE IS ENOUGH.; *end-papers*: 1 free end and paste-down, plain white and blank, front and back; *binding*: in red, blue, purple, or green cloth, otherwise as in A-8.02.

Publication: '1873', [issued 18–23 Jan.] (published simultaneously with A-8.02 (see 'Books Just Published', *Pub. Weekly*, No. 54 (23 Jan. 1873), 94); RB Cost Book C records 16 Dec. 1872, which may refer to the completion of printing; *print run*: 1,500 copies; *price*: $1.50 (Longmans Arch.).

Register of Copies Examined: TxU (base copy: 2 copies: HRCMin 29, 377 and PR 5078 L5 1873); BGR.

A-8.04:* Love is Enough [and] Poems by the Way (PW)

POEMS BY THE WAY | & LOVE IS ENOUGH | BY | WILLIAM MORRIS | NEW EDITION | LONGMANS, GREEN, AND CO. | 39 PATERNOSTER ROW, LONDON | NEW YORK AND BOMBAY | 1896 | *All rights reserved*

Edition: 'Poetical Works Edition' [1st impression, 3rd edn., 2nd English of *Love is Enough*]. This combined vol., one of the series PW, is described as a new title in A-81.01.

Publication: 1896 [issued 20–4 July] ('Publications of the Week', *Pub. Circ.*, 65/1569 (25 July 1896), 84); *print run*: 500 copies; *price*: 6s.

Register of Copies Located: ICU; CabVaU.

A-8.05: Love is Enough (KP)

LOVE IS ENOUGH, OR THE FREEING OF | PHARAMOND: A MORALITY. WRITTEN | BY WILLIAM MORRIS

Edition: 'Kelmscott Press Edition' [1st impression, 4th edn., 3rd English].

Collaborators, Editors, and Illustrators: seen through the Press by S. C. Cockerell, acting for the Trustees of the Morris Estate.

Series: 52nd title, 22nd by Morris, pbd. by the KP.

Colophon: [printer's leaf ornament No. 2] Here ends Love is Enough, or The Freeing of | Pharamond, written by William Morris, with two | pictures designed by Sir Edward Burne-Jones, & | engraved on wood by W. H. Hooper. The picture | on the opposite page was not designed for this edi- | tion of Love is Enough, but for an edition pro- | jected about twenty-five years ago, which was never | carried out. Printed at the Kelmscott Press, Up- | per Mall, Hammersmith, & finished on the 11th day | of December, 1897. [¶] | Sold by the Trustees of the late William Morris | at the Kelmscott Press.

Collation: large 4° in 8s: [a]^4 b–f^8 g^6 [$4 (–b1 c1 d1 e3 f1) signed] 50 leaves pp. [8] [1–2] 3–90 [91–2] [= 100].

Contents: pp. [1–4], blank; p. [5], title page; p. [6], dramatis personæ; p. [7], blank; p. [8], frontis.; p. [1], text begins; pp. 2–90, text completed with the colophon; p. 91, illustration; p. [92], blank.

Technical Notes: *paper*: Batchelor's hand-made Kelmscott Perch paper; *leaf size*: deckled edges, avg. 292 x 213 mm.; *printing*: done in 3 colours: red for stage directions and names of speakers in dialogue; blue for floriated initials in 'the Music' sections; *end-papers*: standard KP handling, i.e. 3 free ends and paste-down, all plain white and blank, front and back, made of the same paper as the body of the book; *binding*: plain unblocked limp natural vellum, with green silk ties, gilt-stamped up the *spine*: LOVE IS ENOUGH; *ornamentation*: 2 full-page pictures designed by Burne-Jones; Morris borders 6a and 7; 5 corner pieces; 12 half borders; 10 small borders; 7 black 8-line initials; 9 blue 6-line initials; 12 black 6-line initials; and 27 blue 3-line initials.

Publication: 11 Dec. 1897 [finished printing, issued 24 Mar.

1898] (Cockerell, p. 171); *print run*: 300 copies on paper, 8 copies on vellum; *price*: 2*gns.* and 10*gns.*, respectively.
Register of Copies Examined: BL (base copy: C.43.f.15.); VU (19M); CU-B (TYP AA4 A3. M58 1873), one of 4 vellum copies, this one 'bound by T. J. Cobden-Sanderson in morocco covered with red silk over which has been hand sewn an embroidery . . . by May Morris . . . .' Five letters relating to this volume have been removed and shelved separately, with this collection (CU-B Cat.).

A-8.06: Love is Enough [and] Poems by the Way (*CW* IX)

THE COLLECTED WORKS | [title details common to the set, see A-126.01] | VOLUME IX | LOVE IS ENOUGH | POEMS BY THE WAY | [publisher's imprint, see A-126.01] | MDCCCCXI.
Edition: [1st impression, 5th edn., 4th English] For detail common to the set—paper, leaf size, printing, type area, headlines or shoulder notes, end-papers, binding, print run, and price—see the entry for *CW*, A-126.01. Details specific to this vol.—*Collation*, *Contents*, and *Technical Notes*—are recorded in the entry for *Poems by the Way*, A-59.06.
Publication: 1911 [issued 11 Dec.] (Longmans Arch.); *print run* and *price*: see this field in A-126.01.
Register of Copies Examined: see this field in A-126.01.

A-9.01: Northern Love Stories

THREE NORTHERN | LOVE STORIES, | AND OTHER TALES. | TRANSLATED FROM THE ICELANDIC | BY EIRÍKR MAGNÚSSON AND WILLIAM MORRIS | [thin rule] | LONDON: | ELLIS & WHITE, 29 NEW BOND STREET. | 1875.
Edition: [1st impression, 1st edn.] 25 LP copies on Whatman paper; 'The Saga of Gunnlaug the Worm-tongue and Rafn the Skald' had been previously published in *The Fortnightly Review* for Jan. 1869 (see D-20); 'The Story of Frithiof the Bold' appeared in 2 parts in *Dark Blue*, Mar. and Apr. 1871 (see D-29). The other tales—'The Story of Viglund the Fair', 'The Tale of Hogni and Hedinn', 'The Tale of Roi the Fool', and 'The Tale of Thorstein Staff-smitten'—appear here for the first time.
Translation: from the Icelandic by E. Magnússon and W. Morris (on the nature of the collaboration, see the *Notes* to A-5.01).
Collation: cr. 8°: π² a⁴ (± a2) B–R⁸ 134 leaves pp. [i–v] vi–vii [viii–xii] [1–3] 4–256 [= 268].
Contents: p. [i], half title; p. [ii], blank; p. [iii], title page; p. [iv], blank; p. [v], headed: PREFACE. | [text begins]; pp. vi–vii, preface completed; p. [viii], blank; p. [ix], headed: CHRONOLOGY | IN | *The Story of Gunnlaug the Worm-tongue.* | [thin rule] | [list of 17 major incidents with dates]; p. [x], blank; p. [xi], headed: CONTENTS. | [list of 3 'stories' and 3 'Tales', plus 'Notes' and 'Index']; p. [xii], blank; p. [1], 2nd half title; p. [2], blank; p. [3], 1st chapter head with subtitle in hanging indent format, text begins; pp. 4–63, text, divided into 18 chapters; p. [64], blank; p. [65], 3rd half title for 'Frithiof the Bold'; p. [66], blank; p. [67], heading, text begins; pp. 68–114, text, divided into 15 chapters; p. [115], 4th half title for 'Viglund the Fair'; p. [116], blank; p. 117, heading, text begins; pp. 118–86, text, divided into 22 chapters; p. [187], 5th half title, for 'Hogni and Hedinn'; p. [188], blank; p. [189], headed: [thin rule] | CHAPTER I. | Of Freyia and the Dwarfs. | [text begins]; pp. 190–210, text, divided into 9 chapters; p. 211, 6th half title, for 'Roi the Fool'; p. [212], blank; p. [213], head title; pp. 214–29, text, divided into 5 chapters; p. [230], blank; p. [231], 7th half title, to 'Thorstein Staff-smitten'; p. [232], blank; p. [233], heading, thin rule, text begins; pp. 234–43, text; p. [244], blank; p. [245]: NOTES | [thin rule] | pp. 246–7, notes conclude; p. [248], blank; p. 249: INDEX | TO THE | STORY OF GUNNLAUG THE WORM-TONGUE.; pp. 250–2, Index concluded; p. 253: INDEX | TO THE STORIES OF | FRITHIOF THE BOLD, VIGLUND THE FAIR, | HOGNI AND HEDINN, ROI THE FOOL, | AND | THORSTEIN STAFF-SMITTEN. | [thin rule]; pp. 254–6, Index concluded: [thin rule] | LONDON: | PRINTED BY JOHN STRANGEWAYS, | Castle St. Leicester Sq.
Technical Notes: *paper*: cream machine-laid, dandy roll laid lines, no watermark; *leaf size*: ordinary copies: lightly trimmed, avg. 190 x 125 mm., LP: avg. 206 x 136 mm.; *printing*: type area: 131 x 80 mm., excluding head and direction lines; *lines-to-page*: set solid, 32 lines; *headlines*: running titles: all versos, 1st 3 stories: THE STORY OF [last 3 stories] THE TALE OF | [all rectos, short title of the relevant story]; all 6 narratives have separate half titles and start new pages; *end-papers*: single free end and paste-down, plain white and blank, front and back; *binding*: plain dark green unblocked cloth; *spine*: printed label: [within thin-rule compartment] THREE | NORTHERN | LOVE | STORIES, | AND | OTHER TALES. | [thin rule] | E. MAGNÚSSON | AND | W. MORRIS. | [thin rule] | 10*s*. 6*d*.
Publication: 1875 [issued 1–15 July] (*Pub. Circ.*, 38/908 (16 July 1875), 497). Morris wrote in a letter of 28 Nov. 1874, that 'Ellis has promised to publish the saga [*Three North-*

ern Love Stories*] on the day after the poems [*The Defence of Guenevere*, 2nd edn.] come out, as a reward of industry you see' (*Letters*, i. 240). On the evidence available it seems that, though *The Defence* was issued on 1 May, *Three Northern Love Stories* did not appear until July. Morris says (see *Notes*, below) that the LP copies were delayed, but he had a copy to his mother on 17 July; *print run*: 500 copies; *price*: 10*s*. 6*d*. regular, 16*s*. 6*d*. for the LP copies.

Register of Copies Examined: LeM (base copy); BGR; VU (B339.6308/M199); CtY

Notes: on Morris's collaboration with Eiríkr Magnússon in the translations from Icelandic, see this field in A-5.01.

The 'Three Northern Love Stories' of the title are distinguished from the 'other Tales' only by being longer. Morris decided to add the 'tales' to the 'Stories' not only because they too showed the qualities he admired in Icelandic literature, but also to eke out the collection sufficiently to make a book to be priced at 10*s*. 6*d*. He wrote to Buxton Forman in 1873 that he would add *Viglund the Fair* to the already published *Gunnlaug* and *Frithiof*, together with 3 other tales 'to make up', he said, 'a book big enough for Ellis's purposes' (*Letters*, i. 205–6). A measure of lavishness in the printing betrays Ellis's efforts to give the book still more bulk: all 6 narratives, and the 'Notes' and 'Index' as well, have separate half-title leaves with blank versos, and most of the half titles face blank versos from the previous sections. But the market was not very interested in the book at the initial price, and until 1901 no reprints were required beyond the 1st print run of 500 copies. When Longmans issued their new edn. in 1901, the price was lowered to 6*s*. though the book had to be reset, there being evidently no moulds or plates made from the 1st edn. All the largesse of Ellis's production is preserved in the Longmans, plus an addition of some 44 pages by changing the type from Caslon's Small Pica to Pica (a change initially resisted by Cockerell). A larger leaf size is negated by larger margins reducing the type area, which, together with the change in type resulted in a book larger in all respects than its predecessor. 1,000 copies were printed on this occasion, and though moulds were made, no use was made of them during the period covered here, further edns. being limited to the Golden Type quarto, vol. 4 of the set of 8, and the *CW*, vol. X.

All 6 narratives were translated by Morris and Magnússon during the early 1870s, in the period immediately following the completion of *EP* and *Love is Enough*.

A-9.02: Northern Love Stories

THREE NORTHERN | LOVE STORIES | AND OTHER TALES | TRANSLATED FROM THE ICELANDIC | BY EIRÍKR MAGNÚSSON AND | WILLIAM MORRIS | NEW EDITION | LONGMANS, GREEN, AND CO. | 39 PATERNOSTER ROW, LONDON | NEW YORK AND BOMBAY | 1901

Edition: New Edition [1st impression, 2nd edn.] Of a size and binding to range with the 1st edn. of *The Sundering Flood* (see *Notes*, below, and A-86.01); for previous pbn. of the 1st 2 stories, see this field in A-9.01.

Collation: cr. 8° (Imperial 16°): [a]⁴ b² A–R⁸ S⁴ 146 leaves pp. [i–iv] v–xi /xii] [1–2] 3–278 [279–80] [= 292].

Contents: p. [i], half title; p. [ii], blank; p. [iii], title page; p. [iv], bibliographic note; p. v, section dropped head: PREFACE; pp. vi–vii, text completed; p. [viii], blank; p. ix, headed: CHRONOLOGY | IN THE STORY OF GUNNLAUG THE | WORM-TONGUE. | [list of 17 major incidents with dates]; p. [x], blank;

Figure 21. A-9.01: *Three Northern Love Stories* (1st edn.) title page

p. xi, headed: CONTENTS | [list of 3 'stories' and 3 'Tales', plus 'Notes' and 'Index']; p. [xii], blank; p. [1], 2nd half title: THE STORY OF | GUNNLAUG THE WORM-TONGUE | AND RAVEN THE SKALD; p. [2], blank; pp. 3–68, headed as the half title; p. [69], 3rd half title: THE STORY OF | FRITHIOF THE BOLD; p. [70], blank; pp. 71–121, text, headed as the half title; p. [122], blank; p. [123], 4th half title: THE STORY OF | VIGLUND THE FAIR; p. 124, blank; pp. 125–200, text, headed as the half title; p. [201], 5th half title: THE TALE OF | HOGNI AND HEDINN; p. [202], blank; pp. 203–25, headed: THE TALE OF | Hogni And Hedinn; p. [226], blank; p. [227], 6th half title: THE TALE OF | ROI THE FOOL; p. [228], blank; pp. 229–47: text, headed as the half title; p. [248], blank; p. [249], 7th half title: THE TALE OF | THORSTEIN STAFF-SMITTEN; p. [250], blank; pp. 251–62, text, headed as the half title; p. [263], 8th half title: NOTES; p. [264], blank; pp. 265–6, headed: NOTES | THE TALE OF HOGNI AND HEDINN; p. [267], headed: NOTE TO PAGE 54, *l*. 28]; p. [268], blank; p. [269], 9th half title: INDEX; p. [270], blank; pp. 271–4, headed: INDEX | TO THE STORY OF GUNNLAUG THE | WORM-TONGUE. | [note to the reader] *The number signifies the page*; pp. 275–7, headed: INDEX | [in hanging indent] TO THE STORIES OF FRITHIOF THE BOLD, | VIGLUND THE FAIR, HOGNI AND HEDINN, | ROI THE FOOL, AND THORSTEIN STAFF- | SMITTEN; p. 278, text ends with explicit: THE END | Printed by BALLANTYNE, HANSON & Co. | Edinburgh & London; pp. [279]–80, ads for: WORKS BY WILLIAM MORRIS.

Technical Notes: *paper*: cream-white 'Antique Wove' (Longmans Arch.), i.e. a machine-wove paper with dandy roll laid lines, no watermark; *leaf size*: lightly trimmed, avg. 207 x 137 mm.; *printing*: *type area*: 137 x 84 mm.; *lines-to-page*: set solid, 32 lines; *headlines*: *running titles*: [all versos] THE STORY OF [or] THE TALE OF | [all rectos, title of the relevant narrative in 10-point caps]; *pagination*: arabic numerals at outer margins of headlines, except for chapter head titles, where page numbers are centred on the direction line; *end-papers*: 1 free end and paste-down front and back, plain grey-white and blank; *binding*: plain red unblocked cloth; *spine*: printed paper label: [within thin-rule compartment] THREE | NORTHERN | LOVE | STORIES | [thin rule] | E. MAGNÚSSON | AND | W. MORRIS | [below compartment] *Six Shillings Net*
Publication: Apr. 1901 [issued 29 Apr.] (Longmans *Notes on Books*, 9/185 (31 May 1901), 302–3); *print run*: 1,000 copies (Longmans Arch.); *price*: 6*s*. net.
Register of Copies Examined: LeM (base copy); VU (S839.6308/2)
Notes: C. J. Longman wrote to Cockerell, 5 Dec. 1900 to send a specimen page of the new popular edn. of *Three Northern Love Stories* which is being done on similar terms to 'Grettir the Strong': 10% on the first 500 and after that 2*d*. per shilling. Originally the price was intended to be 6*s*., but Longmans decided to make it 5*s*. net, and to base the royalties on the 6*s*. price (Smith Arch.).

19 Dec. 1900, W. A. Kelk, Longmans editor, wrote to Cockerell, sending 'another' specimen page for *Three Northern Love Stories*, in the new popular edn., 'in a larger Caslon type unleaded'. Cockerell notes his draft reply, which is for the smaller type, which Kelk says is 'uniform with Grettir'. Cockerell's draft says that the small pica should be used, set solid. *The Three Northern Love Stories* was to be added to the standard publication agreement between Longmans and the Estate (Smith Arch.).

Kelk writes again on 4 Jan. 1901, including a new specimen page nearer the right size and style, to make this book uniform with *The Sundering Flood*. A letter from Ballantyne Press to Cockerell, dated 5 Apr. 1901, asks for return of proof sheets R & S, of *Three Northern Love Stories*, which was obviously being printed at the time. Cockerell inserts a note at the end to his fellow trustee, Robert Proctor, to whom the message is obviously being forwarded, a note that makes it clear that the two of them are engaged in proofreading this new edn. (Smith Arch.).
Cost of production (exclusive of binding): £48. 1*s*. 4*d*. (Longmans Arch., H-34, f.31).

A-9.03: Northern Love Stories (Golden 4°)

[aligned left] THREE NORTHERN LOVE STORIES AND OTHER | TALES. TRANSLATED FROM THE ICELANDIC BY EIRIKR MAGNUSSON AND WILLIAM MORRIS.
Edition: 'Golden type quarto edition' [1st impression, 3rd edn.] For previous pbns. of the 1st 2 stories, see this field in A-9.01. Here bound in with *The Volsunga Saga*, this vol., being a collection, is entered in the C-List (see C-13). For details common to the 'Golden type quarto' set, including paper, leaf size, printing, headlines or shoulder notes, endpapers, binding, print run, and price, see A-47.04.
Publication: 9 Nov. 1901 [this colophon date indicates finished printing, issued 20 Nov.] (Longmans Arch.).
Register of Copies Examined: see this field in A-47.04.

A-9.04: Northern Love Stories (*CW* X)

THE COLLECTED WORKS | [title details common to the set, see A-126.01] | VOLUME X | THREE NORTHERN LOVE STORIES | THE TALE OF BEOWULF | [publisher's imprint, see A-126.01] MDCCCCXI

Edition: 'Collected Works edn' [1st impression, 4th edn.] For previous pbn. of the 1st 2 stories in *Three Northern Love Stories*, see this field in A-9.01.

Series: vol. 10 of 24; for series detail, see this field in A-126.01.

Collation: medium 8°: a^8 (a2+1) (a4+1) b^2 B–T^8 [$2 (–B1) signed] 154 leaves pp. [i–vi] vii–xix [xx] [1–2] 3–172 [*Three Northern Love Stories* ends and *Beowulf* begins] [173–4] 175–284 [285–8] [= 308] +2 plates not included in the book's pagination, but here noted in the formula and described in the *Contents* in their appropriate places.

Contents: [of both titles]: p. [i], blank; p. [ii], limitation (see this field in A-126.01); pp. [iii–iv], blank; 1st inserted plate as frontis., a photoengraved reproduction of an original photograph, within blind-stamped compartment, the platemaker's name included, below right: '*Emery Walker, Ph. sc..*' and labelled at the foot in copperplate: *The Burne-Jones and Morris families | Photographed at the Grange in 1874 | by Frederick Hollyer*; p. v, title page; p. [vi], blank; p. vii, headed: CONTENTS | [list completed]; p. [viii], blank; 2nd inserted plate facing p. ix, in blind-stamped compartment, photoengraved reproduction of an original drawing, including, below right, in copperplate, the platemaker's name: *Emery Walker, Ph. sc.*, | [label in copperplate, centred] *One of a series of Angels, | painted on the nave roof of Jesus College Chapel, Cambridge, | from the original cartoon by William Morris belonging to the College*; p. ix: headed: INTRODUCTION | [text begins]; pp. x–xviii, introduction completed; p. xix, headed: BIBLIOGRAPHICAL NOTE | [list of 4 edns. of *Three Northern Love Stories* and 3 edns, 5 issues of *The Tale of Beowulf*; p. [xx], blank; p. [1], 1st half title: THREE NORTHERN LOVE STORIES | AND OTHER TALES TRANSLATED | FROM THE ICELANDIC BY EIRÍKR | MAGNÚSSON AND WILLIAM MORRIS; p. [2], blank; pp. 3–4, headed: PREFACE | [text begins]; p. 5, headed: CHRONOLOGY | THE STORY OF GUNNLAUG | THE WORM-TONGUE | [list of 17 incidents in the story]; p. [6], blank; pp. 7–158, text of 3 stories and 3 tales, each beginning on new pages; pp. 159–72, headed: NOTES | [text begins]; p. [173], 2nd half title: THE TALE OF BEOWULF SOMETIME | KING OF THE FOLK OF THE WEDER | GEATS. TRANSLATED BY WILLIAM | MORRIS AND A. J. WYATT; p. [174], blank; p. 175, headed: THE ARGUMENT; pp. 176–8, Argument completed; p. 179, headed: THE STORY OF BEOWULF | [text begins]; pp. 180–274, text completed; p. 275, headed: PERSONS AND PLACES | [list begins]; pp. 276–82, list completed; p. 283, headed: THE MEANING OF SOME WORDS | NOT COMMONLY USED NOW | [list begins]; p. 284, list completed; p. [285], blank; p. [286], printer's imprint (see this field, A-126.01); pp. [287–8], blank.

Technical Notes: paper, printing, type, position (but not content) of headlines, running titles, shoulder notes, pagination, signatures, end-papers, and binding are all common to the series and are described in this field in A-126.01, the entry for the set, treated as a single work. Included here are only those details that are specific to this particular vol.; *shoulder notes*: used within narratives, with titles of the relevant stories on versos and chapter titles on rectos; same 12-point type, starting at the top margin outside the outer margin; *Beowulf* has both shoulder titles, all rectos and versos except headed pages: Beowulf; and in smaller type, marginal notes referring to the text adjacent; *spine label*: the 1st five lines are common to the set (see A-126.01): THREE | NORTHERN | LOVE STORIES | BEOWULF

Publication: 1911 [issued 12 Dec.] (Longmans Arch.); for *print run* and *price*, see A-126.01.

Register of Copies Examined: see this field in A-126.01.

A-10.01:* England and the Turks

ENGLAND AND THE TURKS. | [thin rule] | *To the Editor of* THE DAILY NEWS.

Edition: [1st impression, 1st edn.] A new-set but unchanged text from that 1st pbd. as a letter to *The Daily News* (see D-33), except for the addition of Morris's address and the date: '26 Queen Square, Bloomsbury, Oct. 24'. The letter is signed, 'William Morris, Author of "The Earthly Paradise"'. Though noted by Forman as a 'letter to the Editor', this separately printed version is not in HBF, and Forman errs in the order of pbn., placing the 1st pbn. in *The Daily News* after the 1st edn. of *Sigurd the Volsung*. Forman does not cite this separate edn. as a pamphlet, but he calls it by the heading used for the separate version. It was later reprinted in MM, ii. 483–5. A leaflet, the heading appears to have originated with the pbd. leaflet described here. According to Graham Pollard, the only copy in leaflet form so far located was in Forman's collection (see *A Catalogue of Books and Pamphlets from the library of Maurice Buxton Forman, with an introduction by Graham Pol-

lard: Cat. No. 926, 15; hereafter referred to as *Quaritch Catalogue*).
Publisher: [The Eastern Question Association (?)].
Printer: [no imprint].
Collation: s. sh. folded to form a pair of 8° leaves; printed on all 4 pages, pp. [1] 2–4.
Contents: p. [1], dropped head title, text begins; pp. 2–4, text completed with signature, indented several spaces from the right margin: WILLIAM MORRIS, | Author of 'The Earthly Paradise' | [indented from the left margin] 26 Queen Square, Bloomsbury, Oct. 24.
Technical Notes: *paper*: white machine-made with dandy roll laid lines; no watermark; *leaf size*: 185 x 124 mm.; *printing*: *lines-to-page*: thin leaded, 40 lines.
Publication: 28 Oct. 1876. 24 Oct. is the date of Morris's letter; its pbn. as a separate issue was probably a day or two after the 1st appearance in *The Daily News*, which was on 26 Oct. 1876 (See *Quaritch Catalogue*, p. 15); *print run*: unknown; *price*: apparently printed for free distribution.
Register of Copies Located: *a copy was among the Maurice Buxton Forman books in the Quaritch sale of 1973 (see *Quaritch Catalogue*, p. 15). Its present whereabouts is not listed in the usual sources; *another copy is at the Humanities Research Centre, TxU (PR 5080 / E53 / HRC) (see *NUC*, vol. 396, p. 142).
Notes: This leaflet is described by Graham Pollard in his notes in the *Quaritch Catalogue*:

> [MORRIS (W.)]. England and the Turks. To the Editors of The Daily News. 1 sheet, 8vo, FIRST EDITION; folded into 4 pp., with a small ink spot in one margin; unbound, as issued. [1876].
>
> This is the first separate edition of William Morris's first public political pronouncement. It was printed in the *Daily News* on 28 [actually 26] October, 1876. This edn. was unknown to H. B. Forman when compiling *The Books of William Morris* in 1897, although he notes the *Daily News* appearance of the text on pp. 93 and 214.
>
> Both acknowledge the Daily News version but make no mention of the leaflet. 'We have been unable to find a record of any other copy. This one was found loosely inserted in M. B. Forman's copy of his father's bibliography of Morris and it has his reference to p. 93 written on it in pencil. (*Quaritch Catalogue*, 15).

The description of the leaflet provided here is based on photocopies of the Forman original referred to by Pollard. It seems likely that this separate edn. of Morris's letter was printed for distribution at one of a number of demonstrations organised at this time by The Eastern Question Association against the threatened war with Russia. One such meeting is referred to by Morris in the text of his letter to the editor.

A-11.01: The Æneids

THE | ÆNEIDS OF VIRGIL | DONE INTO ENGLISH VERSE | BY | WILLIAM MORRIS, | AUTHOR OF 'THE EARTHLY PARADISE.' | LONDON: | ELLIS AND WHITE, NEW BOND STREET. | MDCCCLXXVI.
Edition: [1st issue, 1st impression, 1st edn.] With 25 LP copies demy 8° in 2 vols.
Collation: square cr. 8°: [A]² B–2B⁸ 194 leaves pp. [4] [1] 2–382 [383–4] [= 388].
Contents: p. [1], half title; p. [2], blank; p. [3], title page; p. [4], printer's imprint: LONDON: | Printed by JOHN STRANGEWAYS, | Castle St. Leicester Sq.; p. [1], 1st chapter headtitle: THE ÆNEIDS | OF | VIRGIL. | BOOK I. | ARGUMENT. | [2-line summary, all small caps] | [text]; pp. 2–381, text, divided into 12 books; p. 382, text ends with explicit: THE END | LONDON: | Printed by John Strangeways, Castle St. Leicester Sq.; pp. [383–4], blank.
Technical Notes: *paper*: cream-white machine-laid, with dandy roll laid lines, no watermark; the LP copies are on Whatmans handmade; *leaf size*: ordinary copies: untrimmed, avg. 199 x 141 mm.; *printing*: *type area*: 130 x 102 mm.; *running titles*: all versos: THE ÆNEIDS OF VIRGIL. | [all rectos] BOOK I [II–X]; line numbers by tens within right-hand margins; *end-papers*: 1 free end and paste-down, plain white and blank, front and back; *binding*: plain unblocked red or dark green cloth; *spine*: printed paper label, printed within a thin-rule compartment: THE | ÆNEIDS | OF | VIRGIL. | [thin rule] | W. MORRIS | 14s.; 25 LP copies, demy 8°, in 2 vols. with continuous pagination and bound in grey paper-covered boards with white parchment spine and printed spine labels similar to the ordinary copies but omitting the price and adding after the title: Books I–VI [VII–XII]; this is also added to the specially printed LP title pages.
Publication: 1876 [issued 4 Nov. 1875] (Letter from Morris to Murray, see *Notes*, below); see also *Pub. Circ.*, 38/916 (16 Nov. 1875), 937, which says 1–15 Nov. May Morris appears to accept as the date of issue Forman's comment that he had his copy 'before the month [of October] was out', but the other evidence supporting the later date suggests that Forman's must have been an advance copy (see HBF, p. 83; *CW*, XI. xxxi); *print run*: 1,000 copies and 25 LP copies (HBF, p. 84); *price*: 14s.

Register of Copies Examined: LeM (2 copies: base copy); MU (2 vol. LP copy: Spec.Coll. Pr 5081/V4 / A4 1876); VU; VPar; BL: (two copies: 2280.aa.16. & 2-vol. LP copy: Ashley 3685).

Notes: Morris to Charles Fairfax Murray, 11 Mar. 1875: 'As to my illumination work it don't get on just now, not because I shouldn't like to be at it, but because I am doing something else with Virgil, to wit, doing him into English verse: I have got toward the end of the 7th book, & shall finish the whole thing & have it out by the beginning of June I hope. I shall keep you a big paper copy both of that & my new vol of Icelandic stories & of the new edition of Guenevere' (*Letters*, i. 246).

Morris to Charles Fairfax Murray, 27 May 1875: 'I have somewhat slacked from the Virgil translations, as I found it not possible to get it out this summer, & easy enough to get it out by October' (*Letters*, i. 254).

Morris to C. F. Murray, dated 'Nov. 4th' [1875]: 'the Virgil translation published today & [the] big-paper awaiting you' (*Letters*, i. 274).

Later issues and impressions of this edn.:
1. Ellis: 1876 [issued 1–14 Feb.]: Second Edition. [2nd issue of the 1st edn.]; *print run*: not known; *price*: 14*s*.;
2. R and T: 1889: Second Edition. [3rd or 4th issue, 1st by R and T, 1st edn.]; *print run*: from copies remaining; *price*: 14*s*.;
3. Longmans: 1896 [issued 18–25 July] Second Edition. 'Cheaper Library Edition.', PW, [4th or 5th issue, 1st Longmans, 1st edn.]; *print run*: from copies remaining; *price*: 6*s*.

A-11.02: The Æneids (imported shts. RB)

Title as in the previous entry except for the substitution of the RB imprint: BOSTON: | ROBERTS, [*sic*] BROTHERS | MDCCCLXXVI

Edition: [2nd issue, 1st American, 1st impression, 1st edn.] Made from imported English sheets with the Roberts Brothers imprint and an American binding. Since this impression duplicates A-11.01, only altered fields are included here.

Contents: as for A-11.01, except for the alteration of the publisher's imprint, as above. Note superfluous comma after 'Roberts' in the publisher's imprint (NNBerg copy). The same error is made elsewhere (eg. vol. 1 of the imported sheets of *EP*, 1868) but only where sheets are imported, when the Boston firm's imprint was probably set and imposed in England. The printer's imprint, pp. [4] and 382 (in 2 lines) remains the same: LONDON: | PRINTED BY JOHN STRANGEWAYS, | Castle St. Leicester Sq.

Technical Notes: *leaf size*: 192 x 142 mm.; *binding*: American: reddish-brown or green cloth-covered boards with chamfered edges; blind-stamped floral rules between black bands with gilt-stamped thin rules above and below each border, top and bottom, front and spine; *spine*: gilt-stamped: THE | ÆNEIDS | OF | VIRGIL | [thin rule] | WILLIAM MORRIS | ROBERTS BRO'S | BOSTON; back plain and unblocked; for further details of paper, type, printing, see this field in the record for the 1st impression, 1st edn. (A-11.01).

Publication: 1876 [issued 11 Dec. 1875] (*Pub. Weekly*, 8/204 (11 Dec. 1875), 917); *print run*: an undetermined number of imported English copies, in shts., from the Ellis 1st printing of 1,000; *price*: $3.50.

Register of Copies Examined: BGR (base copy); NNBerg; CaBVaU.

A-11.03: The Æneids (RB)

THE | ÆNEIDS OF VIRGIL | DONE INTO ENGLISH VERSE | BY | WILLIAM MORRIS, | AUTHOR OF 'THE EARTHLY PARADISE.' | BOSTON: | ROBERTS BROTHERS. | 1876.

Edition: Author's Edition. From the 2nd London Edition. 'Cheaper Edition' [1st impression, 2nd edn., 1st American]

Collation: medium square 8°: [1]⁸ 2–21⁸ 22² [$1 (–7 18) signed] 170 leaves pp. [1–5] 6–338 [339–40] [= 340].

Contents: pp. [1–2], blank; p. [3], title page; p. [4]: [RB Aldine mark of boy on globe] | AUTHOR'S EDITION, FROM THE SECOND LONDON EDITION. | Cambridge: | Press of John Wilson and Son.; p. [5], 1st chapter, headed: THE ÆNEIDS OF VIRGIL. | [thin rule] | BOOK I. | ARGUMENT. | [2-line summary of the chapter] | [text begins]; pp. 6–338, text completed with explicit: THE END.; pp. [339–40], blank.

Technical Notes: *paper*: cream-white machine-made with dandy roll laid lines; *leaf size*: trimmed, 192 x 135 mm.; *printing*: lines numbered by 10s at the right-hand margins; *binding*: full russia lthr. with raised bands this copy.

Publication: 1876 [to be issued 15 Mar.] (*Pub. Weekly*, 9/217 (11 Mar. 1876), 339); *print run*: 1,100 copies (Roberts Arch.); *price*: $2.50.

Register of Copies Examined: BGR (base copy); CaBVaU.

Notes: 'List of Books Just Published', *Pub. Weekly*, 9/218 (18 Mar. 1876) refers to Morris's *Virgil* as 'Cheaper Ed. Sq. 12° $2.50'.

From RB Ledger Book: *Æneid* plates 'Sold to Longmans, Green & Co. 5/24/99'.

Later impressions of this edn.:
1. RB: 1896 [issued 25 Mar.]: Author's Edition [2nd impression, 2nd edn., 1st American]; *print run*: 280 copies; *price*: $2.50;
2. Longmans, NY: 1904: New Impression. Author's Edition, from the Second London Edition [3rd impression, 2nd edn., 1st American]; *print run*: unknown; *price*: $2.00.

A-11.04: The Æneids (PW)

THE ÆNEIDS OF VIRGIL | DONE INTO ENGLISH VERSE | BY | WILLIAM MORRIS | AUTHOR OF 'THE EARTHLY PARADISE' | *THIRD IMPRESSION* | LONGMANS, GREEN, AND CO. | 39 PATERNOSTER ROW, LONDON | NEW YORK AND BOMBAY | 1900 | All rights reserved.

Edition: [1st impression, 3rd edn., 2nd English].
Series: The Poetical Works of William Morris (PW). The series is indicated only on the printed paper spine label; one of a uniform set of 10 unnumbered vols. all issued in 1896 when Longmans became Morris's publisher; in 1898 the set increased to 11 vols. with the addition of *The Tale of Beowulf*. In 1900 *The Æneids* is reset; for further series details, see this field in A-4.16.
Collation: imperial 8°: [A]² B–2B⁸ 194 leaves pp. [4] [1] 2–382 [383–4] [= 388].
Contents: p. [*1*], half title; p. [*2*], blank; p. [*3*], title page; p. [*4*], blank; p. [*1*], 1st chapter head: [dropped head] THE ÆNEIDS | OF | VIRGIL. | BOOK I. | ARGUMENT. | [2 lines of prose summary] | [2 couplets printed in italics] | [text begins]; pp. 2–382, text completed with explicit: THE END. | [printer's imprint] Printed by Ballantyne, Hanson & Co. | Edinburgh & London.; pp. [283–4], blank.
Technical Notes: cream-white machine-made 'Antique Wove' (Longmans Arch.), with dandy roll laid lines, no watermark; *leaf size*: this copy trimmed and all edges gilt, 192 x 135 mm.; *printing*: *line count*: by 10s, at the right hand margins. Neither the binding, nor end-papers, nor leaf size of this copy is as the original binding. The special binding on this copy has vellum covers over boards, gold-stamped and all edges trimmed and gilt. The edition binding for the PW series, with which this vol. was designed to range, has a plain, unblocked dark green or black cloth binding and a printed paper spine label (for detail, see A-4.16).
Publication: 1900 [issued 21 Apr.] (Longmans Arch.); *print run*: 750 copies (Longmans Arch.); *price*: 5*s.* net and $2.00 (Longmans Accts.).
Register of Copies Examined: BGR (base copy, London imprint); NN; New York imprint: not seen.

Notes: C. J. Longman to S. C. Cockerell, 17 Jan. 1900:— Proposes, since stocks are running low, to reset and make stereos of *The Æneids*, there being no stereos from the previous edn., created 25 years before. The new edn. is being reset in order to keep the PW complete, and Longman asks Cockerell for any corrections he might wish to make of the previous (English) edn., to be used as copy text (Smith Arch.).

A-11.05: The Æneids (Golden 4°)

[aligned left] THE AENEIDS OF VIRGIL DONE INTO ENGLISH | VERSE BY WILLIAM MORRIS.

Edition: 'Golden type quarto edition' [1st impression, 4th edn., 3rd English].
Collaborators, Editors, and Illustrators: [edited by S. C. Cockerell and Robert Proctor, though their contribution is recorded nowhere in the books of this set].
Series: 'Golden type quarto edition', 6th vol., unnumbered, in the 8-vol. Golden type quarto series. For further series detail see this field, *Technical Notes*, and *Notes* in A-47.04.
Colophon: Here end the Aeneids of Virgil, done into English verse by William | Morris. First printed in 1876, and now reprinted at the Chiswick Press with | the Golden type designed by William Morris for the Kelmscott Press, and | finished on the twenty-fourth day of February, 1902. Published by Long- | mans, Green and Co. of London, New York and Bombay.
Collation: 4°: [a]² b–2h⁴ 122 leaves pp. [i–ii] iii [iv] 1–238 [239–40] [= 244].
Contents: p. [i], top, flush left, half title, which also serves as the title page; p. [ii], blank; p. iii, [top, flush left] CONTENTS. | [12 Books and their titles, as a list]; p. [iv], blank; p. 1, 1st chapter head title, printed from the top, in red, flush left, the general title as on the title page and Virgil's 4-line verse statement of his poetic progress from lyric through the Bucolics and to his present epic theme, followed by the section title: BOOK I. AENEAS & HIS TROJANS BEING DRIVEN | TO LIBYA BY A TEMPEST HAVE GOOD WELCOME | OF DIDO, QUEEN OF CARTHAGE.; the text, in black, follows, with the first 2 words all caps: I SING; pp. 2–238, text completed with colophon (see above); pp. [239–40], blank.
Technical Notes: paper, printing (including colour), type, position (but not content) of shoulder notes, page numbers, end-papers, binding, print run, and price are all common to the series and are described in this field in A-47.04, the record of the 1st book pbd. in the series. Included here are only those details that are specific to this edn.. *printing*:

shoulder notes: outside the outside margin of the 1st line on all rectos (except p. 1) and versos, in red: The Aeneids | of Virgil | Book i [–xii]; *binding*: *spine label*: WILLIAM | MORRIS | THE | AENEIDS | OF | VIRGIL
Publication: 24 Feb. 1902 [finished printing, issued 28 Apr.] (Chiswick Arch.). The Longmans Arch. says 21 Apr.; *print run* and *price*: see this field in A-47.04.
Register of Copies Examined: see this field in A-47.04.

A-11.06: The Æneids (*CW* XI)

THE COLLECTED WORKS | [title details common to the set, see A-126.01] | VOLUME XI | THE ÆNEIDS OF VIRGIL | [publishers imprint, see A-126.01] | MDCCCCXI
Edition: 'Collected Works edition' [1st impression, 5th edn., 4th English].
Series: vol. 11 of 24.
Collation: medium 8°: a⁸ (a3+1) b⁸ (b4+1) (b6+1) B–T⁸ [$2 signed (B2 and D2 read 2B and 2D)] 160 leaves pp. [i–viii] ix–xxxi [xxxii] [1] 2–286 [287–8] [= 320] +3 inserted plates not noted in the book's pagination, but described here in the *Contents* in their appropriate places.
Contents: pp. [i–iii], blank; p. [iv], limitation notice: see this field in A-126.01; pp. [v–vi], blank; 1st inserted plate as frontis., within blind-stamped compartment and facing p. [vii], recto blank, a photo reproduction of an original drawing, initials, below left, of the artist: E. B-J 1873 | [and of the plate maker, below right] E. W. Ph. sc.; labelled: IRIS AND TURNUS | IRIM DE CAELO MISIT SATURNIA JUNO | AUDACEM AD TURNUM . . . . AEN. LIB IX. 2–3 (May Morris says, p. [x], that this illustration was intended for Morris's calligraphic MS book of Virgil in the original Latin); p. [vii], title page; p. [viii], blank; p. ix, section heading: CONTENTS; p. x, Contents completed; p. xi, headed: INTRODUCTION | [text begins]; pp. xii–xxiv, text continues; 2nd inserted plate, facing p. xxv, in blind-stamped compartment, photo reproduction of another original drawing meant to illustrate the MS book of Virgil's *Æneid* and labelled: AENEAS AND THE HARPIES | AT SUBITAE HORRIFICO LAPSU DE MONTIBUS ADSUNT | HARPYIAE . . . . AEN. LIB. III. 225–226; pp. xxv–xxviii, 'Introduction' continues; 3rd inserted plate, facing p. xxviii, photographic colour reproduction within a blind-stamped compartment, of a page from Morris's calligraphic MS book of Horace's *Odes*, labelled below: Q. HORATII FLACCI, LIB. I, CAR. XXVI–XXVII | FROM THE VOLUME WRITTEN AND ILLUMINATED BY WILLIAM MORRIS; p. xxix, Introduction ends; p. [xxx], blank; p. xxxi: [flush left] BIBLIOGRAPHICAL NOTE TO THE ÆNEIDS OF | VIRGIL [note that the 5th line contains an error: the 1900 issue of Morris's translation is a new edition, see A-11.04]; p. [xxxii], blank; p. [1], 1st chapter head title: THE ÆNEIDS OF VIRGIL | BOOK I | THE ARGUMENT | [3 lines of prose] | [in italics, Virgil's 4-line verse account of his poetic progress from his early lyrics, through the Bucolics, to his present epic theme] | [text begins]; pp. 2–286, text completed; p. [287], blank; p. [288], printer's imprint: see this field in A-126.01.
Technical Notes: paper, printing, type, position (but not content) of headlines, running titles, shoulder notes, page numbers, end-papers, and binding are all common to the series and are described in this field in A-126.01, the entry for the *CW* as itself a separate publication. Included here are only those details that are specific to this particular issue; *printing*: *running titles*: all versos: THE AENEIDS OF VIRGIL | all rectos: BOOK I [–XII]; lines numbered by 10s outside the outer margins; *spine label*: [4 lines common to the set] | VOLUME XI | THE ÆNEIDS | OF VIRGIL
Publication: 1911 [issued 12 Dec.] (Longmans Arch.); *print run* and *price*: see A-126.01.
Register of Copies Examined: see this field in A-126.01.

A-12.01: Sigurd the Volsung

THE STORY | OF | SIGURD THE VOLSUNG | AND THE | FALL OF THE NIBLUNGS. | BY | WILLIAM MORRIS, | AUTHOR OF 'THE EARTHLY PARADISE.' | LONDON: ELLIS AND WHITE, NEW BOND STREET. | MDCCCXXVII
Edition: [1st impression, 1st edn.] With 25 LP copies on Whatman paper.
Collation: sq. cr. 8° (Imperial 16°): [A]⁴ B–2B⁸ 2C⁴ 200 leaves pp. [i–v] vi–vii [viii] [1] 2–392 [= 400].
Contents: p. [i], half title; p. [ii], blank; p. [iii], title page; p. [iv], imprint: LONDON: | PRINTED BY JOHN STRANGEWAYS, | Castle St. Leicester Sq.; pp. [v], dropped heading: CONTENTS. | [thin rule] | BOOK I. | SIGMUND. | [list of chapter titles divided into 4 Books with page numbers begins]; pp. vi–vii, 'Contents' concluded; p. [viii], blank; pp. [1]–77, Book I, headed: THE STORY | OF | SIGURD THE VOLSUNG | AND THE | FALL OF THE NIBLUNGS. | BOOK I. | SIGMUND. | [the argument of this Book, 3 lines in caps formatted as hanging indent] | [1-line chapter title in italics] | [text begins]; pp. 78–167,

headed: BOOK II. REGIN. | [text begins]; pp. 168–313, headed: BOOK III. BRYNHILD. | [text begins]; pp. 314–91: BOOK IV. GUDRUN. | [text begins]; p. 392, text completed with explicit: THE END. | [thin rule] | [printer's imprint, duplicates p. [iv].]

Technical Notes: *paper*: cream machine-laid, with dandy roll laid lines, no watermark; *leaf size*: lightly trimmed, avg. 197 x 143 mm.; *printing*: *type area*: 123 x 110 mm., excluding head and direction lines; *lines-to-page*: leaded, 29 lines general maximum, but variable spaces between verse paragraphs; *headlines*: *running titles*: all versos: THE STORY OF SIGURD THE VOLSUNG. | all rectos: BOOK I. SIGMUND.; [etc., for each of the 4 books, except errors, pp. 165, 167, which have BOOK III instead of BOOK II]; *end-papers*: 1 free end and paste-down, plain white and blank, front and back; *binding*: plain dark blue unblocked cloth; *spine*: printed label: [within thin-rule compartment] THE STORY | OF | SIGURD | THE VOLSUNG | AND | THE FALL OF THE | NIBLUNGS. | [thin rule] | W. MORRIS. | [below compartment] 12*s*.

Publication: 1877 [issued 16–30 Nov. 1876] (*Pub. Circ.*, 39/941 (8 Dec. 1876), 973); pbd. 'by the 20th of November 1876' (HBF, p. 87); *print run*: 2,500 copies (HBF, p. 88) of which 1,000 copies were exported to Roberts Brothers of Boston (see the next entry); *price*: 12*s*.

Register of Copies Examined: LeM (base copy); BGR; VPar; VU; VSL; BL (3 copies: 2292.e.24; Ashley 3686, (1877) "crown octavo", Presentation copy to Swinburne; and LP copy: Ashley 3687 (1877).

Notes: Morris's epic version of *Sigurd the Volsung*, written in eighteen months from mid-1875, while he was mastering the art of dyeing, 'he himself regarded as his highest achievement in literature' (Mackail, i. 311). But the public reception of his book did not match his own estimate of it. There were 2,500 copies of the 1st edn., of which 1,000 were exported in sheets to Roberts Brothers of Boston who issued them in American bindings before Christmas in the same year.

In England the 1st edn. was priced at a rather expensive 12*s*., and despite the 1,000 copies exported, stocks were not exhausted until 1887, by which time 10 years had passed as well as 3 issues from the original impression stock. But, as Morris said in a letter, though the book 'did not sell well', he did not want to see what he thought of as his most important poem fall out of print, unknown and unread. So the 'Fourth Edition' (actually the 2nd, but called the 'Fourth' in sequence with the 3 previous issues) was produced by Morris's new publisher, Reeves and Turner (R

Figure 22. A-12.01: Sigurd (1st edn.) title page

and T), in 1887. Its price was half that of the 1st edn., and the number of pages was reduced by 47, as was the 2nd edn., 1st American, by the usual process of compressions that occurs with a 2nd edn. as well as by using slightly larger paper and reducing the leading between lines.

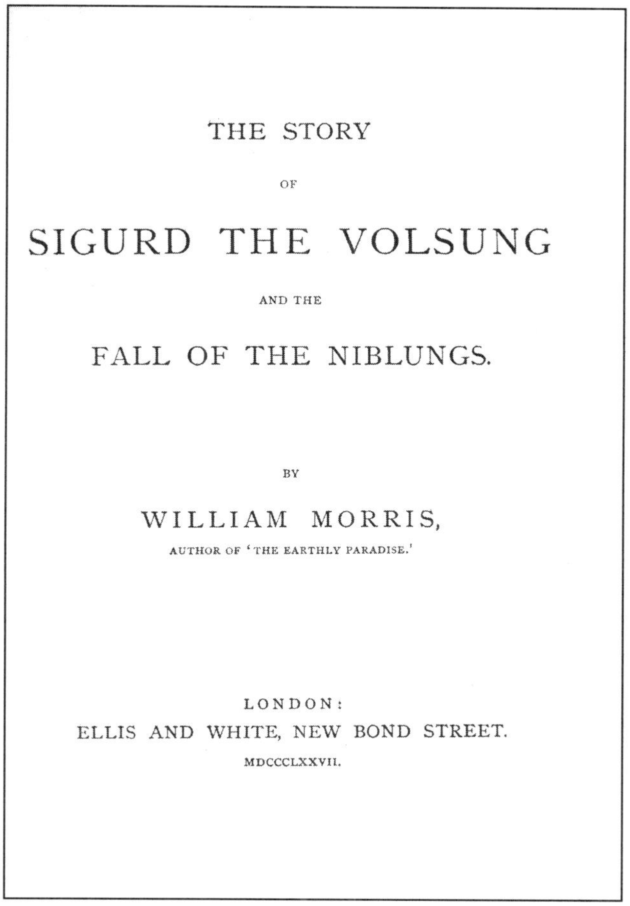

As the frequent later impressions and edns. listed here, and below, show, after its early issues *Sigurd the Volsung* gradually improved its reputation both in England and America and with both the critics and the general audience, which may have needed more time to see the glories of the literature of the North and Morris's response to them.

Later issues of this edn.: Ellis and White:
1. 1877 [issued 1–15 Mar.]: SECOND EDITION [3rd issue, 2nd English, 1st impression, 1st edn.]; *print run*: from stock remaining; *price*: 12*s*.;
2. 1880: THIRD EDITION [4th issue, 3rd English, 1st impression, 1st edn.]; *print run*: from stock remaining; *price*: 12*s*.

A-12.02: Sigurd the Volsung (RB)

THE STORY | OF | SIGURD THE VOLSUNG | AND THE | FALL OF THE NIBLUNGS. | BY | WILLIAM MORRIS, | AUTHOR OF 'THE EARTHLY PARADISE.' | BOSTON: | ROBERTS BROTHERS. | 1877.

Edition: [2nd issue, 1st American, 1st edn.] From English sheets imported by RB and supplied by Ellis and White. Since this issue largely duplicates the 1st English issue (see A-12.01), only fields special to this issue are included here.
Contents: repeats A-12.01, except for the publisher's imprint on the title page.
Technical Notes: as in A-12.01, except: *leaf size*: trimmed, 204 x 142 mm.; *binding*: plain unblocked dark green cloth with champfered edges, front and back; *spine*: gilt-stamped with ornamental border of alternating ovals and dots within thin rules at head and foot, title, author and publisher stamped across the spine: SIGURD | THE | VOLSUNG | [3 groups of 3 short gilt thin rules] | BY | [swash first letter] WILLIAM MORRIS | [gilt fleur-de-lis] | BOSTON | ROBERTS BROTHERS
Publication: 1877; *print run*: 1,000 copies imported from England, given an American binding and an RB imprint; *price*: $3.00 (RB Cost Book D and *Pub. Weekly*, 9/258 (23 Dec. 1876), 1028).
Register of Copies Examined: SSL (base copy: S821/M8773.22); VSL (S821.85S); VPar; NN; SU (R (Q) + 821.85 / M877st).

A-12.03: Sigurd the Volsung (RB)

THE STORY | OF | SIGURD THE VOLSUNG | AND THE | FALL OF THE NIBLUNGS. | BY | WILLIAM MORRIS, | AUTHOR OF "THE EARTHLY PARADISE," "THE LIFE AND DEATH OF JASON," | "THE ÆNEIDS OF VIRGIL," (TRANSLATED.) | BOSTON: | ROBERTS BROTHERS. | 1879.

Edition: '6-quire edition' [1st impression, 2nd edn., 1st American].
Printer: there is no printer's imprint in any issues of this American edn., but the Cost Book lists for this edn., 'T. Monay stereo' with a price ($304.81) that, comparisons suggest, must include setting the type and making stereos, but not printing the book. The stereos were later (4 May 1899) sold by Little, Brown, & Co. to Longmans, Green and Co. NY. *Pub. Weekly* says the 'new edition' comes from 'Wilson's press', but that is probably an error. There being no printer's imprint suggests that John Wilson, who regularly included an imprint, was not used on this occasion. The fact that Monay was used rather than either John Wilson and Son or Welch, Bigelow and Co., till then the main stereo makers and printers of most of Roberts' Morris books, may be related to a coincidence: Wilson was just then engaged in buying out Welch, Bigelow & Co. and their University Press. Wilson announced the takeover in a full-page letter, dated 15 Apr. 1879, complete with a picture of the imposing four-story building which housed the University Press at Cambridge, Mass. (see *Pub. Weekly*, 16/399–400 (Sept. 1879), 326).
Collation: 8°: [1]–22⁸ [$4 signed] 176 leaves [pagination of the book errs in inferred numbers by including in the numbering an extra end paper at the beginning, made of machine-wove paper different from the machine-laid paper used in the body] pp. [i–v] vi–vii [viii]; this should be: [i–iii] iv–v [vi] [1] 2–345 [346] [= 352].
Contents: pp. [i–ii], blank; p. [iii], title page; p. [iv], blank; p. [v], Contents begin; pp. vi–vii, Contents completed; p. [viii], blank; p. [1], head title and text begins; pp. 2–345, text completed with explicit: THE END; p. [346], blank.
Technical Notes: *paper*: cream-white machine-made, no watermark; *leaf size*: 193 x 143 mm.; *printing*: *type area*: 145 x 107 mm.; *lines-to-page*: leaded, 33 lines, not including blanks between verse paragraphs; *headlines*: [all versos] THE STORY OF SIGURD THE VOLSUNG. | [all rectos] BOOK [+ roman book number + relevant book title]; *pagination*: roman numerals at the outer margin of the headline; *end-papers*: 2 free ends, front and back with dark green or brown matt paste-downs and facing free ends, both blank, 2nd free end plain white and blank both sides; *binding*: t.e.g., plain unblocked dark green cloth front and back, with chamfered edges; *spine*: gilt-stamped: [an ornamental border consisting of alternating ovals and lines of 3 vertical dots, between thin rules] | [horizontal title]: SIGURD | THE | VOLSUNG | [ornamental rule] | BY | [swash small caps] WILLIAM MORRIS | [gothic] Boston | [plain type] ROBERTS BROTHERS.
Publication: 1879 [issued 11–17 May] (*Pub. Weekly*, 15/383 (17 May 1879), 553); *print run*: 282 copies (Longmans Arch.); *price*: $2.50.
Register of Copies Examined: CSt (base copy: Spec.Coll. Felton PR5077.Al); BGR.
Notes: The 1000 imported sets of Roberts American issue of the 1st edn. sheets were exhausted by early 1879, having slowly sold out over the previous 2 years. The publisher therefore planned an American setting of the poem. It was probably Thomas Niles, managing director of RB, who thought that a preface or introduction by Morris would

make the new edn. more attractive, perhaps by familiarising the reader with his largely unknown Icelandic sources as he had in the case of his translation of *The Story of the Volsungs and the Niblungs*. Morris's response to Niles' request that he add this new preface to the American edition is dated 4 Mar. 1879. It is one of the very rare direct contacts he had with Roberts Brothers:

> Thanks for your note. I should be happy to write a preface if I thought it would improve the book, but on the contrary I think it would rather *flatten* the whole thing: you have always Mr. Magnusson & my translation of the Icelandic originals to refer to; & the German Nibelungun Noth is well known & has been translated more than once. Of course I should be glad to correct any mistakes that could be pointed out to me: I do not *remember* any at present. (see *Letters*, i. 504).

Later impressions of this edn.:

1. RB: 1881 [issued Apr.–May]: '6-quire Edition' [2nd impression, 2nd edn., 1st American]; *print run*: 315 copies; *price*: $2.50;

2. RB: 1887 [18 Mar., ordered]: FOURTH EDITION [3rd impression, 2nd edn., 1st American]; *print run*: 280 copies; *price*: $2.50;

3.* RB: 1891 [issued 16 Jan.]: FIFTH EDITION. [4th impression, 2nd edn., 1st American]; *print run*: 500 copies; *price*: $2.50;

4.* Longmans NY: 1896 [issued 26 Mar.]: SIXTH EDITION [5th impression, 2nd edn., 1st American]; *print run*: 280 copies; *price*: $2.50;

5.* Longmans, NY: 1900; [6th impression, 2nd edn., 1st American]; *print run*: 270 copies; *price*: $2.50;

6.* Longmans, NY: 1903 [issued late 1902]: [7th impression, 2nd edn., 1st American]; *print run*: 250 copies; *price*: $2.00;

7. Longmans NY: 1906 [8th impression, 2nd edn., 1st American]; *print run*: unknown; *price*: $2.00;

8.* Longmans NY: 1914: New Impression [9th impression, 2nd edn., 1st American]; *print run*: unknown; *price*: $2.00.

A-12.04: Sigurd the Volsung

THE STORY | OF | SIGURD THE VOLSUNG | AND THE | FALL OF THE NIBLUNGS | BY | WILLIAM MORRIS | AUTHOR OF 'THE EARTHLY PARADISE.' | *FOURTH EDITION.* | LONDON: | REEVES AND TURNER, 196 STRAND. | MDCCCLXXXVII.

Edition: [1st impression, 3rd edn., 2nd English] With 50 LP copies in cr. 4° on Dickinson's hand-made paper; 'The 2500 copies printed ten years before must have served for the second and third editions as well as the first; for this one of the new publishers is called the fourth' (HBF, p. 88). But Forman errs in saying 100 LP copies were printed. See Morris's letter in *Notes*, below, where he specifies 50 LP copies.

Collation: square cr. 8° (imperial 16°): [A]⁴ B–Z⁸ 180 leaves pp. [i–v] vi–vii [viii] [1] 2–345 [346] [1]–6, separately paginated 3 leaves of ads. conjunct with the first 3 leaves of the gathering and hence included in the formula and pagination; [=360].

Contents: p. [i], half title; p. [ii], blank; p. [iii], title page; p. [iv], blank; p. [v], headed: CONTENTS | [list begins]; pp. vi–vii, 'Contents' completed; p. [viii], blank; pp. [1]–345, text completed with explicit: THE END | London: Printed by STRANGEWAYS AND SONS, Tower Street, Cambridge Circus, W.C.; p. [346], blank; separately paginated, but conjunct with the text, pp. [1]–6 ads headed: A SELECTION | FROM | REEVES AND TURNER'S PUBLICATIONS.

Technical Notes: *paper*: as in A-12.01, except the dandy roll chain lines here are horizontal; *leaf size*: untrimmed, avg. 199 x 144 mm.; *binding*: (standard Morris English Style) plain dark red or green unblocked cloth; *spine*: printed label: [in thin-rule compartment] THE STORY | OF | SIGURD | THE VOLSUNG | AND | THE FALL OF THE | NIBLUNGS. | [thin rule] | W. MORRIS. | [below compartment] 6s.; LP copies (according to HBF, p. 88), were printed on 'Dickinson's hand-made paper' in cr. 4°, and were 'half-bound in vellum with cloth sides flowered all over in green and gold, and with printed back-labels reading "THE STORY | OF SIGURD | THE VOLSUNG | AND | THE FALL OF THE | NIBLUNGS. | W. MORRIS."'

Publication: 1887 [issued 1–15 June]; *print run*: unknown; *price*: 6s (*Pub. Circ.*, 50/1194 (16 June 1887), 629).

Register of Copies Examined: LeM (base copy); BGR; NNPM (2109/M; this copy has presentation inscription from Morris to Ellis, dated 29 June 1887).

Notes: Morris to Walter Theodore Watts-Dunton, 16 Dec. 1886: 'Item I am bringing out a cheap Edition of Sigurd 6s/0: since the old one did not sell. That last seems a rash speculation; but I did not want it to be out of print, and that plan seemed the best for getting over the difficulty' (*Letters*, ii. 602–3).

It is clear that by the late 1880's Morris viewed the production of LP copies as a matter of business rather than the production of a few presentation copies for friends and associates. Note, for example, that during his years with

Ellis as his publisher, the standard number of LP copies remained at 25 for each 1st edn.. But the 2-vol. 1st edn. of *The Odyssey*, Apr. and Nov. 1887, was made up entirely of 2-vol. LP versions, the popular edn. not being released until the end of Dec. The direction of Morris's thinking on this matter is evident in his note to Reeves regarding LP copies of this 2nd English edn. of *Sigurd*, 13 June 1887: 'I am very pleased with the large paper Sigurd; I think it would be a pity to sell it too cheap, as I believe you will find no difficulty in getting rid of the 50 copies' (*Letters*, ii. 666).

Later issues and impressions of this edn.:
1. R and T: 1893: FIFTH EDITION. [2nd impression, 3rd edn., 2nd English]; *print run*: unknown; *price*: 6s;
2. Longmans: 1896 [issued 18–25 July]: 'Cheaper Library Edition', 'The Poetical Works' [2nd issue, 2nd impression, 3rd edn., 2nd English]; *print run*: from stock remaining when Longmans took over as Morris's publisher; *price*: 6s.;
3.* 1898 [issued 16 July]: 'The Poetical Works' [3rd impression, 3rd edn., 2nd English]; *print run*: 500 copies; *price*: 5s. net;
4.* 1901 [issued 27 Mar.]: 'The Poetical Works' [4th impression, 3rd edn., 2nd English]; *print run*: 500 copies; *price*: 5s. net;
5. 1904 [issued 9 Apr.]: EIGHTH IMPRESSION 'The Poetical Works' [5th impression, 3rd edn., 2nd English]; *print run*: 1,000 copies; *price*: 5s. net;
6.* 1910 [issued 31 Dec. 1909]: [6th impression, 3rd edn., 2nd English]; *print run*: 1,000 copies; *price*: 5s. net.

A-12.05: Sigurd the Volsung (KP)

THE STORY OF SIGURD THE VOLSUNG AND THE | FALL OF THE NIBLUNGS [printer's leaf ornament No. 1] BY WILLIAM MORRIS

Edition: 'Kelmscott Press Edition.' [1st impression, 4th edn., 3rd English].
Collaborators, Editors, and Illustrators: [the text was seen through the press by S. C. Cockerell].
Series: 50th title, 20th by Morris, pbd. by the KP.
Colophon: Here ends The Story of Sigurd the Volsung and the Fall of the Niblungs, written | by William Morris. With two pictures designed by Edward Burne-Jones and | engraved by W. H. Hooper. It was printed at the Kelmscott Press, Upper Mall, | Hammersmith, and finished on the 19th day of January, 1898. | [¶] Sold by the Trustees of the late William Morris at the Kelmscott Press.
Collation: sm. 2°, in 8s: a⁴ b–o⁸ p² [$4 (–a2–4 g1 k4 p1) signed] 110 leaves pp. [8] [1] 2–207 [208–212] [= 220].
Contents: pp. [1–2], blank; p. [3], title page; p. [4], blank; pp. [5–6], contents, as a list, headed: [top margin, flush left, Chaucer type] A TABLE OF CONTENTS OF THIS BOOK.; p. [7], blank; p. [8], frontis. photolitho plate from a woodcut designed by E. Burne-Jones of the Branstock in Sigurd's hall, uncaptioned; p. 1, 1st chapter head title, text begins; pp. 2–208, text completed; p. [209], 2nd uncaptioned plate from a Burne-Jones design of Gudrun with the brand, setting the hall, Atli, alight; p. [210], colophon (see above); pp. [211–12], blank;
Technical Notes: *paper*: cream-white Batcholor's handmade KP Apple paper with vertical chain lines; *leaf size*: trimmed, 325 x 232 mm.; *printing*: in red and black with red chapter titles and shoulder notes, all rectos and versos; *type area*: varies considerably with the length of Morris lines which are never turned here and hence encroach sometimes on the margins, avg. 217 x 168 mm.; *lines-to-page*: set solid, 48 lines; *type face*: Chaucer type, except Troy type on title page and titles of each book; *shoulder notes*: Book [+ roman number and title]; *pagination*: arabic numbers set 12 mm. inside the outer margins on the direction line; *end-papers*: the standard KP treatment, i.e. 3 free ends and paste-down, plain white and blank, front and back, on the same paper; *binding*: 2 bindings: blue paper-covered boards with holland spines and cream-white limp vellum with dark green silk ties, gilt-stamped up the spine: SIGURD; *ornamentation*: 2 plates from E. Burne-Jones' design; 2 full borders: 33a & 33, both rptd. at the end; 21 part borders; 10 corner ornaments; one 22-line initial; one 14-line initial; three 10-line initials; 38 6-line initials; 151 4-line initials; 684 3-line initials.
Publication: 19 Jan. 1898 [colophon date indicates finished printing, issued 25 Feb.] (Cockerell, p. 170); *print run*: 160 copies on paper, 6 on vellum; *price*: 6gns. paper, 20gns. vellum (Cockerell, p. 170).
Register of Copies Examined: VU (base copy: Bail RB); BL (C. 43. g. 9.); CSt (Z239.2/K29M87ss); MU (RB 43 D).
Notes: there was an earlier abortive KP *Sigurd*, which Temple Scott described in his list of 'Books in the Press': 'the original announcement of "Sigurd" stated that the new edition would have 40 woodcuts designed by Sir E. Burne-Jones. Mr. Morris had intended to make a sumptuous book of this poem, and was engaged in designing new borders for it. Its price was advertised at £12 12s each for the 325 copies on paper, and £52 10s each for the 6 on vellum' (Scott, p. 111).

But this large, fully illustrated version could not be completed by Morris's death in 1896, though 32 copies of 2 folio pages were printed and distributed as keepsakes to

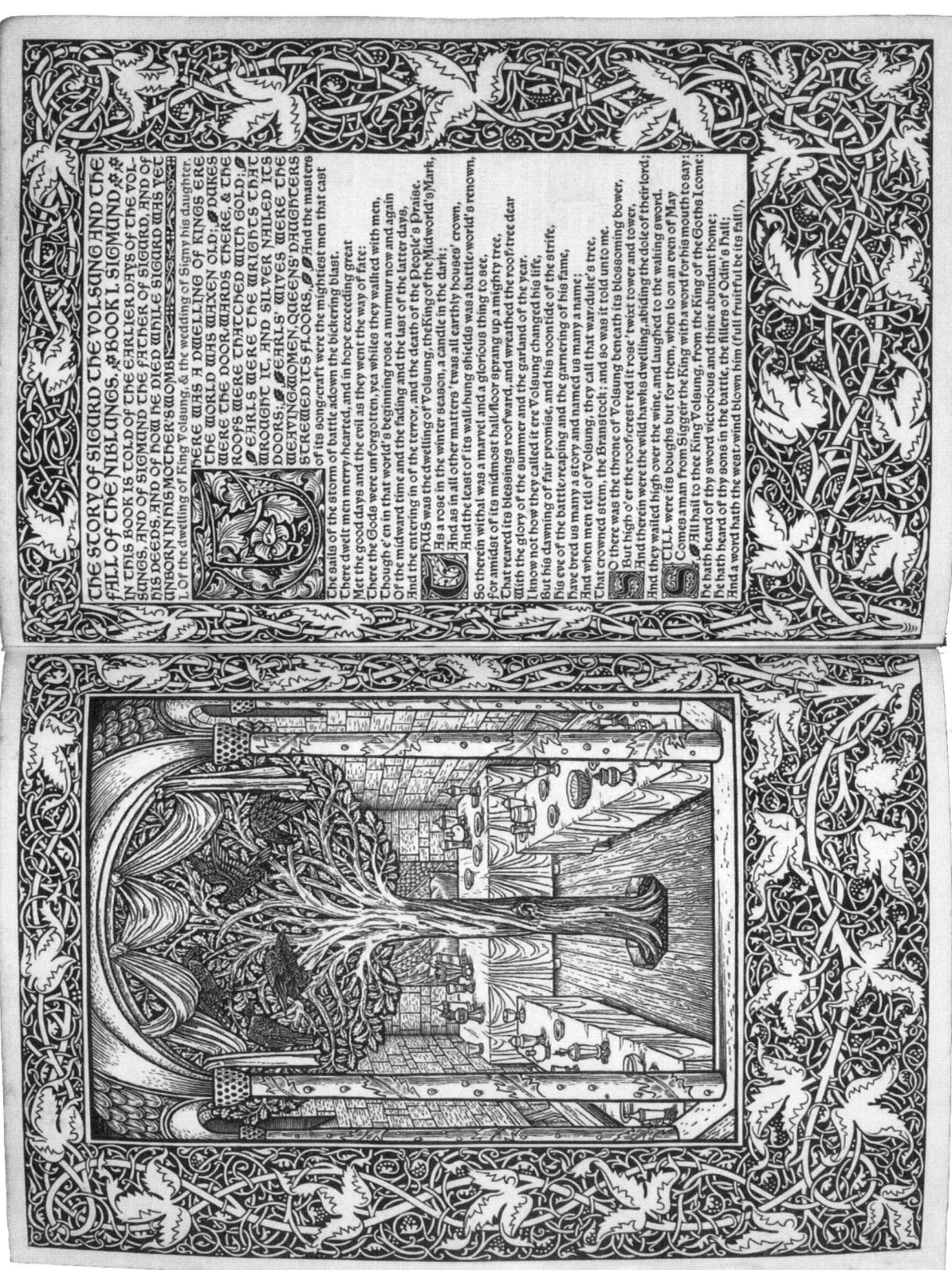

Figure 23. A-12.05: *Sigurd* (KP edn.) opening: frontis. & head title

Morris's friends and associates in Jan. 1897 (see Appendix II-10).

S. C. Cockerell wrote to Robert Proctor, 4 Mar. 1898, to express his satisfaction that the 2nd woodcut in *Sigurd* is to Proctor's liking, as is the book itself, which Cockerell considered among the best of the KP books (Cockerell Papers, BL (Add.) MS 52743).

A-12.06: Sigurd the Volsung (*CW* XII)

THE COLLECTED WORKS | [title details common to the set, see A-126.01] | VOLUME XII | THE STORY OF SIGURD THE VOLSUNG | AND THE FALL OF THE NIBLUNGS | [publisher's imprint, see A-126.01] | MDCCCCXI

Edition: [1st impression, 5th edn., 4th English] Included here are only those details that are specific to this edn.
Series: Vol. 12 of 24; for series detail, see this field in A-126.01.
Printer: See A-126.01.
Collation: medium 8°: a² b⁸ (b1+1) c⁸ B–U⁸ X⁴ [$2 (–a2 b2) signed] 174 leaves pp. [4] [i–iv] v–xxxi [xxxii] [1] 2–306 [307–12] [= 348] +1 inserted plate not counted in the book's pagination, but noted in the formula and described here in the appropriate place in the *Contents*.
Contents: pp. *[1–3]*, blank; p. [4], notice of limitation (see this field in A-126.01); pp. [i–ii], blank; inserted plate as frontis. facing p. [iii], inserted plate, reproduction of a portrait-photograph in a blind-stamped compartment, with the photographer's name, below left: *Abel Lewis, photographer* | [and the plate maker, below right] *Emery Walker Ph. sc.* | [labelled in copperplate, centred] *William Morris | 1880*; p. [iii], title page; p. [iv], blank; pp. v–vi, headed: CONTENTS | [list of 4 books, each with chapters]; pp. vii–xxxi, headed: INTRODUCTION; p. [xxxii], blank; p. 1, 1st chapter head and text begins; pp. 2–306, text completed with explicit: THE END; p. [307], blank; p. 308, printer's imprint (see this field in A-126.01); pp. [309–12], blank.
Technical Notes: paper, printing, type, position (but not content) of headlines, running titles, shoulder notes, endpapers, and binding are all common to the series and are described in this field in A-126.01, the entry for the set, treated as a single work. *Headlines*: *running titles*: [all versos] THE STORY OF SIGURD THE VOLSUNG | [all rectos] BOOK I. [II–IV.] SIGMUND [REGIN, BRYNHILD, GUDRUN]; *binding*: *spine label*: [following 4-line general title of the set] VOLUME XI | SIGURD THE | VOLSUNG.
Publication: 1911 [issued 12 Dec.] (Longmans Arch.); *print run* and *price*: see A-126.01.
Register of Copies Examined: see this field in A-126.01.

A-13.01: SPAB Manifesto

[heading in gothic type] Society for the Protection of Ancient Buildings. | [plain type] OFFICES:—9 BUCKINGHAM STREET, ADELPHI, LONDON, W.C.

Edition: [1st impression, 1st edn.] The text, as a later edn. makes clear, was 'written by Morris and [printed thereafter] without alteration' from the 1st edn., being constantly kept in print by the Society. What is often called the 'Manifesto', 'Principles', or the 'Prospectus' of the SPAB remains exactly the same in each reprint, but naturally there are changes to the attached lists of members of 'The Committee', and the 'Honorary Secretaries', such variations being no doubt one of the reasons for the nearly annual reprints. The records here devoted to this title are intended merely as a sample wherein Morris's contribution remains the same; they obviously do not constitute a complete record of its many impressions and edns. Such manifestoes were pbd. in French and Italian as well as English, but those versions were not always by Morris (see *Notes*, below), and in any case there is no attempt here to list translations of Morris's texts into other languages.
Collation: s. sh., post quarto, folded to form 2 leaves printed on pp. 1–4, pp. [1] 2–3 [4] [= 4] Later edns. sometimes have longer texts, due to the varying number of Committee members and local correspondents, but Morris's text remains the same.
Contents: p. [1], title-heading, see above | [list of names headed in gothic type] Committee. | [double-column list of 22 names, columns separated by a vertical thin rule] | [in gothic type] Honorary Secretary, WILLIAM MORRIS, Esq. | [double thin rule] | [text begins]; pp. 2–3, text of manifesto completed, no rules used; p. [4], blank. In later edns. a list of 'Local Correspondents' was included.
Technical Notes: *paper*: thin moulded, parchment-style, with high onion content; *leaf size*: 210 x 116 mm.; *printing*: *pagination*: arabic numbers in parentheses centred on the headline; no wrapper.
Publication: [issued 18 Apr.–22 May 1877] (see *Notes*, below).
Register of Copies Examined: Fdmn (base copy); NNBerg (1899 edn).
Notes: Morris to Thomas Wardle of Leek, 25 Mar. [1877]: 'We held the first meeting of the Society for the Protection of Ancient Buildings at Queen Sq: on Thursday

last, at which I was appointed Honorary Secretary; and I with Webb and George [Wardle, foreman of the Firm] are to draw up a program setting forth our views and aims, to submit to a meeting on Thursday next; the said program having been agreed upon we shall ask the world in general to join: I think we shall make the program explicit enough to keep out pretenders' (*Letters*, i. 357–8).

A letter dated 3 Apr. from Morris to Rossetti, asking him to join the Committee of the Society, indicates that the 'program' has been accepted: 'I send with this a copy of the paper we intend putting forward to express our views and aims in the matter. There are a few verbal alterations to be made in it, but it is substantially the document agreed upon' (*Letters*, i. 359).

Morris probably refers to the printing and publication of the manifesto in his letter to George Howard, also a member of the SPAB Committee, on 18 Apr. 1877: 'I am getting them printed and will send you them today, I hope. Meantime, I *am* an inefficient secretary: I am looking about for a new one, and am thinking of proposing *you*—' (*Letters*, i. 366). The Manifesto was certainly pbd. by 22 May, when Morris sends a copy to a correspondent (*Letters*, i. 373). Rptd. MM, i. 109–12.

A-13.02: SPAB Manifesto (1896)
THE SOCIETY FOR THE PROTECTION OF ANCIENT BUILDINGS. | OFFICES—10 BUCKINGHAM STREET, STRAND, W. C. | *MINIMUM ANNUAL SUBSCRIPTION, HALF-A-GUINEA, LIFE MEMBERS TEN GUINEAS.*
Edition: [2nd edn. (?)] It is certain that the edns. described in this section are not the only edns. between 1877 and 1899. The text is 'Written by Morris and without alteration' from the 1876 edn. in each case, but there are changes to the membership of the Committee and a list of 'Local Correspondents' was added in the interval, which probably necessitated resetting each annual publication. The manifesto was published simultaneously in French and Italian, at least in some edns. Since this largely duplicates the 1st edn., only details of altered fields are included here.
Series: New impressions of Principles, without a series designation, were issued at intervals from the 1st pbn. in 1877. Others appeared besides those described here from the 1877, 1896, and 1899 versions. But these provide a representative selection.
Collation: folio size s. sh., printed on both sides.
Contents: A 3-part broadsheet made up of the list of Committee Members, the Principles, and the list of Local Correspondents. p. [1], title-heading: 1st section headed 'COMMITTEE', gives names of members of the governing body, followed by 3 'HONORARY SECRETARIES', then the 'TREASURER', 'BANKER', and 'SECRETARY'; below a thin rule is the 2nd part heading, in square brackets, formatted in hanging indent: [*THE FOLLOWING ARE THE PRINCIPLES OF THE SOCIETY FOR* | *THE PROTECTION OF ANCIENT BUILDINGS AS SET FORTH* | *UPON ITS FOUNDATION IN 1877, AND WHICH ARE HERE* | *REPRINTED IN 1896 WITHOUT ALTERATION.*]; the 3rd section, on the verso and also following a thin rule, is headed: *LOCAL CORRESPONDENTS*. Naturally, the names of the officers, committee members, and local correspondents vary from one edn. to the next.
Technical Notes: *paper*: thin moulded, parchment-style, with high onion content; *leaf size*: 332 x 211 mm., no wrapper.
Publication: 1896 [issued Apr.] 'Reprinted in 1896 without alteration'.
Register of Copies Examined: BL (base copy: Cup.502.f.11.[8]); NN Berg; Fdmn).
Notes: Morris's text rptd. in MM, i. 109–12.

A-13.03: SPAB Manifesto (1899)
Title as in the previous entry, but with a change of issue date to 1899.
Edition: 'Written by Morris and without alteration' (from the 1896 impression) [3rd edn.] The text of the Principles remains exactly the same in each reprint, but there are changes to the memberships of the Committee and the List of Local Correspondents, which necessitated resetting in each case. Only details of altered fields are included here.
Series: New impressions of Principles, without a series designation, were issued at intervals from the 1st publication in 1877.
Printer: not known.
Collation: folio size s. sh., printed on both sides.
Contents: recto as in the previous entry, with the minor changes only to the prologue to the Principles: THE FOLLOWING ARE THE PRINCIPLES OF THE SOCIETY FOR | THE PROTECTION OF ANCIENT BUILDINGS AS SET FORTH | UPON ITS FOUNDATION IN 1877, AND WHICH ARE HERE | REPRINTED IN 1899 WITHOUT ALTERATION; verso: with adjustments of date and changes to the lists of Committee members and local correspondents.
Technical Notes: *paper*: thin white machine-moulded,

parchment-style, with vegetable content; *leaf size*: 332 x 211 mm.; *print area*: 282 x 132 mm.; *printing*: broadsheet printed on both sides as in previous entry.
Publication: 1899; *print run*: unknown; *price*: for free distribution.
Register of Copies Examined: BL (base copy: Cup. 502. f. 11.); NN Berg.

A-14.01: Unjust War

[head title] UNJUST WAR: | To the Working-men of England.
Edition: [1st impression, 1st edn.] A handbill, signed 'A Lover of Justice', and Forman says only that it 'is attributed to Morris's pen', but Morris's authorship is certain. Mackail does not question it, and the MS, in Morris's hand, is in the WMG. The BL Catalogue description, '8vo: s. sh.', refers to this flysheet, which is also of a size to admit of being a handbill. Forman says the text was issued in 2 forms: as a 'placard' for posting, and then, 'of this copies were reprinted on a slip [i.e. a handbill] for hand to hand distribution' (HBF, p. 94). The copy described here is the placard version. It has a heading: 'The following placard is being largely posted in London.' It is not clear whether the printed handbill (unseen) has the same setting as the placard or is a new edn.. It would seem likely that if printed especially for posting on a hoarding a placard would have larger paper and type than a handbill, which would require a new setting. Placards of the size of this one were not unusual in Victorian London, and its size would not inhibit its being printed as a handbill. There may never have been 2 different edns. of this text, but the same setting, used perhaps on different size, weight, and coloured papers.
Publisher: [The Eastern Question Association?].
Printer: [no printer's imprint].
Collation: folio s. sh. placard printed on one side; a poster that was also issued as an 8° leaflet.
Contents: title-heading: UNJUST WAR | To the Working Men of England | [text begins with salutation, flush left] Friends and fellow citizens. | [text]; text ends with explicit: UNJUST WAR | [flush right] A LOVER OF JUSTICE
Technical Notes: placard, printed on one side; *paper*: thin moulded paper; *leaf size*: 316 x 125 mm.; *type area*: printed as a single column, 286 x 97 mm.
Publication: [issued on or shortly before 3 May 1877] The date is from the postmark on the envelope in which Morris posted the MS to Georgiana Burne-Jones. Philip Henderson, *The Letters of William Morris to his Family and Friends* (hereafter referred to as Henderson) reprints Morris's text (388–9), and says, 'Morris issued this Manifesto on 11 May 1877', but he gives no source for his date, which does not sort well with Morris sending the MS to Georgiana Burne-Jones on 3 May. The most likely source of the 11 May date would be the list of letters loaned to Mackail in aid of his work on the *Life*. This one is recorded in his 1st Notebook under the sub-heading 'Letters to Georgiana B-J': '11/5/77 (Queen Sq.) [a letter addressed in Morris's hand and postmarked 'My 3 77'] sending MS of the Eastern Question Poster'. It is now in the WMG, along with what appears to be the envelope in which it was sent (WMG, J 163. 49). According to Mackail, Mrs Burne-Jones received it on 11 May 1877. A delay in delivery may be explained by re-posting, the envelope in the WMG being addressed, 'Mrs Burne-Jones | care of A. Baldwin Esq. Wildon House | nr. Stourport'. Either Mackail erred in his dating of the letter or his date in the notebook indicates not posting but reception, which could have been delayed by a re-posting from Wildon House. If she received it as a gift (according to Henderson, 388, the MS was presented to the library by Georgiana) it must have been sent after publication. It is worth noting that in his biography of Morris, Mackail dates the piece simply as having been issued in May (i. 348–9). Pbn. must have been on the day, or before, Morris sent it to Georgiana in an envelope post-marked 'My 3 77'.
Register of Copies Examined: BL (2 copies: base copy: Cup. 502. f.11. [22] & Add. MS. 52772).
Notes: 'A placard headed UNJUST WAR, which was posted about London at the same period, is attributed to Morris's pen and of this copies were reprinted on a slip for hand to hand distribution' (HBF, pp. 93–4).

A-15.01: Wake, London Lads!

[head title] Wake, London Lads! | *Air, The Hardy Norseman's home of yore.*| [thin rule] | [text begins]
Edition: [1st impression, 1st and 2nd edns] Folio poster and a fly-sheet handbill, the text being a 5 stanza lyric for the audience to sing at a public meeting.
Publisher: [The Eastern Question Association].
Collation: Single demy 8° and cr. 8° sheets, printed on one side.
Contents: title and text printed only on recto.
Technical Notes: *paper*: handbill: plain, machine-made, printed in various colours; folio poster copy: cream machine-made; *leaf size*: handbill: 220 x 141 mm.; poster 299 x 221 mm.; *print area*: handbill: 174 x 79 mm.; poster: 235 x 149 mm.
Publication: [issued 16 Jan. 1878]; Forman and Scott differ on the date of this publication, but Morris's 19 Jan. 1878

Wake, London Lads!

Air, The Hardy Norseman's home of yore.

1. Wake, London Lads, wake, bold and free!
    Arise, and fall to work,
   Lest England's glory come to be
    Bond-servant to the Turk!
   Think of your Sires! how oft and oft
    On freedom's field they bled,
   When Cromwell's hand was raised aloft,
    And Kings and scoundrels fled.

2. From out the dusk, from out the dark,
    Of old our fathers came,
   Till lovely freedom's glimmering spark
    Broke forth a glorious flame :
   And shall we now praise freedom's dearth
    And rob the years to come,
   And quench upon a brother's hearth
    The fires we lit at home?

3. O, happy England, if thine hand
    Should forge anew the chain,
   The fetters of a tortured land,
    How were thy glory vain!
   Our starving men, our women's tears,
    The graves of those we love,
   Should buy us curses for all years,
    A weight we might not move.

4. Yea, through the fog of unjust war
    What thief on us might steal,
   To rob us of the gifts of yore,
    The hope of England's weal?
   The toilsome years have built and earned,
    Great men in hope have died;
   Shall all the lesson be unlearned,
    The treasure scattered wide?

5. What! shall we crouch beneath the load,
    And call the labour sweet,
   And, dumb and blind, go down the road
    Where shame abides our feet?
   Wake, London Lads! the hour draws nigh,
    The bright sun brings the day;
   Cast off the shame, cast off the lie,
    And cast the Turk away!

                                    WILLIAM MORRIS.

Figure 24. A-15.01: Wake, London Lads (1st edn.) fly sheet

letter to Mrs Morris makes it clear that the date given here, also given in Scott (p. 6), is correct. The lyrics were sung at an Eastern Question Association meeting. Forman says the song was for a meeting in Islington Hall on 14 May 1877 (HBF, p. 93), but Mackail says: 'At a meeting held in Exeter Hall on the 16th [Jan. 1878] to protest against the threatening attitude of the Government, Morris appeared for the first time as a writer of political verse. "Wake, London Lads!" a stirring ballad written by him for the occasion, was distributed in the hall and sung with much enthusiasm' (Mackail, i. 350–1). The latter account is confirmed by Morris's letter to Mrs Morris, 19 Jan. 1878 (*Letters*, i. 434–5).

Register of Copies Examined: LeM (base copy); Bass; BL (3 copies: Cup. 502. f. 11. [21]); Shaw Papers, Add. Ms. 45338, f.93.; Ashley Library 3682).

Notes: Morris to Jane Morris, 19 Jan. 1878: 'I send you enclose [*sic*] 3 "London Lads": I have a bundle here, & if you want more for the Howards I will send on again' (*Letters*, i. 435).

A-16.01: Decorative Arts

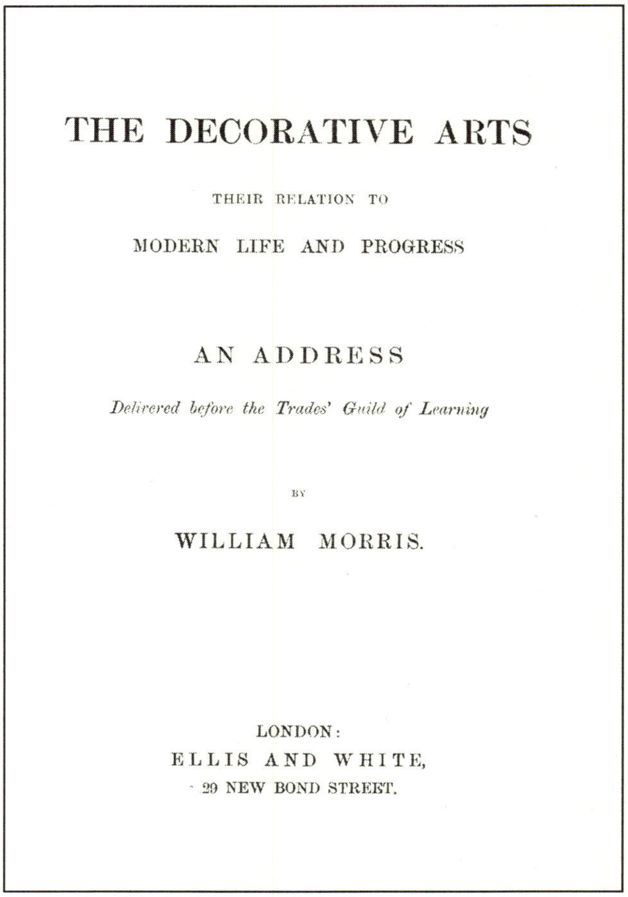

THE DECORATIVE ARTS | THEIR RELATION TO | MODERN LIFE AND PROGRESS | AN ADDRESS | *Delivered before the Trades' Guild of Learning* | BY | WILLIAM MORRIS. | LONDON: | ELLIS AND WHITE, | 29 NEW BOND STREET.

Edition: [1st impression, 1st edn.] 1st pbd. as 'The Decorative Arts' in *The Architect*, 8 Dec. 1877 (see D-45); following the pamphlet version described here, it was retitled 'The Lesser Arts' and published in *Hopes and Fears for Art* (A-21.01).

Collation: 16°: [A]¹⁶ [A5ʳ signed A2], 16 leaves pp. [1–3] 4–32 [= 32] + wrapper.

Contents: p. [1], title page; p. [2], blank; p. [3], chapter head title, text begins; pp. 4–32, text completed: [thin rule] | [imprint] London: Printed by John Strangeways, Castle St. Leicester Sq.

Technical Notes: *paper*: cream-white machine laid, no watermark; *leaf size*: cut flush, 178 x 123 mm; *printing*: *type area*: 139 x 89 mm.; *lines-to-page*: thin leading, 32 lines, excluding head and direction lines; *headlines*: all rectos and versos: *The Decorative Arts*.; chapter head title, dropped 3 lines to title: THE DECORATIVE ARTS | [thin rule] | [text begins]; *wrapper*: plain light grey paper, sewn to the body, printed only on the front, p. [1], the same letterpress as the title page; all within a thin rule compartment, 156 x 111 mm.; pp. [2–4], blank.

Figure 25. A-16.01: *The Decorative Arts* (1st edn.) title page

Publication: [issued 4 Feb. 1878] (HBF, p. 96); 1st issued without an imprint date either on the wrapper title or the title page. According to HBF (p. 96), it was sold later the same year with a new wrapper dated '1878', but the title page remained undated; see also *BSR*, No. 245 (3 Apr. 1878), 306. But the undated wrapper has not been seen and the undated BL copy has no wrapper; *print run*: 2,000 copies; *price*: 1d.

Register of Copies Examined: BL (base copy: Cup. 502. f.11.[45.], with wrapper; 3044. e. 41. [10.], without wrapper); LeM; CSt (Spec. Coll.Rare Books NK1132.M8).

Notes: this lecture, 1st delivered at a hall just off Oxford Street, behind St. George's Church, was Morris's 1st public performance, as it was also his 1st published lecture. As his letter of 10 Aug. 1880 indicates, he had a series of lectures to deliver, and by that time had conceived a plan to collect them into a vol.: 'I will be as serious as I can over them, and when I have these last two done, I think of making a book of the lot, as it will

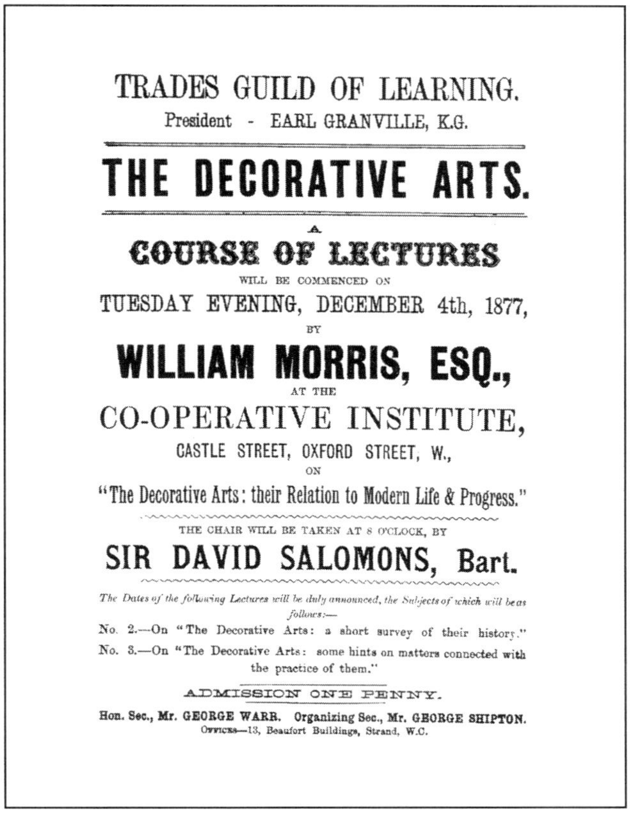

Figure 26. A-16.01: *The Decorative Arts* (1st edn.) handbill ad for the lecture

be about what I have to say on the subject, which still seems to me the most serious one that a man can think of; for 'tis no less than the chances of a calm, dignified, and therefore happy life for the mass of mankind' (*Letters*, i. 579). The fact that a reporter from *The Architect* got to the lecturer immediately after this 1st lecture's delivery was later a source of some regret since it prevented publication in *Fraser's Magazine*. He wrote to William Allingham, then editor of *Fraser's*, on 14 Dec. 1877, to explain that, 'I was stupid enough to let a man from the "Architect" collar my lecture on the spot; so that the affair is at an end: otherwise I should have been glad to let Fraser have it. I am however going to publish it myself later on' (*Letters*, i. 419). Morris carried out his own intent, but it did mean that the full text of this lecture appeared 1st in *The Architect* (see D-45), as was the case with several later lectures.

As a publication, with a print run of 2,000 copies, and an American edn. of 1,000 copies, preceded by the printing in *The Architect*, the text reached a considerable audience and gave Morris an entrance to even larger audiences when he spoke on similar subjects in the months and years that followed.

Morris to Jenny Morris on 7 Dec. 1877: 'Yes I gave my lecture on Tuesday & I have only got your letter today—Friday: it went off very well, and I was not at all nervous, but made myself well heard: I send you the Architect which has got it all in: but I intend publishing it again myself' (*Letters* i. 418).

Morris to Jane Morris, on 28 Dec. 1877: 'I am going to have a quiet evening over the proofs of my last lecture. And then I must set to at the next' (*Letters*, i. 428).

A-16.02: Decorative Arts (RB)

THE DECORATIVE ARTS | THEIR RELATION TO | [gothic type] Modern Life and Progress | [plain type] *AN ADDRESS* | DELIVERED BEFORE THE TRADES GUILD OF LEARNING, | OF LONDON | BY | WILLIAM MORRIS | AUTHOR OF "THE EARTHLY PARADISE" ETC. | BOSTON | ROBERTS BROTHERS | 1878

Edition: [1st impression, 2nd edn., 1st American] Stereos were made of *The Decorative Arts* (1 Feb. 1878) but sales were not such as to require a reprint (Roberts Arch., Cost Book C). Retitled 'The Lesser Arts' in *Hopes and Fears for Art* (1882).

Collation: 8° printed and gathered in 12s, 2 sigs.: [1]–2¹² 3⁸ [signatures are [1], 1*, 2, 2*, 3, with asterisked signatures starting the 2nd half of the gathering] 32 leaves pp. [2] [4] [1–3] 4–50 [51–64] [= 64] + wrapper.

Contents: pp. [1–2], ads; [1–4] Tributes to William Morris; p. [1], title page, as above, ; p. [2], printer's imprint: Cambridge: | Press of John Wilson & Son.; p. [3], dropped head: THE DECORATIVE ARTS | [french rule] | [text begins]; pp. 4–50, text completed; pp. [51–64], ads.

Technical Notes: *paper*: plain white machine-made; *leaf size*: cut flush, 168 x 116 mm.; *running heads*: [all rectos and versos] THE DECORATIVE ARTS; *wrapper*: no wrapper on this copy; details here from Pye (p. 41) taken from the Boston Public Library copy which has the original wrapper bound in: p. [1]; wrapper title, reproduces title page within a thin-rule border, with printer's ornaments at each corner; p. [2], ads headed: MR. WILLIAM MORRIS'S WORKS; pp. [3–4], Roberts Bros. ads.

Publication: 1878 [issued 20 Feb.] (RB ad, *The Bookseller* (US), 13/318 (16 Feb. 1878), 200); hereafter referred to as BSR (US) *print run*: 1,000 copies; *price*: 30 cents.

Register of Copies Examined: CSt (base copy: 821.6 M87d);

with additional detail from Pye, pp. 41–2, and the Roberts Arch. (Book C, p. 52).

Notes: The only copy seen of this rare pamphlet (the Stanford U. copy) is missing the wrapper and perhaps other parts. Pye includes a description (but without a collation). The collation made here from the pamphlet itself is reinforced by the Roberts Archive account of the printing, which specifies that there were '2 1/2 sigs', the half gathering being described with a latitude common to these details in the archival accounts.

A-16.03: Decorative Arts

Title as in A-16.01 except for the addition of the date of publication at the foot: 1878
Edition: [2nd impression, 1st edn.] 1st pbd. as 'The Decorative Arts' in *The Architect*, 8 Dec. 1878 (see D-45); Later retitled 'The Lesser Arts' and published in *Hopes and Fears for Art* (1882). Since this impression largely duplicates A-16.01, only details of altered fields are included here.
Publication: 1878 [issued May] (*BSR*, No 247 (3 June 1878), 492); *print run*: unknown; *price*: 1d.
Register of Copies Examined: LeM (base copy, with dated wrapper); BL (2 copies: Cup. 502. f. 11. [45] & 7801. a. 19., both with dated wrappers).

A-17.01: Art of the People

[wrapper title in gothic] Birmingham | Society of Arts and School of Design. | [thin rule] | ADDRESS | DELIVERED IN | THE TOWN HALL, BIRMINGHAM, | ON THE 19th OF FEBRUARY, 1879, | BY WM. MORRIS, M.A., | PRESIDENT. | BIRMINGHAM: | PRINTED BY E. C. OSBORNE, 84, NEW STREET.
Edition: [1st impression, 1st edn.] 1st published without a title in *The Birmingham Daily Post* (see D-46). Delivered under the above title, but later retitled 'The Art of the People' and included in *Hopes and Fears for Art* (1882).
Series: this is the 1st of 2 Morris lectures delivered to and issued as pamphlets by the Birmingham Society of Arts and School of Design, to record the annual prize-giving with the speeches thereat delivered. Morris served a 2-year term as President, delivering the prize-day addresses for 1879 and 1880 (see also *The Beauty of Life*, A-18.01).
Collation: long 8°, [1¹²], 12 leaves pp. [1–4] 5–23 [24] [= 24]. Self-wrappered, i.e. without a separate wrapper, the first and last leaves, being integral and of course conjunct, provide both the title page and the end of the text.
Contents: p. [1], title page; p. [2], blank; p. [3], text begins: [dropped head] ADDRESS. | [french rule] | [text begins]; pp. 4–23, text completed with thin rule: [printer's imprint] E. C. OSBORNE, Printer, 84, New Street, Birmingham.; p. [24], blank.
Technical Notes: *paper*: plain white machine-made, no watermark; *leaf size*: cut flush, 210 x 128 mm.; *lines-to-page*: thin leaded: 37 lines; *pagination*: arabic numerals centred on the headline.
Publication: 1879 [issued in May] ('Books of the Month', *BSR* (2 June 1879), 518).
Register of Copies Examined: VU (base copy: Ba RB); CSt (Spec. Coll. Felton PR5080.A4. 1879).

A-17.02: Art of the People (Seymour)

[1st 2 lines in neo-Gothic display type] The Art of the | People | An Address delivered before the Birmingham | Society of Arts, February 19th, 1879 | [in red] By WILLIAM MORRIS | [in black, within thin-rule compartment, bookmark of Ralph Fletcher Seymour with that name at the top] | Ralph Fletcher Seymour, Publisher | Fine Arts Building, Chicago | [in red] MDCCCCII
Edition: [1st impression, 2nd edn., 1st American] Text 1st pbd. without a title in *The Birmingham Daily Post*, 20 Feb. 1879, p. 5 (see D-46).
Colophon: [in red] THIS EDITION OF 'THE ART OF THE | PEOPLE' BY WILLIAM MORRIS, IS THE | FIRST BOOK IN WHICH IS USED THE | TYPE DESIGNED & CAST FOR MR. | SEYMOUR; TWO HUNDRED & FIFTEEN | COPIES ON PAPER & TEN ON JAPAN VELLUM | HAVE BEEN PRINTED BY GEO. | F. MCKIERNAN & CO. IN CHICAGO FOR | THE PUBLISHER RALPH FLETCHER | SEYMOUR, & THE TYPE DISTRIBUTED | NOVEMBER, MDCCCCII.
Collation: 4°: a–e⁴ f² 22 leaves pp. [1–7] 8–41 [42–4] [= 44].
Contents: p. [1], half title; p. [2], blank; p. [3], title page; p. [4], copyright note: Copyright 1902 | Ralph Fletcher Seymour; p. [5], 2nd half title; p. [6], epigraph, 7 lines from Daniel Defoe, the same passage that is used in the 1st edn. of *Labour and Pleasure versus Labour and Sorrow* (1880), which Morris switched to this lecture when including it in *Hopes and Fears for Art*; p. [7], chapter head title: full border compartment, floriated woodcut scroll-work border around an inner thin-rule compartment within which are the head-title and commencement of text: [in neo-Gothic 3-line display type, as above] | An Address by WILLIAM MORRIS | Author of 'The Earthly Paradise', Etc. | [text begins with a 9-line floriated initial 'I' in red]; pp. 8–[42], text completed with frequent 4-line black and 6-line

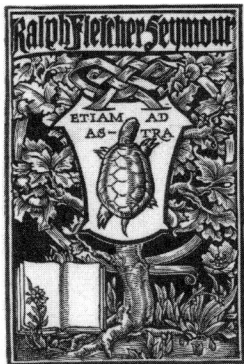

Figure 27. A-17.02: The Art of the People (Seymour edn.) title page

red floriated initials; p. [43], blank; p. [44], colophon (see above).

Technical Notes: *paper*: hand-laid paper made by L. L. Brown; watermarked: W. King (bottom, verso) Alton Mill (bottom, recto); *type face*: English (14 point) Alderbrink font, cut by Robert Weibking of Chicago; *printing*: printed in black and red (red for 9 of the floriated capitals, the epigraph, colophon, and shoulder notes); *end-papers*: 3 free ends and paste-down front and back, plain white and blank; *binding*: tan quarter lthr. with plain unblocked grey paper-covered boards gilt-stamped on front: THE ART OF THE PEOPLE | BY WILLIAM MORRIS; and the same words down the spine.

Publication: Nov. 1902 [colophon date, date of issue unknown]; *print run*: 215 copies on paper, 10 on japan vellum; *price*: $5.00 and $15.00 respectively.

Register of Copies Examined: LeM (base copy); J-F V.

Notes: from Ralph Fletcher Seymour's autobiography:

With Goudy's help and Weibking's matrices I got my first face of type designed, cut and finally cast. The next step was to make use of it in a book. I knew a long nosed printer named McKiernan who had no fine art printing to his credit but to offset that disadvantage he had no notion of what it should be. He said that he had never seen any printed job that he could not beat or at least duplicate. I made a deal with him for the printing of my first book printed from type [Seymour had previously made and sold hand-written books]. It was "The Art of the People." I saw to it that the text was to be hand set and the printing done on dampened hand-made paper by going to his shop and taking part in the work. The ink for the job came from Germany and the paper from the only firm then making hand-made paper in the United States, the L. L. Brown Company. I tried to get McKiernan to print the sheets on an old Washington proofing press, but he had used, so he assured me, a Washington hand press for the last time. So we had to use a pony cylinder, but even at that the printing was good. A. J. Cox & Company bound the edition and Dr. Gunsaulas and Fred Goudy said the books were O.K. (*Some Went This Way: A Forty years pilgrimage among Artists, Bookmen and Printers* (Chicago: R. F. Seymour, 1945), 118–19).

A-17.03: Art of the People (Hillacre)

[all within olive-green Oxford (i.e. double thick-thin rule) compartment, letterpress printed in black and formatted in hanging indent] THE ART OF THE | PEOPLE [in red] *By* WILLIAM | MORRIS | [black] Hillacre Press mark] | [imprint formatted in hanging indent] PRINTED & PUBLISHED BY | FREDERICK C. BURSCH AT | HILLACRE RIVERSIDE CON- | NECTICUT [in red] MCMXIV

Edition: [1st impression, 3rd edn., 2nd American] 1st published without a title in *The Birmingham Daily Post*, 20 Feb. 1879, p. 5 (see D-46) and then as a pamphlet (see A-17.01). Later retitled *The Art of the People* for inclusion in *Hopes and Fears for Art* (1882, see A-21.01).

Collation: sm. 8°: [1⁴ 2–5⁸] 36 leaves pp. [1–4] 5–71 [72] [= 72].

Contents: p. [1], half title; p. [2], blank; p. [3], title page; p. [4], blank; p. [5], dropped head: THE ART OF THE PEOPLE. | [text begins with 2 1/2 line red drop cap initial 'I']; pp. 6–71, text completed; p. [72], blank.

Technical Notes: *paper*: cream-white machine-laid, with dandy roll laid lines and false deckled edges; watermarked: 'Utopian' bottom recto; *leaf size*: 141 x 98 mm.; *pagination*: arabic numbers within the inner margins on the direction line; *end-papers*: 2 free ends (no paste-down), plain white

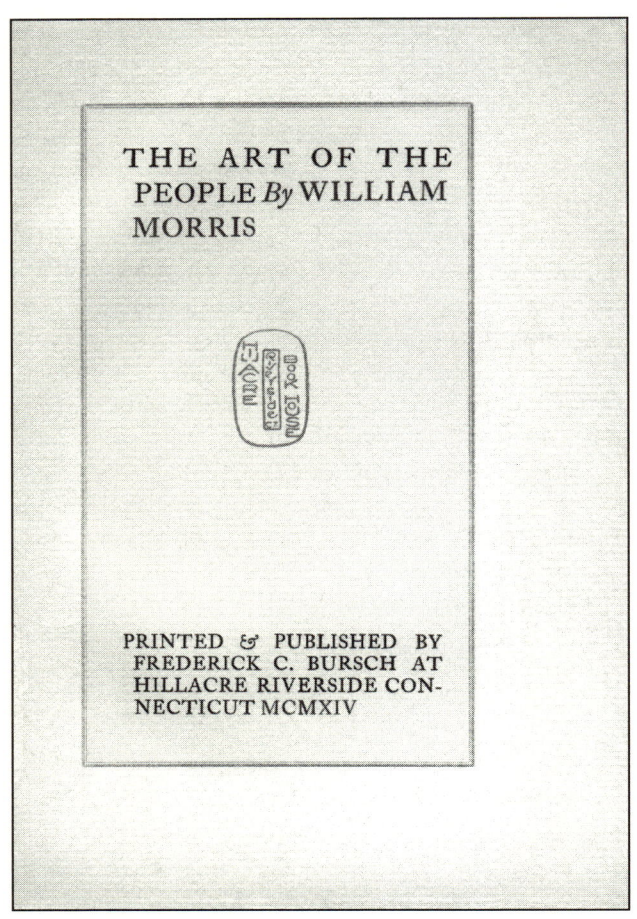

Figure 28. A-17.03: *The Art of the People* (Hillacre edn.) title page

and blank, front and back; *binding*: dark brown rough paper jacket over boards and spine, with printed paper label on jacket front: [within red thin-rule compartment] THE ART OF THE PEOPLE | BY | WILLIAM MORRIS; issued in a plain dark-brown cardboard slipcase with paper labels on spine and slip case, printed in Caslon type (front label), and Della Robbia (slip case) (see Thomas Larremore, 'An American Typographical Tragedy', p. 158; hereafter referred to as Larremore). For additional information on Bursch and his Morris books, see A-120.01.
Publication: 1914; *print run*: John J. Walsdorf. says 'unlimited' (see *William Morris in Private Press and Limited Editions: A Descriptive Bibliography of Books By and About William Morris, 1891—1981*, p. 231; hereafter referred to as Walsdorf); *price*: unknown.
Register of Copies Examined: LeM (base copy); NN.

A-18.01: The Beauty of Life

[ornament] BIRMINGHAM [ornament] | [ornament] SOCIETY OF ARTS AND SCHOOL OF DESIGN. [ornament] | [ornamental rule] | [swash caps] LABOUR AND PLEASURE, | *VERSUS* | [swash caps] LABOUR AND SORROW. | [ornamental rule] | — AN — | [ornament] ADDRESS [ornament] | BY | [swash caps] William Morris, Esq., M. A., | PRESIDENT, | [ornament before and after each word] IN THE TOWN HALL, BIRMINGHAM, | [ornaments before and after text] 19th FEBRUARY, 1880. | [ornamental rule] | [ornaments before and after] BIRMINGHAM: | [ornaments before and after each word] CUND BROS., PRINTERS. LONDON WORKS, MOOR STREET.
Edition: [1st impression, 1st edn.] Issued with an undetermined number of LP copies (see *Notes*, below). Included as *The Beauty of Life* in *Hopes and Fears for Art* (1882, see A-21.01).
Series: Morris's 2nd annual prize-day address of his 2-year term as President of the Birmingham Society of Arts and School of Design.
Collation: 8°: [1]^{18} 18 leaves pp. [2] [1–3] 4–31 [32–4] [= 36].
Contents: p. [1], title page; p. [2], blank; p. [1], half title: LABOUR AND PLEASURE, | *VERSUS* | LABOUR AND SORROW. | [thin rule] | [in italics, 7-line epigraph in hanging indent, in italics, enclosed in quotation marks, labelled below right] | *DANIEL DEFOE*.; p. [2], blank; p. [3], dropped head title: ADDRESS. | [swelled rule] | [text begins] | pp. 4–31, text completed; p. [32], printer's imprint: [thin rule] | BIRMINGHAM | CUND BROTHERS, PRINTERS, LONDON WORKS, PATERNOSTER ROW, | MOOR STREET. | [thin rule]; pp. [33–4], blank.
Technical Notes: *paper*: plain white machine-made; *leaf size*: cut flush, 206 x 136 mm.; *printing*: *type area*: excluding head and direction lines, 154 x 94 mm.; *lines-to-page*: leaded, 34 lines; *pagination*: arabic numbers centred between margins on headlines; *wrapper title*: prtd. on p. [1]; pp. [2–4], blank.
Publication: 1880 [issued 16–23 May] (see Morris's letter to his mother in *Notes*, below, and *Pub. Circ.*, 43/1025 (1 June 1880), 418); *print run*: unknown, but Forman says it is 'very scarce' (p. 98); *price*: for free distribution.
Register of Copies Examined: VU (base copy: Ba RB); Bass; CSt (Spec.Coll Felton PR5080.L3); CSmH.
Notes: letter from Morris to his mother, dated 23 May 1880: 'the Birmingham people have paid me the compliment of printing some copies of my last address on large paper, & have sent me 3 copies. . . . when you have read it, if you will let me have it back I will get it nicely bound for you, which

I would have done before sending it only they have but just come' (*Letters*, i. 568–9).

A-19.01: Speech . . . at the Kyrle Society

SPEECH OF MR WILLIAM MORRIS AT A MEETING OF THE KYRLE | SOCIETY, HELD IN THE KENSINGTON VESTRY HALL, | January 27th, 1881.
Edition: [1st impression, 1st separate edn.] A broadsheet reprinted from *The Woman's Union Journal*, Feb. 1881 (see D-62). Also rptd. in MM, i. 192–7.
Publisher: The Kyrle Society.
Printer: Women's Printing Society, Limited, 21B Great College Street, Westminster, London, S.W.
Collation: Single sheet, printed on one side.
Technical Notes: *paper*: a single sheet of cream machine-made; *leaf size*: 374 x 263 mm.; *print area*: 340 x 194 mm., printed on one side in three columns, each 63 mm. wide, with columns separated by 2.5 mm. margins.
Publication: Feb. 1881; *print run* and *price*: unknown.
Register of Copies Examined: BL Add. MS. 52772 (base copy: Cockerell Papers: printed copy bound in with miscellaneous MS items).

A-20.01: Art and the Beauty of the Earth

[wrapper title] THE | WEDGWOOD INSTITUTE. | REPORTS | OF THE | [in gothic] SCHOOLS OF SCIENCE & ART, | [plain type] FOR THE | YEAR | 1880–81, | WITH THE | ADDRESS DELIVERED | BY | MR WILLIAM MORRIS, | *at The Twelfth Annual Meeting*, | HELD IN THE BURSLEM TOWN HALL, | *OCTOBER 13th, 1881* | Warwick Savage, Printer, Burslem.
Edition: [1st impression, 1st edn.] Text 1st pbd. as 'The Condition and Prospects of Art' in *The Architect*, 29 Oct., 5 Nov. 1881 (see D-65). Later retitled *Art and the Beauty of the Earth*.
Collation: cr. 8°: a single gathering of 14 leaves, stitched through the centrefold, pp. [1–4] 5–23 [24–8] [= 28] self-wrappered, i.e. without a separate wrapper, the first and last leaves, being integral and of course conjunct, provide both the title page and the end of the text.
Contents: p. [1], title page; p. [2], blank; p. [3], list of Committee members; p. [4], chapter head title: [title repeated, all caps] | Committee's Report | [text begins]; pp. 5–8, various reports; p. 9, Report ends, signed: HARRY T. DAVENPORT, | [flush right] Treasurer | ADDRESS | [Morris text begins]; pp. 10–23, text completed with an ornamental tail-piece; p. [24–5], prize list; p. 26, annual accounts; p. 27, headed: ANNUAL SUBSCRIPTIONS; p. 28, course list.
Technical Notes: *paper*: plain white machine-made; *leaf size*: cut flush, 207 x 135 mm.; *type area*: 165 x 102 mm.; *lines-to-page*: set solid, with half-line spaces between paragraphs counted here, 48 lines; *pagination*: arabic numbers centred on the headlines; *binding*: self-wrappered.
Publication: 1881; *print run* and *price*: unknown.
Register of Copies Examined: BL (2 copies: base copy: C.60.i.20, Robert Proctor's copy, and Cup. 502. f. 11. [5], Cockerell's copy); NNPM.

A-20.02: Art and the Beauty of the Earth (Golden 8°)

ART AND THE BEAUTY OF THE | EARTH. BY WILLIAM MORRIS.
Edition: 'Golden type octavo edition' [1st impression, 2nd edn.] 1st pbd. in *The Architect* as 'The Condition and Prospects of Art' (see D-65). Only details specific to this issue are provided here.
Collaborators, Editors, and Illustrators: [edited by S. C. Cockerell, assisted by Robert Proctor, though their part is not noted in the book].
Series: 2nd of a 5-vol. octavo series of 6 fugitive lectures and 1 essay printed in Golden type. For series detail, see this field in see A-71.02.
Colophon: Printed at the Chiswick Press with the Golden | type designed by William Morris for the Kelm- | scott Press, and finished on the sixth day | of December, 1898. Published by Longmans & Co. | 39 Paternoster Row, London.
Collation: cr. 8° prtd. and gathered in 4s: [a]² b–e⁴ 18 leaves pp. [4] 1–31 [32] [= 36].
Contents: pp. [1–2], blank; p. [3], title page; p. [4], blank; p. 1, headed, flush left: ART AND THE BEAUTY OF THE | EARTH. A LECTURE DELIVERED | BY WILLIAM MORRIS AT BURSLEM | TOWN HALL ON OCTOBER 13, 1881. | [text begins]; pp. 2–31, text completed with colophon (see above); p. [32], blank.
Technical Notes: for detail common to the series—paper, printing, type, leaf size, type area, position (but not content) of shoulder notes, pagination, and binding (except for letterpress)—are all common to the series and are described in this field in A-71.02, the entry for the 1st vol. of the set; *shoulder notes*: [all rectos and versos] Lecture II | Art and the | Beauty of | the Earth.; *end-papers*: 1 free end and paste-down, plain white and blank, front and back; *binding*: title printed on front cover: [at the top margin, formatted flush left] ART AND THE BEAUTY OF THE | EARTH. BY WILLIAM MORRIS.
Publication: 6 Dec. 1898 [colophon date, issued 25 Jan. 1899]

(Longmans *Notes on Books*, 9/179 (28 Feb. 1899), 144); *print run*: 1,500 copies, 1,000 copies bound; the binding of the last 500 copies (17 Feb. 1899, 'doing up', as recorded in the Chiswick Arch.) does not constitute a new issue since there was no attempt to specify the new copies as a new and separate issue of the title; the new copies are in no way identified as a group, being merely the means of replenishing existing stocks; and no change is made in the colophon, as there are in the reprints of this series; *price*: 2s. 6d.

Register of Copies Examined: BL (2 copies: base copy: K.T.C. 8. a. 20., and Ashley Library 3698); LeM; SSL (700/M877Sp); VU (2 copies: L & E 704 / M877A); SU (2 copies: 704/M87ar).

Notes: see A-133.01, *The Unpublished Lectures of William Morris*, 296 (hereafter referred to as *Unpublished Lectures*). S. C. Cockerell's diary, on Thursday, 27 Oct. 1898, notes his delivery of the Burslem lecture text to the Chiswick Press, printers of the 'Golden type octavo edn' (Cockerell Papers, BL (Add.) MS 52634); Chiswick Arch. notes that in Dec. 1898 Chiswick printed 1,500 copies of the Prospectus for *Art and the Beauty of the Earth* and 1,500 copies of the book itself.

Letter from C. J. Longman to S. C. Cockerell, 5 Dec. 1898: Longmans urges a delay in the publication of *Art and the Beauty of the Earth* to avoid the rush of Christmas literature, which distracts the public and the booksellers. On 9 Dec. he writes again of his plan to issue the new lecture early in Jan. (Smith Arch.).

S. C. Cockerell to Mrs Morris, 1 Jan. 1899, informs her that *Art and the Beauty of the Earth* in the Golden 8° series is finished at the Chiswick Press. He asks her for any additional names of those who should get presentation copies (Cockerell Papers, BL (Add.) MS 52738).

F. S. Ellis to Cockerell, 18 Apr. 1899: has found a package of 10 copies of Lecture II, which arrived at his house on 1 Jan. 1899 (ibid.).

Longmans Accts. show that in the 6 months after issue, to 1 June 1899, *Art and the Beauty of the Earth* sold nearly 1,000 copies, producing an income for the estate of £78. 2s. 7d. from sales worth £92. 0s. 11d. (Smith Arch.).

An entry in the Chiswick Arch. 'Sold Book' includes payment of a 'fee paid to typewriter (at cost)' which suggests that a new typescript text was prepared for this edn. by Proctor from his own copy of the 1st edn., the original pamphlet version of 1881, the new typescript allowing some sub-editorial changes to be introduced. References by Robert Proctor to preparing text on a typewriter appear in his letters to his co-editor, S. C. Cockerell. See the *Notes* field in the record of *The Hollow Land and Other Contributions to The Oxford and Cambridge Magazine*, C-20.

Later impression from this edn.: Longmans:
1. 16 Aug. 1899 [colophon date, issued after 21 Aug.] (Chiswick Arch.): 'Golden type octavo edition' [2nd impression, 2nd edn.]; *print run*: 500 copies; *price*: 2s. 6d.

A-21.01: Hopes and Fears for Art

HOPES AND FEARS | FOR ART. | FIVE LECTURES DELIVERED IN BIRMINGHAM, | LONDON, AND NOTTINGHAM, | 1878–1881. | BY | WILLIAM MORRIS, | AUTHOR OF 'THE LIFE AND DEATH OF JASON,' | 'THE EARTHLY PARADISE,' &c. | LONDON: | ELLIS & WHITE, 29 NEW BOND STREET | 1882.

Edition: [1st impression, 1st edn.] With 25 LP copies on Whatman Paper. This collection reprints the texts of *The Decorative Arts* as 'The Lesser Arts' | (A-16.01); 'The Art of the People' which was 1st published as the *Address delivered in the Town Hall, Birmingham* in *The Birmingham Daily Post* (see D-46) and as a pamphlet following its delivery (see A-17.01), and later retitled for inclusion here. *Labour and Pleasure* versus *Labour and Sorrow* was issued as a pamphlet, 'The Beauty of Life' (A-18.01). The text of 'Making the Best of It' had previously appeared as 'Hints on House Decoration' in *The Architect* (Dec. 1880, see D-61). 'The Prospects of Architecture in Civilization' was 1st prtd. here. In 1912 it was reprinted separately by Frederick C. Bursch under the title *Not for Leisure Alone* (1912, see A-121.01).

Collation: cr. 8°: [A]² B–O⁸ P⁶ 112 leaves pp. [4] [1] 2–217 [218–20] [= 224].

Contents: p. [1], half title; p. [2], blank; p. [3], title page; p. [4], printer's imprint: LONDON | PRINTED BY STRANGEWAYS & SONS, | Tower Street, Upper St. Martin's Lane.; pp. [1] 2–37: THE LESSER ARTS.*; pp. [38] 39–70: THE ART OF THE PEOPLE*; pp. [71] 72–113: THE BEAUTY OF LIFE*; pp. 114–68: MAKING THE BEST OF IT*; pp. 169–217: THE PROSPECTS OF ARCHITECTURE IN CIVILIZATION*; p. [218], printer's imprint: as on p. [4]; p. [219–20], ads headed: Mr. Morris's Works. * = cues for footnotes.

Technical Notes: *paper*: cream machine-laid, with dandy roll laid lines, no watermark; *leaf size*: lightly trimmed, avg. 193 x 126; *printing*: type area: 130 x 80 mm. excluding head and direction lines; *lines-to-page*: leaded, 30 lines; *headlines*: *running titles*: of each lecture, in italics, all rectos and versos; *pagination*: arabic numerals set at the outer margin of headlines, except on last 2 chapter heads, pp.

114 and 169, where numbers are centred between margins on headlines; *end-papers*: 1 free end and paste-down, plain white and blank, front and back; *binding*: plain dark green unblocked cloth; *spine*: printed paper label: [within thin-rule compartment] MORRIS'S | LECTURES | ON | ART. | [below frame] 4s. 6d.; 25 LP copies on Whatman's Paper, demy octavo with light blue paper-covered boards and cream-white holland spine with bands and printed paper label, text as the ordinary copies.
Publication: 1882 [issued 1–15 Feb.] *Pub. Circ.*, 45/1066 (15 Feb. 1882), 155; *print run*: 1,000 copies (HBF, p. 99); *price*: 4s. 6d.
Register of Copies Examined: SU (base copy: 704/M87H); LeM; NPar; NNPM; BL Ashley (3688).
Notes: of the 5 edns. of *Hopes and Fears for Art* described here, only 2 were issued (along with several rpts.) in Morris's lifetime, the 1st English and the American, and this despite the fact that it was one of his more popular titles. A collection of public lectures given over the previous 4 years, the vol. seems never to have required authorial revision except for the few notes added by Morris in preparing the texts for the printer. By 1882, when the 1st edn. appeared, the publishers were alert to the likely sales and so prudently ordered stereotyped plates for later impressions. The reception of the book was solid, though not startling. In both Britain and America, despite sizeable 1st impression print runs, and despite this being Morris's 1st book-length venture into non-fictional prose, where he could not summon his customary fluency, 2nd impressions were required within the year of its 1st appearance.

Various posthumous groupings of Morris's prose pieces, lectures, and essays, were made after Forman, and something should be said of their history. In vols. 22 and 23 of the *CW*, both exclusively devoted to Morris's lectures and essays, May Morris follows the scheme that was adopted originally by the trustees in 1897. Then the Morris fugitive and unpublished pieces, those not previously published in the 2 vols. Morris himself collected, *Hopes and Fears for Art* (1882) and *Signs of Change* (1888), were divided into those on art and those on socialism, for possible publication in 2 separate vols. The manuscripts were submitted to 2 different authorities for selection, editing, and arrangement. G. B. Shaw was to select and edit the socialist lectures and W. R. Lethaby those on art. But both took the view that the best lecture material had already been published by Morris, and the publication of the remaining materials would inevitably involve a considerable amount of repetition. So

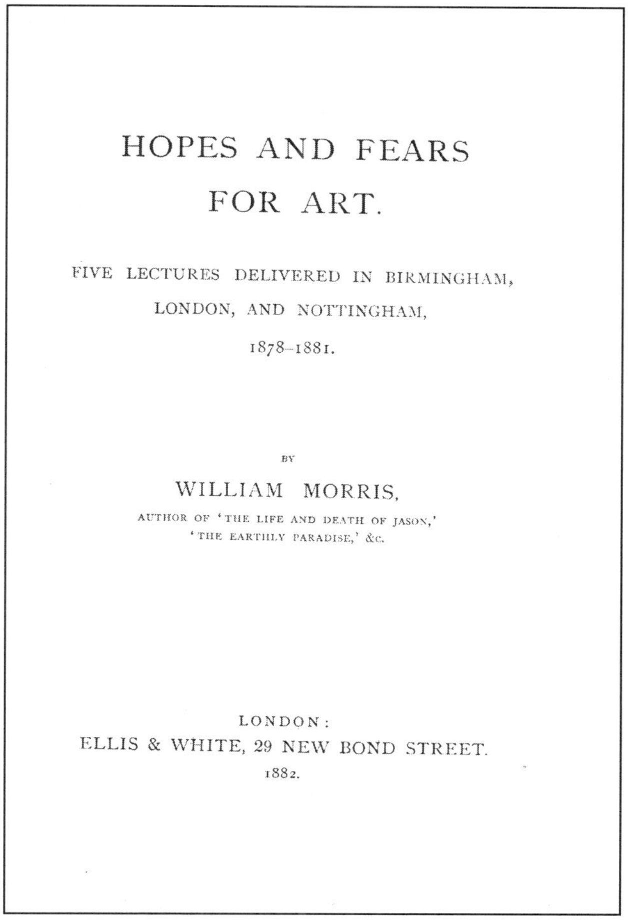

Figure 29. A-21.01: (1st edn.) title page

the plan was abandoned around the turn of the century, though Shaw did edit the lecture *Communism* as a Fabian Tract in 1903 (see A-104.01). Starting in 1898, Sydney Cockerell, with some help from Robert Proctor, produced the 5-vol. 'Golden type octavo' series. Immediately thereafter Cockerell and Proctor selected a mixed batch from the socialist and art papers for their 'Golden-type quarto edition', *Architecture, Industry, and Wealth* (1902, see C-18.01). But in *CW*, vols. 23 and 24, May Morris divides the fugitive pieces as originally planned in 1897: 'Lectures on Art and Industry' and 'Lectures on Socialism'. The reason for her abandoning the Cockerell-Proctor collection is the added scope that made available to her in vols. 23 and 24 of the *CW*, as she explains to Emery Walker in correspondence now at the University of Texas. That enabled her to include more than twice as many of the fugitive and unpublished texts, 23 in fact, with particular emphasis on the Socialist texts, as are in *Architecture, Industry, and Wealth*, which has 11, only 3 of which are overtly Socialist. She did not entirely agree with Cockerell, who advised her in letters of 25 Aug. and 2 Sept. of 1913, when she was making up vols. 22 and 23. In the 1st of these he recommends that the unpublished material be not published both because it repeats the ideas of the already published work and bulks out a canon already very large. A week later, apparently in reply to her claims for the quality of the unpublished work, he suggests again the dangers of bulk for the *CW* and advises that she use a critical eye and publish only that which would be a serious fault to omit.

In fact, May Morris seems to have accepted Cockerell's advice to a considerable degree. While she managed in the *CW* to add the equivalent of another vol. of the uncollected or unpublished prose pieces, there were many left, not all of which made their way into her 2-vol. 1936 edn., *William Morris: Artist, Writer, Socialist.* 10 of those that remained both unpublished and uncollected are included in *Unpublished Lectures* (1969, see A-133.01). Another was subsequently discovered by Paul Meier at the International Institute of Social History (IISH) in Amsterdam (1971), and pbd. as An Unpublished Lecture of William Morris: 'How Shall We Live Then?' (see A-135.01 and D-600). See also 'The Society of the Future' (D-445), the basic text on which the recently discovered MS of 'How Shall We Live Then?' was built.

Later issues and impressions of this edn.:
1. Ellis & White: 1882: Second Edition. [2nd impression, 1st edn.]; *print run*: 1,000 (HBF, p. 100); *price*: 4s. 6d.;
2. Ellis & White: 1883: Third Edition. [3rd impression, 1st edn.]; *print run*: 1,000 copies (HBF, p. 100); *price*: 4s. 6d.;
3. R and T: 1889: Fourth Edition. [4th impression, 1st edn.]; *print run*: unknown; *price*: 4s. 6d.;
4. Longmans: 1896: Fourth Edition. [2nd issue, 4th impression, 1st edn.]; *print run*: copies remaining from R and T, with new title pages with the new publisher's imprint; *price*: 4s. 6d.

A-21.02: Hopes and Fears for Art (RB)

HOPES AND FEARS FOR | ART. | BY | WILLIAM MORRIS, | AUTHOR OF | 'THE LIFE AND DEATH OF JASON,' 'THE EARTHLY PARADISE,' ETC. | BOSTON: | ROBERTS BROTHERS. | 1882.

Edition: [1st impression, 2nd edn., 1st American] Reset from advance sheets of the English 1st edn. In America 'The Lesser Arts' was 1st pbd. separately in 1878 as *The Decorative Arts: Their Relation to Modern Life and Progress* (see A-16.02).

Collation: 8°: π^4 1–13^8 14^6 114 leaves pp. [8] [1] 2–217 [218–20] [= 228].

Contents: p. [1], ads for: MR. WILLIAM MORRIS'S WORKS; p. [2], blank; p. [3], half title; p. [4], bibliographical note: Of the five lectures constituting 'Hopes and Fears | for Art,' only the first has heretofore been printed. [this is an error: the first 4 of the 5 lectures had been previously published in England, see the *Edition* field in A-21.01]; p. [5], title page; p. [6], printer's imprint: UNIVERSITY PRESS: | JOHN WILSON AND SON, CAMBRIDGE.; p. [7]: CONTENTS. [for lecture titles included, see this field in the previous entry]; p. [8], blank; p. [1], dropped heading: HOPES AND FEARS FOR ART | [french rule] | THE LESSER ARTS. | [text begins]; pp. 2–217, text completed; pp. [218–20], blank.

Technical Notes: *paper*: plain white machine-made; *leaf size*: trimmed, 175 x 123 mm.; *printing*: *type area*: 130 x 82 mm.; *lines-to-page*: leaded, 28 lines excepting head and direction lines; *running titles*: lecture titles in italic caps, all rectos and versos; *end-papers*: 3 free ends and paste-down in front, 2 free ends and paste-down in back; facing paste-downs and free ends in tan or dark green matt with floral ornament; *binding*: green or blue cloth with elaborate borders in blue and purple at head and foot of the front and spine (back plain and unblocked): top border triple rules, a Greek style design rule above the gilt-stamped title: • Hopes • and • Fears • for • Art • | [formal pattern of alternating fleurons and circles with dots inside] | [bottom border with alternating thick and thin rules] | [a line of evenly spaced rectangles] | [a series of fan-shaped ornaments alternating with flowers] | [multiple rule of 8 lines] | [a wood-grain pattern with (in some copies) the author's name between 2 fleurons] William Morris; *spine*: gilt-stamped below top border: HOPES | AND | FEARS | FOR | ART | [horizontal rule] | [publisher's monogram within wood-grained foot border] R [superimposed on] B.

Publication: 1882 [issued 24 Feb.–3 Mar.] ('Weekly Record of New Publications', *Pub. Weekly*, 21/529 (4 Mar. 1882), 216); *print run*: 800 copies (Roberts Arch., Cost Book D); *price*: $1.25.

Register of Copies Examined: BGR (base copy); MU; TxU.

Later issues and impressions of this edn.:
1. RB: 1882 [June]: [2nd impression, 2nd edn., 1st American]; *print run*: 280 copies; *price*: $1.25;
2. RB: 1897 [Apr.]: [3rd impression, 2nd edn., 1st American]; *print run*: 280 copies; *price*: $1.25;
3. Longmans NY: 1901: [4th impression, 2nd edn., 1st

American] (Longmans Accts.); *print run*: 250 copies; *price*: $1.25;
4. Longmans NY: 1905: [5th impression, 2nd edn., 1st American]; *print run*: unknown; *price*: $1.25;
5. Longmans NY: 1908: [6th impression, 2nd edn., 1st American]; *print run*: unknown; *price*: $1.25;
6. Post-1915: Micropublished as no. 801 on Reel 59 of 'American Architectural Books' in 1972.

A-21.03: Hopes and Fears for Art

HOPES AND FEARS | FOR ART [2 fleurons] | FIVE LECTURES | DELIVERED IN BIRMINGHAM | LONDON, AND NOTTINGHAM | 1878–1881 | BY | WILLIAM MORRIS | AUTHOR OF | 'THE LIFE AND DEATH OF JASON,' 'THE EARTHLY PARADISE,' ETC. | FIFTH EDITION | LONGMANS, GREEN, AND CO. | 39 PATERNOSTER ROW, LONDON | NEW YORK AND BOMBAY | 1898 | *All rights reserved*
Edition: FIFTH EDITION. [1st impression, 3rd edn., 2nd English] Of the earlier pbns. of the various lectures, see this field in A-21.01.
Collation: quad cr. 8°: π² A–N⁸ O⁶ 112 leaves pp. [4] [1] 2–217 [218–20] [= 224].
Contents: p. [1], half title; p. [2], ad headed: MR. WILLIAM MORRIS'S WORKS.; p. [3], title page; p. [4], blank; p. [1], dropped head: HOPES AND FEARS FOR ART | THE LESSER ARTS* | [text begins]; pp. 2–218, text completed with explicit: THE END | [printer's imprint] Printed by BALLANTYNE, HANSON & CO. | Edinburgh & London; p. [219], the later version of the three-musicians woodcut vignette, within multiple thin-rule compartment; p. [220], blank.
Technical Notes: *paper*: cream-white machine laid, with dandy roll laid lines, no watermark; *leaf size*: 157 x 105 mm.; *printing*: type area: 131 x 81 mm., excluding head and direction lines; *lines-to-page*: thin leaded, 30 lines; *headlines*: running titles: specific lecture titles, all rectos and versos, centred italic caps; *end-papers*: one free end and pastedown, front and back, plain white and blank; *binding*: plain unblocked black cloth; *spine*: printed paper label, 44 x 25 mm.: WILLIAM | MORRIS | HOPES | AND | FEARS | FOR | ART
Publication: 1898 [issued 9 Mar.] (Longmans Arch.); *print run*: 500 copies (Longmans Arch.); *price*: 4s. 6d.
Register of Copies Examined: SU (base copy: 704 M87h.5).
Later impressions of this edn.: Longmans:
1. 1903 [issued 31 Oct.] (Longmans Arch.): [2nd impression, 3rd edn., 2nd English]; *print run*: 800 copies; *price*: 4s. 6d.;
2. 1911 [issued 5 May] (Longmans Arch.): [3rd impression, 3rd edn., 2nd English]; *print run*: 250 copies; *price*: 4s. 6d.; See the Pocket Library entry (A-21.06) for further issues from this setting.

A-21.04: Hopes and Fears for Art (+ Signs of Change, Golden 4°)

[aligned left] HOPES AND FEARS FOR ART. FIVE LECTURES DELIVERED | IN BIRMINGHAM, LONDON & NOTTINGHAM, BY WILLIAM | MORRIS.
Edition: 'Golden type quarto edition' [1st impression, 1st edn. of this combined title] This title is here bound in with *Signs of Change*; but each of the two collections' constituent titles has its own title page, gatherings, pagination and pbn. history. For *Hopes and Fears for Art* this is the 1st impression, 4th edn., 3rd English. For previous publications of the various lectures, see A-21.01 and A-46.01 for *Signs of Change*. This is a cross-reference entry: the details of this book are given in C-17, where this combination of the 2 titles is described. For details common to the Golden 4° set see A-47.04.

A-21.05: Hopes and Fears for Art (+ Lectures on Art and Industry, *CW* XXII)

THE COLLECTED WORKS | [title details common to the set, see A-126.01] | VOLUME XXII | HOPES AND FEARS FOR ART | LECTURES ON ART AND INDUSTRY | [printer's imprint, see A-126.01] | MDCCCCXIV
Editions: *Hopes and Fears* only [1st impression, 5th edn., 4th English] The second title pbd. here, 'Lectures on Art and Industry', is a collection of fugitive pieces that was never pbd. separately. The details of that section is covered here in the *Collation*, *Contents*, and *Technical Notes* fields.
Collation: medium 8°: a⁸–b⁸ (b6+2) c² B–2E⁸ 2F⁴ [$2 signed -a2 c2 B1] 238 leaves pp. [i–viii] ix [x] xi–xxxvi [1–2] 3–152 [*Hopes and Fears* ends and 'Lectures on Art and Industry' begins] [153–4] 155–437 [438–40] [= 476] +1 inserted sh. folded to form 2 leaves not included in the pagination of the book, but noted in the formula and described here under *Contents*.
Contents: pp. [i–iii], blank; p. [iv], limitation note (see this field in A-126.01); pp. [v–vi], blank; p. [vii], title page; p. [viii], blank; p. ix, headed: CONTENTS; p. [x], blank; p. xi, headed: INTRODUCTION | [text begins]; pp. xii–xxviii, Introduction continues; inserted 2-leaf plate between p. xxviii and xxix, a single sheet folded to form 2 leaves of which the 1st and last pages are blank, a black-

and-white photographic reproduction of an opening from a book, labelled below in copperplate: *Pages from Fitzgerald's Rubaiyát of Omar Khayyam written and illuminated by William Morris*; pp. xxix–xxxiv, Introduction concluded; pp. xxxv–xxxvi, headed: BIBLIOGRAPHICAL NOTE | [lists the previous issues of each item included, divided into 2 groups under the 2 main titles]; p. [1], 1st half title: [top left] HOPES AND FEARS FOR ART; p. [2], blank; p. 3, headed: THE LESSER ARTS. DELIVERED BEFORE THE | TRADES GUILD OF LEARNING, DECEMBER 4, | 1877. | [text begins]; pp. 4–152, text completed; p. [153], 2nd half title: [top left] LECTURES ON ART AND INDUSTRY; p. [154], blank; p. 155, headed: ART AND THE BEAUTY OF THE EARTH. A | LECTURE DELIVERED AT BURSLEM TOWN | HALL ON OCTOBER 13, 1882. | [text begins]; pp. 156–437, text concluded; pp. [438–9], blank; p. [440], printer's imprint, see A-126.01. For the Contents of *Hopes and Fears* see this field in A-21.01; 'Lectures on Art and Industry' include: pp. 155–74: Art and the Beauty of the Earth (1881, A-20.01); pp. 175–205: Some Hints on Pattern-Designing (1881, D-69); pp. 206–34: The History of Pattern-Designing (1902, C-18.01); pp. 235–69: The Lesser Arts of Life (1902, C-18.01); pp. 270–95: Textile Fabrics (1884, D-111); pp. 296–317: Architecture and History (1900, C-7); pp. 318–30: The Revival of Architecture (1888, D-372); pp. 331–41: The Revival of Handicraft (1888, D-414); pp. 342–55: Art and Its Producers (1888, D-426); pp. 356–74: The Arts and Crafts of To-day (1889, D-492); pp. 375–90: Art and Industry in the Fourteenth Century (1887, D-491); pp. 391–405: The Influence of Building Materials upon Architecture (1892, D-536); pp. 406–9: The External Coverings of Roofs (1887?, A-44.01); pp. 410–20: Westminster Abbey (1893, A-65.01); and pp. 421–37: An Address . . . at . . . the Birmingham Municipal School of Art (1894, A-71.01).

Technical Notes: for details common to the set see A-126.01, the entry for the *CW*. Included here are only those details that are specific to this particular vol.: *shoulder notes*: all rectos and versos except section heads: the relevant titles of each text; *spine label*: [lines 1–4, see A-126.01] | HOPES AND | FEAR FOR | ART | LECTURES ON | ART AND | INDUSTRY

Publication: 1914 [issued 10 Dec.] (Longmans Arch.); *print run* and *price*: see A-126.01.

Register of Copies Examined: see this field in A-126.01.

A-21.06: Hopes and Fears for Art (LPL)

HOPES & FEARS FOR | ART. FIVE LECTURES | BY WILLIAM MORRIS | *POCKET EDITION* | NEW IMPRESSION | LONGMANS, GREEN, AND CO. | 39 PATERNOSTER ROW, LONDON | FOURTH AVENUE & 30TH STREET, NEW YORK | BOMBAY, CALCUTTA, AND MADRAS | 1919

Edition: Pocket Edition. New Impression [4th impression, 3rd edn., 2nd English] Though published after the 1915 limit for separate recording of books other than 1st edns, this entry is included in order to provide a complete account of the Pocket Library series. For previous pbns. of the various lectures, see A-21.01. Since this impression is the same setting as A-21.03, only details of altered fields are included.

Series: Longmans Pocket Library. For further series detail, see this field in the record of the 1st book in the series, *The Life and Death of Jason*, A-3.09.

Collation: fcap 8°: printed and gathered as a 16°: [A]¹⁶ B–G¹⁶ 112 leaves pp. [6] [1] 2–218 [= 224].

Contents: as A-21.03, except: p. [1]: half title; p. [2], blank; p. [3], title page; p. [4], bibliographic note lists 7 'Editions' plus this 1st Pocket Library version of Feb. 1919; p. [5], headed: CONTENTS | [as a list, flush left, titles + pages of 5 titles]; p. [6], blank; thereafter as A-21.03, until p. 218, text ends with a changed printer's imprint: *Printed at* THE BALLANTYNE PRESS | SPOTTISWOODE, BALLANTYNE & CO. LTD. | *Colchester, London & Eton, England*; pp. [219–20] omitted in the new format.

Technical Notes: *paper*: plain white machine-made; *leaf size*: trimmed, 157 x 106 mm.; *type area*: 131 x 80 mm., *lines-to-page*: leaded, 30 lines; pagination, headlines, etc., as in this field in A-21.03; *binding*: see this field, A-3.09, except gilt-stamped title at head of spine: HOPES | & FEARS | FOR ART | [rule of repeated ornamental circles] | WILLIAM | MORRIS

Publication: 1919 [issued 20 Mar.] (Longmans Arch.); *print run*: 1,000 copies; *price*: 2s. cloth, 3s. lthr.

Register of Copies Examined: LeM (base copy).

Later impressions of this version, after 1915: Longmans:
1. Oct. 1921; *print run*: 1,000 copies; *price*: as above;
2. 1929; *print run*: 1,000 copies; *price*: as above.

A-22.01: Art, Wealth, and Riches

[wrapper title] [REPRINTED FROM THE 'MANCHESTER QUARTERLY, No. VI. Apr., 1883.] | [french rule] | ART, WEALTH, AND RICHES. | BY | WILLIAM MORRIS. | An Address delivered at a Joint Conversazione of the Manchester Literary Club, | the Manchester Academy of Fine Arts, and the Manchester Art Museum | Committee, in the Royal Institution, March 6th, 1883. | Manchester: | 1883.

Edition: [1st impression, 1st edn.] Produced as an offprint of the article pbd. in *The Manchester Quarterly* (see D-77). The article was later (1902) included in *Architecture, Industry, and Wealth*, see C-18.01.

Collaborators, Editors, and Illustrators: [William Edward Armytage Axon, Editor of *The Manchester Quarterly*].

Printer: John Heywood, Manchester.

Collation: large 8°: [1¹²] 12 leaves pp. [153] 154–75 [176] [= 24] + green paper wrapper.

Contents: pagination is that of the journal article, and there is no title page (see wrapper as title, above); p. [153], 2-line dropped head, to ornamental head-piece, circular wreath with floral offshoots, left and right, all within a double thin-rule compartment | drop-head title, in caps, as on wrapper (see above) asterisk, with footnote repeating the names of sponsoring groups as on wrapper, see above] | BY WILLIAM MORRIS. | [text begins]; pp. 154–75, text completed with a tail-piece, an inverted floral triangle; p. [176], blank.

Technical Notes: *paper*: plain white machine-made; *leaf size*: cut flush, 221 x 175 mm.; *printing*: *type area*: 161 x 95 mm.; *lines-to-page*: leaded, 34 lines; *headlines*: all rectos and versos: ART, WEALTH, AND RICHES.; *end-papers*: not used; *binding*: *wrapper*: for contents, see title, p. [1], above; heavy olive green paper with p. [1], details of the original pbn. printed within square brackets; pp. [2–4], blank.

Publication: Apr. 1883 [this offprint was issued at the same time as the Apr. 1883 number of the journal; the lecture was delivered on 6 Mar. 1883]; *print run*: not known; *price*: 'not for sale'.

Register of Copies Examined: BL (base copy: Cup. 502. f. 11. [41], S. C. Cockerell's copy); MH (FC85 M6348 D312); Bass.

Notes: Morris to Thomas Coglan Horsfall, 31 Dec. 1882, on the subject of his coming lecture:

> The point I should try to drive home would be the old one, to wit, that there can be only one foundation for real art, the desire of the whole people to have it; that this desire cannot exist while they are divided into 'cultivated' and 'uncultivated, i.e. degraded' clases [sic]. This is what I must say if I am to speak in public on matters of art *generally*; but it will sound horribly revolutionary, I fear, to many people: now I am not afraid or ashamed of speaking my mind in any audience, but I want to know if you think that weighty matters would be over serious for the occasion in question. If I may do what I should really like, I might call my paper "Art, Wealth and Riches" (*Letters*, ii. 145).

To Jenny Morris, 14 Mar. 1883:

> I have just got back from my lecture with the proofs as they are going to print it: so I shall be able to bring it down & read it to you: a letter from one of my friends there says that the philistines are much moved by it, that there have been 2 leading articles about it in the papers already, and a correspondence beginning: so you see one may yet arrive at the dignity of being hissed for a Socialist down there: all this is encouraging (*Letters*, ii. 174–5).

For a description of the Press controversy, see E. P. Thompson, *William Morris: Romantic to Revolutionary* (308–9; hereafter referred to as Thompson).

A-23.01: Chants for Socialists

DEMOCRATIC FEDERATION. | [french rule] | **CHANTS FOR SOCIALISTS**: | No. I. | THE DAY IS COMING. | BY | WILLIAM MORRIS, | *Author of "The Earthly Paradise," etc.,* | [ornamental rule] | LONDON: | REEVES, 185, FLEET STREET, E.C.

Edition: [1st impression, 1st edn.] Because the various pamphlet versions of the *Chants for Socialists* constitute a single series of the same texts, with later edns. including all the previously published poems plus any additional poems, the pbd. texts are treated here as a single title with successive edns., the distinction depending of course on whether the text is less or more than half reset.

When completed *Chants for Socialists* included 7 poems, 5 of which were originally printed in Socialist periodicals: (1) *The Day is Coming*, 1st pbd. as the pamphlet described in this entry; (2 and 3) 'The Voice of Toil' and 'All for the Cause' were 1st pbd. in *Justice* (see D-98 and D-100). The separate pamphlet pbn. combining these 2 and titled, *The Voice of Toil: All for the Cause. Two Chants for Socialists*, is a forgery, discussed in Section E: Forgeries, Piracies, and Sophistications (see E-2); (4) 'No Master', 1st pbd. in *Justice* (see D-106); (5) 'The March of the Workers', 1st pbd. in *Commonweal* (see D-132); (6) 'The Message of the March Wind', 1st pbd. in *Commonweal* (see D-134), where it became the 1st instalment of *The Pilgrims of Hope*, Morris adopting that title when deciding to make a story from the material introduced in the poem; (7) 'Down among the Dead Men', initially issued. in the complete *Chants* collection, 1885 (see A-23.03).

During Morris's lifetime the poems accumulated in 3

successive separate publications, 4 if one counts the forged edn., which however seems to have made no public appearance until after Morris died. The 3 legitimate original separate issues are *No. I, The Day is Coming* (1883) with only the title poem; the 1st collected edn. of 6 *Chants for Socialists* (1885), and the 2nd collection of 7 poems, published later the same year, using the same setting but adding 'Down among the Dead Men' which completes the series.

Collation: s. sh. cr 8°: [1]⁴ 4 leaves; pp. [1–2] 3–8 [= 8] + wrapper.

Contents: p. [1], title page; p. [2], blank; p. 3, dropped head: CHANTS FOR SOCIALISTS | [french rule] | THE DAY IS COMING. | [text begins]; pp. 4–8, text completed with: [thin rule] | [imprint] Printed at The Modern Press, 13 & 14, Paternoster Row, London, [*sic*]

Technical Notes: *paper*: white machine-made; *leaf size*: 181 x 120 mm.; *printing*: *type area*: 132 x 84 mm.; *lines-to-page*: leaded, 29 lines counting blanks between stanzas; *running titles*: all versos: CHANTS FOR SOCIALISTS. | [all rectos] THE DAY IS COMING.; *wrapper*: BL Ashley 1222 has a plain blue paper wrapper around the original wrapper. BL Cup. 502.f.11 (39) has the original cream-white wrapper: p. [1], duplicates the title page above except for introducing the price below 'Author of "The Earthly Paradise," etc.': [between thin rules, in fat-face type] **Price One Penny**.; p. [2], blank; p. [3], headed: Social Programme of the Democratic Federation.; p. [4], ad for the DF's social and political manifesto, *Socialism Made Plain*.

Publication: n.d. [issued 11 Sept. 1883] The poem was written in early Sept. 1883 (see Morris's letter to Jenny Morris, 4 Sept. 1883, in *Notes*, below). The Reeves and Turner Arch. includes a ledger book of William Reeves, 185, Fleet Street, the son of William Reeves of Reeves and Turner. This records 500 copies of this pamphlet sent to the younger Reeves for distribution. Reeves received these, presumably from the printer, on 11 Sept. 1883, which seems the mostly likely date of issue. Forman's positioning of this pamphlet in his chronological sequence implies it was not pbd. until the following year. But that date, considering both Morris's 4 Sept. letter to Jenny (see *Notes*, below) and the Reeves ledger, is obviously wrong. Either date, of course, is consistent with the pamphlet being advertised, as it was, in the 1st number of *Justice*, 19 Jan. 1884, p. 8, as being available through William Reeves, 185, Fleet Street, E.C. This the first of several Morris socialist pbns., identifiable by the publisher's address, in which the younger William Reeves took a hand as either publisher or distributor. *Print run*: unknown, but at least 500 copies were sent to Reeves; *price*: 1d.

Register of Copies Examined: CtY Beinecke (base copy: Tinker 1612); BL (3 copies: Ashley Library 1222 (9:103); Cup. 502. f. 11. [39.]; and 11652. cc. 51.; MH (*EC85. M8348. 884c).

Notes: It is clear that the younger William Reeves was here, as often in the case of Morris's socialist publications, a distributor rather than the publisher. The true publisher, who initiated the enterprise and guaranteed the costs involved, was the DF, possibly subsidised by Morris himself.

Morris to Jenny Morris, 4 Sept. 1883: 'Item I have made a little poem for them [the DF], a copy of which I would have sent you, my dear, but that it has gone to the printer straight' (*Letters*, ii. 223–4). This lyric was 1st pbd. as a separate pamphlet, *Justice* having not yet begun publication.

A-23.02: Chants for Socialists

[self-wrapped; 1st line within Walter Crane's SL headpiece] THE SOCIALIST | LEAGUE | [below the headpiece] CHANTS FOR SOCIALISTS | BY | WILLIAM MORRIS. | [wavy rule] | Contents: | [titles, in single column, centred] 1. The Day is Coming. | 2. The Voice of Toil. | 3. All for the Cause. | 4. No Master. | 5. The March of the Workers. | 6. The Message of the March Wind. | [thin rule] | PRICE ONE PENNY. | [thin rule] | PUBLISHED AT | THE SOCIALIST LEAGUE OFFICE, 27 FARRINGDON STREET, | LONDON. E.C. | [thin rule] | 1885.

Edition: [1st impression, 2nd edn.; 1st collected edn.] (2nd edn. because more than half is reset) This account does not include the forged *Two Chants for Socialists*, for which see E-2. For previous pbns. of the individual poems, see *Notes* in A-23.01.

Collaborators, Editors, and Illustrators: Walter Crane designed 3 line-block head-pieces associated with a number of Morris publications. Each incorporates the label as part of the design: 'The Commonweal', 'The Socialist League', and 'The Hammersmith Socialist Society'.

Printer: [The International Publishing Company, 35 Newington Green Road, N.] (from an invoice in the Socialist League Archive, The International Institute of Social History, Amsterdam, Reel 7. Hereafter referred to as SLA).

Collation: demy 8°: a single gathering of 8 leaves pp. [1–3] 4–15 [16] [= 16] self-wrapped, but some copies have an illegitimate red wrapper (see E-3).

Contents: p. [1], title page; p. [2], 17-line epigraph, unsigned, by Morris, quoted from his lecture *Art and Socialism* (see

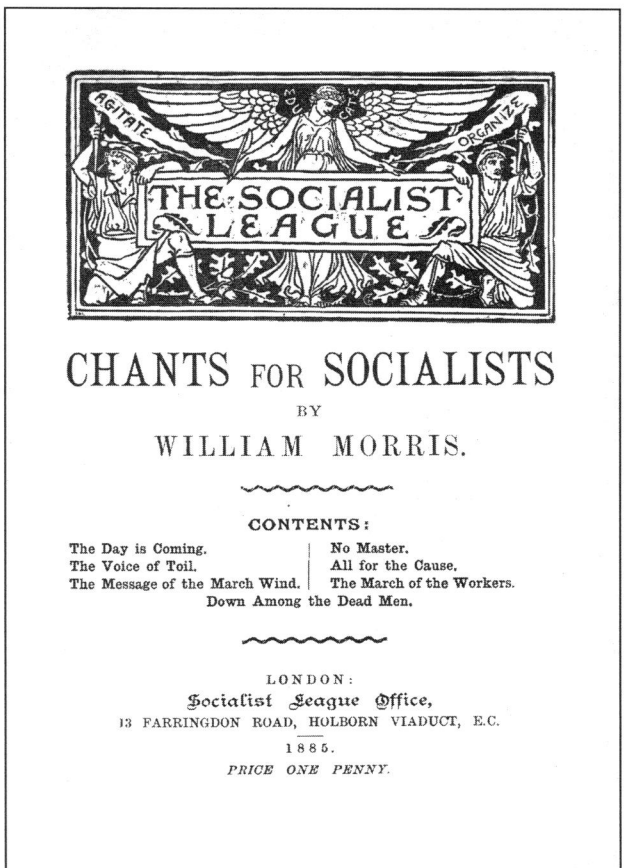

Figure 30. A-23.03: *Chants for Socialists* (2nd edn., 1st complete) wrapper title

CW, xxiii. 194); p. [3], dropped-head title: CHANTS FOR SOCIALISTS | [french rule] | THE DAY IS COMING | [text begins]; pp. 4–15, text completed; p. [16], ads for *Commonweal* and *The Socialist Platform*, a series of SL pamphlets (1885–90) hereafter referred to as SP: [headed with Walter Crane's *Commonweal* head-piece reproduced in HBF, p. 113] | [printer's imprint at the foot below thin rule] Printed and Published by W. Morris and J. Lane at 27 Farringdon St., London, E.C.
Technical Notes: *paper*: plain white machine-made; *leaf size*: 224 x 145 mm.; *printing*: type area: 124 x 103 mm.; *lines-to-page*: leaded, counting extra spaces between verses, 36; *binding*: wrapper: see E-3.
Publication: 1885 [issued Apr.] (see 'Monthly Report', *Commonweal*, I/4 (1 May 1885), 36), and the bill for the printing from The International Publishing Company is dated '30 April 3 1885' (see *Notes*, below); *print run*: 3,000 copies; *price*: 1d.
Register of Copies Examined: MH (base copy: 2 copies, one with and one without the wrapper: *EC85. M8348. and B898p); BL (Cup. 502. f. 11.[40.])
Notes: Forman enters the *Socialist Manifesto* and *Constitution and Rules* pamphlets between *Chants for Socialists No. 1—The Day is Coming* and the remaining edns. of the *Chants*. Since the League shifted its headquarters from 27 Farringdon Street to 13 Farringdon Road on 6 July 1885, the publisher's address in the imprint on this *Chants* pamphlet is another indication that it was issued before *The Manifesto of the Socialist League*.
16 pp. demy 8°; cost for setting and printing the 2nd edn. of *Chants* in 3,000 copies: £4. 15s. 0d. (SLA, Reel 7).

A-23.03: Chants for Socialists

[self-wrappered: 1st line within W. Crane's SL head-piece] THE SOCIALIST | LEAGUE | [below head-piece] CHANTS FOR SOCIALISTS | BY | WILLIAM MORRIS. | [wavy rule] | CONTENTS: | [7 titles, 6 titles in 2 columns of three and a 7th centred below them, columns divided by a vertical rule, left col.:] The Day is Coming. | The Voice of Toil | The Message of the March Wind. | [right] No Master. | All for the Cause. | The March of the Workers. | [centred] Down Among the Dead Men. | [wavy rule] | LONDON: | [in gothic] Socialist League Office, | [plain type] 13 FARRINGDON ROAD, HOLBORN VIADUCT, E.C. | [thin rule] | 1885. | *PRICE ONE PENNY*.
Edition: [2nd impression, 2nd edn.] With 'Down among the Dead Men' added; comparison with the 1st impression indicates the text is the same setting as this, except for minor changes to the title page and the added 7th lyric printed on p. 16, used for ads in the prior version. For 1st pbns. of these poems, see this field in A-23.01. Since this is a 2nd impression of the edn. described in A-23.02, only details of altered fields requiring amendment are included here.
Printer: no printer's imprint is included in either this 1885 or the 1892 impressions of this edn. It is possible that the printing was done by the League's own *Commonweal* printing press. The address in the publisher's imprint ensures that it was done after 6 July 1885, and by Oct. of that year, the League's press was in operation. But it could also have been done by a jobbing press, several of which were, as shown in the SLA, doing work for the League at about this time.
Collation: s. sh. cr. 8°: [1⁸] 8 leaves pp. [1–3] 4–16 [= 16] neither trimmed nor sewn, sold in folded sheets, self-wrappered, i.e. without a separate wrapper, the first and last leaves, being integral and of course conjunct, provide both the title page and the end of the text.

Contents: as in the previous entry except for the addition of 'Down among the Dead Men' on p. 16.
Technical Notes: *paper*: plain white machine-moulded, no watermark; *leaf size*: untrimmed and unbound, avg. 190 x 127 mm.; when, as in some copies, cut flush, 183 x 126 or 186 x 125 mm.; *printing*: *type area*: 140 x 83 mm.; *lines-to-page*: leaded, 33 lines; *running heads*: [all versos] CHANTS FOR SOCIALISTS. | [all rectos, the relevant poem title in caps]; *pagination*: arabic numbers at the outer margins of headlines, except pp. 11 and 13, centred.
Publication: 1885 [issued sometime after 6 July] (see *Printer*, above); *print run*: unknown; *price*: 1d.
Register of Copies Examined: LeM (base copy); Fdmn; BL (4 copies: 11652. cc. 51. [2.];11602. ee. 43. [2.]; Cup. 502. f. 11. [37]; and Ashley 1224); NN (SFC. n.c.1); MH (2 copies: *EC85. M8348. B898p, and Typ 8304. 85.15).
Later impression of this edn.:
1. SL: 1892: [3rd impression, 2nd edn.], imprint address changed to 40, Berner Street, Commercial Road, E.; *print run*: unknown; *price*: 1d.

A-23.04: Chants for Socialists (+ Pilgrims of Hope, LPL)

THE PILGRIMS OF HOPE | AND | CHANTS FOR SOCIALISTS | BY | WILLIAM MORRIS | LONGMANS, GREEN [swash ampersand] & COMPANY | 39 PATERNOSTER ROW, LONDON | FOURTH AVENUE & 30TH STREET, NEW YORK | BOMBAY, CALCUTTA, AND MADRAS | 1915 | All rights reserved
Edition: Pocket Edition. This is a reference entry: for details of this pbn., see the main entry for *The Pilgrims of Hope and Chants for Socialists* in Collections, C-33.
Publication: 1915 [issued 11 Sept.] (Longmans Arch.).
Register of Copies Examined: see this field in C-33.

A-24.01: A Summary of the Principles of Socialism

A | SUMMARY | OF THE | PRINCIPLES OF SOCIALISM | *Written For The Democratic Federation,* | H. M. HYNDMAN AND WILLIAM MORRIS. | [thin rule] | LONDON: THE MODERN PRESS, | 13 AND 14 PATERNOSTER ROW, E.C. | 1884.
Edition: [1st impression, 1st edn.] This 1st impression was printed on FP. The 2nd impression has thinner paper and a smaller price. See *Technical Notes*, below.
Collaborators, Editors, and Illustrators: the text is a collaboration by H. M. Hyndman and William Morris, with a wrapper designed by Morris.
Collation: cr. 8°: [A–B]⁴ C–E⁸ 32 leaves pp. [1–3] 4–62 [63–4] [= 64] sewn to a Morris-designed wrapper (HBF, pp. [103–4]).
Contents: p. [1], title page; p. [2], blank; p. [3], head title: [4-line dropped head] A SUMMARY | OF THE | PRINCIPLES OF SOCIALISM. | [thin rule] | [text begins]; pp. 4–62, text completed: [signed flush left] EXECUTIVE COMMITTEE OF THE DEMOCRATIC FEDERATION, | [16 names arranged in 2 columns]; pp. [63–4], blank.
Technical Notes: *paper*: cream machine-made, no watermark; *leaf size*: cut flush 185 x 120 mm.; *type area*: 141 x 85 mm.; *lines-to-page*: leaded, 32 lines, excluding head and direction lines; *pagination*: arabic numbers centred on the headlines; *wrapper*: cream-white paper; p. [1], floral design, 2/3, one-third each, top and bottom; middle third without ornament and printed in sans serif type, all within a thin-rule compartment, letterpress entirely within the central unornamented band: A SUMMARY | OF THE PRINCIPLES | OF | [3-line pica] SOCIALISM | WRITTEN FOR | THE DEMOCRATIC FEDERATION, | BY | H. M. HYNDMAN & WILLIAM MORRIS.; pp. [2–4], blank.
Publication: 1884 [issued 1–15 Jan.] (the 1st number of *Justice*, 19 Jan. 1884, p. 8, announces the pamphlet as 'Just Published'); *print run*: unknown; *price*: 1s.
Register of Copies Examined: BL (2 copies: base copy: 08275. ee. 76. [2.] and Cup. 502.f.11 [27]); CSt.
Notes: this very early pamphlet published by the DF has given rise to some disagreement as to the relative contributions of Morris and Hyndman to its joint authorship. In a footnote in the 1st edn. of his *William Morris: Romantic to Revolutionary* (deleted from the 2nd edn.) E. P. Thompson quotes Hyndman's correspondence with Alf Mattison to the effect that Hyndman wrote all but one and a half pages, for which Morris was responsible. But Thompson casts doubt on Hyndman's testimony, citing the *Joint Manifesto of English Socialists* as an instance where Hyndman also claimed the main authorship and was gainsaid by one of his collaborators, George Bernard Shaw (Thompson, 387). But on this question see also a letter from Morris to Jane Cobden, 12 Jan. 1884: 'I will send you our last pamphlet, in which I have had a small share' (*Letters*, ii. 255–6).

A 2nd problem has to do with dating the various impressions and at least one variant, all of which issue from the same setting, but do not always have dates. Forman reproduces the 2 versions of the printed wrapper, but not in their original colours. Both from Morris designs, the 1st impression wrapper is printed on cream-white paper and the 2nd and all later impressions in the period of our concern on pink paper (HBF, pp. 104–5): the 1st, which limits the ornaments to the top and bottom thirds of the wrapper title, has all the letterpress in the central third in sans serif type, and the second, printed on pink paper has Morris's ornamental border entirely surrounding the letterpress, which extends into the top and bottom thirds, here in a mixture of type designs. Forman says the 1st wrapper was for the 'first edition' and the 2nd, i.e. A-24.02, 'for the second and later issues' (HBF, p. 105). Some copies of the 2nd impression with the pink paper wrapper also differ from the 1st in that some of the copies left over from the Modern Press printing, also on the pink paper and without advertising, were transferred to William Reeves who printed a single line through the Modern Press imprint and inserted below it the Reeves imprint (see the SSL copy in the *Register of Copies* for A-24.02). Another distinguishing detail is cited by HBF (p. 108). the first impression is sewn, the 3rd is 'wire stitched', i.e. stapled, and the 3rd, entirely manufactured by Reeves, is stabbed and sewn with thread through the holes thus provided. In all 3 cases, the wrapper is glued on after the stapling or sewing was done. All were printed from the same plates. The copies after the first issue, on thinner paper, were reduced in price to fourpence.

Morris to William James Linton, 26 Oct. 1883: '. . . I did not write Socialism made plain, though I fully agree with it. Before long we hope to have a more extended pamphlet [described here] on Socialism published which I don't doubt would interest you' (*Letters*, ii. 241).

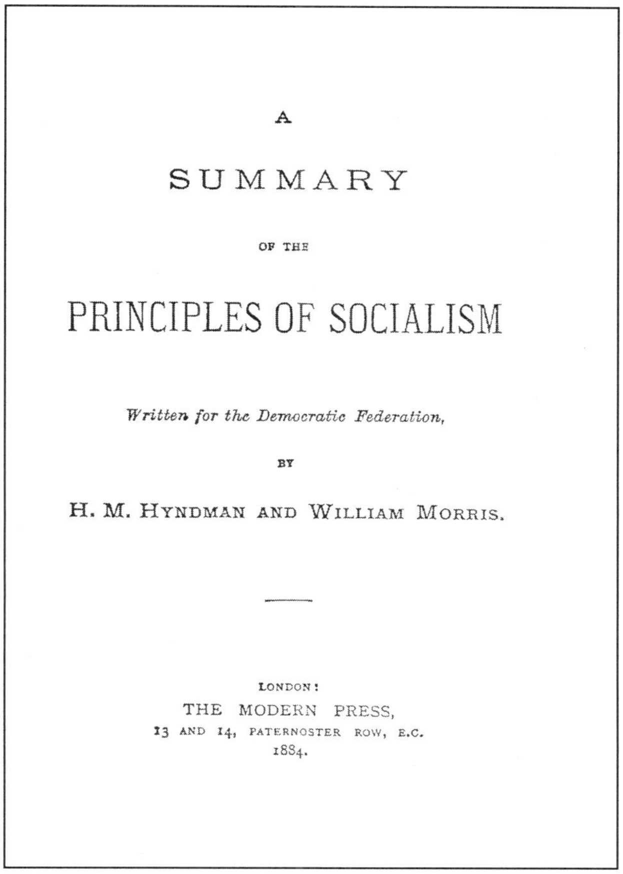

A-24.02: A Summary of the Principles of Socialism

Title: as in A-24.01.
Edition: [2nd impression, 1st edn.] This impression includes an unknown number of variant copies with an altered imprint on the title page (copy in SSL, 335/ P). The original version is: THE MODERN PRESS, | 13 AND 14, PATERNOSTER ROW, E.C. | 1884. In the variant copies all of this is ruled out with a straight line printed through the letterpress and a new imprint printed below: WILLIAM REEVES, 185, FLEET STREET, LONDON, E.C. Since this entry is largely a duplicate of the 1st impression, A-24.01, only detail of altered fields is included here.
Contents: as in A-24.01, except for the variant imprint on the title page (see above).
Technical Notes: *paper*: printed on cheaper, machine-moulded pink paper. Otherwise the same as the 1st impression, A-24.01, except the 2nd wrapper is used (HBF, p. [105]) with the price printed above the compartment, p. [1]: Price FOURPENCE; ads for Modern Press Socialist

Figure 31. A-24.01: Summary. . . Principles of Socialism (1st edn.) wrapper title

pbns. on pp. 2–4 of the pink wrapper and pp. [63–4] of the body; thinner paper in the body.
Publication: 1884 [issued 15 Oct.– 1 Nov.] (announced in *Justice* on 25 Oct. as 'in press', and on 1 Nov. as 'Now Ready. Price Fourpence' 1/41 and 42 (25 Oct., 1 Nov. 1884), 8, 8); *print run*: unknown; *price*: 4d.
Register of Copies Examined: BL (2 copies: base copy: 08275. ee. 76. [2.] and Cup. 502.f.11 [28])); Bass; NPar; SSL (Pamphlet section, no. 335); CSt (335/H9975)
Notes: Morris to Arthur Spencer, 5 Mar. 1884: 'I am writing to our office to bid them send you literature for distribution: I will send you 6 of a pamphlet which has been published at rather a high price, but which will soon come out in a cheap edition (*Letters*, ii. 267). HBF says (p. 108): 'There is an issue of the same year on slightly thinner paper, differing from the first in that it is wire-stitched, with a pink wrapper of which the ornamentation is rearranged as is shown opposite [i.e. the 2nd version], and the 2nd, 3rd and 4th pages filled with ads, as is the last leaf (pp. 63 and 64).'

A-24.03:* A Summary of the Principles of Socialism

Title: as in A-24.01, varied as described in A-24.02, except for the change of date: 1896.

Edition: [3rd impression, 1st edn.] Since this is largely a duplicate of the 1st impression, A-24.01, only details of altered fields are included here.

Collaborators, Editors, and Illustrators: Morris and H. M. Hyndman collaborated in this book (but see the *Notes* to A-24.01).

Publisher: W. Reeves, 185, Fleet Street, E.C.

Printer: William Reeves? The present Mr William Reeves, full name William Arnold Reeves, grandson of William Reeves of 185 Fleet Street and great-grandson of William Dobson Reeves of Reeves and Turner, says that his grandfather acquired a printing press in 1885, a fact corroborated by the presence of that imprint on several pbns. of the time, and operated it well into the 20th Century. It is possible that the Reeves imprint on the title page of this impression is intended to replace that of the Modern Press as printer, but the imprint is the only evidence of relevance to that so far found.

Publication: 1896: Forman had, or used, a copy so dated on the title, but a copy from CSt has no date, nor does BL Cup 502.f.11.(28), in which internal evidence shows that it must be 1891 or later. An ad on p. [63] (hence integral to the text) lists Morris's *Under an Elm Tree*, which was 1st separately pbd. by James Leatham in 1891. *Print run*: unknown; *price*: 4d.

Register of Copies Examined: CSt (base copy: 335/H9975); BL (2 copies: Cup. 502.f.11. [28]) compared with BL (Cup. 502.f.11. [27]): this later version (later is 28, earlier 27) cut flush, size: 186 x 125 mm, has new Wm. Reeves' advertisements both on the last leaf (pp. *63-4*) and on the wrapper (it is at least possible that Reeves was also the printer, having acquired a press in 1885 which he named The Temple Press and operated from his usual address, 185 Fleet Street).

A-25.01: Art and Socialism

[all within thick-thin ruled compartment, type aligned left, in gothic] Art and Socialism: [plain type] a | Lecture delivered [January | 23rd, 1884] before the Sec- | ular Society of *Leicester*, | by William Morris, | author of *"The Earthly | Paradise,"* etc. | [thin rule]. | And *Watchman: What of the Night?* | [thin rule] | Cum Privilegio Auctoris. | [2 columns, on either side of a central sun face within circumambient rays: left of sun ornament] Imprinted for | E. E. M. and W. L. S. | Anno 1884 | [right of sun ornament] Sold by W.

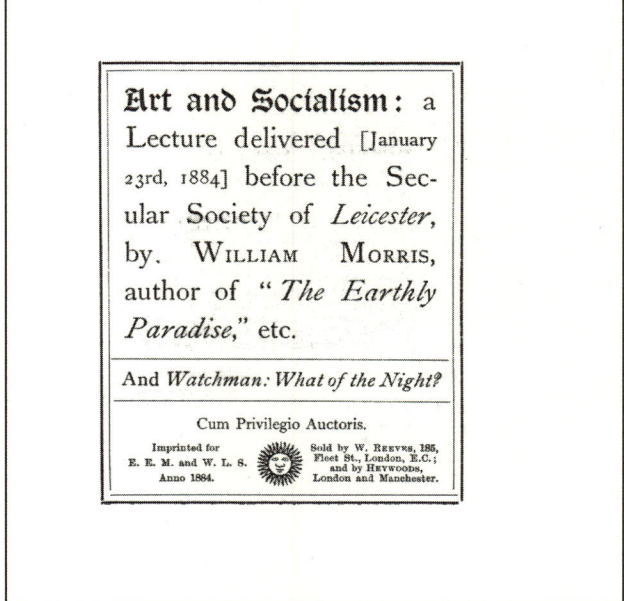

Figure 32. A-25.01: *Art and Socialism* (1st edn.) title page

Reeves, 185, | Fleet St. London, E.C.; | and by Heywoods, | London and Manchester.

Edition: [1st impression, 1st edn.] Forman says nothing of variants other than the 1st ordinary and LP impression of this pamphlet. But considerable variation has been noted in the copies seen, particularly in the wrappers: Though all imprint dates seen are the same, '1884', later impressions seem likely, given that the pamphlet was in print from 20–25 May 1884 until at least 20 May 1890, when *Commonweal* declared it out of print and appealed for clean copies for purchase (p. 152). But no direct or collateral evidence has been found for more than the 2 impressions entered here. Several copies include different combinations of head and tail-pieces, but the reversal of head and tail-piece blocks (see *Technical Notes*, below) may indicate the 1st and 2nd impressions. The imprint suggests that Reeves was a distributor, like Heywood, while the publishers were Sugden and Minton. No printer's imprint appears on any copies seen, but all the copies seen contain the same imprint date, 'Anno 1884.' No other publisher issued this pamphlet in the period 1884–1915.

This lecture was later included in a collection of Morris's fugitive pieces— *Architecture, Industry, and Wealth*— edited by S. C. Cockerell and R. Proctor and issued in 1902 (see C-18.01).

Series: Leek Bijou Reprints, No. VII. This series is obviously conceived as a vehicle of 'free thought', at the time

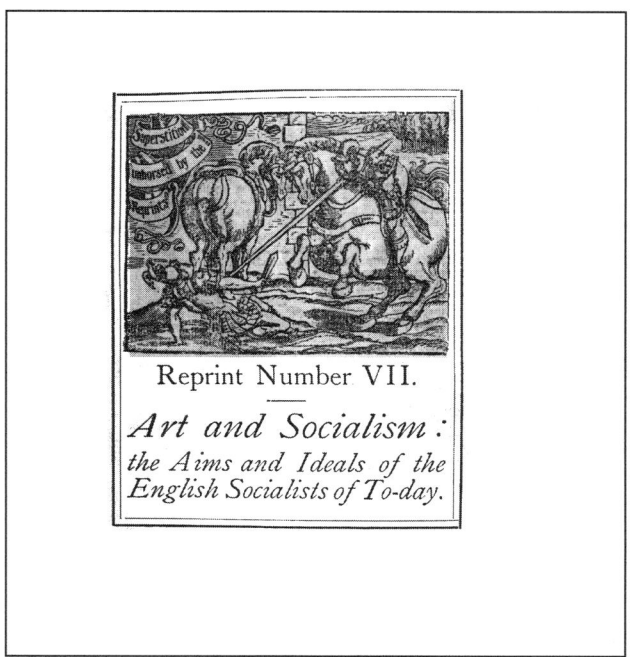

Figure 33. A-25.01: *Art and Socialism* (1st edn.) wrapper front cover

the primary concern of the National Secular Society, the Leek branch of which arranged Morris's lecture.
Publisher: Imprinted for E. E. M. and W. L. S. [Ethelbert Edward Minton and Warner Larner Sugden (see *Notes*, below)].
Printer: no printer's imprint, but the printer was probably the Freethought Publishing Company, whose address was the same as the pamphlet's 'publishing office': 29 Queen Street, Leek, Staffordshire. See this field in A-25.02.
Collation: cr. 16°: [1]⁴⁴, conjugate pairs inserted inside previous ones in sequence, hence a single gathering sewn to the wrapper through the centrefold, 44 leaves pp. [1–5] 6–56 [59–60] 61–72 [73–88] [= 88]. Since this is a 16°, the 44 leaves are printed on 2 and 3/4 sheets (not '3 3/4' as in HBF, p. 111).
Contents: p. [1], half title: [within a thick-thin rule compartment, the Bijou Reprint bookmark, 'Superstition Unhorsed by the Reprints'] | [below woodcut] Reprint Number VII. | [thin rule] | *Art and Socialism:* | *the Aims and Ideals* | *of the English Socialists of To-day.*; p. [2], 18-line epigraph signed, below right: John Ruskin: | Stones of Venice, II, Ch. 6.; p. [3], title page; p. [4]: [14 lines of verse] | [signed below right] Wordsworth: | Sonnet xxxiii; p. [5], head title with ornamental head-piece, a late classical design of verdure coiling around a double pediment with 2 birds, one each side, and a central vase as the source of the verdure, all within a double thin-rule compartment with printer's flowers between the rules | ART | and | SOCIALISM. | [thin rule] | [text begins]; pp. 6–58, text completed with floral tail-piece; p. 59, 2nd half title: "*Watchman, What of* | *the Night?*" | [ornamental tail-piece, direct contrast to the head-piece, with floral forms only, much closer to what Morris did, but certainly not Morris; the contrasting head and tail-pieces are reversed in some copies of the second printing and may be a means of distinguishing the two printings]; pp. [60]–72: [text, quotations from English and American writers, followed by tail-piece]; p. [73], 3rd half title: [within thin-rule compartment] THE | *Bijou Advertiser.* | [ornamental tail-piece]; pp. [74–88], ads, ending with tail-piece and: [ENTERED AT STATIONERS' HALL].
Technical Notes: *paper*: LP copies: cream-white hand-laid, Van Gelder watermark, foot of leaf at centrefold; the paper of the BL and LeM LP copies are uncut, with deckled edges; *leaf size*: avg. 143 x 132 mm.; *paper*: ordinary copies: cream-white machine-wove; *leaf size*: trimmed, avg. 130 x 93 mm.; *printing*: type area: 75 x 68 mm., excluding head and direction lines; *lines-to-page*: set solid, 22 lines, omitting head and direction lines but counting single blank lines separating all paragraphs; *pagination*: arabic numerals centred on headline and enclosed between parentheses; *wrapper*: ordinary copies: printed in red on machine-made paper, pink outside, white inside; wrapper p. [1]: LEEK BIJOU REPRINTS, NO. VII | [floral head-piece] | [text as on the title page (above) but with no compartment] | [leaf and vine ornamental border] | PRICE 3d.; wrapper p. [2]: PUBLISHER'S NOTE. | A few large paper copies have been pulled | on hand-made Dutch paper, and | may be obtained | —post free 1/- each —from the Publishing Office, | 29 Queen Street, Leek. | [entered at Stationers' Hall]; p. [3], ad for *To-Day*; p. [4]: ad for *Justice*; the square brackets on p. [2] of wrapper are in the original.
Publication: 1884 [issued between 20 and 24 May] The lecture was first delivered on Jan. 23 1884 (See *Justice*, 1.3 (2 Feb., 1884, 7. On the date of pbn., see Morris's letter to Mahon and the date of the *Justice* ad, 24 May 1884, both quoted in *Notes*, below); *print run*: unknown; *price*: ordinary copies 3d., LP copies 1s.
Register of Copies Examined: BL (4 copies: base copy: Cup.502.f.11.[16], 4017.a.8. [LP copy], 4017.a.6 [first of the two copies bound in a single volume, the second, BL 4017.e.6, being the "Second Edition," (see 26.02) which is actually the first reprint of the 1st edn.); CSt (V 335/ M877ar/ Rare Book Room); Fdmn (2 copies)

Notes: the pamphlet was not yet published when Morris wrote to J. L. Mahon, 20 May [1884]: 'Larner Sugden is publishing one of my lectures [Art and Socialism] as perhaps you know: perhaps it might sell with you, though 'tis not as good as the one I gave at Edinburgh', i.e. *Useful Work* versus *Useless Toil* (*Letters*, ii, 282).

A *terminus ad quem* for the issue date is provided by the 1st notice of the pamphlet in a Reeves ad in *Justice*, 1/19 (24 May 1884), 8: 'Leek Bijou Reprints. No. 7. 80th Thousand [this figure probably refers to the whole 1st series of Leek Bijou Reprints]. price 3*d*.'

Kelvin also provides a note: 'William Larner Sugden (1850–1901), [was] an architect at Leek who was on the committee of the SPAB. In 1896 he founded the William Morris Labour Church at Leek' (*Letters*, ii. 282, note). 'E. E. M.', Sugden's collaborator, is identified in a signed declaration of membership in the SL: 'Ethelbert Edward Minton, Rudyard Near Leek, Banker's Accountant, 4 May 1885 (Staffordshire)' (SLA, Reel 4).

A-25.02: Art and Socialism

Title: as in A-25.01.

Edition: 2nd Edition 'Popular Edition' [2nd impression, 1st edn.] This issue includes both the cheaper 'Popular' or ordinary edn. and the LP variant. The BL collection of Morris pamphlets from Cockerell (BL Cup. 502.f.11) also includes a copy designated '2nd Edition' (actually the 2nd impression of the lecture portion) ornamental device at the foot of the wrapper, which has been reset, though the pale pink colour is retained. The 2nd title on the 2nd impression wrappers, p. 1, has been changed, omitting 'Watchmen: What of the Night' and inserting in its place a new title: 'With Parallel Passages from Poets and Philosophers' (the contents of the section remain the same). Some copies of the 2nd impression also have reversed the head-piece and tail-piece of the 1st impression. This printing, like the 1st, includes LP copies on Van Gelder handmade paper with pale yellow (primrose) wrappers printed in red; as with the 1st impression, as announced on the respective wrappers, the ordinary copies were priced at 3*d*, the LP copies 1*s*. Since this impression largely duplicates A-25.01, only contents of altered fields are included here.

Series: The Leek Bijou Reprints, No. VII.

Printer: [Freethought Publishing Company, 29 Queen Street, Leek, Staffordshire] (see *Publication* field).

Contents: this second impression reverses the head and tailpieces of the 1st impression of Morris's text.

Technical Notes: as A-25.01, except the ordinary wrapper: same pink outside, white inside, wove paper printed in red, same ornamental borders, top and bottom; wrapper, p. [1], same imprint, but the main title and 'Watchman, What of the Night' are changed: ART AND | SOCIALISM: | by William Morris, | Author of 'The Earthly Paradise,' etc. | With Parallel Passages from Poets | and Philosophers | [below the bottom border] 2nd Edition. PRICE 3d.; the other three pages of the wrapper are identical with the 1st printing except the shifting of the formula '[ENTERED AT STATIONERS' HALL]' from the wrapper to the last line of the body, below the tail-piece (p. 88). Ornamental borders, pp. 5 and 58 have changed places, the 1st becoming last and the last 1st in the reprint.

Publication: 1884 [issued June] (an ad for this edn. appears in *Justice*, 28 June 1884 as 'Second Edition, Dutch paper 1/-. Popular Edition 3*d*. Art and Socialism by William Morris. William Reeves, 185, Fleet Street, E.C.: Heywoods, London and Manchester; Freethought Publishing Company, 29 Queen Street, Leek, Staffordshire'). Both wrappers of the '2nd Edition' are reset. *Print run*: unknown.

Register of Copies Examined: LeM LP (base copy, without wrapper); Cst (with Morris autograph "2nd Edition" wrapper); BL (4017.a.6. second copy).

A-26.01: [Hammersmith Manifesto] (DF)

[head title spaced across the top] <u>Agitate. Educate. Organize.</u> | THE | DEMOCRATIC FEDERATION, | HAMMERSMITH BRANCH. | *Temporary Premises:—Kelmscott House, Upper Mall, Hammersmith.* | [text begins]

Edition: [1st impression, 1st edn.] Though the title given in the heading above was never used on the leaflets on which it was printed, this is the name which the DF and the SL and their associates used among themselves to identify it. This 1st edn. was printed both as a poster and a leaflet, both printed on one side only. But the leaflet went through 3 more issues, roughly doubling in size and finally being included as *What Socialists Want*, No. 11 in the Socialist League Leaflet series (see the 3 following entries).

Collation: s. sh., 8°, printed on one side, also printed as a poster, folio size.

Contents: *heading*: see above; text begins: Fellow Workers,; text ends at the foot with notice of Branch meeting times and Secretarial address; ad: "JUSTICE," *the organ of the Social Democracy,* ONE PENNY WEEKLY, | to be had of all newsmen. | [aligned left, thin-rule] | Churchman, Printer, Hammersmith.

Technical Notes: *paper*: white machine-made; *leaf size*: fly sheet, 186 x 124 mm., printed on one side; duplicated as a folio poster, 342 x 213 mm.

Publication: [issued 16–23 June 1884] (The Hammersmith Branch was formed on Saturday, 14 June 1884, and the manifesto written and pbd. by Morris in the days shortly thereafter (see *Justice*, 1/23 (21 June 1884), 5; and The Hammersmith Branch Minute Book (BL (Add.) MS 45891; hereafter referred to as Ham. Min. Book).

Register of Copies Examined: WMG (2 base copies, folio and 8vo: K 1562); BL (Cup. 502.f.11. (12.)

Notes: Sydney Cockerell's collection once had at least 2 copies of this text, both as pbd. by the SL in a version issued after the break with the DF. One is now in a collection he gave to the BL in 1957 (now catalogued as Cup. 502.f. 11.) and the other in the Huntington Library. To the BL copy (Cup. 502.f.11. (12.)) Cockerell added a longhand note: 'Printed from Draft in William Morris's handwriting of first Socialist manifesto issued in Hammersmith.' To the one in the Huntington Library, San Marino (HM 36915), he has added 2 notes. On the margin at the foot of this copy he writes: 'Written by W. M. The first manifesto, originally issued by the Hammersmith Branch of the Democratic Federation'. The 2nd, on the mounting sheet where the verso of the original leaflet is attached, refers to Morris's handwritten notes, drawings, doodles, on the originally-blank verso of the leaflet: 'These were notes made by Morris during the discussion following a lecture by him at Kelmscott House, Hammersmith, I think in 1886. They are on the back of a leaflet which is now very scarce, written by Morris for the Hammersmith branch of the Democratic Federation and here reprinted for the newly formed Socialist League'. The 1st edn. described in this entry was issued in mid-1884 when the Hammersmith Branch was affiliated with the DF. Copies of the 1884 (or 1st) edn., in both poster and handbill versions, are kept at Walthamstow (WMG K 1562). The texts, though reset for the Branch's SL version of the leaflet, vary only in details, eg. the references to the DF change to SL, meeting times are changed, and advertising for *Justice* changes to *Commonweal* in the later version.

Justice, 1/23 (21 June 1884), 5: 'Hammersmith: A Branch of the Federation was formed here on Saturday last [i.e. 14 June]. The temporary place of Meeting is at Kelmscott House, Upper Mall. The Secretary, pro tem, is Mr. E. Walker, 3 Hammersmith Terrace W. who will be glad to receive the names of all who desire to become members.'

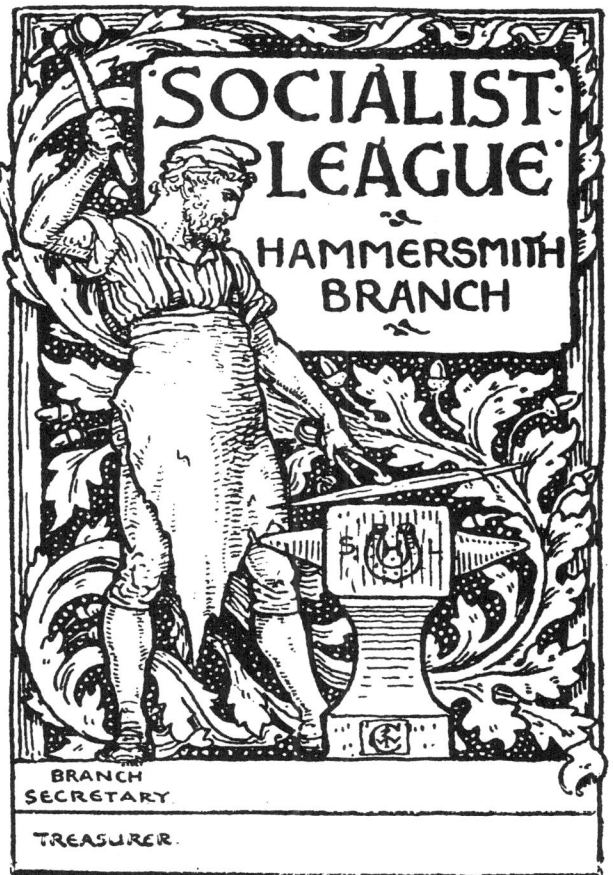

Figure 34. A-26.02: membership card, Hammersmith Branch, SL (Socialist League)

A-26.02: [Hammersmith Manifesto] (SL)

Title: as in A-26.01, except references to the DF change to Socialist League, and references to *Justice* have changed to *Commonweal*, etc. (see *Contents*, below).

Edition: [1st impression, 2nd edn.] Comparison of the 2 texts and their settings confirm that the text of the 'manifesto',1st issued by the Branch in June 1884, is the same, but it has been reset in the SL version. Later, in Jan. 1887, Morris wrote a 'New Manifesto' for the Branch, double the length of the original, which was published by both the Hammersmith and Norwich Branches of the SL and later, as Socialist League Leaflet No. 11, *What Socialists Want* (for this 2nd Manifesto, see A-26.04).

Collation: 8°, s. sh., printed on one side only, though League Branches sometimes printed advertising or lecture schedules on the blank verso of these manifestoes.

Contents: as A-26.01, except the lines 2–5 of the heading change to: THE | SOCIALIST LEAGUE | HAMMER-

SMITH BRANCH | Kelmscott House, Upper Mall, Hammersmith. The text that follows duplicates that of the previous impression, except for the Branch information at the foot of the page: [indent] Members of the Branch meet every Sunday, at 7 p.m., for business at Kelmscott House, | Upper Mall, (notice the board on the gate). All information can be obtained there as to meetings, | lectures and literature of the Socialist League. Lectures of the Hammersmith Branch (every Sunday | at 8 p.m.) are announced in "The Commonweal." | [¶] All communication to be addressed to the Secretary, Hammersmith Branch of the Socialist | League, 3, Hammersmith Terrace, W. | [formatted in hanging indent] Read 'The Commonweal' the official organ of the Socialist | League, ONE PENNY, monthly, to be had of all Newsmen | [thin rule] | Churchman, Printer, Hammersmith.
Technical Notes: as in A-26.01, though no evidence has appeared that indicates this edn. was also done as a poster.
Publication: n.d. [issued 1 June–5 July 1885] The Hammersmith Branch reported at the First General Meeting of 5 July 1885, that its manifesto had been issued (see *Commonweal*, 1/7 (Aug. 1885), 73); *print run*: unknown; *price*: printed for free distribution.
Register of Copies Examined: BL (base copy: Cup. 502. f. 11. [12]).

A-26.03: [Hammersmith Manifesto] (SL)

[Morris-designed masthead block in 4-line Old Face with oak-branch ornament from a central stem] THE | SOCIALIST LEAGUE | [below the block] HAMMERSMITH BRANCH. | [text begins]
Edition: [1st impression, 3rd edn.] Textually, this leaflet is clearly the successor to the original Branch Manifesto (see A-26.01). None of these issues (A-26.01, 2, 3, and 4) was ever printed with 'Manifesto' in the title. The text described here, like A-26.04, is a successor to the earlier 'Manifesto'. It is treated here as a new edn., being a thorough revision of the original text, ending more than twice as long as the 1st 'Manifesto', but addressing the same audience and retaining both the outline and much of the wording of the original.
Collation: s. sh. 8°, printed on both sides. Some copies of this are folded to form a 4-page leaflet with advertising on the last 2 pages.
Contents: imprint at the bottom of the 2nd page: [text ends, followed by a thin rule] | Issued by the Socialist League, 13 Farringdon Road, London, E.C. | The 'Commonweal', Journal of the Socialist League. 1d. weekly.

Technical Notes: *paper*: plain white machine-made; *leaf size*: 215 x 135 mm. In other respects, such as type area, type, and setting, the text duplicates the 1st Hammersmith and the subsequent Norwich versions.
Publication: [issued 9 Jan.–14 Apr. 1887] (see *Notes*, below); *print run*: unknown; *price*: for free distribution.
Register of Copies Examined: BL (3 copies: base copy).
Notes: the 2 preceding impressions help establish the authorship and approximate date of issue of the Branch version and the SL Leaflet titled *What Socialists Want* (see the next entry):

1. The Ham. Min. Book entry for the meeting of 9 Jan. 1887, refers to this leaflet: 'W. Morris read a new manifesto which he had written for the branch to publish.'

2. Morris to John Glasse, 14 Apr. 1887: 'I send you the leaflet you mentioned by me; Binning at the League will deal with you if you want any; it is now called: What the Socialists want' (*Letters*, ii. 640).

Later impression of this version:

1. Norwich Branch, SL: [1887]: [2nd impression, 2nd edn.]; *print run*: unknown; *price*: for free distribution. This impression differs only in the substitution of the branch name in the heading: NORWICH BRANCH.; and a new ad at the foot of p. 2: [thin rule] | Free Lectures are given every Sunday at the Gordon Cafe, Duke St., | See the 'Commonweal', Journal of the Socialist League, 1d. weekly.

A-26.04: [Hammersmith Manifesto] (SL)

[head title:] No. 11.] | WHAT SOCIALISTS WANT. | [wavy rule] | [text begins]
Edition: [2nd impression, 3rd edn.]There are only minor changes in this impression from A-26.03, see *Contents*, below.
Series: Socialist League Leaflets No. 11 [the last pbn. in this series; for series detail see A-33.01].
Collation: a single demy 8° leaf, printed on both sides; but sometimes this leaflet appears as a folded sh. of two 8° leaves: pp. [1–2] being the text and [3–4] ads.
Contents: as in the previous entry, except for the headings (see above and in the previous entry); the text is divided at the foot one line further on than in the Hammersmith and Norwich impressions; and the imprint and ads at the foot of the verso differ here: *Issued by the Socialist League, 13 Farringdon Road, London, E.C.* | The 'COMMONWEAL,' Journal of the Socialist League. 1d. weekly.
Technical Notes: see this field in the previous entry; same setting, except for heading and imprint, as the Hammer-

Original and Posthumous Editions

smith Branch version; both printed on both sides from the same setting.

Publication: [issued between 14 Apr. and 24 June 1887] For this 2nd impression, the interval of issue is between Morris's mention of the SL version in his letter to Glasse and the 1st public record of its issue. This League version was deposited in the BM and has an accession date of 24 June 1887, along with a number of other League publications that required deposit under copyright law. But, as frequently with these leaflets, it is not possible to account for all the times and numbers of reprints.

Register of Copies Examined: BL (base copy, with accession stamp dated '24 JU 87'); IISH Amsterdam.

Later impressions of this version:

1. SL: [issued shortly after 11 June 1888]: [3rd impression, 3rd edn.]: it was agreed 20,000 of leaflets 'What Socialists Want' were to be printed (from 'Weekly Letter', an internal SL report of the Council Meeting of 11 June 1888, SLA, Reel 3); *price*: for free distribution;

2. SL: [issued after 11 Nov. 1889]: [4th impression, 3rd edn.] (when the League moved to offices at 24 Great Queen St., Lincoln's Inn Fields W.C.); *print run*: not known; *price*: for free distribution;

3. HSS: [issued sometime after the HSS was formed in 1891: 5th impression, 3rd edn.]; Same as the SL version, but without the series announcement and with a new imprint: [below a thin rule] Issued by the Hammersmith Socialist Society, Kelmscott House, Upper Mall, | Hammersmith, W. Lectures and discussion every Sunday evening at | 8 o'clock. Open free to all; *leaf size*: 223 x 141 mm.

A-27.01: Textile Fabrics

International Health Exhibition. | LONDON, 1884. | [thin rule] | TEXTILE FABRICS | A LECTURE | DELIVERED IN THE | LECTURE ROOM OF THE EXHIBITION, | *JULY* 11th, 1884. | BY | WILLIAM MORRIS. | PRINTED AND PUBLISHED FOR THE | [gothic type] Executive Council of the International Health Exhibition | and for the Council of the Society of Arts, | [plain text] by | WILLIAM CLOWES AND SONS, LIMITED, | INTERNATIONAL HEALTH EXHIBITION, AND 123, CHARING CROSS, S.W. | 1884.

Edition: [1st impression, 1st edn.] This lecture was 1st pbd. as an article in *The Architect*, 19 and 26 July 1884 (see D-111), this is the 1st of 2 lectures written by Morris with similar titles and subject matter. This one was printed both in the record of proceedings, *International Health Exhibition Literature* (vol. 12, part 3: see D-111) and separately as one of the pamphlet series of lectures delivered at the conference. This separate pbn. appears to be an offprint of the Health Exhibition Literature version. The 1st of the 2 lectures by Morris both at one time titled 'Textiles', this one was included by Cockerell and Proctor when they collected and edited certain of Morris's fugitive pieces in *Architecture, Industry, and Wealth*, in 1902 (see C-18.01). The second, initially titled 'Tapestry and Carpet Weaving', when printed in *The Arts and Crafts Exhibition Society. Catalogue of the First Exhibition, 1888* (see D-410), was retitled 'Textiles', causing some confusion when reprinted in *Arts and Crafts Essays by Members of the Arts and Crafts Exhibition Society*, edited by Morris (see B-15).

Series: Morris's lecture was the 23rd in the lecture series.

Collation: 8°: B¹⁶ 16 leaves pp. [1–3] 4–29 [30–2] [= 32] + grey paper wrapper. The conjugate leaves are folded one inside the other to form a single gathering of 16 leaves, sewn to the wrapper through the centrefold.

Contents: p. [1], title page; p. [2], printer's imprint: LONDON: | PRINTED BY WILLIAM CLOWES AND SONS, LIMITED, | STAMFORD STREET AND CHARING CROSS.; p. [3], head title: International Health Exhibition | LONDON, 1884 | [thin rule] | July 11th, 1884. | [thin rule] | LECTURE ON 'TEXTILE FABRICS.' | By WILLIAM MORRIS. | [thin rule] | [text begins, first 2 words in caps]; pp. 4–29, text completed; p. [30], blank; p. 31, printer's imprint, as above; p. [32], blank.

Technical Notes: *paper*: plain white machine-made; *leaf size*: cut flush, 212 x 137 mm.; *printing*: type area: 161 x 93 mm.; *lines-to-page*: leaded, 38 lines; *running titles*: all rectos and versos: TEXTILE FABRICS.; *wrapper*: printed in brown on pale green paper: p. [1], 3-rule compartment, with Celtic designs at each corner and a crown centred at the top of the compartment border flanked on the left with: ISSUED BY; and on the right: AUTHORITY and at the foot, below the compartment: PRICE: SIXPENCE.; inside the compartment: [3-line display types in an arc] INTERNATIONAL | [4-line display types] HEALTH | [3-line display type] EXHIBITION | [swelled rule] | [2-line letters] LECTURES. | [french rule] | [2-line letters, in sans serif type] TEXTILE FABRICS | *A Lecture delivered in the Lecture Room of the* | *Exhibition, July 11th, 1884.* | BY WILLIAM MORRIS. | *PRINTED AND PUBLISHED FOR THE* | [in gothic type] Executive Council of the International Health Exhibition, | and for the Council of the Society of Arts, | BY | WILLIAM CLOWES & SONS, LIMITED, | INTERNATIONAL HEALTH EXHIBITION,

| AND 13, CHARING CROSS, S.W. | 1884.; p. [2], list of 'Conferences in connection with the International Health Exhibition.'; p. [3], 'Lectures delivered in connection with the International Health Exhibition.' [here Morris's lecture is titled 'Textiles Generally'; p. [4], a list of 'Official Publications . . . cognate to the International Health Exhibition.'
Publication: 1884 [issued c. July–Aug.] (i.e. after the 11 July delivery at the Conference). This dating alters the sequence of Forman's chronology, where this lecture is placed before 6 different titles previously pbd.: *A Summary of the Principles of Socialism*; the first of the *Chants for Socialists*; 2 of Forman's inventions: *Two Chants for Socialists* and *The God of the Poor*; the pamphlet *Art and Socialism*; and the *Manifesto of the Hammersmith Branch*. As Forman assumes in the case of *Art and Socialism* (p. 111), it is reasonable to expect this lecture to have been issued in print shortly after its delivery; *print run*: unknown; *price*: 6d.
Register of Copies Examined: BL (base copy: 7959. cc. 2.); Fdmn; NPar; VSL; MH (*EC85. M8348. B898p).

A-28.01: To Socialists

[head title with dropped head, with ornamental rules as line fillers before and after the title and others before and after each word, in swash caps:] • TO • SOCIALISTS •¨ | [thin rule] | [text begins]
Edition: [1st impression, 1st edn.] A printed circular letter addressed to all socialists and intended to explain the secession of the majority from the SDF and the formation of The Socialist League. On Morris's authorship, see *Notes*, below.
Printer: [Empire Printing and Publishing Co. Ltd., 25 Salisbury Court, E.C.] (see *Notes*, below).
Collation: s. sh. folded once to form two 8° leaves pp. [1] 2–3 [4] [= 4].
Contents: p. [1], dropped head, see above; pp. 2–3, text completed: [date, left, indented] 13th January, 1885. [signed, as a list] Edward Aveling. | Eleanor Marx Aveling. | Robert Banner. | E. Belfort Bax. | J. Cooper. | W. J. Clark. | Joseph Lane. | S. Mainwaring. | J. L. Mahon. | William Morris. | [indented] *Issued from the offices of* | "THE SOCIALIST LEAGUE," 27, *Farringdon Street, London, E.C.*; p. [4], blank.
Technical Notes: *paper*: plain white machine-moulded with dandy roll laid lines, no watermark; *leaf size*: cut flush, 193 x 130 mm.; *type area*: 153 x 90 mm.; *lines-to-page*: leaded, 34 lines; *pagination*: centred on headlines in arabic numbers.
Publication: 13 Jan. 1885; *print run*: 2,000 copies ?; *price*: printed for free distribution (SLA, Reel 8).
Register of Copies Examined: BL (base copy: 8275.dd.22); Bass.
Notes: 'It [i.e. the 'letter of explanation'] declared . . . that there was in the S. D. F., 'a tendency towards National assertion, the persistent foe of Socialism'. The quotation is taken from this pamphlet (see *Letters*, ii. 373 note 2). For a complete text of the 'letter of explanation', see *Tom Mann's Memoirs* (1923, rptd. by Macgibbon and Kee, 1967), 30–1.

Referring to what seems likely to have been the 1st printing of the *To Socialists* leaflet, M. Hare of the Empire Printing and Publishing Co. Ltd., 25 Salisbury Court, E.C., sends a note to the SL, dated 4 Jan. 1885, saying: 'Herewith proof of 4pp. leaflet, please sign one authorizing us to proceed, and correct for size of paper, etc.
Later impressions of this edn.:
1.* SL: 1885 [issued 20 Jan.]: [2nd impression, 1st edn.]; print run: 2,000 copies; price: for free distribution. Printed by Perkins, Bacon & Co. of 36–40 Whitefriars Street, Fleet Street (SLA, Reel 8);
2.* SL: 1885 [issued 30 Jan.]: [3rd impression, 1st edn.]; print run: 2,000 copies; price: for free distribution (SLA, Reel 8).

A-29.01: The Socialist League Manifesto (1st edn.)

[head title aligned flush left, dropped head:] PRICE ONE PENNY] | THE | MANIFESTO | OF | THE SOCIALIST LEAGUE | [text begins]
Edition: [1st impression, 1st edn.].
Collaborators: Morris and E. Belfort Bax were co-authors (see *Notes*).
Collation: 8° half sh. [1]⁸ 4 leaves pp. [1] 2–7 [8] [= 8]; self-wrappered, the first and last leaves, being integral and of course conjunct, provide both the title and the beginning and end of the text.
Contents: p. [1], head title as above, text begins; pp. 2–7, text completed: Signatures Provisional Council of the Socialist League. | [19 names in small caps] | [double thin rule] | [publisher's note:] Those who accept the principles herein stated are requested to communicate | with the Secretary, Office of THE SOCIALIST LEAGUE, 27, Farringdon | Street, London, E.C.; p. [8], ad for forthcoming 1st number of *Commonweal*, to be 'Ready on January 28th', and the printer's imprint: [thin rule] | Printed by ARTHUR BONNER, 63, Fleet Street, London, E.C.— 1885.
Technical Notes: *paper*: plain white machine-made, no watermark; *leaf size*: 186 x 129 mm.; *printing*: type area: 141 x 85 mm.; *lines-to-page*: set solid, 44 lines; *pagination*: ara-

bic numbers centred on the headline; *binding*: no separate wrapper, but with dropped-head title, above, pp. [2-3], text; p. [4], blank.

Publication: 1885 [issued 12–19 Jan.] (2 letters, both in SLA, the first from A. Scheu to SL Secretary, dated 11 Jan., indicates the *Manifesto* had not yet been issued by that date; and the second, a letter from C. J. Faulkner to J. L. Mahon, dated 20 Jan., establishes that copies had been received in Oxford by then, copies which must have been sent by the 19th). Thus this separate pamphlet version appeared shortly before the text appeared in the 1st number of *Commonweal*, 30 Jan. (masthead date: Feb.), 1885, pp. 1–2 (see D-131). An ad on p. [8] of this 1st issue says *Commonweal* will be, 'Ready on January 28th'; *print run*: not known; *price*: one penny.

Register of Copies Examined: MU, (base copy: Spec. Coll PR 5080/M3, 1885, 1st ed. without wrapper, identical with the MH copy); MH (*48-895); BL (8275.dd.22.); Bass.

Notes: Morris to Andreas Scheu, 4 Jan. 1885: '. . . I am anxious to hear what you think of the manifesto, it is Bax and I conjointly' (*Letters*, iii. 370).

Morris to William Sharman, 6 Jan. 1885: 'in a few days we shall have our manifesto and a letter of explanation of our secession printed, which of course will be sent to you' (*Letters*, ii. 372).

Later impressions from this edn.: SL:

1. see the next entry, A-29.02;
2.* 1885 [Apr.]: [3rd impression, 1st edn.]; *print run*: 4,000 copies (bill from Progressive Publishing, see SLA, Reel 8); *price*: 1d.;
3.* 1885 [issued c. 23 May] (bill from Progressive Publishing, see SLA, Reel 8): [4th impression, 1st edn.]; *print run*: 4,000 copies; *price*: 1d.

A-29.02:* The Socialist League Manifesto (2nd impression, 1st edn.)

[wrapper title] THE MANIFESTO | OF | [within no. 2 woodcut block by Walter Crane] THE SOCIALIST | LEAGUE | [below the woodcut] WRITTEN BY WILLIAM MORRIS, | SIGNED BY THE PROVISIONAL COUNCIL, AT THE FOUNDATION OF THE | LEAGUE ON 30TH DEC. 1884, AND ADOPTED AT | THE GENERAL CONFERENCE | *HELD At FARRINGDON HALL, LONDON, on July 5th, 1885.* | [wavy rule] LONDON: | [in gothic] SOCIALIST LEAGUE OFFICE, | 13 FARRINGDON ROAD, HOLBORN VIADUCT, E.C. | [thin rule] 1885.

Edition: [the 2nd impression of the 1st edn.] This is a genuine pamphlet. But the white wrapper with the title as above is fraudulent (perhaps printed here by a confusion with the superfluous 'Turner-grey' wrapper described by Forman as for the 'New Edition' (see A-29.03) he describes on the next page. Such a confusion is possible if it is remembered that Forman's versions of title pages are not limited to photographic reproduction. He had the services of a printer able to reproduce in his own type the titles supplied by Forman. That way wherever necessary title pages could be shrunk without a corresponding shrinking of the letterpress, by reducing the spacing between lines. Where duplication was not possible, such as in the case of the Socialist League blocks by Walter Crane, they could be borrowed and photographic reproductions made. And there are places where comparison of the title pages in HBF with copies of the originals exposes many instances where the printer's resources failed to produce a facsimile).

The fact is that this Manifesto was not 'written by William Morris' but jointly by Morris and Bax, as were the annotations later added to the 2nd edn. Remembering Morris's niceness of conscience in matters of authorship (see *Notes* in A-5.01 and 29.01), it is safe to conclude that neither of the wrappers for this pamphlet Forman cites as having a line 'WRITTEN BY WILLIAM MORRIS' on the title page is genuine (see E-6).

The pamphlet, however is genuine, and it is therefore described here. Other than the added wrapper, this impression of the pamphlet duplicates A-29.01.

Publication: 1885 [issued 19 Mar.]: [2nd impression, 1st edn.] (see bill from Progressive Publishing Co. for *Manifesto*, SLA, Reel 8). Forman says for this impression, 'a white wrapper was added' with a new title page printed thereon with Walter Crane's The Socialist League woodcut, this being, Forman implies, the 1st use of that woodcut; *print run*: 10,000 copies; *price*: 1d.

Register of Copies Examined: none with the 'Turner-grey' wrapper have been seen or located, otherwise as for A-29.01.

A-29.03: The Socialist League Manifesto (2nd edn.)

[wrapper title] THE MANIFESTO | OF | [Walter Crane's vignette SL head-piece block incorporating a label:] THE SOCIALIST | LEAGUE | [below woodcut block] SIGNED BY THE PROVISIONAL COUNCIL AT THE FOUNDATION OF THE | LEAGUE ON 30TH DEC. 1884, AND ADOPTED AT | THE GENERAL CONFERENCE | *Held at FARRINGDON HALL, LON-*

DON, on JULY 5, 1885 | [thin rule with central circle] | A New Edition, Annotated by | WILLIAM MORRIS AND E. BELFORT BAX. | [wavy rule] | LONDON: | [in gothic] Socialist League Office, | [plain type] 13 FARRINGDON ROAD, HOLBORN VIADUCT, E.C. | [thin rule] | 1885. | *PRICE ONE PENNY.*

Edition: A New Edition. [1st impression, 2nd edn.] Though reset, the original text remains the same in this 2nd edn., but the annotations by Morris and Bax roughly double the original Manifesto's length.

Printer: [Progressive Printing Co., 28 Stonecutter Street, E.C.] (SLA, Reel 8).

Collaborators, Editors, and Illustrators: [The 1st edn. was written by Morris and Bax (see *Notes* to A-29.01)]. Annotated by William Morris and E. Belfort Bax.

Collation: single 8°: [1]⁸ 8 leaves pp. [1–3] 4–7 [8–9] 10–14 [15–16] [= 16] self-wrappered, i.e. without a separate wrapper, the first and last leaves, being integral and of course conjunct, provide both the title page and the end of the text; but some copies have a forged wrapper added by Forman. Of this wrapper, Forman says (p. 115): 'Though generally circulated without a wrapper, there are copies—but these are rare—in a Turner-grey wrapper on which the title is repeated with an additional line below the design, "WRITTEN BY WILLIAM MORRIS," and the words "price one penny" omitted'. But see Morris to Scheu, January 4, 1885: "… I am anxious to hear what you think of the Manifesto, it is Bax and I conjointly" (*Letters*, ii. 370). This is sufficient proof that Morris had nothing to do with this wrapper. But the wrapper may prove to be a chimera in its other sense of a will-o'-the-wisp. Collins was unable to find even a single copy.

Contents: p. [1], title page; p. [2], headed: PREFATORY NOTE. | [thin rule] | [12 lines of text] | [signed, below right] E. BELFORT BAX. | WILLIAM MORRIS. | [aligned left] *October, 1885*.; p. [3], dropped head: THE MANIFESTO | OF | THE SOCIALIST LEAGUE | [french rule] | [text begins]; pp. 4–8, text; p. [9], dropped head: NOTES ON THE MANIFESTO | [swelled rule] | Notes begin, arranged alphabetically; pp. 10–13, Notes continue; p. 14, Notes end with signatures: [below right] E. BELFORT BAX. | WILLIAM MORRIS. | [thin rule] | [formatted in hanging indent] *Those who accept the principles herein stated are requested to communicate | with the Secretary, Office of* THE SOCIALIST LEAGUE, *13 Farringdon | Road, London, E.C.*

Technical Notes: *paper*: plain white machine-made; *leaf size*: 182 x 121 mm.; *printing*: type area: 142 x 84 mm.; *pagination*: arabic numbers centred on the headlines; *lines-to-page*: hair leads, 36 lines; *binding*: self-wrappered.

Publication: 1885 [issued 13 Oct.] The verso of the 2nd edn. title page has an editorial note by Morris and Bax dated 'October, 1885.' In the Oct. number of *Commonweal* (pbd. 30 Sept., p. 92), Morris responded to a letter from W. Cabell, saying, 'part of W. Cabell's inquiries will be answered in the Notes to the Manifesto of the Socialist League by Bax and Morris, which are going though the press'. In a letter to H. H. Sparling (dated by Kelvin as 'October 13, 1885') Morris mentions that 'May will fetch away mani: tonight' (*Letters*, p. 465), which, considering the other evidence, suggests that as the probable day of issue.

Register of Copies Examined: LeM (base copy); MU (Spec. Coll PR 5080/M3, 1885, 1st ed. without wrapper); ANL (RB Ec 4319).

Later impression of this edn.: SL:

1.* Mar. 1886: [2nd. impression, 2nd edn.]; *print run*: 150 copies; *price*: 1d. The 'Manager's Report' (i.e. H. A. Barker's), 29 Mar. 1886, lists 13 doz. copies of the Manifesto among 'pamphlets issued during month' (SLA, Reel 3).

A-30.01: The Commonweal

THE | [masthead] COMMONWEAL. | [left of the single line that follows and with only the closing square bracket] REGISTERED | FOR] [6-line caps] THE OFFICIAL JOURNAL OF THE SOCIALIST LEAGUE. [right of the single line that precedes and with only the opening square bracket] [Transmission | Abroad. | [thick-thin rule] | [aligned left] Vol. I — No. 1 [centred] FEBRUARY, 1885 [aligned right] ONE PENNY. | [thin-thick rule] | [text begins, in 2 cols.].

Edition: [1st impression, 1st edn.] There was a 'Second Edition', i.e. a 2nd impression of the 1st number, after the 1st printing of 5,000 was exhausted (see *Notes*, below). These copies carry above the masthead, aligned right, the words: <u>SECOND EDITION.</u> The square brackets in the 3rd and 4th lines of the title are in the original. These 4 bracketed words (to be read together) are single spaced at the right margin. The concern here is with vols. 1–6, Feb. 1885 to 15 Nov. 1890, the period of Morris's direct involvement as editor, contributor, and—with Joseph Lane—proprietor of record.

Collaborators, Editors, and Illustrators: William Morris was appointed editor from 6 Jan. 1885, with Edward Aveling as sub-editor; and both were formally elected at the 1st Annual Conference on 5 July 1885. Morris was re-elected at annual conferences, with a series of different assistants, until May 1890. After losing the editorship election to D.

J. Nichol at the Conference of 25 May 1890, he continued to make contributions until after the concluding instalment of *News from Nowhere* was issued on 4 Oct. 1890, ending his connection with the paper with an article titled 'Where Are We Now?' published on 15 Nov. 1890 (see D-525). As editor, he worked with 4 sub- or assistant, editors: Edward Aveling (6 Jan. 1885–13 June 1886); the end of Aveling's term came on 1 May 1886, with the transition to a weekly (see *Commonweal* of that date, p. 36), Bax replacing him as sub-editor pro tem until the Annual Conference on 13 June; E. Belfort Bax (13 June 1886–Jan. 1887, when he resigned); and Henry Halliday Sparling, who was appointed to replace Bax in Jan. 1887, elected at the 3rd annual conference, 29 May 1887, and re-elected at the conferences of 1888 and 1889. On 9 June 1889, the Annual Conference elected D. J. Nichol as a second assistant editor. Morris and Sparling were replaced, respectively, by D. J. Nichol and F. Kitz at the annual conference of 25 May 1890. Besides the Assistant Editors, there was a 'Manager' (equivalent to the modern 'Managing Editor') of *Commonweal* through the middle 1880s, beginning with J. L. Mahon in 1885.

Series: Begins as a monthly, from Feb. 1885, through Apr. 1886. Weekly pbn. begins with the 1 May issue, 1886, but the last 4 monthly issues contained 4-page supplements.

Place: The original address was '27 Farringdon Street, London, E.C.' In the 6th issue, July 1885, this alters to '13 Farringdon Road, London, E.C.' In the issue of 2 Nov. 1889, *Commonweal* announced, 'On and after Monday, November 11th, the Editorial and Publishing Offices of the 'Commonweal' will be removed to 24 Great Queen Street, Lincoln's Inn Fields, London, W.C.' This was the address of the issue of 16 Nov. 1889, when Morris ended his connection with the paper.

Publisher: Printed and published by William Morris and Joseph Lane, 27 Farringdon Street, London, E.C. This publisher's imprint, required under UK law, always appears as the last item on p. 8. It altered with the issue of 16 Nov. 1889, when the publisher's imprint became 'Frank Kitz at 24 Great Queen St., Lincoln's Inn Fields'.

Printer: The 1st numbers of *Commonweal* were printed by Ramsey and Foote, Printers, the Progressive Publishing Co., first address, 28 Stonecutter Street, E.C. and, later, 14 Clerkenwell Green, E.C. This press, with other commercial printers doing some jobbing work, produced *Commonweal* until the League acquired its own press in Sept. 1885, and started to use it the next month to print *Commonweal*. At that point the press was established, with type and cases supplied by Miller & Richard, at the League headquarters, 13 Farringdon Road (see SLA, Reel 7). After Morris left the Socialist League, the printing press followed the movement of the League offices until it was confiscated by the police at the time of the arrest of the editors, D. J. Nichol and C. W. Mowbray, in Apr. 1892. But at the point it ceased to have connections with Morris it ceases to be relevant to our history.

Collation: Each issue, and the supplementary issues of 1886, was of 4 leaves, unsewn, leaves 2 and 3 folded inside 1 and 4, pp. [1] 2–8 [= 8]. The 1st issue had a 'SECOND EDITION' with the same *Contents*.

Contents: p. [1], masthead, 1st issue, see above; the mastheads in later issues have uniform Old Face type and a willow pattern background; 2 head-piece line-blocks 1-column wide designed by Walter Crane, 'THE COMMONWEAL' and 'THE SOCIALIST | LEAGUE,' came into use in no. 3, Apr.; but after 3 issues the latter block was reserved for separate pbns. 'THE COMMONWEAL' block appeared above League reports, usually on the 4th page of the issue. It carried the date below its banner from its beginning until May 1886, when *Commonweal* became a weekly and the formula below the banner changed to 'ONE PENNY, WEEKLY'; p. 8, imprint below column 2, until June 1885: Printed and Published by William Morris and Joseph Lane at 27 Farringdon Street, London, E.C.; from July 1885, the address changes to: 13 Farringdon Road, London, E.C.; on 16 Nov. 1889, the imprint changes again: Frank Kitz at 24 Great Queen St., Lincoln's Inn Fields.

For Morris's 342 contributions to *Commonweal*, see the D-List: Morris in Periodicals. His essays on political subjects and his comments on current events have been collected in 2 vols., *Political Writings: Contributions to Justice and Commonweal, 1883–1890* and *Journalism: Contributions to Commonweal, 1885–1890*, edited by Nicholas Salmon (see C-36 and 37).

Technical Notes: *paper*: ordinary newsprint, folio, i.e. tabloid size; *printing*: printed in 2 columns throughout; *type face*: types used in *Commonweal* were all purchased from the Miller and Richard's Foundry, who supplied the new SL printery with all the necessary cases, frames, blanks, cutters, etc. (SLA, Reel 5); *pagination*: arabic numbers at the outer margins of the headlines, continuous through each year, issue numbers are continuous through the entire run; vol. numbers are assigned to each year's collected issues, for which 'the title page, index, and covers for binding . . . can be obtained from the manager . . . for 2s.' (*Com-

monweal, 2/12 (Jan. 1886), 8). Vol. and issue numbers are printed, flush left, below the masthead.

Publication: [1] Feb. 1885–15 Nov. 1890 [the period of Morris's active involvement as contributor ended with an article 'Where Are We Now?' (see D-525). For the 15 monthly issues from 1 Feb. 1885, through Apr. 1886, the magazine was, according to its letterhead notepaper (SLA), 'issued on the First of Each Month' (actually the Wednesday preceding or coinciding with the 1st day of the month). When it became a weekly, in May 1886, each issue had a printed issue date as part of the masthead, always the relevant Saturday. But actual issue, earlier than the printed masthead issue, was at 10 a.m. on the preceding Thursday, when copies went out to subscribers and dealers (see *Commonweal*, 2/17 (8 May 1886), 48). But this day of issue may have changed later; Morris wrote his daughter Jenny on 16 Jan. 1889, saying: 'It is publishing day at the League' (*Letters*, iii. 12), and in 1889 16 January fell on a Wednesday, but the difference may be that the printing was finished on Wednesday and copies available late on that day for those able to get one from the *Commonweal* office, but the day of issue, the mailing out of copies, coming on the following morning. That would be consistent with Thursday as the day of issue; *print run* and *price*: see *Notes*, below.

Register of Copies Examined: BL (2 copies: base copy: from Hendon, i.e. Colindale, NR 104, the 2nd BL copy, consulted originally in the North Library, seems to have disappeared).

Notes: Morris to A. Scheu, 16 July 1885: 'Last Monday [13 July] it was settled that Binning should print the Com[monweal]: though he doesn't think it possible to get out the Sept. one as it takes time to prepare. He is to be my man you understand, & I am to be the capitalist printer: this he insisted on. We shall scheme out for beginning the weekly in Jan: 1886, but think it would be rash to attempt it before' (*Letters*, ii. 443). In September Morris, Bax, and Theodore announced the coming change from a monthly to a weekly:

> Steps have been taken by the Council towards realizing this resolution [to change *Commonweal* from a monthly to a weekly]. A printing plant has been bought, a practical printer and compositor [Thomas Binning] has been engaged, thus enabling the Socialist League to print the next monthly issue of the Commonweal on the premises of the League, and so all preliminary conditions are fulfilled for changing the monthly paper into a weekly one. (Signed,) 'E. Belfort Bax, William Morris, C. Theodore. Farringdon Road, Sept. 1, 1885' (*Commonweal*, 1/8 (Sept. 1885), 84).

'This number constitutes the first of the weekly series, and with it is given a cartoon [W. Crane's 'Mrs Grundy Confronting Her Shadow']. In future the Commonweal will be ready every Thursday at 3 o'clock' (*Commonweal*, 2/15 (1 May 1886), 40).

At the 'General Meeting of London Members', 26 July 1886, the 'Commonweal Manager's Report' shows the numbers of copies printed in May, June, and July varied from 3,500 (8 issues) to 4,000 (4 issues), and to 5,000 (1 issue); but copies sold only averaged 2,678 (SLA, Reel 2).

Accounts for *Commonweal* submitted to the 4th Annual Conference of the SL in May 1888, show that in the previous 52 weeks, 163,500 copies were printed, at an average of 3,134 per week. The costs of production, postage, etc. were £594. 12s. 0d. Receipts from sales, contributions, etc., failed by £83. 7s. 10 1/4d. to cover the costs. The paper lost money the previous year as well. And in 1888 an article titled 'Police Spies Exposed', signed 'The Editors', evoked a suit for libel by Charles Theodore Reuss against the proprietors, apparently settled out of court by Morris for £1,000 (SLA, Reel 2).

'Weekly Letter', dated 8 Nov. 1888, notes that 5,000 copies of *Commonweal* were ordered to be printed that week, the week of the execution of the 'Chicago Martyrs' (SLA, Reel 3). The same issue notes that under new arrangements, the cost of producing *Commonweal* had reduced [per week] from £10. 9s. 6d. to £8. 13s. 10 1/2d.

A fortnight after Morris's farewell article 'Where are We Now?' was published, the weekly *Commonweal* became a monthly, and its title altered in early 1891 to *Commonweal, A Revolutionary Journal of Anarchist Communism*.

A-31.01: Useful Work v. Useless Toil (SP)

[wrapper title:] THE SOCIALIST PLATFORM.— No. 2. | [thin rule] | [Walter Crane's SL woodcut headpiece containing label:] 'THE SOCIALIST LEAGUE' | [below block] USEFUL WORK | *V.* | USELESS TOIL | BY | WILLIAM MORRIS | [swelled rule] | PRICE ONE PENNY. | [swelled rule] | LONDON: | SOCIALIST LEAGUE OFFICE, | 13 FARRINGDON ROAD, HOLBORN VIADUCT, E.C. | 1885.

Edition: [1st impression, 1st edn.] A lecture first delivered before The Hampstead Liberal Club, 16 Jan. 1884, but for reasons still obscure not pbd. until a year and a half later. Subsequently pbd. in *Signs of Change*, 1888. Forman's claim (HBF, p. 121) that this lecture was 'printed in Justice' is not true, nor is it noted in Forman's list of

Morris's contributions to that journal (HBF, pp. 196–7).
Collaborators, Editors, and Illustrators: 2 woodcut headpieces—'The Socialist League' and 'The Commonweal'—were designed by Walter Crane and used, respectively, on the title page and heading the ads on p. [40]; and both are rptd. in HBF, p. [113].
Series: The Socialist Platform, No. 2: a numbered series of 7 pamphlets, 3 of which were written by Morris: No. 2, *Useful Work versus Useless Toil*; No. 6, *True and False Society*, and No. 7, *Monopoly* (the last in the series). Besides these, Morris, Bax, and Victor Dave collaborated on No. 4, *A Short Account of the Commune of Paris*. The series was planned and edited by Morris and Bax, as Morris's undated MS report to the SL Executive Council (signed by him and Bax, but in Morris's hand) makes clear. Plans for the new series were announced in *Commonweal*, 1/4 (May 1885), 36; and the 1st 2 pamphlets of the Series—Bax's *An Address to Trades Unions*, and Morris's *Useful Work versus Useless Toil*—were pbd. in June and announced as ready in the issue of July 1885, p. 56.

A preface, signed by the co-editors, Morris and Bax, was printed on the verso of the title page of the earlier issues of pamphlets in the series, but the idea advanced there of a combined vol. of the 'Platform' lectures, the SL *Manifesto*, and *Chants for Socialists*, came to nothing but a spurious entry by Forman (HBF, p. 138); and references to it, along with continuous pagination of successive pamphlets, were discontinued by the time in 1888 when *True and False Society* was added to this series. But the design of the first 5 pamphlets in the series was consistent with the notion of a collected vol.

Morris and Bax's prefatory note says:

> It is designed by the Socialist League to issue a series of pamphlets in exposition of the principles of Socialism. The series will be partly historical, that is to say noteworthy periods of history which form epochs in social evolution will be dealt with, while the direct statement of the economic principles upon which that evolution rests—together with the action and reaction of those principles upon politics, ethics and religion—will receive due attention. The anomalies in the present system will thus be pointed out as the result of an historic development and the earnest of a change for the better will be shown to lie in the issue of the development itself.
>
> These publications will to some extent assume the form of a commentary on the original manifesto of the Socialist League, as it is hoped in the course of the series to devote one or more numbers to the subject-matter of each of its paragraphs; although it may not always be possible to do this in their order.
>
> The pamphlets will be of a uniform size of page, with a view to their ultimately forming a compact volume. They will, as a rule, consist of 16 pages and be published at one penny, but the Editors do not bind themselves to either of these conditions, as it may be found desirable on occasion to issue double or even treble numbers at a somewhat higher price.
>
> In conclusion, the Editors trust to have the support of the public interested in Socialism in this venture; since, to judge by the numerous applications received for instructive literature on the subject it is really likely to meet a want felt by many persons unable to read French or German with ease.

Printer: Printed and published by William Morris and Joseph Lane, at 13 Farringdon Rd. London (the same imprint as that of *Commonweal* at the same time).
Collation: 1 1/2 sheets of small 8°, folded as a single gathering of 12 leaves, sewn through the centrefold, pp. [17–19] 20–39 [40] [= 24], self-wrapped; pagination continuous with the 1st pamphlet in the series, *An Address to Trades Unions*.
Contents: p. [17], title page; p. [18], prefatory note, headed: THE SOCIALIST PLATFORM. | [french rule] | [text begins] | [text ends with 2 sigs., aligned right] ERNEST BELFORT BAX | WILLIAM MORRIS [names joined with 2-line close brace-end bracket] } *Editors.*; p. [19], dropped head: USEFUL WORK VERSUS USELESS TOIL. | [french rule] | [text begins]; pp. 20–39, text completed with sig., aligned right: WILLIAM MORRIS | [thin rule]; p. [40], ads for SL pbns., with Walter Crane's 'The Commonweal' woodcut as a head-piece.
Technical Notes: *paper*: plain white machine-made, no watermark; *leaf size*: cut flush, 185 x 125 mm.; *printing*: *lines-to-page*: set solid, 41 lines; *headlines*: *running titles*: [all versos] *The Socialist Platform.* | [all rectos:] *Useful Work v. Useless Toil.*
Publication: 1885 [announced issue 13 June] 'Will be ready on June 13th' (ad on the back of *Address to Trade Unions*, p. 16, and announced as published in *Commonweal*, 1/6 (July 1885), 56). A deposit copy was lodged with the BM on 30 June 1885; *print run*: 3,800 copies; *price*: 1d. (SL Accounts: June 1885, SLA, reel 8).
Register of Copies Examined: BL (3 copies: base copy: Cup. 502. f. 11 [25.]; 8275.dd.15; and Ashley Lib. 1223) BGR; Bass.
Notes: Morris began this lecture in Nov. 1883, and had it ready for its 1st delivery on 16 January 1884. It became one

of the most popular of Morris's Socialist texts, being rptd. not only in London but also Chicago, Sydney, Moscow and New York (the last 3 being after 1915). Morris's own political organisations, the Socialist League and the Hammersmith Socialist Society, issued it a total of 5 times.

Later (before 1916) issues and impressions from this edn.: SL:
1. 1886: SP [2nd impression, 1st edn.]; *print run*: 3,000 copies; *price*: 1d. (SLA, Reel 8);
2. 1891: SP [4th impression, 1st edn.]; *print run*: unknown; *price*: 1d.;
3. 1896: [2nd issue, 4th impression, 1st edn.]; *print run*: copies remaining; *price*: 1d. (SLA, Reel 8).

A-31.02: Useful Work versus Useless Toil (FL)

USEFUL WORK | *VERSUS* | USELESS TOIL. | [Walter Crane's line block, 'VIVE LA COMMUNE!' [centred between 2 sets of 2 vertical thin rules, the series title repeated, forming 2 side borders either side of the block and containing within the rules, reading up on the left and down on the right:] The "Freedom" Library. | [ordinary horizontal orientation resumes] BY | WILLIAM MORRIS. | [thin rule] | PRICE ONE PENNY.
Edition: [3rd impression, 1st edn.] Printed from plates of the SL edn., retaining the continuous pagination from the 1st title in the series and 'The Socialist Platform' as a running title on all versos. The only changes are the title page, p. [1], p. [2], and p. [40]. See *Contents*, below. Since this impression largely reproduces A-31.01, only the details of altered fields are included.
Collaborators, Editors, and Illustrators: wrapper title woodcut block: "VIVE LA COMMUNE!" designed by Walter Crane.
Series: The "Freedom" Library (hereafter referred to as *FL*). The 1st number of *FL* was issued, 18–25 Sept. 1886 (see *Commonweal*, 2/35 (25 Sept. 1886), 201).
Publisher: [The Freedom Press, with *The Clarion* and William Reeves, 185 Fleet Street, as principal distributors].
Contents: as in A-31.01, except for those changes required to identify the new publisher: p. [1], title page, see above; p. [2], blank; p. [40], ad for 'Freedom, A Journal of Anarchist Communism' and for the 'Freedom Pamphlets' | [imprint below typographical border consisting of double rules made with alternating 'A' and 'V' letters across the page] | Printed by T. Cantwell, 127 Ossulston Street, London, N.W.
Publication: [1890]; *print run*: unknown; *price*: 1d.
Register of Copies Examined: LeM (base copy); ICN; BL ("Freedom" library 1509/1910.)

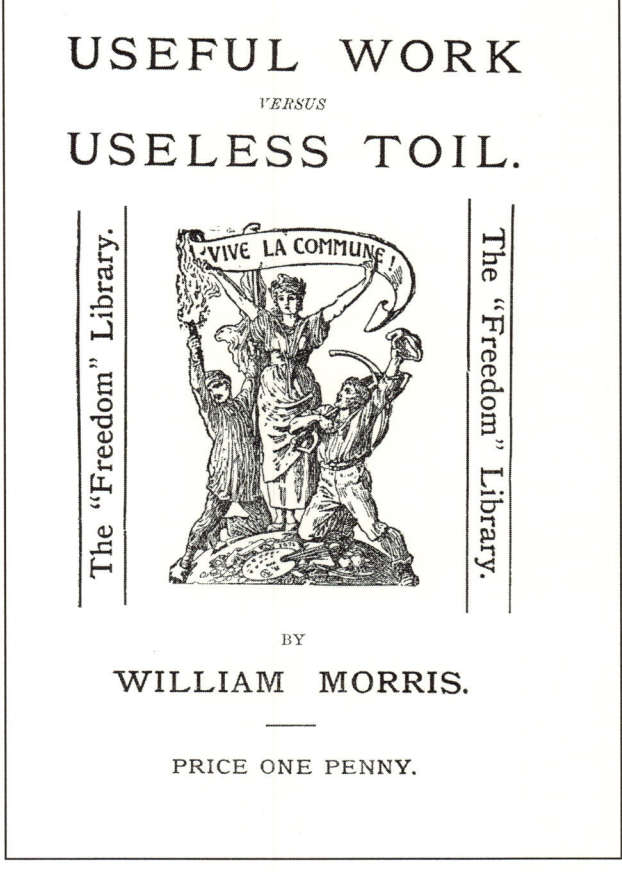

Figure 35. A-31.02: *Useful Work v. Useless Toil* (Freedom Library) wrapper title

Later impressions of this version: FL:
1. 1891: [5th impression, 1st edn.]; *print run*: unknown; *price*: 1d.;
2. 1897: [7th impression, 1st edn.]; *print run*: unknown; *price*: 1d.;
3. [c. 1900]: [8th impression, 1st edn.]; *print run*: unknown; *price*: 1d.

A-31.03: Useful Work versus Useless Toil (HSL)

[Walter Crane's woodcut head-piece incorporating the name of the publisher:] THE | HAMMERSMITH | SOCIALIST SOCIETY | [plain text] USEFUL WORK | VERSUS | USELESS TOIL | BY | WILLIAM MORRIS | Price One Penny | PUBLISHED BY | THE HAMMERSMITH SOCIALIST SOCIETY | KELMSCOTT HOUSE, UPPER MALL, HAMMERSMITH | LONDON, W. | 1893
Edition: [1st impression, 2nd edn.] 2 versions of the back

page of this pamphlet exist, one (BGR) with an ornamental device of a vase and flowers and another with an ad for Hammersmith Socialist Society publications and a map of Hammersmith Mall.
Collaborators, Editors, and Illustrators: head-piece from a design by Walter Crane (rptd. HBF, p. 113).
Series: Hammersmith Socialist Library.
Collation: 8°: single gathering of 10 leaves, no signatures, pp. [1–2] 3–19 [20] [= 20] self-wrappered; all leaves are conjunct, folded and sewn at the fold.
Contents: p. [1], title page; p. [2], blank; p. 3, text begins: [dropped head] USEFUL WORK VERSUS USELESS TOIL. | [thin rule] | [text begins]; pp. 4–19, text completed; p. [20], vase and flowers ornament; some copies (Fdmn copy) have ads for HSS publications, with a map locating Kelmscott House, Hammersmith, and the site of Sunday morning meetings | [thin rule] | [printer's imprint:] LABOUR LITERATURE SOCIETY, LTD, PRINTERS, 105 LONDON ST., GLASGOW.
Technical Notes: *paper*: plain white machine-made; *leaf size*: 182 x 129 mm.; *printing*: *type area*: 141 x 99 mm.; *lines-to-page*: set solid, 44 lines; *running titles*: all rectos and versos, on headline: USEFUL WORK V. USELESS TOIL.; self-wrappered.
Publication: 1893; *print run*: unknown; *price*: 1d.
Register of Copies Examined: CSt (base copy: V335/M877u); Fdmn; BGR (3 copies).

A-31.04: Useful Work versus Useless Toil (TL)

[wrapper title] USEFUL WORK | *VERSUS* | USELESS TOIL | [Walter Crane's woodcut vignette: VIVA LA COMMUNE! flanked left and right by vertical flaming torches within thin rules] | BY | WILLIAM MORRIS. | [thin rule] | Price One Penny.
Edition: [6th impression, 1st edn.].
Series: The Torch Library No. 1 (hereafter referred to as TL). There were, it seems, only 3 pamphlets in this series: Prince Kropotkin's *Appeal to the Young*, Morris's *Monopoly: Or, How Labour Is Robbed*, for which see A-49.03, and the one described here.
Publisher: F. Macdonald at 1 Arlington Terrace, Arlington Road, Camden Town, N.W.
Printer: The Metropolitan Co-operative Printing Works. 127 Ossulston Street, London, N.W.
Collation: as in A-31.01, including self wrapper.
Contents: as in A-31.01, except for title page, p. [2], and printer's imprint (see *Printer*, above).
Publication: [issued 18 Dec. 1894] *The Torch*, n.s. 7 (18 Dec.

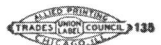

Figure 36. A-31.05: *Useful Work v. Useless Toil* (Kerr edn.) wrapper title

1894); *print run*: unknown; *price*: 1d.
Register of Copies Examined: MH (base copy: *EC85 M8348 B898p).

A-31.05: Useful Work versus Useless Toil (Kerr)

[wrapper title] Useful Work | *Versus* | Useless Toil | By WILLIAM MORRIS | Pocket Library Of Socialism | No. 48 | [trades union label] | CHICAGO | CHARLES H. KERR & COMPANY | 118 West Kinzie Street.
Edition: [1st impression, 3rd edn., 1st American].
Printer: printer and publisher are the same (see title page, above).
Collation: 16°: single gathering of 16 leaves stapled twice in the middle, pp. [1–3] 4–30 [31–2] [= 32]; self-wrappered.
Contents: p. [1], title page; p. [2], blank; p. [3], head title: [dropped head] USEFUL WORK VERSUS USELESS

TOIL. | [thin rule] | [text begins]; pp. 4–30, text completed; pp. [31–2], ads for Socialist publications available from Charles H. Kerr & Company.
Technical Notes: *paper*: plain cream machine-made; *leaf size*: cut flush 144 x 88 mm.; *printing*: type area: 113 x 67 mm.; *lines-to-page*: hair leading, 38 lines; *running heads*: all versos and rectos: USEFUL WORK VS. USELESS TOIL;
Publication: [1909] (internal evidence: 'We intend to sell more than a million [of the Pocket Library] during the campaign of 1910', p. [31]; *print run*: unknown; *price*: 2 cents.
Register of Copies Examined: LeM (base copy).

A-32.01: For Whom Shall We Vote

[head title, aligned left] PRICE ONE HALFPENNY. | FOR WHOM SHALL WE VOTE? | [wavy rule] | *ADDRESSED TO THE WORKING-MEN ELECTORS | OF GREAT BRITAIN.* | [wavy rule] | [text begins]
Edition: [1st impression, 1st edn.].
Collation: half sheet of demy 8°, folded to form 4 leaves pp. [1] 2–8 [= 8], issued unsewn, self-wrappered.
Contents: p. [1], head title, text begins; pp. 2–8, text completed: [aligned right] THE COUNCIL OF THE SOCIALIST LEAGUE | [aligned left] *November, 1885* | [thin rule] | Printed and Published at the 'Commonweal' Office, 13 Farringdon Road, London, E.C.
Technical Notes: *paper*: plain white machine-made, no watermark; *leaf size*: 189 x 119 mm.; *printing*: type area: 141 x 92 mm.; *lines-to-page*: thin leaded, 40 lines; *pagination*: arabic numbers centred on the headline.
Publication: Nov. 1885 [issued a few days after 15 Nov.] (see Morris's letter of 14 Nov., *Notes*, below) and Cash Accts., SLA, Reel 6: 'Saturday Nov. 14 | 85: To composition, etc. of "For Whom Shall We Vote?" . . . 15s. od. [signed] W. Blundell' (Literary Secretary, SL); *print run*: unknown; *price*: 1/2 penny. unsewn, self-wrappered.
Register of Copies Examined: Bass (base copy); NN (SFC. n.c.1).
Notes: Morris to the Chairman of the Meeting of the Executive of the Socialist League, 9 Nov. 1885:

> I was told that something was said last Monday about an election manifesto. I was so much impressed with the necessity of our bringing one out, that, as time presses, I have written one myself in the form of a short pamphlet. This I send in for the consideration of the Council. I think if there is any idea of printing it, it ought to be read at the meeting as it commits us to Abstention from the Poll. For my part I feel very strongly on this point, and have done all along; even when I was in the S. D. F. and before any signs of splitting showed in that body (*Letters*, ii. 486–7).

Morris to Henry Halliday Sparling, [Tues.] 10 Nov. 1885:

> Since the Don't Vote Manifesto is to be printed it should be done *at once* or we shall lose the opportunity. May says it was proposed to put ᵈ1/2 on it: I suppose in any case it would be largely *given* away: but no doubt it ought to have a price on it, and if it makes a small pamphlet it had better be ᵈ1/2. Could it be brought out this week? I wish we could get someone to distribute it in Edinburgh & Glasgow now that that old villain has started his thrice accursed slack-jaw.
> Please see to this, as it will be no use bringing the thing unless we have it out at once—Strax, as the Danes say . . . . P.S. If Binning finds any difficulty in getting the thing out, it had better be done outside rather than delay it (*Letters*, ii. 488).

A-33.01: Home Rule and Humbug

[heading] SOCIALIST LEAFLETS. — No. 7.] | HOME RULE AND HUMBUG. | *TO THE WORKING-PEOPLE OF GREAT BRITAIN AND OF IRELAND.* | [text begins]
Edition: [1st impression, 1st edn.].
Series: Socialist League Leaflets, No. 7. The SL considered the Leaflets series, of which there were 11 titles, to be among the basic statements of its policy (see Eugene D. LeMire, 'The Socialist League Leaflets and manifestos: An Annotated Checklist'. *The International Review of Social History*, 22/1 (1977), 21–9; hereafter referred to as 'SL Leaflets'). Of the 11 leaflets produced, Morris wrote at least 3 for which his authorship is certain: *No. 7: Home Rule and Humbug, No. 9: Shall Ireland be Free?*, and *No. 11: What Socialists Want*. It is possible he wrote others in the series, but as with other uncertain items, unless there is a substantial reason for thinking Morris the author, such items are not included here.
Publisher: Issued by the Socialist League, 13 Farringdon Road, London, E.C.
Printer: [Empire Printing and Publishing Co., 15 Salisbury Court, London, E.C.] (named in SLA Accts.).
Collation: s. sh. 8° printed on one side. SL Branches often printed lecture announcements, etc., on the blank side for local distribution.
Contents: below heading the text begins: FELLOW WORKERS, —; the text is divided by a heading about

half way: You must be free from RENT!; text ends with the Marxist slogan: WAGE-WORKERS OF ALL COUNTRIES UNITE! | [thin rule] | [imprint line] *Issued by the Socialist League, 13, Farringdon Road, London, E.C., January, 1886.* | *Read* The Commonweal, *Official Journal of the League, price One Penny.*

Technical Notes: *paper*: plain white machine-made, no watermark; *leaf size*: 230 x 125 mm. (BL copies, 220 x 141 mm. and 227 x 122 mm.); *type area*: 206 x 105 mm.

Publication: Jan. 1886 [issued prior to 27 Jan.] ('"Home Rule and Humbug" is now ready', *Commonweal*, 2/13 (Feb. 1886), 16). While the published date of issue of the monthly *Commonweal* was the 1st of the month, actual issue of the Feb. 1886 number would have been on the previous Wednesday, 27 Jan.; SLA Accts. entry dated 'January 30, 1886' (SLA, Reel 7); *print run*: 500 copies (SLA Accts., Reel 7); *price*: for free distribution.

Register of Copies Examined: BL (2 copies: base copy: Cup. 502.f.11 [10]; 1882.C.2 [48]); SLA; LSE.

Notes: 'To Correspondents': Morris to 'Irish Socialist.—Thanks for suggestion. A leaflet dealing with the Irish question has been prepared, and will shortly be ready for distribution', *Commonweal*, 2/13 (Feb. 1886), 12. The same issue, p. 16, announces: 'No. 7. 'Home Rule and Humbug' is now ready. Copies may be had on application to the secretary. Supplied for distribution at 2*s*. per 100.'

'Socialist League. Monthly Report': 'Two new leaflets have been issued. One entitled "Home Rule and Humbug," has been widely circulated and generally criticized by the press; the other, upon the topic of the day, is entitled "The Unemployed and Rioting." Of these there have been several thousands distributed and more are being sent out' (*Commonweal*, 2/14 (Mar. 1886), 24).

The MS of this pamphlet, in Morris's hand, is in the Huntington Library, HM6464.

Later impressions of this edn.: (the impressions are in some cases indistinguishable; the details of these entries depend entirely on the SLA Accts., Reel 7; so it remains uncertain whether the following entries are separate issues or merely routine restocking to replenish the supply):

1.* Jan. 1886 [issued 1 Feb.]: [2nd impression, 1st edn.]; *print run*: 1,400 copies printed by Empire Printing and Publishing Co., 15 Salisbury Court, London, E.C.;

2.* Jan. 1886 [issued early Feb.] (invoice dated 5 Feb.): [3rd impression, 1st edn.]; *print run*: 4,600 copies; *price*: for free distribution;

3.* 1886 [issued late Feb., early Mar.?] (17 Mar. is the date of printer's bill): [4th impression, 1st edn.]; *print run*: 4,000 copies; *price*: for free distribution; Empire Printing and Publishing Co., 15 Salisbury Court, London, E.C. (named in print order).

A-34.01: Socialism

[head title] SOCIALISM. | [ornamental rule] | A LECTURE delivered under the auspices of the Norwich Branch of the Socialist League, at | the Victoria Hall, Norwich, on Monday evening, March 8th, 1886, by | Mr. William Morris. | [thin-thick rule] | Reprinted from "Daylight" | [text begins]

Edition: [1st impression, 1st edn.] Also reprinted in a Norwich *Daylight Supplement*, 13 Mar. 1886 (see D-175); portions were rptd. in MM, ii. 193–7.

Collation: s. sh. folio printed in 4 columns each side.

Contents: p. [1], heading, see above; p. [2], text concluded, no imprint.

Technical Notes: *paper*: ordinary white machine-made newsprint; *leaf size*: 434 x 275 mm.; *printing*: 4 columns, separated by 3 vertical thin rules, recto and verso; *type area*: 326 x 220 mm. (including thin rules); *lines-to-page*: 117 lines per column except the last: ll. 114.

Publication: 1886 [issued 13 Mar.]: printed from a lecture delivered on 8 Mar. and appearing in Norwich *Daylight* on 13 Mar. The off-print was probably issued at the same time. The text was completed and 1st delivered at Oxford in June 1885.

Register of Copies Examined: LeM (base copy); BL (Cup. 21. g. 1. (51.); Bass.

A-35.01: The Commune of Paris

[wrapper title] THE SOCIALIST PLATFORM.—No. 4. | [Walter Crane's 'THE SOCIALIST LEAGUE' woodcut block as head-piece] | A SHORT ACCOUNT | OF THE | COMMUNE OF PARIS. | BY | E. BELFORT BAX, VICTOR DAVE | AND | WILLIAM MORRIS. | [thin rule] | PRICE TWOPENCE. | [thin rule] | LONDON: | SOCIALIST LEAGUE OFFICE, | 13 FARRINGDON ROAD, HOLBORN VIADUCT, E.C. | 1886.

Edition: [1st impression, 1st edn.].

Collaborators, Editors, and Illustrators: For a discussion of Bax's contribution, see Dave's letter in *Notes*, below.

Series: SP, No. 4. For further detail on this series, see this field in A-31.01.

Printer: [Empire Printing and Publishing Co., 15 Salisbury

Court, London, E.C.] (printer's bill, SLA, Reel 7).
Collation: 8°: [1]⁶ 6 conjunct pairs folded one within the other to form 12 leaves pp. [57–9] 60–79 [80] [= 24]; pagination continues the sequence from SP No. 3, which ended on p. [56]; self-wrappered.
Contents: p. [57], title page; p. [58], epigraph, a sonnet from George Meredith's *Poems and Lyrics of the Joy of Earth*.; p. 59, headed: A SHORT ACCOUNT | OF THE | COMMUNE OF PARIS OF 1871. | [double thin rule] | [text begins]; pp. 60–79, text completed: double thin rule; p. [80], ads, headed: LITERATURE OF THE SOCIALIST LEAGUE.
Technical Notes: *paper*: plain white machine-made; *leaf size*: 185 x 128 mm.; *type area*: 146 x 93 mm.; *lines-to-page*: leaded, 36 lines; *running titles*: all versos: *The Socialist Platform.* | [all rectos] *The Paris Commune*
Publication: 1886 [issued 15 Mar.]: 'Socialist League. Monthly Report': '"A History of the Commune of Paris" in pamphlet form, will be issued about the middle of March in order in some measure to meet the blundering lies of capitalistic historians and commentators'; also 'Ready by 15th March', *Commonweal*, 2/14 (Mar. 1886), 24, and Morris to Mahon in *Notes*, below; *print run*: 2,000 copies (SLA, 2 bills, for 1,000 copies each, from Empire Printing and Publishing, dated 16 and 17 Mar. 1886); *price*: 2d.
Register of Copies Examined: BL (2 copies: base copy: Ashley 1225 and 8275. dd. 15.); CSt (944.0-8 / B355).
Notes: Morris to J. L. Mahon, 20 Feb. 1886: 'am desperately busy: have got the job of writing a pamphlet on the Commune to appear by March 18, which I find not a little troublesome' (*Letters*, ii. 527).

Letter from Victor Dave to H. H. Sparling, dated (by Sparling?): '[day illegible] March 1886 re Commune of Paris pamphlet' says,

> Confidential
> Dear Sparling,
>> I cannot correct the pamphlet, as I have not the manuscript, and I am not able to do it without :— Let Morris have the proofs rather than Bax, who has not written <u>one single word</u> on the whole pamphlet.
>> 'You will see that on the title-page, my name (if names are to be inserted) should be printed correctly, as Dave and not Davé, as is often the case.
> 'Your friend, Victor Dave (SLA, Reel 16).

This pamphlet is not to be confused with the 2 Socialist League leaflets both titled *The Paris Commune, March 18th, 1871* and both of uncertain authorship.

A-36.01: Shall Ireland Be Free?

[head title] No. 9.] Shall Ireland be Free? | [thick wavy rule] | TO THE WORKING PEOPLE OF GREAT BRITAIN AND IRELAND. | [thick wavy rule] | [text begins]
Edition: [1st impression, 1st edn.] On Morris's authorship, see *Notes*, below.
Series: Socialist Leaflets, No. 9 (for further detail about this series, see this field and the *Notes* to A-33.01).
Printer: [Empire Printing and Publishing Co., 15 Salisbury Court, London, E.C.] (named in SLA print order).
Collation: s. sh. long 8°, printed on one side.
Contents: heading, see above; the text is divided by frequent sub-heads in bold type, 7 in all; imprint at foot of page, below thick rule: Issued by the Socialist League, 13, Farringdon Road, London, E.C., April, 1886. | The Commonweal, Official Journal of the League, One Penny Weekly.
Technical Notes: *paper*: plain white machine-made, no watermark; *leaf size*: 210 x 137 mm. (SLA copy, 224 x 130 mm.); *type area*: set solid, 195 x 105 mm.
Publication: Apr. 1886 [issued 19–29 Apr.] see *Notes*, below; *print run*: 5,000 copies (see *Notes*, below); *price*: for free distribution. There were several reprints of *Shall Ireland be Free*, but in most of them the leaflets themselves are indistinguishable and it is not certain that they were separately issued. Consequently, the facts given here come mainly from the SLA, Reels 7 and 8.
Register of Copies Examined: BL (base copy: 1882.c.2. [48]); SLA.
Notes: A note from Morris, lecturing at the time in Leeds and Bradford, to Sparling, [17 Apr. 1886] (this date can be inferred from other details in the letter), with Morris's report for the SL Council and a list of enclosed documents for Sparling's attention, among which is, 'a new leaflet as bidden by the W & M [Ways and Means] Committee which please produce at Monday's meeting' (*Letters*, ii. 543–4). In 1886, the Monday after 17 Apr. would have been 19 Apr.. That being the date of approval of the leaflet text, it provides a *terminus a quo* for the date of issue. The 1 May masthead date of the *Commonweal* issue wherein the leaflet was announced implies an actual date of 29 Apr., when the *Commonweal* was issued, hence the *terminus ad quem* of 29 Apr. is established.

Morris's authorship is confirmed by the Rosenbach Library holograph MS (shelf mark: EL3 f. M877 MS 1) which is entirely in Morris's hand.
Later reprintings of this edn. (it is doubtful that these are formally reissued impressions): SL:

1.* 1886 [29 Apr.] (bill dated 29 Apr. for 'Ireland' leaflets from W. A. Ramsay, 14 Clerkenwell Green, E.C.): [2nd impression, 1st edn.]; *print run*: 10,000 copies; *price*: for free distribution;

2.* 1886 [May] (bill dated 27 May for 'Ireland' leaflets from W. A. Ramsay, 14 Clerkenwell Green, E.C.): [3rd impression, 1st edn.]; *print run*: 4,000 copies; *price*: for free distribution;

3.* 1886 [June]: [4th impression, 1st edn.] (bill dated 26 June 1886); *print run*: 10,000 'Ireland' leaflets; by the printer, W. A. Ramsey, 14 Clerkenwell Green E.C.; *price*: for free distribution;

4.* 1887 [Apr.] (bill dated 1 Apr. 1887 for 'Ireland' leaflets, printed by W. A. Ramsey, 14 Clerkenwell Green E.C.: [5th impression, 1st edn.]; *print run*: 2,000 copies; *price*: for free distribution.

A-37.01: True and False Society

[wrapper title] CLAIMS OF LABOUR LECTURES— No. 5. | [thick rule] | THE LABOUR QUESTION | FROM THE | SOCIALIST STANDPOINT. | By William Morris. | EDINBURGH | CO-OPERATIVE PRINTING COMPANY LIMITED, | BRISTO PLACE | 1886. | PRICE ONE PENNY.

Edition: [1st impression, 1st edn.] This pamphlet of a lecture later re-titled *True and False Society* is the 1st printing of Morris's contribution to *The Claims of Labour*, a course of lectures on various aspects of the labour problem delivered in Scotland in the summer of 1886. The lecture course, and hence the 2 publications of this text—this separate pamphlet and the text prtd. in the collected vol. of the series of lectures entitled *The Claims of Labour*, the 1st recorded here and the 2nd in the B-List, Morris's Contributions to Books—grew out of discussions at The Industrial Remuneration Conference at Prince's Hall, Piccadilly, in Jan. 1885. For this lecture as part of the collected vol., see B-7.

Collaborators, Editors, and Illustrators: edited by James Oliphant, who contributes a prefatory note on p. [2], see *Contents*, below.

Series: The Claims of Labour Lectures—No. 5. This was a course of 6 Lectures on 'Various Aspects of the Labour Problem', financed by Robert Miller of Edinburgh, organised by Frederic Harrison, and delivered in Edinburgh, Glasgow, and Dundee on the 23, 24, and 25 June 1886. The lectures were, 'By John Burnet, Secretary of the Amalgamated Society of Engineers; Benjamin Jones, Manager of the Co-operative Wholesale Society, London Branch; Patrick Geddes, F.R.S.E.; Alfred Russell Wallace, LL.D. F.L.S., &c.; William Morris; and Herbert Somerton Foxwell, Professor of Economics, University College, London'. James Oliphant, trustee and editor, states the purpose of the course on the verso of the wrapper title: 'This course of lectures has been arranged on the basis of representing all important sections of opinion on labour questions, and while the lectures will afterwards be published in a collective form, it is understood that each writer has no responsibility for any opinions contained in them beyond those expressed in his own lecture.'

When stocks of the initial Edinburgh edn. of the pamphlet were exhausted in 1888, it was retitled *True and False Society* and rptd. by the SL as part of its pamphlet series, SP No. 6, 1888.

Collation: double cr. 8°: one 8° sheet folded to form a single gathering of 16 leaves pp. [1–3] 4–29 [30–2] [= 32] self-wrapped.

Contents: p. [1], title page; p. [2], editorial note signed by James Oliphant, quoted in *Series* notes, above; p. [3], dropped head: THE LABOUR QUESTION FROM THE | SOCIALIST STANDPOINT | [ornamental rule] | [text begins]; pp. 4–29, text completed with double thin rule; pp. [30–1], blank; p. [32]: ad headed: CLAIMS OF LABOUR LECTURES.

Technical Notes: *paper*: plain white machine-wove; *leaf size*: 181 x 123 mm.; *type area*: 140 x 85 mm.; *lines-to-page*: set solid, 38 lines.

Publication: 1886 [issued July–Aug.]: the lecture was delivered 3 times during the Industrial Remuneration Conference. The 1st ad appeared in *Commonweal*, 2/34 (4 Sept. 1886), 184; *print run*: not known; *price*: 1d.

Register of Copies Examined: BL (base copy: Cup. 502. f. 11. [43.]); MH; BGR.

Notes: John S. Common of the Co-operative Printing Company wrote to F. Charles, Manager of *Commonweal*, on 21 June 1888, in response to a request for more copies of this pamphlet: 'Mr. Morris's Lecture is out of print as a separate publication. It can still be had in volume form ('Claims of Labour') at 1/-' (SLA, Reel 15).

Forman gives separate entries to this pamphlet and *True and False Society* (pp. 123, 132), apparently unaware that the 2 pbns. are the same text under 2 titles (see A-37.02, below).

A-37.02: True and False Society (SP)

[wrapper title] "The Socialist Platform." — No. 6. | [thin rule] | [Walter Crane's woodcut head-piece incorporating as a banner:] THE SOCIALIST | LEAGUE | [plain text]

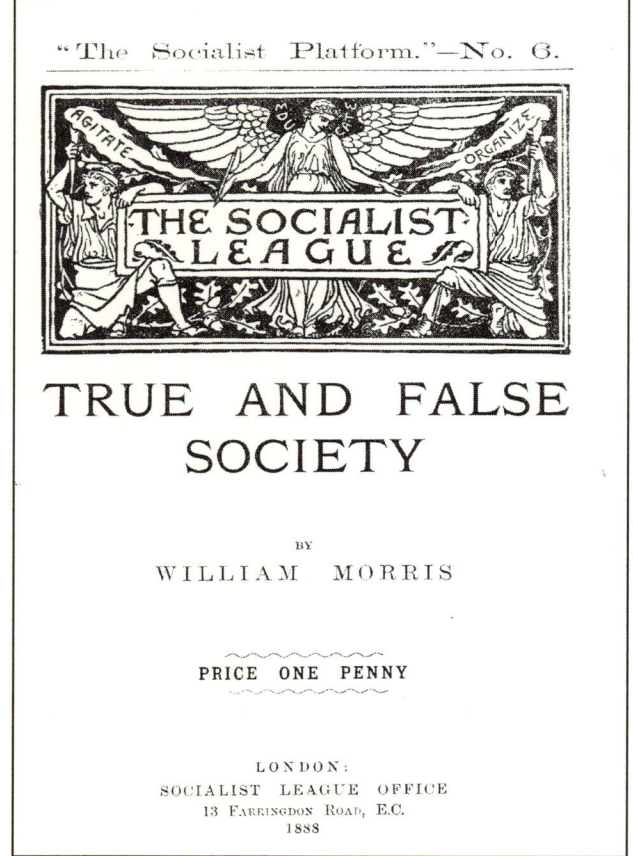

Figure 37. A-37.02: *True and False Society* (2nd edn.) wrapper title

TRUE AND FALSE | SOCIETY | BY | WILLIAM MORRIS | [wavy thin rule] | PRICE ONE PENNY | [wavy thin rule] | LONDON: | SOCIALIST LEAGUE OFFICE | 13 FARRINGDON ROAD, E.C. | 1888

Edition: [1st impression, 2nd edn.] This is the 1st issue using this title, the text being 1st pbd. in 1886 as *The Labour Question from the Socialist Standpoint* (see previous record). This 1st SL printing, under this new title, was made necessary by the exhaustion of copies available from the 1st impression, 1st edn. (see *Notes*, below).

Collaborators, Editors, and Illustrators: The Socialist Platform Series was edited by E. Belfort Bax and William Morris.

Series: SP, No. 6 (for further detail on this series, see A-31.01 and SP, E-10.

Collation: 1 and 1/2 sheets of cr. 8°, folded inside one another to form a single gathering of 12 leaves, sewn through the centrefold pp. [1-3] 4-22 [23-4] [= 24] self-wrappered.

Contents: p. [1], title page; p. [2], blank; p. [3], dropped head: TRUE AND FALSE SOCIETY. | [wavy thin rule] | [text begins]; pp. 4-22, text completed with thin rule; p. [23], blank; p. [24], ads for SL pbns., headed: SOCIALIST LITERATURE. | [thin rule] | [printer's imprint at the foot, below thin rule] SOCIALIST LEAGUE OFFICE, 13 Farringdon Road, London, E.C.

Technical Notes: For details common to the SP Series, see this field in A-31.01, except: *paper*: *leaf size*: cut flush, 184 x 124 mm.; *pagination*: in this case page numbers start from 1, i.e. they are not continuous with any previous pamphlet in the series, indicating that by this time the original project of doing a single combined vol. to be titled 'The Socialist Platform' had been dropped.

Publication: 1888 [issued 21-8 July] (The 1st ad for this pamphlet appeared in *Commonweal*, 4/133 (28 July 1888), 240: 'Just Published, 24 pp., 1d. True and False Society'); *print run*: unknown; *price*: 1d.

Register of Copies Examined: LeM (base copy); Fdmn; BL (3 copies); An-C-TU (M677 T78 1888).

Notes: Morris's letter of 10 July 1890 to Mrs E. D. Hartley describes the lecture as 'in the press' (see *Letters*, ii. 790). From the *Commonweal* 'Weekly Letter': 'It is hoped that branches will order Morris's pamphlet "True and False Society," a large number of which have been printed, and specimen copies sent to the branches' (dated by Kelvin 2 Aug. [1888?], reporting on the Council Meeting of the previous Monday, 31 July 1888. SLA, Reel 3). Forman dates this pamphlet, 'about the 24th of July 1888' (HBF, p. 132).

Later impression from this edn.:
1. SL: 1890 [issued June 7-14] (advertised in *Commonweal*, 6/231 (14 June 1890), 192): SP [2nd impression, 2nd edn.]; *print run*: unknown; *price*: 1d.

A-37.03: True and False Society (HSL)

[wrapper title] [Walter Crane's woodcut head-piece incorporating the label:] THE | HAMMERSMITH | SOCIALIST SOCIETY | [below woodcut] TRUE AND FALSE | SOCIETY | BY | WILLIAM MORRIS | Price One Penny | PUBLISHED BY | THE HAMMERSMITH SOCIALIST SOCIETY | KELMSCOTT HOUSE, UPPER MALL, HAMMERSMITH | LONDON, W. | 1893

Edition: [1st impression, 3rd edn.] The text was originally pbd. as *The Labour Question from the Socialist Standpoint* (see A-37.01). This retitled version was later pbd. in *CW*, xxiii. 215-37.

Series: Hammersmith Socialist Library.

Collation: 8°: single gathering of 10 leaves, pp. [1-2] 3-19 [20] [= 20] self-wrappered, all the leaves are folded and stapled once at the centrefold.

Contents: p. [1], title page; p. [2], head title and text begins; pp. 3–19, text completed; p. [20], ads for HSS publications, with a map locating Kelmscott House, Hammersmith, and the site of Sunday Morning meetings marked, and printer's imprint: [thin rule] | LABOUR LITERATURE SOCIETY, LTD, PRINTERS, 105 LONDON ST., GLASGOW.
Technical Notes: *paper*: plain white machine-made; *leaf size*: cut flush 182 x 129 mm.; *printing*: *type area*: 146 x 93 mm.; *lines-to-page*: set solid, 44 lines; *running titles*: all rectos and versos, on headline: TRUE AND FALSE SOCIETY.; *binding*: self-wrappered.
Publication: 1893; *print run*: unknown; *price*: 1d.
Register of Copies Examined: CSt (base copy: 385/M877t); BGR; An-C-TU (M677 T78 1893): MH (* 78-2491).

A-38.01: All for the Cause

[head title] ALL FOR THE CAUSE | [thick-thin rule with central ornamental device extending downwards separating the authorial notes] | [aligned left] Words by | WILLIAM MORRIS. [aligned right] Music by | E. BELFORT BAX. | [centred] SOCIALIST LEAGUE OFFICE. [aligned right] *Price 6d*. | [centred] 13 Farringdon Road. LONDON. E C | [text and music begin]
Edition: [1st impression, 1st separate edn.] The text was 1st printed as 'Chants for Socialists, No. 3' in *Justice*, 19 Apr. 1884 (see D-100); later included in *Poems by the Way* (1891).
Collation: a single sheet folded to form a pair of 4° leaves pp. [1] 2–4.
Contents: p. [1], head title, see above; pp. 2–4, text completed, no printer's imprint or colophon.
Technical Notes: *paper*: plain white machine-made; *leaf size*: 254 x 190 mm.; *type area*: 212 x 156 mm., includes the music and 4 stanzas of lyric.
Publication: 1887 [issued 26–31 Dec. 1886] (1st ad in *Commonweal*, 3/51 (1 Jan. 1887), 8).
Register of Copies Examined: NNBerg (base copy); BL (E. 270. a.)
Notes: IISH, Letter from May Morris to A. Scheu, 15 Dec. 1886: 'Do you know Bax's new Song to the "All for the Cause" words? If not, and if you consent to come [to a New Year's night party at the Hammersmith Branch], please learn it for the occasion.' She writes again on Dec. 19 to say, 'I will send tomorrow a copy of Bax's song.'

A-39.01: The Aims of Art

THE AIMS OF ART | BY | WILLIAM MORRIS | AUTHOR OF "THE EARTHLY PARADISE" ETC | LONDON | OFFICE OF "THE COMMONWEAL" | 13 FARRINGDON ROAD | 1887
Edition: [1st impression, 1st edn.] Besides the ordinary copies, priced at 3d., there were LP copies for 6d. on Whatman's hand-made paper with dust jackets; rptd. in *Signs of Change* (1888); portions of the text appeared in *The Artist*, 8 (Sept., Oct., Nov. 1887), 283–5; 316–18, 346–8.
Publisher: printed by Strangeways for Morris, who published the pamphlet himself, despite the Socialist League publisher's imprint. The League imprint is true only in that, as the SLA indicates, the League acted as a dealer in respect of this title, buying copies from Morris when supplies ran low.
Collation: demy 16° gathered in 8s: [A]–B⁸ C⁴ 20 leaves pp. [1–3], 4–39 [40] [= 40] + wrapper.
Contents: p. [1], title page; p. [2], blank; p. [3], dropped head: THE AIMS OF ART. | [text begins]; pp. 4–39, text completed: [thin rule] | LONDON: | STRANGEWAYS AND SONS, Tower Street, St. Martin's Lane, W.C.; p. [40], blank.
Technical Notes: *paper*: FP copies: cream hand-laid, 'J. Whatman' watermark and date, '1882' on Proctor copy ('1883' on Cockerell and CtY copies), watermark on outer margin of the 1st gathering,; 'J. Whatman' in last half-sheet gathering; *leaf size*: 144 x 115 mm.; *printing*: *type area*: 89 x 63 mm., not including head or direction lines; *lines-to-page*: leaded, 22 lines; *running titles*: italic capitals, all rectos and versos; *THE AIMS OF ART*; *wrapper*: light blue handmade paper, deckled edges; p. [1] duplicates the title page; the remaining three sides of the wrapper are blank.
Publication: 1887 [issued 12–19 Feb.] (1st advertised as 'Now Ready' in *Commonweal*, 3/58 (19 Feb. 1887), 8); HBF says it, 'was on sale by the middle of February' (p. 126); *print run*: unknown for either version; *price*: 3d. ordinary copies, FP copies 6d.
Register of Copies Examined: VMoU (base copy: *820.8 M877 AG/A); CSt (Spec.Coll. Gunst Z239.2.K29Z8A3t); ANL; Fdmn.; BL (2 copies, both F.P.: 7808.de.5, Proctor's copy, and Cup. 502.f.11.[17.] Cockerell's copy).
Notes: Morris sold the SL 500 copies of *The Aims of Art* on 10 Feb. 1887, for £4. (SLA Accts.).

A-40.01: The Odyssey (2 vols.)

THE | ODYSSEY OF HOMER | DONE INTO ENGLISH VERSE | BY | WILLIAM MORRIS | AUTHOR OF THE EARTHLY PARADISE. | *IN TWO VOLUMES*. | VOL. I. [II.] | LONDON: | REEVES & TURNER, 196

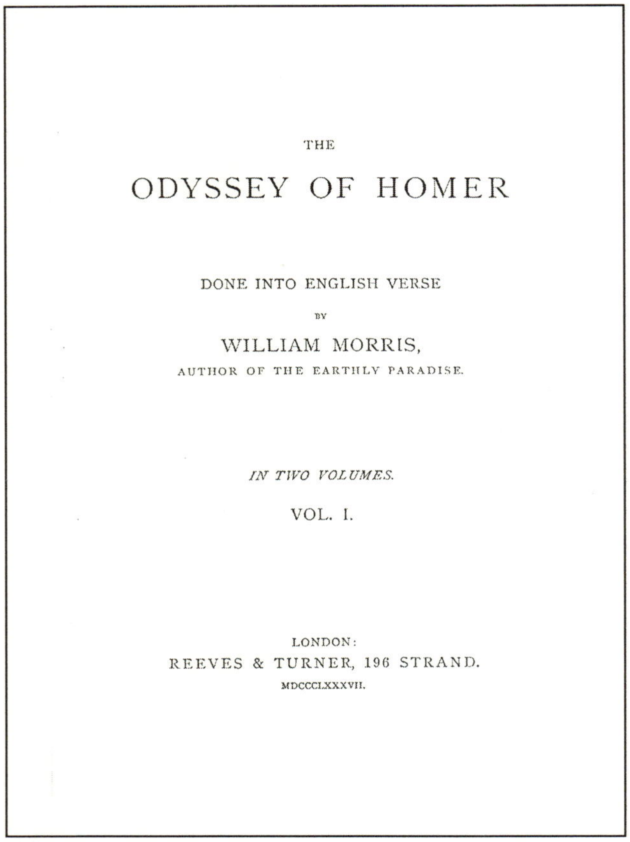

Figure 38. A-40.01: *The Odyssey* (1st edn. vol. 1 of 2) title page

STRAND. | MDCCCLXXXVII.

Edition: [1st impression, 1st edn.] This book is Morris's 1st experiment with a view to producing a combination of the best quality materials with artistic design. This 1st impression is comprised of 2 special variants, with the true ordinary or popular copies being printed months after vol. I was issued in Apr.. Here the issue includes 50 (nominal) LP copies and 250–500 'ordinary' copies, so-called, though both variants are F.P. and LP in comparison to the 1-vol. trade or 'popular' edn., for which see the next entry.

Printer: Printed by Strangeways & Sons, Tower Street, Cambridge Circus. (imprint from the 2nd vol., p. 450).

Collation: vol. I.: fcap 4° printed and gathered in 8s: [A]⁴ B–P⁸ Q⁴ 120 leaves pp. [i–v] vi–vii [viii] [1] 2–230 [231–2] [= 240].

vol. II.: fcap 4° printed and gathered in 8s: π⁴ R–2F⁸ 2G⁶ 114 leaves pp. [i–v] vi–vii [viii] [231] 232–450 [= 228]. Note that the signing and the pagination continue in sequence from the end of vol. I. The 'LP' and 'ordinary' copies are the same except that the 'LP' copies are prtd. on cr. 4° paper and have de luxe bindings.

Contents: vol. I.: p. [i], half title; p. [ii], blank; p. [iii], title page; p. [iv], blank; p. [v], dropped head: CONTENTS | [thin rule] | BOOK I. | [list of 12 books, with book numbers, summaries, and page numbers; pp. vi–vii, Contents completed; p. [viii], blank; p. [1], dropped head: THE | ODYSSEY OF HOMER. | BOOK I. | ARGUMENT. | [5 lines of prose summary formatted in hanging indent] | [text begins]; pp. 2–230, text completed; pp. [231–2], blank.

vol. II.: pp. [i–iv], as in vol. I. except title page changes to vol. II.; p. [v], dropped head: CONTENTS | [thin rule] | BOOK XIII. | [list of 12 books, with book numbers, summaries, and page numbers; p. vi, contents continue; p. vii, contents end; p. [viii], blank; p. [231], dropped head: THE | ODYSSEY OF HOMER. | BOOK XIII. | ARGUMENT. | [6 lines of prose summary in hanging indent] | [text begins]; pp. 232–450, text completed with explicit: THE END. | [thin rule] | [printer's imprint] LONDON | Printed by STRANGEWAYS & SONS, Tower Street, Cambridge Circus.

Technical Notes: *paper*: 'ordinary' copies: cream-white Van Gelder hand-made paper; *leaf size*: trimmed 200 x 142 mm.; LP copies: cream-white Dickinson's hand-made with deckled edges and vertical chain lines; *leaf size*: deckled avg. 225 x 168 mm.; *printing*: *type area*: 137 x 102 mm.; *lines-to-page*: leaded, 31 lines excluding head and direction lines; *line numbering*: by 10s with numbers at the right-hand margins; *pagination*: continuous through the 2 vols.; *end-papers*: 1 free end and pastedown, plain white and blank, front and back; *binding*: 'ordinary' copies: quarter blue holland with light-blue paper covered boards; *spine*: printed paper label: [within fine-rule compartment] THE | ODYSSEY | OF | HOMER. | W. MORRIS. | VOL. I [II] | [below compartment] *Price*: 12*s*.; LP copies: quarter parchment with mottled olive-drab paper-covered boards with printed paper spine label that duplicates the 'ordinary' copy label, but without the price line.

Publication: 1887: vol. I.: [issued 1–15 Apr.] (*Pub. Circ.*, 50/1190 (15 Apr. 1887); vol. II.: [issued 1–15 Nov.] (*Pub. Circ.*, 50/1204 (15 Nov. 1887), 1388); see also *Notes*, below; *print run*: 'ordinary' copies: [500 copies? over 250], LP copies: 50; *price*: 'ordinary' copies 12*s*. per vol., LP copies: unknown.

Register of Copies Examined: CaBVau (base copy: Colbeck Coll: PR10 P4 M6 1887 03); BL (2 copies: LP 2 vols. 11335. i. 18. and Ashley Lib. 3689 LP 2 vols. [1887]; An-C-TU (2 vols: L Gr H766nx .Em, and ordinary edn: LGr H766nx .Em 2).

Notes: on 16 Apr. 1887 Morris writes Mrs Jane Morris to say

> There has been no review of Homer yet except one in 'The Scotsman' (Edinburgh) which was good; but it is selling well enough: 250 had gone off by yesterday, and all the large paper: (I have kept one for you, my dear). So I shall hope to make a few pounds by it, though I have given away a many . . . . I am well on now with the 19th book: so, bar accident, I am sure to finish by October: I am keeping the MS. for you [to do] my dear: fair copying has become rather wearisome to me since I have passed the first vol. through the press (*Letters*, ii. 644).

See also Morris's letter to Ford Madox Brown, 11 Nov. 1887: 'I send you herewith vol 2 of Odyssey which is just out' (*Letters*, ii. 709).

A-40.02: The Odyssey ('Popular' edn.)

For the title page, see A-40.01. The only difference in the title pages of the 1st and 2nd impressions of this title is the removal in the latter of: IN TWO VOLUMES | VOL. I. [II.] and consequent changes in spacing.
Edition: 'Popular Edition' [2nd impression, 1st edn.] In one vol., done from the plates used in the 2-vol. 1st issue, which was paginated continuously over the 2 vols. in anticipation of this 1-vol. popular edn.
Collation: cr. 8°: [A]⁶ B–2F⁸ 2G² 232 leaves; pagination is continuous as in A-40.01.
Contents: contents as in the previous entry, except for omission of vols. notice on title page and omission of some repetitive preliminary leaves of Vol. II.
Technical Notes: paper, format, leaf size, binding, etc. uniform with *Sigurd* and *Æneids*; *binding*: plain unblocked dark blue cloth; *spine*: printed paper label: [within thin-rule compartment] THE | ODYSSEY | OF | HOMER | BY | WILLIAM MORRIS | Price: 6s. 6d.
Publication: 1887 [issued 15–31 Dec.] (*Pub. Circ.*, 50/1027 (31 Dec. 1887), 1858); *print run*: unknown; *price*: 6s. 6d.
Register of Copies Examined: An-C-TU (base copy: ordinary edn. in 1 vol: LGr H766nx .Em 2).

A-40.03:* The Odyssey (PW)

THE | ODYSSEY OF HOMER | DONE INTO ENGLISH VERSE | BY | WILLIAM MORRIS, | AUTHOR OF 'THE EARTHLY PARADISE.' | LONGMANS, GREEN, AND CO. | LONDON, NEW YORK, AND BOMBAY. | 1896. | *All rights reserved*.
Edition: 'Cheaper Library Edition' [2nd issue of 2nd impression, 1st edn.] Unsold Reeves and Turner copies in sheets, acquired by Longmans along with the plates, appear here in a 2nd issue with a new title page displaying the new publisher's imprint.
Series: 'The Poetical Works of William Morris' (PW). This series, indicated in the copies only by the printed paper spine label, is one of a uniform set of 10 unnumbered vols., all issued in 1896 when Longmans became Morris's publisher. In 1898 the set increased to 11 vols. with the addition of *The Tale of Beowulf* (for series details, see this field in A-4.16).
Printer: Strangeways & Sons, Tower Street, Cambridge Circus.
Collation: As in A-40.02.
Contents: only prelims vary from the original 'Popular Edn.': pp. [1–2], blank; p. [i], half title; p. [ii], blank; p. [iii], title page.
Publication: 1896 [issued 18–25 July] (*Pub. Circ.*, 65/1569 (25 July 1896), 84).
Register of Copies Examined: as indicated above, this impression has not been seen, but the SU copy of Jan. 1897 (base copy: 1897: 88 / H80. E mo) is a new impression of the same setting as the 1896 PW volume and of the 1st edn. of 1887.
Later impressions of this title in this series: Longmans:
1. 1897 [issued Jan.] (Longmans Arch.): [3rd impression, 1st edn.] PW 'Popular Edition'; *print run*: 500 copies; *price*: 6s. (all 10 titles in this series were sold for 6s., see *Eng. Cat.*, V (Jan. 1890– Dec. 1897); this one was also imported and sold in the USA for $2.00;
2.* 1904 [issued Apr.] (Longmans Arch.): PW, 'Popular Edition' [4th impression, 1st edn.]; *print run*: 500 copies; *price*: 5s.

A-40.04: The Odyssey (Golden 4°)

[aligned left] THE ODYSSEY OF HOMER DONE INTO ENGLISH | VERSE BY WILLIAM MORRIS.
Edition: 'Golden type quarto edition' [1st impression, 2nd edn.].
Collaborators, Editors, and Illustrators: [Edited by S. C. Cockerell and Robert Proctor] (as disclosed in their unpublished correspondence).
Series: 5th vol., unnumbered, in the 8-vol. Golden type quarto series. For further series detail see this field and *Notes* in A-47.04
Colophon: Here ends the Odyssey of Homer, done into English verse by William | Morris. First printed in 1887, and now reprinted at the Chiswick Press with | the Golden

Type designed by William Morris for the Kelmscott Press, and | finished on the Thirtieth day of December, 1901. Published by Longmans, | Green and Co. of London, New York and Bombay.

Collation: 4°: a–2p⁴ 152 leaves pp. [2] [i–ii] iii–v [vi] 1–293 [294–6] [= 304].

Contents: pp. [1–2], blank; p. [i], title page; p. [ii], blank; p. iii–v, headed: [top, flush left] CONTENTS | [chapter titles, with several lines of summaries for each, as a list]; p. [vi], blank; p. 1, headed: [title, repeated in black] | [in red caps] BOOK I [and a 7-line summary-title] | [text begins]; pp. 2–293, text completed with colophon (see above); pp. [294–6], blank.

Technical Notes: paper, leaf size, printing (including colour), position (but not content) of shoulder notes, pagination, end-papers, and binding are all common to the series and are described in this field in A-47.04, the 1st pbn. of the series. Included here are only those details that belong to this particular edn.: shoulder notes and all chapter titles in red, chapter titles in caps; *type area*: 202 x 142 mm.; *lines-to-page*: set solid, 42 lines; *shoulder notes*: all rectos and versos, in red: The Odyssey | of Homer | Book i [–xxiv]; *spine label*: [across the spine] WILLIAM | MORRIS | THE | ODYSSEY | OF | HOMER

Publication: 30 Dec. 1901 [this colophon date indicates finished printing, but binding had still to be done, so the issue date is likely to be at least 2 weeks later]; *print run*: 315 copies, 299 for sale; *price*: 16gns. the set.

Register of Copies Examined: LeM (base copy); BL (C.43.f.11); CSt (Spec. Coll Gunst Z239.2.C54.H760 1901); VU (L).

A-40.05: The Odyssey (*CW* XIII)

THE COLLECTED WORKS | [title details common to the set, see A-126.01] | VOLUME XIII | THE ODYSSEY OF HOMER DONE | INTO ENGLISH VERSE | [publisher's imprint, see A-126.01] | MDCCCCXII

Edition: [1st impression, 3rd edn.].

Series: vol. 13 of 24; for series details, see this field, *Technical Notes*, and *Notes* in A-126.01.

Collation: medium 8°: a⁸ (a3+1) b⁸ (b1+1) c⁴ B–2A⁸ [$2 (–a2) signed] 204 leaves pp. [i–vi] vii–xxxix [xl] [1] 2–362 [363–8] [= 408] +2 inserted plates not counted in the book's pagination, but noted in the formula and described here in their appropriate places under *Contents*.

Contents: p. [i], blank; p. [ii], limitation notice (see this field in 126.01); pp. [iii–iv], blank; facing p. [v], 1st inserted plate as frontis., vertically-oriented reproduction of a photograph signed by the maker, below right: *Emery Walker photographer and engraver* | [captioned in copperplate, centred] *The Library, Kelmscott House, Hammersmith*; p. [v], title page; p. [vi], blank; p. vii–x, headed: CONTENTS | [each of the 24 books has a heading] BOOK I [II–XXIV], followed by the prose 'argument' in hanging indent; p. xi, headed: ILLUSTRATIONS | [contents completed]; p. [xii], blank; p. xiii, headed: INTRODUCTION | [text begins]; pp. xiv–xviii, text continues; 2nd inserted plate facing p. xviii, from a drawing, with the artist's name below left: *F. L. Griggs dd. 1910* | [below right the plate maker's name] *Emery Walker Ph. sc.* | [captioned in copperplate, centred] *Kelmscott House, Hammersmith, | from the garden*; pp. xix–xxxvii, Introduction concluded; p. [xxxviii], blank; p. xxxix, headed: BIBLIOGRAPHICAL NOTE; p. xl, blank; p. [1], headed: THE ODYSSEY OF HOMER | BOOK I | THE ARGUMENT | [flush left, 7-line prose summary] | [text begins with 3-line drop cap initial 'T']; pp. 2–362, text completed with explicit: THE END; pp. [363–8], blank.

Technical Notes: paper, printing, position (but not content) of headlines, running titles, shoulder notes, pagination, end-papers, and binding are all common to the series and are described in this field in A-126.01. Only those details specific to this issue are included here: *running titles*: all versos: THE ODYSSEY OF HOMER | [all rectos] BOOK I [–XXIV].

Publication: 1912 [issued 31 Oct.] (Longmans Arch.); *print run* and *price*: see A-126.01.

Register of Copies Examined: see this field in A-126.01.

A-41.01:* Appeal for . . . Inglesham Church

Title: Appeal for the Preservation of Inglesham Church. 1887

Edition: [1st impression, 1st edn.] Leaflet.

Collaborators, Editors, and Illustrators: [Rev. O. Birchall acted as editor, consulting with Morris]. (see the *Notes*, below).

Place: London.

Publisher: The Rev. Oswald Birchall, but Morris wrote the appeal, as he had offered to do earlier (see *Notes*, below).

Printer: [Messrs Bridge of Oxford].

Collation: 8° fly leaf printed on only one side, omitting the author's name.

Publication: [June 1887].

Register of Copies Located: 1st edn. neither seen nor located; rptd. London, 1898: MH Houghton (EC 85 / 18348 / B898P); CtY.

Notes: Morris delivered a report to the SPAB at the Society's 10th Annual Meeting (1887) in which he said that Micklethwaite, an SPAB member, had submitted an architect's report, and he,

> . . . estimates the cost of a thorough repair at about £550. The Vicar and Churchwardens have the active sympathy of the Bishop and Archdeacon of Bristol, on the understanding that nothing is to be done against the views of the Society. With a like understanding, and with the sanction of the Society, Mr. Birchall has had an appeal for funds printed by Messrs. Bridge of Oxford, including M. Micklethwaite's report, letters from the Bishop and Archdeacon, &c. This will be circulated widely as soon as replies have been received from the only wealthy landowners of the parish, viz., New College, Oxford, and the Earl of Radnor (*SPAB. 10th Annual Meeting . . . Report, p. 24*).

Rptd. in MM, i. 160.

Three related Morris comments on Inglesham Church are entered in 10th, 11th, and 12th SPAB AGMs., June 1887, 1888, and 1889 9see D-312, 399, 468).

A-41.02: Appeal for . . . Inglesham Church

[heading] THE SOCIETY FOR THE PROTECTION OF ANCIENT BUILDINGS. | [title, aligned flush left] AN APPEAL FOR THE PRESERVATION OF | INGLESHAM CHURCH. BY WILLIAM | MORRIS, 1887. | [text begins]

Edition: [1st impression, 2nd edn.] Notes at the end dated 1898.
Publisher: SPAB.
Printer: [Women's Printing Society, Ltd., 66, Whitcomb Street, W.C.].
Collation: s. sh. folded to form 2 leaves, each 204 x 129 mm.; printed only on pp. 1 and 4, pp. [2–3], blank.
Contents: p. [1]: [title and publisher's imprint at head, then text begins]; pp. [2–3], blank; p. 4, text ends, followed by 'Notes' dated: 1898. It seems likely that the text is the same as the first edn. except for the end note dated 1898.
Technical Notes: *paper*: cream machine-made paper; uniform in size, paper, type, and design with the pamphlet *On the External Coverings of Roofs* (see A-44.01); *type area*: 156 x 92 mm.; *lines-to-page*: leaded, 34 lines; printed only on pp. 1 and 4, pp. [2–3], blank.
Publication: 1898.
Registry of Copies Examined: BL (base copy: Cup. 502. f. 11. [29]); CtY (IP M834 898s); MH Houghton (EC 85 / 18348 / B898P)

A-42.01: The Tables Turned

[wrapper title: all within a typographical compartment:] THE | TABLES TURNED; | OR, NUPKINS AWAKENED | [in gothic] A SOCIALIST INTERLUDE | [plain text] BY | WILLIAM MORRIS | AUTHOR OF 'THE EARTHLY PARADISE.' | *As for the first time played at the Hall of the Socialist League | on Saturday October 15, 1887* | LONDON: | OFFICE OF "THE COMMONWEAL" | 13, FARRINGDON ROAD, E.C. | 1887 | All Rights Reserved

Edition: [1st impression, 1st edn.] Reprinted in MM, ii. 528–67.
Printer: Printed and Published at the Commonweal Office, 13 Farringdon Road. London, E.C.
Collation: dbl. cr. 8°: [1]¹⁶ 16 leaves pp. [1] 2–32 [= 32] + a light green wrapper, sewn.
Contents: p. [1], dropped head: THE TABLES TURNED; | OR, | NUPKINS AWAKENED. | [french rule] | PART I. | SCENE.—A Court of Justice. | [3 lines of scene setting] | [dialogue begins]; pp. 2–22, dialogue continues; p. 23, 2nd chapter head title: dropped head: Part II. | [1 line of scene setting] | [text resumes]; pp. 23–32, text completed with explicit: THE END. | [imprint, see *Printer* field, above]
Technical Notes: *paper*: plain white machine-moulded; *leaf size*: cut flush, 186 x 125 mm.; *printing*: type area: 155 x 95 mm., not including headlines; *lines-to-page*: set solid, 45 lines; text divided into PART I and PART II; all speakers names or initials in italics; *running titles*: [all versos] The Tables Turned; or, | [all rectos] Nupkins Awakened.; *wrapper*: light blue-green machine-made paper; wrapper title page: see above; wrapper p. [2], list of 'ORIGINAL CAST.' divided into Part I and Part II; wrapper p. [3], ad for 'WORKS OF WILLIAM MORRIS.'; wrapper p. [4], ads for Socialist League pbns.
Publication: 1887 [issued 22 Oct.] (on that date, *Commonweal* notes for the 1st time that it 'has been printed and can be had at the Commonweal Office, price 4d.' Performances were scheduled for 3 successive Saturdays following the 1st on 15 Oct.; 22 Oct., at Farringdon Hall (again), 29 Oct. at the Athenæum Hall, Bloomsbury, and at Kelmscott House, Hammersmith, on 5 Nov.
Register of Copies Examined: BL (5 copies: base copy: Cup.502.f.11. (23 and 24); Ashley 1230; 11781. D. 39, and 11779. bb.43; CSt (Rare Book Room: 821.6/M87t); Fdmn.
Notes: the minutes of the 4th Annual Conference of the SL, 20 May 1888, include in the Annual Report remarks on the first successful performance of *The Tables Turned*

at the Hall of the SL on 15 Oct. 1887, adding, 'the play has been translated into French and its performance in America inhibited [*sic*].'

A-43.01: A Death Song

[wrapper title: all within a thick-rule compartment:] SOLD FOR THE BENEFIT OF LINNELL'S ORPHANS. | [thin rule] | ALFRED LINNELL | [within a thin-rule compartment, Walter Crane's 'Justice & Liberty' block, hand-labelled below left 'IN MEMORIAM | ALFRED LINNELL'] | [below thin-rule compartment] *Killed in Trafalgar Square,* | NOVEMBER 20, 1887. | [thin rule] | A DEATH SONG, | BY MR. W. MORRIS. | Memorial Design by Mr. Walter Crane. | [thin rule] | PRICE ONE PENNY.

Edition: [1st impression, 1st edn.]

Collaborators, Editors, and Illustrators: Words by Morris, music by Malcolm Lawson; memorial design by Walter Crane.

Publisher: Richard Lambert [acting for The Law and Liberty League].

Collation: royal 8° (half-sheet): [1]⁴, this copy not stapled or sewn, self-wrappered, 4 leaves pp. [1] 2–8 = [8].

Contents: p. [1], title page, see above; p. [2], begins unsigned memoir, all within thick-rule compartment, headed: ALFRED LINNELL | [thin rule] | text begins in 2 columns; pp. 3–4, memoir completed; p. 5, music of 'A Death Song' begins: [headed, in gothic] A Death Song | (Words by William Morris. Music by M. Lawson); pp. 6–8, musical notation completed with a thin rule: [heading]: [in gothic] A DEATH SONG | *(Words written by Mr. William Morris. Music composed by | Mr. Malcolm Lawson.)* | [4 stanzas, each with a quatrain and a couplet refrain] | [thin rule] | Printed and Published by Richard Lambert, at 2, Northumberland-street, Strand, in the Parish of St. Martin's-in-the-Fields.

Technical Notes: *paper*: plain white machine-made; *leaf size*: 261 x 173 mm.; *printing*: *type area*: 2 cols. in the same thick-rule compartment (HBF calls them 'mourning borders'): 220 x 156 mm.; *headlines*: above a thin rule, versos: ALFRED LINNELL.; recto: KILLED IN TRAFALGAR SQUARE; pp. 5–6: A DEATH SONG; *wrapper*: self wrappered.

Publication: 1887 [issued 18 Dec.] (Mackail, ii. 192); *print run*: unknown; *price*: 1d.

Register of Copies Examined: CSt (base copy: Spec. Coll Felton PR5078.A8); BL (2 copies: Cup. 502.f.11. (34) and Ashley Library (No. 3690, 3:173); Fdmn; LeM copy from Bass.

Notes: rptd., *Commonweal*, 5/202 (23 Nov. 1889), 371.

A-44.01: On the External Coverings of Roofs (SPAB)

[heading, aligned flush left] THE SOCIETY FOR THE PROTECTION | OF ANCIENT BUILDINGS. | ON THE EXTERNAL COVERINGS OF | ROOFS.

Edition: [1st impression, 1st edn.] Later rptd. in *Architecture, Industry, and Wealth* (see C-18.01).

Publisher: SPAB.

Printer: [no imprint].

Collation: cr. 8° leaflet formed by folding a single sheet once, forming 2 leaves pp. [1–4], self-wrappered.

Contents: p. [1], head title, text begins; pp. [2–4], text completed with double column list of 'Good' and 'Bad' roof coverings, list ends with the SPAB address: 9, Buckingham Street, Strand.

Technical Notes: uniform with *An Appeal for the Preservation of Inglesham Church* (see A-41.01); *paper*: plain white machine-made, no watermark; *leaf size*: 205 x 135 mm.; *printing*: type area: 155 x 92 mm.; *lines-to-page*: hair lead, 39 lines; no pagination; self-wrappered.

Publication: [1887 ?] (from Cockerell's longhand date on his copy (BL Cup. 502.f.11.(31.)) HBF, by positioning in his sequence, suggests a pbn. date of 1896 (pp. 188–9), but he offers no evidence for this date. The editors of *Architecture, Industry, and Wealth*, Cockerell and Proctor, place this item last in a sequence where the pieces are arranged otherwise in a consistently chronological order, i.e. the editors imply that this piece appears after 'The Influence of Building Materials on Architecture' of Jan. 1892. But the editors give no more reason for their putting this essay last than Forman for putting it in 1896, or Cockerell for the pencil date on his copy, which he may have entered before or after the *Architecture, Industry and Wealth* vol. was published in 1902. The *British Library Catalogue* (hereafter referred to as *BLC*) uses Cockerell's longhand date, with a query, as is done here. Temple Scott, in his entry on this title in his chronology (Scott, p. 20), positions it in a way consistent with Cockerell's date, which is used here as the most authoritative available; *print run* and *price*: unknown.

Register of Copies Examined: BL (base copy: Cup. 502. f.11.(31.) Cockerell's copy with Morris's signature in ink); NNBerg (copy from Pierce Collection).

A-45.01: John Ball and a King's Lesson

A DREAM OF JOHN BALL | AND | A KING'S LESSON. | *(REPRINTED FROM 'THE COMMONWEAL.')* | BY | WILLIAM MORRIS, | AUTHOR OF | 'THE

EARTHLY PARADISE,' ETC. | With an Illustration by EDWARD BURNE-JONES. | LONDON: | REEVES & TURNER, 196 STRAND. | MDCCCLXXXVIII.
Edition: [1st impression, 1st edn.] Both stories first appeared in *Commonweal*; for *John Ball*, see D-240; *A King's Lesson* was 1st titled 'An Old Story Retold' (see D-227); 50 LP copies on Dickinson's hand-made paper were produced in pott quarto as a variant of this 1st impression.
Collation: royal 16° in 8s: [A]⁴ (A4+1) B–K⁸ (K8+1) 76 leaves pp. [i–vii] viii [1] 2–129 [*John Ball* ends] [130–2] [*A King's Lesson* begins] 133–43 [144] [= 152] + 2 inserts noted in the formula but not included in the book's pagination. Each is described in the *Contents* in its proper place.
Contents: pp. [i–ii], blank; p. [iii], half title; p. [iv], blank; p. [v], title page; p. [vi], blank; pp. [vii]–viii, headed: CONTENTS. | [list of 12 chapters and 'A King's Lesson'; inserted leaf facing p. [1], photogravure illustration from a drawing by Burne-Jones, blank on recto, in blind-stamped compartment, labelled (in letterpress): When Adam delved and Eve span [printer's flower] | who was then the gentleman [printer's flower]; p. [1], text begins; pp. 2–129, text completed; p. [130], blank; p. 131, second half title; p. [132], blank; p. 133, text of *A King's Lesson* begins; pp. 134–43, text completed: [thin rule] | LONDON | Printed by STRANGEWAYS & SONS, Tower Street, Cambridge C.; p.[144], blank; inserted leaf, recto advertising WORKS OF WILLIAM MORRIS.; verso blank; this inserted ad. is at the front in the Cst copy, but at the back in LeM copy).
Technical Notes: *paper*: cream machine wove, no watermark, t.e.g.; *leaf size*: (ordinary copies) untrimmed, avg. 166 x 125; *LP copies: 226 x 177 mm. (see Coupe, p. 138); *printing*: type area: 99 x 68 mm., excluding head and direction lines; *lines-to-page*: 29; *headlines*: running titles: pp. 2–129, all versos and rectos: A DREAM OF JOHN BALL; pp. 134–43, all versos and rectos: A KING'S LESSON; *end-papers*: plain white end-papers, free end and pastedown blank, front and back; *binding*: [Forman's and Cst copies had no gilt stamping but a printed paper spine label (see HBF, p. 139)] plain unblocked dark red cloth; printed *spine label*: 53 x 22 mm.: [within a thin-rule compartment] A | DREAM | OF | JOHN | BALL & c. | BY | W. MORRIS | [below compartment] 4s. 6d.; LeM copy is gilt-stamped, front and spine: front: [aligned left] *A DREAM OF* | [aligned right] *JOHN BALL* | [at the foot] *W. MORRIS*; spine: A | DREAM | OF | JOHN | BALL | [thin rule] | W. MORRIS; LP *binding*: half vellum with marbled paper boards.
Publication: 1888. [issued 1–15 Mar.] (*Pub. Circ.*, 51/1212 (15

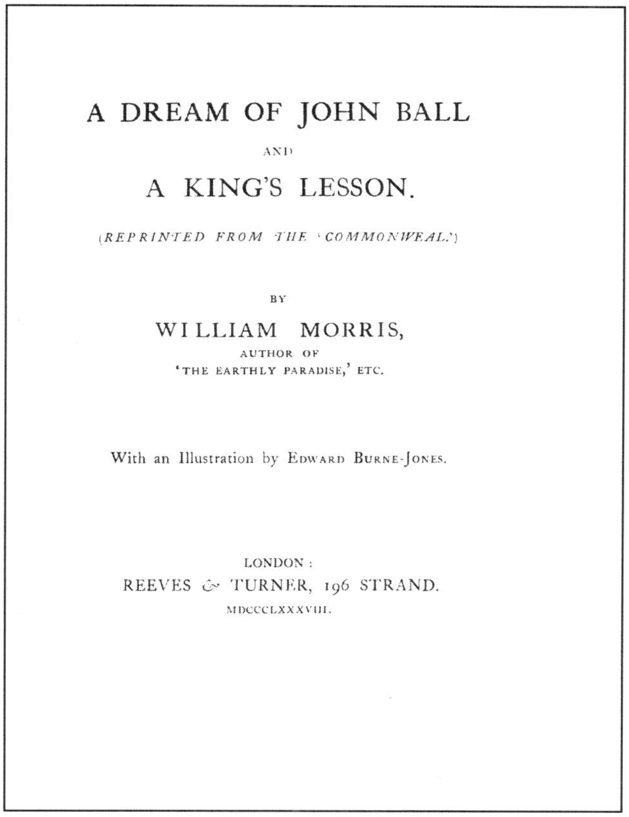

Figure 39. A-45.01: *John Ball and . . .* (1st edn) title page

Mar. 1888), 307); but the same book is listed in the next issue for the period 16–31 Mar.); Mackail (ii. 205) says Mar., but HBF (p. 138) and Kelvin (*Letters*, ii. 594) say Apr. The 1st ad, saying the book is 'Now Ready', appeared in *Commonweal*, 17 Mar. 1888, p. 88. Hence, the date given here, on which *Commonweal, Pub. Circ.*, the earliest reviews, and Mackail agree, seems most likely. This is confirmed by Morris's letter to Charles Rowley, dated 17 Mar.: '. . . as to the large paper John Ball Reeves & Turner 196 Strand are the only people but perhaps the copies are all sold; there are only 50 printed' (*Letters*, ii. 756). To Emma Shelton Morris, 19 Mar. 1888. : 'I send herewith my new little book, which I hope you will like. . . (*Letters*, ii. 757). *Print run*: not known; *price*: regular copies: 4s. 6d., LP copies: 9s.
Register of Copies Examined: Cst (base copy: Spec.Coll Felton PR5079 | D77); LeM; SU (823 | M87); ANL (823,7 | M877d); MU (Spec Coll. 5079 | D8); BGR.
Later issues and impressions of this edn.:
1. R and T: 1889 [issued 16–23 Nov.]: 'Cheap Edition', without illus. [2nd impression, 1st edn.]; *print run*: unknown; *price*: 1s. paper, 1s. 6d. cloth;

2. R and T: 1890 [issued Jan.]: Third Edition, 'Cheap Edition', without illus. [3rd impression, 1st edn.]; *print run*: unknown; *price*: 1*s*. paper, 1*s*. 6*d*. cloth;

3. R and T: 1892 [issued Sept.]: Fourth Edition. 'Cheap Edition', without illus. [4th impression, 1st edn.]; *print run*: unknown; *price*: 1*s*. paper, 1*s*. 6*d*. cloth;

4. R and T: 1895 [issued Mar.]: Fifth Edition. 'Cheap Edition' [5th impression, 1st edn.] without illus.; *print run*: unknown; *price*: 1*s*. 6*d*. cloth, 1*s*. paper;

5. Longmans: 1896 [issued July]: Fifth Edition. 'Cheap Edition' [2nd issue, 5th impression, 1st edn.] without illus. (see the entry A-45.03); *print run*: copies remaining after Longmans replaced R and T as Morris's publisher [hence 3rd issue, 5th impression, 1st edn.; *price*: 1*s*. 6*d*. cloth, 1*s*. paper;

6. Longmans: 1898 [issued 2 July]: Sixth Edition. 'Cheap Edition' [Sixth impression, 1st edn.]; *print run*: 1,000 copies printed by Ballantyne Press; *price*: 1*s*. 6*d*. cloth, 1*s*. paper;

7. Longmans: 1900 [issued 5 Sept.]: Seventh Impression. 'Cheap edition' [7th impression, 1st edn.]; *print run*: 1,000 copies; *price*: 1*s*. 6*d*. cloth, 1*s*. paper.

A-45.02: John Ball and a King's Lesson (KP)

[head title, top, flush left:] A DREAM OF JOHN BALL AND | A KING'S LESSON. BY WILLIAM | MORRIS.
Edition: 'Kelmscott Press Edition' [1st impression, 2nd edn.] For details of 1st publication of both stories, see this field in A-45.01.
Collaborators, Editors, and Illustrators: woodcut illustration from a design by E. Burne-Jones, borders and lettering designed by Morris and, with the Burne-Jones drawing, engraved by W. H. Hooper.
Series: 6th title, 4th by Morris, pbd. by the KP.
Colophon: [printer's leaf ornament No. 1] | This book, a Dream of John Ball and a King's | Lesson, was written by William Morris, and | printed by him at the Kelmscott Press, Upper | Mall, Hammersmith, in the County of Middle- | sex; and finished on the 13th day of May, 1892. | Sold by Reeves & Turner, 196, Strand, London.
Collation: cr 8°: [a]⁴ b–h⁸ i⁶ [$4 (–b1 c1 c2 i1) signed] 66 leaves pp. [8] [1] 2–111 [*John Ball* ends] [112–13] [*A King's Lesson* begins] 114–23 [124] [= 132].
Contents: pp. [*1–4*], blank; p. [*5*], title page; pp. [*6–7*], blank; p. [*8*], frontis. to face p. [1], woodcut of Adam, Eve, and their 2 children, designed by E. Burne-Jones, all within a full border, No. 3a, captioned below (quoted from p. 21) flush left, in letters designed by Morris: WHEN ADAM DELVED | AND EVE SPAN | WHO WAS THEN THE | GENTLEMAN; p. [1], 1st head title, within full border, No. 4: [top flush left] A DREAM OF JOHN BALL. | [in red] CHAPTER I. THE MEN OF | KENT. | [text begins with 10-line floriated initial 'S']; pp. 2–111, text completed with explicit, flush left: HERE ENDS A DREAM OF JOHN | BALL.; p. [112], blank; p. [113], 2nd head title, within full border, No. 2: [top, flush left] A SHORT TALE OF A KING'S | LESSON. | [text begins with 10-line floriated initial 'I']; pp. 114–23, text completed with explicit, flush left: THE END OF A KING'S LESSON. | [KP mark No. 1, followed by the colophon, see above]; p. [124], blank.
Technical Notes: *paper*: Batchelor's hand-made KP Flower paper 1; *leaf size*: untrimmed deckled edges, avg. 203 x 140 mm.; *printing*: *type face*: Golden Type; printed in black and red, red for chapter titles in *John Ball* and general title in *King's Lesson*, for all shoulder notes, red also in a quotation on p. 21, an explanatory shoulder note on p. 40, and a footnote on p. 91; *type area*: 140 x 92 mm.; *lines-to-page*: set solid, 30 lines; *pagination*: arabic, 5 mm. in from the outer margin on the direction line; *end-papers*: standard KP: 3 free ends and 1 pastedown, all plain white and blank, front and back; *binding*: limp white vellum with gold silk ties; *spine*: gilt-stamped title across: JOHN | BALL; *ornamentation*: illus. by Burne-Jones; 1 smaller KP mark; 3 full borders, 3a, 4, and 2; 13 floriated 10-line initials; 74 floriated 6-line initials.
Publication: 13 May 1892 [this colophon date indicates finished printing, issued 24 Sept.] (see Cockerell, p. 150); *print run*: 300 paper copies and 11 on vellum; *price*: 30*s*. and 10*gns*., respectively.
Register of Copies Examined: VU (2 copies: base copy: L and 19F:); CSt (Z239.2/K29/M87dr).

A-45.03:* John Ball and a King's Lesson

A DREAM OF JOHN BALL | AND | A KING'S LESSON. | (*REPRINTED FROM 'THE COMMONWEAL.'*) | BY | WILLIAM MORRIS, | AUTHOR OF | 'THE EARTHLY PARADISE,' ETC. | FIFTH EDITION. | LONGMANS, GREEN, AND CO. | 39 PATERNOSTER ROW, LONDON | NEW YORK AND BOMBAY | 1896 | *All rights reserved*.
Edition: Fifth Edition. [2nd issue, 5th impression, 1st edn.] without illus. This is Longmans re-issue, with a new title page with the new publisher's imprint, of copies purchased from Reeves and Turner when Longmans became Morris's

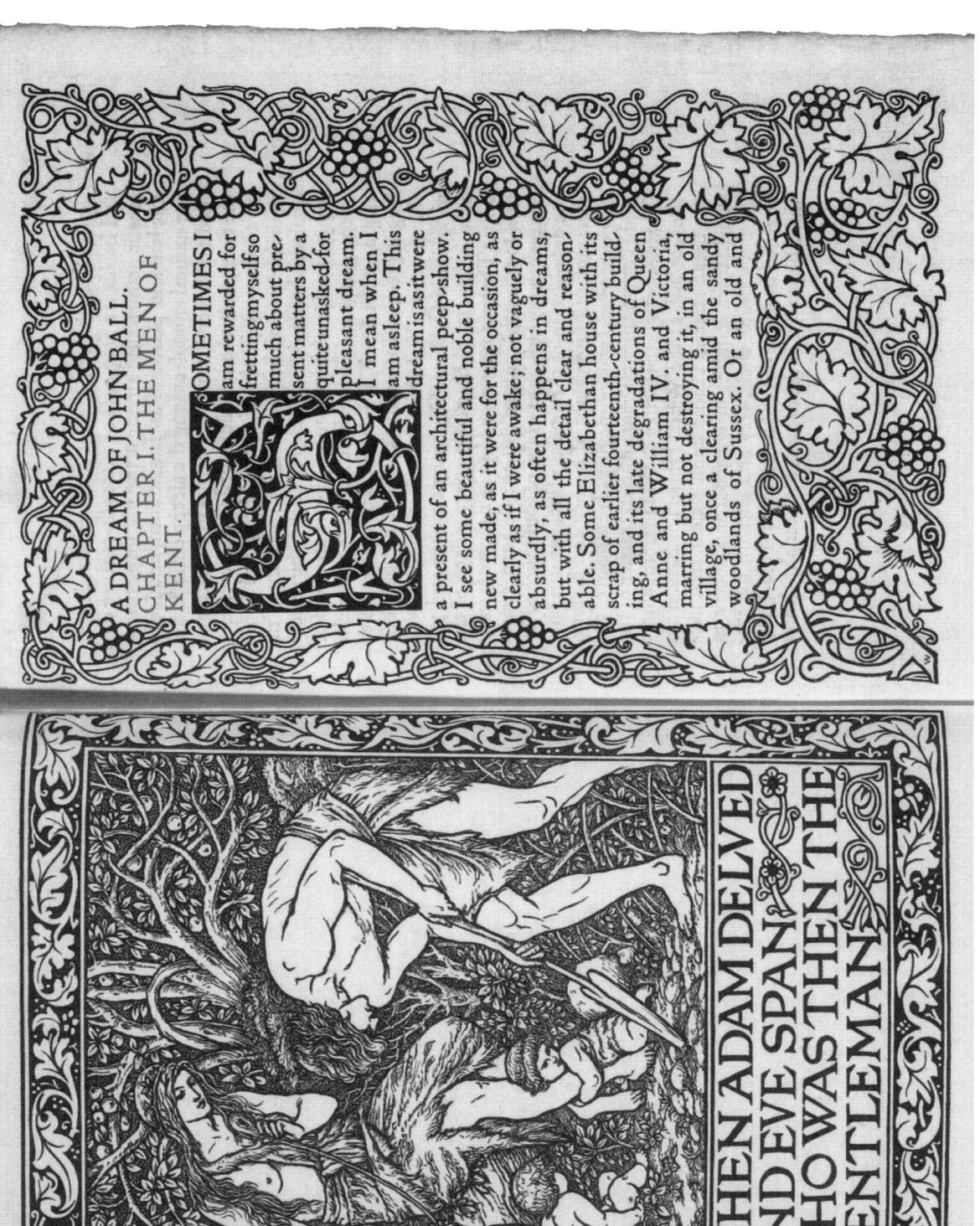

Figure 40. A-45.02: *John Ball and...* (KP edn.) engraved title & facing head title

publisher in mid-1896. For details of 1st pbn. of both stories, see this field in A-45.01.
Publication: 1896 [issued July] (*Eng. Cat.*, 5 (Jan. 1890–Dec. 1897), 689); *print run*: from copies remaining; *price*: 1s. paper, 1s. 6d. cloth.
Register of Copies Located: CSt (base copy: 821.6/M87db); NN.

A-45.04: John Ball and a King's Lesson (Mosher)

[title and date in red] A DREAM OF | JOHN BALL | BY | WILLIAM MORRIS | [Chiswick Press Aldine mark (Bishop No. 2)] | Portland, Maine | [ital. swash caps] *THOMAS B. MOSHER* | [in red] M*dccccij*

Edition: [1st impression, 4th edn., 2nd American of *John Ball*] without illus. For the 1st American edn. (1st edn. done by the Roycroft Press, see A-89.01. For details of the 1st pbn. of both stories, see, respectively, D-240 and D-227.

Series: Mosher's Old World Series—28. This is the only Morris book in this series.

Collation: long 8°: [1–9⁸ 10⁴] 76 leaves pp. [i–iv] v [vi] [1–2] 3–129 [130], *John Ball* ends and *A King's Lesson* begins; [131–2] 133–42 [143–6] [=152]

Contents: p. [i], half title: [top left, in gothic] Old World Series | [thin-thick rule] | [a Chiswick-Jenckes designed head-piece] | A DREAM OF JOHN BALL | [Chiswick-Jenckes tail-piece]; p. [ii], blank; p. [iii], title page; p. [iv], statement of limitation: *This First Edition on | Van Gelder paper con- | sists of 925 copies*; p. v, headed: [Chiswick-Jenckes head-piece] | CONTENTS | [list begins]; p. [vi], contents completed: [Chiswick-Jenckes tail-piece]; p. [1], 2nd half title, duplicates the 1st, without the series name and with different head and tail pieces; p. [2], blank; p. 3, 1st chapter heading: [head-piece] | A DREAM OF JOHN BALL | I | THE MEN OF KENT | [text begins]; pp. 4–[130], text completed with Chiswick-Jenckes tail-piece; p. [131], 3rd half title, head and tail-pieces as for 1st, with the new title between: A KING'S LESSON; p. [132], blank; p. 133, 2nd head title: [Chiswick-Jenckes head-piece] | A KING'S LESSON | [text begins]; pp. 134–[143], text completed with Chiswick-Jenckes tail piece; p. [144], printer's imprint: [at the foot, aligned right] *PRINTED BY | SMITH & SALE | PORTLAND | MAINE*; pp. [145–6], blank.

Technical Notes: *paper*: Van Gelder hand-laid with vertical chain lines, watermarked near the foot of the page: VAN GELDER ZONEN; *leaf size*: deckled edges, lightly trimmed, avg. 180 x 96 mm.; *bindings*: advertised: 'Japan

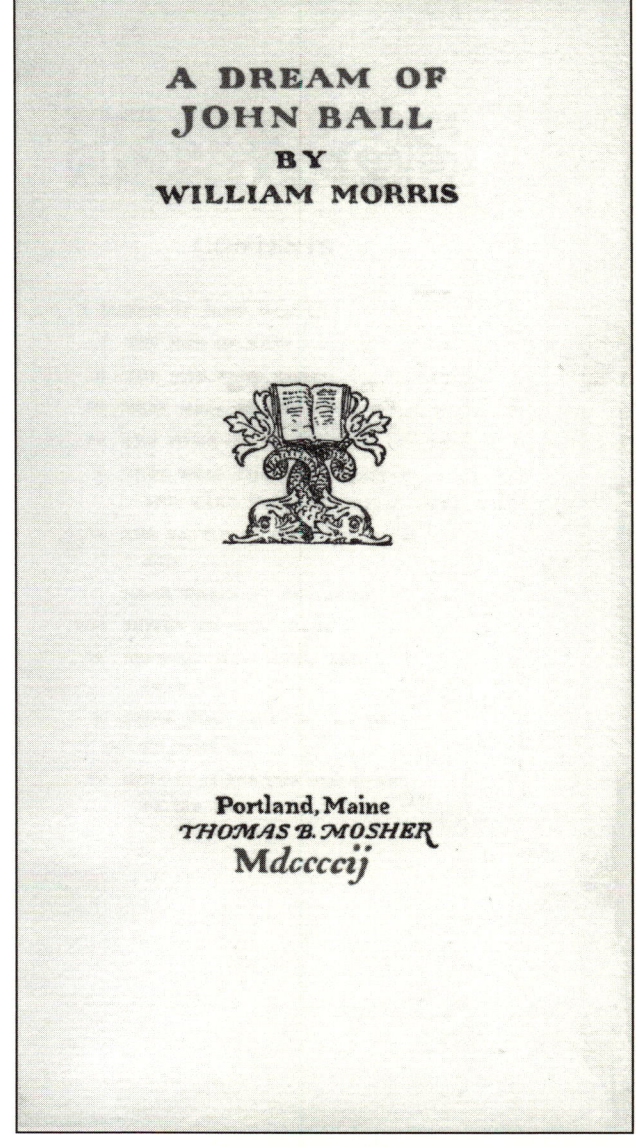

Figure 41. A-45.04: *John Ball and . . .* (Mosher edn.) title page

vellum covers, flexible, with turned down [i.e. yapp] fore-edges, $1.25 net.; Old-style blue paper boards, white back and label, $1.50 net.; flexible lthr., smooth, dark olive colour, gilt tops, $1.75 net.; Japan vellum edition (numbered), $2.50 net.' (Mosher's annual catalogue: *The Mosher Books: A List of Books in Belles Lettres issued in Choice and limited editions MDCCCXCI–MDCCCCXIV*). The copy described here has yet another binding option: blue paper-covered boards with japan vellum (parchment) spine with 4 raised bands and a printed paper label: [thick-thin rule] A | DREAM | OF | JOHN | BALL | [thin rule] | MORRIS

| [thin-thick rule]; *price*: $1.25. But note that Mosher varied the ornaments on occasion (see the cover illustrated in Bishop, p. 130, which is not in any of the copies used for this description. But it may belong to the 2nd edn., not seen).

Publication: 1902; *print run*: 925 copies on Van Gelder paper; 100 numbered copies on japan vellum; *price*: Van Gelder copies $1.00; in blue paper-covered boards $1.25; in lthr. $1.50; japan vellum copies $2.50.

Register of Copies Examined: LeM (base copy); Bsp.

Later impression of this edn.:

1.* Mosher: 1908: Old World Series—28 [2nd impression, 4th edn., 2nd American (*John Ball* only)]; *print run*: 925 copies on Van Gelder paper only; *price*: $1.00.

A-45.05: John Ball and a King's Lesson

A DREAM OF JOHN BALL | AND A KING'S LESSON | BY WILLIAM MORRIS | LONGMANS, GREEN, AND CO. | 39 PATERNOSTER ROW, LONDON | NEW YORK & BOMBAY | 1903

Edition: New Edition. 'Cheap Edition' [1st impression, 5th edn., 3rd English] For details of 1st pbn. of both stories, see this field in A-45.01.

Collaborators, Editors, and Illustrators: The original 1888 1st edn. photogravure woodcut illustration, labelled 'When Adam delved and Eve span | Who was then the Gentleman', as originally drawn by Burne-Jones, is here reintroduced on a smaller scale after being recut by Robert Catterson-Smith, reproduced by Emery Walker as a photo relief block, and moulded by Ballantyne, Hanson & Co. (Smith Arch. and Longmans Arch.).

Collation: royal 16°, printed and gathered in 8s: π⁴ A–K⁸ L⁴ M² 90 leaves pp. [i–vi] vii–viii [1] 2–153 [*John Ball* ends] [154–6, *A King's Lesson* begins] 157–68 [169–72] [= 180].

Contents: p. [i], half title; pp. [ii–iii], blank; p. [iv], frontis. labelled (but not with Morris's original lettering): [below, flush left] WHEN ADAM DELVED AND EVE SPAN | WHO WAS THEN THE GENTLEMAN?; p. [v], title page; p. [vi], bibliographical note of 5 lines; p. vii, dropped head: CONTENTS | [list begins]; p. viii, Contents concluded; p. [1], dropped head: A DREAM OF JOHN BALL | CHAPTER I | THE MEN OF KENT | [text begins]; pp. 2–153, text completed; p. [154], blank; p. [155], 2nd half title: 'A KING'S LESSON'; p. [156], blank; p. 157, dropped head to general title, text of *A King's Lesson* begins; pp. 158–[69], text completed; p. [170], printer's imprint: [at the foot] Printed by BALLANTYNE, HANSON & CO. | Edinburgh & London; pp. [171–2], ads, headed: WILLIAM MORRIS'S WORKS | [list begins].

Technical Notes: *paper*: plain white 'Antique' machine-moulded, t.e.g.; *leaf size*: trimmed, 150 x 120 mm.; *print: type area*: 98 x 80 mm.; *lines-to-page*: set solid, 23 lines, excluding head and direction lines; *running titles*: except chapter titles, all versos and rectos, pp. 2–153: 'A DREAM OF JOHN BALL'; pp. 158–[69],all rectos and versos: 'A KING'S LESSON'; *end-papers*: one free end and paste-down, plain white and blank, front and back; *binding*: plain unblocked dark red or green cloth; *spine*: a printed paper label: [double thin rule] A | DREAM | OF JOHN | BALL | AND A | KING'S | LESSON | WILLIAM MORRIS | [thin rule] | LONGMAN | [double thin rule]

Publication: 1903 [issued 17 Jan.] (Longmans Arch.); *print run*: 2,000 copies; *price*: 2s. net.

Register of Copies Examined: LeM (base copy); CtY; MH; BGR.

Notes: C. J. Longman wrote to S. C. Cockerell, 24 Dec. 1902, about the new cheaper edn. of *A Dream of John Ball and A King's Lesson*. Longman proposed the price be 2s. net with Longman paying for the resetting of the type, for making plates, and for payment to R. Catterson-Smith for re-cutting the frontis. Royalties, he proposed, should be increased from 2d. to 3d. on all copies sold, and that the first 500 copies be free of royalty, or 1,000 at half royalty. But it is clear that even with a standard royalty agreement, the Trustees decided all questions relating to production: type, paper, spacing, etc., and a letter from the New York Longmans office makes it clear that the same understanding applied there (correspondence in the Smith Arch.)

On Catterson-Smith's other contributions, notably to the KP books, see the *Notes* in A-4.17.

Later impressions of this edn.: Longmans:

1. 1903 [issued 28 Apr.]: 'Special Edition' (see the next entry, A-45.06);

2.* 1907 [issued 25 June]: New Edition. [3rd impression, 5th edn., 3rd English] (Longmans Arch.); *print run*: 1,250 copies; *price*: 2s. net;

3. 1910 [issued 29 Jan.]: [4th impression, 5th edn., 3rd English] with frontis. (Longmans Arch.); *print run*: 1,250 copies; *price*: 2s.;

4. 1912 [issued 30 Dec. 1911]: [5th impression, 5th edn., 3rd English] (Longmans Arch.); *print run*: 1,500 copies with woodcut frontis.; *price*: 2s. net.

A-45.06: John Ball and a King's Lesson (FP)

Title: as in the previous entry.

Edition: 'Special Edition' [2nd impression, 5th edn., 3rd

English] Limited to 250 copies on Kelmscott hand-made paper. Though printed from the same plates as A-45.05, and issued at the same time, hence a paper variant, this book was called 'Special Edition' by Longmans. That plus the larger number printed suggests it deserves to be treated as a special issue, and hence it is given a separate entry here. For details of the 1st publication of both stories, see this field in A-45.01. Since this 2nd impression largely duplicates A-45.05, only details of altered fields are provided here.

Collaborators, Editors, and Illustrators: regarding the frontis., see A-45.05.

Technical Notes: *paper*: Batchelor's KP hand-made Hammersmith paper with horizontal chain lines; watermark: hammer and anvil with stream below, oriented vertically at the centrefold, pp. i and iv; *leaf size*: untrimmed deckled edges, avg. 160 x 120 mm.; *binding*: quarter dark blue holland with light blue paper-covered boards; *spine*: a printed paper label: A | DREAM | OF JOHN | BALL | AND A | KING'S | LESSON | WILLIAM MORRIS

Publication: 1903 [issued 28 Apr.] (Longmans *Notes on Books*, 10/193 (30 May 1903), 19); *print run*: 250 copies; *price*: 6s. net.

Register of Copies Examined: BL (2 copies: base copy: 012612. df.39. and Proctor's copy, presented to the BL by Cockerell: C. 130.a.19.); BGR; Fdmn; An-C-TU (Morris M677 D75 1903).

Notes: the 'hand-made paper' impression of *The Dream of John Ball and A King's Lesson* is discussed in a letter dated 7 Mar. 1903 from W. A. Kelk, an editor for Longmans, to Cockerell. In this same letter (now in the Smith Arch.) Longmans proposes a royalty to the Executors of 25% on the published price of this version. The Estate, in other words, received 3d. for each copy of the 'cheap edn' sold and 1s. 6d. per copy for this 'Special Edition'.

An earlier letter from Kelk to Cockerell, dated 13 Jan. 1903, makes clear that the paper being considered early on in the 'Special Edition' project was leftover KP paper still in Executors' hands, hence the Flower 2 paper previously used for *The Hollow Land* and the 8° lecture series in Golden type. Kelk thanks Cockerell for sample sheets of the Kelmscott paper for the better edn., and returns one sheet cut to size and one uncut—to show the waste. He also asks if there is a smaller size, eg. royal, available, that being the size used for the 'cheap' edn.. In the event, the waste must have proved too much because a new order of paper was manufactured in royal size (this impression is printed and bound as a royal 16°), and since the original KP forms had been acquired by the Trustees and permanently retired, the new issue is printed on Batchelor's Kelmscott paper, made with the old recipe but with a new watermark. Longmans' notice of this book says: 'Special Edition, 16mo. pp. viii+170, PRICE 6s. net. [28 April 1903.[single bracket in the original] Printed in Pica type. ***This edition is restricted to 250 copies. . . . The present is a Special Edition, printed on hand-made paper from old-faced type, with a reproduction of the frontispiece from the Kelmscott Edition' (Longmans *Notes on Books*, 10/193 (30 May 1893), 19).

A-45.07: John Ball and a King's Lesson (*CW* XVI)

THE COLLECTED WORKS | [title details common to the set, see A-126.01] | VOLUME XVI | NEWS FROM NOWHERE | A DREAM OF JOHN BALL | A KING'S LESSON | [publisher's imprint, see A-126.01] | MDCCCCXII

Edition: 'Collected Works edn' [1st impression 6th edn., 4th English of this combined title] For details of 1st pbn. of both stories, see this field in A-45.01. For the full title and all details common to the set, particularly *Technical Notes*, see the entry for the *CW*, A-126.01. Only details specific to this title are listed here.

Series: vol. 16 of 24; for series details, see this field in A-126.01.

Collation, *Contents*, and *Technical Notes*: for detail common to the set, see these fields in A-126.01. For those aspects special to the *CW* edn., see A-50.08.

Publication: 1912 [issued 31 Oct.] (Longmans Arch.); *print run* and *price*: see this field in A-50.08.

Register of Copies Consulted: see this field in A-126.01.

A-45.08: John Ball and a King's Lesson (LPL)

A DREAM OF JOHN BALL | AND A KING'S LESSON | BY WILLIAM MORRIS | POCKET EDITION | LONGMANS, GREEN AND CO. | 39 PATERNOSTER ROW, LONDON | NEW YORK, BOMBAY, AND CALCUTTA | 1913

Edition: Pocket Edition [1st impression, 7th edn., 5th English] For details of the first pbn. of both stories, see this field in A-45.01.

Collaborators, Editors, and Illustrators: frontis. (see this field in A-45.05).

Series: Longmans Pocket Library (for further series detail, see this field in the record of the 1st book in the series, *The Life and Death of Jason*, A-3.09).

Collation: fcap 8°: π⁴ A–L⁸ M⁴ 96 leaves pp. [i–vi] vii [viii] [1] 2–170 [*John Ball* ends] 171–84 [text of *A King's Lesson*] [= 192]

Contents: pp. [i–ii], ad for: WILLIAM MORRIS'S WORKS; p. [iii], blank; p. [iv], electrotyped frontis. from a woodcut as in A-45.05; p. [v], title page; p. [vi], headed: BIBLIOGRAPHICAL NOTE | [list of previous issues of this title]; p. vii: CONTENTS; p. [viii], blank; p. [1], text begins; pp. 2–170, text of *John Ball* completed; pp. 171–84, text of *A King's Lesson* completed, printer's imprint: Printed by BALLANTYNE, HANSON & CO. | at Paul's Work, Edinburgh

Technical Notes: for technical detail common to this series, see this field in the 1st Morris entry in this series, *Jason*, A-3.09; *binding*: *spine*: gilt-stamped at head of spine: A DREAM | OF | JOHN BALL | [the remainder is as in A-3.09]

Publication: 1913 [issued 28 Sept.–4 Oct.] ('Books of the Week', *Pub. Circ.*, 99 (4 Oct. 1913), 471); *print run*: 3,000 copies; *price*: 2s. cloth; 3s. lthr.

Register of Copies Examined: LeM (base copy); BGR.

Notes: Longmans Arch. notes in an entry dated 30 Aug. 1913 that the 1st impression of the Pocket Library Edition was printed in 3,000 copies from a new setting and at a total cost of £30. 9s. 1d., not including cloth binding which cost 32s. per 100 copies.

Later impressions of this edn., all after 1915: Longmans:

1.* 15 June 1918: [2nd impression, 6th edn., 4th English]; *print run*: 1,500 copies; *price*: as above; printed by Neill.

2.* 14 May 1920: [3rd impression, 6th edn., 4th English]; *print run*: 2,000 copies; *price*: as above; printed by Neill.

A-46.01: Signs of Change

SIGNS OF CHANGE | [in modern gothic] Seven Lectures | [plain type] *DELIVERED ON VARIOUS OCCASIONS* | BY | WILLIAM MORRIS | AUTHOR OF | *"THE EARTHLY PARADISE"* | LONDON | REEVES AND TURNER | 196 STRAND | 1888

Edition: [1st impression, 1st edn.] In addition to an unknown number of ordinary copies printed there were LP copies, also of an unknown number. Until this time, Morris and his publishers' practice, dating back to Ellis's first issues of *Jason* and *EP*, was to issue 25 LP copies of each 1st impression, 1st edn.. But, with *The Odyssey* and *John Ball*, the numbers of LP copies tended to increase. 5 of the lectures here collected were 1st pbd. elsewhere: *Useful Work* versus *Useless Toil* and *The Aims of Art* 1st appeared as pamphlets published by the Socialist League, in 1885 and 1887, respectively. 'How We Live and How We Might Live' (1887), 'Whigs, Democrats, and Socialists' (1886), and 'Feudal England' (1887) appeared 1st in *Commonweal* (see D-289, 204, and 308, respectively). 'The Hopes of Civilization' and 'The Dawn of a New Epoch' were 1st pbd. in this vol.

Collation: cr. 8°: [A]⁶ B–N⁸ O⁶ [$2 signed] 108 leaves pp. [2] [i–v] vi–viii [ix–x] [1] 2–202 [203–4] [= 216].

Contents: p. [1], blank; p.[2], ads. headed in gothic: By the same Author. p. [i], half title; p. [ii], blank; p. [iii], title page; p. [iv], blank; p. [v], headed: PREFACE. | [text begins]; pp. vi–viii, preface completed, signed: [below right] WILLIAM MORRIS. | [aligned left] Hammersmith, | *March*, 1888.; p. [ix], headed: CONTENTS. [with list]; p. [x], blank; p. [1], 1st head title, text begins; pp. 2–202, text completed with: [thin rule] PRINTED BY BALLANTYNE, HANSON AND CO. | LONDON AND EDINBURGH; pp. [203–4] ads.

Technical Notes: *paper*: ordinary copies: cream-white machine-moulded with dandy roll laid lines; according to Forman, LP copies were printed on demy 8° hand-made paper and bound in cream buckram; *leaf size*: ordinary copies: untrimmed, avg. 193 x 126 mm.; *printing*: *type area*: 131 x 81 mm.; *running heads*: [all versos] *Signs of Change*. | [all rectos: title of the relevant lecture or essay, in italics]; *end-papers*: single free end and paste-down, front and back, paste-down and facing free end printed in light green floral design, reverse free ends plain white and blank; *binding*: dark red cloth-covered boards with thick rule blind-stamped border front and back; ordinary copies: *spine*: gilt-stamped in san serif: [thick rule] SIGNS | OF | CHANGE | [thin rule] | W. MORRIS | Reeves & Turner | [thick rule]; LP *spine*: paper label: SIGNS | OF | CHANGE | Seven Lectures | by | W. MORRIS | Large Paper; (HBF, pp. 137–8).

Publication: 1888 [issued 19–26 May] Mackail (ii. 205) says May, and the 1st ad in the weekly *Commonweal*, saying the book is 'Now Ready' appeared on 26 May, p. 168; *print run*: unknown; *price*: 4s. 6d.

Register of Copies Examined: CSt (base copy: Felton PR5079 | D77 | 1888); MU (Spec.Coll. PR5079 | D8 | 1888; Forman's copy, with his bookplate, signature, and date: '12. 4. 88'); SU (330.4 | M87); LeM.

Later issues and impressions of this edn.: Longmans:

1. 1896 [issued 2 Dec.]: 'New Edition' [2nd impression, 1st edn.]; *print run*: 500 copies; *price*: 4s. 6d.;

2. 1903 [issued 13 Dec. 1902]: 'New Impression' [3rd impression, 1st edn.]; *print run* and *price*: as above;

3. 1913 [issued 23 Aug.]: 'New Impression' [4th impression, 1st edn.]; *print run*: 250 copies; *price*: 4s. 6d.

A-46.02: Signs of Change (Golden 4°)
[aligned left] SIGNS OF CHANGE. SEVEN LECTURES DELIVERED | ON VARIOUS OCCASIONS BY WILLIAM MORRIS.
Edition: 'Golden type quarto edition' [For *Signs of Change* this is the 1st impression, 2nd edn.] This edn. is bound in with *Hopes and Fears for Art*; but each of the 2 titles has its own pbn. history (see A-21.01 and A-46.01), and in this combined edn. each has its own collation and pagination. for *Hopes and Fears for Art* this is the 1st impression, 4th edn., 3rd English. Except for details in common (paper and binding) this entry is concerned with *Signs of Change* only.
Series: 'Golden type quarto edition' The 7th in the unnumbered series, consisting of 8 quarto vols., all printed in 1901–2 as part of the Morris Trustees' project to complete the printing of Morris's own books in his own types. For further detail on this series, see this field and *Notes* in A-47.04.
Colophon: Here ends Signs of Change, by William Morris. First printed in 1888, | and now reprinted at the Chiswick Press with the Golden type designed | by William Morris for the Kelmscott Press, and finished on the first day | of May, 1902. Published by Longmans, Green and Co. of London, New | York and Bombay.
Collation: (*Signs of Change* only): 4°: A–N⁴ O² 54 leaves pp. [2] [i–ii] iii [iv–vi] 1–100 [= 108].
Contents: pp. [*1–2*], blank; p. [i], title page; p. [ii], blank; p. iii, headed: [aligned left] PREFACE. | [text begins]; p. [iv], text ends: [signed, lower right] WILLIAM MORRIS | [aligned left] Hammersmith, March 1888; p. [v], headed: [left] CONTENTS | [list]; p. [vi], blank; p. 1, text begins; pp. 2–100, text completed with colophon: see above.
Technical Notes: paper, printing (including colour), position (but not content) of shoulder notes, page numbers, and binding are all common to the series and are described in this field in A-47.04, the 1st pbn. of the series. Included here are only the details specific to this edn.: *shoulder notes*: [all versos] Signs of | Change | [all rectos, the appropriate lecture title]; *spine label*: WILLIAM | MORRIS | HOPES | AND | FEARS | FOR | ART | SIGNS | OF | CHANGE
Publication: 1 May 1902 [colophon date indicates finished printing; probably issued in June] (320 slips, to be enclosed in the copies, were printed on 14 June 1902 (Longmans Arch.)); *print run* and *price*: see this field in A-47.04.
Register of Copies Examined: LeM (base copy); VU (Baillieu: L).

A-46.03: Signs of Change (+ 'Lectures on Socialism', *CW* XXIII)
THE COLLECTED WORKS | [title details common to the set, see A-126.01] | VOLUME XXIII | SIGNS OF CHANGE | LECTURES ON SOCIALISM | [publisher's imprint, see A-126.01] | MDCCCCXV
Edition: 'Collected Works edn' [1st impression, 3rd edn. of *Signs of Change*] Bound in with 8 miscellaneous 'Lectures on Socialism'.
Collaborators, Editors, and Illustrators: 2 reproductions of Kelmscott House photographs by Emery Walker.
Series: vol. 23 of 24. For details common to this set, see the entry for *CW*, A-126.01.
Collation: medium 8°: a⁸ (a3+1) b⁶ (b1+1) B–T⁸ [$2 (–b) signed] 158 leaves pp. [i–viii] ix [x] xi–xxvi [xxvii–xxviii] 1–140 [*Signs of Change* completed] [141–2] 143–281 ['Lectures on Socialism' completed] [282–8] [= 316] +2 inserted plates not counted in the book's pagination, but noted in the formula and described here in their appropriated places under *Contents*.
Contents: pp. [i–iii], blank; p. [iv], statement of limitation (see this field in A-126.01); pp. [v–vi], blank; 1st inserted plate as frontis. facing the title page (recto blank), within a blind-stamped compartment, vertically oriented reproduction of a photograph with identification below right in copperplate: *Kelmscott House* | [and the plate maker] *Emery Walker Ph. sc.* | [labelled in copperplate, centred] *The Upper Mall, Hammersmith, in 1895*; p. [vii], title page; p. [viii], blank; p. ix, headed: CONTENTS | [list of 15 titles, divided according to the 2 main titles of the vol.]; p. [x], blank; p. xi, headed: INTRODUCTION | [text begins]; pp. xii–xviii, text; 2nd inserted plate to face p. xix, photo reproduction within a blind-stamped compartment, oriented vertically with the name of the plate maker below right in copperplate: *Emery Walker Ph. sc.* | [label centred] *The Drawing Room, Kelmscott House, Hammersmith*; pp. xix–xxiii, Introduction concluded; p. [xxiv], blank; pp. xxv–xxvi, headed: BIBLIOGRAPHICAL NOTE | [list of issues in sequence of all the titles included]; p. [xxvii], 1st half title; p. [xxviii], blank; p. 1, headed, PREFACE | [text begins]; p. 2, Preface ends, signed: [below right] WILLIAM MORRIS. | [left] Hammersmith, March 1888.; p. 3, headed: [aligned left] HOW WE LIVE AND HOW WE MIGHT | LIVE | [text begins]; pp. 4–140, texts of *Hopes and Fears* concluded; for the other titles included, see the *Edition* field in A-46.01; p. [141], 2nd half title: [aligned left] LECTURES ON SOCIALISM; p. [142], blank; pp. 143–63,

headed: ART, WEALTH, AND RICHES: AN ADDRESS | DELIVERED AT A JOINT CONVERSAZIONE OF | MANCHESTER SOCIETIES AT THE ROYAL IN- | STITUTION, MANCHESTER, 6TH MARCH 1883. (D-77); pp. 164–91, 'Art under Plutocracy' (1884, D-90); pp. 192–214, 'Art and Socialism' (1884, A-25.01); pp. 215–37, 'True and False Society' (1886, A-37.01); pp. 238–54, 'Monopoly' (1899, D-486); pp. 255–63, 'The Socialist Ideal. Art' (1891, D-527); pp. 264–76, 'Communism' (1903, A-104.01); pp. 277–81, 'How I became a Socialist' (1894, D-563); pp. [282–3], blank; p. [284], printer's imprint, see this field, A-126.01; pp. [285–8], blank.

Technical Notes: for details common to the set—paper, leaf size, printing, type area, lines-to-page, running titles, endpapers, and binding—see A-126.01. Here are given only those details specific to this vol.: *shoulder notes*: all versos, 1 of the 2 half titles; rectos: the lecture or essay title; *spine label*: [begins with 4 lines common to the set] | SIGNS OF | CHANGE | LECTURES ON | SOCIALISM

Publication: 1915 [issued 10 Dec.] (Longmans Arch.); *print run* and *price*: see this field in A-126.01.

Register of Copies Examined: see this field in A-126.01

Notes: the 2nd title of this vol. is one made up for the purpose, and it has never been published separately. May Morris's choice here of collecting the 'Lectures on Socialism' completes a design started in the previous vol., where *Hopes and Fears* is combined with 'Lectures on Art and Industry', another collection that appears only in *CW*. Her intent is clearly related to the earlier attempt of the Trustees to divide the fugitive essays and lectures into 2 groups—on Art and on Socialism—for editing, respectively, by W. R. Lethaby and G. B. Shaw (for details see this field in A-21.01). Her selection of the pieces to include differs from that of S. C. Cockerell and R. Proctor, the editors of the Golden type quarto vols., who selected the pieces for *Architecture, Industry, and Wealth* (see C-18.01) from all the fugitive and unpublished lectures and essays then known and available, without distinguishing the political from the aesthetic.

A-47.01: The House of the Wolfings

A TALE OF THE HOUSE OF THE | WOLFINGS AND ALL THE KIND- | REDS OF THE MARK WRITTEN | IN PROSE AND IN VERSE | BY WILLIAM MORRIS. | [16-lines of original verse as an epigraph, in smaller type]

    WHILES IN THE EARLY WINTER EVE
    WE PASS AMID THE GATHERING NIGHT
    SOME HOMESTEAD THAT WE HAD TO LEAVE
    YEARS PAST; AND SEE ITS CANDLES BRIGHT
    SHINE IN THE ROOM BESIDE THE DOOR
    WHERE WE WERE MERRY YEARS AGONE
    BUT NOW MUST NEVER ENTER MORE,
    AS STILL THE DARK ROAD DRIVES US ON.
    E'EN SO THE WORLD OF MEN MAY TURN
    AT EVEN OF SOME HURRIED DAY
    AND SEE THE ANCIENT GLIMMER BURN
    ACROSS THE WASTE THAT HATH NO WAY;
    THEN WITH THAT FAINT LIGHT IN ITS EYES
    A WHILE I BID IT LINGER NEAR
    AND NURSE IN WAVERING MEMORIES
    THE BITTER-SWEET OF DAYS THAT WERE.

LONDON 1889: REEVES AND TURNER 196 STRAND.

Edition: [1st impression, 1st edn.] Besides the ordinary copies, there was an LP version: 'One hundred copies of this Large Paper Edition have been printed, of which Eighty-nine are for sale' (from the limitation statement tipped in to the special copies).

Collation: cr. 8°: A⁴ B–N⁸ O⁴ 104 leaves pp. [8] [1] 2–199 [200] [= 208].

Contents: pp. [1–2], blank; p. [3], half title; p. [4], blank; p. [5], title page; p. [6], imprint: CHISWICK PRESS:— CHARLES WHITTINGHAM AND CO. | TOOKS COURT, CHANCERY LANE.; p. [7], headed: [in swash caps] *CONTENTS*. | [31 numbered chapter titles with page numbers]; p. [8], blank; p. [1], 1st chapter, dropped head: THE HOUSE OF THE WOLFINGS. | CHAPTER I. | THE DWELLINGS OF MID-MARK. | [text begins]; pp. 2–199, text completed with formulaic explicit: [indented] AND THIS IS ALL THE TALE HAS TO TELL CON- | CERN- | ING THE HOUSE OF THE WOLFINGS AND THE KINDREDS OF | THE MARK. | THE END; p. [200], printer's imprint: [Chiswick Press mark of anchor, dolphin, and lion] | CHISWICK PRESS:— CHARLES WHITTINGHAM AND CO. | TOOKS COURT, CHANCERY LANE.; added 16° quire (not integral) of Reeves & Turner monthly advertising pamphlet, dated 'July, 1889', separately paginated pp. 1–32, ad section on Morris, p. 9. There were copies with the pamphlet dated 'Decmber, 1888'. This later version seems to indicate a later batch for binding.

Technical Notes: *paper*: cream machine-laid, with dandy roll laid lines; *leaf size*: untrimmed, avg. 198 x 138 mm.; LP copies: hand-made paper, deckled edges, watermarked, middle: John Dickinson & Co.; *leaf size*: avg. 267 x 200 mm.; *printing*: *type face*: set solid in the 10–11 point Venetian old face 'Basle' roman type, modelled and cast by William Howard for Charles Whittingham at the Chiswick Press in the 1840s, and adapted by Morris, using the modern rather than Howard's long 's' and using an oblique stressed lower case 'e', otherwise identical with that used in Rev. W. Calbert's *The Wife's Manual* (Longman, 1854); *type area*: 136 x 106 mm. not including head and direction lines; *lines-to-page*: 37 lines for a full page of prose, but blank spaces between verse paragraphs; *running titles*: all versos: THE HOUSE OF THE WOLFINGS | [rectos: various, each title being a gloss of its opening of text]; *end-papers*: 1 free end and paste-down, plain white and blank, front and back; *binding*: ordinary copy: plain, unblocked dark red cloth; *spine*: printed paper label: The House | of the | Wolfings. | [thin rule] | William | Morris. | Price 6s.; LP label the same except without the price; LP *binding*: red buckram with inserted certification slip tipped inside the front end paper: see *Edition*, above.

Publication: 1889 [issued 15 and 31 Dec. 1888] HBF says the trade copies were issued 'by the 15th of December', 1888, and 100 LP copies 'by the 31st of the same month' (p. 140). These dates are the same as those in the Chiswick Arch., but it is not clear whether these are 'finished printing' dates or the dates of issue. NNPM copy (76886/M) is a presentation copy by Morris to E. Burne-Jones, hence probably an LP copy, dated 'January 6th 1889'; *Pub. Circ.* announces publication as between 17 and 31 Dec. 1888 (51/1231 (31 Dec. 1888), 1140). The dates cited by HBF seem likely, being a close fit with the *Pub. Circ.*; *print run*: 1,000 ordinary copies and 100 LP copies; *price*: ordinary, 6s., LP, unknown.

Register of Copies Examined: LeM (base copy); NNPM (2 copies: 53303, inscribed by Morris to Philip Webb, and 7688 M, presentation inscription to E. Burne-Jones); VU (2 copies: E, ordinary and large paper); MU (Special Coll.: PR5079 T3 1889a, LP copy).

Notes: Morris to Chiswick Press, 3 Oct. 1888: 'I have as yet not received any proof of "The House of the Wolfings". Please send it on here (the above address) *at once* as it is important for me to get the proofs early and regularly since they have to be read for an illustration or two . . .'. Kelvin's Note 2: 'Morris may have referred here to the woodcut block originally intended for the title page, to be placed between the title and the imprint. In the event, there was no illustration, but a poem, "written to the exact measure of the blank to be filled," was used instead' (*Letters*, ii. 827; see also letter No. 1530, n.1, and Henry Halliday Sparling, *The Kelmscott Press and William Morris Master-Craftsman*, 52 (hereafter referred to as Sparling)).

Reed and Johnson say that Morris had his prose romance *A Tale of the House of the Wolfings* set in Basle roman, but discarded the long 's' of the original design. It was used also for another romance by Morris, *The Roots of the Mountains*, dated 1890 but, issued in 1889 (*A History of the Old English Letter Foundries*. 2nd Edn. (London: Faber and Faber Limited, 1952), 365).

Morris to Jenny Morris. 4 Dec. 1888: ' I have now seen my book through the press all but the title-page, so I shall soon be able to send a copy of the ordinary impression to you my dear; I think the large paper will be some time longer before it comes out. It will be a pretty piece of typography for modern times' (*Letters*, ii. 839).

Morris to Reeves and Turner, 17 Dec. [1888]: I am in receipt of your cheque for £50, for which accept my thanks. I called on Mr. Jacoby [sic] last week, but found I could not press successfully any reduction of his bill. As to the small paper edition I agree to your proposition as to my receiving 1/6 per copy for this thousand; but that not to apply to future editions if such are produced (*Letters*, ii. 842).

The date must be 1888 and the book discussed *The House of the Wolfings*, since Jacobi ran the Chiswick Press, and Morris had no other book printed there at the end of 1888.

> Morris to Ellis, [21 Jan. 1889]:
> I am very glad that you like the new book. I quite agree with you about the type; they have managed to knock the guts out of it somehow. Also I am beginning to learn something about the art of type-setting; and I now see what a difference there is between the conceited numskulls of to-day and that of the 15th and 16th century printers merely in the arrangement of the words, I mean the spacing out: it makes all the difference in the beauty of a page of print. If I ever print another book I shall enter into the conflict on this side also. However this is all the grief that comes of fresh knowledge and I am pretty well pleased with the book as to its personal appearance (*Letters*, iii. 14–15).

Later impressions and issues from this edn.:

1. R and T: 1890 [issued 22 Apr.]: Second Edition [2nd impression, 1st edn.]; *print run*: 1,000 copies; *price*: 6s.; new title page (Chiswick Arch.);

2.* Longmans 1896 [issued 1–8 Aug.]: Second Edition [2nd issue, 2nd impression, 1st edn.]; *print run*: 600 copies; on 10 June the Chiswick Arch. reports printing 100 cancel title pages and on 9 Oct. another 500 for the reissue, with the new Longmans imprint and date and bound in black cloth, of remaining copies purchased from Reeves and Turner; *price*: 6s.;

Original and Posthumous Editions

3. Longmans: 1904 [issued 25 June]: [3rd impression, 1st edn.] (Longmans Arch.); *print run*: 250 copies; *price*: 6s.;
4. Longmans: 1909 [issued 20 Aug.]: [4th impression, 1st edn.] (Longmans Arch.); *print run*: 250 copies; *price*: 6s.

A-47.02: The House of the Wolfings (RB)

Title: reset, but as in the previous entry, except for the changed publisher's imprint and date: PUBLISHED BY ROBERTS BROTHERS, | AT THEIR HOUSE, 3 SOMERSET | STREET, BOSTON, 1890.
Edition: 'Edition de Luxe' [1st impression, 2nd edn., 1st American] This 1st American impression is composed of 500 LP copies. For the 1st American ordinary copies, issued in May 1890, see A-47.03. Details of this book come from the entry in Pye, p. 45, and Roberts Arch. (Costbook E). The letterpress, of course, duplicates the ordinary edn..
Collaborators, Editors, and Illustrators: [frontis. photogravure from an F. Hollyer photograph; American binding designed by J. A. Schweinfurth].
Collation: cr. 8°: [1]⁸ ([1]1+1) 2–25⁸ [26]² [$1 (–2) signed] 202 leaves pp. [i–v] vi [7] 8–387 [388] [1] 2–16 [= 404]. + inserted frontispiece, not part of the book's pagination, but integral to the book, and 16 pages of a separate gathering of comment on the tale, separately printed and paginated and described under *Contents* in their appropriate positions.
Contents: p. [i], half title; p. [ii], LP copies only, a statement of limitation certification, in gothic: The printing of this book was begun by the University Press, Cambridge, USA, in January, MDCCCXC, and was finished in February of the same year. Five hundred copies were printed on large paper. [this limitation notice does not apply, of course to the ordinary copies published later (see A-47.03). There this page is used for ads]; frontis. inserted to face title page, recto blank, photogravure portrait of Morris made by A. W. Elson & Co., Boston, from a photograph by F. Hollyer; p. [iii], title page; p. [iv], blank; pp. [v]–vi: headed: CONTENTS | [list begins]; p. [7], dropped head: THE HOUSE OF THE WOLFINGS. | [french rule] | CHAPTER I. | THE DWELLINGS OF MID-MARK. | [text begins]; pp. 8–387, text completed with explicit: [indented 1st line] AND THIS IS ALL THAT THE TALE HAS TO | TELL CONCERNING THE HOUSE OF THE WOLF- | INGS AND THE KINDREDS OF THE MARK.; p. [388], blank; pp. [1]–16, extra advertising gathering in at the end, printed separately and with separate pagination, reprints the review from *The Athenæum*.
Technical Notes: *paper*: cream machine-laid, t.e.g., with dandy roll laid lines, no watermark; *leaf size*: trimmed, avg. 209 x 146 mm.; *printing*: *type area*: 31 x 80 mm. exclusive of head and direction lines; *lines-to-page*: 28 lines; *headlines*: *running titles*: all versos: THE HOUSE OF THE WOLFINGS | [all rectos: chapter titles, in caps]; *end-papers*: 1 free end and paste-down, pale brown and grey floral design on paste-down and facing free end, opposite sides of free ends plain white; *binding*: Schweinfurth design (RB Cost Book E), three-quarter white holland, on spine and extending 54 mm. over olive or tan boards; front, on white cloth, a vertical gilt sword, brown runic initial, and vertical rule of spear heads; front, olive boards, gilt ornamental titling: • THE • HOUSE • OF • | THE • WOLFINGS • | • WILLIAM • MORRIS • [with brown printed figures scattered over the front representing hunting horsemen, animals, spear heads, and a Viking ship; *spine*: gilt-stamped: • THE • HOUSE • | • OF • THE • | • WOLFINGS • | • WILLIAM • | • MORRIS • | [spear-heads rule] | • ROBERTS • BROS •
Publication: 1890 [issued 10 Mar.] (RB Cost Book E and RB announcement in *Pub. Weekly*, No. 944 (1 Mar. 1890), 340). That the date RB announces for the issue of the book is the same as that in Cost Book E suggests that the dates of the Cost Book were at least intended to be dates of issue.
Print run: 500 copies; *price*: unknown.
Register of Copies Examined: CSt (2 copies: base copy: Spec. Coll.Felton PR5079. T14 1890a, LP, and 821. | M87tw); MU (Spec.Coll PR5079/T3, 1890a, LP, inscribed: 'To Prof. Henry M. Whitney in memory of his cousin Dwight Whitney Marsh. July 20 1896'.); LeM.
Notes: Kilgour: '"The House of the Wolfings" . . . he completed in 1889 and published in December of the same year. Roberts Brothers published it in March 1890, in a de luxe edition limited to 500 copies, handsomely bound in white, "in antique style"' (246).
Bill dated 8 Feb. 1890: 'Dec. 1889'; from T. Burleigh for supplying 'Morris's Wolfings' 6s. + postage. This probably indicates that RB had an agreement with Burleigh to supply English books and magazines to RB at the trade rate (this bill is reduced by 25% from the usual retail price) so Messrs Roberts, i.e. Thomas Niles, could read them for possible pbn. Hence this would have been a standing order requiring no correspondence beyond billing and payment (MS from NNC Butler: Roberts Bros. Box l).

A-47.03: The House of the Wolfings (RB)

Title: as in A-47.02.
Edition: 'Cheap Edition' 'Ordinary edn' [2nd impres-

sion, 2nd edn., 1st American] without frontis. Since this is another impression of A-47.02, only details of altered fields are included here.

Technical Notes: *paper*: *leaf size*: trimmed, 188 x 129 mm.; *end-papers*: 1 free end and paste-down, plain white and blank, front and back; *binding*: plain dark red unblocked cloth; *spine*: printed paper label: [within thin-rule compartment] THE HOUSE | OF | THE WOLFINGS. | [thin rule] | BY | WM. MORRIS.

Publication: 1890 [issued 19 May] (RB Cost Book E); *print run*: 280 copies; *price*: $2.00.

Register of Copies Examined: LeM (base copy); SU; BGR

Later impressions of this version of the American edn.:

1. RB: 1890 [issued 23 Oct.]: 'Cheap Edition' [3rd impression, 2nd edn., 1st American] (RB Cost Book E); *print run*: 280 copies; *price*: $2.00;

2.* RB: 1890 [issued 15 Dec.]: 'Cheap Edition' [4th impression, 2nd edn., 1st American] (RB Cost Book E); *print run*: 280 copies; *price*: $2.00;

3.* RB: 1891 [issued 11 Jan. 1892] (the date in the Cost Book—Jan. 1891—is obviously an error): 'Cheap Edition' [5th impression, 2nd edn., 1st American] (RB Cost Book E); *print run*: 280 copies; *price*: $2.00;

4.* Longmans, NY: 1900: 'Cheap Edition' [6th impression, 2nd edn., 1st American] (Longmans Accts.); *print run*: 270 copies; *price*: $2.00;

5. Longmans, NY: 1906: 'Cheap Edition' [7th impression, 2nd edn., 1st American]; *print run*: unknown; *price*: $2.00.

A-47.04: The House of the Wolfings (Golden 4°)

[aligned left] A TALE OF THE HOUSE OF THE WOLFINGS AND ALL | THE KINDREDS OF THE MARK WRITTEN IN PROSE | AND IN VERSE BY WILLIAM MORRIS.

Edition: 'Golden type quarto edition' [1st impression, 3rd edn., 2nd English].

Collaborators, Editors, and Illustrators: [edited by S. C. Cockerell and Robert Proctor].

Series: This is the 1st vol. of an 8-vol. set (unnumbered) done in quarto in Morris's Golden type. Longmans *Notes on Books* (30 Nov. 1901), p. 351, provides the Prospectus of the series under the heading 'Literary Intelligence':

> Messrs. Longmans, Green and Co have the pleasure of announcing that they have arranged with the Trustees of the late William Morris for the publication of a limited edition of the following eight volumes in the Golden Type of the Kelmscott Press:—
>
> 1. A TALE OF THE HOUSE OF THE WOLFINGS.
> 2. THE ROOTS OF THE MOUNTAINS.
> 3. GRETTIR THE STRONG.
> 4. THE VOLSUNGA SAGA AND THREE NORTHERN LOVE STORIES.
> 5. THE ODYSSEY OF HOMER.
> 6. THE AENEIDS OF VIRGIL.
> 7. HOPES AND FEARS FOR ART, AND SIGNS OF CHANGE.
> 8. LECTURES. [issued under the title *Architecture, Industry, and Wealth*].

> It was Mr. Morris's intention to print the full series of his works at the Kelmscott Press, but his death on October 3, 1896, led to the closing of the Press in March, 1898, before the project was completed. The wood-blocks for the initials and other ornaments designed by Mr. Morris were presented to the British Museum, the type alone being reserved for future use by the Trustees. The success of the five small volumes of Mr. Morris's lectures, hitherto the only books printed with it since the closing of the Kelmscott Press, has prompted the publishers to carry out this larger scheme.

> The new volumes are uniform in size with 'Love is Enough,' 'The Well at the World's End,' and the other large quarto volumes of the Kelmscott Press. They are being printed at the Chiswick Press in double columns with the Golden Type, under the immediate direction of the Trustees, no pains being spared to make them worthy of a place beside the Kelmscott Press volumes which are now so widely sought after. The handmade paper is identical in all respects with that of the Kelmscott Press, being made at the same mill, of the same materials, and from the same moulds, with the daisy watermark familiar to collectors. The binding is grey paper boards with linen backs, in the style of 'The Golden Legend.'

> The edition is limited to 315 copies, of which only 300 are offered for sale, and the whole edition will be subscribed for. The eight volumes were offered in sets only at the net price of sixteen guineas per set. As each volume is printed the type will be distributed.

> The first volume, 'The House of the Wolfings,' was published on the 15th of November, 1901, and the remainder will be issued at intervals of about a month, beginning in January, 1902.

For details common to this set of vols.—such as paper, type, formatting, etc— see *Technical Notes*, below.

Colophon: Printed at the Chiswick Press with the Golden type designed by William | Morris for the Kelmscott Press, & finished on the 28th day of January, 1901. | Published by

Longmans, Green and Co of London, New York & Bombay.

Collation: 4°: [a]² b–x⁴ y² 84 leaves pp. [4] 1–161 [162–4] [= 168].

Contents: p. [1], title page; p. [2], blank; p. [3], headed: [top margin, all flush left] CONTENTS. | [list of 31 chapters begins, each with number, title, and page]; p. [4], in red, a 16-line poem, untitled and unsigned, as an epigraph to the book [see title of A-47.01]; p. 1, 1st chapter head: [top, 1 column, in red] A TALE OF THE HOUSE OF THE WOLFINGS AND ALL | THE KINDREDS OF THE MARK. BY WILLIAM MORRIS. | [text begins, in double column, as do all vols. of this set, headed, flush left] CHAPTER I. THE DWELL- | INGS OF MID-MARK.; pp. 2–162, text completed with explicit in the right column: AND THIS IS ALL THAT | THE TALE HAS HERE TO | TELL CONCERNING THE | HOUSE OF THE WOLF- | INGS AND ALL THE KIN- | DREDS OF THE MARK. | [colophon, single column, see above]; pp. [163–4], blank.

Technical Notes: details common to the set: *paper*: cream-white Kelmscott hand-made Flower 2; *leaf size*: deckled edges, lightly trimmed, avg. 288 x 207 mm.; *printing*: *type face*: Golden type; *type area*: double columns, except verse and titles, total type area: 197 x 142 mm.; columns: each 197 x 68 mm., separated by a 6 mm. space; *lines-to-page*: set solid, 42 lines, excluding direction line; printed in red and black, red for epigraph lyric, title on p. 1, and footnote, p. 8; *pagination*: arabic numerals 15 mm. inside the outer margins on the direction line; *shoulder notes*: used throughout (in some vols with marginal notes in smaller type below the shoulder notes, for which see individual entries), here starting at the top line of text, all rectos and versos: The House of | the Wolfings | Chapter i [–xxxi]; *end-papers*: standard KP: 3 free ends and paste-down, front and back, all plain white and blank; *binding*: three-quarter mid-blue holland, with light blue paper-covered boards; *spine*: printed paper labels: WILLIAM | MORRIS | THE | HOUSE | OF THE | WOLF- | INGS

Publication: 28 Jan. 1901 [colophon date indicates finished printing, issued 15 Nov.] Though finished by the end of Jan. 1901, and 31 Jan. is recorded in the Longmans Arch. Impression Book, correspondence in the Smith Arch. discloses that Cockerell and C. J. Longman were still considering the binding, consulting about whether to use bands or not, on 5 June 1901, a decision that would have effected the entire series. On 12 July Longman accepted Cockerell's proposal to give the new vols. plain blue linen spines with printed paper spine labels. So there was obviously a delay between printing and issue, and Longmans Accts. make it clear that the issue date was before the end of 1901. The Longmans prospectus (see the *Edition* field in A-47.04), quoted above, specifies the date given here; *print run*: 315 copies, 300 being for sale (including the 60 sets exported to the USA); *price*: 16*gns*. the set.

Register of Copies Examined: LeM (base copy); BGR; CSmH; NN.

Notes: C. J. Longman wrote to Cockerell, 4 Sept. 1900, to propose a royalty of 20 per cent on all copies of the 8-vol. Golden type quarto set sold in Britain and America. He was considering selling the sets at £12. In the event the price was fixed at 42*s*., i.e. 2*gns*. per vol. but sold only in sets at 16*gns*. All copies were sold by subscription. 60 copies of the sets were exported for sale in the US at an equivalent price (and royalty).

But there were difficulties and delays with the printing. C. J. Longman wrote to Cockerell, 29 Jan. 1901, complaining about these delays, caused, it appears, by text preparation and proof reading. The printing cost increased because of corrections in proof and because of an unauthorised introduction of printing in red, Longman complained, into nearly all the forms (cost of corrections for *The House of the Wolfings* was £14. 5*s*. 0*d*.), though the book was set from typed copy (it may be an indication of the extent to which Cockerell and Proctor amended the text that Proctor re-typed the text rather than using one of the several printed versions available). So, Longman 'stopped the working' and awaited an explanation. Two days later Cockerell sent his answer, indicating a compromise: Longman agreed that the red was worth the extra expense in several places mentioned, but the use of red printing was reduced to 3 pages in each vol. (cited above in *Technical Notes*). Later, with the last vol. of the set, the Longmans over-stiff binding became a problem, as Cockerell writes to Mrs Morris on 17 June 1901. Cockerell carried his point by using a dummy copy of the *Golden Legend* which Mrs Morris lent to him to demonstrate how the binding should be done.

Further to Cockerell and Proctor's editing of this series, part of a letter, in Mrs Morris's hand, to S. C. Cockerell, received 27 Oct. 1902, shows Mrs Morris reconsidering the fee for Cockerell and Proctor's editing of this 8-vol. set. She decides that the amount should be raised by 25 %, i.e. to £100 instead of the £80 previously agreed (Smith Arch.)

A-47.05: The House of the Wolfings (*CW* XIV)

THE COLLECTED WORKS | [title details common to

the set, see A-126.01] | VOLUME XIV | THE HOUSE OF THE WOLFINGS [for full title with lyric epigraph, see A-47.01] | THE STORY OF | THE GLITTERING PLAIN | [publisher's imprint, see A-126.01] | MDCCCCXII

Edition: [1st impression, 4th edn., 3rd English of *Wolfings*]. For previous pbn. and edn. status of this issue of *The Glittering Plain* see this field in A-54.08. The *Collation*, *Contents*, and *Technical Notes* specific to both titles are provided here.

Series: vol. 14 of 24; for series detail, see this field in A-126.01.

Collation: medium 8°: a⁸ (a4+1) b⁸ (b6+1) B–X⁸ Y⁴ [\$2 (–a2) signed] 180 leaves pp. [i–x] xi–xxxi [xxxii] [1–3] 4–208 [end of *Wolfings* text and beginning of the *Glittering Plain*] [209–11] 212–324 [325–8] [= 360] +2 inserted plates not included in the book's pagination, but noted in the formula and described here in their appropriate places under *Contents*.

Contents: pp. [i–v], blank; p. [vi], limitation notice (see this field in A-126.01); pp. [vii–viii], blank; 1st inserted plate as frontis., in a blind-stamped compartment, a reproduction of a photograph with, printed in copperplate, below left: Frederick Hollyer photographer | [and the plate maker, below right, in copperplate] *Emery Walker Ph. sc.* | [label centred in copperplate] *William Morris | 1887*; p. [ix], title page; p. [x], blank; pp. xi–xiii, headed: CONTENTS | [list begins]; p. [xiv], blank; pp. xv–xxviii, headed: INTRODUCTION; facing p. xxviii, 2nd inserted plate, in a blind-stamped compartment: photo-litho reproduction of a photo labelled: *Cabinet, the marriage gift of Edward Burne-Jones | to William Morris and his wife* | [in smaller type] *Emery Walker Ph. sc*; p. xxix, introduction completed; p. [xxx], blank; p. xxxi, headed BIBLIOGRAPHICAL NOTE TO THE HOUSE OF THE WOLFINGS | [following the list] BIBLIOGRAPHICAL NOTE TO THE STORY OF | GLITTERING PLAIN; p. [xxxii], blank; p. [1], 1st half title, with the title and a 16-line verse epigraph (see the title page of A-47.01 The House of the Wolfings); p. [2], blank; p. [3], 1st chapter head and text begins; pp. 4–208, text completed with explicit: [aligned left] AND THIS IS ALL THAT THE TALE HAS TO TELL | CONCERNING THE HOUSE OF THE WOLFINGS AND THE KINDREDS OF THE MARK | THE END; p. [209], 2nd half title for *The Glittering Plain*; p. [210], blank; p. 211, 1st chapter head and text begins; pp. 212–324, text completed with explicit: HEREWITH ENDETH THE TALE.; p. [325], blank; p. [326], printer's imprint (see this field in A-126.01); pp. [327–8], blank.

Technical Notes: paper, printing, type, position (but not content) of headlines, running titles, shoulder notes, pagination, and binding are all common to the series and are described in this field in A-126.01, the entry for the set. Included here are only those details that are specific to this particular edition of this title. *Headlines*: for *Wolfings*, all versos: THE HOUSE OF THE WOLFINGS | [all rectos: relevant chapter title]; for *Glittering Plain*: all versos: THE STORY OF THE GLITTERING PLAIN | [all rectos] OR THE LAND OF LIVING MEN; *spine label*: the first 4 lines are common to the set (see A-126.01), then: THE HOUSE | OF THE | WOLFINGS | THE GLITTERING | PLAIN

Publication: 1912 [issued 31 Oct.] (Longmans Arch.); *print run* and *price*: see this field in A-126.01.

Register of Copies Examined: see this field in A-126.01

A-47.06: The House of the Wolfings (LPL)

[title as in A-47.01, except for the edn. note, publisher's imprint, and date, following the epigraph:] POCKET EDITION | LONGMANS, GREEN AND CO. | 39 PATERNOSTER ROW, LONDON | NEW YORK, BOMBAY, AND CALCUTTA | 1913

Edition: Pocket Edition [1st impression, 5th edn., 4th English].

Series: Longmans Pocket Library (for further series detail, see this field in the record of the 1st Morris book in the series, *The Life and Death of Jason*, A-3.09).

Collation: fcap 8°: π⁴ A–P⁸ Q⁴ 128 leaves pp. [i–vi] vii–viii [1] 2–247 [248] [= 256].

Contents: pp. [i–ii], ads headed: WILLIAM MORRIS'S WORKS; p. [iii], half title; p. [iv], ads headed: Longmans' Pocket Library; p. [v], title page; p. [vi], headed: BIBLIOGRAPHICAL NOTE | [list of 9 issues of this title]; pp. vii–viii, dropped head: CONTENTS | [list of 31 chapters]; p. [1], dropped head title: [full title as on title page, but aligned left] | [16-line epigraph, indented left and in italics] | CHAPTER I | THE DWELLINGS OF MID-MARK | [text begins]; pp. 2–247, text completed with explicit: [aligned left] AND THIS IS ALL THAT THE TALE HAS TO TELL CON- | CERNING THE HOUSE OF THE WOLFINGS AND THE KINDREDS OF THE MARK. | THE END | Printed by Ballantyne, Hanson & Co. | at Paul's Work, Edinburgh; p. [248], blank.

Technical Notes: see A-3.09 for detail common to the series. Special to this title: *printing*: type area: 129 x 80 mm.; *lines-to-page*: hair-line leading, 38 lines, text in mixed verse and prose; *headlines*: all versos: THE HOUSE OF THE

WOLFINGS | [all rectos: the relevant chapter title in caps]; *binding*: see A-3.09, but this copy, like several of the later titles issued in the series, has a light grey dust jacket, the front of which has the series name underlined at the top, then the title, author and price; the back has ads headed: Longmans' Pocket Library; *spine*: title and author printed in caps in 2 lines up the spine.

Publication: 1913 [issued 4–11 Oct.] ('Books of the Week', *Pub. Circ.*, 99 (11 Oct. 1913), 502); *print run*: 3,000 copies (Longmans Arch.); *price*: see this field in A-3.09.

Register of Copies Examined: LeM (base copy).

Notes: the entry from Longmans Arch. for 17 Sept. 1913 gives an account that shows the total cost for 3,000 copies, exclusive of binding, was £50. 5s. 10d.

A-48.01: The Roots of the Mountains

THE ROOTS OF THE MOUNTAINS | WHEREIN IS TOLD SOMEWHAT OF | THE LIVES OF THE MEN OF BURG- | DALE THEIR FRIENDS THEIR | NEIGHBOURS THEIR FOEMEN AND | THEIR FELLOWS IN ARMS | BY WILLIAM MORRIS | [indented left and right, aligned left, a 16-line poem as epigraph in smaller type]

WHILES CARRIED O'ER THE IRON ROAD,
WE HURRY BY SOME FAIR ABODE,
THE GARDEN BRIGHT AMIDST THE HAY,
THE YELLOW WAIN UPON THE WAY,
THE DINING MEN, THE WIND THAT SWEEPS
LIGHT LOCKS FROM OFF THE SUN-SWEET HEAPS—
THE GABLE GREY, THE HOARY ROOF,
HERE NOW—AND NOW SO FAR ALOOF.
HOW SORELY THEN WE WANT TO STAY
AND MIDST ITS SWEETNESS WEAR THE DAY,
AND 'NEATH ITS CHANGING SHADOWS SIT,
AND FEEL OURSELVES A PART OF IT.
SUCH REST, SUCH STAY, I STROVE TO WIN
WITH THESE SAME LEAVES THAT LIE HEREIN.
LONDON MDCCCXC: REEVES AND TURNER | CXCVI STRAND

Edition: 'Superior Edition' and 'Ordinary Edition' [both parts of the 1st impression, 1st edn.] The 'Superior Edition' copies were LP copies on Whatman pott quarto paper with a special cloth binding of Morris and Company chintz from either of 2 designs by Morris. The title page served as a prospectus for the book, making that the 1st edn. of the lyric epigraph included on the title page (see Appendix II-3).

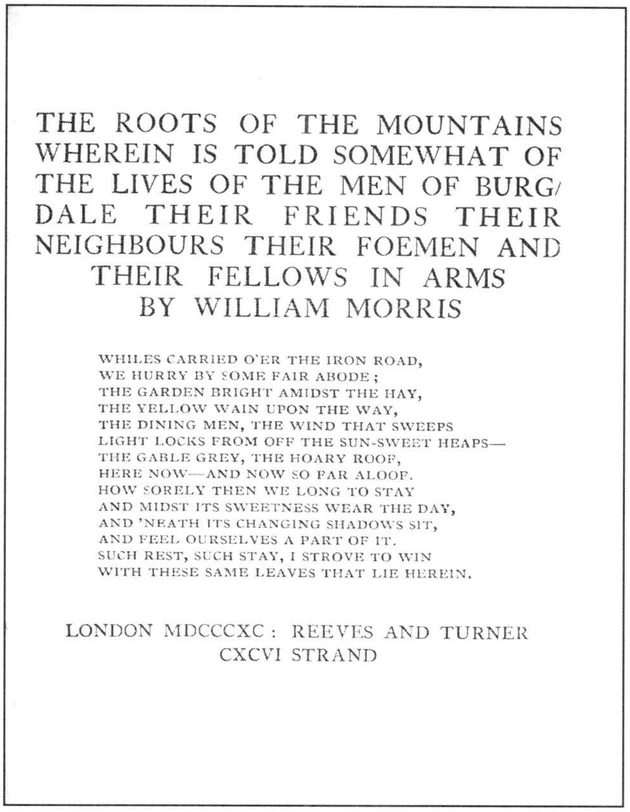

Figure 42. A-48.01: *Roots of the Mountains* ('Superior' edn.) title page

Collation:

1. LP copies: pott 4°: [A]⁴ B–3H⁴ 216 leaves pp. [8] 1–424 [= 432]

2. ordinary copies: sq. cr. 8°: [A]⁴ B–3G⁸ 3H⁴ [4° signatures, 2 for each 8° gathering] 216 leaves. The pagination is the same for both versions, except for a gathering of 16 leaves of Reeves and Turner's monthly *Catalogue of Publications and Remainders*, for Nov., 1889, separately printed and paginated and added to the ordinary copies. These are described in the appropriate place under *Contents*.

Contents: p. [1], blank; p. [2], ad in thin-rule compartment, headed: MR. WILLIAM MORRIS'S WORKS; p. [3], half title; p. [4], blank; p. [5], title page; p. [6], printer's imprint: CHISWICK PRESS:—CHARLES WHITTINGHAM AND CO. | TOOKS COURT, CHANCERY LANE; pp. [7–8]: [headed in italic swash capitals] CONTENTS. followed by a list of 59 chapter titles, each with a roman numeral and a title in the Chiswick Aldine italic font, page nos. in roman; p. 1, text begins; pp. 2–424, text completed with explicit: NO MORE AS NOW TELLETH THE TALE OF THESE | KINDREDS AND FOLKS,

BUT MAKETH AN ENDING. | CHISWICK PRESS: C. WHITTINGHAM AND CO., TOOKS COURT, CHANCERY LANE.
    LP copies as above except for the prelims: in place of the ads on p. [2] is a statement of limitation inserted: *Of this, the superior edition on Whatman paper, only two hundred and fifty | copies are printed.* | [aligned right] CHARLES WHITTINGHAM AND CO.
Technical Notes: *paper*: 'Superior Edition': Whatman's hand-laid paper, specially made in pott quarto: 'thin and tough . . . manufactured especially for this work, of pot-size' (HBF, p. 142); ordinary copies printed on machine-laid paper with dandy roll laid lines, in Imperial 16° size; *leaf size*: untrimmed, avg. 183 x 140 mm.; LP copies: deckled edges, untrimmed, avg. 191 x 160 mm.; *type*: 'Basle' (with two adaptations, the short 's' and the oblique stressed 'e', see *Notes*, A-47.01), with Chiswick Aldine italic and Caslon display types, Contents in italics; *type area*: 123 x 93 mm.; *lines-to-page*: set solid, 34 lines excluding head and direction lines; *shoulder notes*: in outer margins, all rectos and versos, starting level with line 1, a gloss of each page; *pagination*: arabic numerals centred between margins on direction line; *end-papers*: 1 free end and paste-down plain white and blank, front and back; *binding*: 'Superior Edition': boards covered with either of 2 Morris chintz designs, 'Honeysuckle' or 'Little Chintz'; *spine*: gilt-stamped: THE | ROOTS | OF THE | MOUNTAINS | [thin rule] | WILLIAM | MORRIS; the 'Ordinary Edition' is bound in plain dark red unblocked cloth with printed paper spine label: THE | ROOTS | OF THE | MOUNTAINS | [thin rule] | WILLIAM MORRIS | [thin rule] | Price 8*s*.
Publication: 1890 [issued 16 and 21 Nov. 1889] Morris's letters of the time indicate that, contrary to his earlier prediction, the ordinary copies were out by 16 Nov. and the large paper copies on 21 Nov. (see *Notes*, below); *print run*: 1,000 'Ordinary' copies, 250 copies of the 'Superior Edition' (Chiswick Arch.); *price*: 'Ordinary Edition', 8*s*.; Superior Edition, unknown.
Register of Copies Examined: LeM (2 copies, both ordinary: base copy); Fdmn; VU (3 copies: 2 LP (E & L) and 1 ordinary: B821.85 R.M.); SU (823 M87r); BL (C. 109. aaa. 1.)
Notes: Morris to Jenny Morris, 29 Jan. [1889]:

> Did I tell you in my last that I had begun a new tale? I don't know whether it will come to anything, but I have written about 20 p.p. [sic] in the rough. This time I don't think I shall 'drop into poetry' at least not systematically. For one thing the condition of the people I'm telling of is later (whatever their date may be) than that of the Wolfings. They are people living in a place near the great mountains [the Alps?]. I don't think it is worthwhile telling you anything more of it till you hear some of it done; as the telling of the plot of a story in cold blood falls very flat (*Letters*, iii. 24).

Morris to the Chiswick Press, probably Thomas Jacobi, the manager, [15 July 1889]:

> I have seen your note to Mr. Walker; By all means give the order for making the pott [size paper]: there had better be full enough ordered; as we should want end-papers and so forth [in the event, the paper exceeded the needs of the LP issue and was also used for KP drafts and advertising]. I believe you have the sample of quantity & weight & *surface* which I approved of. If not I can let you have the sheet you printed for me (*Letters*, iii. 81).

Morris to Jenny Morris, 17 Oct. [1889]:

> I have had a dummy book bound up in our chintz. It looks so nice and such fun: the gold letters on the back look very well on the linen cloth. The large-papers will be out in a fortnight, the small in three weeks. Reeves says that this will do very well as to time [presumably the coming Christmas season]. The small paper will be thicker than the big; it will in consequence be a chumpy little book: it is to be sold for 8s.—cheap I think. I have begun another story, [*The Glittering Plain* perhaps] but do not intend to hurry it—I must have a story to write now as long as I live (*Letters*, iii. 115).

    Morris approved the preliminaries of *The Roots of the Mountains* and the book went to press on 4 Nov. 1889 (*Letters*, iii. 120).

    Morris to Georgiana Burne-Jones, [16 Nov. 1889]: 'I am so pleased with my book . . .—typography, binding, and I must say it, literary matter—that I am any day to be seen huggling it up, and am become a spectacle to Gods and men because of it' (*Letters*, iii. 122).

Chiswick Arch., Cost Book, vol. 4: 12 Nov. 1889: entry records the cost of paper and printing of the LP copies was £140. 18*s*. 8*d*. Printing the 1,000 ordinary copies and 500 copies Prospectus with original poem on the 1st and 3rd pages cost £44. 19*s*. 9*d*.

Later issues and impressions of this edn.: ordinary copies:
1. R and T: 1893 [finished printing 4 Feb.]: Second Edition. [2nd impression, 1st edn.] (Chiswick Arch.); *print run*: 1,000 copies; *price*: 8*s*.;
2.* Longmans: 1896 [issued July]: Second Edition. [2nd issue, 2nd impression, 1st edn., with new title page] (*Eng. Cat.*, vi. 690, and Chiswick Arch.); *print run*: 400 cancel

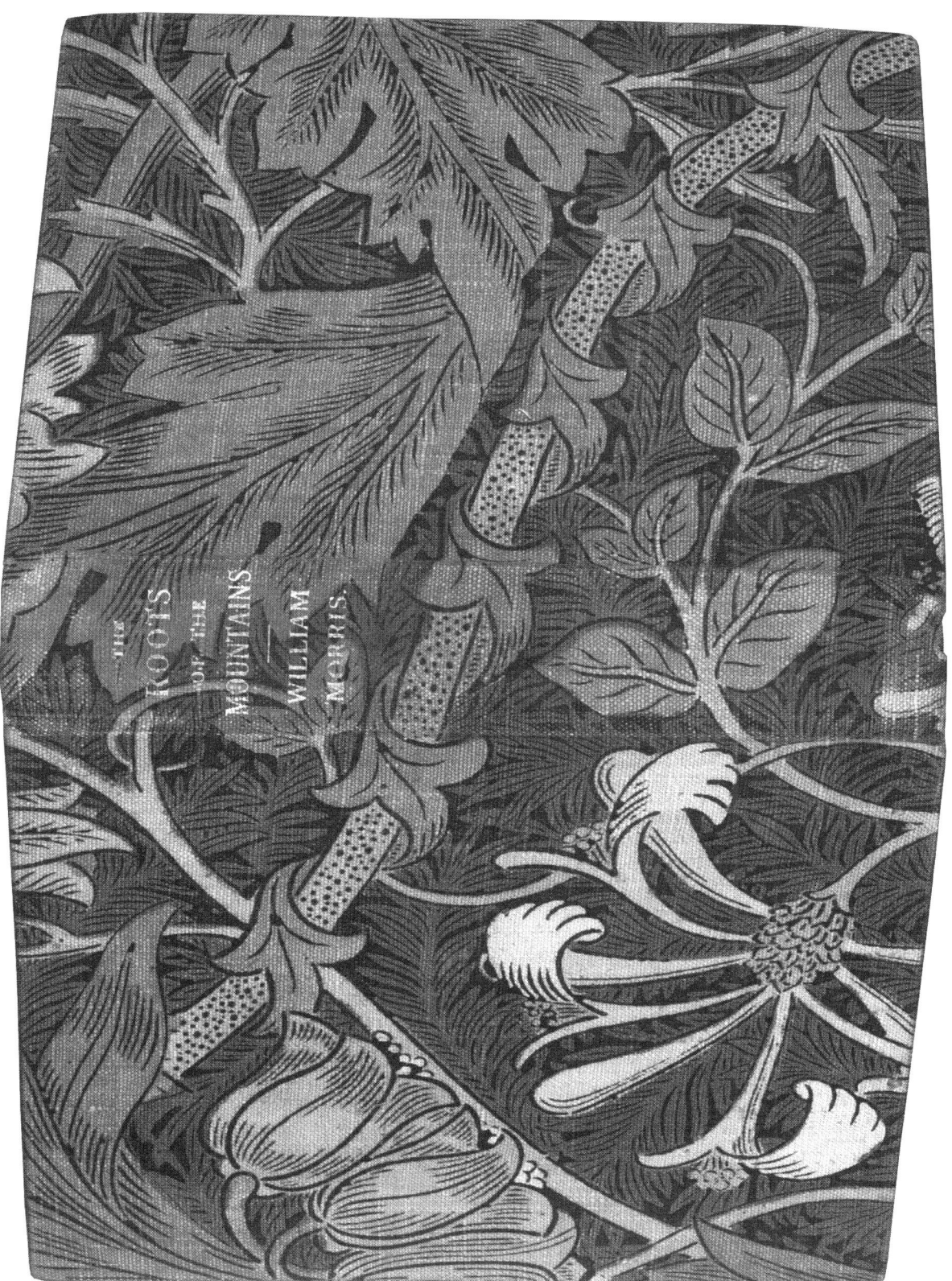

Figure 43. A-48.01: *Roots of the Mountains* ('Superior' edn.) chintz binding

titles printed by Chiswick Press for use with copies remaining of the 2nd impression; *price*: 8*s*.;

3.* Longmans, NY: 1900 [finished printing 13 Mar.]: Second Edition. [3rd issue, 1st American, 2nd impression, 1st edn.] (Chiswick Arch.); *print run*: 400 cancel titles by Chiswick Press for sheets imported by Longmans, NY; *price*: unknown;

4.* Longmans: 1906 [issued 16 Mar.]: Second Edition. [3rd impression, 1st edn.] (Longmans Arch.); *print run*: 500 copies; *price*: 8*s*.;

5. Longmans: 1913 [issued 7 Oct.]: [4th impression, 1st edn.] (Longmans Arch.); *print run*: 500 copies; *price*: 8*s*.

This 4th impression, 1st edn. setting of the text was also rptd. as a facsimile by George Prior Publishers in 1979.

A-48.02: The Roots of the Mountains (Golden 4°)

[aligned left] THE ROOTS OF THE MOUNTAINS: WHEREIN IS TOLD | SOMEWHAT OF THE LIVES OF THE MEN OF BURG- | DALE THEIR FRIENDS THEIR NEIGHBOURS THEIR | FOEMEN AND THEIR FELLOWS IN ARMS BY WILLIAM | MORRIS.

Edition: 'Golden type quarto edition' [1st impression, 2nd edn.].

Collaborators, Editors, and Illustrators: [series edited by S. C. Cockerell and Robert Proctor].

Series: 'Golden type quarto edition.' The 2nd in the series (not numbered) of eight 4° vols. printed as part of the Morris Trustees' project to complete the printing of Morris's own books in his own types. For further detail on this series, see this field and *Notes* in A-47.04.

Colophon: Here ends The Roots of the Mountains. First printed in 1890, and now re- | printed at the Chiswick Press with the Golden type designed by William | Morris for the Kelmscott Press, and finished on the 18th day of April, 1901. | Published by Longmans, Green and Co. of London, New York & Bombay.

Collation: medium 4°: a–2n⁴ 2o² 146 leaves pp. [i–iv] v–vi [vii–viii] 1–284 [= 292].

Contents: pp. [i–ii], blank; p. [iii], title page; p. [iv], blank; pp. v–vi: headed: CONTENTS | [list of 59 chapters]; p. [vii], blank; p. [viii], a lyric of 7 couplets, in red (see the full text in the title, A-48.01); pp. 1–284, text completed with colophon (see above).

Technical Notes: paper, printing (including colour), type, position (but not content) of shoulder notes, page numbers, and binding are all common to the series and are described in this field in A-47.04, the 1st pbn. of the series.

Included here are only those details specific to this edn.: *print*: in red and black, red for verse epigraph, 1st head title, and to identify the singers of verses; *type face*: KP Golden type; *spine*: printed paper label: WILLIAM | MORRIS | THE | ROOTS | OF THE | MOUNT- | AINS

Publication: 1901 [18 Apr., colophon date, issued 30 Apr.] (Longmans Arch.); *print run* and *price*: see this field in A-47.04.

Register of Copies Examined: LeM (base copy); BGR; NN; CSmH.

Notes: Chiswick Arch. Ledger entry, p. 248, Apr. 1900, records the cost of paper and printing of the Golden 4° of *Roots* as £201. 16*s*. 0*d*.

The Longmans Accts. specify 316 copies, 17 being given away (the Chiswick Press had a regular practice of printing one extra copy of every work done to add to its own collection), leaving 299 copies for sale (as part of the same number of 8-vol. sets). 60 bound sets were reserved for export to America, leaving 239 for Britain. The accounts make it clear that even at 2*gns*. a vol. all 299 sets were sold as they were completed and the royalties of the Trustees calculated in the Longmans Accts. for 1902.

A-48.03: The Roots of the Mountains (*CW* XV)

THE COLLECTED WORKS | [title details common to the set, see A-126.01] | VOLUME XV | THE ROOTS OF THE MOUNTAINS [for full title, with lyric epigraph, see A-48.01] | [publisher's imprint, see A-126.01] | MDCCCCXII

Edition: [1st impression, 3rd edn.]

Series: vol. 15 of 24; for details of this set, see this field in A-126.01.

Collation: medium 8°: a⁸ (a2+1) (a8+3) b⁸ c² B–2D⁸ [$2 (–a c) signed] 226 leaves pp. [i–vi] vii–xxxiii [xxxiv–xxxvi] 1–411 [412–16] [= 452] +4 inserted plates not included in the book's pagination, but noted in the formula and described here in their appropriate positions in the *Contents*.

Contents: p. [i], blank; p. [ii], limitation note, see this field in A-126.01; pp. [iii–iv], blank; 1st inserted plate as frontis., in a blind-stamped compartment facing p. [v], photo-litho reproduction of a photograph, labelled in copperplate: *William Morris | from a photograph made on Jan. 19. 1889 by Emery Walker*; p. [v], title page; pp. [vi], blank; pp. vii: headed: CONTENTS | [list begins]; pp. viii–ix: list of 59 chapters concluded; p. x, headed: ILLUSTRATIONS | [list of 4]; pp. xi, headed: INTRODUCTION | [text begins]; pp. xii–xvi, introduction continues, including, pp. xvi–xix, the text of: NOTE BY WILLIAM MORRIS ON HIS AIMS

Original and Posthumous Editions

IN FOUNDING THE KELMSCOTT PRESS; inserted between pp. xvi and xvii: 3 plates printed in red and black as sample leaves illustrating the 3 KP type fonts, 1 leaf and a s. sh. folded to form 2 leaves; pp. xvii–xxxii, Intro. concluded; p. xxxiii, headed: BIBLIOGRAPHICAL NOTE | [list of 6 issues]; p. [xxxiv], blank; p. xxxv: half title, with title and lyric epigraph (see title page of A-48.01); p. [xxxvi], blank; pp. 1, headed: THE ROOTS OF THE MOUNTAINS | [text begins]; pp. 2–411, text completed with explicit: NO MORE AS NOW TELLETH THE TALE OF | THESE KINDREDS AND FOLKS, BUT MAKETH | AN ENDING.; pp. [412–13], blank; p. [414], printer's imprint: see this field in A-126.01; pp. [415–16], blank.

Technical Notes: paper, printing, type, position (but not content) of headlines, running titles, shoulder notes, pagination, end-papers, and binding are all common to the series and are described in this field in A-126.01, the entry for the set. Included here are only those details specific to this edn.: *shoulder titles*: all rectos and versos, in small type, as sub-heads to the adjacent text; *spine label*: [4 lines common to the set, see A-126.01] | VOLUME XV | THE ROOTS | OF THE | MOUNTAINS

Publication: 1912 [issued 31 Oct.] (Longmans Arch.); *print run* and *price*: see A-126.01.

Register of Copies Examined: see this field in A-126.01.

A-48.04: The Roots of the Mountains (2 vols. LPL)

THE ROOTS OF THE MOUNTAINS | WHEREIN IS TOLD SOMEWHAT OF | THE LIVES OF THE MEN OF BURG- | DALE THEIR FRIENDS THEIR | NEIGHBOURS THEIR FOEMEN AND | THEIR FELLOWS IN ARMS | [lyric epigraph in 7 couplets, see A-48.01] | IN TWO VOLUMES—VOL I [II] | POCKET EDITION | LONGMANS, GREEN AND CO. | 39 PATERNOSTER ROW, LONDON | NEW YORK, BOMBAY, AND CALCUTTA | 1913

Edition: Pocket Edition [1st impression, 4th edn.]
Series: Longmans Pocket Library. For further series detail, see this field in the record of the 1st Morris book in the series, *Jason*, A-3.09.
Collation: vol. 1: fcap 8°: π⁴ A–P⁸ Q⁴ 128 leaves pp. [2] [i–iv] v–vi [1] 2–245 [246–8] [= 256].
vol. 2: fcap 8°: π⁴ A–O⁸ P⁶ 122 leaves pp. [i–iv] v–vii [viii] [1] 2–233 [234–6] [= 244].
Contents: vol. 1: pp. [1–2], ads for: WILLIAM MORRIS'S WORKS; p. [i], half title; p. [ii], ad for: Longmans' Pocket Library; p. [iii], title page; p. [iv], headed: [in Bourgeois type] BIBLIOGRAPHICAL NOTE [list of 7 issues]; pp. v–vi, headed: CONTENTS | [lists Chapters 1–28]; p. [1], text begins; pp. 2–245, text; pp. [246–8], blank.
vol. 2: pp. [i–iv], as vol. 1 except the omission of the Bibliographical Note; pp. v–vii, headed: CONTENTS | [lists chapters 29–59]; pp. 1–233, text; p. [234], blank; pp. [235–6], ads for: WILLIAM MORRIS'S WORKS

Technical Notes: For detail common to the series—on paper, binding, etc.—see this field in the first entry for the series, Jason, A-3.09; detail special to this title: *printing*: *type area*: 123 x 76 mm.; *lines-to-page*: set solid, 36 lines.
Publication: 1913 [issued 4 Oct.] (Longmans ad in *Pub. Circ.*, 99 (4 Oct. 1913), 363, says the 2 vols. are 'Ready'); *print run*: 3,000 copies; *price*: see this field in A-3.09.
Register of Copies Examined: LeM (base copy, bookplate of Arthur Odling); VU; BGR.
Notes: entry from Longmans Arch. for 13 Sept. 1913: the account for *The Roots of the Mountains* in 2 vols., specifies the bill for 3,000 copies new set, including paper and moulds made by Ballantyne, but exclusive of binding and dust jacket, was £83. 2s. 0d.

A-49.01: Monopoly (SP)

[wrapper title]"The Socialist Platform."—No. 7. | [thin rule] | [Walter Crane's woodcut head-piece, 'THE SOCIALIST LEAGUE'] | MONOPOLY | OR, | HOW LABOUR IS ROBBED. | BY | WILLIAM MORRIS | AUTHOR OF 'THE EARTHLY PARADISE.' | [thin rule] | PRICE ONE PENNY. | [thin rule] | LONDON: | OFFICE OF "*THE COMMONWEAL*" | 24 GREAT QUEEN STREET, LINCOLN'S INN FIELDS, W.C. | 1890.

Edition: [1st impression, 1st edn.] 1st pbd. in *Commonweal* (see D-486)
Collaborators, Editors, and Illustrators: Arthur Hughes was the artist whose monogram of an 'A' superimposed on an 'H' appears on the cartoon of the wrapper title verso (see Robert Coupe's 'Postscript to The Illustrated Editions of the Books of William Morris: a Descriptive Bibliography', *The Journal of William Morris Studies*, 15/4 (Summer, 2004), 137).
Series: SP—No. 7 (for details of this series, see this field in A-31.01).
Collation: cr. 8°: [1]⁸ 8 leaves pp. [1–3] 4–15 [16] [= 16] self-wrapped and stapled once in the centrefold.
Contents: p. [1], title page; p. [2], cartoon, designer monogram 'A' superimposed on 'H', identified by R. Coupe as Arthur Hughes (see 'A Postscript to Illustrated Editions of the Works of William Morris . . .,' *Journal of William*

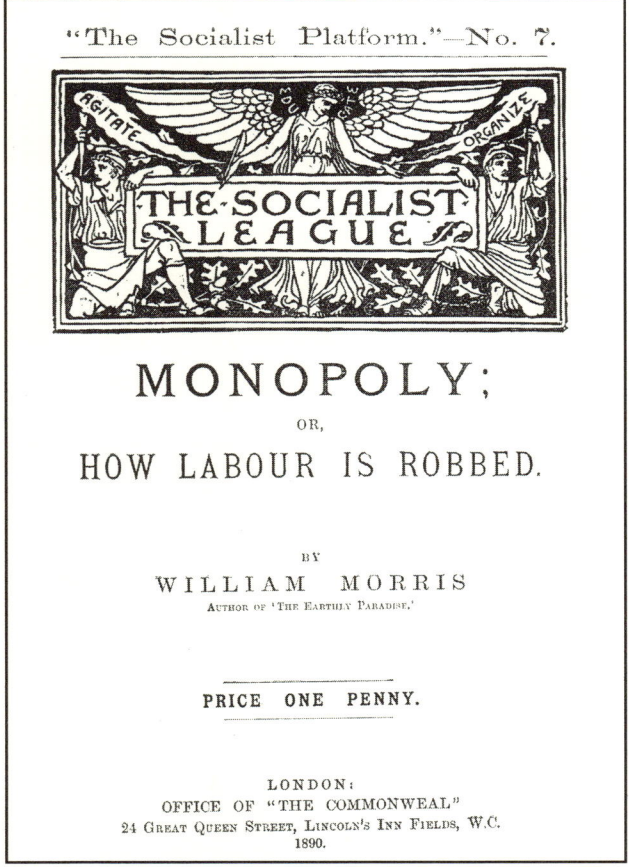

Figure 44. A-49.01: *Monopoly SP* (The Socialist Platform, 1st edn.) wrapper title

Morris Studies, 15.4 (Summer,2004), 136), captioned, top: WHEN WILL HE GET THERE? | [foot] MONOPOLY.; p. [3], headed: MONOPOLY: OR, | HOW LABOUR IS ROBBED. | [wavy rope as a rule] | [text begins]; pp. 4–15, text completed with: [thin rule] | [printer's imprint] SOCIALIST LEAGUE PRINTERY, 24 GREAT QUEEN STREET, W. C.; p. [16], headed: SOCIALIST LITERATURE | [ads]

Technical Notes: *paper*: plain white machine-made; *leaf size*: 185 x 126 mm.; *printing*: *lines-to-page*: set solid, 43 lines; *running titles*: all versos: The Socialist Platform. | [all rectos] Monopoly: or, How Labour is Robbed.; *print run*: not known.; *price*: 1d.

Publication: 1890 [issued 22–9 Mar.] (1st advertised as 'A new pamphlet by William Morris' in *Commonweal*, 6/220 (29 Mar. 1890), 104); *print run*: unknown; *price*: 1d.

Register of Copies Examined: CtY (base copy: Nx16 M73); MH (Typ8304.90.5); LeM; BL (3 copies: 8275. dd. 15.; Cup. 502. f. 11. (47); and Ashley 1226)

Later issues and impressions from this edn.:
1. SL: 1891: SP No. 7 [2nd impression, 1st edn.] Socialist League Printery, 273 Hackney Road, N.E.; *print run*: unknown; *price*: 1d.;
2. TL: 1894 [issued 1 Oct.–18 Dec.] (The 2 issues for these dates of *The Torch, A Revolutionary Journal of Anarchist-Communism*, announce, in the 1st, that the Torch group's 1st pamphlets are 'now being printed' and, in the 2nd, that *Monopoly*, and *Useful Work v. Useless Toil*, 'have been reprinted', forming, with Kropotkin's *Appeal to the Young*, the first 3 numbers of 'The Torch Library' series): [3rd impression, 1st edn.]; *print run*: unknown; *price*: 1d.;
3. 'Freedom' Group: n.d. [this impression of the pamphlet must have been issued after 5 July 1900, when W. Reeves is reported to have moved from his Fleet Street address to 83 Charing Cross Road, the new address appearing on the wrapper title (see *BSR*, No. 510 (5 July 1900), 527)]: FL [4th impression, 1st edn.]; *print run*: unknown; *price*: 1d.

A-49.02: Monopoly (HSL)

[wrapper title headed with Walter Crane's 'HAMMERSMITH SOCIALIST SOCIETY' woodcut head-piece] | MONOPOLY | OR | HOW LABOUR IS ROBBED | BY | WILLIAM MORRIS | Price One Penny | PUBLISHED BY | THE HAMMERSMITH SOCIALIST SOCIETY | KELMSCOTT HOUSE, UPPER MALL, HAMMERSMITH | LONDON, W. | 1893

Edition: [1st impression, 2nd edn.]
Collation: a single 8° gathering: 8 leaves pp. [1–3] 4–15 [16] [= 16] self-wrappered.
Contents: p. [1], wrapper title; p. [2], blank; p. [3], headed: MONOPOLY: OR, | HOW LABOUR IS ROBBED. | [thin rule] | [text begins]; pp. 4–15, text completed; p. [16], ads for HSS pbns. and lectures, with a map of the Upper Mall area, and printer's imprint: [thin rule] | LABOUR LITERATURE SOCIETY, LTD., PRINTERS, 105 LONDON ST., GLASGOW.
Technical Notes: *paper*: plain white machine-made; *leaf size*: cut flush, 179 x 119 mm.; *printing*: *lines-to-page*: set solid, 44 lines, excluding headlines; *running titles*: [all versos] MONOPOLY; OR, | [all rectos] HOW LABOUR IS ROBBED.
Publication: 1893; *print run*: unknown; *price*: 1d.
Register of Copies Examined: Fdmn (base copy); An-C-TU (Morris Pam M677 M65 1893); BGR.

A-49.03:* Monopoly

Monopoly; or How Labour is Robbed [lecture]

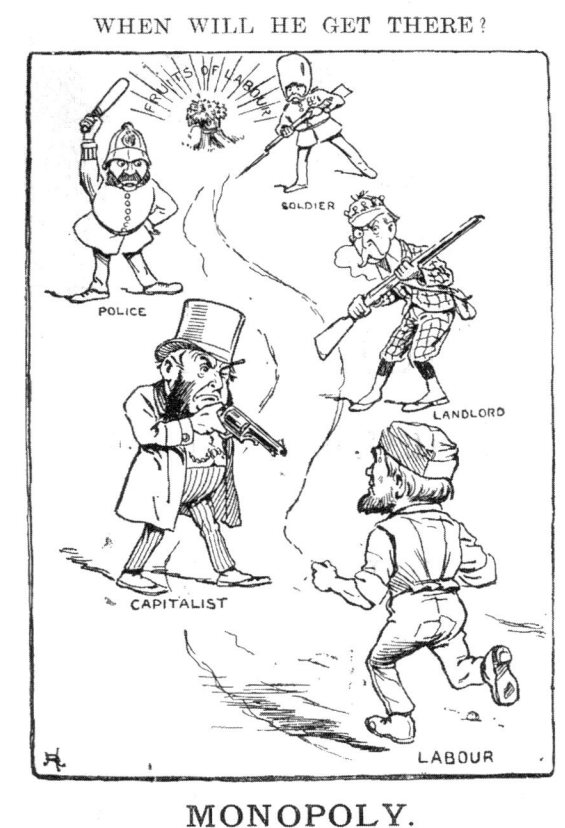

Figure 45. A-49.01: *Monopoly SP* (The Socialist Platform, 1st edn.) opening: cartoon & head title

Edition: [1st impression, 3rd edn.]
Series: Commonwealth Library, No. 8.
Place: New York.
Publisher: Commonwealth Co.
Technical Notes: 21 p. 18 1/2 cm. (*National Union Catalogue*, hereafter referred to as *NUC*).
Publication: 1896.
Register of Copies Located: ICU.

A-50.01: News from Nowhere (RB)

NEWS FROM NOWHERE; | OR, | [in gothic] An Epoch Of Rest. | [plain type] *BEING SOME CHAPTERS FROM A UTOPIAN | ROMANCE.* | BY | WILLIAM MORRIS, | [small type] AUTHOR OF THE EARTHLY PARADISE," [*sic*] "THE LIFE AND DEATH OF JASON," | "THE DEFENCE OF GUENEVERE AND OTHER POEMS," "LOVE IS | ENOUGH," "THE STORY OF SIGURD THE VOLSUNG," "THE | HOUSE OF THE WOLFINGS," "HOPES AND FEARS FOR | ART," "THE AENEIDS OF VIRGIL DONE | INTO ENGLISH VERSE." | [within a thin-rule circle, Aldine 'boy-on-a-globe' publisher's device labelled internally: qui legit regit] | [normal type size] BOSTON: | ROBERTS BROTHERS. | 1890.

Edition: Author's Edition. [1st impression, 1st edn.] This text is unrevised, being taken directly from the 39 weekly instalments previously pbd. in *Commonweal* (see D-493).

Collaborators, Editors, and Illustrators: [Walter Crane's frontis. block 'Solidarity of Labour', here labelled 'Labour's May-Day', was photo-duplicated by Boston Engraving Co.] (Cost Book E, Roberts Arch.)

Collation: cr. 8° printed and gathered in 16s: [1] 2–18⁸ [$1 (−4) signed] 144 leaves pp. [i–v] vi [7] 8–278 [279–88] [= 288].

Contents: p. [i], half title: NEWS FROM NOWHERE; | OR, | AN EPOCH OF REST.; p. [ii], process line block

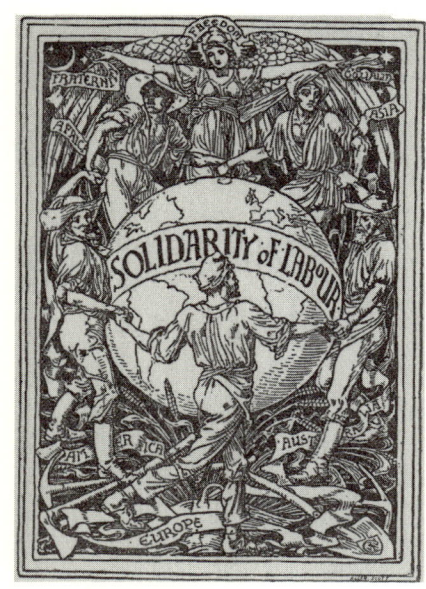

Figure 46. A-50.01: *News from Nowhere* (1st edn., American) opening: frontis. & title page

frontis. within a compartment of 2 sets of double thin rules, a globe surrounded by workmen and surmounted by the angel of Freedom, signed with Walter Crane's monogram and labelled: LABOUR'S MAY DAY.; p. [iii], title page; p. [iv], copyright statement and printer's imprint: *Author's Edition.* | [in gothic] University Press: | [plain text] JOHN WILSON AND SON, CAMBRIDGE.; pp. [v]–vi, headed: CONTENTS | [list of 30 numbered chapter titles]; p. [7], headed: [3 lines as the half title] | [french rule] | CHAPTER I. | DISCUSSION AND BED. | [text begins]; pp. 8–278, text completed with explicit: THE END.; pp. [279–88], ads for Morris books.

Technical Notes: *paper*: plain white machine-made, no watermarks; *leaf size*: trimmed, 179 x 120 mm.; *printing*: type area: 129 x 76 mm., excluding head and direction lines; *lines-to-page*: set solid, 33 lines; *running titles*: [all versos] NEWS FROM NOWHERE | [all rectos] OR, AN EPOCH OF REST.; *end-papers*: 2 free ends and paste-down in front and 1 with paste-down in back, plain white and blank; *binding*: plain unblocked dark red cloth; front: title stamped in grey at the head: • NEWS FROM NOWHERE • | OR | AN EPOCH OF REST | [gilt-stamped globe without the surrounding figures, abstracted from Walter Crane's frontis. (see *Contents*, above), girdled with: SOLIDARITY OF LABOUR] | [below the globe] • WILLIAM MORRIS •; *spine*: gilt-stamped: NEWS | FROM | NOWHERE | OR | AN EPOCH | OF REST | WILLIAM | MORRIS | [monogram of RB]

Publication: 1890 [issued 31 Oct.] (Roberts Arch.); *print run*: 1,500 copies; *price*: $1.00.

Register of Copies Examined: MU (base copy: LP: Spec. Coll. PR5080 N4, 1891c); BGR; MH; LeM (signed in longhand, 'Evelin J. Stanton').

Notes: Kilgour: 'In 1890 Morris wrote *News from Nowhere*, the most famous of his socialist romances. RB published it in November, calling it "a pleasant socialistic novel.".' Kilgour retells story of this being the 1st edn. and asks, 'Why did Niles rush the story into book form in America without waiting for the standard English edition?'. Kilgour says RB were 'counting on the current vogue' of Bellamy's *Looking Backward*. 'The book did sell well, but nothing like Bellamy's (200,000 copies), which was an essentially American work, laid in Boston, whereas Morris' was just as characteristically British' (Kilgour, 247).

Morris writes to Roberts Bros., 3 Feb. 1891: 'Thank you for your account and cheque (other side for formal receipt of latter. I am not much surprised at News from Nowhere not selling well. People would be apt to think it out of my way. The English edition will be out in two to three weeks' (*Letters,* iii. 262).

Later issue and impressions from this edn.:
1.* RB: 1891 [issued 18–25 Apr.] See A-50.03 for the full entry;
2. RB: 1891 [issued 30 July]: Author's Edition. [2nd impression, 1st edn.] (Cost Book E, Roberts Arch.); *print run*: 280 copies; *price*: $1.00;
3. RB: 1892 [issued 7 Nov. 1892] See A-50.04 for the full entry;
4.*.RB: 1894 [issued 4 June]: Author's Edition. [4th impression, 1st edn.] (Cost Book E, Roberts Arch.); *print run*: 280 copies; *price*: 60 cents;
5. RB, but with Little, Brown binding with Little, Brown monograph on spine: 1898 [[issued 16 Oct. 1897]: Author's Edition. [5th impression, 1st edn.] (Cost Book E, Roberts Arch.); *print run*: 280 copies; *price*: $1.00;
6.* Longmans, NY: 1901: Author's Edition. New Impression [6th impression, 1st edn.] (Longmans Accts.); *print run*: 250 copies; *price*: 60 cents;
7. Longmans NY: 1903: New Impression [7th impression, 1st edn.] (Longmans Accts.); 225 copies; *price*: 60 cents;
8.* Longmans, NY: 1906: [8th impression, 1st edn.]; *print run* and *price*: unknown;
9. Longmans, NY: 1913: [9th impression, 1st edn.]; *print run* and *price*: unknown.

A-50.02: News from Nowhere

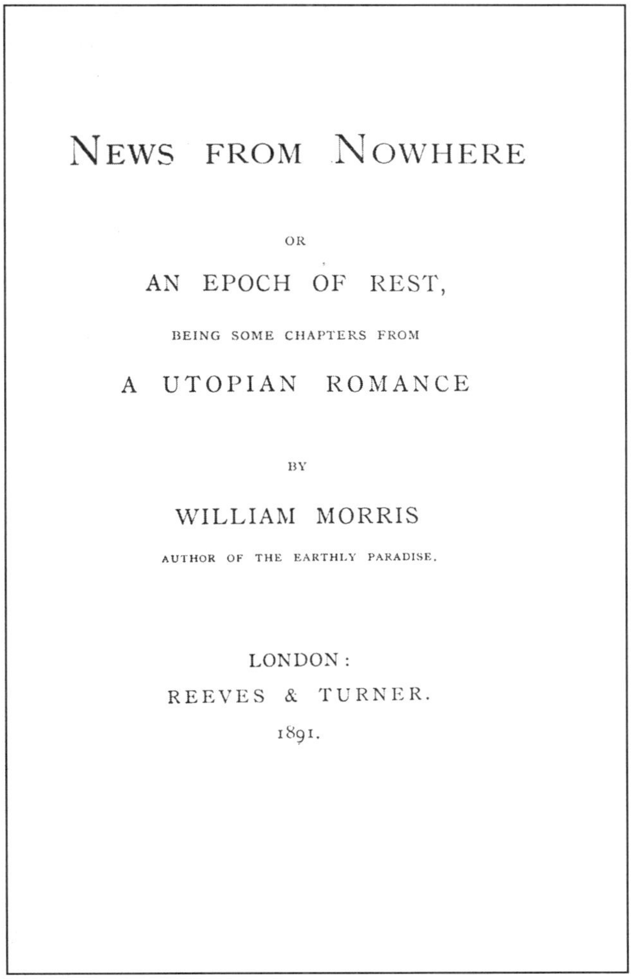

NEWS FROM NOWHERE | OR | AN EPOCH OF REST, | BEING SOME CHAPTERS FROM | A UTOPIAN ROMANCE | BY | WILLIAM MORRIS | AUTHOR OF THE EARTHLY PARADISE. | LONDON: | REEVES & TURNER. | 1891.
Edition: 'Cr. 8vo Edn.' [1st impression, 2nd edn., 1st English] 1st pbd. in *Commonweal* (see D-493), but here extensively revised from the *Commonweal* version. Besides the regular copies, this edn. includes 250 LP copies.
Printer: The book has no printer's imprint, but Bow-

Figure 47. A-50.02: *News from Nowhere* (2nd edn., 1st English) title page

den, Hudson & Co., Printers, Red Lion Street, Holborn, (though not a 'transpontine press', as HBF refers to it) may be inferred from several bits of evidence: the imprint on the ads appended to *The Roots of the Mountains*, 1st edn., 1890, and on the Reeves and Turner dated catalogues of the period, combined with the identification of the Bowden of those earlier imprints with the one named in HBF (p. 149), as the printer of this 1st *News from Nowhere*: 'I believe the book was printed at a small transpontine press by a Mr. Bowden.' The present 'William Reeves: Bookseller', who is the latest (and last) in the 5-generation succession of William Reeves, Bookseller(s), says this Mr Bowden was a relative of his great-grandfather, William Dobson Reeves, the sole proprietor of Reeves and Turner at the time of this *News from Nowhere* edn. This Mr Bowden,

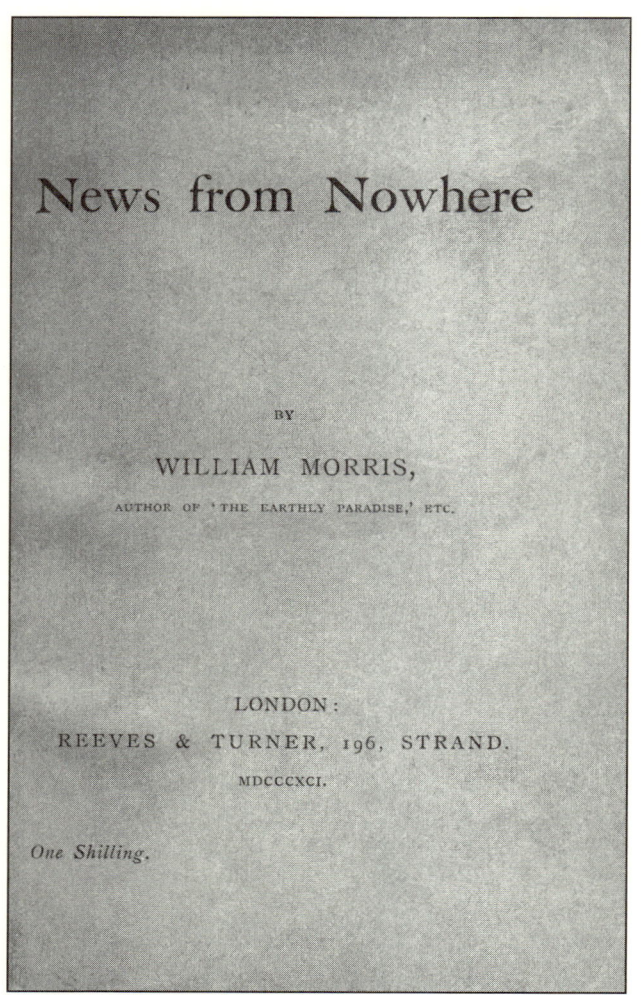

Figure 48. A-50.02: *News from Nowhere* (2nd edn., 1st English) original paper wrapper bound in with the half citron levant binding

the father of another printer also named William Bowden, was the first employee of the Kelmscott Press and helped set it up. His son William H. Bowden, become the 'overseer', i.e. foreman, of the KP printers (see also *KP Biblio.*, p. xxxviii). HBF's comment implies that William Bowden was an obscure figure, but he was well known to most people in the book trade. His death of cholera in 1891, while he was employed at the Kelmscott Press, was noted in America, where he was the subject of an ample obituary: 'He was well known to the English book trade, as he printed practically the whole of the second-hand booksellers' catalogues during a period of over forty years' (see *Pub. Weekly*, 40/1–21 (22 Aug. 1891), 244). The elder Bowden's daughter, Mrs. Pine, the 1st female member of the Printers' Union, was also employed by the Press as a printer and reader (see Sparling, 73). When the press moved from the original cottage at No. 16, Upper Mall, Hammersmith, to larger premises at No. 14, Sparling says, 'William Bowden definitively retired' and his son, William H. Bowden replaced him as overseer (p. 81). This all occurred in 1891.

Collation: cr. 8°: B–Q^8 (–Q8) [$2 signed] 120 leaves pp. [2] [1]–238 [= 240] + inserted title-page leaf and a brown wrapper. This collation is for the *editio princeps* as it is bound with the original wrappers in a half citron levant morocco binding, where the only preliminary leaf is the title page, tipped in.

Contents: p. [1], title page; p. [2], blank, except limitation statement, LP copies only: This Large Paper Edition of 'News from Nowhere' | is limited to Two Hundred and Fifty copies; p. [1], chapter head title: [full title +] CHAPTER I. | DISCUSSION AND BED. | text begins; pp, 2–238, text completed with explicit: THE END.; back paper wrapper inserted, recto blank; verso: WORKS BY WILLIAM MORRIS. The copy described is in the half-citron Levant binding which was one of the edn. bindings, but it contains within it the full text and includes in all copies seen the wrapper of the cheaper paperback edn. sold for 1s.

Technical Notes: *paper*: cream machine-made, no watermark; *leaf size*: trimmed 177 x 118 mm., LP, hand-laid, untrimmed, avg. 192 x 125 mm.; *printing*: type area: 126 x 76 mm.; *lines-to-page*: set solid, 37 lines; *end-papers*: none with the paper wrapper; citron Levant copy: 6 free ends and paste-down, plain white and blank except for thick paper buff paste-down and facing free end, obverse sides plain white, all others plain white and blank, front and back; *binding*: ordinary copies: (1) buff paper wrappers, printed on p. [1]: NEWS FROM NOWHERE | BY | WILLIAM MORRIS, | AUTHOR OF 'THE EARTHLY PARADISE,' ETC. | LONDON: | REEVES & TURNER, 196 STRAND. | MDCCCXCI. | [aligned left] *One Shilling*.; pp. [2–3], blank; p. [4], ads; (2nd binding) half-citron levant morocco with marbled paper-covered boards and red scatter-stained edges, original wrappers bound in (see above), 5 raised bands on spine with gilt thin rules doubled at head and foot, single rule of diagonal gilt strokes in the middle of each band; compartment between top and second band, dyed dark red and gilt-stamped, by hand: [double thin gilt rule,] | NEWS | FROM | NOWHERE | [thin gilt rule] | MORRIS | [double thin gilt rule]; tail has double thin gilt rules above and below a floral ornament; (3rd binding) plain dark green or blue unblocked cloth with printed paper spine labels; (4th binding) LP copies with

Original and Posthumous Editions

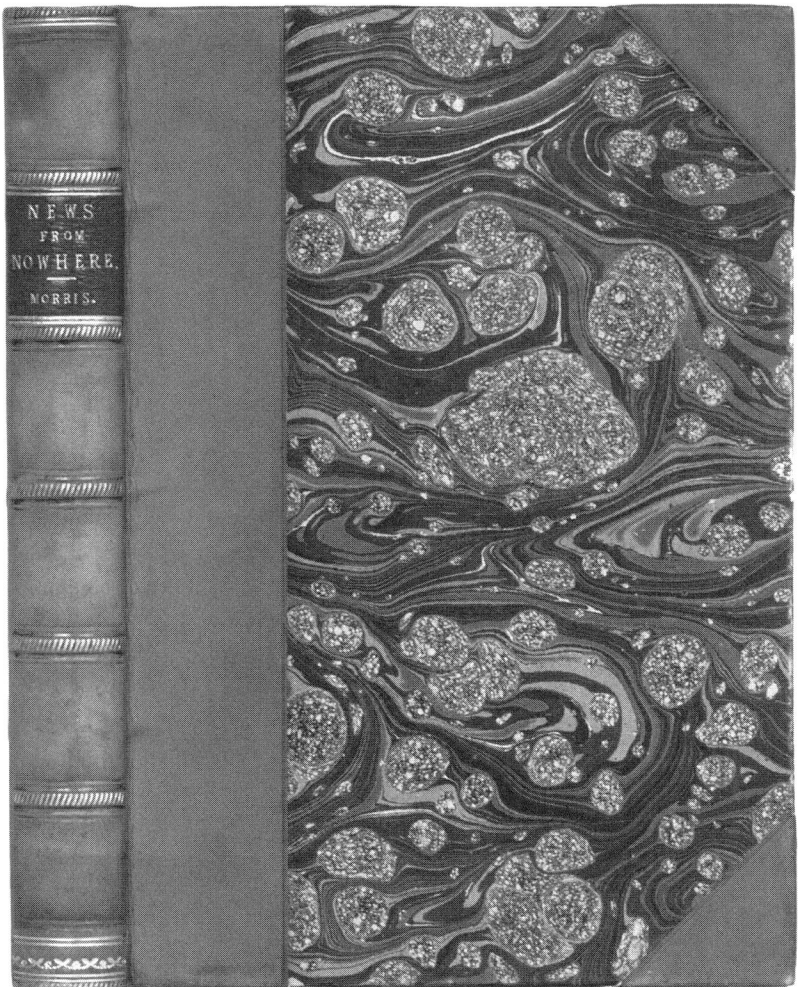

Figure 49. A-50.02: *News from Nowhere* (2nd edn., 1st English) half citron levant binding

machine-made paper and gilt-stamped title and author on front and spine of dark blue cloth binding; and (5th binding) 250 LP copies printed on French hand-made paper, in light-blue paper-covered boards with linen backs and printed paper *spine labels*: NEWS | from | NOWHERE | by | William Morris

Publication: 1891 [issued 21–8 Mar.] ('Publications of the Week', *Pub. Circ.*, 54/1290 (28 Mar. 1891), 336); *print run*: *Reeves and Turner Catalogue for Aug. 1891* says the 'Second Edition', i.e. the 2nd impression, 2nd edn., 1st English was the 'eleventh thousand' implies that the 1st impression was of 10,000 copies. In the context of Morris's books, this is an extraordinary number, but while it should be treated with some caution, Morris's letter (see *Notes*, below) gives it some substance; *price*: 1*s*. 6*d*. cloth, 1*s*. paper, LP copies, 5*s*.; prices of optional fine bindings are not known.

Register of Copies Examined: LeM (base copy: this copy and VSL copy (s 823.89 M83N), bound in half citron levant, are in one of the binding options available for the edition, the original buff wrappers being bound in); Fdmn (2 copies, 1 LP); SU (823 M87n); VMoU (*820.8 M877 A6/n, LP, cloth-bound LP copies have the title page tipped in); VU (4 copies: 821.85 N.n; 11644 15355; 823 M87n; and LP in Special Coll. E); An-C-TU (M677 N48 1891a; has library binding and no half title).

Notes: Morris to J. Bruce Glasier, 7 Oct. [1890]: 'I shall now presently begin to touch up N from N for its book form, & will publish for 1s/o. It has amused me very much in writing it: but you may depend upon it, it wont sell. This is of course my own fault—or my own misfortunes' (*Letters*, iii. 218).

Morris to Reeves and Turner, 22 July [1892?]: 'Thanks for the account and cheque. I understand everything except the account of News from Nowhere. The *first* edition is the large paper copies I suppose: for you have not accounted to me for any other edition but on the other hand I thought you had sold nearly 8000 copies. Kindly explain what the figures mean' (*Letters*, iii. 419–20).

Later issues and impressions from this edn.:

1. R and T: 1891 issued in Apr. (bibliographic note in the book): SECOND EDITION. [2nd impression, 2nd edn., 1st English]; *print run*: unknown; *price*: 1*s*. paper, 1*s*. 6*d*. cloth;

2. R and T: 1891 [issued 31 May–6 June]: SECOND EDITION. [3rd impression, 2nd edn., 1st English]; *print run*: unknown; *price*: 1*s*. paper, 1*s*. 6*d*. cloth;

3. R and T: 1892 [issued Mar.]: THIRD EDITION. [4th impression, 2nd edn., 1st English]; *print run*: unknown; *price*: 1*s*. paper, 1*s*. 6*d*. cloth;

4. R and T: 1895 [issued Mar.]: FOURTH EDITION. [5th impression, 2nd edn., 1st English]; *print run*: unknown; *price*: 1*s*. paper, 1*s*. 6*d*. cloth;

5. Longmans: 1897 [issued 30 Dec. 1896] (Longmans Arch.): [6th impression, 2nd edn., 1st English]; *print run*: 2,000 copies; *price*: 1*s*. paper, 1*s*. 6*d*. cloth. The Longmans Arch. (Index H31, Longmans no. 28) indicates (and inspection of

copies confirms) that with this 1st Longmans impression of *News from Nowhere* the publisher made extensive changes to the prelims of the existing plates, adding a half title, resetting the title page, composing headlines (not previously used) and having them stereotyped and soldered on the plates, and a table of contents composed and inserted. But the body of the book retains the original English setting;

6. Longmans: 1899 [issued 29 Nov.] (Longmans Arch.): SIXTH IMPRESSION [7th impression, 2nd edn., 1st English]; *print run*: 1,500 copies; *price*: 1s. 6d. cloth;

7. Longmans: 1902 [issued 9 Aug.] (Longmans Arch.): SEVENTH EDITION [8th impression, 2nd edn., 1st English]; *print run*: 1,500 copies; *price*: 1s. 6d. cloth;

8. Longmans: 1905 [issued 8 July] (Longmans Arch.): EIGHTH EDITION [9th impression, 2nd edn., 1st English]; *print run*: 1,500 copies; *price*: 1s. 6d. cloth;

9. Longmans: 1907 [issued 26 Dec.] (Longmans Arch.): Ninth Impression [10th impression, 2nd edn., 1st English]; *print run*: 2,000 copies; *price*: 1s. 6d. cloth;

10. Longmans: 1908 [issued 21 Dec.] (Longmans Arch.): Tenth Impression [11th impression, 2nd edn., 1st English]; *print run*: 3,000 copies; *price*: 1s. 6d. cloth;

11. Longmans: Jan. 1910 [issued 25 Dec. 1909] (Longmans Arch.): Eleventh Impression [12th impression, 2nd edn., 1st English]; *print run*: 3,000 copies; *price*: 1s. 6d. cloth.

A-50.03:* News from Nowhere

News from Nowhere; or, an Epoch of Rest.
Edition: [2nd issue, 1st impression, 1st edn.] No copy of this issue has been found, thus the description of edn. is speculative, but such evidence as is available, like the frontis., the number of pages of text, and the date, is consistent with this being another issue of the RB 1st impression.
Series: Unsettled Questions No. 3.
Place: New York, NY
Publisher: Twentieth Century Pub. Co., 23 Warren Street, New York.
Printer: The University Press: John Wilson and Son, Cambridge.
Publication: [issued 18–25 Apr. 1891] ('Publications of the Week', *Pub. Weekly*, 39/1004 (25 Apr. 1891), 591); *print run*: unknown number of copies from the 1,500 of the 1st impression, sold (?) in printed paper covers with an altered title page omitting the date but including a new publisher's imprint; *price*: 50 cents; pp. 278 + 1 il. (*Pub. Weekly*, as above).
Register of Copies Located: none located.

Notes: a copy of this book has not been found, but references to it in the trade journal *Pub. Weekly* suggest that it is another issue from the 1,500 copies printed for RB by John Wilson and Son. So, of course, the text would be as first published in 39 weekly instalments in *Commonweal* (see D-493). This issue could be another instance, as with Humboldt Publishing, where RB sold sheets to another publisher for sale primarily in New York, but there is no record of such a transaction with the Twentieth Century Press Pub. Co. as there is for the copies sold to Humboldt Publishing, a copy of which is in BGR, and since the Humboldt consignment was specially printed by RB, an entry occurs in the Roberts Arch. The cost of production to RB of the 1,500 copies was 6.5 cents a copy, so the price of 50 cents on the paper-backed Twentieth Century Pub. Co. copies would have allowed a profit for both buyer and seller.

A-50.04: News from Nowhere

[title page as for A-50.01, except for the imprint:] NEW YORK: | THE HUMBOLDT PUBLISHING CO. | 19 ASTOR PLACE.
Edition: [3rd impression, 1st edn.] 1st pub. in *Commonweal* (see D-493).
Collation: see this field in A-50.01.
Contents: as the 1st impression, A-50.01, except publisher's imprint.
Technical Notes: *binding*: terra cotta red cloth, blind-stamped front and back with ornamental triple `thin-rule border, ornamented at each corner with a flower; *spine*: white-stamped in swash caps: NEWS FROM | NOWHERE
Publication: [issued 7 Nov. 1892] (Roberts Arch.); *print run*: 500 copies; *price*: 50 cents.
Register of Copies Examined: BGR.

A-50.05: News from Nowhere (KP)

[flush left, printer's leaf ornament No. 2] NEWS FROM NOWHERE: OR, | AN EPOCH OF REST, BEING SOME | CHAPTERS FROM A UTOPIAN RO- | MANCE, BY WILLIAM MORRIS.
Edition: 'Kelmscott Press Edition' [1st impression, 3rd edn., 2nd English] The author 'made a few slight corrections' in the text for this edn. (Cockerell, p. 153). 1st pbd. in *Commonweal* (see D-493).
Collaborators, Editors, and Illustrators: frontis., based on Kelmscott Manor, designed by C. M. Gere and engraved by H. E. Hooper with ornamental border by Morris; captioned in Golden type (see *Contents*, below).

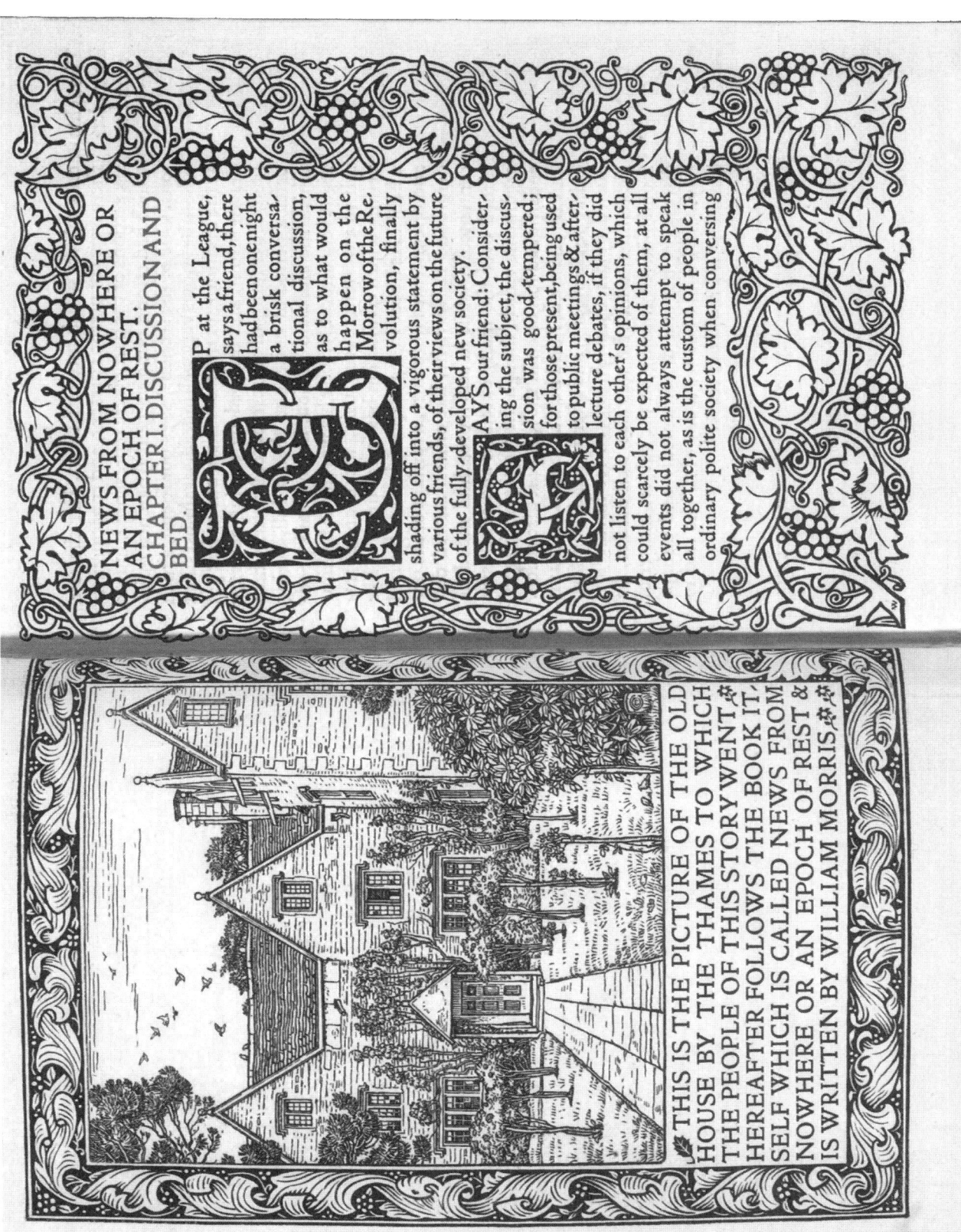

NEWS FROM NOWHERE OR AN EPOCH OF REST. CHAPTER I. DISCUSSION AND BED.

UP at the League, says a friend, there had been one night a brisk conversational discussion, as to what would happen on the Morrow of the Revolution, finally shading off into a vigorous statement by various friends, of their views on the future of the fully-developed new society.

SAYS our friend: Considering the subject, the discussion was good-tempered; for those present, being used to public meetings & after-lecture debates, if they did not listen to each other's opinions, which could scarcely be expected of them, at all events did not always attempt to speak all together, as is the custom of people in ordinary polite society when conversing

Figure 50. A-50.05: *News from Nowhere* (KP) opening: frontis. & head title

Series: 12th title, 5th by Morris, pbd. by the Kelmscott Press.

Colophon: This book, News from Nowhere or an Epoch | of Rest, was written by William Morris, and | printed by him at the Kelmscott Press, Upper | Mall, Hammersmith, in the County of Middle- | sex, and finished on the 22nd day of November, | 1892. Sold by Reeves & Turner, 196, Strand, | London. | [printer's mark 1]

Collation: cr. 8°: [a]⁴ b–u⁸ x⁴ [$2 (– b1 x2) signed] 160 leaves pp. [8] [1] 2–305 [306–12] [= 320].

Contents: pp. [1–2], blank; p. [3], title page; p. [4], blank; pp. [5–6], headed: A LIST OF CHAPTERS OF THE | BOOK. | [32 chapter titles with roman page numbers, arranged as a list]; p. [7], blank; p. [8], frontis. woodcut of Kelmscott Manor House, from a drawing by C. M. Gere, captioned: [printer's leaf ornament No. 1] THIS IS THE PICTURE OF THE OLD | HOUSE BY THE THAMES TO WHICH | THE PEOPLE OF THIS STORY WENT [printer's flower ornament No. 3] | HEREAFTER FOLLOWS THE BOOK IT- | SELF WHICH IS CALLED NEWS FROM | NOWHERE OR AN EPOCH OF REST & | IS WRITTEN BY WILLIAM MORRIS [2 printer's flower ornaments No. 3, all within border 9a]; p. [1], headed with general title, chapter title in red, and text begins, all within border 4; pp. 2–305, text completed; p. 306, colophon (see above), followed by printer's mark 1; pp. [307–12], blank.

Technical Notes: *paper*: (this base copy is specially bound by the Doves Press and the binding, noted here, is not typical) cream-white Batchelor's hand-made KP Flower paper 2, vertical chain lines; *leaf size*: this copy: a.e.g., hence trimmed, 200 x 140 mm; regular copies are untrimmed deckled edges, avg. 207 x 142 mm.; *printing*: in black and red, with the 1st chapter title, shoulder notes, footnotes, asterisks, speakers' initials in red in dialogue passages; *type area*: 140 x 91 mm.; *lines-to-page*: set solid, 30 lines; *type face*: printed in Golden type; *shoulder notes*: sub-heads to the adjacent text, hence unique to the page; *pagination*: 4 mm. in from outer margins on direction line; *end-papers*: standard KP treatment: 3 free ends and paste-down, all plain white and blank, front and back; *binding*: limp natural vellum with two red silk ties (and this copy: with yapp foredges and 5 vellum back strips continued into the front and back by each being rove through to 2 pairs of slits in the front and back within covers); *letterpress*: *spine*: gilt-stamped across: NEWS | FROM | NOWHERE | BY | WILLIAM | MORRIS; *ornamentation*: frontis. designed by C. M. Gere; KP mark No. 1; 2 full borders, 9a and 4; 31 10-line initials, 1 9-line initial, 88 6-line initials.

Publication: 22 Nov. 1892 [this colophon date indicates finished printing, issued 24 Mar. 1893] (Cockerell, p. 153); *print run*: 300 copies on paper, 10 on vellum; *price*: 2gns. and 10gns., respectively.

Register of Copies Examined: VU (base copy: Baillieu RB 19E, with special Doves Press binding); VSL (base copy for ordinary binding: *094/*K29m); CSt (Bender Z239.2 K29M76m); BGR; CSmH.

Notes: Morris to Charles M. Gere, 14 Nov. 1892:

> I have your drawings of the house and think them very good & pretty: but I doubt if any of them will *quite* do for the foundation of our cut.... I should tell you that the one of the entrance front of the house is the only one which is about the right shape for the cut, and I think that this must be the view taken only if something more could be got in of the tapestry block, and of the 2nd gable to the S. it would be better.

Kelvin's note: 'In the event, this drawing was the basis for the one from which the woodcut was made' (*Letters*, iii. 466). Getting this frontis. right delayed the completion of the book well into 1893, though the colophon says the printing was completed before the end of Nov. 1892.

A-50.06:* News from Nowhere

[Title as in A-50.02, except for the edn. notice and the imprint:] FOURTH EDITION. | LONGMANS, GREEN AND CO. | 39 PATERNOSTER ROW, LONDON | NEW YORK, AND BOMBAY | 1896. | All rights reserved

Edition: FOURTH EDITION. [2nd issue, 5th impression, 2nd edn., 1st English] 1st pbd. in *Commonweal* (see D-493). Since this is a reissue of the 5th impression, 2nd edn., only details of altered fields are included. The reissue is the first pbn of the book by Longmans and carries the new publisher's imprint.

Printer: [Printed by Ballantyne, Hanson & Co.] (no imprint, Longmans Arch.).

Technical Notes: repairs to plates and alterations of title page, changing the date and the publisher's imprint to Longmans; otherwise as A-50.02, being made up of copies from Reeves and Turner's 5th impression, acquired by Longmans in sheets from Reeves and Turner, when Morris changed publishers.

Publication: 1896 [issued July]; *print run*: remaining copies acquired from R and T; *price*: 1s. 6d. cloth.

Register of Copies Examined: An-C-TU (base copy: M677 N48 1896); BGR.
Notes: *Eng. Cat.*, 5/689: '*News from Nowhere* 4th ed., post 8vo, pp. 238, 1*s*. 6*d*., Longmans, July '96'.

A-50.07: News from Nowhere (LPL)

NEWS FROM NOWHERE | OR | AN EPOCH OF REST | BEING SOME CHAPTERS FROM | A UTOPIAN ROMANCE | BY | WILLIAM MORRIS | AUTHOR OF "THE EARTHLY PARADISE" | POCKET EDITION | NEW IMPRESSION | LONGMANS, GREEN AND CO. | 39 PATERNOSTER ROW, LONDON | NEW YORK, BOMBAY, AND CALCUTTA | 1912 | All rights reserved

Edition: Pocket Edition. New Impression. [1st impression, 4th edn., 3rd English] 1st pbd. in *Commonweal* (see D-493).
Collaborators, Editors, and Illustrators: Cover illustration of the paper wrapper copied from a drawing of Kelmscott Manor by C. M. Gere, 1st pbd. as the KP edn. frontis. (see A-50.05).
Series: Longmans Pocket Library. This is the only Morris title found in the Pocket Library series to have a paper wrapper as well as the usual choice of cloth or lthr. bindings. For further series detail, see this field in the record of the 1st book in the series, *Jason*, A-3.09.
Collation: fcap 8°: π⁴ A–P⁸ Q⁴ 128 leaves pp. [i–vi] vii–viii [1] 2–247 [248] [= 256].
Contents: pp. [i–ii], ads headed WILLIAM MORRIS'S WORKS; p. [iii], half title; p. [iv], ad headed: Longmans' Pocket Library; p. [v], title page; p. [vi], headed: BIBLIOGRAPHICAL NOTE [with a list, in hanging indent, of 8 issues]; pp. vii–viii, headed: CONTENTS | [list of 32 chapter titles]; p. [1], headed: NEWS FROM NOWHERE | CHAPTER I | DISCUSSION AND BED | [text begins]; pp. 2–247, text completed with explicit: THE END | Printed by BALLANTYNE, HANSON & Co. | Edinburgh & London; p. [248], blank.
Technical Notes: details of paper, type, printing, end-papers, and binding, are common to the series; see this field and the *Series* field in A-3.09. What follows is limited to what is specific to this edn. of this title: *running titles*: [all versos] NEWS FROM NOWHERE | [all rectos, the appropriate chapter titles]; *binding*: *wrapper*: this being the only vol. in the series available in paperback as well as cloth and lthr. bindings (for the cloth and lthr. bindings, see A-3.09, making appropriate adjustments for the present title; also sold in a grey paper wrapper: printed on the front, blank on the other 3 sides; front, title: NEWS FROM NOWHERE | OR AN EPOCH OF REST | BEING SOME CHAPTERS FROM | A UTOPIAN ROMANCE BY | WILLIAM MORRIS | [process line block illus., front view of Kelmscott Manor, within a thin-rule compartment, from a drawing signed by C. M. Gere, but without the Morris border or the label of the original KP edn. version, from which this is taken] | LONGMANS, GREEN AND CO. | 39 PATERNOSTER ROW, LONDON | NEW YORK, BOMBAY, AND CALCUTTA | *Price One Shilling Net*; *spine*: [reading up] NEWS FROM NOWHERE
Publication: 1912 [issued 30 June–6 July] (Longmans ad in *Pub. Circ.*, 97 (6 July 1912), 12. In the next issue of *Pub. Circ.*, a notice says, 'This volume will also shortly be issued in Paper Covers, price One Shilling net'); the paperback edn. was issued the following week, 7–13 July ('Publications of the Week', *Pub. Circ.*, 97 (13 July 1912), 36, 44); *print run*: 3,000 copies; *price*: 1*s*. paper, 2*s*. cloth, 3*s*. lthr.
Register of Copies Examined: LeM (2 copies: base copy: one cloth and one paper binding).
Notes: *The Bookseller* commented: 'Messrs. Longmans, Green & Co. have added to their Pocket Library, 'News from Nowhere . . . by William Morris. It is now being reprinted for the sixteenth time, and will no doubt be in even greater demand than hitherto' ('Trade and Literary Gossip', *BSR*, 58/184 (5 July 1912), 908).
Later issues and impressions from this edn.: Longmans:
1. 1913 [issued 26 Mar.] (Longmans Arch.): LPL [2nd impression, 4th edn., 3rd English]; *print run*: 3,000 copies; *price*: 1*s*. paper, 2*s*. cloth, 3*s*. lthr.;
2. 1914 [issued 14 Feb.] (Longmans Arch.): LPL [3rd impression, 4th edn., 3rd English]; *print run*: 5,000 copies; *price*: 1*s*. paper, 2*s*. cloth, 3*s*. lthr;
3. Impressions issued after 1915: 16 Feb. 1918 (2,000 copies by Neill); 21 Feb. 1919 (5,000 copies by Neill); 14 May 1920 (5,000 copies by Neill); Oct. 1924 (by Neill).

A-50.08: News from Nowhere (+ John Ball and A King's Lesson *CW* XVI)

THE COLLECTED WORKS | [title detail common to the set, see A-126.01] | VOLUME XVI | NEWS FROM NOWHERE | A DREAM OF JOHN BALL | A KING'S LESSON | [printer's imprint, see A-126.01] | MDCCCCXII

Edition: vol. XVI of 24 [1st impression, 5th edn., 4th English, of *News from Nowhere*] 1st pbd. in *Commonweal* (see D-493). For the full title, collation, and all details common to the set, particularly *Technical Notes*, see the entry for the

CW, A-126.01. The *Collation, Contents* and *Technical Notes* provided here cover all 3 titles combined in this vol. For any details specific to *A Dream of John Ball and A King's Lesson*, see A-45.07.

Collation: medium 8°: a⁸ (a2+1) (a8+1) b⁸ B⁸–U⁸ [$2 (–a2) signed] 168 leaves pp. [i–viii] ix–xxxii [1–2] 3–297 [298–304] [= 336] +2 inserted plates not counted in the book's pagination, but noted in the formula and described here in their appropriate places under *Contents*.

Contents: pp. [i–iii], blank; p. [iv], limitation statement, see this field in A-126.01; pp. [v–vi], blank; 1st inserted plate as frontis. facing p. [vii], within blind-stamped compartment, reproduction of a photograph, with the plate maker's name, below right, in copperplate: *Emery Walker Ph. sc.* | [captioned in copperplate, centred] *William Morris's bed at Kelmscott | From a photograph by Mr. F. H. Evans*; p. [vii], title page; p. [viii], blank; pp. ix–x, headed: CONTENTS; p. xi–xxix, headed: INTRODUCTION | [text begins]; pp. xii–xvi, text; 2nd inserted plate, to face p. xvi, photo- reproduction in a blind-stamped compartment of a painting, with the plate maker's name below right: Walker & Boutall ph. sc. | [label in copperplate, centred] *La Belle Iseult | from the picture painted by William Morris in 1858.*; pp. xvii–xxix, introduction concluded; p. [xxx], blank; p. xxxi–xxxii, headed: BIBLIOGRAPHICAL NOTE | [list of the successive issues of 3 titles combined here] | p. [1], 1st half title: [top, flush left] NEWS FROM NOWHERE; OR, AN | EPOCH OF REST: BEING SOME | CHAPTERS FROM A UTOPIAN ROMANCE; p. [2], blank; p. 3, 1st chapter head title and text begins; pp. 4–211, text completed with explicit: THE END OF NEWS FROM NOWHERE; p. [212], blank; p. 213, 2nd half title: [top, flush left] A DREAM OF JOHN BALL; p. [214], blank; p. 215, headed: CHAPTER I. THE MEN OF KENT. | [text begins]; pp. 216–88, text completed; p. 289, 3rd half title: A KING'S LESSON; p. [290], blank; p. 291, headed: A KING'S LESSON | [text begins]; pp. 292–7, text completed; pp. [298–9], blank; p. [300], imprint, common to the series, see A-126.01; pp. [301–4], blank.

Technical Notes: paper, printing, type, position (but not content) of headlines, running titles, shoulder notes, pagination, end-papers, and binding are common to the series and are described in this field in A-126.01. Included here are only those details that are specific to this particular edn. of this title: *headlines*: *running titles*: of the 1st title: [all versos] NEWS FROM NOWHERE | [all rectos, chapter title]; 2nd title, all rectos and versos: A DREAM OF JOHN BALL; 3rd title, all rectos and versos: A KING'S LESSON; *spine label*: [4 lines common to the set, see A-126.01] | VOLUME XVI | NEWS FROM | NOWHERE | JOHN BALL | A KING'S | LESSON

Publication: 1912 [issued 31 Oct.] (Longmans Arch.); *print run* and *price*: see this field in A-126.01.

Register of Copies Examined: see this field in A-126.01.

A-51.01: Gunnlaug Worm-Tongue

[head title] *The Story of Gunnlaug Worm-Tongue and | Raven the Skald. Even as Ari Thorgilson the | learned / the priest / hath told it / who was the man | of all Iceland most learned in tales of the land's | inhabiting and in lore of time agone.* | [text begins, slanted strokes in the original]

Edition: [1st impression, 1st separate edn.] 1st pbd. as 'The Story of Gunnlaug the Worm-Tongue and Rafn the Skald', in *Fortnightly Review* (see D-20); reprinted as the 1st tale in *Three Northern Love Stories* (1875; see A-9.01).

Collaborators, Editors, and Illustrators: translated from the Icelandic by William Morris and Eiríkr Magnússon. For a note on Morris's English translations from the Icelandic and the role in them of E. Magnússon, see this field in A-5.01.

Colophon: Printed at the Chiswick Press | for William Morris. Mdccclxli

Collation: pott 4°: a–h⁴ i⁴ [$2 signed] 36 leaves no pagination, pp. [1–72] [= 72].

Contents: No preliminary leaves, half title, or title page; p. [1], headed, as title above plus: *Chapter i. Of Thorstein Egilson & His Kin.* | [space for illuminated initial T, with 8 lines of text to the right, for an intended 8-line initial, with full lines below]; pp. [2–70], text completed with colophon (see above); pp. [71–2], blank.

Technical Notes: *paper*: cream hand-laid Whatman paper, horizontal chain lines, Whatman's watermark mid-way of the centrefold, with date, '1889'; *leaf size*: untrimmed, 275 x 142 mm.; TxU copy on vellum, *leaf size*: varies, avg. 238 x 262 mm.; *printing*: *type*: Caxton type #2 as reproduced by William Howard for the Chiswick Press, this being the only book published entirely in this font (see Talbot Baines Reed and A. F. Johnson, *A History of the Old English Letter Foundries*, 365); *type area*: 203 x 174 mm. exclusive of head and direction lines; *lines-to-page*: set solid, 26 lines, including blank lines before and after chapter titles; no pagination; *catchwords*: all rectos and versos, at the right margin on the direction line; *end-papers*: 2 free ends and a paste-down, plain white and blank, front and back; *binding*: plain blue paper-covered boards with white holland hollow back.

Publication: 1891 [1 Nov. 1890, finished printing] Though this is the date of the Chiswick Arch. record of printing, there is no issue date for this book. It was made available to the public over some years, through sale and gift. The imprint date from the colophon is 1891. The date used here, 1 Nov. 1890, is the date of completion of printing (the customary practice is to advance the imprint date to the year following when a book is issued near the end of the year); and the 1890 date is from the Chiswick Arch. Paul Needham says, 'though dated 1891 in the colophon Sydney Cockerell records that printing was finished in November 1890, at the time Morris's Golden type was nearing completion (*William Morris and the Art of the Book* (hereafter referred to as *Art of the Book*), 121). The Chiswick Press Account Book records, as usual, 2 dates, one at the beginning and one at the end of the entry. In this particular case, the 1st date is 'Nov.1, 1890', and the 2nd is '19-12-90'; the 1st probably indicates the date of completion of printing (there being no 'issue' or offer for public sale at the time, and the copies were not bound at this time); the 2nd the date of billing or payment. The date that seems closest to an 'issue' date is 22 Aug. 1902, from Mrs. Morris's letter of that date to Cockerell thanking him for finding buyers for the remaining copies (Smith Arch., see also *Notes*, below). In 1897, while having Leighton bind them, Cockerell's correspondence indicates that, besides the vellum copies, 64 paper copies then remained, with 6 more in which Morris had painted in the initials; but, except for the copy that May Morris gave to John Quinn (see the *Notes*, below) none of these 6 copies have been seen or located; *print run*: 75 paper copies and 3 on vellum; since there was no issue, properly speaking, no price was advertised (but see *Notes*).
Register of Copies Examined: St. Bride's (base copy); BL; TxU (1 of the 3 copies printed on vellum: PT 7262 G9 A5 1891; with bookplate of Fairfax Murray and a Leighton red leather binding); NNPM (65857 M; with letter from S. C. Cockerell to Alfred H. Higgins tipped in).
Notes: Morris's MS note attaching to the 'Memorandum about the proposal of Mr. Bernard Quaritch to publish some of my saga translations' (NNBerg) in The Saga Library, mentions the Gunnlaug as using the text as printed earlier in *Three Northern Love Stories* and explains that the 1890 separate edn. is a limited edn. With no more than 50 copies to be sold, it would not encroach on the Saga Library's sales (The Saga Library, which though projected to extend to 15 vols. stopped after Morris's death at 6 vols.), all copies being in the Chiswick Press copy of the Caxton type and rubricated by hand and therefore very expensive. While Morris illuminated the initials in 6 copies, the bulk of the rest remained unilluminated at his death. This may explain why there was no publication: most copies remained unfinished and for some years unsold.

HBF (p. 193) says he never saw a complete copy, only 'some pages in the Arts and Crafts Exhibition of 1890'; and because he did not realise a whole book had been printed, he did not include it in its proper place in his account of Morris's books.

The TxU copy has the bookmark of 'Ch. Fairfax Murray' inside the front cover of a red full-calf binding done by 'Leighton, Brewer St. W.', later the regular binder of the KP books. Below his bookmark, Murray has pencilled his initial, 'CFM' and dated it 'Jan 1896': he says that the 3 copies printed on vellum were all presentation copies, his being selected from the best shts. of all 3. In Nov., 1897, Cockerell wrote to Leighton about binding the remaining copies of which there were then 64 unilluminated and the 6 copies illuminated by Morris (see John Johnson Collection of MSS., Ms. Johnson. e.3., New Bodley Library, Oxford).

May Morris wrote to James Leatham, 25 Sept. 1925, explaining that she is sending him an unilluminated copy of the *Gunnlaug* which was meant to have the capitals drawn in by hand in red and blue (Leatham Arch., Aberdeen University Library). But Leatham understood by her words that Morris meant the reader to illuminate the capitals. He wrote in 'What does it Mean to be Didactic?': 'the other day I got from May Morris a privately printed book of her father's in which the chapter initials were left blank, with the intention that they should be printed in.' (*The Gateway*, 14/164 (Apr. 1926), 15). Leatham of course immediately set to work to illuminate the letters with his own watercolours.

May Morris provided the background of this book in the following inscription in a copy she gave to John Quinn:

> To J. Q. from M. M., Sept. 21st, 1912 . . . The paper of this Gunnlaug is the Whatman paper made for "The Roots of the Mountains." There was a good deal left over, and the little book was printed on purpose to use it up. The type—belonging to the Chiswick Press—is the reproduction of a Caxton fount. The letters are all by W. M.'s hand' *Complete Catalogue of the Library of John Quinn, Sold by Auction in Five Parts*, ii. 679 (hereafter referred to as *Quinn Catalogue*).

A-52.01: Saga Library (vol. I)

THE SAGA LIBRARY. | VOL. I. | THE STORY OF

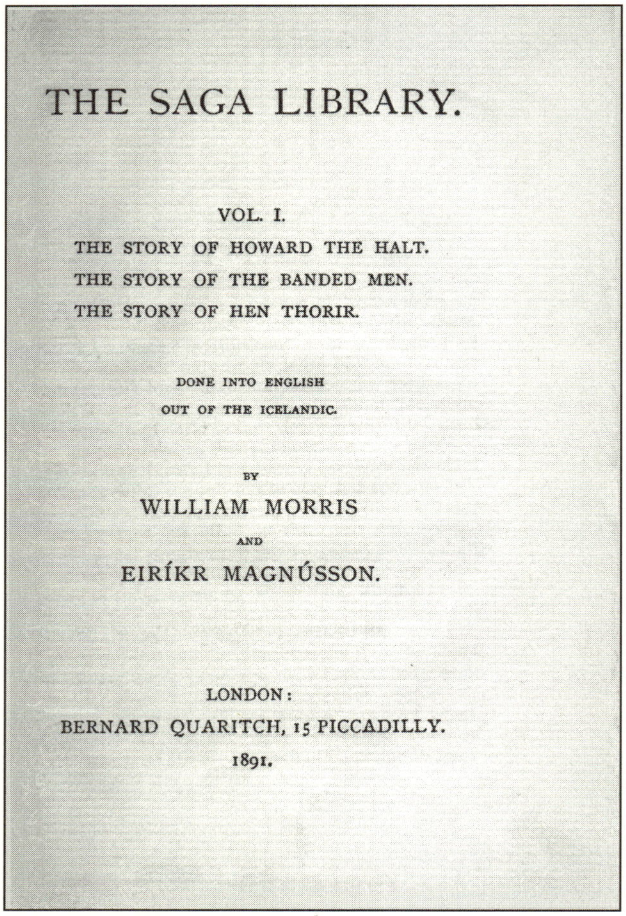

Figure 51. A-52.01: *The Saga Library* (1st edn., vol. 1 of 6) title page

HOWARD THE HALT. | THE STORY OF THE BANDED MEN. | THE STORY OF HEN THORIR. | DONE INTO ENGLISH | OUT OF THE ICELANDIC. | BY | WILLIAM MORRIS | AND | EIRÍKR MAGNÚSSON. | LONDON: | BERNARD QUARITCH, 15 PICCADILLY. | 1891.

Edition: [1st impression, 1st edn.] Here, as with all 6 vols. of the Saga Library, in addition to the ordinary copies, there were 125 LP copies, all numbered, on Whatman handmade paper.

Series: The Saga Library vol. I [–VI]. Magnússon explains the division of the collaborators' contributions:

> The Saga Library was an idea conceived by William Morris, suggested to and taken up by the late Mr. Quaritch. The work on it was divided between Morris and myself in the following manner: Having read together the sagas contained in the first three volumes, Morris wrote out the translation and I collated his MS. with the original. For the last two volumes of the Heimskringla the process was reversed, I doing the translation, he the collation; the style too he emended throughout in accordance with his own ideal. Morris wrote pp. v–xvii of the preface to vol. i; the rest of it was drawn up by me, as was also the preface to the second volume and submitted to Morris' revision. Indexes, notes, genealogical tables I took in hand, also the drawing of the maps which Morris had printed in his own way' (*Saga Library*, vi. p. vii).

The terms of the contract for this series, copies now in the NNBerg and the Quaritch archive involve two 'Memoranda of Agreement', both rptd. in *Letters*, iii. 172–3 note, 231 note. It provided for Quaritch to own the copyright of the translations printed in the series in return for payments to be made, some immediately (for titles already translated) and others at various stages of production, with 12 gratis copies (6 ordinary and 6 LP) to Morris. Morris had control of choice of type, and style of printing. 15 vols. were projected in the original prospectus (Quaritch archive), but only 6 were produced, of which Morris's contribution was limited to the first 5, Magnússon being the sole author of the last or Index vol., published 10 years after Morris's death. All copies, both ordinary and LP, were issued in Roxburghe-style bindings (see *Technical Notes*, below).

Arrangements between Morris and Magnússon for payment for this 1st vol. were between the two of them and, it seems, informal, with Morris forwarding a payment to his collaborator as he received payments from Quaritch. Neither the contract nor available references in letters between Quaritch, Morris, and Magnússon give details of the collaborators' individual shares (see the final 'Agreement' for publication of the Saga Library, rptd. in *Letters*, iii. 231), but Morris wrote Magnússon regarding the 2nd vol. on 16 Dec. 1890: 'I have much pleasure in enclosing a cheque for £50, your half of the 1st payment made by Q. He will pay the other £100, of which you will have half, when the book is printed' (*Letters*, iii. 245).

Collation: cr. 8°: [a]⁸ b–c⁸ d² (± d2) B–F⁸ (F4+1) G–I⁸ (I6+1) K–P⁸ Q² 140 leaves pp. [i–v] vi–xlvii [xlviii–lii] [1] 2–227 [228] [=280] + 2 inserted maps not counted in the book's pagination but noted in the formula and both described in their appropriate places in the *Contents*. The cancel marks the insertion of the 1st map in the place of d2.

Contents: p. [i], half title for: THE SAGA LIBRARY.; p. [ii], blank; p. [iii], title page; p. [iv], printer's imprint: CHISWICK PRESS:—C. WHITTINGHAM AND CO., TOOKS COURT, | CHANCERY LANE.; p. [v],

Original and Posthumous Editions

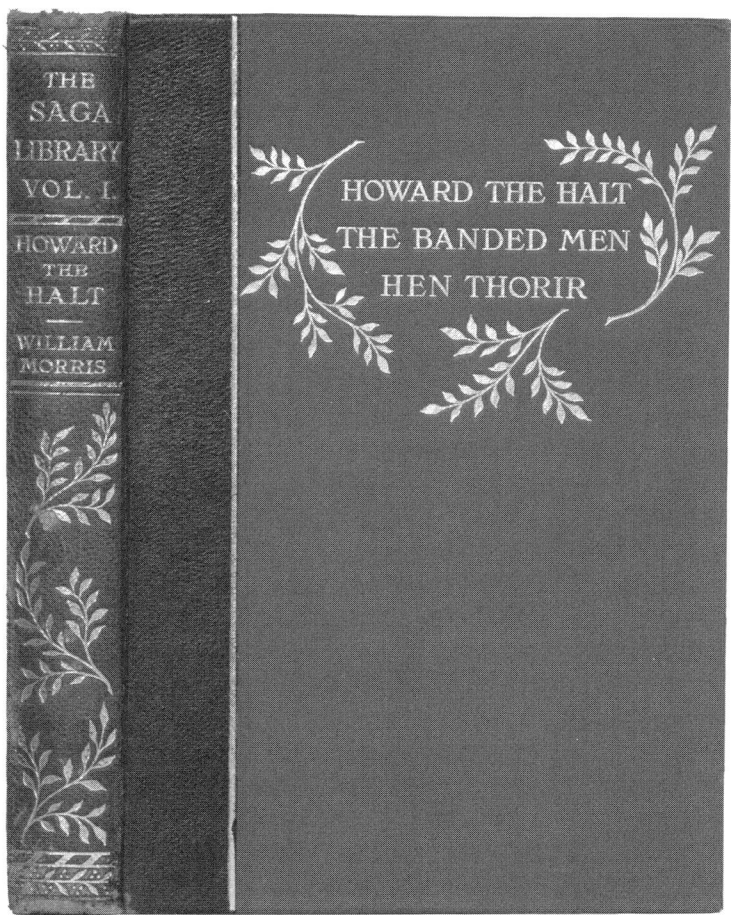

Figure 52. A-52.01: *The Saga Library* (1st edn., vol. 1 of 6) binding

dropped head: PREFACE. | [text begins]; pp. vi–xlvii, Preface concluded; inserted half title for: THE STORY | OF | HOWARD THE HALT.; inserted leaf to face verso of half title, headed CORRIGENDA, verso blank; inserted engraved map, blank on recto, facing p. 1 of the text, captioned in a compartment, upper left: MAP OF THE | COUNTRY OF | THE HOWARD'S | SAGA; p. [1], dropped head, 1st chapter: THE STORY | OF | HOWARD THE HALT. | [flush left] CHAPTER I. OF THORBIORN AND THE ICEFIRTHERS. | [text begins]; pp. 2–69, text concluded; p. [70], blank; p. [71], half title for: THE STORY | OF | THE BANDED MEN.; p. [72], blank; inserted engraved map captioned in a compartment, upper right: MAP OF THE | COUNTRY OF | THE BANDED | MENS' SAGA; p. [73], dropped head: THE STORY | OF | THE BANDED MEN. | [flush left] CHAPTER I. OF UFEIG AND ODD HIS SON. | [text begins]; pp. 74–121, text concluded; p. [122], blank; p. [123], half title for: THE STORY | OF | HEN THORIR. | p. [124], blank; inserted engraved map to face p. [125], recto blank, captioned in a compartment, upper left: MAP OF THE | COUN | TRY OF THE HEN | THORIR SAGA; p. [125], dropped head: THE STORY | OF | HEN THORIR. | [flush left] CHAPTER I. OF MEN OF BURGFIRTH. | [text begins]; pp. 126–63, text concluded; p. [164], blank; p. 165, half title for: APPENDIX.; p. [166], blank; p. [167], dropped head: APPENDIX. | AN ADVENTURE OF ODD UFEIGSON WITH KING | HAROLD HARDRADI. | [text begins]; pp. 168–75, text concluded; p. [176], blank; p. [177], half title for: NOTES.; p. [178], blank; p. [179], dropped head: NOTES. | [text begins]; pp. 180–93, Notes concluded; p. [194], blank; p. [195], half title for: INDEX.; p. [196], blank; p. [197], dropped head: INDEX. | PERSONS. | [text begins]; pp. 198–227, Index completed: [thin rule] | [printer's imprint] CHISWICK PRESS:— C. WHITTINGHAM AND CO., TOOKS COURT, CHANCERY LANE.; p. [228], blank. *Technical Notes*: this being the 1st vol. of the set, this entry includes all items common to the set as well as details specific to this vol.: *paper*: cream-white 'antique' machine-moulded paper with dandy roll laid lines and false deckled edges; *leaf size*: lightly trimmed, avg. 189 x 127 mm.; LP copies on Whatman hand-made with deckled edges; *printing*: *type area*: 140 x 89 mm.; *lines-to-page*: set solid, 33 lines; *running heads*: all versos (except the Preface): *The Saga Library*. | [all rectos, in italics, tale or section title]; *end-papers*: one free end and paste-down, plain white and blank, front and back; *binding*: all vols. of this set, both ordinary and LP, were issued in Roxburghe bindings, with gilt top, 3-quarter-bound style with dark green lthr. spine with a single vertical thick gilt rule on the lthr. at the seam joining it with olive-green cloth-covered boards; front and lower half of the spine gilt-stamped with myrtle branches designed by Morris; front: branches surround the three titles: HOWARD THE HALT | THE BANDED MEN | HEN THORIR; *spine*: [top, myrtle border between thin rules] | THE | SAGA | LIBRARY | VOL. I | [ornamental rule] | HOWARD | THE | HALT | [thin rule] | WILLIAM | MORRIS | [thick-thin rule] | [myrtle design] | [myrtle border between ornamental and thin rules]; all bindings with dust wrappers of pale blue paper, with duplicate titles and floral ornaments by Morris on front and spine, gilt on binding, printed black on dust wrappers.

Publication: 1891 [after 12 Dec. 1890] (Chiswick Arch. says 20 Nov. 1890, but this is probably the date when printing was finished); the book was reviewed in *The Pall Mall Gazette*, 13 Dec. 1890. Morris had his copy by 1 Dec., but that could have been an advance copy, sent because he earlier expressed a wish to see one as soon as possible (see *Notes*, below); *print run*: 1,000 regular and 125 LP copies on Whatman paper; *price*: unknown.

Register of Copies Examined: (applies to the full set of 6 Vols.) LeM (base copy); NNPM (3 sets, including G A 34.01: Vols. I and II are inscribed by Morris to Sydney C. Cockerell); SSL (S859.3a); VU (two sets: 839.608 / S129 & B); VSL (S823.89 M83R); SU (839.6 S12).

Notes: Morris wrote to Georgiana Burne-Jones on 8 July 1890: 'I have undertaken to get out some of the Sagas I have lying about. Quaritch is exceedingly anxious to get hold of me, and received with enthusiasm a proposal to publish a Saga Library: item he will give me money (or perhaps I ought to say old books)' (quoted in Mackail, ii. 247). The phrase 'anxious to get hold of me' is probably a reference to Quaritch's desire to become Morris's publisher, replacing Reeves and Turner, it having become known that Morris was intending to make a change consequent upon the increasing age and imminent retirement from business of William Dobson Reeves, the sole surviving partner of Reeves and Turner after the death of Osborne Turner in 1887.

Morris to Quaritch, 13 July [1890]:

> In case I was not definite enough yesterday I write to say that the size & kind of type which I think would suit the Saga Library best would be Caslon's Pica: The next size smaller would bring you to the same as the Earthly Paradise [i.e. the 1st edn.] is printed with.
>
> I note also that the large paper copies should be printed with the handpress, so as to get the impression black enough'
(*Letters,* iii. 179).

The Chiswick accounts show the total cost of production, ordinary and LP copies, with stereo moulds: £85. 13*s*. 0*d*. (Ledger entry for Nov. 1890, Chiswick Arch., p. 259).
Morris to Quaritch, [1 Dec. 1890]: 'Thank you for the copy of vol. I. It looks very well I think: only I rather wish you hadn't stuck my name outside on the back [only Morris's name appears on the spine, Magnússon's being omitted]: it would have been better to put yours as publisher. The binder has put in map No III upside down in the copy which you have sent me: I hope he has not done it in other copies' (*Letters,* iii. 236–7).

Because some errors appeared in a *Pall Mall Gazette* review of The Saga Library, vol. I, Morris replied in a letter to the editor on 13 Dec. His letter was published on 15 Dec. 1890 (see D-518).

Later impressions of this edn.: Quaritch:
1. 1891 [1 Feb. 1891] (Chiswick Arch.): [2nd impression, 1st edn.]; *print run*: 500 copies; *price*: unknown;
2. 1894 [after 29 Nov.] (this is probably the day printing was finished, binding was still to come) (Chiswick Arch.): [3rd impression, 1st edn.]; *print run*: 500 copies; *price*: unknown.

A-53.01: Principles of the HSS

[wrapper title, gothic type] Statement of Principles of | The Hammersmith Socialist | Society | [plain type] Published by the Society at Kelmscott House, Upper Mall, | Hammersmith, W. | PRICE ONE PENNY

Edition: [1st impression, 1st edn.] Text reprinted as Appendix A, *Letters,* iii. 489–92.

Collation: half of a cr. 8° [1]⁴, 2 pairs of conjunct leaves folded inside one another to form 4 leaves pp. [1–3] 4–8 [= 8] self-wrappered, sewn through the centrefold.

Contents: p. [1], title page; p. [2], headed: RULES OF THE HAMMERSMITH | SOCIALIST SOCIETY. | [series of 5 rules, numbered, + (this copy) stamped notice of lecture time and venue]; p. [3], dropped head title: STATEMENT OF PRINCIPLES | OF THE | HAMMERSMITH SOCIALIST SOCIETY. | [text begins]; pp. 4–8, text completed: [dated, left] December, 1890. | [thin rule] | [printer's imprint] Co-operative Printing Society Limited, 6, Salisbury Court, Fleet Street, and 35, Russell Street, Covent Garden, London. (15,183.)

Technical Notes: *paper*: cream-white machine-made, no watermark; *leaf size*: cut flush, 181 x 122 mm.; *printing*: *type area*: 141 x 89 mm., excluding headlines; *lines-to-page*: set solid, 39 lines.

Publication: Dec. 1890. (so dated on the last page); *print run*: 15,183 (see p. [8] under *Contents*); *price*: 'one penny', but by Oct. 1891, Morris wrote in the 1st issue of *The Hammersmith Socialist Record* that this Statement of Principles was 'free of charge'.

Register of Copies Examined: BL (2 copies: base copy: 8277.de.29.[7], and Cup. 502.f.11.[32]); NNBerg.

Notes: Morris to [Georgiana Burne-Jones, 9 Dec. 1890]: 'I have got to rewrite the manifesto for the new Hammersmith Society, and that I must do this very night: it is a troublesome and difficult job, and I had much rather go on with my Saga work' (*Letters*, iii. 241).

A-53.02: Principles of the HSS (HSL)

[wrapper title: Walter Crane's woodcut head-piece including name of the Society:] THE | HAMMERSMITH | SOCIALIST SOCIETY | STATEMENT OF PRINCIPLES | Price One Penny | PUBLISHED BY | THE HAMMERSMITH SOCIALIST SOCIETY | KELMSCOTT HOUSE, UPPER MALL, HAMMERSMITH | LONDON, W. 1893

Edition: [1st impression, 2nd edn.] Text reprinted as Appendix A, *Letters*, iii. 489–92.
Collaborators, Editors, and Illustrators: Masthead design by Walter Crane.
Collation: half of a cr. 8° [1]⁴, 2 pairs of leaves folded inside one another to form 4 leaves pp. [1–3] 4–7 [8] [= 8] self-wrapped, leaves stapled once through the centrefold.
Contents: p. [1], title page; p. [2], headed: RULES OF THE HAMMERSMITH | SOCIALIST SOCIETY. | [series of 5 rules, numbered, + this copy, stamped notice (in different type) of lecture time and venue]; p. [3], dropped head: STATEMENT OF PRINCIPLES | OF THE | HAMMERSMITH SOCIALIST SOCIETY. | [text begins]; pp. 4–7, text completed, dated below left: December, 1890. | [thin rule] | LABOUR LITERATURE SOCIETY, LTD., PRINTERS, 105 LONDON ST., GLASGOW.; p. [8], blank.
Technical Notes: *paper*: cream-white machine-made, no watermark; *leaf size*: cut flush, 181 x 122 mm.; *printing*: *type area*: 141 x 89 mm., excluding headlines; *lines-to-page*: set solid, 38 lines; *headlines*: *running titles*: all rectos and versos, pp. 4–7: STATEMENT OF PRINCIPLES
Publication: 1893; *print run*: unknown; *price*: see this field in A-53.01.
Register of Copies Examined: Bass (base copy).

A-54.01: The Glittering Plain (KP)

THE STORY OF THE GLITTERING | PLAIN. WHICH HAS BEEN ALSO | CALLED THE LAND OF LIVING | MEN OR THE ACRE OF THE UN- | DYING. WRITTEN BY WILLIAM | MORRIS.
Edition: 'Kelmscott Press Edition' [1st impression, 1st edn.] 1st pbd. in 4 instalments as 'The Glittering Plain; or, the Land of the Living Men', in *The English Illustrated Magazine* (1890, see D-513). The magazine version serving as copytext for this edn., Cockerell says, some authorial emendations of the copytext version were required: 'some of the chapter headings were rearranged, and a few small corrections were made in the text' (Cockerell, p. 148).
Collaborators, Editors, and Illustrators: Morris's border 1 was engraved by W. H. Hooper.
Series: The 1st book and the 1st Morris title pbd. by the KP.
Colophon: HERE endeth the Glittering Plain, printed by | William Morris at the Kelmscott Press, Up- | per Mall, Hammersmith, in the County of | Middlesex: and finished on the 4th day of | April of the year 1891. | [¶] Sold by Reeves & Turner 196 Strand London.
Collation: small 4°: a² b–2a⁴ 2b² (±2b²) [$2 (–b1) signed] 96 leaves pp. [4] [1] 2–188 [= 192]. Peterson finds a cancelled last gathering in a BL copy (see *KP Biblio.*, p. xxxii,), and explains that 2b² was 'reset in order to achieve tighter word-spacing'.
Contents: p. [1–2], blank; p. [3], title page; p. [4], headed: A Table of the Chapters of this Book | [contents printed continuous, not as a list, using the KP paragraph symbol to separate the 22 chapter titles]; p. 1, chapter head title, enclosed in border No. 1 and with a 10-line initial | [text begins]; pp. 2–187, text completed; p. 188, colophon.
Technical Notes: *paper*: Batcholor's hand-made Flower paper 1; *leaf size*: untrimmed deckled edges, avg. 193 x 142 mm.; *printing*: *type face*: Golden type; paragraph mark or 6-line initials indicate paragraphing throughout; *pagination*: arabic numbers at the outer margin on direction line; *end-papers*: 3 free ends and paste-down, plain white and blank, front and back; *binding*: limp natural vellum (4 of the vellum copies dyed green, see Cockerell, p. 148) with 2 wash lthr. ties (the only KP book with lthr. ties, see *KP Biblio*, p. 4); *spine*: gilt-stamped across (Golden type caps): THE | STORY | OF | THE | GLIT- | TER- | ING | PLAIN | BY | WIL- | LIAM | MORRIS | [at foot] 1891; *ornamentation*: 1 full border (No. 1); 10-line ornamental initials begin each of the 22 chapters; 30 6-line initials.
Publication: 4 Apr. 1891 [this colophon date indicates finished printing, issued 8 May] (Cockerell, p. 148); *print run*: 200 copies on paper (180 for sale), 6 on vellum; *price*: paper 2*gns.*, vellum: 12 and 15 *gns*.
Register of Copies Examined: VU (L, base copy: bookplate of Oliver Brett, 3rd Viscount Esher); BL (3 copies: Ashley 3692; C. 43. e. 1.; and C. 102. a. 19.); CSt (Gunst Z239.2/K29/M87sq).
Notes: in her bibliographical note on the publication of poems included in *Poems by the Way*, May Morris says the poem 'The Hall and the Wood' was written for the English Illustrated Magazine (Feb. 1890) at the request of Emery Walker, who was then one of the editors' (*CW*, IX.

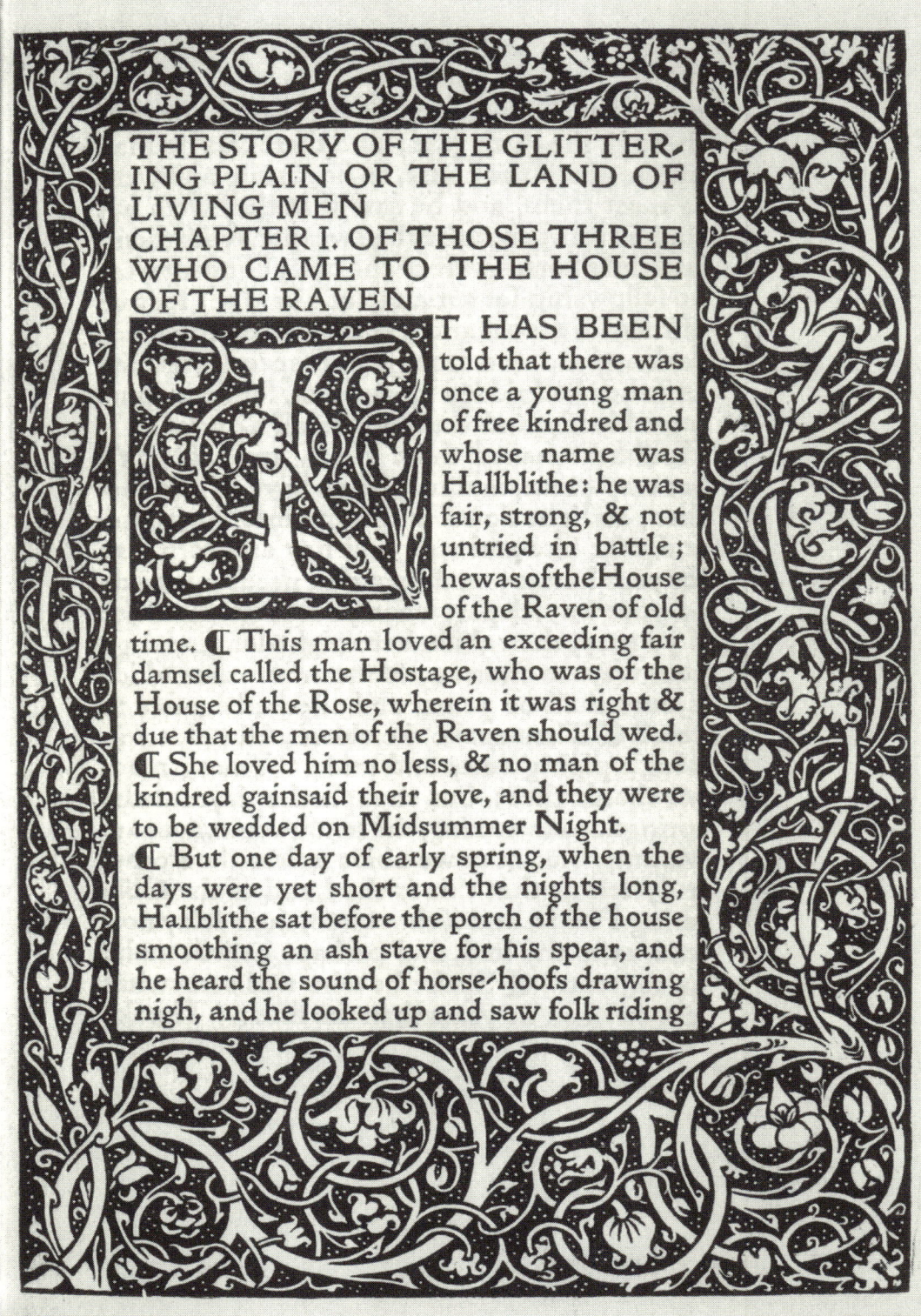

Figure 53. A-54.01: *The Glittering Plain* (KP edn.) head title

xxxiv–xxxv). From this, it seems likely that Walker was also important to Morris's decision to publish his *Story of the Glittering Plain* 1st in *The English Illustrated Magazine*. Peterson notes (*KP Biblio.*, p. 3) that the original plan was to publish *The Golden Legend* as the first KP book, but that was changed when the first shipment of Batchelor's paper proved to be not well enough sized for that purpose, which involved 4 full borders, elaborate ornaments and 2 Burne-Jones illus. In consequence a rather plain *Glittering Plain* was done instead. Later a much more elaborate edn.—this is the only title that appears in 2 KP edns—was illustrated by Walter Crane with 23 pictures (see A-54.05).

Later impression of this edn.: in the period covered here (to 1915), there was only one more impression of this edn., a facsimile; and that is described in A-54.03.

A-54.02: The Glittering Plain

THE STORY OF THE GLITTER-/|ING PLAIN WHICH HAS BEEN | ALSO CALLED THE LAND OF | LIVING MEN OR THE ACRE OF | THE UNDYING WRITTEN | BY WILLIAM MORRIS | LONDON: REEVES AND TURNER | MDCCCXCI

Edition: 'Popular Edition' [1st impression, 2nd edn.] For the 1st printing of this text in *The English Illustrated Magazine*, see D-513.

Collation: sq. post 8°, in 4s: A–Y⁴ Z² 90 leaves pp. [8] 1–172 [= 180].

Contents: p. [*1*], blank; p. [*2*], ad headed: MR. WILLIAM MORRIS'S WORKS.; p. [*3*], half title; p. [*4*], blank; p. [*5*], title page; p. [*6*], printer's imprint: CHISWICK PRESS:— C. WHITTINGHAM AND CO., TOOKS COURT, | CHANCERY LANE.; p. [*7*], headed: CONTENTS. | [22 chapter titles, as a list]; p. [*8*], blank; p. 1, general title, 1st chapter head title, and text begins; pp. 2–172, text completed with explicit: THE END. | [thin rule] | [imprint, as above]

Technical Notes: *paper*: cream-white machine-wove with dandy roll laid lines and no watermark; *leaf size*: untrimmed, avg. 182 x 142 mm.; *printing*: *lines-to-page*: set solid, 29 lines; *end-papers*: single free end and paste-down, plain white and blank, front and back; *binding*: dark green, cherry red or dark blue buckram with title gilt-stamped on front, duplicating that of the title page, and across the spine: THE STORY | OF THE | GLITTER- | ING PLAIN | [thin rule] | WILLIAM | MORRIS | [at foot] 5/- Net | REEVES | &. | TURNER

Publication: 1891 [issued Oct.] ('Publications of the Month', *BSR*, No. 404 (7 Nov. 1891), 1159); *print run*: 1,000 copies (Chiswick Arch.); *price*: 5s. net.

Register of Copies Examined: LeM (2 copies: base copy: blue binding); SSL (S823/M877); VSL (S823.89/M83S); CSt (Spec. Coll.Felton PR5079.S88); BL (12651. f. 76.)

Later issues and impressions of this edn.:

1. R and T: 1892 [issued 23–30 Apr.] (*Pub. Circ.*, 56/1348 (30 Apr. 1892), 485): 'Popular Edition' [2nd issue, 1st impression, 2nd edn.]; *print run*: copies remaining; *price*: 5s. net;
2. Longmans: 1896 [issued July]: 'Popular Edition'; see A-54.06;
3. Longmans: 1898 [issued 15 Feb.] (Longmans Arch.): NEW EDITION 'Popular Edition' [2nd impression, 2nd edn.]; *print run*: 500 copies; *price*: 5s. net;
4. Longmans: 1904 [issued 26 Aug.] (Longmans Arch.): NEW EDITION 'Popular Edition' [3rd impression, 2nd edn.]; *print run*: 500 copies; *price*: 5s. net;
5. Longmans: 1914 [6 Feb.] (Longmans Arch.): 'Popular Edition' [8th impression—this counts all the impressions in the Longmans' Class Books of English Literature series; hereafter referred to as LCBEL (see below, A-54.07) from this same 2nd edn.]; *print run*: 500 copies; *price*: 5s. net.

A-54.03: The Glittering Plain (RB)

[the first 6 lines of the title as in A-54.02, followed by the new edn. statement, publisher's imprint and date:] REPRINTED IN FAC-SIMILE | PUBLISHED BY ROBERTS BROTHERS, | AT THEIR HOUSE, 3 SOMERSET | STREET, BOSTON, 1891.

Edition: [2nd impression, 1st edn., 1st American] Since this is a facsimile reproduction of the book first issued by the Kelmscott Press, this is a 2nd impression of the 1st edn., 2nd in being issued well after the 1st, but a duplicate in all respects except the certificate of limitation, title page, printer's imprint, paper, end-papers, and binding, using the photo-electrotyping process to reproduce the letterpress. For the first printing of this text in *The English Illustrated Magazine*, see D-513.

Printer: plates produced by Gill Engraving Co. of New York (Roberts Arch.); machining by The University Press (see *Contents*, below).

Collation: small 4°: a² b–2a⁴ 2b² [$2 (–b1) signed] 96 leaves pp. [*4*] [1] 2–188 [=192].

Contents: p. [*1*], blank; p. [*2*], certificate of limitation: Limited Edition, Five Hundred Copies; p. [*3*], title page, as above; pp. [*4*], [1] 2–187, text completed; p. [188], printer's imprint: University Press:—John Wilson and Son, Cambridge, U. S. A.

Technical Notes: as in the 1st KP edn., A-54.01, except: *paper*: machine-made; *leaf size*: 225 x 148 mm.; *end-papers*: 1 free end and paste-down, plain white and blank, front and back; *binding*: tan 'vegetable parchment' covered boards, printed in gilt on front: [3-line ornamental red-on-gilt initial 'T'] THE STORY OF THE GLITTERING | PLAIN [3-line red-on-gilt ornamental initial 'W' with 4 fleurons to the right of the upper part of the 'W'] | [ornament leading to lower half of the initial 'W'] WHICH HAS BEEN ALSO | CALLED THE LAND OF THE LIVING MEN | OR THE ACRE OF THE UNDYING [fleuron] | [thin rule] | • WRITTEN BY [1 1/2-line red-on-gilt initial 'W' and 'M'] WILLIAM MORRIS •; *spine*: gilt-stamped across: THE | STORY | OF | THE | GLIT- | TER- | ING | PLAIN | BY | WILL- | IAM | MORRIS

Publication: 1891 [issued 7 Nov.–5 Dec.] (*Pub. Weekly*, Nos. 1030, 1036 (7 Nov., 5 Dec. 1891), 686, 930); *print run*: 550 copies of which 500 were for sale; *price*: $2.50.

Register of Copies Examined: MU (base copy: Spec.Coll PR 5079/S7, 1891a); NN.

Notes: William S. Peterson, in *KP Hist.* (196), quotes a letter from Morris to Reeves (16 June 1891) in response to Roberts' request to have copies of the KP. first edn. of *The Glittering Plain*, and asking permission to print an American edn. of *Poems by the Way* from an advance copy. Morris replied to Reeves that he would send them sheets if they agreed not try to reproduce the KP edition. This didn't and couldn't prevent RB from producing the photographic facsimile of *The Glittering Plain*, but that was the only KP reproduction they did, with the exception of the frontis. for *The Wood beyond the World*, which also appears as the frontis. to Roberts' 1st American edn. of that book.

A-54.04: The Glittering Plain (RB)

THE STORY OF THE GLITTER- | ING PLAIN WHICH HAS BEEN | ALSO CALLED THE LAND OF | LIVING MEN OR THE ACRE OF | THE UNDYING. WRITTEN | BY WILLIAM | MORRIS. | [fleuron] | PUBLISHED BY ROBERTS BROTHERS, | AT THEIR HOUSE, 3 SOMERSET | STREET, BOSTON, 1892.

Edition: 'Popular Edition' 'Cheap Edition' [1st impression, 3rd edn., 1st American] For the 1st printing of this text in *The English Illustrated Magazine*, see D-513.

Collation: 12°, printed, gathered, and sewn as 4° but signed as an 8°: [1]⁸ 2–14⁸ 112 leaves pp. [i–v] vi [vii] 8–220 [221–4] [= 224].

Contents: p. [i], half title; p. [ii], blank; p. [iii], title page; p. [iv], printer's imprint: [gothic type] University Press | [plain type] JOHN WILSON AND SON, CAMBRIDGE, U.S.A.; p. [v]–vi, headed: CONTENTS. | [as list, 22 chapter titles]; p. [7], 1st chapter head title, and text begins; pp. 8–220, text completed with explicit: THE END.; pp. [221–3], RB ads, headed: MR. WILLIAM MORRIS'S WORKS.; p. [224], blank.

Technical Notes: *paper*: cream-white machine-wove, with dandy roll laid lines, no watermark, t.e.g.; *leaf size*: lightly trimmed, avg. 186 x 131 mm.; *printing*: *type area*: 132 x 81 mm.; *headlines*: [all versos] THE STORY OF THE GLITTERING PLAIN | [all rectos, after the first] OR, THE LAND OF LIVING MEN.; *end-papers*: 1 free end and paste-down, plain white and blank, front and back; *binding*: plain unblocked dark red cloth, front gilt-stamped with duplicate title as in this field in A-54.03; *spine*: gilt-stamped across: THE | STORY | OF THE | GLITTERING | PLAIN | [fleuron] | WILLIAM | MORRIS | [publisher's monogram, 'R' interwoven with 'B']

Publication: 1892 [issued Jan.] (Cost Book E, Roberts Arch.); *print run*: 500 copies; *price*: $1.50.

Register of Copies Examined: LeM (2 copies: base copy); BGR; MH; NjR.

Notes: the Roberts Arch. shows that there were 12 sets of Morris stereos involving 11 titles (there being both an 8° set, the American facsimile, and a 12° set of *The Glittering Plain*, both described here). The stereos were all sold to Longmans by Little, Brown and Company on 24 May 1899.

Later issues and impressions of this edn.:

1.* RB: 1896 [issued Jan.] (Cost Book E, Roberts Arch.): 'Popular Edition' [2nd impression, 3rd edn., 1st American]; *print run*: 280 copies; *price*: $1.50;

2.* Longmans, NY: 1900 (*NUC*, cccxcvi. 161): 'Popular Edition' [2nd issue, 2nd impression, 3rd edn., 1st American]; *print run*: 188 copies remaining 'transferred from Messrs. Little, Brown, & Co., Boston' and given Longmans title pages and binding; *price*: $1.50;

3.* Longmans, NY: 1905 (*NUC*, cccxcvi. 161): 'Popular Edition' [3rd impression, 3rd edn., 1st American]; *print run* and *price*: unknown.

A-54.05: The Glittering Plain (2nd KP)

THE STORY OF THE GLITTERING | PLAIN. WHICH HAS BEEN ALSO CALLED | THE LAND OF THE LIVING MEN OR THE | ACRE OF THE UNDYING. WRITTEN BY | WILLIAM MORRIS.

Edition: 2nd 'Kelmscott Press Edition' [1st impression, 4th edn., 3rd English] This is the only book produced in 2

Kelmscott Press edns. For the 1st, see this field in A-54.01. The work was 1st pbd. in *The English Illustrated Magazine* (see D-513).

Collaborators, Editors, and Illustrators: 23 woodcut pictures by Walter Crane were cut by A. Leverett, with ornamental frames for each designed by William Morris.

Series: 22nd book, 9th Morris book, 2nd edn. of this title pbd. by the KP.

Colophon: HERE ends the tale of the Glittering Plain, writ-ten | by William Morris, & ornamented with 23 pictures | by Walter Crane. Printed at the Kelmscott Press, | Upper Mall, Hammersmith, in the County of Mid- | dlesex, & finished on the 13th day of January, 1894. | [KP mark No. 2] | Sold by William Morris, at the Kelmscott Press.

Collation: large 4° printed and gathered in 8s: [a]⁴ b–m⁸ n⁴ [$4 (–b1–3, c1 d3 e4 f4 h4 m2 n2–4) signed] 96 leaves pp. [8] [1] 2–177 [178–84] [= 192].

Contents: pp. [1–4], blank; p. [5], title page; p. [6], headed: [in Chaucer type] A LIST OF THE CHAPTERS OF THIS BOOK. | [22 chapter titles as a list]; p. [7], blank; p. [8], frontis., engraved title within border No. 12a: The Story | of the | Glittering | Plain | or the | Land of | Liv-ing | Men; p. [1], 1st chapter head, with full Morris border, No. 12, forming a compartment containing a head title, and an illus. with a full vine border, the head title, in red: Chapter I. Of those Three who came unto Hallblithe | to the House of the Raven [2 printer's flower ornament No. 3] | [text begins with 18-line initial 'I' as part of the border followed by a 5-line initial 'T' within the text compart-ment; pp. 2–178, text continues, with 21 further chapter head titles, each with an illus.; p. 179, text ends, with colo-phon (above); pp. [180–4], blank.

Technical Notes: *paper*: Flower paper No. 2 (BL copy); *leaf size*: deckled edges, avg. 289 x 209 mm.; *type face*: Troy type, contents page in Chaucer type; *printing*: printed in red and black, red for all chapter head titles; *type area*: set solid, 200 x 130 mm.; *end-papers*: usual KP treatment: 3 free ends and paste-down, all plain white and blank, front and back; *binding*: limp natural vellum with 3 pairs of green silk ties, gilt-stamped title in Troy type up the spine: THE GLITTERING PLAIN; *ornamentation*: 23 illus. by Walter Crane, each with a floral frame by Morris, one on each chapter head, plus one at the end of Chapter I, p. 4; 2 full borders by Morris: 12a and 12 and 7 frames for pic-tures; 20 half borders; 5 corner pieces; 13 full side borders; 26 part side borders; floriated initials: one 18-line 'I'; 16 8-line initials; 41 6-line initials; two 5-line initials; and 160 3-line initials.

Publication: 13 Jan. 1894 [this colophon date indicates fin-ished printing, issued 17 Feb.] (Cockerell, p. 156); *print run*: 250 copies on paper, 7 on vellum; *price*: 5gns. paper, vellum £20.

Register of Copies Examined: BL (2 copies: base copy: C. 43. f. 8.; and C. 69. h. 9.); NNBerg (presentation copy from Morris to E. Burne-Jones, dated by Morris, 'April 6th 1894'); NjP (Rosenwald Coll. PR 5079. 87 | 1894).

Notes: Kelvin's note on Morris's letter to Walter Crane of 24 Sept. [1891] quotes in full the agreement between Mor-ris and Crane on the division of any future profits from this KP edn.. It specifies equal shares (*Letters*, iii. 356).

A-54.06:* The Glittering Plain

Title: [as in A-54.02, except the new publisher's imprint:] LONGMANS, GREEN, AND CO. | LONDON, NEW YORK, AND BOMBAY. | 1896. | *All rights reserved*.

Edition: 'Popular Edition' [3rd issue, 1st impression, 2nd edn.] For the 1st printing of this text in *The English Illus-trated Magazine*, see D-513. Since this is another issue of the 2nd edn., only details of altered fields are included here.

Printer: Chiswick Press:—Charles Whittingham and Co., Tooks Court, Chancery Lane.

Technical Notes: *print run*: 200 copies of a cancel title page only, altered to include Longmans' imprint and the date '1896'; hence this is another issue, not a new impression or edn. (details otherwise as A-54.02).

Publication: 1896 [issued July] (*Eng. Cat.*, 5 (Jan. 1890–Dec. 1897), 690); *print run*: remaining Reeves and Turner copies for which 200 new cancel titles were printed (Chis-wick Arch.); *price*: 5s. net.

Register of Copies Examined: CSt (821.6/M87sp); BGR.

Notes: For Longmans, Green and Co.: 'Printing cancel titles to 4 books 4 pages each with paper for same pressing & folding viz: 400 Roots of the Mountains 200 Glittering Plain 100 House of the Wolfings 100 Poems by the Way' (Chiswick Arch., ledger for 1896, p. 601).

A-54.07: The Glittering Plain (LCBEL)

THE STORY OF THE GLITTER/ | ING PLAIN WHICH HAS BEEN | ALSO CALLED THE LAND OF | THE LIVING MEN OR THE ACRE OF | THE UNDYING WRITTEN | BY WILLIAM MORRIS | NEW IMPRESSION | LONGMANS, GREEN, AND CO. | LONDON, NEW YORK, BOMBAY, AND | [aligned flush left] CALCUTTA [aligned flush right] MCMV

Edition: NEW IMPRESSION. 'School Edition' [4th

impression, 2nd edn.] Here there are new preliminaries, including an Introduction, Notes, and a 2-page glossary at the end; but the text reproduces the 'Popular Edition' (the 2nd edn.), with signatures altered to suit the new format. Mackail's Introduction, except for its last 2 pages, devoted specifically to this title, is an anonymous version of the Introduction to the Silver Library Edition of *EP*.
Collaborators, Editors, and Illustrators: [edited with Introduction, notes, and a glossary by J. W. Mackail].
Series: LONGMANS' CLASS BOOKS OF ENGLISH | LITERATURE [on half title; for series details, see this field in A-110.01].
Collation: dbl. small. imperial, in 8s: [A]⁸ B–M⁸ 96 leaves pp. [i–iv] v–xvi [xvii–xviii] 1–173 [174] [= 192].
Contents: p. [i], half title; p. [ii], blank; p. [iii], title page; p. [iv], headed: BIBLIOGRAPHICAL NOTE. | [7 lines recording the 4 previous issues of this title]; p. v, headed: [flush left] INTRODUCTION.; pp. vi–xvi, introduction completed; p. [xvii], headed: [swash caps] CONTENTS | [22 chapter titles]; p. [xviii], blank; p. 1, 1st chapter head: [aligned left] THE STORY OF THE GLITTERING | PLAIN OR THE LAND OF LIVING | MEN. | CHAPTER I. OF THOSE THREE WHO | CAME TO THE HOUSE OF THE RAVEN. | [text begins]; pp. 2–172, text completed with explicit: THE END.; p. 173, headed: [flush left] GLOSSARY.; p. [174], glossary completed: [thin rule] | [printer's imprint] CHISWICK PRESS: PRINTED BY CHARLES WHITTINGHAM AND CO. | TOOKS COURT, CHANCERY LANE, LONDON.
Technical Notes: for detail common to the series—paper, leaf size, type area, headlines, pagination, end-papers, and binding—see this field in A-110.01.
Publication: Feb. 1905 ['Bibliographical Note' and 'Publications of the Month', *BSR*, No. 569 (5 Apr. 1905), 348]: 'LCBEL edition.'; *print run*: 2,000 copies; *price*: 2*s*. 6*d*.
Register of Copies Examined: BL (base copy: 012273.e.1/2.); LeM.
Notes: Chiswick Arch. Ledger (Jan. 1905) confirms that the 1st issue of this title in the LCBEL series was done from stereo plates.
Later impressions from this version: Longmans:
1. 1906 [issued 13 Sept.]: New Impression ' LCBEL' [5th impression, 2nd edn.]; *print run*: 2,000 copies; *price*: 2*s*. 6*d*.;
2. 1908 [issued 16 Sept.] (Longmans Arch.): New Impression 'LCBEL' [6th impression, 2nd edn.]; *print run*: 3,000 copies; *price*: 2*s*. 6*d*.;
3. 1912 [issued 20 July] (Longmans Arch.): New Impression 'LCBEL' [7th impression, 2nd edn.]; *print run*: 3,000 copies; *price*: 2*s*. 6*d*.;
Post-1915 impressions: 1918 [issued 9 May]; 1,000 copies printed by Clay; 1919 [issued 5 Dec.]; 2,000 copies by Clay.

A-54.08: The Glittering Plain (*CW* XIV)

THE COLLECTED WORKS [title details common to the set, see A-126.01] | VOLUME XIV | THE HOUSE OF THE WOLFINGS | THE STORY OF THE GLITTERING PLAIN | [publisher's imprint, see A-126.01] MDCCCCXII
Edition: 'Collected Works Edition' [1st impression, 5th edn., 4th English] For the 1st pbn. of *The Glittering Plain* in *The English Illustrated Magazine*, see D-513. The details specific to this edn. of this title—*Collation*, *Contents*, and *Technical Notes*—are entered under A-47.05: *The House of the Wolfings*. For details common to the *CW*, see A-126.01.
Publication: 1912 [issued 31 Oct.] (Longmans Arch.); *print run* and *price*: see A-126.01.
Register of Copies Examined: see this field in A-126.01.

A-54.09: The Glittering Plain (LPL)

THE STORY OF THE GLITTER- | ING PLAIN WHICH HAS BEEN | ALSO CALLED THE LAND OF | THE LIVING MEN OR THE ACRE OF | THE UNDYING WRITTEN | BY WILLIAM MORRIS | POCKET EDITION | LONGMANS, GREEN AND CO. | 39 PATERNOSTER ROW, LONDON | NEW YORK, BOMBAY, AND CALCUTTA | 1913
Edition: Pocket Edition [1st impression, 6th edn., 5th English] For the 1st pbn. of *The Glittering Plain* in *The English Illustrated Magazine*, see D-513.
Series: Longmans Pocket Library [for further series detail, see this field in the record of the 1st book in the series, *Jason*: A-3.09].
Collation: fcap 8°: π⁴ A–I⁸ K¹⁰ [$1 (+K5 signed K2) signed] 86 leaves pp. [2] [i–iv] v–vi [1] 2–161 [162–4] [= 172].
Contents: pp. [1–2], Longmans ads; p. [i], half title; p. [ii], blank; p. [iii], title page; p. [iv], headed: BIBLIOGRAPHICAL NOTE | [list of 7 issues of this title]; pp. v–vi, headed: CONTENTS | [list of 22 chapters]; p. [1], 1st chapter head title; pp. 2–161, text completed with explicit: Herewith Endeth the Tale. | [printer's imprint] Printed by Ballantyne, Hanson & Co. | at Paul's Work, Edinburgh; pp. [162–4], blank.
Technical Notes: for points common to the series—paper, leaf size, type area, position of headlines, running titles,

shoulder notes, end-papers, and binding—see this field in A-3.09, the entry for *Jason*, the 1st title in this series. Details specific to this particular edn.: *printing*: *running heads*: all versos: THE STORY OF THE GLITTERING PLAIN | [all rectos:] OR THE LAND OF LIVING MEN.
Publication: 1913 ['to be issued' 17 Nov.] (Longmans ad, *Pub. Circ.* 99 (5 Nov. 1913), 646); *print run*: 3,000 copies (Longmans Arch.); *price*: cloth 2*s*., lthr. 3*s*.
Register of Copies Examined: LeM (base copy).
Notes: total cost of production, not including binding = £30. 9*s*. 11*d*. (Longmans Arch.).

A-55.01: A King's Lesson (Leatham, 1st edn.)

Reprinted in this form by the kind permission of Messrs. Reeves | & Turner, Publishers of Mr. Morris's Works. | A KING'S LESSON | BY | WILLIAM MORRIS | *Author of "The Earthly Paradise," etc.* | [in gothic] **Aberdeen:** | [plain text] PRINTED AND PUBLISHED BY JAMES LEATHAM | 15 ST. NICHOLAS STREET | [thin rule] | 1891

Edition: [1st impression, 1st separate edn.] 1st pbd. Sept. 1886, in *Commonweal*, as 'An Old Story Retold' (see D-227), then, in 1888, in *A Dream of John Ball and A King's Lesson*. This 1st separate impression was also pbd. in an LP variant with a heavy light-grey paper wrapper with letterpress that duplicates the title page, except for omitting the permission notice at the top.
Series: Penny Pamphlet series.
Collation: demy 16°, printed and gathered as a single 8° sht. [1]⁸: 8 leaves pp. [1–3] 4–16 [= 16] + grey paper wrapper stapled in the centre fold. Similar in format, size, paper, and style of binding to such SL pamphlets as *The Aims of Art* (1887).
Contents: p. [1], title page; p. [2], ad for 3 pamphlets, all 'price one penny'; p. [3], head title: [in gothic] A King's Lesson. | [thin ornamental rule] | [3-line drop to text, which begins with an ornamental initial drop cap 'I']; pp. 4–14, text completed; pp. [15–16], ads for 33 'Books for Sale' and 'to be had from J. Leatham, 15 St. Nicholas Street, Aberdeen.'
Technical Notes: *paper*: cream-white machine-made; *leaf size*: BL LP copy is trimmed for a library binding, 141 x 112 mm., ordinary copy trimmed: 136 x 109 mm.; *printing*: type area: 85 x 68 mm.; lines-to-page: set solid, 25 lines; *pagination*: arabic numbers centred on headline; *binding*: *wrapper*: light-grey machine-made paper, p. [1], duplicate of title page except omitting the permission note; p. [2], ads headed: **Penny Pamphlets**; p. [3]: 'List of Works by Mr. William Morris published by Reeves and Turner, 196 Strand, London. W.C.' followed by a list of 11 Morris books; p. [4]: ad for *The Roots of the Mountains*.
Publication: 1891 [issued before 3 May] (the BL copy—012629.e.2—has an accession date of '3 My 91'); *print run*: not known; *price*: 1*d*.
Register of Copies Examined: BL (base copy: 012629.e.2.; Bass; TxU; MH (EC85 M834 B898p); Fdmn; IISH (E1780/87a).
Notes: this pamphlet in its various edns.—and each new printing is reset, as was characteristic of Leatham, perhaps because he, a self-employed printer, found that cheaper, and more fun, than making stereotype plates—marks the many stages of Leatham's career as a Socialist printer and publisher. The 1st edn. issued from his 1st print shop, established in Aberdeen in 1889, with later edns. being produced in the various places in which he later set up shop: the 2nd and 3rd edns. produced in Peterhead, northern Scotland, in 1901 and 1902; the 4th in Cottingham. The BLC says '1910?', but Leatham owned and operated The Cottingham Press between 1912 and 1916. The 5th and 6th edns. were produced at his last printing business, the Deveron Press, at Turriff, where Leatham lived from 1916 until his death in 1945. As indicated in the ads in his journal, *The Gateway*, the Morris pamphlets Leatham pbd.—*A King's Lesson*, *Under an Elm-Tree*, and *The Revolt of Ghent*—he kept in print until he died. He wrote an introduction for another Morris pamphlet, *A Factory as it Might Be* (1907, see A-108.02), but that was commissioned and the pamphlet pbd. in London by the Twentieth Century Press.

There is some difficulty determining which title—*A King's Lesson* or *Under an Elm-Tree*—came 1st. Three factors suggest that *A King's Lesson* had priority: (1), it was advertised in the 1st edn. of *Under an Elm-Tree*, but the latter is not mentioned in the first edn. of *A King's Lesson*; (2nd), the order suggested here is the order in which Leatham put them in his Bijou series; and (3rd), the earliest ad. found for either is from *The Workers' Herald*, Jan. 16 1891, and that is for *A King's Lesson*.

A-55.02: A King's Lesson (Leatham, 2nd edn.)

[wrapper title, swash caps, flush left] A KING'S LESSON. | [plain type] BY | WILLIAM MORRIS, | AUTHOR OF "THE | EARTHLY PARADISE." | [flush right, opposite the title] Second | Edition. | Cum privilegio auctoris. | [flush left] ONE . . | PENNY. [opposite, flush right] PETERHEAD: SENTINEL OFFICE. | LONDON: TWENTIETH CENTURY PRESS. | 1901

Edition: Second Edition. [1st impression, 2nd edn.] 1st pbd. Sept. 1886 in *Commonweal*, as 'An Old Story Retold' (see D-227), then, in 1888, in *A Dream of John Ball and A King's Lesson*.
Series: Though the 'Leek Bijou Reprints' name is not used here, that Leek series' characteristics—derived from the series as issued by Wm. Larner Sugden and Ethelbert Edward Minton in the 1880s—are prominent here, including the formulaic permission: <u>Cum privilegio Auctoris</u>, the elaborate design of the wrapper title, and the printing of the wrapper in colored ink on colored paper. The 1st in Leatham's 'Bijou Reprint' series, described in the next entry, is the 2nd edn. of this title, uses the original series name (see the next entry). The Bijou Reprint No. 2, the 3rd edn. of *Under an Elm-Tree; Or, Thoughts in the Country-Side*, issued in 1902, advertises this pamphlet version of *A King's Lesson* as 'Uniform with this booklet'.
Collation: demy 16°: [1]⁸ 8 leaves, folded in sequence and sewn through the fold to the wrapper, pp. [1] 2–16 [= 16] + yellow wrapper with the title.
Contents: p. [1], dropped head: A KING'S LESSON. | [text begins]; pp. 2–16, text completed with explicit: THE END.
Technical Notes: *paper*: cream machine-moulded 'antique' paper, with dandy roll laid lines, no watermark, vertical chain lines; *leaf size*: cut flush, 133 x 125 mm.; *printing*: *type area*: 77 x 59 mm. excluding head and direction lines; *lines-to-page*: set solid, 22 lines; *pagination*: arabic numbers centred on headline; *binding*: *wrapper*: pale yellow 'antique' machine-moulded paper, printed in brown, with dandy roll laid lines; p. [1], wrapper title, as above; pp. [2–4], ads, headed: Sentinel Publications
Publication: 1901; *print run*: not known; *price*: 1d.
Register of Copies Examined: BL (base copy: Proctor's copy: Cup.503. a. 3.); MU (Spec. Coll. PR 5079 K5 1901).

A-55.03:* **A King's Lesson (Leatham, 3rd edn.)**

[wrapper title and other details deduced from A-55.01, *NUC*, and A-56.04] <u>The Bijou Reprints, No. 1.</u> | [flush left, plain type] <u>A KING'S LESSON.</u> [flush right, opposite title] <u>Third</u> | <u>Edition.</u> | [flush left, gothic] <u>Cum privilegio</u> | <u>Auctoris.</u> [flush right, italic, opposite permission notice] <u>ONE</u> | <u>PENNY.</u> | [centred] PETERHEAD: *SENTINEL* OFFICE. | LONDON: TWENTIETH CENTURY PRESS, LTD. | 1902.
Edition: [1st impression, 3rd edn.] for the earliest pbn. of this text in *Commonweal*, see D-227.

Collation: s. sht. 8°: [1]⁸ 8 leaves sewn through the centrefold, pp. [1–4] 5–16 [= 16] + coloured wrapper.
Contents: p. [1], half title; p. [2], imprint: IMPRINTED AT THE | OFFICE OF THE | "PETERHEAD SEN- | TINEL," IN THE | TOWN OF PETER- | HEAD. MCMI.; p. [3], head-title: [below ornamental head-piece] A KING'S LESSON | [text begins]; pp. 4–16, text completed with tail-piece.
Technical Notes: *paper*: cream machine-made; *leaf size*: 129 x 96 mm.; *printing*: *type area*: 69 x 60 mm., excluding head and direction lines; *pagination*: arabic numbers centred on headlines; *binding*: *wrapper*: pale yellow with red letterpress; p. [1], wrapper title; pp. [2–4], ads, each wrapper page: [in gothic] Sentinel Publications
Publication: 1902; *price*: 1d.; *print run*: not known.
Register of Copies Located: CSmH.
Notes: ads in the 'Third Edition' of *Under an Elm-Tree*, 'The Bijou Reprints No. 2' (A-56.04), refer on the verso of the wrapper title to this version of *A King's Lesson* as 'uniform with this booklet'.

A-55.04: A King's Lesson (+ News from Nowhere and John Ball *CW* XVI)

THE COLLECTED WORKS | [title details common to the set, see A-126.01] | VOLUME XVI | NEWS FROM NOWHERE | A DREAM OF JOHN BALL | A KING'S LESSON | [publisher's imprint, see A-126.01] MDCCCCXII
Edition: 'The Collected Works Edition' [1st impression, 5th edn.] For the earliest pbn. of this text in *Commonweal*, see D-227. Here bound in a composite vol. with *News from Nowhere* and *A Dream of John Ball*. For all details common to the set, particularly *Technical Notes*, see the entry for the *CW*, A-126.01. For the *Collation* and *Contents* of this vol. see A-50.08. Only details of altered fields are included here.
Series: vol. 16 of 24. For series details, see this field in A-126.01.
Publication: 1912 [issued 31 Oct.]; *print run* and *price*: see A-126.01.
Register of Copies Examined: see this field in A-126.01.

A-55.05: A King's Lesson (Leatham, 4th edn.)

[wrapper title:] A King's Lesson | BY | WILLIAM MORRIS | [typographical rule] | COTTINGHAM | THE COTTINGHAM PRESS
Edition: Fourth Edition. [1st impression, 6th edn.] For the earliest pbn. of this text in *Commonweal*, see D-227.

Original and Posthumous Editions

Collation: 16°: [1]⁶ 6 leaves pp. [1] 2–12 [= 12] + a coloured paper wrapper stapled twice to the leaves through the centrefold.

Contents: p. [1], head title: [ornamental head piece] | [dropped head title] A King's Lesson. | [text begins]; pp. 2–12, text completed.

Technical Notes: *paper*: cream machine-wove; *leaf size*: 163 x 104 mm.; *printing*: type area: 117 x 71 mm.; *lines-to-page*: set solid, 28 lines; *running titles*: [all versos] A KING'S | [all rectos] LESSON; *binding*: wrapper: rough tan paper: p. [1], wrapper title, see above; pp. [2–3], blank; p. [4], ads, headed: Publications by James Leatham

Publication: [1912–16] (the period of Leatham's Cottingham Press); *print run*: unknown; *price*: 1d.

Register of Copies Examined: BL (base copy: 072629.e.13); IISH (E1780/87c); An-C-TU (Morris Pam M677 K55 1910).

Later editions: After 1916 at least 2 further edns. of this title were issued during Leatham's time in Turriff (1916–45), where he established the Deveron Press.

A-56.01: Under An Elm-Tree (Leatham 1st edn.)

[wrapper title, above the top border:] **Sold by William Reeves. 185. Fleet Street, E.C.** | (Where all J. Leatham's pamphlets are now to be had.) | [below top ornamental border] | PRICE ONE PENNY | [thin rule] | [in neo-gothic, formatted hanging indent] **Under an Elm-Tree;** | [plain type] *Or, Thoughts in the* | *Country-side. By* | *Wm. Morris, Author* | *of "The Earthly Paradise,"* | *&c., &c.* | [thin rule] | ABERDEEN: | PRINTED AND PUBLISHED BY JAMES LEATHAM, | 15, ST. NICHOLAS STREET. | [thin rule] | 1891. | [typographical border at the bottom]

Edition: [1st impression, 1st edn.] Originally published in *Commonweal*, in July 1889 (see D-465). This pamphlet was sophisticated by the addition of a 'pale green printed wrapper' created by H. B. Forman (see E-12), but copies with the wrapper seem never to have reached the sale room (see *Sequel*, 212). On the question of the sequence of this title relative to *A King's Lesson*, see the *Notes* field in *A King's Lesson* (A-55.01).

Series: Penny Pamphlets.

Collation: 16°: [1]⁸ 8 leaves folded in sequence and sewn through the centre, pp. [1–3] 4–16 [= 16] self-wrappered.

Contents: p. [1], title page; p. [2], ads, headed: PENNY PAMPHLETS; p. [3], dropped head, general title and text begins; pp. 4–16, text completed.

Technical Notes: *paper*: cream machine-made, no watermark; *leaf size*: 146 x 114 mm.; *printing*: type area: 91 x 59

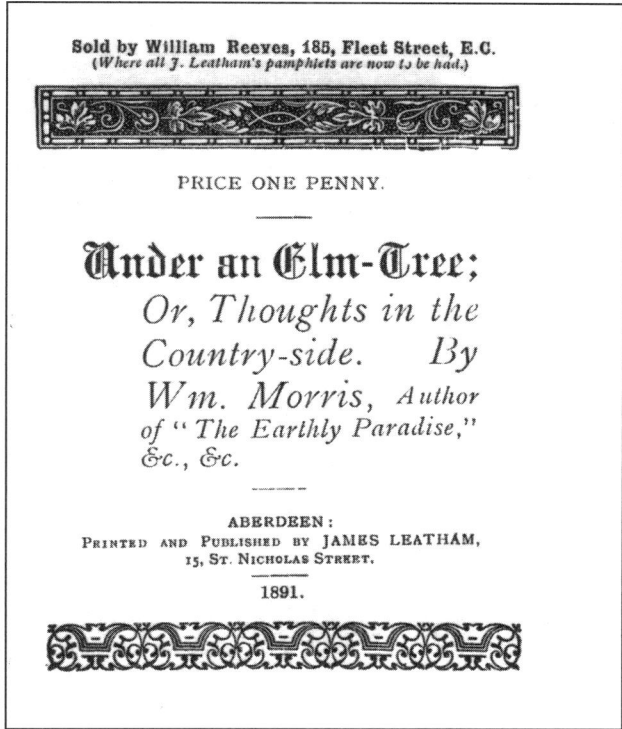

Figure 54. A-56.01: *Under an Elm-Tree* (1st edn.) wrapper title

mm.

Publication: 1891. James Leatham pbd., with Morris's authorisation, the 1st separate edns. of this text. The 2 earliest edns., both dated 1891 on the wrapper title (Fdmn, An-C-TU, and BL have both these edns.) present a problem as to which is the 1st edn.. Some of the following comparisons (including collation by means of transparencies) suggest that the 2 edns.—A-56.01 and A-56.02, called here 'A' and 'B'—are, respectively, the 1st and 2nd edns. (see *Notes*, below).

Register of Copies Examined: BL (6 copies of this title, of which 2 are dated 1891: base copy: Cup. 502. f.11. (19) & (20) the latter here placed as 2nd edn. and called here 'B', the 1st edn. being called here 'A'); Fdmn (2 bound copies, both 1st & 2nd edns); CaBVau; TxU; MH; Bass; An-C-TU (1st & 2nd edns); LeM (2nd edn.)

Notes: as is customary with Leatham, the 2 pamphlets are different settings, i.e. 2 edns., done with different type fonts, including different display type and ornaments on the title pages. Though the type faces are similar, one, 'B', has a narrower 'A-to-Z' measure than 'A'; the text is divided at exactly the same point on each page, suggesting that one is set from the other. But neither is a 'facsimile reprint' edn., the 2nd having, as well as a different font, different ornamental borders on the title-wrapper, top and bottom.

Different type and typographical errors in both versions would appear at first glance to tell us only that these are different settings, not that one is a corrected version of the other. A lower-case 's' on the title page and in the running title 'Country-side' on p. 9 of 'A', an inconsistent 'Under the Elm-Tree' in the running title on p. 16, these are all correct in 'B'; but 'B' has two errors not found in 'A': an ungrammatical 'than' replaces 'that' in the 5th line from the bottom of p. 7, and a superfluous 'he' is repeated in the next line. While in general one would expect errors to be corrected in later edns., resetting always opens the possibility of new errors. Thus, priority is not firmly established by any of these differences in the text. But the change in the capitalisation to 'Country-Side' in B seems more like a correction of the 'A' (or 1st) edn. because it is maintained consistently through B and through all subsequent edns. There are fewer errors in 'B'. Further, since 'A' lists William Reeves as the London distributor, a unique feature of this version compared to all the rest of the series, but a feature that also distinguishes the 1st, that appears to be an experiment abandoned by Leatham thereafter, for all his productions. Such at least are here the grounds, and they are only probabilities, on which 'A' is given precedence over 'B'.

A-56.02: Under An Elm-Tree (Leatham 2nd edn.)

[wrapper title, typographical border] | PRICE ONE PENNY. | [thin rule] | [in neo-gothic, formatted as a hanging indent] **UNDER AN ELM-TREE;** | [plain text] *Or, Thoughts In The* | *Country-Side. By* | *Wm. Morris, Author* | *Of "The Earthly Paradise," | &c. &c.* | [thin rule] | [in neo-gothic] **Aberdeen:** | [plain text] PRINTED AND PUBLISHED BY JAMES LEATHAM, | 15 ST. NICHOLAS STREET. | [thin rule] | 1891. | [typographical border repeated]

Edition: [1st impression, 2nd edn.] Originally pbd. in *Commonweal*, in July 1889 (see D-465). This is the 2nd of 2 different but similar edns. of this pamphlet in the same year. For the reasons for the precedence used here, see this field in A-56.01.

Series: Penny Pamphlets.

Collation: demy 16°: [1]⁸ 8 leaves pp. [1–3] 4–16 [= 16] self-wrappered, single gathering sewn through the centrefold.

Contents: p. [1], title page; p. [2], ad for Leatham's 'PENNY PAMPHLETS', including a listing of *A King's Lesson*; p. [3], head title and text begins: [dropped head, in hanging indent:] UNDER AN ELM-TREE; | OR, THOUGHTS ON THE COUNTRY-SIDE | [thin rule] | [text begins]; pp. 4–16, text completed.

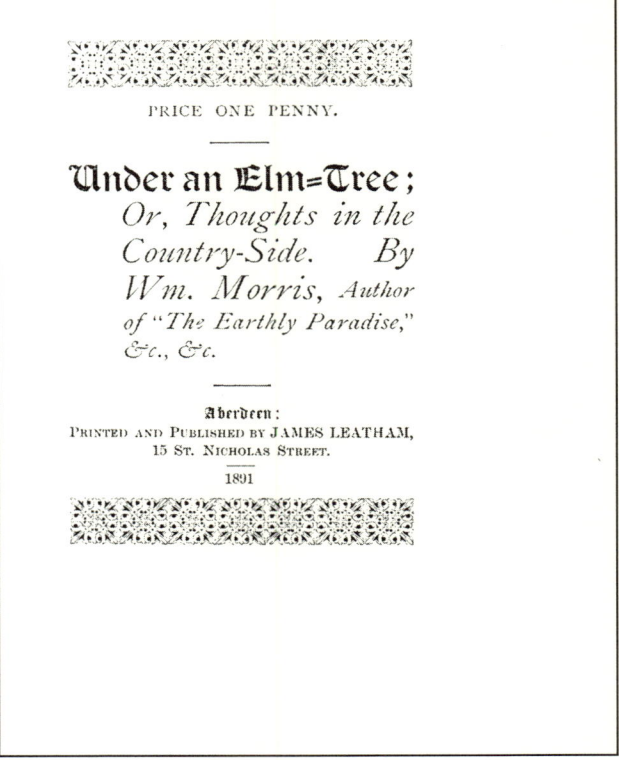

Figure 55. A-56.02: *Under an Elm-Tree* (2nd edn.) wrapper title

Technical Notes: *paper*: cream machine-made, no watermark; *leaf size*: uncut, 144 x 110 mm.; *printing*: *type area*: 82 x 59 mm., excluding head and direction lines; *running titles*: pp. 5–16: [versos] Under an Elm-Tree | [rectos] Or, Thoughts in the Country-Side.; *binding*: self-wrappered.

Publication: 1891 [since *A King's Lesson* was issued sometime before 3 May (see A-55.01), and it was the 1st pbd., probably late May or early June 1891]; *print run*: unknown; *price*: 1d.

Register of Copies Examined: BL (2 copies: Proctor's copy: (Cup. 503. a. 3. and Cockerell's copy: Cup. 502. f. 11 (20); Fdmn (bound copy); CaBVau; TxU; MH; Bass; An-C-TU.

A-56.03:* Under An Elm-Tree (Burke)

UNDER AN ELM-TREE; OR, THOUGHTS IN THE COUNTRY-SIDE

Edition: New Edition. [1st impression, 3rd separate edn.] Originally published in *Commonweal*, see D-465.

Collaborators: With a foreword by Horace Burke.

Place: Hammersmith.

Publisher: Printed at the Liberty Press for the Liberty Group of Anarchist-Communists.

Publication: 1893? (*NUC*, cccxcvi. 163).
Register of Copies Located: IEN (305 M87un 1893).

A-56.04: Under An Elm-Tree (Leatham 3rd edn.)

[wrapper title, part double underlined] The Bijou Reprints, No. 2. | [aligned left] UNDER AN ELM-TREE; | • OR, THOUGHTS IN • | THE COUNTRY-SIDE • | BY WILLIAM MORRIS, | • AUTHOR OF "THE • | EARTHLY PARADISE •" | [aligned right, opposite lines 3–4 of the title] Third | Edition. | [aligned left, in gothic] Cum privilegio | Auctoris. [aligned right] ONE | PENNY. | [imprint, centred at the foot] PETERHEAD: *SENTINEL* OFFICE. | LONDON: TWENTIETH CENTURY PRESS, LTD. | 1902.

Edition: [1st impression, 3rd edn.] Originally published in *Commonweal*, for publishing history see D-465.

Collation: 16°: [1]⁸ 8 leaves; pp. [1–3] 4–16 [= 16] + coloured paper wrapper stitched through the centrefold to the body.

Contents: p. [1], half title; p. [2], imprint: IMPRINTED AT THE | OFFICE OF THE | "PETERHEAD SEN- | TINEL," IN THE | TOWN OF PETER- | HEAD. MCMII.; p. [3], [ornamental head-piece] | [flush left, formatted in hanging indent] UNDER AN ELM-TREE; | OR, THOUGHTS IN THE | COUNTRY-SIDE. [printer's flower] | [text begins with a 2-line illuminated initial 'M']; pp. 4–16, text completed.

Technical Notes: as in the entry for Bijou Reprints No. 1, *A King's Lesson*, A-55.02, with adjustments for the change of title; *wrapper*: printed dark brown on light-brown laid paper; wrapper p. [1], title, as above; pp. [2–4], headed *Sentinel* Publications | [list completed].

Publication: 1902; *print run*: unknown; *price*: 1d.
Register of Copies Examined: ABCL (base copy: LoP 828+20 | 739y); BL 8290.a.15.)

A-56.05: Under An Elm-Tree (Leatham 4th edn.)

[thick-thin rule] | [title in hanging indent] Under an Elm-Tree; | or, Thoughts in the | Country-Side. . By | William Morris. . | with a Foreword by James | Leatham. Fourth Edition. . | Imprinted and Sold at the | Clerkhill Press, Peterhead. . | [double thick-thin rule]

Edition: Fourth Edition. [1st impression, 4th edn.] Originally published in *Commonweal*, 6 July 1889. For full pbn. history, see D-465.

Collation: square 16°: [1]⁸ 8 leaves pp. [1–2] 3–4 [5] 6–16 [= 16] + light green paper wrapper stitched to the body through the centrefold,.

Contents: p. [1], title page, see above; p. [2], [abstract ornamental head-piece] | [headed] FOREWORD. | [text begins]; pp. 3–4, Foreword completed with initials: J. L.; p. [5], headed: [ornamental leaf-and-vine head-piece] | Under an Elm-Tree; | or, Thoughts in the | Country-Side | [text begins]; pp. 6–16, text completed with abstract ornamental tail-piece.

Technical Notes: *paper*: plain cream machine-made, no watermark; *leaf size*: cut flush, 145 x 95 mm.; *binding*: *wrapper*: printed black on light green machine-made paper: p. [1]: Under an Elm-Tree; | Or, Thoughts in the Country-Side | [Hollyer photograph of Morris, within a thin rule box] | FOURTH EDITION. PRICE ONE PENNY; pp. [2–4] are devoted to ads for Leatham's pamphlets.

Publication: n.d. (between 1902, the date of the 3rd edn. and 1908, when Leatham left Peterhead for Huddersfield] (*BLC* proposes '[1910 ?]'; but that is after Leatham's time at Peterhead).

Register of Copies Examined: BL (2 copies: base copy: 8290. a. 15. and 08275. de. 32.)

A-56.06: Under An Elm-Tree (*Bib.*)

[wrapper title, above the compartment, top left] VOL. XVIII. [top right] No. 4 | [within thin-rule compartment, top left] | *APRIL* [top right] *MDCCCCXII* | [for title details common to the series, see A-83.01] | [below compartment, aligned right, in red] UNDER AN ELM-TREE | BY WILLIAM MORRIS | THE HAPPIEST OF POETS | BY W. B. YEATS

Edition: [1st impression, 6th edn., 1st American] Originally published in *Commonweal*, see D-465. Here Morris's text is followed by an extract from W. B. Yeats's 'The Happiest of Poets', an essay on Morris that serves as an afterword to the Morris text. On pagination and ads, see *Series* and *Collation* fields in A-83.01.

Collaborators, Editors, and Illustrators: foreword [unsigned by the editor, T. B. Mosher], and an extract from W. B. Yeats's 'The Happiest of Poets' as an afterword.

Series: The Bibelot: A Reprint of Poetry and Prose for Book Lovers, chosen in part from scarce editions and sources not generally known (hereafter referred as Bib.), 18/4 (Apr. 1912), 103–11. For detail common to this series, see this field in A-83.01.

Place, Publisher, and Printer: see the wrapper transcriptions in A-83.01.

Collation: 12°: [1]²⁰ 20 leaves pp. [4] [97–102] 103–28 [4] [= 40] + a light blue machine-laid paper wrapper sewn to the body through the centrefold. The separate issue of this title has not been seen. Certain details of pagination and contents have been supplied by Mr Philip Bishop, Mosher's bibliographer. On pagination, see this field and *Series* in A-83.01.

Contents: p. [*1–4*], ads. pp. [97–100], unsigned and untitled foreword (by the editor, T. B. Mosher); p. [101], half title: [top, aligned left] UNDER AN ELM-TREE | *By* | WILLIAM MORRIS. | [thin rule] | THE HAPPIEST OF POETS | *By* | W. B. YEATS.; p. [102], blank; p. 103, headed, flush left: UNDER AN ELM-TREE; OR, | THOUGHTS ON THE COUNTRY- | SIDE | [text begins]; pp. 104–11, Morris text completed; p. 112, headed, flush left: THE HAPPIEST OF POETS; pp. 113–28, Yeats text completed.

Technical Notes: for details common to the series—paper, leaf size, printing, type area, lines-to-page, pagination, and binding—see this field in A-83.01; details specific to this issue: *running titles* (for Yeats's essay only): [flush to the inner margin, all rectos and versos] THE HAPPIEST OF POETS; wrapper: printed in red and black, p. [*1*], wrapper title, see above; pp. [*2–4*] common to the series, see A-83.01.

Publication: Apr. 1912 [masthead date, issued 25 Mar.]; *print run* and *price*: see this field in A-83.01.

Register of Copies Examined: Bsp (base copy).

A-57.01: Saga Library (vol. II)

THE STORY OF THE | ERE-DWELLERS | (EYRBYGGJA SAGA), | WITH | THE STORY OF THE HEATH-SLAYINGS | (HEIðARVÍGA SAGA) | AS APPENDIX | DONE INTO ENGLISH | OUT OF THE ICELANDIC | BY | WILLIAM MORRIS | AND | EIRÍKR MAGNÚSSON | LONDON | BERNARD QUARITCH, 15 PICCADILLY | 1892

Edition: [1st impression, 1st edn.] As with all 1st issues of the 6 vols. of the Saga Library, in addition to the ordinary edn. there was a LP variant of 125 copies on Whatman's hand-made paper, all numbered.

Series: The Saga Library, vol. II. For further series detail, see this field in A-52.01, the 1st vol. in the set.

Collation: cr. 8°: [a]⁸ b–c⁸ d² (d2+1) B–N⁸ (N7+1) O–2C⁸ 2D⁶ 232 leaves pp. [i–v] vi–lii [1–3] 4–190 191–410 [411–12] [= 464] + 2 inserted leaves noted in the formula but not counted in the book's pagination. They are described in their appropriate places under *Contents*.

Contents: p. [i], half title: THE SAGA LIBRARY | EDITED BY | WILLIAM MORRIS | AND | EIRÍKR MAGNÚSSON | VOL. II | EYRBYGGJA SAGA; p. [ii], blank; p. [iii], title page; p. [iv], printer's imprint: CHISWICK PRESS:—C. WHITTINGHAM AND CO., TOOKS COURT, | CHANCERY LANE.; p. [v], dropped head: CONTENTS. | [list begins of 65 chapter titles + Appendices A and B]; pp. vi–ix, Contents completed; p. [x], blank; p. xi, dropped head: PREFACE. | [text begins]; pp. xii–xlviii, Preface completed; p. xlix, dropped head: CHRONOLOGICAL LIST | [list begins]; pp. l–lii, list completed; inserted leaf tipped in to face p. lii, list printed on recto headed: ADDENDA AND CORRIGENDA. | [22 corrections, as a list], verso blank; p. [1], 2nd half title: THE STORY | OF | THE ERE-DWELLERS.; p. [2], map, to face head title, oriented vertically, with caption within a small inset compartment, upper left: [aligned left] MAP OF THE | COUNTRY OF | THE ERE-DWEL- | LERS' STORY; p. [3], dropped head title: THE STORY | OF | THE ERE-DWELLERS. | [flush left] CHAPTER I. HEREIN IS TOLD HOW KETIL FLATNEB | FARES TO WEST-OVER-SEA. | [text begins]; pp. 4–186, text completed with explicit: AND HEREWITH ENDETH THE | STORY OF THE THORSNESSINGS, THE ERE-DWELLERS AND THE SWANFIRTHERS.; p. [187], section half title: APPENDIX.; p. [188], blank; p. [189], dropped head: APPENDIX A. | THE CHILDREN OF SNORRI THE PRIEST. | [reference to source] | [text begins]; p. 190, text completed; inserted map facing p. 191, recto blank [not counted in pagination or gathering], with caption on smaller internal compartment: MAP FOR THE | STORY OF THE | HEATHSLAYINGS; p. 191, dropped head: APPENDIX B. | THE STORY OF THE HEATHSLAYINGS, OF WHICH | ONLY A PART IS LEFT. | [text begins]; pp. 192–259, text completed with formulaic explicit: And there endeth this story.; p. [260], blank; p. [261], half title: NOTES.; p. [262], blank; p. [263], dropped head: NOTES. | [Notes begin]; pp. 264–304, Notes completed; p. [305], half title: GENEALOGIES.; p. [306], blank; p. [307], dropped head: GENEALOGIES. | [diagrams of family trees begin]; pp. 308–15, genealogies completed; p. [316], blank; p. [317], half title: INDEX.; p. [318], blank; p. [319], dropped head: INDEX. | I. PERSONS | [list begins; pp. 320–64, Index I. completed; followed by a new heading: Index II. Places | [list begins]; pp. 365–85: list completed, followed by a new heading: III. SUBJECT MATTER. | [list begins]; pp. 386–410, Index III. subject-matter completed; p. [411], printer's imprint: CHISWICK PRESS:—C. WHITTINGHAM AND CO., TOOKS COURT, | CHANCERY LANE.; p. [412], blank.

Technical Notes: for details common to this series—paper, leaf size, printing, type area, lines-to-page, type face and size, running heads, pagination, end-papers, and binding—see this field in A-52.01; only detail specific to this vol. is included here. *Running heads*: all versos: *The Saga Library*. | [all rectos: section head or saga title]; *binding*: as in A-52.01, except titles, the change in vol. no. on the spine, and the title on front: THE STORY | OF THE | ERE- DWELLERS; and on the *spine*: THE | ERE- | DWELL- ERS | [thin rule] | MORRIS | MAGNÚSSON | [thick- thin rule]; note that Morris's complaint about his name only on the spine of vol. I has wrought a correction on the spine of vol. II.
Publication: 1892 [finished printing 23 Sept. 1891] (Chiswick Arch.); *print run*: 1,000 ordinary and 125 LP copies; *price*: unknown.
Register of Copies Examined: see this field in A-52.01.
Notes: total cost of producing vol. II, exclusive of binding = £152. 10s. 5d. (Chiswick Arch.).
See the 'Agreement' between Morris and Bernard Quaritch for the publication of vol. II of the Saga Library, rptd. in *Letters*, iii. 230–1.

There is some difficulty establishing the time Morris and Magnússon did the original translation of this saga. Mackail wrote that the Eyrbyggja Saga was 'the first book translated by Morris from the Icelandic. In the beautiful manuscript of his translation, which he had executed in the previous Apr. [i.e. 1870], he had written some verses . . .' (Mackail, i. 262–3).

Buxton Forman, however, seems to date Morris's translation and manuscript of the saga in Dec. 1873 or Jan. 1874 (HBF, p. 83). Alfred Fairbank clarifies the matter by listing (pp. 65, 67 of *The Story of Kormak*) 2 illuminated MS by Morris of this work: the 1st prepared in 1865 and the 2nd, seemingly the one to which Mackail refers, in 1870 (*Letters*, i. 154). Clearly the translation was done before the 1st illuminated MS of 1865, probably in 1864 or 1865.

Magnússon to Quaritch, 16 Sept. 1891: 'I write to let you know that I have passed for Press the last sheet of the present vol. [i.e. vol. II] of the Saga Library' (clearly a reference to proof reading, quoted from the Quaritch archive in *Letters*, iii. 351 note).
Later impressions of this edn.: Quaritch:
1.* 1891 [finished printing 16 Oct.] (Chiswick Arch.): [2nd impression, 1st edn.]; *print run*: 500 copies; *price*: unknown;
2.* 1906 [finished printing 31 July] (Chiswick Arch.): [3rd impression, 1st edn.]; *print run*: 500 copies; *price*: unknown.

A-58.01: Hammersmith Socialist Record

[heading in gothic] **The Hammersmith Socialist Record.** | [thick-thin rule] | [plain type] OCTOBER, 1891 [–June 1893]. No. 1 [–21]. | [thin-thick rule] | HAMMERSMITH SOCIALIST SOCIETY, | [aligned right] KELMSCOTT HOUSE.
Edition: [1st impression, 1st edn., 21 monthly issues pbd.] The monthly news sheet of the Hammersmith Socialist Society, 'to assist in the Socialist Propaganda as far as possible, and to contain a list of proposed Lectures of Sunday evenings, fixtures and arrangements for ensuing month, and such other information as may from time to time be thought advisable' (p. 1 of No. 1).
Collaborators, Editors, and Illustrators: edited by Sam Bullock.
Printer: [Co-operative Printing Society Limited, 6, Salisbury Court, Fleet Street, and 35 Russell Street, Covent Garden].
Collation: each issue a single sheet folded to form 2 demy 8° leaves, 4 pages, no wrapper. Not issued in a collected bound version.
Contents: p. [1], masthead, see above: [below left] Friends and Comrades, | [text begins]; pp. 2–4, editorial and advertising material. After the 1st few issues, editorial notes are usually initialled: H. B. T. = H. B. Tarleton; S. B. = Sam Bullock; R. C. S. = R. Catterson-Smith; C. E. R. = C. E. Rice; A. S. = Andreas Scheu; W. M. = William Morris; J. B. G. = John Bruce Glasier; A. B. = A. Beasley. Morris is the most frequent contributor; for his contributions, see D-533–4, 540–1, 543–5, 547, and 548.
Technical Notes: *paper*: plain white machine-made; *leaf size*: cut flush, 217 x 134 mm.; *printing*: *type area*: 170 x 102 mm.; *lines-to-page*: sometimes leaded, 33 lines, subjects sometimes separated by a thin rule; *running titles*: [all rectos and versos, above thin rule] HAMMERSMITH SOCIALIST RECORD.; *pagination*: separate for each issue; though usually initialled, articles are occasionally signed in full.
Publication: monthly: No. 1, Oct. 1891–No. 21, June 1893, uninterrupted; *print run*: unknown; *price*: for free distribution.
Register of Copies Examined: BL (base copy: P.P. 3558. i)., contains all, Nos. 1–21, Oct, 1891–June, 1893).
Notes: the draft 1st issue of the *HSR* was read and approved at the HSS meeting of 17 Sept. 1891 (Ham. Min. Book, III, BL (Add.) MS 45893).

A-59.01: Poems by the Way (KP)

[flush left] POEMS BY THE WAY. WRITTEN | BY WILLIAM MORRIS.

Edition: 'Kelmscott Press Edition' [1st impression, 1st edn.] Peterson notes a variant BL copy with a 'different initial and looser word-spacing' in the last gathering (*KP Biblio.*, pp. xxxii, xxxiv). Though this vol. comprises mainly unpublished poems, many of the lyrics had been issued previously: 'Error and Loss' first appeared as 'The Dark Wood' in *Fortnightly Review* (1871, see D-28); 'The Burghers' Battle' in *The Athenæum* (1888, see D-382); 'The Hall and the Wood' in *The English Illustrated Magazine* (1890, see D-495); 'The Day of Days' in *The Humane Review* and *Time* (1890, see D-522); 'The Muse of the North' as the epigraph to *The Grettis Saga* (1869, see A-5.01); 'Of the Three Seekers' in *To-day* (1884, see D-85); 'Love's Gleaning-tide' in *The Athenæum* (1874, see D-31); 'The Message of the March Wind' in *Commonweal* (1889, see D-134; later this became Chapter 1 of *The Pilgrims of Hope*); *A Death Song* was first pbd. as a 4-page leaflet with musical notation (1887, A-43.01); 'Meeting in Winter' in *The English Illustrated Magazine* (1884, see D-95); 'The Two Sides of the River' in *The Fortnightly Review* (1868, see D-19); 'The King of Denmark's Sons' in *Scribner's Monthly, An Illustrated Magazine for the People* (1873, see D-30); 'On the Edge of the Wilderness' in *The Fortnightly Review* (1869, see D-22); 'A Garden by the Sea' was first pbd. as 'The Nymph's Song to Hylas' in *The Life and Death of Jason* (see A-3.01); 'The God of the Poor' in *The Fortnightly Review* (1868, see D-18); 'Mother and Son', as Chapter 4 of *The Pilgrims of Hope*, in *Commonweal* (1885, see D-134); 'The Voice of Toil', 'Chants for Socialists, No. 2' in *Justice* (1884, see D-98); 'The Day is Coming', appeared first as a pamphlet, *Chants for Socialists, No. 1* (1883, see A-23.01); 'All for the Cause', 'Chants for Socialists, No. 3' in *Justice* (1884, see D-100); 'Drawing near the Light', first appeared as a poem of 3-stanzas without a title in *Commonweal* (1888, see D-371); 'Verses for Pictures' appeared first as 'The Seasons' in *The Academy*, the annual Catalogue of the Royal Academy Exhibition (1871, see D-27); 'For the Briar Rose' in *The Legend of "The Briar Rose"* (1890, see B-9); 'The Half of Life Gone', as Chapter 8 of *The Pilgrims of Hope*, first pbd. in *Commonweal* (1885, see D-134); and 'Mine and Thine', a translation of a 14th century poem from Flanders, appeared first in *Commonweal* (1889, see D-439).

Series: 2nd book and the 2nd Morris title pbd. by the KP.

Colophon: HERE endeth Poems by the Way, written | by William Morris, and printed by him at the | Kelmscott Press, Upper Mall, Hammersmith, | in the County of Middlesex; and finished on | the 24th day of September of the year 1891. | [¶] Sold by Reeves & Turner, 196, Strand, London. | [KP printer's mark, No. 1]

Collation: small 4° in 8s: [a]² b⁸ (± c⁸) d–n⁸ o⁴ [$4 (–b2) signed] 102 leaves pp. [4] [1] 2–196 [197–200] [= 204]. The cancel of c⁸ seems, from Emery Walker's evidence and his correspondence with Morris (see *KP Biblio.*, p. 7), to have been to correct an error, 'those' for 'thou' on p. 19, i.e. c2r.

Contents: p. [1], title page; p. [2], blank; p. [3–4], headed: A TABLE OF THE CONTENTS | OF THIS BOOK. | [55 poem titles, ending with the KP mark No. 1]; p. [1], 1st section head: [all within border No. 1] HERE BEGIN POEMS BY THE | WAY. WRITTEN BY WILLIAM | MORRIS. [in red] AND FIRST IS THE | POEM CALLED FROM THE UP- | LAND TO THE SEA. | [text begins]; pp. 2–196, text completed; p. [197], colophon (see above), followed by KP mark No. 1; pp. [198–200], blank.

Technical Notes: *paper*: Flower paper No. 1; *leaf size*: untrimmed deckled edges, avg. 202 x 143 mm.; *printing*: 1st KP book printed in black and red, with shoulder-notes, refrain lines, and speakers' names in dramatic poems in red; *type face*: Golden type; *type area*: 146 x 88 mm.; *lines-to-page*: set solid, 31 lines; *shoulder titles*: used as running titles for each poem, all rectos and versos; *pagination*: arabic numbers 5mm. inside the outer margin on direction line; *end-papers*: standard KP practice: same paper as the text: 3 free ends and paste-down, plain white and blank, front and back; *binding*: plain unblocked stiff natural vellum with green silk ties; *spine*: gilt-stamped across in Golden type: POEMS | BY | THE | WAY | BY | WILL- | IAM | MORRIS | [at the foot] 1891; *ornamentation*: border No. 1; 2 of KP mark No. 1; 55 10-line initials (heading of each poem); 96 6-line initials.

Publication: 24 Sept. 1891 [this colophon date indicates finished printing, issued 20 Oct.] (Cockerell, p. 149); *print run*: 300 copies on paper, 13 on vellum; *price*: 2gns. and c. 12gns., respectively (Cockerell, pp. 148–9).

Register of Copies Examined: VU (base copy: Baill.: L, Poynton Coll.); CSt (Spec.Coll. Felton PR5078.P74); SU (821.85/M877po); BL (2 copies: Ashley 3693 & C. 43.e 2.); Mu (Spec. Coll. PR 5078 /P6 1891, with variant binding).

Notes: see also the notes in *KP Biblio.* (pp. 6–7). According to Cockerell, Morris originally intended to title this book *Flores Atramenti* (quoted in Sparling, 149). In his 'Annotated List of the Books Printed at the Kelmscott Press',

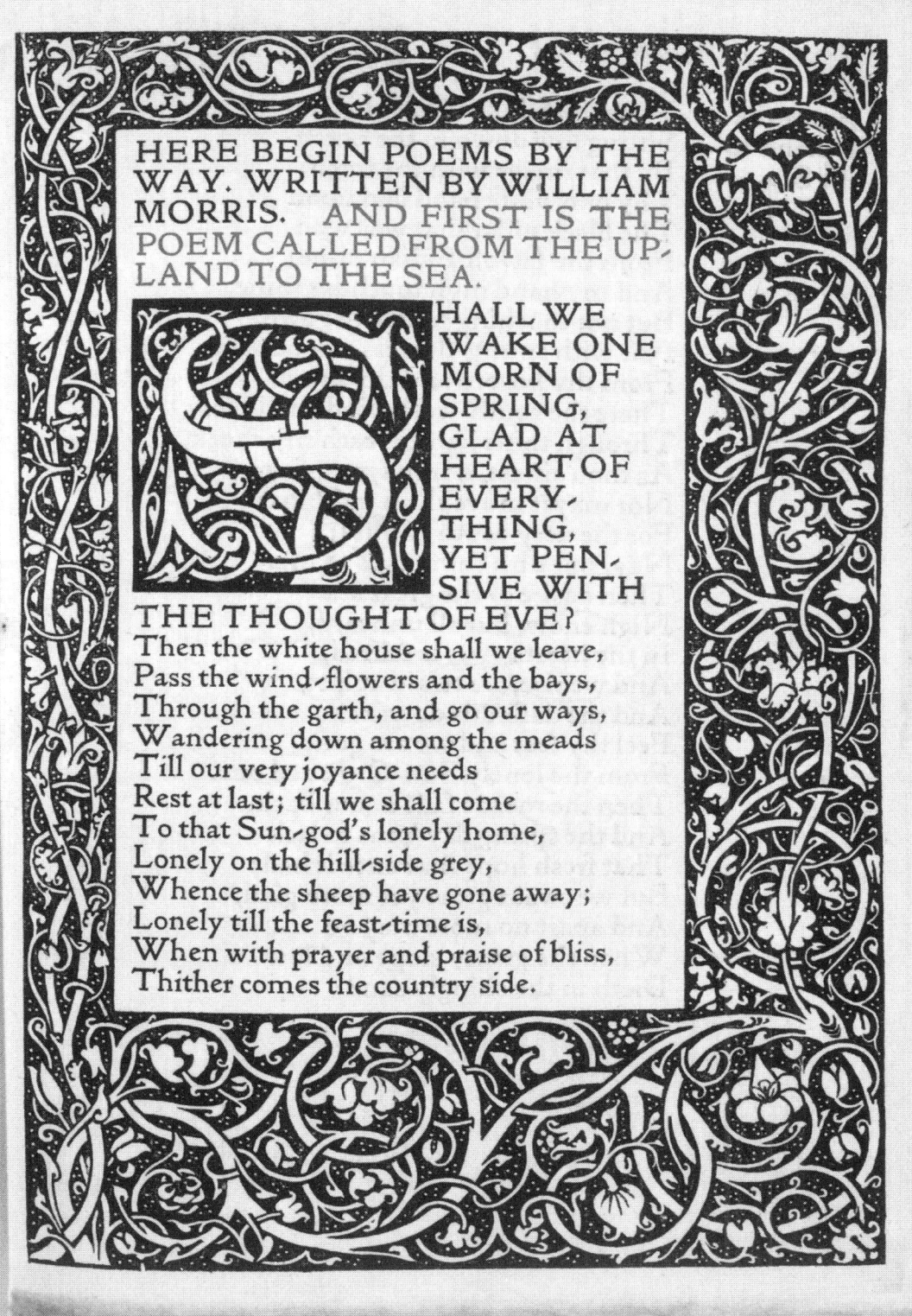

Figure 56. A-59.01: Poems by the Way (KP edn.) head title in Border 1

Cockerell says that 'Goldilocks and Goldilocks' was written in order to increase the bulk of the vol. See May Morris's account of the writing of this poem (*CW*, IX. xxxvii). Mackail quotes a letter from Morris commenting on the composition of the added 'Goldilocks and Goldilocks': 'I am writing', he says, 'a short narrative poem to top up my new book with. My wig! but it is garrulous' (Mackail, ii. 257).

In relating price to the amount of text, Morris felt constrained by what he had already done with *The Glittering Plain* (KP edn.) to provide an equal amount of verse in *Poems by the Way*, the earlier book having also been priced at 2*gns*. (see *Letters*, iii. 313).

The vellum bindings on some copies were dyed red, yellow, indigo, or dark green, but Morris did not think them successful (Cockerell, p. 149).

In a letter of 14 July [1891] to Emery Walker, Morris agrees that Walker was right to order a reprinting of a sheet from the KP *Poems by the Way* because it had a misprint, probably corrected by substituting 'those' for 'thou' on p. 19 (see *KP Biblio.*, p. 7). He also notes Reeves' comment that 'he has subscribed all the 250 [KP paper copies of *Poems by the Way*]. Also '. . . Cornish of Birmingham is weeping & moaning that he can only have 6 copies. Really my cupidity is rising & I begin to regret that I didn't put the book at £5' (*Letters*, iii. 318).

In a prefatory note on the fly-leaf of his MS Diary for 1897 Cockerell gives the dates of composition (most taken directly from Morris's notes on the original holographs) of certain poems in *Poems by the Way*: 'Loves Reward' dated Kelmscott, 21 Apr. 1871; 'Mine and Thine', 2 Mar. 1889; 'The Folkmote by the River' and 'Goldilocks' 'recent'; 'Hildebrand & Hillilel', 'Wed Mar 1 1871'.

Temple Scott says: 'Since going to press I learn that two poems, "The Voice of Toil" and "The Day of Days," both in "Poems by the Way" were reprinted as a leaflet and distributed to those attending a meeting of the South Place Ethical Society on February 21 1897; on that occasion Dr. Stanton Coit lectured on William Morris.' (Scott p. 60). To date no copy of the leaflet or other confirming record of it has been found.

A-59.02: Poems by the Way

POEMS BY THE WAY | WRITTEN BY WILLIAM | MORRIS | LONDON: REEVES AND TURNER | MDCCCXCI

Edition: 'Crown Octavo Edition' 'Trade Edition' [1st impression, 2nd edn.] 100 numbered LP copies in post quarto. For previous publications of some of these poems, see this field in A-59.01.

Collation: small 4° (HBF says 'Imperial 16mo'): A–2B^4 2C^2 102 leaves pp. [8] 1–196 [= 204].

Contents: p. [*1*], blank; p. [*2*], LP copies: certificate: Only One Hundred copies printed. | This is No. 72 [no. entered in longhand]; ordinary copies: R and T ad, headed MR. WILLIAM MORRIS'S WORKS.; p. [*3*], half title; p. [*4*], blank; p. [*5*], title page; p. [*6*], blank; p. [*7*], headed: CONTENTS. | [55 poem titles as a list, in italic]; p. [*8*], contents end; p. 1, headed: HERE BEGIN POEMS BY THE WAY. | WRITTEN BY WILLIAM MORRIS. | AND FIRST IS THE POEM CALLED | FROM THE UPLAND TO THE SEA. | [text begins]; pp. 2–196, text completed with: [thin rule] | CHISWICK PRESS:—C. WHITTINGHAM AND CO, TOOKS COURT, | CHANCERY LANE.

Technical Notes: *paper*: LP copies: cream-white hand-made with deckled edges; *watermark*: VAN GELDER ZONEN; *leaf size*: avg. 220 x 176 mm.; ordinary copies: untrimmed, avg. 187 x 135 mm. including head and direction lines; *printing*: *type area*: 128 x 94 mm.; *lines-to-page*: 29 lines; *shoulder titles*: all rectos and versos, relevant poem titles in smaller type, Long Primer, 10 pt.; *pagination*: arabic numbers centred on the direction line; *end-papers*: ordinary copies: 1 free end and paste-down, plain white and blank, front and back; LP copies: 3 free ends and a paste-down in front, 1 free end and paste-down in back, all plain white and blank; *binding*: LP: plain unblocked cream buckram gilt-stamped on front to duplicate the title and author of the title page; *spine*: gilt-stamped across: POEMS BY | THE WAY | WILLIAM | MORRIS | [at foot] REEVES | & | TURNER; ordinary copies: plain dark red unblocked cloth-covered boards, gilt-stamped on front and spine as the LP copies.

Publication: 1891 [issued 14–18 Dec.] (*Pub. Circ.*, 54/1329 (19 Dec. 1891), 695); *print run*: 1,000 ordinary copies, LP: 100 numbered copies (Chiswick Arch.); *price*: ordinary copies 6*s*., LP copies price unknown.

Register of Copies Examined: LeM (base ordinary copy); CSt (base LP copy: Felton PR5078/P74 1891, copy 72 of 100 copies issued, and ordinary copy: 821.7/M87pw); BGR (LP copy, no. 92 of 100 copies issued).); VU (LP copy, E); MU (LP copy: Spec. Coll. PR5078 P6 1891a; no. 2 of 100 copies); VSL (ordinary copy, S821.85P); SU (821.85 M877po).

Notes: Morris to E. Walker, 16 Aug. [1891]: 'Jacoby [*sic*] has sent me two sheets of the cheap By the Way: it looks well'

(*Letters*, iii. 343). The Chiswick Arch. records the cost of production, excluding the prospectus and binding but including the LP copies, total = £49. 7*s*. 3*d*.
Later issues and impressions from this edn.:
1. R and T: 1892 [Aug.]: Second Edition [2nd impression, 2nd edn.]; *print run*: 1,000 copies (Chiswick Arch.); *price*: 6*s*.;
2. Longmans: 1896 [June]: Second Edition [2nd issue, 2nd impression, 2nd edn.]; *print run*: copies remaining, 100 cancel titles ordered (Chiswick Arch.); *price*: 6*s*.;
3. Longmans: 1899 [18 Feb.]: Second Edition [3rd issue, 2nd impression, 2nd edn.]; *print run*: copies remaining, 500 sets of cancel prelims ordered (Chiswick Arch.); *price*: 5*s*.

A-59.03: Poems by the Way (RB)
POEMS BY THE WAY | WRITTEN BY WILLIAM | MORRIS. | [fleuron] | PUBLISHED BY ROBERTS BROTHERS, | AT THEIR HOUSE, 3 SOMERSET | STREET, BOSTON, 1892.
Edition: [1st impression, 3rd edn., 1st American] Comparison of this with the English 2nd edn. shows the American version to be nearly a facsimile reprint of the English version. The type used is not the same, though the differences are small; running heads are used rather than shoulder notes; signatures differ as does the position of page numbers, and the paper size and format are different. But the American compositors worked closely from the English popular edn., their copytext, duplicating on a line-for-line basis. The entry in RB Cost Book E provides details of the reprint. For previous pbns. of some of these poems, see this field in A-59.01.
Collation: 4°, with irrelevant 8° sigs. in numbers: [a–2a⁴ 2b⁶] 102 leaves pp. [i–v] vi 1–196 [197–8] [= 204].
Contents: p. [i], half title; p. [ii], blank; p. [iii], title page; p. [iv], printer's imprint: [in gothic] University Press: | [plain type] JOHN WILSON AND SON, CAMBRIDGE, U.S.A.; p. [v]–vi, headed: CONTENTS. | [list of 55 poem titles]; p. 1, head title: HERE BEGIN POEMS BY THE WAY. | WRITTEN BY WILLIAM MORRIS. | AND FIRST IS THE POEM CALLED | FROM THE UPLAND TO THE SEA. | [text begins]; pp. 2–196, text completed with explicit: THE END.; pp. [197–8], Roberts Bros. ads, headed: MR. WILLIAM MORRIS'S WORKS.
Technical Notes: *paper*: cream-white machine-wove with dandy roll laid lines, t.e.g.; *leaf size*: edges lightly trimmed, avg. 183 x 129 mm.; *printing*: type area: 123 x 85 mm.; *lines-to-page*: set solid, 29 lines; *headlines*: running titles: relevant poems in italic caps, all versos and rectos; *end-papers*: 1 free end and paste-down, plain white and blank, front and back; *binding*: plain unblocked dark red or green cloth (darker than the English 2nd edn.), gilt-stamped, front: [enlarged and ornamented gilt relief block with initial letter 'P' and ornament in relief to show the binding colour, the reverse of normal letterpress] POEMS BY THE WAY • [thin rule] | • WRITTEN BY [enlarged neo-gothic Morris initials 'W' and 'M' done with relief block, see above] WILLIAM MORRIS •; *spine*: gilt-stamped across: POEMS | BY THE | WAY | [printer's leaf] | WILLIAM | MORRIS | [publisher's monogram at the foot, 'R' intertwined with 'B']
Publication: 1892 [issued 29 Mar.–6 Apr.].(*The International Bookseller* (NY) I (9 Apr. 1892); *print run*: 500 copies (Cost Book E, Roberts Arch.); *price*: $1.25.
Register of Copies Examined: LeM (base copy); CSt. (Spec. Coll Felton PR 5078.P74; NNPM.
Later issues and impressions from this edn.:
1. RB: 1896 [20 Oct.]: [2nd impression, 3rd edn., 1st American]; *print run*: 500 copies (Cost Book E, Roberts Arch.); *price*: $2.00;
2. Longmans NY: 1900: [2nd issue, 2nd impression, 3rd edn., 1st American]; *print run*: 388 copies remaining with Little Brown were purchased by Longmans NY and issued with a new title page indicating the new publisher and date (Longmans (NY) Arch.); *price*: $1.25.

A-59.04: Poems by the Way and Love is Enough (PW)
POEMS BY THE WAY | & LOVE IS ENOUGH | BY | WILLIAM MORRIS | NEW EDITION | LONGMANS, GREEN, AND CO. | 39 PATERNOSTER ROW, LONDON | NEW YORK AND BOMBAY | 1896 | *All rights reserved*
Edition: New Edition [1st impression, 1st edn., considered as a new title; 4th edn., 3rd English of *Poems by the Way*, and 6th edn., 5th English of *Love is Enough*] This is a reference entry: for details of this book, see the main entry for it as new, combined title, A-81.01.
Publication: 1896 [issued 20–4 July] ('Publications of the Week', *Pub. Circ.*, 65/1569 (25 July 1896), 84); *print run*: 500 copies; *price*: 6*s*.
Register of Copies Examined: BL (base copy, 2292.e. 28.)

A-59.05: Poems by the Way (LPL)
POEMS BY THE WAY | BY | WILLIAM MORRIS | NEW EDITION | LONGMANS, GREEN AND CO. | 39 PATERNOSTER ROW, LONDON | NEW YORK, BOMBAY, AND CALCUTTA | 1910 | *All rights reserved*

Edition: New Edition. Pocket Edition. [1st impression, 5th edn., 4th English].
Series: Longmans Pocket Library (for further series detail, see this field in A-3.09. For previous pbns. of some of these poems, see this field in A-59.01).
Collation: fcap 8°: π⁴ A–P⁸ 124 leaves pp. [i–iv] v–vii [viii] [1] 2–236 [237–40] [= 248].
Contents: p. [i], half title; p. [ii], Longmans ad, headed: 'Longmans' Pocket Library'; p. [iii], title page; p. [iv], headed: *BIBLIOGRAPHICAL NOTE* | [list of edns. and rpts. of this title, with month and year of issue]; p. v, headed: CONTENTS | [in caps, titles of 55 poems + page numbers, as a list]; pp. vi–vii, Contents completed; p. [viii], blank; p. [1], dropped head title: POEMS BY THE WAY | FROM THE UPLAND TO THE SEA | [text begins]; pp. 2–236, text completed with printer's imprint: Printed by BALLANTYNE, HANSON & Co. | Edinburgh & London; pp. [237–8], Longmans ad, headed: William Morris's Works; pp. [239–40], blank.
Technical Notes: paper, leaf size, printing, headlines, pagination, end-papers, and binding are common features of the series, for details of which see this field and the *Series* field for the 1st vol. for the series, A-3.09; detail specific to this vol.: *type area*: 117 x 62 mm., excluding head and direction lines; *lines-to-page*: leaded, 28 lines; *headlines*: running heads, all versos (except on chapter heads): POEMS BY THE WAY | [all rectos except chapter heads: the title of the relevant poem].
Publication: 1910 [issued 21–8 Oct.] ('Publications of the Week', *BSR*, n.s. 55/96 (28 Oct. 1910), 1491); *print run*: 3,000 copies (Longmans Arch.); *price*: 2s. cloth, 3s. lthr.
Register of Copies Examined: SU (base copy: Store G, 40838); LeM; BGR.
Notes: the Longmans Arch. records the total cost of producing the 3,000 copies as £41. 4s. 8d., exclusive of binding and dust jacket. Dust jacket not seen.
Later reprints from this edn. (all post-1915): Longmans:
1. 1917 [7 Mar.]: Pocket Edition (1,120 copies printed by Neill);
2. 1920 [28 May]: Pocket Edition (2,000 copies printed by Neill).

A-59.06: Poems by the Way (+ Love is Enough *CW* IX)

THE COLLECTED WORKS | [title details common to the set, see A-126.01] | VOLUME IX | LOVE IS ENOUGH | POEMS BY THE WAY | [publisher's imprint, see A-126.01] | MDCCCCXI
Edition: [1st impression, 6th edn., 5th English] For all details common to the set, particularly *Technical Notes*, see the entry for the *CW*, A-126.01. Only details specific to this vol. are listed here, where the *Collation, Contents, and Technical Notes* cover both of the texts combined here.
Collation: medium 8°: a⁴ b⁸ (b1+1) (b6+1) c⁸ (c4+1) B–R⁸ [$2 (–a a2 +a3 –b2 B2) signed] 148 leaves pp. [i–xii] xiii–xxxix [xl] [1–2] 3–89 [*Love is Enough* ends, *Poems by the Way* begins] [90–2] 93–248 [249–56] [= 296] +3 inserted plates not included in the book's pagination, but noted in the formula and described here in their appropriate places in the *Contents*.
Contents: pp. [i–vii], blank; p. [viii], limitation note; pp. [ix–x], blank; 1st inserted plate as frontis., reproduction inside a blind-stamped compartment of a drawing signed by the plate maker, below right: *Emery Walker Ph.sc.* and labelled below in copperplate: *Artemis | drawn by William Morris*; p. [xi], title page; p. [xii], blank; p. xiii, headed: CONTENTS | [list begins]; p. xiv, Contents completed; p. xv, headed: INTRODUCTION | [text begins with 9-line ornamental initial 'L' by Morris]; pp. xvi–xx, text; 2nd inserted plate, recto blank, a facsimile reproduction, facing p. xxi of a Morris calligraphic MS, oriented vertically and labelled: FACSIMILE FROM A PAGE [p. 25] OF LANCELOT DU LAC.; pp. xxi–xxxii, text; 3rd inserted plate, facing p. xxxii, labelled: BORDERS [3] DESIGNED AND ENGRAVED BY WILLIAM MORRIS FOR | "LOVE IS ENOUGH."; p. xxxiii, text, with a Morris woodcut border along the outer margin; p. xxxiv, text, with, top left, a Morris ornamental initial L; p. xxxv, text, with a woodcut outer margin border of 4 amoretti designed by Burne–Jones and cut by Morris both whose initials are added, below, the border, left: E. B.-J. DEL | [right] W. M. sc., and labelled below: A BORDER FOR LOVE | IS ENOUGH; pp. xxxvi–xxxvii, text; p. xxxviii, text, with a photo reproduction of a Morris handwritten presentation to Emery Walker, with signature, of his copy of Morte d'Arthur; p. xxxix, headed: BIBLIOGRAPHICAL NOTE; p. [xl], blank; p. [1], 1st half title: [flush left] LOVE IS ENOUGH; OR, THE FREEING | OF PHARAMOND; p. [2], dropped head: DRAMATIS PERSONÆ | [list of 13 characters]; p. 3, headed: LOVE IS ENOUGH | THE ARGUMENT | [8 lines of prose summary] | text begins; pp. 4–89, text completed; p. [90], blank; p. [91], 2nd half title; p. [92], blank; pp. 93–248, text of *Poems by the Way* completed; p. [249], blank; p. [250], printer's imprint (see this field in the entry for the set, A-126.01); pp. [251–6], blank.
Technical Notes: paper, printing, type, position (but not

content) of headlines, running titles, shoulder notes, endpapers, and binding are all common to the series and are described in this field in A-126.01, the entry for *CW*. Included here are only those details that are specific to this particular edn.: *shoulder titles*: [all rectos and versos to p. 89]: Love is | Enough; from p. 94, all rectos and versos except head titles: the relevant poem title; *spine label*: 1st 4 lines as in A-126.01, then: LOVE | IS ENOUGH | POEMS BY THE | WAY

Publication: 1911 [issued 11 Dec.] (Longmans Arch.); *print run* and *price*: see this field in A-126.01.

Register of Copies Examined: see this field in A-126.01.

A-60.01: Address . . . Pre-Raphaelite School

[wrapper title] CITY OF BIRMINGHAM | MUSEUM AND ART GALLERY. | [arms of the City] | ADDRESS | ON THE | COLLECTION OF PAINTINGS, | OF THE | ENGLISH PRE-RAPHAELITE SCHOOL, | DELIVERED BY | MR. WILLIAM MORRIS, | IN THE MUSEUM AND ART GALLERY, | *ON FRIDAY, OCTOBER 2nd, 1891.* | BIRMINGHAM: | E. C. OSBORNE AND SON, 84, NEW STREET. | [flush left] PRICE ONE PENNY.

Edition: [1st impression, 1st edn.]

Collation: cr. 8°: [1]⁸ 8 leaves pp. [1–3] 4–16 [= 16], self-wrapped.

Contents: p. [1], title page; p. [2], blank; p. [3], text begins below an ornamental head-piece; pp. 4–16, text completed with triangular printer's flower as tail-piece.

Technical Notes: *paper*: plain white machine-made; *leaf size*: cut flush, 209 x 135 mm.; *printing*: *type area*: 162 x 96 mm.; 20 section titles, in caps, divide the text; *lines-to-page*: set solid, 45 lines excluding head and direction lines; *pagination*: arabic numerals centred on the headline; *binding*: self-wrapped, the single gathering being stapled once in the middle of the centrefold.

Publication: pbd. 1891 [October-December] (reviewed in *Journal of Decorative Art*, 11 (Nov., 1891): 171

Register of Copies Examined: BL (two copies: base copy: Cup. 502.f.11.(30); and 7813. aa. 5.); TxU; MH; CSmH; CaBVaU; Fdmn; NNPL (SFC. n.c. 1).

Notes: rptd. in MM, i. 296–310, with the date of delivery incorrectly printed as 'October 24, 1891'.

Mackail describes this speech as impromptu:

> It perhaps expresses his views not the less exactly because it was spoken on the spur of the moment, and was the imperfect but immediate utterance of his habitual feelings. The curiously halting sentences and inconclusive termination are accounted for very simply. He had meant to think out what he would say on the journey down to Birmingham, but fell asleep in the train and arrived with nothing prepared (Mackail, ii. 270).

If Mackail's information is accurate—and there is no reason to doubt it—this printed version, including its section headings, must derive from a shorthand report.

A-61.01: The Reward of Labour: A Dialogue

[wrapper title] THE REWARD OF LABOUR: A | DIALOGUE BY WILLIAM | MORRIS, AUTHOR OF "THE | EARTHLY PARADISE." | BEING NO. 1 OF THE HAMMERSMITH | SOCIALIST LIBRARY. | ONE PENNY.

Edition: [1st impression, 1st edn.] 1st pbd. in *Commonweal* (21, 28 May 1887), 165, 170 (see D-287).

Collation: 8°: [1]⁶ 6 leaves, with title, stapled once at the centrefold; pp. [1] 2–12 [= 12] + coloured paper wrapper.

Contents: p. [1], dropped head title: **THE REWARD OF LABOUR:** | A DIALOGUE BY WILLIAM MORRIS. | [swelled ornamental rule] | [list of 'Persons'] | [thin rule] | ['Scene' described] | [thin rule] | [text begins]; pp. 2–12, text completed: [double thin rule] | [thin rule] | [printer's imprint] HAYMAN, CHRISTY & LILLY, LTD., PRINTERS 20 & 22 ST. BRIDE ST., E.C.

Technical Notes: *paper*: cream machine-moulded, no watermark; *leaf size*: cut flush, 182 x 125 mm.; *printing*: *type area*: 129 x 93 mm.; *lines-to-page*: set solid, 38 lines, not including head and direction lines; *headlines*: *running titles*: [all versos] The Reward of Labour. | [all rectos] A Dialogue.; *binding*: *wrapper*: thick light blue-grey machine-made paper; p. [1], title page, as above; pp. [2–3], blank; p. [4], headed: THE | HAMMERSMITH SOCIALIST SOCIETY | [information regarding the weekly lecture series]

Publication: n.d. [issued by 10 Dec. 1892] One BL copy, 011652.k.73, has a useful accession stamp dated '10 De 92'. By the placing of their entries both Scott and Forman suggest 1893 for this pamphlet; *print run*: unknown; *price*: 1d.

Register of Copies Examined: BL (three copies: base copy: Cup. 502.f.11.[33], Cockerell's copy; Ashley 1227; & 011652. K. 73). Fdmn; Bass; NNPL (SFC. n.c. 1).

Notes: '*Conclusion*: A genuine pamphlet with an apparently chimerical but legitimate wrapper' (*Sequel*, 208). Neither Cockerell's copy of the pamphlet, which has the wrapper (BL Cup. 502.f.11.(33)), nor his copy of HBF (pp. 166–7) express any scepticism regarding the wrapper.

The decision to publish this pamphlet was taken at the

HSS weekly meeting of Friday, 10 July 1891 (Ham. Min. Book III, BL (Add.) MS 45893).

A-62.01: Saga Library, vol. III
THE STORIES OF THE | KINGS OF NORWAY | CALLED THE ROUND | WORLD | (HEIMSKRIN-GLA) | DONE INTO ENGLISH | OUT OF THE ICE-LANDIC | BY | WILLIAM MORRIS | AND | EIRÍKR MAGNÚSSON | VOL. I [–IV] | *WITH A LARGE MAP OF NORWAY* | LONDON | BERNARD QUARITCH, 15 PICCADILLY | 1893

Edition: [1st impression, 1st edn.] As was the case with the 1st issue of each of the 6 vols. of the Saga Library, there was an LP variant on Whatman hand-made paper (royal 8°) of 125 copies, all numbered. All vols., both ordinary and LP, were issued in Roxburghe bindings, with t.e.g.

Collaborators, Editors, and Illustrators: Eiríkr Magnússon made the map of Norway (stored in a pocket inside the back cover) for which the plate was prepared by Walker & Boutall.

Series: The Saga Library, vol. 3; Heimskringla, vol. I. (For further series detail, see A-52.01).

Collation: cr. 8°: [A]⁴ B–2C⁸ 2D⁴ 2E² (–2E2) 209 leaves pp. [8] [1–3] 4–410 [= 418] + a map of Norway folded and inserted in an envelope attached inside the back cover. The last signature is on a single leaf containing the last 2 pages of the Explanations and the printer's imprint.

Contents: p. [1], 1st half title, 1st 5 lines as in vol. 1 (A-52.01), last 3 lines: VOL III | HEIMSKRINGLA | VOL. I; p. [2], blank; p. [3], title page; p. [4], printer's imprint, as in vol. 1 (A-52.01); p. [5], dropped head: CONTENTS. | [titles of 9 sections with page nos.]; p. [6], blank; p. [7], dropped head: TRANSLATORS' NOTE. [9 lines of prose] | [signed, lower right, by both translators]; p. [8], blank; p. [1], 2nd half title; p. [2], blank; p. 3, dropped head: THE STORIES | OF THE | KINGS OF NORWAY, | CALLED THE ROUND WORLD. | [flush left] THE PREFACE OF SNORRI STURLU- | SON. | [text begins]; pp. 4–7, Preface completed; p. [8], blank; p. [9], 3rd half title; p. [10], blank; p. [11], dropped head: THE STORY OF THE | YNGLINGS. | [flush left] CHAPTER I. HEREIN IS TOLD OF | THE PARTS OF THE EARTH. | [text begins]; pp. 12–73, Yngling story completed; p. [74], blank; p. [75], 4th half title; p. [76], blank; p. [77], dropped head: THE STORY OF | HALFDAN THE BLACK. | [flush left] CHAPTER I. HALFDAN FIGHTS WITH | GANDALF AND SIGTRYGG. | [text begins]; pp. 78–87, Halfdan story completed; p. [88], blank; p. [89], 5th half title; p. [90], blank; p. [91], dropped head: THE STORY OF | HARALD FAIRHAIR. | CHAPTER I. HAROLD'S FIGHT WITH | HAKI AND GANDALF HIS FATHER. | [text begins]; pp. 92–145, Harald's story completed; p. [146], blank; p. [147], 6th half title; p. [148], blank; p. [149], dropped head: THE STORY OF | HAKON THE GOOD. | pp. 150–93, Hakon's story completed; p. [194], blank; p. [195], 7th half title; p. [196], blank; p. [197], dropped head: THE STORY OF KING | HARALD GREYCLOAK AND | OF EARL HAKON THE | SON OF SIGURD. | [flush left] CHAPTER I. THE UPRIS-ING OF ERIC'S | SONS: AND OF EYVIND SKALD-SPILLER. | [text begins]; pp. 198–220, Greycloak story completed; p. [221], 8th half title; p. [222], blank; pp. [223], [dropped head] THE STORY OF KING OLAF | TRY-GGVISON. | CHAPTER I. THE BIRTH OF OLAF TRYGGVISON. | [text begins]; pp. 224–378, Olaf's story completed; p. 379, 9th half title; p. [380], blank; p. [381], dropped head: EXPLANATIONS | [text begins]; pp. 382–410, text completed with explicit: THE END. | [thin rule] | CHISWICK PRESS:—C. WHITTINGHAM AND CO., TOOKS COURT, CHANCERY LANE.

Technical Notes: for details common to this series—paper, leaf size, printing, type area, lines-to-page, running heads (form and position), pagination, end-papers, and binding—see this field in A-52.01; only details specific to this vol. appear here: *spine*: gilt-stamped title: THE | SAGA | LIBRARY | VOL. 3 | [thin rule] | THE | HEIMS- | KRIN-GLA | VOL. 1 | [thin rule] | MORRIS | MAGNÚSSON [double thick-thin rule]; front title also changed on binding and dust cover: THE | HEIMSKRINGLA | VOL. 1.

Publication: 1893 [8 Feb.] [indicating finished printing, issue being some time later] (Chiswick Arch.); *print run*: 1,250 copies + 125 LP copies; *price*: unknown.

Register of Copies Examined: see this field in A-52.01.

Notes: Chiswick Arch. indicates that the total cost of producing this vol. was £143. 19s. 7d., including LP copies and stereo moulds, but excluding binding.

Morris to Magnússon, 25 Feb. [1892]:

> I hope the printers will have sent you a proof of the first sheet of Heimskringla. If you will kindly send me your corrections I will embody them in my proof, & you can see the revise the cleaner and we can fight over that if there is any difference of opinion. Which is not like to be I think. I am now ready to go strait on ahead with the book and will keep no one waiting.
>
> As to map. Would it not be enough for this vol: to have

a small map in the usual place in these vols: with just the districts marked; and then in the 4th vol: a bigger folding one. please tell me what you think (*Letters*, iii. 379).

Obviously, Magnússon's preference for a single large map for the 1st vol. of *Heimskringla* was acted upon.

Morris to Quaritch, 7 Oct. 1892: 're the new vol: of the Saga Library it is nearly ready but not quite. It will make about 400 pp. . . . This first vol [of the Heimskringla] is of the greatest possible interest: mythologically, historically, and artistically' (*Letters*, iii. 450–2).

Morris to Quaritch, 1 Dec. 1892: '*Heimskringla* I am waiting for one more interview with Magnússon to settle the corrections of the last sheets, which will take place in about a week; and also for the map, which I think *ought* to be in the 1st volume. The said map has been in the hands of the engraver for about 3 weeks & will soon be done. The whole book should be out early in January. Also we have begun on the 2nd vol.' (*Letters*, iii. 476–8).

A-63.01: The Order of Chivalry (KP)
[aligned left, in Morris-designed gothic] THE | ORDER OF | CHIVALRY
Edition: 'Kelmscott Press Edition' [1st impression, 1st edn.] This book is a Morris title because one of its parts is his verse translation of *L'Ordene de Chevalerie*, a French poem of the 13th century. The 1st part of the KP book is Caxton's English translation of the French 14th-century prose; the 2nd part, with a separate half title, is the 13th-century poem 'L'Ordene de Chevalerie' in French; and the 3rd part, also with a separate half title, is Morris's verse translation thereof. The 4th part is Ellis's 'Memoranda'.
Collaborators, Editors, and Illustrators: Caxton's translation and the French version of the poem are edited, with 'Memoranda', by F. S. Ellis. Illustrated by E. Burne-Jones.
Series: 13th title, 6th by Morris, pbd. by the KP.
Colophon: [No. 1, at the end of the Caxton translation, in Chaucer type:] The Order of Chivalry, translated from | the French by William Caxton, edited by | F. S. Ellis, & printed by me William Morris | at the Kelmscott Press, Upper Mall, Ham- | mersmith, in the County of Middlesex, & | finished on the 10th day of November, 1892 | [paragraph mark] Sold by Reeves and Turner, 196 Strand, | London. | [small KP mark]
[2nd colophon, p. 151, at the end of Ellis's 'Memoranda . . .': flush left] THIS Ordination of Knighthood was | printed by William Morris at the Kelms- | cott Press, Upper Mall, Hammersmith, | in the County of Middlesex; finished on | the 24th day of February, 1893. | [small KP mark]
Collation: small 4° in 8s: [a]² b–g⁸ h⁴ i–l⁸ [$4 (–b1 h3–4 i1) signed] 78 leaves pp. [4] [1] 2–150 [151–2] [= 156].
Contents: p. [1], title page; pp. [2–3], contents of the text as translated by Caxton, headed: [flush left, printer's leaf ornament] Here beginneth the Table of this pre- | sent book Intytled the Book of the Ordre | of Chyualry or Knyghthode.; p. [4], frontis. within border 9a, woodcut of a knight and lady designed by E. Burne-Jones with caption: THE | ORDRE OF | CHIVALRY; p. [1], engraved title within border 4, at top, in red: [printer's leaf ornament] Here after foloweth the mater and | tenour of this said Booke. And the | fyrst chapyter saith hou the good He- | rmyte deuysed to the Esquyer the | Rule & Ordre of Chyualrye [printer's flower ornament No. 3] | [text begins]; pp. 2–101, text completed; p. 102, colophon (see above) and small KP mark; pp. [103–4], blank; p. [105], 2nd half title: L'ORDENE DE CHEVALERIE, WITH | TRANSLATION BY WILLIAM MORRIS.; p. [106], blank; p. [107], 1st chapter head title: [within vine half border by Morris, French title repeated, flush left] | [French text begins]; pp. 108–25, French text completed with closing formula: [aligned right] Explicit l'Ordene de Chevalerie.; p. [126], blank; p. [127], 3rd half title: THE ORDINATION OF KNIGHTHOOD.; p. [128], Morris's translation begins: [vine half-border with general title as heading] THE ORDINATION OF KNIGHTHOOD. | [text begins]; pp. 129–47, text completed with explicit: THE end of the Ordination of Chivalry.; p. [148], head title of the 4th section: [vine half-border with title at top] MEMORANDA CONCERNING THE | TWO PIECES HERE REPRINTED. | [text begins]; pp. 149–51, text concluded: [below right, Ellis's initials] F. S. E. | [2nd colophon, see above] | [small KP mark]; p. [152], blank;
Technical Notes: *paper*: Flower paper 1, 1st part; Flower paper 2, 2nd part; *leaf size*: lightly trimmed, avg. 201 x 137 mm.; *printing*: printed in red and black, red being used for the argument at the head of p. [1], the 8 chapter titles, and the printer's flowers at the head of the French poem text (p. 107); *type area*: 131 x 88 mm.; *lines-to-page*: set solid, 28 lines; *type*: Chaucer type; *end-papers*: the usual KP treatment: 3 free ends and paste-down, front and back, all plain white and blank; *binding*: limp natural vellum with green silk ties; *spine*: title gilt-stamped vertically up the spine: THE ORDER OF CHIVALRY; *ornamentation*: frontis. designed by E. Burne-Jones; full-page Morris borders 9a and 4; 3 half-page vine borders; 10 floriated 10-line initials;

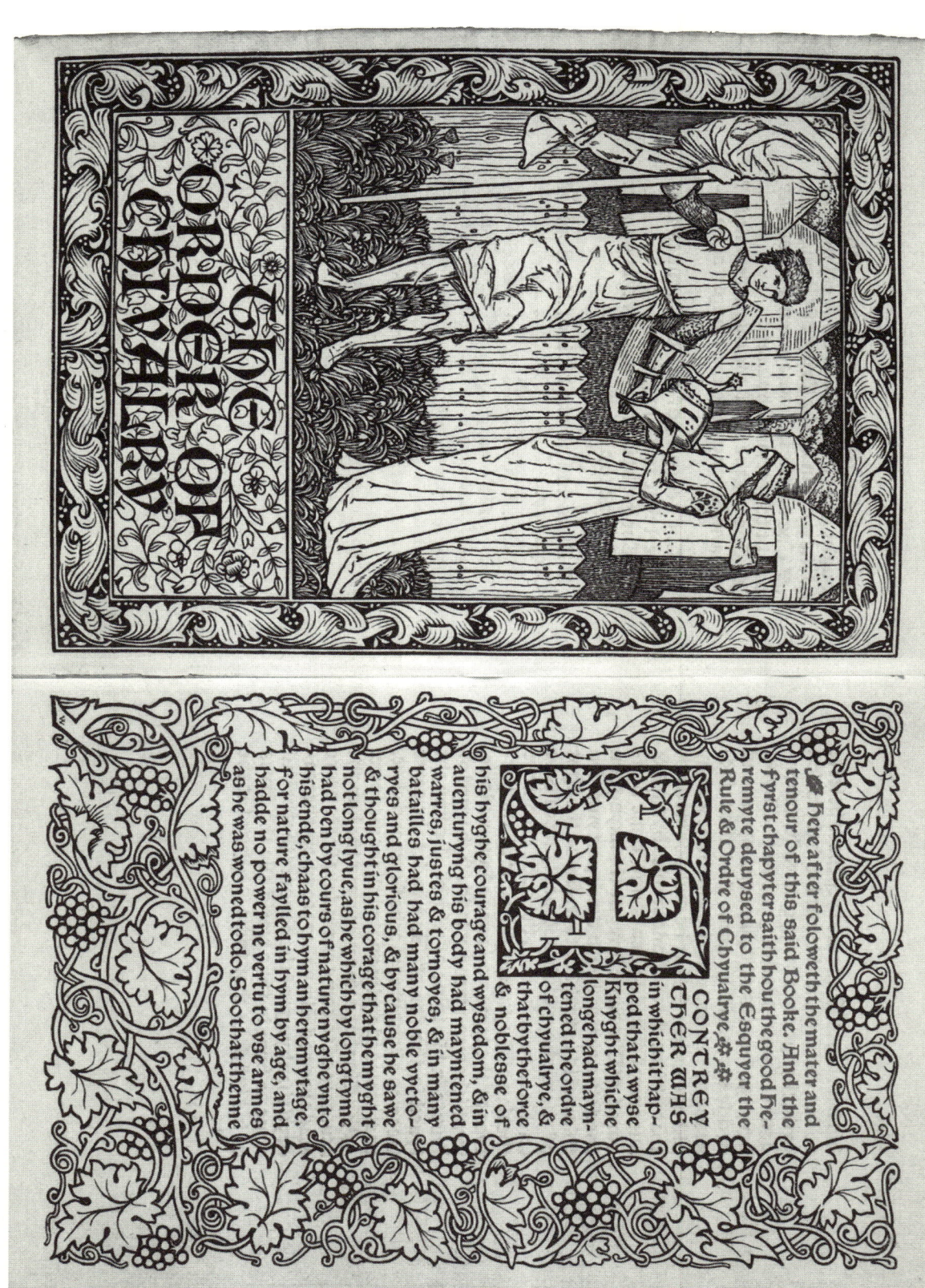

Figure 57. A-63.01: *The Order of Chivalry* (KP edn.) frontis. & head title

123 floriated 6-line initials; and 3 floriated 3-line initials.
Publication: 10 Nov. 1892 [colophon date indicates finished printing, issued 12 Apr. 1893] (Cockerell, p. 154); *print run*: 225 paper copies, 10 vellum; *price*: 30s. paper, 10gns. vellum.
Register of Copies Examined: VU (2 copies: base copy: Special Coll.: 19F and L); BL (3 copies: C.43.e.10.)
Notes: Ellis's 'Memoranda Concerning the Two Pieces Here Reprinted' explains this book's relation to its sources:

> The 'Order of Chivalry' was translated by Caxton from the French original, of which there are many early manuscripts in existence . . . . A strange confusion has been made by various writers and bibliographers between this [14th c.] treatise and a charming little French poem of the 13th century entitled 'L'Ordene de Chevalerie.' This was first printed at Paris in 1759 . . . and again in the 'Fabliaux et Contes.' Paris, 1808 . . . . The poem is here reprinted from the text given in the 'Fabliaux et Contes', 1808 (The Order of Chivalry, (and) L'Ordene de Chevalerie), p. 14).

So Morris's translation is of the 13th century poem, 'L'Ordene de Chevalrie'. The *Fabliaux et Contes* text of this precedes Morris's translation, and both follow Caxton's translation of the prose text, entitled 'The Order of Chivalry', edited by Ellis. Ellis also wrote a prose translation of the poem 'L'Ordene de Chevalerie', but it was not used because Morris suddenly remembered that the Press 'kept a poet of its own', i.e. himself.

A-63.02: The Order of Chivalry (+ News from Nowhere, John Ball, and A King's Lesson *CW* XVI)

THE COLLECTED WORKS | [for title details common to the set see A-126.01] | VOLUME XVII | [publisher's imprint, see A-126.01] | MDCCCCXIII
Edition: 'Collected Works edn' [1st impression, 2nd edn.] This version differs from the KP in that Morris's translation is the only part of the original text rptd. For details common to the set, see A-126.01, and for details specific to this *CW* vol., see A-74.04. Morris's text occupies pp. 353–66.
Publication: 1912 [31 Oct.] (Longmans Arch.); *print run* and *price*: see this field in A-126.01
Register of Copies Examined: see this field in A-126.01.
Notes: Cockerell writes to May Morris on 21 May 1912, to remind her that the verse *L'Ordene de Chevalerie*, in English titled *The Ordination of Chivalry*, must be included somewhere in the *CW* as a Morris translation (Cockerell Papers, BL (Add.) MS 52740).

A-64.01: Manifesto of English Socialists

[wrapper title] MANIFESTO | OF | ENGLISH | SOCIALISTS | PRICE ONE PENNY. | MAY 1, 1893. | Printed By The Twentieth Century Press Limited, 44, Gray's Inn Road, Holborn, W.C.
Edition: [1st impression, 1st edn.] The title varies in the pamphlet itself. The 1st page of text is headed: Manifesto of the Joint Committee of Socialist Bodies.
Collaborators, Editors, and Illustrators: This pamphlet is a collaborative effort of Morris with Henry M. Hyndman and George Bernard Shaw. As an indication of its official status, it ends with the 15 names of the Joint Committee, and the names of the secretaries of the 3 organisations joined in the enterprise, Edward R. Pease for The Fabian Society, H. W. Lee for the SDF, and Emery Walker for the Hammersmith Socialist Society. For more detail on the authorship, see *Notes*, below.
Publisher: Joint Committee of the English Socialists.
Collation: half sht. of cr. 8°: [1]⁴ 2 conjunct pairs folded to form 4 leaves, pp. [1] 2–8 [= 8] + red wrapper stapled to the body.
Contents: p. [1], dropped head: MANIFESTO | OF THE | JOINT COMMITTEE OF SOCIALIST BODIES. | [french rule] | [text begins]; pp. 2–8, text completed with 15 signatories (see above).
Technical Notes: *paper*: plain white machine-moulded; *leaf size*: cut flush, 215 x 138 mm.; *print*: *type area*: 161 x 93 mm.; *lines-to-page*: set solid, 38 lines; *pagination*: arabic numbers centred on the headline; *binding*: *wrapper*: plain red moulded paper stapled to the body twice in the fold, p. [1], title page (see above); p. [2], blank; p. [3], ads for the pbns. of each of the 3 participating groups; p. [4], blank.
Publication: 1 May 1893 (the 1st comment on this pamphlet in *Justice* did not appear until 1 July 1893; so it is possible the issue may have been later than the date on the wrapper, but it is more likely that the issue would have been made to coincide with May Day); *print run*: not known; *price*: 1d.
Register of Copies Examined: BL: (three copies: base copy: Cup.502.f.11 [13], a proof copy; Ashley 3694, and 8282.ff.11 [8]); TxU.
Notes: The Shaw Papers (BL (Add.) MS 50541) has correspondence between G. B. Shaw and Emery Walker regarding the roles of the three authors—Shaw, Hyndman, and Morris—in creating this text. Shaw gave his account of the authorship in his essay, 'Morris as I Knew Him', first pbd. as the introduction to vol. 2 of May Morris's *William Morris, Artist, Writer, Socialist*:

In drafting the manifesto Morris had taken care to give some expression to both the Fabian policy and the Social-Democratic Federation policy. Hyndman immediately proposed the omission of the Fabian program of municipal Socialism, and its explicit denunciation as 'gas and water Socialism.' I was equally determined not to endorse the policy of the S. D. F. Morris soon saw that we were irreconcilable. There was nothing for it but to omit both policies and substitute platitudes that any Church Congress would have signed. Morris's draft, horribly eviscerated and patched, was subsequently sold for a penny as the Joint Manifesto of the Socialists of Great Britain. It was the only document any of the three of us had ever signed and published that was honestly not worth a farthing (MM, ii. pp. xxxv–xxxvi).

A-65.01: Concerning Westminster Abbey

[wrapper title]THE | SOCIETY FOR THE PROTECTION | OF ANCIENT BUILDINGS. | CONCERNING | WESTMINSTER ABBEY. | LONDON | 9, BUCKINGHAM STREET, ADELPHI, W.C.

Edition: [1st impression, 1st edn.] Later, as 'Westminster Abbey', combined with 'Architecture and History' in the 4th vol. of the 'Golden type 8°' series; sometimes this pamphlet occurs with a wrapper manufactured by H. B. Forman (see E-13).

Collation: 8°: [1]⁸ 8 leaves pp. [1–4] 5–14 [15–16] [= 16] self-wrapped. Sometimes sophisticated by an additional separate smooth grey wrapper created by H. B. Forman (see E-13).

Contents: p. [1], title page, see above; p. [2], blank; p. [3], text begins; pp. [4]–14, text completed: [thin rule] | WOMEN'S PRINTING SOCIETY, LTD., 66 Whitcomb Street, W.C.; pp. [15–16], blank.

Technical Notes: *paper*: plain white machine-made; *leaf size*: cut flush, 183 x 124 mm.; *printing*: type area: 129 x 103 mm.; *lines-to-page*: set solid, 38 lines; *pagination*: arabic numbers centred on the headline; *binding*: for details of the forged wrapper, see E-13.

Publication: June 1893 [this date appears only on the grey (T. J. Wise calls it 'lavender', Forman calls it 'grey') paper wrapper, along with a doubtful statement of limitation] (see E-13). But the SPAB Annual Report of July 1893 confirms the date of the original pamphlet is correct; *print run*: unknown; *price*: for free distribution.

Register of Copies Examined: BL (3 copies: base copy: Cup. 502. f. 11. (46.), without separate wrapper; 7808.df.16. (6.), without separate wrapper; and Ashley 1233), with separate wrapper; NNBerg (without separate wrapper).

Notes: S. C. Cockerell's MS Diary for 7 Mar. 1893 says Morris finished the text of *Westminster Abbey* on this day (Cockerell Papers, BL (Add.) MS 52772).

A-66.01: Gothic Architecture (KP)

GOTHIC ARCHITECTURE: | A LECTURE FOR THE ARTS | AND CRAFTS EXHIBITION | SOCIETY [printer's leaf ornament No. 2] BY WILLIAM | MORRIS.

Edition: 'Kelmscott Press Edition' [1st impression, 1st edn.] A lecture 1st delivered at the 1889 Exhibition and printed as one of the displays during the 1893 Exhibition (only the presswork was done at the New Gallery, the composition being previously completed at Hammersmith). There are 3 textual variants brought about by corrections introduced during the printing, but it is not clear whether the revisions were coterminous with the 'reprints' so called by Cockerell. The 1st variant state has 2 errors: 'gilds' for 'Guilds' on p. 41 and 'Van Eyk' for 'Van Eyck' on p. 45; the 2nd state has only the 1st error corrected; and the 3rd state has both errors corrected.. The 4th state involves a deliberate 'paper' variant, consisting of 45 copies printed on vellum. S. C. Cockerell says, 'The first copies were ready on October 21, and the book was twice reprinted before the exhibition closed' (quoted in Sparling, 155). Treating the changes as they are treated here contradicts Cockerell's calling them separate 'reprints', assuming rather that the brief stoppage of the press between sessions justifies classing the different versions as variants of the same impression rather than reprints. The stoppages at 500 and 1,000 on the way to 1500 look like quite deliberate stages of a single printing, the unusual aspect of which is that the demand during the printing happened in this special case so as to bring about an increase in the number of copies being printed.

Series: 18th title, 7th by Morris, pbd. by the KP.

Colophon: This paper, first spoken as a lec- | ture at the New Gallery, for the | Arts & Crafts Exhibition Society, | in the year 1889, was printed by the | Kelmscott Press during the Arts | and Crafts Exhibition at the New | Gallery, Regent Street, London, | 1893. | [¶] Sold by William Morris, Kelms- | cott Press, Upper Mall, Hammer- | smith.

Collation: 16° in 8s: a–d⁸ e⁴ [$2 (–e2) signed] 37 leaves pp. [2] [1] 2–68 [69–72] [= 74] + the title page inserted after the front free end paper, noted in the formula, but not counted in the book's pagination.

Contents: p. [1], title page (tipped in); p. [2], blank; p. [1], head title: [in red] GOTHIC ARCHITECTURE. | [text begins]; pp. 2–68, text completed, with colophon (see

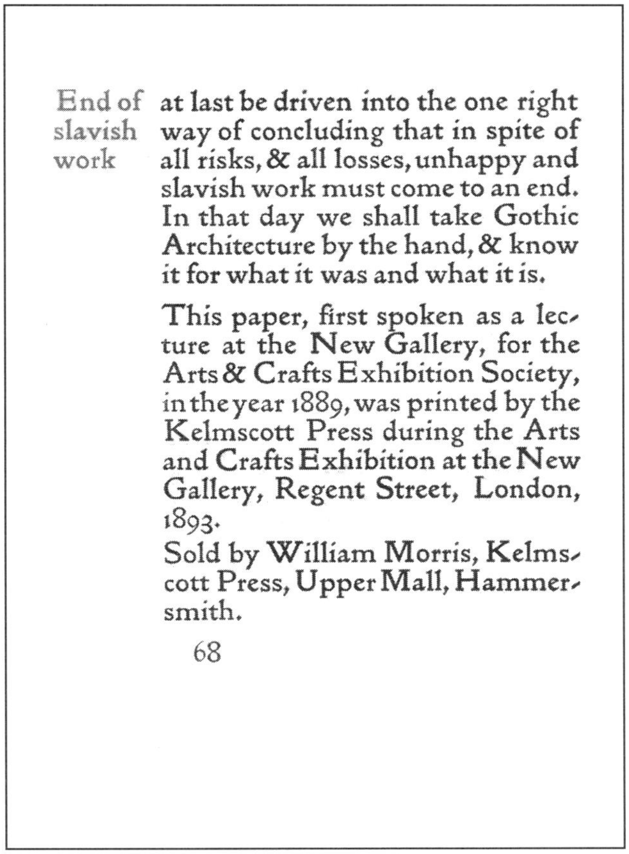

> End of slavish work at last be driven into the one right way of concluding that in spite of all risks, & all losses, unhappy and slavish work must come to an end. In that day we shall take Gothic Architecture by the hand, & know it for what it was and what it is.
>
> This paper, first spoken as a lecture at the New Gallery, for the Arts & Crafts Exhibition Society, in the year 1889, was printed by the Kelmscott Press during the Arts and Crafts Exhibition at the New Gallery, Regent Street, London, 1893.
> Sold by William Morris, Kelmscott Press, Upper Mall, Hammersmith.
>
> 68

Figure 58. A-66.01: *Gothic Architecture* (KP edn.) last page, with colophon

above); pp. [69–72], blank.
Technical Notes: *paper*: Kelmscott Flower paper 2; *leaf size*: trimmed, 144 x 103 mm.; *printing*: printed in red and black: shoulder notes and short title (p. [1]) printed in red; *type area*: 89 x 65 mm., excluding head and direction lines; *lines-to-page*: set solid, 19 lines; *type face*: Golden type; *shoulder notes*: all versos and rectos after p. 1: sub-head to the adjacent text; *end-papers*: front: 1 free end and paste-down; back has a 2nd free end tipped in, corresponding to the title page tipped in at the front; *binding*: quarter white holland with grey paper-covered boards with full title printed on the front, duplicate of title page, except that the printer's leaf is KP no. 1; *ornamentation*: 4 floriated 6-line and 23 floriated 4-line initials (the 1st use of the latter), 1 at the beginning of each paragraph, 43 of printer's leaf ornaments Nos. 1 and 2, usually alternating; no indents used.
Publication: 1893 [issued 21 Oct.] (According to S. C. Cockerell's 'Annotated List of All the Books printed at the Kelmscott Press in the Order in which they were issued', the composition having been done in Hammersmith, issue began with the 1st impression of 500 copies which were ready on 21 Oct. for sale during the exhibition, which ran from 5 Oct. to 5 Dec. Sales continued through the exhibition, with 2 more sessions of printing, each adding 500 copies to the original 500 (Cockerell, p. 155); *print run*: 1,500 paper copies printed in three 500-copy lots and sold at the exhibition; *price*: 2s. 6d.; 45 vellum copies sold for 10s. during the exhibition, 15s. thereafter (see Cockerell, p. 155).
Register of Copies Examined: VSL (2 copies: base copy: *094 K29m; and S723.5/M33); LeM; SSL (728.5Sp); ANL (AB MOO 1851); Fdmn.; CSt (Z239.2/K27M87g Gunst); VU (Baill.: 3 copies, 46 B).
Notes: S. C. Cockerell confirms the various textual emendations, the sequence of the 3 lots of printing, and the number and price of the paper and vellum copies (Cockerell, p. 155).

The British Bookmaker: 'the next issue of the Kelmscott Press will be Mr. William Morris's lecture on "Gothic Architecture" delivered before the Arts and Crafts Society in 1889. This will be the first of what may be called popular editions, as it will be issued in paper boards, 16 mo, at the price of 2/6' ('Home Notes' 7/76 (Oct. 1893), 91).

A-67.01: Help for the Miners

[head title] HELP FOR THE MINERS. | [thin rule] | *Daily Chronicle,* Nov. 10th, 1893. | **THE DEEPER MEANING OF THE STRUGGLE.** | To the Editor. | [text begins]
Edition: [1st impression, 1st edn.] This handbill is the 1st separate edn., reprinted from *The Daily Chronicle* of 10 Nov. 1893, see D-554. The handbill is reset, but the text is indistinguishable from the newspaper version.
Publisher: [The Hammersmith Socialist Society].
Collation: a single cr. 8° leaf, printed on both sides.
Contents: p. [1], head title, text begins; p. [2], text ends with Morris signature: [1st line centred, 2nd indented from 1st, 3rd ending flush right] I am, Sir, | Yours obediently, | WILLIAM MORRIS. | [flush left] KELMSCOTT HOUSE, | [indented] UPPER MALL, HAMMERSMITH. | [further indented] *November 9th*, 1893. | [thin rule] | Baines & Scarsbrook, Printers, 75, Fairfax Road, South Hampstead.
Technical Notes: *paper*: plain white machine-made; *leaf size*: 219 x 124 mm.; *printing*: type area: 191 x 102 mm., leaded.
Publication: 1893 [issued Nov.] (shortly after the *Daily Chronicle* pbn.); *print run*: unknown; *price*: probably for free distribution.
Register of Copies Examined: NNBerg; WMG.

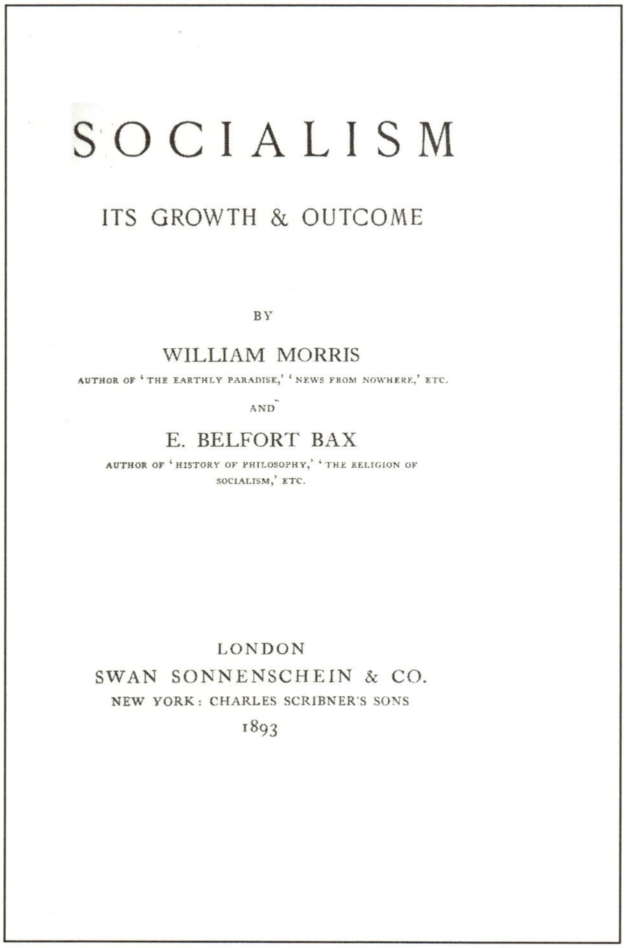

Figure 59. A-68.01: *Socialism: Its Growth & Outcome* (1st edn.) title page

A-68.01: Socialism: Its Growth and Outcome

SOCIALISM | ITS GROWTH & OUTCOME | BY | WILLIAM MORRIS | AUTHOR OF 'THE EARTHLY PARADISE,' 'NEWS FROM NOWHERE,' ETC. | AND | E. BELFORT BAX | AUTHOR OF 'HISTORY OF PHILOSOPHY,' 'THE RELIGION OF | SOCIALISM,' ETC. | LONDON | SWAN SONNENSCHEIN & CO. | NEW YORK: CHARLES SCRIBNER'S SONS | 1893

Edition: [1st impression, 1st edn.] 1st pbd. in *Commonweal* as 'Socialism from the Root Up', in instalments printed at irregular intervals from 15 May 1886 to 19 May 1888 (see D-190). Revised by the two original authors for this separate edn. Besides the ordinary edn., there was a LP 'special edition' of 250 copies (limitation notice says 275 copies, but see an interview with Swan Sonnenschein in *Justice*, 10/511 (28 Oct. 1893), 3).

Collaborators, Editors, and Illustrators: '. . . the work has been, in the true sense of the word, a collaboration, each sentence having been carefully considered by both the authors in common, although now one, now the other, has had more to do with initial suggestions in different parts of the work' (from the 'Preface', p. vi).

Series: Social Science Series.

Collation: cr. 8°: [A]⁴ B–Y⁸ 172 leaves pp. [i–v] vi–viii [1] 2–335 [336] [= 344].

Contents: p. [i], half title; p. [ii], blank; LP has limitation notice: Large Paper Edition | Only two-hundred and seventy-five copies printed for Great Britain and America, of which this is No. 78 [BGR copy]; p. [iii], title page; p. [iv], blank; p. [v], dropped head: PREFACE | [text begins]; p. vi, text ends with initials: [below right] W. M. | E. B. B.; p. [vii], dropped head: CONTENTS | [21 chapters listed]; p. viii, Contents completed; p. [1], 1st chapter head title: SOCIALISM | ITS GROWTH AND OUTCOME | INTRODUCTION | [text begins]; pp. 2–[328], text completed; p. [329], dropped head: INDEX | [list begins]; pp. 330–4, index continues, in 2 cols., divided by vertical thin rule; p. 335, index ends: [printer's imprint] Printed by R & R Clarke, *Edinburgh*.; p. [336], blank.

Technical Notes: *paper*: plain white machine-moulded paper; *leaf size*: 189 x 124 mm.; *printing*: type area: 118 x 67 mm.; *lines-to-page*: set solid, 28 lines; *running heads*: all versos: SOCIALISM | [all rectos, relevant chapter short title]; *end-papers*: single free end and paste-down, plain white and blank, front and back; *binding*: plain unblocked dark red cloth, gilt-stamped on spine: SOCIALISM | ITS GROWTH | AND OUTCOME | [rule] | WILLIAM MORRIS | [thin rule] | E. Belfort Bax | [thick rule] | [printer's leaf] | [at foot] SONNENSCHEIN; LP copies bound in plain unblocked dark red buckram with printed paper spine label, titling as in the ordinary copies.

Publication: 1893 [issued 11–18 Nov.] (*Pub. Circ.*, 59/1429 (18 Nov. 1893), 603); *print run*: 1,000 ordinary and 250 LP copies; *price*: ordinary copies: 6*s*. cloth, and 3*s*. 6*d*. paper; LP copies, 15*s*. ('Publications of the Month' [of Nov.] *Christmas BSR*, No. 433 (15 Dec. 1893), 1185). The American issue was copyright there by Scribner's. The American copyright law at the time required simultaneous issue.

Register of Copies Examined: BL (base copy: 08276.g.60.); VU (2 copies: 335/M877 and 110706); SU (335/M87s Store XG 3624); LeM; BGR ('Large Paper Edition | Only two-hundred and seventy-five copies printed for Great Britain and America, of which this is No. 78').

Notes: the Swan Sonnenschein & Co. Archive at the University of Reading (hereafter referred to as Sonnenschein

Arch.) has correspondence which provides further details of this book: (a) royalties, divided equally between the two authors, were 25% on the LP edn., 22 1/2% on the 1,000 ordinary copies, and 15% for the cheap edn., to be priced at 3*s*. 6*d*.; (b) on 23 Mar. the last proofs were sent to Morris, with a request for any prefatory matter and asking whether an index was planned. The publisher, thinking it would be desirable that one be included, offered the firm's services in providing one; a draft prospectus was sent to Morris on 11 Apr., describing 2 'editions', i.e. LP and ordinary.

E. Belfort Bax, 'Preface to the Third and Revised Edition' (1908):

> As the surviving author of the present book, it has devolved on me to make a few corrections of misprints and slips that had crept into the work in its original form.
>
> Save in one case, that of p 228, in which a paragraph has been rewritten in accordance with the expressed wishes of my lamented collaborator, the late William Morris, no substantial alteration has been made. The book thus remains to all intents and purposes the same as it originally left our hands in the year 1893' [p. vii].

Later impressions from this edn.: Swann Sonnenschein:
1.* 1896 [issued 31 Oct.–7 Nov.] (Sonnenschein Arch.): Second Edition [2nd impression, 1st edn.]; *print run*: unknown; *price*: cloth 6*s*., paper 3*s*. 6*d*.;
2.* 1908 [issued Mar.] (Sonnenschein Arch.): Third Edition [3rd impression, revised, 1st edn.]; *print run*: unknown; *price*: 3*s*. 6*d*.

A-68.02: Socialism: Its Growth and Outcome

SOCIALISM | *ITS GROWTH AND* | *OUTCOME* | BY | WILLIAM MORRIS | AUTHOR OF "THE EARTHLY PARADISE," "NEWS FROM NOWHERE," ETC | AND | E. BELFORT BAX | AUTHOR OF "HISTORY OF PHILOSOPHY," "THE RELIGION OF | SOCIALISM," ETC. | [thin rule] | CHICAGO | CHARLES H. KERR & COMPANY | 1909
Edition: [1st impression, 2nd separate edn., 1st American] 1st pbd. as 'Socialism from the Root Up' in *Commonweal* (see D-190), but revised by the 2 original authors for the 1st separate edn..
Collation: 12°: [1-15$^{6/10}$ 16^8] 126 leaves pp. [1–6] 7–244 [245–8] [= 252].
Contents: [1], title page; p. [2], union-made logo and printer's imprint: JOHN F. HIGGINS, PRINTER AND BINDER | 278–285 MONROE STREET | CHICAGO, U. S. A.; p. [3], dropped head: CONTENTS | [thin rule] | [21 chapter titles, as a list]; p. [4], blank; p. [5], dropped head: PREFACE | [text begins and ends, initialled, below right] W. M. | E. B. B.; p. [6], blank; p. 7, dropped head: SOCIALISM | ITS GROWTH AND OUTCOME | [thin rule] | INTRODUCTION | [text begins]; pp. 8–244, text completed; pp. [245–52], publisher's ads.
Technical Notes: *paper*: plain white machine-made; *leaf size*: trimmed, 167 x 104 mm.; *printing*: *type area*: 118 x 76 mm.; *lines-to-page*: set solid, 33 lines; *end-papers*: one free end and paste-down, plain white and blank, front and back; *binding*: olive green ribbed cloth (Tanselle 1, No. 102) with 2 separate thick-rule compartments black-stamped head and foot on the front, the 1st with title: [aligned left] SOCIALISM | [indented] ITS GROWTH | [further indented] AND OUTCOME; the 2nd compartment, at the foot, has the authors' names: WILLIAM MORRIS | ERNEST BELFORT BAX; a circular blind-stamped compartment with arm and torch design within separates the 2 compartments; *spine*: 4 blind-stamped false bands border the 2 compartments: [top, black stamped] SOCIALISM | ITS | GROWTH | AND | OUTCOME | [thin rule] | MORRIS | AND BAX; [lower compartment, publisher's monogram, intertwined] CHK
Publication: 1909; *print run* and *price*: unknown.
Register of Copies Examined: LeM (base copy); CSmH.
Later reprint of this edn.: Kerr.
1.* 1913: [2nd impression, 2nd edn., 1st American]; *print run*: unknown; *price*: unknown.

A-69.01: King Florus and Fair Jehane (KP)

THE TALE OF KING FLORUS | AND THE FAIR JEHANE.
Edition: 'Kelmscott Press Edition' [1st impression, 1st edn.]
Series: 21st title, 8th by Morris, pbd. by the KP; also the 1st of 3 uniform KP books comprising 4 tales, all translations from the same source—L. Moland and C. D. Hericault, *Nouvelles Françaises en prose du xiiiiéme siècle* (Paris, 1856)—and all later combined in a single vol. (not pbd. by the KP) titled *Old French Romances* (see A-79.01).
Colophon: Printed by William Morris at the | Kelmscott Press, Upper | Mall, Hammersmith, in the | County of Middlesex, & fin- | ished on the 16th day of De- | cember, 1893. | [¶] Sold by William Morris at the Kelmscott Press.
Collation: 16mo in 8s: [a]^4 (a4+1) b–g^8 (g8+1) [$2 (–b1) signed] 52 leaves + 2 tipped in counted in the pagination [=54] pp. [*10*][1] 2–96 [*97–8*] [=108] the front end papers

must be counted here as part of the first gathering, the first leaf being the pastedown, is conjunct with a4, which is the half title. The 2 inserted leaves, as shown in the *Contents*, are the engraved title and the colophon respectively. The last leaves are the typical end-paper gathering of the KP books: 3 free ends and a pastedown.

Contents: pp. [*1–6*], blank; p. [*7*] half title; p. [*8*], blank verso of half title; p. [*9*], blank recto of frontispiece; p. [*10*], frontispiece: engraved title in 3-line gothic letters with an ornamental background designed by Morris: of | KING | FLORUS | and the | FAIR JEHANE; with full border (KP no. 11a); p. [*1*], chapter head: : in red, within border No. 11: The Tale of King Florus | and the Fair Jehane | [text begins, in black]; pp. 2–96, text completed with explicit, in red: Here endeth the tale of King | Florus and the Fair Jehane.; p. [*97*], colophon, see above; p. [*98*], blank.

Technical Notes: this vol. is uniform with the KP issues of *Gothic Architecture, Amis and Amilie* and *The Emperor Coustans and Over Sea*, all 1st edns. Details specific to each title are noted under the relevant title, but the series is uniform for all 3 vols. in the following: *paper*: Perch paper; *leaf size*: 144 x 105 mm.; *printing*: *type face*: Chaucer type, in red and black, red for head title, shoulder notes, and explicit; *shoulder notes*: all rectos and versos: sub-heads of adjacent text; *end-papers*: see the *Collation* and note attached; *binding*: quarter white holland with blue paper-covered boards, title printed on front duplicates title page; specific to this title: *type area*: 92 x 63 mm.; *lines-to-page*: set solid, 22 lines; *ornamentation*: 2 borders—11a and 11— the same for all 3 of the KP French romance vols., each of which has its own engraved title by Morris; *King Florus* also has a 6-line floriated initial, and 56 3-line floriated initials.

Publication: 16 Dec. 1893 [colophon date indicates printing finished, issued 28 Dec.] (see Cockerell, p. 156); *print run*: 350 copies on paper and 15 copies on vellum; *price*: 7s. 6d. and 30s., respectively.

Register of Copies Examined: BL (2 copies: base copy: C. 43. dd. 3., and Ashley 1234)

Notes: Cockerell says eighty-five copies of *King Florus* were bought by J. and M. L. Tregaskis, who had them bound in all parts of the world. These are now in the Rylands Library at Manchester (Cockerell, p. 156, and 'A Memorable Exhibit of Bookbinding', *British Printer*, 7 (July–August 1894), 13.).

Peterson also quotes from the *Amis and Amilie* announcement (see Appendix II-8) a passage which he says is 'probably by Morris': 'this tale dates from about the same period as that of King Florus, and its literary & historical value is equally high. As in the case of King Florus, the Englishing is literal' (*KP Biblio.*, p. 63.)

A-69.02: Old French Romances (Florus, etc.)

Edition: [1st impression, 2nd edn.] For details of the *Old French Romances* vol., see A-79.01.

A-69.03: King Florus and the Fair Jehane (Broc.)

[aligned left, lines 1, 2, and the last line in red] THE TALE OF KING FLORUS | AND THE FAIR JEHANE | [in black, flush left] DONE OUT OF THE ANCIENT | FRENCH INTO ENGLISH BY WILLIAM MORRIS | [Chiswick Press book mark, Bishop No. 2] | [aligned left] PORTLAND MAINE | THOMAS B. MOSHER | MDCCCXCVIII

Edition: 'Brocade Edition' [1st impression, 3rd edn., 1st American] Text 1st pbd. in a KP edn., see A-69.01.

Collaborators: foreword from Joseph Jacobs' Introduction to *Old French Romances* (see A-79.01).

Series: The Brocade Series (hereafter referred to as Broc.).— 11 (minor series: Old French Romances. 2—Morris) For more detail on this series, see this field, *Contents,* and *Technical Notes* in A-70.03.

Colophon: FOUR HUNDRED AND TWEN- | TY-FIVE COPIES OF THIS | BOOK HAVE BEEN | PRINTED | ON JAPAN VELLUM, AND | TYPE DISTRIBUTED, IN THE | MONTH OF SEPTEMBER, A.D. | MDCCCXCVIII. AT THE PRESS | OF GEORGE D. LORING, PORT- | LAND, MAINE.

Collation: 16° in 4s: [1–10]⁴ 40 leaves pp. [1–8] 9–72 [73–80] [= 80].

Contents: p. [1], half title; p. [2], edn. statement, lists the 2 previous Morris pbns. of this title; p. [3], title page; p. [4], blank; p. [5], headed: FOREWORD | [text begins]; p. [6], Foreword ends: [signed, below right] Old French Romances; p. [7], 2nd half title; p. [8], blank; p. 9, dropped head: [below Chiswick Press head piece] | THE TALE OF KING FLORUS | AND THE FAIR JEHANE | [text begins]; pp. 10–[73], text completed with Chiswick Press tail piece; p. [74], colophon, see above; pp. [75–80], blank.

Technical Notes: for details common to the series—paper, leaf size, printing, type area, lines-to-page, pagination, and binding—see this field in A-70.03; details specific to this issue: *running titles*: [all versos, flush left] THE TALE OF KING FLORUS | [all rectos, flush left] AND THE

FAIR JEHANE; *end-papers*: 2 free ends and paste-down, plain white and blank, front and back; *binding letterpress*: title prtd. on front: [4-line red floriated initial 'T']: THE TALE OF | KING FLORUS | AND THE FAIR | JEHANE DONE | OUT THE ANCIENT | FRENCH INTO ENGLISH | BY WILLIAM MORRIS [fleuron]; title (1st 2 lines from title page) printed down the spine; on the back upper right a caduceus designed by Bruce Rogers (see Bishop, p. 53), sold in slip cases with brocade designs, from which the series takes its name.
Publication: Sept. 1898 (colophon date): 'Brocade Series'; *print run*: 425 copies; *price*: 75 cents net, and $3.00 net as a 4-vol. boxed set of Old French Romances, combining *King Coustans, Amis and Amile, King Florus*, and *The History of Over Sea* in cabinet box.
Register of Copies Examined: BL (base copy: 1606/1570); Bsp
Later impressions (or edns?) *from this edn.*: (see also the *Edition* field in A-70.03):
1.* 1898 [Nov.] (Brenton L. Hatch, *A Checklist of Publications of Thomas Bird Mosher*, No. 100; hereafter referred to as Hatch): SECOND EDITION [2nd impression, 3rd edn., 1st American]; *print run* and *price*: see above;
2.* 1904 [Jan.] (Hatch, No. 309): THIRD EDITION [3rd impression, 3rd edn., 1st American]; *print run* and *price*: see above;
3.* 1915 [Dec.] (Hatch, No. 632): FOURTH EDITION [4th impression, 3rd edn., 1st American]; *print run* and *price*: see above.

A-70.01: Amis and Amile (KP)

OF THE FRIENDSHIP | OF AMIS AND AMILE
Edition: 'Kelmscott Press Edition' [1st impression, 1st edn.] For the details of the original, of which this is a translation, see the *Series* field in A-69.01.
Translation: Done into English out of the ancient French by William Morris.
Series: 23rd title, 10th by Morris, pbd. by the KP, and one of 3 vols., not numbered, comprising 4 titles, translated from the same source and uniformly printed and bound.
Colophon: [in red, aligned flush left] Here ends the Story of Amis | & Amile, done out of an- | cient-French into English, by | William Morris, and printed | by the said William Morris | at the Kelmscott Press, 14, | Upper Mall, Hammersmith, | in the County of Middlesex; | finished on the 13th day of | March, of the year 1894. | [¶, in black] Sold by William Morris, at | the Kelmscott Press

Collation: 16° in 8s: a⁴ b–e⁸ f⁴ [$2 (–a1–2 b1 f2) signed] 40 leaves pp. [8] [1] 2–67 [68–72] [= 80].
Contents: pp. [1–4], blank; p. [5], title page; pp. [6–7], blank; p. [8], engraved title in Morris-designed gothic letters as frontis., in border No. 11a: of the | FRIEND | SHIP | of | AMIS | and | AMILE; p. [1], head title, within border No. 11: [in red] The Friendship Of Amis And | Amile [printer's flower ornaments No. 3] | [text begins with 13-line ornamental initial 'I']; pp. 2–66, text completed with explicit: [flush left] Reigning our Lord Jesus | Christ, who liveth & reigneth | without end with the Father | & the Holy Ghost. AMEN.; p. 67, colophon: see above; pp. [68–72], blank.
Technical Notes: in paper, leaf size, type, printing, shoulder notes, pagination, signatures, and binding, the 3 KP vols. of old French romances are uniform, see this field in A-69.01; details specific to this book: *type area*: 83 x 59 mm.; *end-papers*: 2 free ends and paste-down, plain white and blank, front and back; *ornamentation*: 2 Morris borders, 11a and 11; *Amis and Amile* has also 1 13-line floriated initial, 5 6-line initials; and 72 3-line initials.
Publication: 13 Mar. 1894 [colophon date indicates finished printing, issued 4 Apr.] (see Cockerell., 157); *print run*: 500 paper copies and 15 on vellum; *price*: 7s. 6d. and 30s. respectively.
Register of Copies Examined: VU (2 copies: base copy: ER and 46A); BL (2 copies: C. 43. dd. 4. and Ashley Library 1235); MU.
Notes: See also the reference to Peterson in A-69.01, *Notes*.

A-70.02: Old French Romances (Amile, etc.)

Edition: [1st impression, 2nd edn.] This is a reference entry. For details of this vol., see *Old French Romances*, A-79.01.

A-70.03: Amis and Amile (Broc.)

[hanging indent, 1st and last lines in brown] THE STORY OF AMIS & AMILE | DONE OUT OF THE ANCIENT | FRENCH INTO ENGLISH BY | WILLIAM MORRIS | [Chiswick Press book mark, Bishop No. 2] | PORTLAND MAINE | THOMAS B. MOSHER | M*dcccxcvi.*
Edition: [1st impression, 3rd edn., 1st American] It should be noted that Mosher's use of the term 'edition' and his statements of limitation may best be approached with some caution. The 1st and 2nd 'editions' of *Amis and Amile*, issued in Aug. and Dec. 1896, are identical, even to the reproduction of a broken type (p. 40, 'good') in both texts.

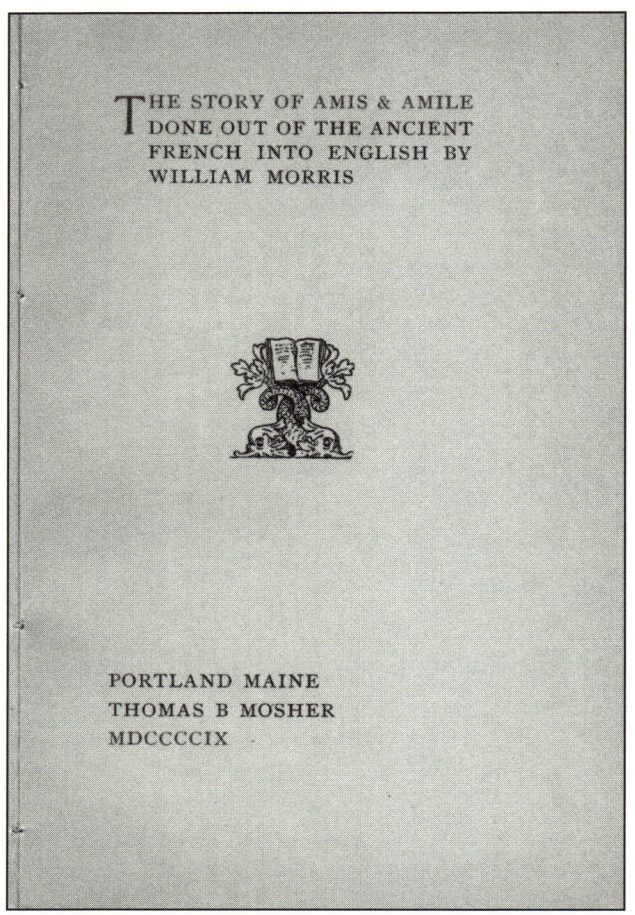

Figure 60. A-70.03: *Amis & Amile* (3rd edn., Broc.) title page

This anomaly, which was pointed out by Philip Bishop, Mosher's bibliographer, makes it impossible to say the texts are different settings, hence different edns, as both Mosher's phrase 'and type distributed' and his naming of subsequent printings as SECOND EDITION, etc., seem to imply (see *Colophon*, below, and the later printings). There has been no attempt here to submit all of the Mosher 'editions' to close comparison to test the edn. statements made or implied in their colophons, but the duplications are so close between the multiple 'editions' that space is saved by describing those after the 1st as later impressions, perhaps made with stereotype plates, while drawing attention to Mosher's attempt in each colophon to imply resetting. It certainly was not so where the *editio princeps* of *Amis and Amile* was concerned. The repeated broken type casts a shadow over past, present, and future proceedings.

Collaborators, Editors, and Illustrators: Foreword, unsigned [by the editor, T. B. Mosher].

Series: This is the 1st Mosher publication of Morris, this title being issued in the 'Brocade Series—3'. As a rule, the series title and number are not printed in any of these books, being designated only in Mosher's advertising lists and catalogues. A total of 9 titles related to Morris (in 27 issues) appeared in the Brocade Series, within which Mosher created 2 subsets or minor series of 4 Morris books each, sold individually or in boxed sets. Later issues were embellished with a contents page prtd. within a reproduction of the title borders of the KP *Amis and Amile*. The first subset is called 'Old French Romances' comprising, besides *Amis and Amile*, *The Tale of King Florus*, *The History of Over Sea*, and *The Tale of King Coustans*, all reprinted by Mosher from the 1896 London vol., *Old French Romances*, a collection of the 4 Morris translations 1st pbd. in 3 vols. at the KP. A 2nd Morris subset of 4 original prose tales, titled by Mosher 'Old English Romances', included *The Hollow Land*, *Gertha's Lovers*, *Golden Wings*, and *The Story of the Unknown Church*, all reprinted from *The Oxford and Cambridge Magazine* (1856). Morris's *The Churches of North France. No. 1—Amiens*, 1st pbd. separately by Mosher as an issue under the *Bibelot* masthead (see A-98.01), then appeared with Morris's essay on Alfred Rethel in the series Reprints from "The Bibelot"—9 (see C-12). Brocade Series—39, *Some Great Churches in France*, where Morris's 'Amiens' essay is combined with 2 essays by Henry James, is neither a Morris title nor a Morris collection, hence it is not included here.

Sold separately as well as in sets and sub-sets, the Brocade Series books are uniform in several respects; their avg. size is 135 x 90 mm.; the price 75 cents each or $3.00 for a minor series 4-vol. boxed set; the print run for each title was 425 copies. All are printed on 'japan vellum' (actually japan paper, an ivory-coloured, thin, silky, parchment paper), and all are set with the same type. They are bound in boards with thin japan vellum wraps glued on at the spine. The title is printed on the front wrap and a caduceus on the back. Individual copies were each sold in a slip-case covered with a brocade-design paper.

Colophon: FOUR HUNDRED AND TWEN- | TY-FIVE COPIES OF THIS | BOOK HAVE BEEN PRINTED | ON JAPAN VELLUM, AND | TYPE DISTRIBUTED, IN THE | MONTH OF AUGUST, A. D. | MDCCCX-CVI, AT THE PRESS | OF GEORGE D. LORING, | PORTLAND, MAINE.

Collation: 16° in 4s: [1–6]⁴ 24 leaves pp. [1–8] 9–46 [47–8] [= 48].

Contents: pp. [1–2], blank; p. [3], half title; p. [4], bibliographical note lists the 2 previous pbns. of this title; p. [5],

Original and Posthumous Editions

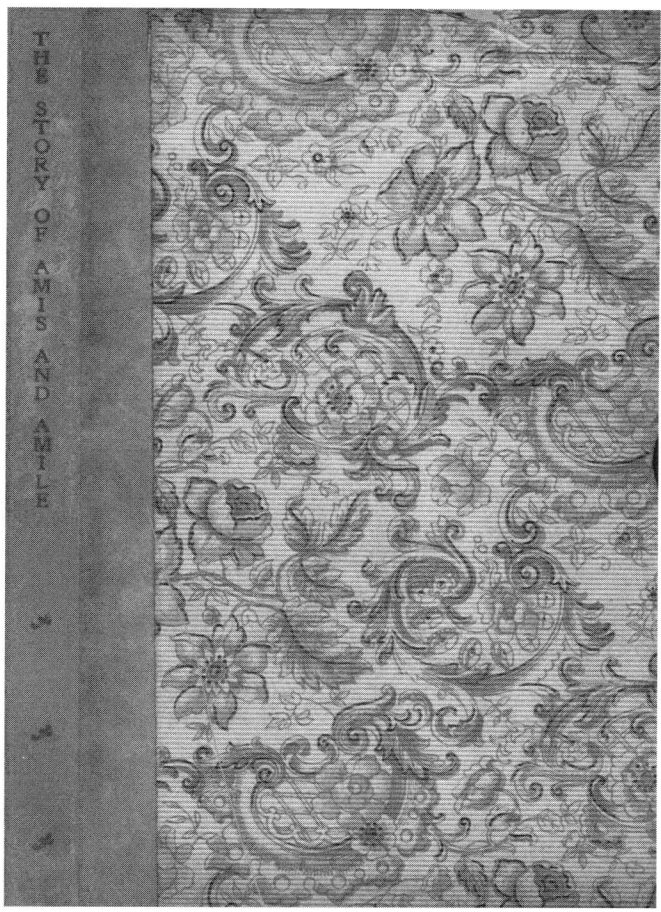

Figure 61. A-70.03: *Amis & Amile* (3rd edn., Broc.) binding

headed: Foreword | [text begins]; p. [6], Foreword ends; p. [7], 2nd half title; p. [8], blank; p. 9, headed: The Story of | Amis & Amile | [text begins]; pp. 10–[47], text completed with printer's leaf as tail piece; p. [48], colophon, see above.

Technical Notes: items common to the Brocade series: *paper*: cream machine-made japan vellum, no watermark; *leaf size*: (all issues): avg. 135 x 90 mm.; *type area*: avg. 85 x 50 mm.; *lines-to-page*: 24 lines set solid; *printing*: in brown (or red) and black, brown or red on binding and the title page, usually the 1st and last lines only; *running titles*: used in all books seen in this series, plain caps aligned to the inner margin; *binding*: cut flush, stiff japan vellum boards covered with japan vellum wraps that carry the letterpress: front: full title with red 4-line ornamental drop initial 'G', rest in black, and short title in black down the spine with letters aligned vertically, one above the other, in brown down the slipcase spine; back upper right has a caduceus, designed by Bruce Rogers (see *Bishop*, p. 53); *ornamenta-*

tion: brocade designs on slip cases; later versions provided optional matching designs on both the boards (some from the KP) and the slip cases; Chiswick Press head and tail-pieces; details specific to this issue: *end-papers*: 4 free ends (a full gathering) plain white and blank, front and back, no paste-downs; *binding*: letterpress: front: [title, with 4-line ornamental initial 'T' in red] THE STORY OF | AMIS AND AMILE | BY WILLIAM | MORRIS [2 fleurons]; *spine*: short title in brown down the spine, letters aligned vertically one above the other: THE STORY OF AMIS AND AMILE [3 fleurons]; back, upper right: caduceus with a flame rather than wings at the top.

Publication: Aug. 1896 (the colophon date indicates finished printing; issue is usually later); *print run*: 425 copies; *price*: 75 cents net; $3.00 as a boxed set of 4 Old French Romances.

Register of Copies Examined: LeM (base copy), Bsp

Notes: Some copies of this 1st American edn. lack the portions printed in brown on the title page, i.e. the title and the date (see *Bishop*, p. 289).

Later impressions (or editions?) from this edn.: Mosher:

1. Dec. 1896: SECOND EDITION [or 2nd impression, 3rd edn., 1st American]; *print run*: 425 copies; *price*: 75 cents net, or $3.00 for the boxed set of Old French Romances;

2.* Oct. 1897: THIRD EDITION [or 3rd impression, 3rd edn., 1st American]; *print run* and *price*: as above;

3.* Nov. 1898: FOURTH EDITION [or 4th impression, 3rd edn., 1st American]; *print run* and *price*: as above;

4.* Nov. 1899: FIFTH EDITION [or 5th impression, 3rd edn., 1st American]; *print run* and *price*: as above;

5.* Feb. 1909: SIXTH EDITION [or 6th impression, 3rd edn., 1st American]; *print run* and *price*: as above.

A-71.01: Birmingham Address 1894

[arms of the City of Birmingham] | **CITY OF BIRMINGHAM** | [thin rule] | MUSEUM & SCHOOL OF ART COMMITTEE. | [thin rule] | **AN ADDRESS** DELIVERED BY | WILLIAM MORRIS, | AT THE | DISTRIBUTION OF PRIZES TO STUDENTS OF THE | BIRMINGHAM MUNICIPAL SCHOOL OF ART, | ON THE 21st OF FEBRUARY, 1894

Edition: [1st impression, 1st edn.]

Printer: [Osborne ?].

Collation: demy 8°: [1]^{12} 12 leaves pp. [1–3] 4–21 [22–4] + wrapper.

Contents: p. [1], title page; p. [2], blank; p. [3], headed, flush left: MR. MAYOR, LADIES, AND GENTLEMEN,; pp. 4–21, text completed; pp. [22–4], blank.

Technical Notes: *paper*: white machine-made; *leaf size*: cut flush, 211 x 139 mm.; *printing*: *type area*: 167 x 99 mm. inc. head line; *lines-to-page*: 37 lines, leaded, with double spaces between paragraphs; *pagination*: arabic numbers, centred on headline; *binding*: *wrapper*: plain white paper, sewn to the body through the centrefold; p. [*1*], duplicate of the title page (above); wrapper pp. [*2–4*], blank. The wrapper is separate, though it need not have been, the text ends on p. 21, leaving 2 blank leaves.

Publication: 1894 [issued before 8 July] (BL copy accession stamp); *print run*: unknown; *price*: probably for free distribution.

Register of Copies Examined: SFU (base copy: p 701 M877a); BL (012301. f. 75.)

A-71.02: Birmingham Address 1894 (Golden 8°)

AN ADDRESS DELIVERED BY WIL- | LIAM MOR- RIS AT THE DISTRIBU- | TION OF PRIZES TO STUDENTS | OF THE BIRMINGHAM MUNICIPAL | SCHOOL OF ART ON FEB. 21, 1894.

Edition: 'Golden type octavo edition' [1st impression, 2nd edn.] Though the last 500 copies of this edn. (see *Notes*) were separately bound, or 'done up', that is not taken here to constitute a separate issue since there was no attempt to register with the public that this title was to be marketed anew or changed in any way. Sales were continuous, with no distinctions either internal or external between the copies of the 1st impression issued in 1898 and 1901. As intended from the beginning, the 'doing up' of the last copies was intended merely to replenish dwindling stocks from warehoused copies in shts.

Collaborators, Editors, and Illustrators: [edited by Sydney C. Cockerell].

Series: This is the 1st of a 5-book set, called by May Morris the 'Golden Type octavo edn', all cr. 8°, uniformly printed and bound, with KP Golden type and KP paper. Though the vols. are not numbered, the lectures—the contents of the set being 6 fugitive Morris lectures and an essay—are, except for the 1st, numbered continuously, Lecture II–VI through the last 4 vols. Vols. IV and V, since they contain more than a single text, are entered here in the C-List (see C-7 and C-11). The series was published by Longmans 'on commission', that is by an agreement with the publisher who received a set percentage or 'commission' on all expenses incurred in producing and marketing the books for the Trustees of the Morris Estate. Cockerell's note, on a slip loosely inserted in this 1st vol., announces the series:

> It is hoped that this lecture, which is printed in the 'Golden' type designed by William Morris for the Kelmscott Press, will be followed by other lectures in the same form, and at the same price, 2s. 6d. net. The Kelmscott Press is now closed, and all the wood blocks of the initials and ornaments have been given to the British Museum. The type still remains under the control of the Trustees, for whom the book was printed at the Chiswick Press.

Colophon: Printed at the Chiswick Press, and finished on | the 18th day of April, 1898. Published by | Longmans & Co., Paternoster Row, London.

Collation: cr. 8° in 4s: a–d⁴ 16 leaves pp. [4] 1–25 [26–8] [= 32].

Contents: p. [*1–2*], blank; edn. note on a slip loosely inserted facing the title page (see *Notes*, below); p. [*3*], title page; p. [*4*], blank; p. 1, head title, with title as on title page, and text begins; pp. 2–25, text completed with colophon (see above); pp. [*26–8*], blank.

Technical Notes: details common to the set: *paper*: cream hand-laid Batchelor's KP Perch paper with deckled edges and fish watermark; *leaf size*: lightly trimmed, 211 x 144 mm.; *printing*: *type face*: Morris's Golden type; *type area*: 141 x 93 mm. excluding direction line; *lines-to-page*: 30 lines set solid; *pagination*: arabic numerals set 10 mm. in from outer margins on the direction line; *end-papers*: vols. I–III and the end of vol. V: 1 free end and paste-down, plain cream and blank; front and back, but the end-paper gatherings in vol. IV and those at the beginning of vol. V, contain letterpress and are counted as part of the body (same paper as the body); *binding*: quarter blue holland with light blue paper-covered boards with duplicated title printed on front; details specific to this issue: *shoulder notes*: all rectos and versos: Birming- | ham School | of Art, 1894.; *binding letterpress*: front has the full title, duplicating the title page (see above).

Publication: 18 Apr. 1898 [this colophon date indicates finished printing, issued 1 June 1898] (Longmans *Notes on Books*, 9/173 (31 May 1898), 84); but see also 2 June 1898, cited in C. J. Longman's letter to Cockerell in *Notes* below); *print run*: 2,000 copies printed, of which only 1,500 were bound for the 1st issue date, the remaining 500 were bound in 1901 for 3*d*. a copy, recorded thus: 'Trustees of the Late William Morris. Doing up 500 copies Lecture I. viz; Birmingham Address. @ 3*d*.' (Chiswick Arch., vol. 10, p. 261 Ledger 30 July 1901); *price*: 2*s*. 6*d*.

Register of Copies Examined: VU (base copy: 2 copies of the

set, both 1st impression: L & E 704 / M877A, + various odd copies); LeM (2nd impression); BL (2 copies: K.T.C. 8. a. 20.; Ashley Library 3698); SU (2 copies: 704/M87ar).
Notes: letter from Cockerell to Mrs Morris, 9 Mar. 1898 with an enclosed copy of the text of this lecture and an explanation of the arrangements for the remaining KP assets, including type, ornaments, etc., with a report of the proposal Cockerell had made to Ellis to do a series of similar short fugitive lectures as small books to be sold at 2*s*. 6*d*. (Cockerell Papers, BL (Add.) MS 52738). Cockerell puts to her the alternatives for financing such a project and suggests that she might prefer to take the risk and dispose of any profits that might accrue. It seems likely that this suggestion as to risk and profits was chosen since later correspondence between Cockerell and Mrs Morris indicates that she, as distinct from the estate, was responsible for the editing expenses and Cockerell was paid a fee for his editing.

This series begins a larger project of the Trustees: to complete the printing in Morris's own type of all of his titles that had not been issued from the Kelmscott Press. Including this set of 5 books, the Trustees had 14 vols. printed in the 'Golden' type between 1898 and 1903, these being in addition to the Morris books pbd. posthumously as KP books during the last years of the Press's production. The 1903 pbn. of *The Hollow Land and Other Contributions to 'The Oxford and Cambridge Magazine'* (see C-20) ranges with this octavo set, but it is printed on Flower paper 2. The remaining 8 vols. are a set called 'Golden type quarto', also printed on Flower paper 2. All 14 Golden type vols. are bound in blue paper-covered boards with darker blue holland spines, one of the 2 main KP bindings, but the KP spines are white rather than blue holland.

In the Chiswick Arch. 'Cost Book' the entry for this 1st book in the series is headed, 'Kelmscott Press. Trustees of the late Wm. Morris', and the entry itself says the book was printed 'from set-up type supplied'. This refers to the fact that the KP compositors actually prepared the type forms for the 1st book of the series, the Chiswick Press being responsible only for the machining and the binding. By Dec. of the same year, the Golden type having by then been moved from Hammersmith to the Chiswick Press in Tooks Court, the 2nd book of this series, *Art and the Beauty of the Earth*, was produced there, the setting as well as the printing, as thereafter were the remaining 3 books of this series.

Cockerell to Mrs Jane Morris, 20 May 1898, explains that 10 gift copies will be going to Mrs Morris, Ellis, Cockerell, and Walker, the latter having worked with the press while Cockerell was on holiday in Italy (Cockerell Papers, BL (Add.) MS 52738).

C. J. Longman to S. C. Cockerell, 10 June 1898, indicates that copies of the Birmingham Lecture were sent to booksellers and issued to the Press on the 2 June (Smith Arch.)

A-72.01: Saga Library, vol. IV

THE STORIES OF THE | KINGS OF NORWAY | CALLED THE ROUND | WORLD | (HEIMSKRINGLA) | BY SNORRI STURLUSSON | DONE INTO ENGLISH | OUT OF THE ICELANDIC | BY | WILLIAM MORRIS | AND | EIRÍKR MAGNÚSSON | VOL. II [of IV] | LONDON | BERNARD QUARITCH, 15 PICCADILLY | 1894

Edition: [1st impression, 1st edn.] As is the case with all the 6 vols. of the Saga Library, in addition to the ordinary 1st issue there was an LP variant on Whatman's hand-made paper (royal 8°) of 125 copies, all numbered.
Series: The Saga Library, vol. IV. [For further series detail, see A-52.01].
Place: London.
Collation: cr. 8°: [A]⁴ B–2H⁸ 2I² 246 leaves pp. [8] [1–3] 4–467 [468–71] 472–84 [= 492].
Contents: pp. [1–2], blank; p. [3], 1st half title, as for vol. 3, allowing for obvious changes in the set and subset vol. nos.; p. [4], blank; p. [5], title page; p. [6], printer's imprint: CHISWICK PRESS:—CHARLES WHITTINGHAM AND CO. | TOOKS COURT, CHANCERY LANE, LONDON.; p. [7]: CONTENTS. | [titles and page nos. of the 2 sections of the book]; p. [8], blank; p. [1], 2nd half title: THE STORY OF OLAF THE HOLY | THE SON OF HARALD.; p. [2], blank; p. [3], dropped head: THE STORY OF OLAF THE | HOLY, THE SON OF HARALD. | CHAPTER I. THE BRINGING UP OF | OLAF THE HOLY, SON OF HARALD. | [text begins with 3-line drop-cap initial 'O']; pp. 4–467, Olaf's story completed; p. [468], blank; p. [469], 3rd half title: EXPLANATIONS OF THE | METAPHORS IN THE | VERSES.; p. [470], blank; p. [471], dropped head: EXPLANATIONS | [2-line note] | [text begins with 3-line drop-cap initial 'S']; pp. 472–84, text completed with explicit: END OF VOL. II. | [thin rule] | [printer's imprint, as on p. [6]].
Technical Notes: for details common to this series—paper, leaf size, printing, type area, lines-to-page, type face and size, running heads, pagination, end-papers, and binding—see this field in A-52.01; binding and 1st half title

altered to show VOL. IV. of the Saga Library, VOL. II. of Heimskringla.
Publication: 1894 [printing finished, issued 26 July] (Chiswick Arch.); *print run*: 1,500 copies + 125 LP copies; *price*: unknown.
Register of Copies Examined: see this field in A-52.01.
Notes: Chiswick Arch.: Bernard Quaritch Ledger book, July 1894, indicates the total cost, including LP copies and making stereo moulds = £160. 2s. 8d.

A-73.01: The Emperor Coustans and Over Sea (KP)

[aligned flush left, 2 of printer's flower ornaments No. 3] THE TALE OF THE | EMPEROR COUSTANS | AND OF OVER SEA.
Edition: 'Kelmscott Press Edition' [1st impression, 1st edn.] A 2nd edn. of this text was included in Joseph Jacobs' collection of the 4 KP prose tales as *Old French Romances* (see A-79.01). The 2 stories of this vol. were later pbd. separately by Mosher in his Brocade Series (see A-92.01 and 93.01). For details of the original French texts of this series of 4 tales, see this field in A-69.01. The 1st of the 2 tales told here is the basis for the story told in the *EP* under the title 'The Man Born to Be King'.
Series: 26th title, 11th by Morris, pbd. by the KP.
Colophon 1 (at the end of *King Coustans*): [in red except for the drop initial 'h' in black] HERE withal endeth the | Story of King Coustans | the Emperor. | [paragraph, with printer's flower ornament No. 1] The said story was done | out of the ancient French into | English by William Morris.
Colophon 2 (at the end of *The History of Over Sea*): [in red except for the last 2 lines and the drop initial 'h', in black] HERE ends the Story of | Over Sea, done out of | ancient French into Eng- | lish by William Morris. [¶] This book, the Stories of the | Emperor Coustans, and of | Over Sea, was printed by Wil- | liam Morris at the Kelmscott | Press, Upper Mall, Hammer- | smith, in the County of Mid- | dlesex, & finished on the 30th | day of August, 1894. [¶] Sold by William Morris at the | Kelmscott Press.
Collation: 16° in 8s: [a]⁴ b–i⁸ k⁴ [$2 (–b k2) signed] 72 leaves pp. [8] [1] 2–38 [*King Coustans* completed] [39–41] [*The History of Over Sea* begins] 42–130 [131–6] [= 144].
Contents: pp. [1–4], blank; p. [5], title page; pp. [6–7], blank; p. [8], engraved title as frontis. with full border 11a, text in 3-line caps: THE TALE | OF KING | COUS- | TANS EM | PEROR OF | BYZANCE; p. [1], headed, in red, within full border 11: The Tale of King Coustans | the Emperor [with 5 fleurons, printer's flower ornaments No. 3] | [text begins, in black, with 6-line ornamental initial 'T']; pp. 2–38, text completed with colophon 1 (see above); p. [39], half title: [top, flush left] THE HISTORY OF OVER | SEA [printer's flower ornament No. 3]; p. [40], border 11a enclosing an engraved title: A TALE | OF | OVER | SEA; p. [41], border 11 enclosing the title, in red: The History of Over Sea [printer's flower ornament No. 3] | [text begins]; pp. 42–130, text completed with 2nd colophon (see above); pp. [131–6], blank.
Technical Notes: *paper*: Batchelor's KP Perch paper; *leaf size*: lightly trimmed deckled edges, avg. 145 x 108 mm.; *printing*: in red and black: red for shoulder notes, head titles, colophons, and the quoted text of a letter (p. 27); *type area*: 93 x 62 mm., excluding shoulder notes and head and direction lines; *lines-to-page*: set solid, 22 lines; *type face*: Chaucer type; *shoulder notes*: all rectos and versos, in red, as marginal sub-heads to the adjacent text; *pagination*: arabic numbers set 7 mm. in from the outer margins on the direction line; *end-papers*: 2 free ends and paste-down, plain white and blank, front and back; *binding*: quarter white holland with blue paper-covered boards, title on the front duplicates the title page; *ornamentation*: 2 full borders, 11a and 11, the same for all 3 of the KP Old French romance vols. and each 11a with its own engraved title by Morris. In this book each full border is used twice, once for each of the 2 tales; the book has 11 6-line ornamental initials and 161 3-line ornamental initials.
Publication: 30 Aug. 1894 [printing finished, issued 26 Sept.] (Cockerell, p. 158); *print run*: 525 copies on paper, 20 on vellum; *price*: 7s. 6d. and 2gns., respectively.
Register of Copies Examined: LeM (base copy); CSt (Z239.2;K29M87t); BL (2 copies); VU (2 copies).

A-73.02: Old French Romances (Florus etc.)

Edition: [1st impression, 2nd edn.] This is a reference entry. For details of this vol., see *Old French Romances* A-79.01.

A-74.01: The Wood beyond the World (KP)

[half title, Chaucer type, flush left] THE WOOD BEYOND THE WORLD. | BY WILLIAM MORRIS.
Edition: 'Kelmscott Press Edition' [1st impression, 1st edn.].
Collaborators, Editors, and Illustrators: [frontis. from a drawing by Sir Edward Burne-Jones, engraved by W. Spielmeyer] (Cockerell, 158).
Series: 27th title, 12th by Morris, pbd. by the KP.
Colophon: HERE ends the tale of the Wood beyond | the World, made by William Morris, and | printed by him at

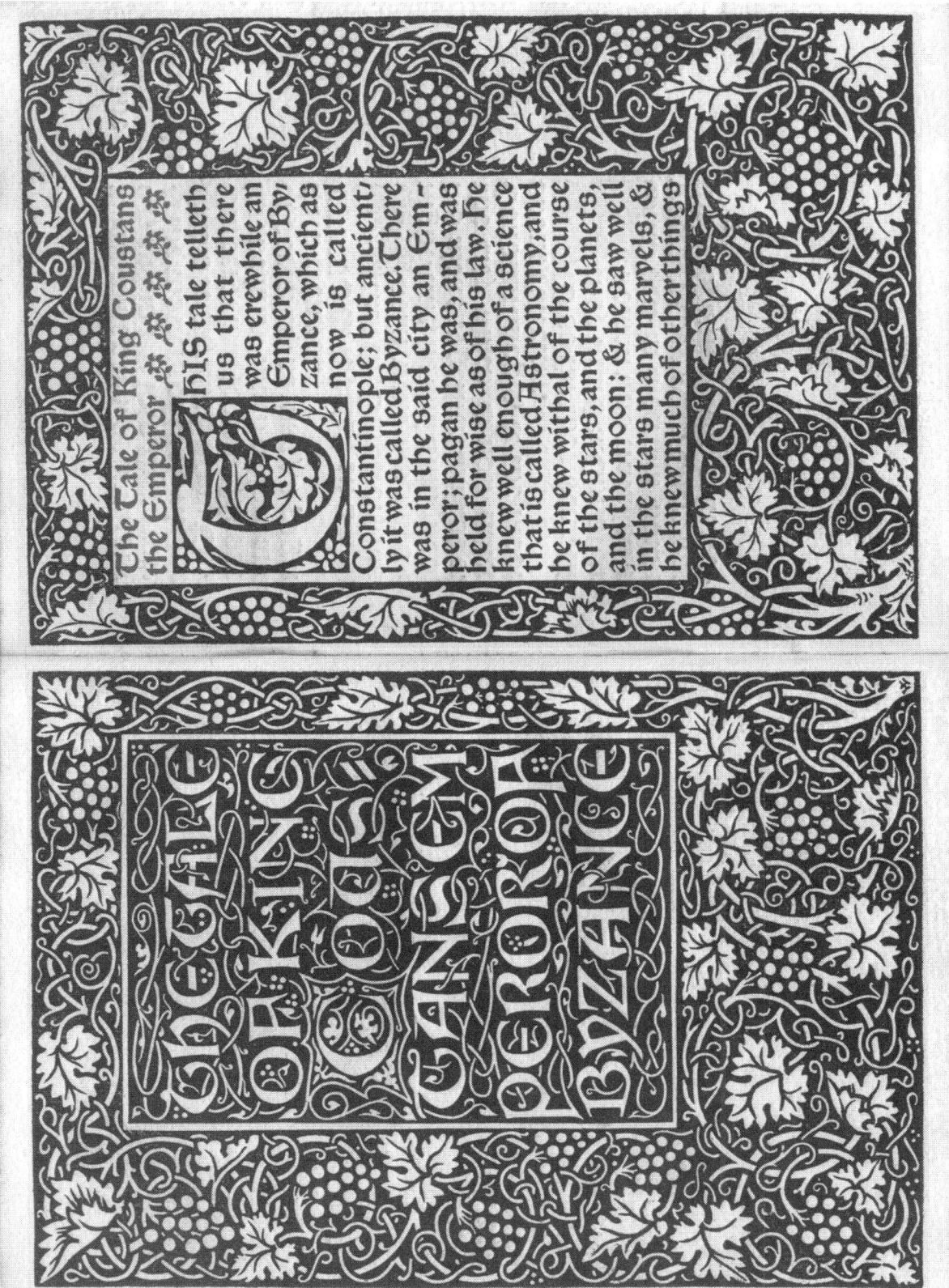

Figure 62. A-73.01: *Emperor Coustans and . . .* (KP edn.) opening; engraved title & head title

the Kelmscott Press, | Upper Mall, Hammersmith. Finished the | 30th day of May, 1894. | [printer's mark 1] | Sold by William Morris, at the Kelmscott | Press.

Collation: 8°: [a]⁴ b–r⁸ s⁴ [$2 (–b1 d1 l2 o2 s2) signed] 136 leaves pp. [*8*] [*1*] 2–261 [262–4] [= 272].

Contents: pp. [*1–4*], blank; p. [*5*], title page; pp. [*6–7*], blank; p. [*8*], frontis., figure called only the Maid in the Wood in the text, a Flora figure designed by Edward Burne-Jones, in border 13a; p. [*1*], 1st chapter head and text begins with 10-line ornamental initial 'A' within compartment surrounded by full border 13; pp. 2–260, text completed; p. 261, colophon, see above; pp. [*262–4*], blank.

Technical Notes: *paper*: Batchelor's KP Flower paper 2; *leaf size*: lightly trimmed deckled edges, avg. 207 x 141 mm., excluding head and direction lines; *printing*: in red and black, all chapter headings and shoulder notes in red; *type face*: Chaucer type; *type area*: 127 x 80 mm.; *lines-to-page*: set solid, 27 lines; *pagination*: set 8 mm. in from outer margins on direction line; *end-papers*: 3 free ends and a paste-down, plain white and blank, front and back; *binding*: cream-white limp vellum with olive-green silk ties; *spine*: gilt-stamped across in Golden type: THE WOOD | BEYOND | THE WORLD | BY | WILLIAM | MORRIS; *ornamentation*: woodcut frontis. designed by Burne-Jones; borders 13a and 13; 35 6-line initials and a part border begin each chapter after the 1st, which has a 10-line initial and full border 13; 200 3-line initials.

Publication: 30 May 1894 [colophon date indicates finished printing, issued 16 Oct.] (Cockerell, p. 158); *print run*: 350 copies on paper, 8 on vellum; *price*: 2gns. and 10gns., respectively. Rptd. in photo-facsimile by Dover Press, NY, in 1972.

Register of Copies Examined: VU (base copy: E, Poynton Coll.); CSt (Gunst: Z239.2/K29/M87wo); BL (C.43.e.17.)

Notes: William S. Peterson notes: '*The Wood Beyond the World* was written by Morris specifically for the KP: hence in the MS . . . he indicated the positions of decorated initials and leaf ornaments. The book was printed during the spring of 1894 but was not issued until the following autumn because of a delay in completing the frontispiece (Ledger; Sparling, 79)' (*KP Biblio.*, p. 71).

When the *Spectator*'s reviewer discovered a Socialist allegory in the story, Morris replied immediately:

> I had not the least intention to thrust an allegory into the Wood beyond the World; it is meant for a tale pure and simple, with nothing didactic about it. If I have to write or speak on social problems, I always try to be as direct as I possibly can be. On the other hand, I should consider it bad art in any

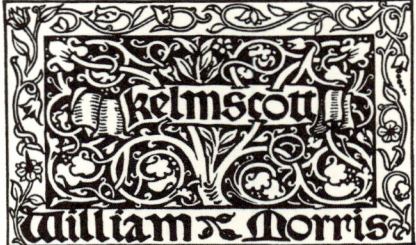

Figure 63. A-74.01: *Wood beyond the World* (KP edn.) colophon & 1st KP mark

one writing an allegory not to make it clear from the first that this was his intention, and not to take care throughout that the allegory and the story should interpenetrate, as does the great master of allegory, Bunyan. (*Letters*, iv. 291).

Morris probably began the story in Nov. 1893 (see *Letters*, iv. 108–9).

A-74.02: The Wood beyond the World (trade edn.)

[aligned left] THE WOOD BEYOND THE | WORLD. BY WILLIAM | MORRIS. | [Lawrence and Bullen monogram bookmark designed and initialled by Walter Crane] | LONDON: LAWRENCE AND BULLEN, | 16 HENRIETTA STREET, COVENT | GARDEN. | MDCCCXCV.

Edition: 'Cheap Edition' [1st impression, 2nd edn.] Besides the ordinary edn., 50 LP copies were issued.

Collation: square cr. 8°: A⁴ B–Q⁸ R⁴ S² 130 leaves pp. [*2*] [*i–iv*] v–vi 1–250 [251–2] [= 260].

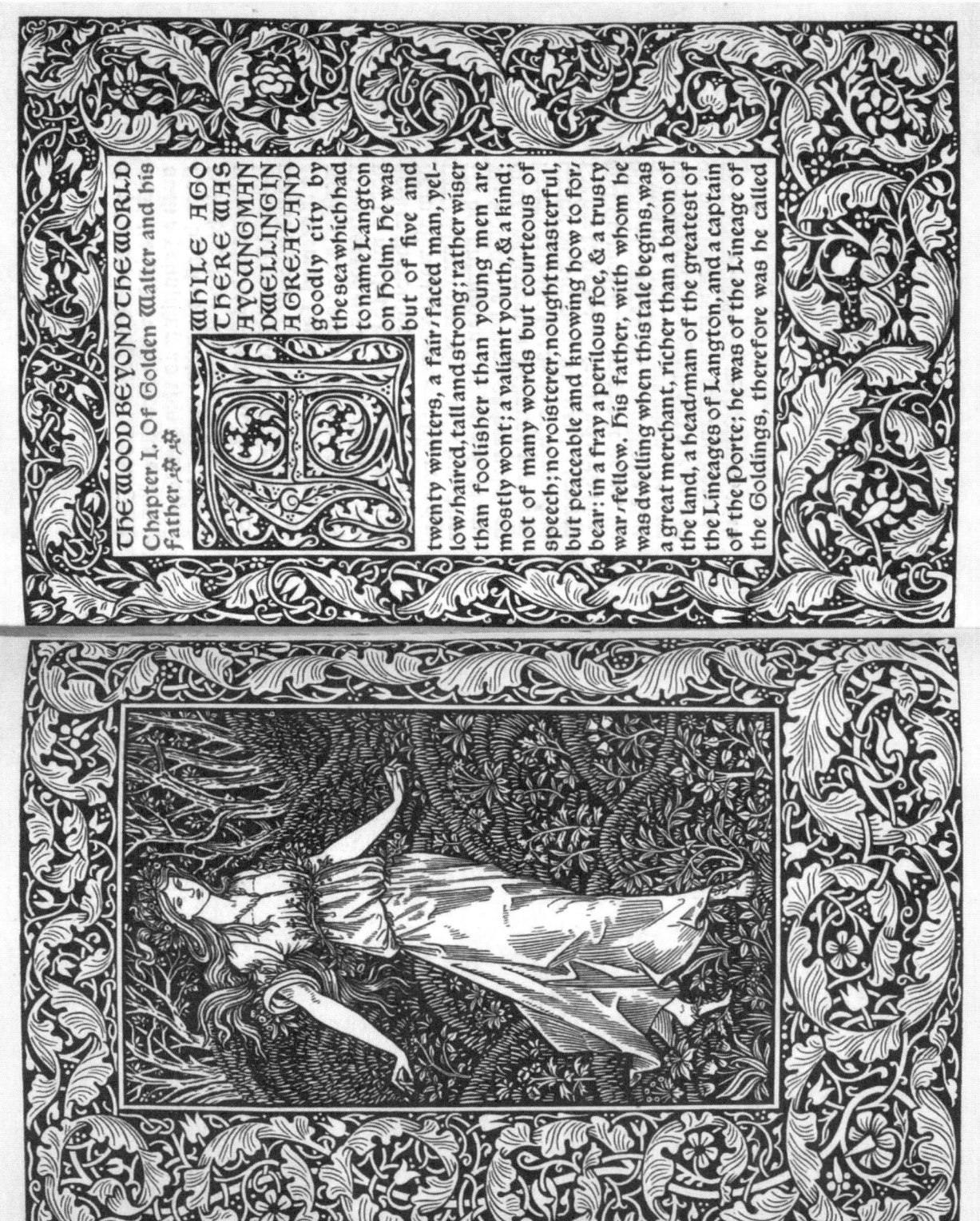

Figure 64. A-74.01: *Wood beyond the World* (KP edn.) opening: frontis. & head title

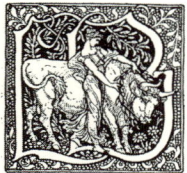

Figure 65. A-74.02: *Wood beyond the World* (trade edn.) title page

Contents: pp. [1–2], blank; p. [i], half title; p. [ii], blank; LP p. [ii], statement of limitation: *Fifty copies printed on Whatman's Paper. | No.* [no. entered in longhand]; p. [iii], title page, LP copies have the title, publisher's name, and year in red; p. [iv], printer's imprint: CHISWICK PRESS:—CHARLES WHITTINGHAM AND CO. | TOOKS COURT, CHANCERY LANE, LONDON.; p. v, dropped head: CONTENTS. | [as a list, 36 chapter titles numbered in roman]; p. vi, Contents completed; p. 1, dropped head: [flush left] THE WOOD BEYOND THE | WORLD. | CHAPTER I | OF GOLDEN WALTER | AND HIS FATHER. | [text begins]; pp. 2–250, text completed; p. [251], printer's imprint: [Chiswick Press Aldine mark of lion, dolphin and anchor] | CHISWICK PRESS:—CHARLES WHITTINGHAM AND CO. | TOOKS COURT, CHANCERY LANE, LONDON.; p. [252], blank.

Technical Notes: *paper*: machine-wove 'antique' laid paper with dandy roll laid lines and false deckle edges; LP copies on Whatman hand-made paper; *leaf size*: ordinary copies: untrimmed, avg. 194 x 139 mm.; *printing*: LP copies printed in red and black, with red on title page (see *Contents*, above); *type area*: 131 x 85 mm. excluding head and direction lines; *lines-to-page*: set solid, 28 lines; *pagination*: centred between margins on the direction lines; *endpapers*: 1 free end and a paste-down, plain white and blank, front and back; *binding*: LP copies: bound in olive-green art linen with a spine label printed with 'special green ink' (Chiswick Arch.); text of label as for ordinary copies; ordinary copies: plain dark-red unblocked buckram; *spine*: gilt-stamped: THE WOOD | BEYOND | THE WORLD | WILLLIAM | MORRIS | [at foot] LAWRENCE | & BULLEN

Publication: 1895 [issued 24 May] (S. C. Cockerell, MS Diary, Cockerell Papers); *print run*: 1,500 ordinary and 50 LP copies; *price*: 6s. ordinary copies, LP copies unknown.

Register of Copies Examined: LeM (base copy); VU (2 copies: E and L); BGR (2 copies, 1 LP); BL (012628.h.1.); MU; NjP; CSt (2 copies: 821.6.M87ww and Spec.Coll.Felton PR5079.W87); SU (823/M87 wo).

Notes: HBF (p. 178) says this is printed from Imperial sheets cut in two and worked as an 8°. This is confirmed by the Chiswick Arch. Ledger Book for 1894–5 (BL (Add.) MS 50915).

Later issues and impressions from this edn.: Longmans:
1. 1900 [issued 17–24 Nov.] (Chiswick Arch.): [2nd issue, 1st impression, 2nd edn.]; *print run*: 173 copies remaining were transferred to Longmans in 1900, and the title pages were rptd. to introduce the Longmans imprint and a new date; *price*: 6s. net;

2.* 1904 [issued 3 Nov.] (Longmans Arch.): [2nd impression, 2nd edn.]; *print run*: 250 copies; *price*: 6s. Printed by William Brendon and Son, Ltd., Plymouth, using plates made earlier by Chiswick Press (Longmans Arch.);

3.* 1911 [issued 29 Aug.] (Longmans Arch.): [3rd impression, 2nd edn.]; *print run*: 250 copies; *price*: 6s. Prtd. by Brendon and Son;

Rptd. in facsimile, London, 1979, by George Prior Publishers, as one of a series called 'The Prose Romances of William Morris'.

A-74.03: The Wood beyond the World (RB)

[aligned left] THE WOOD BEYOND THE WORLD | BY WILLIAM MORRIS | [centred] PUBLISHED BY THE ROBERTS | HOUSE, 3 SOMERSET STREET | BOSTON, 1895

Edition: [1st impression, 3rd edn., 1st American].

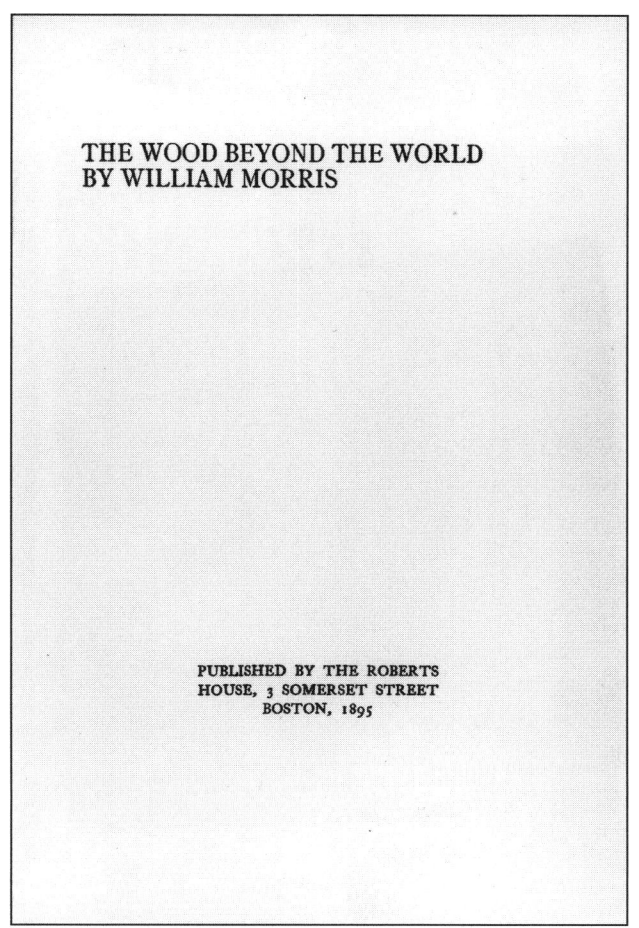

Figure 66. A-74.03: *Wood beyond the World* (RB edn.) title page

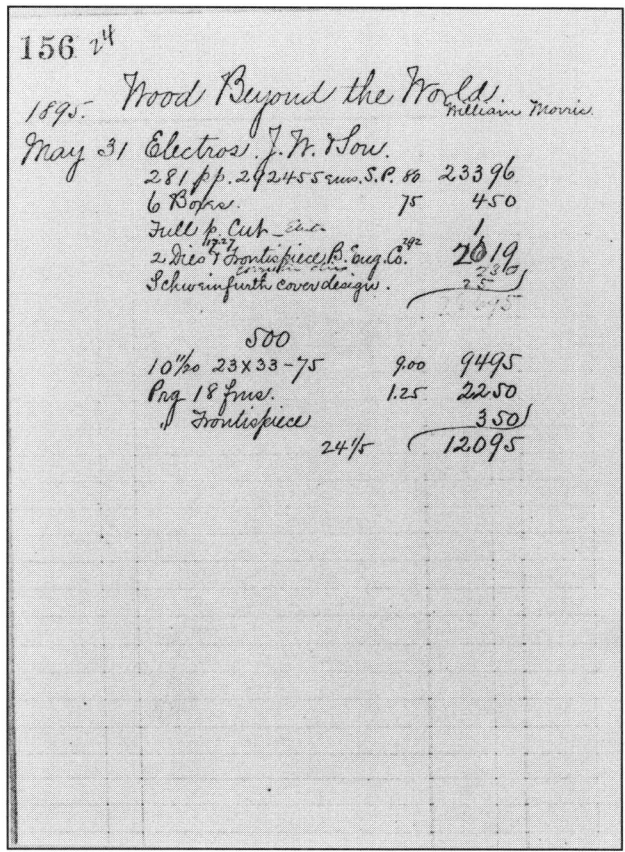

Figure 67. A-74.03: *Wood beyond the World* (RB edn.) RB ledger entry

Collaborators, Editors, and Illustrators: besides a binding designed by Schweinfurth, this American edn. includes a facsimile of the Burne-Jones KP frontis. for this title with its Morris border, 13a, from the KP edn. of the same book. A similar Morris border was adapted as an ornament on the front and spine of this American edn.

Colophon: [1st line indented] Here ends the tale of the Wood beyond | the World, made by William Morris, and | printed by the University Press at Cam- | bridge, U.S.A. Finished the eleventh | day of May, one thousand eight hundred | and ninety-five. | [printer's mark of John Wilson and Son]

Collation: 8°: π⁴ (π1+1) 1–17⁸ [18]² 142 leaves pp. [i–v] vi–vii [viii] 1–273 [274–6] [= 284] + inserted frontispiece not counted in the pagination, but described in its appropriate place in the *Contents*.

Contents: p. [i], half title; p. [ii], statement of limitation: [gothic type] **This Edition is limited to Five Hundred Copies**; inserted leaf, blank verso of frontispiece with, on the recto a photolitho reproduction of the KP edn. frontispiece, within the Morris full border (KP no. 13a); p. [iii], title page; p. [iv], printer's imprint: [gothic type] University Press: | [plain type] JOHN WILSON AND SON, CAMBRIDGE, U.S.A.; p. [v], dropped head: CONTENTS. | [thin french rule] | [list begins of 36 chapter titles]; pp. vi–vii, Contents completed, with running heads: *CONTENTS.*; p. [viii], blank; p. 1, dropped head: THE | WOOD BEYOND THE WORLD. | [french rule] | CHAPTER I. | OF GOLDEN WALTER AND HIS FATHER. | [text begins with drop cap 'A']; pp. 2–272, text completed; p. 273, colophon and printer's mark, see above; pp. [274–6], blank.

Technical Notes: *paper*: cream-white machine-made 'antique wove' with dandy roll laid lines; t.e.g.; *leaf size*: 211 x 142 mm.; *print. type area*: 128 x 78 mm.; *lines-to-page*: leaded, 26 lines; *shoulder notes*: used throughout, as in KP edn., except printed here in black; *pagination*: arabic numbers set 8 mm. in from the outer margin on the direction

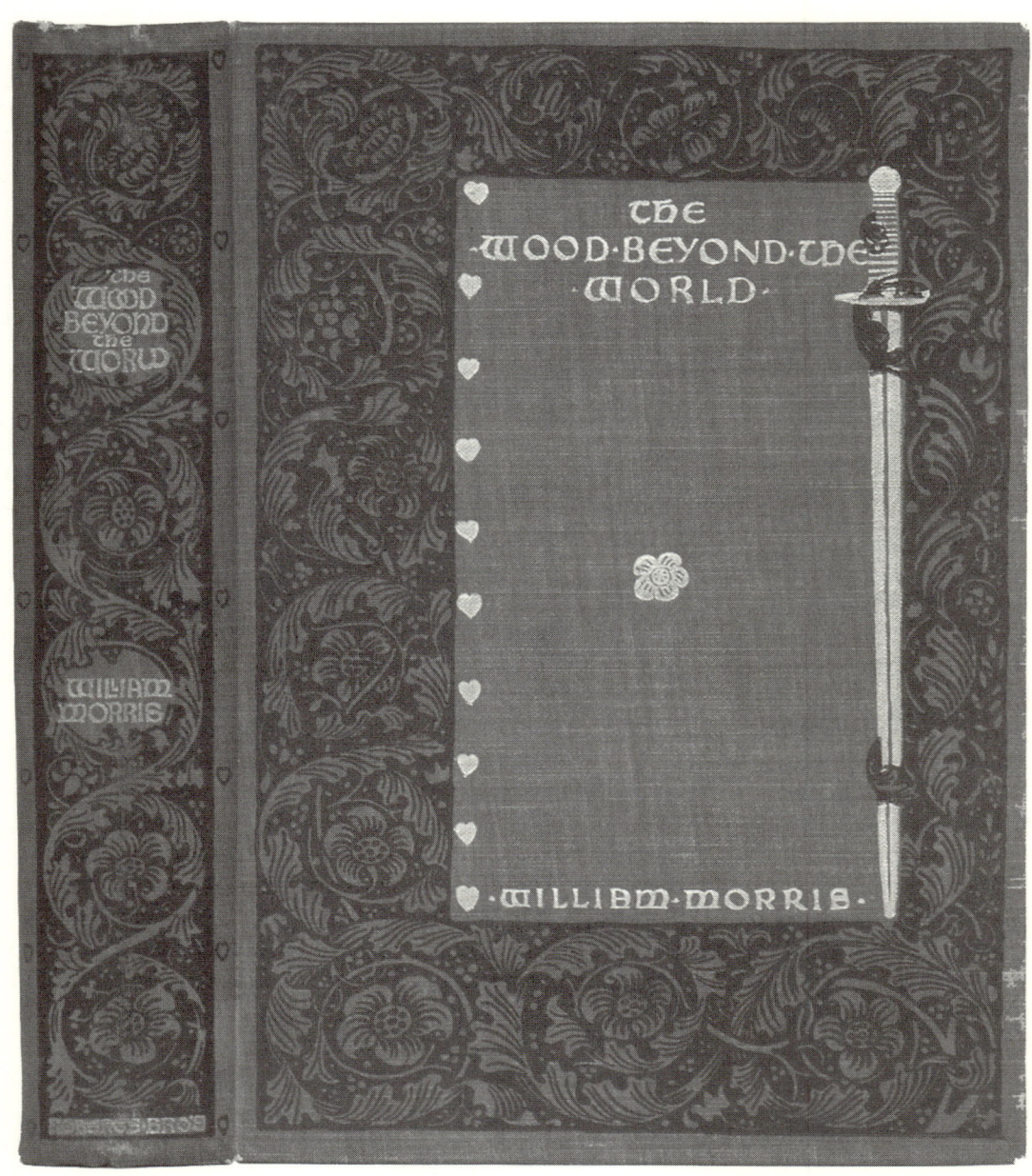

Figure 68. A-74.03: *Wood beyond the World* (RB edn.) binding

line, except where the text ends above the bottom line, where the p. number is on the line following the text; *endpapers*: 1 free end and paste-down, plain white and blank, front and back; *binding*: sage green cloth with adapted Morris border 13a, front and spine, taken from the frontispiece, printed in dark green ink, front border enclosing a compartment, sage green with gilt-stamped ornaments: hearts down left margin and vertical sword along the right margin, letterpress in imitation Morris-design type: [head of compartment] THE | • WOOD • BEYOND • THE | • WORLD • | [central floral ornament] | [foot of the compartment]] • WILLIAM • MORRIS •; *spine*: lettered across in gilt Morris-design type: THE | WOOD | BEYOND | THE | WORLD | WILLIAM | MORRIS | ROBERTS • BRO'S; back plain and unblocked.
Publication: 1895 [issued 31 May] (Roberts Arch.); *print run*: 500 copies; *price*: $3.00.
Register of Copies Examined: LeM (base copy) BGR; MU (Spec Coll. PR5079, W6, 1895b).
Notes: from RB Electro Ledger 1894–99: shows the plates, along with all the other RB Morris plates, were sold to Longmans, Green on 24 May 1899.
Later impression from this edn.: Longmans NY:
1.* 1902 (Longmans Accts.): [2nd impression, 3rd edn., 1st American]; *print run*: 250 copies; *price*: $2.50.

A-74.04: The Wood beyond the World (+ Child Christopher and Old French Romances *CW* XVII)

THE COLLECTED WORKS | [title details common to the set, see A-126.01] | VOLUME XVII | THE WOOD BEYOND THE WORLD | CHILD CHRISTOPHER | OLD FRENCH ROMANCES | [publisher's imprint, see A-126.01] | MDCCCCXIII
Edition: [1st impression, 4th edn., 3rd English of *The Wood beyond the World*] Also contains—besides *Child Christopher* and *Old French Romances*—Morris's translation of *The Ordination of Knighthood* from the KP edn. All the romances rptd. here except *Old French Romances* (itself a reprint of 3 KP books) had KP 1st edns. Details of all 4 titles combined in this vol. are provided here in the *Collation*, *Contents*, and *Technical Notes*. For further details specific to *Child Christopher*, *Old French Romances*, and *The Order of Chivalry*, see A-78.03, 79.02, and 63.02 respectively.
Translation: the *Old French Romances* and *The Ordination of Knighthood* are, 'done out of ancient French into English by William Morris', the latter title translated in verse from a 13th-century French poem, 'L'Ordene de Chevalerie'.

Child Christopher is no translation but Morris's re-creation of the medieval English romance *The Lay of Havelok the Dane*.
Series: vol. 17 of 24. For details common to this series, see this field in A-126.01.
Collation: medium 8°: [a]⁸ (a3+1) b⁸ (b2+1) c⁸ B–2A⁸ [$2 (–K2) signed] 208 leaves pp. [i–viii] ix–xlvi [xlvii–xlviii] 1–130 [*The Wood beyond the World* ends] [131–2] 133–261 [*Child Christopher* ends] [262–4] 265–351 [*Old French Romances* ends] [352] 353–66 [*The Ordination of Knighthood* ends] [367–8] [= 416] +2 inserted plates not included in the book's pagination, but noted in the formula and described here under *Contents* in their appropriate places.
Contents: pp. [i–iii], blank; p. [iv], notice of limitation (see A-126.01); pp. [v–vi], blank; 1st inserted plate, as frontis., reproduction of a drawing in a blind-stamped compartment, with the plate maker identified, below right, in copperplate: *Emery Walker Ph. sc.* | [label centred in copperplate] *William Morris* | *a pencil study for the altar-picture* | *at Llandaff Cathedral, by D. G. Rossetti*; p. [vii], title page; p. [viii], blank; p. ix, headed: CONTENTS | [list begins]; pp. x–xii, Contents completed; p. xiii, headed: INTRODUCTION | [text begins]; pp. xiv–xx, text continues; 2nd inserted plate to face p. xx, photo reproduction of a drawing, labelled below in copperplate: *Mrs. William Morris* | *a pencil study for the head of the Virgin* | *in the Altar-picture at Llandaff Cathedral, by D. G. Rossetti* | [name of the plate maker, in copperplate] *Emery Walker Ph. sc.*; pp. xxi–xliii, Introduction completed; p. [xliv], blank; p. xlv, headed: BIBLIOGRAPHICAL NOTE; p. xlvi, Bibliographical Note completed; p. [xlvii], 1st half title; p. [xlviii], blank; p. 1, text begins; pp. 2–366, text completed; p. [367], blank; p. [368], printer's imprint, see A-126.01.
Technical Notes: paper, printing, type, position (but not content) of headlines, running titles, shoulder notes, pagination, and binding are all common to the set and are described in this field in A-126.01. Details specific to this vol.: *shoulder notes*: used throughout, except in *The Ordination of Knighthood*, as sub-heads to the adjacent text; *spine labels*: [1st 4 lines common to the set] VOLUME XVII | THE WOOD | BEYOND THE | WORLD | CHILD | CHRISTOPHER | OLD FRENCH | ROMANCES
Publication: 1913 [issued 31 Oct.] (Longmans Arch.); *print run* and *price*: see this field in A-126.01.
Register of Copies Examined: see this field in A-126.01.

A-74.05: The Wood beyond the World (LPL)

THE WOOD BEYOND | • • THE WORLD • • | BY

WILLIAM MORRIS | POCKET EDITION | LONGMANS, GREEN AND CO. | 39 PATERNOSTER ROW, LONDON | NEW YORK, BOMBAY, AND CALCUTTA | 1913

Edition: Pocket Edition. [1st impression, 5th edn., 4th English].

Series: Longmans Pocket Library. For further series detail, see this field in *The Life and Death of Jason*, A-3.09.

Collation: fcap 8°: π⁴ A–K⁸ L⁴ 88 leaves pp. [2] [i–iv] v–vi [1] 2–167 [168] [= 176].

Contents: pp. [1–2], ads headed: WILLIAM MORRIS'S WORKS; p. [i], half title; p. [ii], blank; p. [iii], title page; p. [iv], Bibliographical Note; pp. v–vi, Contents; pp. [1]–167, text completed with printer's imprint: Printed by BALLANTYNE, HANSON & CO. | at Paul's Work, Edinburgh; p. [168], blank.

Technical Notes: for details common to this series—paper, leaf size, printing, pagination, end-papers, and binding—see the entry for the 1st Morris book of the series, *The Life and Death of Jason*, A-3.09. Details specific to this issue: *printing*: *type area*: 123 x 76 mm.; *lines-to-page*: set solid, 36 lines; *spine title*: [gilt stamped across] THE • WOOD | • BEYOND • | THE • WORLD | [rule of 3 ornamental circles] | WILLIAM | MORRIS | [the rest as in A-3.09]

Publication: Nov. 1913 [issued 22–29 Nov.] ('Books of the Week', *Pub. Circ.*, 99 (29 Nov. 1913), 712); *print run*: 3,000 copies (Longmans Arch.); *price*: cloth, 2s. net, lthr., 3s. net.

Register of Copies Examined: LeM (base copy); BGR; Fdmn.

Notes: an entry from Longmans Arch. for 22 Oct. 1913, indicates the print run and that the book was new set, moulds made, and printed by Ballantyne for a total cost of £30. 11s. 5d, not including binding @ 31s. 9d. per 100. On 15 Feb. 1938, the plates were melted down and sold as scrap.

A-75.01: Saga Library, vol. V

THE STORIES OF THE | KINGS OF NORWAY | CALLED THE ROUND | WORLD | (HEIMSKRINGLA) | BY SNORRI STURLUSON | DONE INTO ENGLISH | OUT OF THE ICELANDIC | BY | WILLIAM MORRIS | AND | EIRÍKR MAGNÚSSON | VOL. III [of IV] | LONDON | BERNARD QUARITCH, 15 PICCADILLY | 1895

Edition: [1st impression, 1st edn.] As is the case with all 6 vols. of the Saga Library, in addition to the ordinary issue there was a LP variant (royal 8°) of 125 copies, all numbered.

Series: for details of the authorship, origin, and production of the series, see the *Series* field in A-52.01.

Collation: cr. 8°: [A]⁴ B–2I⁸ 2K⁴ 2L² (–2L2) 257 leaves pp. [8] [1–3] 4–505 [506] [= 514] including one inserted leaf signed 2L, included in the formula and pagination.

Contents: p. [1], 1st half title, as for vol. IV, allowing for obvious changes in the set and subset vol. nos.; p. [2], blank; p. [3], title page; p. [4], printer's imprint: CHISWICK PRESS:—CHARLES WHITTINGHAM AND CO. | TOOKS COURT, CHANCERY LANE, LONDON.; p. [5], dropped head: NOTE. | [8 lines on the contents of the forthcoming volume VI]; p. [6], blank: p. [7], dropped head: CONTENTS. | [list begins of 9 stories and section on 'Explanations' each with a half title page included here with page numbers]; p. [8], blank; pp. 1–54, THE STORY OF MAGNUS THE GOOD.; pp. 55–188, THE STORY OF HARALD THE | HARD-REDY.; pp. 189–202, THE STORY OF OLAF THE QUIET.; pp. 203–[44], THE STORY OF KING MAGNUS | BAREFOOT.; pp. [245]–[310], THE STORY OF SIGURD THE | JERUSALEM-FARER, EYSTEIN, | AND OLAF.; pp. [311]–344, THE STORY OF MAGNUS THE BLIND AND HARALD | GILLI.; pp. [345]–96, THE STORY OF INGI, SON OF | HARALD, AND HIS BRETHREN.; pp. [397]–[432], THE STORY OF HAKON SHOULDER–BROAD.; pp. [433]–[88], THE STORY OF KING MAGNUS, | SON OF ERLING.; pp. [489]–504, text begins, headed: EXPLANATIONS OF THE | METAPHORS IN THE | VERSES.; p. 505, text ends with explicit: END OF VOL. III. | [thin rule] | [printer's imprint, as p. 2]; p. [506], blank.

Technical Notes: for details common to this series—paper, leaf size, printing, type area, lines-to-page, running heads, pagination, end-papers, binding and dust wrappers—see this field in A-52.01; details special to this vol.: gilt titling on front within the standard ornaments: THE | HEIMSKRINGLA | VOL. 3 [4]; *spine*: the same, with HEIMS- | KRINGLA thus divided.

Publication: 1895 [24 Dec. 1894, printing finished] (Chiswick Arch.); *print run*: 1,500 ordinary copies, 125 LP copies; *prices*: unknown.

Register of Copies Examined: see this field in A-52.01.

Notes: for 'Memorandum' and 'Agreement' between Morris and Quaritch for publication of Saga Library, see *Letters*, iii. 172, 174, 230–1.

Chiswick Arch. Bernard Quaritch Ledger Book entry, Dec. 1894, shows that the total cost for this vol., including LP copies and stereo moulds, was £167. 13s. 6d.

A-76.01: Letters on Socialism

LETTERS | ON SOCIALISM. | BY | [in gothic] William Morris. | [plain type] *London: Privately Printed* | 1894

Edition: [1st impression, 1st edn.] This is a collection of 4 sequential Morris letters on Socialism to The Rev. George Bainton, dated 2, 4, and 10 Apr. and 6 May 1888. Later, in 1890, Bainton edited and compiled a book, *The Art of Authorship*, to which Morris contributed a letter (see B-10).

Collaborators, Editors, and Illustrators: [Edited by Thomas J. Wise].

Publisher: Privately printed [for T. J. Wise]. This project was authorised by Morris (though he did not initiate it), through Charles Fairfax Murray, who acted for Morris in dealing with Wise, and complained afterwards to Wise for editing the text 'with some variation' (see *Notes* below).

Collation: crown 8vo printed and gathered in 2s: [A]^6 (A3+1) B–I^2 K^2 [$1 (–K) signed] 24 leaves pp. *[12]* [1–3] 4–30 *[31–36]* [= 48] + an inserted leaf as frontispiece, not counted in the pagination, but described in its appropriate place under *Contents*.

Contents: pp. *[1–4]*, blank; p. *[5]*, half title; p. *[6]*, blank; inserted frontis.: photographic facsimile of MS Letter II from series; p. *[7]*, title page; p. *[8]*, blank; p. *[9]*, limitation note: THE IMPRESSION | OF THIS BOOK IS LIMITED TO THIRTY-FOUR COPIES | FOR PRIVATE CIRCULATION ONLY.; p. *[10]*, blank; p. *[11]*: NOTE | [5 lines on the authority of the letters published here]; p. *[12]*, blank; p. [1], 2nd half title: LETTERS.; p. [2], blank; p. [3], 1st chapter head title: 3-line drop to general title: LETTERS ON SOCIALISM. | [french rule] | Letter I. | [thin rule] | [flush right, Morris's Kelmscott House letterhead and date] April 2nd, 1888. | [text begins]; pp. 4–30, text completed; p. [31], The Ashley Library bookmark; pp. *[32–6]*, blank.

Technical Notes: *paper*: cream hand-laid with deckled edges, watermarked, top, centre of leaf: J. Whatman | 1894; *leaf size*, deckled edge, avg. 204 x 124 mm.; *printing*: *type area*: 99 x 55 mm.; *lines-to-page*: leaded, 24 lines, excluding head and direction lines; *running titles*: [all rectos and versos] LETTERS ON SOCIALISM; *end-papers*: 1 free end and paste-down (same paper as the body), plain white and blank, front and back; *binding*: plain, unblocked japan vellum-covered boards, gilt-stamped up the spine: LETTERS ON SOCIALISM—WILLIAM MORRIS—1894

Publication: 1894; *print run*: 34 copies, of which 4 were prtd. on vellum (but these figures on print run are doubtful, see *Notes*, below); *price*: not known.

Register of Copies Examined: BL (base copy: Ashley 1237.); MU (Spec. Coll PR50809/L4, 1894, with bookplate of Edwin B. Holden); CSt (Spec. Coll.Felton PR5080.L65).

Notes: 'The letters were written in 1888. In a note addressed to the editor (Mr. Thomas J. Wise) since the volume was put into type, Mr. Morris states that they [i.e. the ideas of the letters] are quite in accord with his present views' ('News Notes', *The Bookman*, 6/36 (Sept. 1894), 167). This notice, appearing when it does, as well as the existence of C. F. Murray's letters to Wise, listed in the Parisser Catalogue, establishes the authority of the publication. But Wise's editing of the letters did not elicit a very positive response from Murray who, as Barker and Collins say, wrote 'a seven-page letter castigating his editorial errors and misdeeds' (*Sequel*, 147).

'Of the 34 copies 4 were printed on fine writing vellum' (HBF, p. 180). But the limitation statement, the obvious foundation for Forman's numbers, should be taken with some scepticism. John J. Walsdorf has found 36 copies of this pamphlet, and we cannot be sure that his census is exhaustive (see Walsdorf, pp. 137–8).

Morris also wrote another series of letters on Socialism, but directed more to the political affairs of the Socialist movement. Written in 1884 and 1885 to Robert Thomson, before he emigrated to the US, they were published by Elbert Hubbard in *This Then Is a William Morris Book: Being a Little Journey by Elbert Hubbard, & Some Letters, Heretofore Unpublished, Written to His Friend & Fellow Worker, Robert Thomson, All Throwing a Side-Light, More or Less, on the Man and His Times* (East Aurora, NY: The Roycrofters, 1907). There being no evidence that Morris ever formed the intent to publish these letters, this book is not included here as a Morris title.

A-77.01: Beowulf (KP)

THE TALE OF BEOWULF.

Edition: 'Kelmscott Press Edition' [1st impression, 1st edn.]

Series: 32nd title, 13th by Morris, prtd. at the KP.

Colophon: Here endeth the Story of Beowulf, done out of the Old | English tongue by William Morris & A. J. Wyatt, and | printed by the said William Morris at the Kelmscott | Press, Upper Mall, Hammersmith, in the County of | Middlesex, and finished on the 10th day of January, | 1895. | [3 ornaments, KP no. 3] | [KP printer's mark no. 2] | Sold by William Morris at the Kelmscott Press.

Collation: large 4° in 8s: [a]^4 b–h^8 i^4 [$4 (–b1, 4 c1 d2 e1, 4 f3–4 g1 h3–4) signed] 64 leaves pp. [i–iii] iv–vi [vii–viii] [1–3] 4–119 [120] [= 128].

Contents: pp. [i–ii], blank; inserted slip, Peterson says, 'before the title page in some copies' (*KP Biblio*, p. 84): NOTE TO READER. | In this translation of Beowulf, the final ed, where the e is not elided " by the printer, is intended to be pronounced in every case; p. [iii], title page; p. iv, headed: [Chaucer type caps, aligned left] ARGUMENT | [text begins with 8-line floriated drop initial 'H']; pp. v–vi, Argument concluded; p. [vii], blank; p. [viii], engraved title within border 14a: the tale of | Beowulf | sometime | king of the | Folk of the | Weder | Geats; p. [1], 1st chapter head title: Chaucer type] THE STORY OF BEOWULF [4 ornaments, KP no. 3] | 1. And first the kindred of Hrothgar [2 ornaments, KP no. 3] | [text begins with 8-line ornamental drop initial 'W']; all within border 14; pp. 2–110, text completed; p. 111, colophon, see above; p. 112, headed: [top flush left, Chaucer type caps] PERSONS AND PLACES. | [index list begins]; pp. 113–17, 1st index concluded; p. 118, headed: [top flush left] THE MEANING OF SOME WORDS NOT COMMONLY | USED NOW. | [index begins]; p. 119, 2nd index completed; p. [120], blank.

Technical Notes: *paper*: Batchelor's KP Perch paper; *leaf size*: deckled edges, avg. 289 x 210 mm.; *type face*: text, Troy type; Chaucer type for the 'Argument', shoulder and side notes, list of persons and places, and glossary; *printing*: printed in red and black, red for all chapter titles and shoulder notes and once for a printer's leaf, p. 41; *type area*: 188 x 144 mm. (but lines frequently extend beyond the margin); *lines-to-page*: set solid, 32 lines; *shoulder notes*: all rectos and versos, starting at the top at the outer margin, but frequently also lower down the page, as sub-heads to adjacent text; *pagination*: arabic numbers set 10 mm. in from the outer margin on the direction line; *end-papers*: usual KP treatment: 3 free ends and one paste-down, plain white and blank, front and back; *binding*: limp natural vellum with 3 green silk ties; *spine*: gold-stamped in 18-point Golden type up the spine: BEOWULF; *ornamentation*: 2 full borders, 14a and 14 (all smaller marginal ornamentation is reserved to chapter heads); 1 KP mark No. 2; 36 half borders; 1 side border; 1 part border; 2 corner pieces; floriated initials: one 8-line, 42 6-line, and 134 3-line initials.

Publication: 10 Jan. 1895 [colophon date indicates printing finished, issued 2 Feb.] (Cockerell, p. 159); *print run*: 300 on paper, 8 on vellum; *price*: 2gns. paper, vellum £10 (ibid.).

Register of Copies Examined: BL (base copy: C. 43. f. 9.); CSt (Spec. Coll.Gunst Z239.2.K29.B4 f); CSmH.

Notes: Morris to A. J. Wyatt, 28 Aug. [1892]:

> I should be very pleased to work with you if we could hit upon some plan together.... I should be very pleased if we could have some talk together. I do not think I should be able to set to work at once, so full as my hands are of work: but my hope is to tackle Beowulf, which no one can appreciate in the present versions I think. Of course I am well aware of the great difficulty of dealing with it because every word which it is necessary to substitute for the old one (every word that is which has not its exact equivalent in modern English) *must* be weakened and almost destroyed. Still as the language is a different language from modern English and not merely a different form of it, it can, I would hope be *translated* and not paraphrased merely. Anyhow I intend to try if I can get anyone to help me who knows Anglo-Saxon (as I do not) and could also set me right as to the text and its grievous gaps.
>
> I should much like to know what you think of the adventure. (*Letters,* iii. 436–76, *passim*).

S. C. Cockerell's MS Diary (see Cockerell Papers) for 1893 records that Morris did his first section of *Beowulf* on 21 Feb. 1893. The next year's diary says he finished his translation on 10 Mar. 1894 (Cockerell Papers, BL (Add.) MS 52772). From then until 10 Dec., when Morris finished the argument, completing the MS, he and Wyatt worked at revision.

A-77.02: Beowulf (PW)

THE TALE OF BEOWULF | SOMETIME KING OF THE | FOLK OF THE WEDER | GEATS TRANSLATED BY | WILLIAM MORRIS AND A. J. WYATT | LONGMANS, GREEN, AND CO. | 39 PATERNOSTER ROW, LONDON | NEW YORK AND BOMBAY | MDCCCXCVIII

Edition: New Edition 'Trade Edition'[1st impression, 2nd edn.]

Series: The Poetical Works of William Morris (PW). The series, indicated only on the printed paper spine label, originally comprised a uniform set of 10 unnumbered vols. all issued in July 1896 when Longmans became Morris's publisher. In 1898 the set increased to 11 vols. with the addition of this new popular edn. of *The Tale of Beowulf*. For further series details, see this field in A-4.16.

Collation: cr. 8°: π⁶ A–M⁸ 102 leaves pp. [2] [i–iv] v–x [1] 2–191 [192] [= 204].

Contents: pp. [1–2], blank; p. [i], half title; p. [ii], heading:

> THE TALE OF BEOWULF
> SOMETIME KING OF THE
> FOLK OF THE WEDER
> GEATS TRANSLATED BY
> WILLIAM MORRIS AND
> A. J. WYATT
>
>
>
> LONGMANS, GREEN, AND CO.
> 39 PATERNOSTER ROW, LONDON
> NEW YORK AND BOMBAY
> MDCCCXCVIII

Figure 69. A-77.02: *Beowulf* (2nd edn.) title page

BIBLIOGRAPHICAL NOTE | [lists 2 edns, the KP edn. and the present one]; p. [iii], title page; p. [iv], printer's imprint: Printed by BALLANTYNE, HANSON, & Co. | At the Ballantyne Press; p. v, dropped head: ARGUMENT | [text begins with drop cap initial 'H']; pp. vi–x, Argument completed; p. [1], dropped head, 1st fitt title: THE STORY OF BEOWULF | [flush left] I. AND FIRST OF THE KINDRED OF | HROTHGAR. | [text begins with drop cap 'W']; pp. 2–179, text completed; p. [180], blank; p. 181, [dropped head] PERSONS AND PLACES | [alphabetical list begins in smaller, Bourgeois, type]; pp. 182–9, list completed; p. 190, dropped head: THE MEANING OF SOME WORDS | NOT COMMONLY USED NOW | [list begins]; p. 191, list completed, printer's imprint rptd., as above; p. [192], blank.

Technical Notes: *paper*: cream-white 'antique wove' machine-made quad cr., with dandy roll laid lines; *leaf size*: untrimmed, 190 x 126 mm.; *type area*: 133 x 84 mm., excluding head or direction lines; *lines-to-page*: leaded, 27 lines, both prose and poetry; *running heads*: all rectos and versos: THE TALE OF BEOWULF, except dropped section heads; *line numbers*: every 10 lines inside the outer margin; *end-papers*: one free end and paste-down, front and back, plain white and blank; *binding*: plain black unblocked cloth: *spine*: printed paper label: THE | POETICAL | WORKS OF | WILLIAM | MORRIS | [thin-rule] | BEOWULF | TRANSLATED BY | W. MORRIS | AND | A. J. WYATT [all within a thin-rule compartment] | [below compartment] *Price Six Shillings*

Publication: 1898 [October 31 (*Longmans Notes on Books*, 9.175 (Nov.30, 1898): 125); this is a later date than the "August 1898" printed on the verso of the title page, but it is the date given by the publisher, and it is nearer those in the 2 major trade journals, *BS* and *Pub. Circ.*, both of which say November, and to the Longmans Arch. which says Oct. 12]; *print run*: 1,000 copies; *price*: 6s.

Register of Copies Examined: LeM (base copy).

Notes: in a letter from C. J. Longman, to S. C. Cockerell, 2 June 1898 (Smith Arch.) an agreement is being struck between the Trustees and Longmans to include Beowulf in The Poetical Works of William Morris. Cockerell insists on 10% royalties, half of the full royalty on the first 500 copies rather than 250 copies being free of royalty. Letter from Longmans to Cockerell, 10 June 1898, indicates that half of the *Beowulf* royalties will go to A. J. Wyatt.

Later impressions of this edn.: Longmans:

1. 1904 [issued 6 Aug.] (Longmans Arch.): 'The Poetical Works' [2nd impression, 2nd edn.]; *print run*: 500 copies; *price*: 6s.;

2. 1910 [issued 10 Aug.] (Longmans Arch.): 'The Poetical Works' [3rd impression, 2nd edn.]; *print run*: 500 copies; *price*: 6s.

A-77.03: Beowulf (+ *Three Northern Love Stories CW* X)

THE COLLECTED WORKS | [title details common to the set, see A-126.01] | VOLUME X | THREE NORTHERN LOVE STORIES | THE TALE OF BEOWULF | [publisher's imprint, see A-126.01] | MDCCCCXI

Edition: [1st impression, 3rd edn.] For details specific to this vol., see A-9.04, especially *Collation, Contents*, and *Technical Notes*, where both the titles combined here are provided; for details common to the set, see A-126.01.

Technical Notes: only details specific to this edn. are included here: *shoulder notes*: in Long Primer; *binding*: *spine label*: [1st 4 lines common to the set] | VOLUME X |

THREE NORTHERN | LOVE STORIES | BEOWULF
Publication: 1911 [issued 12 Dec.] (Longmans Arch.); *print run* and *price*: see this field in A-126.01.
Register of Copies Examined: see this field in A-126.01.

A-78.01: Child Christopher and Goldilind the Fair (2 vols. KP)

CHILD CHRISTOPHER AND | GOLDILIND THE FAIR BY | WILLIAM MORRIS [vol. II, last line extended to WILLIAM MORRIS. VOL. II]
Edition: 'Kelmscott Press Edition' [1st impression, 1st edn.] Morris's tale is based on *The Lay of Havelock the Dane*.
Collaborators, Editors, and Illustrators: [Engraved title and borders designed by Morris, with border of p. [1] engraved by C. E. Keates].
Series: the 35th title, 15th by Morris, prtd. at the KP.
Colophon: [aligned left, printer's leaf ornament in red (KP no. 3)] Here ends the Story of | Child Christopher & Gol- | ilind the Fair; made by Wil- | liam Morris, and printed by | him at the Kelmscott Press, | Upper Mall, Hammersmith, | in the County of Middlesex | [printer's leaf, KP no. 1] Finished the 25th day of | July, 1895. | [¶] [in black] Sold by William Morris at | the Kelmscott Press.
Collation: vol. I: 16° in 8s: [a]⁴ b–r⁸ [$2 (–b) signed] 132 leaves pp. [8] [1] 2–256 [= 264].
vol. II: 16° in 8s: [A]⁴ B–Q⁸ [$2 signed] 124 leaves pp. [8] 1–239 [240] [= 248].
Contents: vol. I: pp. [1–4], blank; p. [5], title page; p. [6–7], blank; p. [8] border 15a, with engraved title within designed by Morris in gothic style: of Child | Christo- | pher and | Fair Gold- | ilind; p. [1], heading, within border 15: head title: [in red] Chapter 1. Of the King of | Oakenrealm, & his wife and | his child [2 printer's flower ornaments No. 3] | [in black, text begins with 7-line initial 'O']; pp. 2–256, text completed with explicit: The end of the first volume; Henderson reports an inserted errata slip, 'inserted in some copies following r8' (*KP Biblio.*, p. 90): [aligned left] Erratum. | Page 18, line 14: for 'two' read | 'four.'
vol. II: pp. [1–6], blank; p. [7], title page; p. [8], blank; p. [1], headed: [flush left, in red] Chapter XXI. Of the wed- | ding of those twain [2 printer's flower ornaments, No. 3] | [text begins with a 6-line initial 'N']; pp. 2–238, text completed; p. 239, colophon, see above; p. [240], blank.
Technical Notes: *paper*: Batchelor's hand-made KP Flower paper 2; *leaf size*: untrimmed deckled edges, avg. 142 x 102 mm.; *printing*: printed in red and black, chapter titles and shoulder notes in red; *type face*: Chaucer type (Pica); *type area*: 85 x 60 mm., excluding head and direction lines;

lines-to-page: unleaded, 20 lines; *end-papers*: (both vols.) standard KP practice: 3 free ends and paste-down, plain white and blank, front and back; *binding*: quarter holland, blue paper-covered boards with printed paper spine labels: [in Golden type]: CHILD | CHRISTO- | PHER | I [II]; *ornamentation*: vol. I: 2 full borders, 15a and 15; 20 7-line initials, one to head each chapter; and 170 3-line initials; vol. II: 1 side border; 18 7-line initials, one for each chapter head; and 187 3-line initials.
Publication: 25 July 1895 [colophon date indicates printing finished, issued 25 Sept.] (Cockerell, p. 161); *print run*: 600 copies on paper, 12 on vellum; *price*: paper 15s., vellum 4gns. (ibid.)
Register of Copies Examined: SSL (base copy: Rare Books: 823 M877); CSt (Z239.2/K29/M87 cc.); BL (2 copies: Ashley 1238 & C. 43. dd. 6.); VU (Bail RB); BGR (also includes a book made up of the proofs).
Notes: except for Mosher's legal but unauthorised edn. (see below), this title was not rptd. until May Morris included it in vol. XVII of the *CW*, pbd. in 1913. The reason was that Morris's tale grew under his hand until it would no longer fit the original plan for pbn. in a single small vol. and had to be printed in two. To defray the additional expense without raising the announced price of 15s. he more than doubled the usual print run to 600 copies and announced, as May Morris says, 'that he undertook not to reprint it in any cheaper edition' (*CW*, XVII. xlj). Since the *CW* were only sold as 24-vol. sets at 12gns. the set, Morris's promise not to publish a cheaper edn. was kept.

A-78.02: Child Christopher (Mosher)

[within a thin rule compartment and a 2nd compartment within that formed by thin rules, Chiswick Press headpiece] | [double thin rule] | [in red] CHILD CHRISTO-PHER | AND GOLDILIND | THE FAIR | BY | WILLIAM MORRIS | [Chiswick Press mark, Bishop No. 2] | [double thin rule] | PRINTED FOR THOMAS B. MOSHER and published | by him at XLV Exchange Street | Portland Maine | [in red] MDCCCC
Edition: [1st impression, 2nd edn., 1st American].
Collaborators, Editors, and Illustrators: [unsigned prefatory bibliographical note by Thomas B. Mosher].
Series: Miscellaneous Series-12. From Bishop's account of this series (it ran from 1895 to 1923) it seems that the only thing that the 98 books included in it have in common is the series title, which, as usual, does not actually appear anywhere in the books themselves.
Colophon: REPRINTED BY THOMAS B. MOSHER

| AT XLV EXCHANGE STREET, PORT- | LAND, MAINE. FINISHED ON THE | XXIVTH DAY OF NOVEMBER, | MDCCCC.
Printer: printed at the press of George D. Loring, Portland, Maine.
Collation: medium 8°: [1–14⁸ 15⁴] 116 leaves pp. [i–v] vi–ix [x] [1–3] 4–218 [219–22] [= 232].
Contents: all pages are printed within thin rule compartments by 'old style rules' forming a single compartment which, from the contents, pp. [vii]– ix and p. [3]–218 is subdivided into 4 internal compartments by 1 vertical and 1 horizontal rule at the right and head respectively, the larger head compartment contains the running titles, the smaller head compartment at the right margin the page numbers, the larger outer margin compartment the side notes, and the main compartment the text: p. [i], half title within thin rule compartment, aligned left; p. [ii], statement of limitation: [within thin-rule compartment] 450 copies of this book have been printed on Van Gelder hand-made paper and the type distributed; p. [iii], title page; p. [iv], blank; p. [v], edn. note, unsigned [by T. B. Mosher], headed: NOTE; p. vi, headed: CONTENTS. | [list begins]; pp. vii–ix, Contents completed; p. [x], blank; p. [1]: [criblé headpiece reproduced from Chiswick Press] | [dropped head]: CHAPTER I. OF THE KING OF OAK- | ENREALM, AND HIS WIFE AND HIS | CHILD | [text begins with 8-line Chiswick Press criblé initial 'O']; pp. [2]–218, text completed with triangular Chiswick Press tail-piece.
Technical Notes: *paper*: 2 versions: Van Gelder hand-made with deckled edges and japan vellum; *leaf size*: both papers avg. 235 x 155 mm.; *printing*: printed in red and black, red in titles, ornamental initials, and side notes used as subheads to adjacent text; *type area*: 142 x 87 mm.; *lines-to-page*: leaded, 30 lines; *running titles*: [all versos] CHILD CHRISTOPHER | [all rectos] AND GOLDILIND THE FAIR; *end-papers*: the same paper as the body: 3 free ends and a paste-down in front, 1 free end and pastedown in back, all plain white and blank; *binding*: quarter white parchment with plain unblocked blue paper-covered boards and printed paper *spine label*: [thick-thin rule] | CHILD | CHRISTOPHER | AND | GOLDILIND | THE FAIR | [thin rule] | [name in red] WILLIAM | MORRIS | [thin-thick rule]; japan vellum copies bound in japan vellum wrappers with a brocade design underlay over boards with titles printed on the front as well as the spine, in 2 colours, with on the spine, green lthr. labels, the head being as above, and at the foot the date: 1900. All copies provided with slip cases.
Publication: 1900 [issued Nov.] (Hatch, item 142; but see also 22–9 Dec. in 'Publications of the Week', in *Pub. Weekly*, 58/1509 (29 Dec. 1900), 1758); *print run*: 450 copies on Van Gelder hand-made and 50 numbered copies on japan vellum (Bishop, p. 114); *price*: Van Gelder copies, $3.50, japan vellum, unknown.
Register of Copies Examined: BL (base copy: Cup. 500. c. 39.); Bsp.
Notes: Mosher changed the text from the small 2-vol. Kelmscott format to that of a larger 1-vol. edn. Chiswick format with old-style rules. He corrected the errors on the errata sheet in vol. I and corrected p. 18 to read 'some four years' rather than 'some two years', as on the KP version's erratum slip. Each ampersand is changed to 'and', and he continued the use of shoulder notes in the margin with some revisions. He exchanged 2 misplaced notes in vol. I of the KP edn.: 'Goldilind waxeth very fair' on p. 41 here follows 'She makes the best of it' on page 42. Then he shifted the shoulder note of p. 80, 'They are bound for the Tofts' of the KP vol. I, by putting it between 'Simon will not fight' and 'Of Jack o' the Tofts'. Other changes to the shoulder notes included changing 'Of Christopher's aspect' (vol. I, p. 228) to 'Of Christopher's aspects'; Mosher omitted 'Comes in Goldilind' (vol. II, p. 2); and revised Morris's colophon. Mosher worked from his own copy of the KP edn., which is now in the Bishop collection (see Bishop, p. 114, where he lists the detailed corrections given here).

A-78.03: Child Christopher (+ Wood Beyond the World *CW* XVII)

THE COLLECTED WORKS | [for title details common to the set, see A-126.01] | VOLUME XVII | THE WOOD BEYOND THE WORLD | CHILD CHRISTOPHER | OLD FRENCH ROMANCES | [publisher's imprint] | MDCCCCXIII
Edition: 'Collected Works edn' [1st impression, 3rd edn., 2nd English] This is a reference entry. For details specific to this version of this title, see A-74.04; for details common to the series, see A-126.01.

A-79.01: Old French Romances (Allen)

OLD FRENCH | [in red] ROMANCES | [in black] DONE INTO ENGLISH | BY | WILLIAM MORRIS | WITH AN INTRODUCTION BY | JOSEPH JACOBS | [printer's acorn] | LONDON | GEORGE ALLEN, RUSKIN HOUSE | 1896 | *All rights reserved*
Edition: [1st impression, 1st collected edn., 2nd edn. of each of the individual tales] This book is the 1st popular col-

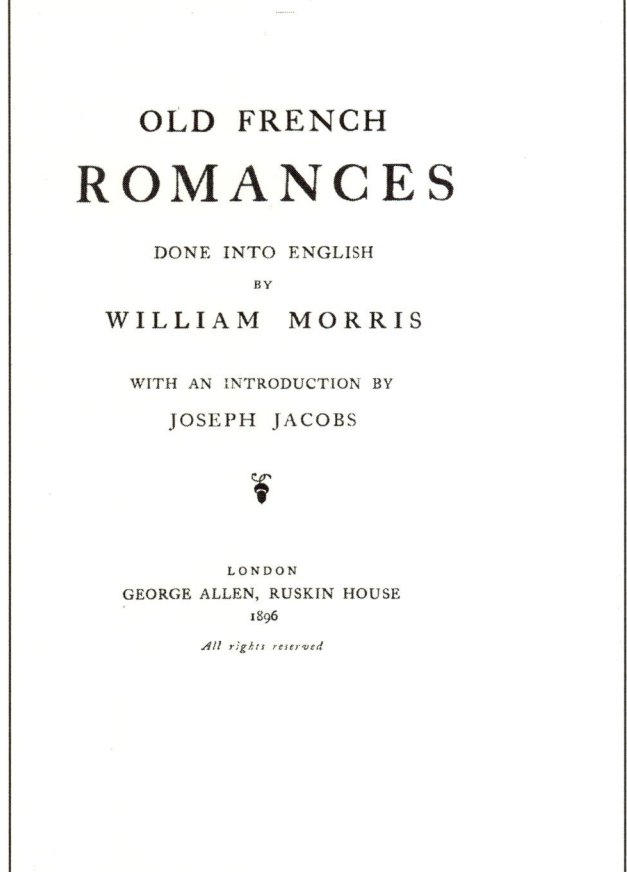

Figure 70. A-79.01: *Old French Romances* (Allen edn.) title page

lected edn. of the 4 medieval prose romances earlier translated by Morris and issued in 3 vols. by the Kelmscott Press (see A-69.01, 70.01, and 75.01). The texts are entirely reset.
Collation: cr. 8°: [a]–b⁸ A–K⁸ L⁴ M² 102 leaves pp. [i–iv] v–xxxii [1–2] 3–169 [170–2] [= 204].
Contents: p. [i], half title; p. [ii], George Allen's publisher's device of St. George slaying the dragon, signed by Walter Crane; p. [iii], title page; p. [iv], printer's imprint: Printed by Ballantyne, Hanson & Co. | At the Ballantyne Press; p. v, dropped head: INTRODUCTION | [text begins]; pp. vi–xxv, Introduction completed; p. [xxvi], blank; p. xxvii, dropped head: CONTENTS | [list of the 4 titles, with Morris's KP edn. shoulder notes collected under each (but not used in the text of the tales)]; pp. xxviii–xxxi, contents continue; p. xxxii, contents end; p. [1], 2nd half title: [top, flush left] THE TALE OF KING COUS- | TANS THE EMPEROR; p. [2], blank; p. 3, text begins with title as shoulder note; pp. 4–24, text completed; p. [25], 3rd half title: [top, flush left] THE FRIENDSHIP OF | AMIS AND AMILE; p. [26], blank; p. 27, text begins with shoulder title; pp. 28–58, *Amis and Amile* completed; p. [59], 4th half title: [top, flush left] THE TALE OF KING FLORUS | AND THE FAIR JEHANE; p. [60], blank; p. 61, text begins with shoulder title; pp. 62–115, text completed; p. [116], blank; p. [117], 5th half title: [top, flush left] THE HISTORY OF | OVER SEA; p. [118], blank; p. 119, text begins with shoulder title; pp. 120–69, text completed with explicit: [flush left, ¶] Here ends the Story of Over Sea | done out of ancient French into | English by William Morris.; p. [170], printer's imprint: Printed by Ballantyne, Hanson & Co. | London & Edinburgh; pp. [171–2], blank.
Technical Notes: *paper*: cream machine-laid with dandy roll laid lines, no watermark, t.e.g.; *leaf size*: untrimmed, avg. 188 x 125 mm.; *printing*: type area: 118 x 73 mm. excluding direction lines; *shoulder titles*: all rectos and versos: titles of adjacent tale or section in italics; *end-papers*: single free end and paste-down, plain white and blank, front and back; *binding*: plain dark red unblocked cloth, *spine*: gilt-stamped: [within thin-rule compartment] OLD | FRENCH | ROMANCES | [below compartment] W. MORRIS | [foot] GEORGE ALLEN
Publication: 1896 [issued 2 Apr.] ('just out' (*BSR*, no. 461 (2 Apr. 1896), 403); *print run*: unknown; *price*: 4s. 6d.
Register of Copies Examined: LeM (base copy); VU (2 copies: Bail.E, and B 821.85O.j; these two copies are duplicates, one from Poynton Coll, one from Scott Coll.); CSt (2 copies: Green Stacks 841.108.M717m; Spec. Coll Felton Pr5081.04).
Notes: Besides the reprints of the collected Old French Romances, the 4 tales were pbd. separately by T. B. Mosher (several times each), and individual tales by various other publishers, British and American. See under the titles of the individual tales.

From the introduction by Joseph Jacobs: 'Mr Morris has . . . consented to allow his versions of the Romances to be combined into one volume in a form not unworthy of their excellence but more accessible . . . He has honoured me by asking me to introduce them to that wider public to which they now make their appeal' (p. vi).

Jacobs' introduction is almost wholly concerned with the origins of the tales. He claims that Morris originated a special 'style' for the writing of romance, and that it has been adopted since 1869 by all who write English translations of medieval or classic romance.
Later issues and impression of this edn.: George Allen.
1.* 1914 [issued 23–30 May] ('Books of the Week', *Pub.*

Circ., 101 (30 Mar. 1914), 693): New Edition. [2nd impression, 1st edn.]; *print run*: unknown; *price*: 4*s* 6*d*.;
2.* Scribners, NY: c. 1914: New Edition [1st American issue, 2nd impression, 1st edn.]; *print run*: probably imported sheets of the English 2nd impression; *price*: unknown.

A-79.02: Old French Romances (+ Child Christopher and Wood Beyond the World *CW* XVII)

THE COLLECTED WORKS | [for title detail common to the set, see A-126.01] | VOLUME XVII | THE WOOD BEYOND THE WORLD | CHILD CHRISTOPHER | OLD FRENCH ROMANCES | [publisher's imprint, see A-126.01] | MDCCCCXIII
Edition: the *CW* edn. of *Old French Romances* [1st impression, 2nd collected edn.] This is a reference entry. For each of the individual tales it is the 3rd edn.. For details such as *Contents* and *Technical Notes* specific to this version of this title see A-74.04, and for details common to the set, see A-126.01.
Publication: 1913 [issued 31 Oct.] (Longmans Arch.); *print run* and *price*: see this field in A-126.01.
Register of Copies Examined: see this field in A-126.01.

A-80.01: The Well at the World's End (KP)

[Troy type] THE WELL AT THE WORLD'S END [printer's leaf ornament No. 1] BY | WILLIAM MORRIS.
Edition: 'Kelmscott Press Edn.' [1st impression, 1st edn.] While the Kelmscott Press edn. was the 1st version of this tale issued, it is not '1st' in reference to its setting: 'The text was set from the sheets of the Longmans edition, printed at the Chiswick Press, which was simultaneously in production' (*KP Biblio.*, p. 98). The KP edn. was delayed because of Morris's abortive attempt to have the book illustrated by Arthur Gaskin, whose pictures were finally rejected after a number of trials. Finally, 4 woodcut illus. by Burne-Jones were used and the book issued in 1896. The ordinary 2-vol. Chiswick Press edn. was set by the end of 1892, but it had to be held up in order that the KP edn., as was the understanding with subscribers, could be issued as the 1st edn.. Naturally, printers much preferring to compose from a printed original, the KP quarto was set not from the original MS fair copy but from the printed sheets of the Longmans-Chiswick Press 2-vol. octavo. In the bibliographic sense, that gives the Chiswick Press version a claim to be the 1st edn., the special textual value of the 1st edn. being that it is the version the author is most likely to have revised carefully for 'accidentals', punctuation, paragraphing, spelling, etc., as well as substantives. But the case for seeing the KP version as the 1st edn. has substance still, it being, quite deliberately, the 1st to be issued. Morris was never very careful about accidentals, but the sheer expense of cancelling KP pages and the damage to the reputation if the Press issued faulty texts would have lent a greater than usual urgency to the requirement of careful proofreading. In any case, priority and the niceties of terminology probably count less in this case than the substance of what was done.
Series: 39th title, 16th by Morris, prtd. by the KP.
Colophon: top, flush left, in 2 columns, with drop cap initial 'H': HERE ends the Well at | the World's End, writ- | ten by William Morris, | with four pictures designed by | Sir Edward Burne-Jones [printer's leaf ornament, KP no. 1] | Printed by William Morris at | the Kelmscott Press, 14, Up- | per Mall, Hammersmith, in the | County of Middlesex, and fin- | ished on the 2nd day of March, | 1896. | [¶] [aligned left, full single column, in red] Sold by William Morris at the Kelmscott Press.
Collation: large 4° in 8s: [a]⁴ b–2i⁸ [$4 (–b d2 f3 i3 m1,3 n3 o1–3 p2–4 q3 r3 t2, 4 u3–4 y4 z1 2a3 2b2–3 2d1 2f1 2g3) signed] 252 leaves pp. [8] [1] 2–496 [= 504].
Contents: pp. [*1–4*], blank; p. [*5*], title page; pp. [*6–7*], blank; p. [*8*], within KP border 16a, engraved frontis., top, within thick-rule compartment, designed by E. Burne-Jones, with caption lower compartment in 4-line floriated characters, designed by Morris: HELP IS TO | HAND IN THE | WOOD | PERILOUS; p. [1], head title, within KP border 16, headed: BOOK I. THE ROAD UNTO LOVE. | [in red] CHAPTER I. THE SUNDERING OF THE WAYS | [text begins with drop ornamental word 'Long']; pp. 2–115, text; p. [116], within KP border 17a, 2nd Burne-Jones illus. The design of the engraved frontis. is repeated in the other 3 Burne-Jones illus., within text in Morris's design in the lower part of the illus., the whole facing the head titles that introduce each of the 4 books. This 2nd engraved illus. is captioned, below: THE CHAMBER | OF LOVE | IN THE | WILDERNESS; p. [117], within KP border 17, headed, in red: BOOK II. THE ROAD UNTO TROUBLE. | CHAPTER I. RALPH MEETS WITH LOVE | IN THE WILDERNESS | [text begins with ornamental drop initial word 'He']; pp. 118–285, text; p. [286], within KP border 18a, 3rd Burne-Jones illus., captioned: FRIENDS | IN NEED MEET | IN THE | WILD-WOOD; p. [287], within KP border 18, headed, in red: BOOK III. THE ROAD TO THE WELL AT THE WORLD'S END. | CHAPTER I. AN ADVENTURE IN THE WOOD UNDER THE MOUNTAINS. | [text

begins]; pp. 288–361, text; p. 362, within KP border 19a, 4th Burne-Jones illus., captioned: THE LAST | TIME OF THE | LONG CHAMPION; p. 363, within KP border 19, headed, in red: BOOK IV. THE ROAD HOME. | CHAPTER I. RALPH AND URSULA COME BACK AGAIN THROUGH THE GREAT MOUNTAINS. | [text begins with ornamental drop initial word 'ON']; pp. 364–495, text completed with colophon (see above); p. 496, KP mark No. 2.

Technical Notes: ranges as a KP book with *The Water of the Wondrous Isles* (see A-84.01); *paper*: Batchelor's KP Flower paper 2 with deckled edges; *leaf size*: lightly trimmed, avg. 285 x 206 mm.; *printing*: in double columns in red and black, red for all chapter titles, shoulder titles, and last line of the colophon; *type face*: Troy type for display type on title page, text in Chaucer type; *type area*: each column 187 x 63 mm., with a 9 mm. gap between columns, except single column for the lyrics and the last line of the colophon; overall type area: 187 x 136 mm.; *lines-to-page*: set solid, 41 lines, excluding head and direction lines; *shoulder notes*: all rectos and versos, in red, indicate each of the books of the story and chapter titles; *end-papers*: the standard arrangement for KP books, 3 free ends and a paste-down, plain white and blank, front and back, sewn in with the body of the book and of the same paper; *binding*: limp white vellum with green silk ties, gilt-stamped across the spine: THE WELL | AT THE | WORLD'S END | BY | WILLIAM | MORRIS; *ornamentation*: 8 full borders: 16a, 16, 17a, 17, 18a, 18, 19a and 19, 2 facing each other being used for the 4 illus. designed by E. Burne-Jones and the head title page of each of the 4 books; 4 14-line floriated initials; 1 8-line initial; 105 6-line initials; one 5-line initial; 654 3-line initials; 49 vine column dividers; 63 half borders; 9 small margin ornaments.

Publication: 2 Mar. 1896 [colophon date indicates finished printing, issued 4 June] (Cockerell, p. 162); *print run*: 350 paper copies, 8 on vellum; *price*: 5*gns.* and 20*gns.*, respectively.

Register of Copies Examined: National Gallery, Canberra (base copy); VU (4 copies; 19 H and L); NNPM (20117: inscribed by Morris to Swinburne '9 June 1896').

Notes: Morris's letter to Jenny on 22 Oct. [1891] establishes that Morris began *The Well at the World's End* shortly before that date (*Letters*, iii. 361), and Cockerell's diary entry for 7 Aug. 1892 (see Cockerell Papers) shows the composition was still going on, then in a late stage. Since the Chiswick Press printing of it was completed before the end of Dec., composition must have been completed by Nov. 1892. On the delay in pbn., see the *Edition* note, above.

('Home Notes', *The British Bookmaker*, 6/67 (Jan. 1893), 148):

> A new book from the Kelmscott Press, which will be ready shortly, is Mr. Morris's new story 'The Well at the World's End'. This volume will be the first of a new size, large Quarto, and will be printed in double columns with his 'Chaucer' type; his earlier productions—a page of one of which we gave in our journal—were printed in 'Golden Type'; while a third kind, the 'Troy' has so far only been used for the Caxton reprints.

S. C. Cockerell's Diary for 19 Oct. 1892 (see Cockerell Papers) says he had read that day some 200 pages of Chiswick Press proofs of *The Well* and found many corrections by Morris, made for the KP version, which was set from those same Chiswick Press sheets, described in the next entry.

A-80.02: *The Well at the World's End* (2 vols. Trade Edn.)

THE WELL AT THE | WORLD'S END A TALE | BY WILLIAM MORRIS | VOLUME I [II] | LONGMANS, GREEN, AND CO. | LONDON, NEW YORK, AND BOMBAY | MDCCCXCVI

Edition: 'Ordinary edn' 'Trade edn' [1st impression, 2nd edn.] 2 vols. On the relation of this edn. to the 1st edn., see this field in the previous entry. Though Forman says (HBF, p. 184) that only one bound copy survives with the Reeves and Turner imprint, the BL copy cited here has both sets of preliminaries, with the Reeves and Turner and the Longmans imprints (though set under Reeves and Turner, the book was not issued until Longmans had taken over). It was S. C. Cockerell's copy, received by the BL in 1957 (see also Robert Proctor's MS 'Odds and Ends' Notebook for a Morris Bibliography (BL Case 43, hereafter referred to as Proctor)).

Collation: vol. I: cr. 8°: [a]⁴ B–2A⁸ 2B⁶ [$1 signed (2B3 as 2B2)] 194 leaves pp. [i–iv] v–vii [viii] 1–378 [379–80] [= 388].

vol. II: cr. 8°: a⁴ B–S⁸ T⁴ 144 leaves pp. [2] [i–iv] v–vi [1–2] 3–279 [280] [= 288].

Contents: vol. I: p. [i], half title; p. [ii], blank; p. [iii], title page; p. [iv], printer's imprint: CHISWICK PRESS:— CHARLES WHITTINGHAM AND CO. | TOOKS COURT, CHANCERY LANE, LONDON.; p. v–vii, headed: CONTENTS. | [list of 2 Books and 65 chapter heads completed]; p. [viii], blank; p. 1, dropped head title: THE WELL AT THE WORLD'S END. | BOOK I. THE

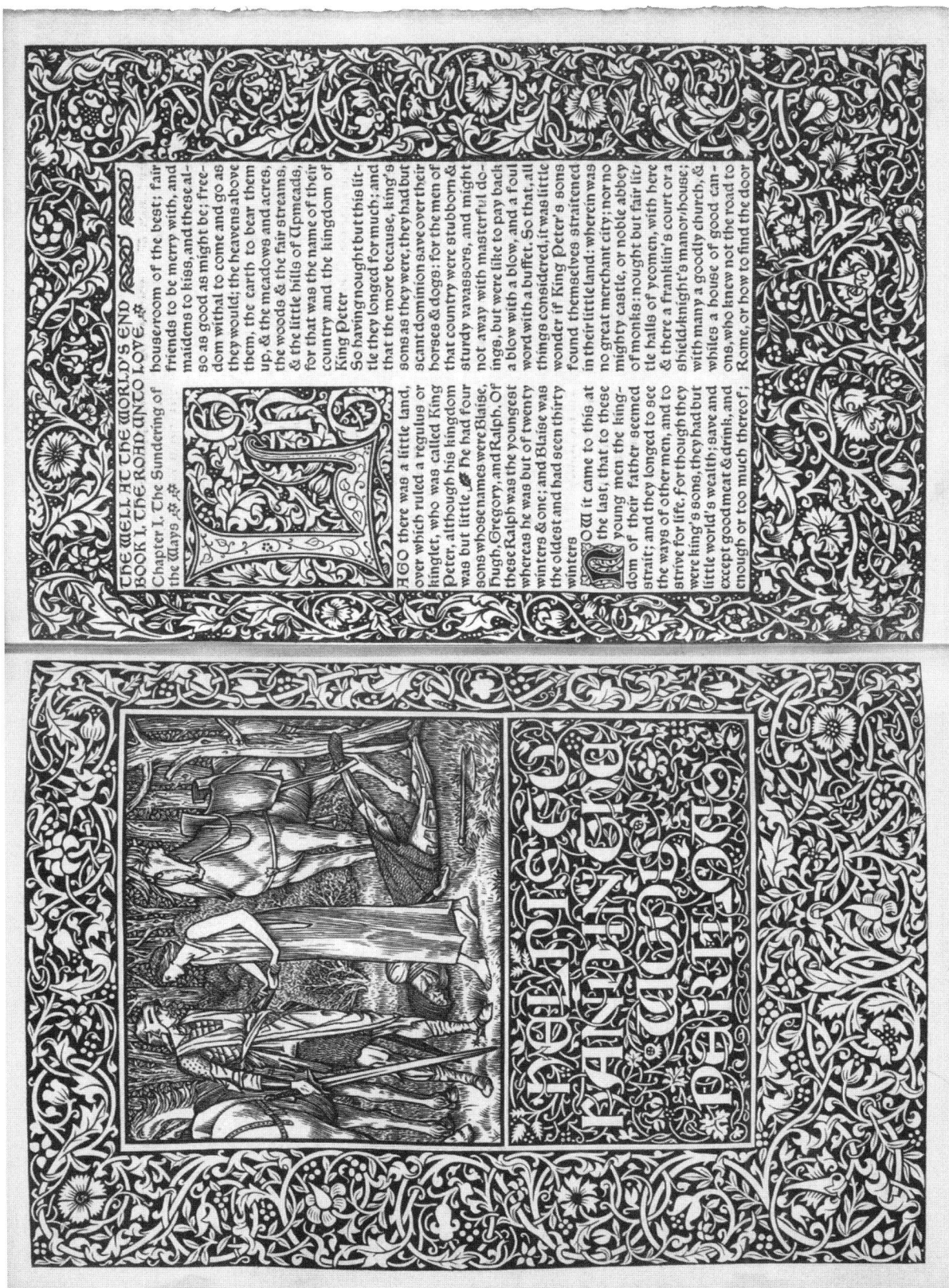

Figure 71. A-80.01: *Well at the World's End* (KP edn.) opening; frontis. & head title

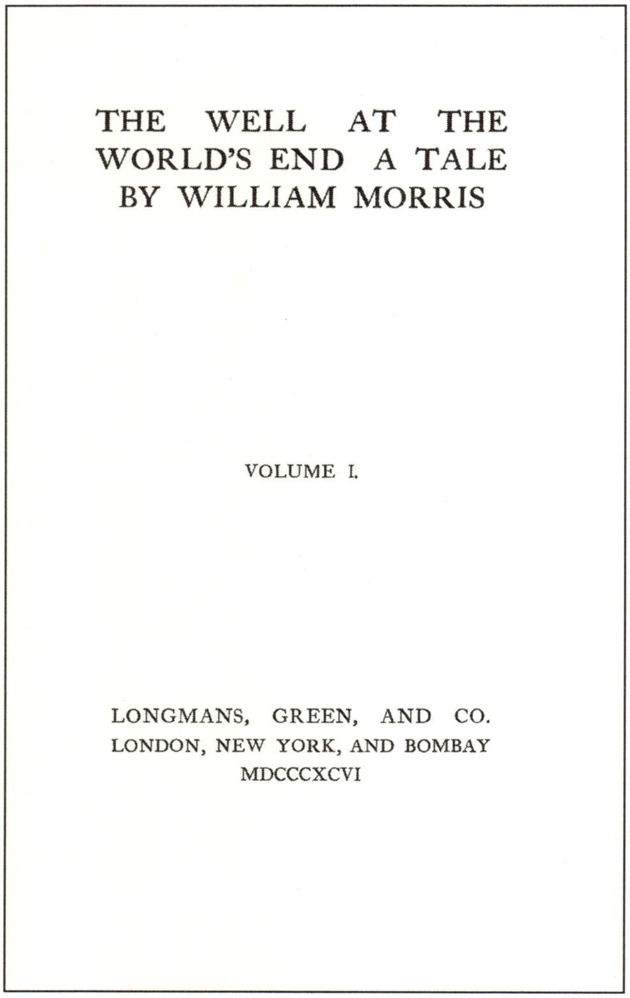

```
THE WELL AT THE
WORLD'S END A TALE
BY WILLIAM MORRIS




            VOLUME I.






LONGMANS, GREEN, AND CO.
LONDON, NEW YORK, AND BOMBAY
          MDCCCXCVI
```

Figure 72. A-80.02: *Well at the World's End* (2nd edn., vol.1 of 2) title page

ROAD UNTO LOVE. | Chapter I. THE SUNDERING OF THE | WAYS. | [text begins]; pp. 2–155 text completed; p. [156], blank; p. [157], Book II half title; p. [158], blank; p. 159, dropped head title: BOOK II. THE ROAD UNTO TROUBLE. | CHAPTER I. RALPH MEETS WITH LOVE | IN THE WILDERNESS.; pp. 160–378, text completed with explicit: END OF VOL. I.; p. [379]: Chiswick Press lion-dolphin-anchor mark, above printer's imprint, as above on p. [iv]; p. [380], blank.
vol. II: pp. [1–2], blank; p. [i], general half title; p. [ii], blank; p. [iii], title page, as above with change of vol. to II; p. [iv], printer's imprint, as vol. I; pp. v–vi, [dropped head title]: CONTENTS. | [list of 2 Books and 54 chapter heads completed]; p. [1], half title; p. [2], blank; p. 3, dropped head: THE WELL AT THE WORLD'S END. | BOOK III. THE ROAD TO THE WELL AT | THE WORLD'S END. | CHAPTER I. AN ADVENTURE IN THE | WOOD UNDER THE MOUNTAINS. | [text begins]; pp. 4–99, text completed; p. [100], blank; p. [101], half title; p. [102], blank; p. 103, dropped head title: BOOK IV. THE ROAD HOME. | CHAPTER I. RALPH AND URSULA COME | BACK AGAIN THROUGH THE GREAT | MOUNTAINS. | [text begins]; pp. 104–279, text completed with explicit: [formatted with text] AND HERE ENDS THE | TALE OF THE WELL AT THE WORLD'S | END; p. [280], printer's mark and imprint as at the end of vol. I.

Technical Notes: *paper*: cream hand-laid, vertical chain lines, deckled edges, and watermark: device and initial of French company 'B A S' on top near inner fold; *leaf size*: deckled edges lightly trimmed, avg. 221 x 136 mm.; *printing*: *type area*: 157 x 89 mm.; *lines-to-page*: set solid, 37 lines; *pagination*: arabic numbers centred on the direction line; *end-papers*: both vols.: 3 free ends and paste-down, plain white and blank, front and back; *binding*: quarter holland (cream) with blue paper-covered boards and printed paper spine labels: MORRIS | THE | WELL | AT THE | WORLD'S | END | VOL. I [II]; an optional de luxe binding: royal blue dyed 1/2 calf with marbled paper-covered boards; *spine*: gilt-stamped with title, author, and vol. between 1st and 2nd of 5 raised bands.

Publication: 1896 [issued 26 Sept.–3 Oct.] (*Pub. Circ.* 65/1579 (3 Oct. 1896), 393); *print run*: 1,000 copies (Longmans Arch.); *price*: 28s. the set.

Register of Copies Examined: LeM (base copy); BL (3 copies, including: Cup. 510. av.14.; this copy, once S. C. Cockerell's, has both the Reeves and Turner and Longmans preliminaries bound in; K.T.C. 101. a. 5.); VSL (S823.89 | M83W); VU (Bail.: 2 copies: Spec. Coll. E, and B821.85 W).

Notes: Chiswick Arch. vol. 7, p. 601, confirms that Longmans had 1,000 copies of the cancel title printed for this edn.

Morris to the Chiswick Press, 31 Dec. [1892]: 'I see that I have made a mistake: the first vol: should end at the end of the *2nd part*. The 2nd vol: beginning with the 3rd part. viz the *Road to the Well at the World's End*' (*Letters*, iii. 486).

Later impressions. from this edn.: Longmans:
1.* 1903 [16 June] (Longmans and Chiswick Archs.): 'Ordinary Edition' [2nd impression, 2nd edn.]; *print run*: 250 copies; *price*: 28s. for the 2 vols.;
2. 1910 [24 Mar.] (Longmans and Chiswick Archs.): 'Ordinary Edition' [3rd impression, 2nd edn.]; *print run*: 250 copies; *price*: 28s. the 2 vols.

A-80.03: The Well at the World's End (*CW* XVIII–XIX)

THE COLLECTED WORKS | [title details common to the set, see A-126.01] | VOLUME XVIII [XIX] | THE WELL AT THE WORLD'S END | VOLUME I [II] | [publisher's imprint, see A-126.01] | MDCCCCXIII

Edition: 'Collected Works Edn.' [1st impression, 3rd edn.]

Series: vols. 18 and 19 of 24. For series information, see this field in A-126.01.

Collation: vol. XVIII, Books 1–2; medium 8°: [a]⁸ (a4+1) b⁸ (b6+1) c⁴ B–Y⁸ Z⁴ [$2 (–b2 c2 Z1–2) signed] 192 leaves pp. [i–x] xi–xxxvii [xxxviii–xl] 1–335 [336–44] [= 384] + 2 inserted plates noted in the collation and described here in their appropriate places under *Contents*, but not included in the book's pagination.

vol. XIX, Books 3–4: medium 8°: [a]⁸ (a4 +1) b⁸ (b2 +1) (b5 + 1) c⁴ B–Q⁸ R⁴ [$2 signed] 147 leaves pp. [i–x] xi–xiii [xiv] xv–xxxvii [xxxviii–xl] 1–245 [246–8] [= 294] including 3 inserted plates noted in the collation but not in the pagination; described here under *Contents*.

Contents: vol. I, pp. [i–v], blank; p. [vi], statement of limitation (see A-126.01); pp. [vii–viii], blank; 1st inserted plate as frontis. within a blind-stamped compartment, verso blank, recto facing p. ix, photo reproduction, oriented vertically, with the plate maker's name below right, in copperplate: *Emery Walker Ph. sc.* | [caption in copperplate, centred]: *Tithe Barn at Great Coxwell, Berkshire* | *from a photograph by Mr. F. H. Evans*; p. [ix], title page; p. [x], blank; pp. xi–xiii, headed: CONTENTS | [list of chapters in Books I and II]; p. xiv, blank; pp. xv–xxviii, headed: INTRODUCTION | [text begins]; 2nd inserted plate, blank on recto, photo reproduction (of interior) in blind-stamped compartment to face p. xxix, with the plate maker's name below right in copperplate: *Emery Walker Ph. sc.* | [captioned in copperplate, centred] *Tithe Barn at Great Coxwell, Berkshire* | *from a photograph by Mr. F. H. Evans*; pp. xxix–xxxvi, Introduction completed; p. xxxvii, headed: BIBLIOGRAPHICAL NOTE; p. [xxxviii], blank; p. [xxxix], half title; p. [xl], blank; p. 1, headed: BOOK I. THE ROAD UNTO LOVE | CHAPTER I. THE SUNDERING OF THE WAYS. | [text begins]; pp. 2–[336], text completed with explicit: END OF VOLUME I.; pp. [337–44], blank.

VOL. II, Books III and IV: pp. [i–v], blank; p. [vi], statement of limitation (see A-126.01); pp. [vii–viii], blank; 1st inserted plate, recto blank, as frontis. within a blind-stamped compartment and facing p. ix, photo reproduction of a drawing, with the plate maker's name below right, in copperplate: *Emery Walker Ph. sc.* | [caption in copperplate, centred] *M*ʳˢ. *William Morris* | *circa 1865* | *from a drawing by D. G. Rossetti*; p. [x], blank; pp. xi–xiii, headed: CONTENTS | [list completed]; p. [xiv], blank; pp. xv–xx, headed: INTRODUCTION | [text begins]; 2nd inserted plate (verso blank), recto a woodcut printed in black with a red oak tree as background and captioned below: MEMBERSHIP CARD FOR DEMOCRATIC FEDERATION | DESIGNED BY WILLIAM MORRIS | FROM THE ORIGINAL BLOCKS; pp. xxi–xxvi, introduction continues; 3rd inserted plate, verso blank, oriented vertically, reproduction of a photograph within a blind-stamped compartment, with the plate maker named, below right, in copperplate: *Emery Walker Ph. sc.* | [vertical caption, centred, in copperplate] *The Meeting Room, Kelmscott House 1896*; p. xxvij–xxxvi, Intro. concluded; p. [xxxviii], blank; p. [xxxix], half title; p. [xl], blank; p. 1, text begins; pp. 2–245, text completed, with explicit formatted as a continuation of the text, but in caps: AND HERE ENDS THE TALE | OF THE WELL AT THE WORLD'S END.; pp. [246-7, blank; p.[248], printer's imprint, see this field in A-126.01.

Technical Notes: paper, leaf size, printing, type area, lines-to-page, position (but not content) of headlines, running titles, shoulder notes, pagination, end-papers, and binding are all common to the series and are described in this field in A-126.01, the entry for the set treated as a single work. Included here are only those details that are specific to this issue: *shoulder notes*: all rectos and versos of the text: BOOK [+ no. in roman caps] | Chap. [+ no. in arabic]; *spine label*: [first 4 lines standard for *CW*, see A-126.01] | VOLUME XVIII [XIX] | THE WELL | AT THE | WORLD'S END | VOLUME I [II].

Publication: 1913 [issued 31 Oct.] (Longmans Arch.); *print run* and *price*: see this field in A-126.01.

Register of Copies Examined: see this field in A-126.01.

A-80.04: The Well at the World's End (2 vols. LPL)

THE WELL | AT THE WORLD'S END | BY WILLIAM MORRIS | IN TWO VOLUMES | VOL. I [II] | POCKET EDITION | LONGMANS, GREEN AND CO. | 39 PATERNOSTER ROW, LONDON | NEW YORK, BOMBAY, AND CALCUTTA | 1913

Edition: Pocket Edition. vol. I [II]. [1st impression, 4th edn.]

Series: Longmans Pocket Library (for series detail, see this field in the record of the 1st book in the series, *Jason*, A-3.09).

Collation: vol. I.: fcap 8°: π⁴ A–T⁸ U⁶ [$1 signed (U3 as U2)] 162 leaves pp. [i–v] vi–vii [viii] [1] 2–316 [= 324].
vol. II: collation duplicates vol. I.
Contents: vol. I: p. [i], half title; p. [ii], blank; p. [iii], title page; p. [iv], dropped head: CONTENTS | BOOK I | [list begins]; pp. v–vii, Contents concluded; p. [viii], blank; p. [1], dropped head title: THE | WELL AT THE WORLD'S END | BOOK I | THE ROAD UNTO LOVE | CHAPTER I | THE SUNDERING OF THE WAYS | [text begins]; pp. 2–316, text completed with explicit: END OF VOL. I | [printer's imprint]: Printed by BALLANTYNE, HANSON & CO. | at Paul's Work, Edinburgh
vol. II as vol. I, except for the vol. no. on the title page, the changes of contents to cover the rest of Book II (chapters 33 to 41), Book III (22 chapters), and Book IV (32 chapters), ending on p. viii; p. [1], dropped head | [text begins]; pp. 2–316, text completed with explicit, formatted as part of the text: AND HERE ENDS THE TALE OF THE WELL AT | THE WORLD'S END. | [printer's imprint as in vol. I.].
Technical Notes: for details common to the series—paper, printing, type, pagination, chapter headings, binding, and end-papers—see this field in A-3.09; details specific to this issue: *type area*: 123 x 76 mm.
Publication: Nov. 1913 [noted as 'Ready' on 1 Nov.] (Longmans *Notes on Books*, 11/225 (Nov. 1913), 279); *print run*: 2,050 copies of 2 vols.; *price*: 2s. cloth, 3s. lthr.
Register of Copies Examined: CaBVaU (base copy: PR 5078 W4 1896A v.1 & 2 STOR); Fdmn; BGR; BL (012203. e. 17/25).
Notes: entry from Longmans Arch. for 8 Nov. 1913 confirms that *The Well at the World's End* was new set and printed in 2,050 copies, with moulds made and printing by Ballantyne. The price of binding was 75s. per 100 copies and the total cost, not including binding, was £115. 8s. 3d.

A-81.01: Poems by the Way [and] Love is Enough (PW)
POEMS BY THE WAY | & LOVE IS ENOUGH | BY | WILLIAM MORRIS | NEW EDITION | LONGMANS, GREEN, AND CO. | 39 PATERNOSTER ROW, LONDON | NEW YORK AND BOMBAY | 1896 | *All rights reserved*
Edition: New Edition [1st impression, 1st edn., considered as a new title; 4th edn., 3rd English, of *Poems by the Way*, and 6th edn., 5th English, of *Love is Enough*] For earlier pbns. of poems in *Poems by the Way* see this field in A-59.01.
Series: The Poetical Works of William Morris (PW) but only indicated as such on the spine label. This is the only new title in the series as 1st pbd., made by combining 2 earlier titles. For further series details, see this field in A-4.16; for *Love is Enough* see A-8.01.
Collation: cr. 8°: π⁴ A–X⁸ Y⁴ 176 leaves pp. [2] [i–iv] v–vi [1–2] 3–222 [223–4] (*Poems by the Way* ends and *Love is Enough* begins) 225–343 [344] [= 352].
Contents: pp. [1–2], blank; p. [i], half title; p. [ii], blank; p. [iii], title page; p. [iv], printer's imprint: Printed by BALLANTYNE, HANSON & CO. | At the Ballantyne Press; p. v, headed: Contents | [list begins]; p. vi, contents completed; p. [1], 2nd half title: POEMS BY THE WAY; p. [2], blank; p. 3, dropped head: FROM THE UPLAND TO THE SEA | [text begins]; pp. 4–222, text of *Poems by the Way* completed; p. [223], 3rd half title: LOVE IS ENOUGH; p. [224], dropped head section title: *DRAMATIS PERSONÆ* | [cast of 13 characters, as a list]; p. 225, dropped head: LOVE IS ENOUGH | ARGUMENT | [4-line prose precis, in hanging indent | [2-line scene direction in italics and hanging indent] | [text begins with speakers' names centred above their lines]; pp. 226–343, text completed with explicit: THE END | Printed by BALLANTYNE, HANSON & CO. | Edinburgh & London; p. [344], blank.
Technical Notes: *paper*: plain white machine-laid 'laid quad cr' (Longmans Arch.) with dandy roll laid lines; *leaf size*: trimmed, 190 x 128 mm.; *printing*: type area: 132 x 88 mm., excluding head and direction lines; *lines-to-page*: leaded, 30 lines; all poems (except 'The Lion' and 'The Orchard') begin new pages; *headlines*: *running titles*: pp. 2–222, all versos except those with headings: POEMS BY THE WAY | [all rectos except those with headings use the poem title or a shortened version thereof]; pp. 226–343, all rectos and versos: LOVE IS ENOUGH; *end-papers*: 1 free end and paste-down, plain white and blank, front and back; *binding*: plain black unblocked cloth-covered boards with a printed paper *spine label*: [within a thin-rule compartment] THE | POETICAL | WORKS OF | WILLIAM MORRIS | [thin rule] | POEMS BY | THE WAY | AND | LOVE IS | ENOUGH | [below compartment] *Six Shillings Net*
Publication: 1896 [27 June–3 July] ('Publications of the Week', *Pub. Circ.*, 65/1569 (25 July 1896), 84); Longmans Arch. says 17 June which may not be a date of issue but the date printing was finished); *print run*: 500 copies; *price*: 6s.
Register of Copies Examined: CSt (base copy: 821.6 M87pwa); BL (2292.e. 28); CaBVaU; SU (821.85 | M877 poe, this being the 2nd impression).
Notes: this is the 1st Morris book recorded in Longmans

Arch. as printed under Longmans direction (Longmans No. 28, Index H31). For details of the series of which this title is a part, see the *Series* field in A-4.16. The cost of production, exclusive of binding, was £49. 14*s*. 5*d*.
Later impressions of this edn.: Longmans:
1. 1898 [9 Mar.] (Longmans Arch.): New Edition 'The Poetical Works' [2nd impression, 1st edn.]; *print run*: 500 copies; *price*: reduced to 5*s*. net on spine label;
2. 1902 [15 May] (Longmans Arch.): New Edition 'The Poetical Works' [3rd impression, 1st edn.]; *print run*: 500 copies; *price*: 5*s*. net;
3. 1907 [6 July] (Longmans Arch.): New Impression 'The Poetical Works' [4th impression, 1st edn.]; *print run*: 500 copies; *price*: 5*s*. net;
4. 1912 [17 Jan.] (Longmans Arch.): New Impression 'The Poetical Works' [5th impression, 1st edn.]; *print run*: 500 copies; *price*: 5*s*. net.

A-81.02: Poems by the Way (+ Love is Enough *CW* IX)
THE COLLECTED WORKS | [title details common to the set, see A-126.01] | VOLUME IX | LOVE IS ENOUGH | POEMS BY THE WAY | [publisher's imprint, see A-126.01] | MDCCCCXI
Edition: 'Collected Works edn' [1st impression, 2nd edn.] For the full title and details common to the set, especially *Technical Notes*, see the entry for the *CW*, A-126.01. For other details of this *CW* issue, see *Collation, Contents, Technical Notes,* and *Publication* in A-59.06.
Publication: 1911 [issued 11 Dec.] (Longmans Arch.); *print run* and *price*: see this field in A-126.01.
Register of Copies Examined: see this field in A-126.01.

A-82.01: How I Became a Socialist
HOW I BECAME A SOCIALIST | [ornamental thin rule] | [oval Hollyer portrait]-photograph in black-and-white] | WILLIAM MORRIS | [flush right] Price One Penny.
Edition: [1st impression, 1st edn.] The title piece is reprinted from *Justice* (see D-563), along with passages from two of Morris's May Day contributions to *Justice*, 'Change of Position—Not Change of Condition', May Day 1895 (see D-571) and 'The Promise of May', May Day 1896 (D-592), and a memorial of Morris by H. M. Hyndman, here pbd. shortly after Morris's death on Oct. 3, 1896 . Some time after pbn. of Morris's essay in *Justice*, the Twentieth Century Press, which belonged to the SDF, combined Morris's contribution with 10 others from the same *Justice* series in a book entitled *How I Became a Socialist: A Series of Biographical Sketches* (see B-18).
Collaborators, Editors, and Illustrators: With an unsigned 'Introduction', [by Harry Quelch] and, as a foreword titled 'William Morris', H. M. Hyndman's account of Morris's connection with the SDF.
Collation: single 8° sheet folded 3 times to form 8 leaves pp. [1–4] 5–16 [= 16] (this pamphlet is sometimes sophisticated by the addition of a spurious wrapper. See *Notes*, below, B-18, and E-15).
Contents: This copy without Forman's manufactured wrapper. p. [1], title page; p. [2], blank; p. [3], headed: INTRODUCTION. | [thin rule] | [text begins]; p. [4], [Introduction concludes with a 4-line stanza from Walter Savage Landor] | [thin rule] | WILLIAM MORRIS | [text of Hyndman's obit. of Morris begins]; pp. 5–7, Hyndman continues; p. 8, Hyndman ends: [signed, flush right] H. M. HYNDMAN. [flush left] October 6th, 1896. | Reprinted from Justice.; p. 9, headed: [as running head] HOW I BECAME A SOCIALIST. | How I Became a Socialist. | [thin rule] | By William Morris. | [thin rule] | [text begins]; pp. 10–13, text completed and the new text begins, headed: Change of Position—Not Change of Condition; pp. 14–15, text completed, signed flush right: WILLIAM MORRIS. | [aligned left] Justice, May Day, 1895. | [ornamental thin rule, as on title page] | The Promise of May. | [thin rule]; p. 16, Morris text ends, with reference: [flush left] Justice, May Day, 1896. | [ornamental rule] | [thin rule] | [imprint] London: printed and published by the Twentieth Century Press, Limited, | 37a. Clerkenwell Green, E.C.
Technical Notes: *paper*: plain white machine-made, no watermark; *leaf size*: cut flush, 180 x 124 mm.; *printing*: *running titles*: pp. 4–8, all rectos and versos: WILLIAM MORRIS; pp. 9–12, rectos and versos: HOW I BECAME A SOCIALIST; pp. 13–14, all rectos and versos: CHANGE OF POSITION—NOT CHANGE OF CONDITION.; pp. 15–16, rectos and versos: THE PROMISE OF MAY; *binding*: see E-15 on the introduction by Forman of a stiff green paper wrapper.
Publication: Oct. 1896 [issued after 6 Oct. and before 3 Nov.] (the date on Hyndman's obituary note is 6 Oct. Forman's note of 3 Nov. 1896 (see the *Notes*), admitting that the green wrappers were his own creation, confirms the pamphlet's earlier issue); *print run*: unknown; *price*: 1*d*.
Register of Copies Examined: LSE (base copy, without the spurious wrapper); ANL (2 copies: 335.0942 MOR (in pams) and C 2030 | 272, Copy A, wanting pp.15 & 16; BL (3 copies: Cup. 502. f. 11. (44); 08282. h. 21. (10.); and Ashley 1239, with Forman's green wrapper).

Notes: for further detail relating to the fraudulent wrapper, see E-15.

A-83.01: The Hollow Land (*Bib.*, tale only, in 2 parts)
[wrapper title, above thin-rule compartments, top left] VOL. III. [top right] NO. 7 [8] | [within thin-rule compartment, top left] *JULY.* [*AUGUST.*] [top right] MDCCXCVII | [thin rule] | [within the main compartment, 1st and last lines in red, 1st in 3-line neo-gothic] The Bibelot | [black neo-gothic, normal size] A Reprint of Poetry | and Prose for Book | Lovers, chosen in part | from scarce edns and | sources not generally | known • • • • | Printed for Thomas B. Mosher | and Publish'd by him at 45 Ex- | change Street, Portland, Maine | [in red] Current Numbers 5 cents | [below compartment, right, in red] THE HOLLOW LAND: | A TALE. PART I [II] | BY WILLIAM MORRIS

Edition: [1st impression, 1st separate edn.] 1st pbd. in 2 parts in *The Oxford and Cambridge Magazine*, Sept. and Oct. 1856 (see D-13). Mosher's versions of *The Hollow Land* began with this separate edn., for sale both to subscribers to *The Bibelot* and the general public as a separate standalone text under *The Bibelot* masthead, with the wrapper title transcribed above. Then in the following January it appeared in the collected annual vol. of *The Bibelot*, issued on 25 Jan. of the following year. As with all Morris items in *The Bibelot*, the A-List entry provides finding-list information for both the separate and the periodical versions (for the latter, see also the *Series* field, below). On Mosher's *Bibelot* pbn. of this title, and its appearance here rather than in the D-List, Morris in Periodicals, see the *Series* field, below.

Collaborators, Editors, and Illustrators: untitled and unsigned foreword [by the editor, T. B. Mosher].
Series: *The Bibelot . . .*, 3/7, 8 (July and Aug. 1897), 205–47, [249–81]. 12 of the 20 Morris titles pbd. by Mosher were 1st issued as separates under *The Bibelot* masthead. Besides *The Hollow Land*, they included *Browning's 'Men and Women'* (Mar. 1898); *Gertha's Lovers* (in 2 parts, Jan., Feb. 1899); *The Two Sides of the River and Other Poems* (Sept. 1899, see C-8.01); *Golden Wings* (Apr. 1900); *Svend and His Brethren* (Sept. 1900); *The Churches of North France—No. 1, Amiens* (Mar. 1901); *The Story of the Unknown Church: Lindenborg Pool* (Mar. 1902, see C-16.01); *A Dream* (July 1902); *Frithiof the Bold* (in 2 parts, Jan, Feb. 1908); *Under an Elm-Tree* (Mar., 1912); and *Sir Peter Harpdon's End* (in 2 parts, July, Aug. 1914). Except for 2—*The Two Sides of the River* and *Under an Elm-Tree*—these are all 1st separate edns, the exceptions having been previously pbd. by Morris or others. Mosher's remaining 8 Morris titles were: *King Florus, King Coustans, Amis and Amile,* and *Over Sea* (all in the Broc. Series); and *Child Christopher* (Miscellaneous Series), *Pilgrims of Hope* (Rpts. of Privately Prtd. Books), *Defence of Guenevere: A Book of Lyrics* (Bib. Series, see C-5), and *John Ball* (Old World Series).

The Bibelot, which began in 1895 and ceased pbn. at the end of 1914, is both a series of separate monthly pbns., each with light blue laid-paper wrappers, and an annual collection of monthly issues, hence it is both a series of pbns. of separate Morris texts and an annual, or periodical. As a series it consists of pamphlets each one of which is either a complete text or one half of a 2-part complete text. When the 12 monthly pamphlets were collected at the end of each year, uncounted conjunct advertising leaves were removed (all issues of *The Bibelot* were made up as a single gathering sewn through the centrefold). Buyers could purchase each separate pamphlet for 5 cents, or subscribe to receive them monthly for 75 cents for the year, with an additional charge of 50 cents for the covers to bind the annual collection. Buyers also had the option of having the 12 monthly pamphlets bound by the publisher for an additional $1.00 (this was in 1900, but as Mosher warned his customers, the prices were subject to change, especially for back issues, in response to supply and demand, and by 1914, when *The Bibelot* ceased, Mosher was telling the public, via the wrapper title, that purchase was then 'by subscription only'.

One notice Mosher distributed said, 'the January number is not issued before the 15th of that month. All other numbers are sent out on or about the 25th of each month preceding date of issue' (quoted in Bishop, p. 63). According to Philip Bishop, the 'standing order to the printer was 5,000 of which 1,000 were delivered in sheets for later issue in sets'. The high point of circulation, both the separate issues and the annual vol., 1907–9, was 4,000 (Bishop, p. 63).

Generally, scholars—including Bishop—have treated the separate issues as parts, i.e. as fascicles or instalments of a periodical. But as pamphlets they are designed to stand alone, being complete texts in a single cover or a complete text issued in 2 parts. Any other material occasionally included—such as bibliographical notes, introductions, afterwords, and epigraphic quotations from critics or poets—is relevant to that text as it would be in a separate edn. of a text. This contrasts with the standard fascicles or separate 'issues' or 'numbers' of a magazine, which normally reflect the varied nature of a magazine's contents, with serialised material deliberately extended over a number of issues. *The Bibelot* issues are separates before being collected into the annual vol., but they are paginated continuously through each year's issues (despite some errors in page numbering in the various collected vols.) in anticipation of the collected annual vol.

The compiler of the *Quinn Catalogue* was referring to Mosher's series Reprints from "The Bibelot" when he said, 'These scarce little booklets are not the regular Mosher publications, but are separates in book form from the original setting in the *Bibelot*. They constitute the First Editions of these pieces in book form, being mainly Morris's contributions to *The Oxford and Cambridge Magazine*, discerned by Mosher to be writings meriting a more permanent dress than the pages of a magazine' (quoted in Bishop, p. 162).

Except for the blanket claim of 'First Editions', or *editio princeps*, status for all these bibelots (which must be qualified for *Under an Elm-Tree* and *The Two Sides of the River and Other Poems*) everything said here applies with an equal force to *The Bibelot* separates. But it is worth noting that the separates, the annual collected volume, and the 6 later rpts. for Reprints from "The Bibelot" are the same edn., all printed from the forms 1st used for the separates. And all of these are small books, 'miniature book' being one meaning of 'bibelot'.

Here *The Bibelot* separates are listed in the A-List rather than the D-List, Morris in Periodicals, not only because they are mostly 1st separate edns. but also because they were originally, many years before Mosher entered the scene, contributions by Morris to periodicals, and their first appearances are all recorded in the D-List (exceptions to this are Mosher's collections and selections of Morris, listed here in the C-List). The D-List is designed and limited, in other words, to those periodical pbns. that add to the Morris canon. Most of *The Bibelot* issues of Morris titles, considered as fascicles in an annual, are reprints of texts that 1st appeared in 1856 in *The Oxford and Cambridge Magazine*, hence none of the Mosher items add to the Morris canon. Mosher, as he states on the wrapper of The Bibelot, chooses 'from scarce edns and sources not generally known'. Finding-list information for them (as well as the other Bibelot items) as journal items is included in the A-List entries.

Collations and contents descriptions provided here of the Morris titles issued under *The Bibelot* masthead are based on the original, separately pbd. versions where those versions have been located and examined. Collections of the annual vols. are usually without the separate issue wrappers and without the conjunct pairs of advertising leaves that contain no reference to the text, these being excised in the preparation of the annual collections. But those leaves are included here in order to provide the (normal) complete account of every page in each book, that being the only way of describing in a clear and complete form the make-up of a book. Some separate issues have not been seen. Where that is the case, as indicated by an asterisk preceding the collation, I am indebted for the necessary details to Philip Bishop, Mosher's bibliographer and owner of perhaps the most comprehensive of all Mosher collections. Here the base copy is always a separate issue.

Collation: Part I:* standard Bibelot separate format: 12°: [1]^{26} 26 leaves pp. [2] [201–4] 205–46 [247–8] [2] [= 52]; the 13 conjunct pairs are sewn at the fold into a light blue paper wrapper.

Part II:* 12°: [1]^{20} 20 leaves, 10 conjunct pairs, pp. [2] [249–50] 251–80 [281–2] [4] [= 40] + wrapper; pagination is continuous through the year's 12 issues, but conjunct leaves at the beginning and end containing only advertising were omitted from the separate issues when they were bound into the annual vol.

Contents: Part I: pagination continuous with the previous issue: pp. [*1–2*], ads; p. [201], Mosher's unsigned foreword begins; p. [202], foreword ends with leaf ornament as tail-piece and contents of the forthcoming Aug. number; p. [203], half title: THE HOLLOW LAND. | A TALE. | PART I. | [17-line lyric epigraph signed, below right] FRANCIS SHERMAN.; p. [204], bibliographical note on Morris's contributions to *The Oxford and Cambridge Magazine* 'upon the authority of a note printed in *The Athenæum* for October 17th, 1896', taken, says Mosher, from 'a copy . . . now before us, and marked, we are informed, by his own hand' (this list includes 'Ruskin and the Quarterly' and 'A Night in a Cathedral' as being by Morris, a position that Mosher abandoned after seeing Mackail's list of Morris's contributions in *The Life of William Morris* (see also the *Notes* to A-1.01)); p. 205, dropped head title: THE HOLLOW LAND. | Chapter 1. | STRUGGLING IN THE WORLD. | [text begins]; pp. 206–[47], text completed with a leaf ornament as tail-piece; p. [248], blank; pp. [*1–2*], ads.

Part 2: pp. [2], ads; p. [249], half title: [top, flush left] THE HOLLOW LAND | A Tale | By William Morris. | Part II; p. [250], blank; p. 251, headed: CHAPTER III. | LEAVING THE WORLD. | Fytte the First | [text begins]; pp. 252–81, text completed with printer's flower as tail-piece; p. [282], ads; pp. [2], ads.

Technical Notes: details common to the series: *paper*: machine-laid paper, with dandy roll laid lines; *leaf size*: uncut, 153 x 116 mm.; *printing*: type area: 95 x 55 mm.; *lines-to-page*: leaded, 27 lines; *pagination*: arabic numbers centred on direction line, continuous through the 12 separate issues of each year, with added title and contents pages in the annual vol., but usually minus the wrappers and any conjunct extra leaves of advertising matter originally pbd. in the separate monthly issues; *binding*: *wrapper*: blue hand-made paper, sewn, no end-papers; p. [*1*], wrapper title, see above; wrapper: p. [*2*], statement of subscription rates and copyright notice; wrapper p. [*3*], ad for *The Bibelot* and printer's imprint: PRINTED BY | SMITH AND SALE | PORTLAND, MAINE; p. [*4*], reproduction in red of a Florentine 16th-century fleur-de-lis device (the Florentine Lilly, see Bishop No. 14) in double thin-rule compartment; annual vols. bound in blue paper-covered boards or blue buckram, the paper covering being the same used for the wrappers of the monthly issues. The round spine is of cream japan vellum with 4 ornamental raised bands and a printed paper *spine label*: [in gothic] The Bibelot; details specific to this issue: *running titles*: [all rectos and versos, flush to inner margin on the headline] THE HOLLOW LAND

Publication: July and Aug. 1897 [issued 25 June and 25 July]; *print run*: 5,000 copies on paper, including 1,000 in sheets for use in sets and 12 copies of vols. I–XV, the annual collection, on japan vellum; *price*: separate issues 5 cents, by subscription 75 cents per year (12 issues; see more about prices under *Series*, above).

Register of Copies Examined: Fdmn (base copy); Bsp; VU (Testimonial Edn); BL (P.P.8001.ea. (1.))

A-83.02:* The Hollow Land (Rpts. Bib.)

[first and last lines in red] THE HOLLOW LAND | A TALE BY WILLIAM | MORRIS | [reproduction of the Chiswick Press mark, Bishop No. 2] | Portland, Maine | Thomas B. Mosher | M*dcccxcvii*

Edition: [2nd impression, 1st separate edn.] 1st pbd. in 2 parts, in *The Oxford and Cambridge Magazine* in numbers 9 and 10, for Sept. and Oct. 1856 (see D-13).

Collaborators, Editors, and Illustrators: unsigned Introduction and a note on *The Oxford and Cambridge Magazine* [by the editor, T. B. Mosher] with 'an original poem by Francis Sherman' as epigraph (Bishop, p. 162).

Series: Reprints from "The Bibelot"—2 (hereafter referred to as Rpts. Bib.). Mosher says in his bibliography of R. L. Stevenson, included in his edn. of *Father Damien: An Open Letter*, that the Reprints from "The Bibelot", including Father Damien, were 'printed from the same forms [as *The Bibelot* versions], only reimposed and with new pagination' (quoted in Bishop, p. 140). Hence, bibliographically—except for their binding, pagination, and their japan vellum paper—the first 2 Reprints from "The Bibelot"— *The Hollow Land* and *Gertha's Lovers*—are new impressions of the separates 1st pbd. under *The Bibelot* masthead. The 4 remaining Morris titles in the Reprints from "The Bibelot" series combine 2 or more Morris texts: No. 6, *The Two Sides of the River and Other Poems*, a rpt. of the Wise-Forman forgery of that title (for the forgery, see E-4), with Mosher adding the poem 'Winter Weather' from *The Oxford and Cambridge Magazine*; No. 8—*Golden Wings* [with] *Svend and His Brethren*—combines 2 previously pbd. separate Morris titles from *The Bibelot*; No. 9, *The Churches of North France: Amiens*, adds a 2nd essay on 'Death the Avenger and Death the Friend', never pbd. in *The Bibelot*; No. 11, *The Story of the Unknown Church and Other Tales* adds 'Lindenborg Pool' and 'A Dream'. Another Mosher title, *The Defence of Guenevere: a Book of Lyrics Chosen from the Works of William Morris* (The Bibelot Series—8) is a selection of lyrics from 4 different Morris works. All these collected Morris items issued by Mosher are here entered in the C-List of Collections.

The Reprints from "The Bibelot" are distinguished by their relatively high price, $4.00, and their small print runs: issues 2, 5, 6, and 8 were limited to 25 copies, of which only 20 were for sale, nos. 9 and 11 to 35 copies, 30 for sale. This scarcity of copies has made it impossible to inspect most of the Morris books in this series. Where that is the case, as indicated by an asterisk preceding the collation, I am indebted to Philip Bishop, Mosher's bibliographer, for the necessary details, particularly with regard to the collations and paginations provided here.

The Reprints from "The Bibelot" are 12° in size, like *The Bibelot* separates, but the Reprints are printed and gathered in 8s.

Collation: 12° in 8s: [1⁴ 2–6⁸ 7⁴] 48 leaves pp. [*8*] [1–4] 5–78 [*79–88*] [= 96].

Contents: p. [*1*], half title; p. [*2*], blank; p. [*3*], certificate of limitation: Twenty-five copies of this book | printed on japan vellum, of | which twenty only are for sale. | This is no. [number in longhand]; p. [*4*], blank; p. [*5*], title page; p. [*6*], blank; p. [*7*], epigraph: [untitled sonnet signed, below right] Francis Sherman; p. [*8*], blank; pp. [1–2], Mosher's unsigned foreword; p. [*3*], 2nd half title; p. [*4*], blank; p. 5, text begins; pp. 6–78, text completed; pp. [*79–80*], blank;

p. [81], headed: NOTE | [Mosher's bibliographical note on *The Oxford and Cambridge Magazine*]; p. [82], blank; pp. [83–4], notes; pp. [85–8], blank.
Technical Notes: details common to the series: *paper*: Mosher's version of 'Japanese vellum' (vegetable parchment); *leaf size*: 155 x 115 mm.; *printing*: type area: 96 x 55 mm.; *lines-to-page*: leaded, 27 lines; *pagination*: arabic numbers centred on the direction line; *end-papers*: one free end and paste-down, plain white and blank, front and back; *binding*: japan vellum wraps over flexible boards; detail specific to this issue: *running heads*: [aligned to the inner margins, rectos and versos] THE HOLLOW LAND; *binding letterpress*: front: THE HOLLOW LAND | A TALE | BY WILLIAM MORRIS; *spine*: running up: THE HOLLOW LAND: A TALE
Publication: 1897; *print run*: 25 copies of which 20 were for sale; *price*: $4.00.
Register of Copies Examined: CSfU (base copy: PR 5079.H6 1897); CtY (X178 M895d 2 vols.)

A-83.03: The Hollow Land (Broc.)

[flush left, in hanging indent, 1st and last lines in red] THE HOLLOW LAND | A TALE | BY WILLIAM MORRIS | [Chiswick Press mark, Bishop No. 2] | PORTLAND MAINE | THOMAS B. MOSHER | MDCCCC
Edition: [1st impression, 2nd separate edn.] 1st pbd. in 2 parts in *The Oxford and Cambridge Magazine* in the numbers for Sept. and Oct. 1856 (see D-13).
Collaborators, Editors, and Illustrators: unsigned introduction and a bibliographical note on *The Oxford and Cambridge Magazine* [by the editor, T. B. Mosher] with 'an original poem by Francis Sherman' as epigraph (Bishop, p. 162).
Series: Brocade Series—22; this book is also the 1st Morris title in a minor series, a 4-vol. subset within the Broc. Series called 'Old English Romances—1. Morris'. For detail common to this series, and the minor series, see this field, *Contents*, and *Technical Notes* in A-70.03.
Colophon: Four hundred and twen- | ty-five copies of this | book have been printed on | Japan vellum, and type | distributed, in the month | of August, a. d. Mdcccc, at | the press | of George D. | Loring, Portland, Maine.
Collation: 16° in 4s: [1–13]⁴ 52 leaves pp. [1–10] 11–96 [97–104] [= 104].
Contents: p. [1], half title; p. [2], blank; p. [3], title page; p. [4], blank; pp. [5–6], Mosher's unsigned Foreword; p. [7], 2nd half title; p. [8], blank; p. [9], verse epigraph signed: Francis Sherman.; p. [10], blank; pp. 11–[97], text completed with reproduction of a Chiswick Press tail-piece; p. [98], blank; p. [99], colophon: see above; pp. [100–4], blank.
Technical Notes: detail common to the series—paper, leaf size, printing, type area, lines-to-page, pagination, end-papers, binding, and slip cases are common to the series and are covered in this field in the record for the first Morris pbn. in this series, A-70.03; details specific to this issue: *binding letterpress*: front: printed title: [4-line ornamental initial 'T' in red] THE HOLLOW | LAND: A TALE | BY WILLIAM | MORRIS [2 fleurons]; short title down the spine in red or brown: [horizontal letters aligned vertically one above the other] THE HOLLOW LAND [5 fleurons as line fillers].
Publication: Aug. 1900 (colophon date); *print run*: 425 copies on japan vellum; *prices*: 75 cents per copy in a slip case, or $3 net as one of a boxed set of 4 vols. of Old English Romances, combining *The Hollow Land* with *Gertha's Lovers*, *Golden Wings*, and *The Story of the Unknown Church and Other Tales*.
Register of Copies Examined: SU (base copy: RC 820.8 M); Bsp; CUSf (PR 5079 H6 1900).
Later impressions [or edns?] from this edn.: Mosher:
1. Jan. 1903 (colophon date): SECOND EDITION [2nd impression 2nd separate edn. (or 3rd separate edn.?)]; *print run*: 425 copies on japan vellum; *price*: 75 cents;
2. Dec. 1908 (colophon date): THIRD EDITION [3rd impression, 2nd separate edn. (or 4th separate edn.?)]; *print run*: 425 copies on japan vellum; *price*: 75 cents.

A-83.04: The Hollow Land (Goudy)

[within Goudy-designed vine border, 4-line gothic type] The | Hollow Land | [thick ornamental rule] | BY WILLIAM | MORRIS
Edition: [1st impression, 3rd separate edn.] 1st pbd. in 2 parts in *The Oxford and Cambridge Magazine* in the numbers for Sept. and Oct. 1856 (see D-13).
Collaborators, Editors, and Illustrators: see the *colophon*, below. Robert Wiebking designed, cut, and cast the initial 'L' on p. 7 and cut and cast the maple leaf ornament.
Colophon: Here ends THE HOLLOW LAND, A TALE, BY | WILLIAM MORRIS. Reprinted from The Oxford and Cam- | bridge Magazine. Printed by hand at The Village Press | Hingham, Massachusetts, by Frederick W. & Bertha M. | Goudy, from the Village type, and finished this second | day of October, 1905. Frontispiece illustration from | drawing by Walter J. Enright; illustration on page 43 | from drawing by Bror. [*sic*] J. Olsson Nordfeldt; the Note

by | Cyrus Lauron Hooper; and double border, title and ini- | tial by Mr. Goudy, the designer of the fount. Composition | by Mrs Goudy. | [2nd Village Press mark] | Two hundred twenty copies. Sold at the Village Press | [signed in longhand by] *Fred W Goudy* | *Bertha Goudy*

Collation: 4°: [a]⁴ b–g⁴ h⁶ [$1 (+f2 g2 h2) signed] 34 leaves pp. [1–7] 8–67 [68] [= 68].

Contents: p. [1], half title; pp. [2–3], blank; p. [4], woodcut frontis. with a full border by Goudy, signed by 'W. J. Enright' and captioned in gothic: A ringing and glittering of Steel; p. [5], title page; p. [6], blank; p. [7]–8, introductory note initialled 'C. L. H.', i.e. Cyrus Lauron Hooper; pp. 9–67, text completed; p. [68], colophon, see above.

Technical Notes: *paper*: Whatman cream-white machine-made with false deckled edges and no laid lines (see *Notes*, below); *watermark*: Whatman | 1896; *leaf size*: 229 x 175 mm.; *printing*: in red and black, 10-line initial 'D' of Chapter 1 is in black with a red background; all other chapters begin with a plain roman 4-line initial; *type face*: the Village type, designed by F. W. Goudy; *pagination*: arabic numbers in shoulder note position; *end-papers*: 3 free ends and a paste-down, plain white and blank, front and back; *binding*: quarter holland with coarse light blue paper-covered boards with the title printed on the front, top left, in red 2-line gothic.

Publication: 2 Oct. 1905 (colophon date); *print run*: 220 copies (200 announced for sale); but Melbert B. Cary, *A Bibliography of the Village Press . . . including an account of the Genesis of the Press by Frederic W. Goudy and a Portion of the 1903 Diary of Will Ransom, Co-Founder* (hereafter referred to as Cary) says (69), that a fire destroyed Goudy's press in New York and all but about 85 copies of this book; *price*: $4.00 (see Ransom, 438).

Register of Copies Examined: CU-B (Bancroft: base copy: Z.239.2 Y55 1905 m).

Notes: Frederic W. Goudy:

> We had much better luck with a small sheet of Whatman, another English paper, which I found at an art store: it was whiter and stronger sized. We could get a sheet that seemed to suit The Hollow Land layout—or maybe we made The Hollow Land layout fit the paper, I don't recall—anyway it was quite satisfactory for hand-press work.
>
> The third [book from The Village Press], The Hollow Land, was undertaken primarily because Mr. Millard of McClurg's [a Chicago bookstore] was kind enough to lend us the bound volume of the rare Oxford and Cambridge Magazine in which Morris's story first appeared (Goudy, 'The Village Press: An Introduction', in Cary, 30–2).

Will Ransom's Diary records that he started the composition of *The Hollow Land* on 25 Sept. 1903 at Park Ridge, Illinois. 'The title page section was printed on Thanksgiving Day 1903, at Park Ridge, Ill., but the balance of the book, beginning on p. 17, was printed at Hingham, Mass' (see Cary, 41, 69). This earlier Chicago portion of the printing had a notable consequence: 'A dummy copy, consisting of three or four printed sections and blank leaves, bound in vellum, was exhibited at the Louisiana Purchase Exposition in St. Louis, 1904' (*American Book Design*, 131–2).

A-84.01: The Water of the Wondrous Isles (KP)

[Troy type, top aligned left] THE WATER OF THE WONDROUS ISLES | BY WILLIAM MORRIS

Edition: 'Kelmscott Press Edition' [1st impression, 1st edn.].

Collaborators, Editors, and Illustrators: see *colophon*, below. [The book, 1st pbd. posthumously, was seen through the press by S. C. Cockerell, with assistance from May Morris].

Series: 45th title, 18th by Morris, pbd. by the KP.

Colophon: Here ends The Water of the Wondrous Isles, written | by William Morris. It was printed at the Kelmscott | Press, Upper Mall, Hammersmith, in the County of | Middlesex, & finished on the first day of April, 1897. | [printer's leaf ornament No. 2] The borders and ornaments were designed entirely | by William Morris, except the initial words Whilom | & Empty, which were completed from his unfinished | designs by R. Catterson-Smith. | [p. 341, KP mark No. 2] | [Troy type, aligned left] Sold by the Trustees of the late William Morris | at the Kelmscott Press; p. [342], blank.

Collation: large 4° in 8s: [a]⁴ b–y⁸ z⁴ [$4 (–b1,4 d1 f2,4 g2 h4 i1,3 k2–4 l3 p1,4 q4 s2 t4 u2 x2 z3–4) signed] 176 leaves pp. [8] [1] 2–340 [341–4] [= 352].

Contents: pp. [1–6], blank; p. [7], title page; p. [8], blank; p. [1], 1st chapter head title, text begins with an ornamental initial word in a single block: Whilom; pp. 2–340, text completed, followed by the colophon (see above); p. [341]: [large KP mark 2] | Sold by the Trustees of the late William Morris at the Kelmscott Press.; pp. [342–4], blank.

Technical Notes: made to range with the KP *Well at the World's End*; *paper*: Batchelor's KP Flower paper 2; *leaf size*: lightly trimmed, avg. 285 x 200 mm.; *printing*: in double columns, in red and black, red for all chapter titles, shoulder notes, and the endings of each of the 7 sections; *type face*: Troy type on title page, closing formula at the end of each part, and in the colophon, text in Chaucer type;

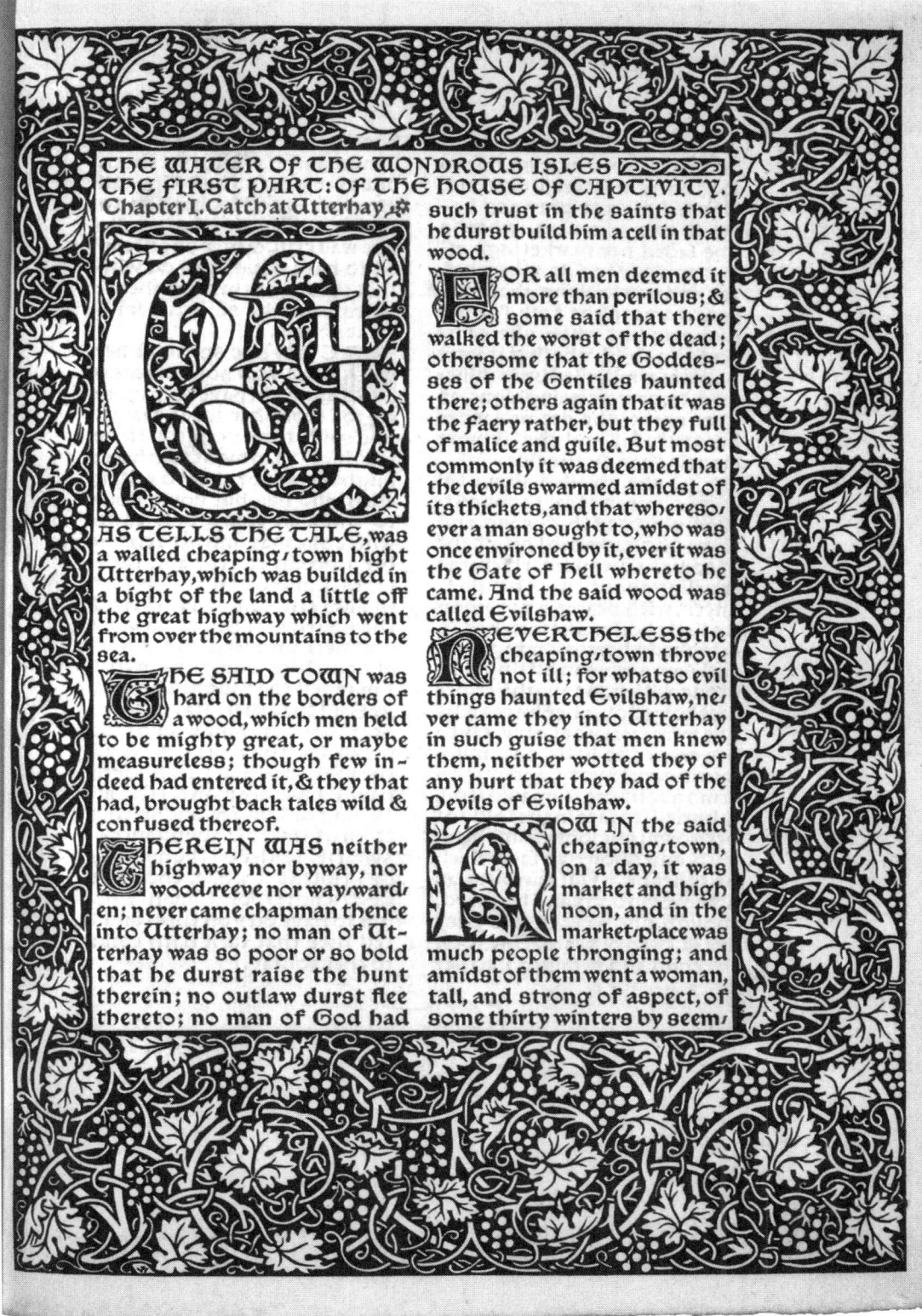

Figure 73. A-84.01: *Water of the Wondrous Isles* (KP edn.) head title

type area: each column 181 x 63 mm.; overall type area: 181 x 135 mm.; *line-to-page*: set solid, 40 lines; *shoulder notes*: identify each of the 7 'Parts' of the story; *pagination*: arabic numbers set 9 mm. in from the outer margin on the direction line; *binding*: limp white vellum with green silk ties; *spine*: title gilt-stamped across: THE WATER | OF THE | WONDROUS | ISLES | BY | WILLIAM | MORRIS; *end-papers*: standard KP practice: 3 free ends and paste-down, plain white and blank, front and back; *ornamentation*: 5 complete borders: 16a, 17a, 18a, 19, and 19a used for the head title of each of 7 parts; 56 vine column dividers, 6 floriated 14-line initial words, 1105 floriated 3-line initials, 106 floriated 6-line initials, 34 half borders, 10 small margin ornaments, 8 corner devices, and 1 KP mark No. 2.
Publication: 1 Apr. 1897 [this colophon date indicates finished printing, issued 29 July] (Cockerell, p. 167); see also the *Notes*, below; *print run*: 250 copies on paper, 6 on vellum; *price*: 3gns. and 12gns. respectively.
Register of Copies Examined: VU (2 copies: base copy: L, from Poynton Collection, and 821.85 W.l.); National Gallery, Canberra; SU (823 | M87w 1897 RB | a); CSt (Gunst: Z239.2/K29M87w); BL (2 copies: C. 43.f. 13, and Ashley 4906).
Notes: S. C. Cockerell, MS Diary for 1895, Mon. 4 Feb., notes that Morris has begun a new romance in verse, i.e. *The Water of the Wondrous Isles*. On 8 Feb. he begins again, having decided to write in prose and verse. Ten days later Cockerell notes that, after some trouble over the metre of the verse parts, leading him to jettison the verse, Morris has started to make significant progress writing exclusively in prose (see Cockerell Papers, BL (Add.) MS 52772).

Correspondence between C. J. Longman and S. C. Cockerell in the Smith Arch. shows that the New York branch of Longmans wished to print and copyright their own copies of this title. But the US International Copyright Act of 1891 required the deposit in the Library of Congress of 2 copies, printed in the US, and that the US copyright copies be submitted no later than pbn. elsewhere. Besides, Longmans of London had to ensure copyright in both countries without jeopardising the British *editio princeps* status of the KP edn., as previously promised to its subscribers. Since Britain had a similar no-prior-publication rule, simultaneous publication was arranged. the issue in London of the KP edn., which finished printing in Apr., had to be 'held back' until 29 July, when copyright on the American 2nd or 'trade' edn. was achieved by the submission of advance copies (public issue was delayed until 1 October). Other consequences of these arrangements were that the American print runs of this book and the following title, *The Sundering Flood*, were enlarged to supply both the British and American markets.

A-84.02: The Water of the Wondrous Isles (Trade Edn)

THE WATER OF THE | WONDROUS ISLES BY | WILLIAM MORRIS | LONGMANS, GREEN, AND CO. | NEW YORK, LONDON, AND BOMBAY | MDCCCXCVII
[the Longmans of London imprint for the UK issue] LONGMANS, GREEN, AND CO. | LONDON, NEW YORK, AND BOMBAY | MDCCCXCVII
Edition: 'Popular Edition' '1st trade edn' [1st impression, 2nd edn.] Printed in the USA for sale in Britain as well as the US. Longmans of London imported 1,006 copies in quires from Little, Brown and Co. of Boston, ordering also new prelims with the London Longman imprint and a page of ads at the end (Longmans Arch.). The spine label and ads were ordered from Ballantynes. This is the 1st Morris title issued by Morris's new American publisher, Longmans of New York, who registered the book for US copyright under the provisions of the Chace International Copyright Act of 1891 (see *Notes* in A-84.01).
Collation: large cr. 8°: 1–35^8 [36]^4 [7^r only signed] 284 leaves pp. [2] [i–v] vi–x [1] 2–553 [554–6] [= 568].
Contents: pp. [*1–2*], blank; p. [i], half title; p. [ii], blank; p. [iii], title page; p. [iv], copyright register: [top] Copyright, 1897, by Longmans, Green, and Co.; p. [v], dropped head: *CONTENTS* | [contents begin, as a list, divided into 7 'Parts', each with a separate series of chapters; pp. vi–x, contents completed; p. [1], dropped head: [top margin, flush left] THE WATER OF THE WONDROUS | ISLES. THE FIRST PART: OF THE | HOUSE OF CAPTIVITY. | CHAPTER I. CATCH AT UTTERHAY. | [text begins, the 1st word being all in caps]; pp. 2–553, text completed with explicit as part of the last paragraph: So here is an end.; p. [554], printer's imprint: Printed by John Wilson and Son at the | University Press in Cambridge, U. S. A. | [printers leaf]; p. [555], Longmans (London) ad headed: MR. WILLIAM MORRIS'S WORKS.; p. [556], blank.
Technical Notes: *paper*: cream-white machine-made 'antique wove' with dandy roll laid lines, no watermark; *leaf size*: UK issue: untrimmed false deckled edges, avg. 205 x 136 mm.; US issue: trimmed, 199 x 132 mm.; *printing*: *type area*: 135 x 85 mm. excluding head and direction lines; *lines-to-page*: 32 lines set solid; *running titles*: all rectos and versos, except chapter head titles: THE WATER OF THE WONDROUS ISLES; *end-papers*: 1 free end and paste-

down, plain white and blank, front and back; *binding*: plain unblocked dark red cloth with printed paper spine label: [within thin-rule compartment] THE WATER | OF | THE | WONDROUS | ISLES | WILLIAM | MORRIS

Publication: 1897 [issued 1 Oct.] (Longmans *Notes on Books*, 9/171 (30 Nov. 1897), 45). The American trade edn. copies were released simultaneously with the English issue (see *Notes* in A-84.01); *print run*: 1,984 copies, 1,006 exported from New York to London in quires, @ 10 cents per copy plus packaging and postage (Smith Arch.); *prices*: $2.50 and 7s. 6d.

Register of Copies Examined: LeM (2 copies: base copy); CSt (2 copies: Green Stacks 821.6.M87wi, and Spec. Coll Felton PR5079.W3); SU (2 copies: 823/M87wSSL; 823/M877); VU (Bail: B821.85 W.I.)

Later impressions from this edn.: Longmans:

1.* 1902 [issued Dec.] ('Bibliographical Note', *CW*, XX. lix): 'trade edn' 'ordinary edn' [2nd impression, 2nd edn.]; *print run*: 475 copies, 100 exported to London (Longmans Accts. for 1902); *price*: $2.50 and 7s. 6d. Printed in the US for sale in Britain as well as the US;

2.* 1909 [issued Apr.] ('Bibliographical Note', *CW*, XX. lix): 'trade edn' 'ordinary edn' [3rd impression, 2nd edn.]; *print run*: unknown; *price*: see above.

A-84.03: The Water of the Wondrous Isles (*CW* XX)

THE COLLECTED WORKS | [title detail common to the set, see A-126.01] | VOLUME XX | THE WATER OF THE WONDROUS ISLES | [publisher's imprint, see A-126.01] | MDCCCCXIII

Edition: 'The Collected Works edn' [1st impression, 3rd edn., 2nd English].

Collaborators, Editors, and Illustrators: 3 reproductions of photographs, 2 by F. Hollyer and the 3rd by R. Faulkner and Co.

Series: vol. 20 of 24; for details common to the set, see this field in A-126.01.

Collation: medium 8°: [a]⁸ (a4+1) b⁸ (b1+1) c⁸ d⁶ (d5+1) B–2B⁸ 2C⁴ [$2 signed] 226 leaves pp. [i–x] xi–lvii [lviii–lx] 1–387 [388–92] [= 452] + 3 inserted illus. noted in the formula and described under *Contents*, below, but not included in the book's pagination.

Contents: pp. [i–v], blank; p. [vi], statement of limitation, see A-126.01; pp. [vii–viii], blank; 1st inserted plate as frontis., facing title page (recto blank), in blind-stamped compartment, reproduction of a photograph, photographer named in copperplate, below left: *F. Hollyer, photo.* | [plate maker, below right: *Walker and Boutall, ph. sc.* | [subject's reproduced signature, centred]: *William Morris* | [in copperplate] *aet 53*; p. [ix], title page; p. [x], blank; p. xi, headed: CONTENTS | [begins list divided into 7 'Parts']; pp. xii–xvi, Contents completed; p. xvii, dropped head: INTRODUCTION | [text begins]; pp. xviii, text continues; 2nd plate inserted, facing p. xviii, within a blind-stamped compartment with photographer named in copperplate below left: *Robert Faulkner & Co, photographers* | [below right the plate-maker] *Emery Walker, Ph. sc.*; reproduction of a photograph, labelled in copperplate: *Mrs Morris, senior* | *1879*; verso blank; pp. xix–lvii, Introduction completed; p. [lviii], blank; 3rd inserted plate, facing p. [lviii], within a blind-stamped compartment, reproduction of a photograph with the photographer's name lower left, in copperplate: *Frederick Hollyer, photographer.* | [lower right the plate maker] *Emery Walker, Ph. sc.* | [label centred in copperplate] *Edward Burne-Jones* | *1896*; verso, blank; p. [lix], headed: BIBLIOGRAPHICAL NOTE | [list of 3 issues]; p. [lx], blank; p. 1, headed: [top margin, flush left] THE WATER OF THE WONDROUS | ISLES. THE FIRST PART: OF THE | HOUSE OF CAPTIVITY. | CHAPTER I. CATCH AT UTTERHAY. | [text begins]; pp. 2–387, text completed with explicit: SO HERE IS AN END.; pp. [388–9], blank; p. [390], printer's imprint, see A-126.01; pp. [391–2], blank.

Technical Notes: paper, leaf size, printing, type area, lines-to-page, pagination, position (but not content) of headlines, running titles, shoulder notes, pagination, end-papers, and binding are all common to the series as described in this field in A-126.01, the entry for the set; details specific to this issue: *shoulder notes*: [all rectos and versos] PART I [II–VII] | Chap. [+ arabic number]; *binding letterpress*: *spine label*: [first 4 lines common to the set] | VOLUME XX | THE WATER | OF THE | WONDROUS | ISLES

Publication: 1913 [issued 31 Oct.] (Longmans Arch.); *print run* and *price*: see A-126.01.

Register of Copies Examined: see this field in A-126.01

Notes: S. C. Cockerell to May Morris, 14 Sept. 1912: pursuant to her preparation of the CW edn. of *The Water of the Wondrous Isles*, she has asked him how much of the proof reading of *The Water of the Wondrous Isles* was done by her father. He thinks Morris probably read more than the 1st two of the total of 7 parts (Cockerell Papers, BL (Add.) MS 52740).

A-84.04: The Water of the Wondrous Isles (2 vols. LPL)

THE WATER OF | THE WONDROUS ISLES | BY

WILLIAM MORRIS | IN TWO VOLUMES | VOL. I [II] | LONGMANS, GREEN, AND CO. | 39 PATER-NOSTER ROW, LONDON | NEW YORK, BOMBAY, AND CALCUTTA | 1914

Edition: Pocket Edition [1st impression, 4th edn., 3rd English].

Series: Longmans Pocket Library. For further series detail, see this field in *Jason*, A-3.09.

Collation: vol. I: fcap 8°: π^6 A–P^8 Q^4 130 leaves pp. [2] [i–iv] v–ix [x] [1] 2–246 [247–8] [= 260].

vol. II: duplicate of vol. I, except page numbers: pp. [2] [i–iv] v–ix [x] [1] 2–247 [248] [= 260].

Contents: vol. I: pp. [1–2], Longmans ads, headed: WILLIAM MORRIS'S WORKS; p. [i], half title; p. [ii], blank; p. [iii], title page; p. [iv], dropped head: BIBLIOGRAPHICAL NOTE | [lists the 4 edns. of this title]; p. v, dropped head: CONTENTS | BOOK I | THE FIRST PART | OF THE HOUSE OF CAPTIVITY; pp. vi–ix, Contents continue as a list, chapter number in italic roman numbers, chapter titles in italic, and page numbers in arabic, covering 'Parts' 1–4 and 3 chapters of the 5th Part; p. [x], blank; p. [1], dropped head: THE WATER OF | THE WONDROUS ISLES | THE FIRST PART | OF THE HOUSE OF CAPTIVITY | CHAPTER I | CATCH AT UTTERHAY | [text begins]; pp. 2–246, text completed with explicit: END OF VOL. I | [printer's imprint] Printed by BALLANTYNE, HANSON & CO. | at Paul's Work, Edinburgh; p. [247], Longmans ad, headed: Longmans' Pocket Library; p. [248], blank.

vol. II: prelims, as vol. I, except no bibliographical note, title page change to: vol. II; pp. [1–2], ads; p. [i], half title; p. [ii], blank; p. [iii], title; p. [iv], blank; pp. v–ix: [headed] CONTENTS | [completes the list in vol. I layout]; p. [x], blank; p. [1], as vol. I except for the change of title, part and chapter: THE WATER OF | THE WONDROUS ISLES | THE FIFTH PART—*continued* | Chapter IV | OF THE SLAYING OF FRIEND AND FOE | [text begins]; pp. 2–247, text completed with explicit: SO HERE IS AN END | [printer's imprint, as in vol. I]; p. [248], blank.

Technical Notes: for technical details common to the Pocket Library series—paper, leaf size, printing, type area, pagination, end-papers, and binding—see under the 1st Morris book in the series, *Jason*, A-3.09; details specific to this issue: *type area*: 124 x 77 mm.; *lines-to-page*: leaded, 32 lines, excluding head and direction lines. The copy described here has the original grey dust wrappers with the engraving of Kelmscott Manor on the front designed by C. M. Gere for the KP *News from Nowhere* frontis: wrapper p.[1, all in blue ink]: LONGMANS' POCKET LIBRARY | THE WATER OF THE | WONDROUS ISLES | VOLUME ONE [TWO] | [within a thin rule compartment, a woodcut of Kelmscott Manor, duplicating the design of the frontispiece of *News from Nowhere*] | By WILLIAM MORRIS | [thin rule] | IN TWO VOLUMES FOUR SHILLINGS NETT; wrapper pp. [2–3] and their adjacent flaps are blank; wrapper p. [4], headed: Longmans' Pocket Library; followed in both vols. by a list of the titles and authors included in the series.

Publication: Jan. 1914 [issued 17–24 Jan.] ('Books of the Week', *Pub. Circ.*, 100 (24 Jan. 1914), 87); *print run*: 2,000 copies; *price*: for the pair, cloth 4s. net, lthr 6s. net.

Register of Copies Examined: LeM (base copy).

Notes: entry from Longmans Arch.: 'Dec. 20, 1913: Water of Wondrous Isles, 2 vols. Pocket Library, 2,000 copies, new set, moulds made, & printed by Ballantyne'. Longmans Arch. indicates that binding cost 72s. 6d. per 100 cloth copies, 166s. 8d. per 100 lthr. copies. Total cost, for 2,000 copies, not including binding = £73. 13s. 11d.

A-85.01: Some German Woodcuts of the Fifteenth Century (KP)

[half title, top margin, flush left] SOME GERMAN WOODCUTS OF THE FIFTEENTH | CENTURY

Edition: 'Kelmscott Press Edition' [1st impression, 1st edn.] Morris's text, the 'Preface' to this book, comprises selected passages from his article (also a lecture) on 'The Early Woodcut Books of Ulm and Augsburg', published in *Bibliographica* (1895, see D-585). It is accompanied here by 35 woodcut illus., 6 used in the original article and a further 29 from the projected Catalogue of Morris's library, which was never completed.

Collaborators, Editors, and Illustrators: Edited, compiled, and Foreword written by Sydney C. Cockerell.

Series: 49th title, 19th by Morris, prtd. by the KP.

Colophon: [in red] Here ends Some German Woodcuts of the Fifteenth Century, for | which the blocks (with one exception) were prepared by Walker | and Boutall under the direction of the late William Morris. Now | edited by S. C. Cockerell, and printed at the Kelmscott Press, Upper | Mall, Hammersmith. Finished on the 15th day of December, 1897. | [p. 37, in black] Sold by the Trustees of the late William Morris at the Kelmscott Press.; p. [38], blank.

Collation: large 4° in 8s: a^6 [b–d^8 e^6] (only 1 signature, on a2^r, signed a3] 36 leaves pp. [i–ii] iii [iv] v–xi [xii] pp. [1–46], being plates, are numbered as folios 1–23. Thereafter normal pagination returns, but starts continuous with the preceding folio numbers: 24–36 [37–38] [= 72].

PREFACE, BEING EXTRACTS FROM AN ARTICLE BY WILLIAM MORRIS ON THE ARTISTIC QUALITIES OF THE WOODCUT BOOKS OF ULM AND AUGSBURG IN THE FIFTEENTH CENTURY.

THE invention of printing books, & the use of wood-blocks for book ornament in place of hand-painting, though it belongs to the period of the degradation of mediæval art, gave an opportunity to the Germans to regain the place which they had lost in the art of book decoration during the thirteenth & fourteenth centuries. This opportunity they took with vigour and success, and by means of it put forth works which showed the best and most essential qualities of their race. Unhappily, even at the time of their first woodcut book, the beginning of the end was on them; about thirty years afterwards they received the Renaissance with singular eagerness and rapidity, and became, from the artistic point of view, a nation of rhetorical pedants. An exception must be made, however, as to Albert Durer; for, though his method was infected by the Renaissance, his matchless imagination and intellect made him thoroughly Gothic in spirit.

Amongst the printing localities of Germany the two neighbouring cities of Ulm and Augsburg developed a school of woodcut book ornament second to none as to character, and, I think, more numerously represented than any other. I am obliged to link the two cities, because the early school at least is common to both; but the ornamented works produced by Ulm are but few compared with the prolific birth of Augsburg. It is a matter of course that the names of the artists who designed these wood-blocks should not have been recorded, any more than those of the numberless illuminators of the lovely written books of the thirteenth and fourteenth centuries; the names under which the Ulm and Augsburg picture-books are known are all those of their printers. Of these by far the most distinguished are the kinsmen (their degree of kinship is not known), Gunther Zainer of Augsburg and John Zainer of Ulm. Nearly parallel with these in date are Ludwig Hohenwang & John Bämler of Augsburg, together with Pflanzmann of Augsburg, the printer of the first illustrated German Bible. Anthony Sorg, a little later than these, was a printer somewhat inferior, rather a reprinter in fact, but by dint of reusing the old blocks, or getting them recut and in some cases redesigned, not always to their disadvantage, produced some very beautiful books.

The earliest of these picture-books with a date is Gunther Zainer's

Figure 74. A-85.01: *Some German Woodcuts* (KP edn.) head title of Preface

Contents: p. [i], title page; p. [ii], blank; p. iii, note of 26 lines, headed in red: FOREWORD [see *Notes*, below] | [text] | [signed, below right] S. C. COCKERELL; p. [iv], blank; p. v, headed in red: [flush left] PREFACE, BEING EXTRACTS FROM AN ARTICLE | BY WILLIAM MORRIS ON THE ARTISTIC QUALI- | TIES OF THE WOODCUT BOOKS OF ULM AND | AUGSBURG IN THE FIFTEENTH CENTURY. | [text begins, in black, with a 6-line floriated initial 'T']; pp. vi–ix, Preface completed with date: [below, flush left] Nov. 5, 1894; pp. x–[xi], Contents: [heading in red, top, flush left] A LIST OF THE WOODCUTS OF THE FIFTEENTH | CENTURY REPRODUCED IN THIS BOOK. [text formatted as a list, with page numbers in red]; p. [xii], list of woodcuts completed; pp. 1–46 numbered as folios 1–23, the woodcuts reproduced in electrotype plates; pp. 24–34 [48–58 counting pages throughout], headed: [flush left, top, ornament 2] A LIST OF THE PRINCIPAL BOOKS OF THE | FIFTEENTH CENTURY, CONTAINING WOOD- | CUTS, IN THE LIBRARY OF THE LATE WILLIAM | MORRIS, ARRANGED ALPHABETI- | CALLY ACCORD- | ING TO TOWNS, WITH THE NUMBER OF CUTS | IN EACH, AND REFERENCES TO HAIN'S REPER- | TORIUM BIBLIOGRAPHI- | CUM. [town names and references in red]; p. 35, section headed: [flush left, top, in red] ANALYSIS OF THE WOODCUTS IN THE LATIN | EDITION OF THE NUREMBERG CHRONICLE.; p. 36, Analysis ends with colophon (see above); p. [37], printer's mark 2 and the last line of the colophon; p. [38], blank.

Technical Notes: *paper*: Batchelor's KP Perch paper; *watermark*: fish outline with initials 'W' before and 'M' after, in the middle of the centrefold; *leaf size*: trimmed, 290 x 212 mm.; *printing*: in red and black, headings, shoulder notes, page references in contents, and the 1st part of the colophon in red; *type face*: Golden type; *type area*: 197 x 123 mm.; *lines-to-page*: 42 lines set solid; *shoulder notes*: at top margin, 5 mm. outside outer margin; *pagination*: arabic numbers set 5 mm. inside the outer margin on the direction line; *endpapers*: 2 free ends and paste-down, plain white and blank, front and back; *binding*: quarter white holland with blue paper-covered boards; front: title, duplicating that of the title page but on one line; *ornaments*: 6-line floriated initials to begin paragraphs, printer's mark No. 2.

Publication: 15 Dec. 1897 [this colophon date indicates finished printing, issued 6 Jan. 1898] (Cockerell, p. 170); *print run*: 225 copies on paper, 8 copies on vellum; *price*: paper 30s., vellum 5gns.

Register of Copies Examined: VSL (base copy: *aF 769 C64); VU (2 copies: 19H and L).

Notes: S. C. Cockerell, MS Diary for 21 May 1894 notes that Morris began on this day to make notes concerning his incunabula for a prospective catalogue to be illustrated from his own collection (see Cockerell Papers, BL (Add.) MS 52772). Cockerell to Proctor, 10 Dec. 1897, records that the *German Woodcuts* was finished that day except for the binding and that would be finished by Christmas (Cockerell Papers, BL (Add.) MS 52743).

From S. C. Cockerell's 'Foreword' (p. iii):

> Of the 35 reproductions of German woodcuts here given, 29 are all that were done of a series chosen by Morris to appear in the Catalogue of his library, which was to have been written by him and printed at the Kelmscott Press. The other six were made for his article in the 4th number of Bibliographica on the Early Woodcut books of Ulm & Augsburg, and thanks are due to Messrs. Kegan Paul, Trench, Trübner & Co. for the loan of the blocks, as well as for permission to quote the portions of the article which serve as an introduction to this book. These quotations will show the nature of the remarks that Mr. Morris intended to write for the Catalogue, of which they would have been the most interesting feature. A minor feature was to have been a statement of the number of different cuts, and the number of cuts including repetitions, in the principal illustrated books. For this purely scientific side of the work I was made responsible, and as the early printers usually repeated their cuts, and no one has hitherto troubled to count them in this way, it has seemed worth while to preserve these few statistics now that the original design of the Catalogue has fallen through. They are accordingly printed as an appendix in a list of the more important woodcut books that the library contained. For some particulars in this section I am indebted to my friend Mr. Robert Proctor, who has kindly looked over the proofsheets, and pointed out errors and omissions.
>
> I have been tempted to add a list of the manuscripts, which, though comparatively few in number (112) were the most notable part of the library; but without a full description of each volume such a list would be meaningless, and anything more than a list would be out of place. S. C. COCKERELL

A-86.01: The Sundering Flood (KP)

[Chaucer type] THE SUNDERING FLOOD WRITTEN BY | WILLIAM MORRIS

Edition: 'Kelmscott Press Edition' [1st impression, 1st edn.]

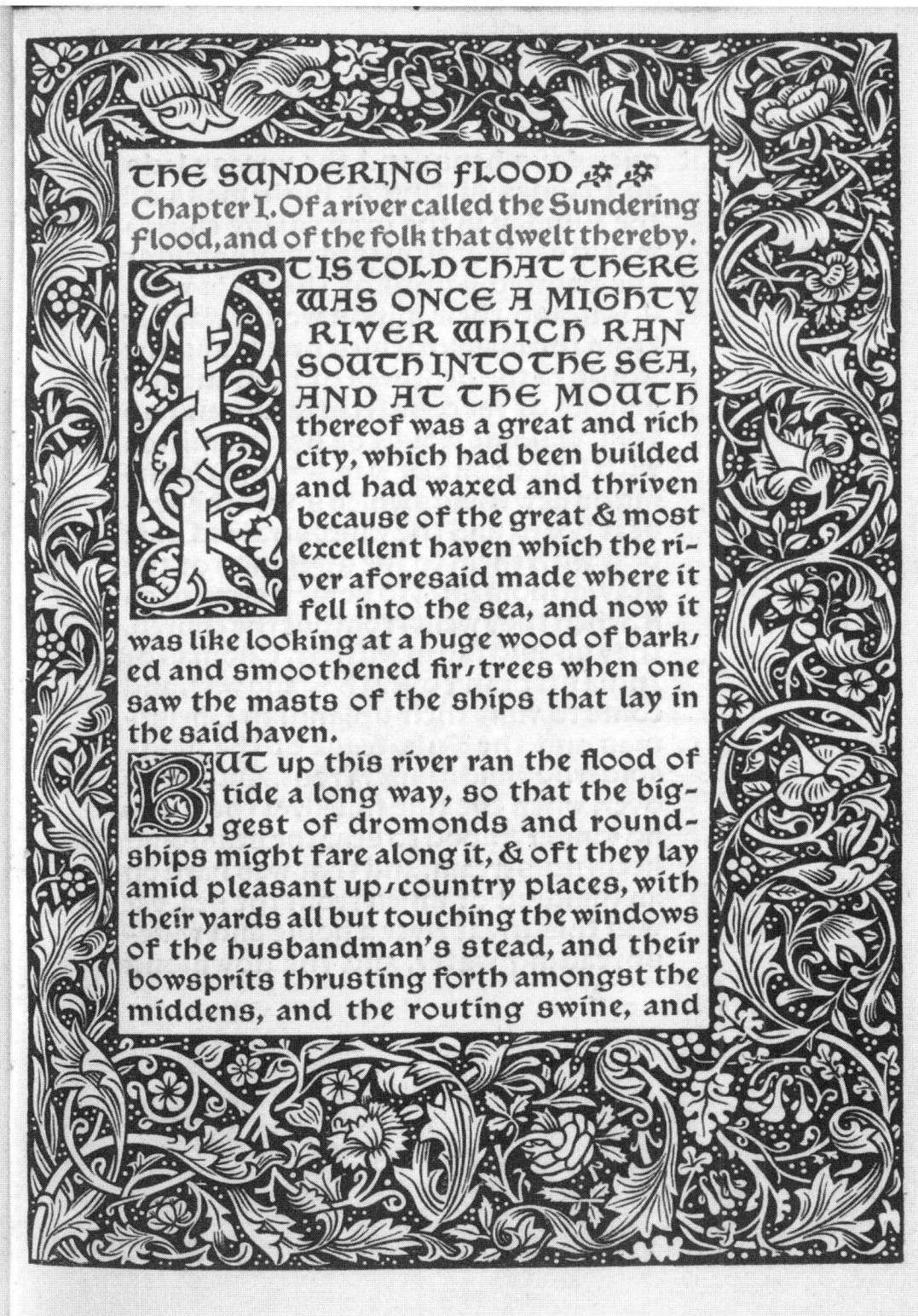

Figure 75. A-86.01: *The Sundering Flood* (KP edn.) head title

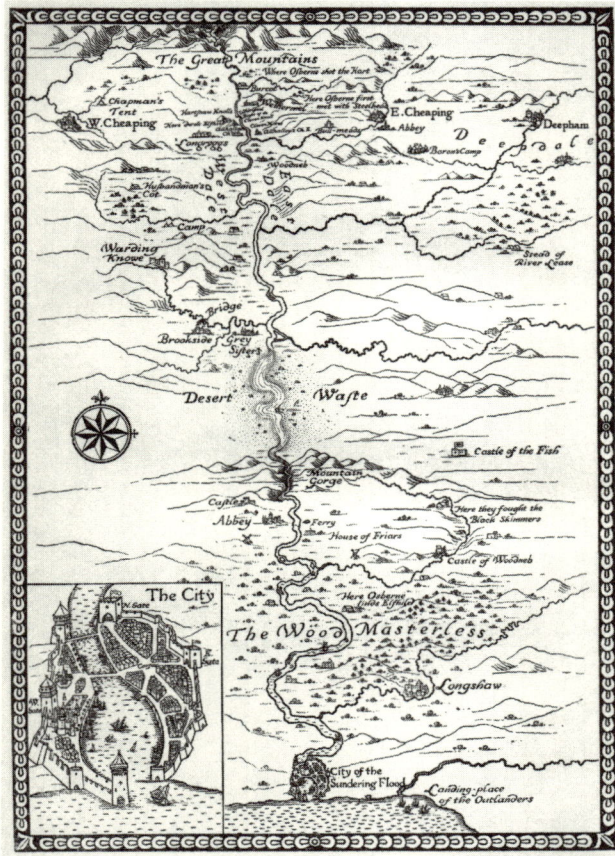

Figure 76. A-86.01: *The Sundering Flood* (KP edn.) map as paste-down inside the front cover

Collaborators, Editors, and Illustrators: [line-block map (on front paste-down) designed by H. Cribb from a rough sketch, probably by Morris, with plate made by Walker and Boutall, who produced the line block] (Cockerell, p. 171).

Series: 51st title, 21st by Morris, produced by the KP.

Colophon: [printer's leaf ornament No. 1] Here ends the story of the Sundering | Flood, the last romance written by William | Morris [printer's leaf ornament No. 2]. It was overseen by May Morris, | and printed at the Kelmscott Press, Upper | Mall, Hammersmith. Finished on the 15th | day of November, 1897. | [KP pressmark, No. 1] | Sold by the Trustees of the late William | Morris at the Kelmscott Press.

Collation: 8°: [a]⁴ b–2i⁸ 2k⁶ [$2 (–b1 h1 k1 m2 p2 t1 2k2) signed] 258 leaves pp. [8] [1] 2–507 [508] [= 516].

Contents: pp. [1–6], blank; p. [7], title page; p. [8], blank; p. [1], 1st chapter head: border No. 10 with letterpress within internal compartment: [top, flush left] THE SUNDER-ING FLOOD [2 fleurons] | [in red] Chapter I. Of a river called the Sundering | Flood, and of the folk that dwelt thereby. | [text begins with 12-line ornamental drop-cap 'I']; pp. 2–507, text completed with explicit: [drop cap initial 'N']: Now is there no more to say con- | cerning the Sundering Flood & | those that dwelt thereby.; p. [508], colophon, see above.

Technical Notes: *paper*: Flower paper 2 with watermark centred on the bottom of the page; *leaf size*: deckled edges, lightly trimmed, avg. 206 x 142 mm.; *printing*: in black and red, red for chapter titles and shoulder notes; *type area*: 127 x 80 mm.; *lines-to-page*: 27 lines set solid; *type face*: Chaucer type; *shoulder notes*: in red, as sub-heads to the adjacent text; *pagination*: arabic numbers set 9 mm. in from the outer margins on the direction line; *end-papers*: 2 free ends and 1 paste-down, front and back, front paste-down having the map mentioned by S. C. Cockerell (see *Notes*, below), note also that the map's spelling of 'Skinners' should be 'Skimmers'; the remaining end-papers are plain white and blank; *binding*: quarter white holland with blue paper-covered boards with title printed in Chaucer type on the front: THE SUNDERING FLOOD. WRITTEN | BY WILLIAM MORRIS; and a printed paper spine label in Golden type: THE | SUNDERING | FLOOD | BY | WILLIAM | MORRIS; *ornamentation*: border No. 10; heading of each chapter has ornamental 3/4 border = 66 such borders; one 12-line initial; 67 6-line initials; 399 3-line initials.

Publication: 15 Nov. 1897 [this colophon date indicates finished printing, issued 25 Feb. 1898]; *print run*: 300 paper copies, 10 vellum; *price*: paper 2*gns*., vellum 10*gns*. (Cockerell, p. 171)

Register of Copies Examined: VU (Bail: 3 copies: base copy, [L], from the Poynton Coll.; + 2 in blue paper-covered boards. The base copy is one of the 10 copies printed on cream-white vellum with green silk ties, but with a special binding (pigskin) differing from that regularly used on KP books, either vellum or blue boards. Cockerell's record notes that originally this edition was "bound in half holland" (Sparling, p. 127), this being Cockerell's way of describing what modern convention would call quarter holland. This copy presents a problem in that it would seem to have been awarded as a prize to A. J. Wyatt of Christ College, Oxon, in '1892', according to the date on the award mark inside the back cover, but this is obviously impossible: the book not being published until 1898. The award mark may be transferred from another book to give this copy an added value (Wyatt being Morris's collabora-

tor in the verse translation of *Beowulf*); BL (2 copies: C. 43. c. 15. and Ashley 3697).
Notes: S. C. Cockerell, MS Diary for Sat. 2 Dec. 1895, records the beginning of Morris's composition of *The Sundering Flood* (Cockerell Papers, BL (Add.) MS 52772). The diary entry for Tues. 8 Sept. 1896 records Morris's dictation of the last dozen lines of *The Sundering Flood* to Cockerell from his deathbed.

Cockerell to Jenny Morris, 28 Feb. 1898: Cockerell explains that he has had a few complaints about the placing of the map, originally intended as a frontis., on the front paste-down. He explains that the map did not harmonise in colour or type with the title page originally intended to face it (see Cockerell Papers, BL (Add.) MS 52739).

A-86.02: The Sundering Flood (trade edn)

THE SUNDERING FLOOD | BY WILLIAM MORRIS | LONGMANS, GREEN, AND CO. | [American issue only] NEW YORK | LONDON AND BOMBAY | MDCCCXCVIII [London issue] LONDON, NEW YORK, AND BOMBAY | MDCCCXCVIII

Edition: 'trade edn' [1st impression, 2nd edn.] 1st printed in Cambridge, Mass., for sale in both the US and Britain, but with different title page imprints to distinguish the British and American issues.
Collaborators, Editors, and Illustrators: [on the line-block map by H. Cribb of the firm of Walker and Boutall, see this field in the previous entry].
Collation: large cr. 8°: 1^8 (1_4+1) $2-24^8$ [5^r signed] 192 leaves pp. [i–v] vi–vii [viii] 1–373 [374–6] [= 384] + 1 inserted leaf noted in the formula and described here in the correct position under *Contents*, but not counted in the book's pagination.
Contents: p. [i], half title; p. [ii], blank; p. [iii], title page; p. [iv], copyright notice: Copyright, 1897, by Longmans, Green, and Co.; p. [v], dropped head: CONTENTS | [list begins of 66 chapters]; pp. vi–vii, Contents completed; p. [viii], blank; inserted engraved map (untitled) of the country of *The Sundering Flood* as frontis. to face p. 1, recto blank; p. 1, dropped head: [flush left] THE SUNDERING FLOOD. | CHAPTER I. OF A RIVER CALLED | THE SUNDERING FLOOD, AND OF | THE FOLK THAT DWELT THEREBY. | [text begins]; pp. 2–373, text completed with explicit: [¶, formatted as text] Now is there no more to say concerning the | Sundering Flood and those that dwelt thereby.; p. [374], printer's imprint: [at the head] Printed by John Wilson and Son at the | University Press in Cambridge U. S. A. | [fleuron as tail-piece]; p. [375], ad headed: MR. WILLIAM MORRIS'S WORKS.; p. [376], blank.
Technical Notes: trade edn. made to range with *The Water of the Wondrous Isles*: *paper*: 'antique' machine-moulded paper with dandy roll laid lines; *leaf size*: UK issue: untrimmed false deckled edges, avg. 205 x 136 mm.; US issue: trimmed, 199 x 132 mm.; *type area*: 136 x 85 mm. exclusive of head and direction lines; *lines-to-page*: 31 lines set solid; *running heads*: all rectos and versos: THE SUNDERING FLOOD; *end-papers*: 1 free end and paste-down, front and back, both plain white and blank; *binding*: plain dark red unblocked cloth with printed paper spine label: [within a thin-rule compartment] THE | SUNDERING | FLOOD | WILLIAM | MORRIS
Publication: 1898 [issued 25 Feb.] (Longmans *Notes on Books*, 9/172 (28 Feb. 1898), 65); Longmans Arch. records 4 Jan. 1898 as a date for importing copies from the US, but there would have been several considerations making for a deliberate delay before issue: the need for simultaneous pbn. of the KP version in Britain and this 'Trade edition' in the US to obtain copyright in both countries while retaining the KP version as the *editio princeps* (for details of this, see this field in A-84.01). Note that the KP edn. of *The Sundering Flood* was also issued on 25 Feb. 1898; *print run*: 2,030, with 1,004 exported to London (Longmans Accts. for 1898); *price*: $2.25 and 7s. 6d.
Register of Copies Examined: English imprint: LeM (base copy); SSL (Y9064); VSL (S823.89 | M83su); SU (823 | M87 su); BL (012623. g. 13.); US imprint: LeM; CSt (2 copies: Green Stacks 821.6.M87sf; and Spec.Coll Felton PR5079.S9, 1898 XL).
Notes: Ballantyne and Hanson printed the back labels and copies of the map for the UK books (Longmans Arch.).
Later impression from this edn.: Longmans:
1.* 1910 [issued Jan.] (CW, XXI. xxxvii): 'Trade edn' [2nd impression, 2nd edn.]; *print run*: unknown; *price*: $2.50, 7s. 6d.

A-86.03: The Sundering Flood (2 vols. LPL)

THE SUNDERING FLOOD | BY WILLIAM MORRIS | IN TWO VOLUMES | VOL. I [II] | POCKET EDITION | LONGMANS, GREEN, AND CO. | 39 PATERNOSTER ROW, LONDON | NEW YORK, BOMBAY, AND CALCUTTA | 1914

Edition: [1st impression, 3rd edn., 2nd English] Though the editor of the *CW* edn., May Morris, says she 'retained the chapter headings and shoulder notes added to the Kelmscott Press edition', there are significant changes in the latter part of the Pocket Library text, which also apply to the *CW* edn..

Collaborators, Editors, and Illustrators: [the text generally conforms to the KP edn. as overseen by May Morris (but see the *Edition* field, above). KP line-block map, here folded and attached to the recto of the back free end paper, vol. I, by H. Cribb of the firm Walker and Boutall, which produced the plate] (see this field in A-86.01).

Series: Longmans Pocket Library. The 11th Morris title of 14 in this series; for detail common to the series, see this field in the 1st of the series, *Jason*, A-3.09.

Collation: vol. I: fcap 8°: π⁴ A–I⁸ K⁴ 80 leaves pp. [2] [i–iv] v–vi [1] 2–152 [= 160].

vol. II: fcap 8°: π⁴ A–K⁸ 84 leaves pp. [i–iv] v–vii [viii] [1] 2–157 [158–60] [= 168].

Contents: vol. I: pp. [1–2], ads, headed: WILLIAM MORRIS'S WORKS; p. [i], half title; p. [ii], blank; p. [iii], title page; p. [iv], dropped head: BIBLIOGRAPHICAL NOTE | [5-line list of pbns. of this title]; pp. v–vi, list, headed: CONTENTS; p. [1], dropped head: THE SUNDERING FLOOD | CHAPTER I | [2 lines in hanging indent] OF A RIVER CALLED THE SUNDERING FLOOD, AND | OF THE FOLK THAT DWELT THEREBY | [text begins]; pp. 2–152, text completed with explicit: END OF VOL. I | [printer's imprint] Printed by BALLANTYNE, HANSON & CO. | at Paul's Work, Edinburgh; with an engraved map of the setting, 201 x 132 mm. folded and glued to the recto of the free end paper.

vol. II: as vol. I, except no ads leaf, no 'Bibliographical Note'; pp. v–vii, headed: CONTENTS; p. [viii], blank; p. [1], dropped head: THE SUNDERING FLOOD | CHAPTER XXXIII | OSBERNE SEEKS TIDINGS OF ELFHILD | [text begins]; pp. 2–157, text completed with explicit: [¶, formatted as text] Now is there no more to say concerning the Sunder- | ing Flood and those that dwelt thereby. | THE END | [printer's imprint, as above]; p. [158], blank; pp. [159–60], ads, headed: WILLIAM MORRIS'S WORKS

Technical Notes: for details common to the series—paper, leaf size, printing, pagination, end-papers, and binding—see this field in *Jason*, A-3.09, the 1st title in this series. Points specific to this edn. of this title: *printing*: type area: 126 x 75 mm.; *lines-to-page*: thin leading, 34 lines; *running heads*: [all rectos and versos] THE SUNDERING FLOOD; *spine*: gilt-stamped across: THE | SUNDERING | FLOOD | VOL. I [II].

Publication: Feb. 1914 ('Bibliographical Note', p. iv); *print run*: 2,000 copies; *price*: for the 2 vols. cloth 4s. net, lthr 6s. net.

Register of Copies Examined: LeM (base copy); Fdmn; BGR; CaBVaU;

Notes: entry from Longmans Arch. for 3 Dec. 1913 shows the book was new set, moulds made, and printed by Ballantyne, in 2,000 copies; binding: 65s. 6d. per. 100 cloth sets; 166s. 8d. per 100 leather sets; total cost not including binding = £49. 18s. 6d.

A-86.04: The Sundering Flood (+ Unfinished Romances *CW* XXI)

THE COLLECTED WORKS | [title details common to the set, see A-126.01] | VOLUME XXI | THE SUNDERING FLOOD | UNFINISHED ROMANCES | [publisher's imprint, see A-126.01] | MDCCCCXIV

Edition: 'The Collected Works edn' [1st impression, 4th edn., 3rd English] Bound in with four 'Unfinished Romances' (for the titles of which see *Contents*, below) all previously unpublished. In this respect this book is the 1st impression, 1st edn. of these romances. On the editor's alterations to the original version of the title text as regards chapter titles and numbers, see this field in A-86.03.

Collaborators, Editors, and Illustrators: edited and introduced by May Morris. KP line-block map by H. Cribb of the firm Walker and Boutall, which produced the plate (see Cockerell, p. 171).

Series: vol. 21 of 24; for details common to the set, see this field in A-126.01.

Collation: medium 8°: a⁸ (a2+1) (a7+1) b⁸ c⁴ (c4+1) B–Y⁸ Z⁴ [$2 (–a2) signed] 192 leaves pp. [i–vi] vii–xxxvii [xxxviii–xl] 1–340 [341–4] [= 384] +3 inserted plates noted in the formula but not counted in the book's pagination. They are described here under *Contents*.

Contents: p. [i], blank; p. [ii], limitation notice (see A-126.01); pp. [iii–iv], blank; 1st inserted plate as frontis. to face title page, recto blank, reproduction in a blind-stamped compartment of a drawing, with the designer named, below left in copperplate: *Philip Webb inv. et del.* | [lower right the plate maker] *Emery Walker Ph. sc.* | [captioned, below, in copperplate] *The Grave at Kelmscott*; p. [v], title page; p. [vi], blank; p. vii, headed: CONTENTS; pp. viii–x, Contents concluded; pp. xi–xiv, headed: INTRODUCTION; 2nd inserted plate to face p. xiv (verso blank), photographic reproductions of 2 woodcut initial words—'Empty' and 'Whilom' captioned: Facsimiles of the last blocks designed for the | Kelmscott Press. [verso blank]; May Morris says (p. x) that 'The word "Empty" was finished but "Whilom" was only drawn in and was completed by Mr. Catterson Smith'; pp. xv–xxxvi, Introduction completed; p. xxxvii, headed: [flush left] BIBLIOGRAPHICAL NOTE TO THE SUNDER- | ING | FLOOD | [list of 5 issues]; p. [xxxviii], blank; p. [xxxix], half title; p. [xl], blank; 3rd inserted plate to face p. 1, uncaptioned engraved map of the Sundering Flood with an inserted detail of 'The City of the Sundering Flood', recto blank; p. 1, headed: [flush left, top margin: THE SUNDERING FLOOD | CHAPTER I. OF A RIVER CALLED THE SUN- | DERING FLOOD, AND OF THE FOLK THAT | DWELT THEREBY. | [text begins]; pp. 2–250, text completed with explicit: [formatted as continuation of the text] Now is there no more to say concerning the Sundering | Flood and those that dwelt thereby.; p. [251], 2nd half title: [top margin] UNFINISHED ROMANCES; p. [252], blank; pp. 253–95, headed: [top margin] KILIAN OF THE CLOSES | [text completed]; p. 296, headed: THE FOLK OF THE MOUNTAIN DOOR; pp. 297–309, text completed; p. 310, headed: THE STORY OF DESIDERIUS; pp. 311–22, text completed; p. 323, headed: [top margin] THE STORY OF THE FLOWER; pp. 324–40, text, extracts in verse completed with prose transitions supplied by the editor, completed; p. [341], blank; p. [342], printer's imprint (see A-126.01); pp. [343–4], blank.

Technical Notes: paper, leaf size, printing, type area, lines-to-page, running titles, shoulder notes, pagination, endpapers, and binding are all common to the series and are described in this field in A-126.01; details specific to this issue: *side notes*: pp. 1–250: all rectos and versos, distributed outside the outer margins, in smaller type as sub-heads to adjacent text; *shoulder titles*: all rectos and versos, for each of 'unfinished romances', pp. 253–340.

Publication: 1914 [issued 10 Dec.] (Longmans Arch.); *print run* and *price*: see this field in A-126.01.

Register of Copies Examined: see this field in A-126.01.

A-87.01: Browning Review (*Bib.*)

[wrapper title, above the compartment, top left] VOL. IV. [top right] No. 3 | [within thin-rule compartment, top left] | *MARCH.* [top right] *MDCCCXCVIII.* | [details common to the series wrapper titles, see A-83.01] | [below the compartment, right, in red] BROWNING'S "MEN AND WOMEN" | A REVIEW BY | WILLIAM MORRIS

Edition: [1st impression, 1st separate edn.] On this article's appearance here rather than in the D-List, Morris in Periodicals, see this field and the *Series* field, A-83.01). This review was 1st pbd. in *The Oxford and Cambridge Magazine*, Mar. 1856 (see D-5).

Collaborators, Editors, and Illustrators: unsigned foreword [by the editor, T. B. Mosher].

Series: *The Bibelot*, 4/3 (Mar. 1898), 85–122.

Place, Publisher, and *Printer*: see wrapper transcriptions in A-83.01.

Collation: 12°: [1]^{22} 22 leaves pp. [4] [85–8] 89–121 [122] [2] [= 44] + the blue wrapper; pagination is continuous through the year's 12 issues, but conjunct leaves at the beginning and end containing only advertising were omitted from the separate issues when they were bound into the annual vol. Here the base copy is always the separate issue.

Contents: pp. [1–4], ads; pp. [85–6], headed: [3-line gothic] The Bibelot | [unsigned prefatory notes by T. B. Mosher]; p. [87], half title: [top right] MEN AND WOMEN. By | ROBERT BROWNING. | [swash caps] *A Review by* | [plain type] WILLIAM MORRIS | [epigraph, aligned left, 4 lines from Browning, with source, below right] | ONE WORD MORE, TO E. B. B.; p. [88], contents of Browning's *Men and Women*, from *Literary Anecdotes of the Nineteenth Century*; p. 89, headed: [top, flush left] "MEN AND WOMEN" | By ROBERT BROWNING. | [text begins]; pp. 90–[122], text completed with printer's flower as tail-piece; pp. [2], ads.

Technical Notes: for details common to the series—paper, leaf size, printing, type area, lines-to-page, pagination, and binding—see this field in A-83.01; details specific to this issue: *running titles*: [flush to the inner margin, all rectos and versos except prelims and postlims] MEN AND WOMEN

Publication: Mar. 1898 [masthead date, issued 25 Feb.] (see *Series* field in A-83.01); *print run* and *price*: see this field in A-83.01.

Register of Copies Examined: LeM (base copy); Bsp; Fdmn.

A-88.01: Note by William Morris on His Aims in Founding the KP (KP)

[half title] A NOTE BY WILLIAM MORRIS ON HIS | AIMS IN FOUNDING THE KELMSCOTT | PRESS [printer's leaf ornament No. 1] TOGETHER WITH A SHORT | DESCRIPTION OF THE PRESS BY S. C. | COCKERELL, & AN ANNOTATED LIST | OF THE BOOKS PRINTED THEREAT.

Edition: 'Kelmscott Press edn' [1st impression, 1st edn.] This 'Note' was originally written in response to a query from Carl Edelheim. Edelheim gave Morris's reply as the body of a paper read to the Philobiblon Club of Philadelphia on 29 Jan. 1896. Thereafter he pbd. it headed 'The Kelmscott Press' in the Boston journal *Modern Art* (see D-590). The paper includes 'in toto' Morris's previously unpublished account of the press (comparison of the magazine and KP texts confirms this journal version originates from the same text as the *Note*. The MS includes an address and date at the end: 'Kelmscott House, Upper Mall, Hammersmith, 11 November, 1895' (see Christie's Catalogue, Doheny VI. 79).

Collaborators, Editors, and Illustrators: edited by S. C. Cockerell, with a short history and description and an annotated list of the books pbd. thereat.

Series: 53rd (and last) title and 23rd (and last) Morris book pbd. by the KP (*The Glittering Plain*'s 2 editions and the translation of *The Order of Chivalry* each counting as separate Morris titles).

Colophon: THIS WAS THE LAST BOOK PRINT- | ED AT THE KELMSCOTT PRESS. IT | WAS FINISHED AT NO. 14 UPPER | MALL, HAMMERSMITH, IN THE | COUNTY OF LONDON, ON THE | FOURTH DAY OF MARCH, MDCCCX- | CVIII. SOLD BY THE TRUSTEES OF | THE LATE WILLIAM MORRIS AT | THE KELMSCOTT PRESS.

Collation: 8°: [a]⁴ b–d⁸ e⁸ (±) f⁴ [$2 (–b f2) signed] 40 leaves pp. [8] [1] 2–70 [71–2] [= 80]. The evidence of the cancellation of gathering e (see *KP Biblio.*, p. 141) seems to rest entirely on Cockerell's letter to Leighton of 7 Mar. 1898 (see *Notes*, below). The letter implies that only part of sheet e was cancelled, but no evidence has been found that indicates which part.

Contents: p. [1–4], blank; p. [5], half title; pp. [6–7], blank; p. [8], frontis.: woodcut illus., in border 4a, with label: [printer's flower ornament No. 1] PSYCHE BORNE OFF BY ZE- | PHYRUS, DRAWN BY EDWARD | BURNE-JONES & ENGRAVED | BY WILLIAM MORRIS [printer's flower ornament No.3]; p. [1], headed, within border No. 4: [top, printed in red] NOTE BY WILLIAM MORRIS | ON HIS AIMS IN FOUNDING | THE KELMSCOTT PRESS [2 printer's leaf ornaments No. 3] | [text begins with 6-line drop initial 'I']; pp. 2–70, text completed with large KP printer's mark No. 2; p. [71], colophon, in red: see *Colophon*, above; p. [72], blank.

Technical Notes: *paper*: cream, hand-laid KP Flower paper, No. 2, with untrimmed deckled edges; *watermark*: primrose with initials 'W' before and 'M' after, centred on the leaf; *leaf size*: 206 x 143 mm.; *printing*: prtd. in black and red: red for labels of illus., chapter head titles, titles of books, and the colophon; *type face*: Golden type, with 5 pages in Troy and Chaucer types; *type area*: 141 x 93 mm.; *lines-to-page*: 30 lines set solid; *pagination*: arabic numerals set 10 mm. in from the outer margin on the direction line; *end-papers*: 2 free ends and paste-down, plain white and blank, front and back; *binding*: quarter holland with blue paper-covered boards, printed on the front, replicating the title in black (see above) and (this copy) lettered by hand in black up the spine: Morris on His Aims in Founding the Kelmscott Press; but other copies are not lettered on the spine, suggesting that this was not the book as issued.

Publication: 4 Mar. 1898 [this colophon date indicates finished printing, issued 24 Mar.] (Cockerell, p. 172); *print run*: 525 copies on paper, 12 on vellum; *price*: 10s. and 2gns., respectively (Cockerell, p. 172).

Register of Copies Examined: VSL (base copy: *094/K29); VU (19H).

Notes: S. C. Cockerell's transcript of Morris's autograph MS ('now unlocated', having been sold in the Christie's Doheny VI sale (see Pearson, 715) includes an address and date at the end of Morris's *Note*: 'Kelmscott House, Upper Mall, Hammersmith, 11 November, 1895' (see Pearson, 715). Morris's *Note* was reprinted by May Morris in the 'Introduction' to vol. XV of the *CW*; and the entire text of this book was reprinted as four appendices in Sparling, 135–74, and in *Letters,* iii. Appendix B.

S. C. Cockerell's MS Diary for 11 Nov. 1895 says that on this day Morris began his account to Carl Edelheim of the origin of the KP (see Cockerell Papers, BL (Add.) MS 52772).

S. C. Cockerell noted to Robert Proctor, 4 Mar. 1898, that the last sheet of the *Note* was to be printed that day; but Cockerell noticed (letter of 23 Mar.), too late, i.e. just after printing finished, that in the *Note* the date of the Chaucer is erroneously given as 1893 instead of 1896 (BL (Add.) MS 52743), so an erratum slip was added to 'some copies' headed: 'MISPRINT. | p. 44, l. 12. Please alter 1893 to 1896' (see *KP Biblio.*, p. 141).

This is clearly not the cancel Cockerell refers to in his letter to J. J. Leighton on 7 Mar. 1898 (p. 44 would be in sheet d, not e): 'the Note [*A Note by William Morris . . .*] will be ready for you on the 15th. Will it not be best to fetch the first sheet[s] and begin folding? There will be a cancel in sheet 'e' & sheet 'f' will be a good while drying, as there are some heavy initials in it. Sheets a to e (except the cancel) are now ready' John Johnson Collection (JC).

A-89.01: A Dream of John Ball (title tale only, Roycroft)

A DREAM OF JOHN BALL | BEING AN IDYLL IN

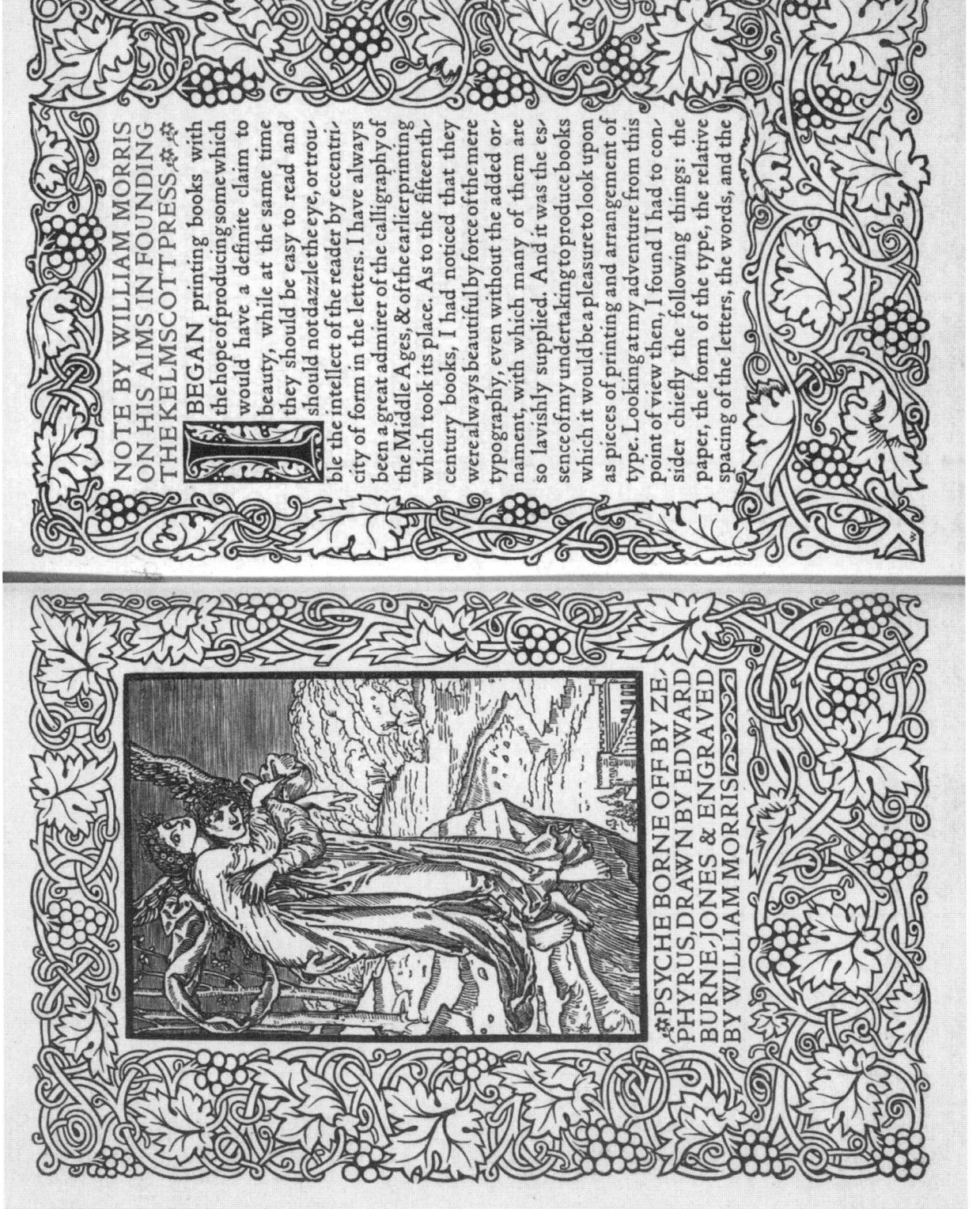

Figure 77. A-88.01: *A Note by Morris . . .* (KP edn) opening: frontis. & head title

PROSE BY WILLIAM MORRIS. | DONE INTO A BOOK BY THE ROYCROFTERS AT | THE ROY-CROFTER SHOP | THAT IS IN EAST AURORA, NEW YORK, U.S.A. | MDCCCXCVIII

Edition: [1st impression, 1st separate edn.] The title story is printed here without its usual companion piece, *A King's Lesson*. In addition to the ordinary copies, 100 LP copies were printed on Whatman paper. For details of the 1st book pbn. of *A Dream of John Ball and A King's Lesson*, see A-45.01. The 1st pbn. of *John Ball* was in *Commonweal* (1886, see D-240).

Colophon: [in red:] SO HERE ENDETH A DREAM OF JOHN | BALL: BEING AN IDYLL IN PROSE BY | WILLIAM MORRIS & DONE INTO A | BOOK BY ME, ELBERT HUBBARD. | AT THE ROYCROFT SHOP [printer's leaf] | WHICH IS IN EAST AU- | RORA, N.Y., U.S.A. | MDCCCXCVIII | [2 printer's leaves]

Collation: 8°: [1⁴ 2–9⁸ 10⁶] 74 leaves pp. [1–8] 9–146 [147–8] [= 148].

Contents: p. [1], half title; p. [2], blank; p. [3], title page; p. [4], blank; p. [5], limitation notice: 'Of this edition six hundred and fifty copies were printed [+ 100 FP copies] and the types then distributed. This book is No. 402' (number in longhand); p. [6], blank; pp. [7–8], headed: Contents; p. 9, text begins with 6-line illuminated initial 'A'; pp. 10–[147], text completed; p. [148], colophon (see above).

Technical Notes: *paper*: cream-white machine-made; *leaf size*: 220 x 136 mm.; *printing*: in red and black, with red shoulder titles, all rectos and versos, and illuminated initials in red; *end-papers*: grey hand-laid paper, 1 free end and paste-down, plain grey and blank, front and back; *binding*: quarter tan suede leather with grey paper-covered boards. Gilt-stamped on front with title: A DREAM OF JOHN BALL; *spine*: gilt-stamped against a dark brown background: A DREAM OF JOHN BALL—MORRIS

Publication: 1898; *print run*: 650 copies and 100 copies on Whatman hand-made paper; *price*: unknown.

Register of Copies examined: BGR (base copy: 2 copies, standard and LP); J-F V.

Notes: John Walsdorf says that besides the 650 copies, 'there was also another limited edition of 100 copies on Whatman paper' (Walsdorf, p. 153).

A-89.02: A Dream of John Ball (only, Little Leather Library)

A DREAM OF | JOHN BALL | By WILLIAM MORRIS | [4 dots in diamond shape] | LITTLE LEATHER LIBRARY | CORPORATION NEW YORK

Figure 78. A-89.02: *John Ball* (only, Little Leather edn.) binding, front cover

Edition: [1st impression, 2nd separate edn.] For details of earlier pbns. of *A Dream of John Ball*, see A-89.01.

Series: Miniature Library and Little Leather Library.

Collation: 24° in 16s: [1–4]¹⁶ 64 leaves pp. [1–3] 4–128 [= 128].

Contents: p. [1], title page; p. [2], blank; p. [3], 1st chapter head and text begins; pp. 4–128, text completed.

Technical Notes: *paper*: plain cream-white machine-made; *leaf size*: trimmed, 95 x 74 mm.; *printing*: *type area*: 81 x 61 mm.; *lines-to-page*: 29 lines set solid; *running titles*: all rectos and versos: A DREAM OF JOHN BALL; *end-papers*: 1 free end and paste-down; mid-grey and blank, front and back; *binding*: soft tan calfskin, deeply embossed in brown on front, spine, and back: *front*: [within a printer's border] A DREAM | OF | JOHN BALL | • • • | WILLIAM | MORRIS; *back*: logo for the Little Leather Library, with the 3-word name placed within a single 3-line initial 'L'; *spine*: title only down the spine.

Publication: [n.d., c. 1915] (*NUC* says '191?'); *print run* and *price*: unknown.

Register of Copies examined: LeM (base copy).

Original and Posthumous Editions

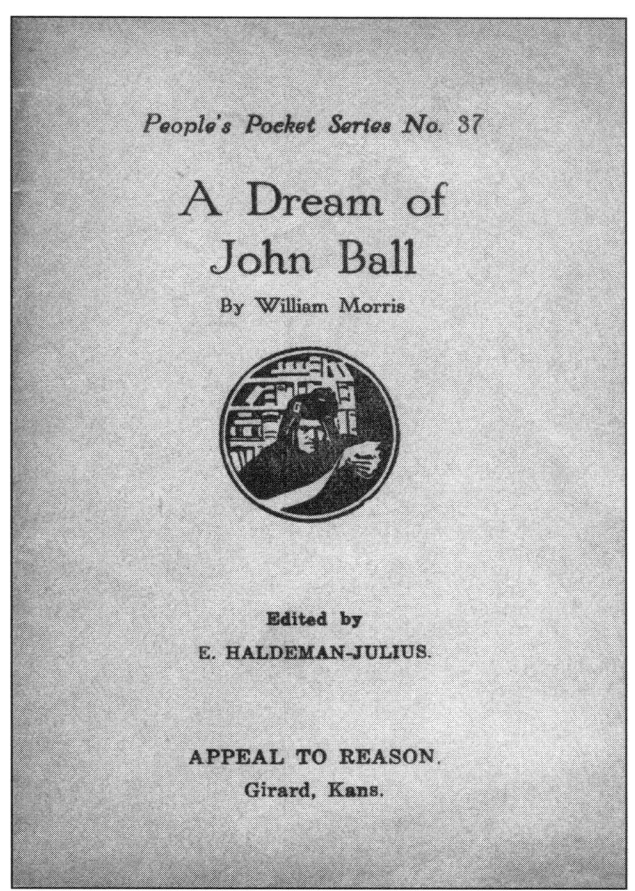

Figure 79. A-89.03: *John Ball* (only, Haldeman-Julius) wrapper title

A-89.03: A Dream of John Ball (title story only)

[wrapper title] *People's Pocket Series No. 37* | A Dream of | John Ball | By William Morris | [circular printer's mark, 25 mm. dia., reader with a background of bookshelves] | edited by E HALDEMAN-JULIUS. | APPEAL TO REA-SON | Girard, Kans

Edition: [1st impression, 3rd separate edn., 3rd American] The 1st pbn. of *John Ball* was in *Commonweal* (1886, see D-240).
Series: 2 series that include this title have been seen: the Ten Cent Pocket Series (with title page) and The People's Pocket Series No. 37 (without title page).
Collation: 18°: [1]⁴⁰ 40 leaves pp. [1] 2–80 [=80] 20 conjunct leaves folded inside each other and stapled twice through the centre-fold to grey-green wrapper of heavier paper.
Contents: p. [1], head title; pp. 2–80, text completed.
Technical Notes: *paper*: plain white machine-made, no water mark; *leaf size*: cut flush: 128 x 91 mm.; *type area*: 102 x 67 mm., not counting headlines; *lines to page*: set solid, 40 lines; *running titles*: all rectos and versos: A Dream of John Ball; *binding*: wrapper: p. [1] wrapper title, as above; pp. [2-3], blank; p. [4] ad for a weekly titled *Appeal to Reason* also pbd. in Girard, Kans.
Publication: n.d. [c. 1915]; *print run* and *price*: unknown.
Register of Copies Examined: LeM (base copy); BGR has 2 copies from the 2 different series cited above.

A-90.01: Gertha's Lovers (*Bib.* in 2 parts)

[wrapper title, top left] VOL. V. [top right] NO. 1 [2] | [within thin-rule compartment, top left] *JAN.* [*FEB.*] [right] *MDCCCXCIX.* | [title detail common to Bibelot issues, see A-83.01] | [below the compartment, right, in red] GERTHA'S LOVERS: A TALE PART I [II] | BY WILLIAM MORRIS

Edition: [1st impression, 1st separate edn.] On this tale's appearance here rather than in the D-List, Morris in Periodicals, see this field and the *Series* field in A-83.01. This A-List entry provides finding-list information for both versions (see the *Series* field, below). *Gertha's Lovers* was 1st pbd. in 2 parts (5 chapters), in *The Oxford and Cambridge Magazine*, in July and Aug. 1856 (see D-8).
Collaborators, Editors, and Illustrators: unsigned foreword [by the editor, T. B. Mosher], with an excerpt from William Sharp's *Atlantic Monthly* article on Morris as an epigraph.
Series: *The Bibelot . . .*, 5/1, 2 (Jan., Feb. 1899), 5–54, 55–102. For detail common to the series, see this field in A-83.01.
Place, Publisher, and *Printer*: see wrapper-title transcriptions in A-83.01.
Collation: Part I: 12°: [1]³⁴ 34 leaves, 17 conjunct pairs, pp. [6] [1–4] 5–53 [54] [8] [= 68] + Bibelot wrapper sewn to the body through the centrefold.
Part II: 12°: [1]³⁰ folded as in Part I, 30 leaves, 15 conjunct pairs, pp. [6] [55–6] 57–101 [102] [6] [= 60] + the usual Bibelot wrapper sewn to the body through the centrefold; on pagination, see this field in A-83.01.
Contents: Part I: pp. [*1–6*], ads later deleted for the annual collection; p. [1], unsigned foreword [by the editor, T. B. Mosher], headed: [modern gothic as on the wrapper title but in black] The Bibelot | [Mosher's foreword begins]; p. [2], foreword ends; p. [3], half title: [flush upper right] GERTHA'S LOVERS. | A TALE. | PART I. | [16-line epigraph aligned flush left with source printed below right] THE EARTHLY PARADISE.; p. [4], 2nd epigraph, 24 lines of prose, signed: [below right] WILLIAM SHARP, | (*Atlantic Monthly*, Sept., 1898.); p. 5, headed: GERTHA'S LOVERS. | CHAPTER I. | BY THE RIVER. | [text begins

with a 4-line quotation from Coleridge]; pp. 6–[54], text of part I concluded with the conclusion of Chapter III and a printer's leaf as tail-piece; pp. [1–8], ads.
Part II: pp. [1–6], ads, deleted for the annual vol.; p. [55], half title: [flush upper right] GERTHA'S LOVERS, | A TALE BY WILLIAM MORRIS. | PART II; p. [56], blank; p. 57, headed: CHAPTER IV. | GERTHA THE QUEEN. | [text begins]; pp. 58–101 [102], text completed with printer's leaf as tail-piece; pp. [1–6], ads.
Technical Notes: for details common to the series—paper, leaf size, printing, type area, lines-to-page, pagination, and wrapper—see this field in A-83.01; details specific to this issue: *running titles*: flush to the inner margin, all rectos and versos: GERTHA'S LOVERS
Publication: Jan., Feb. 1899, issued in 2 parts: [issued 15 and 25 Jan.] (for evidence of issue dates, print run, and price, see *Series* field in A-83.01).
Register of Copies Examined: BL (2 parts: base copy: PP. 8001. ea.120, (121)) Bsp (2 parts).

A-90.02:* Gertha's Lovers (Rpts. Bib.)

[1st and last lines in red] GERTHA'S LOVERS | A TALE BY WILLIAM | MORRIS | [Chiswick Press Aldine mark, Bishop No. 2] | Portland, Maine | [swash ital. caps] *Thomas B. Mosher* | Mdcccxcix
Edition: [2nd impression, 1st separate edn.] Here published in 1 vol. 1st pbd. in 2 parts (5 chapters), in *The Oxford and Cambridge Magazine*, in July and Aug. 1856 (see D-8). Mosher explains that the same forms were used for the original issues under *The Bibelot* masthead and for the series Reprints from "The Bibelot", with new pagination (see Bishop, p. 140). The resultant book, described here, is printed on japan vellum, has a new format, is printed and gathered in 8s, has a conventional title page, eliminates the uncounted conjunct leaves devoted solely to ads before and after the *Bibelot* texts, and adds a limitation statement and revised prelims.
Collaborators, Editors, and Illustrators: unsigned introduction [by the editor, T. B. Mosher].
Series: Reprints from "The Bibelot"—5. For details common to this series, see A-83.02.
Collation: *12° in 8s: [1⁴ 2–7⁸ 8²] 54 leaves pp. [6] [1–5] 6–99 [100–2] [= 108].
Contents: p. [1], half title; p. [2], blank; p. [3], limitation notice: Twenty-five copies of this book | printed on Japan vellum, of | which twenty only are for sale. | This is No. [no. added in longhand]; p. [4], blank p. [5], title; p. [6], blank; pp. [1–2], unsigned foreword [by the editor, T. B. Mosher]; p. [3], 16-line epigraph aligned flush left with source printed below right: THE EARTHLY PARADISE.; p. [4], 2nd epigraph, 24 lines of prose, signed: [below right] WILLIAM SHARP, | (*Atlantic Monthly*, Sept. 1898.); p. [5], blank; p. 6, headed: GERTHA'S LOVERS. | CHAPTER I. | BY THE RIVER. | [text begins after a 4-line quotation from Coleridge]; pp. 7–[100], text completed with printer's leaf as tail-piece; pp. [101–2], blank.
The text of the tale is in the same setting as A-90.01, the Reprints from the "Bibelot", being printed from the same forms (see Bishop, p. 140).
Technical Notes: for details common to the series—paper, leaf size, printing, type area, lines-to-page, pagination, and binding—see this field in A-83.02; detail specific to this issue: *end-papers*: 3 free ends and paste-down, plain white and blank, front and back; *binding letterpress*: front cover: GERTHA'S LOVERS; up the spine: GERTHA'S LOVERS | A TALE BY WILLIAM | MORRIS
Publication: 1899; *print run* and *price*: see this field in A-83.02.
Register of Copies Examined: Bsp.

A-90.03: Gertha's Lovers (Broc.)

[1st half line to the colon, and last line in red, drop 3-line initial 'G'] GERTHA'S LOVERS: [in black] A TALE | BY WILLIAM MORRIS | [Chiswick Press Aldine mark, Bishop No. 2] | [flush left] PORTLAND MAINE | THOMAS B. MOSHER | MDCCCCII
Edition: [1st impression, 2nd separate edn.] 1st published in 2 parts (5 chapters), in *The Oxford and Cambridge Magazine*, in July and Aug. 1856 (see D-8).
Collaborators, Editors, and Illustrators: unsigned foreword [by the editor, T. B. Mosher].
Series: Brocade Series.—32; this book is also the 2nd of a 4-vol. subset within the Brocade series titled, 'Old English Romances—Morris' and including, No.1, The Hollow Land, No. 3, Golden Wings and Svend and His Brethren, and No. 4, The Story of the Unknown Church. Mosher sold these subset books either singly in individual slip cases or by the set in cabinet cases of 4-vols. For further series detail, see this field in A-70.03.
Colophon: FOUR HUNDRED AND TWEN- | TY-FIVE COPIES OF THIS BOOK | HAVE BEEN PRINTED | ON JAPAN VELLUM, AND TYPE | DISTRIBUTED, IN THE MONTH | OF JUNE, A.D. MDCCCCII, | AT THE PRESS OF GEORGE D. | LORING, PORTLAND, MAINE.
Collation: 16° gathered in 4s: [1–16]⁴ 64 leaves pp. [1–10]

Original and Posthumous Editions

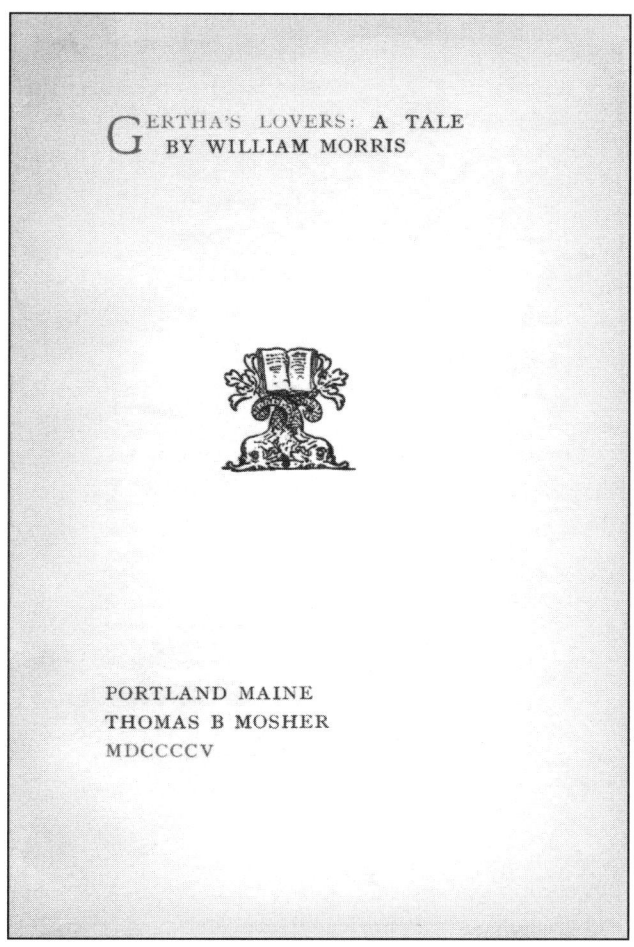

Figure 80. A-90.03: *Gertha's Lovers* (Broc. edn.) title page

11–123 [124–8] [= 128].
Contents: p. [1], half title; p. [2], blank; p. [3], title page; p. [4], blank; pp. [5–7], Mosher's unsigned Foreword heading below a Chiswick Press head-piece; p. [8], blank; p. [9], 2nd half title (as the 1st); p. [10], an epigraph of 16 lines from *EP*, signed: [below right] THE EARTHLY PARADISE.; p. 11, headed: [Chiswick Press head-piece] | GERTHA'S LOVERS | Chapter I | BY THE RIVER | [text begins with 4-line quotation, signed] *Coleridge*; pp. 12–[124], text completed with Chiswick Press tail-piece; p. [125], colophon; pp. [126–8], blank.
Technical Notes: for details common to the series—paper, leaf size, printing, type area, lines-to-page, running titles, pagination, binding, and slip cases—see this field in the record for the 1st Morris publication in this series, *Amis and Amile*, A-70.03; detail specific to this issue: *running titles*: [to the inner margin on headlines, all rectos and versos] GERTHA'S LOVERS; *end-papers*: 4 free ends, no pastedown, plain white and blank, front and back; *binding*: *letterpress*: title printed on the front: [4-line floriated drop initial 'G' in red] GERTHA'S [fleuron] | [fleuron] LOVERS | A TALE BY | WILLIAM | MORRIS [5 fleurons as line fillers]; title printed in black on spine, brown on slipcase, with letters aligned horizontally down the spine one above the other: GERTHA'S LOVERS [with 5 fleurons as line fillers]; back: upper right: Mosher's adaptation of the caduceus designed by Bruce Rogers with a torch rather than wings at the top.
Publication: 1902 [June]: 'First Brocade Edition' [1st impression, 2nd separate edn.] (Hatch, item 217; Bishop, item 134); *print run*: 425 copies on japan vellum; *price*: 75 cents net.
Register of Copies Examined: LeM (base copy); Bsp.
Later impression from this Mosher edn.:
1. 1905 [issued Oct.] (Hatch, No. 343) SECOND EDITION. [2nd impression (or edn.?), 2nd separate edn.]; *print run*: 425 copies; *price*: 75 cents.

A-91.01: The Ideal Book (Broughton)

[all within a typographical border formed of printer's flowers] The Ideal Book | An Address | By | William Morris | [cross formed of 5 fleurons] | New York | Mdcccxcix
Edition: [1st impression, 1st separate edn.] 1st pbd. in the *Transactions of the Bibliographical Society*, 1893 (see D-555); see also Collections, C-14, *The Art and Craft of Printing*, text reprinted in MM, i. 310–18; and in Peterson, pp. 67–73.
Collaborators, Editors, and Illustrators: unsigned Foreword [by George H. Broughton Jr.?]
Colophon: Printed for George H. Broughton Jr. at the Calumet Press in JANry Mdcccxcix. Two hundred and fifty copies on deckle-edge paper. Fifty copies on Japan vellum. This is copy No. [no. in longhand]
Collation: Crown 8° in 4s: [A–B⁴ C² D⁴] 14 leaves, pp. [1–7] 8-20 [21–2] [23–8] [=28] C² is an unsewn inserted conjunct pair, but A, B, and D are sewn in the standard way, between the 2nd and 3rd leaves.
Contents: p. [1], title page; p. [2], blank; p. [3], half title; p. 4, blank; 5 FOREWORD [text begins]; p. [6], blank; p. [7], headed: THE IDEAL BOOK | [text begins with a drop cap 'B' in red with the rest of the initial word in black caps]; pp. 8–20, text completed; pp. [21], colophon (see above) and, printed: copy number: this copy is [number in longhand]; pp. [22–8], blank.
Technical Notes: *paper*: hand-made with deckle edges (250 copies) and japan vellum (50 copies); *leaf size*: vellum: cut

flush, paper: deckle edge, avg. 217 x 134 mm.; *printing*: in red and black; paragraphs begin with red drop cap initial and black cap initial word; running heads: all rectos and versos: THE IDEAL BOOK; *end papers*: front, 5 free ends and pastedown, plain white and blank; back has 1 free end and pastedown; *binding*: quarter holland with blue-grey paper-covered boards and (in J-F V copy) spine label: [in red, three thin-rule compartments] WILLIAM MORRIS | [KP mark No. 1] | [in red gothic] The Ideal Book; at least one copy (VMoU) has no spine label, but a printed paper label on the front: 3 red thin-rule compartments: [within no.1, in black] WILLIAM MORRIS | [no.2, neo-gothic type with black Morris design as background] kelmscott | [red thin rule] | William Morris | [no. 3, in red neo-gothic] The Ideal Book

Publication: Jan. 1899 (colophon date); *print run*: see *colophon*, above; *price*: unknown.

Register of Copies Examined: J-F V (base copy); VMoU (*686 | M877.I, paper copy numbered '237').

A-91.02: The Ideal Book (LCC Arts and Crafts)

THE IDEAL BOOK | A PAPER BY WILLIAM MORRIS | Read before the Bibliographical Society, London, June 19, 1893 | L.C.C. Central School of Arts & Crafts, Regent St. | 1907

Edition: [1st impression, 2nd separate edn., 1st English] 1st pbd. in *Transactions of the Bibliographical Society*, 1893 (see D-555). See also Collections, C-14, *The Art and Craft of Printing*.

Colophon: Printed at the L.C.C. Central School of Arts and Crafts, Regent St., W. Set in type by Leonard Jay. Instructor: J. H. Mason. Finished February, 1908

Collation: pott 4°: [1–2]⁴ 8 leaves pp. [1] 2–13 [14–16] [= 16].

Contents: p. 1, title page; p. 2, text begins; pp. 3–13, text completed with colophon (see above); pp. [14–16], blank.

Technical Notes: *paper*: cream white machine-made; *leaf size*: 206 x 143 mm.; *type area*: 136 x 93 mm.; *lines-to-page*: 28 lines set solid; *end-papers* (specific to this copy, originally issued without end-papers or binding): of KP hand-made Flower paper: 2 free ends and paste-down, plain white and blank, front and back; *binding*: see *Notes* for details of this copy.

Publication: Feb. 1908 (colophon date); *print run* and *price*: unknown; on *print run*, see *Notes*, below.

Register of Copies Examined: VMoU (base copy); BL (K.T.C. 33. a. 24., Cockerell's copy); WMG (K. 773); St. Bride's (18935).

Notes: Cockerell's copy, presented to him by Emery Walker on Christmas, 1909, contains notes on both paste-downs and the title page in Cockerell's hand to the effect that there were very few copies printed, between 12 and 20 (letter dated 23 July 1911), and that Katherine Adams of Broadway, Worchestershire, was the binder of his copy.

A-92.01: King Coustans (only, Broc.)

[1st line, part of the 2nd line, and last line in red] THE TALE OF KING COUSTANS | THE EMPEROR [in black] DONE OUT | OF ANCIENT FRENCH | INTO ENGLISH BY WILLIAM | MORRIS | [Chiswick Press Aldine mark (Bishop No. 2)] | THOMAS B. MOSHER | PORTLAND, MAINE | MDCCCXCIX

Edition: [1st impression 1st separate edn.] Originally published as a KP book, where it is bound in with *The History of Over Sea* (see A-73.01) and later (1896) included with 3 other translations in *Old French Romances* (see A-79.01).

Collaborators, Editors, and Illustrators: unsigned introduction and bibliographic note [by T. B. Mosher]; 2nd introduction is from that written by Joseph Jacobs for *Old French Romances*.

Series: The Brocade Series—13. This book is also the 3rd in the 4-vol. Morris Broc. subset called 'Old French Romances'. The subset also includes *Amis and Amile, King Florus,* and *The History of Over Sea*, available as individual titles in brocade slip-casings or in the 4-vol. set in a cabinet box. For detail common to the Brocade series, see this field, *Contents,* and *Technical Notes* in A-70.03.

Colophon: FOUR HUNDRED AND TWEN- | TY FIVE COPIES OF THIS | BOOK HAVE BEEN PRINTED | ON JAPAN VELLUM, AND TYPE | DISTRIBUTED, IN THE MONTH | OF APRIL, A. D. MDCCCXCIX, | AT THE PRESS OF GEORGE D. | LORING, PORTLAND, MAINE.

Collation: 16° in 4s: [1–9]⁴ 36 leaves pp. [i–viii] ix–xxxvi [xxxvii–xxxviii] [1–2] 3–27 [28–34] [= 72].

Contents: [i–ii], blank; p. [iii], half title; p. [iv], bibliographical note [by Mosher]; p. [v], title page; p. [vi], blank; p. [vii], headed: INTRODUCTION | [Mosher's text]; [viii], blank; p. ix, dropped head: INTRODUCTION | [Jacobs' text begins]; pp. x–xxxvi, text completed and signed, below right: JOSEPH JACOBS.; pp. [xxxvii–xxxviii], blank; p. [1], 2nd half title; p. [2], blank; p. 3, [dropped head title:] THE TALE OF KING COUSTANS | THE EMPEROR | [text begins]; pp. 4–[28], text completed with explicit: HERE withal endeth the Story of | King Coustans the Emperor. | [¶] THE SAID Story was

Original and Posthumous Editions

done out of the | ancient French into English by William | Morris | [tail-piece]; p. [29], colophon (see above); pp. [30–4], blank.
Technical Notes: for technical details common to the Brocade series—paper, leaf size, printing, type area, lines-to-page, and binding—see this field in the 1st entry for the series, A-70.03; detail specific to this issue: *end-papers*: no paste-downs, 2 free ends, plain white and blank, front and back; *binding*: *letterpress*: front: title beginning with a 4-line ornamental drop initial 'T' in red: THE TALE OF | KING COUS- | TANS THE EMP- | EROR DONE | OUT OF THE ANCIENT FRENCH INTO ENG- | LISH | BY WILLIAM MORRIS [a printer's leaf as line filler]; *spine*: letters, black on spine, red on slipcase, oriented horizontally, one above the other: THE TALE OF KING COUSTANS THE EMPEROR [2 printer's leaves as line fillers]
Publication: Apr. 1899 (colophon date); *print run*: 425 copies; *price*: 75 cents net.
Register of Copies Examined: SU (820.8 M); Bsp.
Later impressions (or edns.) of this text: Mosher: (on whether these are rpts. or edns., see the *Edition* field in A-70.03) :
1.* Aug. 1900 (colophon date): SECOND EDITION [2nd impression (or 2nd edn.?), 1st separate edn.]; *print run* and *price*: as above;
2.* June 1912 (colophon date): THIRD EDITION [3rd impression (or 3rd edn.?), 1st separate edn.]; *print run* and *price*: as above.

A-93.01: History of Over Sea (only, Broc.)

[top left, hanging indent, short title and last line in red, dropped cap initial 'T'] THE HISTORY OF OVER SEA | DONE OUT OF THE ANCIENT | FRENCH INTO ENGLISH By | WILLIAM MORRIS | [Chiswick Press Aldine mark (Bishop No. 2)] | [aligned left] PORTLAND MAINE | THOMAS B. MOSHER | MDCCCXCIX
Edition: [1st impression, 1st separate edn.] Originally included in a KP book, where it is bound in with *The Tale of the Emperor Coustans* (see A-73.01); later (1896) included with 3 other French tales in *Old French Romances* (see A-79.01).
Collaborators, Editors, and Illustrators: bibliographical note [by T. B. Mosher].
Series: The Brocade Series—14; minor series: Old French Romances. 4—Morris. For further series and minor series detail, see this field in A-70.03.
Colophon: FOUR HUNDRED AND TWEN- | TY-FIVE COPIES OF THIS | BOOK HAVE BEEN PRINTED |

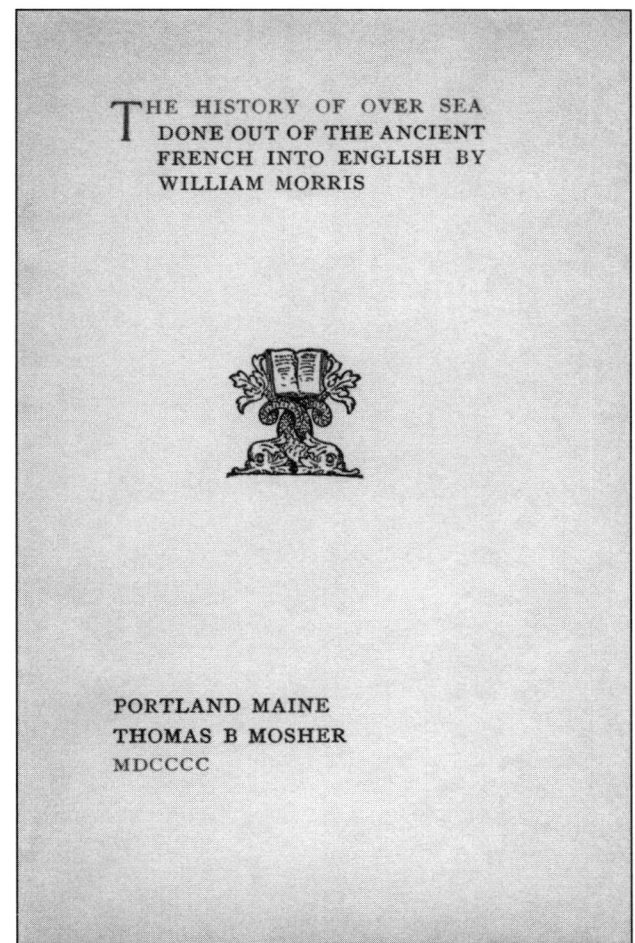

Figure 81. A-93.01: *History of Over Sea* (Broc. edn.) title page

ON JAPAN VELLUM, AND TYPE | DISTRIBUTED, IN THE MONTH | OF JUNE, A.D. MDCCCXCIX, | AT THE PRESS OF GEORGE D. | LORING, PORTLAND, MAINE.
Collation: 16° in 4s: [1–9]⁴ 36 leaves pp. [1–6] 7–66 [67–72] [= 72].
Contents: p. [1], half title; p. [2], bibliographical note; p. [3], title page; p. [4], blank; p. [5], 2nd half title; p. [6], blank; p. 7, dropped head title: THE HISTORY OF OVER SEA | [text begins]; pp. 8–[67], text completed with explicit: HERE ends the story of Over Sea, | done out of ancient French into | English by William Morris. | [tail-piece]; p. [68], blank; p. [69], colophon, see above; pp. [70–2], blank.
Technical Notes: for details common to the Brocade series—paper, leaf size, printing, type area, lines-to-page, pagination, and binding—see this field in the 1st entry for

the series, A-70.03; details specific to this issue: *running titles*: all rectos and versos: THE HISTORY OF OVER SEA; *end-papers*: no paste-down, 2 free ends, plain white and blank, front and back; *binding: letterpress*: front title: [4-line dropped-cap ornamental initial 'T' in red, rest in black] THE HISTORY | OF OVER SEA | DONE OUT OF | THE ANCIENT | FRENCH INTO ENGLISH | BY WILLIAM MORRIS [printer's leaf as line-filler]; *spine*: letters, black on spine, red on slipcase: letters printed horizontally, but oriented vertically, one above the other: THE HISTORY OF OVER SEA [4 printer's leaves as line fillers]; *ornamentation*: see A-70.03.
Publication: June 1899 (colophon date); *print run*: 425 copies; *price*: 75 cents per copy.
Register of Copies Examined: LeM (base copy); SU (RC 820.825 M).
Later impressions (or edns.?) from this edn.: Mosher:
1. July 1900 (colophon date): SECOND EDITION [2nd impression (or 2nd edn.?), 1st separate edn.; *print run* and *price*: as above;
2.* Nov. 1909 (colophon date): THIRD EDITION [3rd impression (or 3rd edn.?), 1st separate edn.; *print run* and *price*: as above.

A-93.02:* History of Over Sea (Russell)

[in red] THE HISTORY OF OVER SEA | [black] DONE INTO ENGLISH BY WILLIAM MORRIS | WITH DECORATIONS BY LOUIS RHEAD | NEW YORK [red] R. H. RUSSELL | [black] PUBLISHER MCMII
Edition: [1st impression, 2nd separate edn.] The text was first issued as a KP book, bound in with *The Tale of the Emperor Coustans* (see A-73.01); and later (1896) combined with 3 other tales in *Old French Romances* (see A-79.01).
Printer: John Wilson and Son, Cambridge, USA (*American Book Design*, 143).
Collation: 4°: [1]¹⁴ 14 leaves pp. [1–4] 5–28, + inserted frontis. and 1 inserted illus. (Coupe, p. 169).
Contents: for details see Coupe, p. 169.
Technical Notes: *paper*: clay-coated (*American Book Design*, 143); *printing*: in red and black, full printer's borders on frontis., title page (Hodgkins Cat. 80, 1995, item 219), and around each illus. and the facing page; *type face*: title page in gothic, body in Bookman type; *binding*: paper-covered boards printed in red and green fleur-de-lis pattern, with 2 silk ties.
Publication: 1902; *print run* and *price*: unknown.
Register of Copies Located: Coupe; MU; IEN, NjP (notes in Hodgkins Cat. 80, 1995, item 219).

Later reprint: Coupe (p. 170) reports that 500 copies of this edn. were photographically reproduced as a keepsake in 'about 1982' by the Library Binding Company of Waco, Texas.

A-94.01: Some Hints on Pattern Designing (Golden 8°)

SOME HINTS ON PATTERN DE- | SIGNING. BY WILLIAM MORRIS.
Edition: 'Golden type octavo edition' [1st impression, 1st edn.] 1st printed in 2 instalments in *The Architect* (1881, see D-69).
Collaborators, Editors, and Illustrators: [edited by Sydney C. Cockerell, assisted by Robert Proctor].
Series: No. 3 in the 'Golden type octavo' edn. of 5 unnumbered vols. containing 6 fugitive lectures and 1 essay by Morris. For more details common to the series, see this field in A-71.02.
Colophon: Printed at the Chiswick Press with the Golden | type designed by William Morris for the Kelms- | cott Press, and finished on the fourth day of | October, 1899. Published by Longmans & Co., | 39, Paternoster Row, London.
Collation: cr. 8°: [a]² b–g⁴ 26 leaves pp. [4] 1–45 [46–8] [= 52].
Contents: pp. [1–2], blank; p. [3], title page; p. [4], blank; p. 1, head title: SOME HINTS ON PATTERN-DE- | SIGNING. A LECTURE DELIVERED | BY WILLIAM MORRIS AT THE | WORKING MEN'S COLLEGE, LON- | DON, ON DECEMBER 10, 1881 | [text begins]; pp. 2–45, text completed with colophon, see above; pp. [46–8], blank.
Technical Notes: for detail common to the series—paper, leaf size, printing, type, type area, lines-to-page, position (but not content) of shoulder notes, pagination, binding (except the letterpress), see this field in A-71.02, the entry for the 1st vol. of the set; details specific to this issue: *shoulder notes*: all rectos and versos except p. 1: Lecture III. | Some Hints | on Pattern- | Designing.; *binding letterpress*: printed front title duplicates the title page (see above).
Publication: 4 Oct. 1899 [colophon date indicates finished printing, issued 25 Oct.] (Longmans *Notes on Books*, 9/129 (30 Nov. 1899), 206); *print run*: 2,000 copies (but only 1,500 bound, the remaining 500 being bound on 30 July 1901 (Chiswick Arch.); *price*: 2s. 6d.
Register of Copies Examined: BL (2 copies: base copy: K.T.C. 8. a. 20. and Ashley Library 3698); VU (2 copies: L & E 704\M877A); SU (2 copies: 704/M87ar); LeM.

Notes: 'Composing Lecture III Some Hints on Pattern Designing by Wm. Morris. 6 1/2 half sheets demy 8° with side notes; Proof in slips with marking up into pages & corrections & alterations'; and 'Printing 2,000 copies of 6 1/2 = 7 half sheets working on 14 reams. Demy in your Handmade paper. Printing 2,100 copies of Front cover for above, 1 leaf to form side of book with blue handmade paper for same including paper for plain backs; binding in boards 1500 copies blue linen backs; (end-papers from own stock) a thicker volume this time; Postages paid on various presentation copies including packing (20-10-99)' (Chiswick Arch. (Oct. 1899, p. 545, in Ledger).

Cockerell wrote to Mrs Morris on 18 Dec. 1899 to inform her that, having done the 1st 3 vols. of the 8° series, he proposed to charge a fee of 2*gns*. for his work in editing and seeing the books through the press, those duties being extra to the ordinary work of a trustee. He also listed the names of all those receiving presentation copies: the executors, Mr Pierce of Philadelphia, Philip Webb, Lady Burne-Jones, Emery Walker and May Morris (Cockerell Papers, BL (Add.) MS 52738).

A-95.01:* Golden Wings: A Tale (*Bib.*)

[*Bibelot* wrapper title, above the compartment, top left] VOL. VI. [top right] No. 4 | [within thin-rule compartment, top left] | APRIL. [top right] MDCCCC. | [title details common to the series wrapper titles, see A-83.01 | [below the compartment, right, in red] GOLDEN WINGS: A TALE BY | WILLIAM MORRIS
Edition: [1st impression, 1st separate edn.] Originally pbd. in *The Oxford and Cambridge Magazine*, Dec. 1856 (see D-16).
Collaborators, Editors, and Illustrators: unsigned foreword [by the editor, T. B. Mosher].
Series: (as in the annual vol.) *The Bibelot* . . . , 6/4 (Apr. 1900), [103–40]. For series detail see this field in A-83.01.
Place, Publisher, and *Printer*: see full wrapper transcription in A-83.01.
Collation: 12°: [1]²⁴ 24 leaves, 12 conjunct pairs, pp. [4] [103–6] 107–38 [139–40] [6] [= 48] + the usual blue Bibelot wrapper sewn to the body at the centrefold; The separate issue of this title has not been seen. Certain details of pagination and contents have been supplied by Mr Philip Bishop, Mosher's bibliographer.
Contents: pp. [*1–4*], unpaginated ads.; pp. [103–4], headed, in 3-line black letter: The Bibelot | [text of Mosher's unsigned foreword]; p. [105], half title; p. [106], blank; p. 107, headed: Golden Wings | [text begins with 4-line epigraph from *Sir Percival*]; pp. 108–[139], text completed with fleuron as tail-piece; p. [140], blank; pp. [*1–6*], unpaginated ads.
Technical Notes: for details common to the series—paper, leaf size, printing, type area, lines-to-page, pagination, binding, and full wrapper title transcription—see this field in A-83.01; details specific to this issue: *running titles*: [all rectos and versos, aligned to the inner margin on headline] GOLDEN WINGS
Publication: Apr. 1900 [masthead date, issued 25 Mar.]; *print run* and *price*: see this field in A-83.01.
Register of Copies Located: BL (PP. 8001.ea.[19.]); Bsp.

A-95.02: Golden Wings: A Tale (Finch)

[ornamental border, 1st and last lines in red] GOLDEN WINGS | BY | WILLIAM MORRIS | London | JAMES FINCH & CO. LTD. | 33 Paternoster Row | 1905
Edition: [1st impression, 2nd separate edn., 1st English] 1st pbd. in *The Oxford and Cambridge Magazine*, Dec. 1856 (see D-16).
Series: This book is one of 4, one of which, *The Unknown Church*, contains two stories, all pbd. by James Finch in 1905, and seeming to have in common their paper, leaf size, printing (in red and black), end-papers, and binding. So, though there is no indication of a formal or named series in the books themselves, they constitute a uniform set (except for differences noted in specific entries). Besides *Golden Wings*, the titles are: *Svend and His Brethren* (A-96.03), *A Dream* (A-101.03), and *The Story of the Unknown Church* (C-16.05) which also contains 'Lindenborg Pool'.
Collation: 12° in 4s: π² A–E⁴ F² 24 leaves pp. [4] 1–43 [44] [= 48].
Contents: p. [*1*], half title; p. [*2*], blank; p. [*3*], title page; p. [*4*], blank; p. 1, headed: GOLDEN WINGS | [3-line epigraph from *Sir Percival*, in quotation marks] | [text begins with 6-line ornamental initial 'I']; pp. 2–43, text completed; p. [*44*], printer's imprint: The Riverside Press Limited | Edinburgh
Technical Notes: details common to the set: *paper*: cream 'antique' machine-wove with dandy roll laid lines, no watermark, t.e.g.; *leaf size*: 137 x 76 mm.; *printing*: in red and black, red for title on title page, publisher's name, and the 1st initial of the text; *type area*: 85 x 34 mm.; *lines-to-page*: set solid, 31 lines; *pagination*: arabic numbers centred on the direction line; *end-papers*: 1 free end and pastedown, plain white and blank, front and back; *binding*: dark red or blue soft morocco with title gilt-stamped up the spine and on the front, between gilt art nouveau head and tail-pieces; detail specific to this issue: *binding*: letter-

press: *front*: *Golden Wings,* otherwise plain and unblocked; *spine*: title upwards.
Publication: 1905; *print run* and *price*: unknown.
Register of Copies Examined: BL (base copy: 012635. a. 30.)

A-96.01*: Svend and His Brethren (*Bib.*)

[*Bibelot* wrapper title, above the compartment, top left] VOL. VI. [top right] No. 9 | [within thin-rule compartment, top left] SEPTEMBER. [top right] MDCCCC. | [title details common to the series wrapper titles, see A-83.01] | [below the compartment, right, in red] SVEND AND HIS BRETHREN | A TALE BY | WILLIAM MORRIS
Edition: [1st impression, 1st separate edn.] Like all *The Bibelot* texts this edn. appeared 1st as a separate edn. issued to subscribers and the general public under *The Bibelot* masthead. See also this field in A-83.01. As with all Morris items in *The Bibelot*, the A-List entry provides finding-list information for both the separate and the periodical versions. This tale was 1st prtd. half a century earlier in *The Oxford and Cambridge Magazine*, this one in Aug. 1856 (see D-11).
Collaborators, Editors, and Illustrators: unsigned foreword [by the editor, T. B. Mosher].
Series: (as in the annual vol.) *The Bibelot . . .*, 6/9 (Sept. 1900), [291]–[330]. For detail common to the series, see this field in A-83.01.
Place, Publisher, and *Printer*: see wrapper transcriptions in A-83.01.
Collation: 12°: [1]²⁰ 20 leaves folded and sewn through the middle: pp. [291–4] 295–328 [329–30] [= 40] + *Bibelot* wrapper sewn to the body through the centrefold. On pagination and ads. see A-83.01 The separate issue of this title has not been seen. Certain details of pagination and contents have been supplied by Mr Philip Bishop, Mosher's bibliographer.
Contents: p. [291], Mosher's unsigned foreword, headed: [in 3-line gothic] The Bibelot | [text begins]; p. [292], Mosher's foreword ends, with printer's leaf as tail-piece; p. [293], half title; p. [294], blank; p. 295, headed: SVEND AND HIS BRETHREN | [text begins]; pp. 296–[329], text completed with printer's leaf as tail-piece; p. [330], blank.
Technical Notes: for details common to the series—paper, leaf size, printing, type area, lines-to-page, pagination, binding: and wrapper title—see this field in A-83.01; details specific to this issue: *running titles*: [flush to the inner margins on the headline, all versos and rectos:] SVEND AND HIS BRETHREN
Publication: Sept. 1900 [masthead date, issued 25 Aug.]; *print run* and *price*: see *Series* field in A-83.01.

Register of Copies Located: BL (base copy: P.P. 8001.ea.[21.]); Bsp.
Later impression from this Mosher edn.:
1. 1900: [2nd impression, 1st separate edn.] combined with *Golden Wings* as the Reprints from "The Bibelot"—8. This selection is a re-formatted impression of the original Bibelot forms of both tales. This and 2 issues of the same combination of texts in the Mosher 2nd edn., done in the Brocade series in [July] 1902 and [Nov.] 1906, are described in Collections, C-10.01; *print run*: 425 copies; *price*: 75 cents.

A-96.02: Svend and His Brethren (Palmetto)

[within full border and double thin rule compartment] SVEND & HIS BRETH- | REN [2 printer's leaves as line fillers] A TALE | BY WILLIAM MORRIS | [thin rule] | [Palmetto Press mark] | [thin rule] | Printed By The Palmetto Press | Which Is In Aiken, South Caro- | lina, U.S.A., in the | Year MCMI.
Edition: [1st impression, 2nd edn., 2nd American] 1st printed in *The Oxford and Cambridge Magazine*, Aug. 1856, see D-11.
Series: 4th book issued from the Palmetto Press (according to Ransom, 374).
Colophon: This little book was printed and bound by W. L. Washburn at The Palmetto Press, Aiken, S.C., in the summer of the year MCMI, the title page being designed by Miss A. T. Colcock. Dedicated to all lovers of William Morris and his books.
Collation: small sq. 16° in 4s: [a]⁴ b–f⁴ g² 26 leaves pp. [1–8] 9–50 [51–2] [= 52].
Contents: p. [1], notice of limitation: This is No. [no. in red, longhand] of Seventy-nine copies printed on Kelmscott paper [signed longhand] W. L. Washburn; p. [2], blank; p. [3], half title; p. [4], blank; p. [5], title page; p. [6], blank; p. [7], epigraph from *EP*; p. 8, blank; p. 9, text begins; pp. 10–50, text completed; p. [51], colophon; p. [52], blank.
Technical Notes: *paper*: 'Kelmscott paper'; *leaf size*: 151 x 110 mm.; *type face*: Bradford type; *binding*: quarter holland with blue paper-covered boards, with title printed on front.
Publication: Summer, 1901 (colophon date); *print run*: 79 copies on Kelmscott paper, 2 on vellum; *price*: $2 paper, $6 vellum.
Register of Copies Examined: J-F V (base copy); MU.

A-96.03: Svend and His Brethren (Finch)

[within ornamental border, lines 1–3 and 7 in red] SVEND

| AND HIS | BRETHREN | By | WILLIAM MORRIS | London | JAMES FINCH & CO. LTD | 33 Paternoster Row | 1905

Edition: [1st impression, 3rd separate edn., 1st English] 1st pbd. in *The Oxford and Cambridge Magazine*, Aug. 1856 (see D-11).

Series: see this field in A-95.02.

Collation: 12° in 4s: π² A–F⁴ 26 leaves pp. [4] 1–47 [48] [= 52].

Contents: p. [1], half title; p. [2], blank; p. [3], title page; p. [4], blank; p. 1, dropped head: SVEND AND HIS | BRETHREN | [text begins with a 6-line ornamental initial 'A' outlined in red]; pp. 2–47, text completed; p. [48], printer's imprint: *The Riverside Press Limited | Edinburgh*

Technical Notes: see this field in A-95.02, making adjustments to titles and page nos.; details specific to this issue: *binding*: letterpress: *front*: [between art nouveau head and tail-pieces, in a gilt embossed design] SVEND | AND | HIS BRETHREN; *spine*: [upward] SVEND AND HIS BRETHREN

Publication: 1905; *print run* and *price*: unknown.

Register of Copies Examined: LeM (base copy).

A-96.04: Svend and His Brethren (Burr)

SVEND AND HIS BRETHREN. | A TALE OF THE ANCIENT DAYS BY WILLIAM MORRIS. | PRINTED AT THE HILLSIDE PRESS | ENGLEWOOD, NEW JERSEY. | M.CM.VI.

Edition: [1st impression, 4th separate edn., 3rd American] 1st printed in *The Oxford and Cambridge Magazine*, Aug. 1856 (see D-11).

Series: [The second book issued from the Hillside Press].

Colophon: Here ends the curious and moving tale of Svend and His Brethren as told by William Morris. Set up and printed from the type by Frederick M. Burr at The Hillside Press, Englewood, New Jersey. Presswork finished in the month of July, M-CM-VI. Fifty-five copies on French hand-made paper.

Collation: cr. 8° in 4s: [1–6⁴ 7²] 26 leaves pp. [4] [1–4] 5–43 [44–8] [= 52].

Contents: pp. [1–4], blank; p. [1], half title; p. [2], blank; p. [3], title page in red and black; p. [4], blank; p. 5, text begins; pp. 6–44, text completed; p. 45, colophon, see above; pp. [46–8], blank.

Technical Notes: *paper*: hand laid paper with vertical chain lines; *leaf size*: deckled edges, avg. 204 x 130 mm.; *binding*: blue paper-covered boards and spine, with printed spine label (short title only) and front label: SVEND AND HIS BRETHREN | A TALE OF THE ANCIENT DAYS | BY WILLIAM MORRIS

Publication: Sept. 1906 (see Burr's presentation note, below); *print run*: 55 copies; *price*: $2.50.

Register of Copies Examined: J-F V (base copy, see *Notes*, below); CtY; BL (X.950/33572).

Notes: Burr's undated presentation note in longhand (J-F V copy): 'To Belle. From Fred. This is the second publication from the "Hillside Press". Presswork finished in July, 1906, bound in September.'

Note from *American Book Design*: 'again in Jenson on French laid paper [? Van Gelder], this book has an unexceptionable but weak title page within panels. Burr's presswork is faulty: the Register of the red and black title at the text opening is not exact' (204).

A-97.01: Gossip about an Old House (Hill)

[in orange] GOSSIP ABOUT AN | OLD HOUSE ON THE | UPPER THAMES [printer's leaf as line filler] | [black] BY WILLIAM MORRIS | [floral device within a compartment, initialled below:] JEH | [orange]FLUSHING [fleuron] QUEENS BOROUGH | NEW YORK | [black] MDCCCCI.

Edition: [1st impression, 1st legitimate separate edn., 1st American] An earlier English edn. is a fraudulent hybrid, probably invented by Forman (see this field in E-14). The text was 1st published in *The Quest*, the magazine of the Birmingham Guild of Handicraft, Nov. 1895 (see D-579). This 1st separate edn. is legitimate, there being no Morris copyright on this title in America, and permission was granted by one of the proprietors of *The Quest*, D. B. Updike.

Colophon: The illustration used as the frontispiece here is by C. M. Gere, & was used in the Kelmscott Press edition of *News from Nowhere*. The other 2 illustrations are by E. H. New, & the initial letters were designed & engraved on wood by J. E. Hill. Reprinted from the 'Quest,' by permission of the publisher, D. B. Updike, Boston, by J. E. Hill, at Flushing, Queens Borough, New York, and finished on the twenty-third day of February, 1901.

Collation: small sq. 8° printed and gathered in 4s: [1–4]⁴ 16 leaves pp. [1–8] 9–25 [26–32] [= 32].

Contents: p. [1], half title; p. [2], limitation notice: One hundred copies of this book have been printed on Japan Vellum, of which seventy-five are for sale. This is No. [no. in longhand]; p. [3], blank; p. [4], frontis. woodcut of Kelmscott Manor House, originally used as the frontis. to *News from Nowhere*, signed with the monogram of C. M. Gere; p. [5], title page; p. [6], blank; p. [7]: FOREWORD;

p. [8], blank; p. 9, text begins; pp. 10–26, text completed; p. [27], colophon; pp. [28–32], blank.
Technical Notes: *paper*: japan vellum; *leaf size*: 163 x 126 mm.; *print*: in orange and black; *binding*: quarter vellum with green-marbled paper-covered boards, printed in green up the spine: GOSSIP ABOUT AN OLD HOUSE BY WILLIAM MORRIS
Publication: 23 Feb. 1901 (colophon date); *print run*: 100 copies on japan vellum; *price*: unknown.
Register of Copies Examined: CtY (Base copy: IP M834 895g); TxU; CaBVaU; CSt (Spec. Coll Felton PR5080. G6); BL (Ashley 3696).

A-98.01:* Churches of North France (*Bib.*)

[*Bibelot* wrapper title, above the compartment, top left] Vol. VII. [top right] No. 3 | [within thin-rule compartment, top left] MARCH. [top right] MDCCCCI. | [title details common to the series wrapper titles, see A-83.01] | [below the compartment, right, in red] THE CHURCHES OF NORTHERN FRANCE. NO. I | BY WILLIAM MORRIS
Edition: [1st impression, 1st separate edn.] This essay was 1st pbd. as 'The Churches of North France. No. 1.— Shadows of Amiens' in *The Oxford and Cambridge Magazine*, Feb. 1856 (see D-3). Like all the *Bibelot* texts, this edn. appeared 1st as a separate edn. issued to subscribers and the general public under *The Bibelot* masthead, with a title-page wrapper; it then appeared in Jan. of the following year in a combined annual vol. titled *The Bibelot*, vol. VII. As with all Morris items under *The Bibelot* masthead, this A-List entry provides finding-list information for both the separate and the periodical versions (see also the *Series* field, below and in A-83.01). Mosher rptd. this text in the Reprints from "The Bibelot" series, with Morris's essays on '"Death the Avenger" and "Death the Friend"' though these never appeared in *The Bibelot* (see C-12).
Collaborators, Editors, and Illustrators: unsigned foreword [by the editor, T. B. Mosher].
Series: *The Bibelot* . . ., 7/3 (Mar. 1901), 83–117. For detail common to this series, see this field in A-83.01.
Place, Publisher, and *Printer*: see wrapper transcriptions in A-83.01.
Collation: 12°: [1]²² 22 leaves pp. [2] [79–82] 83–116 [117–18] [2] [= 44] + the usual light blue *Bibelot* paper wrapper sewn to the body through the centrefold; on pagination and ads. see *Series* field in 83.01. After this issue the essay was incorporated into the annual vol. and rptd. in the Reprints from "The Bibelot" series. The separate issue of this title has not been seen. Certain details of pagination and contents have been supplied by Mr Philip Bishop, Mosher's bibliographer.
Contents: pp. [1–2], ads; pp. [79–80], headed: [in 3-line gothic] The Bibelot | [text of Mosher's unsigned foreword (mainly composed of quotations from Mackail, i. 96, 97)]; p. [81], half title; p. [82], page-long epigraph from Mackail's *Life*; p. 83, headed: [top, aligned left] THE CHURCHES OF NORTH | FRANCE. | I. | SHADOWS OF AMIENS. | [text begins]; pp. 84–[117], text completed with fleuron as tail-piece; p. [118], blank; pp. [1–2], ads.
Technical Notes: for detail common to the *Bibelot* separates—paper, leaf size, printing, type area, pagination, binding, and wrapper title—see this field in A-83.01; specific to this issue: *running heads*: [all rectos and versos] THE CHURCHES OF NORTH FRANCE
Publication: Mar. 1901 [masthead date, issued 25 Feb.]; *print run* and *price*: see A-83.01.
Register of Copies Located: Bsp; BL (P.P. 8001. ia. 25., this is bound in the annual collected volume for 1891, issued in Jan., 1892).
Later impression of this Mosher edn:
1.* Later in 1901, as one of his Reprints from 'The Bibelot' series, Mosher combined this essay with a 2nd and 3rd, neither of which ever appeared in *The Bibelot*. They concern Morris's comments on a pair of 19th-century woodcuts by Alfred Rethel: 'Death the Avenger' and 'Death the Friend'. For details of this selection, see C-12.

A-99.01: Pilgrims of Hope (Mosher)

THE | PILGRIMS OF HOPE | A POEM IN XIII BOOKS | BY | WILLIAM MORRIS | AUTHOR OF THE EARTHLY PARADISE | [Mosher's Chiswick Press Aldine mark, Bishop No. 2] | PORTLAND MAINE | THOMAS B. MOSHER | MDCCCCI
Edition: [1st impression, 1st legitimate separate edn., 1st American] An earlier separate edn., used by Mosher as the copy text for this edn., was a piracy created by H. Buxton Forman, who claimed in his Preface an authorisation by Morris (unverifiable, see the E-List entry for this title, E-9). But this Mosher edn. required no authorisation, there being no copyright on this title registered in the US.
Collaborators, Editors, and Illustrators: an unsigned prefatory note [by T. B. Mosher, editor and publisher], quotes extensively from Forman's introduction to his edn. and his description of that in HBF.
Series: Reprints of Privately Printed Books—8. This is the only appearance of Morris in this series, in which the main

distinguishing characteristic is the variety of sizes, design, type, bindings, print runs and prices.

Collation: 4°: [1–8]⁴ 32 leaves pp. [i–vii] viii [1–3] 4–53 [54–6] [= 64].

Contents: p. [i], half title; p. [ii], limitation notice: 400 copies of this book have | been printed on Van Gelder | handmade paper and the type distributed.; p. [iii], title page; p. [iv], blank; p. [v], Contents; p. [vi], blank; pp. [vii]–viii, unsigned Preface, [by T. B. Mosher]; p. [1], 2nd half title; p. [2], blank; pp. [3]–53, text completed with explicit: THE END.; p. [54], printer's imprint: [bottom right, aligned to inner margin] *PRINTED BY* | *SMITH & SALE* | *PORTLAND* | *MAINE*; pp. [55–6], blank.

Technical Notes: *paper*: Van Gelder hand-laid; *leaf size*: deckled edges, avg. 222 x 172 mm.; *printing*: type area: 142 x 102 mm.; *lines-to-page*: 34 lines, counting blanks between verse paragraphs; *end-papers*: same paper as the body: 5 free ends and paste-down in front, 3 free ends and paste-down in back, all plain white and blank; *binding*: paper copies: light blue paper-covered boards with parchment spine, green silk page marker, and printed paper *spine label*: [thick-thin rule] | THE | PIL- | GRIMS | OF | HOPE | [thin rule] | 1901 | [thin-thick rule]; 12 japan vellum copies have japan vellum wrapper with the title printed on the front.

Publication: 1901; *print run*: 400 copies on Van Gelder hand-made paper, + 50 copies, numbered, on japan vellum (see Walsdorf, p. 187 and Bishop, p. 238); 4 on vellum folded but unbound, signed by the publisher (Hatch, item 195); *prices*: Bishop says books in this series were priced from $1.00–$5.00 per ordinary copy, $2.00–$20 for the japan vellum copies.

Register of Copies Examined: CSfU (3 copies: base copy: PR 5078 P35); Bsp.

A-99.02: Pilgrims of Hope (+ Chants for Socialists LPL)

THE PILGRIMS OF HOPE | AND | CHANTS FOR SOCIALISTS | BY | WILLIAM MORRIS | LONGMANS, GREEN & COMPANY | 39 PATERNOSTER ROW, LONDON | FOURTH AVENUE & 30TH STREET, NEW YORK | BOMBAY, CALCUTTA, AND MADRAS | 1915 | All rights reserved

Edition: Pocket Edition. This is a reference entry. For details of this pbn., see the main entry for *The Pilgrims of Hope and Chants for Socialists* in Collections, C-33.

Publication: 1915 [issued 11 Sept.] (Longmans Arch.).

Register of Copies Examined: see this field in C-33.

A-100.01: The Doom of King Acrisius (Russell)

[within a multiple thin-rule rectilinear border with leaves within at each corner, swash caps, title and publisher's name in red] THE DOOM OF KING | ACRISIUS BY [3 printer's leaves] | WILLIAM MORRIS | ILLUSTRATED WITH | PICTURES BY SIR ED- | WARD BURNE-JONES | [publisher's device of rose with centred RHR monogram, 1st R reversed] NEW YORK R • H • RUSSELL | PUBLISHER MCMII

Edition: [1st impression, 1st separate edn.] Printed and bound as the 1st of 2 vols. of Morris texts not previously pbd. with their Burne-Jones illus. See also the same publisher's *Pygmalion and the Image* (1903, A-107.01).

Collaborators, Editors, and Illustrators: illus. with 12 large and 4 small pictures by Sir Edward Burne-Jones reproduced in black and white, introduction by Fitzroy Carrington.

Series: This tale is the 1st of 2 intended to make available the only 'two series [of pictures to illustrate stories in the *EP*] which are in any way complete in themselves, and which are available for reproduction, namely, those for "Pygmalion and the Image" and those for the story of Perseus entitled "The Doom of King Acrisius" in "The Earthly Paradise",' (editorial note). These were thought to be the only stories and pictures that Morris and Burne-Jones completed in their abortive project to produce a fully illustrated edn. of *EP*. The editorial statement seems to be made in ignorance of the illus. for 'Cupid and Psyche' (see Carrington's introduction, p. x, and A-137.01). The illus. are here reproduced in half-tone plates from photographs made by Frederick Hollyer of the Burne-Jones pictures. The pictures originated in the 2 Perseus story projects of Burne-Jones (1) for the *Earthly Paradise* illus. and (2) for the interior decoration of Arthur Balfour's drawing room in Carleton Gardens.

Printer: unknown, possibly John Wilson and Son, Cambridge, Mass., previously used by Russell.

Collation: small 4°: [1⁴ (1₁ + 1) 2⁴ (2₂ +1) (2₃ +1) 3–7⁴ (7₁ +1) (7₂ +1) (7₄ +1) 8⁴ (8₂ +1) (8₃ +1) 9⁴ (9₁ +1) (9₃ +1) 10⁴ (10₁ +1) (10₂ +1) 11–13⁴] 52 leaves pp. [i–viii] ix--xvi [mis-numbered, 2 pages omitted from count, should be [i]–x and xi–xviii [xix–xx] 1–82 [83–4] [= 104] + 12 inserted plates indicated here in the formula but not included in the book's pagination. They are described in their appropriate places under *Contents*.

Contents: p. [i] blank but for a photo-reproduction of a drawing of Morris pasted on an integral leaf and labelled:

WILLIAM MORRIS | From a drawing by C. Rowe; p [ii], blank; p. [iii], half title, top left; p. [iv], blank; inserted frontis., The Garden of the Hesperides, facing p. [v], recto blank; p. [v], title page; p. [vi], copyright notice: *Copyright, 1902, by Robert Howard Russell*; p. [vii], LIST OF ILLUSTRATIONS | BY SIR EDWARD BURNE-JONES, BART. [list of 12 inserted plates; 5 smaller photo-reproductions not listed [pasted on pp. [i] [ix] xiii xv, xvii; p. [viii], blank; p. [ix] illus. of 'Perseus and the Graiæ' pasted on an integral leaf with a Latin superscription; p. x, blank; p. xi (mis-numbered ix), text of unheaded introduction commences with a 15-line drop initial 'I'; p. xii (mis-numbered x), text continues; p. xiii (mis-numbered [xi], text continues with photo-reproduction of Burne-Jones painting of Perseus about to slay Medusa, pasted in space left blank in the type area, on an integral leaf; p. xiv (mis-numbered xii), text continues; p. xv, (mis-numbered xiii) text continues with illus. of Perseus fleeing from the Gorgons' pasted on an integral leaf; p. xvi (mis-numbered xiv), text continues; p. xvii (mis-numbered xv) text continues with pasted-in reproduction of Burne-Jones painting of Pegasus and Chrysador springing from the headless Medusa's body; p. xviii (mis-numbered xvi) Introduction ends, signed: [below right] FITZROY CARRINGTON. | MAMARONECK, NEW YORK. | [and dated] FEBRUARY, 1902; p. [xix], epigraph from 'The Idle Singer', beginning with a 9-line drop illuminated initial 'D'; p. [xx], blank; inserted illus. facing p. 1, reproduction of Burne-Jones' 'Danae'; pp. 1–2, text of *Acrisius* begins; inserted illus. facing p. 2 'The Building of the Brazen Tower'; pp. 3–29, text continues; inserted illus. facing p. 30 'The Call of Perseus', pp. 30-2, text continues; facing p. 32, inserted illus. 'Perseus and the Sea Maidens', pp. 33–6, text continues; inserted to face p. 36, illus. 'The Graiæ'; pp. 37–40, text continues; illus. inserted to face p. 40, 'Perseus and Medusa'; pp. 41–2, text continues; illus. inserted to face p. 43, 'The Escape with Medusa's Head', pp. 43–6, text continues; inserted illus. to face p. 46, 'Atlas Turned to Stone', pp. 47–50, text continues; inserted illus. to face p. 50, 'Andromeda Chained to the Rock'; pp. 51-4, text continues; illus. inserted to face p. 54 'The Killing of the Monster'; pp. 55–6, text continues; inserted illus. to face p. 56, 'Perseus Showing the Head to Andromeda'; pp. 57–82, text completed; pp. [83–4], blank.

Technical Notes: *paper*: white machine-moulded paper with false deckled edges; *leaf size*: lightly trimmed, avg. 215 x 170 mm.; *printing*: in red and black, red only on the title page; *type area*: 157 x 120 mm.; *lines-to-page*: 32 lines set solid; *pagination*: at the inner margin on the direction line; *endpapers*: one free end and paste-down, light tan and blank, front and back; *binding*: white buckram cloth-covered boards with gilt-stamped ornaments and lettering; *front*: repeats in a larger version the title page border and title; *back*: plain except the publisher's monogram lower right; *spine*: double thin rule, top and bottom: THE | DOOM | OF | KING | ACRISIUS | [publisher's monogram of 2 Rs with 'H' in the middle, the 1st R reversed and connected to the 2nd letter]; *ornamentation*: large drop illuminated initials, from 9–15 lines, on pp. xi, 1, 14, 24, 43, 62, and 71.

Publication: 1902 (copyright date); *print run* and *price*: unknown.

Register of Copies Examined: LeM (base copy); BGR; CSt (Spec Coll Gunst NC975.B96.M67).

A-101.01:* A Dream (*Bib.*)

[*Bibelot* wrapper title, top left, above compartment] VOL. VIII. [top right] No. 7 | [within thin-rule top compartment, left] *JULY.* [top right] *MDCCCCII.* | [within main compartment: detail common to all wrapper titles in this series, see A-83.01] | [below compartment, right, in red] A DREAM | BY WILLIAM MORRIS

Edition: [1st impression, 1st separate edn.] 1st pbd. in *The Oxford and Cambridge Magazine* (1856, see D-4). On Mosher's Bibelot pbn. of this title, and its appearance here rather than in the D-List, Morris in Periodicals, see the *Series* and *Notes* fields in A-83.01.

Collaborators, Editors, and Illustrators: untitled and unsigned introductory note [by the editor, T. B. Mosher], where he explicitly accepts the authority of J. W. Mackail over that of H. B. Forman as to what Morris contributed to *The Oxford and Cambridge Magazine*.

Series: The Bibelot..., 8/7 (July 1902). For detail common to this series, see this field in A-83.01.

Place, Publisher, and *Printer*: see wrapper transcriptions in A-83.01.

Collation: 12°: [1]²² 22 leaves, 11 conjunct pairs [2] [227–32] 233–62 [263–4] [4] [= 44] + the usual light blue *Bibelot* wrapper sewn to the body through the centrefold; on pagination and ads. see this field in A-83.01. The separate issue of this title has not been seen. Certain details of pagination and contents have been supplied by Mr Philip Bishop, Mosher's bibliographer.

Contents: pp. [2], ads; pp. [227–9], headed: [in 4-line gothic] The Bibelot | [Mosher's unsigned foreword, consisting mainly of quotations from Mackail, i. 96, 97]; p. [230], blank; p. [231], half title; p. [232], blank; p. 233, text begins; pp. 234–[63], text completed with printer's leaf as

Original and Posthumous Editions

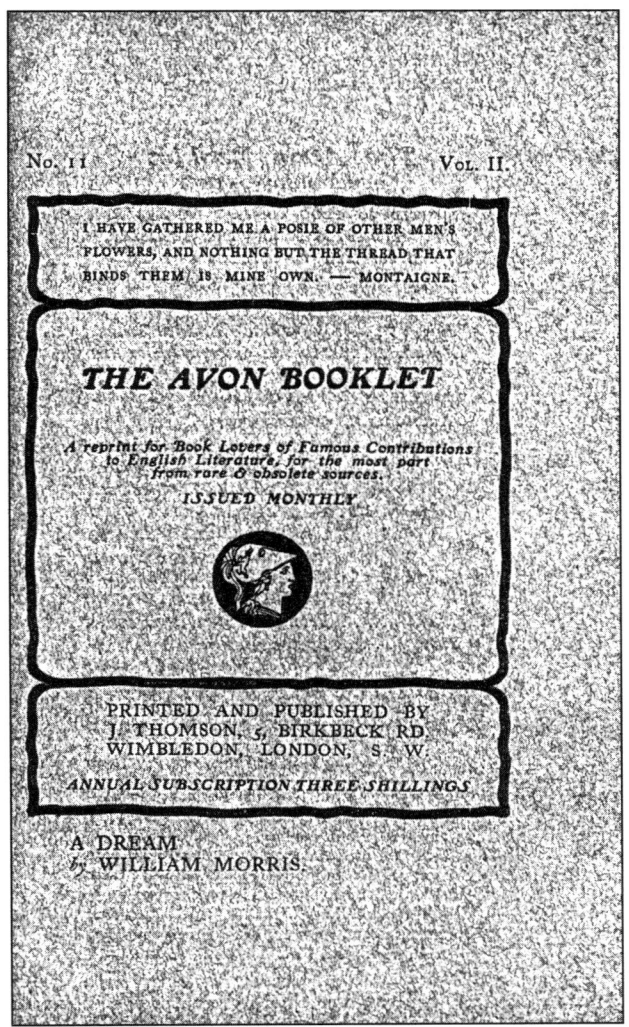

Figure 82. A-101.02: *A Dream* (Avon edn.) wrapper title

tail-piece; p. [264], blank; pp. [4], ads.
Technical Notes: for detail common to *The Bibelot* separates—paper, leaf size, printing, type area, pagination, binding, and wrapper title—see this field in A-83.01.
Publication: July 1902 [masthead date, issued 25 June]; *print run*: 5,000 copies printed, 4,000 for subscribers and retail sales, 1,000 for sets; *price*: 5 cents per copy or 75 cents for a year's subscription.
Register of Copies Examined: Bsp (base copy); BL (P.P. 8001. ea. [31.])

A-101.02: A Dream (Avon)

[Avon wrapper title with 3-part (one above the other) thick-rule compartment; above the compartment, left] No. 11 [right] Vol. II. | [within top compartment, 3-line epigraph signed below right:]—MONTAIGNE. | [2nd compartment, swash caps] THE AVON BOOKLET | *A reprint for Book Lovers of Famous Contributions | to English Literature, for the most part | from rare and obsolete sources.* | ISSUED MONTHLY | [medallion head as press mark] | [bottom compartment] PRINTED AND PUBLISHED BY | J. THOMSON, 5, BIRKBECK RD. | WIMBLEDON, LONDON, S. W. | [swash caps] *ANNUAL SUBSCRIPTION THREE SHILLINGS* | [below compartment] A DREAM | *by* WILLIAM MORRIS.
Edition: [1st impression, 2nd separate edn., 1st English] 1st pbd. in *The Oxford and Cambridge Magazine* (1856, see D-4).
Series: vol. 2, No. 11 (May 1904) of The Avon Booklet. 'Issued Monthly'. Like Mosher's *Bibelot* pbns., this pamphlet was separately issued 1st but paginated consecutively with others for later collection in annual vols. called *The Avon Booklet*.
Printer: Printed at the private press of the publisher, and supplied to subscribers only.
Collation: small 8°: [1]^{16} 16 leaves, pp. [107–10] 111–38 [= 32] + Avon paper wrapper sewn to the body through the centre fold.
Contents: pp. [107–8], headed: [top, flush left] THE | AVON | BOOKLET | [unsigned foreword by J. Thomson, text begins with 4-line ornamental initial 'O']; p. [109], half title: [swash caps] A DREAM | [bottom left, epigraph, 5 lines of verse, unsigned]; p. [110], 5 stanzas of 8 lines signed A. C. Swinburne, from his tribute to Morris; p. 111, headed: A DREAM. | [text begins]; pp. 112–38, text completed with printer's flower as tail-piece.
Technical Notes: *paper*: plain white machine-moulded, with dandy roll laid lines, chain lines vertical; *leaf size*: 175 x 115 mm.; *printing*: type area: 98 x 61 mm.; *lines-to-page*: set solid, 28 lines; prtd. in red and black only on the wrapper title; *running heads*: [all rectos and versos, set adjacent to the inner margins] A DREAM; *pagination*: arabic numbers centred on the direction line; *binding*: sewn into a light-blue laid-paper wrapper; *letterpress*: p. [1], wrapper title, as above; wrapper pp. [2–4], ads for Thomson's pbns.
Publication: May 1904 (masthead date); *print run*: the verso of the wrapper title page says 'limited to 1200' copies, but an Avon ad of the same period (both 1903), *The Story of the Avon Booklet*, says 'limited to 1000 copies'; *price*: 'supplied to subscribers only'; 'subscription three shillings'.
Register of Copies Examined: BL (base copy: 012208. f. 34 | 8.); ABCL.

A-101.03: A Dream (Finch)

[within vine border, 1st and 5th lines in red] A DREAM | By | WILLIAM MORRIS | London | JAMES FINCH & CO. LTD. | 33 Paternoster Row | 1905
Edition: [1st impression, 3rd separate edn., 2nd English] 1st pbd. in *The Oxford and Cambridge Magazine* (1856, see D-4).
Series: see this field in A-95.02.
Collation: 16° in 4s: [A]⁴ B–F⁴ 24 leaves pp. [4] 1–42 [43–4] [= 48].
Contents: p. [1], half title; p. [2], blank; p. [3], title page; p. [4], blank; p. 1, dropped head: A DREAM | [text begins with a white 6-line ornamental initial 'I' on red background]; pp. 2–42, text completed; p. [43], printer's imprint: *The Riverside Press Limited | Edinburgh*; p. [44], blank.
Technical Notes: for detail common to the series, see A-95.02; *leaf size*: trimmed, 136 x 76 mm.; *type area*: 85 x 34 mm.; *lines-to-page*: 31 lines set solid, not including direction or headlines; *end-papers*: 1 free end and paste-down, plain white and blank, front and back; *binding*: smooth dark red full calf; *binding letterpress*: title gilt-stamped in swash caps on front, no ornaments except the entire binding has a single compartment formed by a black thin rule around the edge of the front, back, and spine.
Publication: 1905; *print run* and *price*: unknown.
Register of Copies Examined: VU (base copy: BX 821.85D. f).

101.04:*A Dream (Northend)

[half title] A Dream, Being a Romance | By William Morris | Contributed to the *Oxford and Cambridge Magazine*, 1856
Edition: [1st impression, 4th separate edn.] (details of this book are from Coupe, pp. 27–9)
Colophon: Here ends A Dream, written by William Morris, with a frontispiece and ornaments designed by William F. Northend. Printed by the same at the School of Art Press, Sheffield, and finished this 14th day of March 1908.
Collation: pp. [i–vi] 1–49 [50].
Contents: p. [i], limitation statement: This edition is limited to twenty copies of which this is number [number entered in longhand]; p. [ii], blank; p. [iii], half title; p. iv, blank; p. [p. [v], blank iv], frontispiece; pp. 1–46, text completed; p. 47, colophon; pp. 48–50, blank.
Technical Notes: *paper*: hand-made, with deckled edges; *leaf size*: 150 x 115 mm.; *end papers*: 1 free end and paste-down, front and back, plain white and blank; *binding*: quarter holland with blue paper-covered boards, title printed on the front above a design of grapes and vines; *ornamentation*: 'a marginal floral ornament adorns almost every double page of the text, and each paragraph begins with a large decorated capital' (Coupe, p. 29); text ends with tail-piece.
Publication: 14 March 1908 (colophon date); *print run*: 20 numbered copies; *price*: not known.
Register of Copies Located: CSmH (copy No. 11 inscribed by Northend to Edwina Curwen) (Coupe, p. 29).

A-102.01: Sir Galahad (Elston)

[half title] Sir Galahad, A Christmas Mystery, By William Morris
Edition: [1st legitimate separate edn., 1st American] An earlier edn. is the Wise-Forman forgery (see E-1). Text 1st pbd. in *The Defence of Guenevere and Other Poems* (1858, see A-2.01). Some of these details are from Coupe (pp. 54–6)
Collaborators, Editors, and Illustrators: 4 full borders, ornaments and 2 illus. by H. M. O'Kane, i.e. Mrs Clarke Conwell.
Colophon: [1st and last lines in red] Here endeth this book, | Sir Galahad, a Christmas Mystery, by William Morris. | One hundred and eighty copies, with decorations by H. M. | O'Kane, have been printed by me, Clarke Conwell, at the | Elston Press in New Rochelle, New York, and | are to be sold thereat. Finished this | Tuesday the second day of | December, | MDCCCCII.
Collation: large folio: [1–7]² 14 leaves, 7 conjunct pairs, pp. [1–28] [= 28] [no pagination].
Contents: p. [1], half title; p. [2], copyright notice; p. [3], 2nd half title; p. [4], engraved title with full border in red and black (large caps in red), complementary to that on p. 5; p. [5], 1st line of text, engraved with large caps in red with full border; p. [6], text continues; p. [7], 1st illus. with full border: 'A damozel' farewells her knight; pp. [8-22], text continues; p. [23], full border with illus.: 'Galahad, rise and be armed'; pp. [24-5], text concluded; p. [26], blank; p. [27], colophon; p. [28], blank.
Technical Notes: *paper*: cream-white American hand-made, no watermark; *leaf size*: untrimmed deckled edges, avg. 320 x 240 mm.; no pagination; *printing*: Gothic type in black and red; *binding*: quarter holland with blue paper-covered boards; *spine*: printed paper label: [in gothic, horizontally oriented letters printed down the spine] Sir Galahad, A Christmas Mystery, by William Morris; *ornamentation*: an engraved title and 4 full borders, with many ornamental initials in red.

Original and Posthumous Editions

Publication: 2 Dec. 1902 (colophon date); *print run*: 180 copies; *price*: $10.00 (see 'Checklist of Elston Press Books', in *Notes on the Elston Press* (Wilmington: Douglas M. Harris, Publisher, 1997), item 17).
Register of Copies Examined: base copy: BL (Cup. 510); BGR; NjP; CSmH.

A-102.02: Sir Galahad (Blue Sky)

[neo-gothic caps, with floral rules head and foot, 1st, 2nd, and 6th lines in red] SIR | GALAHAD | A CHRIST- | MAS MYSTERY | WILLIAM | MORRIS | [circular monogram 'BS', centred within a floral border].
Edition: [1st impression, 2nd edn., 2nd American] An earlier edn. is a Wise-Forman forgery, see E-1. The text was 1st pbd. in *The Defence of Guenevere and Other Poems* (see A-2.01). 25 copies of an FP variant are noted in the *Colophon* (below) and described under *Technical Notes*.
Collaborators, Editors, and Illustrators: frontis. from a painting by Walter H. Hinton.
Colophon: Here endeth the poem Sir | Galahad, a Christmas Mys- | tery by William Morris. | ¶ This book was designed by | Thomas Wood Stevens and let- | tered under his direction. The | frontispiece is from a painting by | Walter H. Hinton. Of this edition | there have been printed and pub- | lished by the Blue Sky Press in | Chicago, five hundred copies on | paper and twenty-five copies on | Japan vellum, this being no . . . [no. added in longhand].
Collation: long 8° in 4s: [1–8]⁴ 32 leaves pp. [1–64] [= 64] no pagination, french fold, i.e. printed on only one side of the sheet so printed pages always face each other with blanks between printed openings.
Contents: pp. [1–8], blank; p. [9], half title; pp. [10–11], blank; p. [12], frontis. detail from a painting of a lady arming Galahad; p. [13], title page; pp. [14-15], blank; pp. [16], copyright notice, bottom, flush right: Copyright 1904 | The Blue Sky Press | Chicago; p. [17], text begins; pp. [18–57], text completed; pp. [58–9], blank; p. [60], colophon; pp. [61–4], blank.
Technical Notes: *paper*: hand-made with vertical chain lines and deckled edges; *watermark*: crown placed below the centrefold; 25 copies on Japan vellum, otherwise identical with the paper copies; *leaf size*: 209 x 126 mm.; *printing*: leaves prtd. on one side only, in red and black, red on the title page and running titles; *headlines*: [in red, all versos, in neo-gothic caps] SIR GALAHAD | [all rectos] A Christmas Mystery; *end-papers*: 1 free end and paste-down of dark green paper printed with a black floral border extending over the entire opening of the free end and its facing paste-down, front and back; *binding*: dark green quarter holland with blue paper-covered boards, plain on the back, black floral border printed on the front, with short title gilt-stamped in gothic on the front.
Publication: 1904 (copyright date); *print run*: 500 paper copies, 25 on japan vellum, numbered; *price*: paper $5.00, vellum price unknown.
Register of Copies Examined: CSt (base copy: Gunst Z 239. B66M87); BL (Cup. 510. sbe. 1.); TxU.

A-102.03:* Sir Galahad (Burr)

Sir Galahad. A Christmas Mystery | By William Morris | Hillside Press | Englewood, New Jersey | MCMXV
Edition: [3rd edn., 3rd American] text 1st published in *The Defence of Guenevere and Other Poems* (see A-2.01). Details provided here are from Walsdorf and Coupe.
Collaborators, Editors, and Illustrators: front cover illus. by an unnamed artist
Colophon: Here ends *Sir Galahad, A Christmas Mystery*, a poem by William Morris. Set up and printed from the type by Frederic M. Burr at the Hillside Press, Englewood, New Jersey. Press work finished in December, MCMXV. One hundred and fifty copies on Van Gelder Zonen handmade paper.
Collation: sewn, [1]¹⁸ 18 leaves, pp. [1–36] (no pagination) + a dark green wrapper
Contents: p. [1], half title; p. [2], blank; p. [3], title page, with title, floral ornament, and Hillside Press monogram in red; p. [4], blank; pp. [5–35] text of the poem completed (printed only on rectos); p. [36], colophon.
Technical Notes: *leaf size*: 189 x 115 mm.; *printing*: in red and black, but only on rectos, versos blank; *wrapper*: thick dark green paper title with a photograph of a knight and his horse glued on the front within a triple thin-rule compartment; *running heads*, all rectos and versos, the title in red.
Publication: Dec. 1915 (colophon date); *print run*: 150 copies (Walsdorf, p. 235, Coupe, pp. 61–2); *price*: $2.50.
Register of Copies Located: CtY (Ip M854 1, from NUC, vol. 396, p. 156).

A-103.01:* In Praise of My Lady (Morris Press)

IN PRAISE OF MY LADY BY WILLIAM MORRIS
Edition: [1st impression, 1st separate edn.] text 1st pbd. in *The Defence of Guenevere and Other Poems* (1858, see A-2.01).
Collaborators, Editors, and Illustrators: the title page and border were designed by William Edward Davidson.
Place: St. Charles, Illinois.

Publisher: William Edward Davidson.
Printer: The Morris Press, St. Charles, Illinois.
Technical Notes: limitation statement of NN copy: 'No. 221 of 400 copies printed on outside of doubled leaves uncut at the top. The title page and border were designed by William Edward Davidson'; *print run*: 400 copies; *type face*: Jenson; *leaf size*: 120 mm. (quoted in *NUC*, cccxcvi. 145).
Publication: 1902.
Register of Copies Located: NN; CLSU (from NUC, vol. 396, p. 145).
Notes: Davidson's border, 'is repeated on each page', according to Susan Otis Thompson, and 'the cover has a woodcut title and ornament in the manner of Blue Sky books. The title page and borders have the same flower printed in green and orange (the type is black). The title is on a scroll, with a flower impinging on the words "By William Morris" asymmetrically placed . . .. The printer's device at the end contains a smoking lamp and the motto: "Love and Art are Life"' (*American Book Design*, 105).

A-104.01: Communism (Fabian Society)

[wrapper title] Fabian Tract No. 113. | [thin rule] | **COMMUNISM** | A LECTURE BY | WILLIAM MORRIS. | PUBLISHED AND SOLD BY | THE FABIAN SOCIETY. | **PRICE ONE PENNY.** | LONDON: | THE FABIAN SOCIETY, 3 CLEMENTS INN, STRAND, W.C. | MARCH 1903.
Edition: [1st impression, 1st edn.]
Collaborators, Editors, and Illustrators: edited and introduced by George Bernard Shaw, who initials the 'Editor's Note', 'G. B. S.'
Collation: s. sh. demy 8°: [1]⁸ 8 leaves pp. [1–3] 4–15 [16] [= 16] self-wrappered.
Contents: p. [1], title page; p. [2], blank; p. [3], headed: EDITOR'S NOTE. | [text begins]; pp. 4–5, text completed: [initialled by G. B. Shaw] G. B. S.; p. 6, facsimile from the MS, oriented vertically; p. 7, dropped head: COMMUNISM. | [text begins]; pp. 8–15, text completed; p. [16], ad for Fabian pbns. | [thin rule] | [imprint] Printed by G. Standring, 7 Finsbury St., London, E.C., and published by the Fabian Society, | 3 Clement's Inn, Strand, London, W.C.
Technical Notes: *paper*: plain white machine-made; *leaf size*: cut flush, 215 x 137 mm.; *printing*: *lines-to-page*: set solid, 50 lines; *type area*: 170 x 102 mm.; *pagination*: arabic numbers centred on the headlines.
Publication: Mar. 1903; *print run*: unknown; *price*: 1d.
Register of Copies Examined: LeM (base copy); BL (2 copies: Cup. 502. f. 11. (48.) and 113.7.)

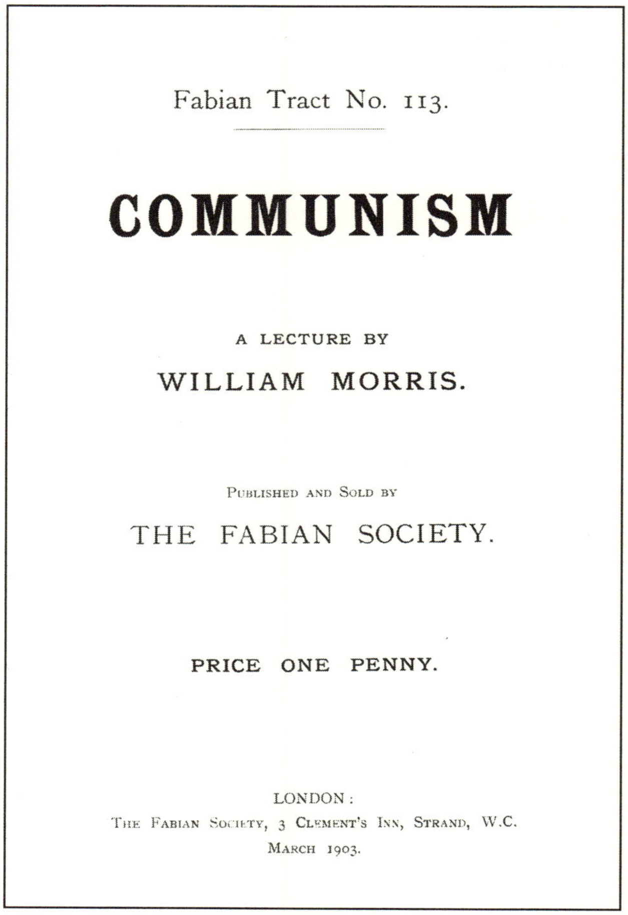

Figure 83. A-104.01: *Communism* (Fabian Tract) wrapper title

Later issues and impressions of this edn.:
1. 1907: Fabian Tract No. 113 [2nd impression, 1st edn.]; *print run*: unknown; *price*: 1d.
2. 1923: Fabian Tract No. 113 [3rd impression, 1st edn.]; *print run*: unknown; *price*: 1d.
3. Jan. 1968: *The Socialist Leader*, 11 (18 Jan. 1968); *print run* and *price*: not known.

A-105.01: Printing, An Essay (Goudy)

[1st line in 3-line type and, with the fleuron, in red] PRINTING | AN ESSAY BY WILLIAM MORRIS & EMERY | WALKER. FROM 'ARTS AND CRAFTS ESSAYS | BY MEMBERS OF THE ARTS AND CRAFTS | EXHIBITION SOCIETY' | [fleuron] | PARK RIDGE | THE VILLAGE PRESS | M CM III
Edition: [1st impression, 1st separate edn.] A lecture originally written by Emery Walker and 1st delivered under the title 'Printing' at the 1st exhibition of the Arts and Crafts Exhibition Society in 1888, it was later almost completely

rewritten by Morris for pbn. in the collection *Arts and Crafts Essays by Members of the Arts and Crafts Exhibition Society*, edited by Morris in 1893 (see B-15).
Collaborators, Editors, and Illustrators: Illustrations by W. J. Enright and B. J. O. Nordfeldt. See also *Colophon*, below.
Colophon: Here ends 'Printing,' an essay by William Morris | and Emery Walker, reprinted from 'Arts and Crafts Essays | by Members of the Arts and Crafts Exhibition | Society.' Designed, printed in the Village Type, and | bound by Fred. W. Goudy and Will H. Ransom at the | Village Press, Park Ridge, Illinois, in the month of | August, 1903. [fleuron] Of 231 copies (200 for sale), this is | number [no. hand written in arabic] Published & for sale by the Village Press. | [printer's mark]
Collation: fcap 4°: [a1] b–c⁴ 9 leaves [title leaf tipped in] pp. [1–3] 4–16 [17–18] [= 18].
Contents: p. [1], title page, title only in red 3-line caps; p. [2], blank; p. [3], text begins with an ornamental 11-line drop initial 'P', below repeat of title in 3-line type in red; pp. 4–16, text completed with repeat of printer's flower from the title page, this time as tail-piece in black; p. [17], colophon, see above; p. [18], blank.
Technical Notes: *paper*: cream-white Alton Mill hand-made paper with deckled edges; *watermark*: centred at bottom of sheet: 'W. King Alton Mill'; no chain or wire lines; *leaf size*: 230 x 177 mm.; *printing*: *type face*: 1st use of Goudy's Village Type; printed in red and black; *end-papers*: front 3 and back 2 free ends and paste-down, plain white and blank; *binding*: beige cloth with title printed in 3-line roman caps in red on front upper left.
Publication: Aug. 1903 [colophon date, issued after 16 Sept. when, Will Ransom's Diary says, he and the Goudys were still binding the books] (quoted in Cary, 41); *print run*: 231 copies, 200 for sale; *price*: $3.00 (see Ransom, 437).
Register of Copies Examined: CU-B (base copy: TYP AA4 A3 M65 1903); CSmH.
Notes: Frederic W. Goudy said: 'The first book [from the Village Press], Printing, was intended as a tribute and acknowledgment of obligation to William Morris' (quoted in Cary, 31). This Goudy edn. won a prize at the Louisiana Purchase Exposition of 1904 (see Cary, 62, Ransom, 437).

A-106.01: The Saga of Hen Thorir (Goetting)

[border in red, black, and gold, consisting of vine and ancient weapons around a thick-thin rule compartment, with letterpress centred within in neo-gothic type] The Saga Of | Hen Thorir | Done into English | Out of The Icelandic. | by | William Morris | and | Eíríkr Magnusson. | With Decorations by | A. E. Goetting. | Byway Press. | Cincinnati, Ohio.
Edition: [1st impression, 1st separate edn.] 1st pbd. in The Saga Library, vol. I (1891, see A-52.01).
Colophon: [in neo-gothic type, aligned as an upturned isosceles triangle] HERE ENDETH THIS EDIT- | ION OF THE SAGA OF | HEN THORIR PRINT- | ED AT THE BYWAY | PRESS IN THE | MONTH OF SEP- | TEMBER, | 1903.
Collation: sq. 12° printed and gathered in 4s: [1–12]⁴ 48 leaves pp. [8] [1] 2–87 [88] [= 96].
Contents: pp. [1–6], blank; p. [7], title page; p. [8], statement of limitation: [in neo-gothic] Edition limited to 350 copies, printed from type on M.B.M. French hand made paper, of which this is No. [no. in longhand, red ink]; p. [1], headed: The Saga of Hen Thorir. | Chapter I. Of The Men of Burgfirth. | [text begins]; pp. 2–87, text completed with explicit: Thus endeth the story of Hen Thorir. | [colophon]; p. [88], blank.
Technical Notes: *paper*: French hand-made; *leaf size*: untrimmed deckled edges, avg. 159 x 128 mm.; *printing*: *lines-to-page*: set solid, 20 lines; *running heads*: [all versos, aligned right] The Saga of Hen Thorir | [all rectos, chapter title or short title]; *binding*: quarter holland with red and blue marbled boards, or quarter tan canvas spine with plain tan paper covered boards and printed paper spine label; quarter holland with brown paper boards printed in red and brown on the *front*: [upper right, each word begins with a red capital] The Saga Of Hen Thorir.; *ornamentation*: 1 full border, 12 tail pieces, 17 floriated 8-line initials, one at the head of each chapter.
Publication: Sept. 1903 (colophon date); *print run*: 350 numbered copies; *price*: $2.50 (Ransom, 224).
Register of Copies Examined: BL (base copy: 12411. aa. 21.); J-F V.

A-107.01: Pygmalion and the Image (Russell)

[within a multiple thin-rule rectilinear border with leaves at each corner within the border, swash caps, title and publisher's name in red] PYGMALION AND [printer's leaf] | THE IMAGE BY [3 printers' leaves] | WILLIAM MOR- RIS | ILLUSTRATED WITH | PICTURES BY SIR ED- | WARD BURNE-JONES | [publisher's device of rose with centred RHR monogram, 1st R reversed] | NEW YORK R • H • RUSSELL | PUBLISHER MCMIII
Edition: [1st impression, 1st separate edn.] This is a companion vol. to the same publisher's *The Doom of King Acri-*

sius (1902, see A-100.01). *Pygmalion and the Image* was also 1st pbd. in *EP*, vol. I (1868).

Collaborators, Editors, and Illustrators: illus. by Sir Edward Burne-Jones, originally done as part of a project, abandoned earlier, to produce a copiously illustrated version of *EP*. the originals of the 4 pictures used here were exhibited in the Grosvenor Gallery Summer Exhibition in 1879. In the book these are reduced productions from photographs by Frederick Hollyer. Morris wrote a quatrain to accompany the 4 pictures on exhibition, 4 lines that each provided the caption for a painting, but read in sequence constitute themselves a poem, one that was subsequently pbd. as such in *Grosvenor Notes* (see D-49). The frontis. of this separate edn. is a photographic reproduction of G. F. Watts' portrait of Morris, now displayed in the National Portrait Gallery.

Series: this is the 2nd in a set of 2 vols. devoted to combining Morris's *Earthly Paradise* tales with the drawings made by Burne-Jones for 'the book that never was', i.e. the illustrated *Earthly Paradise*. The books range together and have the same paper, binding, ornamentation, and end papers.

Printer: unknown, possibly John Wilson and Son, Cambridge, Mass., previously used by Russell.

Collation: 4°: [1⁴ (1₄+1) 2–3⁴ (3₄+1) 4⁴ (4₄+1) 5⁴ (5₄+1) 6⁴ (6₄+1) 7²] [5₁] signed 2, [7₁] signed 3] 26 leaves pp. [i–vi] vii–xiii [xiv–xvi] 1–34 [35–6] [= 52] + 5 inserted plates indicated in the formula but not included in the book's pagination. They are described under *Contents*.

Contents: p. [i], half title; p. [ii], blank; inserted frontis. to face p. [iii], captioned (as all 5 illus. are) on an inserted protective tissue: *William Morris | From the painting by G. F. Watts, R. A.*; p. [iii], title page; p. [iv], copyright notice: *Copyright, 1903 | By* ROBERT HOWARD RUSSELL | [thin rule] | *Published October, 1903*; p. [v], headed: LIST OF ILLUSTRATIONS | By SIR EDWARD BURNE-JONES, BART. | [list of 5 pictures, including the frontis., with Morris's captions]; p. [vi], blank; p. vii, untitled introduction, text begins with 15-line ornamental drop 'W'; pp. viii–[xiv], introduction completed and signed, below right: FITZROY CARRINGTON. | [below left] ORIENTA COTTAGE, | MAMARONECK, NEW YORK, | DECEMBER ELEVENTH, 1902; p. [xv], Morris's prose argument for the story, begins with a 10-line ornamental initial 'A' and is signed at the end, below right: *WILLIAM MORRIS*; p. [xvi], blank; p. 1, text begins with 10-line ornamental initial 'A'; pp. 2–34, text continues, with the 4 Burne-Jones illus.: to face p. 8: *The Heart Desires*; to face p. 16: *The Hand Refrains*; to face p. 24: *The Godhead Fires*; to face p. 32: *The Soul Attains*; p. [35], text ends with explicit: THE END; p. [36], blank.

Technical Notes: *paper*: white machine-moulded paper with false deckled edges; *leaf size*: lightly trimmed, avg. 215 x 170 mm.; *printing*: in red and black, red only on the title page; *type area*: 144 x 113 mm.; *lines-to-page*: 21 lines, leaded; *pagination*: at the inner margin on the direction line; *end-papers*: one free end and paste-down, light tan and blank, front and back; *binding*: white buckram cloth-covered boards with gilt-stamped ornaments and lettering; *front*: repeats in a larger version the title page border and title; *spine*: [double thin rule at the top, above letterpress printed across] PYGMAL- | ION | AND | THE | IMAGE | [publisher's mark of rose with at the centre the monogram RHR, joined, with the 1st R reversed], bottom with thin rule and line of triangles; *back*: blank and unblocked.

Publication: Oct. 1903; *print run* and *price*: unknown.

Register of Copies Examined: LeM (base copy); WMS (dated 1903); BGR; MU.

Notes: in the description from Blackburn's *Grosvenor Notes*, 1879, Morris's titles for the 4 paintings are deliberately cast as a quatrain. For the text, see under *Contents*, above.

A-108.01:* Factory Work As It Might Be (Buzz Saw)

FACTORY WORK AS IT IS AND MIGHT BE. A SERIES OF FOUR PAPERS

Edition: [1st impression, 1st separate edn.] Taken from a 3-part article in *Justice*, 1 (May and June), 1884 (see D-102, 105, and 107), where part 1 is titled 'A Factory as It Might Be', parts 2 and 3 titled 'Work in a Factory as It Might Be. II [III]'.

Series: Buzz Saw Series, vol. 1, no. 8.

Place: New York.

Publisher: New York Labour News.

Publication: 1904 (rptd. in 1922); *print run* and *price*: unknown.

Register of Copies Located: NIC (HD 4815 B99 v.1, no. 8); DLC; NN (from NUC, v. 396, p. 142).

A-108.02: A Factory As It Might Be (Leatham)

[wrapper title] **A FACTORY AS IT MIGHT BE.** | **By WILLIAM MORRIS.** | **With PREFACE by JAMES LEATHAM.** | [double thin rule] | [reproduction of a Hollyer photograph of Morris, signed, lower right, this copy only, Morris's longhand] William Morris | [double thin rule] | **PRICE ONE PENNY.** | [double thin rule] | [in gothic] London: | [plain type] TWENTIETH CENTURY PRESS, LIMITED | (Trade Union and 48 Hours), | 37a & 38, CLERKENWELL GREEN, E.C. | [left] 5000/7/07.

Edition: [1st impression, 2nd separate edn., 1st English] 1st pbd. in *Justice* in 3 parts: part 1 titled 'A Factory As It Might Be', parts 2 and 3 titled 'Work in a Factory As It Might Be. II [III]' (1884, see D-102, 105, and 107). An article in *Justice* preliminary to this, 'Why Not?' (see D-99), makes Morris's case against the notion that large cities are a necessity for modern manufacture; the 1st exposition of ideas later developed into the 3-part article described here.
Collaborators, Editors, and Illustrators: edited by Harry Quelch, editor of *Justice*, who made minor textual changes to accommodate the change from the original 3-instalment form to a single essay without any division into parts.
Publisher: the SDF, through its subsidiary The Twentieth Century Press.
Collation: cr. 8°: [1]⁸ 8 leaves pp. [1] 2–15 [16] [= 16] + mid-grey wrapper stapled to the body at the centrefold.
Contents: p. [1], headed: PREFACE. | [thin rule] | [text begins]; pp. 2–3, text; p. 4, preface ends, signed below right: JAMES LEATHAM | [below left] Westerton-of-Clerkhill, Peterhead, | June, 1907; p. [5], headed: A FACTORY AS IT MIGHT BE. | [thin ornamental rule] | [text begins]; pp. 6–15, text completed with double thin rule; p. [16], ads for 'Socialist Literature' in a thin-rule compartment.
Technical Notes: *paper*: plain white machine-made; *leaf size*: cut flush, 204 x 131 mm.; *lines-to-page*: leaded, 36 lines; *type area*: 161 x 105 mm.; *binding*: *wrapper*: p. [1], title page; p. [2], blank; pp. [3–4], ads; on the wrapper title is a prtd. note: 5000/7/07; this indicates that 5,000 copes were printed in July 1907, see also Leatham's account of the first pbn.: '5000 of a first edition' (*The Gateway*, 8/85 (Sept. 1919), 18–19); *price*: one penny.
Publication: July 1907 (printing finished); *print run*: 5,000 copies; *price*: 1d.; text rptd., MM, ii. 130–40.
Register of Copies Examined: SSL (base copy: 338.65P); IISH (E1780/96); MH (*EC85. M8348. B898p); BL (YA.1994. a. 3680).
Notes: in response to a derogatory comment by Harry Quelch, editor of *Justice*, Leatham wrote 'A Reply to *Justice*' in *The Gateway* (8/85 (Mid Sept. 1919), 18–20). There he gives a history of his publications in *Justice* or rptd. as pamphlets by the Twentieth Century Press, giving actual print runs and prices, but asserting he was never paid and never asked for payment: 'When Mr. Harry Quelch proposed to publish Morris's 'What A Factory Might be', he wrote and asked me for an introduction to it. The introduction occupies about half the pamphlet, and Mr. Quelch was pleased to say that he was very glad to have it—as he might well be, considering the price! [presumably it too was free] Again 5000 of a first edition. For all these and other services I never fingered a penny, never asked for it, and did not expect it' (pp. 18–19).

A-109.01:* The Writing on the Image

THE WRITING ON THE IMAGE, BY WILLIAM MORRIS
Edition: [1st impression, 1st separate edn.] A tale 1st pbd. in *EP*, vol. I. Detail from the *NUC*, cccxcvi. 166.
Series: Vest Pocket Series, 6.
Place: New York and London.
Publisher: George Putnam's Sons.
Technical Notes: pp. 77, 11 x 4 cm.; text, in verse, runs parallel with the spine.
Publication: 1904.
Register of Copies Located: DLC (NUC, v. 396, p. 166).

A-109.02: The Writing on the Image

William Morris | [thin rule] | THE WRITING ON | THE IMAGE | AND OTHER PASSAGES FROM | 'THE EARTHLY PARADISE' | EDITED BY | EDITH FRY, M.A. | Teacher of English literature at St. Monica's School, Epsom | BLACKIE AND SON LIMITED | 50 OLD BAILEY LONDON | GLASGOW AND BOMBAY | 1912
Edition: [1st impression, 2nd separate edn.] The 'other passages' are sections from 'The Apology', and 'The Wanderers' to introduce the tale, which is complete. It is included here rather than in the C-List, Collections and Selections, because the focus of the book is its presentation of the single text, *The Writing on the Image*.
Series: Blackie's English Classics.
Collation: 8°: [1]¹⁶ 16 leaves pp. [i–ii] iii–vi 7–32 [= 32] + wrapper.
Contents: p. [i], title page; p. [ii], blank; pp. iii–vi, Introduction; pp. 7–32, text completed.
Technical Notes: *paper*: plain white machine-made; *leaf size*: cut flush, 166 x 108 mm.; *printing*: *lines-to-page*: hair lead, 33 lines; *binding*: *wrapper*: light brown fabric backed with heavy paper, title printed on the front: [3 parallel thin rules] | Blackie's English Classics | [thin rule] | THE WRITING | ON THE IMAGE | AND OTHER PASSAGES FROM | 'THE EARTHLY PARADISE' | BY | WILLIAM MORRIS | Threepence | [2nd set of 3 thin rules, as above]; wrapper, pp. [2–4], blank.
Publication: 1912; *print run*: unknown; *price*: 3d.
Register of Copies Examined: BL (base copy: 012200. E. 3 | 69).

A-110.01: The Man Born to Be King (LCBEL)

THE MAN BORN TO | BE KING | (*FROM "THE EARTHLY PARADISE"*) | BY | WILLIAM MORRIS | EDITED WITH AN INTRODUCTION AND NOTES | FOR THE USE OF SCHOOLS AND COLLEGES | LONGMANS, GREEN AND CO. LTD. | 39 PATERNOSTER ROW, LONDON | NEW YORK AND BOMBAY | 1905

Edition: [1st impression, 1st separate edn.] This book might be described as the 2nd impression of the 5th edn., 4th English, since its setting, including most of J. W. Mackail's introduction, is from that made for the Silver Library Edition of the *EP*, printed and issued at the same time. This tale, 1st pbd. in the *EP*, is Morris's re-telling of the medieval French prose romance, *The Emperor Coustans*, his translation of which was printed by the KP in 1894 (see A-73.01).

Collaborators, Editors, and Illustrators: Edited with an Introduction and Notes [by J. W. Mackail] for the use of Schools and Colleges (for detail on Mackail's introductions, see *Notes*, below).

Series: Longmans Class Books of English Literature. This is the first of 5 Morris titles in a series which, when complete, included over 70 works by standard authors. The other Morris titles in the series were: *The Glittering Plain* (1905, A-54.07); *Atalanta's Race and The Proud King* (1912, this being a selection of 2 stories, see C-29); *The Wanderers* (1923, A-128.01); and *The Story of Sigurd the Volsung*, the last 'with portions condensed into prose by Winifred Turner and Helen Scott' (hence it is not included here). Longmans gave notice of the Class Books as: 'A new series, edited, and with Introductions and Notes, for the use of Schools and Colleges . . . . Each of the vols. contains a prefatory note on the life and work of William Morris, together with a résumé of the narrative and short notes and bibliography' (Longmans *Notes on Books*, 10/199 (Mar. 1905), 128). Perhaps to avoid any suggestion of a conflict of interest between his role in a textbook for schools and his position at that time in the Education Department, Mackail's name does not appear in any of these books, though his introductions, the biographical part being derived from his Silver Library introduction, are included in all of them.

For the sake of completeness, an attempt is made here, as with the Pocket Library, to list both pre- and post-1915 re-issues and reprints from this series at the end of the entry for the 1st issue of each title. For other details common to this series, see *Contents* and *Technical Notes*, below. The texts were all taken from previous edns: the 4 from the *EP* are from the Silver Library Edition of 1905, and *The Glittering Plain* from the 2nd, or 'Popular' edn. of 1891.

Collation: 8°: π^{10} A–D^8 E^6 F^4 52 leaves pp. [i–iv] v–xx 1–83 [84] [= 104].

Contents: p. [i], half title; p. [ii], blank; p. [iii], title page; p. [iv], BIBLIOGRAPHICAL NOTE; p. v–xx, INTRODUCTION; pp. 1–73, text completed; pp. 74–6, NOTES; pp. 77–83, EXAMINATION QUESTIONS; p. [84], imprint: Printed by BALLANTYNE, HANSON & Co. | Edinburgh & London

Technical Notes: *paper*: plain white machine-made; *leaf size*: trimmed, 185 x 123 mm.; *printing*: *running heads*: all versos: THE EARTHLY PARADISE | [all rectos] THE MAN BORN TO BE KING; line count by 10s at the right margin; *end-papers*: a single free end and paste-down, plain white and blank, front and back; *binding*: varied over the years of production, the 1st being red cloth-covered boards, plain on the back, with a 9-part compartment black-stamped on the front combining, top: 2 black swans with flower between; middle: 2 sets of Ionic pillars with the title between; and bottom: 2 standard roses with Longmans ship and series title between; *spine*: black-stamped, oriented vertically, with author and title. Later bindings were plain red cloth-covered boards with thin-rule border around the edges, front and back, and a blind-stamped Longmans ship lower right on the front, and title and author gilt-stamped up the spine.

Publication: 1905 [issued 11–18 Feb.] ('Publications of the Week', *Pub. Circ.*, 82 (18 Feb. 1905), 183); *print run*: 2,000 copies, of which 260 copies were exported to Longmans of New York (Impression Book, Longmans Arch.); *price*: 1s. 4d. net.

Register of Copies Examined: BL (base copy: 012273. e. 1 | 2.); LeM (2 copies).

Notes: In June 1904, Longmans proposed school edns. of individual tales from the *EP*. Cockerell and his co-trustees declined on the ground that Morris often expressed the view that poetry studied in school was ever thereafter disliked by the student. But Longmans persisted, and J. W. Mackail, then working in the department of education, took up the case, offering to write introductions for each vol. So it was done.

Mackail wrote to Cockerell, 15 June 1904, to say that he approved of the proposal to have some selected stories of the *EP* published separately and sold at a shilling for schools and for the general reader. At that point he approved of introductions but had reservations about adding notes to the text. But eventually he agreed on annotations to the text and they were added, largely in the form of glosses on Morris's vocabulary. Shortly after this, on 17 June 1904, Cockerell wrote to agree with school edns. (Smith Arch.)

Mackail to Cockerell, 12 Oct. 1904: Here Mackail agrees to write introductions for each vol., each consisting of a biographical section of approximately one-third of the total and common to all the books. The remainder would be devoted to the particular title. For the *EP* stories— only 2 were planned at this time—another third would be devoted to the *EP* in general and the rest to the tale. As to his payment, Mackail proposed 10*gns.* for the 2 *EP* stories, *The Man Born to be King* and *Atalanta's Race* (the latter was not pbd. until 1912, when it was combined with *The Proud King*).

Later issues and impressions of this edn.: Longmans:
1. 1906 [Oct.] (6 Dec. in Impression Book, Longmans Arch.); *print run*: 2,000 copies; *price*: 1s. 4d.;
2. 1911 [21 Jan.] (Longmans Arch.); *print run*: 1,000 copies; *price*: 1s. 4d.;
3. 1911 [19 Apr.] (Longmans Arch.); *print run*: 1,500 copies; *price*: 1s. 4d.;
4. 1911 [12 Aug.] (Longmans Arch.); *print run*: 2,000 copies; *price*: 1s. 4d.;
5. 1912 [27 Nov.] (Longmans Arch.); *print run*: 2,000 copies; *price*: 1s. 4d.;
6. post-1915 printings were issued [15 Apr.] 1918: 2,500 copies; [7 May] 1919: 2,000 copies; [22 Oct.] 1921: 2,000 copies; Sept. 1924; Aug. 1926; and Jan. 1929 (Longmans Arch.).

A-111.01: The Defence of Guenevere (title poem only, Parnassus)

[all within thin-rule compartment] THE DEFENCE OF GUENE- | VERE. BY WILLIAM MORRIS. | WITH ILLUSTRATIONS [flower ornament] BY JESSIE M. KING [3 flower ornaments] | JOHN LANE: PUBLISHER | LONDON AND NEW YORK | 1905

Edition: [1st impression, 1st separate edn.] Consists of title poem only from the John Lane edn. of *The Defence of Guenevere and Other Poems* (see A-2.07).
Collaborators, Editors, and Illustrators: F. B. Money-Coutts was the series general editor.
Series: Flowers of Parnassus No. 22.
Collation: 8°: [1–3]⁸ 24 leaves pp. [1–8] 9–43 [44–8] [= 48].
Contents: p. [1], half title: FLOWERS OF PARNASSUS— XXII | THE DEFENCE OF GUENEVERE; pp. [2–3], blank; p. [4], frontis.: [engraving, titled] SHE THREW HER WET HAIR BACKWARD FROM HER BROW; p. [5], title page; p. [6], printer's imprint: Wm. Clowes and Sons, Limited, Printers, London.; p. [7], headed: Illustrations | [list of 8 engraved line-drawing illus. in black and white, including head and tail-pieces]; p. [8], blank; p. 9, head-piece illus., head title and text begins; pp. 10–43, text completed; p. [44], blank; p. [45], tail-piece illustration; p. [46], blank; pp. [47–8], ads for the Parnassus series.
Technical Notes: *paper*: cream glossy machine-made; t.e.g.; *leaf size*: trimmed, 141 x 111 mm.; *type area*: 79 x 81 mm., excluding head and direction lines; *running heads*: [between thin rules, rectos and versos] THE DEFENCE OF GUENEVERE; *pagination*: arabic numerals centred on the direction line; *end-papers*: 1 free end and paste-down, plain white and blank, front and back; *binding*: choice of olive green cloth or green morocco-covered boards with blind-stamped compartments, front and back; front: gold-stamped title in floral oval compartment; spine: gilt title stamped vertically.
Publication: 1905 (accession date on the BM copy is '6 Fe 1905'); *print run*: unknown; *price*: 1s. net cloth, 1s. 6d. net lthr.
Register of Copies Examined: BL (base copy: 11607. aaaa. 2/22)

A-112.01: Saga Library, vol. VI

THE STORIES OF THE | KINGS OF NORWAY | CALLED THE ROUND | OF THE WORLD | (HEIMSKRINGLA) | BY SNORRI STURLUSSON, DONE INTO ENGLISH | OUT OF THE ICELANDIC | BY WILLIAM MORRIS | AND | EIRÍKR MAGNÚSSON | VOL. IV. BY EIRÍKR MAGNÚSSON | LONDON | BERNARD QUARITCH, 15 PICCADILLY | 1905

Edition: [1st impression, 1st edn.] Though Morris had no part in this vol., having died some 9 years before it was issued, it is included here to complete the description of the set in which Morris had an equal part with his collaborator, Eiríkr Magnússon. As was the case with all 6 vols. of the Saga Library, in addition to the ordinary edn. there were 125 LP copies in royal 8°, all numbered.
Collaborators, Editors, and Illustrators: though Morris's name appears on the dust jacket, binding, and titles, as in the previous 5 vols., Eiríkr Magnússon is sole author of this vol., which is made up of an 'Introduction' to the life of Snorri Sturlusson (original author of the Heimskringla), with notes and indexes to the entire Heimskringla series.
Series: for series detail, see this field in A-52.01.
Printer: Chiswick Press:—C. Whittingham and Co., Tooks Court, Chancery Lane.

Collation and *Contents*: not needed since this is not a Morris book.
Technical Notes: see this field in A-52.01.
Publication: 1905 [issued 18 Nov.] (Chiswick Arch.) Magnússon's Preface is signed and dated 'October, 1895'; *print run*: 1,500 copies + 125 LP copies on Whatman paper; pp. xcii + [520] + genealogies as inserts.
Register of Copies Examined: see this field in A-52.01.

A-113.01: Art, Labour, and Socialism (SPGB)

[title aligned left, underlined and in swash neo-gothic type] Art, Labour, | & Socialism. | [aligned right] By William Morris. | [thin rule] | [centred] *REPRINTED FROM "TO-DAY."* | [thin rule] | [in gothic] London : | [plain type] Published by | THE SOCIALIST PARTY OF GREAT BRITAIN, | 22, GREAT JAMES STREET, W. C. | 1907.

Edition: [1st impression, 1st separate edn.] A lecture 1st delivered as 'Art under Plutocracy' at University College Hall, Oxford, on 14 Nov. 1883; 1st prtd. entire in *To-Day* (1884, see D-90), from which the text of this edn. is taken. Morris's abstract of the original was pbd. in *The Cambridge Review* and in *The Cambridge Chronicle and University Journal* (1883, see D-84). The present text is from the *To-Day* version but with a new title and without the beginning and ending paragraphs.

Collaborators, Editors, and Illustrators: Foreword [signed]: The Executive Committee of the | Socialist Party of Great Britain.
Series: S.P.G.B. Library, No. 3.
Printer: Printed by John Lewis & Compy., | The Selkirk Press, | 5, Bridewell Place, London, E.C.
Collation: 12°: [1]¹² 12 leaves pp. [1–3] 4–8 [9] 10–24 [= 24] + wrapper stapled to the body through the centrefold.
Contents: p. [1], title page; p. [2], printer's imprint (see *Printer* field, above); p. [3], dropped head: FOREWORD. | [thin rule] | [text begins]; pp. 4–8, foreword completed: signature: [aligned right] THE EXECUTIVE COMMITTEE OF THE | SOCIALIST PARTY OF GREAT BRITAIN.; p. [9], dropped head: ART, LABOUR, AND SOCIALISM. | BY WM. MORRIS. | [thin rule] | *Reprinted from "To-Day."* | [thin rule] | [text begins]; pp. 10–24, text completed with printer's flower as tail-piece.
Technical Notes: *paper*: plain white machine-moulded; *leaf size*: cut flush, 179 x 108 mm.; *type area*: 136 x 67 mm.; *pagination*: centred on headline; *binding*: *wrapper*: plain heavy tan machine-made paper, printed on pp. [1] and [4] only; p. [1]: [flush right] S.P.G.B. Library, No. 3. | [title in 3-line swash neo-gothic type, aligned left] Art, Labour, | &

Figure 84. A-113.01: *Art, Labour, and Socialism* SPGB (Socialist Party of Great Britain)

Socialism. | By . . . . | [aligned right, 2-line type] William Morris. | [globe, northern hemisphere encircled by] THE SOCIALIST PARTY [southern hemisphere] OF GREAT BRITAIN | Price One Penny. | [centred] Reprinted and Published with **Special Introduction** | by **The Socialist Party of Great Britain**, | 22, Great James Street, Bedford Row, London, W. C. | **Trade Agent:** HENDERSONS, 15a, Paternoster | Row, E.C., and 66, Charing Cross Road, W.C.; p. [4], ads for Socialist Party pbns.
Publication: 1907; *print run*: unknown; *price*: 1d.
Register of Copies Examined: LeM (2 copies: base copy); Fdmn.
Later impressions. of this text: Socialist Party of Great Britain (SPGB):

1. 1911: SECOND EDITION; *print run* and *price*: unknown;

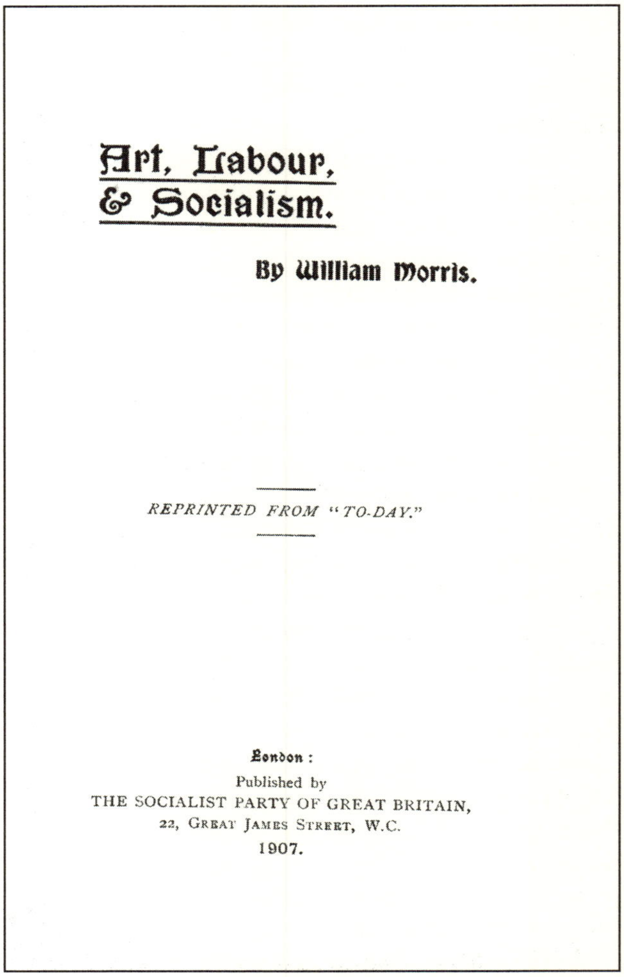

2. Post-1915: 1962: with 'a Modern Assessment'.

A-114.01: Frithiof the Bold (*Bib.* in 2 parts)

[*Bibelot* wrapper title, above compartment, top left] VOL. XIV. [top right] No. 1 [2] | [within small thin-rule top compartment, left] *JANUARY.* [*FEBRUARY.*] [top right] MDCCCCVIII. | [thin rule] | [main compartment: detail common to all wrapper titles in this series, see A-83.01] | [below the compartment, right, in red] THE STORY OF FRITHIOF THE BOLD | TRANSLATED FROM THE ICELANDIC | BY WILLIAM MORRIS [or, in Part II:] THE STORY OF FRITHIOF THE BOLD | (CONCLUDED.) | BY WILLIAM MORRIS

Edition: [1st impression, 1st separate edn.] 1st pbd. in 2 parts in *Dark Blue* under Morris's name only (1871, see D-29), but included in *Three Northern Love Stories* under the names of both the collaborators, Morris and Magnússon. On the nature of their collaboration, see Morris's letter to the *Athenæum* listed in D-51 and rptd. in *Letters*, i. 512, and in part here (see *Notes* in A-5.01). T. B. Mosher's unsigned and untitled foreword makes it clear that his copytext for this separate edn. was the version in *Dark Blue*.

On later edns., the arrangement of pagination and ads, see this and the Series fields in A-83.01. As with all Morris items in *The Bibelot*, this A-List entry provides finding-list information for both the separate and the periodical versions (see the *Series* field, below). On Mosher's *Bibelot* publication of this title, and its appearance here rather than in the D-List, Morris in Periodicals, see this field in A-83.01.

Collaborators, Editors, and Illustrators: unsigned and untitled foreword [by the editor, T. B. Mosher].
Series: *The Bibelot . . .*, 14/1 and 2 (Jan. and Feb. 1908), [1]–34 and [35]–64. For detail common to the series, see this field in A-83.01.
Place, Publisher, and *Printer*: see wrapper transcriptions in A-83.01.
Collation: Part 1: 12°: [1]²⁰ 20 leaves, 10 conjunct pairs, folded to form a single gathering pp. [2] [1–6] 7–32 [33–4] [4] [= 40] + the usual blue Bibelot wrapper sewn to the body through the centrefold.
Part 2: 12°: [1]¹⁶ 16 leaves, 8 conjunct pairs pp. 35–63 [64] [2] [= 32] + the usual Bibelot wrapper sewn to the body through the centrefold; on pagination and ads, see this field and *Series* in A-83.01 The separate issue of this title has not been seen. Certain details of pagination and contents have been supplied by Mr Philip Bishop, Mosher's bibliographer.

Contents: Part 1: pp. [*1–2*], ads; p. [1], T. B. Mosher's unsigned foreword begins, headed: [modern gothic] The Bibelot | I. | [text begins]; pp. [2–4], [text of foreword completed with printer's leaf as tail-piece | [contents of Feb. and Mar. numbers]; p. [5], half title; p. [6], 10-line epigraph, + 3 lines for the source reference: Preface to *Three Northern Love Stories*; pp. 7–[34], text completed; pp. [*1–4*], ads.
Part 2: pp. 35–63, text completed with printer's leaf as tailpiece; p. [64], blank; pp. [2], ads.
Technical Notes: for detail common to this series, see this field in A-83.01; detail specific to this issue: *running heads*: [all rectos and versos, aligned to the inner margins] THE STORY OF FRITHIOF THE BOLD
Publication: Jan., Feb. 1908 [masthead date, in 2 parts, issued 15 and 25 Jan.] (see *Series* field in A-83.01); *print run* and *price*: see this field in A-83.01.
Register of Copies Examined: this title seen only in the Testimonial Edition of *The Bibelot* (all of these titles have been examined in that edn., pbd. in 1925 by Wm. H. Wise and Co., New York); VU (Ba RB 45A); additional detail from Bsp.

A-115.01: Journals of Travel in Iceland (*CW* VIII)

THE COLLECTED WORKS | [title details common to the set, see A-126.01] | VOLUME VIII | JOURNALS OF TRAVEL IN ICELAND | 1871 1873 | [publisher's imprint, see A-126.01] | MDCCCCXI

Edition: 'Collected Works edn' [1st impression, 1st edn.]
Collation: medium 8°: a⁸ (a3+1) b⁸ c² B–H⁸ (H1+1) I⁸ (I8+1) K–R⁸ (R6+1) [$2 (–b2 c2) signed] 146 leaves pp. [i–viii] ix–xxxv [xxxvi] 1–251 [252–6] [=292] + 4 inserted plates noted in the formula but not included in the book's pagination. All are described here in the *Contents*.
Contents: pp. [i–iii], blank; p. [iv], limitation notice (see A-126.01); pp. [v–vi], blank; inserted plate as frontis. photo reproduction in a blind-stamped compartment with the photographer's name below left: *Elliot & Fry photo.* | [plate maker, in copperplate, below right] *Emery Walker Ph. sc.* | [labelled in copperplate] *William Morris* | *(March 21, 1877)*; p. [vii], title page; p. [viii], blank; p. ix, headed: CONTENTS | [list begins, divided into: A JOURNAL . . . 1871 [and] A DIARY. . . 1873; p. x–xiii, Contents completed; p. [xiv], blank; p. xv, headed: INTRODUCTION; pp. xvi–xxxv, Intro. completed; p. [xxxvi], reproduction of the Arms of Iceland; p. 1, headed: A JOURNAL OF TRAVEL IN ICELAND | 1871 | CHAPTER I. LONDON TO REYKJAVIK | [text of Journal begins]; pp. 2–98, text con-

tinues; 2nd inserted plate, to face p. 98, oriented vertically and labelled: A facsimile page of the first Journal of Travel in Iceland.; pp. 99–128, text continues; 3rd inserted plate, map facing p. 128, with the plate maker's name lower right outside an ornamental border: *Emery Walker sc.*, labelled lower left within border: Map to illustrate | Author's journey of 1873; pp. 129–185, text of Journal completed; p. 186, text of Diary begins; pp. 187–251, Diary completed; p. [252], printer's imprint, see A-126.01; 4th inserted plate, between pp. [252 and 253], a foldout map s. sh. folded 3 times (2 vertical and 1 horizontal) to form a single plate, 316 x 390 mm., labelled, upper left within an ornamental border: WEST ICELAND | to illustrate the Author's journey of 1871 [with the 1871 journey traced in red]; pp. [253–6], blank.

Technical Notes: paper, printing, type, position (but not content) of headlines, running titles, shoulder notes, pagination, and binding are all common to the series and are described in this field in A-126.01, the entry for the set; details specific to this issue: *shoulder notes*: all rectos and versos other than section heads, serving as sub-heads to adjacent text; *binding*: *printed spine label*: [4 title lines common to the set, see A-126.01] | VOLUME VIII | JOURNALS | OF TRAVEL | IN ICELAND | 1871 1873

Publication: 1911 [issued 14 June] (Longmans Arch.); for details of print run, price, etc., see the entry for *CW*, A-126.01.

Register of Copies Examined: see this field in A-126.01.

A-116.01: Two Red Roses Across the Moon (Feather Weights)

TWO RED ROSES ACROSS THE MOON [title within a rose-vine border] | BY | WILLIAM MORRIS | LONDON: | HODDER & STOUGHTON

Edition: [1st separate edn.] 1st pbd. in *The Defence of Guenevere and Other Poems*, see A-2.01.

Collaborators, Editors, and Illustrators: Designs for the series by L. A. Govey, illus. signed by Anne Anderson.

Series: Feather Weights [a series of 4 un-numbered booklets, 2 being Morris texts, all 'printed by the Edinburgh Press in the City of London', all bearing the same series title and device, a girl with butterfly wings blowing the petals from a flower, petals which in turn form a heart-shaped frame to the device on p. 4 of the wrapper. The series, while it looks like Children's literature, has a satirical point to make to adults regarding Morris's poetry and his politics. This is suggested by (1) the selection of the two Morris poems for reprinting, both being among the most mysterious, indeed opaque (and childish?) verse from Morris's earliest compositions, (2) the title 'Featherweights' and the device associated with it suggest a *reductio ad absurdum*, treating the poems as an excursion into childish sentimental obscurity, and (3) Matthew Browne's verses in *Lilliput Land*, the first of the series of booklets, the first 2 stanzas of which indicate the point of the exercise:

> Where does the Pinafore Palace stand?
> Right in the middle of Lilliput-Land!
> There the Queen eats bread and honey,
> There the King counts up his money!
> Oh, the glorious Revolution!
> Oh, the Provisional Constitution!
> Now that the children, clever bold folks!
> Have turned the tables on the old folks!

The 2nd of the 4 series titles, *The Grey Squirrels* by William Howitt, is a (supposed) children's tale of courageous triumph over difficulties, but the triumph is for some, not all. For some courage and strength and skill are rewarded, but not for others, who lose their lives despite their best efforts. It is a tale of the way things are in the real world.

The 3rd and 4th booklets are separate edns. of the 2 Morris poems: 'Two Red Roses across the moon' and 'Summer Dawn.'

Collation: 12°: [1]⁶ (1₂ +1) 6 leaves pp. [1–12] [=12] (no pagination) + an inserted illus. noted in the formula but not counted in the pagination + a stiffer paper cover, or flaps, glued on and folded over the first and last leaves.

Contents: pp. [1–2], blank; p. [3], title page, ornamented with rose garland; p. [4], blank, followed by an inserted illus. (108 x 54 mm.) with part rose border and caption, in swash lettering, below: There • Was • a Knight | Came • Riding • By • •; pp. [5–10], text, with ornamental devices on each page; text of Morris's poem reprinted as in *The Defence of Guenevere and Other Poems*, pp. [11–12], blank.

Technical Notes: *paper*: stiff glossy cream-white linen paper; *printing*: printed in olive green with display caps in red; *leaf size*: cut flush, 150 x 81 mm.; *ornamentation*: ornamental devices of roses on each page and back cover; illus., in colour, on front cover (54 x 45 mm.) and verso of title page (108 x 54 mm); *binding*: *wrapper*: letterpress, caps in red, within a red-lined compartment on front, with separate internal compartments top (title) and bottom (author's name); the centre has a woman's head in a coif and a rose vine.

Publication: [by 28 Sept. 1911] (accession stamp on BL copy); *print run* and *price*: unknown.

Register of Copies Examined: BL (base copy: 11601. cc. 28. (3).)

A-117.01: Summer Dawn (Feather Weights)
SUMMER DAWN | BY | WILLIAM MORRIS | LONDON: | HODDER & STOUGHTON
Edition: [1st separate edn.] 1st pbd. in *The Defence of Guenevere and Other Poems* (1858, see A-2.01).
Collaborators, Editors, and Illustrators: Designs and Illustrations by L. A. Govey.
Series: Feather Weights [a series of 4 booklets, 2 being Morris texts reprinted from *The Defence of Guenevere*]. For further detail on this series, see this field in the previous entry.
Printer: Edinburgh Press, London.
Collation: 12°: [1]⁶ 6 leaves pp. [1–12] (no pagination), sewn, with a stiff matte paper cover, or flaps that fold over the 1st and last blank leaves, glued on and bearing a colour picture glued on the front.
Contents: pp. [1–2], blank; p. [3], title page; p. [4], colour illus. glued to blank verso of the title page, of a woman in pink among the clouds; pp. [5–9], text, rectos have ornamental devices on each page, versos have various designs: a potted plant, a rose, and a village with a hill and the sun behind; p. [10] has only the Feather Weights device. Morris's poem is reprinted as it is in *The Defence of Guenevere and Other Poems*.
Technical Notes: *paper*: printed in olive green on cream linen paper; *leaf size*: cut flush, 150 x 81 mm.; *binding*: *wrapper*: an illus. in colour pasted on the front of a wrapper that folds over the 1st and last blank leaves, of a woman in a red dress, a flowered crown and playing a lute looks out a window at a flying bird, all within a compartment of flowers and brown rules; this all above title and author which is ornamented with a dove-within-a-cloud below and to each side of the author's name; *ornamentation*: flower designs on title and between each 2 stanzas on each recto, versos with various designs, including a tail-piece to follow the last stanza, 2 Viking ships with low sun below cloud.
Publication: n.d. [by 28 Sept. 1911] (accession stamp on BL copy); *print run* and *price*: unknown.
Register of Copies Examined: BL (base copy: 11601. cc. 28. (4).)

A-118.01: Near Avalon (Fowler)
NEAR AVALON | BY | WILLIAM MORRIS
Edition: [1st separate edn.] A lyric of four 4-line stanzas, taken from *The Defence of Guenevere and Other Poems*.
Place: Kansas City, Kansas.
Publisher: H. A. Fowler.
Colophon: Imprinted by H. Alfred Fowler, at Kansas City, in December of 1911.
Collation: s. sh. 8°: [1]⁴ 4 leaves pp. [1–2] 3 [4] 5 [6–8] [=8].
Contents: pp. [1–2], blank; p. 3, text; p. [4], blank; p. 5, colophon and notice of limitation, in longhand: 'Number 6 of forty copies'; pp. [6–8], blank.
Technical Notes: *paper*: hand-laid paper, watermarked: 'PM Handmade in Italy'; *binding*: *wrapper*: blue hand-made paper printed with title and author on front; *end-papers*: 1 free end, front and back of imitation watered-silk paper, unmarked.
Publication: Dec. 1911 (colophon date); *print run*: 40 copies; *price*: unknown.
Register of Copies Examined: J-F V (base copy).

A-119.01: The Revolt of Ghent (Leatham)
[2-line caps] THE REVOLT | OF GHENT | By WILLIAM MORRIS | HUDDERSFIELD: | "THE WORKER" OFFICE | LONDON: | TWENTIETH CENTURY PRESS | MANCHESTER: | NATIONAL LABOUR PRESS
Edition: [1st impression, 1st separate edn.] The 4th instalment of the *Commonweal* version (No. 133 (28 July 1888), 234) is omitted, probably deliberately, from this edn., James Leatham's pamphlet version. But Leatham also creates 2 chapters by dividing the 7th instalment, so his version also has 8 parts or chapters (including Leatham's introduction), consistent with the original. 1st pbd. (complete) in *Commonweal* in 7 instalments (1888, see D-391).
Collaborators, Editors, and Illustrators: [edited and] introduced by James Leatham.
Printer: [James Leatham at] "The Worker" Office, Huddersfield.
Collation: 8°: [1⁸ (1₂+1) 2–3⁸ 4⁴] 28 leaves pp. [1–5] 6–55 [56] [= 56] with 1 inserted plate noted in the formula and described under *Contents*, but not counted in the book's pagination, + gray paper wrapper sewn to the body.
Contents: p. [1], half title; p. [2], blank; inserted frontis., a Hollyer portrait photo of Morris, within thin-rule compartment, with caption in gothic: William Morris; p. [3], title page; p. [4], blank; p. [5], dropped head title: THE REVOLT OF GHENT | [white-on-black 5-line ornamental drop initial 'I'] text begins; pp. 6–54, text continues with chapters divided by Roman numerals; p. 55, text ends with explicit (square brackets in the original): [The End], p. [56], blank.

Technical Notes: *paper*: cream moulded 'antique' paper, with dandy roll laid lines, no watermark; *leaf size*: cut flush, uncut size avg. 192 x 129 mm.; *printing*: *type area*: 121 x 76 mm., not including headlines; *lines-to-page*: 30 lines, with various spacing before and after numbered divisions; *running titles*: [all rectos and versos] THE REVOLT OF GHENT.; *wrapper*: p. [*1*]: thin-rule compartment with 11 smaller internal boxes aligned left vertically down the left margin with a flower in each and a vertical rule forming the 4th side of the boxes; *letterpress*: centred in the rest of the larger compartment: THE . . . | REVOLT | OF . . . . . | GHENT. | [flower ornament] | [aligned left] By | [centred] WILLIAM MORRIS | [flower ornament repeated] | [aligned left] SIXPENCE; wrapper p. [*2*], ads. for 'Worker Publications'; wrapper p. [*3–4*], ads. concluded.
Publication: [1910] The IISL copy is dated '[1910]', in pencil, which fits the known circumstances of its publication. Leatham was in Huddersfield from 1908–1912 (see James Leatham, 'Sixty Years of World-Mending', in *The Gateway*, 30/359 (Sept.–Oct. 1944), 7–11). In establishing the date of this pamphlet, for which there are no references so far found in the usual trade journals, two things may be observed: (1) given Leatham's habit of numbering edns. after the 1st, the absence of any indication of edn. suggests that this is the 1st edn. (and no other separate edn. has been found), and (2) on the wrapper of the 1st number of *The Gateway*, published from Cottingham in July 1912, this pamphlet is advertised as 'The Revolt of Ghent. By William Morris. Antique paper, broad margins, 6*d*.' The elaborately designed wrapper, the fine paper, and the larger format explain the higher price, which in turn suggests a slower sale. This may explain why sufficient copies remained to be advertised in July, 1912. *Print run*: unknown; *price*: 6*d*.
Register of Copies Examined: IISH (base copy: E 1780/17); MML.

A-120.01:* Paying for Art (Hillacre)

PAYING FOR ART BY WILLIAM MORRIS PRIVATELY PRINTED THE HILLACRE BOOKHOUSE RIVERSIDE, CONN. 1911
Edition: [1st separate edn.] The text of this pamphlet is from Morris's letter to *The Star*, T. P. O'Connor's London newspaper, in defence of the pricing of his books. Morris's letter was in reply to a letter in which he was mentioned by name in an attack on book prices (see D-136). The original Morris letter (not included in the *Letters*) was headed 'Poet's Prices' by the editor. No copy available: title transcript and other details from Walsdorf, p. 231, and Larremore, 151.
Series: The Wallet Books, Second Series.
Publisher: Frederick C. Bursch.
Colophon: OF THIS BOOK 250 COPIES HAVE BEEN PRINTED AT THE HILLACRE BOOKHOUSE
Collation: fcap 8°: [1]⁸ 8 leaves, unpaginated, + a wrapper sewn to the body at the centrefold.
Contents: half title, title, text, and colophon.
Technical Notes: *leaf size*: 152 x 102 mm. (Walsdorf, p. 231); *type*: 'Missal' initial; *binding*: stiff paper wrapper with a brown cover and a printed paper label on the front printed in black and orange: PAYING FOR ART BY WILLIAM MORRIS
Publication: 1911: *print run*: 250 copies; *price*: unknown.
Register of Copies Located: NN (*NUC*, v. 396, p. 153).
Notes: Frederick C. Bursch, the printer-publisher of this book at the Hillacre Bookhouse, is the subject of Thomas Larremore's *An American Typographical Tragedy–the Imprints of Frederick Conrad Bursch*, not to be confused with Frederic M. Burr who pbd. *Svend and His Brethren* and *Sir Galahad* at the Hillside Press, Englewood, New Jersey.

Bursh produced 6 Morris titles. Besides *Paying for Art*, see *The Art of the People* (A-17.03); *Not for Leisure Alone* (or *The Prospects of Architecture in Civilization*, A-121.01); *How We Live and How We Might Live* (A-123.01); *The Hopes of Civilization* (A-124.01); and *The Idle Singer* (A-127.01).

A-121.01:* Not for Leisure Alone (Hillacre)

NOT FOR LEISURE ALONE BY WILLIAM MORRIS
Edition: [1st separate edn.] A pamphlet, originally a lecture titled 'The Prospects of Architecture in Civilization', 1st pbd. in *Hopes and Fears for Art* (see A-21.01). No copy being available, the title and other information is from Walsdorf, p. 232, and Larremore, 168.
Series: The Wallet Books, Third Series: 'According to Mr. Bursch's Catalogue of 1915, Hillacre Books, p. 10, the Wallet Books . . . were printed from hand-set Caslon type . . . on good deckle-edge paper, hand-stitched into heavy brown paper wrappers with protective flap' (Larremore, 167).
Place: Riverside, Conn.
Publisher and *Printer*: Printed and published by Frederick C. Bursch at The Hillacre Bookhouse.
Collation: 16°: [1]⁸ 8 leaves, unpaginated, + a brown wrapper sewn to the body at the centrefold (Walsdorf, p. 232).
Contents: half title, title, and text.

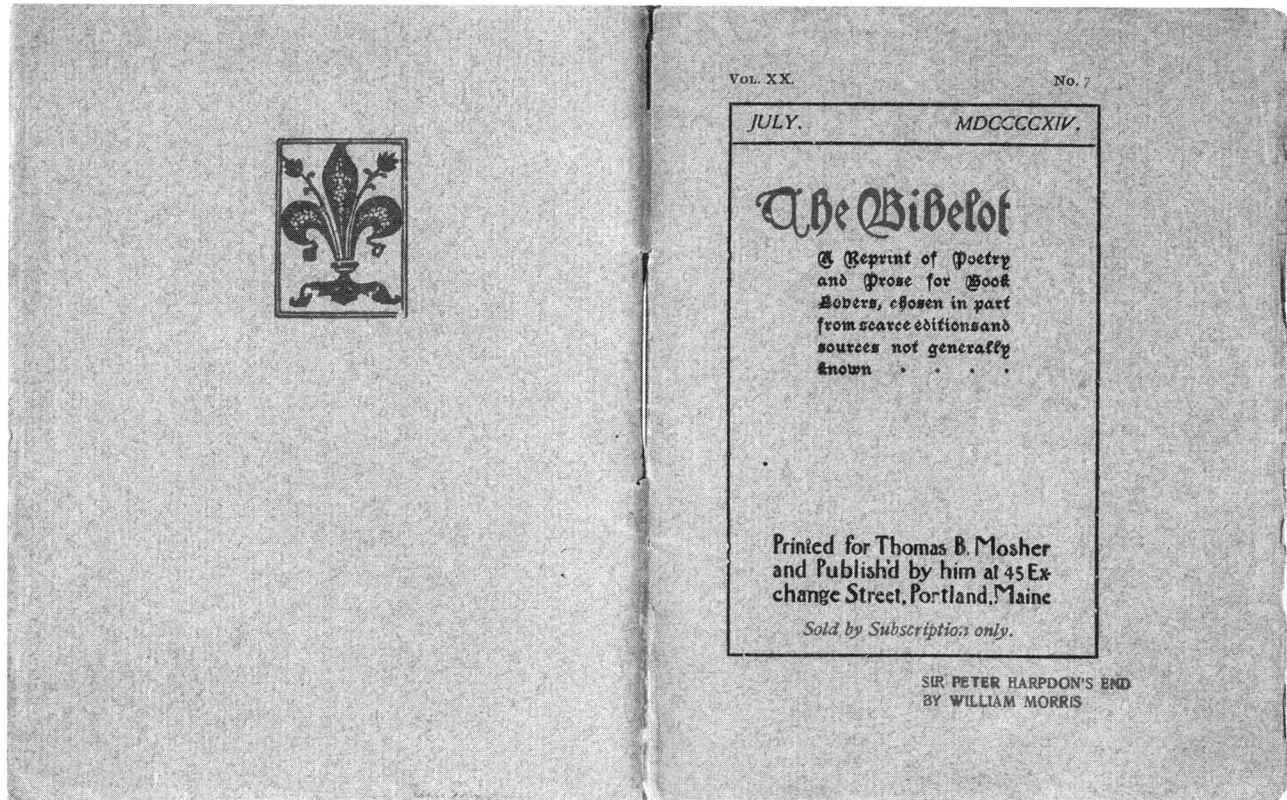

Figure 85. A-122.01: *Sir Peter Hardon's End* (Bib. edn.) wrapper, outer pages

Technical Notes: *paper*: hand-made; *leaf size*: deckled edges untrimmed, avg. 153 x 103 mm.; *type*: 'Missal' initials; title page and label in black and orange with orange device (Larremore, 168).
Publication: 1912; *print run* and *price*: unknown.
Register of Copies Located: none.

A-122.01: Sir Peter Harpdon's End (*Bib.* 2 parts)

[wrapper title, above compartment, top left] VOL. XX. [top right] NO. 7 [8] | [within thin-rule top compartment, left] JULY. [AUGUST.] [top right] MDCCCCXIV. | [thin rule] | [main compartment: detail common to all wrapper titles of this series, see A-83.01] | [below compartment, right, in red, Part 1] SIR PETER HARPDON'S END | BY WILLIAM MORRIS [or, Part 2] SIR PETER HARPDON'S END | (CONCLUDED). | BY WILLIAM MORRIS
Edition: [1st impression, 1st separate edn.] Pbd. here in 2 parts and with the 4th scene, excised from the 1st pbn. in *The Defence of Guenevere and Other Poems* (1858), pbd. here in the text for the 1st time. The missing text is supplied from that printed in May Morris's Introduction to her edn. in vol. I of the *CW*.

As with all Morris items in *The Bibelot*, the A-List entry provides finding-list information for both the separate and the annual versions (see also the *Series* field, below). For details of pbn., pagination, etc., see the *Series* field in A-83.01.
Collaborators, Editors, and Illustrators: introduction, untitled and unsigned [by T. B. Mosher]; epigraph from Alfred Noyes; and an extract from John Drinkwater's *William Morris: A Critical Study*.
Series: *The Bibelot . . .*, 20/7 and 8 (July and Aug. 1914), 247–72 and 273–89. For detail common to the series see this field in A-83.01.
Place, Publisher, and *Printer*, see wrapper title transcriptions in A-83.01.
Collation: Part 1: 12°: [1]²⁰ 20 leaves, 10 conjunct pairs, folded inside one another to form a single gathering pp. [4] [241–6] 247–72 [4] [= 40] + the usual grey-blue Bibelot wrapper sewn to the body through the centrefold.
Part 2: 12°: [1]²⁰ 20 leaves, 10 conjunct pairs, pp. [4] 273–303 [304] [4] [= 40] + the usual light blue Bibelot wrapper sewn to the body through the centrefold; on pagination and ads. in later issues, see A-83.01

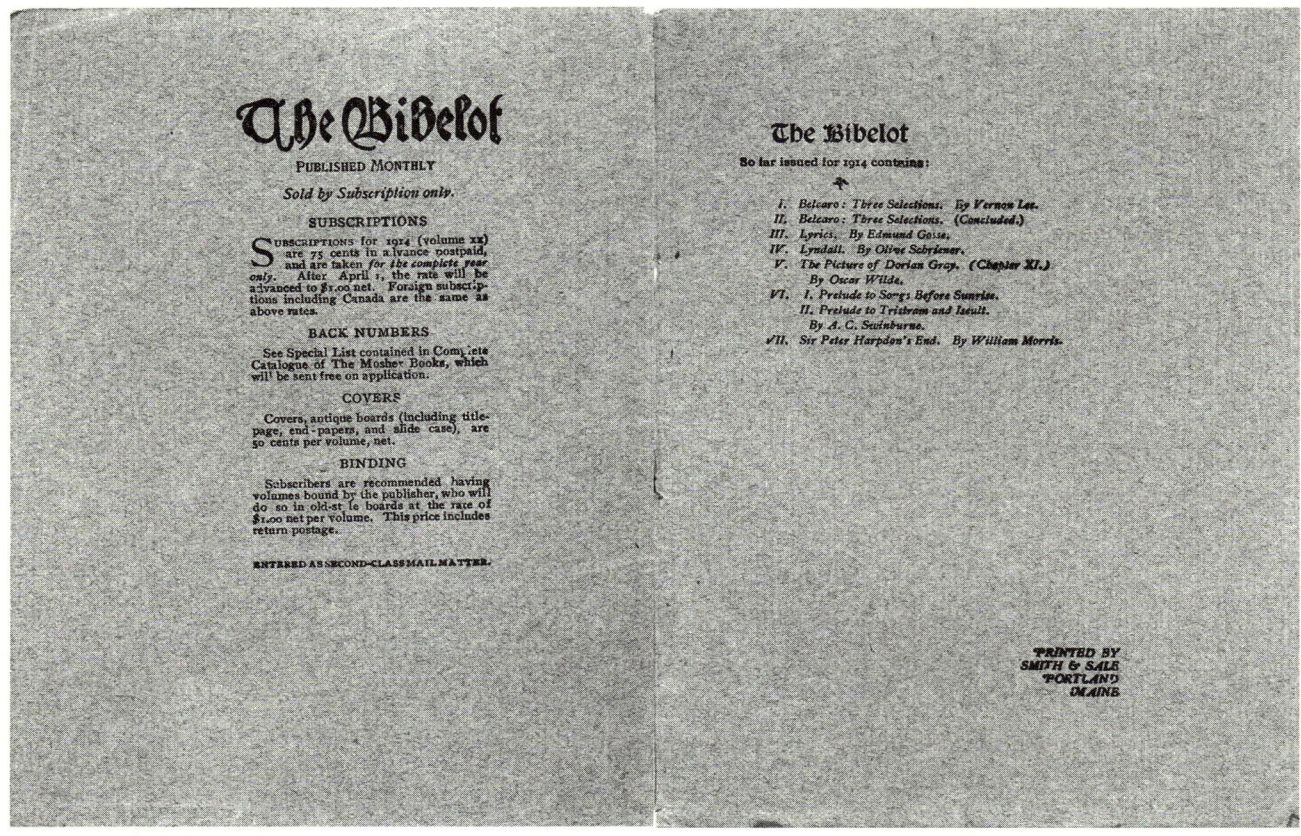

Figure 86. A-122.01: *Sir Peter Hardon's End* (Bib. edn.) wrapper, inner pages

Contents: Part 1: pp. [1–4], ads; p. [241], T. B. Mosher's unsigned foreword, headed: [3-line modern gothic] The Bibelot | [text begins]; p. [242–4], Mosher's introduction completed with printer's leaf as tail-piece and, below right, contents of the next issue; p. [245], half title: [upper right] Sir Peter Harpdon's End | By | William Morris.; p. [246], epigraph, 18 lines of prose signed, below right: Alfred Noyes.; p. 247, headed: [top, aligned left] Sir Peter Harpdon's End. | I. | [stage direction] | [text begins]; pp. 248–72, Part 1 text completed, including 2 footnotes (pp. 258, 272) from May Morris's edn.; pp. [1–4], ads.

Part 2: pp. [1–4], ads; pp. 273–89, Morris's text concluded; p. [290], blank; p. 291, dropped head: [aligned left] A Critical Estimate of | Sir Peter Harpdon's End. | [text begins]; pp. 292–[304], text completed with a bibliographical reference to Drinkwater's *William Morris: A Critical Study* and a printer's leaf as tail-piece; pp. [1–4], ads.

Technical Notes: for detail common to the series—paper, leaf size, printing, type area, lines-to-page, pagination, and wrapper title, see this field in A-83.01; items specific to this issue: *headlines*: only in Drinkwater's text, pp. 292–[304], aligned against the inner margins: [all versos] A CRITICAL ESTIMATE OF | [all rectos] SIR PETER HARPDON'S END

Publication: July and Aug. 1914 [actual issue 25 June and 25 July 1914]; *print run* and *price*: see this field in A-83.01.

Register of Copies Examined: LeM (base copy); BL (PP. 8001.ea.[94.])

Notes: the publisher's unsigned and untitled foreword disagrees with H. B. Forman's adverse judgement of the drama and adds as an afterword John Drinkwater's more favourable one. Mosher also explains why and how he has restored the 4th scene, earlier rejected by Morris when he pbd. the rest of the text in *The Defence of Guenevere*.

A. C. Swinburne writes to Morris, 3 June 1892, having just received his presentation copy of the KP *Defence of Guenevere*:—'I only wish you had inserted the admirable additional scene to "Sir Peter Harpdon's End" which you read to me so many years ago at the old "Red House", and in which the character of John Curzon was developed with such excellent humour and pathos' (Morris Papers, BL (Add.) MS 45345).

A-123.01: How We Live and How We Might Live (Hillacre)

[hanging indent] HOW WE LIVE AND | HOW WE MIGHT LIVE | By WILLIAM MORRIS | [Hillacre Bookhouse press mark] | PRINTED & PUBLISHED BY | FREDERICK C. BURSCH AT | HILLACRE RIVERSIDE CON- | NECTICUT [in red] MCMXIV

Edition: [1st separate edn.] A lecture 1st pbd. in *Commonweal*, June and July 1887 (see D-289) and later included in *Signs of Change* (see A-46.01).
Collation: small 8° gathered in 4s: [1–8]⁴ 32 leaves pp. [1–4] 5–63 [64] [= 64].
Contents: p. [1], half title; p. [2], blank; p. [3], title page; p. [4], blank; p. 5, text begins; pp. 6–63, text completed; p. [64], blank.
Technical Notes: *paper*: hand-laid, with vertical chain lines; *leaf size*: deckled edges, avg. 145 x 96; *type area*: 111 x 55 mm.; *binding*: stiff tan paper boards with dark brown machine-laid paper jacket with printed front paper label with red compartment and black letterpress: HOW WE LIVE AND | HOW WE MIGHT LIVE | BY | WILLIAM MORRIS; sold with slip case; printed in red and black.
Publication: 1914; *print run*: Walsdorf says 'unlimited' (p. 231); *price*: unknown.
Register of Copies Examined: J-F V (base copy) (see also *NUC*, Vol. 396, p. 145).
Notes: for more details on the Hillacre Morris books, see A-120.01.

A-124.01:* The Hopes of Civilization (Hillacre)

THE HOPES OF CIVILIZATION | [in red] By WILLIAM MORRIS | [publisher's device of the Hillacre Bookhouse] | [hanging indent] PRINTED & PUBLISHED BY | FREDERICK C. BURSCH AT | HILLACRE RIVERSIDE CON- | NECTICUT [in red] MCMXIV

There being no copy of this book available, this title transcript and collation are conjectural, based on the Bursch imprint as seen in the *NUC*, the Hillacre edn. of *The Art of the People*, A-17.03, and details in Larremore, 158.
Edition: [1st impression, 1st separate edn.] A lecture 1st pbd. in *Signs of Change* (see A-46.01).
Collation: small 8° printed and gathered in 4s: [1–9]⁴ 36 leaves pp. [1–4] 5–71 [72] [= 72].
Technical Notes: *paper*: machine-made; *watermark*: Utopian; *leaf size*: deckled edges, 145 x 96 mm. (details from Larremore, 158).
Publication: 1914; *print run*: Walsdorf says 'unlimited' (p. 231); *price*: unknown
Register of Copies Located: NN (NUC, Vol. 396, p. 145).
Notes: for more details on the Hillacre Morris books, see A-120.01.

A-125.01: Scenes from Fall of Troy and Other Poems and Fragments (*CW* XXIV)

THE COLLECTED WORKS | [title detail common to the set, see A-126.01] | VOLUME XXIV | SCENES FROM THE FALL OF TROY | AND OTHER POEMS | AND | FRAGMENTS | [publisher's imprint, see A-126.01] | MDCCCCXV

Edition: [1st impression, 1st edn. of the Troy poems and others previously unpublished, printed here from manuscript]. For previous pbns. see *Contents* field.
Collation: medium 8°: a⁸ (a2+1) (a6+1) b⁸ c² B–F⁸ *F⁴ G–2D⁸ [$2 (−a2) signed] 230 leaves pp. [i–vi] vii–xxxv [xxxvi] 1–51 [*Scenes from The Fall of Troy* ends and *Other Poems* begin] 52–417 [418–24] [= 460] + 2 inserted plates noted in the formula, but not counted in the book's pagination; described here in their appropriate places under *Contents*.
Contents: p. [i], blank; p. [ii], limitation notice (see A-126.01); pp. [iii–iv], blank; facing p. [v], 1st inserted plate as frontis. photo reproduction within a blind-stamped compartment, with the plate maker, in copperplate, below right: *Walker & Boutall, ph. sc.* | [label in copperplate, centred]: *William Morris | aet 23.*; p. [v], title page; p. [vi], blank; p. vii, headed: CONTENTS | [list begins]; p. viii, Contents completed; p. ix, headed: INTRODUCTION | [chapter list divided into 4 sections, being Early Poems, Poems of the Earthly Paradise Time (About 1865–1870), Late Poems, and Illustrations]; pp. x–xii, text continues; 2nd inserted plate facing p. xiii, labelled in copperplate: *Reduced page from the Kelmscott Chaucer* | [plate maker] *E. W. Ph.sc.*; pp. xiii–xxxiv, Introduction completed; p. xxxv, headed: BIBLIOGRAPHICAL NOTE | [list of previously pbd. poems included, with their 1st pbns.]; p. [xxxvi], blank; p. 1, half title: EARLY POEMS; p. [2], blank; pp. 3–51, 'Scenes from The Fall of Troy'; pp. 52–7, 'Once My Fell Foe'; pp. 58–62, 'The Long Land'; pp. 63–7, 'The Romance of the Three Wooer's'; pp. 68–9, 'St Agnes Convent'; pp. 70–1, 'Palomydes' Quest'; pp. 72–3, 'Ballad'; p. 74, 'We have done all that men could do'; p. 75, 'Saint George'; pp. 76–7, 'Twas in Church on Palm Sunday'; pp. 78–80, 'Blanche'; pp. 81–3, 'Winter Weather' (1st pbd. in *The Oxford and Cam-

bridge Magazine, 1856, see D-2); p. [84], blank; p. [85], 2nd half title: [top, aligned left] POEMS OF THE EARTHLY PARADISE | TIME (About 1865–70); 2nd section begins, p. 85: Poems of the Earthly Paradise Time (About 1865–1870): pp. 87–170, 'The Wanderers'; pp. 171–238, 'The Story of Aristomenes' (pbd. in a forged pamphlet, see E-4); pp. 239–80, 'The Story of Orpheus and Eurydice'; pp. 281–315, 'The Wooing of Swanhild'; pp. 316–28, 'In Arthur's House'; pp. 329–42, [Anthony]; pp. 343–4, 'Written in a copy of The Earthly Paradise'; pp. 345–6, 'Verses for the Months Earthly Paradise March, April, May'; pp. 347–51, 'Hapless Love' (pbd. in a forged pamphlet, see E-4); pp. 352–5, 'The Mother under the Mould'; p. 356, 'Sad-eyed and soft and grey'; p. 357, 'Rhyme slayeth shame' (pbd. in 1870, see D-24); p. 358, 'May grown a-cold' (pbd. in 1870, see D-25); p. 359, 'As this thin thread'; pp. 360–1, 'Song: Twas one little word'; pp. 362–3, 'Why dost thou struggle'; p. 364, 'O Far away to seek'; p. 365, 'Our hands have met'; p. 366, 'Fair Weather and Foul'; p. 367, 3rd half title: [top] LATE POEMS; p. [368], blank; pp. 369–408, section begins: 'The Pilgrims of Hope' (unauthorised pbn., see E-9); p. 409, 'No Master' (see A-23.03); pp. 410–11, 'The March of the Workers' (see A-23.03); p. 412, 'Down among the Dead Men' (see A-23.03); pp. 413–14, 'May Day' (see D-539); pp. 415–16, 'May Day, 1894' (see D-562); p. 417, 'For the Bed at Kelmscott' (see D-551); pp. [418–19], blank; p. [420], printer's imprint (see A-126.01); pp. [421–4], blank.

Technical Notes: paper, printing, type, position (but not content) of headlines, running titles, shoulder notes, page numbers, and binding are all common to the series and are described in this field in A-126.01, the entry for the set. Included here are only the details specific to this issue: *shoulder notes*: pp. 4–50: [all versos] Scenes | from the | Fall of | Troy; | [all rectos, sub-heads of text below]; pp. 52–417, all rectos and versos: title of adjacent poems; *printed spine label*: [4 lines common to the set] | VOLUME XXIV | SCENES FROM | THE FALL OF | TROY AND | OTHER POEMS

Publication: 1915 [issued 30 Jan.] (Longmans Arch.); for *print run* and *price*, see A-126.01.

Register of Copies Examined: see this field in A-126.01.

Notes: at the end of the project, while vols. XXIII and XXIV were in press, Longmans announced that: 'The last volume consists of over four hundred pages of new material selected from the MSS. in the possession of the Editor. 'Scenes from the fall of Troy', an early draft of 'The Wanderers' (*Earthly Paradise*), 'The Story of Aristomenes', and others, the whole representing Morris's poetical work from his early writing days almost to the end of his career' (Longmans *Notes on Books*, 11/228 (Mar. 1915), 311).

A-126.01: The Collected Works (I–XXIV)

THE COLLECTED WORKS | OF WILLIAM MORRIS | WITH INTRODUCTIONS BY | HIS DAUGHTER MAY MORRIS | VOLUME I [–XXIV] | THE DEFENCE OF GUENEVERE | THE HOLLOW LAND | LONGMANS GREEN AND COMPANY | PATERNOSTER ROW LONDON | NEW YORK BOMBAY CALCUTTA | MDCCCCX [–MDCCCCXV]

Edition: This is the standard edn. of Morris's works, and it includes 2 vols. that are 1st edns. of their individual titles—*Journals of Travel in Iceland in 1871 and 1873* (vol. VIII), and *Scenes from the Fall of Troy and Other Poems* (vol. XXIV). As 1st edns., these are treated as separates of those titles and introduced in their proper places in the general chronology, each having its own date of issue. To avoid needless repetition the details specific to the titles of each vol. of this set are provided under each title where there is only one title in the vol. and under the major title where there is more than one title in a vol. Title detail common to all vols. of the set is reserved for this entry where the set itself is considered as a title. The texts of the *CW* titles, except the two already mentioned, are new edns. of already published books for which a heading and cross reference is made at the appropriate place in the chronology of each title's successive edns., specifying the place of the *CW* edns. in the chronology of each title, and directing the reader to this entry for details common to the set. *CW* also contains 2 new collections of fugitive pieces: 'Lectures on Art and Industry' (vol. XXII) and 'Lectures on Socialism' (vol. XXIII). But these titles never have had an existence as separately pbd. entities and require no separate treatment.

May Morris's introductions were collected in 2 vols. as *May Morris: The Introductions to The Collected Works of William Morris,* with a Preface by Joseph Riggs Dunlap (New York: Oriole Editions, 1973).

Collaborators, Editors, and Illustrators: besides writing the introduction to each vol., May Morris edited every text, considering both the extant manuscripts and the previously printed versions.

Series: when the first 4 vols had been published, in Nov. 1910, Longmans advertised the set in these terms:

> The Collected Works of William Morris. Edited by Miss May Morris. 24 Vols. Medium 8°. Bound in paper boards, with

linen back. Price: Twelve Guineas net. A Prospectus with specimen pages and Illustrations will be sent on application.

This edition will be limited to 1,050 copies, of which 1,000 only will be for sale, and the 24 volumes will be sold, in sets only, at the price of 12 guineas the set. As each volume is printed the type will be distributed. It is proposed to publish the set in six quarterly instalments of four volumes each, the first instalment being now ready.

The edition which it is now proposed to issue includes some unpublished matter of great interest as well as various lectures, letters to the press and other fugitive pieces, many of which have never been reprinted. The order of issue will be mainly chronological, but in a few cases it has been found more convenient to depart from the proper sequence.

Among the works wholly or in part unpublished, the most important is the Journal kept during William Morris's first visit to Iceland in the year 1871, though of considerable interest are some lyrics and extracts from the Earthly Paradise tale 'Orpheus' and some fragments of a poem in the poet's earlier manner entitled 'Scenes from the Fall of Troy.' Each volume will be preceded by an introduction and biographical notes by the poet's daughter, Miss May Morris.

As frontispieces, in addition to the better-known portraits of the Author and some that have not been published, it is proposed to include one or two of his own Drawings and others by Dante Gabriel Rossetti, reproduced in photogravure by Mr. Emery Walker, specimens of Mr Morris's own textile designs, including the tapestry made by himself (in colour); a page of the illuminated Horace (in colour), and an example of the Cupid and Psyche series of wood-engravings, most of which Morris cut with his own hand after the designs of Sir Edward Burne-Jones. Besides these, there will be an illustration of the cabinet painted with pictures of Chaucer's 'Prioress's Tale,' which was Burne-Jones's wedding-gift to the Poet. Three portraits of Mrs. Morris will also be reproduced' (Longmans *Notes on Books*, Nov. 1910, p. 78).

At the end of the project, while vols. XXIII and XXIV were in press, Longmans announced that:

The issue of 'The Collected Works of William Morris' is now complete. Of the last four volumes, two, Volumes 21 and 22, were sent out to subscribers on the 14th of December. The first of these contains 'The Sundering Flood,' the last of the author's romances, completed except for a song and an unrevised sentence here and there, together with some unfinished romances hitherto unpublished, which will interest the student of Morris's mind and art. Volumes 22 and 23 are devoted to 'Hopes and Fears for Art,' together with Morris's lectures and papers on Architecture, Industry and Socialism. Some of these are reprinted for the first time from Justice, The Commonweal, and other sources, and are surprisingly full of actuality twenty years after (Longmans *Notes on Books*, 11/228 (Mar. 1915), 311).

Collations: see the main entry for the vol. in which the particular text appears.

Contents: See this field in the main entry for each of the vols. The sequence of prelim and postlim matter is common to all vols., but the number of blank pages before the limitation note and after the text ends varies according to the make-up of the vol.

Inserted plates in the *CW* are noted, as usual for all volumes with plates, in the collation and described in the *Contents*. Those in the *CW* that are produced from plates made by Emery Walker, which includes almost all of the frontispieces, are enclosed in blind-stamped compartments, with the plate maker's name in copperplate, below right. Composite vols. such as this 1st one, i.e. those containing more than one title, have half-title leaves preceding the text of each title. End-matter is also common, with a varied no. of blanks between the end of text and the end-papers. The printer's imprint appears on an otherwise blank leaf: PRINTED BY W. H. SMITH AND SON AT | THE ARDEN PRESS LETCHWORTH.

The remaining vols. are uniform with these details.

Technical Notes: *paper*: cream-white machine-made 'Antique Wove' (Longmans Arch.); *leaf size*: untrimmed, avg. 230 x 158 mm.; *printing*: *shoulder notes*: usually in Pica but sometimes in Long Primer; *lines-to-page*: set solid, 37 lines; *end-papers*: 3 free ends and paste-down, front and back, plain white and blank; *end-papers* for each vol. constitute a separate gathering of 4 leaves of the same 'Antique Wove' paper, sewn in as a regular gathering, front and back; *binding*: quarter holland with plain unblocked light blue paper-covered boards with white holland spines and printed paper labels: COLLECTED | WORKS | OF WILLIAM | MORRIS | VOLUME I [II–XXIV] | THE DEFENCE OF | GUENEVERE | THE HOLLOW | LAND

Publication: 1910–15: vols. 1–4, 4 Nov. 1910; vols. 5–6, 28 Mar. 1911; vols. 7–8, 14 June 1911; vol. 9, 11 Dec. 1911; vols. 10–12, 12 Dec. 1911; vols. 13–16, 31 Oct. 1912; vols. 17–20, 31 Oct. 1913; vols. 21–2, 10 Dec. 1914; vols. 23–24, 30 Jan. 1915. These dates are from Longmans Arch. and Longmans *Notes on Books*. Comments in S. C. Cockerell's diary for 1915 (see Cockerell Papers, BL (Add.) MS 52652) make it clear that the last 2 vols. of the *CW* were in fact published on the day,

30 Jan. 1915, recorded in the Longmans Arch. This strongly suggests that the dates in the Longmans Arch., at least for the *CW*, are dates of issue. The entire set was reprinted in facsimile in 1968 by Russell and Russell, New York, and in 1992 (in reduced facsimile) by Thoemmes Press, Bristol. *Print run*: 1,050 numbered sets printed, 1,000 for sale; *price*: 12*gns*. the set.

Register of Copies Examined: LeM (base copy: copy no. 709); VU (2 copies, nos. 25 and 499); VSL (copy no. 498): BGR; Fdmn; BL (012273. g. 2.)

Notes: after a proposal for a uniform collected works edn. in 1904 was declined mainly because of the fears of the American branch of Longmans that it would not sell there, C. J. Longman reintroduced the proposal on 4 May 1909, in a letter to Cockerell. His idea was for a limited edn., i.e. 1,500 sets at 10*s*. 6*d*. net per vol.: 'If such an edition as this is ever to be put on the market, it ought to be put on very shortly, as the Copyrights are beginning to run out' (Smith Arch.). On 26 Aug. 1909, Longman wrote to propose that the Trustees hire an editor, for which Longmans would put up the money, but take it out of the Trustees' share of the profits. This was agreed (ibid.) The profits were to be evenly divided.

After the W. H. Smith bid for the printing of the set came in some £400 more than Ballantyne's, Longman wrote to Charles St. John Hornby, who was both a Morris Estate trustee and a director of W. H. Smith and Son, on 28 Aug. 1909, to say that he would prefer to give the printing to The Arden Press if only a reasonable part of the gap between the Ballantyne and Arden estimates could be made up (Smith Arch.). This was accomplished, and by 6 Sept. 1909, Longmans produced a draft agreement providing that May Morris edit the entire set, with W. H. Smith's printery, The Arden Press, doing the printing.

With agreement from America this time, Longman proposed 1,050 sets be printed, with 1,000 for sale at 10*s*. 6*d*. per vol., 12*gns*. the set. Longmans undertook to put up the capital required with an arrangement for the Firm and the Estate sharing equally in the profits, the Estate's half being charged for half of the expenses. All expenses attaching to preparing the text and proofreading were the responsibility of the Estate, including the 15*gns*. per vol. for May Morris and whoever contracted to do the proofreading, that being Mr Kelk of Longmans.

A-127.01:* The Idle Singer (Hillacre)

THE IDLE SINGER | FROM 'THE EARTHLY PARADISE.' | BY WILLIAM MORRIS

Edition: [1st impression, 1st separate edn.] This book has not been seen; details here are from Walsdorf, p. 236, and Larremore, 151.
Series: Hillacre Broadsides.
Publisher: Frederick Conrad Bursch.
Collation: s. sh. broadside, printed only on one side.
Colophon: HILLACRE BROADSIDES THE EDITION OF THIS BROADSIDE CONSISTS OF 100 COPIES, PRINTED ON TUSCANY HAND MADE PAPER, AT HILLACRE, RIVERSIDE, CONN.
Contents: reprint of verses of 'An Apology', usually prefixed to the 'The Earthly Paradise'.
Technical Notes: *paper*: hand-made Tuscany paper; *leaf size*: 330 x 254 mm.; *type*: 'Missal' initials.
Publication: 1915; *print run*: 100 copies; *price*: unknown.
Register of Copies Located: NN (NUC, v. 396, p. 145).
Notes: for more details on the Hillacre Morris books, see A-120.01.

A-128.01: The Wanderers (only, LCBEL)

LONGMAN'S CLASS BOOKS OF ENGLISH LITERATURE | [thin rule] | [flush left] THE WANDERERS • BEING THE PROLOGUE TO THE | EARTHLY PARADISE • BY | WILLIAM MORRIS | WITH NOTES | LONGMANS, GREEN AND CO. | 39 PATERNOSTER ROW, LONDON, E.C. 4 | NEW YORK, TORONTO | BOMBAY, CALCUTTA AND MADRAS | 1923 | Made in Great Britain

Edition: New Impression [1st impression, 1st separate edn.] The setting is from moulds of the Silver Library Edition of 1905, i.e. 5th edn., 4th English (see A-4.18).
Collaborators, Editors, and Illustrators: Edited, with Introduction and Notes for the Use of Schools and Colleges [by J. W. Mackail, whose Introduction includes portions of his previous Introduction to the Silver Library Edition of *EP* (1905)].
Series: Longmans Class Books of English Literature. This is the last Morris book pbd. in this series, and included here (though published after 1915) to complete the account of the Morris 'Class Books'. For further series detail, see this field in *The Man Born to Be King*, A-110.01.
Collation: 8°: π⁶ A–F⁸ G⁴ 58 leaves pp. [i–iv] v–xii 1–95 [96] 97–104 [= 116].
Contents: pp. [i–ii], ads, headed: LONGMAN'S CLASS BOOKS OF | ENGLISH LITERATURE; p. [iii], title page; p. [iv], printer's imprint: Printed in England at THE BALLANTYNE PRESS | Spottiswoode, Ballantyne & Co. Ltd. | Colchester, London & Eton; p. v, headed: INTRODUC-

TION | [text begins]; pp. vi–xii, Introduction completed; p. 1, section head title and text begins; p. 2, L'Envoi ends; p. 3, headed: PROLOGUE: THE WANDERERS | ARGUMENT [6-line prose summary of the tale, in hanging indent] | [text begins]; pp. 4–95, text completed; p. [96], blank; p. 97, headed: NOTES | [glossary, entries ordered by page number]; pp. 98–104, Notes completed.
Technical Notes: for details common to this series, see A-110.01.
Publication: 1923 [issued July] (Longmans Arch.); *print run*: 3,000 copies; *price*: 1s. 6d.
Register of Copies Examined: BL (base copy: 012273. e. 1 / 57.)

A-129.01: Ornamented MSS of Middle Ages (Woolly Whale)

[within full typographical border] Some Thoughts on | the Ornamented MSS. | of the Middle | Ages | [thin rule] | BY | [in gothic] William Morris | Printed | on his Albion Hand Press, with an Account | of Its Travels from the Closing | of the Kelmscott Press | to the Present | Day. | [printer's leaf ornament] | ISSUED ON THE ONE-HUNDREDTH ANNIVERSARY | OF WILLIAM MORRIS'S BIRTH | March 24th, 1934. | [thin rule] | [swash caps] *Privately Printed* | [plain type] PRESS OF THE WOOLLY WHALE | [swash caps] *New York*
Edition: [1st impression, 1st edn.] Besides Morris's previously unpbd. fragmentary essay, printed from the manuscript in the Huntington Library, San Marino, California, this includes an essay by Melbert B. Cary, Jr., on the history of the Albion Press, No. 6551, once owned by the KP, here used for the printing of this 1st edn.
Colophon: This memorial volume, commemorating the one-hundredth | anniversary of the birth of William Morris, March 24th, | 1934, is the first book to be hand printed on his Kelmscott | 'Chaucer' Press by the Press of the Woolly Whale. The il- | lustration of the Press is from a careful drawing by Warren | Chappell. Set by hand in the original English Caslon Old | Face 16 point, a modest number of copies (besides four on | vellum) have been printed damp on Arnold Unbleached | by George W. Van Vechten, Jr.
Collation: 4°: [1]¹⁴ 14 leaves pp. [6] [1] 2–20 [21–2] [= 28].
Contents: p. [1], title page: p. [2], printer's imprint; p. [3], acknowledgment identifying the source of the Morris MS as The Huntington Library, San Marino; p. [4] blank; p. [5] half title; p. [6], blank; pp. [1] 2–12, headed: SOME THOUGHTS ON THE ORNAMENTED MANUSCRIPTS OF THE MIDDLE AGES | [text completed]; pp. 13–20, headed: A BRIEF ACCOUNT OF THE WANDERINGS OF THE ALBION PRESS NO. 6551, ITS VARIOUS OWNERS AND THE WORK IT HAS DONE | [signed below right] Melbert B. Cary, Jr.; p. 21, blank; p. 22, colophon, see above.
Technical Notes: *paper*: Arnold Unbleached; *leaf size*: 240 x 150 mm.; *end papers*: 2 free ends and a pastedown, plain white and blank, front and back; *binding*: blue paper-covered boards with vellum spine with gilt-stamped name of the author oriented vertically down the spine: WILLIAM MORRIS, with on the front a stamped illus. of the press.
Publication: 24 Mar. 1934 (see the title page transcription, above, and Peterson, 121, note). Cary's account of the travels of the Albion hand press says (p. 20) that it 'arrived and was installed in New York on March 24, 1932. Only later was it realized that this was Morris's birthday'; *print run*: 'a modest number' on paper, 4 on vellum; *price*: $5.00 for the paper copies (quoted in Walsdorf, p. 293, from a pamphlet, *Excerpts from the work of The Press of the Woolly Whale*); vellum, price unknown.
Register of Copies Examined: MU (base copy: PR 5080. S78 1934); MH (Typ 970 34-5800); CSmH; CaBVaU; IEN.
Notes: rptd., Peterson, 1–6.

A-130.01 : William Morris: Artist, Writer, Socialist (2 vols.)

[common to both vols.] WILLIAM MORRIS | ARTIST WRITER SOCIALIST | BY MAY MORRIS | [vol. I] VOLUME THE FIRST | THE ART OF WILLIAM MORRIS | MORRIS AS A WRITER | [epigraph] *Waneth wealth & fadeth friend | And we ourselves shall die | but fair fame dieth nevermore | If well ye come thereby* | [signed, below right] Hávamál | [imprint] OXFORD: BASIL BLACKWELL | MCMXXXVI | [vol. II, lines 1–3, as in vol. I] VOLUME THE SECOND | MORRIS AS A SOCIALIST | WITH AN ACCOUNT OF | WILLIAM MORRIS AS I KNEW HIM | BY BERNARD SHAW | [imprint common to both vols.]
Edition: [1st impression, 1st edn.] This is a collection of many fugitive pieces by Morris, along with many that were never published before and are here printed from the original MS. It is therefore supplementary to the *CW*, intended to make available items originally printed in out-of-the-way places and to further extend the Morris canon by including unpbd. works. For titles and 1st pbns., see *Contents*, below.
Collaborators, Illustrators, and Editors: Index, covering both

these vols. and the *CW*, prepared by Christine Blackwell. *Limitation notice*: SEVEN HUNDRED AND FIFTY COPIES | OF THIS EDITION HAVE BEEN PRINTED | AND MADE IN GREAT BRITAIN | AT THE SHAKESPEARE HEAD PRESS [some copies say: THE KEMP HALL PRESS] | ST. ALDATES OXFORD | JUNE, MDCCCCXXXVI

Collation: vol. I: medium 8°: [A]⁴ (A1+1) B–2A⁸ (2A6+1) 2B–2C⁸ (2C8+1) 2D–2T⁸ 2U¹⁰ [$1 (+2U2) signed] 342 leaves pp. [i–iv] v–vii [viii] 1–673 [674–6] [= 684] + 3 inserted plates noted in the formula and described here under *Contents*, but not included in the book's pagination.

vol. II: medium 8°: π⁴ (π1+1) a–b⁸ B–2T⁸ 2U⁴ 352 leaves pp. [i–viii] ix–xl 1–661 [662–4] [= 704] + 1 inserted plate noted in the formula but not included in the book's pagination.

Contents: The list that follows is different from the usual Section A *Contents* field in that it not only accounts for all the pages in these volumes, also but focuses on what Morris texts, complete or fragmentary, are included and whether and where they were previously pbd. The titles are as May Morris has them, but the titles as pbd. are noted in the Sections A and D references provided.

vol. I: p. [i], half title; p. [ii], blank; inserted plate as frontispiece, portrait drawing of Morris, labelled: [in copperplate] *William Morris* | *Drawn by C. Fairfax Murray from a photograph. c. 1870* | *Emery Walker Ltd. Ph. sc.*; p. [iii], title page; p.[iv], statement of limitation: SEVEN HUNDRED AND FIFTY COPIES | OF THIS EDITION HAVE BEEN PRINTED | AND MADE IN GREAT BRITAIN AT | THE SHAKESPEARE HEAD PRESS | SAINT ALDATES OXFORD | JUNE MCCCCVI; pp. v–vii, headed: THE CONTENTS OF VOLUME I | [list completed]; p. [viii], unheaded acknowledgments initialled below right: M. M.; pp. 1–99, headed: THE ART OF WILLIAM MORRIS | INTRODUCTION; p. [100], blank; pp. 101–5: 'Review of Dante Gabriel Rossetti's Poems' in *The Academy* (1870, see D-26); pp. 106–7: untitled appeal for the formation of 'an association' which became the SPAB, pbd. in *The Athenæum* (1877, see D-34); pp. 107–9: 'Restoration', a letter to *The Athenæum* on restorations at Tewksbury Abbey (1877, see D-35); pp. 109–12: Manifesto of the Society for the Protection of Ancient Buildings, originally pbd. as a quarto leaflet (1877, see A-13.01); pp. 112–19: 'The Report' at the 1st annual meeting of the SPAB (1878, see D-43); pp. 119–24: 'Address at the Second Annual Meeting' of the SPAB (1879, see D-50); pp. 124–45: 'Paper Read at the Seventh Annual Meeting of the S.P.A.B.' (1884, see D-116); pp. 146–57: 'Address at The Twelfth Annual Meeting' of the SPAB (1889, see D-468); pp. 157–8: 'Canterbury Cathedral', a letter to *The Times* (1877, see D-36); pp. 158–60: untitled, on Canterbury Cathedral, a letter to *The Times* (1877, see D-37); p. 160: Appeal for the Preservation of Inglesham Church, originally pbd. as an SPAB leaflet (1887, see A-41.01); pp. 161–2: 'Notes on the Churches of Inglesham and Kelmscott' in 'The Report' of the Twelfth Annual Meeting of the SPAB (1889, see D-468); pp. 163–5: 'Destruction of City Churches', a letter to *The Times* (1878, see D-40); pp. 165–7: 'St. Albans Cathedral', a letter to *The Times* (1878, see D-44); p. 167: 'Ashburnham House', a letter to *The Daily News* (1881, see D-66); pp. 167–9: 'High Wycombe Grammar School', a letter to *The Athenæum* (1881, see D-68); pp. 169–70: 'Blundell's School, Tiverton', a letter to *The Daily News* (1883, see D-75); pp. 170–1: 'The Vulgarisation of Oxford', a letter to *The Daily News* (1885, see D-164); pp. 171–3: 'Monuments in Westminster Abbey', a letter to *The Daily News* (1889, see D-432); pp. 173–4: untitled, a 2nd letter on monuments in Westminster Abbey to *The Daily News* (1889, see D-450); pp. 174–81: 'Westminster Abbey and Its Monuments', an article pbd. in *The Nineteenth Century* (1889, see D-437); pp. 181–3: 'Peterborough Cathedral', a letter to *The Pall Mall Gazette* (1889, see D-473); pp. 183–5: 'The Proposed Addition to Westminster Abbey', a letter to *The Times* (1891, see D-529); pp. 185–6: a letter opposing a proposal for an extension to Westminster Abbey for the housing of funereal monuments, *The Daily Chronicle* (1894, see D-560); pp. 186–8: 'The Royal Tombs in Westminster Abbey', a letter to *The Times* (1895, see D-573); pp. 188–90: 'The Restoration of Rouen Cathedral', a letter to *The Athenæum* (1895, see D-577); p. 190: 'Peterborough Cathedral', a letter to *The Daily Chronicle* (1895, see D-581); pp. 191–2: 'Chichester Cathedral', a letter to *The Times* (1895, see D-583); pp. 192–7: 'Speech at a Meeting of the Kyrle Society, Kensington Vestry Hall, 27 January, 1881', 1st pbd. in *The Women's Union Journal* (1881, see D-62); pp. 197–205: 'Nottingham Kyrle Society, 1881', a speech at The Castle, Nottingham, on 16 Mar. 1881: not previously pbd.; pp. 205–25: 'Technical Instruction: Royal Commission on Technical Instruction ... William Morris examined', Morris's testimony before the Royal Commission was pbd. in *Evidence before The Royal Commission on Technical Education. Second Report of the Commissioners*. vol. 3 (1884, see Appendix I-2); pp. 225–41: 'The Exhibition of the Royal Academy (By a Rare Visitor)', an article in *To-Day* (1884, see D-108); pp. 241–66: *Arts and Crafts Essays*, with the texts of Morris's contributions: the 'Preface', 'Textiles', 'Printing', and 'Of Dyeing as an Art' (1893, for the publishing history of Morris's contributions, see B-15); pp. 266–86: *Gothic Architecture* (a KP book, 1893, see A-66.01); pp. 286–9: 'Preface to *Medieval Lore* by Robert Steele' (1893, see B-13); pp. 289–92: 'More's Utopia: Foreword by William Morris' (a KP book, 1893, see B-14); pp. 292–5: 'Preface to *The Nature of Gothic* by John Ruskin' (a KP book, 1892, see B-12); pp. 295–6: 'Introductory Note to *Good King Wenceslas*, by Dr. Neale' (1894, see B-16.01); pp. 296–310: 'Address on the Collection of Paintings of the English Pre-Raphaelite School in the City of Birmingham Museum and Art Gallery on Friday, October 24, 1891', 1st pbd. as a pamphlet by the Birmingham Museum and Art Gallery (1891, see A-60.01); pp. 310–18: 'The Ideal Book. A Paper read before the Bibliographical Society', 1st pbd. as an article in *Transactions of the Bibliographical Society* (1893, see D-555); pp. 318–38: 'The Woodcuts of Gothic Books. A Paper read before The Society of Arts', pbd. as an article in *The Journal of the Society of Arts* (1892, see D-538); pp. 338–45: 'Some Notes on the Illuminated Books of the Middle Ages', pbd. in *The Magazine of Art* (1894, see D-557); pp. 346–56: 'On the Artistic Qualities of the Woodcut Books of Ulm and Augsburg in the Fifteenth Century', pbd. in *Bibliographica* (1895, see D-585); pp. 356–64: 'Stained Glass', an article for *Chamber's Encyclopædia* (1890, see B-11); inserted plate from a woodcut, signed lower left corner: F. L. G. 1936; and labelled below: THE MEMORIAL HALL KELMSCOTT | *Drawn by F. L. Griggs R.A.* | [below right]: *Vol. I, to face page 364*; verso blank; pp. 364–71: [headed] Gossip about an Old House on the Upper Thames | [text completed], an article written for *The Quest* (1894, see D-579 and E-14); pp. 377–82: passages from an untitled and unpublished poem written for the Oxford Prize Poem competition of 1853 on the subject 'The Dedication of the Temple' (1853) pbd. entire in *The Juvenilia of William Morris: with a Checklist and Unpublished Early Poems* (1983, see A-140.01; hereafter referred to as *Juvenilia*); pp. 382–400, editorial comment; inserted plate facing p. 401, within a thick-rule border, labelled below: SYRINX & PSYCHE | *Engraved on wood by William Morris* | *from a drawing by E. Burne-Jones* | *for The Earthly Paradise* | [below left] *Vol. I, to face page* 401; pp. 401–4, more editorial comment and quotation; pp. 405–11, 414–22, 424–5, 426–7, 435–6: draft passages from stories later revised for *EP*; pp. 449–53: untitled passages from 'an unpublished lecture', later pbd. in full as 'The Early Literature of the North—Iceland' in *Unpublished Lectures* (1969, see A-133.01); pp. 462–7: 4 unpbd. Norse-inspired poems of the 1870s and 80s: 'State-aided Emigration in 889' and 3 untitled; pp. 484–8: rejected (and unpbd.) passage intended for *Sigurd the Volsung*; pp. 517–32: 'Juvenilia' section of 8 previously unpbd. poems: (1) p. 517: 'Ballad: Where have you been so long to-day?'; (2) pp. 517–18: 'Ballad: Malmston had a dream in the night'; (3) pp. 518–23: 'Fame'; (4) pp. 523–4: 'The Abbey and the Palace'; (5) pp. 525–9: 'The Night-Walk'; (6) p. 530: 'The Fen River'; (7) p. 531: 'The Banners'; (8) pp. 531–2: 'Drowned'; pp. 532–43: a new section titled 'Poems of about the Earthly Paradise Period': pp. 532–4: translation of a 'French Noel', originally pbd. in a *Collection of Antient Christmas Carols* (1860, see B-1); pp. 534–5: 'Song for Orpheus', previously unpbd.; pp. 535–6: 'Song for Orpheus' (2), previously unpbd.; pp. 536–8: 'Song for Cupid and Psyche' previously unpbd.; pp. 538–9: 'Near but far away', previously unpbd.; p. 539: 'The Doomed Ship', previously unpbd.; pp. 539–40: 'What All Men Long for & What None Shall Have', previously unpbd.; pp. 541–3: 'Praise of Wine', previously unpbd.; p. 543: 'Verses for Pictures', comprising 2 lyrics, each a quatrain', 'The Pilgrim at the Gate of Idleness' and 'The Heart of the Rose', both for an exhibition in the New Gallery Summer Exhibition, 1893 (may have been pbd. in the catalogue) of 2 Burne-Jones pictures illustrating scenes from The Romance of the Rose; pp. 543–63: translations 'From the Icelandic', comprising Morris's previously unpbd. and 'unrevised' draft translations from 'The Prophecy of the Vala', in 71 stanzas of irregular length; and pp. 565–636: 'The Story of Egil the Son of Scaldgrim' (Egilssaga) previously unpbd. fragment in 40 chapters. The letters included at the end of this vol., pp. 639–73, are omitted here as there is no indication that Morris intended any of these to be pbd. They are included in Kelvin's edn. of the *Letters*.

vol. II: p. [i], half title; p. [ii], blank; inserted engraved plate as frontispiece, labelled below in copperplate: [below left *F. L. Griggs del. 1911* [right] *Emery Walker Ltd.ph.lc.* | [centred] William Morris's Grave in Kelmscott Churchyard; p. [iii] title page; p. [iv], statement of limitation, as in Vol. I; pp. v–vii, headed: THE CONTENTS OF VOLUME II | [list completed]; p. [viii], blank; pp. ix–xl, headed: MORRIS AS I KNEW HIM | [text completed and initialled below right] G. B. S.; pp. 1–53, editorial introduction; pp. 53–62: Extended passages from a previously unpbd. lecture entitled 'War and Peace', signed 'W. M. Jan. 30. 1880. 2.30 a.m. Kelmscott House, Upper Mall, Hammersmith'; pp. 63–72: extensive passages thought to be from a previously unpbd. lecture, said by May Morris to have been 'written in 1880', and on the MS of which Morris wrote, 'Queen Sq: to Men and Women's College' (but see 'Some Hints on Pattern Designing', D-69); pp. 114–49: passages from early Socialist articles by Morris in *Justice* and elsewhere, comprising: 'An Old Fable Retold' (see D-86); pp. 116–17: 'The Way Out: An Appeal to Genuine Radicals' (see D-93); pp. 118–19: 'Uncrowned Kings' (see D-117); pp. 120–2: 'The Dull Level of Life' (see D-101); pp. 122–8: 'Philanthropists' (see D-127); pp. 128–30: 'Why not?' (see D-99); pp. 130–40: the 3-part article on 'A Factory as It Might Be' (see D-102, 105, and 107); pp. 140–2: 'Individualism at the Royal Academy' (see D-104); pp. 143–7: 'The Lord Mayor's Show' (see D-125); pp. 150–69: several texts under 'Morris as a Lecturer': pp. 150–64: extensive passages from the previously unpbd. 'Misery and the Way Out' (see D-119); pp. 165–9: passages from a previously unpbd. and untitled lecture at a picture-show at the Whitechapel Art Gallery (for a 2nd such lecture, see pp. 406–19); passages from a lecture, 'Socialism' (unpbd. in May Morris's view, but see A-34.01 and D-175); pp. 197–203: several passages from a previously unpbd. lecture on 'Equality'; pp. 230–5: a *Commonweal* leader on 'Our Policy' (see D-176); pp. 237–40: untitled excerpts from Morris's *Commonweal* article, 'Free Speech in the Streets' (see D-214); pp. 243–4: untitled excerpts from Morris's article, 'Coercion for London' (see D-286); pp. 245–6: an untitled excerpt from Morris's 'Free Speech in America' article in *Commonweal* (see D-320); pp. 251–5: from *Commonweal*, Morris's article on 'London in a State of Siege' (see D-333); pp. 268–72: excerpts from Morris's article, 'A Triple Alliance' (see D-361); pp. 275–6: untitled excerpts from Morris's article 'Socialism and Politics' (see D-149); pp. 277–87: an edited version of a previously unpbd. 1886 lecture, 'The Political Outlook' (see A-133.01); pp. 289–92: excerpts from the *Commonweal* article 'The Skeleton at the Feast' (see D-384); pp. 292–4: from his *Commonweal* 'Notes on Passing Events', an excerpt on the proposal to turn Beaumont Hall into a 'People's Palace' (see D-238); pp. 294–5: excerpts from *Commonweal* 'Notes on News' in which Morris comments on a Guinness Trust proposal for an exhibition of the 'Garments of the Poor' (see D-484); p. 297: a passage from 'Notes on News' on vegetarianism as a cure for poverty (see D-411); pp. 298–9: untitled excerpt from a previously unpbd. 1885 lecture, [The Depression of Trade] (see A-133.01); pp. 299–300: a comment in 'Notes on News' on the inadequacy of the co-operative movement as a response to the labour question (see D-290); pp. 300–1: 'Notes on News', comment on the superiority of Socialism to the Co-operative Movement as a response to the class-war conditions (see D-379); pp. 301–2: untitled letter from *Commonweal*, where it is titled 'Correspondence. Christianity and Socialism' in which Morris responds to a letter by Rev. J. Rickarby (see D-501); pp. 305–7: passages from a *Commonweal* article, 'On Some "Practical" Socialists' (see D-359); pp. 308–10: passages from 'The Policy of the Socialist League', as written by Morris and pbd. in *Commonweal* (see D-380); p. 311: a passage from a previously unpbd. lecture, 'Commercial War' (see A-133.01); pp. 312–17: a letter, complete as pbd. in *Commonweal* under the heading 'Correspondence', continues a discussion of Anarchism and Socialism (see D-458); pp. 317–21: a *Commonweal* letter, complete except for the 1st paragraph, headed 'Communism and Anarchism', continues the previous discussion (see D-470); pp. 330–3: untitled passages run together from 3 different *Commonweal* 'Notes on News' columns, all on the Dockers' Strike of 1889 (see D-471, 474, and 477); pp. 341–3: a previously unpbd. lecture on 'Socialism Up-to-date' (see A-133.01); pp. 345–52: passages from a previously 'unpublished lecture on Communism' (see A-133.01); pp. 355–7: passages from a previously unpbd. lecture, largely notes, titled 'What Is: What Should Be: What Will Be: What May Be' (see A-133.01); pp. 358–61: excerpts from a previously unpbd. lecture, 'What We Have to Look For' (see A-133.01); pp. 361–3: an article for *Justice*, May Day, 1896 (see D-592); pp. 367–606: under the heading 'Lectures, Articles and Letters' are a number of complete items, pbd. or previously unpbd.: pp. 370–82: a previously unpbd. lecture, 'Address to English Liberals' (see A-133.01); pp. 382–406: 'Art and the People: A Socialist's Protest against Capitalist Brutality; Addressed to the Working Classes' (see A-133.01); pp. 406–19: a previously unpbd. lecture, 'At a Picture Show' (see A-133.01); pp. 420–34: a lecture pbd. in Norwich *Daylight*, here titled 'The End and the Means' (see D-233); pp. 434–53: a previously unpbd. lecture, 'The Policy of Abstention' (see A-133.01); pp. 453–68: a pbd. lecture, 'The Society of the Future' (see D-445); pp. 469–83: a previously unpbd. lecture, 'Makeshift' (see A-133.01); pp. 483–7: a letter to *The Daily News* on 'England and the Turks' (see D-33); pp. 488–92: a *Commonweal* article, 'The Reward of Genius' (see D-229); pp. 492–6: a letter pbd. in *Commonweal*, titled 'Artist and Artisan: As an Artist Sees It' (see D-315); pp. 496–500: a *Commonweal* article titled 'Thoughts on Education under Capitalism' (see D-389); pp. 501–7: a review of Bellamy's 'Looking Backward' (see D-462); pp. 507–12: an article 'Under an Elm-Tree; or, Thoughts on the Country-Side' (see D-465); pp. 512–18: 'Where Are We Now?' Morris's farewell to the SL (see D-525); pp. 519–21: an article, pbd. by *The Sun*, on 'The Coal Struggle, Some Obvious Thoughts Thereon' (see D-552); pp. 522–4: a letter to *The Daily Chronicle*

on 'The Deeper Meaning of the Struggle' (see D-554); pp. 524–7: an article for *Liberty* titled 'As to Bribing Excellence' (see D-570); pp. 528–67: a play, *The Tables Turned; or, Nupkins Awakened* (see A-42.01); pp. 568–606, section of 'Personal Letters', pbd. in *Letters*, not detailed here; pp. 607–11: an 'Appendix. List of drafts, &c.'; pp. 612-25 :'Appendix. Inconsequences'; pp. 625–7: 'Socialists at Play' (see E- 8); pp. 627–31: a list of his 'Likes and Dislikes'; pp. 632–7: a 'Calendar of the Principal Events in Morris's Life'; pp. 638–40: a 'List of the Principal Lectures Delivered by William Morris'; p. 641: an Errata sheet; and, pp. 642–61: an 'Index to the Collected Works', by Christine Blackwell, which indexes both of these vols. and the 24-vol. *CW*.
Technical Notes: these vols. are obviously designed to range with the *CW*; paper, leaf size, printing, lines-to-page, type face, shoulder notes, and binding are all the same, for which see this field in A-126.01; *end-papers* differ: 1 free end and paste-down, plain white and blank, front and back; *spine labels*: [common to both vols.] WILLIAM | MORRIS | ARTIST WRITER | SOCIALIST | BY MAY MORRIS | [specific to] VOLUME I | THE ART OF | WILLIAM | MORRIS | MORRIS AS A | WRITER [specific to] VOLUME II | MORRIS AS A | SOCIALIST | INTRODUCTION BY | BERNARD | SHAW
Publication: 1936 [issued mid-Aug.] (Cockerell wrote two letters to May Morris, 16 and 25 Aug. 1936, the 1st saying the 2 vols are out but complaining he has not yet seen his copy. His copy arrived by 25 Aug. (see Cockerell Papers, BL (Add.) MS 52740); *print run*: 750 copies; *price*: unknown.
Register of Copies Examined: LeM (base copy); BL (010821. ff. 7.)
Notes: S. C. Cockerell to May Morris, 13 July 1932:—Cockerell refers to this work, and extends his sympathies to her because Longmans has rejected the 2 vols. for pbn., on economic grounds, a decision he and Walker had already discussed and found reasonable. In the midst of the depression such books would be unlikely to have good sales (Cockerell Papers, BL (Add.) MS 52740). On the involvement of Sir Basil Blackwell in this pbn., see his introduction to G. B. Shaw's *Morris as I Knew Him* (London: Morris Society, 1966), 6–7.

A-131.01: William Morris and His Praise of Wine

[ornamental device of vine and grapes] WILLIAM MORRIS | and his 'Praise of Wine' | [aligned right] Los Angeles | 1958
Edition: the title poem is bound in with a previously unpublished, untitled sonnet, beginning 'Ah, shall this day be e'en as morn of yesterday?' Thus this pamphlet contains the 1st pbn. of an untitled sonnet as well as the 1st separate edn. of Morris's 'In Praise of Wine', previously printed in MM, i. 541–43. The presence of the sonnet makes this pamphlet a 1st edn.
Collaborators, Editors, and Illustrators: [edited and introduced by] Ward Ritchie.
Colophon: 300 copies | have been printed for | Theodore Lilienthal | and | Ward Ritchie | for distribution | to the members of the | Roxburghe Club | and the | Zamorano Club | [swelled rule] The Ward Ritchie Press | September 21, 1958
Collation: long 8°: [1]⁸ 8 leaves pp. [2] [1–4] 5–11 [12–14] [= 16] + a blue paper wrapper stapled to the body through the centrefold.
Contents: pp. [1–2], blank; p. [1], title page; p. [2], blank; p. [3], text of 'In Praise of Wine' begins, no title, 3-line initial 'T'; p. [4], text concludes; p. 5, Ward Ritchie's commentary begins with 3-line initial 'W', no title; pp. 6–8, commentary continues; p. 9, unpbd. text of sonnet, 'What change is this since morn of yesterday?'; pp. 10–11, Commentary completed with signature, flush right: Ward Ritchie; p. [12], blank; p. 13, colophon (see above); p. [14], blank.
Technical Notes: *paper*: plain white bond machine-made; *leaf size*: cut flush, 220 x 122 mm.; *pagination*: centred on direction line; *binding*: plain unblocked blue hand-made paper wrapper with printed paper label on upper front: [within thick rule compartment] WILLIAM MORRIS | and his | PRAISE OF WINE
Publication: 21 Sept. 1958 (colophon date, the date of issue was probably shortly thereafter).
Register of Copies Examined: Fdmn (base copy); J-F V.

A-132.01: Mr. William Morris on Art Matters (WMS)

[wrapper title, in red] Mr. William Morris on Art Matters | [in black] from *The Manchester Guardian* 21 October 1882 | WILLIAM MORRIS SOCIETY | LONDON | 1961
Edition: [1st separate edn.]
Collaborators, Editors, and Illustrators: [edited for the Society by Ronald Briggs, Hon. Sec.]
Collation: s. sh. 4°: [1]⁴ 4 leaves pp. [1] 2-7 [8] self-wrappered and stapled at the centrefold.
Contents: [1], wrapper title (see above); p. 2, head title, top, repeats lines 1 and 2 of the title page | text begins; pp. 2–7, text completed; p. [8], imprint: [in red] June, 1961 | [black] Printed in Great Britain
Technical Notes: *paper*: cream-white machine-wove, no water mark; *leaf size*: cut flush, 254 x 159 mm.; *print: type*:

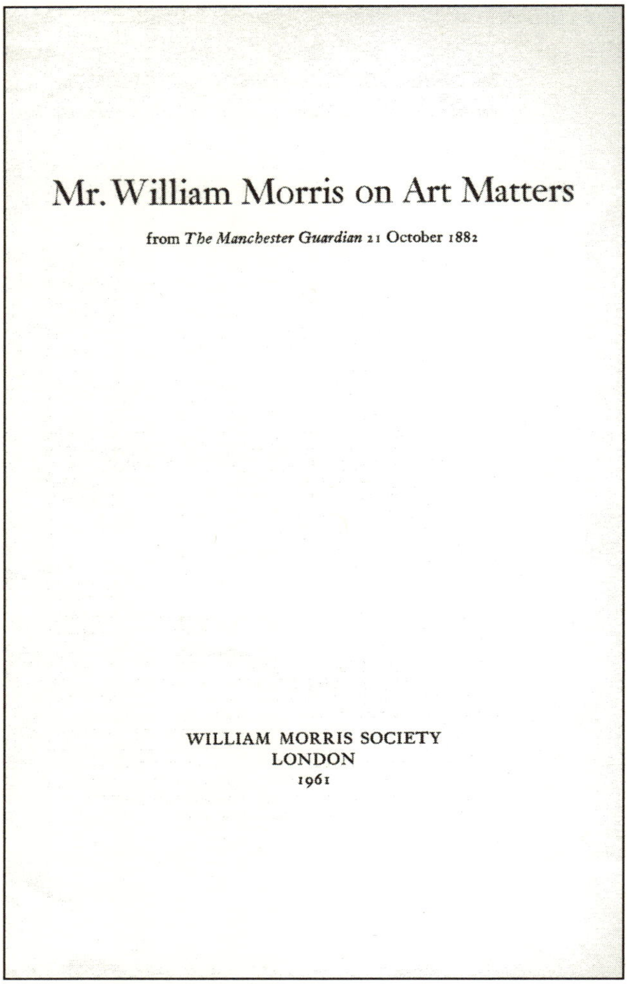

Figure 87. A-132.01: *Morris on Art Matters* (1st edn.) wrapper title

Times New Roman ; *pagination*: Arabic numbers at the outer matgin on the direction line; *binding*: *wrapper*: self-wrapped, printed as described in *Contents*
Publication: dated June, 1961 in the imprint; *print run* and *price*: unknown.
Register of Copies Examined: LeM (base copy)
Notes: This pamphlet makes available a fugitive piece Morris wrote as a speech for delivery at the opening of The Fine Art and Industrial Exhibition at St. James's Hall, Manchester on 20 Oct. 1882. It was published in full in both *The Architect*, 28 Oct., and *The Manchester Guardian*, 21 Oct. (see D-73).

A-133.01: Unpublished Lectures of William Morris

the unpublished | lectures of | [neo-gothic] William Morris | [plain text] edited and compiled by | EUGENE D. LEMIRE | UNIVERSITY OF WINDSOR | [1st, smaller, KP pressmark, reduced] | Wayne State University Press | Detroit / 1969
Edition: [1st impression, 1st edn.] A collection of lectures previously either entirely or mainly unpublished; thus this edn. of Morris is supplementary to the *CW* and MM, i and ii. For earlier pbn of portions, see *Contents*, below.
Collation: large 8° printed and gathered as 16°: [1–9^{16} 10^8 11^{16}] 168 leaves pp. [1–6] 7–331 [332–6] [= 336].
Contents: 10 lectures are here published entire, all taken from MS in the British Library. Included here are the titles, and whether and where items were, in part, previously published:
1. [Art: A Serious Thing], pp. 36–53, was pbd. in part in *The Leek Times*, 16 Dec. 1882;
2. 'The Gothic Revival [part 1]', pp. 54–73; a excerpt was pbd. in MM, ii. 629–30;
3. 'The Gothic Revival [part 2]', pp. 74–93;
4. 'Art and Labour', pp. 94–118;
5. [The Depression of Trade], pp. 119–35; an excerpt was pbd. in MM, ii. 298–9;
6. 'Of the Origins of Ornamental Art', pp. 136–57; excerpts were pbd. in The *Manchester Guardian*, 27 Sept. 1886, p. 6, and in *The American Architect*, Dec. 1886, pp. 288–9;
7. 'Early England', pp. 158–78;
8. 'The Early Literature of the North—Iceland', pp. 179–98; previously unpbd., except for the 1st page, set up as a sample of KP printing (see Appendix II-5);
9. [The Present Outlook in Politics], pp. 199–216;
10. 'What Socialists Want', pp. 217–33.
Besides these Morris texts, the *Unpublished Lectures* provides an Introduction, pp. 14–32, Editor's Note, pp. 33–5, and 2 appendices: 'A Calendar of William Morris's Platform Career', pp. 234–90, and 'A Bibliographical Checklist of Morris's Speeches and Lectures', pp. 291–322.
Technical Notes: *leaf size*: trimmed, 228 x 152 mm.; *endpapers*: single free end and paste-down, plain brown and blank, front and back; *running titles*: all versos except titles, etc., aligned to the inner margins: *The Unpublished Lectures of William Morris* | [all rectos, titles of the relevant lectures in italics]; *binding*: plain unblocked brown cloth gilt-stamped on spine: [horizontal at the head] LEMIRE | [vertical orientation, two lines down the spine] *the unpublished lectures of* | [in modern gothic] William Morris | [horizontal, at the foot, in swash letters] wayne; *dust covers*: light grey heavy paper with full ornamental borders front and back, within which on the back is an engraved pen-and-ink drawing of Morris; *letterpress*: within the bor-

der on the front: [2-line italics] *the unpublished* | *lectures of* | [neo-gothic 3-line type] William Morris | edited and compiled by | EUGENE D. LEMIRE; spine lettering reproduces the binding spine, above.
Publication: 1969; *print run*: 2,000 copies; *price*: $9.95.
Register of Copies Examined: LeM (4 copies: base copy); SU; VU; SSL, BL

A-134.01: The Story of Kormak

THE STORY OF | KORMAK | THE SON OF OGMUND | by William Morris | and Eiríkr Magnússon | *With an Introduction* | *by Grace J. Calder* | *and a Note on the manuscript* | *work of William Morris* | *by Alfred Fairbank* | [ornamental rule] *1970* | WILLIAM MORRIS SOCIETY | *LONDON*
Edition: [1st impression, 1st edn.].
Translation: Trans. from the Icelandic with Eiríkr Magnússon.
Colophon: This book was printed by Nordlundes Bogtrykkeri, Copenhagen. | The plates were printed by The Meriden Gravure Company, Meriden, Connecticut. | The binding was done by the Kemp Hall Bindery, Oxford. | The work was completed in September 1970.
Collation: 4° in 8s: [1–6⁸ (6$_4$+6) 7–9⁸ 10⁶] 78 leaves pp. [2] [i–iv] v [vi] vii [viii]–xiii [xiv] 1–139 [140] [= 156] + a 6° gathering of plates sewn, and consisting of 12 pages of illus., noted in the formula and described in the *Contents*, but not counted in the pagination.
Contents: pp. [*1–2*], blank; p. [i], half title; p. [ii], blank; p. [iii], title page; p. [iv], imprint; p. v, Foreword, by Basil Blackwell; p. [vi], blank; p. vii, headed: CONTENTS | [list completed]; p. [viii], blank; pp. ix–x, Acknowledgments; p. xi, List of Illustrations; pp. [xii], blank; p. xiii, List of Abbreviations; p. [xiv], blank; pp. 1–44, Introduction; pp. 45–6, Bibliographical Note; pp. 47–51, A Note on Dróttkvætt; p. [52], blank; pp. 53–64, A Note on the Manuscript Work of William Morris; pp. 65–9, An Annotated List of the Manuscript Work of William Morris [initialled at the end] 'A. F./' [Alfred Fairbank]; p. [70], blank; p. 71, half title: THE PLATES; p. [71], blank; inserted between pp. [71] and 73 are 12 unnumbered pages of plates: I–III: 3 from Kormak MS; IV: from The Dwellers at Eyr MS; V: from Morris's A Book of Verse MS; VI: from the Rubáiyát; VII from the Dwellers at Eyr; VIII: from Hen Thorir MS; IX: from Hig Hafbur MS; X: from The Odes of Horace; XI: from the Virgil MS; XII: some experimental scripts; p. 73, 3rd half title: THE STORY OF KORMAK | NOTE ON THE TEXT | [note completed], p. [74], blank; pp. 75–[134], the text of The Story of Kormak completed with explicit: AND SO HERE ENDED THE STORY.; pp. [135–6], blank; pp. 137–9, Index; p. [140], colophon.
Technical Notes: *paper*: cream-white machine-made, no watermark; *leaf size*: 272 x 184 mm.; *binding*: 3/4 calf binding with dark green calf spine and beige cloth-covered boards separated by a gilt vertical thick rule; gilt-stamped down the spine: [printer's ornament before and after] THE STORY OF KORMAK | [horizontal orientation] WILLIAM | MORRIS | SOCIETY
Publication: 1970 [issued Sept.–Dec.] (printing and binding were completed in Sept.); *print run*: unknown; *price*: £5.25
Register of Copies Examined: LeM (base copy); CSt (2 copies: Green Stacks PT7269.K7E56 and Spec.Coll Felton PR5081. K6); VU (B f 839.6/K84); SU (RC 839.608/K84Q).

A-135.01: How Shall We Live Then?

[wrapper title] AN UNPUBLISHED LECTURE OF WILLIAM MORRIS: | 'HOW SHALL WE LIVE THEN?' | Edited by Paul Meier | *International Review of Social History, Vol. XVI (1971), Part 2*
Edition: [1st impression, 1st separate edn.] The lecture here published is an offprint from *The International Review of Social History* (see D-600).
Collaborators, Editors, and Illustrators: Edited, annotated, and introduced by Paul Meier.
Place: Amsterdam.
Collation: a single gathering of 12 conjunct leaves pp. [1] 2–24 [= 24] + wrapper, folded at the centre and stapled twice at the fold.
Contents: p. [1], headed DOCUMENTS | [aligned left] *Paul Meier* | AN UNPUBLISHED LECTURE OF WILLIAM MORRIS | [text begins]; pp. 2–24, text completed.
Technical Notes: *leaf size*: cut flush, 239 x 157 mm.; *wrapper*: stiff white paper p. [1], title; pp. [2–4], blank.
Publication: 1971; *print run* and *price*: not known, probably for free distribution by the author.
Register of Copies Examined: LeM (base copy); BL; IISH (2 copies: Br0498/6 & 3052-6.

A-136.01: Justice and Socialism

'Justice and Socialism' (extensive notes for a lecture), first pbd. in *LA PENSÉE UTOPIQUE DE WILLIAM MORRIS*, by Paul Meier (Paris: Editions Sociales, 1972); pp. 835–40.
Edition: Though not a separate edn., nor in any sense a periodical article, this pbn. is the only existing version of

a significant part of a lecture, printed from a MS in the library of Chimen Abramsky of London. Since it is the only known source of this lecture, it is included here.
Publication: 1972; Morris's lecture was originally delivered to the Bloomsbury Branch of the SL on 1 Oct. 1885 (see Paul Meier, *William Morris: the Marxist Dreamer*, ii. 579).
Register of Copies Examined: LeM (base copy)
Notes: Meier's book has been translated into English by Frank Gubb as *William Morris: The Marxist Dreamer* (2 vols. Hassocks, Sussex: The Harvester Press, 1978). Here, as in the French original, the lectures notes are printed entire as an appendix, in ii. [579]–84.

A-137.01: Cupid and Psyche (2 vols.)

[the text is in vol. 2, title page: flush left, on a grey background, printer's leaf] WILLIAM MORRIS: The Story of | Cupid and Psyche, with wood-engravings designed by | Edward Burne-Jones and mostly engraved by | William Morris, with an Introduction by A. R. Dufty; | published by Clover Hill Editions, London | and Cambridge 1974;
Edition: [1st separate edn.] The tale 1st appeared in *EP*, Part 1, the 1st of the tales for May (see A-4.01). Though a 2 vol. set, Morris's entire text with the Burne-Jones illus. is contained in the 2nd vol., the 1st being A. R. Dufty's introduction and editorial machinery.
Collaborators, Editors, and Illustrators: Douglas Cleverdon, General Editor.
Publisher: Clover Hill Editions: Will and Sebastian Carter, joint publishers with Douglas Cleverdon, 12 Chesterton Road Cambridge CB4 3AB.
Colophon: The Story of Cupid and Psyche, Volume 2. | The text with the engravings was designed | and printed by Will and Sebastian Carter | at the Rampant Lions Press, Cambridge, | in the Kelmscott Troy Types cast at the foundry | of the Oxford University Press from the | original matrices in the possession of | the Cambridge University Press, | on paper made by J. Barcham Green. | Bound by John P. Gray, Cambridge.
Collation: (vol. 2 only) large 4°: [1–13]⁴ 52 leaves pp. [8] [1–2] 3–92 [93–6] [= 104].
Contents: (vol. 2 only): pp. [1–2], blank; p. [3], half title: [flush left, printer's leaf] The Story of Cupid and Psyche, Volume Two: | the poem with the engravings; p. [4], large display-type title as frontis.: [printed on grey background in a double thick-thin ruled compartment] The | Story | of | Cupid | and | Psyche; p. [5], title page; p. [6], copyright statement and a note on the Morris attributions for the woodcuts; p. [7], 2nd half title: THE ENGRAVINGS; p. [8], blank; p. [1], [ornamental head-piece] | [flush left] THE ARGUMENT | [11-line precis]; p. [2], blank; p. 3, woodcut head-piece: [Venus on left, Psyche on right] | [text begins with 9-line ornamental initial 'I']; pp. 4–92, text completed; pp. [93–4], blank; p. [95], colophon, as above; p. [96], blank.
Technical Notes: *paper*: white, hand-made, with deckled edges, no watermark; *binding*: 3/4 leather with a reduced version of Morris's Willow paper, white leaves against a dark blue background, covering the boards; title and author gilt-stamped down the spine.
Publication: 1974; *print runs* and *prices*: 400 copies total, divided into 2 lots: 130 numbered copies (2 vols., numbered I–CXXX) with portfolio of the plates: *price*: £450 (£405 for subscribers); 270 copies of the 2 vols. (numbered 1–270); *price*: £120 (£108 for subscribers).
Register of Copies Examined: SSL (base copy: 821 M877c).

A-138.01: A Book of Verse

A BOOK OF VERSE | A facsimile of the manuscript | written in 1870 by | WILLIAM MORRIS | London | Scolar Press | 1980 [1981]
Edition: [1st and 2nd impressions, 1st edn.] Facsimile copied from the original calligraphic book presented as a birthday gift to Georgiana Burne-Jones in 1870. The book includes 25 poems in all, some of which had previous pbns., for which see *Contents*, below.
Collaborators, Illustrators, and editors: see *Colophon*, below.
Colophon: [from the facsimile of Morris's longhand colophon]: As to those who have had a hand in | making this book, Edward Burne-Jones | painted the picture on Page 1: the other | pictures were all painted by Charles F. | Murray, but the minstrel figures on | the title page, and figures of Spring | Summer and Autumn on page 40, he did | from my drawings. | [¶] As to the pattern-work, George Wardle | drew in all the ornament on the first ten | pages, and I coloured it; he also did | all the coloured letters both big and | little; the rest of the ornament I did, | together with all the writing. | [¶] Also I made all the verses; but two | poems, the Ballad of Christine, and the | Son's Sorrow I translated out of Icelandic. | [below right] William Morris | 26 Queen Sq. Bloomsbury, London | August 26th 1870.
Collation: 8°: [1–5]⁸ 40 leaves pp. [24] 1–51 [52–6] [= 80].
Contents: the only page nos. in the book are those printed in the MS. All the others are constructed, hence in italics and in square brackets: pp. [1–2], blank; p. [3], half title: [top] A BOOK OF VERSE; p. [4], blank; p. [5], title page; p. [6], copyright notice and printer's imprint:

The Scolar Press, Ilkley, Yorkshire; p. [7], headed: Contents | [list completed]; p. [8], frontis., photograph by Hollyer, captioned: The Morris and Burne-Jones families [etc.]; p. [9], introduction by Roy Strong, headed: William Morris 1834–1896; pp. [10–12], photo reproductions of Morris (by Hollyer), a painting of Georgiana Burne-Jones, and a specimen of Morris's handwriting; pp. [13–15], 2nd intro. by Joyce Irene Whalley, headed: William Morris: A Book of Verse 1870; p. [16], headed: BIBLIOGRAPHY | [list completed]; pp. [17–18], blank; p. [19], facsimile title page of the original MS: [against background of green leaves, mostly willow] A BOOK OF VERSE | BY | WILLIAM MORRIS | [portrait head of Morris in a thick-thin circular rule] | [line of 4 minstrels separated by single trees across the page] | WRITTEN IN LONDON | 1870; p. [20], blank; pp. [21–2], headed: [with floral background] A TABLE OF CONTENTS | [list completed]; p. [23], 2nd half title (as the first, but in facsimile); p. [24], blank; pp. 1–6: 'The Two Sides of the River', from the rejected version of 'The Man Who Never Laughed Again', was 1st pbd. in *The Fortnightly Review* (1868, see D-19) and rptd. in *Poems by the Way* (1891, see A-59.01); p. 7: 'The Shows of May'; p. 8: 'The Fears of June'; p. 9: 'The Hopes of October'; p. 10: 'The Weariness of November'; pp. 11–12: 'Love Fulfilled', was apparently written for this vol. and later rptd. in *Poems by the Way* (A-59.01); pp. 13–14: 'Rest from Seeking'; pp. 15–16: 'Missing' was pbd. as 'The Dark Wood' in *The Fortnightly Review* (1871, see D-28) and in *Poems by the Way* as 'Error and Loss'; pp. 17–18: 'Prologue to the Volsung Tale' was 1st pbd. as 'A Prologue in Verse' set before the beginning of the Morris and Magnússon translation of *The Völsunga Saga* (1870, see A-6.01); pp. 19–20: 'Love and Death'; p. 21: 'Guileful Love' and p. 22: 'Summer Night' were apparently written for this vol. and not pbd. until K. L. Goodwin included the texts of both in an article, 'Unpublished Lyrics of William Morris', *Yearbook of English Studies* (1975, see D-602); pp. 23–5: 'Hope Dieth Love Liveth'; pp. 26–7: 'Love Alone'; pp. 28–30: 'Meeting in Winter' was originally part of the rejected EP 'Tale of Orpheus', later revised and pbd. in *The English Illustrated Magazine* (see D-95) and rptd. in *Poems by the Way*; pp. 31–2: 'A Garden by the Sea' is from *Jason*; this poem was later revised and included in *Poems by the Way*; pp. 33–5: 'The Ballad of Christine', translated by Morris from the Icelandic; p. 36: 'To Grettir Asmundsen' was pbd., without a title, as the epigraph to *The Story of Grettir the Strong* (1869, see A-5.01); pp. 37–9: 'The Son's Sorrow', translated by Morris from the Icelandic; p. 40: 'The Lapse of the Year'; pp. 41–2: 'Sundering Summer'; p. 43: 'To the Muse of the North' was originally planned, according to May Morris, as an epigraph to be placed at the beginning of *The Story of Grettir the Strong* (see *CW*, IX. xxxv). Since the epigraph beginning that vol. is 'To Grettir Asmundson', this lyric was presumably rejected; pp. 44–6: 'Lonely Love and Loveless Death' was not pbd. until 1965, when David Delaura printed it from a MS in the Miriam Lutcher Stark Library, The University of Texas. It appeared as an article titled 'An Unpublished Poem of William Morris' in *Modern Philology*, with added editorial notes and commentary (see D-599); pp. 47–8: 'Birth of June'; pp. 49–51: 'Praise of Venus'; p. [52], blank; p. [53]: Morris's longhand colophon.

Technical Notes: *paper*: *leaf size*: LP copies: 275 x 210 mm.; 1981 ordinary copies: trimmed, 236 x 164 mm.; *running titles*: all rectos and versos of the original text have the titles of the relevant poems; *binding*: The 1st impression was issued in 2 forms, according to the prospectus: 'This edition is limited to 300 numbered copies. 62 copies, one for each year of Morris's life, are bound in a facsimile of the original Riviére binding, in vellum blocked with gold fleurons. 238 copies are bound in cloth.' The 1981 cheaper edn. is bound in light green cloth, plain and unblocked front and back, gilt-stamped down the spine: [leaf ornament] A BOOK OF VERSE *by* WILLIAM MORRIS [leaf ornament] [at foot] SCOLAR; the ordinary issue has a cream paper dust wrapper with the front having a green thin-rule compartment within which the letterpress is: A BOOK OF VERSE | *by* William Morris | INTRODUCED BY | ROY STRONG AND JOYCE IRENE WHALLEY | [repeat of the ornament from p. 20 of the text, 'Love and Death']; the spine reprints the binding spine, the back being blank and the two fold-overs having notes on Morris and his calligraphic work and on the provenance of the book reproduced here.

Publication: 1980; *print runs*: limited edn.: 300 copies in 2 variants; the number of the smaller rpt., 1981, is unknown; all are facsimiles of the hand-written and ornamented vol. Morris presented as a birthday gift to Georgiana Burne-Jones in 1870. The 1980 variants differ from the 1981 only in their paper, bindings (vellum vs. cloth), and size—275 x 210 mm. compared with 238 x 164 mm. for the 1981 version, and the 1980 variants differ from each other only in their binding: a modern reproduction of the Riviere vellum original, now in the Victoria and Albert Museum (V and A), used here for the first 62 copies and cloth for copies 63–300 (the 1980 versions are limited edns., all numbered). *price*: copies 1–62: £300 / $675; copies 63–300: £195 / $440. The 1981 version was priced at £7. 95. The type area, of course, is the same in all 3 versions, as are the ornaments and rubrications.

Register of Copies Examined: SU (base copy: Special collection, Rare books: 821.85 M8776 D); BL (X950/8213).

Later issues and impressions of this edn. by the Scolar Press:
1. 1981: see differences listed above;
2. *1982: a paper-back variant of the ordinary copy as described above, manufactured in Britain but pbd in New York by Clarkson N. Potter, Inc., Publishers, and distributed by Crown Publishers, Inc. (see Coupe, p. 114).

A-139.01:* Socialist Diary

SOCIALIST DIARY | WILLIAM MORRIS | FLORENCE S. BOOS / EDITOR | MCMLXXXI | THE WINDHOVER PRESS AT IOWA CITY

Edition: [1st separate edn.]. This privately printed pamphlet is the 1st of 3 versions edited by Florence S. Boos, the latter 2 (see A-139.02 and D-604) being much enlarged in the introduction and annotation. Detail used here of the 1st edn. for the conjectural title and collation are derived from the BLC Supp. for 1982–6, p. 577 and the library catalogue of the University of Iowa, Iowa City.

Colophon: William Morris's Diary has been set by hand in Dante | types, with Bembo Titling for display, and printed on Barcham Green's Windhover paper. Of the 400 copies printed, | 200 are published by the Windhover Press in the United | States of America and 200 by the William Morris Society in | England. Different case-bindings for each part of the edn. | have been designed and executed at the Black Oak Bindery.

Collation: medium 8° in 4s: [1–5⁴ 6⁶ 7⁴] 30 leaves pp. [4] i–ix [x–xii] 1–35 [36–44] [=60].

Contents: p. [1] half title; p. [2], blank; p. [3], title page; p. [4], copyright notice; pp. i–viii, headed: Preface | [text begins]; p. ix, preface completed; p.[x], blank; p. [xi] 2nd half title; p. xii, blank; pp. 1–35, text of Morris's diary for 25 Jan. to 25 Apr. 1887 completed; p. [36], blank; p. [37, list of newspaper clippings inserted in the MS diary; p. [38] colophon; pp. [39–44], blank (pp.[43–4] being the pastedown).

Technical Notes: *paper*: see *Colophon*; *leaf size*: trimmed, 197 x 146 mm.; *end papers*: front, 3 free ends and pastedown, plain white and blank; the last gathering has letterpress on the 1st leaf, the last leaf being the pastedown; *binding*: USA copies: quarter black holland with blue paper covered boards and printed paper spine label: [vertical orientation down the spine] SOCIALIST DIARY—MORRIS

Publication: 1981; *print run*: 400 copies, 200 for sale in the USA and 200 for England by the William Morris Society (WMS); *print run* and *price*: unknown.

Register of Copies Located: U. of Iowa Libraries (Spec. Coll. Z239.W5 M67); CSt (Spec. Coll Gunst Z239.W695M67).

Notes: Morris wrote to Jenny Morris, 9 Mar. 1887, remarking in passing that he was starting a diary of his Socialist activities in expectation that it might be useful to later generations of Socialists to have a record of the early days of the movement as seen by someone on the inside, 'Jonah's view of the Whale, you know, my dear' (*Letters*, ii. 624)

A-139.02: Socialist Diary

William Morris's | SOCIALIST DIARY | *edited and annotated by* | *Florence Boos* | Journeyman, *London and New York* | London History Workshop Centre

Edition: [2nd impression of the article pbd. in *History Workshop: A Journal of Socialist and Feminist Historians* (see D-604)] With minor changes this separate version is printed from the same setting as the *History Workshop* article of earlier the same year, 1982, to which were added annotations and biographical notes not present in the original Windhover Press 1st separate edn. in 1981 (see A-139.01).

Collation: 8° no sigs. or gatherings indicated: 40 leaves pp. [4] [1] 2–75 [76] [= 80] + wrapper

Contents: p. [1], half title; p. [2], blank; p. [3], title page; p. [4], copyright notice; p. [1], head title with oval portrait photo reproduction of Morris, text begins with an Introduction by the editor; pp. 2–18, Introduction completed; pp. 19–56, text of the Diary, with footnotes by the editor; pp. 57–75, Biographical Notes; p. [76], blank.

Technical Notes: *paper*: cream-white machine-made; *leaf size*: 207 x 142 mm.; *printing*: *running heads*: all rectos: *William Morris's Socialist Diary* | [all versos: blank]; *end-papers*: single red free end and pastedown, blank front and back; *binding*: stiff dark red paper wrapper, glued on, with p. [1] title duplicating the title page, but without the imprint, with a reproduction of a pen-and-ink drawing by Walter Crane, labelled, by hand on the original: William Morris | speaking from | a wagon in Hyde | Park May 1 1894; pp. [2–3], blank; p. [4], ads.

Publication: 1985; *print run* and *price*: unknown.

Register of Copies Examined: LeM (base copy).

A-140.01: The Novel on Blue Paper

THE NOVEL ON BLUE PAPER BY | WILLIAM MORRIS. EDITED AND | INTRODUCED BY PENELOPE

| FITZGERALD. | WILLIAM MORRIS SOCIETY
Edition: [1st edn.] After this book was issued, later in the same year, 1982, Penelope Fitzgerald's transcription in type of the original MS (BL (Add.) MSS 45328) appeared in the *Dickens Studies Annual* (see D-605). This 1st edn. is a reading copy, with appropriate editorial corrections to the text, chapter titles supplied, etc.
Series: Journeyman Chapbook 6.
Printer: The Journeyman Press, 97 Ferme Park Road, Crouch End, London; limitation notice, p. [iv]: This limited edition of 400 copies has been printed by special arrangement with the publisher for the exclusive use of the William Morris Society, Kelmscott House, 26 Upper Mall, Hammersmith, London W6 9TA
Collation: 8°: 48 leaves pp. [i–iv] v–xv [xvi] 1–79 [80] [= 96] + blue paper wrapper.
Contents: p. [i], half title; p. [ii], frontis., E. H. New's drawing of Elm House, Walthamstow, unlabelled, in thin-rule compartment; p. [iii], title page; p. [iv], copyright and limitation notices, see *Printer*, above; p. v, headed: INTRODUCTION | [text begins]; pp. vi–xv, Introduction completed, signed, below right: *Penelope Fitzgerald*; p. [xvi], headed: Note | [explains the editing practices used]; p. 1, dropped head title: CHAPTER I | THE VILLAGE OF ORMSLADE | [text begins]; pp. 2–76, text completed with explicit in sq. brackets: [The Manuscript ends here]; pp. 77–9, headed: THE CONCLUSION | [the editor provides the evidence of Morris's plan for the direction of the uncompleted narrative, mainly from Morris's working notes on the back of the MS, and details the narrative-time difficulties Morris had created for himself]; p. [80], blank.
Technical Notes: *paper*: white machine-made; *leaf size*: cut flush, 195 x 123 mm.; *binding*: plain unblocked stiff light-blue paper wrapper, glued on, with a reduced reproduction of Morris's binding ornament for *Love is Enough* (see this field in A-8.01), here the background to the letterpress of title and author (the title being, as noted, the invention of the editor); at the foot, below the ornament: EDITED AND INTRODUCED BY | PENELOPE FITZGERALD; prtd. down the spine: THE NOVEL ON BLUE PAPER WILLIAM MORRIS WILLIAM MORRIS SOCIETY
Publication: 1982; *print run*: 400 copies (see *Printer*, above).
Register of Copies Examined: LeM (base copy).
Notes: Penelope Fitzgerald, editor, says:

> In this version I have corrected spelling, punctuation, omissions, and repetitions and regularised the names, ages and place-names. I have also paragraphed the story, which has meant cutting out one or two of the mediaevalising, 'and so's', divided it into short chapters and given them chapter headings, but I have left the story itself without a title, as Morris did. I have altered one word (p. 67) for consistency's sake. Arthur cannot start rowing at this point without in every sense rocking the boat.

A-141.01: The Juvenilia of William Morris

THE JUVENILIA OF WILLIAM MORRIS | With a Checklist and | Unpublished Early Poems | Florence S. Boos | New York and London | The William Morris Society | 1983
Edition: [1st edn., contains the 1st pbns. of several early poems].
Collation: medium 8° prtd. and gathered in 16s: [1–3]¹⁶ 48 leaves pp. [i–iv] v [vi] 1–90 [= 96].
Contents: p. [i], title page; p. [ii], copyright notice; p. [iii], headed: CONTENTS | [list completed]; p. [iv], blank; p. v, headed: PREFACE | [preface completed with background of the book and acknowledgments, signed below right] Florence S. Boos | Cambridge, Massachusetts, | and Iowa City, Iowa | June, 1981; p. [vi], a note on the handling of references; p. 1, headed: William Morris's Juvenilia: preparation | for <u>The Defence of Guenevere</u> | [the editor's introduction begins]; pp. 2–29, introduction completed; p. 30, text of a letter from Morris to Murray, 1 May 1891; p. 31, headed: Checklist | of | Surviving Early Morris Poems, and Poetic and | Prose fragments Not Published in <u>The Defence of Guenevere and Other Poems</u> | [list begins with 'Sources cited']; pp. 32–41, list completed; pp. 42–90, texts of 9 unpbd. poems or fragments: pp. 42–4, 'The Ruined Castle'; pp. 45–55, 'The Dedication of the Temple'; pp. 55–64, 'The Blackbird'; pp. 65–70, [The Lady of Havering]; pp. 71–81, 'The Sleeve of Gold'; p. 82, [The Lady of the Wasted Land]; pp. 83–4, [Untitled—1st line: 'Lo Sirs a desolate Damozel']; pp. 84, Introduction to the 'Story of the Flower'; pp. 85–9, [Sir Richard]; p. 90, [untitled—1st line: 'Dear friends, I lay awake in the night']
Technical Notes: *paper*: plain white machine-made; *leaf size*: 227 x 150 mm.; *printing*: *type area*: this being a 'camera ready' copy of typescript, photographically reproduced, margins vary, especially at the head and foot: 193 x 100 mm., including head and direction lines; *lines-to-page*: single-spaced, varies, avg. 41 lines; *pagination*: arabic numbers centred on the direction line; *end-papers*: 1 free end and paste-down, cream-white and blank, front and back;

binding: beige cloth-covered boards, plain and unblocked, front and back, *spine*: gilt-stamped downwards: The Juvenilia of William Morris Boos William Morris Society
Publication: 1983; *print run* and *price*: unknown.
Register of Copies Examined: LeM (base copy); Fdmn.

A-142.01: The Widow's House by the Great Water

[aligned left] WILLIAM MORRIS | THE WIDOW'S HOUSE BY THE | GREAT WATER | Edited and with an introduction by Helen | A. Timo | William Morris Society in the United | States | 1990
Edition: [1st impression, 1st edn.] An unpublished prose tale, fragmentary, which Morris later developed into *The Water of the Wondrous Isles*.
Place: Iowa City, Iowa.
Publisher: WMS in the United States.
Collation: 8°: [1]^{32} 32 leaves, 16 conjunct pairs stapled at the centrefold; pp. [1–4] 5–64 [= 64] + wrapper stapled to the body at the centrefold.
Contents: p. [1], title page; p. [2], statements of copyright, permission, and limitation (200 copies); p. [3], dedication to St. Hugh's College, Oxford; p. [4], frontis. photo from the MS, labelled: First page of the autograph manuscript of *The Widow's House by the Great Water*. Reproduced by permission of the British Library.; p. 5, introduction begins (no dropped head); pp. 6–16, introduction completed; pp. 16–17, EDITOR'S NOTE; pp. 18–64, headed: CHAPTER I. OF THE SAID HOUSE AND ITS NEIGH- | BORS. | text completed.
Technical Notes: *paper*: plain white machine-made; *leaf size*: 228 x 145 mm.; *printing*: *type area*: 192 x 104 mm. excluding direction line; *lines-to-page*: 39 lines; *pagination*: centred between margins on the direction line; *binding*: *wrapper*: heavy grey paper; p. [1], Morris wallpaper design ('Apple', 1877) in darker grey with the title page reproduced thereon in black; pp. [2–4], blank.
Publication: 1990; *print run*: 200 copies; *price*: unknown.
Register of Copies examined: LeM (base copy).
Notes: from Timo's introduction, ' "The Widow's House by the Great Water": A Literary Enigma: . . . "The Widow's House by the Great Water" . . . is manifestly an early version of the tale which was finally published in 1897 as The Water of the Wondrous Isles' (p. 6).

A-143.01: Cambridge Speech, 23 Feb. 1878

A SPEECH BY MR. W. MORRIS FROM THE CAMBRIDGE CHRONICLE, 23 FEBRUARY 1878
Edition: [1st impression, 1st separate edn.] Text from *The Cambridge Chronicle and University Journal*, 23 Feb. 1878 (see D-39).
Collaborators, Editors, and Illustrators: Preface by Prof. Ian Gordon. Edited with Introduction, 'William Morris in Cambridge', by Fiona MacCarthy. Book designed by Kelvyn Laurence Smith.
Publisher: One Horse Press, The Front Room 46 Church Crescent. London N10 3NE.
Printer: Collins and Waltestow.
Collation: 8° gathered in 4s: [1–5]^4 20 leaves pp. [I–IV] V–XVII [XVIII] 1–21 [22] [= 40]
Contents: p. [I], half title; p. [II], blank; p. [III], title page; p. IV, imprint information; pp. V–VII, Preface; pp. IX–XVII, 'William Morris in Cambridge'; pp. 1–12, Morris's speech; pp. 13–21, particulars of the distribution of prizes; p. [22], blank.
Technical Notes: *paper*: cream-white 'Hi-Speed Fawn 200gsm'; *binding*: stiff purple paper covers, plain and unblocked, with a reproduction, within a thin-thick rule compartment, purple on white, of a Burne-Jones cartoon of Morris reading a paper, and above the compartment the title, also purple on white.
Publication: Sept. 1996; *print run*: 2,000 copies; *price*: unknown.
Register of Copies Examined: An-C-TU (base copy: NK 942 M6A35 1969X ROBA).

B

Morris's Contributions to Books

This list is limited to contributions deliberately undertaken by Morris and 1st pbd. in their intended works. It ends with Morris's death. Except in B-16.02, the issues described are 1st edns.

B-1: 'Masters in This Hall' (ed. Sedding)

'VIII.—FRENCH NOËL: MASTERS IN THIS HALL' [in] A COLLECTION OF ANTIENT CHRISTMAS CAROLS
Edition: [1st impression, 1st edn.] A lyric poem of 12 quatrains with a 4-line chorus to be sung after each. 'The english words written expressly by william morris, esq., B.A.' (from the headtitle, p. 16).
Translation: translated from Old French by William Morris.
Collaborators: [Edited and] 'arranged for four voices by Edmund Sedding, Precentor of S. Raphael the Archangel, Bristol; Sometime Organist of S. Mary, B.V. Soho'.
Printer: J. Alfred Novello, Typographical Music and General Printer, Dean Street, Soho.
Contents: Morris's contribution is on pp. 16–17.
Publication: A.D. 1860 (rptd. 1864, 1867); *print run*: unknown; *price*: 18d.
Notes: From the editor's Preface:

> This collection . . . comprises melodies and words chiefly composed and in use since the time of the Reformation, and it will be a matter of congratulation to many, I feel sure, to see how the simplicity of construction, quaintness of expression, and, what is of more importance still, the grand conception of Catholick Truth, have never been allowed to die out in these precious compositions (p. ix).

Morris to G. W. Kirby, Jr., 21 June 1870: 'I have forgotten the title of the book, which however was a little book of old French Carol music, edited by a Mr. Sedding (now dead I think) and published by Novello where I should think you would get it' (*Letters*, i. 122).

Edmund Sedding (1836–68), architect and musician, composer of carols and other pieces. He and Morris met while they were both apprentices in G. E. Street's office. See HBF, p. 216 and W. R. Lethaby, *Philip Webb and His Work* (16, 17; hereafter referred to as Lethaby). Forman says:

> In *Ancient Christmas Carols* by Edward Sedding (London, 1860) is a poem of twelve quatrains with a chorus which is to be sung after each. It is entitled "Masters in this Hall"; and we are told that "The English Words" were "written expressly by William Morris, Esq., B.A." It is a quaint production, sincere enough, and by no means without beauty; but the poet did well not to challenge, by reprinting it, a comparison with his treatment of the same theme—the birth of Christ—in *The Earthly Paradise*. See "The Land East of the Sun and West of the Moon." (HBF, p. 216).

Forman seems unaware that this carol is translated by Morris from Old French.

B-2: 'Hammersmith Carpets' (in) The Morris Exhibit (Boston)

THE | MORRIS EXHIBIT | AT | *THE FOREIGN FAIR,* | BOSTON, 1883–84. | [decorated rule] | BOSTON: | ROBERTS BROTHERS. | 1883.
Edition: [1st impression, 2nd edn.] The 1st edn. of Morris's essay on carpet-weaving and its history was issued as a leaflet by Morris and Co. dated 24 May 1880, then rptd. and issued in a 2nd impression in Oct. 1882. It was finally reset as part of this catalogue of the *Morris Exhibit at the Foreign Fair, Boston* in 1883, where it is quoted in full.
Contents: Morris's note is on pp. 9–10.
Collaborators, Editors, and Illustrators: George Wardle was

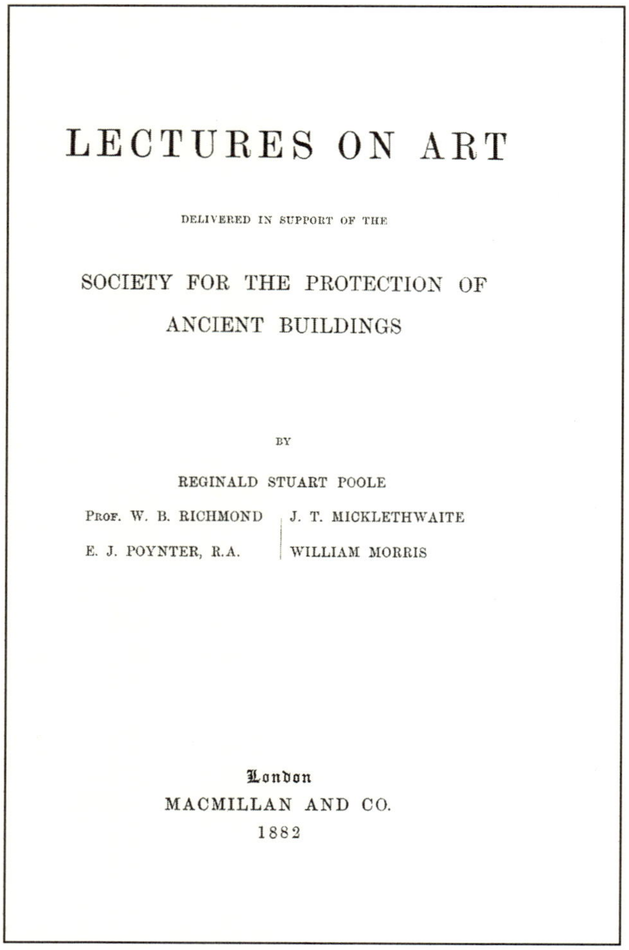

Figure 88. B-3: *Lectures on Art* (1st edn.) title page

the editor as well as the writer of the greater part of the booklet (see HBF, p. 195), which has sections on all the crafts exhibited by the Firm.
Publication: 1883 [21 Nov.] (Roberts Arch.); *print run*: 5,000 copies; *price*: this pamphlet was done on commission for the Firm, and it was probably distributed without cost.

B-3: 'History of Pattern Designing' (and) ' Lesser Arts of Life' (in) *Lectures on Art Delivered in Support of The SPAB*

LECTURES ON ART | DELIVERED IN SUPPORT OF THE | SOCIETY FOR THE PROTECTION OF | ANCIENT BUILDINGS | BY | REGINALD STUART POOLE | [last 4 names printed in 2 columns divided by a vertical thin rule] | PROF. W. B. RICHMOND [rule] J. T. MICHLETHWAITE | E. J. POYNTE R, R.A. [rule] WILLIAM MORRIS | [gothic] London | [plain type] MACMILLAN AND CO. | 1882
Edition: Morris's lecture, 'The History of Pattern Designing', was pbd. previously as, 'Mr. William Morris on Egyptian, Greek, and Roman Art' in *The Architect* (see D-48), and 'The Lesser Arts of Life', previously unpbd. Both were later included in the collection, *Architecture, Industry, and Wealth* (see C-18.01).
Collaborators, Editors, and Illustrators: 'Preface' [initialled] J. H. M. [John Henry Middleton]. Forman says J. T. Micklethwaite wrote the 'Preface' (HBF, p. 100), but Middleton is the only contributor whose initials match those following the text of the 'Preface'.
Printer: R. & R. Clark, Edinburgh.
Contents: Morris's contributions appear as 'Lecture V . . . The History of Pattern Designing' on pp. [127]–73, and 'Lecture VI . . . The Lesser Arts of Life' on pp. [174]–232.
Technical Notes: *paper*: plain white machine-moulded; *leaf size*: trimmed, 191 x 123 mm.; *running titles*: all rectos and versos, lecture titles of individual lectures in caps with the lecturer's surname aligned to the inner margins in smaller type; *end-papers*: a single free end and paste-down, plain white and blank, front and back; *binding*: plain dark green cloth over boards with blind-stamped thin-rule border, front and back; *spine*: gilt-stamped across: Lectures | on | Art | Poole | Richmond | Poynter | Micklethwaite | Morris | [at foot] MACMILLAN & Co.
Publication: 1882; *print run* and *price*: unknown.
Notes: all 6 lectures were delivered in a series sponsored by the SPAB at The Kensington Vestry Hall in 1881–2, but Morris's were delivered elsewhere as well (see *Unpublished Lectures*). As Forman says, Morris's essays total 'not far short of half the book' (HBF, p. 100).

B-4: 'Introduction' to *A Review of European Society*

A REVIEW OF EUROPEAN SOCIETY, | WITH AN | EXPOSITION AND VINDICATION OF | THE PRINCIPLES OF SOCIAL DEMOCRACY. | BY J. SKETCHLEY, | Author of "Popery, its Supporters and Opponents," "The Irish Question," "The Funding System," "German Democracy," &c. | [epigraph from Carlyle] | PRICE EIGHTEENPENCE. | LONDON: | W. REEVES, 185, FLEET STREET, E.C. | BIRMINGHAM: | J. SKETCHLEY, 348, CHEAPSIDE. | [ALL RIGHTS RESERVED.]
Edition: [1st impression, 1st edn.]
Contents: Morris's Introduction is on pp. 7–8.
Publication: 1884 [issued 15 Nov.] (see *Justice*, 8 Nov. 1884, p. 8); Morris's Introduction is dated 'September 29th, 1884.'

Notes: HBF says, p. 109, that there were 2 different wrappers used on copies of the 1st edn.: one printed in black, one in dark blue, with only the Reeves imprint. But this may be because there was a 2nd impression. It seems likely that the change of wrapper occurred with a new impression. William Reeves of 75 Fleet Street is probably noted in the title page for his role of distributor rather than publisher.

B-5: 'Mural Decoration' (in) *Encyclopædia Britannica*

'MURAL DECORATION' [illustrated essay in] ENCY-CLOPÆDIA BRITANNICA.
1st pbn. of this text is in the 9th edn., xvii. 34–48.
Collaborators, Editors, and Illustrators: signed, 'W.Mo.—J.H.M.' i.e. the article is a collaboration of William Morris and J. H. Middleton.
Place: Edinburgh.
Publication: 1884.
Notes: at this time J. H. Middleton was a London architect.

B-6: 'The Socialist Platform' (a prefatory note to) *An Address to Trades Unions*

THE SOCIALIST PLATFORM.—NO. 1 | [Walter Crane's Socialist League block] | ADDRESS TO | TRADES' UNIONS | ISSUED BY THE | [in gothic] The Council of the Socialist League. | [french rule] | [plain type] PRICE ONE PENNY. | [french rule]
Edition: [1st impression, 1st edn.]
Collaborators: 'The Socialist Platform' is signed: E. Belfort Bax | William Morris [names bracketed together and labelled] Editors. As co-editors of the pamphlet series so named, here they explain the nature, format, and program of the series. The pamphlet itself is by Bax.
Series: SP, No. 1. 'The Socialist Platform' is a name that refers to 3 things: (1) the note described here, placed before the text of the pamphlets No. 1 and 2 of the series; (2) the series of 7 numbered SL pamphlets so named, and (3) the wrapper-title of a planned 'compact volume' (so-called by the editors in their note described here) in which all of the pamphlets were to be collected in a single vol. with The Manifesto of the Socialist League added. The evidence now available suggests that a single vol. collection of Socialist League pamphlets never was issued. But the title page exists as 2 entries in H. B. Forman's *The Books of William Morris* (p. 133, which provides the title-page transcription used here, and p. 145, where *Monopoly* is said to have been added to the 6 pamphlets and the SL *Manifesto* of the original series). The cream of the jest is that the title also exists as a set of 6 proofs of forged wrapper-titles found in 1972 among the books of Forman's library. These last were described by Graham Pollard in the *Quaritch Catalogue* of the 1973 Forman sale.

For further detail on this forged wrapper-title for which there is no book, see E-10.
Contents: 'The Socialist Platform' editorial note appears on pp. [iii–iv] of the *Address to Trades Unions* and on p. [ii] of *Useful Work v. Useless Toil*.
Publication: The series of pamphlets started in 1885 [May–June]. *Commonweal* (1 (May 1885), 36), notes that the 1st pamphlet of 'The Socialist Platform' is about to appear; in the July number, p. 56, the 1st 2 numbers had been issued; *print run*: unknown; *price*: 1d. each for the pamphlets containing this note.
Notes: a set of MS notes on the SP, in Morris's hand, survives, signed by both Bax and Morris and listing 16 prospective titles for the series and their nominated authors (SLA, Doc. 119, Reel 3).

B-7: 'The Labour Question' (in) *The Claims of Labour*

'THE LABOUR QUESTION FROM THE SOCIALIST STANDPOINT' [in] THE CLAIMS OF LABOUR: A COURSE OF LECTURES DELIVERED IN SCOTLAND IN THE SUMMER OF 1886, ON VARIOUS ASPECTS OF THE LABOUR PROBLEM. | Edinburgh | Co-operative Printing Company Limited, | Bristo Place. | 1886
Edition: [1st impression, 1st edn.] This lecture was later retitled *True and False Society* (see A-37.02) and included under that title in *CW*, vol. XXIII. The lecture course, and hence the 2 pbns. described here—the separate pamphlet (see A-37.01) and this collected vol. of all the lectures—grew out of discussions at The Industrial Remuneration Conference at Prince's Hall, Piccadilly, in Jan. 1885. The book chapter is the same setting as the pamphlet, but the forms have been opened and lines rearranged to suit the design of the book, that is, the page breaks come at different points in the text, so it is a new impression, but no other difference is discernible in the body of the text (but see other differences under *Technical Notes*, below). Hence the pamphlet is not a straightforward offprint, and the pamphlet came 1st.
Collaborators, Editors, and Illustrators: edited by James Oliphant who contributes a 'Preface', signed and dated 'September, 1886' explaining the origin of the collection:

The present volume has arisen out of the Industrial Remuneration Conference held in the Prince's Hall . . . . It will be enough to repeat here that the general question proposed in the inquiry was, *Is the present system whereby the products of industry are distributed between the various persons and classes of the community satisfactory? or, if not, are there any means by which that system could be improved?*

Series: The Claims of Labour Lectures—No. 5. A course of 6 Lectures financed by Robert Miller of Edinburgh (who remained anonymous at the time) and organized by Frederick Harrison, on 'Various Aspects of the Labour Problem', and delivered, respectively, in Edinburgh, Glasgow, and Dundee on 23, 24, and 25 June, 1886. The lectures were, 'By John Burnet, Secretary of the Amalgamated Society of Engineers; Benjamin Jones, Manager of the Co-operative Wholesale Society, London Branch; Patrick Geddes, F.R.S.E.; Alfred Russell Wallace, LL.D. F.L.S. , &c.; William Morris; and Herbert Somerton Foxwell, Professor of Economics, University College, London.' The editor states the purpose of the course on the verso of the pamphlet's wrapper-title: 'This course of lectures has been arranged on the basis of representing all important sections of opinion on labour questions, and while the lectures will afterwards be published in a collective form, it is understood that each writer has no responsibility for any opinions contained in them beyond those expressed in his own lecture.'

When stocks of the initial impression of the pamphlet were exhausted in 1888, Morris retitled it *True and False Society*, and it was later rptd. by the SL as No. 6 of the pamphlet series, SP 1888 (see A-37.02).

Contents: Morris's lecture is on pp. 155–85.

Technical Notes: *paper*: plain white machine-wove; *leaf size*: 181 x 120 mm.; *running titles*: all versos: THE LABOUR QUESTION; all rectos: FROM THE SOCIALIST STANDPOINT; *binding*: cloth-covered boards.

Publication: 1886. Morris delivered his lecture 3 times, each time in a different city, for the Industrial Remuneration Conference, after which it was printed both separately and in this collected vol. of the Conference. The pamphlet was 1st advertised in *Commonweal*, 2/34 (4 Sept. 1886), 184, and it probably precedes the collected vol. since the last page of the pamphlet wrapper advertises the 1st 4 lecture pamphlets, including Morris's, as 'just published' but the last 2 as 'Will shortly be published'; *print run*: unknown; *price*: 1s.

B-8: 'Preface' to Fairman's *Principles*

THE | PRINCIPLES OF SOCIALISM | MADE PLAIN; AND | OBJECTIONS, METHODS & QUACK RE- | MEDIES FOR POVERTY CONSIDERED. | BY FRANK FAIRMAN. | WITH | PREFACE BY WILLIAM MORRIS | [in gothic] London: | [plain type] WILLIAM REEVES, 185, Fleet Street, E.C. | 1888.

Series: this book was later added to Reeves' series The Bellamy Library.

Printer: The Temple Press (?) The absence of a printer's imprint and the inclusion of an ad for Reeves' series The Bellamy Library suggests that William Reeves, the younger, (son of William Dobson Reeves of R and T), may have used his own Temple Press (acquired in 1885) at 185 Fleet Street to produce the book.

Contents: Morris's Preface is on pp. iii–vi, and it is signed and dated, 'London, Dec. 5th, 1887'.

Technical Notes: Forman says, 'The original wrapper was primrose-coloured: the same edition is still on sale [1897], but with a pale blue wrapper' (HBF, p. 131). The Monash copy has a grey paper wrapper (which may be what Forman calls 'blue') printed in blue, bearing the imprint date of 1888; so there may have been several different coloured wrappers or bindings, perhaps used in sequence for successive printings. The BL copy is bound with an edn. binding of tan textured cloth with ornamental blind stamps, front and back, and gilt-stamped titles on front and spine and author's name on the front.

Publication: 1888 [issued 24–31 Mar.] (see *Commonweal*, for those dates, pp. 96 and 104, the earlier number saying the book is 'nearly ready' and the later saying 'Now Ready'); the accession stamp of the BL copy is dated '16 Ap 88'; *print run* and *price*: unknown.

B-9: [Verses for Pictures] (in) *The Legend of the Briar Rose*

THE LEGEND | OF | [in gothic] "The Briar Rose." | A SERIES OF PICTURES | PAINTED BY | E. BURNE JONES, A.R.A. | [swash caps] *EXHIBITED AT* | THOS. AGNEW & SONS' GALLERIES, | 39, OLD BOND STREET, W. | 1890

Edition: [1st impression, 1st edn. with a 2nd edn. also noted] A series of 4 Morris verses in the catalogue of an exhibition of pictures painted by E. Burne-Jones. 2 versions of the catalogue were printed, one presumably free, and the 2nd, double in size, priced at 6*d*. The latter version (not seen) may have been for the 2nd exhibition of the same pictures held in Whitechapel in the year following. Morris wrote these 4 quatrains, each with the title of a Burne-Jones painting: 'The Briar Wood', 'The Council

Room', 'The Briar Court', and 'The Rosebower', each illustrating a scene from *The Sleeping Beauty*.
Collaborators, Editors, and Illustrators: Besides the 4 quatrains by Morris, the catalogue has a prose account of the legend of the Sleeping Beauty supplied by an unknown writer. In the 2nd, longer, version (not seen) E. J. Milliken provides the prose summary.
Contents: 1st version: Morris's verses: pp. 10, 11: 2 titles each page: 'The Briar Wood', The Council Room', 'The Garden Court' and 'The Rosebower' are underlined and each followed by a quatrain, in quotation marks, the last followed by a printed signature: WILLIAM MORRIS.; p. 12, ad for the photogravures of the series to be prepared and sold by Agnew & Sons.
Technical Notes: *paper*: hand-laid paper, deckled edges, with horizontal chain lines; Van Gelder watermark; *leaf size*: untrimmed, avg. 146 x 110 mm.; *printing*: running titles: [swash italic caps, all rectos and versos] THE BRIAR ROSE; *binding*: self-wrappered.
Publication: 1890 [issued Apr.] (see Martin Harrison and Bill Waters, *Burne-Jones* (New York: G. P. Putnam's Sons, 1973), 149). This was the date of the Exhibition at Agnew's. The 2nd exhibition, in Whitechapel, was mounted in Apr. 1891.
Notes: there are 2 versions of this pamphlet, as is evident in Robert Proctor's note in his MS list of Morris's books: '118 Briar Rose 1st version'. Forman says, 'six demy 16mo leaves sewn together' (HBF, p. 151). The 2nd version is an 'extended pamphlet of 24 pages' in fcap. 8° (HBF, p. 151). The 2nd differs only in that the prose version of the story is different and E. J. Milliken is identified as the author of descriptions of the pictures.

Morris rptd. this series of quatrains in *Poems by the Way* as 'For the Briar Rose', with each verse separately headed with the Burne-Jones title. He also prts. there a 2nd version of the 4 quatrains, but without the titles (see A-59.01).

B-10:* [advice to aspiring writers] in *The Art of Authorship*

THE | ART OF AUTHORSHIP | LITERARY REMINISCENCES, | METHODS OF WORK, AND ADVICE TO YOUNG BEGINNERS, | PERSONALLY CONTRIBUTED BY | LEADING AUTHORS OF THE DAY. | COMPILED AND EDITED BY | GEORGE BAINTON. | LONDON: | JAMES CLARKE & CO., 13 & 14, FLEET STREET. | [rule] | 1890. [or] NEW YORK: | D. APPLETON AND CO. | [rule] | 1890.

Morris's untitled letter of advice to young men aspiring to write professionally, pbd. in a collection of 178 such letters solicited, compiled, and edited by George Bainton.
Printer: W. Speaight and Sons, Printers, Fetter Lane.
Contents: Morris's contribution, introduced by the editor, is on pp. 59–61.
Notes: the editor is the same Reverend George Bainton to whom Morris wrote the 4 *Letters on Socialism*, in 1888 (*Letters*, ii. 763–88, *passim*) afterwards printed as a pamphlet by Thomas J. Wise (1894, see A-76.01).

Two public controversies followed the pbn. of Bainton's book. Morris's contribution touched on restoration to Oxford University buildings and referred to Oxford dons as 'blackguards', which when the book was reviewed in *The Speaker* (17 May 1890, p. 536) by its editor, Sir Thomas Wemyss Reid, produced some outrage. Morris replied in conciliatory tone in a letter also pbd. in *The Speaker* (see D-512). The editor-compilers of *A Bibliography of Henry James* say (209) that, 'James's statement, like most of the others in the book, was elicited for use in connection with a school course in composition. Publication was unauthorized, and created a controversy, the details of which are recounted in 'The Art of Authorship", *The Author* I (16 June 1890), 44–6.'
Morris's contribution is rptd. in *Letters*, iii. 154–5.

B-11: 'Glass, Painted or Stained' in *Chamber's Encyclopædia*

'GLASS, PAINTED OR STAINED' [in] *CHAMBER'S ENCYCLOPÆDIA*, v. 246–8.
Publication: 1890, New Edition of *Chambers*.
Notes: rptd. in MM, i. 356–64.

B-12: 'Preface' to *The Nature of Gothic* (KP)

Preface to THE NATURE OF GOTHIC: A CHAP- | TER OF THE STONES OF VENICE. | BY JOHN RUSKIN.
Series: The 4th book issued from the KP.
Colophon: HERE ends the Nature of Gothic, by John Rus- | kin, printed by William Morris at the Kelmscott | Press, Hammersmith, and published by George | Allen, 8, Bell Yard, Temple Bar, London, and | Sunnyside, Orpington. | [printer's leaf No. 1]
Contents: Morris's 'Preface' is on pp. i–iv. It is signed and dated: [below right] WILLIAM MORRIS. | [below left] Kelmscott House, Hammersmith. | [indented] Feb 15th, 1892. | [small KP mark, No. 1]
Technical Notes: *paper*: KP Flower paper No. 1; *leaf size*: 200

x 141 mm.; *binding*: limp white vellum with 2 green silk ties; title gilt-stamped across the spine: THE | NATURE | OF | GOTHIC. | BY | JOHN | RUSKIN
Publication: 1892 [issued 22 Mar.] (see *KP Biblio.*, p. 12); *print run*: 500 paper copies ; *price*: 30s.
Later issues of this text:
1.* Allen: 1899 [2nd edn.] with Morris's 'Preface' but without KP ornaments or type, bound in a blue paper wrapper with the title printed in red and black on the front along with the price, 1 shilling); 'Preface' still dated 'February 15, 1892';
2.* 1908: Paris: Hachette;
after 1915:
3.* 1977: [facsimile edn.] New York: Garland Publishing Co.
Also rptd., Preface only, in MM, i. 292–5 as 'Preface to the Nature of Gothic by John Ruskin (1892)'.

B-13: 'Preface' [to] *Medieval Lore* (ed. Steele)

MEDIEVAL LORE: | AN EPITOME OF | *THE SCIENCE, GEOGRAPHY, ANIMAL AND* | *PLANT FOLKLORE AND MYTH OF* | *THE MIDDLE AGE:* | BEING | CLASSIFIED GLEANINGS FROM THE ENCYCLOPEDIA OF | BARTHOLOMEW ANGLICUS | ON THE PROPERTIES OF THINGS. | EDITED BY | ROBERT STEELE. | *WITH A PREFACE BY* | WILLIAM MORRIS, | AUTHOR OF 'THE EARTHLY PARADISE.' | LONDON: | ELLIOT STOCK, 62, PATERNOSTER ROW, E.C. | 1893.
Edition: [1st publication of Morris's Preface] The book itself was written in the 13th century and translated into many languages in the following century. Dr. Robert Steele's edn. was rptd. several times, see *Later issues and rpts.*, below. The base copy described here is the 1893 edn. (BL 12430.k.30.)
Translation: translated from the Latin by John of Trevisa in 1397.
Contents: Morris's 'Preface' is on pp. v–viii, signed: [below right] WILLIAM MORRIS.
Technical Notes: *paper*: machine-laid; *watermarked* centrefold: Abbey Mill | Greenfield; *pagination*: pp. x + 156; *leaf size*: deckled edges lightly trimmed, avg. 230 x 150 mm.; *side titles*: smaller type, outside the outer margins at the beginning of each paragraph as subtitles thereof; *binding*: buff buckram, brown-stamped across the *spine*: MEDIEVAL | LORE | [double thin rule] | STEELE | [printer's leaf] | [foot] PREFACE | BY | Wm. MORRIS
Publication: 1893 [issued Feb.] ('Publications of the Month [of Feb.]'), *BSR*, No. 424 (Mar. 1893), 227); BL Accession stamp dated '14 Fe 93'; *print run*: unknown; *price*: 7s. 6d.
Notes: Morris to Steele, 21 July [1892]: 'As to the Glanville [i.e. Bartholomew Anglicus], I suppose you want me to write a preface; all right, only you will find me a sad procrastinator I fear; also I shall want to see your matter' (*Letters*, iii. 419). Morris to Steele, 13 Nov. [1892]: 'Here you are at last, if the accompanying scrawl will suffice' (*Letters*, iii. 466).
Later issues and rpts. of this Preface:
1. 1895: the entire book was reset and rptd. [1st impression, 2nd edn.] in The King's Classics and pbd. by Alexander Moring.
2. 1905: [March? the BL copy has an accession stamp dated "22 Mh 1905; 2nd impression, 2nd edn.] included in The Medieval Library, ed. Gollancz, and prtd. by R. & R. Clarke, Edinburgh.
Issues after 1915:
3. 1924: [2nd impression, 2nd edn.] as No. 20 of the Medieval Library Series;
4. 1936: Preface only, MM, i. 286–9 (see A-130.01).
5. 1966 [3rd impression, 2nd edn.] New York: Cooper Square Publishers, Inc.

B-14: 'Foreword' to More's *Utopia* (KP)

'FOREWORD' to UTOPIA [leaf ornament No. 2] WRITTEN BY SIR | THOMAS MORE.
Series: the 16th title pbd. at the KP.
Colophon: Now revised by F. S. Ellis & printed again | by William Morris at the Kelmscott Press | Hammersmith, in the County of Middle- | sex. Finished the 4th day of August, 1893. | [smaller KP mark, no. 1] | Sold by Reeves and Turner, 196, Strand.
Contents: Morris's Foreword occupies pp. [iii–viii]: headed: [flush left, in red] Foreword by William Morris [2 printer's flowers] | [text begins with a 6-line floriated initial 'R']; p. viii, text of Foreword concludes.
Technical Notes: *paper*: cream-white KP Flower 2 paper, primrose watermark with W left and M right; *leaf size*: lightly trimmed deckled edges, avg. 205 x 140 mm.; *printing*: *type*: Chaucer type, with 1 transcription in Troy type; printed in red and black; *end-papers*: standard KP: 3 free ends and paste-down, plain white and blank, front and back; *binding*: limp white vellum with silk ties, gilt-stamped across the spine: MORES | UTOPIA
Publication: 4 Aug. 1893 [colophon date, issued 8 Sept.]; *print run*: 300 copies on paper, 8 on vellum; *prices*: 30s. and 10gns., respectively (Cockerell, p. 155).
Notes: also prtd. in MM, i. 289–92 as 'More's Utopia: Foreword by William Morris (1893)'.

B-15: 'Preface', 'Textiles', 'Printing', and 'Of Dyeing as an Art' in *Arts and Crafts Essays*

Arts and Crafts Essays | BY | Members Of The Arts And Crafts | Exhibition Society | With A Preface | By William Morris | [gothic] London | RIVINGTON, PERCIVAL, & CO. | 1893

Collaborators: besides editing this vol. (hereafter referred to as *ACES Essays*), Morris contributed a Preface and 3 essays. Besides Morris's Preface and his essays, this vol. contains 32 essays from previously pbd. catalogues of ACES exhibitions in 1888, 1889, 1890, and 1893: Walter Crane (3), G. T. Robinson (2), W. A. S. Benson, Somers Clarke (3), Steven Webb (3), T. J. Cobden-Sanderson, F. Madox Brown, Heywood Sumner, W. R. Lethaby (2), May Morris (3), Alan S. Cole (2), Reginald Blomfield (2), Lewis F. Day, Edward S. Prior, Halsey Ricardo, J. H. Pollen, T. G. Jackson, Mary E. Turner, John D. Sedding, and Selwyn Image (1). On the nature and extent of the collaboration on Morris's essay on 'Printing,' see *Notes*, below.

Printer: Printed by R. & R. Clarke, Edinburgh.

Contents: Morris's contributions: Preface, pp. v–xii, and three essays : pp. 22–38, 'Textiles' (1st printed in *Catalogue of the First Exhibition of the Arts and Crafts Exhibition Society* (hereafter referred to as *ACES Cat.*), see D-410); pp. 111–33, 'Printing' (Morris's revision of Emery Walker's essay of 1888); and pp. 196–211, 'Of Dyeing as an Art' (see D-480).

Technical Notes: *paper*: 'antique' machine-moulded paper, with dandy roll laid lines, and false deckled edges; *watermark*: at the centrefold, coat of arms: Abbey Mills | Greenfield; *leaf size*: avg. 190 x 127 mm.; *printing*: running titles: all rectos and versos except on titles, both rectos and versos use the relevant essay title; *pagination*: pp. [xviii] + 420; *binding*: plain unblocked dark red buckram-covered boards; *spine*: printed paper label: ARTS & CRAFTS | ESSAYS | PREFACE BY | William Morris

Notes: as President of the Arts and Crafts Exhibition Society for 1893, Morris was editor of this vol.; and 2 of his essays: 'Textiles' and 'Of Dyeing as an Art', were previously pbd. in the *Catalogues* of the 1st and 2nd Arts and Crafts Exhibitions of 1888 and 1889 respectively (see D-410 and 480). The 3rd, Morris's revision of Walker's 'Printing' 1st appears here.

The revised text of the essay on 'Printing' came about because Morris, though much influenced by Walker's lecture, thought it required some expansion to cover the subject when prtd. in this collection. Being the editor of the 1893 vol. of the Society's *Essays*, he undertook the revisions himself after discussion with Walker and agreement as to what needed to be done. Walker left a MS note on the Morris revision, saying that Morris rewrote nearly the entire piece. This is quoted by Peterson, who describes the resulting manuscript thus: 'significantly only this note and the first two paragraphs of the essay are written by Walker; the rest of the essay is in Morris's hand—a useful piece of evidence, since there has been much speculation through the years about their relative contributions to this work of joint authorship' (See William S. Peterson, 'The Library of Emery Walker,' *Matrix*, 12 (Winter 1990), 3–14).

B-16.01: 'Introduction' (to) *Good King Wenceslas* (English edn.)

GOOD KING | WENCESLAS | A CAROL WRITTEN BY DR NEALE AND | PICTURED BY ARTHUR J. GASKIN WITH | AN INTRODUCTION BY WILLIAM MORRIS. | BIRMINGHAM. MESSRS. CORNISH BRS. | NEW STREET MDCCCXCV.

Edition: [1st impression, 1st edn.]

Colophon: GOOD KING WENCESLAS. A CAROL | WRITTEN BY DR. NEALE, WITH AN | INTRODUCTION BY WILLIAM MORRIS. | PICTURED BY ARTHUR GASKIN. AND | PRINTED WITH HIS OWN HAND AT | THE PRESS OF THE GUILD OF HANDICRAFT IN THE CITY OF BIRMINGHAM. | MDCCCXCIV | PUBLISHED BY MESSRS CORNISH BROS. | NEW STREET BIRMINGHAM.

Contents: Morris's 'Introductory Note' is on p. [15]. It is dated and signed: [below right] WILLIAM MORRIS. | [below left] *Sept., 1894*

Technical Notes: *leaf size*: LP, 283 x 225 mm.; *printing*: leaves prtd. on 1 side only; no page nos.; *end-papers*: 3 free ends and a paste-down, plain white and blank, front and back; *binding*: quarter holland with blue paper-covered boards; *binding letterpress*: woodcut ornamental title in 3-line letters printed in black on the front.

Publication: 1895; *print run*: limitation statement on p. [6]: 'This edition is limited to 125 copies of which 113 are for sale'; *price*: unknown;

Notes: Morris's Introduction is rptd. in MM, i. 295–6.

B-16.02: 'Introduction' (to) *Good King Wenceslas* (Goudy)

GOOD KING | WENCESLAS | A CAROL WRITTEN | BY DR NEALE PIC | TURES BY ARTHUR | GASKIN.

WITH AN | INTRODUCTION BY | WILLIAM MORRIS | HINGHAM. MASSACHUSETTS | M.CM.IV.
Edition: [1st impression, 2nd edn., 1st American].
Colophon: Reprinted from the edition issued by Cornish Brothers. Double border and title from drawings by Will Dwiggins. One hundred and eighty-five copies printed by hand at the Village Press, Hingham, Massachusetts, by Fred and Bertha Goudy, and finished on the 19th day of November, 1904.
Contents: Morris's Introduction is in the prelims.
Technical Notes: *paper*: French Arches hand-made paper, 7 on japan vellum; *leaf size*: 156 x 121 mm.; *binding*: plain grey paper-covered boards; *spine*: printed down the paper label: GOOD KING WENCESLAS.
Publication: 19 Nov. 1904 (colophon date); *print run*: limited to 185 paper copies (but see *Notes*, below) 173 for sale; *price*: $1.50 paper, vellum price unknown.
  Morris's Introduction is rptd. in MM, i. 295–6.
Notes: 'About 100 copies were destroyed in the Parker Building fire. The 2-line initials are Cheltenham' (Cary, 64). This book is described here, though it falls outside the limits set for this list, because of its direct relation to the 1st edn. and its intrinsic interest.

B-17: 'Why I Am a Communist' (in) *The Why I Ams*

[wrapper-title] SECOND SERIES | [Walter Crane's 2nd SL block with SL banner changed to] LIBERTY PRESS | THE WHY I AMS. | WHY I AM A COMMUNIST | By WILLIAM MORRIS. | WHY I AM AN EXPROPRIATIONIST, BY L. S. BEVINGTON. | LONDON: | PRINTED AND PUBLISHED BY JAMES TOCHATTI, | at the "LIBERTY" PRESS. | 1894. | PRICE ONE PENNY.
Written as an article for *Liberty*, a Journal of Anarchist Communism, in Feb. 1894 (see D-559).
Series: The Why I Ams, Second Series.
Publication: 1894 [issued Nov.] (1st advertised as 'Just Published' in *Liberty*, 1/12 (Dec. 1894), 96).
Contents: Morris's contribution is on pp. 2–10.
Technical Notes: *paper*: plain white machine-made; *leaf size*: untrimmed, 222 x 145 mm.

B-18:* 'How I Became a Socialist' (in) *How I Became a Socialist: A Series...*

HOW I BECAME A SOCIALIST: A SERIES OF BIOGRAPHICAL SKETCHES
An autobiographical essay, here used as a contribution to a collection. Morris's contribution 1st appeared in *Justice*, 16 June 1894 (see D-563). The same essay was pbd. separately in a memorial pamphlet edited and introduced by H. M. Hyndman and issued in Oct. 1896 shortly after Morris's death (see A-82.01).
Collaborators, Editors, and Illustrators: Harry Quelch, ed., also edited *Justice* and was interviewer for some of the pieces included. The contributions are by H. M. Hyndman, pp. 1–8; E. Belfort Bax, pp. 9–16; Morris, pp. 17–22; Walter Crane, pp. 23–7; J. Hunter Watts, pp. 28–33; J. E. Williams, pp. 34–41; Andreas Scheu, pp. 42–51; H. W. Lee, pp. 52–8; James R. Macdonald, pp. 59–66; Robert Blatchford, pp. 67–9; Harry Quelch, pp. 70–8; and Tom Mann, pp. 79–81.
Series: a collection of *Justice* articles and interviews, all having the same title, 'How I Became a Socialist'. The earliest ones are interviews (but not Morris's) conducted by Harry Quelch, and all are accounts of the way the subjects came to join the Socialist movement. In this collection each article has a portrait of the author opposite the 1st page of text.
Publisher: The SDF.
Printer: probably the Federation's printer, The Twentieth Century Press.
Contents: Morris's 'sketch' is on pp. 17–22. For the rest, see *Collaborators, Editors, and Illustrators*, above.
Publication: [1894] (undated, but probably issued sometime towards the end of 1894, after all these pieces had been pbd. in *Justice*).

B-19: [Seven Verse Scenes for Burne-Jones pictures (of) *The Legend of St. George and the Dragon*]

THE LEGEND OF | [ornamented gothic] St. George and the Dragon | By | SIR EDWARD BURNE-JONES, BART. | [thin rule] | London: | THOMAS McLEAN, | 7 HAYMARKET, | PUBLISHER BY APPOINTMENT TO HER MAJESTY. | [thin rule] | 1895.
Edition: This is an 1895 exhibition catalogue written to accompany paintings done in 1865 by Burne-Jones. The verso of the half title says: 'These pictures were painted by Sir Edward Burne-Jones for his friend, Mr. Birket Foster and have not before been exhibited.' In 1865 Foster's house was decorated by Morris, Marshall, Faulkner and Co., and the paintings were part of the design. The exhibition catalogue described here contains verse quotations selected by Morris to accompany each of the 7 pictures, and that is why the catalogue is described here.
Collation: the collation is included here because of an irregularity: 16° in 8s: a single gathering of 8 leaves stapled twice at the centrefold, pp. [2] [1–5] 6–11 [12–14] [= 16]; the pag-

ination omits one leaf of the unpaginated prelims, indicated here as [2].

Contents: Morris's verse: p. [5], headed: 1. THE KING'S DAUGHTER | [6 lines of verse in couplets]; p. 6, headed: 2. THE PETITION TO THE KING. | [5 lines of verse, 2 couplets and a single line unrhymed (note that though the basic pattern is the couplet, most of the verses have an unrhymed extra line). Here the 1st line begins with an ellipsis, which is also used before or after the verses for pictures 3, 4, 5, 6, and 7, suggesting that the verses either come from a larger whole or that they are left unfinished]; p. 7, headed: 3. THE PRINCESS SABRA DRAWING THE LOT. | [9 lines of verse]; p. 8, headed: 4. THE PRINCESS LED TO THE DRAGON. | [7 lines of verse]; p. 9, headed: 5. THE PRINCESS TIED TO THE TREE. | [2 lines of verse]; p. 10, headed: 6. THE FIGHT. | [6 lines of verse]; p. 11, headed: 7. THE RETURN OF THE PRINCESS. | [7 lines of verse, signed, below right] | WILLIAM MORRIS.

Technical Notes: *paper*: hand-laid with deckled edges, watermarked Van Gelder Zonen; *leaf size*: 153 x 116 mm.; *pagination*: centred on headlines within parentheses; *binding*: self-wrapped.

Publication: 1895; *print run* and *price*: unknown.

Notes: there is a problem with the origin of these verses. The *BLC* describes Morris's lines as, 'verses selected from the poems of William Morris to accompany a series of paintings by Burne-Jones'; and that seems to be confirmed by the liberal use of ellipsis in the text; this description seems to have become universally accepted. It has always been assumed that the verses were from Morris's *The Earthly Paradise* (recently they were described so by John Christian and Stephen Wildman in their catalogue for the most recent Burne-Jones exhibition, see *Edward Burne-Jones, Victorian Artist-Dreamer*. New York: Metropolitan Museum of Art, 1998, 101). But except for a single one-page poem entitled 'Saint George' (see *CW* XXIV. 75), Morris never wrote a complete narrative of the Saint George's rescue of the Princess Sabra, either in the *EP* or anywhere else yet discovered.

The solution to the problem lies in a closer examination of the *EP*. Morris made use of quotations from 2 of the *EP* tales that reproduce quite closely the central action of 'Saint George and the Dragon': a man accomplishes the heroic rescue of a maiden who has been sacrificed to a monster by a terrified community intent on saving itself. The stories involved are 'The Story of Cupid and Psyche' and 'The Doom of King Acrisius', and the lines quoted are from them.

C

Collections, Selections, and Anthologies to 1915

Books that combine two or more titles are listed and described in the C Section. It includes collections and anthologies issued through 1915 with the exception of collections made by Morris (such as *Signs of Change, John Ball and A King's Lesson*, and *Poems by the Way*) which are in Section A as Morris titles. It also excludes *The Collected Works* and *Old French Romances*, both considered 1st edns. and therefore included, with Morris's collections, in the A Section. The C Section also includes collections of fugitive pieces (that is, collections of published items issued from rare and little-known sources) to the present. There being much less emphasis here on textual relationship and book construction and more on contents, a pagination statement is given rather than a full collation, and the *Contents* listed are mainly concerned with the Morris texts included rather than a complete account of all pages.

C-1: Selection From The Poems of William Morris (Tauchnitz)

A SELECTION | FROM | THE POEMS | OF | WILLIAM MORRIS. | EDITED | WITH A MEMOIR | BY FRANCIS HUEFFER. | *COPYRIGHT EDITION.* | LEIPZIG | BERNHARD TAUCHNITZ | 1886. | *The Right of Translation is reserved.*

Series: Collection of British authors. Tauchnitz Edition, vol. 2378. Poems by William Morris. in one volume. [For obvious copyright reasons, the series was legally for sale only outside Britain, the Tauchnitz books being a prohibited import inside Britain. On the influence of Tauchnitz on Roberts Bros. 'Author's Edition' notice, see the Introduction passage leading to footnote 5].

This is the 1st of 4 anthologies of Morris to be published with Morris's knowledge and assistance, the others being the Francis Watts Lee edn. of 1891, *William Morris: Poet, Artist, Socialist* (see C-4); Oscar Fay Adams' edn. of *Atalanta's Race and Other Tales* of 1888 (see C-2); and H. B. Forman's selection in *Poets and Poetry of the Century: William Morris to Robert Buchanan* of 1891. Forman's is not a separate Morris publication, being only some 80 pages in an anthology of over 500 pages of poetry by other authors born in the same decade, from 1830 to 1840, but it is included as a separate entry here (see C-3) because of its size and its concentration on Morris. The many anthologies where a selection of Morris pieces is reprinted along with that of several other authors are not. In other words, in general only Morris books are included here.

Pagination: [2] [1–5] 6–319 [320] [= 322].

Contents: pp. 5–20, 'Memoir of William Morris', signed 'Francis Hueffer'; pp. 23–54, 7 poems from *The Defence of Guenevere*; pp. 55–81, Book XIV from *The Life and Death of Jason*; pp. 82–172, 'An Apology', a selection from the 'Prologue', 'Ogier the Dane', 'The Golden Apples', and 'L'Envoi' from *The Earthly Paradise*; pp. 173–7, 'Interludes' from *Love is Enough*; and pp. 178–319, 'Book II, Regin' from *Sigurd the Volsung*; p. [320] printer's imprint: [between thin rules] PRINTING OFFICE OF THE PUBLISHER.

Technical Notes: *paper*: machine made, t.e.g.; *leaf size*: trimmed: 157 x 116 mm.; *end papers*: 1 free end and paste down front and back, facing free ends and paste downs marbled (red); *binding*: plain unblocked dark red calico cloth (Tanselle I, No. 302) with 4 false raised bands on the spine with title and author between the 1st and 2nd: POEMS | [short thin rule] | MORRIS

Publication: 1886 [issued Oct.] (the Tauchnitz list of 'Latest Volumes,' dated Nov. 1886, records this vol. as available; *print run*: not known; *price*: 1 mark, 60 pfennig.

Register of Copies Examined: LeM (base copy: this copy is defective, missing gathering No. 6); BL (2nd base copy: Tauch. 2378[1]); TxU.

Notes: though Baron Tauchnitz's edns. were done with

the agreement of each individual author (hence the editorial note, 'copyright edition' on the title page), and Morris actively assisted Hueffer—son-in-law of Ford Madox Brown and father of Ford Madox Ford—in the making of this vol. (see *Letters*, ii. 447–9), the Morris copyright in Britain remained the exclusive property of Morris and, later, his Estate. On the original paper wrapper supplied with this edn. is printed the following exhortation: 'This Collection is published with copyright for Continental circulation, but all purchasers are earnestly requested not to introduce the vols. into England or into any British Colony'.

Morris to his publisher's nephew [Gilbert Ifold Ellis] 23 July 1885: 'Dear Sir Please send as soon as possible copies of my poems E.P., Love is Enough, Jason, Guenevere & Sigurd if possible in *sheets* to Francis Hueffer Esqre.' (*Letters*, ii. 447–8). Morris to Francis Hueffer, 23 July: 'Dear Hueffer I enclose all I could think of likely to be of any use to you: I have written to Ellis to send you the poems. I really couldn't write before, I was so busy. Could you come to Merton Abbey tomorrow?' (*Letters*, ii. 448–9).

C-2: Atalanta's Race and Other Tales (ed. Adams)
ATALANTA'S RACE | [in gothic] *And Other Tales from The Earthly Paradise* | [plain text] By WILLIAM MORRIS | EDITED WITH NOTES | BY OSCAR FAY ADAMS | WITH THE CO-OPERATION OF | WILLIAM J. ROLFE, A.M., LITT.D. | *WITH ILLUSTRATIONS* | [Ticknor's mark] | BOSTON | TICKNOR AND COMPANY | 1888

Edition: [1st edn. this anthology] (This book was done with the cooperation of Morris, as is shown by his correspondence with Adams, some of which is included as notes on the texts. The complete texts of the Morris side of the correspondence are rptd. in *Letters*, ii, 670–1).
Collaborators, Editors, and Illustrators: O. F. Adams (Preface initialled and dated 'March 16, 1888'); H. B. Forman, John Skelton, E. C. Stedman, and Oscar Wilde contribute previously pbd. sections to the Introduction.
Printer: The University Press:—John Wilson and Son, Cambridge, U.S.A.
Pagination: [i–vii] viii [ix–xi] 12–242 [243–4] [=244], note that the numbering begins with the half title and continues in sequence from roman continuously through the arabic numerals to the end of the text.
Contents: p. [iv] has frontispiece of Morris in half tone reproduction of an unsigned photograph with Morris's autograph reproduced below; pp. [vii]–viii, Preface by O. F. Adams; pp. 11–21, extracts from Morris scholars and critics, including Oscar Wilde's poem, 'The Charms of Morris's Poetry': p. 24, 2nd frontispiece, engraving of Peterborough Cathedral (later identified in the Notes), facing the 1st page of text; pp. 25–6, [Apology]; pp. 27–112, 'Prologue.—The Wanderers'; p. [114], [the author to the reader]; p. 115, 'March'; pp. 116–18, 'Prelude to Atalanta's Race'; pp. 119–41, 'Atalanta's Race'; p. 142, 'Interlude'; p. 143, 'April'; pp. 144–5, 'Prelude to The Proud King'; pp. 146–74, 'The Proud King'; pp. 174–5, 'Interlude'; p. 176, 'May'; p. 177, 'Prelude to The Writing on the Image'; pp. 178–88, 'The Writing on the Image'; p. 188, 'Interlude'; pp. 189–240, Notes; pp. 241–2, Index of words and phrases explained.
Technical Notes: *paper*: machine made, all edges stained red; *leaf size*: trimmed: 166 x 121 mm.; *illustrations*: besides the 2 frontispieces, there are 13 illustrations in half tone or steel engraving, all of which, Coupe says (83), 'have little or no relevance to the text.' But on close inspection all are of people or scenes directly described in the text, e.g. no. 9, which shows a sunset breaking through clouds, refers directly to p. 118, ll. 69–71:

And as again the sinking sun did break
Through the dark clouds and blazed adown the hall....

And, the 10th illustration, which shows a densely wooded scene, is directly above the first lines of 'Atalanta' on p. 119:

Through thick Arcadian woods a hunter went.

And all the other pictures can be similarly connected to the texts they illustrate. On some occasions the pictures are identified in the Notes.
end papers: front: 2 free ends and paste down; back: 1 free end and paste down; all sides plain white and blank; *binding*: dark green cloth-covered boards, blind-stamped thick-rule compartments, front and back; front gilt-stamped within the compartment: MORRIS'S | ATALANTA'S RACE, ETC | EDITED BY | OSCAR FAY ADAMS AND WILLIAM J. ROLFE | [thin rule]; down the spine: MORRIS'S ATALANTA'S RACE ETC.
Publication: 1888 (Ticknor registered the copyright, 1888, no. 9706).
Register of Copies Examined: LeM (base copy); BGR; MU (Spec. Coll. PP 5057/A2A8, 1888)
Notes: this Adams selection quotes from one or more letters of Morris to the editor on pp. 192–3, 197, 231, 232. Morris wrote to Adams on 17 June 1887:
'I should suggest that one of the lyrical pieces out of "Love is Enough" would be suitable and might take the place of one from the earlier vol: Perhaps "Atalanta's Race" would

be the most pleasing amongst those pieces you mention if it were not too long. I give you formal permission (if that be necessary) to take such pieces as you think fittest for your book.' Kelvin's Note: l. 'Oscar Fay Adams (1855–1919), a Massachusetts author and teacher whose books included *Through the Years with the Poets* (1886) in twelve volumes, and *A Dictionary of American Authors* (1897)' (*Letters*, ii. 670–1).

Morris to Adams, 12 June [1889], probably responds to receipt of a presentation copy of Adams' book: 'I must apologize very much to you for not answering your letter before and acknowledging your kind gift of the annotated extracts from my E.P. I now thank you very much for them, & the pains you have taken with the very interesting notes' (*Letters*, iii. 72). In this letter Morris is at some pains to identify 2 local places, both on the Thames, the 1st above and the 2nd below Oxford, which were the originals for settings used in the intercalary lyric links for June and Aug. in the *EP*.

Later issues or impressions of this edn.:

1.*1888 and 1894: these were either re-issues of unsold copies or rpts. from the Ticknor stereos by Houghton Mifflin and Company, Boston and New York; *print run* and *price*: unknown.

C-3: Morris to Buchanan (ed. Forman)

The | Poets | and the | Poetry | of the | Century | William Morris | to | Robert Buchanan | Edited by | Alfred H. Miles | Hutchinson & Co. | 25 Paternoster Square, London

Edition: [1st impression, 1st edn. this selection] H. B. Forman, editor of the 'William Morris' section, says it is 'another selection made with authority', i.e.; it had Morris's approval (see HBF, p. 219). In a 'Prefatory' Miles notes that the 15 poets represented in this vol., vol. 6 of the series, were all 'born during the fourth decade of the century'.
Pagination: [i–xx] 1–596, with the Morris section being pp. 1–80.
Contents: The Morris Section includes: pp. 1–14, Forman's introductory essay; pp. 15–24, 3 lyrics and scenes 2 and 3 of 'Sir Peter Harpdon's End'; pp. 25–32, from *The Defence of Guenevere*; pp. 35–59, 2 extracts from *The Earthly Paradise*; pp. 60–1, 3 lyrics from *Love is Enough*; pp. 62–8, an extract from *Sigurd the Volsung*; pp. 69–72, 2 *Chants for Socialists*; pp. 75–6, a lyric from *The House of the Wolfings*; and, pp. 77–80, 2 songs from *The Roots of the Mountains*.
Technical Notes: *binding*: original binding not seen.
Publication: [Apr. 1891] (HBF, p. 219); *print run* and *price*: not known.

Register of Copies Examined: BL (base copy 11603.c.c 20/6).
Notes: Forman says, 'It was not quite easy to persuade Morris that *Sigurd the Volsung*, *The House of the Wolfings*, and *The Roots of the Mountains* ought to be represented by extracts; but when I had done my biographical sketch, he waived his objections; and on looking back at the book again I cannot but think he did well . . . . the first edition of this volume came out in April 1891; and a second (revised) was published in May 1896' (HBF, p. 219).

The title page of the 2nd edn., he says, 'is changed only by the alteration of the address to "34 Paternoster Row" and the addition of the date "1896". Both books alike consist of half-title, title pp. iii– xii of preface and "index," a second half-title and 596 pages of text' (HBF, p. 219).

C-4: *W. M. Poet, Artist, Socialist. Selection (ed. Lee)

WILLIAM MORRIS: POET, ARTIST, SOCIALIST. A SELECTION FROM HIS WRITINGS TOGETHER WITH A SKETCH OF THE MAN. EDITED BY FRANCIS WATTS LEE. NEW YORK: THE HUMBOLDT PUBLISHING CO. CLINTON HALL, ASTOR PLACE

Collaborators, Editors, and Illustrators: Introduction by William Clarke.
Series: The Social Sciences Library, [No. 5], ed. by W. D. P. Bliss.
Contents: Introduction: William Morris, By William Clarke; A Dream of John Ball,| A King's Lesson; Signs of Change; How the Change Came; (6) Chants for Socialists.
Technical Notes: *binding*: in buff paper wrapper.
Publication: 1891 (copyright date); *print run* and *price*: unknown.
Register of Copies Located: MU (Spec.Coll. HX 246/M75, 1891); DLC; NN.
Notes: the details provided here are from the *NUC*, vol.196, p. 165, and Scott, pp. 27–8.
Later impression of this edn.: The Twentieth Century Publishers:

1.* 1901 (copyright date): SECOND EDITION; *print run* and *price*: unknown.

C-5: Defence Of Guenevere: A Book Of Lyrics (ed. Mosher)

[aligned left, hanging indent] THE DEFENCE OF GUEN- | EVERE | **A B**ook of **L**yrics | **Chose**n *from the works of* | **W**illiam **M**orris | **P**rinted *for* **T**homas **B. M**osher

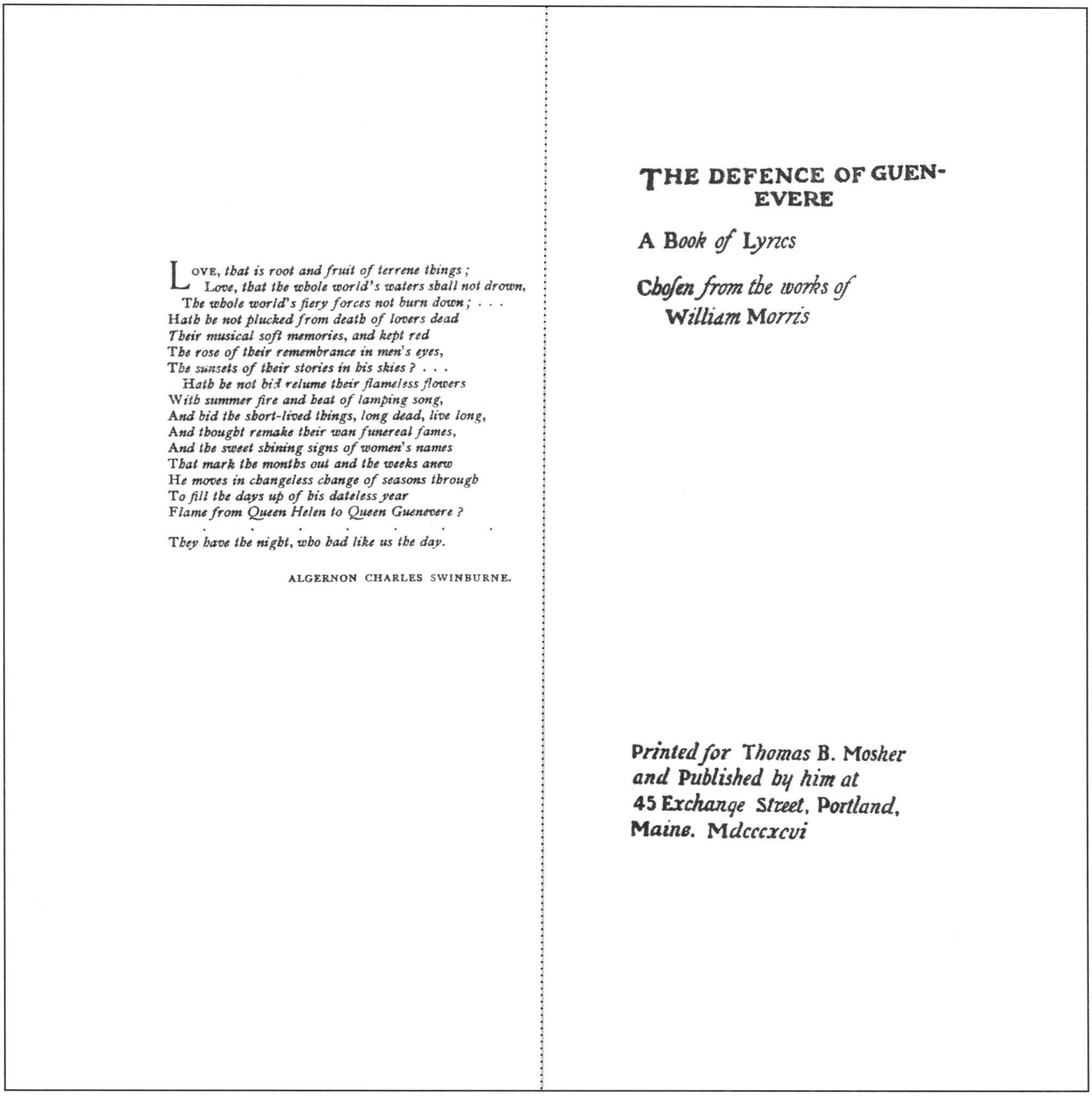

Figure 89. C-5: *Defence of Guen.: A Book of Lyrics* (1st edn.) epigraph & facing title page

| and Published by him at | 45 Exchange Street, Portland, | Maine. Mdcccxcvi

Edition: [1st impression, 1st edn. this collection] A selection of 27 Morris lyrics from his various books (see *Contents*, below).

Series: The Bibelot Series—8. The only Morris title in this series, which Mosher advertises in *The Bibelo*t 2/11 (Nov. 1896) as entirely distinct from both The Bibelot separates and the Reprints from "The Bibelot": 'The Bibelot Series is modelled on an old style format, narrow 8vo, and beautifully printed on Van Gelder's hand-made paper, uncut edges; done up in flexible Japan vellum, with outside wrappers, dainty gold seals, each in a separate slip case. 925 copies, Van Gelder Paper, at $1.00 net. 100 copies on Japan

Vellum $2.50 net.' He also gives series details in his 1902 catalogue: 'the Bibelot Series is modelled on the Aldine format, and like those early books of the great Italian printers, each volume is printed in Italic type throughout. It is the only series of Italic books ever printed in this country' (quoted in Bishop, p. 60). Mosher also printed a notice of 'The . . . new "Bibelots" for 1896 . . . VIII. The Defence of Guenevere. A Book of Lyrics Chosen from the Works of William Morris . . .'. In fact, this collection never appeared in The Bibelot, either as a separate or as a part of the annual vol. In this instance Mosher uses the more general sense of 'bibelot' which distinguishes a collectable 'miniature book', with no reference to the name of his periodical.

Pagination: pp. [2] [i–viii] ix–xcii [xciii–xciv] [= 96].

Contents: p. [4], statement of limitation: This Edition is limited to 925 copies.; pp. [i–viii] ix–xcvi, text: 16 lyrics from *The Defence of Guenevere and Other Poems*; 2 lyrics from *The Life and Death of Jason*; 5 poems from *The Earthly Paradise*; and 4 poems from *Poems by the Way*; p. [xciii], text ends with triangular vine and leaf tailpiece; p. [xciv], printer's imprint: PRINTED BY | SMITH AND SALE | PORTLAND | MAINE; pp. [xcv–vi], blank.

Technical Notes: *paper*: ordinary copies: Van Gelder handmade with deckled edges; FP copies: 100 copies on japan vellum; *leaf size*: ordinary copies: untrimmed deckled edges, avg. 208 x 98 mm.; *type face*: Brevier Elzevir Italic (see Bishop, 60); *pagination*: in lc italic roman numerals throughout; *end-papers*: 1 free end and paste-down, plain white and blank, front and back; *binding*: japan vellum wraps over boards; *spine*: title, series, and date printed across the spine in brown ink: The | Defence | of | Guenevere | BIBELOT | SERIES | 1896; title rptd. on front over leaf design; back: wreath design as circular compartment with letterpress inside: Bibelot | Series

Publication: 1896; *print run* and *price*: see the *Series* field, above.

Register of Copies Examined: CSt: (base copy: Felton PRn 5074/D31 1896); SU; Bsp.

C-6: *A Gilliflower of Gold (Collins)

[A Gilliflower of Gold. London and Glasgow, Collins Clear-Type Press, [18–?]]

Edition: [1st impression, 1st edn. this selection] (details from *NUC*, vol. 396, p. 142)

Pagination: pp. [1] 2–31 [= 31].

Contents: a selection of poems from *The Defence of Guenevere and Other Poems*.

Technical Notes: *end papers*: illus. continuous across the opening, front and back; illus. on front cover, title page, and elsewhere, the first 2 being in colour; each page with ornamental border.

Register of Copies Located: *MH.

C-7: Architecture and History and Westminster Abbey (Golden 8°)

[half title, aligned left] ARCHITECTURE AND HISTORY, | and WESTMINSTER ABBEY. BY | WILLIAM MORRIS.

Edition: 'Golden type octavo edn' [1st impression, 1st edn. of this collection] This combines for the 1st time 2 earlier pbd. papers: the 1st, 'Architecture and History', a paper delivered at the annual meeting of the SPAB on 1 July 1884, was 1st published as 'Paper Read by Mr. Morris', in the annual *SPAB Report, 1884*, (see D-116). The 2nd, 'Westminster Abbey', 1st appeared as a separate pbn. titled *Concerning Westminster Abbey*, published by the SPAB in June 1893 (see A-65.01).

Collaborators, Editors, and Illustrators: [edited by Sydney C. Cockerell assisted by Robert Proctor].

Series: No. 4 in a series of 5 vols. of lectures and papers by Morris. For details of the series, see this field in A-71.02.

Colophon: Printed at the Chiswick Press with the Golden | type designed by William Morris for the Kelms- | cott Press, and finished on the sixteenth day of | September, 1900. Published by Longmans & Co. | 39, Paternoster Row, London.

Pagination: pp. [2] 1–50 [51–4] [= 56].

Contents: pp. [1], title page; p. [2], blank; p. 1, headed: [top, flush left] ARCHITECTURE AND HISTORY. A | PAPER READ BEFORE THE SO- | CIETY FOR THE PROTECTION OF | ANCIENT BUILDINGS, ON JULY 1, | 1884. BY WILLIAM MORRIS. | [text begins]; pp. 2–33, text completed; p. [34], blank; pp. 35–49, 2nd paper, headed: [top, flush left] WESTMINSTER ABBEY. A PAPER | WRITTEN FOR THE SOCIETY FOR | THE PROTECTION OF ANCIENT | BUILDINGS IN JUNE, 1893. | [text begins]; p. 50, text ends with colophon, see above; pp. [51–4], blank.

Technical Notes: items common to the set—paper, printing, type, position (but not content) of shoulder notes, pagination, and binding (except for printed titles)—are described in this field in A-71.02, the entry for the 1st of the 5 vols.; *end papers*: none provided, the front and back paste-downs being part of the first and last gatherings, [a] and h, which also contain letterpress on their conjunct leaves.

Publication: 14 Sept. 1900 [colophon date, issued 17 Oct.]

(Longmans *Notes on Books*, 9/183 (30 Nov. 1900), 268); *print run*: 1,000 copies (Chiswick Arch.); *price*: 2s. 6d.
Register of Copies Examined: VU (base copy: 2 copies of the whole set, both 1st impression: L & E 704 / M877A, + various odd copies); LeM (2nd impression of the 1st edn.); BL (2 copies: K.T.C. 8. a. 20.; Ashley Library 3698); SU (2 copies: 704/M87ar);
Later impression of this edn.: Longmans:
1. 20 Dec. 1900 [finishing printing, issued 27 Dec.] (Chiswick Arch.): [2nd impression, 1st edn.]; *print run*: 500 copies; *price*: 2s. 6d.

C-8.01: *The Two Sides Of The River (etc., *Bib.*)

[wrapper-title, top left] Vol. V. [top right] No. 9 | [within thin-rule compartment, top left] | *Sept.* [right] *MDC-CCXCIX.* | [for title detail common to Bibelot issues, see A-83.01] | [below the compartment, right, in red] THE TWO SIDES OF THE RIVER AND | OTHER POEMS BY WILLIAM MORRIS
Edition: [1st impression, 2nd edn., 1st American] The 1st edn. of this title is the Wise-Forman forgery, for which and for earlier pbns. of the first 2 poems, see E-4. To the 3 poems of the original forged pamphlet, Mosher adds a 4th, the poem 'Winter Weather' from *The Oxford and Cambridge Magazine* (see D-2), because, he explains in his unsigned preface, it had not been reprinted by Morris himself in either *The Defence of Guenevere* or *Poems by the Way*. This Bibelot separate has not been closely examined. The contents and pagination given here have been supplied for the most part by Mr Philip Bishop, Mosher's bibliographer
Series: This is the 4th Morris title pbd. by Mosher both as a separate pamphlet and as part of the annual Bibelot collection (in this case Vol. 5, 1899). For further details of this series arrangement, see this field in A-83.01.
Pagination: pp. [4] [273–6] 277–93 204–7: the last 4 page numbers, from the separate edn., are an error, corrected in the collected annual vol. to 294–7 [298] [2] [= 32]. Pagination in the Bibelot separates is continuous through all the issues of the year, but it does not count conjunct pairs of advertising leaves at the beginning and end of the separate issues, these being excised before binding into the annual vol.
Contents: pp. [1–4], ads; pp. [273–4], headed in 3-line neogothic letters: The Bibelot | [text of Mosher's unsigned foreword completed]; p. [275], half title; p. [276], blank; pp. 277–82, text of 'The Two Sides of the River'; pp. 283–9, text of 'Hapless Love'; pp. 290–6, text of 'The First Foray of Aristomenes'; pp. 297–[298], text of 'Winter Weather'; pp. [1–2], ads.
Technical Notes: *paper*: plain white machine-wove "antique" paper with dandy-roll chain and wire lines; *leaf size*: this copy trimmed for library binding, 142 x 105 mm; *printing*: type: Caslon Brevier; *type area*: 99 x 68 mm; lines to page: leaded, 28 lines (p. 279); running heads: not used; pagination: arabic numbers centred on the direction line; *binding*: wrapper: the usual Bibelot wrapper, with the title in red, lower right, below compartment. For further detail common to this series, see *Collation*, *Series*, and *Technical Notes* fields in A-83.01.
Publication: *print run*: 5000 copies printed; *price*: 5 cents (for further details, see this field in A-83.01) 12 FP copies on japan vellum.
Register of Copies Examined: BL (PP.8001.ea.[16]); Bsp.

C-8.02: Two Sides Of The River (etc., Rpts. *Bib.*)

[1st, 2nd, and last lines in red] THE TWO SIDES OF THE | RIVER AND OTHER POEMS | BY WILLIAM MORRIS | [Chiswick Press Aldine mark, Bishop No. 2].
Edition: [2nd impression of the 2nd edn., 1st American] This pbn. adds 'Winter Weather' from *The Oxford and Cambridge Magazine* to the selection of 3 poems made by Wise and Forman for their forgery, Mosher's obvious source (for which see E-4).
Collaborators, Editors, and Illustrators: edited with an unsigned foreword [by T. B. Mosher].
Series: Reprints from "The Bibelot"—6. Mosher says in his bibliography of R. L. Stevenson, included in his edn. of *Father Damien: An Open Letter*, that the Reprints from 'The Bibelot', of which *Father Damien* was one, were printed on japan vellum in 25 copies and 'printed from the same forms [as the Bibelot versions], only reimposed and with new pagination'. For further series detail, see A-83.02.
Pagination: pp. [6] [1–2] 3–23 [24–6] [= 32].
Contents: p. *[1]*, half title; p. [2], limitation statement: Twenty-five copies of this book | printed on Japan vellum of | which twenty only are for sale. | This is No. [number inserted in longhand]; pp. 3–7, 'The Two Sides of the River'; pp. 8–13, 'Hapless Love'; pp. 14–20, 'The First Foray of Aristomenes'; pp. 21–[4], 'Winter Weather'; pp. [25–6], blank.
Technical Notes: *leaf size*: 152 x 112 mm.; for further detail, see this field in A-83.02.
Publication: 1899 [issued after 25 Aug. 1899, when Mosher issued the Bibelot separate, the plates of which were used for this 2nd impression]; *print run*: 25 copies, 20 for sale;

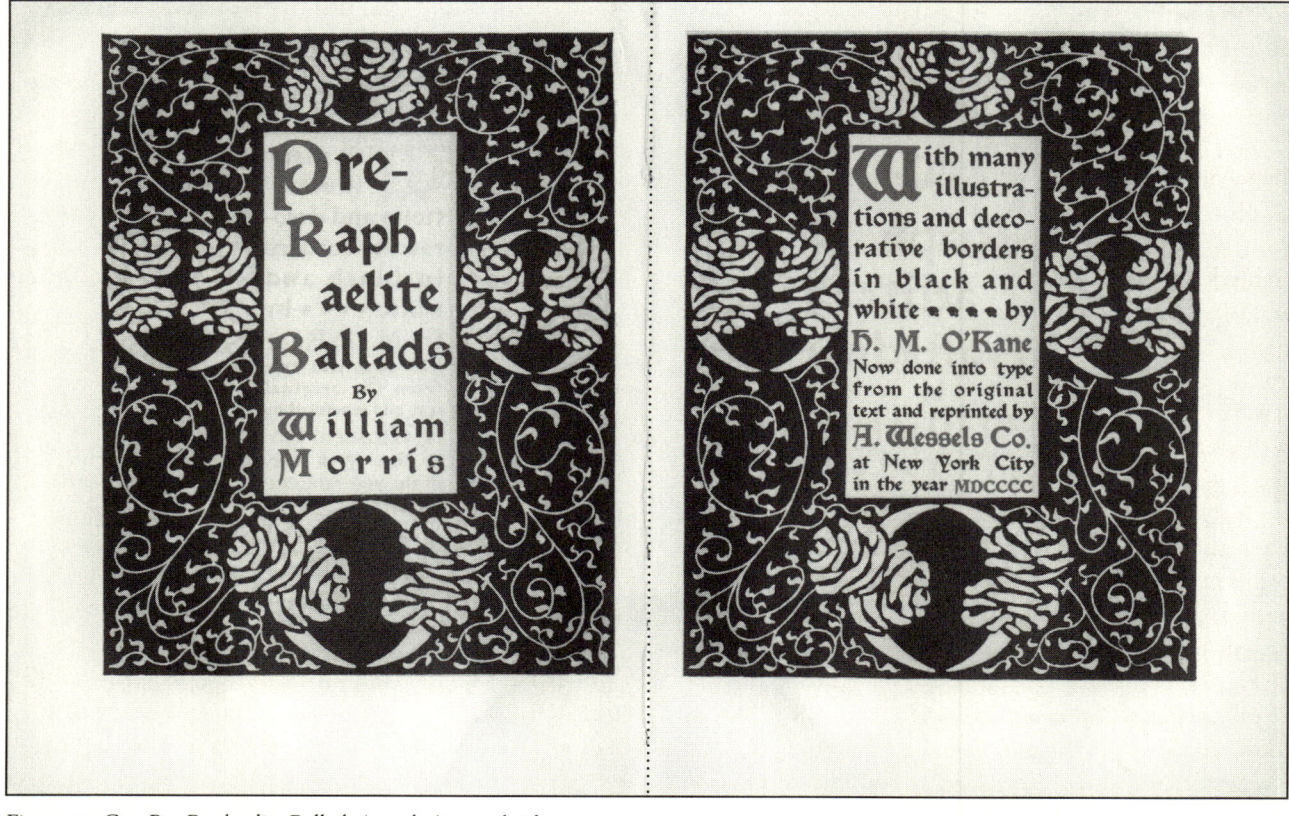

Figure 90. C-9: Pre-Raphaelite Ballads (1st edn.) spread title

price: $4.00. Limitation notice: "Twenty-five copies of this book printed on Japan vellum, of which twenty only are for sale. This is no. [number in longhand]."
Register of Copies Examined: Bsp (base copy).
Notes: this is more than a normal new impression from existing plates, Reprints from the Bibelot being a limited edn., done on 2 varieties of FP, free of advertising, and sold with a more permanent binding (see *Technical Notes* in A-83.02) and at a much higher price.

C-9: Pre-Raphaelite Ballads (Wessels)

[spread title (double title page) with duplicate borders, pp. [12–13], [throughout this entry, underlining indicates letters in red] Pre- | Raph[-]aelite | Ballads | By | William | Morris | [p. [13], With many | illustra- | tions and deco- | rative borders | in black and | white [4 printer's leaves] by | H. M. O'Kane | Now done into type | from the original | text and reprinted by | A. Wessels Co. | at New York City | in the year MDCCCC
Edition: a selection of 4 Morris lyrics, all from *The Defence of Guenevere and Other Poems*. There are 2 different limitation notices in this book, one in the ordinary copies and the other in the LP copies, the latter specifying 250 LP copies, the former only 100 (see *Contents*, below). In fact there were 250 LP copies (see Coupe, 52–3).
Colophon: [begins with a 4-line initial 'H' in red] Here endeth the Book: Pre-Raphaelite | Ballads, written by William Morris, | and now newly done into type from | the original text, being embellished with many decorative borders, illustrations | and initials by H. M. O'Kane, and published by | A. Wessels Company at Nine West Eighteenth | Street in New York City: August, MDCCCC.
Pagination: 32 leaves, no pagination, pp. [1–64] [= 64]. Alternate openings have no verses, but include the titles and line numbers of the verses printed on the reverse side of each leaf.
Contents: p. [1], half title; pp. [2–4], blank; p. [5], [limitation notice in the LP copies]: Of this edition of Pre-Raphaelite Ballads | there have been printed five hundred num- | bered copies on "Old Stratford" paper, and | Two hundred and fifty numbered large paper copies on Imperial Japanese paper, of which numbers | one to ten inclusive have been specially bound | in full English vellum and the initials drawn | in and illuminated by H. M. O'Kane; [in the

ordinary copies only 100 LP copies are specified (thus in my copy); otherwise the notices are the same (see Coupe, 52–3)]. This copy is number [no. added in longhand] of the edition in "Old Stratford" paper.

Clearly, the number of LP copies was changed when the japan vellum copies were printed]; pp. [6–8], blank; p. [9], 2nd half title; pp. [10–11], blank; pp. 12–13, spread title pages with full floral border-compartments in white on black on both pages, title on verso, edn. statement and publisher's imprint on the recto (see above); p. [14], copyright notice; p. [15], 1st poem title, below right; p. [16], frontis. with full border; pp. [17, 20–1], text of 'Two Red Roses Across the Moon' [each poem has a similar sequence with each opening of frontis. and text or text only alternating with an opening blank except for poem titles at the lower right margins]; pp. [25, 28–9, 32–3, 36], 'In Praise of My Lady'; pp. [41, 44–5], 'The Tune of the Seven Towers'; pp. [49, 52–3, 56], 'The Gilliflower of Gold'; p. [57], rose-tree tail piece in red within full decorative border in black; pp. [58–60], blank; p. [61], colophon, see above; pp. [62–4], blank.
Technical Notes: *paper*: see limitation notice in *Contents*, above; *leaf size*: ordinary copies: 192 x 144 mm.; LP copies: 210 x 160 mm.; *end-papers*: 1 free end and pastedown, with facing pages decorated with red rose-tree, the same as the tail piece, otherwise plain white; *binding*: LP: cream japan vellum covered boards, plain and unblocked; *spine*: gilt-stamped across: Pre- | Ra- | pha | elite | Bal | lads | Will | iam | Mor | ris; gilt-stamped on front in modern black letter: Pre-Raphaelite Ballads | By William Morris; ordinary copies: quarter white holland with grey paper-covered boards and printed paper spine label; with full ornamental black border on front with internal compartment with letterpress aligned left and all in red: Pre- | Raphaelite | Ballads | [centred] By | William | Morris | [left oriented] With many illustrations | and decorative borders | in black and white—by | H. M. O'Kane; *ornamentation*: every page of verse has a full white-on-black border, and every poem begins with a full-page illus. within a full border; text begins with a large drop-cap illuminated initial in red within a compartment with a background black-and-white pen drawing. The text appears only on facing pages, each with full border, the ornamentation being oriented to the opening rather than the page, and the reverse of each page of text carries only the title and verse numbers of the poem printed on the obverse page.
Publication: Aug. 1900 [colophon date, issued 13–20 Oct.]

(*Pub. Weekly*, 58/1499 (20 Oct. 1900), 1114); *print run*: 500 ordinary, 250 LP copies including 10 on vellum; *price*: unknown.
Register of Copies Examined: LeM (base copy).
Notes: the type used here was 'Satanick', issued by the American Type Founders Company in 1896 and 'modelled directly on Morris' Gothic font' (*American Book Design*, 213), i.e. the Chaucer type. It seems indistinguishable from Morris's Chaucer type but reduced in size from Pica to Long Primer, 12 to 10 point.

C-10.01: *Golden Wings [with] Svend (Rpts. Bib.)

[1st, 2nd, and last lines in red] GOLDEN WINGS SVEND | AND HIS BRETHREN | BY WILLIAM MORRIS | [Chiswick Press Aldine mark, Bishop No. 2] | Portland, Maine | [swash caps] *THOMAS B. MOSHER* | Mdcccc
Edition: [1st impression, 1st separate edn. of this combined title] Mosher 1st pbd. the texts of these 2 tales separately under the Bibelot masthead, 'Golden Wings' in Apr. and 'Svend and His Brethren' in Sept. 1900 (see A-95.01 and 96.01). Mosher's usual practice, except in the series Reprints from "The Bibelot", was to use new settings for the various series in which the same titles appeared. This being the 1st appearance of this combined title, it is treated as the 1st edn. of a new title, but both tales appear in the same edn., i.e. in the same setting as in the monthly *Bibelot* separates and in the annual *Bibelot* collection. So, though treated here as a new title, this combined edn. is a 2nd impression of both titles. Both of these tales were 1st pbd. in *The Oxford and Cambridge Magazine* (1856, see D-16 and D-11).
Collaborators, Editors, and Illustrators: Introduction [unsigned, by T. B. Mosher].
Series: Reprints from "The Bibelot"—8. For series detail see this field in A-83.02.
Colophon: TWENTY-FIVE COPIES OF THIS BOOK HAVE BEEN PRINTED ON JAPAN VELLUM, OF WHICH TWENTY ONLY ARE FOR SALE. THIS IS NO. [no. in longhand].
Pagination: [i–viii] 1–77 [78] [= 86].
Contents: pp. 5–36, Golden Wings; pp. 37–71, Svend and His Brethren.
Technical Notes: *binding*: flexible japan vellum with yapp edges.
Publication: 1900 [issued after Sept., when *Svend* first appeared separately under *The Bibelot* masthead]; *print run*: 25 copies on japan vellum, 20 for sale; *price*: $4.00.
Register of Copies Located: Bsp (base copy).

C-10.02: *Golden Wings [with] Svend (Broc.)

GOLDEN WINGS [WITH] SVEND AND HIS BRETHREN

Edition: [1st impression, 2nd combined edn.] Both of these tales were 1st pbd. by Morris in *The Oxford and Cambridge Magazine* (1856, see D-16 and D-11). T. B. Mosher 1st pbd. them as separate edns. issued under *The Bibelot* masthead in Apr. and Sept., 1900 (see A-95.01 and 96.01). The detail of this description is supplied by Philip Bishop.

Collaborators, Editors, and Illustrators: foreword in 2 parts, unsigned, [by T. B. Mosher].

Series: Brocade Series—33. For detail common to this series, see this field in A-70.03.

Colophon: FOUR HUNDRED AND TWEN- | TY-FIVE COPIES OF THIS BOOK | HAVE BEEN PRINTED IN JAPAN | VELLUM, AND TYPE DISTRIB- | UTED, IN THE MONTH OF | JULY, A.D. MDCCCCII, | AT THE PRESS OF GEORGE D. | LORING, PORTLAND, MAINE

Pagination: pp. [1] 2–96 [97–8] [=98].

Contents: pp. 13–51, 'Golden Wings'; pp. 55–96, 'Svend and His Brethren'; p. 97, colophon: see above.

Technical Notes: paper, type, printing, binding, and slip cases are common to the series and are covered in this field in the record for the 1st Morris pbn. in this series, A-70.03; *ornaments*: head- and tail-pieces from Chiswick Press: pp. 11, 97.

Publication: July 1902 (colophon date); *print run*: 425 copies on japan vellum; *price*: 75 cents, or as one of a boxed set of 4 vols. of Old English Romances, combining *The Hollow Land, Gertha's Lovers, Golden Wings | Svend and His Brethren*, and *The Story of the Unknown Church and Other Tales*: $3.00 net.

Register of Copies Located: Bsp.

Later impression of this edn.: Mosher:

1.* Nov. 1906 (colophon date): Second Edition: *print run*: 425 copies on japan vellum; *price*: 75 cents.

C-11: Two Addresses . . . before the NAAA (Golden 8°)

[aligned left] ART AND ITS PRODUCERS and THE | ARTS & CRAFTS TODAY: TWO | ADDRESSES DELIVERED BEFORE | THE NATIONAL ASSOCIATION FOR | THE ADVANCEMENT OF ART. BY | WILLIAM MORRIS

Edition: 'Golden type octavo edition' [1st impression, 1st edn.] These 2 addresses were delivered, respectively, at 2 annual conferences of National Association for the Advancement of Art and its Application to Industry (hereafter referred to as NAAA) in 1888 (in Liverpool) and 1889 (in Edinburgh), and pbd. in each case in the Association's *Transactions* (see D-426 and 492, the 2nd being 'The Presidential Address').

Collaborators, Editors, and Illustrators: [edited by Sydney C. Cockerell assisted by Robert Proctor].

Series: the last in the 'Golden type octavo edition' set of 5 vols. of fugitive lectures and papers by Morris. For series details, see this field in A-71.02, the 1st entry for a book in this series.

Colophon: Printed at the Chiswick Press with the Golden type | designed by William Morris for the Kelms- | cott Press, and finished on the twenty-sixth day of | April, 1901. Published by Longmans & Co. 39, | Paternoster Row, London.

Pagination: pp. [8] 1–47 [48] [=56].

Contents: p. 1, lecture V, headed: [top, flush left] ART AND ITS PRODUCERS. A LEC- | TURE DELIVERED IN LIVERPOOL | IN 1888. BY WILLIAM MORRIS. | [text begins]; pp. 2–20, text of lecture completed; p. 21, lecture VI, headed: [top, flush left] THE ARTS AND CRAFTS OF TODAY. | BEING AN ADDRESS DELIVERED IN | EDINBURGH IN OCTOBER, 1889. BY | WILLIAM MORRIS. | [text begins]; pp. 22–47, text completed with a colophon (see above).

Technical Notes: paper, printing, type, position (but not content) of shoulder notes, pagination, signatures, and binding (except for printed titles) are all common to the series and are described in this field in A-71.02, the entry for the 1st vol. in the series. Included here are only those details that are specific to this particular edn. of this title: *binding letterpress*: front, reproduces the title page.

Publication: 26 Apr. 1901 [colophon date, issued 27 June] (Longmans *Notes on Books*, 9/136 (31 Aug. 1901), 316). However Cockerell says 17 June 1901 (Cockerell to Mrs. Morris, 17 June 1901, Smith Arch.). *Pub. Circ.* concurs with the date preferred here ('Publications of the Week', 75 (6 July 1901), 13), which suggests either a rare slip of the pen in Cockerell's date or an unforeseen delay; *print run*: 1,250 copies (all done up, Chiswick Arch.); *price*: 2s. 6d.

Register of Copies Examined: LeM (base copy); BGR; CSt (Spec Coll Gunst Z239.2.C54.M87 art); VU (3 copies: L & E, all with the same 1901 colophon); SU (704/M87a).

C-12:* Churches of North France [+ Rethel essay] (Rpts. Bib.)

[1st, 2nd, and last lines in red] THE CHURCHES OF |

NORTH FRANCE **BY | WILLIAM MORRIS** | [Chiswick Press Aldine mark, Bishop No. 2] | Portland, Maine | [swash caps] THOMAS B. MOSHER | Mdccccj
Edition: [1st impression, 1st edn. of this combined title] As well as the title essay, 'The Churches of Northern France', this includes Morris's essay on 2 engravings by Alfred Rethel: "Death the Avenger" and "Death the Friend". The essay was 1st pbd. in *The Oxford and Cambridge Magazine*, Aug. 1856, respectively (see D-10). Though *The Churches of North France* was 1st pbd. by Mosher as a Bibelot separate, '"Death the Avenger" and "Death the Friend"' never appeared in The Bibelot or in Mosher's other series. The separate issue of this title has not been seen. The details of pagination and contents have been supplied by Mr Philip Bishop, Mosher's bibliographer.
Collaborators, Editors, and Illustrators: the introductory note is an excerpt from Mackail.
Series: Reprints from "The Bibelot"—9. For details common to this series, see this field in A-83.02.
Printer: Smith and Sale, Portland, Maine.
Pagination: 26 leaves pp. [4] [1–4] 5–39 [40] 41–6 [47–8] [= 52].
Contents: p. [2], limitation statement: Thirty-five copies of this book | printed on Japan vellum, of | which thirty only are for sale. | This is No. [number written in longhand]; pp. 5–39, The Churches of North France; pp. 41–[7], '"Death the Avenger" and "Death the Friend"'.
Technical Notes: see this field in A-83.02; *end-papers*: 1 free end and paste-down, plain white and blank, front and back; *binding letterpress*: *front*: title as on title page, but all lines in black; *spine*: title printed down.
Publication: 1901; *print run*: 35 copies of which 30 were for sale; *price*: $4.00.
Register of Copies Examined: Bsp (base copy); MH (Typ 490156).

C-13: Volsunga Saga [and] Three Northern Love Stories (Golden 4°)

[1st of 2 title pages, or, rather, half titles made to serve as title pages, both aligned left]: VOLSUNGA SAGA: THE STORY OF THE VOLSUNGS | AND NIBLUNGS, WITH CERTAIN SONGS FROM THE | ELDER EDDA. TRANSLATED FROM THE ICELANDIC | BY EIRIKR MAGNUSSON AND WILLIAM MORRIS.
[2nd title]: THREE NORTHERN LOVE STORIES AND OTHER | TALES. TRANSLATED FROM THE ICELANDIC | BY EIRIKR MAGNUSSON AND WILLIAM MORRIS.
Edition: 'Golden type quarto edition' [1st impression, 3rd edn. for each of the 2 titles] For previous pbns. of the stories, see this field in A-6.01 and 9.01. Here the expression 'bound in with' is most literally true. Each title is complete and separate in all except sharing the same binding.
Collaborators, Editors, and Illustrators: [edited by S. C. Cockerell and Robert Proctor].
Series: 4th vol. pbd. of the 8-vol. 'Golden-type quarto' series; for series details, see this field in A-47.04.
Colophon: 1st: p. 112, 1st series: Here ends The Story of the Volsungs and Niblungs, with some songs from | the Elder Edda; translated from the Icelandic by Eiríkr Magnússon and | William Morris. First printed in 1870, and now reprinted at the Chiswick | Press with the Golden type designed by William Morris for the Kelmscott | Press, and finished on the 20th day of September, 1901. Published by Long- | mans, Green and Co. of London, New York and Bombay.
2nd *Colophon*: p. 113, 2nd series of page nos.: Here ends Three Northern Love Stories and Other Tales, translated from | the Icelandic by Eiríkr Magnússon and William Morris. First printed in | 1875, and now reprinted at the Chiswick Press with the Golden type de- | signed by William Morris for the Kelmscott Press, and finished on the ninth | day of November, 1901. Published by Longmans, Green and Co. of London, | New York and Bombay.
Pagination: 1st title: 62 leaves, [i–ii] iii–xii 1–112 [=124]; 2nd title: 61 leaves, [i–ii] iii–viii 1–113 [114] [=122].
Contents: 1st title: p. [i], title page; p. [ii], blank; pp. iii–v, headed: [top, flush left] THE NAMES OF THOSE WHO ARE MOST NOTE- | WORTHY IN THIS STORY. | [list begins]; p. viii, list completed; p. ix, headed: CONTENTS; p. x, Contents completed; p. xi, headed: [in red] A PROLOGUE IN VERSE BY WILLIAM MORRIS. | [verses begin]; p. xii, verses completed; p. 1, headed: [in red] THE STORY OF THE VOLSUNGS AND NIBLUNGS, | TRANSLATED BY E. MAGNUSSON & WILLIAM MORRIS. | [text begins]; pp. 3-112, text completed with colophon: Here ends The Story of the Volsungs and Niblungs, with some Songs from | the Elder Edda; translated from the Icelandic by Eiríkr Magnússon and | William Morris. First printed in 1870, and now reprinted at the Chiswick | Press, with the Golden type designed by William Morris for the Kelmscott | Press, and finished on the 20th day of September, 1901. Published by Long- | mans, Green and Co. of London, New York and Bombay.
2nd title.: p. [i], 2nd title page; p. [ii], blank; pp. iii–iv, headed: PREFACE. | [text completed]; p. [v], headed:

[top, flush left] CHRONOLOGY IN THE STORY OF GUNNLAUG | WORM-TONGUE. | [lists 17 major incidents in the story and provides their dates]; p. vi, blank; p. vii, headed: [top, flush left] CONTENTS. | [Contents completed]; p, [viii], blank; p. 1, headed, in red: [flush left] THE STORY OF GUNNLAUG WORM-TONGUE AND | RAVEN THE SKALD, EVEN AS ARI THORGILSON THE | LEARNED, | THE PRIEST, HATH TOLD IT, WHO WAS | THE MAN OF ALL ICELAND MOST LEARNED IN | TALES OF THE LAND'S INHABITING AND IN | LORE | OF TIME AGONE. | [text begins]; pp. 2–113, text completed with 2nd colophon, see above; pp. [114–16], blank.

Technical Notes: paper, printing, type, position of shoulder notes, page numbers, and binding are all common to the series and are described in this field in A-47.04, the 1st pbn. of the series. Included here are only those details specific to this edn.: *running titles*: *shoulder notes*: all rectos and versos, each with the short title of the relevant tale or story.

Publication: 9 Nov. 1901 [colophon date, issued 20 Nov.] (Longmans Arch.); *print run*: 315, copies, 299 for sale including 60 for the US; *price*: 2gns.

Register of Copies Examined: LeM (base copy); BL (C. 43. f. 18.); BGR; CSmH; NN.

C-14: Art and Craft of Printing (Elston Press)

THE ART AND CRAFT OF PRINTING, BY WILLIAM MORRIS.

Edition: [1st edn., this collection] A selection of 3 fugitive Morris essays on printing. *A Note by William Morris . . .* was 1st pbd. by the KP (see A-88.01), 'The Ideal Book' in *Transactions of the Bibliographical Society* (see D-555), and 'Printing' in *Arts and Crafts Essays* (see B-15).

Colophon: Here ends The Art and Craft of Printing: collected essays by William Morris. Of this book there have been printed two hundred and ten copies by Clark Conwell at the Elston Press: finished this thirtieth day of January, MDCCCCII. Sold by Clark Conwell at the Elston Press, Pelham Road, New Rochelle, New York.

Pagination: pp. 1–44, numbering restarts, 1–26 [= 70].

Contents: pp. 1–44: 'A Note by William Morris on His Aims in Founding the Kelmscott Press, Together with a Short Description of the Press by S. C. Cockerell, and an Annotated List of the Books Published Thereat'; pp. 1–8 (pagination restarts): 'The Ideal Book'; and pp. 11–19 (pagination continuous with 'The Ideal Book'): 'Printing'; pp. [20–4], illus. of Morris's Chaucer and Troy types; pp. [25–6], Cockerell's 5 corrections to Conwell's draft 'Notes' to Morris's texts.

Technical Notes: *paper*: *leaf size*: 246 x 166 mm.; *printing*: *type*: Caslon Old Roman (Ransom, 260); *binding*: quarter holland with light blue paper-covered boards and printed paper spine label: THE ART AND CRAFT OF PRINTING: WILLIAM MORRIS. Made to range with *Some Notes on Early Woodcut Books* (see below).

Publication: 30 Jan. 1902 (colophon date); *print run*: 231 copies; *price*: $5.00.

Register of Copies Examined: CtY (base copy); J-F V.

C-15: *Some Notes on Early Woodcut Books (Elston Press)

SOME NOTES ON EARLY WOODCUT BOOKS, WITH A CHAPTER ON ILLUMINATED MANUSCRIPTS, BY WILLIAM MORRIS.

Edition: [1st edn. of this collection] This is a collection of three fugitive Morris essays on early printed books with woodcut illustrations. All were previously pbd.: 'Some Notes on Early Woodcut Books' 1st appeared as 'On the Artistic Qualities of the Woodcut Books of Ulm and Augsburg in the Fifteenth Century', from *Bibliographica* (see D-585); 'The Woodcuts of Gothic Books', is from *The Journal of the Society of Arts* (see D-538); and 'Some Notes on the Illuminated Books of the Middle Ages', from *The Magazine of Art* (see D-557).

Colophon: Here end the Notes on Early Woodcut Books by William Morris. Of this book there have been printed one hundred and twenty copies by Clark Conwell at the Elston Press: finished this twentieth day of February, MDCCCCII. Sold by Clark Conwell at the Elston Press, Pelham Road, New Rochelle, New York.

Pagination: 1–15, numbers restart, 1–17, numbers restart again, 1–8 [= 40].

Contents: pp. 1–10, 'Some Notes on Early Woodcut Books'; pp. [11–15], reproductions of early woodcuts; (pagination restarts) pp. 1–17, 'The Woodcuts of Gothic Books'; (pagination restarts) pp. 1–8, 'Some Notes on the Illuminated Books of the Middle Ages'.

Technical Notes: *paper*: *leaf size*: 248 x 168 mm.; *printing*: printed in red and black, colophon and shoulder notes in red; *pagination*: each of the 3 essays restarts the pagination at 1; *binding*: quarter holland with light blue paper-covered boards.

Publication: 20 Feb. 1902 (colophon date); *print run*: 120 copies; *price*: $5.00.

Register of Copies Located: MU (base copy); CSmH.

Notes: all 3 rptd. in Peterson. The details here come mainly from Walsdorf (p. 197). Will Ransom says there were 120 copies in 8° priced at $5.00 and printed in Caslon Old Roman (Ransom, 260).

C-16.01:* The Story of the Unknown Church [and] Lindenborg Pool (*Bib.*)

[above compartment, left] Vol. VIII. [right] No. 3. | [top left, within compartment] MARCH. [right] MDCCCCII. | [for title details common to the series, see A-83.01] | [below compartment, aligned right, in red] THE STORY OF THE UNKNOWN CHURCH | LINDENBORG POOL | BY WILLIAM MORRIS
Edition: [1st impression, 1st separate edn.] 1st pbd. in *The Oxford and Cambridge Magazine.*
Collaborators: unsigned Introduction [by T. B. Mosher].
Series: *The Bibelot*, 5/9 (March. 1902), 277–98. For more series detail, see this field in A-83.01.
Place, Publisher, Printer: see wrapper transcription in A-83.01.
Pagination: 24 leaves pp. [4] [81–4] 85–102 [103–4] 105–119 [120] [4] [= 48] Pagination in the Bibelot separates is continuous through all the issues of the year, but it does not count conjunct pairs of advertising leaves at the beginning and end of the Bibelot separates, these being excised before binding into the annual vol. They are included here with assigned numbers not related to any number sequence in the text. This Bibelot separate has not been seen. The details of pagination and contents are from Mr Philip Bishop, Mosher's bibliographer.
Contents: p. 85–102, headed: THE STORY OF THE UNKNOWN CHURCH | [text completed]; pp. 105–20, headed: LINDENBORG POOL | [text completed]
Technical Notes: for details common to the series, see A-83.01.
Publication: Mar. 1902 [masthead date, issued on 25 Feb.]; *print run* and *price*: see this field in A-83.01.
Register of Copies Examined: Bsp (base copy).

C-16.02: The Story of the Unknown Church and Other Tales (Rpts. Bib.)

[aligned left, 1st, 2nd, and last lines in red] THE STORY OF THE | UNKNOWN CHURCH | AND OTHER TALES BY | WILLIAM MORRIS | [Chiswick Press Aldine mark, Bishop No. 2] | Portland, Maine | [swash italic caps] THOMAS B. MOSHER | M*dccccij*
Edition: [2nd impression, 1st separate edn., this collection] Comprising 3 texts—'The Unknown Church', 'Lindenborg Pool', and 'A Dream', this, like all the Reprints from "The Bibelot" is printed from the same forms as the original Bibelot separates, except that the Bibelot separate version didn't include 'A Dream' where the 'Reprint' does (taking the text from the July 1902 issue of The Bibelot).
Series: Reprints from "The Bibelot"—11 (for further series detail, see A-83.02.
Collaborators, Editors, and Illustrators: For the 'Preface' to the 1st 2 stories, from the Bibelot separate issue, pp. 1–2, Mosher selects introductory extracts from the Mackail and Vallance biographies of Morris. 'A Dream' also has an unsigned foreword [by T. B. Mosher], pp. 43–5, in which he explicitly accepts Mackail's testimony as to Morris's contributions to *The Oxford and Cambridge Magazine* and abandons the Forman account he had previously used as his guide to the Morris texts.
Pagination: [8] [1–4] 5–76 [77–8] [=86].
Contents: pp. [1–2], unsigned preface; p. 5, limitation statement: Thirty-five copies of this book | printed on Japan vellum, of | which thirty only are for sale. | This is No. [number added in longhand]; pp. 6–22, 'The Unknown Church'; pp. 25–39, 'Lindenborg Pool'; pp. 43–5, unsigned preface; pp. 47–77, 'A Dream'.
Technical Notes: for details common to the series—paper, leaf size, printing, type area, lines-to-page, and binding—see this field in A-83.02.
Publication: 1902; *print run*: 35 copies (30 for sale) on japan vellum; *price*: $4.00 (see Bishop, p. 59).
Register of Copies Examined: Bsp (base copy).

C-16.03: The Story of the Unknown Church and Other Tales (Broc.)

[hanging indent, title and last line in red] THE STORY OF THE UNKNOWN | CHURCH AND OTHER TALES BY | WILLIAM MORRIS | [Chiswick Press Aldine mark, Bishop No. 2] | [last 3 lines aligned left] PORTLAND MAINE | THOMAS B. MOSHER | MDCCCCII
Edition: [1st impression, 2nd separate edn.] All three of the prose tales included—'Unknown Church', 'Lindenborg Pool', and 'A Dream'—were 1st pbd. in *The Oxford and Cambridge Magazine*, respectively in Jan., Sept., and Mar. 1856 (see D-1, 12, and 4).
Series: The Brocade Series—34 [minor series:] Old English Romances—Morris # 4. [For further series detail, see this field in A-70.03].
Pagination: [i–vi] vii–xi [xii–xiv] 15–96 [97–8] [=98].
Contents: 'The Story of the Unknown Church', 'Lindenborg Pool', and 'A Dream'.

Technical Notes: see this field in A-70.03.
Publication: 1902 [issued July] (Hatch, item 219); *print run*: 425 copies; *price*: 75 cents.
Later impression of this selection: Mosher:
1. 1906 [issued July] (Hatch, item 379): Second Edition, 'Brocade Series—34'; *print run*: 425 copies; *price*: 75 cents.
Register of Copies Examined: Bsp (base copy).

C-16.04: The Story of the Unknown Church and Lindenborg Pool (Avon)

[wrapper-title with 3-part (one above the other) thick-rule compartment; above the compartment, left] No. 8 [right] Vol. II. | [for title detail common to the series, see this field in A-101.02] | [below compartment] THE STORY OF THE UNKNOWN CHURCH & LINDENBORG POOL by WILLIAM MORRIS

Edition: [1st impression, 3rd edn. this selection] Both of these tales were 1st pbd. in *The Oxford and Cambridge Magazine*, the 1st in Jan. and the 2nd in Sept. 1856 (see D-1 and 12).
Series: The Avon Booklet, 2/8 (Feb. 1904).
Place, Publisher, and *Printer*: see the full title detail in A-101.02.
Pagination: [i–viii] [1–4] 5–38 [39–40] [=48].
Contents: pp. 1–2, unsigned foreword to Morris's tales [by J. Thomson], headed: [in swash caps, flush left] THE | AVON | BOOKLET | [foreword completed]; pp. 5–21, THE STORY OF THE UNKNOWN | CHURCH. | [text completed]; pp. 23–38, headed: LINDENBORG POOL | [text completed with footnote reference to Morris's source, Thorpe's *Northern Mythology*]; p. 39, text ends with tailpiece design.
Technical Notes: see this field in A-101.02.
Publication: 1 Feb. 1904 (masthead date); *print run* and *price*: see this field in A-101.02.
Register of Copies Examined: BL (base copy: 012208.f.34/5.); ABCL.

C-16.05: The Story of the Unknown Church [+ Lindenborg Pool] (Finch)

[within a full leaf-and-vine border, lines 1–4 and 8 in red] THE STORY | OF THE | UNKNOWN CHURCH | By | WILLIAM MORRIS | London | JAMES FINCH & CO. LTD. | 33 PATERNOSTER ROW | 1905

Edition: [1st impression, 4th edn.] Though not indicated on the title page, this tale is bound in with 'Lindenborg Pool'. Both stories were 1st pbd. in *The Oxford and Cambridge Magazine,* Jan. and Sept. 1856 (see D-1 and D-12).

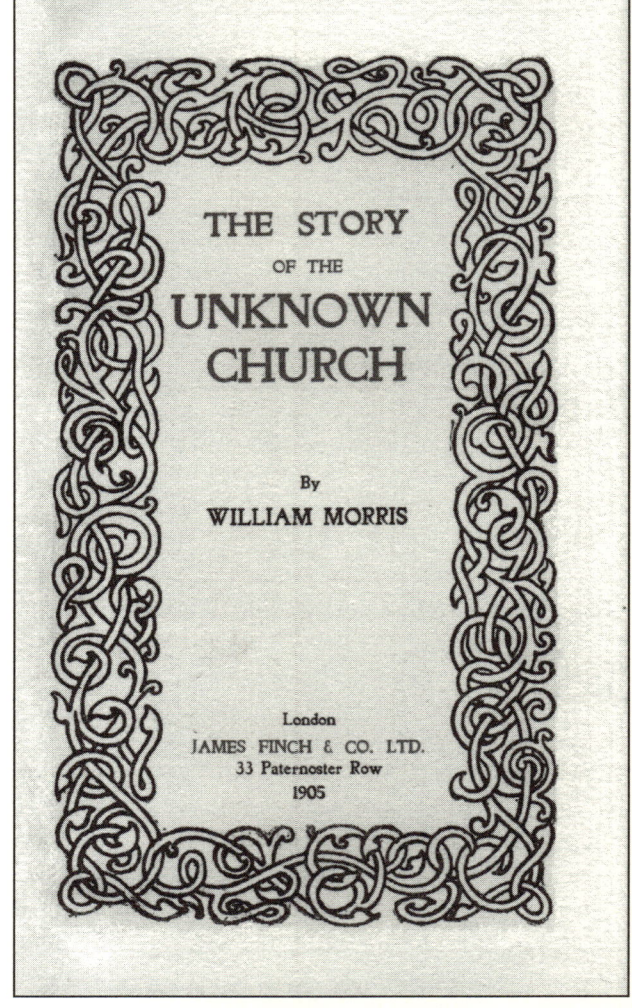

Figure 91. C-16.05: *Story of the Unknown Church* (Finch edn.) title page

Series: one of 4 Finch productions; for series detail see this field in A-95.02
Pagination: 1–47 [48] [=48].
Contents: pp. 1–25, 'The Story of the Unknown Church'; pp. 26–47, 'Lindenborg Pool'.
Technical Notes: for detail common to this Finch series, see this field in A-95.02; detail specific to this issue: *binding*: *letterpress*: *front*: *The Story of the Unknown Church,* otherwise plain and unblocked; *spine*: gilt title upwards.
Publication: 1905; *print run* and *price*: unknown.
Register of Copies Examined: LeM (base copy).

C-17: Hopes and Fears for Art [and] Signs of Change (Golden 4°)

[combined vol., with 2 title pages, both aligned left, 1st:]

HOPES AND FEARS FOR ART. FIVE LECTURES DELIVERED | IN BIRMINGHAM, LONDON & NOTTINGHAM, BY WILLIAM | MORRIS.
[2nd title page] SIGNS OF CHANGE. SEVEN LECTURES DELIVERED | ON VARIOUS OCCASIONS BY WILLIAM MORRIS.

Edition: 'Golden type quarto edition' [1st impression, 1st edn. of this combined title] But each of these constituent titles also have their own publishing histories, see A-21.01 and 46.01. Though bound in the same binding, each title has its own title page, colophon, pagination, etc.

Collaborators, Editors, and Illustrators: [edited by S. C. Cockerell and R. Proctor].

Series: 'The Golden type quarto edition' (not numbered), the 7th of eight quarto vols. printed as part of the Morris Trustees' project to complete the printing of Morris's books in his own type. For further detail on this series, see this field and *Notes* for *The House of the Wolfings*, A-47.04.

Colophon (p. 106, 1st title): Here ends Hopes and Fears for Art, by William Morris. First printed | in 1882, and now reprinted at the Chiswick Press, with the Golden type de- | signed by William Morris for the Kelmscott Press, and finished on the | seventh day of April, 1902. Published by Longmans, Green and Co. of | London, New York and Bombay.

Colophon (p. 100, 2nd title): Here ends Signs of Change, by William Morris. First printed in 1888, | and now reprinted at the Chiswick Press with the Golden type designed | by William Morris for the Kelmscott Press, and finished on the first day of May, 1902. Published by Longmans, Green and Co. of London, New | York and Bombay.

Pagination: (1st title) [i–ii] iii [iv] 1–106 [107–8] [=112]. (2nd title) [2] [i–ii] iii–v [vi] 1–100 [=106].

Contents: (1st title) this vol. has no general title page, having instead 2, one for each of the 2 titles (see above): 1st title: pp. 1–18, headed: LECTURE I. THE LESSER ARTS; pp. 19–34, LECTURE II. THE ART OF THE PEOPLE; pp. 35–55, LECTURE III. THE BEAUTY OF LIFE; pp. 56–82, LECTURE IV. MAKING THE BEST OF IT; pp. 83–105, LECTURE V. THE PROSPECTS OF ARCHITECTURE IN CIVILIZATION; p. 106, text ends with 1st colophon, in single column, see above.

Contents: (2nd title) p. [i], second title page, see above; p. [ii], blank; pp. iii–iv, headed: [flush left] PREFACE. | [text completed]; pp. 1–18, LECTURE I. HOW WE LIVE AND HOW WE MIGHT LIVE; pp. 19–27, LECTURE II. WHIGS, DEMOCRATS, AND SOCIALISTS; pp. 28–41, LECTURE III. FEUDAL ENGLAND; pp. 42–57, LECTURE IV. THE HOPES OF CIVILIZATION; pp. 58–69, LECTURE V. THE AIMS OF ART; pp. 70–85, LECTURE VI. USEFUL WORK VERSUS USELESS TOIL; pp. 86–99, LECTURE VII. THE DAWN OF A NEW EPOCH; p. 100, text ends with 2nd colophon, in single column, see above.

Technical Notes: for details common to the series—paper, leaf size, type area, lines-to-page, printing, type face, pagination, end-papers, and binding—see this field in A-47.04. Only details specific to this vol. are given here: *printing*: *pagination*: 2 sequences of page numbers, one for each title, both having lc roman for prelims; *shoulder notes*: start at top margin, all versos, either: Hopes and | Fears for Art [or] Signs of | Change; all rectos, the relevant lecture title; *spine*: printed paper label: WILLIAM | MORRIS | HOPES | AND | FEARS | FOR | ART | SIGNS | OF | CHANGE

Publication: *Hopes and Fears*, 7 Apr. 1902; *Signs of Change*, 1 May 1902 (both colophon dates) [the combined vol. was issued June 1902] (320 slips, to be enclosed in the copies, were printed on 14 June 1902, see Longmans Arch.); *print run*: 315 copies, 299 for sale (60 exported to the US); *price*: 2*gns*. per vol., but sold only as sets at 16*gns*.

Register of Copies Examined: LeM (base copy); NN; CSmH; VU.

C-18.01: Architecture, Industry, and Wealth (Golden 4°)

[aligned left] ARCHITECTURE, INDUSTRY, AND WEALTH: | COLLECTED PAPERS BY WILLIAM MORRIS.

Edition: [1st impression, 1st edn. of this collection] A collection of fugitive lectures and essays [edited by Cockerell and Proctor]. After a failed attempt to have G. B. Shaw edit a vol. of Socialist lectures and essays and W. R. Lethaby another on art and industry, both from the extant prtd. and MS papers, the executors decided to commission Cockerell and Proctor to prepare a single vol. of those texts that would merit republication., that being the recommendation of those first consulted.

All the texts included were set from previously prtd. versions (see *Notes*, below): 'The History of Pattern Designing' and 'The Lesser Arts of Life', lectures written for the SPAB and pbd. by the Society in 1882 in *Lectures on Art Delivered in Support of the Society for the Protection of Ancient Buildings* (see B-3); 'Art, Wealth, and Riches', a lecture to the Joint Conversazione of Manchester Societies and pbd. by them in 1883 in their journal *The Manchester Quarterly* and as an offprint (see A-22.01); *Art and*

Socialism, a lecture to the Leicester Secular Society, was pbd. by them as a pamphlet in 1884 (see A-25.01); *Textile Fabrics*, a lecture delivered at the International Health Exhibition and pbd. both as a separate pamphlet (1884, see A-27.01) and in the proceedings of the Conference (see D-111); 'Art under Plutocracy', a lecture delivered at University College, Oxford, and pbd. in Feb. and Mar. 1884 in *To-Day*, the Socialist monthly (see D-90); 'The Revival of Architecture', an essay written for *The Fortnightly Review* (1888, see D-372); 'The Revival of Handicraft', a 2nd essay for *The Fortnightly Review* (1888, see D-414); 'Art and Industry in the Fourteenth Century', an essay for *Time: a Monthly Magazine*, pbd. by Swan Sonnenschein (Jan. 1890, misdated 'Nov.' in *CW* and in both edns. of this collection, see D-491); 'The Influence of Building Materials upon Architecture', a lecture delivered to The Art Workers' Guild and pbd. in *The Century Guild Hobby Horse* (1892, see D-536); and *On the External Coverings of Roofs*, a leaflet written for and pbd. by the SPAB (1887? see A-44.01).

Collaborators, Editors, and Illustrators: [ed. S. C. Cockerell and Robert Proctor].

Series: 'Golden type quarto edition' No. 8 in a series of 8 quarto vols., unnumbered, pbd. as part of an effort to complete the printing in Morris's own Golden type of any Morris books not already produced by the KP. The title of this collection was invented by the editors (for further series detail, see this field in A-47.04).

Colophon: Here ends Architecture, Industry, & Wealth, Collected Papers by Wil- | liam Morris. Now first gathered together & printed at the Chiswick Press | with the Golden type designed by William Morris for the Kelmscott | Press, and finished on the 23rd day of June, 1902. Published by Longmans, | Green and Co. of London, New York and Bombay.

Pagination: [i–ii] iii [iv] 1–163 [164] [=168].

Contents: pp. 1–21, I. The History Of Pattern Designing.; pp. 22–47, II. The Lesser Arts Of Life.; pp. 48–62, III. Art, Wealth, And Riches.; pp. 63–79, IV. Art And Socialism: The Aims and Ideals of The English Socialists of To-Day.; pp. 80–98, V. Textile Fabrics.; pp. 99–119, VI. Art Under Plutocracy.; pp. 120–9, VII. The Revival of Architecture.; pp. 130–7, VIII. The Revival of Handicraft.; pp. 138–49, IX. Art and Industry in the Fourteenth Century.; pp. 150–60, X. The Influence of Building Materials upon Architecture.; pp. 161–3, XI. On the External Coverings of Roofs.; p. 163, text ends with colophon, see above.

Technical Notes: paper, printing, type, position of shoulder notes, page numbers, and binding are all common to the series and are described in this field in A-47.04, the 1st vol. pbd. of the series. Included here are only those details that belong to this particular edn. of this title: *printing*: in black and red, red for all chapter titles, for a footnote (p. 95), and 2 passages (p. 75); *shoulder notes*: all versos: vol. title; all rectos: essay or lecture title; *spine*: a printed paper label: WILLIAM | MORRIS | ARCHI- | TECTURE | INDUSTRY | AND | WEALTH

Publication: 23 June 1902 [colophon date, issued July 1902] (Longmans *Notes on Books*, 9/191 (29 Nov. 1902), 421); *print run*: 315 copies (including 60 exported to the US); *price*: 16gns. the set; rptd. (in facsimile?): New York: Garland Publishing Co., 1978.

Register of Copies Examined: (complete sets) LeM (base copy); SSL (S704); SPar; VMoU; BL.

Notes: in a letter to May Morris of 25 Mar. 1912, S. C. Cockerell tells her that he has looked at the lectures pbd. in this book and in the 5 separate vols. in Golden type, and they were all set from previously printed copies, with nothing set from MS (Cockerell Papers, BL (Add.) MS 52740).

C-18.02: Architecture, Industry, and Wealth (trade edn.)

ARCHITECTURE IN- | DUSTRY & WEALTH | COLLECTED PAPERS | BY WILLIAM MORRIS | LONGMANS, GREEN, AND CO. | 39 PATERNOSTER ROW, LONDON | NEW YORK AND BOMBAY | 1902

Edition: New Edition 'Trade edn.' [1st impression, 2nd edn.] For the 1st pbns. of the contents titles, see this field in the previous entry.

Collaborators, Editors, and Illustrators: [ed. S. C. Cockerell and Robert Proctor].

Pagination: [i–vi] vii–viii 1–268 [269–72] [=280].

Contents: p. [I], blank; p. [ii], ads; p. [iii], half title; p. [iv], blank; p. [v], title page; p. [vi], bibliographical note; pp. vii–viii, headed: CONTENTS | [list completed]; pp. 1–36, headed: Architecture, Industry & Wealth | I | THE HISTORY OF PATTERN-DESIGNING | A LECTURE DELIVERED IN SUPPORT OF THE SOCIETY FOR | THE PROTECTION OF ANCIENT BUILDINGS | [text completed]; pp. 37–79: THE LESSER ARTS OF LIFE; pp. 80–104: ART, WEALTH, AND RICHES; pp. 105–32: ART AND SOCIALISM; pp. 133–63: TEXTILE FABRICS; pp. 164–97: ART UNDER PLUTOCRACY; pp. 198–213: THE REVIVAL OF ARCHITECTURE; pp. 214–27: THE REVIVAL OF HANDICRAFT; pp. 228–46: ART AND INDUSTRY IN THE FOURTEENTH CENTURY; pp. 247–64: THE INFLUENCE OF

BUILDING MATERIALS UPON ARCHITECTURE; pp. 265–9: ON THE EXTERNAL COVERINGS OF ROOFS; p. [269], text ends with printer's imprint: Printed by BALLANTYNE, HANSON & CO. | Edinburgh & London
Technical Notes: *paper*: machine-made 'Antique Wove' (Longmans Arch.), no watermark; *leaf size*: untrimmed, avg. 205 x 137 mm.; *running titles*: all rectos and versos, short titles of the individual pieces, in Pica caps; *pagination*: arabic numbers centred on the direction line; *endpapers*: 1 free end and paste-down, front and back, both plain white and blank; *binding*: plain unblocked dark red cloth-covered boards; *spine label*: [thin rule] | ARCHITECTURE | INDUSTRY | AND | WEALTH | [thin rule] | WILLIAM MORRIS | [thin rule] | *Six Shillings Net*
Publication: Nov. 1902 [issued 4 Nov.] (Longmans *Notes on Books*, 9/191 (29 Nov. 1902), 421); but Cockerell's diary says 3 Nov. (see Cockerell Papers, BL (Add.) MS 52639); *print run*: 1,500 copies; *price*: 6s. net.
Register of Copies Examined: LeM (base copy); BGR.
Notes: C. J. Longman to Cockerell, 18 July 1902 (W. H. Smith Bequest): Longmans agrees on a royalty of 20% on all copies of this book sold either in Britain or the US. He adds a note that 6s. 6d. should be a good price both as to income (covering costs) and popularity (encouraging sales). The price was later set at 6s.

C-19: Five Arthurian Poems (Elston Press)

FIVE ARTHURIAN POEMS BY WILLIAM MORRIS: THE DEFENCE OF GUENEVERE. KING ARTHUR'S TOMB. SIR GALAHAD, A CHRISTMAS MYSTERY. THE CHAPEL IN LYONESS. A GOOD KNIGHT IN PRISON.
Edition: [1st impression, 1st edn. of this collection] All the poems were 1st pbd. in *The Defence of Guenevere and Other Poems* (see A-2.01).
Colophon: HERE ENDETH THIS BOOK OF FIVE ARTHURIAN POEMS BY WILLIAM MORRIS. ONE HUNDRED AND SEVENTY-EIGHT COPIES HAVE BEEN PRINTED, WITH INITIALS FROM DESIGNS BY H. M. O'KANE. PRINTED AND SOLD BY CLARKE CONWELL, AT THE ELSTON PRESS, NEW ROCHELLE, NEW YORK. FINISHED THIS ELEVENTH DAY OF SEPTEMBER, MDCCCCII.
Contents: pp. 1–11, 'The Defence of Guenevere'; pp. 13–27, 'King Arthur's Tomb'; pp. 29–36, 'Sir Galahad'; pp. 37–40, 'The Chapel in Lyoness'; pp. 41–5, 'A Good Knight in Prison'.
Technical Notes: *paper*: *leaf size*: 237 x 158 mm.; *printing*: colophon and 5 initials by O'Kane, in red; *binding*: plain unblocked black cloth gilt-stamped down the spine: FIVE ARTHURIAN POEMS BY WILLIAM MORRIS
Publication: 11 Sept. 1902 (colophon date); *print run*: 178 copies; *price*: $5.00 (Ransom, 260, other details from Walsdorf, item 95).
Register of Copies Examined: J-F V (base copy); TxU; MU; NjP.

C-20: The Hollow Land and Other Contributions ... (Golden 8°)

THE HOLLOW LAND AND OTHER | CONTRIBUTIONS TO THE OXFORD | AND CAMBRIDGE MAGAZINE BY | WILLIAM MORRIS
Edition: [1st impression, 1st edn. this collection] On the question of Morris's authorship of contributions to the Oxford and Cambridge Magazine, see the *Notes* to A-1.01. For a more detailed treatment, see the Introduction to the reprint of this title (Bristol: Thoemmes Press, 1996), v–xxx.
Collaborators, Editors, and Illustrators: [ed. S. C. Cockerell and Robert Proctor].
Series: This is the last vol. of 14, comprising 17 Morris titles, published as part of a project to print in the Golden type any Morris works not already published by the KP. The project involved the 5-vol. 8° set of lectures, the 8-vol. 4° set of miscellaneous titles, and this book, which is bound in the same fashion as the other 13 and sized to range with the set of five 8° lecture vols.
Colophon: These first writings of William Morris were | printed in The Oxford and Cambridge Magazine | in 1856, when the author was twenty-two years | old, and are now reprinted at the Chiswick Press | with the Golden type designed by William Morris | for the Kelmscott Press, and finished on the tenth | day of July, 1903. Published by Longmans, Green | & Co., 39, Paternoster Row, London.
Pagination: [4] [i–ii] iii [iv] 1–332 [333–6] [=344].
Contents: p. [i], title page; p. [ii], blank; p. iii, headed: [flush left] CONTENTS | [as a list, 12 titles headed in red:] PROSE [and 5 titles headed in red:] VERSE; p. [iv], blank; pp. 1–15, headed: [flush left, in red] THE STORY OF THE UNKNOWN | CHURCH. | [text completed]; pp. 16–39: A DREAM; pp. 40–112: GERTHA'S LOVERS; pp. 113–40: SVEND AND HIS BRETHREN; pp. 141–53: LINDENBORG POOL; pp. 154–208: THE HOLLOW LAND; pp. 209–34: GOLDEN WINGS; pp. 235–58: FRANK'S SEALED LETTER; pp. 259–88: 'MEN AND WOMEN.' BY ROBERT BROWNING; pp.

289–316: THE CHURCHES OF NORTH FRANCE. SHADOWS OF AMIENS; pp. 317–20: DEATH THE AVENGER & DEATH THE FRIEND; pp. 321–4: WINTER WEATHER; pp. 325–6: RIDING TOGETHER; p. 327: HANDS; pp. 328–31: THE CHAPEL IN LYONESS; p. 332: PRAY BUT ONE PRAYER FOR US; p. [333], colophon, see above.

Technical Notes: *paper*: Batchelor's Flower paper No. 2; *watermark*: Primrose watermark centred on the 1st 2 leaves of each gathering, inverted on the recto; *leaf size*: deckled edges, lightly trimmed, avg. 207 x 145 mm.; *lines-to-page*: set solid, 30 lines; *type face*: Golden type; *printing*: red and black: red for all titles, for 'PROSE' and 'VERSE' in the Contents, for epigraphs, for speakers' names in 'A Chapel in Lyoness', and for shoulder titles of the relevant items, all rectos and versos; *end-papers*: 3 free ends and a paste-down, plain white and blank, front and back; *binding*: quarter blue holland with blue paper-covered boards and printed *spine label*: WILLIAM | MORRIS | THE | HOLLOW | LAND

Publication: 10 July 1903 [colophon date, issued 12 Aug.] (Longmans *Notes on Books*, 10/194 (31 Aug. 1903), 26); *print run*: 316 copies; *price*: 25s. net. This vol. was rptd. in slightly reduced facsimile by Thoemmes Press, Bristol, Mar. 1996.

Register of Copies Examined: LeM (base copy); CSt (Z239.2/C54M87h Gunst); VU (L).

Notes: Cockerell to Mrs Morris, 27 Jan. 1903: tells Mrs Morris that while the project to collect Morris's contributions was being printed, George Bell proposed to reprint the entire text of *The Oxford and Cambridge Magazine*. Cockerell recommended Cormell Price as the best editor available for that job (see Cockerell Papers, BL (Add.) MS 52738). No rpt. appeared until the AMS Press Inc., NY, facsimile reprint of 1972.

Letter from S. C. Cockerell to C. J. Longman, 24 June 1903: here Cockerell summarizes *The Hollow Land* project, now complete, saying that 315 copies had been prtd. (actually 316: the Chiswick Press seems always to have printed one extra copy for their own archive) of a book containing 331 pp. (*sic*, actually 334 counting the colophon leaf); of the 315 copies, 300 copies were for sale. The Trustees proposed a price of 25s. net, or sale of the 300 copies to Longmans at 17s. 6d. per copy with Longman setting his own price. Longman replied two days later, accepting the commission offer. As the Longmans Accts. show, all copies were sold (except 23 given away) by 19 Dec., with Longmans receiving £25. 2s. 1d. and the Trustees £261. 9s. 2d. from which they paid the Chiswick Press £134. 10s. 10d. for the printing and binding (correspondence in the Smith Arch.). So, Longmans here was acting as the agent of the Morris Estate.

On the controversy over whether Morris or someone else contributed three pieces to the *Magazine* — 'Ruskin and the Quarterly,' 'The Two Partings,' and 'A Night in a Cathedral — see *Notes* in A-1.01 or the Introduction to the Thoemmes Press edn. of this title (1996).

C-21: Golden Wings: A Prose Romance and a Poem (Harrap)

[3-part thick-rule compartment, divided twice horizontally, top compartment] GOLDEN WINGS | *A Prose Romance | and a Poem* | [middle compartment, in red, heraldic sign] | [in red] *William Morris* | [bottom compartment, in black] George G. Harrap & Co. | London: 15 York Street, Covent Garden

Edition: [1st impression, 1st edn. of this selection] (though this English edn. is unseen, the American issue, noted below, which Coupe (p. 25) says is identical, except for a different series and publisher's imprint, has been examined. The English could have been 1st pbd. since the Morris material used here became public domain in England in 1903. The detail referring to the English 1st edn. is taken from Coupe, pp. 25–6).

Series: The King's Treasury of Literary Masterpieces.

Pagination: pp. [1–8] 1–66 [= 74].

Contents: p. [1] series title: The King's Treasury of Literary Masterpieces; p. [2] blank; p. [3] inserted frontispiece leaf recto blank; p. [4], frontis. within a decorative oval border, an engraving of a court scene, signed A. D. Marcel; p. [5], title page; p. [6], blank; p. [7], half title: Golden Wings; p. [8], blank; pp. 1–50, text of 'Golden Wings' prose romance; pp. 51–66, text of 'Golden Wings' poem.

Technical Notes: *paper*: plain white machine-made; t.e.g.; *leaf size*: 142 x 99 mm.; *end-papers*: 1 free end and pastedown, plain white and blank, front and back; *binding*: (de luxe edn.) red morocco with front gilt-stamped thick-rule compartment divided horizontally into 3 by thin-rules, with title in the top, an Aldus press mark in the middle; and in the bottom: MORRIS; *spine*: gilt-stamped across: GOLDEN | WINGS— | WILLIAM | MORRIS

Publication: [1903] (this being the year that copyright on Morris's contributions to the *Oxford and Cambridge Magazine* entered the public domain); *print run* and *price*: unknown.

Register of Copies Examined: VSL (base copy: American issue: S. 823.89 | M83G); (Coupe describes the English edn. of this book, pp. 25-6).

Later issue of this edn.:
1904: (copyright date) H. M. Caldwell Co., New York and Boston:. *Series*: The Remarque Series, No. 33.; pp. [vi] 166 + [1–3 on 2 leaves of tipped in ads for the Remarque Editions of Literary Masterpieces series, of which this is no. 33]; *binding*: ordinary copies: light blue cloth with a picture of a tree in a mountain scene pasted on the front cover; deluxe copies: red morocco, otherwise as the English issue; *print run and price*: unknown.

C-22: Poems of William Morris (Crowell)

THE POEMS OF | WILLIAM MORRIS | SELECTED AND EDITED BY | PERCY ROBERT COLWELL | [printer's leaf ornament] | NEW YORK | THOMAS Y. CROWELL & COMPANY | PUBLISHERS
Edition: [1st impression, 1st edn. of this collection].
Series: The Astor Editions [and] Gladstone Edition (this copy).
Pagination: [i–vi] vii–xxxiv [1–2] 3–360 [=394].
Contents: p. [ii], inserted half-tone reproduction, on special coated photographic paper, of a photo portrait of Morris, facing engraved title; p. [iii], engraved title with full floral border in white on black; p. [v], title page (see above); p. [vi], copyright notice: COPYRIGHT, 1904 | BY THOMAS Y. CROWELL & CO.; pp. xi–xiv, Bibliography; pp. xv–xxxiv, Introduction: [text completed and signed, below right] PERCY ROBERT COLWELL | [left] LAWRENCEVILLE, N.J., Jan. 13, 1904; pp. 3–88: EARLY ROMANTIC POEMS | [16 poems of the *Defence of Guenevere* period]; pp. 89–102, THE LIFE AND DEATH OF JASON (Selection of [6] Songs); pp. 105–215, THE EARTHLY PARADISE ([11] Selections); pp. 219–85, SIGURD THE VOLSUNG ([3] Selections); pp. 289–347, [19] POEMS BY THE WAY. SOCIALISTIC, ROMANTIC, AND ICELANDIC.; pp. 349–58, NOTES; pp. 359–60, INDEX OF TITLES
Technical Notes: *binding*: dark red diagonally ribbed cloth (Tanselle 1, No. 102, cut on the bias) over boards: front: black double thin-rule border with printer's leaves between the rules at the corners and gilt central tree ornament in double oval thin rule compartment; back: plain and unblocked; spine: gilt-stamped: [thin rules, head and foot] WILLIAM | MORRIS'S | POEMS | [ornament] | [circular ornament with series title] GLADSTONE | EDITION | [at the foot]: T. Y. CROWELL & CO | NEW YORK·
Publication: 1904 (copyright date); *print run and price*: not known.
Register of Copies Examined: LeM (base copy), MU (Special Collection: PR 5074/A2 C6 1904).

Notes: this vol. has an engraved title with full leaf-and-vine border and title in red before the standard title page.

C-23: The World of Romance, Being Contributions . . . (Avon)

[drop-cap initial] T*HE* WORLD OF ROMANCE, *BEING* | *CONTRIBUTIONS TO THE* OXFORD | AND CAMBRIDGE MAGAZINE, 1856 | [swash type] *By* WILLIAM MORRIS | [plain type] L*ONDON: Published by* J. T*homson at* 10, | *CRAVEN GARDENS, WIMBLEDON,* S. W. | MCMVI
Edition: [1st impression, 1st edn. this collection] This vol. was intended to be the 1st of 2 uniform vols. The announcement, facing the title page of this vol. says: UNIFORM WITH THIS VOLUME | GERTHA'S LOVERS and OTHER STORIES | BY WILLIAM MORRIS | ¶ In the above volume together with "The World of | Romance," is contained the entire series of Morris's | contributions to the "Oxford and Cambridge Magazine." Since no evidence has been seen indicating that the 2nd vol. of the pair was ever pbd., this title has become a separate, not part of a complete edn. of Morris's contributions to the *O & C. Magazine*.
Series: The Avon Booklet Series.
Printer: Printed at THE AVON PRESS, *London*.
Pagination: pp. [8] 1–163 [164–8].
Contents: pp. 1–17: THE STORY OF THE UNKNOWN CHURCH; pp. 19–35: LINDENBORG POOL; pp. 37–64: A DREAM; pp. 65–96: GOLDEN WINGS; pp. 97–130: SVEND AND HIS BRETHREN; pp. 131–64: THE CHURCHES OF NORTH FRANCE: I SHADOWS OF AMIENS; p. [164], printer's imprint, see above'; pp. [165–8], blank.
Technical Notes: *paper*: cream-white machine-laid with dandy roll laid lines; *leaf size*: lightly trimmed, avg. 169 x 107 mm.; *pagination*: arabic numbers centred on the direction line; *running titles*: aligned to the inner margins, titles of the pieces printed below, shorter titles ('Lindenborg Pool', 'A Dream', and 'Golden Wings') repeated in full all rectos and versos, longer titles (the rest) divided between recto and verso; *end-papers*: a single paste-down and free end, plain white and blank, front and back; *binding*: plain unblocked dark red cloth front and back, with printed paper spine label: [red thick rule] | [black thin rule] | [swash letters] *The* WORLD | *of* | ROMANCE | [thin rule] | [plain type] Wm. Morris | [red thick rule].
Publication: 1906; *print run* and *price*: unknown.

Register of Copies Examined: LeM (base copy); SU (823 M 87 wor); NjP.

C-24: Early Romances (Everyman's Lib.)

[engraved spread title with a full floral border, with an epigraph from Chaucer on the verso and the title page on the recto] THE EARLY | ROMANCES | of WILLIAM | MORRIS [fleuron] | IN PROSE AND | VERSE [2 fleurons] | [ornamental design] | LONDON: PUBLISHED | by | | J•M•DENT & CO | AND | IN NEW YORK | BY E. P. DUTTON & CO

Edition: [1st impression, 1st edn. this collection].
Collaborators: General Editor: Ernest Rhys; this vol. edited and introduced by Alfred Noyes.
Series: Everyman's Library, Romance, No. 261.
Pagination: pp. [*i–xx*] [1–2] 3–303.
Contents: pp. [ix–xix], Introduction completed, signed, below right: ALFRED NOYES | [below left] 1907; pp. 3–138: headed: THE DEFENCE OF GUENEVERE | AND OTHER POEMS [complete]; pp. 141–302, headed: THE STORY OF THE UNKNOWN | CHURCH | AND OTHER PROSE ROMANCES [complete, from *The Oxford and Cambridge Magazine*]; p. 303, text completed with explicit: THE END | [imprint] Printed by BALLANTYNE, HANSON & Co. | Edinburgh & London.
Technical Notes: *paper*: plain white machine-moulded, top edge stained the colour of the binding; *leaf size*: trimmed, 172 x 106 mm.; *end-papers*: full opening of paste-down and facing free end covered with a single light green design including on the rectos the figure of Good Deeds and on the versos a speech of Good Deeds: EVERYMAN | I WILL GO WITH | THEE | & BE THY GVIDE | IN THY MOST | NEED | TO GO BY THY SIDE; opposite sides of free ends blank; *binding*: ribbed blue cloth-covered (Tanselle I, No. 102) boards with Dent's mark blind-stamped on the front; *spine*: gilt-stamped: [headpiece] | [fleuron] THE | EARLY [fleuron] | ROMANCES | [fleuron] OF | WILLIAM | MORRIS | [3 fleurons and tailpiece]
Publication: [1907] [21–8 Sept.] ('New Books This Week', *Pub. Circ.*, 87 (28 Sept. 1907), 339); *print run* and *price*: unknown.
Register of Copies Examined: SSL (base copy: 823/M877); LeM; VU (821.85 E.n/111005); SU (828 M87e).
Later impressions and new edn. of this book.: Dent:
1. 1910, 1913, 1920, 1925, 1930, and numerous times thereafter;
2. 1973 (copyright date): new edn. [2nd edn.] revised and introduced by Peter Faulkner (with several later rpts).

C-25: Jason [+ The Defence of Guenevere] (Collins)

[title page (and frontispiece on a 2-leaf insert following the half title and not included in the book's pagination) letterpress within an engraved portico as frame, with an interior scene as a vignette, all printed in sepia] THE LIFE AND DEATH | OF JASON | W. MORRIS | ILLUSTRATED BY P. B. HICKLING. | LONDON & GLASGOW | COLLINS' CLEAR-TYPE PRESS

Edition: [1st impression, 1st edn. this collection] Though not mentioned on the title page, this book also includes the complete text of *The Defence of Guenevere and Other Poems*, hence its inclusion here as a collection.
Series: Collins Illustrated Pocket Classics, No. 197.
Collaborators, Editors, and Illustrators: title-page vignette is signed by Malcolm Patterson; 4 black-and-white illustrations for 'Jason' (including the frontispiece) and 4 colour illustrations for the 2nd title (originally done for the Collins edn. of *The Defence of Guenevere*, see A-2.11), are all separate insertions and signed by P. B. Hickling.
Pagination: [4][1–5]; pp. 6–474 [=478] + 8 inserted illustrations and 4 pages of advertisements for Collins' Illustrated Pocket Classics.
Contents: p. [*1*] half title; p. [2], blank; p. [3], blank; p. [4], frontispiece of Hylas meeting the nymph, illustrating a passage from p. 68, quotation as a label: 'Harm not a queen, I pray thee.'; p. [*1*], title page; p. [2], blank; p.[3], Contents; p. [4], blank; p. [5], text begins; pp. 6–299, 'The Life and Death of Jason' completed; pp. 300–[470], 'The Defence of Guenevere and Other Poems' completed; pp. [471–4], Index of First Lines. 4 pp. of advertisements follow.
Technical Notes: *paper*: thin machine-made; t.e.g.; leaf size, trimmed: 152 x 110 mm.; *end papers*: 1 free end and pastedown, dark maroon on facing pages, front and back; *binding*: 2 versions, ordinary and deluxe: ordinary in red ribbed cloth (Tanselle I, No. 102), with a red silk signet (page marker); *spine*: gilt thin rules on top, below letterpress, and above and below the publisher, horizontal title, author, and publisher plus vertical Morris leaf pattern; the deluxe version is bound in maroon leather, embossed to imitate reptile skin, with the same gilt text and ornament on the spine as the cheaper version, but with 'William Morris' in copperplate on the front (see Coupe, 72).
Publication: 1912 [issued 17–24 May] ('Books of the Week', *Pub. Circ.*, 96 (25 May 1912), 704); *print run*: not known; *price*: 1s. net cloth, 2s. lthr.
Register of Copies Examined: SSL (base copy: 821 M8773); LeM (ordinary); (Coupe describes a de luxe copy, p. 72).

Collections, Selections, and Anthologies to 1915

C-26: *Gems from William Morris (Collins)

GEMS FROM WILLIAM MORRIS | [vignette of lilies and hearts] | LONDON & GLASGOW | COLLINS CLEAR-TYPE PRESS

Edition: [1st impression, 1st edn.] Since this book has not been seen, details provided here are taken from Coupe, pp. 47–8.
Collaborators, Editors, and Illustrators: illus. by P. B. Hickling, except title-page vignette by Malcolm Patterson (see Coupe, 48).
Pagination: pp. 1–95 [96].
Contents: p. [1], half title; p. [2], Collins monogram; p. [3], blank; p. [4], frontispiece: 'The Sailing of the Sword'; p. [5], title page with, below the title and above the publisher's imprint, a vignette by P. B. Hickling of Easter lilies with hearts above and a rose-vine border; p. [6], blank; pp. 7–95, text completed of 13 short poems all taken from *The Defence of Guenevere*, p. [96], monogram of WSC Co., Coupe suggests perhaps the initials are of the founder of Collins (Coupe, p. 48).
Technical Notes: *leaf size*: 101 x 74 mm.; *end papers*: one free end and pastedown, front and back, with a picture on the facing sides (done by Malcolm Patterson ?) of an English garden with an Edwardian lady in the front and an old gentleman, also Edwardian, in the back opening; *binding*: cut flush; stiff glossy white paper cover with title up the spine in blue, front full rose vine border as compartment, title within at the top, in the lower portion a vignette with a circular rose-vine border enclosing a picture of a city with mountains in the background, with a lyre between the vignette and the bottom border (see Coupe, 47–8).
Publication: n.d. (c. 1912) (see Coupe, p. 47).
Register of Copies Located: Coupe describes this book, pp. 47–8).

C-27: *Poems by William Morris (Collins)

[half title] Poems by William Morris [title page has the letterpress all within a double thin-rule border with roses between the lines]WILLIAM MORRIS | [vignette of a lady] | LONDON & GLASGOW | COLLINS CLEAR-TYPE PRESS

Edition: [1st impression, 1st edn. of this selection] (since this book has not been seen, detail given here is mainly from Coupe (pp. 45–6). Except for changes in the order of poems, 2 of the headnotes, and the omission of 2 poems—'Sir Peter Harpdon's End' and 'Rapunzel'—from the same publisher's *The Defence of Guenevere*, of which this book is a selection, the similarities suggest a possibility that the forms of the earlier book may have been used here, making this a partial reprint rather than a new edn. Coupe says (p. 46) that 'with the exceptions described above, the illustrations and type of Guenevere . . . and Poems are identical'. But Coupe doesn't raise the question of edn. or rpt., and without having copies of both at hand for comparison the point is moot.
Collaborators, Editors, and Illustrators: AAD (possibly Arthur A. Dixon's) initials are on the title vignette. Otherwise, the illustrations are by P. B. Hickling.
Pagination: pp. 1–127.
Contents: The text consists of 18 poems from *The Defence of Guenevere*. Hence it omits 12 poems from the full text of *The Defence of Guenevere* and alters the order of those included.
Technical Notes: *paper*: t.e.g.; *leaf size*: 149 x 95 mm.; *binding*: red or green suede with 'William Morris' gilt stamped on spine and front, where it is in an oval blind-stamped floral compartment; title page vignette: a lady sitting on a bench at work writing on a sheaf of papers that rest on her knee. The background is a tree, flowers, and seagulls, all enclosed in a double thin-line compartment with roses at intervals between the lines; *end papers*: illustrated with 2 different pictures of sheep, shepherd, and shepherdess: in front both at rest with him playing a pipe; on the back, they and the sheep wander homeward.
Publication: probably in 1912 or shortly thereafter, that year being included in the title-page vignette.
Register of Copies Located: Coupe (2 copies); Bodl.
Later impression [or edition?] of this edn.: Collins:
1. [1924]: Coupe describes a ('new') presentation copy an inscribed date, '1924', with slight differences in the end papers and binding, but with a radically different order of the poems, the result being a reduction by half in the number of pages. [Rather than a mere reprint, this would appear to be a new edition, but this distinction is not one that Coupe would ordinarily make.] Coupe says of this later copy, 'We cannot be sure it was not a later impression' (p. 45).

C-28: *Songs of Chivalry (3rd Collins' selection from Guenevere)

[title page: floral border on left, top, and right, issuing from pots below left and right, title in red] SONGS OF CHIVALRY | [blue] WILLIAM MORRIS | [black] LONDON & GLASGOW | COLLINS' CLEAR-TYPE PRESS

Edition: [1st impression, 1st edn.] (the details regarding this publication are taken mainly from Coupe, 46–7).
Collaborators, Editors, and Illustrators: floral borders signed PJB, probably Percy J. Billinghurst; 4 pictures by P. B. Hickling.
Pagination: pp. [1–40].
Contents: 5 poems from *The Defence of Guenevere*.
Technical Notes: *paper*: t.e.g., beige matte paper; *leaf size*: 149 x 104 mm.; *end papers*: lightly marbled in light brown; *binding*: stiff brown suede with title and author gilt stamped vertically on the spine and blind stamped on the top left of the front, within a floral border; *ornamentation*: head and tailpieces wherever space permits, the same as in the previous Collins issues of *Guenevere* and *Poems*.
Publication: For reasons not disclosed, Coupe says 'after 1912'.
Register of Copies Located: (Coupe describes this book, pp. 46-7).

C-29: Atalanta's Race and the Proud King (LCBEL)

ATALANTA'S RACE | AND | THE PROUD KING | (FROM "THE EARTHLY PARADISE") | BY | WILLIAM MORRIS | EDITED WITH AN INTRODUCTION AND NOTES | FOR THE USE OF SCHOOLS AND COLLEGES | *NEW IMPRESSION* | LONGMANS, GREEN, AND CO. | 39 PATERNOSTER ROW, LONDON | NEW YORK, BOMBAY, AND CALCUTTA | 1912 | All rights reserved

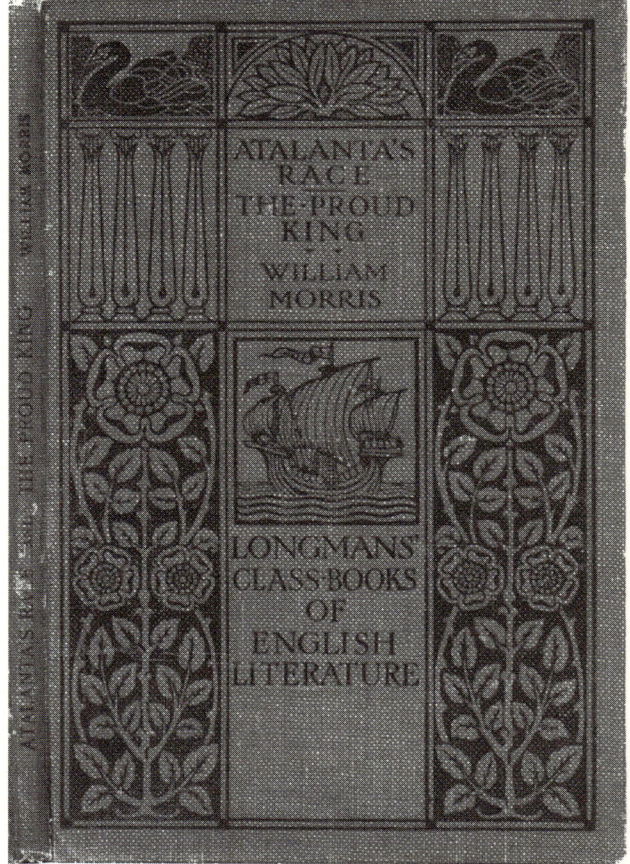

Figure 92. C-29: *Atalanta's Race and . . .* (LCBEL, Longmans Class Books . . .) binding

Edition: New Impression. [1st impression, 1st separate edn.] But this book, like its companion in this series, *The Man Born to be King*, is properly described as the 2nd impression of the 5th edn., 4th English, since it derives its setting from stereos of the Silver Library Edition of 1905. J. W. Mackail's unsigned 'Introduction' is the same as the 1905 Silver Library and 12-part edn. (see A-4.18), except for the 2nd half of the Introduction, pp. xiii–xix, obviously written specially for this title, being devoted to the 2 texts reprinted here.
Series: LCBEL. For further series detail, see this field in the record for the 1st Morris book in the series, *The Man Born to Be King* (A-110.01).
Printer: The Ballantyne Press—Ballantyne, Hanson & Co, Edinburgh & London.
Pagination: [i–iv] v–xix [xx] 1–59 [60].
Contents: p. [i], half title; p. [ii], blank; p. [iii], title page; p. [iv], blank; pp. v–xix, unsigned introduction [by J. W. Mackail]; pp. 1–27, headed: ATALANTA'S RACE [complete]; pp. 28–57, headed: THE PROUD KING [complete]; p. 59, headed: NOTES TO ATALANTA'S RACE; p. [60], headed: NOTES TO THE PROUD KING
Technical Notes: for details common to this series—paper, leaf size, pagination, end-papers, and binding—see this field in A-110.01; specific to this book: *headlines*: versos: THE EARTHLY PARADISE; rectos: relevant section title.
Publication: 1912 [issued 27 July] (Longmans Arch.); *print run*: 3,000 copies; *price*: 1s.
Register of Copies Examined: LeM (base copy); BL (.012273. e. 1/28.); BGR; MU (Spec. Coll. PP 5057/A2A8, 1888).
Notes: J. W. Mackail's role as editor is confirmed by the record in Longmans Arch. His payment of 5*gns*. is listed as the 1st charge on royalties, noted on 27 July 1912.
post-1915 reprints of this title: 'Class Books' series (from the Longmans Arch.):
1. 1920 [9 Aug.]; *print run*: 2,000 copies printed by The Ballantyne Press:—Spottiswoode, Ballantyne & Co.; *price*: 1s. 6d.;

Collections, Selections, and Anthologies to 1915

2. 1921 [17 Nov.]; *print run*: 5,000 copies printed by The Ballantyne Press:—Spottiswoode, Ballantyne & Co.; *price*: 1s. 6d.;

3. 1922 [11 Dec.]; *print run*: 3,000 copies by The Ballantyne Press:—Spottiswoode, Ballantyne & Co.; *price*: 1s. 6d.;

4. 1926: *NEW IMPRESSION*; *print run*: unknown; *price*: 1s. 6d.

C-30: Prose and Poetry (1856–1870) by Wm. Morris (OUP)

PROSE AND POETRY | (1856–1870) | BY | WILLIAM MORRIS | INCLUDING 'THE DEFENCE OF GUENEVERE', 'THE LIFE | AND DEATH OF JASON', PROSE ROMANCES FROM | THE OXFORD AND CAMBRIDGE MAGAZINE | AND OTHER PROSE AND POETRY | [OUP arms as pressmark] | HUMPHREY MILFORD | OXFORD UNIVERSITY PRESS | LONDON EDINBURGH GLASGOW NEW YORK | TORONTO MELBOURNE CAPE TOWN BOMBAY | 1913 [1920 this copy]

Edition: [1st impression, 1st edn. this collection] The text of *Jason* is that prepared by E. Maxwell for his edn. (see A-3.13), including his textual notes.

Series: This appears to be a forerunner of the Oxford Standard Authors Series, though no explicit statement of that appears in the copies seen.

Pagination and *Contents*: 8°: labelled below: WILLIAM MORRIS | *From a photograph by Emery Walker*; p. [iii], title page; p. iv, printer's imprint: OXFORD: HORACE HART | PRINTER TO THE UNIVERSITY; p. v, section heading: CONTENTS | [as a list subdivided under 5 headings, 'Prose Romances from The Oxford and Cambridge Magazine,' 'The Defence of Guenevere,' 'The Life and Death of Jason,' 'Miscellaneous Poems,' and 'Descriptive and Critical Articles'; pp. vi–vii, Contents completed; p. [viii], blank; p. [1], 2nd half title: PROSE ROMANCES | FROM | THE OXFORD AND CAMBRIDGE MAGAZINE | 1856; p. [2], blank; p. [3], 1st chapter head: THE STORY OF THE UNKNOWN | CHURCH | [text begins]; pp. 4–653, text completed; p. [654], blank; pp. [655]–6, headed: INDEX OF FIRST LINES OF POEMS

Technical Notes: *paper*: machine-made, no watermark; *leaf size*: trimmed, 185 x 120 mm.; *printing*: type area: 138 x 86 mm. inc. footnotes, exc. headlines; *lines-to-page*: set solid, 40 lines, excluding head and direction lines; *running titles*: all versos, short title of sub-section, e.g. Prose Romances; all rectos, short titles of the relevant romance; short poems and prose pieces have individual titles on both rectos and versos; *Jason* has the full title on all rectos and versos; *endpapers*: 1 free end and paste-down, plain white and blank, front and back; *binding*: red textured cloth (Tanselle 1, linen No. 304), with blind-stamped double thin rule borders around the front and back and across the head and foot of the spine; *spine*: gilt-stamped: GUENEVERE | JASON | ETC. | WILLIAM | MORRIS

Publication: 1913 [14–21 Nov.] ('Publications of the Week', *BSR*, 60/256 n.s. (21 Nov. 1913), 1636); *print run* and *price*: not known.

Register of Copies Consulted: NNC (base copy); BL (012273. ee. 6., with the BL accession stamp: '27 Sep 13'; LeM (1920 version); SU (828/M87X); NPar; SSL (S821/M8773); MU.

Later impression of this edn.: OUP:

1. 1920: rptd. with 2 additional sonnets first prtd. in *The Atlantic Monthly*: 'Rhyme Slayeth Shame' and 'May Grown A-Cold' (see D-24, 25).

C-31: Guenevere, Jason, and Other Poems (WC)

[2nd title page] THE | DEFENCE OF GUENEVERE |

Figure 93. C-30: *Prose and Poetry* (OUP) title page

THE LIFE AND DEATH OF JASON | AND OTHER POEMS | BY | WILLIAM MORRIS | [typographical design] | HUMPHREY MILFORD | OXFORD UNIVERSITY PRESS | LONDON, EDINBURGH, GLASGOW | NEW YORK, TORONTO, MELBOURNE & BOMBAY

Edition: [2nd OUP collection of Morris texts selected this time from the poetry only (see the previous record). *The Defence* and the *Other Poems* are here printed from the 1st edn. while the text of *Jason,* edited for OUP by E. Maxwell, is based on the 2nd, revised edn., issued in Dec. 1867, but dated '1868'. Alternate readings in footnotes of *Jason* are from the E. Maxwell text (see A-3.13).
Series: The [Oxford] World's Classics (WC), No. 183.
Printer: Horace Hart, Printer to the University.
Pagination and Contents: pp. [3]–150, headed: THE DEFENCE OF GUENEVERE (1858) [complete]; pp. 151–491, headed: THE LIFE AND DEATH OF JASON (1867) [complete]; pp. 493–523, headed: Miscellaneous Poems (1856–69) [9 poems]; p. [524], headed: INDEX OF TITLES | [list completed]; p. [525], headed: INDEX OF FIRST LINES OF | POEMS | [list completed].
Technical Notes: *paper*: plain white machine-made; *leaf size*: 100 x 93 mm.; *running titles*: all rectos and versos, the title of relevant text; *end-papers*: 1 free end and pastedown, front and back, facing paste-down and free end printed in light green of 2 hemispheres of a globe, with surrounding signs of the zodiac; *bindin*g: OUP advertised 7 different bindings for this series, the most common being dark green or blue cloth-covered boards, with blind-stamped borders, front and back, gilt-stamped on the spine: POEMS | BY | WILLIAM | MORRIS | [series of decorative figures] | [at foot] HUMPHREY | MILFORD
Publication: 1914 [issued 15–22 Nov. 1913] ('Books of the Week', *Pub. Circ.*, 99 (22 Nov. 1913), 625).
Register of Copies Examined: LeM (base copy); SSL (821 M8773): BL (012209. df. 104.)
Later impressions of this edn.: OUP:
Rptd. 1919, 1920, 1933 (pbn. history noted on the verso of the 2nd title page of each later issue).

C-32:* Six Poems Selected from the Early Writings (Bubb)

SIX POEMS SELECTED FROM THE EARLY WRITINGS OF WILLIAM MORRIS. IMPRINTED AT THE CLERK'S PRIVATE PRESS, 1915.
Edition: [1st impression, 1st edn., this collection].

Editors, Illustrators, and Collaborators: Charles Clinch Bubb, editor, publisher, and printer.
Colophon: Done into print by Charles Clinch Bubb, clerk in holy orders (*NUC*, cccxcvi. 156).
Technical Notes: *leaf size*: 129 x 104 mm.; *binding*: pink wrappers (information from Ransom, 231–3), and Walsdorf (234).
Publication: 20 Aug. 1915 (collation date); *print run*: 32 copies, all numbered; *price*: unknown.
Register of Copies Located: NN.
Notes: *NUC* quotes the limitation note: 'No. 30 of 32 copies printed' (NN copy); 38p. + press mark. printed in Jensen type, with rose Fabriano wrappers 'stiffened with Bristol board and backs squared, binding hand sewn' (Ransom, 231).

C-33: Pilgrims of Hope and Chants . . . (LPL)

THE PILGRIMS OF HOPE | AND | CHANTS FOR SOCIALISTS | BY | WILLIAM MORRIS | LONGMANS, GREEN [swash ampersand] & COMPANY | 39 PATERNOSTER ROW, LONDON | FOURTH AVENUE & 34TH STREET, NEW YORK | BOMBAY, CALCUTTA, AND MADRAS | 1915 | All rights reserved
Edition: 'Longmans Pocket Library edn' [1st impression, 1st combined edn.] Though both the main titles combined here were previously pbd. separately, this selected edn. is treated here as a new title, new set. *The Pilgrims of Hope* is the 1st impression of the 3rd edn., 2nd English, the 1st edn. being the Forman unauthorized (i.e. piratical) pamphlet (see E-9), the 2nd edn. being Mosher's edn. in the series Rpts. of Privately Printed Books—8 (see A-99.01). For the previous pbns. of *Chants for Socialists*, see A-23.01. The unsigned 'Foreword' [by May Morris, (p. v)] says: '"The Pilgrims of Hope" appeared in *The Commonweal* between March 1885 and July 1886, its title being decided on with the publication of the second part. Sections I, IV, and VIII were included in *Poems by the Way* after the Author had abandoned his intention of revising it as a whole. "To be concluded" stands at the bottom of the last instalment.'

For the early publishing history of *Chants for Socialists*, see this field in A-23.01. *A Death Song*, also included here, was written for the funeral of Alfred Linnell who died from injuries received at a demonstration in Trafalgar Square on 20 Nov. 1887. It first appeared as a pamphlet with a musical setting by Malcolm Lawson, to be sung at Linnell's funeral (see A-43.01). 'May Day' (1892) and 'May Day, 1894,' originally appeared in *Justice* (see D-539 and 562).
Series: LPL. For detail common to the series, see this field

in the record of the 1st book issued in the series, *The Life and Death of Jason*, A-3.09.
Pagination and Contents: p. v, headed: FOREWORD; pp. 3–57, text of 'Pilgrims of Hope'; pp. 61–80, texts of 'Chants for Socialists'; p. 81, text ends with the printer's imprint: PRINTED IN GREAT BRITAIN | BY BALLANTYNE, HANSON & CO. LTD. | EDINBURGH AND LONDON
Technical Notes: for details of paper (except leaf size), pagination, end-papers, and binding, see this field in A-3.09; details specific to this issue: *leaf size*: 157 x 113 mm., larger in width than any other in this series, to accommodate the longer lines of *The Pilgrims of Hope* without turning.
Publication: 1915 [issued 11 Sept.] (Longmans Arch.); *print run*: 2,000 copies; *price*: cloth 2s., lthr. 3s.
Register of Copies Examined: LeM (base copy); SU (821.85/ M877p); BL (012203. e. 17/28.)
Notes: the executors' decision to reprint the full text of *The Pilgrims of Hope*, 1st in 1915 in vol. 24 of *The Collected Works* and, later in the same year in this selection, after they had for years refused permission for others to do reprints, raises questions. The original ground for refusal was that Morris had himself made a final judgement against the poem as a whole when he selected only 3 parts for inclusion in *Poems by the Way*. The *BSR* suggests that the executors might have changed their view in anticipation of demand: 'Messrs Longmans, Green & Co. have arranged to issue in their Pocket Library an edn. of William Morris's poem 'Pilgrims of Hope' which attracted so much attention when it appeared recently in the 24th volume of The Collected Works of William Morris' ('Trade and Literary Gossip,' *BSR*, 63/338 (18 June 1915), 625). Besides, there were already 2 versions in print—Forman's forgery and Mosher's legitimate American edn. using Forman's as its copy-text—thus ensuring eventual passage of the text into the public domain and lending value to the issue of an authoritative, reliable text.

C-34: The Letters of William Morris (ed. Henderson)
THE LETTERS | OF WILLIAM MORRIS | TO HIS FAMILY AND FRIENDS | Edited with Introduction | and Notes by | PHILIP HENDERSON | [Longmans' mark, square-rigged ship with sea and the date of the Company's founding: 1724; all within an oval border] | LONGMANS, GREEN AND CO | LONDON • NEW YORK • TORONTO
Edition: [1st edn. of this collection] The two major collections of Morris's letters, this one and the Kelvin edn. (see C-38) are included here because, despite the fact that most of the letters were not written for pbn., Morris's letters to the press, as well as other public statements—many of them fugitive pbns.—are included in both. This volume contains as well as the personal letters 6 letters pbd. in *The Athenæum*, 7 in *The Daily Chronicle*, 7 in *The Daily News*, 1 in *The Manchester Examiner*, 4 in *The Pall Mall Gazette*, 1 in *The Spectator*, 1 in *The Standard*, and 8 in *The Times*, besides a rpt. of Morris's leaflet for the Eastern Question Association on *Unjust War*, inserted as an appendix.
Printer: RICHARD CLAY AND COMPANY, LTD. | BUNGAY, SUFFOLK
Pagination: [2] [i–iv] v [vi] vii–lxvii [lxviii 1–2] 3–406 [407–8] [=478].
Contents: (restricted to letters written for publication and 1 separately pbd. leaflet): letters to *The Athenæum*, pp. 85–6, 87–9, 127–8, 153–4, 371–3, 374–5; to *The Daily Chronicle*, pp. 355–7, 358, 363–7, 376–8, 379; to *The Daily News*, pp. 80–3, 153, 179, 242–3, 276–7, 309–10, 311–12; to *The Manchester Examiner*, pp. 165–6; to *The Pall Mall Gazette*, pp. 244–7, 261–2, 264–5, 317–191; to *The Spectator*, pp. 370–1; to *The Standard*, pp. 190–1; to *The Times*, pp. 90–3, and for a Morris leaflet (see A-14.01) *Unjust War*, pp. 388–9; all of the pbd. letters cited here are separately listed and annotated in Section D.
Technical Notes: *paper*: cream machine-made; *leaf size*: trimmed, 223 x 148 mm.; *type area*: 170 x 106 mm.; *endpapers*: 1 free end and pastedown, front and back, both plain white and blank; *binding*: plain unblocked dark red cloth-covered boards with gilt letterpress across the spine: THE LETTERS OF | WILLIAM | MORRIS | TO HIS FAMILY | AND FRIENDS | Edited by | PHILIP | HENDERSON | [at foot] LONGMANS; jacket: background pattern on a buff base from a Morris wallpaper, 'Rose and Pink', with letterpress: front: THE LETTERS OF | WILLIAM | MORRIS | TO HIS FAMILY & FRIENDS | EDITED WITH INTRODUCTION | AND NOTES BY | PHILIP HENDERSON; and a spine printed buff-on-black, across: THE LETTERS | OF | WILLIAM | MORRIS | TO HIS FAMILY | AND FRIENDS | + | EDITED BY | PHILIP HENDERSON | [at foot] LONGMANS
Publication: issued 1950; *print run*: unknown; *price*: 25s.
Register of Copies Examined: LeM (base copy); BL (10922. dd. 25.)

C-35: The Ideal Book (ed. Peterson)
[aligned left, first 4 lines in red] THE IDEAL BOOK [KP printer's leaf, No. 1] ESSAYS AND LEC- | TURES ON THE ARTS OF THE BOOK | BY WILLIAM MOR-

RIS [KP printer's leaf, No. 1] EDITED BY | WILLIAM S. PETERSON | [reproduction of a woodcut of an early printing press in operation] | [in black] UNIVERSITY OF CALIFORNIA PRESS | [KP printer's leaf No. 1] 1982
Edition: [1st edn. of this collection] A collection of Morris's fugitive pieces on books and printing, all previously pbd.: 'Some Thoughts . . .' was 1st pbd. as a separate edn. in 1934 (see A-129.01); 'Some Notes on . . . Illuminated Books' was 1st pbd. in *The Magazine of Art*, Jan. 1894 (see D-557); 'The Early Illustration of Printed Books', a lecture printed in summary form in *The British and Colonial Printer*, 9 Jan. 1896 (see D-587); 'The Woodcuts of Gothic Books' a paper delivered to the Applied Arts Section of the Society of Arts and pbd. in *The Journal of the Society of Arts*, June 1892 (see D-538); 'On the Artistic Qualities of the Woodcut Books of Ulm and Augsburg in the Fifteenth Century' was originally written as an article for the Bibliographical Society's journal *Bibliographica* where it was pbd. in the 4th number (1895, see D-585); 'Printing', a paper originally drafted and delivered as a lecture by Emery Walker at the 1st exhibition of The Arts and Crafts Exhibition Society, was almost entirely rewritten by Morris and signed by both himself and Walker when Morris prepared it for his edn., the 1st, of *Arts and Crafts Essays* in 1893 (see B-15); 'The Ideal Book', a lecture, was 1st pbd. in the *Transactions of the Bibliographical Society*, 1893 (see D-555); 'A Note by William Morris on His Aims in Founding the Kelmscott Press' was written in response to a query from Carl Edelheim of Philadelphia, who pbd. the reply as an article in Apr. 1896 in the journal *Modern Art* (Boston, see D-590).
Pagination: iii–xxxix [xl–xlii] 1–134 [=174].
Contents: (Morris texts): pp. 1–6: 'Some Thoughts on the Ornamented Manuscripts of the Middle Ages'; pp. 7–14: 'Some Notes on the Illuminated Manuscripts of the Middle Ages'; pp. 15–24: 'The Early Illustration of Printed Books'; pp. 25–44: 'The Woodcuts of Gothic Books'; pp. 45–58: 'On the Artistic Qualities of the Woodcut Books of Ulm and Augsburg in the Fifteenth Century'; pp. 59–66: 'Printing'; pp. 67–73: 'The Ideal Book'; pp. 74–8: 'A Note by William Morris on His Aims in Founding the Kelmscott Press'; Appendix A, pp. 79–88: (S. C. Cockerell's text) 'Short History and Description of the Kelmscott Press'.

Journalists' interviews with Morris on books and printing are headed: APPENDIX B: FOUR INTERVIEWS WITH WILLIAM MORRIS: pp. 89–95: 'The Poet as Printer' (from *The Pall Mall Gazette*); pp. 95–8: ' "Master Printer Morris" A Visit to the Kelmscott Press' (from *The Daily Chronicle*); pp. 98–106, 'Mr. William Morris at the Kelmscott Press' (from *The English Illustrated Magazine*); and pp., 106–17: 'The Kelmscott Press: An Illustrated Interview with Mr. William Morris' (from *The Bookseller*). For further details on these, see 'Appendix I: Morris's Interviews with the Press' in this vol.
Technical Notes: *paper*: plain white machine-made; *leaf size*: 271 x 185 mm.; *printing*: in red and black, titles and shoulder titles in red in Golden type; margin references to illus. in red in Bembo, text in black Bembo; *binding*: paperback, cut flush, light blue on outer sides, plain white and blank on insides; *letterpress*: *front*: lines 6–7 in red: WILLIAM MORRIS | [printer's leaf, KP, No. 1, in red] THE [printer's leaf, KP No. 1] | IDEAL | BOOK | [reduced reproduction of title page woodcut] | ESSAYS AND LECTURES ON | THE ARTS OF THE BOOK | EDITED AND INTRODUCED BY | WILLIAM S. PETERSON; *spine*: printed down: WILLIAM MORRIS [KP leaf ornament No. 1] THE IDEAL BOOK [across] CAL | 775
Publication: 1982 (copyright date); *print run*: unknown; *price*: $15.95.
Register of Copies Examined: LeM (base copy, the paperback, which lacks the half-title leaf of the cloth-bound version).

C-36: Political Writings, 1883–1890 (ed. Salmon)
POLITICAL | WRITINGS | CONTRIBUTIONS | TO *JUSTICE* AND | *COMMONWEAL* | 1883–1890 | *William Morris* | Edited and Introduced by | Nicholas Salmon | [press mark] | THOEMMES PRESS
Edition: [1st edn., this selection] A selection of Morris's political essays, and his 4 political dialogues, in chronological order as 1st pbd. in *Justice* and *Commonweal*, finishing with the complete text of *Socialism from the Root Up*, taken from the *Commonweal* version, the 1st pbd. text, before it was extensively revised, retitled, and published separately as *Socialism: Its Growth and Outcome*. An appendix supplies a chronological list of Morris's contributions to both papers, but omits his post-1890 contributions to *Justice*, of which there were 9, including 2 *Justice* accounts of lectures otherwise unpbd. (see D-532, 539, 561, 562, 563, 571, 588, 589, and 592).
Series: William Morris Library, First Series [as later named].
Place: Bristol.
Printer: Antony Rowe Ltd. Chippenham.
Pagination: [i–vii] viii–xlviii [xlix–l] 1–3] 4–668 [669–70] [= 720].
Contents: pp. vii–xlviii: INTRODUCTION; pp. 1–77:

CONTRIBUTIONS TO *JUSTICE*: 1884; pp. 81–494, divided by year: CONTRIBUTIONS TO *COMMONWEAL*: 1885–1890; pp. 497–622: *SOCIALISM FROM THE ROOT UP*; pp. 625–68: [appendix, a handlist] WILLIAM MORRIS'S JOURNALISTIC | CONTRIBUTIONS TO *JUSTICE* AND *COMMONWEAL*: 1884–1890; pp. [669–70], prospectus, headed: THE WILLIAM MORRIS SOCIETY | [prospectus completed].

Technical Notes: *paper*: plain white machine-made; *leaf size*: cut flush, 216 x 138 mm.; *binding*: hard back: dark blue cloth-covered boards, plain and unblocked, front and back; *spine*: [gilt-stamped, head, double rule, horizontal orientation] | POLITICAL WRITINGS | *Contributions to JUSTICE and* | *COMMONWEAL 1883–1890* || *William Morris* | [at foot, Thoemmes Press logo, repeated 3 times]; paperback: *wrapper*: p. [*1*], title page text duplicated within full KP border with series title at the foot: WILLIAM | MORRIS | LIBRARY; p. [*2*], ads; p. [*3*] notes on Morris, the editor, and the general editor; p. [*4*], ads; *spine*: title, author and Thoemmes logo, as above.

Publication: 1996; *print run*: unknown; *price*: paper: £16.75, cloth: £60.

Register of Copies Examined: LeM (base copy); BL.

C-37: Journalism: Contributions to *Commonweal* (ed. Salmon)

JOURNALISM | CONTRIBUTIONS TO | *COMMONWEAL* | 1885–1890 | **William Morris** | EDITED AND INTRODUCED BY | NICHOLAS SALMON | [press mark] | THOEMMES PRESS

Edition: [1st impression, 1st edn. this collection] A chronological selection of Morris's political writings as 1st pbd. in *Commonweal*, arranged year by year from 1885 through 1890.

Series: William Morris Library, Second Series [as later named].

Place: Bristol.

Printer: Antony Rowe Ltd, Chippenham.

Pagination: [i–vii] viii–xlv [xlvi 1–3] 4–674 = [720].

Contents: pp. vii–xxxiii: INTRODUCTION, signed, below right: Nick Salmon | Buckinghamshire, 196l; pp. [xxxv]–xlv, CHRONOLOGY: 1885–1890; pp. 1–674, arranged by year: CONTRIBUTIONS TO *COMMONWEAL*: 1885–1890.

Technical Notes: *paper*: plain white machine-made; *leaf size*: cut flush, 216 x 138 mm.; *binding*: paperback: *wrapper*: p. [*1*], duplicate of title within full border, with series below left; p.[*2*], ads.; p.[*3*], note on the editor and the general editor; p. [*4*] ads; hardback: plain, unblocked dark blue cloth, gilt stamped on the spine: [2 lines, printed down] JOURNALISM | Contributions to *Commonweal* 1885–1890 | [raised 3 points] *William Morris* | [across the foot, rule of repeated Thoemmes Press logos]

Publication: 1996; *print run*: unknown; *price*: £18.75.

Register of Copies Examined: LeM (base copy, paperback).

C-38: The Collected Letters of William Morris (4 parts in 5 vols.)

THE COLLECTED LETTERS OF | [in modern gothic] **William | Morris** | [printer's leaf in bold] | [plain type] VOLUME I | 1848–1880 [VOLUME II [a] | 1881–1884; VOLUME II [b] | 1885–1888; VOLUME III | 1889–1892; VOLUME IV | 1893–1896] | [printer's leaf] | PRINCETON UNIVERSITY PRESS

Edition: [1st edn. this collection] The *Collected Letters* is included here because, like The *Letters of William Morris to His Family and Friends*, it contains writings meant by the Author for pbn. The most obvious of these are Morris's letters to the press, but in the letters collections the category includes other fugitive pieces, included as appendices.

Place: Princeton, New Jersey, and Guildford, Surrey.

Colophons: Vol. I: THE COLLECTED LETTERS OF | WILLIAM MORRIS | [printer's leaf] | COMPOSED IN LINOTRON BEMBO AND | PRINTED ON WARREN'S 1854 BY | PRINCETON UNIVERSITY PRESS | BOUND IN HOLLISTON ROXITE BY | SHORT RUN BINDERY | ENDPAPER DESIGN AFTER THE BRUGES WALLPAPER | CREATED BY WILLIAM MORRIS IN 1887 | DESIGNED BY LAURY A. EGAN [p. *627*]

Vol. II [b]: as for Vol. I except: PRINTED ON WARREN'S OLDE STYLE BY | [. . .] | ENDPAPER DESIGN AFTER | THE MARIGOLD WALLPAPER | CREATED BY WILLIAM MORRIS | [. . .]

VOL. III: as for Vol. II except: COMPOSED IN BEMBO BY | PRINCETON UNIVERSITY PRESS | PRINTED IN THE UNITED STATES | OF AMERICA BY | PRINCETON ACADEMIC PRESS | [. . .] | ENDPAPER DESIGN AFTER | THE ROSE AND THE PINK | [. . .]

Vol. IV: as for Vol. III except: [. . .] BOUND IN I.C.G. ARRESTOX BY | [. . .] | ENDPAPER DESIGN AFTER | BIRD AND ANEMONE [. . .]

Pagination:
Vol. I: [2] [i–vi] vii–lxiv [1–2] 3–626 [627–8] [=694].
Vol. II [a]: [i–vi] vii–liii [liv 1–2] 3–365 [366] [=419].

Vol. II [b]: [i–vi] vii [viii–ix] 366–921 [922] [=566; total for [a+b=986].
Vol. III: [2] [i–vi] vii–lxv [lxvi 1–2] 3–537 [538] [=604].
Vol. IV: [2] [i–vi] vii–lvii [lviii 1–2] 3–465 [466] [= 514; total for the work = 3,217].

Contents: approx. 2,400 letters of which 1,500 were unpublished. Separately pbd. items are included as appendices, and the editorial notices from the prelims. Vol. II [a and b] are treated together because they are paginated continuously. All of the pbd. letters are separately listed and annotated in Section D. The separately pbd. Morris items included as appendices to the *Letters* volumes are entered and described in Section A. Only letters written for pbn. are cited in this digest of *Contents*.

Vol. I: editorial notice, p. [ii]: EDITED BY NORMAN KELVIN; letters to *The Architect*, p. 510; to *The Athenæum*, pp. 61, 351–2, 361–2, 513–14; to *The Daily News*, pp. 323, 527–9; to the Italian newspapers, pp. 444–5; to *The Times*, pp. 374–6.

Vol. II [a] and Vol. II [b]: editorial notice (both parts), p. [ii]: EDITED BY NORMAN KELVIN | ASSISTANT EDITOR: GALE SIGAL; letters to *The Athenæum*, pp. 86–7; to *The Daily News*, pp. 83, 117–9, 129–31, 158–9, 216–17, 382, 4546, 493–4, 522–3, 605–6, 700, 702–3; to *The Echo*, pp. 328–9; to *Justice*, p. 331; to *The Manchester Examiner*, pp. 173–4; to *The Manchester Guardian*, pp. 325–8; to *The Nineteenth Century*, p. 107; to *The Oxford Magazine*, p. 397; to *The Pall Mall Gazette*, pp. 55–6; 247; 514–17; 589–90; 600–1; 620–1; 708–12; 714–15; 719; to *The Scotsman*, p. 758; to *The Times*, pp. 107–8. The 1 separately pbd. Morris item in this volume—*The Manifesto of The Socialist League*, by Morris and Bax, pp. 849–58—is described in A-29.02.

Vol. III: editorial notice, p. [ii]: EDITED BY NORMAN KELVIN | ASSISTANT EDITOR: HOLLY HARRISON; letters to *The Commonweal*, pp. 44–6, 62, 85, 146; to *The Daily Chronicle*, p. 462; to *The Daily News*, pp. 25, 53; to *The Liverpool Daily Post*, p. 264; to *The Pall Mall Gazette*, pp. 100, 104, 242, 362; to *The Speaker*, p. 156; to *The Times*, pp. 194, 204, 262. The 2 separately pbd. Morris items rptd. in this volume—*Statement of Principles of the Hammersmith Socialist Society* (pp. 489–92 and *A Note by William Morris on His Aims in Founding The Kelmscott Press* (pp. 493–95) are described as separates in A-53.01 and A-88.01, respectively.

Vol. IV: editorial notice: as for Vol. III (above); letters to *The Athenæum*, pp. 301, 305, 320; to *The Daily Chronicle*, pp. 102, 134, 262, 268, 270, 273, 324, 339, 342, 343; to *The Journal of Derbyshire Archaeological and Natural History Society*, p. 27; to *Liberty*, p. 209; to *The Spectator*, p. 291; to *The Times*, pp. 281, 344. A Morris article rptd. in Vol. IV as Appendix A— 'The Present Outlook of Socialism in England'— as originally pbd. in the American magazine *The Forum,* is described in D-591.

Technical Notes: paper: plain white machine-made; *leaf size*: trimmed, 235 x 155 mm.; *type area*, set solid: 177 x 110 mm.; end papers: 1 free end and pastedown, front and back, facing sides with the wallpaper pattern used on the jacket (see the *Colophons*, above), reverse free end sides plain white and blank; *binding*: unblocked cloth-covered boards, the cloth being fine linen (Tanselle 304 linen), Vol. I in light tan, Vols. II and III in beige, and Vol. IV in light grey; letterpress only across the spine and all within 2 compartments composed of 2 rules, outer dark, inner gilt, printed in gilt on a ground of dark brown (Vol. I), dark green (Vol. II [a and b]), dark red (Vols. III and IV); main compartment, Vol. I: THE | COLLECTED | LETTERS OF | [modern gothic] WILLIAM | MORRIS | [printer's leaf] | [plain type] VOLUME I | 1848–1880 [VOLUME II [a] | 1881–1884; VOLUME II [b] | 1885–1888; VOLUME III | 1889–1892; VOLUME IV | 1893–1896 | [printer's leaf] | KELVIN; smaller compartment formed of 2 rules, one dark, one gilt, enclosing the appropriate dark ground on which is printed: PRINCETON; *dust jackets*: repeat the colours and pattern of the end papers (see the *Colophons*); the letterpress repeats the spines of the binding (but without the gilding) and the division into compartments but with white backgrounds; the fronts have a single three rule (2 dark with one light colour rule between them) border forming a compartment within which the words and spacing are as on the spine but larger, with a background colour that tones with the pattern colour, and with a full editorial notice: EDITED BY | NORMAN KELVIN

Publication: 1984–1996; *print run*: unknown; *price* (US currency): Vol. I: $61; Vol. II [a]: $45, [b] $49.50; Vol. III: $45; Vol. IV: $45.

Register of Copies Examined: LeM (base copy, 2nd copies of Vols. III and IV inscribed to 'Gene' (E. LeMire) by the editor, 'Norman' (Norman Kelvin); BL.

D

Morris in Periodicals

This list is limited to first publications, that is, to items that at the time of issue, from 1856 (*The Oxford and Cambridge Magazine*) to the present, were additions to the Morris canon. In a few cases, where no Morris text has been found for lectures or public speeches known to have been delivered, published accounts of shorthand versions are entered as the nearest approximation to a proper Morris text now known (and indicated as such in the entries).

'Periodicals' should here be understood to encompass anything published at more or less regular intervals, hence anything that might be called a serial, including annual reports of organizations such as the SPAB, or the *Catalogues* of the Arts and Crafts, the exhibitions of which began as annual events.

It is assumed that all the letters listed here are rptd. in Kelvin's edn. of *The Collected Letters of William Morris*. References to rpts. in the *Letters* are included only when special circumstances require them (as for example when a letter has no other printed source than that provided in the *Letters*.)

D-1: 'The Story of the Unknown Church' (prose romance), *The Oxford and Cambridge Magazine*, 1/1 (Jan. 1856), 28–33.
Notes: Morris edited this 1st issue of the *Magazine*, but 'before the second number appeared the editorship had been formally assigned to Fulford, to whom Morris paid a salary of £100 a year for the performance of that duty' (Mackail, i. 88).

D-2: 'Winter Weather' (poem), *The Oxford and Cambridge Magazine*, 1/1 (Jan. 1856), 62–4.

D-3: 'The Churches of Northern France. No. 1—Shadows of Amiens.' (essay), *The Oxford and Cambridge Magazine*, 1/2 (Feb. 1856), 99–110.

D-4: 'A Dream' (prose romance), *The Oxford and Cambridge Magazine*, 1/3 (Mar. 1856), 146–55.

D-5: 'Men and Women'. By Robert Browning (review), *The Oxford and Cambridge Magazine*, 1/3 (Mar. 1856), 162–72.

D-6: 'Frank's Sealed Letter' (prose fiction), *The Oxford and Cambridge Magazine*, 1/4 (Apr. 1856), 225–34.

D-7: 'Riding Together' (poem), *The Oxford and Cambridge Magazine*, 1/5 (May 1856), 320–1.

D-8: 'Gertha's Lovers' (prose romance), *The Oxford and Cambridge Magazine*, 1/7, 8 (July, Aug. 1856), 403–17, 499–512.

D-9: 'Hands' (poem), *The Oxford and Cambridge Magazine*, 1/7 (July 1856), 452.
Notes: incorporated into 'Rapunzel' in *The Defence of Guenevere and Other Poems* (see A-2.01).

D-10: ' "Death the Avenger" and "Death the Friend" ' (essay), *The Oxford and Cambridge Magazine*, 1/8 (Aug. 1856), 477–9.
Notes: an explication of two wood engravings by Alfred Rethel.

D-11: 'Svend and His Brethren' (prose romance), *The Oxford and Cambridge Magazine*, 1/8 (Aug. 1856), 488–99.

D-12: 'Lindenborg Pool' (prose romance), *The Oxford and Cambridge Magazine*, 1/9 (Sept. 1856), 530–4.

D-13: 'The Hollow Land. A Tale' (prose romance), *The Oxford and Cambridge Magazine*, 1/9, 10 (Sept., Oct. 1856), 565–77, 632–41.

D-14: 'The Chapel in Lyoness' (poem), *The Oxford and Cambridge Magazine*, 1/9 (Sept. 1856), 577–9.

D-15: ['Pray but one prayer for me'] (poem), *The Oxford and Cambridge Magazine*, 1/10 (Oct. 1856), 644.
Notes: rptd. as 'Summer Dawn' in *The Defence of Guenevere* (1858, A-2.01). The 'Contents' of '*The Hollow Land*' and Other Contributions to The Oxford and Cambridge Magazine and *The Oxford and Cambridge Magazine* list this poem as 'Pray but one Prayer for Us', but in the original magazine, the text of the poem appears with no title. Since the 'Contents' version of the title has no convincing justification in the text for the pronoun 'Us', the conventional way of identifying untitled poems is employed here, the title being taken, unchanged, from the 1st line of the text.

D-16: 'Golden Wings' (prose romance), *The Oxford and Cambridge Magazine*, 1/12 (Dec. 1856), 733–42.

D-17: [Journal's heading:] 'Mr Morris's new poem' (to the Editor), *The Athenæum*, No. 2113 (25 Apr. 1868), 593. Letter dated 20 Apr. 1868.
Notes: Morris corrects an error made in a review of *Jason*; also includes a note on the projected illus. version of *The Earthly Paradise*.

D-18: 'The God of the Poor' (poem), *Fortnightly Review*, 4, n.s. (1 Aug. 1868), 139–45.
Notes: also rptd. separately as a pamphlet recently proved by Nicolas Barker and John Collins to be an unauthorized, forged 1st separate edn. (see *Sequel*, and E-5).

D-19: 'The Two Sides of the River' (poem), *Fortnightly Review*, 4, n.s. (Oct. 1868), 379–82.
Notes: with 'Hapless Love' and 'The First Foray of Aristomenes', this text was prtd., probably in 1890, in an unauthorized 1st separate edn. pamphlet, falsely dated '1876', and created by H. B. Forman and T. J. Wise (see E-4).

D-20: 'The Saga of Gunnlaug the Worm-tongue and Rafn the Skald', *Fortnightly Review*, 5, n.s. (Jan. 1869), 27–56.
Translation: by Morris and Eiríkr Magnússon from the Icelandic.

D-21: 'Hapless Love' (poem), *Good Words*, 10 (1 Apr. 1869), 264–5.
Notes: a dialogue between 'Hic' and 'Ille'. See also *Notes* to D-19 and E-4.

D-22: 'On the Edge of the Wilderness' (poem), *Fortnightly Review*, 5, n.s. (Apr. 1869), 391–4.

D-23: 'The Death of Paris' (narrative poem), *Every Saturday*, 8 (13 Nov. 1869), 625–30.
Notes: pbd. at about the same time as the 1st tale for Sept. in Part 3, vol. II of *The Earthly Paradise* (issued 15–30 Nov. 1869). This appears to be the only instance in which Morris pbd. a part of *The Earthly Paradise* before the vol. that contains it.

D-24: 'Rhyme slayeth Shame' (sonnet), *The Atlantic Monthly, a Magazine of Literature, Science, Art, and Politics*, 25/148 (Feb. 1870), 144.
Notes: rptd. by Samuel Waddington in 'Sonnets by William Morris', *The Athenæum*, No. 4539 (24 Oct. 1914), 430, as part of his attempt to establish the authorship of this and 'May grown a'cold'. May Morris's reply under the same heading in *The Athenæum*, No. 4541 (7 Nov. 1914), 480, confirms Morris's authorship.

D-25: 'May grown a-cold' (sonnet), *The Atlantic Monthly, a Magazine of Literature, Science, Art, and Politics*, 25/151 (1 May 1870), 553.
Notes: see this field in the previous entry.

D-26: [Journal's heading:] '**General Literature and Art. Poems by Dante Gabriel Rossetti. London: Ellis, 1870**' (review), *The Academy*, 1 (14 May 1870), 199–200.

D-27: 'The Seasons' (poem), *The Academy*, 1 (1 Feb. 1871), 109.
Notes: in this original version, the poem has 4 four-line stanzas, one for each of the seasons. In Morris's later version in *Poems by the Way*, as Temple Scott observes, it 'was republished with a variant in the shape of a new stanza in the place of the original on Winter'. Other changes included the addition of 2 stanzas, one each on 'Day' and on 'Night' at the beginning and the end. 'In this form', Scott continues, 'the poem is titled "Verses for Pictures" so it may well have been printed in an exhibition catalogue before it appeared in *Poems by the Way*' (Scott, p. 39). That catalogue has not yet been found, but it appears more likely if one is aware that the 6 verses as they are in *Poems by the Way* correspond to 6 paintings with the same titles. The pictures were all painted by Burne-Jones for F. R. Leyland of Liverpool

(see M. Harrison and B. Waters, *Burne-Jones* (New York: G. P. Putnam's Sons, 1973), p. 157).

D-28: 'The Dark Wood' (poem), *Fortnightly Review,* Feb. 1871, 219–20.
Notes: 1st titled 'Missing' in *A Book of Verse* (completed in MS in 1870, but not pbd. until 1980) and later rptd. as 'Error and Loss' in *Poems by the Way* (1891).

D-29: 'The Story of Frithiof the Bold' (saga), *Dark Blue,* 1 (Mar., Apr. 1871), 42–58, 176–82.
Translation: By Morris and Eiríkr Magnússon from the Icelandic.

D-30: 'The King of Denmark's Sons' (narrative poem), *Scribner's Monthly, An Illustrated Magazine for the People,* 5/3 (Jan. 1873), 294–7.
Notes: retold from the *Heimskringla* story of King Gorm the Old and his sons, Knut and Harald, written in 67 couplets interspersed with 8 quatrains.

D-31: 'Love's Gleaning-Tide' (poem), *The Athenæum,* No. 2424 (11 Apr. 1874), 492.

D-32: 'The First Foray of Aristomenes' (narrative poem), *The Athenæum,* No. 2533 (13 May 1876), 663–4.
Notes: called 'a fragment of a poem' in Morris's foreword, because it is only a single episode from a longer poem originally planned for inclusion in *The Earthly Paradise* and pbd. in its entirety in the *CW,* xxiv. 171–238). This shorter version was later combined with 'The Two Sides of the River' and 'Hapless Love' in a pamphlet recently demonstrated to be one of the Wise-Forman 'creative forgeries.' See E-4.

D-33: [an unheaded letter] (to the Editor), *The Daily News,* 26 Oct. 1876, p. 93. Letter dated 'October 24'.
Notes: also pbd. as a leaflet and a placard under the title 'England and the Turks' (see A-10.01).

D-34: [Journal's heading:] 'Society for the Protection of Ancient Monuments' (to the Editor), *The Athenæum,* No. 2578 (10 Mar. 1877), 326. Letter dated 'March 5'.
Notes: Morris's initial call for the formation of a society 'to keep watch on old monuments' such as Tewksbury Minster. There is a reply to this letter in *The Athenæum,* No. 2579 (31 Mar. 1877), 425, by Edmund A. H. Lechmere, Chairman of Tewkesbury Abbey Restoration Committee.

D-35: [Journal heading:] 'Restoration' (to the Editor), *The Athenæum,* No. 2580 (7 Apr. 1877), 455. Letter dated 'April 4'.
Notes: a reply to E. A. H. Lechmere's response to Morris's 1st letter on Tewkesbury Minster (see the previous entry).

D-36: [An unheaded letter on restoration of the choir of Canterbury Cathedral] (to the Editor), *The Times,* 4 June 1877.
Notes: written for the SPAB in reply to letters from the Dean and the architect in charge of restoration at Canterbury Cathedral, the letter's date is not known, but a draft MS, in the Berg Collection (NN), is dated 'May 1877'.

D-37: [an unheaded 2nd letter on restoration at Canterbury] (to the Editor), *The Times,* 7 June 1877.
Notes: written for the SPAB on the restoration of the choir of Canterbury Cathedral, this time replying specifically to one from Dean Smith; the letter's date is not known.

D-38: 'To The Very Reverend the Dean & the Reverend the Chapter, of Canterbury Cathedral' (to the Editor), *The Architect,* 8 July 1877.
Notes: written for the SPAB and also prtd. as a news item in *The Times,* 7 July 1877. Letter dated 'June 22'.

D-39: [Journal's heading:] 'Cambridge School of Art' (speech), *The Cambridge Chronicle and University Journal,* 23 Feb. 1878, p. 4. The address was delivered on 21 Feb. 1878.
Notes: recently pbd. separately as *A Speech by Mr. W. Morris from The Cambridge Chronicle 23 February 1878* (see A-142.01).

D-40: [Journal's heading:] 'Destruction of City Churches' (to the Editor), *The Times,* 17 Apr. 1878. Letter dated 'April 15'.
Notes: written on behalf of the SPAB, opposing the planned destruction of Wren's churches in the City.

D-41: [Journal heading:] 'The Threatened Destruction of Blundell's Schools' (to the Editor), *The Athenæum,* No. 2645 (6 July 1878), 24.
Notes: for a 2nd letter on this subject, see D-75. Not rptd. or listed in the standard sources.

D-42: [Journal's heading:] 'St Alban's Abbey' (to the Editor), *The Times,* 2 Aug. 1878, p. 5. Letter dated 'August 1'.

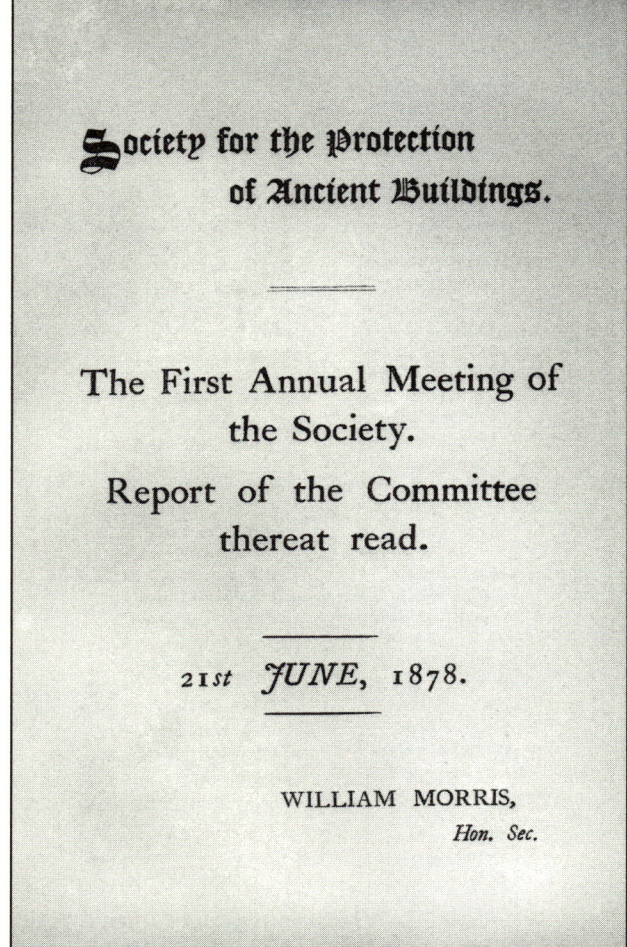

Figure 94. D-43: *1st Annual Report*, SPAB title page

Notes: a letter written on behalf of the SPAB, opposing alterations to the roof of St. Alban's and approving the same views from Lord Carnarvon, President of The Society of Antiquaries.

D-43: 'The [Annual] Report', *Society for the Protection of Ancient Buildings. The First Annual Meeting of the Society. Report of the Committee thereat read. 21st June, 1878.* pp. 9–18.
Notes: written and read by Morris. Printed but not yet issued by 25 Sept. 1878 (see *Letters*, i. 523–4).

D-44: [On the alteration of the roof of St. Alban's Abbey] (to the Editor) originally intended for *The Times*, but not pbd. there. Letter dated 26 Aug. 1878.
Notes: a 3rd letter on this subject to *The Times*. Written on behalf of the SPAB. Kelvin says, 'this letter was apparently never published in *The Times*' (*Letters*, i. 497). But it was intended for publication, and it has been pbd. since at least 3 times: in *Letters*, i. 495–7; MM, i. 165; and in Henderson, pp. 126–7.

D-45: 'The Decorative Arts' (lecture), *The Architect*, 8 Dec. 1877, pp. 308–12. 1st delivered on 4 Dec. 1877.
Notes: prtd. later in the same year as a pamphlet: *The Decorative Arts: Their Relation to Modern Life and Progress* (see A-16.01). Later retitled 'The Lesser Arts' for pbn. in *Hopes and Fears for Art*.

D-46: [Journal's heading:] 'Presidential Address' (lecture), *The Birmingham Daily Post*, 20 Feb. 1879, p. 5. Delivered at the annual prize giving, 19 Feb. 1879.
Notes: Morris's 2nd public lecture, pbd. separately as a pamphlet by the sponsor, the Birmingham Society of Arts and School of Design (see A-17.01). Later retitled and pbd. in *Hopes and Fears for Art* as 'The Art of the People'.

D-47: [Structural repairs to ancient buildings, the principles of the SPAB] (to the Editor), *The Architect*, 19 Apr. 1879, p. 239. Letter dated 'April 8'.

D-48: [Journal heading:] 'Mr. William Morris on Egyptian, Greek and Roman Art' (lecture), *The Architect*, 19 Apr. 1879, pp. 236–7.
Series: One of a 6-lecture series on decorative art sponsored by and in aid of the SPAB, to which Morris contributed 2, this and 'The Lesser Arts of Life'. All were later pbd. in *Lectures on Art in Support of the Society for the Protection of Ancient Buildings* (see B-3).
Notes: Morris's title: 'The History of Pattern Designing'; delivered 8 Apr. 1879.

D-49: [An untitled poem], *Grosvenor Notes: 1879. An Illustrated Catalogue of the Summer Exhibition*, No. II, p. 46.
Notes: 4 lines, each line to accompany a painting by Edward Burne-Jones, the set of 4 paintings titled 'The Story of Pygmalion'. The editor gives the titles of the pictures, which together make up the poem: 'the Titles are as follows:
No. 167. "The heart desires."
No. 168. "The hand refrains."
No. 169. "The Godhead fires."
No. 170. "The soul attains." '
The journal's resumé follows: 'In the first, Pygmalion is seen contemplating a group of three graces; in the

second, he pauses before his unfinished statue; in the third, Venus welcomes the statue to life; in the fourth, Pygmalion kneels before the new creation'.

D-50: [a speech at the Second Annual Meeting of the SPAB], *Society for the Protection of Ancient Buildings. The Second Annual Meeting of the Society. Report of the Committee thereat read. 28th June, 1879*. Report, pp. 8–17; speech, pp. 30–6.
Notes: the 'Report' was read and at least in part composed by Morris, who also made a seconding speech supporting Prof. Byrne's motion against restoration.

D-51: [Journal's heading;] 'English Translations from the Icelandic' (to the Editor), *The Athenæum*, 17 May 1879, pp. 632–3. Letter dated 'May 12'.
Notes: explains and defends Eiríkr Magnússon's role as at least an equal contributor with Morris to the 'English versions of the Grettis Saga and the Gunnlaug Saga'. For the text, see this field in A-5.01.

D-52: [In support of The National Liberal League] (to the Editor), *The Daily News*, 18 Oct. 1879, pp. 527–8. Letter dated 'October 17'.
Signed: 'William Morris, Treasurer to the National Liberal League.'

D-53: [On the restoration of St Mark's Venice] (to the Editor), *The Daily News*, 1 Nov. 1879; and *The Architect*, 8 Nov. 1879; letter dated 'October 31'.

D-54: 'Memorial' (petition), *The Times*, 19 Nov. 1879, p. 8.
Notes: addressed to the Italian authorities against the restorations proposed for St Mark's, Venice, with the signatures of some of the many eminent persons who had signed it: 'William Morris, Hon. Sec. of the S.P.A.B.' is the 1st signature in a long list. This 'Memorial' was prepared by Morris before a series of 3 meetings— London on 6 Nov., Birmingham on 13 Nov., and Oxford on 15 Nov. 1879—where it was discussed (see *Unpublished Lectures*, p. 236).

D-55: [A reply to the Italian Ministry of Public Instruction on the restoration of St Mark's] (to the Editor) *The Times*, 24 Nov. 1879, p. 5. Letter dated 'November 22'.
Notes: a letter on behalf of the SPAB in response to the Italian Ministry's comments as reported on 22 Nov.

D-56: [Morris's reply to the charge of anti-Italian bias in the SPAB's St Mark's protest] (to the Editors of several Italian newspapers). Letter dated 'November 27' 1879.
Notes: a letter on behalf of the SPAB, enclosing copies of the SPAB *Manifesto*. Rptd. *Letters*, i. 544–5.

D-57: [Journal's heading:] 'St. Mark's, Venice' (to the Editor), *The Times*, 29 Nov. 1879. Letter dated 'November 28'.

D-58: 'The Baptistery Ravenna' (to the Editor), *The Times*, 12 June 1880. Letter dated 'June 9'.

D-59: [Morris's Speech seconding a Resolution on Women's Rights] *The Women's Union Journal. The Organ of the Women's Protective and Provident League*, 5 (July 1880), 69–70.
Notes: text from the 'Annual Report of the Women's Protective and Provident League'.

D-60: 'The [Annual] Report' *Society for the Protection of Ancient Buildings. The Third Annual Meeting of the Society. Report of the Committee thereat read. 28 June 1880*. pp. 10–18.
Notes: Issued on 29 Aug. 1880, see Morris's remarks in letters dated 29 Aug. to Henry Wallis and Newman Marks (*Letters*, i. 588–9).

D-61: [Journal's heading:] 'Hints on House Decoration' (lecture), *The Architect*, 18, 25 Dec. 1880, pp. 384–7, 400–2. 1st delivered in London on 13 Nov. 1880.
Notes: Later retitled 'Making the Best of it' for inclusion in *Hopes and Fears for Art* (1882, A-21.01).

D-62: [Journal's heading:] 'The Kyrle Society' (speech), *The Women's Union Journal*, 6/61 (1 Feb. 1881), 13–16. Delivered 27 Jan.
Notes: supporting a resolution calling for public support for the Kyrle Society in its efforts 'to bring art and music within reach of the people'. Rptd. MM, i. 192–7.

D-63: [On the threatened destruction of Magdalen Bridge, Oxford] (to the Editor), *The Pall Mall Gazette*, but not pbd. there; 1st pbd. in *Letters*, ii. 55–7. MS letter dated, 'July 16, 1881'.

D-64: 'The [Annual] Report', *Society for the Protection of Ancient Buildings. Fourth Annual Meeting of the Society. Report of the Committee thereat read. 24th June 1881*. pp. 7–18.

D-65: 'The Condition and Prospects of Art' (lecture), *The Architect*, 29 Oct., 5 Nov. 1881, pp. 282–4, 297–8; delivered 13 Oct. 1881.
Notes: delivered at the annual prize giving of the Burslem School of Art and pbd. there in pamphlet form as *Address Delivered . . . in the Burslem Town Hall* (see A-20.01). Retitled *Art and the Beauty of the Earth* and rptd. in 1899 as the 2nd vol. in the Golden type octavo series (see A-20.02).

D-66: [On Ashburnham House] (to the Editor), *The Daily News*, 29 Nov. 1881; letter dated 28 Nov.

D-67: 'Widening of Magdalen Bridge' (memorial), intended for pbn. in *The Times* or *The Athenæum*, but not published there. Letter dated 10 Nov. [1881].
Notes: 1st pbd. in *Letters*, ii. 77–8. Morris drafted 2 Memorials on this issue (both rptd. In *Letters*) one for circulation and signatures within Oxford, the other for the rest of the country (see Morris to H. G. Woods, *Letters*, ii. 77–8).

D-68: [Journal heading:] 'High Wycombe Grammar School' (to the Editor), *The Athenæum*, No. 2854 (10 Dec. 1881), 785.

D-69: 'Some Hints on Pattern Designing' (lecture) *The Architect*, 17, 24 Dec. 1881, pp. 391–4, 408–10; and *The American Architect*, 2 (1882), 32, 44, 66; delivered 10 Dec. 1881.

D-70: [On the buildings recently 'restored' in the Milan area] (to the Editor), *The Times*, 12 Apr. 1882, p. 10. The letter is undated.

D-71: 'The [Annual] Report' (speech), *Society for the Protection of Ancient Buildings. The Fifth Annual Meeting of the Society. Report of the Committee thereat read. 9th June, 1882.* pp. 46–7.
Notes: Morris seconds a vote of thanks to Hon. James Bryce MP, Chairman of the Annual Meeting, SPAB.

D-72: [Morris's reply to accusations that the Iceland famine is exaggerated] (to the Editor), *The Daily News*, 28 Sept. 1882.; letter dated 'September 27'
Notes: rptd. in *Letters*, ii. 129–31.

D-73: [Journal's heading:] 'Mr. William Morris on Art Matters' (lecture), *The Manchester Guardian*, 21 Oct. 1882, p. 5; as 'Mr. William Morris on English Decorative Art', *The Architect*, 28 Oct. 1882, pp. 262–3; *The American Architect*, 12 (1882), 281.
Notes: Morris's 'The Progress of Decorative Art in England', was delivered under this title at the opening of the Fine Art and Industrial Exhibition at St James Hall, Manchester, 20 Oct. 1882. It was rptd. in part as a separate and issued by the WMS, 1961.

D-74: [Titled in longhand on the MS, possibly by W. R. Lethaby:] 'Art: a Serious Thing' (lecture), portions in *The Leek Times*, 12 Dec. 1882; full text in *Unpublished Lectures*.
Notes: delivered at the annual distribution of prizes at the Leek School of Art, 12 Dec. 1882.

D-75: [On Blundell's Schools] (to the Editor), *The Daily News*, 26 Feb. 1883; letter date not known.

D-76: [Morris's reply to a letter signed 'Verax' and pbd. in *The Manchester Weekly Times*] (to the Editor), *The Manchester Examiner*, 14 Mar. 1883; the letter has the same date.
Notes: a defence of the thesis of Morris's Manchester lecture, 'Art, Wealth, and Riches'.

D-77: 'Art, Wealth, and Riches' (lecture), *The Manchester Quarterly*, Apr. 1883, pp. 153–75.
Notes: delivered at the Manchester Royal Institution before a joint conversazione of Manchester Societies. Besides this article there was a separate offprint, for which see A-22.01.

D-78: 'The [Annual] Report' (speech), *Society for the Protection of Ancient Buildings. The Sixth Annual Meeting of the Society. Report of the Committee thereat read. 6th June, 1883.* pp. 7–29.

D-79:* [On impending famine in Iceland] (to the Editor), *The Daily News*, 8 Aug. 1882, p. 7; letter dated 'August 5'.
Notes: rptd. *Letters*, ii, 17–18.

D-80: 'Art and the People: A Socialist's Protest Against Capitalist Brutality; Addressed to the Working Classes' (lecture), *The North-Western Gazette*, 16, 30 June 1883; delivered on 12, 15 June.
Notes: report of Morris's 2-part lecture at the Vestry Hall, Haverstock Hill, Hampstead.

D-81: [On pollution of the ditch parallel to the towpath near Hammersmith Bridge] (to the Editor), *The Daily News*, 15 Aug. 1883, p. 6; letter dated 'August 14'.

D-82: [A reply to 'One of the audience' at Morris's Oxford lecture] (to the Editor), *The Pall Mall Gazette*, 19 Nov. 1883, p. 2; the letter is dated 'November 17'.
Notes: Morris defends the economic judgments basic to the lecture 'Art under Plutocracy'.

D-83: [A reply to 'M'] (to the Editor), *The Standard*, 22 Nov. 1883; the letter is dated 'November 21'.
Notes: Morris's defence of himself for preaching Socialism while being a capitalist.

D-84: [Journal's heading:] 'Mr Morris on Art under Plutocracy' (lecture abstract), *The Cambridge Review*, 5 Dec. 1883, p. 122; *The Cambridge Chronicle and University Journal*, 7 Dec. 1883, p. 7; delivered 4 Dec. 1883, in the Cambridge University Union, but the 1st delivery was at University College Hall, Oxford, on 14 Nov. 1883.
Notes: from the *Chronicle*'s heading: 'The following abstract of his lecture on this subject at the Union on Monday has been written for us by Mr. Morris himself.' Later delivered as 'Art under the Rule of Commerce'. Under the original title the full text was published in *To-Day* in 1884 (see D-90) and included in *Architecture, Industry, and Wealth*, in 1902 (see C-18.01). In 1907 it was pbd. separately as 'Art, Labour, and Socialism' by SPGB (SPGB Library, No. 3, see A-113.01), and rptd. in 1962 with 'A Modern Assessment'.

D-85: 'The Three Seekers' (narrative poem), *To-Day: The Monthly Magazine of Scientific Socialism*, 1/1 n.s. (Jan. 1884), 25–9.

D-86: 'An Old Fable Retold' (fable), *Justice: The Organ of the Social Democracy*, 1/1 (19 Jan. 1884), 2.
Notes: allegory to show how Socialism enlarges the standard choices presented by the major parties.

D-87: 'The Principles of *Justice*' (editorial), *Justice: The Organ of the Social Democracy*, 1/1 (19 Jan. 1884), 4.
Signed: 'H. M. Hyndman. | William Morris. | J. Taylor.'
Notes: an editorial stating The DF's political purposes in establishing *Justice* as the organ of its programme.

D-88: [Journal's heading:] 'Mr. W. Morris at Hampstead' (lecture), *Justice: The Organ of the Social Democracy*, 1/1 (19 Jan. 1884), 6; 1st delivered 16 Jan. 1884.
Series: No. 2 of The Socialist League Platform.
Notes: 1st report and summary of a lecture on 'Useful work versus Useless Toil'. Rptd. as a pamphlet *Useful Work versus Useless Toil* (1885, see A-31.01), and included in *Signs of Change* in 1888.

D-89: 'Cotton and Clay' (comment), *Justice*, 1/2 (26 Jan. 1884), 2.
Signed: 'M.' Internal evidence establishes that the initial refers to Morris.
Notes: on the government enquiry into the adulteration process of sizing cotton and the effect of the additive on workers set to weaving the product.

D-90: 'Art under Plutocracy' (lecture), *To-Day: The Monthly Magazine of Scientific Socialism*, n.s. 1/2, 3 (Feb., Mar. 1884), 79–90, 159–76; 1st delivered 14 Nov. 1883. An abstract of this lecture was written by Morris and pbd. earlier (see D-84).

D-91: [Journal's heading:] 'The Executive Committee appeal . . . .' (appeal), *Justice*, 1/4 (Feb. 1884), p. 5.
Signed: H. M. Hyndman . . . | William Morris, Hon. Treas. | H. H. Champion'
Notes: call for donations to support Federation propaganda initiatives; 1st in a series of such appeals.

D-92: 'The Bondholder's Battue' (leader), *Justice: The Organ of the Social Democracy*, 1/4 (9 Feb. 1884), 4.
Signed: 'H. M. Hyndman. | William Morris.'
Notes: on British policy in Egypt.

D-93: 'The Way Out. An Appeal to Genuine Radicals' (leader), *Justice*, 1/7 (1 Mar. 1884), 4.

D-94: 'Order and Anarchy' (article), *Justice*, 1/4 (9 Feb. 1884), 2.
Notes: contrasting capitalist *laissez faire* chaos with Socialist order.

D-95: 'Meeting in Winter' (poem), *The English Illustrated Magazine*, 1/3 (Mar. 1884), 339–40.

D-96: 'Art or No Art? Who Shall Settle It?' (lead editorial), *Justice*, 1/9 (15 Mar. 1884), 2.

D-97: 'Henry George' (lead editorial), *Justice*, 1/12 (5 Apr. 1884), 4.

D-98: 'Chants for Socialists No. 2. The Voice of Toil' (poem), *Justice*, 1/12 (5 Apr. 1884), 5.

Notes: rptd. in the collected edns. of *Chants for Socialists*. The 1st of the Chants for Socialists was issued separately as a pamphlet in 1883 before *Justice* was founded on 19 Jan. 1884 (see A-23.01).

D-99: 'Why Not?' (article), *Justice*, 1/13 (12 Apr. 1884), 2.
Notes: makes the case against large cities as a necessity of modern manufacture; the 1st exposition of ideas later developed in a 3-part article, 'A Factory As It Might Be'.

D-100: 'Chants for Socialists No. 3. All for the Cause' (poem), *Justice*, 1/14 (19 Apr. 1884), 5.

D-101: 'The Dull Level of Life' (leader), *Justice*, 1/15 (26 Apr. 1884), 4.
Notes: defends Socialism against the charge it would lead to a dull life.

D-102: 'A Factory As It Might Be' (lead editorial), *Justice*, 1/18 (17 May 1884), 2.
Series: 1st part of a 3-part series contrasting the factory of the future with the present reality. See also D-105 and 107.

D-103: 'The Propaganda Fund' (appeal), *Justice: The Organ of the Social Democracy*, 1/18 (17 May 1884), 5.
Notes: call for donations, several times rptd., along with, from 21 June 1884, a list of donors; 2nd in a series (see D-91).

D-104: 'Individualism at the Royal Academy' (leader), *Justice*, 1/19 (24 May 1884), 4.

D-105: 'Work in a Factory as it Might Be. II.' (lead editorial), *Justice*, 1/20 (31 May 1884), 2.
Series: 2nd part of a 3-part series contrasting the factory of the future with the present reality. See also D-102 and 107.

D-106: 'Chants for Socialists. No. IV. No Master' (poem), *Justice*, 1/21 (7 June 1884), 5.

D-107: 'Work in a Factory as it Might Be. III.' (lead editorial), *Justice*, 1/24 (28 June 1884), 2.
Series: 3rd part of a 3-part series contrasting the factory of the future with the present reality. See also D-102 and 105.

D-108: 'The Exhibition of the Royal Academy (By a Rare Visitor)' (essay), *To-Day: The Monthly Magazine of Scientific Socialism*, 2/7 n.s. (July 1884), 75–91.

D-109: 'The Propaganda Fund' (appeal), *Justice*, (5 July 1884), 5.
Series: 3rd in a series of appeals for donations to a fund established in Feb. 1884, see D-91, 103.

D-110: 'To Genuine Radicals' (editorial), *Justice*, 1/26 (12 July 1884), 4–5.
Notes: article calling upon Radicals to consider whether their 'practical politics' have made, or would make, even if adopted, any substantial gain on their present position.

D-111: 'Textile Fabrics' (lecture), *The Architect*, 19, 26, July 1884, pp. 43–5, 50–3. Also pbd. in *The Health Exhibition Literature*, 12/3 (1884), 173–201; delivered on 11 July.
Notes: on the history of the weaving, dyeing, and design of art textiles, read at a Conference of The International Health Exhibition and pbd. in the official proceedings (see above) and included here as are all 'transactions' pbns. Also pbd. as a pamphlet by the International Health Exhibition, see A-27.01, and later included in the collection *Architecture, Industry, and Wealth*, see C-18.01 and .02.

D-112: 'The Housing of the Poor' (article), *Justice*, 1/27 (19 July 1884), 4–5.

D-113: 'Propaganda Fund' (appeal), *Justice*, 1/27 (19 July 1884), 5.
Series: 4th in a series of appeals, each rewritten, for donations to a fund established in Feb. 1884, see D-91, 103, and 109.

D-114: 'Propaganda Fund' (appeal, rewritten), *Justice*, 1/29 (2 Aug. 1884), 5.
Series: last in a series of 5 appeals, with an updated list of donors, for donations to a fund established in Feb. 1884, see also D-91, 103, 109, and 113.
Signed: 'William Morris. Treasurer of the Democratic Federation'.

D-115: 'Socialism in England in 1884' (editorial), *Justice*, 1/30 (9 Aug. 1884), 4.
Notes: a lead editorial reviewing Socialist political and intellectual progress over the 3 years since modern Socialism was introduced in England.

D-116: [Journal's heading:] 'Paper read by Mr. Morris' (speech), *Society for the Protection of Ancient Buildings. The Seventh Annual Meeting of the Society. Report of the Committee and Paper read by Mr. William Morris. July*

1st, 1884. pp. 49–76.
Notes: later titled 'Architecture and History' and pbd. with 'Concerning Westminster Abbey' (see C-7); extracts appeared as 'Medieval and Modern Craftsmanship', in *The Architect*, 13 Sept. 1884, pp. 171–3; *The Clarion*, Oct. 1884; as 'The Essential Difference between the Work of the Medieval and the Modern Craftsman', *American Architect and Building News*, 16/452 (23 Aug. 1884), 89–91; and *Merry England*, No. 18 (Oct. 1884), 361–77.

D-117: 'Uncrowned Kings' (lead editorial), *Justice*, 1/34 (6 Sept. 1884), 4.
Notes: addressed primarily to radicals and advising they divest themselves of the hero worship of politicians like Palmerston, Beaconsfield, and Gladstone, the 'uncrowned kings' who have dominated all the reformed parliaments without producing genuine benefits for the workers.

D-118: 'The Social Democratic Federation to the Trades Unions of Great Britain, September, 1884' (an open letter), *Justice*, 1/34 (6 Sept. 1884), 5.
Signed: 'The Executive Council of the Social Democratic Federation', inc. among 17 other signatures 'William Morris, Treasurer'.
Notes: suggests that trades unions recognize that without a programme based on the inescapable struggle between capital and labour their palliative parliamentary measures will do nothing to permanently improve the lives of working people.

D-119: [Journal's heading:] 'Monthly Report' (lecture resumé), *Justice*, 1/35 (13 Sept. 1884), 6. Delivered 8 Sept. 1884.
Notes: resumé of Morris's lecture, 'Misery and the Way Out', delivered for the 1st time on this occasion at the Borough of Southwark Branch of the SDF. The complete text, though available in a BL MS, has never been pbd., though generous extracts are prtd. in MM, ii. 150–64.

D-120: 'The Hammersmith Costermongers' (article), *Justice*, 1/36 (20 Sept. 1884), 3.
Notes: on the background and significance of the Hammersmith Board of Works prosecution of the King Street costermongers.

D-121: [On 'Art and Labour'] (to the Editor), *The Manchester Guardian*, 7 Oct. 1884, p. 5; letter dated 'October 4, 1884'; lecture delivered 21 Sept. 1884.
Notes: written after the lecture 'Art and Labour', delivered at Ancoats, Manchester, was attacked by several correspondents in *The Guardian*'s letters column. Rptd. *Letters*, ii. 325–8. The lecture is rptd. entire in *Unpublished Lectures*, pp. 94–118.

D-122: [A reply to criticisms of his lecture 'Architecture and History'] (to the Editor), *The Echo*, 7 Oct. 1884, p. 2; letter dated 'October 4', the lecture was delivered at the SPAB Annual Meeting, 1 July 1884.
Notes: Morris denies both of *The Echo*'s assumptions: (1) that he is interested only in art, and (2) that he authorized *Merry England*'s publication of his lecture.

D-123: 'An Appeal to the Just' (lead editorial), *Justice*, 1/39 (11 Oct. 1884), 4.
Notes: calls for a fair judgment of Socialism for addressing in practical terms the true and present problems of poverty among the working class, as well as proposing a political programme for a fundamental change in the system that inevitably produces that poverty.

D-124: [Journal's heading:] 'Literary Courtesy' (to the Editor), *Justice*, 1/39 (11 Oct. 1884), 6; the date of the letter is not known.
Notes: on the subjects previously covered in a letter to *The Echo*—for which see D-122—'in case a letter which I have written to the Echo . . . should not appear.' But this *Justice* letter is entirely rewritten. Rptd. *Letters*, ii. 331.

D-125: 'The Lord Mayor's Show' (commentary, with a tale), *Justice*, 1/44 (15 Nov. 1884), 2.
Notes: taking his cue from a scene on a pageant wagon in the Lord Mayor's Show depicting the murder of Wat Tyler, Morris retells the entire tale as it is told in Froissart's *Chronicle*, pointing a Socialist moral and anticipating *A Dream of John Ball*. Rptd. MM, ii. 143–6.

D-126: 'The Hackney Election' (lead editorial), *Justice*, 1/46 (Nov. 1884), 4.
Notes: suggests that, having elected a Radical, Prof. Stuart, the electors of Hackney should not expect much.

D-127: 'Philanthropists' (article), *Justice*, 1/49 (20 Dec. 1884), 2.
Notes: describes the various sorts of philanthropists from a Socialist point of view.

D-128: 'The Meaning of Socialism' (Morris's rewriting of the SDF Manifesto), *To-day: The Monthly Magazine of Scientific Socialism*, 3/13 n.s. (Jan. 1885), 1–10.
Notes: Morris to William J. Linton, 26 Oct. 1883: 'I did not write Socialism made plain [the original SDF Manifesto], though I fully agree with it' (*Letters*, ii. 241). Morris to A. Scheu, 8 Oct. 1884: '. . . yesterday I was told off along with Aveling to prepare a new manifesto: my flesh creeps at the difficulties' (*Letters*, ii. 330).
To Scheu, 6 Dec. 1884:

> 'The manifesto got past on Tuesday, but it was declared disappointing: I don't think it what a *manifesto* should be myself, and am sure I could do a better one, if not now, yet soon: however it don't prevent a more distinctly explanatory one being done. You may imagine how *frank* friend Mahon was on the subject: however I owe him no grudge: yet he should make *some* allowances for the weaknesses of human nature' (*Letters*, ii. 343).

Justice, 6 Dec. 1884: '. . . Members of the Executive were requested to return the proofs of the new Manifesto with any amendments to W. Morris not later than Monday December 14th' (p. 6).
Justice, 13 Dec., 1884: 'A proposition that the Manifesto first appear in the January number of To-Day was agreed to' (p. 6).

D-129: [Morris's role as *Commonweal* editor] (to the Editor), *The Daily News*, 27 Jan. 1885, p. 3; letter dated 'January 26'.

D-130: 'Introductory' (editorial), *The Commonweal. The Official Journal of the Socialist League*, 1/1 (1 Feb. 1885), 1.
Signed: 'William Morris'.
Notes: statement of the purpose and the editorial policy of *Commonweal*, pbd. as the 1st item in the 1st issue of the monthly journal. For *Commonweal* as a Morris title, see A-30.01. Morris refers to the 1st issue of *Commonweal* in a letter to Jane Morris, 10 Feb. 1885: 'They . . . sold 5,000 and are in a second edition..' (*Letters*, ii. 386).

D-131: 'The Manifesto of the Socialist League', *Commonweal*, 1/1 (Feb. 1885), 1–2.
Signed: 'Signatures of the Provisional Council of the Socialist League'.
Notes: the Manifesto was drafted by William Morris and E. Belfort Bax (see *Letters*, ii. 370), but signed by 23 members of the Provisional Council of the Socialist League. 1st pbd. as a pamphlet, 11–22 Jan. 1885 (see A-29.01).

D-132: 'The March of the Workers' (lyric), *Commonweal*, 1/1 (Feb. 1885), 4.
Notes: to be sung 'To the tune of "John Brown" '. This became the 5th poem in *Chants for Socialists*.

D-133: 'Comrades,—' (an unheaded appeal for funds), *Commonweal*, 1/2 (Mar., 1885), 12.
Notes: with a list of contributors and their donations; an appeal for funds from members to support the League's various activities, repeated here and in several subsequent numbers of *Commonweal*. Later appearances of the appeal are not listed here.

D-134: 'The Message of the March Wind' (poem, as later designated, Chapter I of *The Pilgrims of Hope*, pbd. in 13 installments, as follows), (1) *Commonweal*, 1/2 (Mar. 1885), 12; (2) 'The Pilgrims of Hope. II.— "The Bridge and the Street" (Being a continuation of "The Message of the March Wind.")', 1/3 (Apr. 1885), 20; (3) 'The Pilgrims of Hope. III.—Sending to the War', 1/4 (May 1885), 32; (4) 'The Pilgrims of Hope. IV.—Mother and Son', 1/5 (June 1885), 44–5; (5) 'The Pilgrims of Hope. V.—New Birth', 1/7 (Aug. 1885), 68–9; (6) 'The Pilgrims of Hope. VI.—the New Proletarian', 1/8 (Sept. 1885), 80–1; (7) 'The Pilgrims of Hope. VII.—In Prison and At Home', 1/10 (Nov. 1885), 96–7; (8) 'The Pilgrims of Hope. VIII.—the Half of Life Gone', 2/12 (Jan. 1886), 4; (9) 'The Pilgrims of Hope. IX.—A New Friend', 2/14 (March 1886), 21–2; (10) 'The Pilgrims of Hope. X.—Ready to Depart', 2/15 (Apr. 1886), 28–9; (11) 'The Pilgrims of Hope. XI.—A Glimpse of the Coming Day', 2/17 (8 May 1886), 45; (12) 'The Pilgrims of Hope. XII.—Meeting the War-Machine', 2/21 (5 June 1886), 75; and (13) 'The Pilgrims of Hope. XIII.—The Story's Ending . . .', 2/25 (3 July 1886), 107.
Notes: this 1st poem was also included as the 6th lyric in *Chants for Socialists*. The last instalment here pbd. ends with '(to be concluded)'. As with all titles pbd. serially in periodicals, only one entry is made here for each such title.

D-135: [unheaded letter on the disturbance at the Socialist meeting in Oxford on 25 Feb. 1885] (to the Editor), *The Oxford Magazine*, 1/3 (4 Mar. 1885), 124;

the letter was probably written 1–3 Mar.
Signed: 'William Morris | Edward Aveling' (Edward Aveling was the 2nd of the 2 League speakers on the occasion). Rptd., *Letters*, ii. 397.

D-136:* **[Journal's heading:] 'Poet's Prices'** (to the Editor), *The Star*, 16 Mar. 1885?
Signed: 'William Morris'.
Notes: Morris defends the pricing of his books. This letter was pbd. as a broadside titled *Paying for Art*, pbd. by Frederick M. Bursch at the Hillacre Press, Riverside, Conn., in 1911 (see A-120.01).

D-137: **'The Worker's Share of Art'** (article), *Commonweal*, 1/3 (Apr. 1885), 18–19.

D-138: **'Signs of the Times'** (comment), *Commonweal*, 1/3 (Apr. 1885), 22.
Series: front page, 1st column headed 'Signs of the Times', a series of editorial notes on current affairs, later retitled 'Notes on News', and later still simply 'Notes', with sections written and initialled by various authors. Morris is usually the main contributor.
Initialled: 'W. M.'
Notes: 2 paragraphs, one questioning the bona fides of a *Daily News* 'interview with a terrorist', the other welcoming the 1st number of *The Anarchist*.

D-139: **'Reviews and Notices. Socialist Rhymes. By J. L. Joynes'** (a complimentary paragraph on J. L. Joynes' anthology, *Socialist Rhymes*), *Commonweal*, 1/3 (Apr. 1885), 23.
Series: the 1st of a series with the title 'Reviews and Notices.'

D-140: **'Signs of the Times'** (comment), *Commonweal*, 1/4 (May 1885), 35.
Notes: Morris quotes Charles Rowley's *Social Politics*, just pbd., as a sign of the turn of the middle classes towards Socialism.

D-141: **'Reviews and Notices. Social Politics. By Charles Rowley, Jun.; John Heywood Manchester'** (comment), *Commonweal*, 1/4 (May 1885), 35.
Notes: a one-paragraph notice, expressing approval of Rowley's analysis of class distinctions, but disagreement with his remedy, emigration.

D-142: **'Monthly Report'** (comment), *Commonweal*, 1/4 (May 1885), 36.
Series: a regular column of various notes on League affairs, here on the conduct of Mr Bradlaugh as chairman of the Sudan War meeting on 2 Apr..
Initialled: 'W. M.'

D-143: **'Unattractive Labour'** (article), *Commonweal*, 1/4 (May Supplement 1885), 37.
Series: 1st of a 2-part series; see also the next entry.
Notes: on the unattractive effects of the capitalist system on the production of wares that were once naturally beautiful and a pleasure to create.

D-144: **'Attractive Labour'** (article), *Commonweal*, 1/5 (June Supplement 1885), 49–50.
Series: 2nd of a 2-part series; see also 'Unattractive Labour' in the entry above.
Notes: capitalism being unnatural, goods and labour will become naturally attractive again when capitalism ceases.

D-145: **[on violence]** (2 unheaded paragraphs), *Commonweal*, 1/5 (June Supplement 1885), 52.
Notes: distinguishes between the violence of the present society and in a revolution, and argues against Lassalle's position 'that to everybody should be secured the fruits of his industry'.

D-146: **[Speech, as Chairman, SPAB]** *Society for the Protection of Ancient Buildings. The 8th Annual Meeting of the Society. Report of the Committee thereat read. 6th June, 1885*. pp. 45–54; delivered 4 June 1885.

D-147: **'Notes on the Political Crisis'** (article), *Commonweal*, 1/6 (July 1885), 53–4.

D-148: **'Socialists at Play. (Prologue spoken at the Entertainment of the Socialist League at South Place Institute, June 11, 1885)'** (poem), *Commonweal*, 1/6 (July 1885), 56.
Notes: later used as the text for an unauthorized pamphlet, see E-8 and *Sequel*, p. 210.

D-149: **'Socialism and Politics. (An Answer to "Another View")'**, *Commonweal*, 1/6 (July Supplement 1885), 61.
Notes: Morris replies to a letter by R. F. E. Willis, who advocates Socialist candidates running for Parliament.

D-150: **'First General Conference of The Socialist League, Sunday, July 5, 1885'**, *Commonweal*, 1/7 (Aug. 1885), 65.
Signed: 'William Morris. | Edward Aveling.'

Notes: 3 paragraphs as introduction to the minutes of the meeting.

D-151: '**Report of the Editors of *Commonweal*'** (part of the report of the First General Meeting), *Commonweal*, 1/7 (Aug. 1885), 66.
Signed: 'William Morris (Editor). | Edward Aveling (sub-editor)'.

D-152: '**Signs of the Times**' (comment), *Commonweal*, 1/7 (Aug. 1885), 72.
Notes: a paragraph on the offer of baronetcies to G. F. Watts and J. E. Millais, with praise to the 1st for refusing, acid for the 2nd for accepting.
Initialled: 'W. M.'

D-153: '**Mr. Chamberlain at Hull**' (lead editorial: comment on a speech), *Commonweal*, 1/8 (Sept. 1885), 77.

D-154: [Journal's heading:] '**Meeting on the Recent Exposures**' (speech), *Commonweal*, 1/8 (Sept. 1885), 78–9.
Notes: includes a resumé of Morris's speech at the public meeting called to discuss W. T. Stead's exposé of child prostitution in London.

D-155: '**Appeal!**' (a call for contributions), *Commonweal*, 1/8 (Sept. 1885), 84.
Signed: 'E. Belfort Bax, William Morris, C. Theodor.'
Notes: report on 'A Weekly *Commonweal* Fund' and on steps made to date to prepare for the change to a weekly.

D-156: '**A New Party**' (lead editorial), *Commonweal*, 1/8 (Sept. Supplement 1885), 85.
Notes: on the coming new party of reaction, and on the futility of Parliamentary politics for Socialist revolutionaries.

D-157: '**Answers to Previous Inquiries**', *Commonweal*, 1/8 (Sept. Supplement 1885), 87.
Initialled: (each of 5 paragraphs) 'W. M.'
Notes: Morris responds to questioners about the efficacy of small Socialist Communities, on the extra-parliamentary process necessary for genuine revolutionary Socialism, on rewards under Socialism, and on the process by which human character may be 'regenerated'.

D-158: [unheaded defence of the accused in the Dod Street Police Court, 21 Sept. 1885] (to the Editor), *The Daily News*, 23 Sept. 1885; the letter is dated 'September 22'.

D-159: '**Ireland and Italy. A Warning**' (comment), *Commonweal*, 1/9 (Oct. 1885), 86–7.
Notes: Morris warns Ireland against independence without consultation with the working class.

D-160: '**Signs of the Times**' (comment), *Commonweal*, 1/9 (Oct. 1885), 91.
Notes: the situation of the radicals in the political manoeuvring of the election campaign.

D-161: '**Inquiry Column. Answers.**' (reply), *Commonweal*, 1/9 (Oct. 1885), 92.
Notes: Morris replies to a query from a reader regarding the Socialist attitude towards the family not being limited 'to blood relations'.

D-162: '**Moves in the Game Political**' (analysis), *Commonweal*, 1/10 (Nov. 1885), 93.
Notes: Morris on moves by each of the major figures—Gladstone, Chamberlain, Churchill, and Lord Salisbury—thus far in the General Election campaign.

D-163: '**Free Speech and the Police**' (report), *Commonweal*, 1/10 (Nov. 1885), 99–100.
Notes: an account, with commentary by Morris, of the struggle with the police over meetings in Dod Street, and with the SDF over the management of the demonstrations.

D-164: [Journal's heading:] '**On the Vulgarization of Oxford**' (to the Editor), *The Daily News*, 20 Nov. 1885; the letter has the same date.
Notes: opposing the destruction of Oxford's ancient buildings and the substitution of modern ones.

D-165: '**On the Eve of the Elections**' (comment), *Commonweal*, 1/11 (Dec. 1885), 101.

D-166: '**To Our Readers**' (comment), *Commonweal*, 1/11 (Dec. 18 William Morris. | Edward Aveling.'
Notes: the editors briefly assess *Commonweal* at the end of the year 1885, vol. 1 of the paper being then complete.

D-167: '**The Morrow of the Elections**' (comment), *Commonweal*, 2/12 (Jan. 1886), 1.
Notes: an explanation of why the election result, a Liberal victory, is satisfactory to Socialists.

D-168: 'Notes' (2 paragraphs of comment), *Commonweal*, 2/12 (Jan. 1886), 4.
Series: 1st of 11 items with this heading.
Initialled: 'W. M.'
Notes: on the challenges facing the new government: writing and enacting a Home Rule bill and pacifying Egypt.

D-169: 'The Husks that the Swine Do Eat' (comment), *Commonweal*, 2/12 (Jan. 1886), 7.
Notes: remarks on a criminal case where a man was sentenced to a month's hard labour for eating refuse food given him by a soldier, because the refuse food had already all been sold to a contractor.

D-170: '*The Commonweal*' (report), *Commonweal*, 2/12, 13 (Jan. 1886), 8; rptd. Feb. 1886, p. 16.
Signed: 'E. Belfort Bax. William Morris. | H. H. Sparling. Carl Theodor.'
Notes: directions for obtaining the bound *Commonweal*, and an explanation of the £100 guarantee fund prerequisite to the paper becoming a weekly.

D-171: 'Notes' (comment), *Commonweal*, 2/13 (Feb. 1886), 12.
Series: 2nd of 11 items with this heading.
Initialled: 'W. M.'
Notes: on Irish, allotment, and Work-house Questions.

D-172: 'A Letter from the Pacific Coast' (article), *Commonweal*, 2/13 (Feb. 1886), 13.
Notes: rpts. a letter from San Francisco on a meeting there to discuss Chinese labour questions, with Morris's analysis and comment that the difficulty originates in the capitalist system, not the Chinese workers.

D-173: [Journal's title for the *Pall Mall* series:] 'The Best Hundred Books' (to the Editor), *The Pall Mall Gazette: An Evening Newspaper and Review*, Extra, No. 24 (2 Feb. 1886), 10–11; this is also the date of the letter.

D-174: [Corrections of *The Daily News*' report of Morris's lecture 'The Political Outlook'] (to the Editor), *The Daily News*, 12 Feb. 1886, p. 6; letter dated 'February 11', lecture delivered at the Hammersmith Liberal Club in the aftermath of the Trafalgar Square Riots of 1886.

D-175: [Journal's heading:] 'Socialism. Mr. William Morris in Norwich' (verbatim report of a lecture), [Norwich] *Daylight Supplement*, 13 Mar. 1886, pp. 1–2.
Notes: also issued as a separate folio sheet for distribution, using the same type setting (see A-34.01), except for the beginning, end, and the display types. Detail is as in the *Daylight Supplement* version, but breaking the columns at different points and omitting the description of the audience, the dignitaries present, and the questions and answers following the lecture.
For additional detail see *Unpublished Lectures*, pp. 253, 303.

D-176: 'Our Policy' (lead editorial), *Commonweal*, 2/14 (Mar. 1886), 17–18.
Notes: on the political significance of the recent unemployed riots in London and Leicester, with an explicit Socialist League policy stance regarding them.

D-177: 'Notes on Matters Parliamentary' (editorial), *Commonweal*, 2/15 (Apr. 1886), 28.
Notes: on the 'small matters' of Parliamentary debate, useless but for the exercise necessarily attaching to 'sitting on two stools'.

D-178: 'Socialism in the Provinces' (report), *Commonweal*, 2/15 (Apr. 1886), 30.
Notes: Morris's report of his lecture tour to Sheffield, Liverpool, and Norwich.

D-179: 'Editorial' (comment), *Commonweal*, 2/16 (1 May 1886), 33.
Signed: 'William Morris. | E. Belfort Bax.'
Notes: written to mark the 1st issue of the weekly *Commonweal*, this article restates the SL position with regard to 'State-Socialism', 'palliative' measures, and parliamentary or constitutional reforms.

D-180: 'Independent Ireland' (article), *Commonweal*, 2/16 (1 May 1886), 36.
Notes: on Gladstone's Home Rule Bill, recently presented, and Socialist policy in relation to it.

D-181: [Unheaded paragraph] (comment), *Commonweal*, 2/16, (1 May 1886), 36.
Initialled: 'W. M.'
Notes: on Socialists acquitted of a charge of obstructing the public right of way.

D-182: [Unheaded Paragraph] (comment), *Commonweal*, 2/16 (1 May 1886), 37.
Initialled: 'W. M.'
Notes: on the 'pit-brow' women's defence of jobs in

D-183: 'Concerning the *Commonweal*' (comment), *Commonweal*, 2/16 (1 May 1886), 38.
Notes: Morris replies to an objection to the subtitle of *Commonweal*, *The Official Journal of the Socialist League*.

D-184: [Unheaded paragraph] (comment), *Commonweal*, 2/16 (1 May 1886), 38.
Notes: Morris denies Chamberlain's assertion that the Irish will reject the Home Rule Bill.

D-185: 'Notes on Passing Events' (lead editorial), *Commonweal*, 2/17 (8 May 1886), 41.
Series: 1st of 22 lead articles with this title pbd. in 1886–7.
Signed: 'William Morris.'
Notes: on reactions by Matthew Arnold and others to the Home Rule Bill.

D-186: 'Socialism in Dublin and Yorkshire' (report), *Commonweal*, 2/17 (8 May 1886), 43.
Notes: Morris reports on a lecture tour.

D-187: [Unheaded paragraph] (comment), *Commonweal*, 2/17 (8 May 1886), 45.
Notes: Morris replies to Sir Michael Hicks Beach regarding his confusion of 'competition' and 'monopoly', with particular reference to railways.

D-188: 'Notes on Passing Events' (lead editorial), *Commonweal*, 2/18 (15 May 1886), 49–50.
Notes: on recent events: the sentencing and final speeches of the Chicago Anarchists, the Queen's Jubilee and Tennyson's Ode thereon, and the harvest of imperialism—all seen from the Socialist perspective.

D-189: '"The Commercial Hearth", by E. Belfort Bax' (footnote), *Commonweal*, 2/18 (15 May 1886), 50.
Notes: Morris defends Ruskin's contribution on 'economical matters', against Bax's negative judgement.

D-190: 'Socialism from the Root Up. Chapter I.—Ancient Society', pbd. in 25 parts: *Commonweal*, 2/18 (15 May 1886), 53; 'Chapter II.— Medieval Society', 2/19 (22 May 1886), 61; 'Chapter III.—The Break-up of Feudalism', 2/20 (29 May 1886), 69; 'Chapter IV.—Modern Society: Early Stages', 2/21 (5 June 1886), 77; 'Chapter V.—Preparing for Revolution—England', 2/22 (12 June 1886), 82–3; 'Chapter VI.—Preparations for Revolution—France', 2/25 (3 July 1886), 108–9; 'Chapter VII.—The French Revolution: Constitutional Stage', 2/28 (24 July 1886), 130–1; 'Chapter VIII.—The French Revolution: The Proletarian Stage', 2/29 (31 July 1886), 138–9; 'Chapter IX.—The Industrial Revolution in England', 2/31 (14 Aug. 1886), 156–8; 'Chapter X.—Political Movements in England', 2/33 (28 Aug. 1886), 170–1; 'Chapter XI.—Reaction and Revolution on the Continent', 2/35 (11 Sept. 1886), 189; 'Chapter XII.—The Paris Commune of 1871, and the Continental Movement following it', 2/38 (2 Oct. 1886), 210; 'Chapter XIII.—The Utopists: Owen, Saint-Simon, and Fourier', 2/42 (30 Oct. 1886), 242–3; 'Chapter XIV.—The Transition from the Utopists to Modern Socialism', 2/56 (5 Feb. 1887), 42–3; 'Chapter XV.—Scientific Socialism—Karl Marx', 3/59 (26 Feb. 1887), 66–7; 'Chapter XVI.—Scientific Socialism—Karl Marx II— Money', 3/61 (12 Mar. 1887), 82; 'Chapter XVII.—Scientific Socialism—Conversion of Capital into Money', 3/63 (26 Mar. 1887), 101; 'Chapter XVIII.—Scientific Socialism—The Production of Surplus Value—That Is, of Rent, Interest, and Profit', 3/68 (30 Apr. 1887), 141; 'Chapter XIX. Scientific Socialism.—Constant and Variable Capital', 3/75 (18 June 1887), 196–7; 'Chapter XX.—Marx's Deduction of the Historical Evolution of Modern Industry', 3/80 (23 July 1887), 234–5; 'Chapter XXI.—Scientific Socialism. Conclusion', 3/82 (6 Aug. 1887), 253; 'Chapter XXII.—Socialism Militant', 4/113 (10 Mar. 1888), 76–7; 'Chapter XXII (cont.).—Socialism Militant', 4/114 (17 Mar. 1888), 82; 'Chapter XXIII.—Socialism Triumphant', 4/121 (5 May 1888), 140–1; 'Chapter XXIII (concluded).—Socialism Triumphant', 4/123 (19 May 1888), 154–5.
Series: 25 instalments on the history and future of Socialism. Revised in 1893 for pbn. as *Socialism: Its Growth and Outcome* (see A-68.01).
Signed: each instalment signed, 'E. Belfort Bax and William Morris.'

D-191: 'Notes on Passing Events' (comment), *Commonweal*, 2/19 (22 May 1886), 57.
Notes: Morris comments on the progress of the Home Rule Bill, the clothing manufacturers' lock out in Chicago, Imperial Federation, and the incompetence of British business managers.

D-192: 'Our Representatives' (editorial), *Commonweal*,

2/20 (29 May 1886), 68.
Notes: comment on the political divisions occasioned by the Home Rule Bill.

D-193: [Unheaded paragraph] (comment), *Commonweal*, 2/20 (29 May 1886), 68.
Notes: on the Teleky expedition to Africa and lock outs of clothing workers in New York.

D-194: 'Notes and Queries. Practical Socialism' (replies), *Commonweal*, 2/20 (29 May 1886), 71.
Notes: Morris responds to practical questions about the working of the future Socialist state.

D-195: 'Branch Reports: Birmingham' (report), *Commonweal*, 2/20 (29 May 1886), 72.
Notes: Morris's account of 2 lectures delivered in Birmingham.

D-196: 'Notes on Passing Events' (lead editorial), *Commonweal*, 2/21 (5 June 1886), 73.
Notes: comment on the progress of the Home Rule Bill in Parliament, and on the current depression of trade.

D-197: 'Instructive Items' (comment), *Commonweal*, 2/21 (5 June 1886), 79.
Notes: Morris finds a useful contradiction between the progress of the shorter hours movement and certain examples of degeneracy and cruelty.

D-198: 'Notes on Passing Events' (lead editorial), *Commonweal*, 2/22 (12 June 1886), 81.
Notes: comment on parliament, unemployment, and the 'right' of working men to sell their labour at their own evaluation of it.

D-199: [Unheaded paragraph] (comment), *Commonweal*, 2/22 (12 June 1886), 83.
Notes: Morris comments on the contradictions of Individualism and Nationalism.

D-200: 'Correspondence' (reply), *Commonweal*, 2/22 (12 June 1886), 86.
Signed: 'eds.' At this time Morris was Editor and E. B. Bax Sub-Editor.
Notes: reply to a correspondent on the inevitable conflict of interest between capital and labour.

D-201: 'Free Speech at Stratford' (report), *Commonweal*, 2/22 (12 June 1886), 87.
Notes: Morris reports on a meeting in Stratford where he, Edward Aveling, and others spoke.

D-202: 'Notes on Passing Events' (comment), *Commonweal*, 2/23 (19 June 1886), 89.
Notes: Morris comments on Gladstone's defeat on Home Rule and the consequent dissolution of Parliament.

D-203: 'Home Rule or Humbug' (article), *Commonweal*, 2/24 (26 June 1886), 100–1.
Notes: though their titles are similar, this article has little in common, other than its subject, with the leaflet *Home Rule and Humbug*, issued in Jan. 1886 (see A-33.01).

D-204: 'Whigs, Democrats, and Socialists' (lecture), *Commonweal*, 2/24, 25 (26 June, 31 July 1886), 97–8, 106–7.
Notes: read at a Conference convened by the Fabian Society at South Place Institute, 11 June 1886.

D-205: 'A Letter from Scotland' (report), *Commonweal*, 2/25 (3 July 1886), 105–6; the letter is dated, 'Glasgow, June 27'.
Notes: Morris's report of the 1st part of his Scottish lecture tour (see also D-207, 208).

D-206: 'Notes on the Elections' (lead editorial), *Commonweal*, 2/26 (10 July 1886), 113.
Notes: the election campaign seen from the Socialist viewpoint, which foresees a coming defeat for the Liberals.

D-207: 'The Sequel of the Scotch Letter' (report), *Commonweal*, 2/26 (10 July 1886), 114.
Notes: Morris continues the report of his lectures in Scotland (see D-205, 208).

D-208: 'Notes' (comment), *Commonweal*, 2/26 (10 July 1886), 116.
Notes: Morris concludes his report of his lectures in Scotland (see D-205, 207).

D-209: 'Review. "Modern Socialism" By Annie Besant', *Commonweal*, 2/26 (10 July 1886), 117.

D-210: 'The Whig-Jingo Victory' (lead editorial), *Commonweal*, 2/27 (17 July 1886), 121.
Notes: on the defeat of the Liberals in the Home Rule election.

D-211: 'An empty pocket is the worst of crimes' (para-

graph), *Commonweal*, 2/27 (17 July 1886), 123.
Notes: on the case of an unemployed youth, wearied by his walk from Fulham to Eastbourne in search of work, who was sent to jail for sleeping in an unused boat.

D-212: 'Review. "Cashell Byron's Profession". By George Bernard Shaw', *Commonweal*, 2/27 (17 July 1886), 126.
Initialled: 'W. M.'

D-213: 'What is to Happen Next?' (lead editorial), *Commonweal*, 2/28 (24 July 1886), 129.
Notes: on the shifts within the Liberal Party that have created the Unionist Movement or Whig-jingoism as Morris calls it, and with that the electoral triumph of reaction.

D-214: 'Free Speech in the Streets' (lead editorial), *Commonweal*, 2/29 (31 July 1886), 137.
Notes: discusses the conflict over street meetings in various places—Stratford, Bell Street, Kilburn—where Socialists have been harried by police. Morris cites evidence of anti-Socialist bias in the courts and police.

D-215: 'Political Notes' (lead editorial), *Commonweal*, 2/30 (7 Aug. 1886), 145.
Series: 1st of 4 lead editorials with this heading.
Notes: on the induction of the new Tory government and its concerns with coercion of the Irish, the gradual loss of the empire, cabinet appointments, and the general decay of civilization.

D-216: [2 paragraphs, the 1st headed 'Workmen and Horses', the 2nd, unheaded] (comment), *Commonweal*, 2/30 (7 Aug. 1886), 147.
Initialled: 'W. M.'
Notes: on the cost of horses to the Paris tramways compared to the cost of workmen (horses are more costly and consequently better treated), and the 2nd responding to an article, 'School in Prison', in *The Daily News*, on rehabilitation.

D-217: 'Mr. Chamberlain's Leader' (lead editorial), *Commonweal*, 2/31 (14 Aug. 1886), 153.
Notes: on the state of politics as the Liberal Party confronts its divisions over Home Rule.

D-218: 'Notes on Passing Events' (comment), *Commonweal*, 2/31 (14 Aug. 1886), 156.
Notes: Morris comments on the 'solemn farce' of the Report of the Commission on the Depression of Trade, and on the practice of Liberal MPs walking out when Chamberlain, or other dissenters from party policy, rise to speak.

D-219: 'The Abolition of Freedom of Speech in the Streets' (lead editorial), *Commonweal*, 2/32 (21 Aug. 1886), 161.
Notes: on the conviction of SL and SDF street speakers for obstruction of the public right of way, which Morris says amounts to banning of all street meetings.

D-220: 'Notes on Passing Events' (editorial), *Commonweal*, 2/32 (21 Aug. 1886), 164.
Notes: Morris's comments on the newspapers' treatment of the Socialist trial for obstruction; on a speech by Lord Salisbury, the new Tory Prime Minister; the disastrous state of the Liberal Party; and on punishments for living without working.

D-221: 'Notes on Passing Events' (lead editorial), *Commonweal*, 2/33 (28 Aug. 1886), 169.
Notes: Morris comments on the biased death sentences passed on the Chicago anarchists, on the equal bias of British courts, on the Tory policy of coercion in Ireland, on gambling on grain futures, and on police interference with religious street meetings as a fig-leaf designed to hide an anti-Socialist bias.

D-222: 'Misanthropy to the Rescue!' (criticism), *Commonweal*, 2/33 (28 Aug. 1886), 172.
Notes: Morris's criticism of Wordsworth Donisthorpe's lecture, delivered at a conference sponsored by the Fabian Society and pbd. in *The Anarchist*, Donisthorpe being Secretary of the Liberty and Property Defence League.

D-223: 'Notes on Passing Events' (lead editorial), *Commonweal*, 2/34 (4 Sept. 1886), 177.
Notes: Morris's comment on speeches by Parnell and Chamberlain and on an article by Annie Besant on 'Why I Am a Socialist', pbd. in *Our Corner*.

D-224: 'Notes on Passing Events' (editorial comment), *Commonweal*, 2/35 (11 Sept. 1886), 185.
Notes: Morris's lead editorial comment on the Bulgarian crisis, parliamentary debate on the Crofter question, and on the unemployed demonstration in Liverpool.

D-225: 'The Paris Trades Union Congress' (reply), *Commonweal*, 2/35 (11 Sept. 1886), 187.

Notes: Morris responds to a trades unionist's account, in the *Pall Mall Gazette*, of the Paris Congress.

D-226: 'Education' (lecture report-summary), *The Architect*, 17 Sept. 1886, pp. 170–1.
Notes: account, with substantial quotation, of a lecture given to the Clerkenwell Branch of the SL on 15 Sept. 1886 (see *Unpublished Lectures*, pp. 257, 307).

D-227: 'An Old Story Retold' (prose tale), *Commonweal*, 2/36 (18 Sept. 1886), 197–8.
Notes: Morris narrates a Hungarian folk tale, later retitled 'A King's Lesson' and pbd. in *A Dream of John Ball and A King's Lesson*, 1888 (see A-45.01). Also pbd. by James Leatham in a separate edn., *A King's Lesson*, Aberdeen: Leatham, 1891 (see A-55.01–.03).

D-228: 'Notes on Passing Events' (lead editorial), *Commonweal*, 2/37 (25 Sept. 1886), 201.
Notes: Morris's comment on Parnell's private-member's Home Rule Bill, on the *Pall Mall*'s greater sympathy with Socialism, which seems to coincide with the editor's (i.e. W. T. Stead's) absences on holiday, and congratulations on the 1st issue of *Freedom*, pbd. by 'Anarchist-Socialists'.

D-229: 'The Reward of "Genius"' (article), *Commonweal*, 2/37 (25 Sept. 1886), 205–6.
Notes: Morris's argument against varying rewards for workers to provide incentives and to avoid the 'dull level of mediocrity'.

D-230: 'The Origins and Subsequent Growth of Ornamental Art' (lecture report-summary), *The Manchester Guardian*, 27 Sept. 1886, p. 6; *The Architect*, 1 Oct. 1886, pp. 197–8; *The American Architect*, 18 Dec. 1886, pp. 288–9.
Notes: for the 1st complete edn., see *Unpublished Lectures*, pp. 136–57.

D-231: [Journal's heading:] 'Fabian Society and Socialist Notes' (speech), *Our Corner*, 8 (1 Oct. 1886), 252–3.
Notes: Morris's speech against involvement by Socialists in Parliamentary elections, in the form of a rider to a resolution of Annie Besant proposing that the Socialists organise themselves into a political party.

D-232: 'Notes on Passing Events' (lead editorial), *Commonweal*, 2/40 (16 Oct. 1886), 225.
Notes: notes on Randolph Churchill's speech at Dartford.

D-233: [Journal's heading:] 'Comrade William Morris on "Socialism: Its Aims and Methods"' (lecture), [Norwich] *Daylight*, 16 Oct. 1886, pp. 2–4; the lecture was delivered on 11 Oct. 1886.
Notes: 1st pbn. of a lecture titled on the MS 'Socialism: The End and the Means'. Substantial sections rptd. in MM, ii. 420–34, as 'The End and the Means'.

D-234: 'Notes on Passing Events' (lead editorial), *Commonweal*, 2/41 (23 Oct. 1886), 233.
Notes: notes on various foreign and domestic news items: Irish politics, Austrian plots, and workplace health and safety.

D-235: 'Notes on Passing Events' (lead editorial), *Commonweal*, 2/42 (30 Oct. 1886), 241–2.
Notes: notes on Irish politics, the Czar and possible European war, the tendency of the economy to disadvantage workers, and The Lord Mayor's Show.

D-236: [Journal's heading:] 'English Literature at the Universities' (to the Editor), *The Pall Mall Gazette: An Evening Newspaper and Review*, 1 Nov. 1886, pp. 1–2; the letter may have had the same date.
Notes: Morris's arguments against formal university study of English literature. The letter arises from a controversy over the appointment of an expert in philology to the Merton Professorship of English Language and Literature (see *The Pall Mall Gazette*, 15 Oct. 1886, p. 11). Rptd., *Letters*, ii. 589–90.

D-237: 'Notes on Passing Events' (lead editorial), *Commonweal*, 2/43 (6 Nov. 1886), 249.
Notes: Morris's lead editorial notes on current news items: Randolph Churchill's speech at Bradford, Russian aggression in Bulgaria, and England's isolationism.

D-238: 'Notes on Passing Events' (lead editorial), *Commonweal*, 2/44 (13 Nov. 1886), 257.
Notes: notes on the Liberal caucus meeting at Leeds (which involved a surrender to the Unionists), Henry George's good showing in the New York election for mayor, and making the Mansion House a 'People's Palace'.

D-239: 'The Moral of Last Lord Mayor's Day' (lead editorial), *Commonweal*, 2/45 (20 Nov. 1886), 265.
Notes: on the Lord Mayor's Parade, the parallel demonstrations against it, and the Socialists' role in the latter.

D-240: 'A Dream of John Ball' (prose romance), here pbd. in 11 instalments: *Commonweal*, 2/44 (13 Nov. 1886), 257–8; (2) 2/45 (20 Nov. 1886), 266–7; (3) 2/46 (27 Nov. 1886), 274–5; (4) 2/47 (4 Dec. 1886), 282–3; (5) 2/48 (11 Dec. 1886), 290–1; (6) 2/49 (18 Dec. 1886), 298–9; (7) 2/50 (25 Dec. 1886), 307; (8) 3/51 (1 Jan. 1887), 3; (9) 3/52 (8 Jan. 1887), 13; (10) 3/53 (15 Jan. 1887), 20–21; and (11) 3/54 (22 Jan. 1887), 28–9.
Series: later pbd. in a book as *A Dream of John Ball and a King's Lesson* (see A-45.01).
Signed: each instalment signed, 'William Morris'.
Notes: as with all larger works pbd. in instalments in a periodical, this citation includes the finding-list information for all the instalments, these issues not being listed here by separate entry

D-241: 'Mr. Jawkins at the Mansion House' (comment), *Commonweal*, 2/45 (20 Nov. 1886), 268–9.
Notes: Morris comments on the speech that Lord Salisbury, as Prime Minister, had given at the Lord Mayor's banquet, 9 Nov. 1886, Morris casting Churchill and Salisbury as the political equivalents of Spenlow and Jawkins from *David Copperfield*.

D-242: 'The Ten Commandments' (reply), *Commonweal*, 2/46 (27 Nov. 1886), 276.
Notes: Morris's answer to a series of articles in *The Pall Mall Gazette*, expressing disquiet as to the future of the Ten Commandments, i.e. orthodox morality, in a Socialist society. Morris shares none of that anxiety, being mindful of how far from present practices the Ten Commandments already are.

D-243: 'Notes on Passing Events' (lead editorial), *Commonweal*, 2/47 (4 Dec. 1886), 281.
Notes: 2 paragraphs by Morris on Mr Labouchere's Manchester speech in support of Home Rule.

D-244: 'Notes on Passing Events' (editorial), *Commonweal*, 2/48 (11 Dec. 1886), 289.
Notes: 3 paragraphs by Morris on the limitations of John Bright's political ideology as seen in a letter by Bright on 'depressed trade and high wages'.

D-245: [Corrections to a published report of Morris's lecture, 'Early England'] (to the Editor), *The Pall Mall Gazette*, 15 Dec. 1886, p. 2.
Notes: The lecture was the 1st in a series of 3 on 'England As It Was, As It Is, and As It May Be'.

D-246: 'Notes on Passing Events' (editorial), *Commonweal*, 2/49 (18 Dec. 1886), 297.
Notes: Morris's comment on the changes in the Liberal Party over the Home Rule question.

D-247: 'Is Trade Recovering?' (comment), *Commonweal*, 2/49 (18 Dec. 1886), 300.
Notes: Morris defines the proper Socialist response to any real or fancied 'good times' coming, i.e. they are merely the 'boom' that precedes the 'bust'.

D-248: '"The Law" in Ireland' (lead editorial), *Commonweal*, 2/50 (25 Dec. 1886), 305.
Notes: on the prosecution of Mr Dillon, an Irish politician, for promulgating the 'Plan of Campaign'.

D-249: 'Political Notes' (lead editorial), *Commonweal*, 3/51 (1 Jan. 1887), 1.
Notes: comment on the meaning and likely result of Lord Randolph Churchill's resignation from the Liberal shadow ministry and on the possibility of a European war.

D-250: 'Editorial', *Commonweal*, 3/51 (1 Jan. 1887), 4.
Signed: 'William Morris. | H. Halliday Sparling.'
Notes: on the beginning of *Commonweal*'s 3rd year.

D-251: 'The Battle of Trafalgar Square—Classes v. Masses' (comment), *Commonweal*, 3/51 (1 Jan. 1887), 5.
Initialled: 'W. M.'
Notes: 2 paragraphs, 1st by J. L. Mahon and 2nd by Morris, on attempts by bankers and tradesmen to close Trafalgar Square to public meetings and demonstrations.

D-252: 'Words of Forecast for 1887' (lead editorial), *Commonweal*, 3/52 (8 Jan. 1887), 9.
Signed: 'E. Belfort Bax. | William Morris.'
Notes: the writers predict European war.

D-253: [Unheaded paragraph], *Commonweal*, 3/52 (8 Jan. 1887), 11.
Initialled: 'W. M.'
Notes: on *The Pall Mall Gazette*'s acceptance of Madame de Novikoff as a source of reliable testimony.

D-254: 'Notes on News' (comment), *Commonweal*, 3/53 (15 Jan. 1887), 17.
Series: 1st of 125 editorial notes with this title.
Initialled: 'W. M.'

Notes: 2 paragraphs of editorial comment on 2 characteristics of middle-class attitudes towards poverty: the tendency to blame the poor for their poverty and to treat begging as a criminal offence, even when it is begging for the survival of their children.

D-255: 'The Political Crisis' (comment), *Commonweal*, 3/53 (15 Jan. 1887), 20.
Notes: on the political compromises over Home Rule.

D-256: 'Notes on Passing Events' (lead editorial), *Commonweal*, 3/54 (22 Jan. 1887), 25.
Notes: on Bismarck's military build-up and its consequences, and on the internal politics of the Liberal Party.

D-257: [on the sentencing of the Socialists of Norwich] (to the Editor), *The Daily News*, 24 Jan. 1887, 33; letter dated 'January 22'.

D-258: 'Notes on Passing Events' (editorial), *Commonweal*, 3/55 (29 Jan. 1887), 33.
Notes: on Justice Grantham's sentences on 2 Norwich Socialists, on Tory moves towards coercion in Ireland, the buying of MP's votes, and the Commission on the Depression of Trade.

D-259: 'The Norwich Socialists. A Town in Turmoil.— Shameful Sentences on Comrades Henderson and Mowbray' (supplementary comment), *Commonweal*, 3/55 (29 Jan. 1887), 37.
Initialled: 'W. M.'
Notes: Morris adds 3 supplementary paragraphs, following the verdict, to an article by J. L. Mahon.

D-260: 'Notes on News' (lead editorial), *Commonweal*, 3/56 (5 Feb. 1887), 41.
Notes: Morris's comment on Chamberlain's 'appeal for the gratitude', of voters, 'for past services', a sad comment on the degradation of 'honour' since the Middle Ages.

D-261: 'The Little Vagabond' (head note), *Commonweal*, 3/56 (5 Feb. 1887), 43.
Initialled: 'W. M.'
Notes: Morris contributes a prefatory note to Blake's poem of this title.

D-262: [On the proper objectives of art education] (letter to A. M. Pearson), *The Architect*, 18 Feb. 1887, pp. 100–2; *The Manchester Guardian*, 11 Feb. 1887, p. 8.

According to Kelvin, the letter was probably addressed between 2 and 5 Feb. Kelvin's notes provide further detail on the controversy (*Letters*, ii. 610).
Notes: a letter, intended for pbn., addressed to Arthur M. Pearson, an art student at the Manchester Art School who solicited comments from various English artists regarding J. H. E. Partington's lecture comparing Belgian art education with the South Kensington System and the Manchester School of Art in England. Pearson submitted this letter (and 3 by other authorities) for publication to both the journals in which it appeared, doing so with Morris's permission.

D-263: 'Notes on News' (lead editorial), *Commonweal*, 3/57 (12 Feb. 1887), 49.
Notes: on British policy in Egypt, unsafe ships, and the Foote-Besant debate, then in progress.

D-264: 'Notes on News' (lead editorial), *Commonweal*, 3/58 (19 Feb. 1887), 57.
Notes: comment on a media-invented conflict between a butcher and the Socialists, on *The Pall Mall's* view of the depression of trade, on the deaths by asphyxiation of 2 children of a family of 7 all asleep in the same bed in an 8 x 9 ft. room, and on Bradlaugh's untenable distinction between crofters and 'working-men'.

D-265: 'Facing the Worst of It' (comment), *Commonweal*, 3/58 (19 Feb. 1887), 60–1.
Notes: on the progress of the historical dialectic toward Socialism.

D-266: [Journal's heading:] 'Against (ii)' (the 2nd in a series of solicited responses on the proposed Ambleside railway in the Lake District), *The Pall Mall Gazette*, 22 Feb. 1887, p. 2.
Notes: Morris's comment against the railway is, as he says, 'the Socialist view' of the proposal.

D-267: 'Notes on News' (editorial), *Commonweal*, 3/59 (26 Feb. 1887), 65.
Notes: on Parliament's mishandling of Irish matters, the release of Indian prisoners on the occasion of the Queen's Jubilee, and on the need to prevent the proposed Ambleside railway.

D-268: 'Fighting for Peace' (article), *Commonweal*, 3/59 (26 Feb. 1887), 68.
Notes: criticising *The Cotton Factory Times'* explanation of recent riots in Lanarkshire, for not understanding

the forces behind the riots, i.e. starvation wages, and the only true remedy for that: labour solidarity to end the capitalist system of unequal competition.

D-269: '**Notes on News**' (editorial paragraph), *Commonweal*, 3/60 (5 Mar. 1887), 73.
Notes: on the necessity of interest in the capitalist system.

D-270: '**Political Notes**' (comment), *Commonweal*, 3/61 (12 Mar. 1887), 81.
Notes: on the parliamentary lead-up to the Coercion Bill.

D-271: '**Notes on News**' (editorial), *Commonweal*, 3/61 (12 Mar. 1887), 84.
Notes: Morris criticizes *Punch*'s cartoon use of Dürer's 'The Knight and Death' as based on the misperception both of Dürer's meaning and of Bismarck's 'victory' over Socialism.

D-272: [Journal's heading:] '**Correspondence. The Ambleside Railway Bill**' (reply), *Commonweal*, 3/61 (12 Mar. 1887), 85.
Signed: 'Ed.'
Notes: Morris's response to a correspondent who argues that the proposed railway would be a useful convenience to workers on holiday. Morris doubts that the limitation of the railway to Ambleside will hold, and sees little use in a convenience which destroys the natural beauty that is, ostensibly, the object of the trip.

D-273: '**Political Notes**' (lead editorial notes), *Commonweal*, 3/62 (19 Mar. 1887), 89.
Notes: on the Tory government's approach to coercion in Ireland and the imminent reunification of the Liberals in opposition to that.

D-274: '**Why We Celebrate the Commune of Paris**' (article), *Commonweal*, 3/62 (19 Mar. 1887), 89–90.
Notes: for the 16th anniversary of the Commune, asserting the Socialist aim of redeeming the Commune from the 'bourgeois legend of history'.

D-275: [An editorial note appended to an article titled '**How Chains are Forged at Cradley Heath**'] (quoted from *The St. James's Gazette*), *Commonweal*, 3/62 (19 Mar. 1887), 91.
Signed: 'Eds.'
Notes: decries the only remedies proposed for unemployed chain-makers: emigration and charity.

D-276: '**Notes on News**' (editorial), *Commonweal*, 3/63 (26 Mar. 1887), 97.
Notes: comment on a recent speech by Gladstone, and its political expediency.

D-277: '**Notes on News**' (lead editorial), *Commonweal*, 3/64 (2 Apr. 1887), 105.
Notes: analysis of the debate in Parliament over the Coercion Bill.

D-278: '**Law and Order in Ireland**' (lead editorial), *Commonweal*, 3/65 (9 Apr. 1887), 113.
Notes: analysis of the political significance of the Coercion Bill.

D-279: '**The Revival of Trade (?)**' (article), *Commonweal*, 3/65 (9 Apr. 1887), 115.
Notes: Morris quotes from a series of newspapers on the 'revival of trade', the quotations selected to show that trade is not reviving. Note that the question mark is part of the title.

D-280: [Unheaded paragraph] (comment), *Commonweal*, 3/65 (9 Apr. 1887), 117.
Notes: on British brutality against rioting villagers in Egypt.

D-281: [Journal's heading:] '**The Socialists and the Miners. The Great Demonstration at Horton. Speeches by Messrs. Morris and Hyndman**', *The Newcastle Chronicle*, 12 Apr. 1887, p. 4; delivery was on 11 Apr..
Notes: Morris wrote in his diary, 'I note that my speech as given in the Chronicle is verbatim almost . . .' (see A-138.02, *William Morris's Socialist Diary*, Florence Boos ed., 53; hereafter referred to as *Socialist Diary*).

D-282: '**Notes on News**' (lead editorial), *Commonweal*, 3/67 (23 Apr. 1887), 129.
Notes: on the resistance to coercion and the positions of the Liberals and Tories.

D-283: '**Notes on News**' (lead editorial), 3/68 (30 Apr. 1887), 137.
Notes: attacks *The Times* for publishing a letter, supposedly written by Parnell, on the Phoenix Park murders.

D-284: '**Notes on News**' (lead editorial), *Commonweal*, 3/69 (7 May 1887), 145.
Notes: on the legal system's prejudice against Socialism in the streets.

D-285: 'Notes on News' (lead editorial), *Commonweal*, 3/70 (14 May 1887), 153.
Notes: on Tory politics, a Tory preacher at the Chapel Royal, and a new Honours school of English at the ancient universities.

D-286: 'Coercion for London' (article), *Commonweal*, 3/70 (14 May 1887), 153–4.
Notes: on the arbitrary exercise of judicial power over innocent people arrested in a police-incited riot at Hyde Park Gate.

D-287: 'The Reward of Labour. A Dialogue' (a one-act comedy), *Commonweal*, pbd. here in 2 parts: 3/71, 72 (21, 28 May 1887), 165, 170–1.
Notes: in the form of a conversation concerning contemporary politics and economics. See also A-61.01.

D-288: 'Notes on News' (editorial notes), *Commonweal*, 3/72 (28 May 1887), 172.
Notes: on the uselessness of Parliament, as demonstrated by the debate and compromises on the Coercion Bill; and on the employment of women in men's jobs—the 'pit brow women' for example—as a capitalist's method of driving wages down, with a warning to feminist seekers after 'equal rights', i.e. the right to compete with men for employment, that 'as long as men are slaves, women can be no better'.

D-289: 'How We Live and How We Might Live' (lecture), *Commonweal*, pbd. in 5 parts: 3/73, 74, 75, 76, and 77 (4, 11, 18, 25 June, and 2 July 1887), 177–8, 186–7, 194–5, 202–3, and 210–211; the 1st verified delivery of this lecture was on 11 Jan. 1885 (see *Unpublished Lectures*, pp. 245, 301–2).
Notes: Morris's footnote: 'This paper has been delivered as a lecture on several occasions, and I have been often asked to reprint it: hence its appearance in "Commonweal"' (p. 177).

D-290: 'Notes on News' (editorial notes), *Commonweal*, 3/74 (11 June 1887), 188.
Notes: on the politics of coercion and the shortcomings of the co-operative system as an alternative to the existing system.

D-291: [Unheaded Paragraph on British Railways in India], *Commonweal*, 3/74 (11 June 1887), 191.
Notes: Morris quotes from an Indian newspaper, the *Bangabasi*, against the proposal that India borrow money for railways from England. Morris agrees, not because the English people only will profit, but because only English capitalists will profit.

D-292: 'Notes on News' (editorial notes), *Commonweal*, 3/75 (18 June 1887), 193.
Notes: on the conflict between William O'Brien and Father McGlynn as the crucial issue of Irish nationalist politics: genuine revolution or capitalist compromises, and on the destruction of the people's rights along with the Westminster Abbey, about to be utterly restored.

D-293: 'Notes', *Commonweal*, 3/75 (18 June 1887), 196.
Notes: Morris corrects the editorial interpretations, printed in *Justice*, of resolutions adopted at the SL 3rd Annual Conference on 29 May, denying any 'anarchist' turn in the League.

D-294: 'Common-sense Socialism. By H. Kempner. A Review', *Commonweal*, 3/75 (18 June 1887), 197.
Notes: Morris approves of Kempner's analysis of the failures of the present system, but not of the proposed remedy: limiting the hours of work in factories.

D-295: [2 paragraphs in the regular 'Labour Struggle' column], *Commonweal*, 3/75 (18 June 1887), 198–9.
Initialled: 'W. M.'
Notes: on the failure of the 'universal' strike of Belgian coal miners.

D-296: 'An Old Superstition—A New Disgrace' (comment), *Commonweal*, 3/76 (25 June 1887), 204.
Notes: Queen Victoria's Golden Jubilee, seen from Morris's Socialist viewpoint.

D-297: 'North of England Socialist Federation' (postscript), *Commonweal*, 3/76 (25 June 1887), 205.
Notes: Morris appends a paragraph of anti-parliamentary advice to the *Commonweal* rpt. of the 'Principles' and 'Programme' of a newly-formed Socialist Federation.

D-298: 'Notes', *Commonweal*, 3/77 (2 July 1887), 212.
Notes: Morris comments on the unlikely prospect of Liberals reuniting, on the Jubilee, and on the failure of the legislation against employment of pit-brow women.

D-299: 'Notes on News' (editorial), *Commonweal*, 3/78 (9 July 1887), 217.
Notes: on the passage of the Coercion Bill, bias in the

justice system's treatment of unionist bouncers at the Kensington Town Hall, on a murder of a Malay by the crew of an English ship, Bradlaugh's attempt at land management, and on the disappearance of the 'revival of trade'.

D-300: 'Notes on News' (editorial), *Commonweal*, 3/79 (16 July 1887), 228.
Notes: on the lessons of the Coercion Bill, passed at 3rd reading: force is the cement of contemporary society, used mainly in defence of property.

D-301: [Untitled note appended to LaFargue's 'The Morrow of the Revolution'], *Commonweal*, 3/79 (16 July 1887), 227.
Notes: Morris objects to LaFargue's description of E. Belfort Bax's view of Socialism, and to the assumption that such is the common view of English Socialists.

D-302: 'Notes on News' (editorial), *Commonweal*, 3/80 (23 July 1887), 236.
Notes: comment on various news items: the Tory Land Bill, the emergence of a new 'National', i.e. unionist, party, and the success of Williams' appeal against a jail sentence for obstruction.

D-303: 'The Boy-Farms at Fault' (dialogue), *Commonweal*, 3/81 (30 July 1887), 241.
Notes: conversation between a father and his son, disclosing the futility both of school and of the adult 'work' of business management.

D-304: 'Notes' (lead editorial), *Commonweal*, 3/82 (6 Aug. 1887), 249.
Notes: on Walter Besant's effort to collect the facts about working women and the probable reformist outcome of that, which will not cure the evils, since those arise from the capitalist system: that will yield only to a revolution. And a note on the destruction of St Alban's Abbey through its 'restoration' by Lord Grimsthorpe.

D-305: 'Bourgeois Versus Socialist' (analysis), *Commonweal*, 3/82 (6 Aug. 1887), 252.
Notes: on the Bradlaugh v. Bax debate, and 2 others preceding it, all pitting Capitalist and Socialist spokesmen against each other. 2 difficulties beset such debates: the Capitalist cannot be brought to say what his position is, and he refuses to think seriously about Socialism, it being 'impractical' in his eyes.

D-306: 'Notes', *Commonweal*, 3/83 (13 Aug. 1887), 257.
Notes: on the quarrel between workers and union leaders over the failed strike at Blyth Links and on H. G. Wells' article on advancing technology in *Contemporary Review*.

D-307: 'Notes on News' (editorial), *Commonweal*, 3/84 (20 Aug. 1887), 265–6.
Notes: notes on the Allotment Bill and Sir William Harcourt's famous saying, on its passage, 'it seems we are all Socialists now'; on Bradlaugh's position on the effects of war on wage earners, and on *The Daily News*' assertions regarding the mere forms of protest.

D-308: 'Feudal England' (lecture), *Commonweal*, pbd. in 4 parts: 3/84, 85, 86, and 87 (20, 27 Aug., 3, 10 Sept. 1887), 266–7, 274, 282, 290–1; lecture first delivered on 13 Feb. 1887 (see *Unpublished Lectures*, pp. 308–9).
Series: this is the 2nd lecture in a trilogy titled 'England, As It Was, As It Is, and As It May Be', the others being 'Early England' and 'Art & Industry in the 14th Century'.
Notes: titled 'Mediaeval England' on the MS, rptd. in *Signs of Change*.

D-309: 'Notes on News' (lead editorial), *Commonweal*, 3/85 (27 Aug. 1887), 271.
Notes: on the police and the justice system, beginning with Mr Pole's sentence and going on to the cases of Mlle Drouin, Mr Justice Field and a 'luckless Welsh girl', and the trial of Lipski. Morris ends with the 'strange thing' of Lord Wemyss conferring honours on Mr Bradlaugh.

D-310: 'A Note on Passing Politics' (analysis), *Commonweal*, 3/85 (27 Aug. 1887), 276.
Notes: on the significance of the Liberal bye-election at Norwich.

D-311: 'Is Lipski's Confession Genuine?' (analysis), *Commonweal*, 3/85 (27 Aug. 1887), 276.
Notes: an argument that in a state where capital punishment is legal, false confessions are often extorted. The system produces the confession.

D-312:* [Morris chairs the 10th Annual Meeting of the SPAB] (2 speeches), *Society for the Protection of Ancient Buildings. 10th Annual Meeting: Report of the Committee thereat read. June 8th, 1887* (Aug. (?) 1887), 23–5, 56–7.
Notes: a verbatim account of Morris's speeches in support of the need for action to gather funds for the vari-

ous activities of the Society, and especially to repair the Church of St John the Baptist, Inglesham, Wilts, near Lechlade. See *Unpublished Lectures*, p. 264.

D-313: 'Notes on News' (lead editorial), *Commonweal*, 3/86 (3 Sept. 1887), 281.
Notes: on 'moderation' as a political virtue or a vice.

D-314: 'Notes on News' (lead editorial), *Commonweal*, 3/87 (10 Sept. 1887), 289.
Notes: on John Bright's idea of peace as the equivalent of bourgeois control, and on Gladstone's Jubilee speech as a repetition of the palliatives that do not approach the central issue of class war.

D-315: 'Artist and Artisan. As an Artist Sees It' (reply), *Commonweal*, 3/87 (10 Sept. 1887), 291.
Notes: Morris replies to a letter by Jim Allman headed 'Artist and Artisan. As a Workman Sees It', Morris insisting that the distinction between artist and artisan is a false one; rptd. in MM, ii. 492–6.

D-316: 'Notes on News' (lead editorial), *Commonweal*, 3/88 (17 Sept. 1887), 297.
Notes: on the killings at Mitchelstown, and on *The Daily News* admonishing unions for forming a separate political party.

D-317: 'Notes on News' (editorial), *Commonweal*, 3/89 (24 Sept. 1887), 305.
Notes: on the Queen's Speech, Balfour on Mitchelstown, the progress of coercion, the British treatment of political prisoners, and the failure of the appeal of the Chicago anarchists.

D-318: 'A Plea for the American Anarchists', *The Pall Mall Gazette*, 28 Sept. 1887, p. 5.

D-319: 'Notes' (lead editorial), *Commonweal*, 3/91 (8 Oct. 1887), 321.
Notes: on the political usefulness of the Irish Question for the major parties, a current example of the workings of coercion, and the aggregation of capital, an issue arising from the Bax-Bradlaugh debate.

D-320: 'Free Speech in America' (analysis), *Commonweal*, 3/91 (8 Oct. 1887), 324.
Notes: Morris undertakes to correct and explain the truths untold or falsified in the press about the Chicago anarchists.

D-321: 'Notes', *Commonweal*, 3/92 (15 Oct. 1887), 329.
Notes: on the Anglican Church Congress, Liberal fear of Socialism among the miners, on the failure of the Tory attempt to unseat the Lord Mayor, Mr Sullivan, and on reported conflict between New York Socialists and the followers of Henry George.

D-322: [on the Police attack on demonstrators at South Place Institute] (to the Editor), *The Daily News*, 18 Oct. 1887, p. 7; the letter is dated 'October 17'.

D-323: 'Notes on News' (lead editorial), *Commonweal*, 3/93 (22 Oct. 1887), 337.
Notes: on police and media attacks on demonstrations by the London unemployed and on the bias of American opinion against the Chicago anarchists.

D-324: 'Notes on News' (editorial), *Commonweal*, 3/94 (29 Oct. 1887), 345.
Notes: on police brutality in the confrontation with unemployed demonstrators, and on recent developments in Ireland.

D-325: 'The Unemployed' (official statement of policy), *Commonweal*, 3/94 (29 Oct. 1887), 348–9.
Signed: 'On behalf of the Council of the Socialist League, Henry A. Barker, Secretary.' But the Houghton Library, Harvard University, has a copy (MH* EC 85.M 8348 B898p.) of the pamphlet *Report of the Fourth Annual Conference of the Socialist League Held at 13 Farringdon Road, London, E.C., on Whitsunday, May 20, 1888*. In this annual report it is recorded that during the year past 'The Unemployed Question specially occupied the attention of the Executive, and in connection therewith a manifesto was written on its behalf by Wm. Morris, setting forth the attitude of the League with regard to it' (p. 4).
Notes: a policy statement aligning the SL with unemployed demonstrators protesting in the streets against their situation as winter approached.

D-326: 'Practical Politics at Nottingham' (report), *Commonweal*, 3/94 (29 Oct. 1887), 349.
Notes: on the Liberal Party Conference at Nottingham.

D-327: 'Notes on News' (editorial), *Commonweal*, 3/95 (5 Nov. 1887), 353.
Notes: on the imprisonment of W. S. Blunt for speaking on home rule in Ireland, and on more local matters.

D-328: 'Honesty is the Best Policy; or, The Inconvenience of Stealing' (dialogue), *Commonweal*, pbd. in 2 parts: 3/95, 96 (5, 12 Nov. 1887), 356–7, 364–5.
Notes: a 2-part, 2-scene dramatic dialogue between 2 neighbours, Mr James Brown, businessman, and Mr Olaf Evans, an artist and writer, talking about the theft of some pears from Mr Brown's tree.

D-329: [Journal's heading:] 'The Chicago Anarchists. English Efforts for Their Reprieve' (to the Editor), *The Pall Mall Gazette*, 7 Nov. 1887, p. 12.
Notes: Morris disputes an editorial paragraph defending the verdict pbd. in *The New York Tribune* and rptd. in *The Pall Mall Gazette*.

D-330: [On free speech and the right of public meeting in Trafalgar Square] (to the Editor), *The Pall Mall Gazette*, 11 Nov. 1887, p. 6; the letter is dated 'November 11'.
Notes: Morris protests against the prohibition of meetings in the Square by Sir Charles Warren, Metropolitan Commissioner of Police.

D-331: 'Notes on News' (editorial), *Commonweal*, 3/96 (12 Nov. 1887), 361.
Notes: on the Chicago anarchists and the struggle for 'free speech' in the form of demonstrations.

D-332: [On the name and intentions of the Law and Liberty League] (to the Editor), *The Pall Mall Gazette*, 18 Nov. 1887, p. 5; the letter is dated 'November 17'.
Notes: Morris subscribes to *The Link*, organ of the League, and agrees with its intentions.

D-333: 'London in a State of Siege' (article), *Commonweal*, 3/97 (19 Nov. 1887), 369–70.
Notes: on the police suppression of demonstrations in Trafalgar Square on 'Bloody Sunday'.

D-334: [Unheaded paragraph] (comment), *Commonweal*, 3/97 (19 Nov. 1887), 375.
Notes: on Gladstone's stand on the right to demonstrate, as revealed in his reply to a Bermondsey radical.

D-335: [the inaugural meeting of the Law and Liberty League] (to the Editor), *The Pall Mall Gazette*, 21 Nov. 1887, p. 3; the letter has the same date.
Notes: Morris compliments the paper on its successful meeting at the Memorial Hall on 18 Nov. in support of those arrested on 'Bloody Sunday'.

D-336: 'Notes on News' (lead editorial), *Commonweal*, 3/98 (26 Nov. 1887), 377.
Notes: on the aftermath of 'Bloody Sunday', including the swearing-in of 'Specials', Sir Frederick Leighton among them.

D-337: 'Insurance Against Magistrates' (editorial), *Commonweal*, 3/98 (26 Nov. 1887), 377.
Notes: on the work of the Law and Liberty League.

D-338: 'The Liberal Party Digging its Own Grave' (article), *Commonweal*, 3/98 (26 Nov. 1887), 380.
Notes: on the political miscalculation of the Gladstonian Liberals in not supporting the radicals and Socialists over Trafalgar Square.

D-339: [Correction of a report of the 'London Sunday Forum'] (to the Editor), *The Pall Mall Gazette*, 1 Dec. 1887, p. 5; letter dated 'November 29'.
Notes: on dates of performance of *The Tables Turned*.

D-340: 'Notes on News' (lead editorial), *Commonweal*, 3/99 (3 Dec. 1887), 385.
Notes: on the lessons learned from the experience of 'Bloody Sunday' and on J. A. Froude's speech to the Liberty and Property Defence League.

D-341: 'Notes on News' (lead editorial), *Commonweal*, 3/100 (10 Dec. 1887), 393.
Notes: on matters arising from 'Bloody Sunday'.

D-342: 'Notes on News' (editorial), *Commonweal*, 3/101 (17 Dec. 1887), 401.
Notes: on speeches by various politicians; a 12-month sentence to Coleman, a demonstrator; and on the response to Alfred Linnell's death from injuries sustained in Trafalgar Square on 20 Nov.

D-343: 'The Conscience of the Upper Classes' (editorial), *Commonweal*, 3/101 (17 Dec. 1887), 404.
Notes: on the response of the middle class to the occurrences of 'Bloody Sunday', with particular attention to the speech of Cardinal Manning at Memorial Hall, Farringdon Street, on 5 Dec.

D-344: 'Notes on News' (editorial), *Commonweal*, 3/102 (24 Dec. 1887), 409.
Notes: on an anarchist alarm in New York; Bismarck's army and anti-socialist legislation; on medals for the police; Justice Stephens' sentence of Harrison, a demonstrator; his interpretation of the law covering such

cases; and the newspaper accounts of Linnell's funeral.

D-345: **'Emigration and Colonisation'** (lead editorial), *Commonweal*, 3/103 (31 Dec. 1887), 417–18.
Notes: occasioned by a speech by Lord Salisbury at Derby.

D-346: [Journal's heading:] **'Correspondence. Empirical Socialism'** (editorial notes in reply), *Commonweal*, 3/103 (31 Dec. 1887), 421.
Signed: 'Ed.'
Notes: a note in opposition to a letter by Reginald A. Beckett on the extinction under Socialism of religion and nationalism, and on the adoption of 'centralisation of production and distribution'.

D-347: **'Notes on News'** (editorial), *Commonweal*, 4/104 (7 Jan. 1888), 1.
Notes: on 'Gladstone-worship' among the Liberals, Gladstone's speech at Dover, the Tory government's reduction of judicial rents in Ireland, and the death of John Frost in Pentonville Prison.

D-348: **'Police Spies Exposed'** (article), *Commonweal*, 4/104 (7 Jan. 1888), 1–2.
Signed: 'Editors' (i.e. Morris and H. H. Sparling).
Notes: this article was the occasion for a lawsuit for libel: Morris to John Glasse, 10 Feb. 1888, '. . . I am to have an action for libel brought against me for that article in the C. by one [Charles Theodore] Reuss who is mentioned there and who was once a member of the S.L. I have no doubt myself of my facts, but proving them in a law Court is a different thing and it will in any case bleed me seriously: hence my wish to spend as little as I can help on my northern tour . . . (*Letters*, ii. 741). According to E. P. Thompson, '£1,000 damages had been mulcted from him in a libel action early in 1888' (Thompson, 611). There is little about the action on the public record since Morris apparently settled out of court. Reuss initiated the action because the article, signed as above and following an account in a Zurich journal, accused him of having been a police spy in England in the pay of the German Police Bureau.

D-349: **'What 1887 Has Done'** (editorial), *Commonweal*, 4/10 4 (7 Jan. 1888), 4–5.
Notes: review of the past year's positive and negative developments in the UK and world politics.

D-350: **'Notes on News'** (editorial), *Commonweal*, 4/105 (14 Jan. 1888), 9–10.
Notes: 3 paragraphs on W. S. Blunt's lost appeal and on the attempt to set aside part of Ravenscourt Park for public meetings.

D-351: **'Radicals Look Around You'** (editorial), *Commonweal*, 4/105 (14 Jan. 1888), 12–13.
Notes: on the lessons Radicals should learn from the victory of the Tories in the Winchester bye-election.

D-352: **'Notes on News'** (editorial), *Commonweal*, 4/106 (21 Jan. 1888), 17.
Notes: on the 'revival of trade', on a speech by J. A. Froude, on Matthew Arnold forced to join the philistines, and a Liverpool speech by Lord Salisbury.

D-353: **'Notes on News'** (editorial), *Commonweal*, 4/107 (28 Jan. 1888), 25.
Notes: on the guilty verdict on Cunningham-Graham and John Burns for their part in the Trafalgar Square demonstration of 13 Nov.

D-354: **[Unheaded Paragraph]**, *Commonweal*, 4/107 (28 Jan. 1888), 29.
Initialled: 'W. M.'
Notes: Morris's response to a speech of Lord Henry Bruce, MP, decrying the 'immigration of Socialists and paupers into England'.

D-355: **'Notes on News'** (editorial), *Commonweal*, 4/109 (11 Feb. 1888), 41.
Initialled: 'W. M.'
Notes: on Lord Salisbury's reception of 2 groups of petitioners, Irish landlords and the London unemployed; on Bismarck's attempt to suppress Socialism; and on an article in *The Nineteenth Century* on 'How to Live on £700 a Year'.

D-356: **'Notes on News'** (editorial), *Commonweal*, 4/110 (18 Feb. 1888), 49.
Initialled: 'W. M.'
Notes: on the slim chance for useful decisions on Home Rule or Trafalgar Square in the new session of Parliament, on Mr Balfour allowing Mr Shaw-Lefevre to hold a meeting which Socialists are prohibited from holding, on the failure of Bismarck's anti-Socialist legislation to gain approval, and on the Bermondsey Board of Guardians making a profit on a local work-for-the-dole scheme, and on the judgment of Arthur Gough for 'assaulting' the police.

D-357: 'On Some "Practical" Socialists' (editorial), *Commonweal*, 4/110 (18 Feb. 1888), 52–3.
Notes: on the need to avoid an over-emphasis on the economic aspects of Socialism.

D-358: 'Notes on News' (editorial), *Commonweal*, 4/111 (25 Feb. 1888), 57.
Initialled: 'W. M.'
Notes: on Commissioner Kerr's sentencing of SL member Arthur Gough, shameful manoeuvres regarding the release of John Burns and Cunningham-Graham, on William O'Brien's speech, the liberal victory in the Southwark bye-election, and the reception of the released Socialists.

D-359: [Journal's heading] 'Correspondence. "Practical" Socialists' (untitled paragraph), *Commonweal*, 4/111 (25 Feb. 1888), 61.
Initialled: 'W. M.'
Notes: a note appended to T. Binning's reply to Morris's 'On some "Practical" Socialists'—for which see entry D-357.

D-360: 'Notes on News' (editorial), *Commonweal*, 4/112 (3 Mar. 1888), 65.
Initialled: 'W. M.'
Notes: on recent debates in Parliament over the crofters, the Irish question, and the lessons of the British penal system.

D-361: 'A Triple Alliance' (editorial), *Commonweal*, 4/112 (3 Mar. 1888), 68.
Notes: on the Liberal Party's lack of response to the violence of 'Bloody Sunday', and the alliance of Radicals, Socialists, and Irish Home Rulers that must bring about change in Liberal policy.

D-362: 'Notes on News' (editorial), *Commonweal*, 4/113 (10 Mar. 1888), 73.
Initialled: 'W. M.'
Notes: on the system of debate and vote in the House, with a comparison of the different attitudes of London and Welsh courts on similar matters.

D-363: 'Dead At Last' (comment), *Commonweal*, 4/114 (17 Mar. 1888), 81.
Initialled: 'W. M.'
Notes: Morris's comment on the death of the German Kaiser, on Mr Snelling's arrest for speaking in Ireland, and on the moves by Labouchere in the House of Commons to end the hereditary seats in the House of Lords.

D-364: 'Notes on News' (editorial comment), *Commonweal*, 4/115 (24 Mar. 1888), 89.
Initialled: 'W. M.'
Notes: editorial comment on the likely behaviour of the new Kaiser Frederick.

D-365: 'A Speech from the Dock' (comment), *Commonweal*, 4/115 (24 Mar. 1888), 93.
Notes: on John Burns' courtroom speech, just printed.

D-366: [Unheaded letter] (to the Editor), *The Scotsman*, 28 Mar. 1888, p. 9; the letter is dated 'March 26'.
Notes: corrects a report that Morris had no audience for a lecture at West Calder.

D-367: 'Notes on News' (editorial notes), *Commonweal*, 4/117 (7 Apr. 1888), 105.
Initialled: 'W. M.'
Notes: on the Local Government Bill and further consequences for the Liberal Party for not taking up the Trafalgar Square issue.

D-368: 'Socialism Militant in Scotland' (report), *Commonweal*, 4/117 (7 Apr. 1888), 106–7.
Notes: Morris's account of his just-completed lecture tour in Scotland.

D-369: 'Notes on News' (lead editorial), *Commonweal*, 4/118 (14 Apr. 1888), 113.
Initialled: 'W. M.'
Notes: notes on continuing controversy about the police interpretation and inconsistent application of the law prohibiting 'obstruction' of the public thoroughfare, the policies of a vestryman, economic analysis as done by *The Daily News*, with a Whiggish twist.

D-370: 'Notes on News' (editorial), *Commonweal*, 4/119 (21 Apr. 1888), 121.
Initialled: 'W. M.'
Notes: on the testimony of Arnold White before the Lords enquiry into 'sweating' as practiced in the East End, Mr Saunder's civil action against the police for abridging free speech in the streets, and *The Daily News* report on the Nan slaves of Siam.

D-371: [Untitled verses], *Commonweal*, 4/119 (21 Apr. 1888), 125.
Notes: later titled 'Drawing Near the Light' and rptd. in

Poems by the Way (see A-59.01).

D-372: 'The Revival of Architecture' (article), *Fortnightly Review*, 43/257 n.s. (1 May 1888), 665–74.
Notes: The 1st part of a 2-part series pbd. in the same journal, the 2nd being 'The Revival of Handicraft' (see D-414). Later rptd. in *Architecture, Industry, and Wealth* (see C-18.01).

D-373: 'Notes on News' (editorial), *Commonweal*, 4/120 (28 Apr. 1888), 129.
Initialled: 'W. M.'
Notes: on the expulsion of *Der Sozial Demokrat* from Zurich, Balfour's coercion of Ireland, the Liberal Party and Trafalgar Square, and 2 civil cases that display the contradictions in the laws of private property.

D-374: 'Notes on News' (editorial), *Commonweal*, 4/121 (5 May 1888), 137.
Initialled: 'W. M.'
Notes: on the Mid-Lanark bye-election and the part played in it by the Irish MPs, what Home Rule should mean, what Socialists should learn from their defeat in the bye-election, on the Pope's banning of the Plan of Campaign and boycotting, and on the decline of charity.

D-375: 'The Reaction and the Radicals' (editorial), *Commonweal*, 4/121 (5 May 1888), 137–8.
Notes: predicting the future of the Liberal Party in the light of the Home Rule Bill forced upon them by the Irish parliamentary party, leading towards the demise of the Liberal Party.

D-376: 'Notes on News' (editorial), *Commonweal*, 4/122 (12 May 1888), 145–6.
Initialled: 'W. M.'
Notes: on the irrelevance of the Pope and on the state of property and sweated labour in Britain as revealed in the House of Lords commission on the poor, where the Rev. W. Adamson—quoted here—gave evidence.

D-377: 'Notes on News' (editorial), *Commonweal*, 4/123 (19 May 1888), 153.
Initialled: 'W. M.'
Notes: on Irish politics and a political argument over defence spending.

D-378: 'Notes on News' (editorial), *Commonweal*, 4/124 (26 May 1888), 153.
Initialled: 'W. M.'

Notes: charges the Liberals with hypocrisy for condemning the government's use of coercion in Ireland while taking no stand on the Bloody Sunday fracas, and recalling that when the Liberals were in power they also used coercion on the Irish.

D-379: 'Notes on News' (editorial), *Commonweal*, 4/125 (2 June 1888), 169.
Initialled: 'W. M.'
Notes: on the Tory loss of the Southampton bye-election, the annual conference of Co-operative Societies, and on Lord Salisbury's refusal to accept official government participation in the Paris Exhibition because it will commemorate the French Revolution.

D-380: 'The Policy of the Socialist League', *Commonweal*, 4/126 (9 June 1888), 180.
Signed: 'Signed by the Council of the Socialist League'.
Notes: Morris's statement of the anti-parliamentary position: Morris to John Bruce Glasier, 29 May [1888]:

> I should say: if the S.L.L.L. [Scottish Land and Labour League] insists of [*sic*] the parliamentary game, let it remain as it is & don't affiliate to it, but work with it cordially from outside: but if it will agree to a new pronunciamento just coming from the Council, (of which more presently; let it be all S.L. The said pron: is meant as a test: I was asked to write it, and I (personally) purposely made it as moderate as was possible; I should recommend branches to use it *as* a test in their own places. (*Letters*, ii. 783–4).

Substantial portions rptd. in MM, ii. 308–10, passim. Comparison of this 'Statement of Policy' with the 'Statement of Principles', pbd. in Commonweal in the next year (see D-453) strongly suggest that the latter was Morris's revised version of the former.

D-381: [Journal's heading:] 'Revolutionary Calendar. Week ending June 16, 1888. Wat Tyler', *Commonweal*, 4/126 (9 June 1888), 182.
Series: at this time, the 'Revolutionary Calendar' was a regular column in *Commonweal*, designed to construct a Socialist history through a series of anniversary accounts of major events and figures.
Initialled: 'W. M.'
Notes: this being the week of Wat Tyler's 1381 rebellion and murder, Morris writes a brief summary of his life and its significance.

D-382: 'The Burghers' Battle', (poem), *The Athenæum*, No. 3164 (16 June 1888), 761.
Notes: The poem is rptd. in *Poems by the Way* (see A-59.01).

D-383: 'Notes on News' (editorial), *Commonweal*, 4/127 (16 June 1888), 185.
Initialled: 'W. M.'
Notes: on the Conservative government's withdrawal of its 'compensation clauses', John Morley's speech at the Liberal-Radical meeting opposing coercion in Ireland but disregarding the same thing in England, and on Lord Wolseley's attempt to get a conscript army.

D-384: 'The Skeleton at the Feast' (comment), *Commonweal*, 4/127 (16 June 1888), 188.
Notes: on the chequered history of Jesse Collings of the Allotment Association and his 'three acres and a cow' proposal in relation to the Liberal policies.

D-385: 'Notes on News' (editorial), *Commonweal*, 4/128 (23 June 1888), 193.
Initialled: 'W. M.'
Notes: on the death of Kaiser Frederick, drawing a distinction between the political and the private man; on the distinction of the unsung Irish prisoners; and on the Liberal victory at Ayr.

D-386: 'Pentonville Prison' (comment), *Commonweal*, 4/128 (23 June 1888), 195.
Notes: Morris introduces and adds a comment to a letter by a former juryman on the living conditions in British prisons.

D-387: 'Counting Noses' (comment), *Commonweal*, 4/128 (23 June 1888), 196.
Notes: reflections, prompted by a Joseph Chamberlain speech, on the machine-politics of the House of Commons.

D-388: 'Notes on News' (editorial), *Commonweal*, 4/129 (30 June 1888), 201–2.
Initialled: 'W. M.'
Notes: on the sentence of Dillon and the debate over its 'legality', on the movement towards rejection of the new 'Kaiser No. 2', the use of Richmond Park for a rifle range, on the imprisonment of Shane O'Donnell, the sweating commission, and court mourning for the late Kaiser.

D-389: 'Thoughts on Education under Capitalism', *Commonweal*, 4/129 (30 June 1888), 204–5.
Notes: comment on education in relation to economics, occasioned by a lecture of Charles Leland describing his experiment in educating American children in the handicrafts.

D-390: 'Notes on News' (editorial), *Commonweal*, 4/130 (7 July 1888), 209–10.
Initialled: 'W. M.'
Notes: on the opposition's, i.e. Liberal's, lack of policy, the futility of the Channel Tunnel debate, the legality of the ban on public meetings in Trafalgar Square, the politics of immigration, and the sweating enquiry.

D-391: 'The Revolt of Ghent' (lecture), *Commonweal*, pbd. in 7 parts: 4/130, 131, 132, 133, 134, 135, and 136 (7, 14, 21, 28 July and 4, 11, and 18 Aug. 1888), 210, 217–18, 226–7, 234, 242–3, 250, 258–9; 1st delivered 29 Jan. 1888 (see *Unpublished Lectures*, pp. 269, 272, 282, 312)
Series: A series of 7 instalments pbd. weekly from 7 July 1888.
Each instalment signed: 'William Morris.'
Notes: rptd. as a pamphlet introduced by James Leatham and pbd. by the Twentieth Century Press, see A-119.01.

D-392: 'Notes on News' (editorial), *Commonweal*, 4/131 (14 July 1888), 217.
Initialled: 'W. M.'
Notes: on *The Times'* war on the Irish, the contradiction in Irish politics between constitutional means and a revolutionary purpose, and the lapse of 3 cases against people charged with assaulting police in Trafalgar Square.

D-393: 'Sweaters and Sweaters. No. 1—Matches by the Factory Drill [and] No. 2—Passing on the Pinch', *Commonweal*, 4/132 (21 July 1888), 225–6.
Signed: 'William Morris.'
Notes: the Socialist view of the struggle against the 'sweating' system, pbd. as a preparation for the 'Anti-Sweating Demonstration' scheduled for Hyde Park, 22 July.

D-394: [Unheaded paragraph], *Commonweal*, 4/132 (21 July 1888), 227.
Initialled: 'W. M.'
Notes: on the failure of newspapers to inform.

D-395: 'Notes on News' (editorial), *Commonweal*, 4/132 (21 July 1888), 228.

Initialled: 'W. M.'
Notes: on the politics behind the make-up of the Commission to enquire into the charges brought against Mr Parnell by *The Times*.

D-396: **[Unheaded paragraph]**, *Commonweal*, 4/132 (21 July 1888), 229.
Initialled: 'W. M.'
Notes: on a member of Bryant and May management asking whether Mrs Besant will be seeking champagne suppers for the match girls in future.

D-397: **'Notes on News'** (editorial), *Commonweal*, 4/133 (28 July 1888), 233.
Initialled: 'W. M.'
Notes: Morris's comments on the match girls' victory over Bryant and May, on Irish politics in Parliament, the defeat of charges of violence against citizens by the police, and on imperialism in Africa.

D-398: **'Notes on News'** (editorial), *Commonweal*, 4/134 (4 Aug. 1888), 241.
Initialled: 'W. M.'
Notes: on the Government's Commission of Enquiry into the political affairs of Charles Parnell, the torture and death of an arrested Irish member in Tullamore Jail, and on the 'swindle' of emigration.

D-399:* **'The [Annual] Report'** (speech), *Society for the Protection of Ancient Buildings. The Eleventh Annual Meeting of the Society. Report of the Committee thereat read. June ?, 1888.* pp. 30–5; pbd. ? Aug., 1888 (see Letters, ii. 581–2).
Notes: another report of progress on Inglesham Church and a speech in support of a fund for the repair of ancient buildings.

D-400: **'Notes on News'** (editorial), *Commonweal*, 4/135 (11 Aug. 1888), 249.
Initialled: 'W. M.'
Notes: on the attitude of the public towards the police, English and Catholic policy on 'civilizing Africa', and on the Bryant and May dispute.

D-401: **[Journal's heading:] 'Revolutionary Calendar . . . Death of W. Stanley Jevons'**, by S. W. (footnote), *Commonweal*, 4/135 (11 Aug. 1888), 251.
Initialled: 'W. M.'
Notes: Morris comments in a footnote.

D-402: **'Notes on News'** (editorial), *Commonweal*, 4/136 (18 Aug. 1888), 257–8.
Initialled: 'W. M.'
Notes: on speeches by Balfour and Lord Salisbury, on the Paris strike and *The Daily News*' reaction to it.

D-403: **'Notes on News'** (editorial), *Commonweal*, 4/137 (25 Aug. 1888), 265.
Initialled: 'W. M.'
Notes: on the suicide of a prison officer, a speech of the new German Kaiser, the closing of a factory of 1,000 workers, the critical reception of Zola's works in Britain, with complimentary reference to *Germinal*, the only one of those novels Morris had read, as a true picture of the working-class way of life.

D-404: **'Socialist Work at Norwich'**, *Commonweal*, 4/137 (25 Aug. 1888), 268.
Notes: Morris's account of a Socialist group of speakers working in Norwich over the previous Sunday and Monday.

D-405: **'Ugly London'**, *The Pall Mall Gazette: An Evening Newspaper and Review*, 48/7322 (4 Sept. 1888), 1–2.
Series: a sequel to an article by Ouida (Marie Louise Ramée, 1839–1908) titled 'The Ugliness of London. A Plea for Beautiful Streets', *The Pall Mall Gazette*, 30 Aug. 1888, p. 11.
By-lined: 'By William Morris.'

D-406: **'Notes on News'** (editorial), *Commonweal*, 4/139 (8 Sept. 1888), 281.
Initialled: 'W. M.' (twice, since his contributions are before and after several paragraphs by E. Belfort Bax).
Notes: on coercion as bad policy, the treatment in British prisons of political prisoners, *The Daily News*' attack on Sir Charles Warren and the proper Socialist response to that, the secularists' treatment of Mr Bradlaugh, and the use of 'obstruction' to muzzle free speech.

D-407: **'Notes on News'** (editorial), *Commonweal*, 4/140 (15 Sept. 1888), 289.
Initialled: 'W. M.'
Notes: answers Lord Bramwell of The Liberty and Property Defence League on the inequities of a rich country containing poor people as an underclass.

D-408: **'Notes on News'** (editorial), *Commonweal*, 4/141 (22 Sept. 1888), 297.
Initialled: 'W. M.'
Notes: on the conflict between Michael Davitt, the Irish

Socialist, and *The Daily News*; on the most recent bad decision from Justice Saunders, 'Nupkins' to Morris; and on the 'purest public spirit' of the newly emerging Salt Trust.

D-409: 'A Modern Midas', *Commonweal*, 4/141 (22 Sept. 1888), 300.
Notes: on making money as a religion.

D-410: 'Textiles', in the 'Notes' section of the *Arts and Crafts Exhibition Society Catalogue of the First Exhibition MDCCCLXXXVIII*, 1 (4 Oct. 1888), 17–29.
Notes: besides the products of Morris and Company, Morris contributed twice to the educative functions of the ACES exhibition in 1888. The 1st, titled 'Textiles', covered the 5 types of decorated woven goods: Tapestry, woven carpet, mechanical weaving, printed or painted cloth, and embroidered cloth. This is the piece of printing Morris refers to in the letter to the Chiswick Press quoted below. The 2nd contribution was a lecture, on 'Tapestry and Carpet Weaving', delivered on 1 Nov., during the exhibition. This seems never to have been pbd. in full, though an account of it appears in *The Pall Mall Gazette*, (48 (2 Nov. 1888), 6). The printed text of 'Textiles' in the *ACES Cat.* indicates by its title a larger scope than the lecture title. For that reason and the lack of a text for the lecture it would probably be a mistake to confuse the lecture with the piece on 'Textiles' or to take 'Textiles' as an earlier version of the lecture. Morris, as editor of *ACES Essays* (1893, see B-15), reprinted his note on 'Textiles' in pp. 17–29, but he seems never to have rptd. the lecture 'Tapestry and Carpet Weaving'.
Morris to Chiswick Press, late Aug. ?1888: 'Sirs, Herewith I send the copy for the paper on Textiles for the Arts & Crafts Exhibition: Kindly send by return or as soon as the copy is set up one proof to me, and one to Ernest Radford, Esqre [secretary-manager of the exhibition] at the New Gallery . . .' (*Letters*, ii. 810).
This *Catalogue* is the 1st of 5 pbd. during the last years of Morris's life. Though the 1st 3 exhibitions were held annually, after 1890, the Society decided to hold the event in 3-year intervals. Consequently, the exhibition catalogues issued in Morris's time were published as follows: 1888, 1889, 1890, 1893, and 1896. 4 Oct. 1888 is cited as the date of issue of this 1st *ACES Cat.* because that coincides with the opening of the exhibition.

D-411: 'Notes on News' (editorial), *Commonweal*, 4/143 (6 Oct. 1888), 313–14.
Initialled: 'W. M.'
Notes: on the politics of the Irish National Party, the bourgeois reaction to the Whitechapel murders and their basis in the capitalist system, and on vegetarianism as a cure for poverty.

D-412: 'Notes on News' (editorial), *Commonweal*, 4/146 (27 Oct. 1888), 337–8.
Initialled: 'W. M.'
Notes: on the likely outcome of the Commission of Enquiry into Parnell's authorship of certain letters, and on the dubious claim to fame of General Gordon, he being a tool of capitalism and of imperialism.

D-413: [unheaded note], *Commonweal*, 4/146 (27 Oct. 1888), 343.
Signed: 'Eds.', i.e. Morris and H. H. Sparling.
Notes: in response to a letter requesting material on socialism.

D-414: 'The Revival of Handicraft' (article), *The Fortnightly Review*, 44/263 n.s. (1 Nov. 1888), 603–10.
Series: The 2nd of a 2-part series pbd. in the same journal, the 1st being 'The Revival of Architecture', for which see D-372.
Signed: 'William Morris'.

D-415: [Journal title:] 'Mr. Morris on Tapestry' (lecture), *The Pall Mall Gazette*, 48 (2 Nov. 1888), 6.
Notes: this is a detailed summary account of Morris's lecture-demonstration on the history of the craft of tapestry-weaving. It was delivered, probably extempore, at the 1st exhibition of The Arts and Crafts Exhibition Society on 1 Nov. 1888. No text or notes have so far been found (for further detail, see D-410).

D-416: 'In Memoriam', *Commonweal*, 4/148 (10 Nov. 1888), 353–4.
Signed: 'Editors', i.e. Morris and H. H. Sparling.
Notes: on the 'Chicago Martyrs'.

D-417: 'Notes on News' (editorial), *Commonweal*, 4/148 (10 Nov. 1888), 356.
Signed: 'William Morris.'
Notes: replies to *The Echo's* condemnation of the Chicago Anarchists, to Balfour and *The Daily News'* views of the relation of Socialism to the cause of Ireland, with some observations on the condemnation of Vizitelly for publishing the books of Zola in England.

D-418: 'Notes on News' (editorial), *Commonweal*, 4/149 (17 Nov. 1888), 361.
Initialled: 'W. M.'
Notes: on Gladstone's politics and on the International Trades Union Congress. Morris says English unions are 'reactionary' and 'conservative'.

D-419: 'Notes on News' (editorial), *Commonweal*, 4/151 (1 Dec. 1888), 380.
Initialled: 'W. M.'
Notes: Morris comments on the Land Act, here called 'The Bill for the Relief of the Irish Landlords', Liberal prospects of election, Henry George, and the injustice of the British judicial system.

D-420: 'Notes on News' (editorial), *Commonweal*, 4/152 (8 Dec. 1888), 385.
Initialled: 'W. M.'
Notes: on the futility of Socialists participating in the London School-Board elections, and on a reactionary speech by Lord Salisbury.

D-421: 'In and About Cottonopolis', *Commonweal*, 4/153 (15 Dec. 1888), 396.
Signed: 'William Morris'.
Notes: Morris's report of his annual trip to Lancashire: to Ancoats, Manchester, Bolton, Blackburn, and Rochdale.

D-422: 'Notes on News' (editorial), *Commonweal*, 4/153 (15 Dec. 1888), 397.
Initialled: 'W. M.'
Notes: on the British war in Suakim, and on Henry James' blinkered view of London—he being 'the clever historian of the deadliest corruption of society, the laureate of the flirts, sneaks, and empty fools of which that society is mostly composed, and into whose hearts (?) he can see so clearly'.

D-423: 'Notes on News' (editorial), *Commonweal*, 4/154 (22 Dec. 1888), 401.
Initialled: 'W. M.'
Notes: Morris's comments on the situation in the Soudan, on Mr Page Hopp's *A Radical's Creed*, on monopoly of the land, a speech by John Morley on Irish land reform, and the politics of *The Star*.

D-424: 'Talk and Art' (report), *Commonweal*, 4/154 (22 Dec. 1888), 404.
Notes: Morris's report on his attendance at the NAAA Art Congress in Liverpool.

D-425: 'Notes on News' (editorial), *Commonweal*, 4/155 (29 Dec. 1888), 409.
Initialled: 'W. M.'
Notes: on Gladstone and the unemployed, and on capital punishment in Zanzibar as a result of western influence.

D-426: 'Art and its Producers' (lecture), *Transactions of the National Association for the Advancement of Art and Its Application to Industry* (Liverpool: The Society, 1888), pp. 228–36; delivered 5 Dec. 1888.
Notes: this lecture was 1st pbd. in the 1st of 2 vols. of *Transactions*, dated 1888 and 1890, the conferences being in 1888 at Liverpool and 1889 at Edinburgh, in which Morris is represented by his 2 talks at the annual meetings of the Association. The 2nd of his talks was the 'Presidential Address' before the Applied Arts Section (D-492). In 1901, S. C. Cockerell combined and edited the 2 talks as a book, *Art and Its Producers* and *The Arts & Crafts Today*, the last vol. in the Golden type octavo series (see C-11).

D-427: 'Notes on News' (editorial), *Commonweal*, 5/156 (5 Jan. 1889), 4–5.
Initialled: 'W. M.'
Notes: Morris responds to a pbd. letter by Mr W. McCree asserting that London is improving with time, and to a comment on the 'police outrage of Christmas Eve', as seen by *The Pall Mall Gazette*.

D-428: 'Notes on News' (editorial), *Commonweal*, 5/157 (12 Jan. 1889), 12.
Initialled: 'W. M.'
Notes: on the new jingoism of *The Pall Mall Gazette*, and on the inconsistency of such chauvinism with its advocacy of Home Rule, and on fraudulent inventions, like the machine to refine sugar without reducing its weight.

D-429: 'Notes on News' (editorial), *Commonweal*, 5/158 (19 Jan. 1889), 17–18.
Initialled: 'W. M.'
Notes: on the incidence of contemporary crime and the inhumanity of contemporary punishment, a view to contrast with that pbd. in *The Daily News*.

D-430: 'Whigs Astray. A Dialogue Between Owen Marx Bakounine Jones, an architect (unsuccessful),

and—the Rev. Swain Stride, a Nonconformist parson, and Mr. Jeremiah Brown, a business man [the last two being] advanced Radicals' (a dramatic dialogue with passages quoted from John Page Hopp's *A Radical's Creed*, pbd. in *The Pall Mall Gazette*, 10 Dec. 1888), *Commonweal*, prtd. here in 2 instalments: 5/158, 159 (19, 26 Jan. 1889), 18–19, 26–7.
Both instalments signed: 'William Morris.'

D-431: 'Notes on News' (editorial), *Commonweal*, 5/159 (26 Jan. 1889), 25.
Initialled: 'W. M.'
Notes: comment on local government elections, with John Burns elected to the London County Council, on the developing Socialism of Col. Ingersoll, and on charity and its relation to poverty and equality.

D-432: [unheaded protest against additions to monuments in Westminster Abbey] (to the Editor), *The Daily News*, 30 Jan. 1889, p. 3; the letter has the same date.
Signed: 'William Morris'.
Notes: rptd. as 'Monuments in Westminster Abbey', in MM, i. 171–3; also in *Letters*, iii. 25–6.

D-433: 'Notes on News' (editorial), *Commonweal*, 5/60 (2 Feb. 1889), 33.
Initialled: 'W. M.'
Notes: on coercion measures in Ireland, the quarrel between *The Star* and *The Pall Mall Gazette*, and their differing versions of reform, on Gordon, and on Boulanger's election to represent Paris.

D-434: 'Notes on News' (editorial), *Commonweal*, 5/161 (9 Feb. 1889), 41.
Initialled: 'W. M.'
Notes: on Mr O'Brien in Clonmel Jail, the punishments of political prisoners, and a better policy for *The Star*.

D-435: 'Notes on News' (editorial), *Commonweal*, 5/163 (23 Feb. 1889), 57.
Initialled: 'W. M.'
Notes: on government housing for the poor.

D-436: [Journal's heading:] 'Mr Morris on Art Education' (speech), *The Macclesfield Courier and Herald*, 23 Feb. 1889, p. 3; delivered on 14 Feb. 1889.
Notes: the 1st and perhaps the only text of Morris's speech at the annual prize giving of the Macclesfield School of Art and Science. It appears to be from a shorthand record, the punctuation differing from Morris's practice (see *Unpublished Lectures*, pp. 277, 314). Morris describes this occasion in a letter to his daughter Jenny, 16 Feb. 1889 (*Letters*, iii. 33–4).

D-437: 'Westminster Abbey and Its Monuments' (article), *The Nineteenth Century*, 25/1 (Mar. 1889), 409–14.
Signed: 'William Morris, Hon. Sec. of the Society for the Protection of Ancient Buildings.'
Notes: rptd., MM, i. 174–81.

D-438: 'Notes on News' (editorial), *Commonweal*, 5/164 (2 Mar. 1889), 65.
Initialled: 'W. M.'
Notes: on the Radicals as an example of the pointlessness of party political 'warfare'; and, in response to an article in *The Daily News*, on the 'beastly corner of the earth', i.e. Australia, where 'workers must be paid for living there' and where the workers have conceived a better future that they can make themselves.

D-439: 'Mine and Thine' (introduction to and translation of a 14th Century poem), *Commonweal*, 5/164 (2 Mar. 1889), 67.
Translation: from the original Flemish.
Notes: rptd. in *Poems by the Way* (see A-59.01).

D-440: 'Notes on News' (editorial), *Commonweal*, 5/165 (9 Mar. 1889), 73.
Initialled: 'W. M.'
Notes: comment on the outcome of the Commission of Enquiry into Charles Parnell's political affairs, a triumph of Parnell over both *The Times* and the Government.

D-441: 'Notes on News' (editorial), *Commonweal*, 5/166 (16 Mar. 1889), 81.
Initialled: 'W. M.'
Notes: on the different views of street demonstrations as either another extension of machine politics or a step towards revolution, a controversy arising from the violence of Trafalgar Square.

D-442: 'Notes on News' (editorial), *Commonweal*, 5/167 (23 Mar. 1889), 89.
Initialled: 'W. M.'
Notes: on the Liberal victory in the Kennington bye-election, with a speech supplied as one preferable to what John Morley actually said at the 'great anti-coer-

cion meeting at St. James Hall'; and on the new MP's view of the Trafalgar Square controversy.

D-443: 'Some Greetings . . . From William Morris' (from a collection of letters of apology for non-attendance at the Celebration of the Commune anniversary, a letter from Morris explaining that his illness prevents his attending and commenting on the relevance of the Paris Commune to the present position of Socialism in Britain), *Commonweal*, 5/167 (23 Mar. 1889), 91.

D-444: 'Notes on News' (editorial), *Commonweal*, 5/168 (30 Mar. 1889), 97–8.
Initialled: 'W. M.'
Notes: on police violence, closed meetings of the London County Council, and on the similar goals of the Liberals and Tories.

D-445: 'The Society of the Future' (lecture), *Commonweal*, Here pbd. in 3 instalments: 5/168, 169, and 170 (30 Mar., 6, 13 Apr. 1889), 98–9, 108–9, 114–15; 1st verified delivery on 20 Nov. 1887 (see *Unpublished Lectures*, pp. 268, 311).
Notes: also sometimes used as the basic text for 'How Shall We Live Then': Morris to Sydney Olivier, 10 Jan. [1889]: 'Would "How shall we live then?" do for the title [see A-134.01]. It would be pretty much my Society of the Future with differences suited to the probable audience' (*Letters*, iii. 9). Rptd. in MM, ii. 453–68.

D-446:* [Journal's heading:] 'Great Men Become Great by Looking at Nature. A Word to Art Students', *The Artist*, 10 (Apr. 1889), 95–6.

D-447: 'Notes on News' (editorial), *Commonweal*, 5/169 (6 Apr. 1889), 105.
Initialled: 'W. M.'
Notes: Morris's comments on the politics of teetotalism and, mostly, on the character and reputation of John Bright, recently deceased.

D-448: 'Ducks and Fools' (fable), *Commonweal*, 5/169 (6 Apr. 1889), 107.
Initialled: 'W. M.'
Notes: based on the Icelanders' exploitation of the eider ducks for their down, with the moral pointing to the exploitation of English working men by their employers.

D-449: 'Notes on News' (editorial), *Commonweal*, 5/170 (13 Apr. 1889), 113.
Initialled: 'W. M.'
Notes: on the survival of Stanley and on his murder of his native bearers by hanging, to show Stanley's enmity to workers in general; and on the pointlessness of Broadhurst's House of Commons discussion of the 'condition of the poor' in the large cities, there being no remedy for that that the parliamentarians are ever likely to adopt.

D-450: [unheaded response to a scheme to admit more monuments to the dead into the cloisters and Chapter House of Westminster Abbey] (to the Editor), *The Daily News*, 17 Apr. 1889, p. 6; the letter bears the same date.
Signed: 'William Morris'.

D-451: 'Notes on News' (editorial), *Commonweal*, 5/171 (20 Apr. 1889), 121.
Initialled: 'W. M.'
Notes: Morris responds in the negative to *The Star's* invitation to Socialists to join forces with radicals to form a single party.

D-452: 'Notes on News' (editorial), *Commonweal*, 5/172 (27 Apr. 1889), 129.
Initialled: 'W. M.'
Notes: Morris replies to the attempt by the National Home Reading Circles Union to encourage reading among the poor, Morris saying that if the poor had a reasonable life, they would read what they like.

D-453: 'Statement of Principles', *Commonweal*, 5/173 (4 May 1889), 137.
Signed: 'Council of the Socialist League', but see below.
Notes: Morris, possibly to forestall internal debate at the coming annual Conference of the SL, scheduled for 9 June, prepared the draft of this 'Statement', subsequently approved by Council and rptd. thereafter as a standard part of the last page of *Commonweal*. The main reasons for attributing this piece to Morris are: (1) that most of it is repeated verbatim in the 1st number of *HSR*, 1 Oct. 1891, well after Morris had resigned from the SL and formed the HSS; and (2) comparison of 'The Policy of the Socialist League' (see D-380) with this 'Statement of Principles', pbd. in *Commonweal* a year later, strongly suggest that the latter was a revised version of the former, of which the text is certainly by Morris (see this field in D-380).

D-454: [Unheaded Paragraph], *Commonweal*, 5/173 (4 May 1889), 137.
Initialled: 'W. M.'
Notes: on the sentencing of Zulu chiefs to be hanged.

D-455: 'Notes on News' (editorial), *Commonweal*, 5/173 (4 May 1889), 140.
Initialled: 'W. M.'
Notes: Morris's comments on Sir Peter Edlin's administration of justice as likely to bring the law into disrepute, on John Morley's opposition to the 8 hours movement, and on *The Pall Mall Gazette's* support for the 'Primrose Ladies'.

D-456: 'Notes on News' (editorial), *Commonweal*, 5/174 (11 May 1889), 145.
Initialled: 'W. M.'
Notes: on the Parliamentary debate on the Leasehold Enfranchisement Bill and on the Vigilance Committee's attack on the publication of Zola, even in expurgated versions.

D-457: 'Notes on News' (editorial), *Commonweal*, 5/175 (18 May 1889), 153.
Initialled: 'W. M.'
Notes: Morris's analysis of the support in and out of Parliament for the 'new flogging bill'.

D-458: [Journal's heading:] 'Correspondence', *Commonweal*, 5/175 (18 May 1889), 157.
Signed: 'William Morris'.
Notes: 'A few thoughts suggested by reading the clauses of the Anarchist Congress at Valentia'. Morris's reply to James Blackwell's invitation (*Commonweal*, 5/170 (13 Apr. 1889), 117) to a discussion of anarchism, Morris opposing anarchist tendencies in the SL on the ground that civilized life requires some degree of authority in the state.

D-459: 'Notes on News' (editorial), *Commonweal*, 5/178 (8 June 1889), 177.
Initialled: 'W. M.'
Notes: on the law as related to the assault on Mr Simms by a Royal Duke and a policeman, who were neither arrested or charged; on the aping of English commercial practice in Servia; on Henry George's notion of competition; and on raj jingoism as seen in *The Pall Mall Gazette*.

D-460: 'Notes on News' (editorial), *Commonweal*, 5/179 (15 June 1889), 185.
Initialled: 'W. M.'
Notes: on the failure of a dam in Johnstown, Pa., as an example of capitalist waste and rapaciousness, and on the tendency among some Radical papers, e.g. *Reynolds* and *The Star*, to omit the usual announcements of Socialist lecture-lists.

D-461: 'Notes on News' (editorial), *Commonweal*, 5/180 (22 June 1889), 193.
Initialled: 'W. M.'
Notes: on the rail disaster in the USA, the strike of the Plumstead tram car men, and a defence of Ibsen's *A Doll's House* against critical attack.

D-462: 'Looking Backward' (a review of Bellamy's utopia of that title), *Commonweal*, 5/180 (22 June 1889), 194–5.
Signed: 'William Morris'.

D-463: 'Notes on News' (editorial), *Commonweal*, 5/181 (29 June 1889), 201.
Initialled: 'W. M.'
Notes: on Bismarck's attempt to end asylum in Switzerland; and on laughter in a courtroom when an environmental matter was introduced, that being 'no laughing matter'.

D-464: 'Notes on News' (editorial), *Commonweal*, 5/182 (6 July 1889), 209.
Initialled: 'W. M.'
Notes: on a police attack on a Salvation Army procession and on the reactions of the political parties both to that and to the question of the Parliamentary delegates discussing the 8-hour day at an inter-government conference in Berne.

D-465: 'Under an Elm-Tree; or, Thoughts in the Country-Side' (essay), *Commonweal*, 5/182 (6 July 1889), 212–13.
Notes: reflections on the effects of capitalism on the countryside and on what the countryside might be like under Socialism. This essay was issued in a long succession of authorized separate edns. by James Leatham starting with A-56.01 (1891). In the US T. B. Mosher of Portland, Maine, rptd. it both as a separate (see A-56.06) and in the annual collection of *The Bibelot: A Reprint of Poetry and Prose for Book Lovers, chosen in part from scarce editions and sources not generally known*, 18/2 (Apr. 1912), 103–11 (see D-596); also rptd. in MM, ii.

507–12.

D-466: 'Impressions of the Paris Congress', *Commonweal*, pbd. in 2 instalments: 5/185, 186 (27 July, 3 Aug. 1889), 234, 242.
Both instalments signed: 'William Morris.'
Notes: Morris's account of the International Guesdist, i.e. Marxist, conference where he was a delegate.

D-467: 'Notes on News' (editorial), *Commonweal*, 5/186 (3 Aug. 1889), 241.
Initialled: 'W. M.'
Notes: Morris's contribution to the annual debate over grants to the Royal Family.

D-468: 'The [Annual] Report', 'Address by Mr. William Morris' and 'Inglesham Church', *Society for the Protection of Ancient Buildings. The Twelfth Annual Meeting of the Society. Report of the Committee and Paper read by Mr. William Morris. 3rd July, 1889*. Aug. (?), 1889, pp. 35–7, 62–76.
Notes: the 'paper' is on how to make the case for the preservation of ancient buildings, the 2nd also by Morris, part of the annual 'report', on the need for repairs to Inglesham Church, with a further report on Kelmscott Church included under the same heading.

D-469: 'Trial by Judge v. Trial by Jury', *Commonweal*, 5/188 (17 Aug. 1889), 257.
Notes: Morris's criticism of the British criminal justice system, occasioned by disturbances in Liverpool when the guilty verdict was announced in the Maybrick case.

D-470: [Journal's heading:] 'Correspondence. Communism and Anarchism', *Commonweal*, 5/188 (17 Aug. 1889), 261.
Signed: 'William Morris'.
Notes: Morris's 2nd reply to correspondence on the issue of anarchism and its relation to communism. See also the entry for 18 May 1889, D-458.

D-471: 'Notes on News' (editorial), *Commonweal*, 5/189 (24 Aug. 1889), 265.
Initialled: 'W. M.'
Notes: on *The Daily News'* treatment of the Maybrick case, and on the Dockers' strike as 'a sign of the times' in that it points towards a greater consciousness of class antagonism.

D-472: 'The Lesson of the Hour', *Commonweal*, 5/191 (7 Sept. 1889), 281–2.
Notes: on the Dockers' strike as an expression of class warfare.

D-473: [Journal's heading:] 'The Preservation of Peterborough Cathedral' (to the Editor), *The Pall Mall Gazette*, 10 Sept. 1889, p. 3; the date of the letter is not known.
Notes: a protest against impending restoration.

D-474: 'Notes on News' (editorial), *Commonweal*, 5/192 (14 Sept. 1889), 289.
Initialled: 'W. M.'
Notes: analysis of various reactions to the dock strike.

D-475: [Journal's heading:] 'Mr. William Morris writes to us as follows:—', *The Pall Mall Gazette*, 20 Sept. 1889, p. 2; the letter bears the same date.
Notes: Morris responds to a correspondent, 'Muratore', who denies the beauty of the west front of Peterborough Cathedral.

D-476: 'Notes on the News', *Commonweal*, 5/193 (21 Sept. 1889), 297.
Initialled: 'W. M.'
Notes: on the dockers' victory as a lesson in Socialist solidarity.

D-477: 'Notes on News' (editorial), *Commonweal*, 5/193 (28 Sept. 1889), 305.
Initialled: 'W. M.'
Notes: on the widespread view, especially after the dockers' win, that Socialism won't mean any very radical change in society, a view that leaves out of consideration the class war.

D-478: 'Notes on News' (editorial), *Commonweal*, 5/197 (19 Oct. 1889), 329.
Initialled: 'W. M.'
Notes: on the threat by the London County Council to censor music hall lyrics, and comparing the Turkish atrocities in Crete and Armenia with the capitalist treatment of the English working class.

D-479: 'Notes on News' (editorial), *Commonweal*, 5/198 (26 Oct. 1889), 337.
Initialled: 'W. M.'
Notes: on the rise of the Liberals, their possibility of election, and the consequences of that for Socialism.

D-480: 'Of Dyeing as an Art' in the '*Notes*' section of *The*

Arts and Crafts Exhibition Society Catalogue of the Second Exhibition MDCCCLXXXIX, (7 Nov. 1889), 56–67.
Notes: for the ACES show of 1889, Morris lectures on 'Gothic Architecture' and writes for the 'Notes' section on 'Of Dyeing as an Art'. This is also the paper 'The Art of Dyeing' delivered at the annual conference of the National Association for the Advancement of Art and Its Application to Industry, 29 Oct. 1889 (see *Unpublished Lectures*, p. 280). As in the case of 'Textiles', Morris reprinted this 'Notes' piece in the *ACES Essays* (1893, see B-15). The date of issue of the *ACES Cat.* is taken in each case as coinciding with the opening of the exhibition.

D-481: **'Notes on News'** (editorial), *Commonweal*, 5/200 (9 Nov. 1889), 356.
Initialled: 'W. M.'
Notes: Morris rewrites Gladstone's Saltney speech to make it clearer to working men; and reports on the Edinburgh Art Congress of the NAAA, at which he gave the Presidential Address (see D-492).

D-482: **'Notes on News'** (editorial), *Commonweal*, 5/201 (16 Nov. 1889), 361.
Initialled: 'W. M.'
Notes: Morris's objections to *The Pall Mall Gazette's* defence of both advertising and the Eiffel Tower.

D-483: **'Notes on News'** (editorial), *Commonweal*, 5/202 (23 Nov. 1889), 369.
Initialled: 'W. M.'
Notes: on the bakers' strike, the partiality of Baron Huddlestone as a judge and its implications for both the civil and criminal law, and the political implications of a speech by Mr Goschen in Cardiff.

D-484: **'Notes on News'** (editorial), *Commonweal*, 5/203 (30 Nov. 1889), 377.
Initialled: 'W. M.'
Notes: on an exhibition of 'Garments for the Poor' and on Guinness's 'magnificent gift to the London poor' of £250,000, on the Brazilian revolution, and on the death of William Sharman, a Unitarian preacher turned Socialist.

D-485: **'Notes on News'** (editorial), *Commonweal*, 5/204 (7 Dec. 1889), 385.
Initialled: 'W. M.'
Notes: comment on how 'charity' can be related to the Queen's clothes, and on Lord Salisbury's speech at Nottingham.

D-486: **'Monopoly'** (lecture), *Commonweal*, pbd. in 3 instalments: 5/204, 205, and 206 (7, 14, and 21 Dec. 1889), 388–9, 394, and 401–2; the 1st confirmed delivery occurred on 13 Mar. 1887 (see *Unpublished Lectures*, pp. 261, 309).
Signed: Instalments 1 and 2: 'William Morris'; instalment 3 initialled: 'W. M.'
Notes: the text of a lecture later pbd. in the pamphlet series, SP, where it was 'No. 7' (see A-49.01).

D-487: **'Notes on News'** (editorial), *Commonweal*, 5/205 (14 Dec. 1889), 393.
Initialled: 'W. M.'
Notes: on the presence and prospects of Socialism in the Radical wing of the Liberal Party.

D-488: **'Notes on News'** (editorial), *Commonweal*, 5/207 (28 Dec. 1889), 409.
Initialled: 'W. M.'
Notes: on strikes as they affect middle-class attitudes, which recently supported the dockers but now turn away from the gas-stokers.

D-489: **[unheaded speech]** (summary), *Protocol of the International Workers' Congress, Paris, Held from 14–20 July, 1889*, pbd. Nuremberg, 1890, p. 17; delivered 16 July 1889.
Notes: against the Possibilists gaining entry to the Congress.

D-490:* **[unheaded speech]**, *Protocol of the International Workers' Congress, Paris, Held from 14–20 July, 1889*, pbd. Nuremberg, 1890, pp. 39–43.
Notes: Morris's main contribution to the International Workers Congress, Paris, reviewing the progress and condition of English Socialism.

D-491: **'Art and Industry in the Fourteenth Century'** (lecture), *Time: a Monthly Magazine*, 1, n.s. (Jan. 1890), 23–36; 1st delivered as a lecture: 15 May 1887 (see *Unpublished Lectures*, p. 264).
By-lined: 'By William Morris'.
Series: last in a series of three lectures: the 1st of the series is 'Early England', the 2nd 'Medieval England' (sometimes called 'Feudal England'), and 3rd the present text. The order of composition of this series is not the historical sequence (see D-558 and 308).

D-492: [Journal's heading:] 'Section of Applied Art. The Presidential Address, By William Morris' (lecture), *Transactions of the National Association for the Advancement of Art and Its Application to Industry*, 2 (? Jan. 1890), 189–207; lecture delivered 30 Oct. 1889 (see *Unpublished Lectures*, pp. 280, 316).
Notes: delivered in Edinburgh on 30 Oct. 1889, and later titled 'The Arts and Crafts of Today' and pbd. with 'Art and Its Producers' as a book, see C-11.

D-493: 'News from Nowhere: or, An Epoch of Rest. Being Some Chapters from a Utopian Romance.', *Commonweal*, pbd. in 39 weekly instalments: (1) 6/209 (11 Jan. 1890), 9–10; (2) 6/210 (18 Jan. 1890), 18–19; (3) 6/211 (25 Jan. 1890), 25–7; (4) 6/212 (1 Feb. 1890), 34–5; (5) 6/213 (8 Feb. 1890), 42–3; (6) 6/214 (15 Feb. 1890), 49–51; (7) 6/215 (22 Feb. 1890), 58–9; (8) 6/216 (1 Mar. 1890), 65; (9) 6/217 (8 Mar. 1890), 74; (10) 6/218 (15 Mar. 1890), 82–3; (11) 6/219 (22 Mar. 1890), 89–90; (12) 6/220 (29 Mar. 1890), 98; (13) 6/221 (5 Apr. 1890), 105–6; (14) 6/222 (12 Apr. 1890), 113–14; (15) 6/223 (19 Apr. 1890), 121–2; (16) 6/224 (26 Apr. 1890), 130–1; (17) 6/225 (3 May 1890), 141–2; (18) 6/226 (10 May 1890), 145–6; (19) 6/227 (17 May 1890), 156–7; (20) 6/228 (24 May 1890), 161–2; (21) 6/229 (31 May 1890), 169–70; (22) 6/230 (7 June 1890), 179; (23) 6/231 14 June 1890), 186–7; (24) 6/232 (21 June 1890), 195; (25) 6/233 28 June 1890), 205; (26) 6/234 (5 July, 1890), 209–10; (27) 6/235 (12 July 1890), 220–1; (28) 6/236 (19 July 1890), 229–30; (29) 6/237 (26 July 1890), 233–4; (30) 6/238 (2 Aug. 1890), 242; (31) 6/239 (9 Aug. 1890), 250; (32) 6/240 (16 Aug. 1890), 257–8; (33) 6/241 (23 Aug. 1890), 266–7; (34) 6/242 (30 Aug. 1890), 274–5; (35) 6/243 (6 Sept. 1890), 284–5; (36) 6/244 (13 Sept. 1890), 292–3; (37) 6/245 (20 Sept. 1890), 298–9; (38) 6/246 (27 Sept. 1890), 306; (39) 6/247 (4 Oct. 1890), 314–15.

10 years later, from October 1901 to September 1903, *News from Nowhere* was serialized again, this time in New York, in 19 instalments in Vols. 1 and 2 of *The Comrade: An Illustrated Socialist Monthly* (for more detail, see Coupe, pp. 153–4).
Series: This 1st pbn. of the novel in *Commonweal* appeared with 30 chapters in 39 instalments; details of each instalment appear in this entry. Note that the 2nd edn., 1st English (see A-50.02) was revised by Morris and has a different number of chapters.
Each instalment signed: 'William Morris.'

D-494: 'Fabian Essays in Socialism' (review), *Commonweal*, 6/211 (25 Jan. 1890), 28–9.
Signed: 'William Morris.'

D-495: 'The Hall and the Wood' (poem), *The English Illustrated Magazine*, No. 77, (Feb. 1890), 351–4.
By-lined: 'By William Morris.'
Notes: in her bibliographical note on the pbn., May Morris says, '"The Hall and the Wood" was written for the *English Illustrated Magazine* (February, 1890) at the request of Emery Walker, who was then one of the editors' (*CW*, IX. xxxiv–v).

D-496: 'Notes on News' (editorial), *Commonweal*, 6/212 (1 Feb. 1890), 33.
Initialled: 'W. M.'
Notes: on current news items: the *Labour Elector* and its attack on Mr Parke, the doubtful 'victory' of the German Socialists over Bismarck, and the article in *The Star* insisting that England has had 'municipal Socialism for over fifty years'.

D-497: 'Notes on News' (editorial), *Commonweal*, 6/213 (8 Feb. 1890), 41.
Initialled: 'W. M.'
Notes: on the changes in attitude of English workers to the Irish Question, and on the war of landowners against public right of way.

D-498: 'Notes on News' (editorial), *Commonweal*, 6/214 (15 Feb. 1890), 49.
Initialled: 'W. M.'
Notes: on Bismarck's struggle with the German Socialists and the reaction of the English public.

D-499: 'Notes on News' (editorial), *Commonweal*, 6/215 (22 Feb. 1890), 57.
Initialled: 'W. M.'
Notes: on the blow to the 'respectables', especially *The Times*, in the Parnell Commission's exoneration of Parnell.

D-500: 'Coal in Kent', *Commonweal*, 6/217 (8 Mar. 1890), 77.
Signed: 'William Morris.'
Notes: responds to the discovery of coal in Kent, asking 'cui bono?'

D-501: [Journal's heading:] 'Correspondence. Christianity and Socialism' (reply), *Commonweal*, 6/217 (8 Mar. 1890), 77.
Signed: 'William Morris.'

Notes: to the readers of *Commonweal*, opposing A. T. Rickarby's argument that Christian belief is consistent with Socialist belief. Morris says Christianity, or whatever of good that religion has, 'will be ... absorbed in Socialism'.

D-502: 'Notes on News' (editorial), *Commonweal*, 6/219 (22 Mar. 1890), 89.
Initialled: 'W. M.'
Notes: on Bismarck's resignation from political office.

D-503: 'The Great Coal Strike', *Commonweal*, 6/219 (22 Mar. 1890), 91.
Notes: on the larger political implications of the general coal strike.

D-504: [Journal's heading:] 'The Class Struggle. Address by Mr. William Morris', *The Leeds Mercury*, 26 Mar. 1890, p. 3; delivered in this instance on 25 Mar. 1890.
Notes: extended portions, possibly from a shorthand transcription, of the lecture Morris titled 'The Class Struggle', which was delivered 5 times in 1889–90 (see *Unpublished Lectures*, pp. 280, 281, 283).

D-505: 'Notes' (editorial), *Commonweal*, 6/220 (29 Mar. 1890), 100.
Initialled: 'W. M.'
Notes: on the sentence of death passed on two boys convicted in Crewe of murdering the man who led them into crime.

D-506: 'Notes on News' (editorial), *Commonweal*, 6/221 (5 Apr. 1890), 105.
Initialled: 'W. M.'
Notes: on Balfour's Land Bill as a canard, on the 'not guilty' verdict for a Socialist prosecuted at Leeds, and calling for leniency for the two boys at Crewe.

D-507: 'Notes on News' (editorial), *Commonweal*, 6/222 (12 Apr. 1890), 116.
Initialled: 'W. M.'
Notes: on a hanging at Knutsford and the meaning of such 'legal murders' for those who accept 'the burden of collective responsibility'.

D-508: 'Labour Day' (article), *Commonweal*, 6/225 (3 May 1890), 137.
Notes: designed to show how the demonstrations of Labour Day reach beyond the call for the 8-hour day where the consciousness of Socialism and the class war is evident.

D-509: 'Notes on News' (editorial), *Commonweal*, 6/225 (3 May 1890), 140.
Initialled: 'W. M.'
Notes: on John Morley's speech against Socialism, on an article in *The Star* advocating profit sharing—which Morris describes as a subterfuge which does not reach the reality of class war—and on the justified attack, also in *The Star*, on H. M. Stanley, explorer and journalist.

D-510: 'The "Eight Hours" and the Demonstration' (lead editorial), *Commonweal*, 6/227 (17 May 1890), 153.
Signed: 'William Morris'.
Notes: distinguishes between British trades unionists and continental Socialists. The 8-hours legislation tends only to state socialism, with which Communists would disagree.

D-511: 'Notes', *Commonweal*, 6/227 (17 May 1890), 157.
Initialled: 'W. M.'
Notes: on the whitewash accorded to prison management by a commission appointed to inquire into instances of bad treatment of prisoners. Morris argues that prisons are instruments of torture for the punishment of those 'enemies of society' that the society itself has created.

D-512: [unheaded response] (to the Editor, Sir Thomas Wemyss Reid), *The Speaker*, 24 May 1890, pp. 559–70; the letter is dated 'May 19'.
Signed: 'William Morris'.
Notes: Morris's original statement (to which Sir Thomas made reply) appeared in a letter printed in *The Art of Authorship*; for further detail see this field in B-10.

D-513: 'The Glittering Plain; or, The Land of the Living Men', *The English Illustrated Magazine*, pbd. here in 4 instalments: 7/81, 82, 83, and 84. Chapters 1–6, 7–12, 13–18, 19–22 (June, July, Aug., and Sept. 1890), pp. 687–98, 754–68, 824–38, and 884–900; with 4 headpiece illus., one for each instalment, three signed or initialled—'R. S.'; 'Henry Ryland'; 'R. H.'; and the 4th anonymous. The 1st part ends with a tail-piece designed by Walter Crane (see Coupe, p. 161).
By-lined: 'By William Morris, Author of "The Earthly Paradise."'
Notes: after this 1st pbn., this tale was issued in book form—8 May 1891—as the 1st production of the KP, titled *The Story of the Glittering Plain. Which has been*

also called the Land of the Living Men or the Acre of the Undying (see A-54.01). Later in the same year a 2nd edn. was issued at a more popular price (see A-54.02). Emery Walker was, about this time, 'one of the editors' of the *English Illustrated*, according to May Morris (*CW*, IX. xxxv).

D-514: 'Anti-Parliamentary', *Commonweal*, 6/230 (7 June 1890), 180–1.
Notes: Morris argues against Socialists entering parliamentary politics.

D-515: 'Notes on News' (editorial), *Commonweal*, 6/232 (21 June 1890), 193.
Notes: on the newly unified Italy, which will be democratic only for the masters, the capitalists, 'like other "civilised" nations'.

D-516: 'Notes on News' (editorial), *Commonweal*, 6/233 (28 June 1890), p. 204.
Initialled: 'W. M.'
Notes: on nationalism and the labour movement, on Stanley, on the competition between Britain and Germany, and on Gladstone's recommendation of 'thrift' to a meeting of railway workmen.

D-517: [Journal's heading:] 'Stratford-on-Avon Church' (to the Editor), *The Times*, 15 Aug. 1890, p. 10; the date of the letter is not known.
Signed: 'William Morris, Hon. Sec. of the Society for the Protection of Ancient Buildings, 9, Buckingham-street, Adelphi'.
Notes: a reply to a letter from the Vicar revealing plans 'to erect a copy' of the missing parts of the reredos in the church.

D-518: [unheaded letter] (to the Editor), *The Pall Mall Gazette*, 15 Dec. 1890, p. 2; the letter is dated 'December 13'.
Signed: 'William Morris'.
Notes: corrections to a review of *The Saga Library*, vol. I. (see A-52.01)

D-519: 'Notes on News' (editorial), *Commonweal*, 6/234 (5 July 1890), 212.
Initialled: 'W. M.'
Notes: Morris's comment on the kidnapping of Signor Arrigo, a gentleman-landowner, by brigands, the captors including one of his own guards. Morris hopes he may have experienced in the course of his extraordinary captivity something of how the poor live ordinarily, enough to try in future to improve the living conditions of his employees.

D-520: 'The Development of Modern Society' (lecture), *Commonweal*, pbd. in 5 weekly instalments: 6/236–40 (19, 26 July, 2, 9, and 16 Aug. 1890), pp. 225–6, 237, 244, 253, and 260–1; delivered 13 Apr. 1890 (see *Unpublished Lectures*, pp. 283, 316).
Each instalment signed: 'William Morris'.
Notes: an expanded version of a lecture 1st delivered in Liverpool.

D-521: 'Notes on News' (editorial), *Commonweal*, 6/237 (26 July 1890), 235.
Initialled: 'W. M.'
Notes: on the 'Peace Conference' then taking place in London where, however, the true cause of war, i.e. capitalism, is not addressed.

D-522:* 'The Day of Days' (poem), *The Humane Review*, July 1890; *Time*, Nov. 1890.
Notes: rptd. in *Poems by the Way* (see A-59.01).

D-523: [Unheaded letter] (to the Editor), *The Times*, 10 Sept. 1890, p. 12.
Signed: 'William Morris, Hon. Secretary of the Society for the Protection of Ancient Buildings'.
Notes: opposing the shifting to Germany of the Hanseatic League Museum at Bergen.

D-524: 'Workhouse Socialism' (article), *Commonweal*, 6/251 (1 Nov. 1890), 345–6.
Notes: criticism of General Booth's 'great scheme' for the 'amelioration of the lot of the poor', which Morris finds to be a degrading stopgap, merely a system of 'workhouse socialism', not a general or permanent improvement.

D-525: 'Where Are We Now?' (lead editorial), *Commonweal*, 6/253 (15 Nov. 1890), 361–2.
Notes: a summing up of the progress of the modern English Socialist Movement during Morris's involvement, and—by implication—Morris's farewell to the SL after 6 years of active work for that organization.

D-526:* 'The Relations of Art to Labour' (lecture revised for an article), *Co-operative Wholesale Societies Annual, 1890*.
Notes: this is an earlier, probably the original, version of the lecture from which came 'Art and Labour' as pbd. in

Unpublished Lectures, pp. 94–118. This version is revised from its lecture form for journal pbn., but it retains its original orientation to a middle-class audience. On the sequence of the 2 manuscript versions, see Alan Bacon, 'William Morris's Lectures and the Question of Audience', *The Yale University Library Gazette*, 58/3, 4 (Apr. 1984), 163–80. On the identification of this 1st journal pbn., see 'Lost Morris Article Pops up at the Co-op!' *William Morris Society Newsletter*, July 1994, pp. 1–2.

D-527: 'The Socialist Ideal. I.—Art' (article), *The New Review*, 4/20 (1 Jan. 1891), 1–8.
Notes: this article was the 1st of a 3-part series on Socialist ideals of art, politics, and literature, by Morris, G. B. Shaw, and H. S. Salt, respectively. A reply to this by Mr W. H. Mallock appeared in *The New Review*, 4 (1 Feb. 1891), 100. This article was later issued in pamphlet form, 'unauthorized' according to S. C. Cockerell's annotation in his copy of HBF (see E-11).

D-528: [Journal's heading:] 'The : "Triumph of the Innocents"' (to the editor), *The Liverpool Daily Post*, 7 Feb. 1891, p. 6; the date of Morris's letter is not given, but Rathbone's (in which Morris's text is included) is dated 'February 4.'
By-lined: 'Mr. William Morris, the Poet of The Earthly Paradise, and decorative inventor'.
Notes: this letter—along with others by Ford Madox Brown, William M. Rossetti, Cosmo Monkhouse, and Dame Millicent Fawcett—is on the importance of Holman Hunt's painting of that name, the letters being solicited for publication, probably by Harold S. Rathbone. All the letters are contained in a letter to *The Liverpool Daily Post* by 'a Liverpool gentleman'. The intention, to acquire the painting for the Walker Art Gallery in Liverpool, was achieved (see *Letters*, iii. 264–5, note).

D-529: [Journal's heading:] 'Westminster Abbey' (to the Editor), *The Times*, 11 Feb. 1891, p. 4; letter dated 'February 5'.
Signed: 'William Morris, Hon. Sec. of the Society for the Protection of Ancient Buildings. Kelmscott House, Upper Mall, Hammersmith'.
Notes: a response to proposals for a memorial chapel connected to Westminster Abbey. This is not the text of 'Westminster Abbey' as ed. by Cockerell and pbd. in 1900 in combination with 'Architecture and History' (for which see C-7).

D-530:* 'The [Annual] Report' (report of a speech), *Society for the Protection of Ancient Buildings. The Fourteenth Annual Meeting of the Society. Report of the Committee and Paper by Mr. W. B. Richmond thereat read. 10th June, 1891*. Pbd. Aug. (?) 1891, pp. 2–45. Another report appeared in *The Trident*, 1 (1 Mar. 1891), 286–7.
Notes: this SPAB 'report' of an address at Trinity College, Cambridge, and the even briefer report in *The Trident* (Trinity College) appear to be the only sources that provide any detail of Morris's text, which concerns the protection and preservation of historic buildings.

D-531:* 'The [Annual] Report' (report of a speech), *Society for the Protection of Ancient Buildings. The Fourteenth Annual Meeting of the Society. Report of the Committee and Paper by Mr. W. B. Richmond thereat read. 10th June, 1891.*
Notes: a speech moving a vote of thanks to Richmond.

D-532: 'Seven Years Ago and Now' (lecture summary), *Justice*, 8/399 (5 Sept. 1891), 1; delivered 30 Aug. 1891, at Kelmscott House, Hammersmith.
Notes: on the progress of modern Socialism in Britain since 1884; the only contemporary account so far discovered of this lecture.

D-533: [Journal's heading:] 'Hammersmith Socialist Society, Kelmscott House. Friends and Comrades' (lead editorial), *HSR*, No. 1 (Oct. 1891), 1.
Notes: statement explaining the nature and purpose of a new 'Monthly Sheet', the *Hammersmith Socialist Record* (*HSR*), on the occasion of its inaugural issue.

D-534: [unheaded 'statement of principles', as referred to on p. 1 of this 1st issue], *HSR*, No. 1 (Oct. 1891), 4.
Notes: on the history of this 'statement', and Morris's authorship, see this field in D-453. The first 3 paragraphs, only slightly changed from the SL 'Statement of Principles', drafted by Morris, signed by the 'Council of the Socialist League', and 1st pbd. on the front page of *Commonweal*, 4 May 1889, and from 5 Oct. of that year intermittently on the last page of individual issues. Despite the resemblances neither of these versions of this text should be confused with the official HSS *Statement of Principles*, printed as an 8-page pamphlet and pbd. in Dec. 1890 (see A-53.01).

Regarding authorship of articles in the *HSR*, unless there is clear collateral information on authorship, the policy here is to accept only signed or initialled contributions as being by Morris. Except for the 1st, unsigned leaders are likely to be by the editor, Sam Bullock, given that there seems to be a practice, established early, that others, including Morris, sign or initial their contributions. For a 'key' to the initials, see the *Contents* field in A-58.01.

D-535: [unheaded protest] (to the Editor), *The Pall Mall Gazette*, 27 Oct. 1891, p. 2; Morris's letter is dated 'October 22'.
Signed: 'on behalf of the Society for the Protection of Ancient Buildings . . . William Morris, Hon. Sec.', along with 3 other signatories: Thackeray Turner, Richard Grosvenor, and J. Hen. Middleton.
Notes: against plans for restorations to Westminster Abbey, with a request to publish previous correspondence between the SPAB and the Dean, Rev. George G. Bradley.

D-536: 'The Influence of Building Materials on Architecture' (lecture), *The Century Guild Hobby Horse*, 7 (Jan. 1892), 1–14; delivered 20 Nov. 1891.
Notes: a lecture originally delivered to the Art Workers Guild at Barnard's Inn (see *Unpublished Lectures*, p. 318).

D-537:* 'The New Year' (poem), *The Artist*, 13 (Jan. 1892), p. 3.
Notes: a fugitive item, not in *CW* or *MM* (i. or index), not mentioned in *Letters*, HBF, or Scott.

D-538: 'The Woodcuts of Gothic Books' (lecture), *Journal of the Society of Arts*, 40 (12 Feb. 1892), 246–60.
Notes: report of a paper read on 26 Jan. 1892 before the Applied Arts Section of the Society of Arts, with 37 lantern slides and including an introduction by Sir George Birdwood, pp. 246–7, text, pp. 247–57, 'Discussion', pp. 257–9, and Morris's response, pp. 259–60; also includes 4 illus. selected from Morris's 37 'limelight' pictures shown at the lecture. According to S. C. Cockerell's diaries, substantially the same lecture with the same illus. was delivered on 28 Feb. 1890 at the Art Workers' Guild (quoted in Peterson, p. 122). Rptd. (without the introduction and the illus.) in 2 parts, *The Architect*, 26 Feb., 4 Mar. 1892, pp. 145–7, 157–9; *The Journal of Decorative Art*, June and July 1892, pp. 82–7, 102–3 (with the same 4 illus. included in *The Journal of the Society of Arts*). Rptd., abridged, as 'The Woodcuts of Old and Modern Books', *Bookworm*, 5 (1892), 193–201, with an editorial head note but without illus. or the discussion.
All 4 journal versions of this text appear to derive, directly or indirectly, from Morris's MS, the paragraphing being Morris's in each case.
A summary account appeared in *The Times* under the heading, 'The Society of Arts', 28 Jan. 1892, p. 8.

D-539: 'May Day' (poem), *Justice*, 9/433 (30 Apr. 1892), 1.
Notes: 10 stanzas, in quatrains, a dialogue between 'The Workers' and 'The Earth'.

D-540: [*HSR* heading:] 'Hammersmith Socialist Society, Kelmscott House. Friends and Comrades' (leader), *HSR*, No. 8 (May 1892), 1–2.
Initialled: 'W. M.'
Notes: on anarchist bombs and bomb plots in Walsall, London, and Paris. Rptd., *The Church Reformer*, 11 (June 1892), 136.

D-541: [*HSR* heading:] 'Hammersmith Socialist Society, Kelmscott House. Friends and Comrades' (leader), *HSR*, No. 9.(June 1892), 1–2.
Initialled: 'W. M.'
Notes: on destitution in Cleveland due to Durham miners' strike.

D-542: 'The [Annual] Report', *Society for the Protection of Ancient Buildings. The Fifteenth Annual Meeting of the Society. Report of the Committee thereat read. 28th June, 1892*. Pbd. Aug. (?) 1892, p. 1.
Notes: opening remarks and the 'annual report'.

D-543: [*HSR* heading:] 'Hammersmith Socialist Society, Kelmscott House. Friends and Comrades' (leader), *HSR*, No. 11 (Aug. 1892), pp. 1–3.
Initialled: 'W. M.'
Notes: on political prospects of the new Parliament, with its 3 labour members.

D-544: [*HSR* heading:] 'Hammersmith Socialist Society, Kelmscott House. Friends and Comrades' (leader), *HSR*, No. 12 (Sept. 1892), 1–2.
Initialled: 'W. M.'
Notes: on the results of the just-ended 'labour war', i.e. a strike and its associated violence.

D-545: [*HSR* heading:] 'Hammersmith Socialist Society, Kelmscott House. Friends and Comrades' (leader), *HSR*, No. 13 (Oct. 1892), 1–2.
Initialled: 'W. M.'

Notes: on parliamentary recess at a time of 'seething ... discontent'.

D-546: [unheaded reply] (to the Editor), *The Daily Chronicle*, 31 Oct. 1892, p. 4; the letter is dated 'October 29'.
Signed: 'William Morris'.
Notes: the whole text of the letter consists of one sentence: 'Dear Sir, Will you kindly contradict the report that I have been offered the Laureateship, as it is not true?' Morris had merely been 'sounded' on whether he would accept if an offer were made.

D-547: [*HSR* heading:] 'Hammersmith Socialist Society, Kelmscott House. Friends and Comrades' (leader), *HSR*, No. 17 (Feb. 1893), 1–2.
Initialled: 'W. M.'
Notes: on the Liberal government's policy failures, and an appropriate Socialist policy with reference to them.

D-548: [*HSR* heading:] 'Hammersmith Socialist Society, Kelmscott House. Friends and Comrades' (leader), *HSR*, No. 19 (Apr. 1893), 1–2.
Initialled: 'W. M.'
Notes: on the contradictions in the criminal justice system in a capitalist state.

D-549: [Journal's heading:] 'Mr. William Morris on "Town and Country"' (lecture notes), *The Journal of Decorative Art*, 13 (Apr. 1893), 106; from a lecture delivered in Jan. 1893, before the Ancoats Brotherhood, New Islington Hall, Manchester (see *Unpublished Lectures*, pp. 286–7, 319).
Notes: a brief summary, probably from Morris's notes, of a lecture covering the origins and development of English towns and their relationship to the countryside, with some reference to what the towns should be like in an enlightened future. This is the only contemporary account so far discovered of the lecture as a whole. Though Mackail quotes from 'a few pages of manuscript' several of which he says had been 'carefully written out', most of the lecture being 'delivered without notes' (see Mackail, ii. 301). But comparison of this journal report of the lecture and the contents of the 'carefully written' passages suggests that the passages are not merely the 1st part of a lecture, as Mackail suggests, but a condensed form of the whole.

D-550: [unheaded letter to Joseph Edwards, a founder of the Labour Church in Liverpool], *The Labour Prophet*, July 1893, p. 60; the letter is dated 'May 5, 1893'.
Signed: 'William Morris'.
Notes: a letter on the favourable prospects for Socialism, this was probably intended by Morris for reading on the May Day celebrations in the Labour Church, Liverpool, and for pbn. in *The Labour Prophet*, the organ of the Labour Church, of which there were a number of parishes. So, being obviously intended by Morris for pbn., it is included here as an initial publication. Both the matter and style suggest that Morris meant it to be so used and published.
Rptd. in *Letters*, iv. 41.

D-551: [Journal's heading:] '200 Curtain and Valance. Part of a bed hanging for Kelmscott Manor, Lechlade. Woolwork on linen'; later pbd. as 'For the Bed at Kelmscott', *Arts & Crafts Exhibition Society. Catalogue of the Fourth Exhibition 1893*, 4 (5 Oct. 1893), 36–7. The date is the date of the Exhibition's opening.
Signed: 'WILLIAM MORRIS'.
Notes: text to accompany the display of the bed hanging on which the poem is embroidered. Rptd. Mackail, ii. 268–9, and in *CW*, XXIV. 417 (where it is divided into 2 stanzas, unlike Mackail's version. This may be because the poem extends over 2 pages in this *Catalogue*, the 1st pbn. of the text. Morris's letter to Cockerell on 2 Oct. [1893] shows his attempt to correct a mistake in the text, 'quiet' having taken the place of the right word, 'grief'. But the *Catalogue* explains why the error occurs also in the printed text (*Letters*, iv. 92).

D-552: 'The Coal Struggle, Some Obvious Thoughts Thereon' (article), *The Sun*, 16 Oct. 1893, p. 6.
By-lined: 'By William Morris'.
Notes: on the political significance of the Yorkshire coal strike and lock-out, apparently written specially for *The Sun*. Rptd. in MM, ii. 519–21.

D-553: [Journal's heading:] 'Mr. William Morris on the Printing of Books' (lecture summary), *The Times*, 6 Nov. 1893, p. 4. A similar but slightly longer report also appears in *The Printers' Register*, 6 Nov. 1893, p. 4; lecture delivered on 2 Nov. 1893.
Notes: Morris wrote to Cobden-Sanderson, who was to chair this lecture, that his text could not be printed, 'as it will be but notes and lantern' (22 Sept. 1893, *Letters*, iv. 88). These reports remain the only indicators of the text found to date.

D-554: 'The Deeper Meaning of the Struggle' (to the Editor), *The Daily Chronicle*, 10 Nov. 1893, p. 4; the letter is dated 'November 9'.
Notes: also issued by the HSS as a fly-sheet, 'Help for the Miners; The Deeper Meaning of the Struggle' (see A-67.01).

D-555: 'The Ideal Book' (lecture), *Transactions of the Bibliographical Society*, 1 (1893), 179–86; originally delivered 19 June 1893.
Notes: read before the Bibliographical Society and also several times issued separately as a demonstration of fine printing by printers involved in what came to be known as 'the revival of printing'; see A-91.01 and *Unpublished Lectures*, p. 320.

D-556:* 'The [Annual] Report', *Society for the Protection of Ancient Buildings. The Sixteenth Annual Meeting of the Society. Report of the Committee thereat read. 18th July, 1893*. Aug. (?), 1893, pp. 53–4; delivered 18 July 1893.
Notes: Morris's remarks as chairman of the 16th annual meeting.

D-557: 'Some Notes on the Illuminated Books of the Middle Ages' (essay), *The Magazine of Art*, 17 (Jan. 1894), 83–9.
Notes: apparently written expressly for *The Magazine of Art*, with the editor of which Morris was in correspondence about this piece as early as 23 May 1890 (see *Letters*, iii. 160).

D-558: [Journal's heading:] 'Early England. Address by Mr. William Morris' (a summary report), *The Daily Chronicle*, 15 Jan. 1894, p. 6; delivered 14 Jan.
Notes: the lecture had been delivered earlier (see *Unpublished Lectures*, p. 260), but this is the only contemporary account of the text delivered at the South London Art Gallery; full text pbd. in *Unpublished Lectures*, pp. 158–78.

D-559: 'Why I Am a Communist' (article), *Liberty: A Journal of Anarchist Communism*, 1/2 (Feb. 1894), 13–15.
Series: The 'Why I Ams'.
By-lined: 'By William Morris'.
Notes: this was also printed at the 'Liberty' Press in a pamphlet titled *The Why I Ams* (2nd series, 1894, see B-17) and pbd. by James Tochatti. There it is combined with L. S. Bevington's 'Why I Am an Expropriationist'.

D-560: [Journal's heading:] 'The Proposed Addition to Westminster Abbey' (to the Editor), *The Daily Chronicle*, 27 Feb. 1894, p. 3; letter dated 'February 26'.
Signed: 'William Morris'.
Notes: a protest against Yates Thompson's proposal to add an extension to the Abbey as a 'mortuary chapel'.

D-561: [Journal's heading:] 'South Salford Branch' (lecture summary), *Justice*, 11/531 (17 Mar. 1894), 3.
Notes: the only report so far discovered of a lecture titled 'Waste' delivered for the South Salford Branch of the SDF at the Large Free Trade Hall, Manchester, 11 Mar. 1894. For detail of deliveries and bibliographical note, see *Unpublished Lectures*, pp. 288, 321.

D-562: 'May-Day, 1894' (poem), *Justice*, 11/538 (5 May 1894), 1.
Signed: 'William Morris'.

D-563: 'How I became a Socialist. III', *Justice*, 11/544 (16 June 1894), 6.
Series: the 3rd in a series titled 'How I became a Socialist' by leading members of the movement. The previous contributions to the series—from H. M. Hyndman and E. Belfort Bax—were interviews conducted by the Editor, but Morris's contribution is entirely his own, as is the 4th, by Walter Crane.
Bye-lined: 'William Morris'.
Notes: an article written in response to a request by the editor of *Justice*, Harry Quelch, for Morris to contribute to the 'How I became a Socialist series'. When the series ended in *Justice* (1894), Morris's essay was collected with the other contributors' in a book with the series name as title (see B-18). When Morris died on 3 Oct. 1896, this contribution was rptd. by the Twentieth Century Press as a memorial pamphlet. This included Hyndman's introduction and memoir and parts of 2 later Morris contributions to *Justice* (see A-82.01).

D-564: [Journal's heading:] 'Mr. Morris's "Chaucer"' (to the Editor), *The Daily Chronicle*, 24 July 1894, p. 3; letter dated 'July 20'.
Signed: 'William Morris'.
Notes: on the plans for issue of the KP edn. in mid-1895.

D-565: [Untitled paragraph in the column 'Between Ourselves'] (to the Editor), *Liberty: A Journal of Anarchist Communism*, 1/10 (1 Oct. 1894), 76.

Notes: Morris's answer to a question from the editor of *Liberty*, James Tochatti, on how work will be organized in a Socialist state, and whether and how provision will be made for artists, painters, and poets.

D-566: **[Unheaded letter]** (to the Editor), *The Clarion*, 3 Nov. 1894, p. 8; letter dated 'October 25, 1894'
Signed: 'William Morris'.
Notes: on behalf of the HSS on the need for a united Socialist party.

D-567: **[Unheaded letter]** (to the Editors of London daily papers), *The Daily News*, *The Daily Chronicle*, *The Standard*, *The Times*, and *The Morning Post*, 2 Apr. 1895 (all papers); letter dated 'April 1'.
Series: The 1st of 3 letters on Peterborough Cathedral. See also D-581 and 582.
Signed: 'William Morris'.
Notes: on necessary repairs, and against the 'restoration', of the west front of Peterborough Cathedral.

D-568: **[Journal's heading:]** 'Tree-felling in Epping Forest' (to the Editor), *The Daily Chronicle*, 23 Apr. 1895, p. 3; letter dated 'April 22'.
Signed: 'William Morris'.
Notes: 1st of 3 letters on this subject, responds to news of the establishment of an 'expert' committee to 'sit in judgment on Epping Forest' (see also D-569 and 572).

D-569: **[Journal's heading:]** 'Epping Forest' (to the Editor), *The Daily Chronicle*, 30 Apr. 1895, p. 3; letter dated 'April 27'.
Signed: 'William Morris'.
Notes: 2nd of 3 letters on this subject, this one responding to objections by Prof. Fisher, chairman of the 'expert committee', to some statements in Morris's previous letter, and stating Morris's intention to visit the Forest and report on what he finds there (see D-572).

D-570: 'As to Bribing Excellence' (article), *Liberty: A Journal of Anarchist Communism*, 2/17 (1 May 1895), 131.
By-lined: 'By William Morris'.
Notes: on the difference between Capitalist and Socialist views of production and rewards.

D-571: 'Change of Position——Not Change of Condition' (article), *Justice*, (Special May Day Edn.) 1 May 1895.
Notes: rptd. in the pamphlet *How I Became a Socialist*, see A-82.01.

D-572: **[Journal heading:]** 'Epping Forest. Mr. Morris's Report' (to the Editor), *The Daily Chronicle*, 9 May 1895, p. 3; letter dated 'May 8'.
Notes: the last of 3 letters on the subject (see also D-568–9). Having completed his inspection trip to the Forest, Morris details what he found there.

D-573: **[Journal's heading:]** 'The Royal Tombs in Westminster Abbey' (to the Editor), *The Times*, 1 June 1895, p. 13; letter dated 'May 31'.
Signed: 'William Morris, Hon. Sec. of the Society for the Protection of Ancient Buildings'.
Notes: a warning against restoration of the tombs in the Abbey.

D-574: **[Journal's heading:]** 'The Wood Beyond the World' (to the Editor), *The Spectator*, 20 July 1895, p. 81; letter dated 'July 16'.
Notes: Morris denies a critic's allegorical interpretation of his prose romance.

D-575: **[Journal's heading:]** 'Casts v. Tapestries' (to the Editor), *The Athenæum*, No. 3539 (24 Aug. 1895), 264–5; letter dated 'August 13'.
Notes: on the substitution of portrait plaster casts of Roman emperors for tapestries in the great hall at South Kensington, the 1st of 2 letters on this subject (see below).

D-576: **[Journal's heading:]** 'Casts v. Tapestries' (to the Editor), *The Athenæum*, No. 3540 (31 Aug. 1895), 298–9; the letter is not dated.
Notes: opposes the replacement of tapestries with plaster casts of portrait busts in the great hall at South Kensington. Morris's second letter on this subject (see also D-575).

D-577: **[Unheaded letter]** (to the Editor), *The Athenæum*.
Notes: on repairs or Restoration of Rouen Cathedral. Kelvin can find no evidence that this letter was actually published in *The Athenæum* (see *Letters*, iv. 321, note). He reconstructs the date as Sept. 1895 for the sending of this letter, there being no date on the rough draft and no evidence of pbn. But a notice 'To Correspondents' has Morris's initials, indicating that Morris's letter might well have been received but a decision not to publish was made.
The text was prtd. for the 1st time from the MS in *Let-*

ters, iv. 320–1.

D-578: [Unheaded letter] (to the Editor), *The Daily Chronicle*, 14 Oct. 1895, p. 3; letter dated '12 October'.
Notes: Morris's 2nd letter on repair or Restoration of Rouen Cathedral (see also D-577). Rptd. in *Letters*, iv. 324–9; also as 'The Restoration of Rouen Cathedral' in MM, i. 188–90.

D-579: 'Gossip about an Old House on the Upper Thames' (essay), *The Quest*, No. 4 (1 Nov. 1895), 5–14; the article is dated at the end: 'Kelmscott, October 25'.
Collaborators, Editors, and Illustrators: 2 illus. of Kelmscott Manor by Edmund H. New. Five 4-line initial letters by E. G. Treglown. Frontis. woodcut of Kelmscott Manor designed by C. M. Gere for *News from Nowhere* and cut by W. Hooper.
Signed: 'William Morris | Kelmscott, October 25.'
Notes: rptd. MM, i. 364–71. Copies of this article were used to create an unauthorized separate version (see E-14). There was also a legitimate separate of the same text pbd. by J. E. Hill in Flushing, NY (1901, see A-97.01). Another American, Will Bradley of the Wayside Press in Springfield, Mass., rptd. this article in 1896 in his art journal, *Bradley His Book*, 1/2 (June 1896), 27–32 (see Scott,. 65, *American Book Design*, 118–19, and Coupe, 187).

D-580: [Journal's heading:] 'Preservation of the Trinity Almshouses. A Ready Response. The Whole Amount Subscribed' (to the Editor), *The Daily Chronicle*, 26 Nov. 1895, p. 6; letter dated 'November 25'.
Signed: 'William Morris'.
Notes: opposing the pulling down of the houses.

D-581: [Unheaded letter] (to the Editor), *The Daily Chronicle*, 7 Dec. 1895, p. 6; letter dated 'December 5'.
Signed: 'William Morris'.
Notes: The 2nd of 3 letters opposing restorations to Peterborough Cathedral. See also D-567 and 582.

D-582: [Unheaded letter] (to the Editor), *The Daily Chronicle*, 13 Dec. 1895, p. 9; letter dated 'December 12'.
Series: The last of 3 letters on Peterborough Cathedral. See also D-567 and 581.
Signed: 'William Morris'.
Notes: on funding restorations at Peterborough Cathedral.

D-583: [Journal's heading:] 'Chichester Cathedral' (to the Editor), *The Times*, 14 Dec. 1895, p. 6; letter dated 'December 12'.
Signed: 'William Morris, Hon. Secretary to the Society for the Protection of Ancient Buildings'.
Notes: opposing the rebuilding of the north-west tower of Chichester Cathedral.

D-584: [Journal's heading:] 'Funeral of Stepniak' (report), *The Times*, 30 Dec. 1895, p. 9; the funeral was on 28 Dec. 1895.
Notes: a one-paragraph summary report of Morris's oration at the funeral of Sergius Stepniak.

D-585: 'On the Artistic Qualities of the Woodcut Books of Ulm and Augsburg in the Fifteenth Century' (lecture), *Bibliographica*, 1/4 (1895), 437–55.
Notes: the MS, in the Huntington, shows that S. C. Cockerell edited Morris's text for pbn. He also selected extracts from the article for use as the introduction to the KP edn. of *Some German Woodcuts of the Fifteenth Century* which is based partly on this article and partly on the *Catalogue* of Morris's library, which was started but never finished.

D-586: [Journal's heading:] 'Between Ourselves' (report of a lecture titled 'One Socialist Party' and the post-lecture discussion), *Liberty: A Journal of Anarchist Communism*, 3/1 (5 Jan. 1896), 7.
Collaborators, Editors, and Illustrators: report by the Editor, James Tochatti, in his column, 'Between Ourselves'. This is the only account so far discovered of this lecture.

D-587:* [Journal's heading:] 'Early Illustration: a Lecture', *The British and Colonial Printer and Stationer*, 37 (9 Jan. 1896), 10–11; Morris's lecture, titled 'The Early Illustration of Printed Books' was delivered 14 Dec. 1895, at the London County Council School of Arts and Crafts, Bolt Court, Fleet Street, where W. R. Lethaby was Principal.
Series: one of a series for the School of Arts and Crafts, the others including T. J. Cobden-Sanderson on 'Bookbinding' and Emery Walker on 'Typography'.
Notes: summary report of a lecture delivered with slides and recorded in shorthand. There may have been no full written text, Morris's later practice with slide presentations being to depend for continuity on his slides and notes. See, for example, the *Notes* to the entry 'On the

Printing of Books', D-553. Rptd., Peterson, pp. 15–24.

D-588: [Journal's heading:] 'William Morris on Socialism and Art' (to the Editors), *Justice*, 13/634 (7 Mar. 1896), 8, and *The American Fabian*, 2/2 (1 Apr. 1896), 12.
Signed: 'William Morris'.
Notes: Morris makes it clear to the general public as well as an unnamed correspondent, identified by Kelvin as Louis Edwin Van Norman, editor of *The American Fabian*, that his view of the relation of art to Socialism has not altered. Morris obviously authorized pbn. in both journals. Rptd. in Mackail, ii. 292–3 and in *Letters*, iv. 350–1.

D-589: [Unheaded letter] (to the Editor), *Justice*, 13/636 (28 Mar. 1896), 4.
Signed: 'William Morris'.
Notes: Morris's letter of thanks to the Executive of the SDF, occasioned by a resolution expressing sympathy and good wishes regarding Morris's illness, pbd. in *Justice* on 21 Mar.; not in *Letters*.

D-590: [Journal's heading:] 'The Kelmscott Press' (report), *Modern Art* (Boston), 4 (1 Apr. 1896), 36–9.
Notes: this journal article is a report of a paper read by Carl Edelheim to the Philobiblon Club of Philadelphia on 29 Jan. 1896. The paper includes 'in toto' Morris's previously unpublished account of the press, written in response to Edelheim's queries. Comparison of the texts shows clearly that this is an earlier version of what became *A Note by William Morris on His Aims in Founding the Kelmscott Press* (KP, see A-88.01). The MS includes an address and date at the end: 'Kelmscott House, Upper Mall, Hammersmith, 11 November, 1895' (see Christie's Catalogue. *Doheny*, vi. 79). Also rptd., perhaps from the KP version, in Sparling, pp 135–8.

D-591: 'The Present Outlook of Socialism in England' (article), *The Forum*, 21 (21 Apr. 1896), 01093–200.
Signed: 'William Morris'.
Notes: rptd. as 'Appendix A' in Kelvin, *Letters*, iv. 393–400.

D-592: 'The Promise of May' (article), *Justice*, Special May-Day Number, 1 May 1896, pp. 5–6.
Signed: 'William Morris'.
Notes: on Socialism as the only true hope of humankind.

D-593: [Journal's heading:] 'The Walsall Anarchists: The Amnesty Agitation' (to the Editor), *Liberty: A Journal of Anarchist Communism*, 3/5 (1 May 1896), 51. The letter was read at a public meeting at the South Place Institute on 22 Apr. 1896.
Headed: 'From William Morris—'.
Notes: written to support a campaign 'in favour of an amnesty being granted to the imprisoned Walsall Anarchists, Charles, Battola, and Cailes'. Not in *Letters*.

D-594: [Unheaded report of a speech], *A Beautiful World*, 3 (Dec. 1896), 16–18; speech delivered on 31 Jan. 1896.
Headed: 'Mr. William Morris: [. . .]'.
Notes: a speech seconding a resolution, 'that it is of national interest to protect rural scenery from unnecessary disfigurement', delivered at the Society of Arts during the annual meeting of The National Society for Checking the Abuses of Public Advertising. The text was included in the minutes of the annual general meeting and pbd. in the Society's journal, *A Beautiful World*.

D-595: [Journal's heading:] 'The Days that Were' (poem), *Eclectic Magazine*, 68/6 n.s. (Dec. 1898), 785.
By-lined: 'By William Morris'.
Notes: this is the 1st periodical appearance of the untitled poem 1st pbd. as an epigraph printed on the title page of *The House of the Wolfings* (see A-47.01). According to HBF (p. 140), Morris said it was, 'written just to fill up the great white lower half' of that page.

D-596: Reference entry, to list the pbns. of Morris in T. B. Mosher's annual collection titled *The Bibelot: A Reprint of Poetry and Prose for Book Lovers, chosen in part from scarce editions and sources not generally known.*
Notes: Most of these items do not fit the requirements of the D Section, not being 1st pbns. in a periodical (all the items taken from *The Oxford and Cambridge Magazine* were issued 50 or more years before the 1st of the Bibelot issues), but because of their inherent interest as well as their impact on Morris's American audience, they are listed here as well as in detailed descriptions in the A Section or, for Mosher's collections, the C Section, in accordance with their pbn. as separate issues of the Bibelot.
Among the 48 Mosher issues of some 20 Morris titles, he pbd. 12 Morris titles as separate Bibelot pamphlets and included each of them in the annual *Bibelot* collections:

1. 'The Hollow Land: A Tale', *The Bibelot*, in 2 parts: 3/1, 2 (July, Aug. 1897), 205–47, 249–81 (see A-83.01).
2. 'Browning's "Men and Women": A Review', *The Bibelot*, 4/3 (Mar. 1898), 87–122 (see also A-87.01).
3. 'Gertha's Lovers: A Tale', *The Bibelot*, in 2 parts: 5/1, 2 (Jan., Feb. 1899), 5–54, 57–102 (see also A-90.01).
4. 'The Two Sides of the River and Other Poems', *The Bibelot*, 5/9 (Sept. 1899), 277–93 204–7 (pagination error, corrected in the annual collection to 294–7) (see also C-8.01).
5. 'Golden Wings: A Tale', *The Bibelot*, 6/4 (Apr. 1900), 107–39 (see also A-95.01).
6. 'Svend and His Brethren', *The Bibelot*, 6/9 (Sept. 1900), 295–329 (see also A-96.01).
7. 'The Churches of North France No. 1', *The Bibelot*, 7/3 (Mar. 1901), 83–117 (see also A-98.01).
8. 'The Story of the Unknown Church: Lindenborg Pool', *The Bibelot*, 8/3 (Mar. 1902), 85–120 (see also C-16.01).
9. 'A Dream', *The Bibelot*, 8/7 (July 1902), 233–63 (see also A-101.01).
10. 'The Story of Frithiof the Bold', *The Bibelot*, in 2 parts: 15/1, 2 (Jan., Feb. 1908), 7–34, 35–63 (see also A-114.01).
11. 'Under an Elm-Tree . . . with an Essay by W. B. Yeats', *The Bibelot*, 18/4 (Apr. 1912), 103–11 (see also A-56.06).
12. 'Sir Peter Harpdon's End' (with 'A Critical Assessment of Sir Peter Harpdon's End' by John Drinkwater), *The Bibelot*, in 2 parts: 20/7, 8 (July, Aug. 1914), 247–72, 273–89 (see also A-122.01).

D-597: [Journal's heading:] 'William Morris: Designer' (2 poems), *The Studio*, Special Winter Number, 1934.
Notes: an article by Gerald Crow, this includes 2 previously unpublished Morris poems, 'Love and Death' and 'Guileful Love', reproduced as photographic facsimiles from Morris's calligraphic gift to Georgiana Burne-Jones, *A Book of Verse* (1st pbd. in 1980, see A-137.01).

D-598: 'An Unpublished Poem by William Morris', *English*, 15/87 (Autumn 1964), 100–2.
Signed: by Morris with an 'Icelandic pseudonym' on the fair copy: 'Vilhjalmr Vandraethaskald', i.e. 'William the troublous skald', (or so Morris translates the second word in *Heimskringla*).
Notes: an untitled poem of 56 lines, edited with introduction and notes by Ruth C. Ellison from the MS at the WMG.

D-599: [Journal's heading, under the general heading 'Notes and Documents':] 'An unpublished Poem by William Morris', *Modern Philology*, 62 (May 1965), 340–1.
Notes: Morris's 'Lonely Love and Loveless Death', was included in the calligraphic *A Book of Verse* of 1870 and presented as a birthday gift to Georgiana Burne-Jones. The book was issued in facsimile in 1980 (see A-137.01). The poem is edited with commentary and notes by David J. DeLaura from a MS in the Miriam Lutcher Stark Library, Humanities Research Centre, University of Texas.

D-600: 'An Unpublished Lecture of William Morris: "How Shall We Live Then?"' *The International Review of Social History*, 16/2 (1971), 217–40.
Signed: 'William Morris'.
Notes: the lecture is edited, annotated, and introduced by Paul Meier from a MS at the International Institute for Social History, Amsterdam (see also D-445).

D-601: 'An Unpublished Tale from The Earthly Paradise', *Victorian Poetry*, 13/3–4 (Autumn–Winter, 1975), 91–102.
Notes: an extensive report and analysis by K. L. Goodwin of Morris's 'The Story of Dorothea', a tale written for *The Earthly Paradise* but finally rejected. With paraphrase and quotation from the BL MS, this is the only readily available account so far pbd. of this tale, though the full text and the other 3 rejected tales are provided in David Latham's unpbd. thesis: 'A Variorum Edition of the Omitted Prologue and Tales of William Morris's *The Earthly Paradise*' (University of York, Ontario, 1981).

D-602: 'Unpublished Lyrics of William Morris', *Yearbook of English Studies*, 5, (1975), 190–206.
Notes: an article by K. L. Goodwin, this includes texts of 5 'unpublished' poems, 2 of which, 'Guileful Love' and 'A Summer Night', are from Morris's calligraphic *A Book of Verses* (for this vol. as pbd. in facsimile in 1980, see A-137.01). 'Dead and gone is all desire', 'Alone unhappy by the fire I sat' (a fragment), 'Dear if God praise thee much for many a thing', 'Peace for the joy abiding', 'Three chances and one answer', 'Everlasting Spring', 'Thy lips that I have touched no more may speak', and 'The world perchance to mock and jest would turn' are included from a group of MS May Morris placed in the 'period of The Earthly Paradise',

but left unpbd. As Goodwin acknowledges, 'Guileful Love' was previously pbd. in an article by G. H. Crow (see D-597).

D-603: '**The Expedition of The Ark**' (article), *The Journal of the William Morris Society*, 3/3 (Spring 1977), 2–11.
Notes: J. M. Baïssus edits and annotates the text of Morris's account, titled 'Description of an expedition by boat from Kelmscott House Upper Mall Hammersmith to Kelmscott Manor Lechlade Oxfordshire with critical notes'. This refers to the 1880 trip up the Thames to Kelmscott Manor. Edited from BL (Add.) MS (45407-vol. XVII 605 h.6).

D-604: [Journal's heading:] '**William Morris's Socialist Diary**', *History Workshop: A Journal of Socialist and Feminist Historians*, No. 13 (Spring 1982), 1–75).
Notes: Morris's unpublished diary of 1887, which begins on 25 Jan. and ends on 25 Apr. 1887; edited and introduced, with annotations and biographical notes by Florence Boos, whose text is from BL (Add.) MS 45335. 1st separate edn. issued in 1981 (see A-138.01).

D-605: [Editor's title, the MS being untitled:] '**The Novel on Blue Paper**' *The Dickens Studies Annual*, 10 (1982), 143–220).

Notes: This version is a literal transcription from Morris's holograph, BL (Add.) MS 45328. This article, produced by Penelope Fitzgerald, includes her introduction, pp. 143–51; a facsimile page from the MS, p. 152; Morris's text, pp. 153–215; and Fitzgerald's 'Conclusion' and her footnotes on the text, pp. 215–20 (see also A-139.01).

D-606: '"**Silence and Pity**"; **an Unpublished Fair Copy**' (poem), *The Journal of the William Morris Society*, 9/2 (Spring, 1991), 12–15.
Notes: this article is by Richard Pearson, who edits this Morris poem for the 1st time in its revised form (for the 1st, untitled version to be pbd., see D-602) and provides its significant background and annotations. The text is from a fair copy in the WMG, MS J149, the 1st line of which is 'Thy lips that I have touched no more may speak'.

D-607: '**Processes of Reproduction**' (essay), *Matrix*, 12/314 (Winter, 1992), 9–11.
Notes: an essay with the above title by Morris pbd. within an article on 'The Library of Emery Walker', by William S. Peterson. The text is from a MS in the Emery Walker Collection in The Cheltenham Museum and Art Gallery.

E

Forgeries, Piracies, and Sophistications

This list records those Morris publications so far discovered to be fraudulent, either creatively forged 1st edns. or genuine Morris pamphlets sophisticated by the addition of wrappers of a later, illegitimate manufacture, being unauthorized by Morris or his estate. 'Forgery' in this context refers to unauthorized publication of a genuine Morris pieces, usually with an invented imprint, with a bogus date, publisher, and printer either stated, as is the case with *Sir Galahad*, or implied, as in *Gossip about an Old House on the Upper Thames*. The object of the exercise in both these cases is to create a false rarity, an invented first edition attractive to the rare book market (at the turn of the century enjoying a heavy demand for modern first editions) or a 'scarce' version of a pamphlet made so by adding a wrapper printed specially for the purpose. The texts used are all genuine Morris texts, but the books that transmit them are fraudulent since they are published without authorization. All such false rarities are also piracies; and when sold within the period of copyright, as the Morris forgeries were, necessarily involve a violation of copyright. As Cockerell and Ellis's letter to *The Athenæum*, Nov. 20, 1897, put the matter:

> Unauthorized reprints of some of his [Morris's] contributions to the weekly and monthly press are now being offered for sale at high prices . . . it would be well for those concerned in the manufacture of these 'rarities' to remember that they are engaged in an act of piracy.

In order to avoid needless repetition, this list provides the only full descriptions of forgeries. They could not appear in Section A, the original editions, being by their nature false as publications of Morris. *The Two Sides of the River | Hapless Love | The First Foray of Aristomenes* has nothing to do with any selection made by Morris. Though his earlier publications supplied the texts, he did not choose to offer this combination of his poems to the public or to issue it in pamphlet form in 1876 (or any other time).

The sophistications are different however, being a mixture of truth and falsehood in their relation to the texts involved. Barker and Collins call these parts of publications 'chimaeras', a biological term to describe something foreign, or false, grafted on to a genuine stem. Here 'sophistication' indicates the attachment of false wrappers to a genuine Morris publication, thus implying an additional rarity and attracting a higher price in the saleroom. To avoid repetition the entries for unauthorized (and deliberately misleading) wrappers often contain cross references to Section A descriptions of the legitimate texts to which such sophistications were attached.

E-1: Sir Galahad: A Christmas Mystery

SIR GALAHAD | A CHRISTMAS MYSTERY. | BY | WILLIAM MORRIS. | LONDON: BELL AND DALDY, 186, FLEET STREET. | 1858

Edition: [1st impression, 1st separate edn.] A forgery, proved so by the presence of esparto grass in its paper (see *Notes*, below). The pamphlet, as Barker and Collins say, agreeing with HBF (p. 34), 'exists in two states: the earlier (A) in a unique copy at Texas, with the reading "hauberk" on p. 16, and a later (B), distinguished by progressive batter of what is clearly the same setting of types as A, and the reading "hauberke" on p. 16' (*Sequel*, p. 114). Obviously the two later researchers differ from Graham Pollard on the types employed. Pollard calls the 2 states 'two editions . . . one printed in modern face small pica . . ., the other printed in modern face pica' (*Quaritch Catalogue*, p. 15). The Barker and Collins description is favoured here, and it follows that a resetting of the later version's title page does not constitute a new edn. (see *Sequel*, 114). The presentation by Morris to 'D. Ward' (TxU copy) is, like the presentation to Ford Madox Brown in the Ashley copy, on an inserted leaf. Both must be considered fraudulent. Comparison of the 4 TxU copies, including the variant 'facsimile reprint' Forman describes, shows that they are all from the same setting of type, and all are fraudulent. In the 'facsimile reprint', though HBF fills nearly a page with its variations, these differences are only details within the original setting.

Publisher and *Printer*: the imprint indicates Bell and Daldy, 186, Fleet Street, but Forman says it, 'cannot be traced in the books of Messrs. George Bell & Sons, the imprint of whose predecessors, Messrs. Bell & Daldy, it bears' (HBF, p. 33). The pamphlet has no printer's imprint, and there is no record of this book in the Chiswick Press Arch. (Chiswick Press was the regular Bell and Daldy printer in 1858 and its records have been deposited in the British Library). HBF says that it was certainly not printed there (p. 33).

Collation: fcap. 8°: single gathering, unsigned, sewn through the centrefold, with a pair of conjunct leaves tipped in at the end to form pp. 17–[20]. 10 leaves pp. [1–5] 6–18 [19–20] [= 20] + a presentation leaf tipped in. The Morris presentation to Ford Madox Brown in the Ashley copy is clearly an additional leaf (making 11 leaves counting the insertion) with a genuine signature probably taken from a legitimate copy of a Morris book with a presentation inscribed to Ford Madox Brown, verso blank.

Contents: p. [1], half title: SIR GALAHAD; p. [2], blank; p. [3], title page; p. [4], blank; p. 5, dropped head title, text begins, 4-line stanzas of verse; pp. 6–18, text completed; pp. [19–20], blank.

Technical Notes: *paper*: white machine-made, no watermark; *leaf size*: 177 x 108 mm.; *printing*: *type area*: 117 x 80 mm.; *lines-to-page*: leaded, counting double spacing between stanzas, 20 lines; *running titles*: all rectos and versos: SIR GALAHAD, A CHRISTMAS MYSTERY; *binding*: no binding or wrapper; *print run* and *price*: not known.

Publication: though the imprint indicates '1858', the forgers' enterprise necessarily involved there being no historically verifiable date of issue. The earliest known public sale of this book occurred on 14 June 1897 (see *Enquiry*, 208), the year both H. B. Forman and Temple Scott described the book in their bibliographies of Morris. Before that the only reference to it appears to be that of T. J. Wise in *The Bookman*, in 1894. No evidence of an earlier date has been so far discovered except for a copy with a presentation inscription in Morris's autograph: 'H. Buxton Forman from William Morris, Nov. 23 1890'. This was part of H. B. Forman's collection sold in 1920, after Forman's death in 1917. It is worth noting that though both Wise and Forman had 'inscribed' copies, neither of these copies was cited as evidence of the pamphlet's authenticity when it was attacked by Proctor's 1898 letter pbd. in *The Athenæum*.

Register of Copies Examined: BL (2 copies: base copy: C.57.i. 33, with 2 bookplates on the front pastedown, one of John Drinkwater, the other of Oliver Brett. It is signed and dated in ink on the half title: *John Drinkwater | 1922*. Just below is a pencilled note in the same hand, presumably Drinkwater's: '*The extremely rare first edition, | perfect. Not to be confused with | the spurious reprint*'. Being both uncut and unbound it is possible to unfold the sheet, which proves to be a straightforward 8vo gathering with an additional pair of conjunct leaves tipped in to the verso of leaf 8 and forming pp. 17-18 and *19-20*); and Ashley 1211, with signed Morris presentation inscription to Ford Madox Brown, and 11 moulded-paper leaves. The leaf of the inscription has a trimmed & gilded top edge, like all the others, but the bottom edge, like the others untrimmed, is on an angle that makes it obviously not conjunct with any of the others. Conclusion: the signature leaf was tipped in after being taken from another source, probably a genuine presentation copy to Brown, whose books—including presentation copies—were sold at a sale from his house after Brown's death). TxU (4 copies: HRC WP M834 D858S, all bound, 3 in full calf by Riviere & Son for J. H. Wrenn).

Notes: suspicion about the authenticity of this pbn. was expressed by Robert Proctor, a typographical expert at the British Museum, a good friend of Sydney Cockerell, and one of the executors of the Morris Estate from F. S. Ellis's death in 1901 until his own death in 1903. Proctor's letter to *The Athenæum*, pbd. on 22 Jan. 1898 (rptd. in *Enquiry*, 208–9), reviewed the evidence—mostly an absence of evidence—and concluded that, 'All that is known about it seems to point to its being itself an unauthorized and later reprint from the "Guenevere" of 1858'.

In 1934, Carter and Pollard proved, by the presence of esparto in its paper, that this pamphlet is a 'forgery', i.e. a book created with a false imprint and so dated as to suggest a rare, previously unknown, 1st edn. Though the date on the title page of this pamphlet is 1858, esparto paper did not come into use in England until 1861. In fact, this pbn. is the 1st separate edn., but not the 1st pbn.: it does not antedate *The Defence of Guenevere and Other Poems* (1858), as Forman implies by his positioning of the entries, since it could not have been printed before 1861.

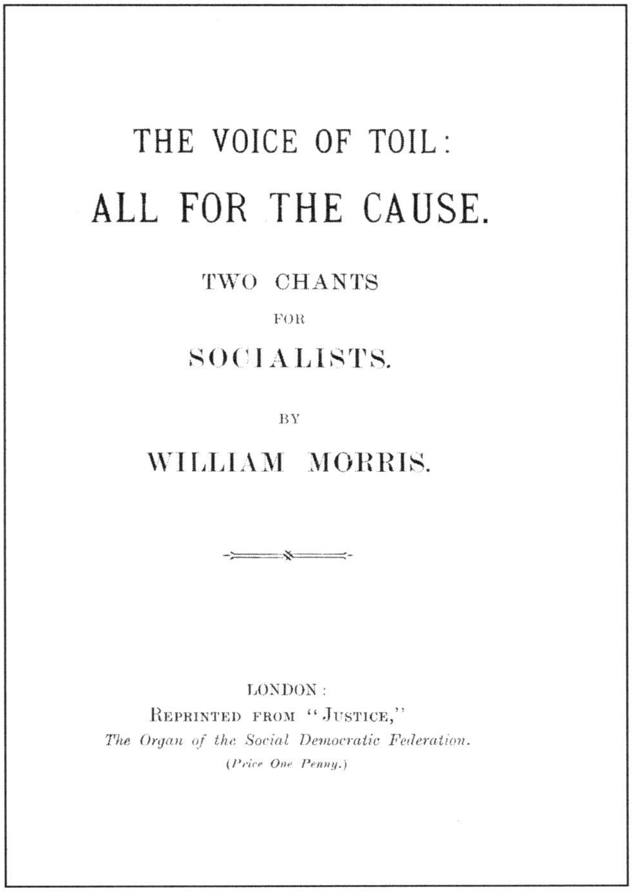

> THE VOICE OF TOIL:
> ALL FOR THE CAUSE.
>
> TWO CHANTS
> FOR
> SOCIALISTS.
>
> BY
> WILLIAM MORRIS.
>
> ———※———
>
> LONDON:
> REPRINTED FROM "JUSTICE,"
> *The Organ of the Social Democratic Federation.*
> (Price One Penny.)

Figure 95. E-2: *All for the Cause . . .* (forgery) wrapper title

E-2: Voice of Toil; All for the Cause: Two Chants

[wrapper title] THE VOICE OF TOIL: | ALL FOR THE CAUSE. | TWO CHANTS | FOR | SOCIALISTS. | [thin rule] | LONDON: | REPRINTED FROM "JUSTICE," | *The Organ of the Social Democratic Federation.* | (Price One Penny.)

Edition: a forgery intended to be taken for the 1st impression, 2nd edn. of *Chants for Socialists*, that being the position falsely implied for this pamphlet in the HBF sequence (see p. 110). Though the 2 poems here are genuine, having been 1st pbd. in *Justice* (see D-98 and 100) and included in the later collected versions of *Chants for Socialists*, this pamphlet is a later forgery, established as such by Barker and Collins on the basis of paper and type common to another forgery, *The God of the Poor*, and also common to the Twentieth Century Press, which did not begin production until 1893 (*Sequel*, 212–13). Forman positioned this pamphlet in his bibliography immediately after the 1st and only separate edn. of a lyric within the sequence. Forman implies publication in 1884 by placing this pamphlet immediately after *No 1. The Day is Coming* and before *The God of the Poor*, after which he says, 'There is one more booklet belonging to 1884', that being *Art and Socialism*. *Chants for Socialists No. 1. The Day is Coming* was actually issued in 1883, before *Justice* commenced publication (see A-23.01), and before the 1st collected edn. of 1885. Thus Forman's forgery takes advantage of a gap in the sequence of numbers implied by the 1st pamphlet in the series.

Series: this pamphlet is made up to look like a pamphlet belonging to a series (here treated as different issues of a single title, *Chants for Socialists*). It appears to come after *Chants for Socialists No. 1, The Day is Coming*, but none of the other *Chants* 1st issued in *Justice* and *Commonweal* as Nos. 2, 3 etc., were issued as separates before they were assembled in 2 collections titled simply *Chants for Socialists*, which were later several times rptd.

Publisher: the imprint is false; this title is never mentioned, much less advertised in *Justice*.

Printer: the printer's imprint (see *Contents*, below) is also a fiction. Comparison of types shows that this pamphlet was printed by the Twentieth Century Press sometime during or after 1893.

Collation: s. half sh. cr. 8°: [1]⁴ 4 leaves; pp. [1] 2–4 [5] 6–8 [= 8] self-wrappered + a red wrapper pasted on, but not on all copies (see *Technical Notes*, below).

Contents: p. [1], dropped head: THE VOICE OF TOIL | [thin rule] | I | [text begins]; pp. 2–8, text completed with 2 thin rules and imprint: PRINTED AT THE OFFICE OF "JUSTICE."

Technical Notes: *paper*: plain white machine-moulded, no watermark; *leaf size*: untrimmed, 193 x 130 mm.; *printing*: type area: 131 x 85 mm., excluding headlines; *lines-to-page*: leaded, 23 lines, including blanks between stanzas but excluding headlines; *headlines*: not used except for pagination, which is in arabic numbers centred on headlines; all stanzas of "The Voice of Toil" are numbered in roman numbers centred between stanzas; *wrapper*: p. [1], title page, see above; pp. [2–4], blank. It is pasted to the body and stapled through the middle with a single staple. Forman describes the wrapper as 'pale primrose', but the base copy used here is in a plain white wrapper. But Forman left hand-written notes among his papers in which he asserts the existence of a red wrapper as well: 'This is the only copy of the "Two Chants" I ever saw in a red wrapper. It was certainly issued in a primrose one like that of "The Day is Coming"'. In the extension of these notes he used the same form of words to describe the wrappers of another 'manufactured rarity', *The God of the Poor*, but the rarer wrapper is there the primrose one, being described in HBF (p. 110) as raising 'the blood-red banner of socialism by means of its wrapper'. In his notes Forman says, 'This is the only copy of "The God of the Poor" that I ever saw in a primrose coloured wrapper' (these hand-written notes are all transcribed in the *Quaritch Catalogue*).

Publication: 1884 is implied by H. B. Forman's positioning, but this is not so. Barker and Collins say, 'Although only one line of this pamphlet is set in type 35, common types and paper confirm that this was printed by the Twentieth-Century Press at the same time as *The God of the Poor*', also a forgery (*Sequel*, p. 213). Since the Twentieth Century Press did not begin production until 1893 (the 'Office of "Justice"' did not have a printing press until then), the conclusion must be that this pamphlet was pbd. some years later than the date implied by Forman's design of its title page, which obviously suggests it is an intended 2nd in the series of *Chants for Socialists*, the successive edns. of which tended to add more lyrics to those already published.

Register of Copies Examined: LeM (base copy: an unopened copy as it was printed on a single sheet and folded, but not stapled or sewn); BL (Ashley Lib. 1219); TxU (3 copies: HRC WP M834 885V, in special binding; another in a red wrapper, otherwise undistinguishable; and the third in a very light buff wrapper of distinctly different body from that of the pamphlet).

Notes: John Collins says in '. . . A Preliminary Enquiry' (hereafter referred to as Collins) that in The Voice of Toil: All for the Cause. Two Chants for Socialists (Forman, [item] 72) the type fount used is the same as the 'spurious wrapper' for *How I Became a Socialist*, a type described in *Enquiry* (pp. 227, 242).

Temple Scott says, '"The Voice of Toil" and "The Day of Days", both in "Poems by the Way" were reprinted as a leaflet and distributed to those attending a meeting of the South Place Ethical Society on February 21st 1897; on that occasion Dr Stanton Coit lectured on William Morris' (Scott, p. 60). Neither a copy nor other evidence has so far confirmed this.

E-3: Chants for Socialists

For all details of this pamphlet, see A-23.02. Only the false wrapper, with the appropriate documentation, is described here.

Edition: [1st impression, 2nd edn.; 1st collected edn.] Some copies of this pamphlet were sophisticated by Forman, who created for them a fraudulent wrapper. Only 1 copy with the forged wrapper has so far come to light, and that was in Forman's library as inherited by his son, Maurice. Barker and Collins find the types of the wrapper indicate that it, unlike the pamphlet itself, was prtd. at the Twentieth Century Press, which began operations in 1893 (see *Sequel*, 204).

Forman described the wrapper in *The Books of William Morris* (item 79): 'Copies are occasionally found in a red wrapper with the legend "CHANTS | FOR | SOCIALISTS | BY William Morris. | 1885."' But he made a long step toward candour (and a revelation of his methods) in a longhand note he left in his personal copy of this edn. of the *Chants*:

> Unlike most of the Socialist penny pamphlets of Morris, the demy 8vo "Chants" [this 6-lyric version] was issued uncut and simply folded with no stitching or metal-sewing. It had no wrapper as <u>published</u>. But I happened to go to the Office of the "Commonweal" just as it had been sold out all but a handful and the second edition with a seventh poem was just ready. I bought the handful and had the red wrapper printed to protect what seems to me still to be a very agreeable and sightly title page. I should not have chosen these ornamental types, but had to have what I could get. I had fifty of these wrappers done, and ultimately got copies enough for all of them (this MS is quoted in *Two Forgers*, pp. 136–7).

Technical Notes: wrapper: red paper introduced by Forman (reproduced in *Two Forgers*, p. [135]): p. [1] in Grecian type: CHANTS | [plain roman] FOR | [2-line Pica, 'Helvetian, 1883', later identified as '*Twentieth-Century Press*. 22', and cast at the Fann St. Foundry (see *Enquiry*, p. 354)] SOCIALISTS | [plain type] BY | William Morris. | 1885. [It should be noted that this wrapper-title has but 7 words, but is printed in 6 quite different fonts, an aesthetic solecism of which Morris would never have been guilty]. Barker and Collins observe that,

> No copies thus bound have been located except one of the two sold in the last Forman sale at Sotheby's, 12 April 1972, lot 251, with the note quoted above. The types, in particular 129 and 140, used for the wrapper suggest that it was printed at the Twentieth-Century Press.
>
> Conclusion: A chimaera, with a false wrapper, intended to 'improve' a genuine pamphlet (*Sequel*, 204).

Register of Copies Examined: see this field in A-23.02.

E-4: Two Sides of the River (+ 2 poems)

THE TWO SIDES OF | THE RIVER | HAPLESS LOVE | AND | THE FIRST FORAY OF | ARISTOMENES | BY

| WILLIAM MORRIS | LONDON | 1876 | [*Not for Sale*]
Edition: [unauthorized 1st impression, 1st edn.] A forged 1st edn., actually a collection invented by Buxton Forman and Thomas J. Wise, as is revealed in the Symington Correspondence now at Rutgers University Library. On 17 Feb. 1890, Forman wrote to Wise, saying, 'the three Morris poems I spoke of are to be found in the Fortnightly for Oct., 1868, Good Words for 1 Apr., 1869, and the Athenæum for 15 May, 1876—probably all easy enough to get' (see *Sequel*, 211). The journal entries Forman cites are the 1st pbns. of the 3 poems included in this pamphlet's title.
Publisher: [a collaborative, clandestine production, i.e. very privately printed, by H. Buxton Forman and T. J. Wise].
Printer: [Richard Clay] (see *Sequel*, 210–12).
Collation: post 8°: [1]¹² 12 leaves pp. [1–5] 6–22 [23–4] [= 24].
Contents: p. [1], half title: THE TWO SIDES OF THE RIVER | HAPLESS LOVE | AND | THE FIRST FORAY OF | ARISTOMENES; p. [2], blank; p. [3], title page; p. [4], blank; p. [5], dropped head: [1st poem head title] | text begins; pp. 6–22, text completed; pp. [23–4], blank.
Technical Notes: *paper*: plain cream-white machine-wove paper with dandy roll laid lines, no watermark; *leaf size*: cut flush, 192 x 123 mm.; *printing*: type area: 125 x 73 mm.; *lines-to-page*: leaded, with extra half spaces between speeches or stanzas counted here, 28 lines; *running heads*: all versos and rectos: relevant poem title in italic caps; *wrapper*: both BL copies have the original wrappers bound in their special bindings: sage-green machine-made paper without marks other than the title, enclosed in a thin-rule compartment on the front, duplicating the half title (see above).
Publication: the imprint date of 1876 is false, and being a 'creative forgery' of a 1st edn., the pamphlet could have no date of issue. The earliest credible evidence of its existence seems to be 30 Apr. 1894, when a Manchester bookseller, J. E. Cornish, bought a copy from Wise which he later sold to the BL (see *Sequel*, 210–12). That copy (one of two in the BL), described here, has its accession date stamped on p. 22: '12 No 94'. And on 18 May 1894 Wise mentions it along with *Sir Galahad* in his *Bookman* review of Slater's *Early Editions* as 'the two most difficult of Mr. Morris's books to procure' (quoted in *Sequel*, 211). But it is of some significance that though Wise had signed copies of *Sir Galahad* and *The Two Sides of the River. . .* , when their legitimacy was brought into question, he made no attempt to claim legitimacy for the pamphlets on the basis of those signatures. Perhaps he knew that they could not stand up to close inspection.

Register of Copies Examined: BL (2 copies: base copy: C. 59. g. 7., with BL accession stamp and date, and Ashley 1217, with Morris's signature on the half title); NNBerg, with blue paper-covered boards and a white cloth spine, and the original wrapper bound in; MU (Spec. Coll. PR 5078 T9 1876).
Notes: Barker and Collins summarize the scholarship on this pbn. in *Sequel*, 210–11. Rptd., and used as copy text in legitimate American edns., both as a 2-part serial separate edn. (see C-8.01 and .02) and as a 2-part item in T. B. Mosher's annual collection *The Bibelot: A Reprint of Poetry and Prose for Book Lovers, chosen in part from scarce editions and sources not generally known*, 5/9 and 10 (Sept. 1899), 277–98 (see D-596). The publisher, T. B. Mosher, was apparently unaware of the fraudulence of the Wise-Forman pamphlet from which he took the 1st 3 poems for his collection.

E-5: The God of the Poor
THE GOD OF THE POOR. | BY | WILLIAM MORRIS, | AUTHOR OF "THE EARTHLY PARADISE." | [decorated thin rule] | ORIGINALLY PUBLISHED IN THE | "FORTNIGHTLY REVIEW," AUGUST 1, 1868.
Edition: [unauthorized 1st impression, 1st separate edn.] Though it is a 1st separate edn., it is also a forgery (see *Notes*, below).
Publisher: 'The Social Democratic Federation', a fictitious imprint.
Printer: Printed at the Office of "Justice", | *The Organ of the Social Democratic Federation*; fictitious printer's imprint (from the wrapper).
Collation: s. half sh. 8° folded to form 4 leaves pp. [1–2] 3–8 [= 8] + paper wrapper.
Contents: p. [1], title page; p. [2], blank; p. 3, dropped head title: THE GOD OF THE POOR. | [text begins]; pp. 4–8, text completed.
Technical Notes: *paper*: plain white machine-made, no watermark; *leaf size*: 193 x 126 mm.; *printing*: type area: 142 x 69 mm.; *lines-to-page*: set solid, 44 lines, including blank lines separating each quatrain; *headlines*: not used except for pagination: arabic numbers centred between margins; *wrapper*: stiff red paper sewn, p. [1]: THE GOD OF THE POOR | BY | WILLIAM MORRIS, | AUTHOR OF "THE EARTHLY PARADISE." LONDON: | PRINTED AT THE OFFICE OF "JUSTICE," | The Organ of the Social Democratic Federation. | (Price One Penny.); pp. [2–4], blank. Forman, in his hand-written notes found after his death among his papers, describes a second wrap-

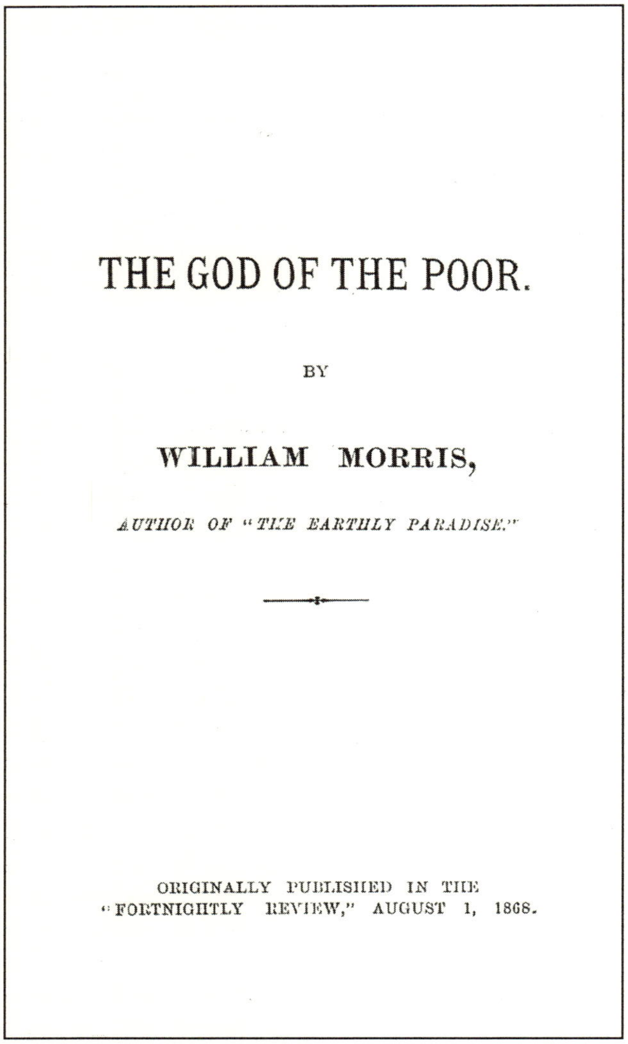

Figure 96. E-5: *The God of the Poor* (forgery) title page

per in 'pale primrose' of which he had seen only a single copy (see this field in E-2).
Publication: [n.d.] 1884 is implied by Forman's placing of this pamphlet in the chronology of his *Books of William Morris Described*. The actual date is more likely to be 1896 or 1897; *print run* and *price*: not known.
Register of Copies Examined: MU (base copy: Spec. coll. PR 5078 G6 1884); BL (Ashley Lib. 1220); NN Berg (binding by Tout for Harold Pierce); TxU (Wp M834 865g); Bass.
Notes: a manufactured rarity exposed as such by S. C. Cockerell's marginal note, '?unauthorized by W. M.', in his copy of Forman's *The Books of William Morris Described* (quoted in *Sequel*, 205). Morris published the poem in *The Fortnightly Review* in Aug. 1868 (see D-18). Cockerell's judgement of the pamphlet is confirmed by Barker and Collins in their *Sequel*, where they cite typographical evidence, saying it is 'condemned as a forgery by the presence of type 35, the Figgins Long Primer 11/15 peculiar to the Twentieth-Century Press' (*Sequel*, 205). That press was not established until 1893. So the publisher and the printer of the imprint on the wrapper, and the implied date are all fictitious. The pamphlet is a forgery, a fabricated relic, as well as a piracy (since it violates the law of copyright). Not only is it unauthorized, but its imprint (quoted in Forman), and its position in the chronology of Forman's narrative suggest a false earlier date, 1884, which if true would have made it a previously unknown 1st edn.

In a hand-written note inserted in his personal copy, Forman again suggests a complication: a second wrapper of a different colour, the only copy of which, it seems, belonged to Forman himself. This device, also deployed in *The Voice of Toil: All for the Cause. Two Chants for Socialists*, may have been introduced as a distraction from more basic questions, the variant for all its differences of detail being also the product of Forman's 'art'. Besides copies 1st issued with a red paper wrapper, there was one, in Forman's collection, with a primrose wrapper. Of it Forman wrote:

> This is the only copy of "The God of the Poor" that I ever saw in a primrose coloured wrapper. This pamphlet and "The Voice of Toil" having both been printed at the office of "Justice", there must have been an accidental transposition of coloured papers through having the two little prints in hand at the same time. This accident tends to fix the date of "The God of the Poor" pamphlet as identical with that of the others (quoted in *Quaritch Catalogue*, p. 16).

Barker and Collins continue:

> The evidence being that the Twentieth Century Press probably produced both the pamphlets, their wrappers, and the variant of the latter as well, it is possible to agree with Forman that the 2 pamphlets probably date from the same time, but it is more likely to be after 1896 than in 1884, the 1st known copies being catalogued in 1897 by a dealer, Jones and Evans' (*Sequel*, 205).

The evidence available leaves no doubt that both the pamphlets and the red and primrose wrappers originated with HBF.

Of *The God of the Poor*, Forman says,

> This again is an untrimmed crown 8vo. of eight pages,

but this time with a regular title page and six pages of text, numbered centrally in arabic figures. It is sewn into a red wrapper on which the upper part of the title[page] is reproduced, with the imprint "London: | PRINTED AT THE OFFICE OF "JUSTICE," *The Organ of the Social Democratic Federation.* | (Price One Penny.)." Pages 2, 3 and 4 of the wrapper are blank. The refrain *Deus est Deus pauperum*, instead of following each of the 52 stanzas as in *The Fortnightly Review* is only printed after the first and last (HBF, p. 111).

These details are all correct, except that the pamphlet could not have been 'printed at the Office of "Justice," ' as the imprints for this pamphlet and *The Voice of Toil: All for the Cause. Two Chants for Socialists* both aver. The DF, and therefore *Justice*, owned no printing press in 1884. Corroboration of this is a resolution of the SDF Executive, reported in *Justice*, 1/49 (20 Dec. 1884), 6, where it was decided to leave the printing of the SDF in the hands of 'Foulger and Co.', the owners of The Modern Press, 13 and 14, Paternoster Row, and printers of *Justice* from Jan. 1884. Their imprint appeared as follows on the last page of each issue of *Justice* they printed: 'London—Printed and Published for the Proprietors at the Modern Press, 13 and 14, Paternoster Row, E.C.' (see *Justice*, 1/2 (26 Jan. 1884), 8).

Thus, it is obvious that the imprint on the pamphlet is false, as is the date, 1884, under which Forman places it, immediately after *The Voice of Toil: All for the Cause. Two Chants for Socialists*. It and *The God of the Poor* were labelled, by Cockerell, '?unauthorized by W. M.' Cockerell also suggested to Forman at the time that: 'if, as you hint in your letter, you are responsible for the existence of some of these (especially *The God of the Poor* and *The Voice of Toil*), I think there ought to be some statement of it in your bibliography or elsewhere, in order to separate these artificial rarities from duly published & authorized reprints—what do you think?' (quoted in *Sequel*, 156–7).

No reply from Forman to this has been found; and, needless to say, he made no such public disclaimer.

E-6: Socialist League Manifesto (2nd impression, 1st edn.)

[2nd impression, 1st edn.] This is a legitimate pamphlet (for details see A-29.02) for which Forman in his handwritten notes asserted the existence of a white paper wrapper (HBF, p. 115) which included the line WRITTEN BY WILLIAM MORRIS (which alone condemns it as a forgery) below Walter Crane's Socialist League block (No. 2). Morris says the authorship was 'conjoint with Belfort Bax' (*Letters*, ii. 370).

E-7: Socialist League Manifesto (1st impression, 2nd edn.)

[forged 'Turner-grey' wrapper title] THE MANIFESTO | OF | [photographic reproduction of Walter Crane's SL line-block no. 2 with masthead: THE SOCIALIST | LEAGUE] | [below the block] WRITTEN BY WILLIAM MORRIS, | SIGNED BY THE PROVISIONAL COUNCIL AT THE FOUNDATION OF THE | LEAGUE ON 30TH DEC. 1884, AND ADOPTED AT | THE GENERAL CONFERENCE | *Held at FARRINGDON HALL, LONDON, ON JULY 5TH*, 1885. | [wavy rule] | LONDON | [gothic] Socialist League Office, | [italic plain type] 13, *FARRINGDON ROAD, HOLBORN VIADUCT, E.C.* | [thin rule] | 1885.

[original title page of the pamphlet] THE MANIFESTO | OF | [Walter Crane's block No. 2, with masthead: THE SOCIALIST | LEAGUE] | SIGNED BY THE PROVISIONAL COUNCIL AT THE FOUNDATION OF THE | LEAGUE ON 30TH DEC. 1885, AND ADOPTED AT | THE GENERAL CONFERENCE | *Held at FARRINGDON HALL, LONDON, on July 5th*, 1885 | [thin rule with a central circle] | A New Edition, Annotated by | WILLIAM MORRIS AND E. BELFORT BAX. | [wavy rule] LONDON: | [in gothic] Socialist League Office, | 13 FARRINGDON ROAD, HOLBORN VIADUCT, E.C. | 1885. | *PRICE ONE PENNY.*

Edition: [1st impression, 2nd edn.] This also has a false wrapper, described by Forman as 'Turner-grey' and 'rare', but it seems to have been designed by Forman himself, though the 'Turner-grey' one has not been found on any copies other than the one included in the Quaritch Catalogue. For descriptions of the original legitimate pamphlet see A-29.01.

Technical Notes: H. B. Forman says, 'though generally circulated without a wrapper, there are copies—but these are rare—in a Turner-grey wrapper on which the title is repeated with an additional line below the design, "WRITTEN BY WILLIAM MORRIS," and the words "price one penny" omitted' (HBF, p. 115). In their *Sequel* (206–7), Barker and Collins find that:

> The wrapper mimics the title exactly . . . except that it adds 'written by William Morris' beneath Walter Crane's woodcut 'The Socialist League' block. But it is set in different types throughout, which can be identified as Billing's by

comparison with *Books of William Morris*, and the block has been photographically copied from the original title-page as a process line-block, with the loss of the two rather indeterminate points between the three words of the title. These were evidently routed away by the engraver with other 'unwanted' details. (Crane, perhaps deliberately, failed to take down the white areas of the block enough) (*Sequel*, 206–7).

They conclude that this wrapper renders the pamphlet 'A chimaera' *(Sequel*, 207).
A chimaera being a true plant with something foreign, hence false, grafted thereto, hence the graft, they say, is 'a false wrapper, probably printed by Billing at the same time as Books of William Morris'. In other words, this is a genuine pamphlet sophisticated by the addition of a manufactured rarity, a false wrapper, probably arranged by Forman himself.

But one of the more serious consequences of this operation is the falsification of the authorship, which, as Morris himself avowed, was in truth a collaborative effort of himself and Bax in both the original text and the annotations (see the *Notes* to the 1st edn., A-29.01). By that standard one must condemn both the white paper wrapper pictured in Forman (p. 115) and the 'Turner-grey' wrapper described but not pictured at the bottom of p. 115, which seems never to have appeared elsewhere than on Forman's own copy as it is described in the *Quaritch Catalogue*, p. 18.
Register of Copies Examined: Bass (base copy, but without the forged wrapper).

E-8: Socialists at Play

SOCIALISTS AT PLAY. | BY | WILLIAM MORRIS. | ***Prologue | Spoken at the Entertainment of | the Socialist League:*** | **SOUTH PLACE INSTITUTE**, | ***June 11***, | 1885.
Edition: [1st impression, 1st separate edn.] A forgery, the text of which was 1st pbd. in *Commonweal*, 1/6 (July 1885), 56. Cockerell condemned it with his usual formula: '? unauthorized by W. M.' (quoted in *Sequel*, 210). Graham Pollard observed that 1 copy differed from the 4 (all printed from the same setting of type) in the Maurice Buxton Forman Sale of 1972. Besides the 3 covered with red paper was one with a brown paper wrapper printed on fine paper and watermarked '1896', undisputable evidence of a forgery. It was produced 'at least eleven years later than the date on the title-page' (Graham Pollard in *Quaritch Catalogue*, p. 19). This copy is in the collection of Sanford Berger, now in the Huntington Library, San Marino, California).
Printer: no printer's imprint, but Barker and Collins establish that the pamphlet was printed at the Twentieth Century Press as is shown by 'the presence of type 32, an American type not advertised there before 1892 and unlikely to have been available in Britain earlier... [which with] other types associate it with other works produced by the Twentieth-Century Press' (*Sequel*, 210).
Collation: small 4° (HBF, p. 117, says 'royal 16mo. of 8 pages (a quarter of a sheet)', hence), 4 leaves pp. [1–5] 6–8 [= 8] + a coloured wrapper.
Contents: p. [1], title page; p. [2], blank; p. [3], half title; p. [4], blank; p. [5], dropped-head title: SOCIALISTS AT PLAY | [thin rule] | [text begins]; pp. 6–8, text completed with thin rule.
Technical Notes: *paper*: 2 papers used in different copies, laid and wove, both white; *leaf size*: cut flush, 163 x 125 mm.; *printing*: *lines-to-page*: leaded, 22 lines including blanks between verse paragraphs and excluding headline; *pagination*: arabic numbers centred between margins on headline; *wrapper*: cut flush, 2 wrappers, red or brown paper; p. [1] reproduces the title page; all other pages blank.
Publication: the title page says 'June 11, 1885', so placed on the title page of the pamphlet as to imply a date of issue. But the '1896' watermark on one of the known copies betrays that implication. The earliest public record of its appearance on the market appears to be 21 Oct. 1901, when it was sold at Bangs (*Sequel*, 210); *print run* and *price*: unknown, those details being among the forger's secrets.
Register of Copies Examined: BL (base copy: Ashley Lib. 1221); NjP; CtY; TxU: MU; Bass.

E-9: Pilgrims of Hope

THE | PILGRIMS OF HOPE | A POEM | IN THIRTEEN BOOKS | Brought together from "The Commonweal" | FOR MARCH, APRIL, MAY, JUNE, AUGUST, SEPTEMBER, & NOVEMBER, 1885, | AND JANUARY, MARCH, APRIL, MAY 8, JUNE 5, & JULY 3, | MDCCCLXXXVI.
Edition: [unauthorized 1st impression, 1st separate edn.] This is the 1st separate edn., but unauthorized, hence a forgery, produced 'privately for friends', according to Forman's prefatory 'Note' (p. 5). Probably produced in the late 1890s by H. B. Forman, with text taken from *Commonweal*. 3 parts—'The Message of the March Wind', 'Mother and Son', and 'The Half of Life Gone'—were reprinted by Morris in *Poems by the Way in 1891*. Forman's 'Note' says,

Forgeries, Piracies, and Sophistications

When a few sections of this poem had appeared in *The Commonweal* many besides myself thought that *The Pilgrims of Hope* was not only a beautiful work, but by its subject and treatment highly important to educated readers. On the appearance of the last part, I tried to persuade Mr. Morris to publish the whole at once as a volume. He demurred, saying that the matter needed consideration and that the poem might want much revision. In several talks I upheld the view that it was not for such a work as this to lie buried in a socialist paper concerned mainly with questions of immediate politics, and so fail to come into the hands of more than a few among the reading classes who have his works in their libraries, as a permanent source of pleasure and profit. Failing to carry the point, I said we must have the poem in book form somehow, and that I would print a short issue in a decent manner privately for friends. Being unforbidden, I have proceeded to carry out my project; and indeed it has not been difficult to persuade the poet that a dozen or two copies cherished in libraries where the rest of his poems are lovingly guarded do not add one whit to the publicity of the book pending the arrival of the time when he may set about revising it for a general circulation. We now have the sketch in book form, and a grand sketch it is. For the elaborated final work we await the poet's leisure and pleasure' (HBF, pp. 15–16).

Barker and Collins conclude:

The title-page is so arranged that the date 'MDC-CCLXXXVI' can be construed in two ways . . . the obvious interpretation—and the one which Buxton Forman himself endorsed by placing the book under this year in his *Books of William Morris*—is that it was printed in 1886. But it could equally refer to the date on which the later instalments of the poem were published in *The Commonweal*. In fact we have been unable to find any evidence for the existence of the book before April 1897. There are four references to it in that year (B.M. reception, Ashley copy bound, the bibliographies of Scott and Forman (*Sequel, 208*).

Forman's claim to authorization from Morris himself raises questions. 1st, Forman's implied dating for his edn. and his supposed discussion of that with Morris conflicts with the evidence of Morris's view as expressed both before and some years after the *Commonweal* version of the poem appeared. The fact is Morris never revised or republished the poem as a whole because he considered it unfinished. The last instalment as it appeared in *Commonweal* ended with the note 'to be concluded', after which no conclusion ever appeared. But he selected 3 parts of the poem for pbn. in *Poems by the Way* (1891): 'The Message of the March Wind', 'Mother and Son', and 'The Half of Life Gone'. Obviously these are the parts he thought justified reprinting. 2nd, though Forman says in his prefatory note that he was 'unforbidden' to reprint the poem, there is no evidence that anyone saw the finished reprint until 4 copies are suddenly recorded in 1897, the year after Morris's death, one being presented by Forman to the British Museum. That copy is accession-stamped '9 April, 1897'. And an earlier copy, inscribed and dated 23 Mar. 1897, was presented by the editor to Edmund Gosse (copy now at MU). But there is no record of any copy being presented to Morris. The posthumous catalogue of his library, prepared by his secretary, S. C. Cockerell, records no copy.

From late 1886 to late 1897 seems a long delay for the pamphlet to make a 1st public appearance, the inscription date of the Gosse copy at the MU, the earliest so far unearthed, being some six months after the death of Morris. It would seem that if Morris gave permission after July 1886, for a private printing to be issued, he would have expected to have a copy before the year was out. But Cockerell wrote to Forman in 1897 to say, 'I have never seen a copy and begin to wonder whether it may not be an unauthorized reprint' (quoted in *Two Forgers*, 139).

Printer: Barker and Collins say: 'No printer's imprint, but printed by Richard Clay. A set of proofs in the 1972 Forman sale (Sotheby's, 12 Apr. 1972, lot 252) bore the initials, Mac G., T. F., A. K. and T. F. P., of compositors and readers employed by Clay' (see *Sequel*, 207).

Collation: sq. cr. 8°: π² [A]⁸ B–D⁸ E⁴ [$2 (–E2) signed] 38 leaves pp. [4] [1–5] 6–69 [70–2] [= 76] + a blue wrapper.

Contents: pp. [1–2], blank; p. [3], half title; p. [4], blank; p. [1], title page; p. [2], blank; p. [3], Contents; p. [4], blank; p. [5], Note begins; p. 6, Note ends; p. [7], 2nd half title, as the 1st; p. [8], blank; p. 9, text begins; pp. 10–69, text completed with explicit: THE END; pp. [70–2], blank.

Technical Notes: *paper*: cream 'antique' machine-moulded, with dandy roll laid lines, no watermark; *leaf size*: cut flush, 191 x 135 mm.; *printing*: type area: 123 x 103 mm. excluding head and direction lines; *lines-to-page*: leaded, generally 28 lines, but with occasional extra spacing between verse paragraphs; *headlines*: all versos: THE PILGRIMS OF HOPE.; all rectos, the relevant chapter titles, all centred; *wrapper*: plain blue-grey paper, 'antique' machine-wove, with title printed on p. [1]: THE | PILGRIMS OF HOPE | BY | WILLIAM MORRIS; pp. [2–4], blank.

Publication: 1886 [this is the date implied by the design of the title-page, by the change in numerals from arabic to roman, centred, by Forman's use of tense in reference to Morris in his prefatory 'Note' to the pamphlet, and by the placing of this entry in the chronology of *The Books of William Morris described*. But the implied date is false. A more likely approximate date would be shortly before 23 Mar. 1897, that being the earliest appearance of the pamphlet recorded so far, but there could be no formal date of issue for a forgery; *print run*: unknown: Forman's 'Note' says 'a dozen or two copies' but more may exist; *price*: no price is specified, nor could it be for a forgery which could never be released in the normal way of a public issue.

Register of Copies Examined: MU (base copy: Spec. Coll.: PR 5078 P5 1886, presentation copy from Forman to Edmund Gosse, dated '23 March 1897', with Gosse's bookplate); NNPM (77555 M); NNBerg; Fdmn; BL (2 copies: Ashley 1228 and 011652.g.55.)

E-10: Socialist Platform (wrapper)

THE SOCIALIST PLATFORM | WRITTEN BY SEVERAL HANDS FOR | [Walter Crane's SL block, No. 2, with masthead design incorporating] THE SOCIALIST | LEAGUE | [below the block] TOGETHER WITH | THE MANIFESTO | AND | CHANTS FOR SOCIALISTS | BY | WILLIAM MORRIS. | [wavy rule] | LONDON: | [in gothic] Socialist League Office | [plain type] 13, FARRINGDON ROAD, HOLBORN VIADUCT, E.C. | 1888. | [thin rule] | *Price One Shilling*.

Edition: the transcribed wrapper title above (based on Forman's bibliography, p. 133) does not exist as part of any book (but see the *Register of Copies Located*, below). 'The Socialist Platform', used as a short title, heads an editorial preface prtd. in the early pamphlets of the series and signed by the co-editors, Morris and Bax (see B-6). The evidence available at present suggests that, so far as a composite vol. of Socialist League publications is concerned, the title 'The Socialist Platform' as transcribed above exists only (1) as a numbered series of Socialist League pamphlets (the early numbers of the pamphlets were produced with continuous pagination, as if for later collection into a vol., but they were never, apparently, so collected); (2) as 2 entries in H. B. Forman's *The Books of William Morris described* (items 102 and 111); and (3) as 6 printed proofs of paper wrappers found among the Forman books and described by Graham Pollard in the *Quaritch Catalogue* (item 92) of the 1973 Forman sale. The idea of a vol. collecting various SL pamphlets was conceived originally by Morris and Bax, who were appointed early in 1885 as editors of the pamphlet series. A set of MS notes in Morris's hand survives in the SLA, signed by both Bax and Morris and listing 16 prospective titles for pamphlets in the series and their nominated authors. But it was Forman, not the SL, that produced wrappers for the composite edn., of which no copy has yet been discovered.

The proofs of 6 forged wrappers Forman left to his son, with the title pages transcribed, essentially, as above, were apparently all printed at the same time, probably by Billings, and under Forman's order, using mostly the same setting of type, though they bear different publication dates: one dated 1885, two dated 1888, and 3 dated 1890. They are described by Graham Pollard in the *Quaritch Catalogue*:

> All six of the wrappers are different: the one for 1885 is on white paper, bears the imprint of the Socialist League Office in gothic type and is priced: the two for 1888 are the same as that for 1885 except for the date and one is on green paper; lastly the three for 1890 all bear the imprint *The Commonweal*, two are on white paper, the other on apricot and of the two white copies one has the price omitted. Quite a few faulty letters indicate that the majority of the setting is the same for all the wrappers, even though the dates printed on them extend over a period of five years [actually 6]. All the wrappers are of similar design using the Socialist League block and on all of them it is the copied block as identified in the *Manifesto of the Socialist League* [see *Technical Notes* in E-7]. The final positive evidence against these wrappers is that three of the pamphlets listed in the contents on the front of the 1885 wrappers were published after that date (*Quaritch Catalogue*, item 92).

The 6 wrappers described in the *Quaritch Catalogue*, Lot No. 926, item 92, p.22, are evidence that Forman took considerable care to take advantage of the possibilities opened to him by the publishing policies and practices of the Socialist organizations to which Morris made literary contributions.

Register of Copies Located: As noted above, no book has been found with the wrapper described here. But the *NUC* (vol. 396, p. 135) registers a copy that may be the book described as having this wrapper. It is described as '6 pamphlets in 1 v., illus.', and it is said to have a 'title on spine: Pamphlets, 1885—1889'. (my queries about this have yielded no response, but one fact may help to identify the collection if it exists: *Monopoly* was 1st pbd. with a cartoon as a frontispiece.) The copy referred to here is at IEN (335.04 / M877c).

E-11: Socialist Ideal of Art

THE SOCIALIST IDEAL | OF ART. | BY | WILLIAM

MORRIS, | *AUTHOR OF "THE EARTHLY PARA-DISE," | "A DREAM OF JOHN BALL," "NEWS FROM | NOWHERE," &c. &c.* | [decorated rule] | LONDON: | REPRINTED FROM "THE NEW REVIEW," | JANUARY, 1891.

Edition: [forged 1st separate edn.] 1st pbd. as 'The Socialist Ideal. 1.—Art' in *The New Review*, 4/20 (Jan. 1891), 1–8 (see D-527).

Series: this article was originally pbd. in *The New Review* as the first of a 3-part series on Socialist ideals of art, politics, and literature, by Morris, G. B. Shaw, and H. S. Salt, respectively.

Publisher: there is no imprint, but the content and design of the title page suggest, falsely, that it was issued by *The New Review*, perhaps as an offprint done at the same time as the original article.

Printer: the pamphlet has no printer's imprint, but Barker and Collins say: 'The presence of type 35, the Figgins Long Primer 11/15 peculiar to the Twentieth-Century Press, shows that it must have been printed in or after 1893 when the Press was founded. The ambiguous style of the imprint (and its position in *The Books of William Morris*) makes it clear that Forman intended the date to be taken as 1891' (*Sequel*, 209).

Collation: 3 conjunct pairs of cr. 8° leaves folded within each other and stapled at the centrefold to form 6 leaves pp. [1–3] 4–12 [= 12] self-wrappered.

Contents: p. [1], title page; p. [2], blank; p. [3], dropped-head title: THE SOCIALIST IDEAL OF ART. | [thin rule] | [text begins]; pp. 4–12, text completed | [thin rule].

Technical Notes: *paper*: plain white machine-made; *leaf size*: cut flush, 191 x 122 mm.; *printing*: *type area*: 133 x 85 mm.; *lines-to-page*: hair leading, 34 lines, excluding headlines; *pagination*: centred on headlines.

Publication: Jan. 1891. This date is implied by Forman; but see the *Printer* field, above; *print run* and *price*: unknown; in order to conceal the forgery the forger announces neither.

Register of Copies Examined: BL (base copy: Ashley 1232); NNBerg.

E-12*: Under an Elm-Tree (wrapper)

[in gothic] **Under an Elm-tree;** | [plain type] *Or, Thoughts in the Country-Side. By* | *Wm. Morris.*

This transcription is taken from Forman's *The Books of William Morris* (p. 163). The pamphlet is legitimate, but some copies were later covered in a forged wrapper. The pamphlet is described in A-56.01; the forged wrapper is the only concern here. It was made for the 1st impression, 1st edn. (see *Notes*).

Register of Copies Examined: only one copy of this wrapper has been found, and that was in Forman's library, sold in 1972. A reason why there were not more is explored below, see the *Notes*.

Notes: H. B. Forman's description of this pamphlet is uncharacteristically brief: 'This is a sixteen-page pamphlet, demy 16 mo., stitched through the middle, uncut. It was sold without a wrapper; but special copies are occasionally found with a pale green printed wrapper added, bearing the words [in gothic] "Under an Elm-tree; | [plain type] *Or, Thoughts in the Country-Side. By* | *Wm. Morris*" (HBF, p. 163).

Forman's MS note, which became public when his library was sold by his son in 1972, not only reveals that the wrappers 'occasionally found' on this pamphlet were his own doing, but also describes his practice as applied to several other wrappers he created for Morris pamphlets: 'Mr. Leatham issued the pretty little pamphlet without any wrapper. Having bought a small parcel of copies for myself and friends, I had 50 wrappers printed as nearly in the style of the pamphlet as I could manage' (quoted in *Sequel*, 212).

So far, one copy only has been found with this 'pale green' wrapper; and that one was Forman's, included in the Solomon Sale. The fact that others have not surfaced may be accounted for by the fact that James Leatham, printer and publisher of the original pamphlet, lived on until 1945 and would have been both able and willing to denounce any such manufactured rarity.

E-13: Concerning Westminster Abbey (wrapper)

See transcription under *Technical Notes*, below.

This is a legitimate pbn. (1st impression, 1st edn.); later, retitled 'Westminster Abbey' and combined with 'Architecture and History' in the 4th vol. of the 'Golden type 8°' series (see C-7). But the original SPAB version sometimes appears with a separate wrapper, transcribed above, manufactured by H. B. Forman. The legitimate pamphlet is described in A-65.01. The original pamphlet is self-wrappered, i.e. the conjunct 1st and last leaves contain the last of the text (on the last leaf) and the title page (on p. [1]).

Technical Notes: *wrapper*: forged, only found on some copies: mid-grey machine-made paper, printed title on front: [alignment top left in hanging indent] THE | SOCIETY FOR THE | PROTECTION | OF ANCIENT BUILDINGS | CONCERNING | WESTMINSTER ABBEY. |

LONDON: JUNE, *1893*. | [flush left] "[250 Copies For The Author" | [indented] WILLIAM MORRIS. This is the wrapper condemned as 'a fabrication' by S. C. Cockerell in his copy of HBF (see *Notes*: below).
Publication: the date, "June, 1893," is confirmed by the *SPAB Annual Report* of July 1893. But this can hardly apply to the separate wrapper and the '250' copies specially printed for the author. Since it is the forger's intent to conceal the true origin of a forgery, it is almost impossible in most cases to know when or by whom forged material originated. In the present case it seems reasonable to assume that the forged wrapper was done shortly before or after the pbn. of Forman's bibliography in 1897. It could hardly have been marketed while Morris was still alive because he would have denounced the forgery, which would have started an investigation of the wrapper's provenance.
Register of Copies Examined: see this field in A-65.01.
Notes: T. J. Wise says: 'Concerning Westminster Abbey (1893?) "Crown octavo". . . . As issued in the original lavender-coloured printed paper wrappers, upon which is the extended imprint, "London: June, 1893. 250 Copies for the Author | William Morris"' (*Catalogue of the Ashley Library*, iii. 175). But Forman (item 138) differs, saying it was issued 'without any wrapper, and without the author's name but . . . also occurs in a smooth grey wrapper.' Collins says that Cockerell marked in his copy of HBF, opposite the '250 copies for the author' his own brusque dismissal: '? a fabrication'. Collins also notes that SPAB pamphlets were distributed without charge and that 250 (or more) copies could easily have been acquired (see Collins, 514–15). It is possible, considering that Wise was once on the Committee of the SPAB, that he could have acquired extra copies.

E-14: Gossip about an Old House

GOSSIP about an Old | House on the Upper | Thames written by | WILLIAM MORRIS | [flush left] November, 1895.
Edition: [unauthorized 1st impression, 1st separate edn.] A 'complex chimaera', according to Barker and Collins (see *Sequel*, 206) meant to be taken as a legitimate offprint of the 1st publication in *The Quest*, Nov. 1895 (see D-579). H. B. Forman says that 'this choice little book' is 'of the same typography as the magazine' (HBF, p. 183). In reality, the text is directly from the magazine, the copies being 'made up' using for its body leaves excised from copies of *The Quest*, combined with newly printed preliminaries and a fictitious colophon which announces that there were 'Fifty Copies Done In This Separate Form' (see *Sequel*, 205–6).
Publisher: not indicated, but the evidence indicates that this separate edn. of the text 1st printed in *The Quest* originated with H. B. Forman.
Printer: the book has a fictitious colophon: PRINTED AT THE PRESS OF THE BIRMING- | HAM GUILD OF HANDICRAFT LIMITED, | PUBLISHED IN "THE QUEST" FOR NOVEM- | BER MDCCCXCV, AND FIFTY COPIES DONE IN | THIS SEPARATE FORM. But the original printer produced only pages 3–14, the 6 leaves that comprise the body of the essay. It is not known where the 4 additional leaves, including the preliminaries and colophon pages, were printed.
Collation: 4°: [1² 2⁶ 3²] 10 leaves pp. [2] [1–4] 5–14 [15–18] [= 20] Barker and Collins describe the make-up of the book: 'The separate copies consist of the original 6 leaves [taken from copies of *The Quest*] with two gatherings of 4 leaves each added before and after; the first consists of endpapers, title and half title; the second, colophon, blank and endpapers' (see *Sequel*, 205–6).
Contents: p. [1], half title: [flush left] GOSSIP ABOUT AN OLD HOUSE.; p. [2], blank; p. [1], title page; p. [2], blank; p. [3], blank; p. [4], frontis. woodcut initialled by C. H. Gere and captioned: A VIEW OF THE MANOR HOUSE AT | KELMSCOTT, IN OXFORDSHIRE FROM | THE GARDEN GATE.; p. 5, headed: [flush left on top margin] GOSSIP ABOUT AN OLD HOUSE ON THE | UPPER THAMES. | [text begins with a 4-line decorated initial 'T']; p. 6–14, text completed with Morris's signature, flush right, and 'Kelmscott, October 25.' and a smaller view of the back of the house.; p. [15], bogus COLOPHON (see under *Printer*, above); pp. [16–18], blank.
Technical Notes: *paper*: both the original and added parts are Van Gelder hand-made, but the added leaves are thinner; *end-papers*: 4 each, front and back, 3 free ends and 1 paste-down; *binding*: grey paper-covered boards, plain and unblocked, title printed on front: [top left:] GOSSIP ABOUT AN OLD HOUSE.
Publication: Nov. 1895; the date is stated in the colophon and on the title page in a way that implies the book was done at the same time as the magazine issue, but H. C. Marillier made enquiries of the Birmingham people involved in the magazine, and they denied that any separate copies were printed at that time or any other. After that he wrote to Forman for information, and his letter was preserved among Forman's books (see *Sequel*, 206); *print run*: Forman's invented colophon says, '. . . Fifty Copies In This Separate Form', but far fewer seem to have made it to

the market (see *Sequel*, 206); *price*: unknown.

Register of Copies Examined: CtY (base copy: IP M834 895g); TxU (PR 5080 G67); CSt (Spec. Coll Felton PR5080.G6); BL (Ashley 3696).

E-15: How I Became a Socialist (wrapper)

[wrapper title] How I became a Socialist. | BY | WILLIAM MORRIS. | *With some account of his connection with the* | *Social-Democratic Federation* | BY H. M. HYNDMAN. | LONDON: OCTOBER, 1896.

Edition: an unauthorized wrapper used on a legitimate pamphlet, hence a sophistication of the 1st impression, 1st edn. For a full description of the pamphlet, see A-82.01.

Technical Notes: *wrapper*: stiff green wrapper, p. [1], printed as above; pp. [2–4], blank.

Register of Copies Examined: BL (base copy: Ashley 1239, with Forman's green wrapper); LSE.

Notes: Forman said in his bibliography of Morris (HBF, p. 190) that as pbd. the pamphlet had 'no other title page' than that transcribed at the head of the A-List entry, A-82.01, 'but there are special copies with a stiff green wrapper . . .'. However, Forman also left a handwritten note with his copy of this pamphlet, saying: 'The special issue of 150 copies with printed wrapper, etc., of which this is one, was done for me. H. B. F. 3 November, 1896' (quoted in *Quaritch Catalogue*, item 105).

Appendix I

Interviews

Including Morris's Testimony before Public Bodies.

Appendix I-1: 'The Earthly Paradise: The Author, Mr. Morris, and His Method of Working', *The London World*, 16 Apr. 1879; rptd. in *The New York Times*, 28 Apr. 1879, p. 27.

Appendix I-2: [the Second Report's heading for Morris's testimony before the Royal Commission on Technical Education:] 'Mr. Morris', *Evidence before The Royal Commission on Technical Education. Second Report of the Commissioners.* (London: Eyre and Spottiswoode, 1884), iii. 150–61; Portions in *The Architect*, 21 Feb. 1884, pp. 120–2, from an interview conducted on 17 Mar. 1882.
Collaborators, Editors, and Illustrators: Bernhard Samuelson, M.P., F.R.S., Chairman.
Notes: rptd. MM, i. 205–25.

Appendix I-3:* 'A Talk with William Morris on Socialism', *The Daily News*, 8 Jan. 1885.
Notes: rptd. *Victorian Institute Journal*, 19 (1991), 189–95.

Appendix I-4:* 'William Morris at Work', *American Architect and Building News*, 20 June 1885, pp. 296–9.

Appendix I-5: [Morris's Testimony on the Restoration of Westminster Hall], *Report from the Select Committee on Westminster Hall Restoration* (London: H. M. Stationer's Office, 1885), pp. 89–92.
Collaborators, Editors, and Illustrators: Shaw-Lefevre, MP, was chairman.

Appendix I-6: 'The Police and the Socialists at the East End', *The Pall Mall Gazette*, 42/6403 (22 Sept. 1885), 7.
Notes: this article on the 'Dod Street affair' includes the testimony of Morris at the Thames Police Court when he was examined by the magistrate, Mr Saunders, about his conduct in the courtroom earlier in the day.

Appendix I-7:* 'The Poet and the Police' (an interview occasioned by Morris's arrest at the Thames Police Court in the 'Dod Street affair'), *The Pall Mall Gazette*, 42/6404 (23 Sept. 1885), 4; rptd. in *The Critic* (NY), 4/93 (10 Oct. 1885), 176–7.

Appendix I-8: 'The Poet as Printer', *The Pall Mall Gazette*, 12 Nov. 1891, pp. 1–2.
Notes: rptd. in Peterson, 89–95.

Appendix I-9: 'Interview with William Morris', *The Clarion*, 19 Nov. 1892, p. 8.
By-line: by Quinbus Flestrin [Robert Blatchford]
Notes: Blatchford urges Morris to contribute something to *The Clarion*

Appendix I-10: 'Master Printer Morris: A Visit to the Kelmscott Press—An Illustrated interview with Mr. William Morris', *The Daily Chronicle*, 22 Feb. 1893, p. 3; rptd. *The British Bookmaker*, 6/69 (18 Mar. 1893), 190; *The British Printer*, 6 (Mar.–Apr.), 97.
Initialled: 'N.' [Henry Norman, interviewer] see *Notes* in the next interview, below.
Notes: rptd. Peterson, 95–8.

Appendix I-11: 'Art, Craft, and Life. A Chat with Mr. William Morris', *The Daily Chronicle*, 9 Oct. 1893, p. 3; also, with additional editorial comment, in *The British Bookmaker*, 7/78 (Dec. 1893), 128.
Collaborators, Editors, and Illustrators: [Henry Norman, interviewer for *The Daily Chronicle*, see *Notes*, below].
Notes: an interview conducted at the Arts and Crafts

Exhibition, in the New Gallery, before (and largely about) the Morris and Co. tapestry, 'The Attainment'. S. C. Cockerell, in his MS Diary for 1893, Thurs. 5 Oct., identifies Henry Norman as the interviewer for the *Chronicle* (see Cockerell Papers, BL (Add.) MS 52772). Rptd. in 'Interviews with William Morris III', *The Journal of the William Morris Society,* 9/2 (Spring, 1995), 2–4.

Appendix I-12: 'A Socialist Poet on Bombs and Anarchism, an Interview with William Morris', *Justice: The Organ of the Social Democracy*, 11/524 (27 Jan. 1894), 6.
Collaborators, Editors, and Illustrators: Harry Quelch, Editor.
Signed: 'Wat Tyler' [Harry Quelch?].
Notes: rptd. in 'Interviews with William Morris I', *The Journal of the William Morris Society*, 10/4 (Autumn, 1993), 2–5.

Appendix I-13: 'A Living Wage for Women', *The Woman's Signal*, 19 Apr. 1894.
Signed: 'Sarah Tooley', the interviewer.
Notes: later rptd. in 'Interviews with William Morris II', *The Journal of the William Morris Society*, 10 (Spring, 1994), 5–8. As explained in the Morris Society's *Journal*, a brief 2nd interview was pbd. by Tooley in a longer article, 'Interviewing as Woman's Work', in *The Young Woman*, 5 (Sept. 1897), and the parts relating to Morris are rptd. here, pp. 8–9.

Appendix I-14: [Testimony as a character witness for Thomas Cantwell at his Old Bailey trial for 'soliciting the murder of members of the Royal Family'], *The Times*, 31 July and 1 Aug. 1894.

Appendix I-15: 'On the Revival of Tapestry-Weaving. An Interview with William Morris', *The Studio*, 3 (July 1894), 98–101.
Signed: 'Aymer Vallance', the interviewer.

Appendix I-16: 'Morning Calls: Mr. William Morris at the Kelmscott Press', *The English Illustrated Magazine*, 13 (Apr. 1895), 47–55.
Initialled: 'A. B.'
Notes: rptd. in Peterson, pp. 98–106.

Appendix I-17: 'Do People Appreciate the Beautiful? A Chat with Mr. William Morris', *London World*, 16 Apr. 1895; rptd. in *Cassell's Saturday Journal*, No. 628 (9 Oct. 1895), 62.

Appendix I-18: 'The Kelmscott Press: An Illustrated Interview with Mr. William Morris', *Bookselling: A Journal for Publishers, Booksellers, Writers, and Readers*, 1/12 (Christmas number, Dec. 1895), 2–14.
Signed: 'I. H. I.' I. H. Isaacs, whose pen name was 'Temple Scott', the interviewer, identifies himself in his *Bibliography of the Works of William Morris*, p. 66.
Notes: rptd. in Peterson, 106–117.

Appendix I-19: 'Representative Men at Home. Mr. William Morris at Hammersmith', *Cassell's Saturday Journal*, No. 368 (18 Oct. 1896).
Series: Representative Men at Home.

Appendix II

Ephemera

Publications having text written by Morris and issued for purposes both transitory and occasional (mostly advertising). William S. Peterson has compiled a substantial list of the notices and advertising issued by the Kelmscott Press, in the section headed 'D. Ephemera' (pp. 171–187 of his *KP Biblio*.) Some of those are of uncertain authorship and therefore are not included here.

Appendix II-1:* 'Prospectus' for The Oxford and Cambridge Magazine

Collaborator(s): Cormell Price and William Fulford worked with Morris on this (see *Notes*, below).
Place: London, Oxford, and Cambridge.
Publisher: Bell and Daldy, 186 Fleet Street.
Printer: The Chiswick Press:—C. Whittingham and Co., Tooks Court, Chancery Lane.
Collation: 'Demy 8vo, 2 pages' (leaves?, Chiswick Press Arch.).
Publication: 1855 [Nov.–Dec.]: the composition took place on 22 Nov.; the printing of 5,000 was ordered on 28 Nov., with a 2nd order of 4,000 on 28 Dec. (Chiswick Press Arch., BL (Add.) MS 41928); *print run*: 9,000; *price*: for free distribution.
Notes: Cormell Price: 'Nov. 22 [1855]. Ground at a prospectus with Top [Morris]: in the evening to Pembroke and go on with the prospectus, Fulford joining in and doing lion's share' (from Price's Diary, as quoted in Mackail, i. 88).

Appendix II-2.01:* The Hammersmith Carpets

[heading] The Hammersmith Carpets
Edition: [1st impression, 1st edn.]
Collation: 4° half sheet, 2 leaves, no wrapper.
Publisher: Morris and Company.
Printer: The Chiswick Press:—Charles Whittingham and Son, Tooks Court, Chancery Lane.
Technical Notes: on 'bluish hand-made paper' (HBF, p. 194).
Publication: 24 May 1880; *print run*: unknown; *price*: free distribution. Mackail provides significant background (see also *Notes*, below).
Later impression: Morris and Co.:
1.* Oct. 1882 [2nd impression, 1st edn.], 'The firm reissued it in the same form in October 1882'; *print run*: unknown; *price*: free distribution to Morris and Co. customers.
Notes: 'During the following winter [1879–80] the manufacture of rugs and carpets went busily on at Kelmscott House. By May enough specimens had been successfully produced to allow of a public exhibition of them. The circular written by Morris and issued by the firm on that occasion states the facts very clearly. This new branch of the business was 'an attempt to make England independent of the East for carpets which may claim to be works of art' (quoted in Mackail, ii. 4). Mackail goes on to quote nearly the entire text of the circular, omitting only the 1st few words and 2 sentences from the end as printed in the 1883 Boston pamphlet described in the next entry.

Appendix II-2.02: The Hammersmith Carpets

[heading] The Hammersmith Carpets [a section of a pamphlet] THE | MORRIS EXHIBIT | AT | *THE FOREIGN FAIR,* | BOSTON, 1883–84. | [decorated short rule] | BOSTON: | ROBERTS BROTHERS. | 1883.
Edition: [1st impression, 2nd edn.]
Collation: 4° half sheet, 2 leaves + wrapper.
Printer: Cambridge, Mass.: | PRINTED BY JOHN WILSON AND SON, | UNIVERSITY PRESS

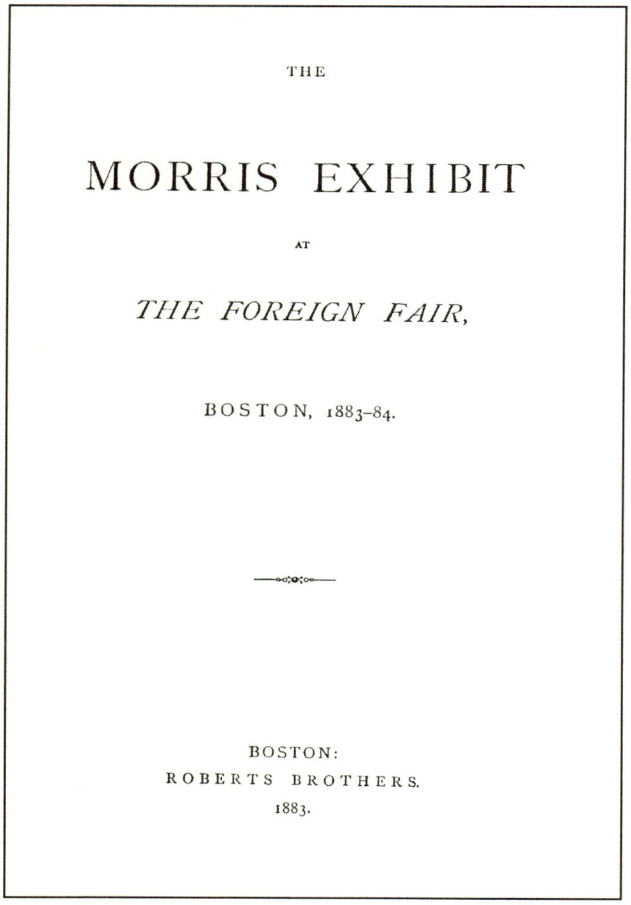

Figure 97. Appendix II-2.02: *Morris Exhibit* (Boston) wrapper title

Technical Notes: grey paper wrapper printed on pp. [1] and [3]: p. [1], lines 1–4 in gothic: The | Morris Exhibit | At | The Foreign Fair, | [plain type] Boston, 1883; p. [3], RB ad for their Morris books.
Contents: the section on 'Carpets' begins on p. 7; the Morris essay is under the heading: The Hammersmith Carpets, pp. 9–10.
Publication: 1883 [printing ordered 4 March] (Roberts Arch.).
Notes: see this field in the previous entry.

Appendix II-3: Prospectus for *The Roots of the Mountains*

[heading] NEW WORK BY MR. WILLIAM MORRIS, | AUTHOR OF "THE EARTHLY PARADISE," ETC. | In small 4to, cloth, 8s. | [thin rule] | [followed by the 1st edn. title page as in A-48.01] | ❋ *A limited number of copies upon Larger (Whatman) paper, bound | in chintz, from a design of the Author*

Edition: the prospectus includes the book's title page (A-48.01) and consequently it also includes the Morris poem beginning, 'WHILES CARRIED O'ER THE IRON ROAD'. This is the 1st edn. of the poem.
Publication: [12 Nov. 1889] (Chiswick Press Arch.); *print run*: 500 copies on 12 Nov., another 500 on 20 Nov.; *price*: free distribution.
Collation: 4°: 2-leaf leaflet, printed on pp. [1] and [3].
Contents: p. [1], prospectus, as above; p. [3], headed: LIST OF OTHER WORKS BY | MR. WILLIAM MORRIS | PUBLISHED BY | REEVES AND TURNER, | 196, STRAND. | [list completed]
Notes: May Morris provides some background to this lyric in her 'Introduction' to *The Roots of the Mountains* in vol. XV of the *CW* and prints an earlier version of the poem (XV. xxxi).

Appendix II-4:* Prospectus for *The Saga Library*

Publisher: Bernard Quaritch.
Printer: [Chiswick Press].
Publication: Sept. 1890; *print run*: unknown; *price*: free distribution.
Notes: Morris to Bernard Quaritch, 2 July 1890: 'I send back your draft agreement [covering the pbn. of *The Saga Library*, vol. I] . . . . I will set to work at once on the prospectus' (*Letters*, iii. 172). Kelvin notes that, 'The prospectus . . . [is] dated September 1890 and issued in Quaritch's name . . .' (iii. 174). Kelvin prints part of the text:

> Henderson is able, in his note to this, to quote from the prospectus: 'The literature of the Sagas is on the one hand the very flower of the medieval, or epical feeling; and on the other it is seldom tainted by any touch of rhetoric . . . at the same time though they sometimes necessarily give us pictures of rude and violent life, they are singularly free from anything that can be called *coarseness*' (quoted in Henderson, 324).

Appendix II-5: Specimens of the three KP type founts

3 untitled page-long samples of Morris's KP types, the texts of each being taken from his own writings, all at the time unpbd., except for the last, 'Acontius and Cydippe'.
Editions: (1) 'The Early Literature of the North-Iceland', the 1st page of a previously unpublished lecture, with the last line in red: 'This is the Golden type'. The lecture is pbd. in full in *Unpublished Lectures* (pp. 178–98); (2) a passage from an unfinished romance, previously unpbd.—'The Folk of the Mountain Door'—

KELMSCOTT PRESS.

SIDONIA THE SORCERESS, translated from the German of William Meinhold, by Francesca Speranza, Lady Wilde. In one volume, quarto, 456 pages, in Golden type, with borders, flowered letters, and other ornaments. In black and red. 300 to be printed. 10 on vellum. To be published by William Morris, at Four Guineas, bound in vellum of extra quality, with silk ties.

SIDONIA THE SORCERESS, the translation of which is now on the point of being issued by the Kelmscott Press, is an Historical Romance, based more or less on fact, concerning the Witch Fever that afflicted Northern Europe during the latter half of the 15th & first half of the 16th centuries. It was written by William Meinhold, a Lutheran minister, dwelling in the island of Rugen, off the shore of Pomerania, a man so steeped in the history and social life of his country during the period above-mentioned, that he might almost be said to have been living in it, rather than in his own, the early part of the present century. The result of his life and literary genius was the production of two books: "The Amber Witch," & "Sidonia the Sorceress," both of which, but, in my judgment, especially "Sidonia," are almost faultless reproductions of the life of the past; not mere antiquarian studies, but presentations of events, often tragic, the actors in which are really alive, though under conditions so different from those of the present day. In short, "Sidonia" is a masterpiece of its kind, and without a rival of its kind. It must be added that it was a great favourite with the more literary part of the pre-Raphaelite artists in the earlier days of that movement. The two beautiful water-colour pictures of Sidonia and of Clara von Dewitz, by Mr. Burne-Jones, which the general public had the opportunity of seeing at the exhibition of his pictures this spring, caused many questions to be asked about this, which the present edition of the book will answer satisfactorily. Lady Wilde's translation, which was the one through which we made acquaintance with Meinhold's genius, is a good, simple, and sympathetic one.

WILLIAM MORRIS.

Figure 98. Appendix II-7: *Sidonia* (prospectus) Morris text

with the last line in red: 'This is the Troy type' (text rptd. in *CW*, XXI. 296–309); and (3) 5 of the 6 stanzas from the prefatory 'Song' to 'The Story of Acontius and Cydippe' (*EP*), with the last line in red: 'This is the Chaucer type'. About the same time as the *EP* version, 1870, Morris included all 6 stanzas as 'Sundering Summer' in the MS 'A Book of Verse'. This was not pbd. until a facsimile of the MS book (original now at the V & A) was issued in a limited edn. in 1980 (see A-137.01). The 3 specimens are rptd. between pp. xvi and xvii in *CW*, XV.
Printer: [the Kelmscott Press].
Collation: from a KP printing on hand-made paper, each specimen on one side of a leaf, the latter 2 of the specimen leaves being conjunct. Printed on pp. [1, 3, and 5], other leaves blank.
Technical Notes: *paper*: KP hand-made Flower paper 2; *leaf size*: 189 x 138 mm. (225 x 158 mm. in *CW*, XV); *type area*: 163 x 105 mm. (*CW*, XV).
Publication: c. mid-1892, after delivery of the Chaucer type. The leaflet was probably done as a specimen for free distribution.

Appendix II-6:* 'Appreciation' of The Recuyell of the Histories of Troy
MR. WILLIAM MORRIS'S PRODUCTIONS OF THE KELMSCOTT PRESS
Editions: pbd. as a 4-page circular with Morris's 'Appreciation' of *The Recuyell of the Histories of Troy*, with reproductions of the KP colophon and Caxton's 'Preface'; Morris's text also used in a Quaritch *Catalogue* of the time, advertising the book under the heading above.
Publisher: Bernard Quaritch.
Printer: KP.
Publication: Feb. 1893; *print run*: 2,000 copies ordered by Quaritch; *price*: free distribution.
Notes: Morris's text is rptd. in *KP Biblio.*, pp. 25–6.

Appendix II-7: Prospectus for Sidonia the Sorceress (KP)
KELMSCOTT PRESS.
Collation: s. sh. folded to form 2 leaves, printed on all 4 pages.
Contents: p. [1], 2 parts: a bibliographical account of the book and Morris's appreciation of its literary qualities, signed below right; p. [2], a specimen page: Chapter III title and 1st page of text, title and marginal note in red; p. [3], sales detail and an order form; p. [4], 2nd

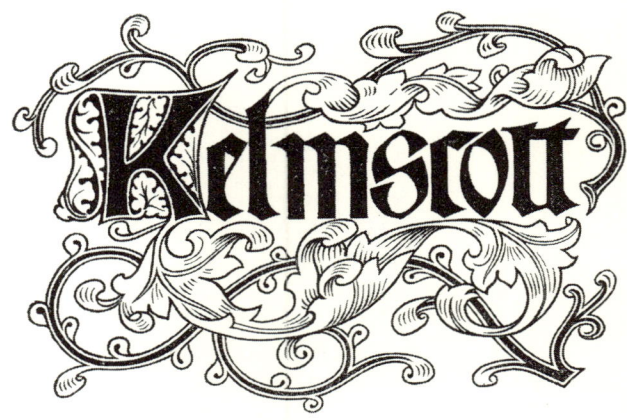

Figure 99. Appendix II-7: *Sidonia* (prospectus) 2nd KP mark

KP mark.
Technical Notes: *paper*: Flower paper 2; *leaf size*: 293 x 206 mm.; *type*: Golden type; *printing*: in black and red; *ornamentation*: a 10-line and a 6-line initial (p. [3]); 2nd KP mark.
Publication: 'probably issued in October 1893' (*KP Biblio.*, p. 159).

Appendix II-8:* announcement of the KP edn. of *Amis and Amile*
Place: 14 Upper Mall, Hammersmith.
Publisher: William Morris, at the Kelmscott Press.
Date: 28 Feb. 1894.
Collation: s. sh. folded to form 2 leaves pp. 4, printed on pp. [2] and [3] only.
Technical Notes: *paper*: Flower paper 2; *leaf size*: 143 x 103 mm.; *type*: Golden type.
Notes: William S. Peterson quotes from this announcement, which he says is 'probably by Morris' (*KP Biblio.*, p. 62). The content and style of the description support that judgement, and it is difficult to imagine Morris delegating this task.

Appendix II-9: Morris's announcement of a change of print run for *The Works of Geoffrey Chaucer*
KELMSCOTT PRESS EDITION | OF CHAUCER'S WORKS.
Edition: A pbd. letter signed by Morris to inform subscribers that the print run of the Chaucer is to be increased from 325 copies to 425 to offset unexpected additional expenses. Morris offers to refund deposits paid by anyone who declines the changes proposed.
Publisher: William Morris.
Printer: KP.

> LETTER FROM WILLIAM MORRIS TO PHILIP WEBB with reference to the books printed at the Kelmscott Press given by the latter to Trinity College, Cambridge, in 1903.
>
> Kelmscott House,
> August 27th, '94.
>
> My dear Fellow,
> A traveller once entered a western hotel in America and went up to the clerk in his box (as the custom is in that country) and ordered chicken for his dinner: the clerk, without any trouble in his face, put his hand into his desk, and drew out a derringer, wherewith he covered the newcomer and said in a calm historic voice: Stranger, you will not have chicken, you will have hash.
>
> This story you seem to have forgotten. So I will apply it, and say that you will have the Kelmscott books as they come out. In short you will have hash because it would upset me very much if you did not have a share in my 'larx.'
>
> As to the Olaf Saga, I had forgotten what you had had; chiefly I think because I did not prize the big-paper copies much. They were done in the days of ignorance, before the Kelmscott Press was, though hard on the time when it began.
>
> You see as to all these matters I do the books mainly for you and one or two others; the public does not really care about them a damn...which is stale. But I tell you I want you to have them, and finally you shall.
>
> Yours affectionately,
> WILLIAM MORRIS.

Figure 100. Appendix II-11: [*Morris to Webb*] (letter, keepsake) Morris text

Collation: a s. sh. folded to form 2 leaves, 1 page printed.
Technical Notes: *paper*: Flower paper; *leaf size*: 143 x 105 mm.; *type*: Golden type.
Publication: 'Nov. 14th, 1894'; *print run*: unknown; *price*: free distribution to all subscribers.
 Notes: Morris gives 2 reasons for the larger print run: the increase of Burne-Jones's illus. from 60 to 70, and the greater demand for copies than had been anticipated.

Appendix II-10: Pbd. Specimen Pages (a Keepsake) from *The Story of Sigurd the Volsung*
The Story of Sigurd the Volsung and the Fall of the Niblungs
Edition: incomplete sheet printed as a keepsake by the Trustees of the Morris estate after Morris's death forced the projected book to be abandoned. This text was later pbd. in full in a less elaborate design under Cockerell's supervision (see A-12.05), a remnant of the original design remains in this 2-page keepsake.
Place: Upper Mall, Hammersmith.
Publisher: Trustees of the Morris Estate.
Colophon: [all in red, printer's leaf No. 1] Incomplete sheet of *Sigurd the Volsung*. 32 copies printed at the Kelmscott Press on | Jan. 11, 1897, before the distribution of type. Not for sale.
Collation: incomplete 2° sheet, folded to form 2 leaves; printed on one side only pp. [1] and [4]; p. [4] is paginated '19', as a specimen of the original planned setting.

Technical Notes: *paper*: Perch paper; *leaf size*: 420 x 280 mm.; type area: ?286 x 190 mm.; *lines-to-page*: leaded, 49 lines; *type*: text in Troy type, colophon in Chaucer type.
Publication: 11 Jan. 1897 [colophon date; issued 22 Jan. 1897] (Cockerell's Diary, see Cockerell Papers); *print run*: 32 copies; *price*: presented to family and friends.

Appendix II-11: A Keepsake Letter from Morris to Philip Webb
[heading] LETTER FROM WILLIAM MORRIS | TO PHILIP WEBB | with reference to the | books printed at the Kelmscott Press given by | the latter to Trinity College, Cambridge, in 1903.
Edition: the letter was produced by the Chiswick Press for the Trustees as a keepsake.
Collation: s. sh. 8°, printed on one side.
Technical Notes: *paper*: Flower paper 2; *type*: Golden type.
Publication: [21 Jan. 1903] (Chiswick Arch.), text from a letter dated 27 Aug. 1894; *print run*: 100 copies (Chiswick Arch.); *price*: free distribution.
Notes: The Trustees—at the time these were Mrs Morris, S. C. Cockerell, and R. Proctor—had this letter printed as a keepsake to mark the occasion of Philip Webb's presentation of his KP collection to Trinity College, Cambridge, with copies of the letter being included in each book and presented to family and guests attending the presentation. The text was 1st pbd. in Mackail, ii. 306–7, and is rptd. in *Letters*, ii. 198–9. A reduced facsimile appears in Walsdorf, p. 10.

Index

Morris's contributions to periodicals are indexed by journal title, with Morris's contributions sub-divided by subject (for or about The Society for the Protection of Ancient Buildings: SPAB) or type. Serialized works are designated by the titles as used in the periodical.

'Abbey and the Palace, The' A-130.01
Abramsky, Chimen A-136.01
Academy of Fine Arts, Manchester A-22.01
Academy, The, reviews: D-26–7
ACES Catalogues: vol. I, 1888: lecture notes on 'Tapestry and Carpet Weaving'; article on 'Textiles': D-410; vol. II, 1889: essay: 'Of Dyeing as an Art': 480; vol. III, a poem: 551
'Acontius and Cydippe' (from *EP*) A-4.12, 13, 17, 18, App II-5
Adams, Oscar Fay, editor and contributor C-2
Address . . . Pre-Raphaelite School A-60.01; see also A-130.01
'Address to English Liberals' A-130.01
[advice to aspiring writers] B-10
Æneids, The xxxv, A-11.01–06; see also under *Series* in A-4.16
Aims of Art, The A-39.01; see also A-46.01, C-17
Alcott, Louisa May xxxv
All for the Cause lxi, A-38.01; see also A-23.01–03, D-100, E-2, 5
Allen, George A-79.01, B-12
Ambleside railway D-266–7, 272
American Architect and Building News, The, interview: App I-4
American Architect, The, lectures: D-69, 73, 230
Amis and Amile, The Story of xlviii–ix, A-70.01–03; see also A-69.03, 79.01, App II-8
'An Empty Pocket is the Worst of Crimes' D-211
'An Old Story Retold' D-227
'An Old Superstition—a New Disgrace' D-296
anarchism A-130.01, D-94, 458, 470
Anderson, Anne, illustrator A-116.01
'Answers to Previous Inquiries' D-157
Antient Christmas Carols, A Collection of B-1
'Anti-Parliamentary' D-514
Appeal for . . . Inglesham Church A-41.01–02; see also A-130.01, D-312, 399, 468
'Appeal to the Just, An' D-123
Architect, The, SPAB: D-38, 45; lectures: D-48, 61, 65, 111, 226, 230, 262, 584; 'The Woodcuts of Gothic Books': 538
Architecture and History and Westminster Abbey C-7; see also A-21.05, D-116, 122, E-13 (wrapper)
Architecture, Industry, and Wealth xlv–lvi, C-18.01–02; see also A-21.05, D-84, 111, 372
'Aristomenes, The First Foray of' D-32
Armfield, Maxwell, illustrator A-3.14
Arnold, Matthew D-185, 352

Art and Craft of Printing A-91.01–02; see also C-14, D-555
Art and Socialism xl–i, A-25.01–02
Art and the Beauty of the Earth A-20.01–02; see also A-21.05, D-65
'Art and the People' A-130.01; see also D-80
Art of Authorship, The B-10
Art of the People, The A-17.01–03; see also A-21.01–06, D-46
'Art or No Art . . .' D-96
'Art under Plutocracy' D-90; see also A-113.01, D-84
Art, Labour, and Socialism A-113.01; see also D-84, 90
Art, Wealth, and Riches A-22.01; see also A-46.03, C-18.01–02, D-76–7
'Art: a Serious Thing' D-74
'Artist and Artisan' A-130.01, D-315
Artist, The: 'to Art Students': D-446; 'The New Year': poetry: 537
artists, see Burne-Jones, Crane, Gaskin, Hunt, Millais, Morris, Northend, O'Kane, Rethel, Rowe, Watts
Arts And Crafts Essays B-15; see also A-130.01
Arts and Crafts Exhibition Society xli, A-66.01, 105.01, B-15
'As to Bribing Excellence' A-130.01, D-570
Astor Editions (Gladstone Edition series) C-22
'At a Picture Show' A-130.01
Atalanta's Race and Other Tales C-2; see also A-4.01–18
Atalanta's Race and the Proud King C-29; see also A-4.01–18
Athenæum, The: reportage: D-17, 51; poetry: 31–2, 41, 382; SPAB: 34–5, 67–8, 577; 3 letters: 575–7
Atlantic Monthly, The: poetry: D-24–5
'Attractive Labour' D-144
Aveling, Edward A-30.01, D-128, 135, 150–1, 166, 201
Avon Booklets series A-101.02, C-16.04, 23
Axon, William E. A., editor A-22.01

Bainton, Rev. George, editor and compiler A-76.01, B-10
'Baldur's Dream' A-5.04
Balfour, Arthur D-317, 356, 373, 402, 417, 506
Banner, Robert A-28.01
Barker, H. A. l, D-325
Barker, Nicholas E-14
'Battle of Trafalgar Square . . .' D-251
Bax, Belfort lvi, lxi, D-189, 301, 305, 319
assistant editor A-30.01, 31.01, 37.02
collaborator A-29.01–03, 35.01, 38.01, 68.01–02, B-6, 18, D-131, 155, 170, 179, 190, 200, 252
Beautiful World, A, speech: D-594
Beauty of Life, The lii, A-18.01; see also C-17
Bell and Daldy xxxii–iv, xxxvi, A-1.01, 2.01–3.03, App II-1
Bell, George, publisher xxxii–iv, C-20, App II-1; see also Bell and Daldy
Bellamy, Edward A-50.01, 130.01, D-462
Beowulf, The Tale of A-77.01–03; see also A-2.05, 9.04

Besant, Annie D-209, 223, 231, 263, 396
Besant, Walter D-304
Bibelot, The: list of Morris pbns. in that annual: D-596
Bibelot: A Reprint of Poetry and Prose . . ., The, see Mosher
Bibliographical Society, Transactions of the, later *Bibliographica*: lecture: 'The Ideal Book': D-555; in *Bibliographica*: 585
Bijou Reprints A-55.03, 56.04; see also Leek Bijou Reprints
Billinghurst, Percy J., designer C-28
Billings, Hammatt, illustrator A-7.01
binders, see Black Oak, Cobden-Sanderson, Kemp Hall, Leighton, Morris
binding, vellum A-2.04, 4.03, 11, 17, 8.05, 11.04, 12.04–05, 45.01–02, 80.01, 83.04, 84.01, 138.01, B-12, 14, C-9
Birchall, Rev. O., editor A-41.01–02
Birmingham Address . . . 1894 A-71.01–02
Birmingham Daily Post, The, lecture: D-46
Bismarck D-256, 271, 344, 355–6, 463, 496, 498, 502
Black Oak Bindery A-139.01
Blackie's English Classics series A-109.02
Blackwell, Christine, indexer A-130.01
Blackwell, Sir Basil, publisher and contributor xxxii, A-130.01, 134.01
Blake, William, poet D-261
Blatchford, Robert, interviewer App I-9
Bliss, W. D. P., general editor C-4
Blundell, W. A-32.01
Blundell's Schools D-41, 75
Blunt, W. S. D-327, 350
'Bondholder's Battue, The' D-92
Book of Verse, A lx, A-138.01; see also D-28, 597, 599, 602, App II-5
Bookman, The E-1, 4
Books of William Morris described, The xlix, E-5, 9, 10
Bookselling: A Journal for Publishers, Booksellers, Writers, and Readers, interview: App I-18
Boos, Florence, editor A-139.01–02, 141.01, D-281, 604
Booth, General Wm. D-524
'Bourgeois Versus Socialist' D-305
Bowden, William (father and son) A-50.02
Bradley, W., publisher D-579
British and Colonial Printer and Stationer, The, lecture summary: D-587
British Bookmaker, interview: App I-11
Brocade Series, see Mosher
Broughton, George Jr., editor A-91.01
Brown, Ford Madox D-528
Brown, L. L., papermaker A-17.02
Browning Review A-87.01, D-5
Browning, Robert A-1.01, 4.20, 87.01, D-5
Bryant and May dispute D-396–7, 400
Buchanan, Robert, poet and critic xxxvii, C-3
Bullock, Sam, editor of *HSR* A-58.01
Burleigh, T. book supplier to Roberts Brothers A-47.02

Burne-Jones, Georgiana xxxix, A-14.01, 138.01, D-597, 599
Burne-Jones, Sir Edward, artist-illustrator xxxiii, A-1.01, 3.04, 07, 4.01, 4.19, 8.05, 9.04, 11.06, 12.05, 45.01, 02, 05, 47.01, 05, 63.01, 74.01, 03, 80.01, 84.03, 88.01, 100.01, 107.01, 126.01, 130.01, 137.01, 138.01, 143.01, B-9, 19, D-27, 49, App II-9
  writer A-1.01
Burr, Frederic M. xlix, A-96.04, 102.03
Bursch, Frederick C. A-17.03, 120.01, 121.01, 123.01, 124.01, D-136
Buzz Saw Series A-108.01
Byfield, Mary, engraver A-1.01

Calder, Grace, editor A-134.01
Cambridge Speech, 23 Feb. 1878 A-143.01; see also D-39
Cambridge Chronicle, The: speech: D-39; lecture: 84
Camelot Series A-6.02
Cameo Poets series A-2.11
Campfield, George, engraver A-3.06, 4.01
cancelled sheets A-1.01, 4.01, 16, 5.04, 52.01, 54.01, 80.01, 88.01
  titles A-47.01, 54.06, 80.01; in *Later Issues* of A-48.01, 59.02
Cantwell, Thomas App I-14
Carrington, Fitzroy, editor A-100.01, 107.01
Carter, John, and Graham Pollard xxviii, xlvi, l; see also *Enquiry* in 'Abbreviations'
Cary, Melbert B., publisher and editor at the Wooly Whale A-129.01
Cassell's Saturday Journal: interview: App I-17, 19
Cathedrals and Abbeys
  Amiens C-20, 23, D-3
  Canterbury D-36–8
  Chichester D-583
  Peterborough C-2, D-473, 475, 567, 577, 581–2
  Ravenna D-58
  St Alban's D-42, 44, 304
  St Mark's, Venice D-53–7
  Tewkesbury Minster D-34–5
  Westminster Abbey A-20.05, 65.01, C-7, D-116, 292, 432, 437, 450, 529, 535, 560, 573, E-13
Catterson-Smith, R., illustrator, rubricator, and engraver A-4.17, 20, 45.05, 84.01, 86.04
  contributor A-58.01
Caxton, William, translator A-63.01–02, App II-6
Central School of Arts & Crafts A-91.02
Century Guild Hobby Horse, The, 'The Influence of Building Materials on Architecture': lecture: D-536
chamfered edges A-2.03, 4.02, 09, 11.02, 12.02–03
'Change of Position—Not Change of Condition' D-571; see also A-82.01
Chants for Socialists A-23.01–04; see also A-99.02, C-3–4, 33, D-98, 100, 106, 132, 134, E-2–3, 5, 10
Chapel in Lyoness, The A-1.01, 2.01–13, D-14
Chappel, Warren, illustrator A-129.01
Chaucer type, see type faces
Chaucer, Geoffrey A-3.12, C-24, App II-9
Chicago Anarchists D-188, 221, 317–8, 320, 323, 329, 331, 416–7
Child Christopher and Goldilind the Fair A-78.01–03; see also A-79.02
chimaera E-3, 7, 14
Chiswick-Jenckes, decorations for *A Dream of John Ball* A-45.04

Christianity and Socialism A-130.01, D-221, 346, 376, 400, 501
Churches of North France, The A-98.01; see also A-1.01, C-12, D-3
Churchill, Randolph D-162, 232, 237, 241, 249
Claims of Labour (lecture series) A-37.01, B-7
Clarion, The: letter: D-566; interview: App I-9
Clarke, William, collaborator C-4
Cleverdon, Douglas, general editor A-137.01
'Coal in Kent' D-500
Coal Struggle, The A-130.01, D-552; see also D-503
Cobden-Sanderson, T., binder A-8.05, D-553, 587
Cockerell, S. C. xxxv, xlii–vii, lvi, lix, A-51.01, 54.01, 77.02, 86.01, 130.01
  as contributor A-85.01, 88.01, C-14, 35
  as editor, see Golden type quarto series, Golden type octavo series and A-2.06, 09, 4.18, 8.05, 9.01–02, 11.04, 12.05, 20.02, 84.01, 85.01, 88.01, C-18.02, D-426, 585
  as Trustee A-21.01, 45.05, 46.03, 63.02, 71.02, 110.01, 126.01, App II-11
  on forgeries E-5, 8, 13
'Coercion for London' D-286
Coit, Dr Stanton E-2
Colbeck, Norman, collector and author A-2.01
Colcock, A. T., designer A-96.02
Coleridge, S. T. A-90.01–03
Collected Letters of William Morris xxviii, C-38
Collected Works of William Morris, The xliv, xlvi–vii, li, lvii, A-126.01; see also A-2.09, 3.10, 4.19, 5.04, 6.06, 8.06, 9.04, 11.06, 12.06, 21.05, 40.05, 45.07, 46.03, 47.05, 48.03, 50.08, 54.08, 55.04, 59.06, 63.02, 78.03, 79.02, 80.03, 81.02, 84.03, 86.04, 115.01, 125.01
Collins Illustrated Pocket Classics series C-25
Collins, John l, E-14
Colwell, Percy Robert, editor C-22
'Commercial War' A-130.01
Commonweal, The xxix, li, A-30.01
  analysis: 'Bourgeois Versus Socialist': D-305; significance of Norwich bye-election: 310; 'Is Lipski's Confession Genuine?': 311; 'Free Speech in America': 320; on emigration: 345; 'Under an Elm-Tree; or, Thoughts on the Country-Side': 465; on immigration: 354, 359; on the parliamentary system: 362; 'The Revival of Architecture': 1st of a 2-part series, 372, with 'The Revival of Handicraft': 414; Gladstone's Saltney speech rewritten to make it clearer to working men: 481;
  appeals: for funds: D-133, 155, for the Chicago anarchists: 318;
  books, some in parts: 'Socialism from the Root Up': 25 parts: 190; 'An Old Story Retold': 227; 'A Dream of John Ball': in 11 parts: 240; 'News from Nowhere', in 39 parts: 493;
  correspondence: D-136; 'Answers to Previous Enquiries': 157; letter from the US: 172; 200; answers social questions: 161; 'Letter from the Pacific Coast': 172; reply on life in the socialist future: 194; reply to a question regarding class war: 200; false distinction between artist and artisan: 315; 'Empirical Socialism': 346; Morris's letter of apology for missing the Commune celebration through illness: 443; Morris's objections to anarchism: 458, 470; 'Christianity

and Socialism': 501;
  dialogues: 'The Reward of Labour. A Dialogue': in 2 parts: 287; 'The Boy-Farms at Fault': 303; 'Honesty is the Best Policy; or, The Inconvenience of Stealing', a dialogue: 328; 'Whigs Astray. A Dialogue . . .': 430; fable: 'Ducks and Fools', 448;
  elections: election campaign, 1885: D-162; the election: 165; election result: 167–8; election debate, 1886: 179–82; reactions to Home Rule Bill: 183–5; Ireland: 202–3; coming election: 206; election result, 1886: 210–11; bye-election at Norwich: 310; Winchester bye-election: 351; Kennington bye-election and Morris supplies a better speech than the one John Morley used at St. James Hall: 442; the fortunes of the Liberals and the consequence for Socialists: 479; Liberal radicals and Socialism: 487;
  foreign affairs: war in Europe?: D-252; 291, 295; continental views of English Socialists; on the death of the German Kaiser: 363–4, 385; 'Impressions of the Paris Congress': 466; Bismarck's resignation: 502; democracy in Italy: 515; on a Spanish kidnapping: 519; on a 'peace conference' in London: 521;
  honours: baronetcies offered: D-152;
  lecture tours: to the west: D-178; to Dublin and Yorkshire: 186; to Birmingham: 195; Scotland: 205, 207–8, 268; 'In and About Cottonopolis': 421
  lectures: 'Whigs, Democrats, and Socialists': in 2 parts: D-204; corrections to an account of a lecture: 245; 'How We Live and How We Might Live', in 5 parts: 289; 'Feudal England': 308, 'The Revolt of Ghent': in 7 parts: 391; 'The Society of the Future': in 3 parts: 445; 'Monopoly': in 3 parts: 486; 'Art and Industry in the Fourteenth Century': 491; 'The Class Struggle': shorthand transcription of parts: 504; 'The Development of Modern Society: in 5 parts: 520;
  legal: legal anomaly: D-169; Dod Street affair: 163; on violence: 145; on Lipski's confession: 311; 196–9; '"The Law" in Ireland': 248; banning public meetings in Trafalgar Sq.: 251; 'Police Spies Exposed' (and consequent lawsuit against Morris): 348; W. S. Blunt's appeal lost: 350; on 'obstruction' and the law: 369–70, 406, 464; Dillon sentence and its legality: 388; on the new Land Act: 419; on 'the new flogging bill': 457; the environment in the courtroom: 463; on the royal stipend: 467; 'Trial by Judge v. Trial by Jury': 469, 471; death sentence on children: 505; various court proceedings: 506; a recent execution: 507;
  local affairs: Norwich Socialists sentenced: 259; against the Ambleside railway: 272; London Socialists guilty: 353, 365; futility of running socialists in the London School Board elections: 420; on London's gradual improvement: 427; local govt. elections, 1889: 431; housing for the poor: 435;
  manifestoes of the Socialist League: D-131; on the unemployed, 325; on the parliamentary system, 380; on engaging in party politics, 453;
  national affairs: Victoria's Jubilee: 296; 'London in a State of Siege' and other reactions to 'Bloody Sunday': 333–8, 340–4, 361, 367; Gladstone

Index

and the Liberals: 347; J. A. Froude on Matthew Arnold: 352; Home Rule and the demise of the Liberal Party: 375, 383; 'Education under Capitalism': 389; a rich country with poor people: 407; Michael Davitt and *The Daily News*: 408; 'A Modern Midas': 409; 'Talk and Art': NAAA Conference, 1888: 424; on fraudulent inventions: 428; inhumanity in the criminal law and its administration: 429, 434; Parnell wins in the Commission findings: 440; demonstrations as revolutionary or merely machine politics in action: 441; on John Bright: 447; on sentencing the Zulu chiefs to be hanged: 454; nationalism and the labour movement: 516

Notes on current affairs: D-171; 188; 189; 191–3; free speech: 201; 228; 232, 234–5, 237–9; Lord Salisbury as Mr. Jawkins: 241; 242–4; 246–7; 253–4; 263–5; 268; 273; 275; 275–80; 282–6; 288; 290; 292; 298–300; 302; failed strike and H. G. Wells on technology: 304; 307; 309; 313–14; 316–17; 319; 324; 327; 355–6; Chicago anarchists: 331; Gladstone on free speech: 334; 347; 358; 366; 376–9; Liberals and the allotment scheme: 384; conditions in Pentonville Prison: 386; debate on the channel tunnel: 390; Irish politics: 392; failure of newspapers to inform: 394; the Parnell Commission: 395, 398, 499; on Zola: 403, 456; various items: 411–13; 423; 425; 433; 444; 455; 460; 'In Memoriam' of the Chicago anarchists: 416; reply to *The Echo* on the Chicago anarchists: 417; on the attempt to encourage the poor to read more: 452; Morris vs. the *PMG*'s defence of advertising and the Eiffel Tower; on Guinness's gift to the London poor and an exhibition of 'Garments for the Poor': 484, 485; German Socialists and Bismarck: 496, 498; the Irish question and British workers: 497; discovery of coal in Kent: 500; 'Labour Day', the meaning of: 508; Morley's speech against Socialism: 509; unionists vs. Socialists: 510; on prisons and punishment: 511

on *Commonweal*: D-129; 130; 138;151; 166; 170; 'Concerning *Commonweal*': 183 196–9; post election, 1886: 213–25; 250;

opinion:, 505–11, 514–16, 519, 521, 524–5; 139, 209, 212, 294, 462, 494; on 'practical' Socialism: 357, 359;

parliamentary: on the 'political crisis': D-147; anti-parliamentary: 149, 177; Chamberlain's speech at Hull: 153: rise of the Unionists: 156; R. Churchill and European War: 249; compromises on Home Rule: 255; 256; 258; anti-parliamentary advice to the North of England Socialists: 297; Liberal Party Conference: 326; on recent debates: 360; on machine politics: 387; the unlikely prospect of parliament doing anything to help the poor: 449; 'Anti-Parliamentary': 514;

poetry: D-132, 134; 148;, headnote to Blake's 'The Little Vagabond': 261; untitled, later 'Drawing Near the Light': 371; 'Mine and Thine' trans. from Flemish: 439;

reviews: *Socialist Rhymes*: D-139; *Social Politics*:141; *Modern Socialism*: 209; *Cashel Byron's Profession*: 212; review of a lecture: 222; *Common-sense Socialism*: 294; general review of 1887: 349; Morris on Henry James: 422; on Ibsen's *A Doll's House*: 461; on Bellamy's *Looking Backward*: 462; *Fabian Essays in Socialism*: 494;

'*Revolutionary Calendar*': Wat Tyler: D-381; Jevons: 401;

SL AGM, and other reports: 'Monthly Report': D-142; 'Impressions of the Paris Congress': 466; Commune celebrations: 274; resolutions of the 3rd AGM: 293; 'Socialist Work at Norwich': 404; Morris declines to form a new party with the radicals: 451;

speeches: W. T. Stead's exposures, resumé: D-154; at Horton: 281

strikes and the labour struggle: Belgian strike fails: D-295; the Bryant and May strike: 397, 400; Paris strike: 402; on English unions: 418; on Australia, 'where workers must be paid to live there': 438; the dockers' strike: 472, 474, 476; on class war: 477; Turkish treatment of Armenians compared with the treatment of the working class in Britain: 478; the bakers' strike: 483; middle-class attitudes to strikes: 488; 'The Great Coal Strike': 503; 'Workhouse Socialism': 524; 'Where Are We Now?': 525

work and employment: 'Unattractive' and 'Attractive Labour': 2-part series: D-142–3; the unemployed: 'The Worker's Share of Art': 137; 'The Reward of "Genius"': 229; NAAA: 'Talk and Art': 424; women and men at work: 288; 'Sweaters and Sweaters': 393

Commonwealth Library series A-49.03
Commune of Paris, The A-35.01; see also D-190, 274
Communism A-104.01; see also A-130.01
'Concerning Geffray Teste Noire' A-2.01
'Concerning *The Commonweal*' D-183
Concerning Westminster Abbey A-65.01; see also C-7, E-13
'Condition and Prospects of Art, The' D-65
'Conscience of the Upper Classes, The' D-343
Conwell, Clarke, of Elston Press xlix, C-14, 15, 19
co-operative movements A-130.01, D-290, 379
Co-operative Wholesale Societies Annual, The, lecture: 'The Relations of Art to Labour': D-526
copyright xxvii, xxix–xxxii, xxxv–vii, xlii, xliv–ix, A-3.12, 4.07, 7.01, 52.01, 68.01, 84.01, 86.02, 97.01, 99.01, C-1, 21
copytext A-3.13, 4.17, 11.04, 54.01, 59.03, 99.01, 114.01, C-33
Cornish, J. E., bookseller E-4
corrections to Morris texts lv, A-2.04, 06, 09, 3.01, 4.01, 05, 5.01, 04, 11.04, 20.02, 47.04, 50.05, 54.01, 57.01, 66.01, 68.01, 78.02, 80.01, 85.01, 140.01
'Cotton and Clay' D-89
'Counting Noses' D-387
Coupe, Robert L. M. A-93.02
Crane, Walter, illustrator, artist, engraver A-23.02–03, 29.02–03, 30.01, 31.01–04, 35.01–02, 37.03, 43.01, 49.01–03, 50.01, 53.02, 54.05, 74.02, 79.01, 139.02, B-6, 17, 18, D-513
Cribb, H., illustrator A-86.01–04
Cupid and Psyche A-137.01; see also A-4.01–20, B-19

Daily Chronicle, The: letter correcting a report on the Laureateship: D-546; opinion: 554; lecture summary: 558; conservation: 3 letters on Epping Forest: 568–9, 572; 4 letters for the SPAB: 578, 580–2; interview: App I-10–11

Daily News, The: opinion: D-33, 52, 72, 81, 158, 257, 322; reportage: 79, 129, 174; letters for the SPAB: 53, 66, 75, 164; objects to additional monuments in Westminster Abbey: 432, 450; letter: 567; interview: App I-3
Daldy, Frederick R., xxxii–iii, xxxv–vi
Dark Blue, saga translation: D-29
'Dark Wood, The' D-28
Dave, Victor, collaborator A-35.01
Davidson, William Edward, publisher, designer A-103.01
'Day is Coming, The' E-2
'Day of Days, The' D-522
Daylight [Norwich], lecture: D-233
'Death of Paris, The' D-23
Death Song, A lxi, A-43.01; see also C-33
'Death the Avenger and Death the Friend' D-10, 596
Decorative Art, The Journal of: lecture: 'The Woodcuts of Gothic Books': D-538; lecture notes: 'Town and Country': 549
Decorative Arts, The xxxv, A-16.01–03; see also 'The Lesser Arts' and D-45
dedications A-2.01–10, 3.11, 4.01–20
'Deeper Meaning of the Struggle, The' A-130.01
Defence of Guenevere, The, xxxi, xxxiii–iv, xlix, lii, lvi, A-111.01; see also A-2.01–13, C-25, 31 selections from C-1, 3, 5–6, 9, 19, 22, 24–8, 30–1, D-15, E-1
Defence of Guenevere, The: A Book of Lyrics C-5
Defoe, Daniel, writer A-17.02
Deighton, Bell & Co., bookstore, xxxii
Deluxe Edition A-2.11, 4.06, C-21, 25
Democratic Federation, publisher of *Justice*, see Social Democratic Federation (SDF)
Depression of Trade, Commission on D-218, 258
'Depression of Trade, The' A-130.01, 133.01
designers of books: see Billinghurst, Colcock, Crane, Davidson, Dwiggins, Goetting, Govey, Hill, Morris, Northend, O'Kane, Patterson, Rhead, Rogers, Smith, Stevens, Treglown, Webb, Whittingham
Dickens Studies Annual, The, fiction, 'The Novel on Blue Paper': D-605
Dickens, Charles xxxi
Dickinson, Emily, xxxv
Dixon, A. A., illustrator A-2.11, C-27
Dod Street affair D-158, 163, App I-6–7
Doom of King Acrisius, The A-100.01; see also A-4.12–13, 17–18, B-19
'Doomed Ship, The' A-130.01
Doughty, Oswald xxxiv
Dream of John Ball, A D-240, A-89.01–3; see also A-45.01–07, C-4, D-125, 227
Dream, A lvi, A-101.01–04; see also A-1.01, C-16.02–03, 20, 23, D-4, 596
Drinkwater, John A-2.10, 3.11, 4.20, 122.01, D-596
'Ducks and Fools' D-448
Dufty, A. R., editor A-137.01
'Dull Level of Life, The' D-101
Dunlap, Joseph R. A-126.01
Dwiggins, Will, designer B-16.02

'Early England' lii, D-558; see also *Unpublished Lectures*
'Early Literature of the North-Iceland' App II-5
Early Romances C-24
Earthly Paradise, The xxxiii–v, xxxviii–ix, xliii, xlv, lvii, lx, A-4.01–20; see also D-17

arrangements in parts A-4.01
Cabinet Edition A-4.13
KP copy text A-4.17
selections A-3.10, 7.10, C-1–3, 22, 29, D-23, 601
Eastern Question Association xxxii, lii, A-10.01, 15.01, C-34
editors: see Adams, Axon, Bainton, Bliss, Boos, Broughton, Bullock, Calder, Carrington, Cary, Cleaverdon, Cockerell, Colwell, Dufty, Eliot, Ellis, Faulkner, Finch, Fitzgerald, Forman, Fry, Fulford, Gordon, Henderson. Hueffer, Jacobs, Kelk, Kelvin, Kitz, Leatham, Lee, LeMire, Mac-Carthy, Mackail, Magnússon, Maxwell, Meier, Middleton, Miles, Money-Coutts, May and William Morris, Mosher, Mowbray, Nicol, Noyes, Oliphant, Pearson, Peterson, Proctor, Quelch, Rhys, Richie, Rolfe, Salmon, Sparling, Steele, Timo, Walker, Wardle, Whalley
Echo, The, opinion: D-122
Eclectic Magazine, The: poem: D-595
Edelheim, Carl A-88.01, C-35, D-590
editiones princepes, discussion of xxxv, xxxviii, xlvii, liii, A-83.01, 84.01, 86.02
Egilssaga A-130.01
'"Eight Hours" and the Demonstration' D-510
Eliot, Charles W., editor A-6.05
Elliot & Fry, photographers A-115.01
Ellis, F. S. as editor xxxi–vii, xlii–iv, xlvi, lx, A-5.02, 63.01, B-14
Ellis, F. S., as publisher, Ellis and White, Ellis and Green, F. S. Ellis (in chron. order), xxxii, lvii
Morris titles pbd. xxxv, A-2.02, 06, 3.01, 04, 06, 4.01–02, 04–05, 08, 12, 5.01–02, 6.01, 8.01, 9.01, 11.01–02, 12.01–02, 16.01, 21.01, C-1
Ellis, Herbert M., illustrator A-2.04
Elson, A. W., & Co., photoengravers A-47.02
'Emigration and Colonisation' D-345
Emperor Coustans, The A-73.01–02; see also *King Coustans*
'End and the Means, The' A-130.01, D-233
England and the Turks A-10.01; see also A-130.01, D-33
English Illustrated Magazine, The: 'Meeting in Winter': D-95, 'The Hall and the Wood': 495; *The Glittering Plain*, in 4 parts: 513; interview: App I-16
English, poem D-598
engravers: see Byfield, Campfield, Catterson-Smith, Crane, Elson, Hill, Hooper, Keates, Morris, Rogers, Spielmeyer, Walker
Enright, Walter J., illustrator A-83.04, 105.01
'Equality' A-130.01
Evans, F. H., illustrator and photographer A-50.08, 80.03
'Eve of the Elections, On the' D-165
Every Saturday, poetry: D-23
Everyman's Library series lvii, A-3.12, C-24
'Exhibition at the Royal Academy …' D-108
exhibition catalogues, contributions and comment on xxxvi, A-130.01, B-2, D-410, 484
'Expedition of The Ark, The' D-603

Fabian Society, publishers A-104.01, D-204, 222, 231, 494
'Facing the Worst of It' D-265
facsimiles
reprints lx, A-126.01, 138.01, C-20, D-599, 602, 605; see also Prior
pages xlix, A-2.09, 3.10, 4.19, 104.01, 115.01
Factory as It Might Be, A A-108.01–02; see also A-130.01, D-102, 105, 107

Fairbank, Alfred, contributor A-134.01
'Fame' A-130.01
Faulkner, C. J. A-29.01
Faulkner, Peter, editor, new edition C-24
Faulkner, Robert, & Co., photographers A-84.03
Feather Weights series A-116.01, 117.01
'Fighting for Peace' D-268
Finch series (James Finch, editor and publisher) xlix, A-95.02, 96.03, 101.03, C-16.05
Finch, James A-95.02, 96.03, 101.03, C-16.05
Fitzgerald, Penelope, editor A-140.01, D-605
Five Arthurian Poems C-19
Flowers of Parnassus series A-111.01
'Folk of the Mountain Door, The' A-86.04, App II-5
For Whom Shall We Vote A-32.01
forgeries xxix, l, lx, C-8.01–02, 33, E-1–15
Forman, Harry Buxton xxxvii, liiie, A-4.14, 10.01, 45.01, 56.01, 99.01, 122.01, C-33
as forger xlix–l; see also Section E
editor C-3
on Morris's authorship A-1.01
Fortnightly Review, The: poetry: D-18–19, 22, 28; saga: 20; 'The Revival of Architecture': 1st of 2 articles, 372; see also 'The Revival of Handicraft: 414
Forum, The (US): reportage: D-591
Franklin, Colin xxxix
'Free Speech and the Police' D-163
Freedom Library series A-31.02, 49.01
Frithiof the Bold A-114.01; see also A-9.01–04, D-29, 596
Fry, Edith, editor A-109.02
Fulford, William, editor and poet A-1.01, App II-1

Gaskin, Arthur, printer and artist A-80.01, B-16.01–02
Gems from William Morris C-26
George, Henry D-97, 238, 321, 419, 459
Gere, C. M., illustrator A-3.09, 50.05, 07, 84.04, 97.01, D-579
Gertha's Lovers A-90.01–03; see also A-1.01, C-20, D-8, 596
Gilliflower of Gold, The C-6
Gladstone, William D-117, 162, 180, 202, 276, 314, 334, 347, 418, 425, 481, 516
Glasier, J. Bruce A-58.01
'Glass, Painted or Stained' *Chamber's Encyclopædia* B-11
Glittering Plain, The A-54.01–09; see also D-513
God of the Poor, The E-5; see also D-18
Goetting, A. E., designer A-106.01
Golden type quarto and octavo editions xlv, lvii; see also Longmans series
Golden Wings: A Tale, A-95.01–02; see also A-1.01, 2.09, C-10.01–02, 20, 21, 23, D-16, 596
Good Words, poetry: D-21
Goodwin, K. L. lxi, D-601–2
Gordon, Prof. Ian, editor A-143.01
Gossip about an Old House A-97.01; see also D-579, E-14
Gothic Architecture liv, A-66.01; see also D-480
Gothic Books, Woodcuts of C-15, 35, D-538
Govey, L. A. designer A-116.01, 117.01
Gresham Book series A-2.12
Grettis Saga xxxv, A-5.01–04, 6.06, D-51
Griggs, F. L., illustrator A-4.19, 40.05, 130.01
Grosvenor Notes, poetry: D-49
groupings of Morris's prose pieces, lectures, essays li, lvi, A-3.13, *Notes* in 21.01, C-18.01–02
Gubb, Frank, translator A-136.01
Gunnlaug Worm-Tongue A-51.01, 9.01–04; see also

C-13, D-20, 51

'Hackney Election, The' D-126
'Hall and the Wood, The' D-495
'Hammersmith Carpets' B-2, App II-2.01–02
'Hammersmith Costermongers, The' D-120
Hammersmith Manifesto A-26.01–04
Hammersmith Socialist Record, The li, A-58.01, Introductory: D-533; statement of principles: 534; current affairs: 541, 543–5, 547–8
contributors to A-58.01; see also Bullock, Catterson-Smith, Rice, Scheu, Morris, Glasier, Beasley, Tarleton
journal items: introductory: D-533; statement of principles: 534; current affairs: 541, 543–5, 547–8
Hammersmith Socialist Society xli, A-26.04, 49.02, 53.01–02, 64.01, 67.01; see also under *Principles of HSS*
as publisher:
Hammersmith Socialist Library A-31.03, 37.03, 61.01
Hammersmith Socialist Record A-58.01, D-533–4, 540–1, 543–5, 547–8
'Hands' (poem, later incorporated in 'Rapunzel') lii, A-1.01; see also A-2.01, D-9
'Hapless Love' D-19, 32, E-4
Hardy, Eugene D., publisher at Roberts Brothers xxxv–vi
Harrison, Florence, illustrator A-2.12
Harrison, Frederick, organiser of 'Claims of Labour' lectures A-37.01, B-7
Hart, Horace, printer to Oxford University A-3.13, C-30–1
Harvard Classics series li, A-6.05
'Havelock the Dane', for Morris's version see A-78.01
'Haystack in the Floods' A-2.01
'Heart of the Rose' A-130.01
Help for the Miners A-67.01
Henderson, Philip, editor xxviii, li, A-14.01, C-34
Hericault, C. D. A-69.01
Hickling, P. B., illustrator A-2.11, C-25–28
Hill, J. E., designer, engraver, publisher A-97.01, D-579
Hillacre, see Bursch under publisher-printers US
Hinton, Walter H., illustrator A-102.02
History of Over Sea, The A-93.01–02; see also A-73.01–02
'History of Pattern Designing, The' B-3, C-18.01–02, D-48
History Workshop: A Journal of Socialist and Feminist Historians, 'William Morris's Socialist Diary': D-604
Hollow Land and Other Contributions…, The xlv–vi, C-20; see also A-1.01, 2.09, 83.01–04, C-10.01–02, D-13, 15, 596
Hollyer, F., photographer A-2.07, 9.04, 47.02, 05, 56.05, 82.01, 84.03, 100.01, 107.01, 108.02, 119.01, 138.01
Home Rule and Humbug A-33.01; see also D-203
Homer, see *Odyssey*, xxxix, A-41.01–05
Hooper, Cyrus Lauron A-83.04
Hooper, William H., engraver A-4.17, 8.05, 12.05, 50.05, D-579
Hopes and Fears for Art xxxv, lvi, A-21.01–06; see also C-17
Hopes of Civilization, The A-124.01; see also A-46.01–03
Hornby, C. H. St. John, trustee xliv, xlvii, A-4.18
House of the Wolfings, The xxxiii, xxxviii–ix, A-47.01–06
'Housing of the Poor, The' D-112
How I Became a Socialist A-82.01; see also B-18, D-563,

Index

571, E-15 (wrapper)
How Shall We Live Then? A-135.01; see also D-445, 600
Howard, George A-13.01
Howard, William A-51.01
Hubbard, Elbert, at the Roycrofters A-76.01, 89.01
Hueffer, Francis, editor C-1
Hughes, Arthur, illustrator A-49.01
Humane Review, The, poem: 'The Day of Days': D-522
Hunt, Holman, artist D-528
'Husks the Swine Do Eat, The' D-169
Huth, Henry and Alfred, collectors xxxiv
Hyndman, H. M.
    as collaborator and contributor A-24.01–03, 64.01, 82.01, B-18, D-87, 91–2, 281, 563

Ibsen, *A Doll's House* D-461
Iceland D-72, 79, 448
Ideal Book, The A-91.01–02; see also C-14, 35, D-555
Idle Singer, The A-127.01
'Illuminated Books of the Middle Ages, Some Notes on the' D-557; see also C-15
illustrators: see Anderson, Armfield, Billings, Burne-Jones, Catterson-Smith, Chappel, Crane, Cribb, Dixon, Ellis, Enright, Evans, Gere, Griggs, Harrison, Hickling, Hinton, Hughes, King, Leverett, Marcel, Morris, Murray, Rogers, Rossetti, Weibking
imported sheets A-2.03, 4.02–03, 05–06, 09, 13, 15, 8.01–02, 11.02, 12.02, 54.03; in *Later Issues*, A-79.01
'Impressions of the Paris Congress' D-466
'In and About Cottonopolis' D-421
'In Praise of My Lady' A-103.01; see also A-2.01–12, C-9
'Independent Ireland' D-180
'Individualism at the Royal Academy' A-130.01, D-104
Industrial Remuneration Conference B-7
'Influence of Building Materials on Architecture, The' C-18.01–02, D-536
'Instructive Items' D-197
'Insurance against Magistrates' D-337
intellectual property, see copyright, xxix–xxx
International Health Exhibition Society, publisher A-27.01, D-111
International Institute of Social History, Amsterdam, publisher A-135.01, D-600
International Review of Social History, The, lecture: 'How Shall We Live Then': D-600
International Workers' Congress D-489–90
interviewers: see Norman, Tooley, 'Temple Scott', Vallance
'Introduction' to *A Review of European Society* B-4
'Introduction' to *Good King Wenceslas* B-16.01–02
'Ireland and Italy. A Warning' D-159
Irish Question D-171, 234–5, 248, 292, 319, 360, 377–8, 385, 392, 398, 408, 411, 497
    Home Rule A-33.01, 36.01, D-184, 267, 361, 374–5
    landlords D-355, 419, 423
'Is Trade Recovering?' D-247
Isaacs, I. H. ('Temple Scott') D-27, E-1–2

Jacobi, Thomas, manager, Chiswick Press A-48.01
Jacobs, Joseph, collaborator, editor A-69.03, 79.01, 92.01
James, Henry, writer B-10, D-422
Jenckes, see Chiswick-Jenckes
John Ball and a King's Lesson A-45.01–08; see also C-4
Journalism: Contributions to Commonweal C-37
Journals of Travel in Iceland A-115.01

Journeyman Chapbooks series A-140.01
Justice and Socialism A-136.01
Justice: opinion: D-86–9, 91–4, 96–7, 99, 101, 110, 112–15, 117–20, 123–7, 571, 592; article: 'A Factory As It Might Be', in 3 parts: 102, 105, 107; manifesto: 128; 2 lectures: 532, summary: 561; poetry: 'Chants for Socialists', Nos. 2–4: 98, 100, 106; 'Seven Years Ago and Now': lecture summary: 532; poems: 562; 'May Day': 539, 562; appeal: 103, 109, 113–14; reviews: 104, 108; reportage: 563, 589, letters: 588–9; interview: App I-12
juvenilia A-130.01, 141.01
Juvenilia of William Morris, The A-141.01

Kaiser Frederick D-363, 385, 388, 403
Keates, C. E., engraver A-78.01
Keats, John xxxvii, A-2.08
Kelk, W. A., Longmans editor A-5.04, 9.02, 45.06, 126.01
Kelmscott House A-31.03, 40.05, 46.03, 80.03, D-603, App II-2.01–02
Kelmscott Manor xxxiv, A-4.09, 19, 50.05, 07, 84.04, 97.01, D-551, 579, 603
Kelmscott Press, publisher and printer xxxiii–iv, xxxviii–xli, xliv–ix, lviii–ix
    later editions with KP corrections A-2.06, 13
    Morris titles (21 titles in 30 vols.) A-2.04, 3.07, 4.17, 8.05, 12.05, 45.02, 54.01, 05, 59.01, 63.01, 66.01, 69.01, 70.01, 73.01, 74.01, 77.01, 78.01, 80.01, 84.01, 85.01, 86.01, 88.01; see also A-50.02, 54.03 (facsimile), 74.03, 86.02, B-12, 14, App II-7, 10, 11
    prices of KP books A-3.07
    type fount samples App II-5
Kelvin, Professor Norman, editor xxviii, li, C-38
Kemp Hall Bindery A-134.01
Kilgour, Raymond L. xxxv–vi
King Coustans, The Tale of A-92.01; see also *Emperor Coustans*
King Florus and Fair Jehane A-69.01–03
'King of Denmark's Sons, The' D-30
King, Jessie, illustrator A-2.07, 111.01
King, W., Alton Mill papermaker A-105.01
King's Lesson, A A-55.01–05; see also A-45.01–08, C-4, D-227
King's Treasury of Literary Masterpieces series C-21
King's Poets series A-2.08
Kingsley, Charles A-1.01
Kitz, F., *Commonweal* assistant editor A-30.01
Kyrle Society, publisher UK xli, A-19.01; see also A-130.01, D-62
Kyrle Society, Speech . . . at the A-19.01

'Labour Day' D-508
Labour Prophet, The, letter: D-550
'Labour Question, The' (later pbd. as *True and False Society*) lii, B-7
Lambert, Richard, Law and Liberty League, A-43.01
Landor, Walter Savage A-82.01
Lang, Andrew xlii
Law and Liberty League D-332, 335, 337; see also A-43.01
Lawson, Malcolm, collaborator lxi, A-43.01
'Lay of Thrym, The' A-5.04
Leatham, James, publisher and printer xl; see also A-51.01, D-227, 391, 465
    at 15, St Nicholas St., Aberdeen A-55.01, 56.01–02
    Clerkhill Press A-56.01

Cottingham Press, A-55.05
Peterhead *Sentinel* Publications A-55.02–03, 56.04
as editor A-108.02, 119.01
lectures xxviii, xlv, lii
    collections of, A-21.01–06, 46.01–03, 130.01, 133.01, B-3, C-7, 11, 17, 18.01–02, 35–6
    separate publications A-16.01–03, 17.01–03, 18.01, 20.01–02, 22.01, 25.01–02, 27.01, 31.01–05, 34.01, 37.01–03, 39.01, 49.01–03, 66.01, 71.01–02, 91.01–02, 94.01, 104.01, 113.01, 123.01, 124.01, 129.01, 132.01, 135.01, 136.01, 143.01
Lee, Francis Watts, editor C-4
Leeds Mercury, The, lecture: D-504
Leek Bijou Reprints series A-25.01–02; see also Leatham's Bijou Reprints A-55.02, 56.04
Leek Times, The, lecture: D-74
Legend of the Briar Rose B-9
Leighton, binder A-51.01
LeMire, Eugene D., editor and compiler A-133.01
'Lesser Arts of Life, The' B-3, A-21.01–06; see also C-17, 18.01–02, D-48 and *The Decorative Arts*
Lethaby, W. R. C-18.01, D-74, 587
'Letter from the Pacific Coast, A' D-172
[Letter to several Italian newspapers]: for the SPAB: D-56
Letters of William Morris to his Family and Friends C-34
Letters on Socialism xxviii, A-76.01
Leverett, A., illustrator A-54.05
Lewis, Abel, photographer A-12.06
libel D-348
'Liberal Party Digging its Own Grave' D-338
Liberty and Property Defence League D-222, 340, 407
Liberty: article: D-559; opinion: 565, letters: 570, 593; lecture summary: 586
Library Edition xxxv, A-4.16, 11.01
Library of Congress, copyright xxx, A-3.12
Life and Death of Jason, The xxix, xxxiii–vi, lii, A-3.01–14; see also C-1, 5, 22, 25, 30, 31 D-17
Lilienthal, Theodore A-131.01
Lindenborg Pool A-1.01, C-16.01–05, 20, 23, D-12, 596
Linnell, Alfred A-43.01, C-33, D-342, 344
'Lipski's Confession Genuine?, Is' D-311
Little Leather Library, Miniature Library series A-89.02
'Little Vagabond, The' D-261
Liverpool Daily Post, The: letter: 'The "Triumph of the Innocents"': D-529
London County Council A-91.02, D-431, 444, 478, 587
'London in a State of Siege' A-130.01, D-333
London World: interview: App I-1, 17
Longman, C. J. xlii, xlvi–vii, A-45.05, 84.01
Longmans of London, publisher
    Morris titles pbd. xlii–iv A-2.05–06, 3.05–06, .08, 4.12–14, 16, 18, 5.02, 6.03, 8.04, 9.02, 04–06, 12.03–04, 06, 21.01–05, 23.04, 40.03–04, 45.01, 03, 05, 07, 47.03, 50.06, 80.02, 81.01, 84.02, 86.02; as *Later issues and impressions*, A-11.01, 48.01, 50.02, 54.02, 59.02–03, 77.02
    collections, see *Collected Works* (A-126.01, 24 vols.), C-7, 11, 13, 17, 18.01–02, 20, 34
    series, Longmans Class Books of English Literature (LCBEL, 4 titles in 4 vols.) A-54.07, 110.01, 128.01, C-29
    series, The Poetical Works of William Morris (PW, 8 titles in 11 vols.) A-2.05, 3.08, 4.16, 8.04, 11.04, 12.04, 77.02, 81.01
    series, Golden type octavo edition (7 titles in 5 vols.) A-20.02, 71.02, 94.01, C-7, 11

series, Golden type quarto edition (10 titles in 8 vols.) A-5.03, 6.03, 9.03, 11.05, 21.04, 40.04, 46.02, 47.04, 48.02, C-13, 17, 18.01
series, Pocket Library (LPL, 14 titles in 18 vols.) lvii, A-2.13, 3.09, 21.06, 45.08, 47.06, 48.03, 50.07, 59.01, 05, 74.05, 80.04, 84.04, 86.03, 99.02, C-33
Longmans, NY xxx, A-84.02, 86.02; in *Later issues and impressions*, A-47.03, 50.01, 74.03
'Lord Mayor's Show, The' A-130.01, D-125, 235, 239
Love is Enough xxxv, xlv, A-8.01–06; see also A-81.01–02, C-1, 3
'Love's Gleaning-Tide' D-31
Lovers of Gudrun, The xxxiv, A-7.01
LP copies liv–v
  25 copy runs xxxv, A-2.02–04, 3.04, 06, 4.01, 08, 5.01, 6.01, 8.01, 9.01, 11.01, 12.01, 04, 18.01, 21.01
  larger runs A-25.01–02, 39.01, 40.01, 45.01, 46.01, 47.01–02, 48.01, 50.02, 52.01, 55.01, 57.01, 59.02, 62.01, 68.01, 72.01, 74.02, 75.01, 89.01, 112.01, 138.01, B-16.01, C-9

MacCarthy, Fiona, editor A-143.01
Macclesfield Courier and Herald, The, speech on art education: D-436
Mackail, J. W., editor and contributor xxxiii–iv, xl–xli, A-4.18, 14.01, 54.07, 98.01, 101.01, 110.01, 128.01, C-12, 16.02, 29, D-551, App II-2.01, 11
  on authorship A-1.01
Magazine of Art, The: reportage: D-557; essay: 557
Magdalen Bridge, Oxford D-63, 67
Magnússon, Eiríkr, collaborator, editor, translator, mapmaker xlvii, A-5.01–6.06, 9.01–04, 51.01, 52.01, 57.01, 62.01, 72.01, 75.01, 106.01, 112.01, 114.01, 134.01, C-13, D-20, 29, 51
Mahon, J. L. A-28.01, 30.01, D-128, 259
'Makeshift' A-130.01
Man Born to Be King, The A-110.01; see also A-4.01–20
Manchester Academy of Fine Arts A-22.01
Manchester Examiner, The, opinion: D-76
Manchester Guardian, The: lectures: D-73, 230; opinion: 262, 266
Manchester Quarterly, The, lecture: D-77
Manifesto of English Socialists A-64.01
maps lviii–ix, A-5.01–04, 31.03, 37.03, 52.01, 62.01, 86.01–04, 115.01
Marcel, A. D., illustrator C-21
'March of the Workers, The' D-132
marketing xxix, xxxi, xxxiii, xl, xlviii
'Masters in This Hall' B-1
Matrix, reportage: D-607
Maxwell, E., editor A-3.13, C-30–1
'May Day' D-539
'May grown a'cold' D-25
'Mayday 1894' D-562
McLean, Thomas, publisher B-19
'Meaning of Socialism, The' xxviii, D-128
'Meeting in Winter' D-95
Meier, Paul, editor A-135.01, D-600
'Men and Women' D-5
Meredith, George xxxv, A-35.01
Meriden Gravure Company, platemakers A-134.01
'Message of the March Wind, The' D-134
Middleton, John Henry, editor B-3, 5
Miles, Alfred, general editor C-3

Millais, J. E., artist D-152
Miller, Robert A-37.01, B-7
Milliken, E. J., writer B-9
'Mine and Thine' D-439
'Misanthropy to the Rescue' D-222
'Misery and the Way Out' A-130.01; see also D-119
Modern Art (Boston): reportage: D-590
'Modern Midas, A' D-409
Modern Philology, poem D-599
moire patterned cloth A-2.01
Moland, L. A-69.01
Money-Coutts, F. B., editor A-111.01
Monopoly A-49.01–03
Moring, Alexander, publisher De la More Press xlix, A-2.08
Morning Post, The, SPAB, letter: D-567
Morris and Company xxxix, D-410, App II-2.01
Morris Estate xxix, xxxii, xxxiv, xxxvi, xli–ii; see also Morris Trustees
  Morris titles pbd. xlv–vii, lii
Morris to Buchanan C-3
Morris Trustees, see also Mrs Jane Morris, S. C. Cockerell, F. S. Ellis, Robert Proctor, C. H. St John Hornby, and May Morris xxxii, xli, xliii–vii, A-4.17, 5.03, 8.05, 9.02, 12.05, 21.01, 45.05–06, 71.02, 77.02, 84.01, 85.01, 86.01, 88.01, 110.01, 126.01, C-20, E-1, App II-10–11
Morris, Jenny xli, A-4.19
Morris, May xxxii, xlv, xlvii, lvi, A-126.01, editor of *CW*, and *William Morris, Artist, Writer, Socialist*, 130.01; see also A-2.04, 2.09, 4.19, 5.10, 04, 11.06, 21.01, 46.03, 51.01, 84.01, 86.04, C-33, D-24, App II-3
Morris, Mrs Jane (nee Burden) xliv, A-3.10, 4.19, 71.02, 74.04
Morris, William
  as artist A-50.08
  and *Commonweal* A-30.01, C-36–7
  as designer, A-84.01, 138.01
  as editor of *Commonweal* A-30.01, Socialist Platform (SP), and *Arts and Crafts Essays* B-15
  as engraver A-4.19
  as illustrator A-54.05, 59.06
  as rubricator A-51.01, 05
  as translator, see translations
  bindings designed by Morris A-4.14, 6.01, 8.01, 52.01
  corrections and revisions, discussions of A-2.04, 06, 09, 3.01, 03, 4.01, 05, 57.01, 59.01, 80.01
  discussion with US publisher RB A-12.03
  essays on textiles, see D-410; see also A-21.05, 27.01, B-15, C-18.01–02, D-111
  lists of lectures and speeches A-130.01, 133.01
  on LP copies A-12.04
  on education A-130.01, D-226, 262, 389, 436, App I-2
  on free speech A-130.01, D-163, 201, 214, 219, 320, 330, 370, 406
  on government D-92, 218, 263, 361, 390, 406, 547
  on Magnússon's role A-5.01
  on poverty A-130.01, D-123, 254, 411, 431
  on Socialists A-130.01, D-176, 180, 325, 380, 453, 534, 547
  publishers, contracts with xxxiii–iv, xlv, A-3.01
'Morrow of the Elections, The' D-167
Mosher, Thomas Bird, editor and publisher xlvii–ix, lvi–vii, lix, E-4
  Bibelot Series C-5

Bibelot: A Reprint of Poetry and Prose ..., The xlviii–ix, lvii, A-56.06, 83.01, 87.01, 90.01, 95.01, 96.01, 98.01, 101.01, 114.01, 122.01, C-8.01, 16.01, D-465, 596
Bibelot, Testimonial Edition of A-114.01
Brocade Series A-69.03, 70.03, 83.03, 90.03, 92.01, 93.01, C-10.02, 16.03
Miscellaneous Series A-78.02
Old World Series A-45.04
Reprints from "The Bibelot" A-83.02, 90.02, C-8.02, 10.01, 12, 16.02
Reprints of Privately Printed Books A-99.01
'Moves in the Game Political' D-162
Mowbray, C. W., assistant editor A-30.01, D-259
'Mr. Chamberlain at Hull' D-153
'Mr. Chamberlain's Leader' D-217
'Mr. Jawkins at the Manor House' D-241
'Mural Decoration' (in *Encyclopædia Brittanica*) B-5
Murray, Charles Fairfax, illustrator A-11.01, 130.01, 138.01
Muses Library series lvii, A-2.10, 3.11, 4.20

National Association for the Advancement of Art and Its Application to Industry C-11, D-426, 480, 492
Near Avalon A-118.01; see also A-2.01–13
'Near but far away' A-130.01
'New Party, A' D-156
New Review, The, 'The Socialist Ideal. I.–Art': D-527; see also E-11
'New Year, The' D-537
New York Times, interview: App I-1
New, E. H., illustrator A-97.01, D-579
Newcastle Chronicle, The: speech: D-281
Newdigate, Bernard, printer xlvii
News from Nowhere xxviii, A-50.01–08, D-493
Nicol, D. J., editor of *Commonweal* A-30.01
'Night in a Cathedral, A' A-1.01; see also *Notes*, C-20
Niles, Thomas xxxv–vi, A-3.02, 12.03
Nineteenth Century, The, on adding monuments to Westminster Abbey: letter for the SPAB: D-437
'No Master' D-106
Nordfeldt, Olsson, illustrator A-83.04, 105.01
Norman, Henry, interviewer App I-10, 11
Norroena series A-6.04
'North of England Socialist Federation' D-297
Northend, William F., publisher, artist and designer A-101.04
Northern Love Stories, Three xxxv, lvi, A-9.01–04; see also A-77.03, C-13
North-Western Chronicle, The, lecture: D-80
Not for Leisure Alone A-121.01
Note by William Morris on His Aims in Founding the Kelmscott Press A-88.01, 48.03; see also C-14, 35, 38, D-590
'Notes of the Political Crisis' D-147, 255
'Notes on Matters Parliamentary' D-177
'Notes on the Elections' D-206
Novel on Blue Paper, The A-140.01; see also D-605
Nowell-Smith, Simon A-3.12
Noyes, Alfred, editor C-24
Nupkins Awakened, The Tables Turned and, A-42.01, 130.01

O'Kane, H. M. (Mrs Clarke Conwell), artist-designer, rubricator A-102.01, C-9, 19
Odyssey, The xxxviii–ix, A-40.01–05
'Of Dyeing as an Art' B-15, D-480

Index

Old English Romances series A-83.03, 90.03
'Old Fable Retold, An' A-130.01, D-86
Old French Romances xl, lvi, A-79.01; see also A-70.01–02
Old World Series, see Mosher
Oliphant, James, editor A-37.01, B-7
'On Some "Practical" Socialists' D-357
'On the Edge of the Wilderness' D-22
On the External Coverings of Roofs A-21.05; see also A-44.01, C-18.01–02
'Order and Anarchy' D-94
Order of Chivalry, The A-63.01–02
'Origins and Subsequent Growth of Ornamental Art' D-230
Ornamented MSS of Middle Ages A-129.01; see also C-35
Osborne, E. C., printer A-17.01, 60.01, 71.01
Our Corner, speech: D-231
'Our Policy' D-176
'Our Representatives' D-192
Oxford and Cambridge Magazine, The xxviii, xxxi–iii, xlv–vi, xlix, li–ii, A-1.01, 83.01–02, D-1–16, App II-1
   reprints from C-10.01–02, 12, 16.01–05, 20, 23–4, 30–1, D-596
   fiction: D-1, 4, 6, 8, 11–13, 16; poetry: D-2, 7, 9, 14–15; reviews: D-3, 5,10
Oxford Magazine, The: letter on the disturbance at a Socialist meeting: D-135

Pall Mall Gazette, The: SPAB letters: D-63, 82, 473, 475, 535; review (of world literature): 173; opinion: 236, 318, 329–30, 332, 335, 339; 'Ugly London': sequel to Ouida's article: 405, 473, 475; reportage: 245; Morris lecture on Tapestry weaving: summary: 415; corrects an account of The Saga Library: 518; interviews: App I-6–8
Palmerston D-117
paper
   Abbey Mills B-13, 15
   Alton Mill A-17.02, 105.01
   American hand-made A-102.01
   Ansell, hand-laid A-4.05
   Apple A-4.17, 12.05
   Arnold A-129.01
   Barcham Green hand-laid A-137.01, 139.01
   Flower A-2.04, 45.02, 47.04, 50.05, 54.01, 05, 59.01, 63.01, 66.01, 74.01, 78.01, 80.01, 84.01, 86.01, 88.01, 91.01, B-12, 14, C-20, App II-5, 7–9, 11
   French hand-made A-50.02, 80.02, 96.04, 106.01
   Hammersmith A-45.06
   Italian hand-laid A-118.01
   japan vellum A-2.08, 45.04, 69.03, 70.03, 78.02, 83.01–03, 90.02–03, 91.01, 97.01, 99.01, 102.02, B-16.02, C-5, 8.01–02, 9, 10.01–02, 12, 16. 02
   John Dickinson & Co. xxxviii, A-12.04, 40.01, 45.01, 47.01
   Old Stratford C-9
   Perch A-3.07, 8.05, 69.01, 71.02, 73.01, 77.01, 85.01, App II-10
   Tuscany handmade A-127.01
   Van Gelder xxxviii, A-25.01–02, 40.01, 45.04, 59.02, 78.02, 99.01, 102.03, B-9, 19, C-5, E-14
   vellum A-8.01, 05, 51.01, 54.01, 59.01, 63.01, 66.01, 69.01, 70.01, 73.01, 74.01, 76.01, 77.01, 80.01, 85.01, 86.01, 88.01, 99.01, 102.02, 129.01
   Warren's Olde Style and 1854 C-38
   Whatman's paper, hand-laid A-2.01–02, 3.04, 4.01, 08, 6.01, 8.01, 9.01, 11.01, 12.01, 21.01, 38.01, 39.01, 48.01, 50.01, 51.01, 52.01, 57.01, 62.01, 72.01, 74.02, 75.01, 76.01, 83.04, 89.01, 112.01, App II-3
'Paris Trades Union Congress, The' D-225
Patterson, Malcolm, designer C-25, 26
Paying for Art A-120.01; see also D-136
Pearson, Richard, lxi, editor D-606
Pease, Edward R. A-64.01
Penny Pamphlets series A-55.01, 56.01–02, E-3 (wrapper)
'Pentonville Prison' D-386
Peterson, William S., editor lviii, C-35, App II headnote
'Philanthropists' A-130.01, D-127
photo-electrotype facsimile A-54.03
photographers: see Elliot and Fry, Evans, Robert Faulkner and Co., Hollyer, Lewis, Walker
Pierce, Harold A-2.02
'Pilgrim at the Gate of Idleness' A-130.01
Pilgrims of Hope A-99.01–02; see also C-33, D-134, E-9
Pine, Mrs A-50.02
piracy xxix, E-5
'Plea for the American Anarchist, A' D-318
Poems by the Way lii, lvi, A-59.01–06; see also 89.01–02, C-5, 22, 33, D-27–8, 371, 382, 439, 522, E-9
Poems by William Morris C-27
Poems of William Morris C-22
Poems of William Morris, A Selection From the C-1
poems, various, inc. posthumous 1st pbns. lii, A-125.01, 126.01, 138.01, 141.01, C-1, 22, 26–33
Poetical Works of William Morris, The, series, see Longmans
'Police Spies Exposed' D-348
'Policy of Abstention, The' A-130.01
'Political Outlook, The' A-130.01, 133.01
Political Writings, 1883–1890 C-36
Pollard, Graham, see also *Enquiry* l, A-10.01
'Practical Politics at Nottingham' D-326
Praise of Wine A-131.01
'Pray but One Prayer for Me' A-1.01, 2.01, C-20, D-15
'Preface' to *More's Utopia* B-14
'Preface' to *Medieval Lore* B-13
'Preface' to *The Nature of Gothic* B-12
Pre-Raphaelite Ballads C-9
'Present Outlook of Socialism in England, The' D-591
Price, Cormell C-20, App II-1
pricing of Morris books A-12.01, 120.01, D-136
'Principles of *Justice*, The' D-87
Principles of Socialism, A Summary of the A-24.01–03
Principles of the HSS A-53.01–02, D-534; see also C-38
printers UK
   Arden Press, W. H. Smith xlvii, A-126.01
   Baines and Scarsbrook A-67.01
   Ballantyne Press xxxii, xxxviii, A-2.06, 3.08–09, 4.14–15, 18, 5.02, 9.02, 11.04, 21.03, 06, 45.01, 05, 08, 47.06, 48.04, 50.06–07, 54.09, 59.05, 74.05, 77.02, 79.01, 80.04, 81.01, 84.04, 86.03, 110.01, 128.01, C-18.02, 24, 29, 33
   Bonner, Arthur A-29.01
   Bowden, Hudson, & Co. A-50.02
   Brendon, William, and Son Ltd. A-3.11, 74.02
   Churchman A-26.01–02
   Clarke, R. & R. A-68.01, B-3, 13, 15
   Clowes, Wm., and Sons A-3.03, 05, 27.01, 111.01
   Collins and Waltestow A-143.01
   Cornish Bros. B-16.01
   Co-operative Printing Company Limited A-37.01, 53.01, 58.01, B-7
   Cund Bros A-18.01
   E. C. Osborne A-17.01, 60.01
   Edinburgh Press A-2.10, 116.01, 117.01
   Elliott Stock B-13
   Empire Printing and Publishing A-28.01, 33.01, 35.01,36.01
   Guild of Handicraft Press B-16.01
   Hayman, Christy & Lilly A-61.01
   Headley Brothers A-3.14
   Heywood, John A-22.01
   International Publishing Company A-23.02
   Journeyman Press A-139.02, 140.01
   Kemp Hall Press A-130.01
   Labour Literature Society A-31.03, 37.03, 49.02, 53.02
   London and Norwich Press A-4.20
   Messrs Bridge of Oxford A-41.01
   Modern Press A-23.01, 24.01
   National Labour Press A-119.01
   Neill, in *Later Issues* A-50.07, 59.05
   Perkins, Bacon & Co. (under *Later Impressions*) A-28.01
   Progressive Printing Company (under *Later Issues*) A-29.01–03, 30.01
   Rampant Lions Press A-137.01
   Riverside Press A-95.02–3, 96.03, 101.03
   Roberts, Robert A-2.02
   Savage, Warwick A-20.01
   Selkirk Press A-113.01
   Sentinel Publications, see Leatham
   Shakespeare Head xxxii, A-130.01
   Socialist League, see Socialist League
   Speaight, W., and Sons B-10
   Standring, G. A-104.01
   Strangeways, Strangeways and Walden, Strangeways and Sons, John Strangeways xxxii, xxxviii, xxxix, A-3.04, 06, 4.01–02, 05–06, 08, 12, 13, 5.01, 6.01, 8.01–02, 9.01, 11.01–02, 12.01, 04, 16.01, 03, 39.01, 40.01, 03, 45.01
   Swarthmore Press A-3.14
   Temple Press, The A-3.12, B-8
   Villafield Press A-2.12
   Whittingham, Charles xxxiii, A-1.01, 2.01, 3.01, App II-1
printers US
   Calumet Press A-91.01
   Dover Press A-74.01
   Gill Engraving A-54.03
   Higgins, John F. A-68.02
   Loring, George D., A-69.03, 70.03, 78.02, 83.03, 90.03, 92.01, 93.01, C-10.02
   McKiernan, Geo. F., & Co. A-17.02
   Smith & Sale A-45.04, 83.01, 99.01, C-5, 12
   Van Vechten, George W. A-129.01
   Ward Richie Press A-131.01
   Welch, Bigelow and Co. A-4.03, 07, 7.01
   Wilson, John, & Son, University Press xxxii, xxxvii, A-3.02, 05, 4.07, 10–11, 8.03, 11.03, 16.02, 21.02, 50.01, 03, 54.03–04, 59.03, 74.03, 84.02, 86.02, 93.02, 100.01, 107.01, C-2, App II-2.02
Printers' Register, The: lecture summary: D-553
Printing, An Essay A-105.01
printing, on B-15, C-14, 35, D-553, 555, 585
Prior, George, (facsimiles) A-5.01, 6.01, 48.01, 74.02
'Processes of Reproduction' D-607
Proctor, Robert
   as Trustee xliv, App II-11

as editor xlvi, lvi, A-5.03, 6.03, 9.02, 11.05, 20.02, 40.04, 44.01, 47.04, 48.02, C-7, 11, 13, 17, 18.01–02, 20
on forgery E-1
'Promise of May, The' D-592
'Propaganda Fund, The' D-103; see also D-91, 109, 113–14
'Prophesy of the Vala' A-130.01
Prose and Poetry (1856–1870) C-30
Prose Romances of William Morris series A-74.02 (facsimile)
Protocol of the International Workers Congress, 2 speeches: D-489, 490
Proud King, The C-29
publisher-printers UK, see also separate entries for Democratic Federation, Kelmscott Press, Socialist League and Tochatti
   Birmingham Guild of Handicraft Limited E-14
   Clay, Richard, & Sons A-2.08, 13, C-34, E-4, 9, *Later Issues* A-54.07
   Collins Clear-Type Press A-2.11, C-6, 25–28
   Freethought Publishing Company A-25.01–02
   Northend, William F. A-101.04
   Novello, J. Alfred, music publisher B-1
   Scolar Press A-138.01
   Twentieth Century Press A-55.02–03, 56.04, 64.01, 82.01, 108.02, 119.01, B-18, E-2–3, 5, 8, 11
   WSC Co. (see Collins) C-26
publisher-printers US
   Blue Sky A-102.02
   Bubb C-32
   Burr, Frederic, at the Hillside Press xlix, A-96.04, 102.03
   Bursch, F. C., at the Hillacre Bookhouse A-17.03, 120.01, 121.01, 123.01, 124.01, 127.01, D-136
   Byway Press A-106.01
   Davidson, William Edward, at the Morris Press A-103.01
   Elston Press xlix, A-102.01, C-14–15,19
   Fowler, H. A. A-118.01
   Kerr, Charles H., A-31.05, 68.02
   Roycrofters A-89.01
   Russell and Russell A-126.01
   Village Press, Goudy, Frederick and Bertha xlix, A-83.04, 105.01, B-16.02
   Washburn, W. L., at the Palmetto Press A-96.02
   Wayne State University Press A-133.01
   Woolly Whale A-129.01
publishers UK
   Agnew, Thos., & Sons' Galleries B-9
   Allen, George A-79.01, B-12
   Blackie & Son Ltd A-2.12, 109.02
   Chatto and Windus A-2.08
   Clarendon Press A-3.13
   Clarke, James, & Co. B-10
   Clover Hill Editions A-137.01
   De la More Press xlix, A-2.08
   Dent, J. M., & Sons A-3.12, C-24
   Freedom Press A-31.02
   Harrap, George, & Co. C-21
   Hodder & Stoughton A-116.01, 117.01
   Joint Committee of the English Socialists A-64.01
   Lane, John, Bodley Head xlix, A-2.07, 111.01
   Lane, Joseph, with William Morris A-28.01, 30.01, 31.01
   Lawrence and Bullen A-74.02
   Law and Liberty League, Richard Lambert A-43.01; see also D-332, 335, 337
   London History Workshop Centre A-139.02, D-604
   Macmillan xxxiii, xli, B-3
   Miller, Robert A-37.01, B-7
   Minton, Edward xli, A-25.01–02
   One Horse Press A-143.01
   Oxford University Press, Humphrey Milford C-30–1
   Routledge & Sons, Ltd A-2.10, 3.11, 4.20
   Scott, Walter xl, A-6.02
   Seymour, Ralph Fletcher, Aldebrink Press xlix, A-17.02
   Sketchley B-4
   Sugden, William Larner, see also Minton, co-publisher xli, A-25.01–02
   Swan Sonnenschein A-68.01
   Thoemmes Press, Bristol A-1.01, 126.01, C-20, 36, 37
   Thomson, James, Avon Press xlix, A-101.02, C-16.04, 23
   Wessels, A. C-9
publishers US, see also separate entries for Mosher and Roberts Brothers
   Appleton, D. and Co., B-10
   Caldwell, H. M., Co. in *Later issues*, C-21
   Clarkson N. Potter, in *Later isssues* A-138.01
   Crowell, Thomas Y., C-22
   Dodge Publishing A-2.12
   Dutton, E. P., & Co. A-2.10, 3.11–12, 4.20, C-24
   Hill, J. E. A-97.01, D-579
   Humboldt and Co., N.Y. A-50.04, C-4
   Jacobs, G. W. A-2.08
   Library Binding Company, in *Later issues* A-93.02
   Lilienthal, Theodore, and Ward Richie A-131.01
   Little, Brown and Company xxx, xxxvi–vii, A-4.15, 7.01
   Luce, John, and Co. A-2.08
   New York Labour News A-108.01
   Princeton University Press C-38
   Putnam's, G., Sons xlix, A-109.01
   Russell, R. H. A-93.02, 100.01, 107.01
   Scribners A-68.01, under *Later Issues*, as imported sheets, A-79.01
   Ticknor and Fields, Ticknor and Company xxxvi, C-2
   Twentieth-Century Publishers A-50.03; under *Later impressions* C-4
   Windhover Press A-139.01
   Wise, Wm. H., and Co. A-114.01
publishers:Editions Sociale, Paris A-135.01
Pygmalion and the Image A-107.01; see also A-4.01–20
Pygmalion, a poem for 4 pictures D-49

Quaritch xxxix–xl, A-52.01, 57.01, 62.01, 72.01, 75.01, 112.01, App II-4, 6; see also A-51.01
Quarterly, The A-1.01
Queen Victoria D-188, 267, 296, 317, 485
Quelch, Harry, editor A-82.01, 108.02, B-18, D-563, App I-12
Quest, The, essay: D-579
Quinn, John (collector) A-51.01

'Radicals Look Around You' D-351
Ransom, Will A-83.04, 105.01
'Rapunzel' lii, A-1.01, 2.01, D-9
'Reaction and the Radicals, The' D-375
'Recuyell of the Histories of' Troy, Appreciation of App II-6

Reeves, Reeves and Turner, publisher and distributor xxxii, xxxvii–ix, lvii
   Morris titles pbd. A-4.13–15, 12.04, 23.01, 24.02–03, 31.02, 40.01–02, 45.01, 46.01, 47.01, 48.01, 50.02, 54.02, 59.02, B-4, 8, 14, App II-3
   in *Later impressions* or issues A-2.02, 8.01
Remarque Series C-21
Reprints from "The Bibelot", see Mosher
restoration, arguments against B-10, D-34–8, 50, 53–8, 64, 304, 473, 535, 567, 573, 577–8, 580–3, App I-5
Rethel, Alfred, artist C-12, D-10; *Later impression* A-98.01
reviews, see D-5, 26, 139, 141; see also this heading under *Commonweal*
'Revival of Architecture, The' C-18.01–02, D-372, 414
'Revival of Handicraft' D-414
'Revival of Trade' D-279
Revolt of Ghent, The A-119.01
'Reward of Genius, The' A-130.01
Reward of Labour: A Dialogue, The A-61.01; see also D-289
Rhead, Louis, designer A-93.02
'Rhyme Slayeth Shame' D-24
Rhys, Ernest, editor A-3.12, 6.02, C-24
Richie, Ward, editor A-131.01
Rickarby, Rev. J. A-130.01, D-501
'Riding Together' A-1.01, 2.01, C-20, D-7
Roberts Brothers xxix–xxxii, xxxv–vii, xlii, liv
   Morris titles pbd. xxxvi, note 22, A-2.03, 3.02, 05, 4.02–03, 06–07, 09–11, 15, 7.01, 8.02–03, 11.02–03, 12.02–03, 16.02, 21.02, 47.02–03, 50.01, 54.03–04, 59.03, 74.03, B-2, App II-2.02
   Author's Editions A-3.05, 4.03, 06–07, 10, 8.03, 11.03, 50.01
Roberts, Lewis A. xxxv
Rogers, Bruce, illustrator, designer and engraver A-70.03, 90.03
Rolfe, William J., assistant editor C-2
Roots of the Mountains, The xxxiii, xxxviii–ix, A-48.01–04; see also C-3, 26, App II-3
Rossetti, Christina and Dante Gabriel xxxv
Rossetti, Dante Gabriel, illustrator xxxiv–v, A-2.01, 08–09, 4.19, 74.04, 80.03, 126.01; see also A-130.01, D-26
Rowe, Antony, printer C-36–7
Rowe, C., artist A-100.01
Rowley, Charles D-140–1
Roxburghe-style bindings, see Saga Library, A-52.01, 62.01
Royal Academy, two articles on A-130.01, D-104, 108
Royal Commission on Technical Education App I-2
Royal family D-467, App I-14
royalties xxx, xxxiii–vi, xlii–iii, lx, A-4.08, 9.02, 45.05, C-18.02
Rubaiyát of Omar Khayyam, The A-21.05
Ruskin, John, writer A-1.01, 25.01, B-12, D-189

Saga Library xxxix–xl, lviii
   sales A-51.01
   vol. I A-52.01, vol. II A-57.01, vol. III A-62.01, vol. IV A-72.01, vol. V A-75.01, vol. VI A-112.01
Saga of Hen Thorir, The A-106.01; see also A-52.01
Salisbury, Lord D-162, 220, 241, 345, 352, 355, 379, 402, 420, 485
Salmon, Nicholas, editor C-36–7
Salt Trust D-408
Samuelson, Bernhard App I-2

Index

Saunders, Mr, magistrate App I-6
Scenes from Fall of Troy and Other Poems and Fragments A-125.01
Scheu, Andreas, SL associate xxxix, A-4.14, 58.01, B-18
Schweinfurth, J. A., binding designs A-47.02, 74.03
Scotland, reports of lecture tour D-205, 207, 368
Scotsman, The, reportage: D-366
'Scott, Temple', I. H. Isaacs, xxvii, D-27, App I-18
Scribner's Monthly: poetry: D-30
'Seasons, The' D-27
Sedding, Edmund, editor B-1
Selection From The Poems of William Morris C-1
serials indexed: ACES Catalogues; American Architect; American Architect and Building News; Architect; Artist; Athenæum; Atlantic Monthly; Beautiful World; Bibelot; Bibliographical Society, Transactions of the, later Bibliographica; Birmingham Daily Post; Bookselling: A Journal for Publishers, Booksellers, Writers, and Readers; British and Colonial Printer and Stationer; British Bookmaker; Cambridge Chronicle; Cassell's Saturday Journal; Century Guild Hobby Horse; Clarion; Commonweal; Co-operative Wholesale Societies Annual; Daily Chronicle; Daily News; Dark Blue; Daylight; Decorative Art; Dickens Studies Annual; Echo; Eclectic Magazine; English; English Illustrated Magazine; Every Saturday; Fortnightly Review; Forum (US); Good Words; Grosvenor Notes; Hammersmith Socialist Record; History Workshop: A Journal of Socialist and Feminist Historians; Humane Review; International Review of Social History; Justice; Labour Prophet; Leeds Mercury; Leek Times; [Letter to several Italian newspapers]; Liberty; Liverpool Daily Post; London World; Macclesfield Courier and Herald; Magazine of Art; Manchester Examiner; Manchester Guardian; Manchester Quarterly; Matrix; Modern Art (Boston); Modern Philology; Morning Post; New Review; New York Times; Newcastle Chronicle; Nineteenth Century; North-Western Chronicle; Our Corner; Oxford and Cambridge Magazine; Oxford Magazine; Pall Mall Gazette; Printers' Register; Protocol of the International Workers Congress; Quest; Scotsman; Scribner's Monthly; Society of Arts; Journal of the, SPAB, The Annual Report; Speaker; Spectator; Standard; Studio; Sun; Time: a Monthly Magazine; Times, The; To-Day; Trans. of the NAAA, 1888; Trident; Victorian Institute Journal; Victorian Poetry; William Morris Society, Journal of the; Women's Union Journal; Woman's Signal; Yearbook of English Studies
series: (in which Morris appears more than once) see Avon Booklet, Bibelot, Blackie's English Classics, Brocade, Buzz Saw, Everyman's Library, Feather Weights, Freedom Library, Longmans Class Books of English Literature, Longmans Pocket Library, Muses Library, Old English Romances, Penny Pamphlets, Poetical Works of William Morris, Rpts. from The Bibelot, Social League Leaflets, SP (Socialist Platform)
'Seven Years Ago and Now' D-532
'Shadows of Amiens' C-20, 23, D-3
Shall Ireland Be Free? A-36.01
Sharp, William A-90.01–02
Shaw, G. B. xxxiv, A-21.01, 24.01, 64.01, 104.01, 130.01, C-18, D-212
Shelley, P. B. xxxvii
Sherman, Francis, epigraph A-83.01–03
shorthand reports A-60.01, D-436, 504, 587
Sidonia the Sorceress App II-7
Signs of Change xxxviii, lvi, A-46.01–03; see also C-17, D-88, 308
Sigurd the Volsung xxxv, xlv, A-12.01–06; see also C-3, 22, App II-10
'Silence and Pity' D-606
Silver Library A-4.18, 54.07
Sir Galahad A-102.01–03; see also A-1.01, 2.01–12, C-19, E-1
Sir Peter Harpdon's End xlix, A-122.01; see also A-2.01–13, C-3, 27, D-596
Six Poems Selected from the Early Writings C-32
'Skeleton at the Feast, The' A-130.01, D-384
Skelton, John, contributor C-2
Smith, Kelvyn Laurence, designer A-143.01
Social Democratic Federation xli, lii, A-23.01–02, 24.01, 26.01–02, 28.01, 82.01, 108.02, B-18, D-118
Social Sciences Library series C-4
Socialism A-34.01; see also D-175
'Socialism from the Root Up' D-190
'Socialism in Dublin and Yorkshire' D-186
'Socialism in England in 1884' D-115
'Socialism in the Provinces' D-178
'Socialism Up-to-date' A-130.01
'Socialism: Its Aims and Methods' D-233
Socialism: Its Growth and Outcome lvi, A-68.01–02; see also C-36, D-190
Socialist Diary A-139.01–02; see also D-281, 604
Socialist Ideal of Art E-11; see also D-527
Socialist League xxxi–ii, xli, lii, A-23.02–03, 28.01, 34.01, 38.01, 42.01–03, 49.01, 130.01, D-525, E-10
Socialist League Manifesto, The A-29.01–03; see also C-38, D-128, 131, 325, E-6–7, 10
Socialist League Leaflets series A-26.02–04, 33.01, 36.01
Socialist Platform series A-31.01, 35.01, 37.02, 49.01, B-6, E-10
Socialist Party of Great Britain (SPGB) A-113.01
'Socialist Work at Norwich' D-404
'Socialists and Politics' D-149
Socialists at Play D-148, E-8
Society for the Protection of Ancient Buildings xxxi, xli, lii, A-65.01, 130.01, B-3, C-7, 18.01–02, D-36–38, 40–44, 47, 55–8, 122, 535, E-13
Annual Reports D-43, 50, 56, 60, 64, 71, 78, 146, 312, 399, 468, 530–1, 542, 556
Manifesto A-13.01–03
occasional pbns. A-41.01–02, 44.01
Society of Arts and School of Design, Birmingham A-17.01–03, 18.01, D-46
Society of Arts, Council of, publisher A-27.01
Society of Arts, The Journal of the, 'The Woodcuts of Gothic Books': lecture: D-538
'Society of the Future, The' A-130.01, D-445
Some German Woodcuts of the Fifteenth Century A-85.01; see also D-585
Some Hints on Pattern Designing A-94.01; see also C-18.01–02, D-69
'Some Notes on Early Woodcut Books' C-15, D-585
'Song for Cupid and Psyche' D-130.01
'Song for Orpheus' A-130.01
Songs of Chivalry C-28
sophistications xxix, xlix, E-3, 6–7, 10–11, 13, 15
South Place Ethical Society A-59.01
SPAB, The Annual Report: D-43, 50, 56, 60, 64, 71, 73, 116, 146, 150; 2 speeches at the 10th AGM: 312; at the 11th AGM: 399; on Inglesham Church at the 12th AGM: 468, 399; speeches: 2 in 312, 399, 468, 530, 531, 542, 556; letters: 560, 564, 567
Sparling, Henry Halliday, assistant editor, contributor xl, A-6.02–04, 30.01, 32.01, 35.01, D-170, 250, 348, 413, 416
Speaker, The, Morris replies to the editor: D-512
Spectator, The: reportage: D-574; letter, reportage: 574
'Speech from the Dock, A' D-365
SPGB Library series A-113.01
Spielmeyer, W., engraver A-74.01
St Alban's Abbey D-42, 44, 304
St Mark's Venice D-53–7
St. George and the Dragon (verses) B-19
Standard, The: opinion: D-83; letter, SPAB: 567
Stead, W. T. D-154, 228
Stedman, E. C., contributor C-2
Steele, Robert, editor A-2.08, B-13
Stepniak, Sergius D-584
Stevens, Thomas Wood, designer A-102.02
Story of Kormak, The A-134.01
Strong, Roy, contributor A-138.01
Studio, The: 2 poems: D-597; interview: App I-15
Summer Dawn A-117.01; see also A-1.01, 2.01–13, D-15
Sun, The, article: D-552
Sundering Flood, The xxxvii, xlv, A-86.01–04
Svend and His Brethren A-96.01–04; see also C-10.01–02, 20, 23, D-11, 596
Swinburne, A. xxxiv, epigraph A-101.02

Tables Turned, The A-42.01
'Talk and Art' D-424
tapestry D-410, 415, App I-11, 15
Tauchnitz, Bernhard, publisher of Tauchnitz International Editions xxxi, C-1
'Ten Commandments, The' D-242
Tewksbury Minster D-34–5
Textile Fabrics A-27.01; see also C-18.01–02, D-111
Theodor, Carl D-155, 170
Thomson, Robert xlix, A-76.01
three musicians vignette A-3.04, 06, 08, 4.01, 04–05, 08, 12–14, 16, 19, 8.01, 21.03
'Three Seekers, The' D-85
Time: a Monthly Magazine: lecture: 'Art and Industry in the Fourteenth Century': D-491; poetry, 522
Times, The: letters for the SPAB: D-36–7, 40, 42, 44, 54–5, 57–8, 67, 70; Stratford-on-Avon Church: 517; against moving to Germany the Hanseatic League Museum at Bergen: 523; on Westminster Abbey: 529; oration at Stepniak's funeral: 584; 'On the Printing of Books': lecture summary: 553; letters: 567, 573, 583
Timo, Helen A., editor A-142.01
To Socialists lxi, A-28.01
Tochatti, James, Liberty Press, publisher and printer A-56.03, B-17, D-559, 565, 586
To-Day, The Monthly Magazine: poetry: D-85; lecture: 90; review: 108; manifesto: 128
Tooley, Sarah, interviewer App I-13
Torch Library series A-31.04, *Later issues* A-49.01
'Town and Country' D-549
Trafalgar Square C-33, D-174, 251, 330, 333, 338, 342, 353,

365, 373, 390, 392, 441–2
Trans. of the NAAA, 1888, lecture: 'Art and Its Producers': D-426; presidential address: 492
translations lvi, lx
   Flemish D-439
   Greek A-40.01–05
   Icelandic A-5.01–04, 6.01–06, 9.01–04, 51.01, 57.01, 62.01, 72.01, 75.01, 114.01, 130.01, 138.01, C-13, D-20, 29, 51, 598
   Latin A-11.01–06
   Old English A-77.01–03
   Old French A-63.01–02, 79.01
translators: see Caxton, Gubb, Magnússon, Morris, Wyatt
Tregaskis, J. and M. L. A-69.01
Treglown, E. G. designer D-579
'Trial by Judge v. Trial by Jury' D-469
Tributes to William Morris xxxi, A-4.07, 11, 7.01, 8.03, 16.02
Trident, The (Trinity College, Camb.), SPAB: D-530
'Triple Alliance, A' A-130.01, D-361
True and False Society lii, A-37.01–03; see also B-7
Two Addresses . . . before the NAAA C-11
'Two Genuine Radicals' D-110
'Two Partings, The' A-1.01, C-20
Two Red Roses Across the Moon A-116.01; see also C-9
Two Sides Of The River, The E-4; see also C-8.01–02, D-19, 32, 596
typefaces
   Aldebrink A-17.02
   Aldine display types A-48.01
   Basle xxxiii, xxxix, A-47.01, 48.01
   Bembo C-35, 38
   Bookman A-93.02
   Bradford A-96.02
   Brevier Italic C-5
   Caslon xxxiii, xlviii, A-17.03, 48.01, 52.01, 121.01, 129.01, C-8.01, 14, 15
   Caxton A-51.01
   Chaucer A-12.05, 63.01, 69.01, 73.01, 74.01, 77.01, 78.01, 80.01, 84.01, 86.01, 88.01, B-14, C-9, 14, App II-5, 10
   Dante A-139.01
   Golden type xlv, lvii, A-2.04, 4.17, 5.03, 6.03, 9.03, 11.05, 20.02, 21.04, 40.04, 45.02, 45.06, 46.02, 47.04, 48.02, 50.05, 54.01, 59.01. 66.01, 71.02, 74.01, 78.01, 77.01, 85.01, 88.01, 94.01, C-7, 11, 13, 17, 18.01, 20, App II-7, 8, 9
   Jenson A-96.04, 103.01, C-32
   Satanick C-9
   Troy A-3.07, 12.05, 54.05, 77.01, 137.01, B-14, App II-5, 10

Village A-83.04, 105.01

'Ugly London' D-405
'Unattractive Labour' D-143
'Uncrowned Kings' A-130.01, D-117
Under An Elm-Tree A-56.01–06, D-465; see also A-130.01, D-596, E-12 (wrapper)
'Unemployed, The' D-325
Unfinished Romances: 'Kilian of the Closes', 'Folk of the Mountain Door', 'Story of Desiderius', 'Story of the Flower' A-86.04
Unjust War A-14.01; see also C-34
Unknown Church, The Story of the C-10.02, 16.01–05; see also A-1.01, D-1, 596
Unpublished Lectures of William Morris A-133.01
Unsettled Questions series A-50.03
Updike, D. B., publisher A-97.01
US International Copyright Act xxx, xlviii, A-84.01–02
Useful Work v. Useless Toil A-31.01–05; see also C-17, D-88

'Verses for Pictures' A-130.01, B-9, D-27
Vest Pocket Series A-109.01
Victorian Institute Journal, interview; App I-3
Victorian Poetry: narrative poetry: D-601
'Voice of Toil, The' D-98, E-2, 5
Volsunga Saga xxxv, xl, li, A-6.01–06, C-13

W. H. Smith & Sons, see also Arden Press and St John Hornby, xliv, xlvii
Wake, London Lads! A-15.01
Walker, Emery xli, xliii
   editor, collaborator A-45.05, 59.01, 02, 06, 64.01, 105.01, 125.01, 130.01, B-15, C-30, 35, D-495, 523, 587, 607
   as photographer A-2.09, 3.10–11, 4.18–19, 40.05, 46.03, 48.03, 115.01, 126.01, 130.01
Walker & Boutall, platemakers A-5.01–04, 9.04, 12.06, 47.05, 50.08, 62.01, 71.02, 74.04, 80.03, 84.03, 85.01, 86.01–04
Wallet Books series A-120.01, 121.01
Wanderers, The (LCBEL) A-128.01; see also C-2
'War and Peace' A-130.01
Wardle, George, rubricator, editor A-138.01, B-2
Water of the Wondrous Isles, The xxxvii, xliii, xlv, A-84.01–04
Watts, G. F., artist A-4.19, 107.01, D-152
'Way Out: An Appeal to Genuine Radicals, The' A-130.01, D-93
Webb, Philip, designer A-5.01–04, 6.01, 86.04, App II-11
Wedgwood Institute A-20.01
Weibking, Robert, illustrator A-17.02, 83.04
Well at the World's End, The xliii, A-80.01–04

Westminster Abbey A-21.05; see also A-65.01, C-7, E-13 (wrapper)
Westminster Abbey, restoration D-292, 432, 437, 450, 529, 535, 560, 573
Weston, Jessie L. A-6.04
Whalley, Joyce Irene, editor A-138.01
'What 1887 has Done' D-349
'What All Men Long for' A-130.01
'What is to Happen Next?' D-213
'What Is: What Should Be' A-130.01
'What We Have to Look For' A-130.01
'Where Are We Now?' D-525
'Whig-Jingo Victory, The' D-210
'Whigs, Democrats, and Socialists' D-204
'Whiles Carried O'er the Iron Road', epigraph App II-3
Whittingham, Charlotte and Eleanor, designers A-1.01
'Why I Am a Communist' B-17, D-559
Why I Ams series B-17, D- 559
'Why not?' A-130.01, D-99
Widow's House by the Great Water, The A-142.01; see also A-84.01–04
Wilde, Oscar C-2
William Morris and His Praise of Wine A-131.01
William Morris Library series C-36–7
William Morris on Art Matters A-132.01; see also D-73
William Morris Society, The Journal of the: diary of 'The Expedition of the Ark': D-603; poem: 606; interviews App I-11–13
William Morris Society, UK and US, publisher, A-132.01, 134.01, 139.01–02, 141.01, 142.01
William Morris: Artist, Writer, Socialist A-130.01
William Morris: Poet, Artist, Socialist. A Selection C-4
'Winter Weather' A-1.01, 125.01, C-8.01–02, 20, D-2
Wise, T. J., publisher UK xxviii, l, liii, D-19, 32
Woman's Signal: interview App I-13
Women's Union Journal, The: speech: D-59; see also A-19.01
Wood beyond the World, The xxix, xl, A-74.01–05; see also D-574
'Words of Forecast for 1887' D-252
'Worker's Share of Art, The' D- 137
'Workhouse Socialism' D-524
'Workmen and Horses' D-216
World of Romance, The C-23
World's Classics series, OUP C-31
wrappers, forged E-3, 10, 12–13
Writing on the Image, The A-109.01–02; see also C-2
Wyatt, A. J., translator A-9.04, 77.01–03

Yearbook of English Studies, The, 5 poems: D-602
Yeats, W. B. A-56.06, D-596

Zola, Emile D-403, 417, 456